A Turbulent Voyage: Readings in African American Studies

EDITED BY

Floyd W. Hayes, III
Purdue University

COLLEGIATE PRESS

Collegiate Press
San Diego, California

Executive Editor: Christopher Stanford
Senior Editor: Steven Barta
Senior Developmental Editor: Arlyne Lazerson
Design: John Odam Design Associates
Cover art: Paul Slick
Typography: ExecuStaff, Campbell, California

Library of Congress Card Number: 91-78104

ISBN: 0-939693-26-7

Printed in the United States of America

10 9 8 7 6 5 4 3

to Harold Cruse,
who dared to analyze the crisis

for Tracy, Keisha, Ndidi, and Kia,
my next generations

Photo Credits

Acknowledgments

Many people contributed to the arrival of *A Turbulent Voyage*. Nancy Elizabeth Fitch, Robert L. Harris, Jr., and Sterling Stuckey served as readers of the manuscript. Their guidance, concern, and suggestions for improvement made the production of this anthology less difficult. I want to express my deep appreciation to Arlyne Lazerson, my editor at Collegiate Press, for it was she who initially asked me to undertake the project, and she has worked patiently with me to bring it to fruition.

I also am indebted to other colleagues who read and commented on parts of the book at various stages of development. They include Samuel Hay, Mack Jones, Ted Kornweibel, and Winston Napier. A special thanks goes to my research assistant, Lois Greene, for her assistance and willingness to engage me in dialogue about trends related to the development of African American Studies and prospects for black educational advancement in the future. I want to thank the numerous San Diego State University and Purdue University students who read and discussed many of this anthology's essays in my introductory courses.

Over the years, my thoughts about African American Studies and related issues have been shaped by conversations, and sometimes fierce intellectual debates, with a number of individuals. Significantly, there is much difference of opinion, but I have learned much from association with them. The list includes Molefi K. Asante, Thais Aubry, Ronald Bailey, Robert Chee-Mooke, John Henrik Clarke, Eugenia Collier, JoAnne Cornwell-Giles, Robert Fikes, Nancy Elizabeth Fitch, Eugene Grigsby, Daphne Harrison, Samuel Hay, Mary Jane Hewitt, Rickey Hill, Njeri Jackson, Caulbert A. Jones (deceased), Charles E. Jones, Edward L. Jones, Mack Jones, Alfred and Bernice Ligon, Maulana Karenga, Eddie Meadows, Boniface I. Obichere, Clovis Semmes, Earl Smith, Carl Spight, James Turner, Seneca Turner, Ronald W. Walters, Herbert West, C. S. Whitaker, Arthur Williams, Sloan Williams, and Alex Willingham. For nearly a decade, I have benefitted enormously from participating in the annual Black Studies conference at Olive-Harvey College in Chicago, Illinois. I want to thank Armstead Allen and his colleagues at that institution for providing a setting in which teachers, students, and local citizens challenge each other regarding the burning issues of the day.

I express to my colleague and friend Nancy Elizabeth Fitch special appreciation for taking time from her busy schedule to accompany me to New York City's Schomburg Center for Research in Black Culture. She assisted me in selecting photographs for this book.

To Jewell R. Crawford Mazique, I am indebted in so many ways. She has willingly shared with me her more than seventy years of accumulated knowledge, wisdom, and experience. She has taught me the value of intellectual growth tempered with a concern for and commitment to the common person and collective social development. She has demonstrated courage in the face of adversity; yet, she possesses a serenity and knowledgeable confidence that I still am unable to understand fully. Jewell is my dearest friend, ever-receptive confidante, and harshest critic; she reads everything I write.

No words can adequately express my appreciation to Charlene Moore Hayes, my adviser, wife, and critic; to Kia-Lillian Nicole Hayes, my daughter and young writer of stories; and to Thelma R. Hayes, my mother who came to visit as I was finishing this book. Each has sustained, strengthened, and nurtured me in ways that have contributed directly to my ability to complete this anthology.

In 1967, with the publication of his book, *The Crisis of the Negro Intellectual,* Harold Cruse intellectually jolted and energized people inside and outside of the American academy. Some thought that Cruse's assessment of the black creative intellectual was too severe. Others were captivated by his independent mind and intellectual courage; many declared that his book was the most daring and insightful examination of the black experience published that year. In some ways, Cruse blazed an independent trail in African American critical scholarship. His early views about the development of African American Studies—its focus, direction, and mode of interpretation—were prescient, and his subsequent contribution to the field has been significant. For these reasons, I dedicate this book to Harold Cruse.

CONTENTS

Preface: To the Student

African American Studies, as an organized academic enterprise, grew out of the late 1960s struggle for black liberation. Before that, only historically black colleges in the South had paid attention to the scholarly examination of Africa and its American legacy, particularly in the discipline of history. The field of Black Studies (as it was originally called) developed simultaneously with the social movements that sought to transform both American society and its academy. By the mid-1960s, the Black Power movement was challenging the cultural and racial exclusivity of American society and its social institutions, including the academic institution. Its accusers said that the policies, practices, and curricula at historically white universities discriminated against African Americans. Consequently, the demand grew for more African American students and faculty and for Black Studies.

In the years since the beginning of African American Studies, American society seems to have come full circle, as symbolized by the 1992 Los Angeles revolt. In the 1960s, African Americans demanded attention to their charges of white racism and economic oppression, but the conventional channels of demand were largely blocked or ineffective for working class and impoverished urban residents. Urban African Americans living in poverty scarcely experienced the tangible benefits of civil rights legislation. As a result, a number of major American cities were engulfed in a rising tide of violent disturbances. The 1965 Watts rebellion signaled the watershed of urban black frustration and anger with racism, police brutality, and economic hardship. The 1992 Los Angeles insurrection (triggered by the exoneration of four white policemen whose brutal beating of a black man was captured on videotape by a local citizen and later shown on television to the nation and to the world) reflected mounting discontent among impoverished Los Angelenos (African American, Latino, and white), who destroyed property throughout much of the city. As in the 1960s, America's cities are becoming the visible terrain of frustration, hopelessness, cynicism, and unrest, brought on by decades of society's indifference to the growing severity of urban economic and political underdevelopment. In contrast to the 1960s, indications are that in the 1990s the feelings of urban cynicism and anger are expanding beyond impoverished African American communities to include Latino and dispossessed white city residents. This is the new urban reality of cultural crosscurrents in America's increasingly multicultural society. If the developing cynicism and impoverishment continue to meet with societal indifference, urban anarchy may be the result.

Since the 1960s and the Great Society programs of the Johnson administration, there has been a progressive economic polarization between more affluent and less affluent Americans. The economic policies of the Reagan and Bush administrations speeded up this process. The effects of this economic development are of particular significance to African Americans. Even though the 1960s breakthroughs resulted in a growing middle class of African American professionals and managers, many other African Americans slid further down the slope toward economic disaster. Trapped by poverty and powerlessness, black residents of the central city remain alienated from America's mainstream, while their institutions are under attack and their children are betrayed in public schools, where the fundamental tools of knowledge building have been discarded. Embittered, angry, and cynical, an expanding underclass struggles to survive in a nation where unemployment is rising steadily. Not surprisingly, crime and other social problems associated with persistent poverty increase. Therefore, whether we speak of the liberal Johnson administration's welfare capitalist state policies or the more recent reactionary Reagan-Bush competitive capitalist state policies, the fundamental social conditions of the African American dispossessed seem to be worsening. The racial division of labor, the social problems of disenfranchisement, and the legacy of racial stereotyping—which have been inherited from the master-slave tradition and which have been employed by America's ruling elite to express effectively their determination to maintain the subordination of the African American masses—remain, and indeed are expanding as we approach the twenty-first century.

If American society continues on its present trajectory toward socioeconomic polarization and cultural clash, this nation cannot hope to remain a great power in the emerging global economic order, which is organized increasingly on the production, distribution, and consumption of knowledge. The earlier social-scientific conception of American society as "melting pot" actually meant the engineering, as closely as possible, of a white Anglo-Saxon Protestant culture; it is not racial and cultural assimilation but racial and cultural domination of diverse groups that historically has characterized the American social order. The result has been the suppression of America's historic multicultural reality. Such practices must give way to practices that acknowledge and encourage the multicultural character of American society.

To achieve this goal, quality education for all is critically important. Educational institutions at all levels must ensure that all students master the fundamental tools of knowledge (reading, writing, computational skills, and critical thinking); gain academic motivation; and receive positive character-building. In an increasingly knowledge-intensive age, advanced learning will constitute the essential ingredient of occupational advancement and robust citizenship. Additionally, the time is now for educational institutions to (re)develop curricula that recognize and respect the historical and contemporary contributions that people of color have made to America's multicultural society. This is the quest of African American Studies, for this field challenges America to refashion its self-understanding.

At the edge of the twenty-first century, African American Studies has the potential for exploring aspects of America's transition toward a postindustrial-managerial society. In this new social order, in which knowledge and managerial skill will be the essential societal resources, professional experts, as the manipulators of new knowledge, will have increasing power and influence in the policy-making process. Governmental and other policy makers more and more are influenced by policy *specialists,* who define complex social problems and provide alternative perspectives for solving them. These specialists, it is expected, will be able to avoid short-sighted solutions, such as the continued insistence on school busing for racial balance or the banning of teenage mothers from high schools. Courses in African American Studies can lay out numbers of social problems that policy makers and citizens will have to try to solve. Such courses can provide the knowledge and viewpoint that can allow policy makers and specialists to come up with creative solutions to pressing social problems. While a single course in African American Studies cannot, of course, give you as a student and as a citizen such knowledge, it can give you quick glimpses of various points of view as a foundation for further learning.

This anthology is designed to introduce the reader to the contours and content of African American Studies. The text and readings included here not only impart information but seek as their foremost goal to precipitate in the reader an awareness of the complex and changing character of the African

American experience—its origins, developments, and future challenges. The book aims to engage readers in the critical analysis of a broad spectrum of subjects, themes, and issues—ancient and medieval Africa, Western European domination and African enslavement, resistance to oppression, African American expressive culture, family and educational policies, economic and political matters, and the importance of ideas. The materials included in this anthology comprise a discussion of some of the fundamental problems and prospects related to the African American experience that deserve attention in a first course in African American Studies.

African American Studies is a broad field concerned with the examination of the black experience, both historically and presently. Hence, the subjects, themes, and issues included in this text transcend the narrow confines of traditional academic disciplinary boundaries. Reality, after all, is not disciplinary. In selecting materials for this text, I was guided by a developmental or historical approach in the general compilation of each section's readings. By so doing, I hope that the reader will be enabled to arrive at a critical understanding of the conditions and forces that have influenced the African American experience.

I need to say something about the scope and limitations of this anthology. I already have suggested that African American Studies includes the global African experience; this means Africa, the Caribbean, Latin America, and any other areas inhabited by African-descended people. However, no single text or African American Studies enterprise can be this expansive. Although African American Studies programs in Africa, Asia, Europe, or the Caribbean might include different emphases, in the United States of America the field has focused largely on the life experiences of African-descended North Americans. This text focuses mainly on the interrelationship between Africa and African America as a basis for understanding developments in the United States of America.

Part I, "African American Studies: Trends, Developments, and Future Challenges," presents ideas that have influenced the genesis and current development of African American Studies. Considered the father of black history, Carter G. Woodson made a classic statement about the role of education that inspired many early formulators of African American Studies. Included here is an excerpt from his 1933 book, *The Mis-Education of the Negro.* James Stewart's examination of W. E. B. Du Bois points up the scholar-activist orientation of the field. Molefi Asante is one of the foremost conceptualizers of Afrocentricity—a theory and method in African American Studies.

Part II is devoted to "The African Background." Although African Americans are descendants largely of the West Africans brought to these shores in chains, their historic efforts to reclaim and reconstruct a positive cultural identity and sense of human worth have resulted in a desire to connect with Africa in all of its diversity. John Henrik Clarke provides an important reconception of the role of Africa in world history. The place of ancient Egypt within the cultural continuity of African history continues to be hotly debated. In discussing ancient Egypt, John G. Jackson examines what might be called the classical age of African history. Often ignored is the extent of the African presence in ancient Greece and Rome. Edward L. Jones examines Lucius Septimius Severus, an African emperor of Rome. Adu Boahen investigates the rise and decline of ancient and medieval West African empires and states.

Part III is a discussion of "Western Europe and the Culture of Domination." How have Africans and their descendants come to be viewed so negatively? This section addresses some of the ideas, strategies, and tactics Western Europeans employed in the process of gaining cultural hegemony over Africa. Dona Richards examines critically the tradition of the Western idea of progress as a dimension of Western cultural and racial domination and exploitation. Cheikh Anta Diop probes in some detail the manner in which French Egyptologists sought to misrepresent the African cultural and racial foundation of ancient Egypt.

Part IV explores "Africa and the Americas: Pre-Columbian Contact, Enslavement, and Resistance." This section provides a broader view of early contacts between Africa and the Americas. It challenges many received ideas, such as the notion that Africans' first contact with the Americas was as chattel slaves or that chattel slavery was a humanizing process, beneficial to happy and passive slaves. LeGrand Clegg explores skeletal and sculptural remains which suggest strongly that Africans made contact with ancient American civilizations long before Christopher Columbus' voyage. In a classic essay, C. L. R. James argues that the Atlantic slave trade and the enslavement of Africans in the Americas not only contributed much to the economic development of modern Western Europe but also influenced the elaboration of the American personality and political culture. Vincent Harding uses David Walker, a free African American, and Nat Turner, a chattel slave, to examine the African American struggle against chattel slavery.

Part V is devoted to "African American Expressive Culture: Music and Literature." Although largely overlooked, the culture of African-descended Americans has directly influenced and enhanced the development of American culture. One could easily argue that without African American expressive culture there would be little American popular culture of significance. The complex character of African American cultural expressions also has served as a mechanism of survival and salvation for an oppressed yet strong-willed people. Portia Maultsby investigates the relationship between African and African American musical traditions. Sterling Brown examines the development, character, structure, and meaning of African American folk culture. Nelson George dissects the complex interaction between the emergence of soul music and the political economy of the American music world in the 1950s and 1960s. Richard Wright offers a conception of the African American writer's role, purpose, and perspective. Bernard Bell discusses the character of African American novels influenced by the Black Power/Black Arts Movements and the Women's Liberation Movement of the 1960s and 1970s.

Part VI addresses "The African American Family: Historical and Policy Issues." The breakdown of the family is a major challenge facing American society today. The crisis of family instability is even greater in many African American communities, which are plagued with impoverishment and resulting hopelessness. How did matters reach this crisis point and what are suggestions for improvement? From the dehumanizing chattel slave experience to the present, African American families have been characterized by cycles of instability and stability. Andrew Billingsley studies the patterns of traditional West African family life and the impact of chattel slavery on the development of the African American family. E. Franklin Frazier investigates the social and economic forces and conditions that shaped the structure and dynamics of African American families from slavery to freedom. The major objective of this section is to engage the reader in a critical dialogue about the growing and complex problem of African American family instability by including competing perspectives. The two articles by Glenn Loury and by William Darity, Jr., and Samuel Myers, Jr., provide conservative and radical policy assessments of this dilemma.

Part VII focuses on "The African American Struggle for Literacy and Quality Education." It is concerned with major trends in the development of African American education; contradictions and dilemmas in the provision of educational opportunity to African Americans; and the effect of desegregation policies on historically black colleges. Frederick Douglass, the slave who became a statesman, describes the challenges he faced as a child learning to read and write and developing an appreciation for knowledge. Jewell Mazique critically analyzes the subversion of urban public school systems during the 1960s. My contribution examines the politics of public school desegregation in Washington, D. C., during the late 1950s and 1960s. John Matlock investigates the role of the courts in desegregating institutions of higher education and the adverse impact on historically black colleges and universities.

Part VIII explores the "Political Economy of the African American Situation." This section examines the changing character of the American political economy and its constraints on the African American struggle for collective survival and economic well-being. Harold Baron investigates America's economic exploitation and racial oppression of African Americans from the Colonial Era to the mid-1960s. Daniel Fusfeld and Timothy Bates analyze the economic condition of African Americans from World War II to the 1980s, suggesting a growing polarization between an emerging middle class and a developing class of urban disinherited.

Part IX is devoted to "Politics and the African American Experience." It is concerned with the African American battle for human rights, political empowerment, and social development within the historic structures and processes of domination. Although articulating lofty democratic principles of liberty, justice, and equality for all of its citizens, the founders of the American system denied the humanity of African slaves and their descendants (and of American Indians) and excluded them from membership in the political community. This legacy of African American subordination and exclusion has become deeply embedded in the fabric of American political culture, continuing to shape individual and institutional attitudes, values, and practices. Milton Morris theorizes about the manner in which the American political system institutionalized the social relations of power between African Americans and whites. Mary Berry and John Blassingame describe the long-standing African

American struggle to gain citizenship rights, from the pre-Civil War era to the end of the 1970s.

Part X addresses "Ideology and the Culture of Ambiguity." It looks at some of the historic and contemporary contradictions faced by African American women and men in their struggle to (re)fashion a sense of identity and community. The text ends with this set of issues because I think that Americans in general and African Americans in particular are moving toward a period of increasing social complexity and ambiguity. In my judgment, uncertainty and paradox will characterize the African American future. W. E. B. Du Bois articulates the fragmented condition of being an African-descended American. Cornel West provides an explanation of the rise to prominence of African American neoconservatives during the age of Reaganism. Patricia Hill Collins articulates an African American feminist perspective on the nature of oppression and women's resistance to it.

The guiding spirit of this volume accepts as an initial educational premise that an introductory text in African American Studies should be broadly based. Hence, the readings that comprise this volume cover a wide range of areas—from history to sociology, from economics to politics, from music to literature, and from education to ideology. Academically, African American Studies is located primarily in the human sciences. Practically, the field deals with social change. This anthology's driving theme centers on the historic black struggle against cultural domination and for human rights, socioeconomic advancement, and collective survival. As you explore the issues raised in this book, you should reflect on the following questions: What does this reality (for example, oppression and resistance or the struggle for identity and community) mean? How did it come into existence? What are its contradictions and dilemmas? How does this reality affect the quality of our lives? How can we change this existing reality? Why does it matter?

The broad purpose of this volume, then, is to pose questions, articulate differing responses, evaluate them, and set the stage for further questions. African American Studies faculty and students need to be engaged in an ongoing struggle for knowledge, the gaining of which will allow the development of wisdom, moral courage, and social responsibility.

Preface: To the Instructor

African American Studies made its appearance with the promise of solving some of the educational problems of African Americans and of challenging the American academy's de facto racial exclusivity. Not only had individuals of African descent been excluded from university faculty and student bodies, the curricula of many disciplines had ignored African and African American achievements and points of view.

The field emerged in the 1960s as part of a larger and turbulent social movement, which was itself a product of a transformation of American society. That transformation—and the field of African American Studies—is more than thirty years old. And now we are facing another transformation, a quiet, progressive one that has profound implications for all Americans: the shift from an industrial-manufacturing to a postindustrial-managerial society. This quiet, all-encompassing change requires us to reconsider the role and place of African American Studies not only within the academy but also in American society.

My intent in this introductory essay is to attempt such a reconsideration. To do this, I must examine the field's major intellectual tendencies—past and present, complementary and contradictory. My concern is to locate the logic and follow the trajectory of this evolving field. In the discussion that follows, I do not purport to provide an exhaustive genealogy of African American Studies; rather, my intention is to examine some of the representative intellectual trends and developments characterizing the field so far. After this examination, I will address the possible future challenges to African American Studies and black educational advancement posed by the current transformation of America from an industrial-manufacturing society to a postindustrial-managerial society. Although the intellectual roots of African American Studies can be traced back to a much earlier period (as shown in several of the readings included here), I will limit the scope of my analysis to the intellectual and social forces that have contributed to the field's development from the 1960s to the present. Having been involved in African American Studies for more than twenty years, I write this essay not as an outsider looking in, but as an insider looking around.

A note on naming: In the early years, African Americanists called the field Black Studies. Later, the terms Afro-American Studies, Pan African Studies, African American Studies, and

Africana Studies also came to be used. Although there might exist some distinctions or variations among these names—particularly regarding the extent of an inclusion of African Studies and Caribbean Studies—for the purposes of this discussion, these titles are interchangeable.

THE TURBULENT EMERGENCE OF BLACK STUDIES

In the late 1950s and the 1960s, after the momentous *Brown* v. *Board of Education* ruling that, in effect, outlawed racial and ethnic segregation in schools, public school systems across the nation tried to find ways to evade the law and continue segregation. In response to such practices by local school boards, a powerful coalition of civil rights leaders, educational experts, and public policy makers was created, and the coalition determined to use all means available, and especially the courts, to make school systems comply with the desegregation orders. Many school systems, black as well as white, were caught in the middle of the war.

Scarce resources—intellectual as well as financial—were allocated to the policy battles and to moving children in buses instead of being allocated to education. Many black community leaders and organizations tried to point this out. They challenged the schools to implement policies and programs that would promote quality education, no matter what a school's racial makeup. But the movement for school integration had gathered such momentum that it could not be stopped by rational argument or even by evidence of blatant failure. As the coalition grew more and more powerful, imposing on urban communities racial integration at any cost, the quality of classroom teaching declined. Parents increasingly were intimidated by and excluded from an urban bureaucracy in which the policy-making process was dominated by a nonlocal elite with its own agenda—an agenda based solely on civil rights, ignoring students' rights to quality education.

As the civil rights movement began to wind down in the mid-1960s, many African American high school and college students looked for an alternative. They found it in the more militant social movements of the late 1960s, particularly the Black Power movement. These powerful, and in some ways anarchic, tendencies, along with resentment toward the educational establishment, served as the crucible for the turbulent appearance of African American Studies.

As an organized academic enterprise, African American Studies emerged at historically white universities and colleges during the late 1960s in the context of complex social changes that affected virtually every sector of American society. The African American Studies movement converged with mass movements of protest against the brutalizing effects of social injustice, socioeconomic inequality, racial antagonism, the Vietnam War, and university paternalism. Militant students challenged the hegemony of traditional modes of thinking and social practice, inaugurating an assault on what they perceived as the hypocrisy and immorality of many of the nation's social institutions. Institutions of higher education became primary targets of criticism as students challenged them to address the burning questions and urgent social problems of the day. Students attacked the university's conventional disregard of their everyday life experiences and demanded, increasingly, that the content of their university education be relevant to the solution of social problems.

While agreeing with the general student demand for a growing interaction between the academy and the world outside of its walls, African American students also audaciously called into question the American academy's dominant Eurocentric perspective—the unchallenged assumption that Western European culture is superior, neutral, and normative. Labeling this orientation ethnocentric, African American students charged that Western education, wittingly and otherwise, diminished, distorted, and, in many instances, obliterated the contributions of African peoples to world development generally and the contributions of African Americans to America's development specifically. Therefore, African American students demanded that the university establish courses of study that provided a systematic examination of African and African-descended peoples' experiences.

Responding to the powerful challenge of these student activists, many institutions of higher learning across the nation hurriedly implemented African American or Black Studies programs as appeasement measures. Under these circumstances, little long-range planning (academic or financial) took place, since many university officials considered the issue an aberration or fad and hoped that it would shortly disappear. Significantly, many universities decided to isolate Black Studies enterprises rather than to force traditional academic departments to transform their curricula to include the study of the black experience. In many instances, early African American Studies units drew on any African American faculty member already at the university—even if the person had no intellectual interest or academic preparation in the area—or any white faculty member who might be interested in race-related issues. More commonly, as African American students demanded that courses on the black experience be taught by black people, universities quickly sought to hire more black faculty members. In that highly charged period, some new faculty possessed Ph.D.s in their fields, but many did not; some well-established black scholars decided not to affiliate with Black Studies; and some well-prepared black intellectuals were overlooked. Consequently, the view emerged in this early period that many African American Studies enterprises were designed to fail.

The eruption of what generally was called Black Studies in the late 1960s can best be understood as an institutional representation of the contemporary African American struggle for collective survival, socioeconomic advancement, and human rights. After having seen the white South's terroristic reaction to civil rights activists' peaceful protests, African Americans found it difficult to believe that the American social order would soon end the oppression of African Americans.

Citing the limitations of the integrationist civil rights philosophy and social practice for bettering the circumstances of black Americans, the Nation of Islam and its chief spokesman, Malcolm X, urged urban African American masses across the nation to unite on the basis of black nationalist ideology and to expand their struggle beyond the narrow confines of the civil rights agenda to the global issue of human rights. Calling on African Americans to take their cause to the United Nations, Malcolm viewed human rights as an overall framework that included a struggle for the following: (1) personal worth and human dignity, (2) family stability and community solidarity, (3) literacy and quality education, (4) economic self-sufficiency and collective well-being, and (5) democratic political rights and self-determination. Malcolm X urged African Americans to take pride in themselves and their African heritage. He argued that black communities should control and support their own political and economic institutions. He admonished black Americans to respect their women and to clean up themselves and their communities by removing the socially destructive evils of family disintegration, alcoholism, drug abuse, and crime. In short, Malcolm challenged African Americans to improve the overall moral character and social stability of their communities.

The rhetoric of civil rights leaders and the decade of actual advances in legal rights had meanwhile fostered hopes in black communities for quick changes in economic and social conditions. Such changes, of course, were not forthcoming, and the dashed hopes for social and political self-determination produced violent revolts in Harlem, Watts, Detroit, Cleveland, Newark, and other cities outside of the American south. These powerful and defiant protests shook the nation and, in the summer of 1966, ushered in a new era, signaled by the discourse of "Black Power" (Forman, 1972; Stone, 1968).

On May 29, 1966, Congressman Adam Clayton Powell, Jr., Chairman of the U. S. House of Representatives' Committee on Education and Labor and one of America's few progressive African American politicians, articulated the need for "black power" in his baccalaureate address at Howard University. He asserted: "Human rights are God-given. Civil rights are man-made. . . . Our life must be purposed to implement human rights. . . . To demand these God-given rights is to seek *black power*—the power to build black institutions of splendid achievement" (Stone, 1968, p. 189). A week later, during the James Meredith protest march in Mississippi, Student Non-Violent Coordinating Committee activists Willie Ricks and Stokely Carmichael led the chant, "We want black power, we want black power" (Carson, 1981; Forman, 1972; Stone, 1968).

As with any political slogan, interpretations of Black Power differed. Although many civil rights leaders criticized the term, others appropriated it for their own agendas by articulating a variety of meanings, including group solidarity, cultural pride, political power, economic power, defensive violence, anti-integrationism, community control, black nationalism, and human rights. In 1967, Stokely Carmichael and Roosevelt University political scientist Charles Hamilton sought to define and clarify this new political vision when they wrote that Black Power

> is a call for black people in this country to unite, to recognize their heritage, to build a sense of community. It is a call for black people to begin to define their own goals, to lead their own organizations and to support those organizations. It is a call to reject the racist institutions and values of this society (1967, p. 44).

This conception of Black Power set forth the vivid necessity for African-descended Americans to center their political outlook and social practice on their own collective concerns. The concentrated focus on Black Power—its accentuation of African American collective interests—characterized the ideological milieu within which African American Studies emerged.

The establishment of African American Studies was insurrectionary and emancipatory in at least two ways. First, as case studies of events at San Francisco State University (Chrisman, 1969; McEvoy and Miller, 1969), Merritt College (Walton, 1969), and Cornell University (Edwards, 1970 and 1980) disclose, African American Studies erupted in the context of university protest. African American students and their supporters sought to challenge and transform the policies and practices of institutional racism.

Second, African American Studies represented a bold movement that undertook to unmask the power/knowledge configuration of Eurocentrism and the white cultural domination characteristic of the American academy. The new field of study sought to resist the rigid barriers between traditional academic disciplines by emphasizing an innovative multidisciplinary approach to teaching and learning. Additionally, African American Studies challenged the ideological basis of the Eurocentric paradigm, which assumes that the Western European structure of knowledge is true, objective, and politically neutral, applicable equally to all peoples and circumstances. This organization of knowledge resulted in a representation of civilization that not only idealizes Western culture and thought but devalues all others. From the standpoint of the Eurocentric knowledge structure, Western European views and values are and should be the human norm; hence, other cultures can be discounted insofar as they deviate from the norm. In this regard, literary scholar Edward Said has observed:

> The entire history of nineteenth-century European thought is filled with such discriminations as these, made between what is fitting for us and what is fitting for them, the former designated as inside, in place, common, belonging, in a word *above*, the latter, who are designated as outside, excluded, aberrant, inferior, in a word *below*. . . . The large cultural-national designation of European culture as the privileged norm carried with it a formidable battery of other distinctions between ours and theirs, between proper and improper, European and non-European, higher and lower: they are to be found everywhere in such subjects and quasi-subjects as linguistics, history, race theory, philosophy, anthropology, and even biology. But my

main reason for mentioning them here is to suggest how in the transmission and persistence of a culture there is a continual process of reinforcement, by which the hegemonic culture will add to itself the prerogatives given it by its sense of national identity, its power as an implement, ally, or branch of the state, its rightness, its exterior forms and assertions of itself: and most important, by its vindicated power as a victor over everything not itself (1983, pp. 13–14).

In similar fashion, Carolyn Gerald, arguing from the stand-point of the Black Aesthetic movement—a cultural and literary movement that paralleled the emergence of African American Studies in the late 1960s—assailed white American racial and cultural projections of its self-image and the historic practice of excluding a projection of the African American self-image. She stated:

> Concomitant with that projection for several hundred years— ever since the black man has come within the sphere of influence of the white—the moral and aesthetic associations of black and white have been mixed up with race. Thus, the negative reflec- tion of ourselves is, in the white man's system, the reverse side of his positive projection of himself. The white man has devel- oped a myth of superiority based on images which compare him symbolically with the black man. The very fact of this inter- connection is at once a holdover from previous bondage and the most effective means of perpetuating that bondage. We realize now that we are involved in a black-white war over the control of image. For to manipulate an image is to control a peoplehood. Zero image has for a long time meant the repres- sion of our peoplehood (1972, pp. 352–353).

Since Eurocentrism lay at the base of most discourse within the American academy, many African American Studies theorists and practitioners saw their task as contesting and transforming the received ideas, entrenched institutions, and questionable values of the Eurocentric tradition. But there was no consensus on what Black Studies programs should attempt. There were differing intellectual and ideological tendencies corresponding largely to the ambiguous interpretations of Black Power. There- fore, during its first decade, Black Studies was characterized by a variety of orientations even while improvising upon the academy's Eurocentric tradition.

The advocacy of a critical approach grounded in black cultural nationalism was a major intellectual tendency during the establishment of African American Studies enterprises. Harold Cruse, author of the widely read and debated book *The Crisis of the Negro Intellectual* (1967) was one of the strongest proponents of this view. At the 1968 Yale University symposium of Black Studies, Cruse attacked the integrationist ethic of American scholarship, arguing that it had precluded the development of a viable black social theory on which to ground Black Studies. For him, any intellectually valid Black Studies curriculum had to rest on the ideology of black cultural nationalism and had to employ a critical historical approach. Cruse remarked:

> It is my belief that cultural nationalism as an ideology, nurturing the whole desire and thrust toward a black studies program, can only be understood if it is approached, first, historically, and then, by analyzing many of the deep problems which enmesh the Negro intelligentsia today. All over the country, in different aspects of the black movement we can see a general thrashing about, a frenetic search for method, and a search for both internal and external criticisms (1968, p. 7).

Cruse suggested that Black Studies should focus its attention on black institutional development on all levels—cultural, political, economic, and social. While he called for a self-critical analysis—that is, investigation of the impact of the Protestant Ethic on African American social development; of W. E. B. Du Bois' talented tenth thesis and the historical origins of the black intellectual class; and of the clash between radical-revolutionary and reformist-gradualist tendencies within the black movement—Cruse cautioned that Black Studies should not be too narrowly conceived. Rather, he argued for a critical investigation of the larger American cultural dynamic:

> Black cultural nationalism has to be seen as an attempt, a necessary historical attempt, to deal with another kind of cultural nationalism that is implied in our society, namely, the cultural nationalism of the dominant white group. You might call it a kind of cultural "particularism" which is found when you examine the cultural particularism of the Anglo-Saxon group or the WASP. . . . I think we find that an ideology exists which *has* to deny the validity of other kinds of cultural values that might compete with its own standards—whether in the social sciences, the arts, literature, or economic activity. We find this particularism of the Anglo-American implicit in all that is done in our society, whether it is done unconsciously or consciously (1968, p. 9).

Cruse goes on:

> Black Studies must make the dominant particularism, the dominant racial creed, more capable of dealing with the internal crises facing us all. . . . I think that those who would institute the black studies program must not only understand their own particular black history but must also grapple with, and understand, the dual tradition that has been nurtured in this society and that has given our society its unique character. I think the question of a black studies program—even if it expresses black particularism—is a kind of particularism which understands its own limits and its social function. Its social function is not to replace one particularism with another particularism but to counterbalance the historical effects and exaggeration of particularism toward a more racially balanced society, a society which would include expectations regarding the democratic creed (1968, pp. 9–10).

For Cruse, then, Black Studies needed to employ a historical approach, grounded in black cultural nationalism, that critically examined both developments and contradictions within the African American population as well as the manifestations of the larger American cultural apparatus and its effects on black consciousness.

Another intellectual tendency during the formative stage of Black Studies was to define the new enterprise as almost solely an examination of the black experience because the white academy had omitted it. Although advocates of this program also sought to break the interpretive domination of the conventional Eurocentric paradigm, the effect ultimately would have been to replace white particularism with the black particularism against which Harold Cruse earlier had cautioned. In an article titled "Toward a Sociology of Black Studies," Maurice Jackson advocated this point of view when he defined the meaning and scope of Black Studies in the following manner:

> Black studies, simply put, is the systematic study of black people. In this sense Black studies differs from academic disciplines which stress white experiences by being based on black experiences. Black studies is an examination of the deeper truths of black life. It treats the black experience both as it has unfolded over time and as it is currently manifested. These studies will examine the valid part that black people have played in man's development in society. In so doing, Black studies will concentrate on both the distinctiveness of black people from, and their interdependence with, other people. To develop this kind of

knowledge, Black studies must extend beyond the limits prejudice has placed on knowledge of black people (1970, p. 132).

By studying African American achievements, Jackson maintained, Black Studies could foster a sense of black pride among African Americans. In the examination of the African American experience, however, Jackson rejected the race-relations and ethnic minority approaches of conventional sociological analysis. Noting that these approaches assumed that black people could or should be studied only in relation to white people, Jackson argued that black people should be studied on their own terms. Because of different life experiences and values, white scholars lacked the necessary sensibility to gather and assess adequately information about the African American experience. Therefore, according to Jackson, black scholars were more appropriate for examining the African American experience, past and present. They would be the best interpreters of that experience.

This intellectual tendency within Black Studies also questions the notion of the political or value neutrality of received knowledge. Jackson pointed out that "cultural values play a dominant part in the selection of problems for study and the application of formulated knowledge" (1970, p. 134). A similar view is expressed by James Turner, of Cornell University's Africana Studies and Research Center, who criticized the idea that scholars have little control over the application of knowledge. Turner wrote:

> For many professional black educators any question of the relationship of ideology to what they teach makes them uneasy. They would most likely be inclined to consider the discussion of black studies . . . as a subjective approach to learning and a sort of sectarian encroachment that would demean the academic quality of their work. But, while it is true that facts must derive from objective discourse, we must not become confused by the facade that education is value-free and above the social system when in fact it is the axis for the development of the ideology of society. Education for blacks must consider the need to break down "false consciousness." It must seek to reveal to black people—by facts, by emotionally powerful experiences and by argument—the machinations of oppression (quoted in Hare, 1974, pp. 256–257).

Although the focus on the "black experience" generally referred to the African American experience, another intellectual tendency defined African American Studies in more global terms. According to this view, the Eurocentric knowledge system is a particularism that is at best fragmented and partial knowledge; at worst, it is fictionalized data that is widely accepted. This more global intellectual perspective sees African American Studies as an expansion of the frontiers of knowledge beyond the singular and limited discourse of Eurocentrism. The original statement of objectives of the African American Studies Program at the University of Maryland, Baltimore County, exemplified this orientation:

> The broad goal of the UMBC African American Studies program is to provide a new horizon in liberal arts education that seeks a reunification of knowledge of the human experience. By broadening the basis of knowledge, it hopes to strike at the narrowness and ethnocentrism of the traditional disciplines which are at the root of much prejudice and racial misunder-standing. Western education developed alongside Western civili-zation and understandably to serve the needs of the West; consequently, it has been one-sided in approach, incomplete in content and culture bound in orientation. In the process, it wittingly and otherwise played down and in places distorted the contributions of other peoples to world development. The African American Studies program thus seeks to provide a center for the systematic study, research and dissemination of informa-tion about the contributions of Africans and peoples of the African diaspora to the development of the world (UMBC, 1973–1974, p. 78).

Finally, African American Studies, from its inception, sought to challenge and change the Eurocentric paradigm's rigid barriers between traditional academic disciplines by emphasiz-ing multidisciplinary and interdisciplinary studies. Not only were African American Studies programs to incorporate courses from many conventional disciplines (multidisciplinary), but faculty and courses would seek to trespass and criss-cross tradi-tional academic disciplinary boundaries. Describing this more global approach, University of Pittsburgh administrator Donald Henderson pointed out:

> The primary goal of this department should be to provide the student with an encompassing knowledge of the history, culture, life-styles and futures of Africans and/or Afro-Americans. Such a department, unlike present substantive departments, would have to be truly interdisciplinary. Its membership would of necessity represent most of the established departments of the social sciences and the humanities. It is conceivable that geolo-gists, biologists, geneticists and others from the natural sciences

might be responsible for certain aspects of this department's program. The department would offer a broad concentration in African and Afro-American studies which would include, for example, surveys of art, literature, history, philosophy, religion, biology, economics, etc., as these areas contribute to an understanding of the world black experience. A student would be able to specialize, for example, in African Studies or Afro-American Studies with emphasis on the black experience in anglo-saxon cultures, or Afro-American Studies with emphasis on the black experience in latin cultures. . . . In short, the student would become reasonably knowledgeable about the experiences of black people in a certain large geographical area and their relations to all other blacks in the world (1971, pp. 15–16).

Summing up this expansive approach to African American Studies, Henderson remarked:

> The Department of African and Afro-American Studies must be truly interdisciplinary and its members must be meta-disciplinarians. They must be academically and intellectually able to range across a variety of traditional areas with facility and sophistication. Obviously the selection of personnel will be a principal factor in the operation of such a department. The traditional and often arbitrary boundaries that divide sociology from history or philosophy from economics will not only be undesirable but dysfunctional in carrying out the mission of this department (1971, pp. 16–17).

Clearly, a number of differing ideological positions found expression in the implementation of early Black Studies enterprises. In addition, depending on local institutional arrangements and circumstances, a variety of organizational designs (programs, centers, departments) characterized the emerging field's formation. The highly charged times of the late 1960s and early 1970s did not promote ideological and organizational uniformity. In light of Black Studies' turbulent implementation process—the often nonnegotiable demands of strident student advocates for Black Studies and the differing definitions of the field by its theorists and practitioners—it was largely inevitable that problems would emerge and that criticisms would arise. The next section addresses these matters.

BLACK STUDIES: CONTRADICTIONS AND DILEMMAS
By the late 1970s, Black Studies began to suffer growing pains resulting from the 1974–1975 economic recession and the repression of black student and other insurgent movements (see

Donner, 1980; 1990; O'Reilly, 1989). Many Black Studies opera-tions, implemented hastily and often without much thought and planning in the late 1960s and early 1970s, closed down. The financial crisis sweeping the nation caused many universities to experience severe financial setbacks. Many universities had to reduce the budget and resource allocations of academic pro-grams. Perhaps hardest hit were disciplines within the human-ities; students reflected the uncertainties of economic crisis by choosing courses of study more immediately job related. Because Black Studies units still were in their infancy, resource and budgetary reductions especially hurt them.

It also was during the mid-1970s and early 1980s that criticism of Black Studies gained increasing professional and public attention. Some critics charged that Black Studies was reverse racism. Others noted that many Black Studies programs suffered because of internal conflicts and poor leadership. Still others maintained that Black Studies was intellectually bankrupt. Additionally, there were critics who both pointed out some weaknesses of Black Studies program and blamed universities for not adequately supporting Black Studies enterprises (Allen, 1974; Colt, 1981; Malveaux, 1980; Poinsett, 1973; *U. S. News and World Report,* 1973). What follows is a brief attempt to capture some aspects of the critical environment surrounding Black Studies at its beginning and later during the 1980s.

At the 1968 Yale University symposium on Black Studies, Harvard political scientist Martin Kilson declared a profound skepticism regarding the establishment of Black Studies as an organized academic unit. Kilson, like many black scholars, chose not to affiliate with Black Studies but to remain in the traditional academic department. He was particularly concerned about what the impact of a "black racialist outlook" would be on the interpretation of the black experience. He argued that black nationalists would be selective in marshalling evidence and historical data in order to fashion an analysis of the black experi-ence that would ipso facto castigate whites and thus endow black people with a special aura of righteousness. Pointing to the African entrepreneurial involvement in the Atlantic slave trade, Kilson contended that oppression has been practiced not only by whites but by human beings everywhere. Therefore, he main-tained, "the black experience is . . . little more than an offshoot of the human experience—no better and no worse" (1968, p. 15). Kilson then rejected "the viewpoint that the black man's experience with white oppression has endowed black men with a special insight into oppression and thus a special capacity to rid human affairs of oppression" (1968, pp. 15–16).

Five years later, in a *Journal of Black Studies* article, Kilson renewed his concern for the future development of Black Studies. He discussed four issues. First, he maintained that because of the interdisciplinary complexity of Black Studies, its faculty should originate from the traditional academic disciplines and that students should receive a sound background in a conventional discipline in addition to coursework in Black Studies. Kilson wrote:

> The significant issue is to guarantee that students—especially those marked for graduate school and professional schools—who pursue Black Studies are simultaneously grounded in an established academic and technical discipline. A Black Studies curriculum, like other interdisciplinary curricula (American Studies, Asian Studies) cannot stand alone: it must, so to speak, be clothed in the tested scholarly and technical garment of an established discipline (1973, p. 307).

Second, in discussing who should major in Black Studies, Kilson soundly criticized the tendency among some militant black students to discourage white students from participating in Black Studies. He condemned this separatist tendency in Black Studies, arguing that in fact most black students should major in the scientific and technical fields. This is the kind of educational preparation required to transform the subordinate economic and political status of the black community, Kilson asserted:

> No amount of psychological, therapeutic, or symbolic dependence upon Black Studies should be permitted to prevent this development; if it does, the road to group suicide awaits us, for in the coming decades American society will be more, not less, dependent upon scientific and technological skills (1973, p. 309).

In Kilson's view, majors in Black Studies should be "those special students, black or white, who have a serious appreciation of and good aptitude for the social sciences and the humanities" (1973, p. 310).

Finally, Kilson called for the depoliticization of Black Studies in order to ensure that the education of students in this field would rest on an academically and technically sound foundation. He charged that white university administrators and faculty members contributed to the academic weakness of Black Studies by yielding to militant student demands and by ignoring usual academic standards and procedures in the organization of Black

Studies units and the appointment of black faculty. Concluding, Kilson issued a major challenge to Black Studies.

> Unless this psychological immaturity, nearly endemic to the militants in the Black Studies movement, soon ceases, a large section of blacks who seek intellectual status will be relegated to the backwaters or the trash-heap of American academic and intellectual life. Perhaps, alas, this is the unconscious wish—a kind of death wish—of large segments of militant black students and intellectuals. Lacking the stamina and special stuff required of first-class students and scholars, these militant black students and teachers sport a fashionable and psychologically gratifying militant style in order to achieve a protected and segregated (but academically undemanding and inferior) educational niche called a Black Studies program (1973, p. 313).

Kilson made his case in the early and heady days of Black Studies. As university campuses quieted down after the turbulent 1960s, a seeming (and probably inevitable) backlash occurred in the late 1970s and 1980s in the form of mounting complaints about the academic and intellectual integrity, viability, and adequacy of the Black Studies enterprise. The youthful field of inquiry was under attack.

Duke University English professor Kenny Williams is representative of this backlash. Writing in a 1981 issue of *Change* magazine, she leveled a harsh critique at the field. Williams contended that the image of Black Studies had come to be confused, wittingly or otherwise, with the relaxation of academic and professional standards. Echoing Kilson's previous concerns, Williams charged that students, faculty, and administrators perceived Black Studies as a collection of easy courses that was intellectually empty and simply gratified political and emotional demands. Examining trends in the development of Black Studies, Williams blamed many universities for yielding to strident black student demands and hastily installing Black Studies curricula taught by newly hired faculty who often lacked conventional academic credentials and preparation. Williams charged:

> Unwittingly colleges and universities that prided themselves on their broadmindedness and their commitment to the "search for truth" supported the notion that Black Studies ought to be a program for black students. Even the academic purists, who insisted upon standards for everyone else, were frequently convinced that this was one area where relaxed standards were acceptable. They were aided in this misconception by students who often found some emotional security in minority-based

social programs passed off as Black Studies. And to make these efforts the more fascinating and visible, many colleges and universities hired popular radicals and "media darlings" to augment the staff. In time few institutions were without their house radical who shouted at them and made them feel guilty, while they themselves dismissed as "inconsequential" such things as academic standards and honest research (1981, p. 31).

According to Williams, many Black Studies enterprises remained unstable because institutions of higher learning employed a revolving door policy in regard to faculty hiring. This instability may have been inevitable, given the impact of the economic challenges and retrenchment of the times and the growth of the other "new studies": Women's Studies, Latino Studies, Asian American Studies, and Native American Studies. Nevertheless, because universities consistently applied the law of publish or perish, many Black Studies faculty were refused tenure and left the department. Black faculty members who could marshal enough protest support from black students and white sympathizers were able to win tenure by way of political bargaining. The outcome of all this was that many Black Studies programs were viewed as temporary while their faculty remained virtual outsiders or invisible within the university community.

Williams leveled a series of additional charges. She attacked university officials for employing budgetary management strategies to constrain Black Studies operations. She criticized black students' contradictory behavior and attitudes with respect to Black Studies. Some of these students, Williams observed, advocated Black Studies but refused to take these courses, not wanting Black Studies courses to appear on their transcripts. Some students enrolled in Black Studies courses seeking racial pride, while others expected African American professors to pass them automatically because of their common racial heritage. Finally, she criticized as racist the academy's rejection of Black Studies as an intellectually sound enterprise but its willing acceptance of the field as academically marginal. Speaking about the foreseeable future, Williams remarked cynically:

There will, of course, remain for some time the brand of academic racism—both intentional and otherwise—that negates Black Studies as a scholarly discipline while accepting the Black Studies syndrome as a substitute. Our colleagues will remain for some time well-meaning and self-serving; continue to smile tolerantly when we speak of literary standards as applied to Afro-American literature; expect all of us to be authorities "on the race"; and in their discussions with us, unwittingly support Du Bois' 1903 declaration that the major problem of the twentieth century will be the color line (1981, pp. 36–37).

With contradictions and dilemmas confronting Black Studies, an awareness emerged about the need to address critics' charges (see Davidson and Weaver, 1985; Farrell and Bridges, 1987). Leading Black Studies professionals and theorists put forward proposals to improve the status and image of the field. Perhaps the major strategies for renewal were efforts to stabilize, standardize, and (re)conceptualize the African American Studies' curriculum and philosophical foundation.

FROM BLACK STUDIES TO AFRICAN AMERICAN STUDIES: TOWARD INSTITUTIONALIZATION

Over the past decade, a major goal of African American Studies practitioners has been to institutionalize the field—to build a permanent foundation within the academy. Although some tensions remain between the university and African American Studies, there has been a gradual shift from the strictly reactive strategies by both parties that characterized the turbulent 1960s to forms of mutual adjustment. This and the desire for a more uniform name of the field might explain why many newer enterprises, developing in the late 1970s and after, called themselves African American Studies.

In its current and still evolving phase, a major strategy to institutionalize African American Studies has been the endeavor to standardize the curriculum. In 1980, the National Council for Black Studies, the field's professional organization, adopted a core curriculum for Black Studies (see Alkalimat and Associates, 1986; and Gordon, 1981). The purpose was to establish a model curriculum that would provide a coherent framework for standardizing African American Studies as a consistent field of study. The model core curriculum includes three broad course areas—social/behavioral studies, historical studies, and cultural studies—with four levels of courses. The first level is an introduction to the three broad course areas. The second level contains courses that review and survey basic literature on the black experience within the categories of social/behavioral studies, historical studies, and cultural studies. The third level includes advanced courses that explore current research methods and analysis on emerging issues within the three broad categories. The fourth level consists of senior seminars that integrate, synthesize, and apply knowledge acquired in previous courses with the goal of reconsidering and reassessing current issues in the field. At this level, students prepare for further research, graduate study, or the work world.

An ongoing issue in the attempts at institutionalization is the search for a philosophical or theoretical grounding for the field of African American Studies. There are a number of competing theoretical, philosophical, and ideological viewpoints in the evolving field. Maulana Karenga, chair of the Pan-African Studies Department at California State University at Long Beach, sets forth a conceptualization of the field in his textbook, *Introduction to Black Studies* (1982). Karenga's contribution is grounded in his long-standing black cultural nationalist theory of Kawaida, which seeks to encompass all aspects of the black experience. As he states:

> The scope of Black Studies as a discipline is the totality of historical and current Black thought and practice, but expresses itself most definitively in seven core subject areas: 1) Black History; 2) Black Religion; 3) Black Social Organization; 4) Black Politics; 5) Black Economics; 6) Black Creative Production (Black Art, Black Music and Black Literature); and 7) Black Psychology. As an interdisciplinary discipline concerned with the coherence and unity of its subject areas, Black Studies, of necessity, has core integrative principles and assumptions that serve as thematic glue which holds together these core subject areas.

Karenga continues by identifying four "integrative principles and assumptions":

> Each subject area of Black Studies is a vital aspect and area of the Black experience and, therefore, contributive to the understanding and appreciation of its wholeness. Secondly, the truth of the Black experience is whole and thus, any partial and compartmentalized approach to it can only yield a partial and incomplete image and understanding of it. Thirdly, effectively integrated into the pattern of the discipline as a whole, each subject area becomes a microcosm of the macrocosm, the Black experience, which not only enriches our knowledge of the Black experience, but also enhances the analytical process and products of the discipline itself. Finally, all the subject areas mesh and intersect not only at the point of their primary focus, i.e., Black people in the process of shaping reality in their own image and interest, but also in their self-conscious commitment and contribution to the definition and solution of the social and discipline problems which serve as the core challenges to Black Studies (1982, pp. 37–38).

Molefi K. Asante, editor of the *Journal of Black Studies* and chair of the Department of African American Studies at Temple University, is another leading African American Studies theorist and well-known formulator of "Afrocentricity" or "Africalogy" (Asante, 1980; 1987; 1990; Asante and Asante, 1990). Afrocentricity is an interpretive strategy and theoretical framework that is directed at the examination of all human phenomena from an African-centered world view. This world view comes out of an exhaustive investigation of African and African American cultural history.

This African-centered standpoint can offer an alternative to the dominant Eurocentric paradigm and reveal its shortcomings by exposing its particularity, ethnocentrism, and subjectivity. While maintaining that the Eurocentric tradition is valid within its own context, Asante asserts that this tradition becomes imperialistic when it is presumed to be objective and equally applicable to all people and circumstances. Hence, Afrocentric criticism emphatically rejects Eurocentrism's representation of its view as universal and absolute. Asante does not arrogantly assert that Afrocentricity is the only interpretation of the world. Afrocentric critical practice is an interpretation of the world, according to Asante, from a particular philosophical and ideological standpoint. For example, Asante suggests that one of Afrocentricity's crucial elements is the notion of harmony and complementarity—the idea that entities can be different and yet complement each other. Asante remarks:

> In the Afrocentric conception of literature and orature, the critical method would be employed to determine to what degree the writer or speaker contributed to the unity of the symbols, the elimination of chaos, the making of peace among disparate views, and the creation of an opportunity for harmony and hence balance. . . . Harmony, in the sense that I am speaking of it, is an equilibrium among the various factors impinging upon communication (1987, pp. 177–178).

Asante points out how much the Afrocentric concept of harmony differs from the conception of oppositional dichotomies so fundamental to Eurocentric consciousness. He notes that dichotomization pervades the Eurocentric structure of knowledge; people and things are generally grouped on the basis of their opposition to each other—for example, European/African, male/female, mind/body, reason/emotion, or science/nature. Moreover, the opposing categories are hierarchically related within the

Eurocentric dualist conception of the world. That is, one of the dichotomous elements is superior to and therefore should dominate or negate the other: European over African, male over female, mind over body, reason over emotion, or science over nature. Parenthetically, this central dimension of the Eurocentric outlook might well be a driving force behind Western cultural aggression and exploitation based on class, race, and gender.

Asante suggests that Afrocentricity should become the theoretical and critical framework of African American Studies:

> As a relatively new field African-American Studies must take steps that might appear rather undramatic to most observers yet these steps are essential for a proper understanding of this novel coalescence within the academy. One of those steps involves the definition of the field in a way that distinguishes it from the study of black people in general by scholars, black and white, in other fields. In other words, the study of black people is not African/African-American Studies. If that were so we could argue that African-American Studies has existed for a hundred years. It is not the study of blacks that is the fundamental issue but the study of blacks and others from an afrocentric perspective; this is the locus of African-American Studies. . . . It is the congruence of object and subject (1986, pp. 258–259).

Another effort to conceptualize and institutionalize African American Studies is found in sociologist Abdul Alkalimat and associates' textbook, *Introduction to Afro-American Studies* (1986). Although the underlying interpretive approach of the text is Marxist, the authors indicate that their aim is to provide a unifying theoretical framework that can incorporate competing ideological tendencies in African American Studies.

> Our text is based on a paradigm of unity for Black Studies, a framework in which all points of view can have the most useful coexistence. While maintaining a dynamic process of debate, everyone involved can remain united and committed to the field. This includes Marxists, nationalists, pan-Africanists, and old-fashioned civil rights integrationists as well. Further, our specific orientation is anti-racist, anti-sexist, and anti-capitalist. We are basing our analysis on most of our Black intellectual tradition and that leads us, as it did Langston Hughes, Paul Robeson, and W. E. B. Du Bois, to a progressive socialist position. This text, therefore, has a definite point of view, but it presents the basis for clarity, understanding, and dialogue between different schools of thought and different disciplines (1986, pp. 21–22).

Besides the competing viewpoints just discussed, there are differences in programs, the organization and curricula of African American Studies, according to their institutional environments. So the outcome of current efforts to standardize the curriculum and to develop a critical theoretical practice of African American Studies is uncertain. Moreover, it is not clear that the National Council for Black Studies can ensure that African American Studies enterprises across the nation will conform to a model core curriculum. In fact, one must ask whether there should be conformity to a model curriculum and a single theoretical or ideological orientation in African American Studies. Most fields of study do not display this kind of uniformity. Perhaps an alternative is to allow a more flexible and innovative atmosphere in which African American Studies can continue to grow and develop.

Clearly, one future challenge for African American Studies is to move beyond its marginal image and status within the academy. An equally if not more important future challenge is to deal with the intellectual and social implications of the changing character of American society as the declining industrial-manufacturing order gives way to a rising postindustrial-managerial order.

CONCLUSION: AFRICAN AMERICAN STUDIES IN THE EMERGING POSTINDUSTRIAL-MANAGERIAL AGE

The postindustrial-managerial transformation of American society is characterized by the transition from a capital-intensive economy based on physical resources, which dominated the first half of this century, to a knowledge-intensive economy based on human resources, which characterizes the last half of this century. The principal resource in America's declining capital-intensive economy has been finance capital, invested in industrial plants, machinery, and technologies to increase the muscle power of human labor. In the emerging knowledge-intensive economy, the decisive resource is cultural capital: the nation's investment in and management of education, knowledge, computers, and other technologies that enhance the mental capacity of workers (Botkin, Dimancescu, and Stata, 1984; Drucker, 1969; Lyotard, 1984; Machlup, 1962, 1980, 1982, 1984; Reich, 1991; Toffler, 1990). Important now are specialized knowledge, communication skills, the capacity to process and utilize collections of information in strategic decision-making processes, and an increasingly professionalized/bureaucratic approach to managing people. With this expanding role for formal or specialized knowledge, professionals and experts—intellectuals and the technical intelligentsia—are becoming a "new class" in the public and private spheres, particularly with regard to policy making (see Bazelon, 1971; Derber, Schwartz, Magrass, 1990; Ehrenreich and Ehrenreich, 1979; Freidson, 1970; Galbraith, 1971; Nachmias and Rosenbloom, 1980; Perkin, 1989).

Mental capacity and managerial skills are supplanting money and manufacturing as the source of power. Learning, therefore, becomes an indispensable investment for social development, and educational credentials are more and more the key to a person's role in society (Collins, 1977). In view of these trends, many parents are becoming preoccupied with the educational advantages they can confer on their children, and many university students are realizing the importance of advanced education.

Society's new power wielders are located in government, elite universities, philanthropic foundations, the mass media, elite law firms, political action committees, and major policy research institutions (see Benveniste, 1972; Burnham, 1960; Fischer, 1990; Keane, 1984; Lebedoff, 1981; Smith, 1991). Their influence comes from the capacity to conceptualize the character of social issues and to design strategies for handling them; they also produce and manage ideas and images that direct the cultural, intellectual, and ideological development of society. For example, the current debate about the urban underclass and social welfare policy reform includes policy intellectuals of various ideological persuasions (see Auletta, 1982; Cottingham, 1982; Jencks and Peterson, 1991; Jones, 1992; Lawson, 1992; Mead, 1992; Murray, 1984; Wilson, 1987). Living by argumentation and persuasion, the new elite is not only a socioeconomic class, but it is also a cultural elite (see Darity, 1986; Fischer, 1990; Gouldner, 1979; Luke, 1989; Majone, 1989; Perkin, 1989).

This new elite does not rise to dominance by itself. To be effective, the new elite must be allied to a political, legal, or organizational base. Their power comes from their access to and their ability to influence policy makers in government and private organizations. They operate at many levels to influence the intellectual direction, content, and contours of public decision making. They may be policy specialists within the offices of political executives, intellectual activists who appear at local school board hearings, renowned university professors who consult with government officials on important policy matters, or social scientists whose research findings contribute to major court rulings.

What role will African American Studies intellectuals and scholars play in the evolving society? I think we need to respond with innovation and a critical consciousness in regard to curriculum development and strategies for social development. African American scholars will be required to pursue new knowledge that can prove useful for handling complex social problems—for example, the progressive impoverishment of urban black communities. Moreover, in the evolving global political economy that is anchored in knowledge production, distribution, and consumption (see Reich, 1991; Toffler, 1990), African American Studies will be compelled to strengthen its transdisciplinary and global thrusts by designing curricula that transgress upon the conventional academic disciplinary boundaries between the humanities and the social, behavioral, biological, and physical sciences. African American Studies needs to destroy old stereotypes, break new ground (conceptually and empirically), and broaden its intellectual scope and horizons to include attention to such areas of study as policy studies and advocacy, critical social theory, critical cultural studies, social and political ethics, futures research, organizational development, and leadership preparation.

In the process, African American Studies theorists, practitioners, and students need to remain skeptical of received knowledge and must continue to disturb the intellectual and ideological hegemony of Eurocentrism and white American chauvinism within the academy. I am not at all suggesting an end to the study of Western culture. However, because the Eurocentric perspective and white American chauvinism continue to set the terms of intellectual discourse and dictate the academy's accepted structure of knowledge, I advocate a more careful and critical investigation of Western European culture and its American legacy—but with a different and even irreverent interpretive lens refracted by African American Studies and the other "new studies" (see Hayes, 1989). Western civilization and its cultural heritage need to be seen and understood not as superior to others but as part of a democratic community of world civilizations and cultures. There is no normative civilization and culture.

Importantly, African American Studies scholars and intellectuals must be determined to grapple with the implications of the emerging postindustrial-managerial estate for African Americans and other historically oppressed peoples. How will this new social order affect such real human concerns as individual dignity and human worth; family stability and community solidarity; literacy and quality education; economic well-being and self-sufficiency; and democratic political rights and self-determination? African American Studies cannot ignore the examination of the consequences of a progressively changing world.

African American Studies, as a critically conscious intellectual endeavor, needs to hammer out a concept of social justice and morality that encompasses the growing multicultural and multiracial nature of America's evolving society. Cultural critic Jim Merod sets forth some guidelines for this project:

> The critic's task is not only to question truth in its present guises. It is to find ways of putting fragments of knowledge, partial views, and separate disciplines in contact with questions about the use of expert labor so that the world we live in can be seen for what it is. Thus the virtue of defining critical work in terms of opposition to the state rather than (or at least alongside) transgression of intellectual norms is that it offers the possibility of defining criticism as an ally of demoted people and of an intensified political process. Critical analysis cannot be relegated to text-bound labor unless critics insist upon fighting among themselves for purely professional authority. That, ironically, is what Foucault's transgressive strategy calls for. The larger authority of the democratic enterprise—to put public needs and general human welfare into open conflict with the depoliticized mystique of Western institutions (the professionalization of expert knowledge in government, science, technology, law, and education)—can be fought for, nevertheless, by critics who work against the authorization of existing power by technical and professional elites. Such work requires not just negational suspicion, rampant skepticism, but proposals and concepts from which more just institutions may emerge. Justice requires that everyone have access to all information in a political system that develops the organized energy of once excluded interests and identities. This access is not wholly a matter of illuminating previously invisible discourse; *it depends on the emergence of previously invisible people and political positions* [emphasis added] (1987, pp. 188–189).

Thus, intellectual work is not apolitical, and African American Studies theorists and practitioners need to consider themselves involved in a struggle for identity and community beyond the domination of manipulative images and exploitative policies. This battle resides in cultural, political, and economic systems and can only culminate in dynamic systems that are not more exclusive but more inclusive.

In the last analysis, African American Studies needs to decide whether it will continue to consume the dominant modes of thinking and knowledge of the academy's intellectual and managerial elites or whether it will engage in new thinking and design an independent critical social theory and practice that will promote the expansion of the frontiers of new knowledge (for example, see Wynter, 1984a; 1984b; 1984c; 1987). These critical and uncertain times demand, therefore, that African American Studies give leadership in the academic and non-academic world by developing new strategies and tactics that could save humanity and thereby save the world African community. As we approach the tweny-first century, African American Studies will continue to develop to the extent that it remains innovative, critical, self-reflective, and emancipatory. The general purpose of this anthology is to contribute to that intellectual and practical project.

References Cited

Alkalimat, Abdul, and Associates, *Introduction to Afro-American Studies: A Peoples College Primer,* Chicago: Twenty-First Century Books & Publications, 1986.

Allen, Robert L., "Politics of the Attack on Black Studies," *The Black Scholar,* Vol. 6, No. 1 (September 1974), pp. 2–7.

Auletta, Ken, *The Underclass,* New York: Random House, Inc., 1982.

Asante, Molefi K., *Afrocentricity: The Theory of Social Change,* Buffalo: Amulefi Publishing Co., 1980.

_____, "A Note on Nathan Huggins' Report to the Ford Foundation on African-American Studies," *Journal of Black Studies,* Vol. 17, No. 2 (December 1986), pp. 255–262.

_____, *The Afrocentric Idea,* Philadelphia: Temple University Press, 1987.

_____, *Kemet, Afrocentricity and Knowledge,* Trenton: Africa World Press, Inc., 1990.

_____ and Kariamu W. Asante, eds., *African Culture: The Rhythms of Unity,* Trenton: Africa World Press, Inc., 1990.

Bazelon, David T., *Power in America: The Politics of the New Class,* New York: The New American Library, 1971.

"Black Studies Run Into Trouble on U. S. College Campuses," *U. S. News and World Report,* Vol. 74, No. 5 (January 29, 1973), pp. 29–32.

Benveniste, Guy, *The Politics of Expertise,* Berkeley: The Glendessary Press, 1972.

Botkin, James, Dan Diamancescu, and Ray Stata, *The Innovators: Rediscovering America's Creative Energy,* New York: Harper & Row, Publishers, Inc., 1984.

Burnham, James, *The Managerial Revolution,* Bloomington: Indiana University Press, 1960.

Carmichael, Stokely, and Charles V. Hamilton, *Black Power: The Politics of Liberation in America,* New York: Random House, 1967.

Carson, Clayborne, *In Struggle: SNCC and the Black Awakening of the 1960s,* Cambridge: Harvard University Press, 1981.

Chrisman, Robert, "Observations on Race and Class at San Francisco State," in James McEvoy and Abraham Miller, eds., *Black Power and Student Rebellion,* Belmont: Wadsworth Publishing Company, Inc., pp. 222–232.

Collins, Randall, *The Credential Society: An Historical Sociology of Education and Stratification,* New York: Academic Press, Inc., 1979.

Colt, George H., "Will the Huggins Approach Save Afro-American Studies?" *Harvard Magazine,* September-October 1981, pp. 38–46, 62 & 70.

Cottingham, Clement, ed., *Race, Poverty, and the Urban Underclass,* Lexington: Lexington Books/D. C. Heath and Company, 1982.

Cruse, Harold, *The Crisis of the Negro Intellectual,* New York: William Morrow and Company, Inc., 1967.

_____, "The Integrationist Ethic as a Basis for Scholarly Endeavors," in Armstead L. Robinson, Craig C. Foster, and Donald H. Ogilvie, eds., *Black Studies in the University: A Symposium,* New Haven: Yale University Press, 1969, pp. 4–12.

Darity, William A., Jr., "The Managerial Class and Industrial Policy," *Industrial Relations,* Vol. 25 (Spring 1986), pp. 217–227.

Davidson, Douglas V., and Frederick S. Weaver, "Black Studies, White Studies, and Institutional Politics," *Journal of Black Studies,* Vol. 15, No. 3 (March 1985), pp. 339–347.

Derber, Charles, William A. Schwartz, and Yale Magrass, *Power in the Highest Degree: Professionals and the Rise of a New Mandarin Order,* New York: Oxford University Press, 1990.

Donner, Frank J., *The Age of Surveillance: The Aims and Methods of America's Political Intelligence System,* New York: Alfred A. Knopf, 1980.

_____, *Protectors of Privilege: Red Squads and Police Repression in Urban America,* Berkeley: University of California Press, 1990.

Drucker, Peter F., *The Age of Discontinuity: Guidelines to Our Changing Society,* New York: Harper and Row, Publishers, 1968.

Edwards, Harry, *Black Students,* New York: The Free Press, 1970.

_____, *The Struggle That Must Be: An Autobiography,* New York: Macmillan Publishing Co., Inc., 1980.

Ehrenreich, Barbara, and John Ehrenreich, "The Professional-Managerial Class," in Pat Walker, ed., *Between Labor and Capital,* Boston: South End Press, 1979, pp. 5–45.

Farrell, Walter C., Jr., and Edgar F. Bridges, "Black Studies at the Crossroads," *Thought & Action: The NEA Higher Education Journal,* Vol. 3 (September 1987), pp. 103–112.

Fischer, Frank, *Technocracy and the Politics of Expertise,* Newbury Park: Sage Publications, 1990.

Forman, James, *The Making of Black Revolutionaries,* New York: The Macmillan Company, 1972.

Freidson, Eliot, *Professional Dominance: The Social Structure of Medical Care,* Chicago: Aldine Publishing Company, 1970.

Galbraith, John K., *The New Industrial State,* Boston: Houghton Mifflin Company, 1971.

Gerald, Carolyn F., "The Black Writer and His Role," in Addison Gayle, Jr., ed., *The Black Aesthetic,* Garden City: Doubleday & Company, Inc., 1971, pp. 349–356.

Gordon, Vivian V., "The Coming of Age of Black Studies," *The Western Journal of Black Studies,* Vol. 5, No. 3 (Fall 1981), pp. 231–236.

Gouldner, Alvin W., *The Future of Intellectuals and the Rise of the New Class,* New York: Seabury Press, 1979.

Hare, Nathan, "The Contribution of Black Sociologists to Black Studies," in James E. Blackwell and Morris Janowitz, eds., *Black Sociologists: Historical and Contemporary Perspectives,* Chicago: The University of Chicago Press, 1974, pp. 253–266.

Hayes, Floyd W. III, "Politics and Education in America's Multicultural Society: An African-American Studies' Response to Allan Bloom," *The Journal of Ethnic Studies,* Vol. 17, No. 2 (Summer 1989), pp. 71–88.

Henderson, Donald, "What Direction Black Studies?," in Henry J. Richards, ed., *Topics in Afro-American Studies,* Buffalo: Black Academy Press, Inc., 1971.

Jackson, Maurice, "Toward a Sociology of Black Studies," *Journal of Black Studies,* Vol. 1, No. 2 (December 1970), pp. 131–140.

Jencks, Christopher, and Paul E. Peterson, eds., *The Urban Underclass,* Washington, D. C.: The Brookings Institution, 1991.

Jones, Jacqueline, *The Dispossessed: America's Underclasses from the Civil War to the Present,* New York: Basic Books, 1992.

Karenga, Maulana, *Introduction to Black Studies,* Inglewood: Kawaida Publications, 1982.

Keane, John, *Public Life and Late Capitalism: Toward a Socialist Theory of Democracy,* New York: Cambridge University Press, 1984.

Kilson, Martin, Jr., "The Intellectual Validity of Studying the Black Experience," in Armstead L. Robinson, Craig C. Foster, and Donald H. Ogilvie, eds., *Black Studies in the University: A Symposium,* New Haven: Yale University Press, 1969, pp. 13–16.

———, "Reflections on Structure and Content in Black Studies," *Journal of Black Studies,* Vol. 3, No. 3 (March 1973), pp. 297–313.

Lawson, Bill E., ed., *The Underclass Question,* Philadelphia: Temple University Press, 1992.

Lebedoff, David, *The New Elite: The Death of Democracy,* New York: Franklin Watts, 1981.

Luke, Timothy W., *Screens of Power: Ideology, Dominance, and Resistance in Informational Society,* Urbana: University of Illinois Press, 1989.

Lyotard, Jean-Francois, *The Postmodern Condition: A Report on Knowledge,* trans. Geoff Bennington and Brian Massumi, Minneapolis: University of Minnesota Press, 1984.

McEvoy, James, and Abraham Miller, "San Francisco State 'On Strike . . . Shut It Down'," in McEvoy and Miller, eds., *Black Power and Student Rebellion: Conflict on the American Campus,* Belmont: Wadsworth Publishing Company, Inc., 1969, pp. 12–31.

Machlup, Fritz, *The Production and Distribution of Knowledge in the United States,* Princeton: Princeton University Press, 1962.

———, *Knowledge and Knowledge Production,* Princeton: Princeton University Press, 1980.

———, *The Branches of Learning,* Princeton: Princeton University Press, 1982.

———, *The Economics of Information and Human Capital,* Princeton: Princeton University Press, 1984.

Majone, Giandomenico, *Evidence, Argument, and Persuasion in the Policy Process,* New Haven: Yale University Press, 1989.

Malveaux, Julianne, "Black Studies: An Assessment," *Essence,* August 1980, pp. 78–79, 95, 98, 103–104.

Mead, Lawrence M., *The New Politics of Poverty: The Nonworking Poor in America,* New York: Basic Books, 1992

Merod, Jim, *The Political Responsibility of the Critic,* Ithaca: Cornell University Press, 1987.

Murray, Charles, *Losing Ground: American Social Policy, 1950–1980,* New York: Basic Books, 1984.

Nachmias, David, and David H. Rosenbloom, *Bureaucratic Government USA,* New York: St. Martin's Press, 1980.

Perkin, Harold, *The Rise of Professional Society: England Since 1880,* New York: Routledge, 1989.

Poinsett, Alex, "The Plight of Black Studies," *Ebony,* Vol. 29, No. 2 (December 1973), pp. 128–134.

Reich, Robert B., *The Work of Nations: Preparing Ourselves for 21st-Century Capitalism,* New York: Alfred A. Knopf, 1991.

Said, Edward W., *The World, the Text, and the Critic,* Cambridge: Harvard University Press, 1983.

Smith, James A., *The Idea Brokers: Think Tanks and the Rise of the New Policy Elite,* New York: The Free Press, 1991.

Stone, Chuck, *Black Power in America,* Indianapolis: The Bobbs-Merrill Company, 1968.

———, "The National Conference on Black Power," in Floyd B. Barbour, ed., *The Black Power Revolt: A Collection of Essays,* Boston: Extending Horizons Books, 1968, pp. 189–198.

Toffler, Alvin, *Powershift: Knowledge, Wealth, and Violence at the Edge of the 21st Century,* New York: Bantam Books, 1990.

UMBC Catalog 1973–1974, Baltimore: University of Maryland Baltimore County, 1973.

Walton, Sidney F., *The Black Curriculum: Developing a Program in Afro-American Studies,* East Palo Alto: Black Liberation Publishers, 1969.

Williams, Kenny J., "The Black Studies Syndrome: Down by One is Still Losing," *Change,* (October 1981), pp. 30–37.

Wilson, William J., *The Truly Disadvantaged: The Inner City, the Underclass, and Public Policy,* Chicago: The University of Chicago Press, 1987.

Wynter, Sylvia, "New Seville and the Conversion Experience of Bartolome de Las Casas," Part One, *Jamaica Journal,* Vol. 17, No. 2 (May 1984), pp. 25–32.

———, "New Seville and the Conversion Experience of Bartolome de Las Casas," Part Two, *Jamaica Journal,* Vol. 17, No. 3 (August 1984), pp. 46–55.

———, "The Ceremony Must Be Found: After Humanism," *Boundary 2,* Vol. XII, No. 1 (Spring/Fall 1984), pp. 19–70.

———, "On Disenchanting Discourse: 'Minority' Literary Criticism and Beyond," *Cultural Critique,* No. 7 (Fall 1987), pp. 207–244.

African American Studies: Trends, Developments, and Future Challenges

Why African American Studies? Why do we study any human experience? We do so in order to learn about ourselves and others. We do so in order to understand the character of social development so that we can improve the human condition. African American Studies, as the study of Africa and its global legacy, developed as a consequence of the historical relationship between Africans and Western Europeans that resulted in the dynamics of slave trading and chattel slavery, imperialism and colonialism, annihilating wars and exploitation, and segregation and racism. The field of study draws its strength from the legacy of African peoples' historic struggle for liberation and self-determination, intellectual and cultural advancement, and socioeconomic and political development. By examining the experiences of African peoples, African American Studies can provide to black students a sense of individual identity and community, and a sense of personal and collective dignity. For both black and non-black students, African American Studies can be of help in understanding other cultures, an ability especially needed in the increasingly multicultural American society. By challenging and correcting the misrepresentations of Africa and Western Europe and their cultural legacies, African American Studies can give students the intellectual tools and the moral courage to improve the human condition.

The essays in this section explore aspects of the background and character of African American Studies—why the field developed, the concern to link scholarship and social practice, and the contemporary quest for a theory and appropriate method of analysis. In his essay "The Study of the Negro," written early in this century, Carter G. Woodson decries American history's treatment of Africans and African Americans and concludes that a study of such "history" can only have a negative psychological impact on African Americans. He puts forward views similar to those employed by the creators of African American Studies in the late 1960s. Woodson, who founded the Association for the Study of Negro Life and History in 1916 and who is often referred to as the father of African American history, argues that the strategy of omitting or misrepresenting the contributions Africans have made to the development of human civilization encourages African-descended people to hate themselves and to worship Europeans. Woodson sees traditional American education as a form of intellectual control, which has behavioral consequences: "The education of the Negro then must be carefully directed lest the race may waste time trying to do the impossible. Lead the Negro to believe this and thus control his thinking. If you can thereby determine what he will think, you will not need to worry about what he will do. You will not have to tell him to go to the back door. He will go without being told; and if there is no back door he will have one cut for his special benefit." Unaware of their past, mis-educated African Americans become the tools of their oppressors and are of little use to the salvation and survival of African-descended people. The alternative to mis-education, according to Woodson, is for African-descended people to think for themselves and to act in their own interests. This requires that they undertake their own systematic study and examination of the African and African American experience.

The article by James B. Stewart, "The Legacy of W. E. B. Du Bois for Contemporary Black Studies," investigates the scholar/activist and suggests that the link between his formidable scholarship and progressive political activities constitutes a foundation and model for contemporary African American Studies.

William Edward Burghardt Du Bois was born in Great Barrington, Massachusetts in 1868, three years after the end of the Civil War; he died in Ghana, West Africa in 1963, in self-imposed exile, at the time of the momentous civil rights March on Washington. He graduated from Fisk University and obtained a Ph.D. degree from Harvard University. A sociologist, historian, essayist, novelist, and poet, Du Bois remains to this day a towering figure in the pantheon of African American intellectuals and leaders. A distinguished scholar and educator, Du Bois also became a political activist by helping to establish the National Association for the Advancement of Colored People and by being the editor of its journal *The Crisis*. A consistent advocate of racial justice, the complex Du Bois was an integrationist and a separatist, a black nationalist and a Pan-Africanist, a socialist and a communist. He championed the development of a black educated elite, the "Talented Tenth." And he opposed the conservative leader Booker T. Washington and the black nationalist leader Marcus Garvey. Du Bois not only studied structures of oppression, he also struggled to dismantle them.

Examining both Du Bois' fiction and his social-scientific work, Stewart argues that Du Bois can serve as an exemplar for today's scholars, particularly Du Bois' interdisciplinary approach to knowledge, his development of new and significant concepts, his effort to use social research to improve the life chances of African Americans, and his willingness to correct his own flawed theoretical positions. Stewart suggests that Du Bois' legacy challenges contemporary African American Studies enterprises to develop an educational method and a critical perspective that are academically sound and socially responsible.

Molefi K. Asante, in "The Search for an Afrocentric Method," seeks to establish a theory and method for examining the African and African American experience that is grounded in an African cultural and historical context. The Afrocentric critical perspective challenges the ideological dominance of the Eurocentric and white American intellectual tradition. While maintaining that the Eurocentric paradigm, or model of scholarship, may be valid within its own cultural and historical context, Asante rejects that tradition's claims to being universally valid. Afrocentric criticism does not assert that it is the sole interpretation of the world. According to Asante, Afrocentric critical practice is an interpretation of the world from a particular philosophical and ideological standpoint; this African-centered paradigm finds its essential foundation in the history, culture, and thought of African and African-descended people. One of its crucial elements is the notion of harmony or complementarity—that is, entities can be different and yet complement each other.

The Afrocentric concept of harmony contrasts sharply with the conception of dichotomies so fundamental to the Eurocentric intellectual tradition, in which people and things generally are grouped on the basis of their opposition to each other, for example, European/African, male/female, mind/body, reason/ emotion, or science/nature. Moreover, the opposing categories generally are hierarchically related; that is, one of the dichotomous elements is viewed as superior to the other and therefore should dominate or exclude it: European over African, male over female, mind over body, reason over emotion, or science over nature. This central dimension of the Eurocentric outlook may well be a driving force behind Western cultural aggression, which finds expression in complex structures of domination and exploitation based on class, race, and sex. In practical and intellectual terms, Afrocentric critical practice, with its interest in harmony and inclusion, seeks an alternative to Eurocentric cultural and intellectual domination.

Taken together, the views put forward in these essays represent progressive expressions of the intellectual vocation and collective concern of African American Studies. Carter G. Woodson's criticism of traditional education's cultural and racial exclusivity and his call for the study of the black experience are at the heart of African American Studies. The conventional academic bias for Western European culture and civilization and against all others initially energized, and continues to inspire, the demand for African American Studies. Although this field is situated within the academy, teachers and researchers in African American Studies are aware of their responsibility to be actively engaged in changing society for the better. This dual responsibility to academic excellence and to social change often is complex, ambiguous, and difficult, as W. E. B. Du Bois found out. Nevertheless, he exemplifies the committed and socially responsible intellectual—the reflective practitioner of social change—that African American Studies faculty and students need to emulate. Finally, African American Studies seeks to challenge the dominance of the Western European and white American cultural perspective as the only grounding for social analysis. Molefi Asante and others have put forth Afrocentricity as a theoretical and methodological alternative. As with any emerging critical perspective, Afrocentricity is controversial within educational institutions and among scholars and intellectuals. It offers a different and important point of view, one from the standpoint of the experience of Africans and their descendants. As a theoretical and methodological orientation in African American Studies, Afrocentricity has the potential for providing a much-needed intellectual direction and scholarly appreciation of the cultural crosscurrents in a multicultural society.

The Study of the Negro

CARTER GODWIN WOODSON

HE FACTS DRAWN FROM AN experience of more than twenty years enable us to make certain deductions with respect to the study of the Negro. Only one Negro out of every ten thousand is interested in the effort to set forth what his race has thought and felt and attempted and accomplished that it may not become a negligible factor in the thought of the world. By traditions and education, however, the large majority of Negroes have become interested in the history and status of other races, and they spend millions annually to promote such knowledge. Along with this sum, of course, should be considered the large amount paid for devices in trying not to be Negroes.

The chief reason why so many give such a little attention to the background of the Negro is the belief that this study is unimportant. They consider as history only such deeds as those of Mussolini who after building up an efficient war machine with the aid of other Europeans would now use it to murder unarmed and defenseless Africans who have restricted themselves exclusively to attending to their own business. If Mussolini succeeds in crushing Abyssinia he will be recorded in "history" among the Caesars, and volumes written in praise of the conqueror will find their way to the homes and libraries of thousands of mis-educated Negroes. The oppressor has always indoctrinated the weak with this interpretation of the crimes of the strong.

The war lords have done good only accidentally or incidentally while seeking to do evil. The movements which have ameliorated the condition of humanity and stimulated progress have been inaugurated by men of thought in lifting their fellows out of drudgery unto ease and comfort, out of selfishness unto altruism. The Negro may well rejoice that his hands, unlike those of his oppressors, are not stained with so much blood extracted by brute force. Real history is not the record of the successes and disappointments, the vices, the follies, and the quarrels of those who engage in contention for power.

From *The Mis-Education of the Negro*, edited by Charles H. Wesley and Thelma D. Perry. Africa World Press, Trenton, New Jersey.

Carter G. Woodson, founder of the Association for the Study of Negro Life and History in 1916.

The Association for the Study of Negro Life and History is projected on the fact that there is nothing in the past of the Negro more shameful than what is found in the past of other races. The Negro is as human as the other members of the family of mankind. The Negro, like others, has been up at times; and at times he has been down. With the domestication of animals, the discovery of iron, the development of stringed instruments, an advancement in fine art, and the inauguration of trial by jury to his credit, the Negro stands just as high as others in contributing to the progress of the world.

The oppressor, however, raises his voice to the contrary. He teaches the Negro that he has no worth-while past, that his race has done nothing significant since the beginning of time, and that there is no evidence that he will ever achieve anything great. The education of the Negro then must be carefully directed lest the race may waste time trying to do the impossible. Lead the Negro to believe this and thus control his thinking. If you can thereby determine what he will think, you will not need to worry about what he will do. You will not have to tell him to go to the back door. He will go without being told; and if there is no back door he will have one cut for his special benefit.

If you teach the Negro that he has accomplished as much good as any other race he will aspire to equality and justice without regard to race. Such an effort would upset the program of the oppressor in Africa and America. Play up before the Negro, then, his crimes and shortcomings. Let him learn to admire the Hebrew, the Greek, the Latin and the Teuton. Lead the Negro to detest the man of African blood—to hate himself. The oppressor then may conquer exploit, oppress and even annihilate the Negro by segregation without fear or trembling. With the truth hidden there will be little expression of thought to the contrary.

The American Negro has taken over an abundance of information which others have made accessible to the oppressed, but he has not yet learned to think and plan for himself as others do for themselves. Well might this race be referred to as the most docile and tractable people on earth. This merely means that when the oppressors once start the large majority of the race in the direction of serving the purposes of their traducers, the task becomes so easy in the years following that they have little trouble with the masses thus controlled. It is a most satisfactory system, and it has become so popular that European nations of foresight are sending some of their brightest minds to the United States to observe the Negro in "inaction" in order to learn how to deal likewise with Negroes in their colonies. What the Negro in America has become satisfied with will be accepted as the measure of what should be allotted him elsewhere. Certain Europeans consider the "solution of the race problem in the United States" one of our great achievements.

The mis-educated Negro joins the opposition with the objection that the study of the Negro keeps alive questions which should be forgotten. The Negro should cease to remember that he was once held a slave, that he has been oppressed, and even that he is a Negro. The traducer, however, keeps before the public such aspects of this history as will justify the present oppression of the race. It would seem, then, that the Negro should emphasize at the same time the favorable aspects to justify action in his behalf. One cannot blame the Negro for not desiring to be reminded of being the sort of creature that the oppressor has represented the Negro to be; but this very attitude shows ignorance of the past and a slavish dependence upon the enemy to serve those whom he would destroy. The Negro can be made proud of his past only by approaching it scientifically himself and giving his own story to the world. What others have written about the Negro during the last three centuries has been mainly for the purpose of bringing him where he is today and holding him there.

The method employed by the Association for the Study of Negro Life and History, however, is not spectacular propaganda or fire-eating agitation. Nothing can be accomplished in such fashion. "Whom the gods would destroy they first make mad." The Negro, whether in Africa or America, must be directed toward a serious examination of the fundamentals of education, religion, literature, and philosophy as they have been expounded to him. He must be sufficiently enlightened to determine for himself whether these forces have come into his life to bless him or to bless his oppressor. After learning the facts in the case the Negro must develop the power of execution to deal with these matters as do people of vision. Problems of great importance cannot be worked out in a day. Questions of great moment must be met with far-reaching plans.

The Association for the Study of Negro Life and History is teaching the Negro to exercise foresight rather than "hindsight." Liberia must not wait until she is offered to Germany before realizing that she has few friends in Europe. Abyssinia must not wait until she is invaded by Italy before she prepares for self-defense. A scientific study of the past of modern nations would show these selfish tendencies as inevitable results from their policies in dealing with those whom they have professed to elevate. For example, much of Africa has been conquered and subjugated to save souls. How expensive has been the Negro's salvation! One of the strong arguments for slavery was that it brought the Negro into the light of salvation. And yet the Negro today is all but lost.

The Association for the Study of Negro Life and History, however, has no special brand for the solution of the race problem except to learn to think. No general program of uplift for the Negroes in all parts of the world will be any more successful than such a procedure would be in the case of members of other races under different circumstances. What will help a Negro in Alabama may prove harmful to one in Maine. The African Negro may find his progress retarded by applying "methods used for the elevation of the Negro in America." A thinking man, however, learns to deal wisely with conditions as he finds them rather than to take orders from some one who knows nothing about his status and cares less. At present the Negro, both in Africa and America, is being turned first here and there experimentally by so-called friends who in the final analysis assist the Negro merely in remaining in the dark.

In the furtherance of the program of taking up these matters dispassionately the Association had made available an outline for the systematic study of the Negro as he has touched the life of others and as others have functioned in

their relation to him, *The African Background Outlined: A Handbook.* This book is written from the point of view of history, literature, art, education, religion and economic imperialism. In seventeen chapters as Part I of the work a brief summary of the past in Africa is presented; and courses on "The Negro in Africa," "The Negro in the European Mind," "The Negro in America," "The Negro in Literature," "The Negro in Art," "The Education of the Negro," "The Religious Development of the Negro," and "Economic Imperialism," follow as Part II with ample bibliographical comment for every heading and subhead of these outlines. This facilitates the task of clubs, young peoples' societies, and special classes organized where the oppressors of the race and the Negroes cooperating with them are determined that the history and status of the Negro shall not be made a part of the curricula.

In this outline there is no animus, nothing to engender race hate. The Association does not bring out such publications. The aim of this organization is to set forth facts in scientific form, for facts properly set forth will tell their own story. No advantage can be gained by merely inflaming the Negro's mind against his traducers. In a manner they deserve to be congratulated for taking care of their own interests so well. The Negro needs to become angry with himself because he has not handled his own affairs wisely. In other words, the Negro must learn from others how to take care of himself in this trying ordeal. He must not remain content with taking over what others set aside for him and then come in the guise of friends to subject even that limited information to further misinterpretation.

The Legacy of W. E. B. Du Bois for Contemporary Black Studies

JAMES B. STEWART

INTRODUCTION

Academic disciplines or enterprises develop a research program or paradigm as they mature. Key elements of a paradigm are exemplars that illustrate the conceptual foundations of the field of inquiry. Often these exemplars incorporate a review of the historical development of the enterprise, with illustrations of the incremental contributions made to the refinement of the conceptual core by successive practitioners building on earlier efforts.

Over the past decade and a half, Black Studies as an academic enterprise has matured rapidly. Much of this maturation has been involuntary, however, constituting a response to continual external threats to its existence. In other words, in the same sense that a child must develop survival skills and adaptive capacities more rapidly in hostile as opposed to nurturing environments, Black Studies has been forced to bypass its adolescent stage.

Even if Black Studies had not been faced with persistent threats of extinction, there are at least three reasons why the type of emerging exemplars would necessarily differ from those generated in the process of maturation of traditional academic disciplines. The first reason is the interdisciplinary nature of the intellectual core of Black Studies. As Karenga has argued:

> As a contribution to a new social science, Black Studies, which is interdisciplinary, becomes a paradigm for the multidimensional approach to social and historical reality. Secondly, it is a model of a holistic social science, not simply focusing on Blacks, but critically including other Third World peoples and whites in appropriate socio-historical periods and places of interaction with Blacks and denying no people its relevance, unlike the case of traditional white studies.[1]

The difficulty of constructing exemplars that reflect this complexity should be obvious enough to require no additional elaboration.

The second reason why Black Studies exemplars cannot resemble those of traditional

W. E. B. Du Bois (1868–1963), distinguished scholar and educator and noted political activist. He helped establish the National Association for the Advancement of Colored People.

disciplines is the explicit linkage between scholarship and praxis. Thus, as Karenga noted "[f]rom its inception, Black Studies has had both an academic and social thrust and mission."[2] Similarly, Allen described one conception of Black Studies as instrumental, in which Black Studies became a vehicle for social change with an integral connection to community-based activities designed to produce social change.[3] Elsewhere, this writer argued that the implication of this wedding of scholarship and praxis is the inappropriateness of the term *discipline* as a descriptor of

the developmental goal of Black Studies.[4] The dual nature of Black Studies complicates the process of exemplar construction because relevant exemplars simply cannot focus on intellectual achievements, but must also examine the political activities of historical figures important to the development of the enterprise.

The third barrier to traditional exemplar construction is the persistent belief that the history of Black Studies as a coherent intellectual enterprise begins with its violent birth in institutions of higher education in the late 1960s. To illustrate, Karenga claims: "Black

Studies, as an academic discipline, began as a political demand which had its origin in both the general Student Movement and the social struggles of the 60's out of which the Student Movement evolved."[5] If this view is valid, it severely restricts the data base from which exemplars can be drawn since there is no long history of continuous intellectual development to trace.

The principal thrust of this analysis is, in fact, to demonstrate that contemporary Black Studies has well defined historical precedents. More precisely, the line of argumentation is that Black Studies can accelerate its maturation rate by recognizing that there are historical Black Studies analysts/activists whose primary efforts included the clear delineation of a research program or paradigm linked to specific implementation strategies that can provide guidance for contemporary development efforts.

To the extent that this claim can be supported, it opens new avenues for the design of exemplars, namely, the comparative content analyses of the writings and political activities of Black Studies pioneers. The scope of the present investigation is more limited, however. Here, attention is restricted to the works and life of W. E. B. Du Bois. Without prejudice, it is easy to identify other viable candidates for similar treatment, including Martin Delany, Carter G. Woodson, and Paul Robeson. At the same time, an initial focus on Du Bois is particularly instructive, not simply because of the comparatively greater magnitude of his contributions but also as a result of the efforts and failures of Du Bois scholars to describe accurately his totality with the use of traditional labels.

This problem has manifested itself in the tendency to resort to anthologies as the chosen mode to capture the complexity of Du Bois. In these anthologies largely unconnected essays each examine his career from a different frame of reference. The persistence of this approach can be seen from the structure of

the workshops associated with the celebration of the opening of the Du Bois papers at Amherst. The shotgun approach of the workshops bore remarkable similarities to that found in the 1970 anthology edited by Clarke, Jackson, Kaiser, and O'Dell.[6]

To place this issue in perspective, we can think of Du Bois as a microcosm of the composite Black experience which traditional academic disciplines have artificially fragmented. The restoration of the wholeness of Du Bois, then, may shed light on how Black Studies in the aggregate should persist in its larger restoration/reconstruction or, as Karenga would argue, corrective project.

A wholly satisfactory restoration of Du Bois cannot be accomplished within the boundaries of this brief analysis. Nevertheless, an attempt will be made to demonstrate the internal coherence of a variety of concepts and activities that generally have been treated in other investigations as either unconnected or only loosely connected. Examples of specific concepts and/or activities of Du Bois critical to this investigation include (a) the variety of "methodologies" utilized in the study of the Black experience, (b) the range of modes utilized to disseminate knowledge, (c) the role of "double-consciousness" as a source of unique insights to produce and disseminate knowledge, (d) the role of the "Talented Tenth" as a producer of knowledge and leader of activities designed to produce social change, (e) mobility between activist and academic settings as a co-ordinating strategy, and (f) the need for a long-range research/activist program.

EARLY DEVELOPMENT OF DU BOIS AS BLACK STUDIES ANALYST/ACTIVIST

As a starting point in the reconstruction of Du Bois, we can point to the assessment by Turner and McGann that Du Bois was engaged in structuring an inter-disciplinary policy-oriented enterprise from 1913 until his death in 1963. The objective of the enterprise was improvement of the conditions faced by Afro-

Americans.[7] There is no doubt that the second decade of the twentieth century was a critical juncture in Du Bois's life. As he recalled in 1944:

> Gradually and with increasing clarity, my whole attitude toward the social sciences began to change: in the study of human beings and their actions, there could be no . . . rift between theory and practice, between pure and applied science, as was possible in the study of sticks and stones. The studies which I had been conducting at Atlanta I saw as fatally handicapped because they represented so small a part of the total sum of occurrences; were so far removed in time and space as to lose the hot reality of real life; and because the continuous, kaleidoscopic change of conditions made their story old . . . before it was analyzed and told. . . . I saw before me a problem that could not and would not await the last word of science, but demanded immediate action to prevent social death.
>
> I realized that evidently the social scientist could not sit apart and study *in vacuo;* neither on the other hand, could he work fast and furiously simply by intuition and emotion, without seeking in the midst of action, the ordered knowledge which research and tireless observation might give him. I tried therefore in my new work not to pause when remedy was needed; on the other hand I sought to make each incident and item in my program of social uplift, part of a wider and vaster structure of real scientific knowledge of the race problem in America.[8]

There are several elements of this quotation that require emphasis. First, Du Bois ascribed a simultaneous role for intuition and science as sources of inspiration for his "program of social uplift." This complementarity between science and other modes of knowledge acquisition and the explicit linkage to efforts to promote social change were exhibited in his own activities in the period preceding 1913 as well as after.

The complementarity of methodologies manifested itself in the co-temporal publication of the Atlanta Studies, *The Souls of Black Folk* (1903) and his first published novel, *The Quest of the Silver Fleece* (1911). The early commitment to social change is evident in the role Du Bois played in the Niagara Movement and later in the founding of the National Association for the Advancement of Colored People (NAACP) in 1909.

One of the more interesting features of *The Souls of Black Folk* was the use of "sorrow songs" as introductions to the various essays. Du Bois saw these songs as an alternative "window" on the Black experience, and, in addition, as an effective way of calling people to take action to foster social uplift, appealing to emotion and innate sensibilities. This theme is projected in one of Du Bois's later novels, *The Black Flame* (1928), in which the protagonist, Matthew Towns, is coerced into singing a slave song at a meeting of representatives of the Third World who are dedicated to the liberation struggle. This experience is the catalyst for Towns to reject his earlier socialization and dedicate his life to the liberation of oppressed people.

Du Bois had, of course, become familiar with the sorrow songs during his sojourn at Fisk University. The "field work" undertaken to collect this "oral history" can be compared to the collection of survey data as part of the research design of the Atlanta Publications, again illustrating the complementarity of methodologies.

The mechanisms that Du Bois saw as necessary to create change agents also included the use of the novel and other creative media as a means of making principles and research findings understandable to the masses. These instruments also allowed him to meld a humanistic focus with a systematic framework of analysis in the same way that participant observation, historical analysis, and pseudo-econometric techniques were integrated in the Atlanta Publications. *Silver Fleece*, in effect, was an alternative mode of presenting Black history, examining the over-arching domination of social forces exercised by the cotton industry in the post-Reconstruction South.[9]

The second aspect of Du Bois's assessment which requires emphasis is his recognition of the limitations of traditional science alone as a vehicle of liberation. This theme is integrally connected (a) to his concepts of the psychic duality of Black Americans and the implications of this "double consciousness" for the range of activities in which a conscious "race man" would be expected to be engaged and (b) to his notion of the "Talented Tenth." An unpublished novel, *A Fellow of Harvard* (circa 1892), was linked temporally and contextually with Du Bois's articulation of the concept of "double consciousness." This novel is, in fact, a loosely veiled biographical statement in which the protagonist finds temporary salvation in an historically black institution following bad experiences at Harvard University. Du Bois's belief at that time about the psychological turmoil emanating from duality manifests itself in the protagonist's eventual loss of sanity.

In *The Quest of the Silver Fleece,* the hero, Blessed Alwyn, is a composite representation of Du Bois's "Talented Tenth." However, it is only through the guidance provided by the heroine, Zora, an uneducated girl raised in the swamp, that he is able eventually to achieve the liberation of his psyche, including access to knowledge not accessible through science.

The third element of Du Bois's own assessment of his direction that necessitates additional consideration is the critical role of research in his overall program of social uplift. Underlying Du Bois's disenchantment with the Atlanta Publications was his failure to set in place his plan to replicate each of the ten studies as part of a one-hundred-year research program. The design of the individual studies, although seemingly loosely connected, was in fact, an expansion of the holistic methodology of *The Philadelphia Negro.*[10]

When examined in a broader context, Du Bois's first stint with the NAACP provided an alternative environment to higher education where the desired type of research could be pursued. In fact, his official title was Director of Publicity and Research. The *Crisis* (the NAACP magazine) became an outlet for dissemination of research findings as much as a general source of relevant information. The move into this arena was necessitated, in part, by obstacles that he faced in seeking continued support for his research plan from the University of Pennsylvania.

One of the more interesting activities in which Du Bois was engaged during this period was the publication of *The Brownie's Book,* a precursor to the call of contemporary Black Studies proponents for special efforts targeted at the public school population to foster self-knowledge, academic excellence, and social responsibility. Earlier in his career, he had founded several other periodicals, including *The Moon* (1906) and *The Horizon* (1907). In each of these efforts his experience as a journalist enhanced the effectiveness of these communication vehicles. Du Bois was a correspondent for several periodicals between 1883 and 1885 and joined the editorial board of the Socialist organ, *The New Review,* in 1913.

If, as has been argued to this point, it is possible to observe Du Bois's early rejection of his socialization as a classicly trained traditional Western scholar and the subsequent self-definition of an alternative program bearing strong similarities to contemporary Black Studies, what accounts for this transformation? One obvious answer is the increasing exploitation faced by Black Americans. A less obvious connecting thread is Du Bois's early and continuing commitment to the liberation of the Third World, and in particular Africa. This commitment is evidenced in his involvement in the early Pan-African Congresses. His interest in Africa was codified in his book, *The Negro.*[11] One of Du Bois's most ambitious efforts to portray the beauty and potential of

Africa to the masses was his theatrical production, *Star of Ethiopia,* an output of the Negro Theatre he organized in Harlem, the Krigwa Players. For present purposes, it is instructive to note that Du Bois saw the first Pan-African Congress (1900) as a vehicle for reform utilizing history, organization, and protest in a way that bore remarkable similarities to his view of the function of the Atlanta Conferences for Black Americans.[12]

The usefulness of the preceding examination of the early transformation of Du Bois into a Black Studies analyst/activist hinges on the ability to demonstrate the refinement of the hypothesized Black Studies research program over time as the primary thrust of Du Bois's later activities. It is to this issue that the analysis now turns.

MATURATION OF DU BOIS AS A BLACK STUDIES ANALYST/ACTIVIST

There is a wealth of evidence that demonstrates Du Bois's increasing belief in the complementarity of methodologies in the analysis and portrayal of the Black experience. In the postscript to the first volume of his trilogy, *The Black Flame* (1957, 1959, 1961), Du Bois provided a clear indication of the critical role which he ascribed to imagination in intellectual inquiry. He argued that although *The Black Flame* was not history in the strict disciplinary sense, limitations in terms of time and money had forced him to abandon pure historical research in favor of the method of historical fiction "to complete the cycle of history which (had) for a half century engaged (his) thought, research and action."[13] At the same time, Du Bois indicated that the foundation of the book was "documented and verifiable fact" although he freely admitted that in some cases he had resorted "to pure imagination in order to make unknown and unknowable history relate an ordered tale to the reader" and in other cases small changes had been made in the exact sequence of historical events.[14] Du Bois claimed that this

methodology was superior to the tendency of historians to "pretend we know far more than we do" provided that the methodology was explicitly acknowledged beforehand.[15]

The notion of a gray area between history and fiction also arises in his work entitled *The World and Africa* (1946). Du Bois characterized the book as history even though he admitted that "The weight of history and science support me only in part and in some cases appears violently to contradict me."[16] The upshot of these examples is that the method of counter-factual history can be said to be a critical component of the methodology that Du Bois used in both his fiction and his nonfiction. The appreciation of this fact is critical for understanding the general methodology that Du Bois applied in incorporating his social ontology into his major works and for understanding the relevance of this methodology for contemporary Black Studies.

Du Bois perceived that certain methodologies of analysis and styles of presentation were more appropriate than others for capturing the complexity of the Black experience and for communicating that complexity in a manner that generated new insights for non-Blacks and self-reflection among Blacks leading to social action. There is no doubt that Du Bois's methodological predilections violated traditional standards of historical research. As noted by Aptheker, Du Bois's historical works utilized already published sources and graduate papers rather than manuscript materials as references.[17] The tone of the presentation of his research was also at variance with accepted procedures, manifesting itself in what Aptheker has characterized as a "literary tendency . . . which took the form of rather exaggerated assertions or a kind of symbolism that in the interest of effect might sacrifice precision."[18]

To understand Du Bois's methodology it is necessary to examine the connotation of the word "fact" as it relates to social science. What constitutes fact in social science is that which can be verified with respect to a particular paradigm. Throughout his career, Du Bois operated from a mind-set that posited the existence of systematic biases in the determination of what constituted "fact" with respect to the Black experience. Consequently, to seek substantial correspondence between his interpretation and the conventional wisdom was necessarily self-defeating. A more salient strategy was to construct alternative explanations and subject them to testing procedures that were indigenous to the alternative paradigm. This is what Du Bois did. At the same time, Du Bois was always concerned with preserving his reputation as a bona fide scholar among traditionalists. This accounts in part for his extensive use of the novel to complement his "scientific" efforts—the method of counter-factual history was more acceptable in literary spheres.

The creation of characters in his novels provided Du Bois a means for developing a correspondence system between participant observation methodologies and representative depictions of the everyday life of Black people. This linkage simply reflects his acceptance of a variant of phenomenological sociology as a critical element in his research design. Thus, the characters in his novels become manifestations of his concern with resurrecting the history of common folk: "We have the record of kings and gentlemen *ad nauseam* and in stupid detail; but of the common run of human beings, and particularly of the half or wholly submerged working group, the world has saved all too little of authentic record and tried to forget or ignore even the little saved."[19]

Du .Bois's attempts to meld fiction and nonfiction in the study of history and society suggests that there should be an organic connection between the images or metaphors in his fiction and the models found in his nonfiction. He was an early proponent of the idea of a "Black Aesthetic," i.e., the position that art must be appropriate for Black culture and its value must be defined according to an indigenous concept of beauty. As an example, Du Bois argued in 1925 that there was undoubtedly a certain group expression of Negro art which included essays examining Black life, aspirations and the problems of the color line, autobiographies of former slaves and notable Blacks, poetry, novels, paintings, sculpture, music, and plays which emerged organically from the collective experience.[20]

Du Bois's increasing disenchantment with the methodology of the traditional social sciences took a variety of forms which included (a) criticism of the evolution of sociology and the portrayal of history as a superior intellectual enterprise, (b) a re-assessment of his notion of the "Talented Tenth," and (c) increasing criticism of the curriculum of historically Black institutions. Du Bois's growing dissatisfaction with sociology is shown most clearly in a 1944 review essay co-authored with the philosopher-anthropologist, Rushton Coulburn:

> Sociologists exist because they think that economists and political scientists are too one-sided, historians too conventional, philosophers too vague. But we think that Sorokin's procedure in this work advertises the limitations of sociology. If sociology describes and classifies more fully, realistically, and accurately than the other social sciences, let it describe only that which is susceptible of full and realistic classification. How far, then, can sociology comprehend society and history? In the last analysis the answer depends upon belief rather than fact: a sociologist who has been trained in the natural sciences and regards sociology as one of them firmly believes—or at least dares not deny the conviction—that eventually all the facts of human action can be so measured and classified as to conform to natural law. On the other hand, the historian believes that creative human initiative, working outside mechanical sequence, directs and changes the course of human action and so of history.

If now the area of human initiative is as broad and decisive as history has assumed, then the realm of sociology is the comparatively narrow one of the measurable in human action. On the other hand, if physical, chemical, and biological law and but partially known determinants in the fields of psychology so condition human action that little or nothing is left for human initiative —which is from the point of view of orthodox science, chance—then the sociologist becomes everything and the historian simply his recorder. . . . Change and movement have to be further explained; but the sociologist, even the sociologist who has conceived a meaningful causal system, dare not be too clear that it is man who causes movement and change; that would so constrict the validity of sociology.[21]

Thus, Du Bois rejected the fragmentation of experience into disciplinary compartments, the attempt by the social sciences to use the natural sciences as a developmental model, because he believed that it was, in fact, man who causes "movement and change."

As early as 1898, Du Bois noted that "scientific work must be sub-divided, but conclusions that affect the whole subject must be based on study of the whole."[22] For him, history was an enterprise that could integrate science and tuition. As such, it was a forward-looking as well as a backward-looking enterprise. Its usefulness lay not only in preserving tradition, but also in facilitating the prediction of future events. This requires that one "tamper" with history by using the method of counter-factual history to ask the question of what would have been the outcome if this had happened instead of what actually occurred. Thus Du Bois wrote in 1905: "We can only understand the present by continually referring to and studying the past; when any one of the intricate phenomena of our daily life puzzles us; when there arises religious problems, political problems, race problems, we must always remember that while their solution lies in the present, their cause and their explanation lie in the past."[23]

Du Bois's modification of his conception of the "Talented Tenth" grew out of his growing realization that transformation of the economic system de-activated many of the sources of social unity among Blacks which he had assumed earlier to be inviolable. Du Bois had originally seen the emergence of the Negro group leader which, in the aggregate, comprises his "Talented Tenth" as a potential substitute for the submerged African heritage of Blacks thrust into the American capitalist environment. Because of the isolation of Blacks, Du Bois insisted that the Black mass:

. . . gets it ideals; its larger thoughts, its notions of life, from these local leaders; they set the tone to that all-powerful spiritual world that surrounds and envelopes the souls of men; their standards of living, their interpretation of sunshine and rain and human hearts, their thoughts of love and labor, their aspirations and dim imaginings—all that makes life *life*.[24]

Du Bois saw these leaders as servants of the people who would serve as catalysts for the resolution of the problems arising in respect of the duality of the Black psyche, and he saw himself as part of this group. Du Bois's conception of the "Talented Tenth" was built on an historical analysis of the liberated house servant and his view of the special preparation of this class to assume group leadership following emancipation. Reminiscing in 1948, he noted; "I never for a moment dreamed that such leadership could ever be for the sake of the educated group itself, but always for the mass. Nor did I pause to enquire in just what ways and with what technique we would work—first, broad, exhaustive knowledge of the world; all other wisdom, all method and application would be added onto us."[25]

Once the criticality of continuity in experiences as a necessary condition to insure continued cultural cohesiveness became apparent to Du Bois, the flaws in his original conception of the "Talented Tenth" also became evident. His increased understanding of the writings of Karl Marx helped him to conceptualize the forces that could transform the consciousness of Black elites in ways that weakened their subjective identification with the Black masses. Thus, in re-examining his original premises he noted; "I assumed that with knowledge, sacrifice would automatically follow. In my youth and idealism, I did not realize that selfishness is even more natural than sacrifice."[26] Continuing this train of thought he indicated:

> My Talented Tenth must be more than talented, and work not simply as individuals. Its passport to leadership was not alone learning, but expert knowledge of modern economics as it affected American Negroes; and in addition to this and fundamental, would be its willingness to sacrifice and plan for such economic revolution in industry and just distribution of wealth, as would make the rise of our group possible.[27]

The alterations in his theoretical constructs, as indicated above, led Du Bois to advance a new conception of the Talented Tenth— The Guiding Hundredth—to be implemented through secret fraternal orders or similar entities with an international as well as a domestic focus.

The societal changes that Du Bois perceived signaled to him the need for historically Black institutions to assume responsibility for providing a nontraditional program of instruction for the preparation of Blacks to perform their role as change agents. Reflecting on the classic Du Bois-Washington debate in 1930, Du Bois criticized the Negro colleges for not "establishing that great and guiding ideal of group development and scholarship."[28] At the same time, he criticized the industrial school as a "gift of capital and wealth" which "looked upon the worker as one to be adapted to the demands of those who conducted industry."[29] Scoring students for their gullibility, he noted; "The average Negro undergraduate has swallowed hook,

line, and sinker, the dead bait of the white undergraduate who, born in an industrial machine, does not have to think and does not think."[30]

To correct this situation Du Bois saw the need for a new type of educational institution with a curriculum that integrally linked preparation for manual and intellectual labor in an Afro-centric perspective and whose scope of activities included direct involvement in the processes that produce social change:

> The university must become not simply a center of knowledge but a center of applied knowledge and guide of action. And this is all the more necessary now since we easily see that planned action especially in economic life is going to be the watchword of civilization . . . starting with present conditions and using the facts and the knowledge of the present situation of American Negroes, the Negro university expands toward the possession and the conquest of all knowledge. It seeks from a beginning of the history of the Negro in America and in Africa to interpret all history; from a beginning of social development among slaves and freedmen in America and Negro tribes and kingdoms in Africa, to interpret and understand the social development of all mankind in all ages. It seeks to reach modern science of matter and life from the surroundings and habits and attitudes of American Negroes and thus lead up to understanding of life and matter in the universe.[31]

The maturation of Du Bois's rational enterprise emerged not only out of conscious reflection but also from his concrete efforts to synthesize theory and praxis. Thus, in 1933 he played a prominent role in efforts to produce an encyclopedia of the Negro. This initiative eventually culminated in his acceptance of an invitation from President Nkrumah in 1961 to reside in Ghana and direct the Encyclopedia Africana Project. Between these events, his continuing commitment to a structured research program took a variety of forms. The arena of higher education again became the principal locus of his struggle to establish a long-term research agenda in 1934 when, after resigning his position with the NAACP, he became chairman of the Department of Sociology at Atlanta University.

During the decade of his tenure at Atlanta, Du Bois attempted to resurrect his idea of a one-hundred-year research program and in 1943 he organized the First Conference of Negro Land-Grant Colleges as a possible vehicle for its implementation. He also founded the journal *Phylon* in 1940. The philosophical underpinnings of *Phylon* articulated by Du Bois clearly reflect the ontology of contemporary Black Studies, whereby the immigration of Blacks to America from the fifteenth through the nineteenth centuries was described as "the greatest social event of modern history" leading, in Du Bois's view, to the foundation of modern capitalism and the evolution of democracy in the U.S. and providing the basis for "the greatest laboratory test of the science of human action in the world."[32]

Forced again to abandon academe in 1944, Du Bois rejoined the NAACP to pursue his program as director of special research. During the four years in which he held this position he presided at the fifth Pan-African Congress, participated in the founding convention of the United Nations, and helped to prepare and present an appeal to that body in protest of Jim Crow segregation of Blacks in the United States.

The ultimate manifestation of his charge to utilize the Black experience as a bridge to the problems of all mankind in all ages was his involvement in the Peace Movement beginning in 1949. Du Bois's view of the necessity of moving into this arena is reflected in the plot of *The Black Flame* in which the heroine, Jean Du Bignon, achieves complete psychological liberation despite previous activity as a prototype Black Studies analyst/activist only after she attended an international peace conference. One ramification of this perspective

on the likely end result of the continuing personal development of Black Studies professionals is the suggestion of a framework from which the continuing development of important figures like Paul Robeson, Malcolm X, and Martin Luther King can be gauged.

Careful scrutiny of the continuing evolution of Du Bois's views will demonstrate the explicit connection of each successive conceptual refinement to particular practical concrete experiences in attempts to operationalize his ontology. Particular emphasis on the symbiosis of theory and praxis must be a critical consideration in subsequent efforts to reconstruct Du Bois and other Black Studies pioneers as part of the continuing Black Studies development process.

IMPLICATIONS FOR CONTEMPORARY BLACK STUDIES

The continuing reconstruction/restoration of Du Bois is not only important for the further development of Black Studies, but also for the realization of its full potential to contribute to global concerns. Du Bois's bequest to Black Studies is, at the same time, a bequest to Freire's search for a pedagogy of the oppressed which recognizes that words invariably embody both reflection and action, the implication of which is that "those who have been denied their primordial right to speak their word must first reclaim this right."[33] Du Bois's legacy is also complementary to Habermas's struggle to define a critical social theory that is an alternative to both the "systematic sciences of social action" (e.g., economics, sociology, and political science) and purely intuitive understanding."[34]

Even though the analysis presented in this investigation is contingent upon further reconstruction/restoration efforts, several specific directions for contemporary Black Studies development efforts can be ascertained. First, Black Studies cannot be an enterprise that is housed solely in academe if it is to be true to its historical legacy, nor can it be simply a domestic enterprise. Complementary nonacademic entities must be structured both to allow the entire spectrum of Black Studies activities to be pursued as well as to protect the enterprise from strangulation at the hands of inimical controlling forces inside the Academy. Such complementary organizations should include research institutes, media outlets, publishing houses, political action committees, and organizations with direct linkages to African institutions where Black Studies type activities transpire. Extra-academic entities are particularly critical for the development of long-term research and "community education" activities of the type Du Bois attempted to implement. Even given the successful organization of extra-academic support bases, the question of the organization of Black Studies within American academe is critical. Du Bois's ideal model of the Black college[35] can be applied to Black Studies. This application would suggest that a possible long-term goal of the Black Studies movement should be the organization of an entire institution as a Black Studies university. This could be accomplished through the "rescue" of an existing historically Black institution faced with the prospect of closing due to financial pressures. One of the paradoxes of the contemporary Black Studies movement is its relative weakness in traditionally Black institutions at a time when severe restrictions are imposed on the operation of Black Studies units in predominantly white institutions. At the same time, however, Black Studies advocates in predominantly white universities have not, in many cases, taken full advantage of available options. To illustrate, even in Black Studies departments curriculum is typically organized along traditional disciplinary lines. In a similar vein, in most institutions where journalism, mass media, social work, technology, and science programs exist, Black Studies units have not

developed formal linkages to provide opportunities for students to learn how to translate theory into praxis.

The successful implementation of the above suggestions presumes the existence of a coherently articulated inter-disciplinary or non-disciplinary paradigm that gives direction to teaching, research, and social change activities—unfortunately, such a paradigm has not yet been fully developed and the specification of the content of the requisite core constructs is a complex undertaking. Fortunately, continued success in the restoration/reconstruction of Du Bois can provide guidance here as well. To illustrate, one of the current barriers to paradigm development is the absence of a synthesis of the Nationalist and Marxist approaches to Black Studies. While the precise delineation of the elements of Du Bois's ontology that provide the foundations for such a synthesis is beyond the scope of the present analysis, suffice it to say that he does achieve a reconciliation that can guide contemporary theorists.

This analysis should lay the groundwork for identification and scrutiny of early Black Studies practitioners such that both their theoretical contributions and their efforts to synthesize theory and praxis can be eventually incorporated into Black Studies texts. Given, however, that tracing the lineage of theoretical development is a more difficult task than describing the relatedness of scholarship and activism (because of the interdisciplinary nature of the conceptual foundations of Black Studies), it may be necessary to phase appropriate materials into textbooks, focusing first on the aggregate parameters of the enterprise, in the spirit of the present analysis, and later integrating detailed analysis of the evolution of paradigm content.

Given the importance of history to Black Studies, it is paradoxical that Black Studies practitioners have failed to complete the cycle of this field's history. It is hoped that this analysis will begin to close the gap, recognizing the continuing relevance of Du Bois's 1897 injunction:

> For the development of Negro genius, of Negro literature and art, of Negro spirit, only Negroes bound and welded together, Negroes inspired by one vast ideal, can work out in its fullness the great message we have for humanity. We cannot reverse history; we are subject to the same natural laws as other races, and if the Negro is ever to be a factor in the world's history—if among the gaily-colored banners that deck the broad ramparts of civilization is to hang one uncompromising black, then it must be placed there by black hands, fashioned by black heads and hallowed by the travail of two hundred million black hearts beating in one glad song of jubilee.[36]

Notes

1. Maulana Karenga, *Introduction to Black Studies* (Los Angeles: Kawaida Publications, 1982), p. 31.

2. Ibid., p. 17.

3. Robert Allen, "Politics of the Attack on Black Studies," *Black Scholar,* 6 (1974), 2.

4. James B. Stewart, "Alternative Models of Black Studies," *UMOJA,* 5 (1981), 19–20.

5. Karenga *Introduction to Black Studies,* p. 17.

6. John Henrik Clarke, Esther Jackson, Ernest Kaiser, and J. H. O'Dell, eds., *Black Titan: W. E. B. Du Bois* (Boston: Beacon Press, 1970).

7. James Turner and C. Steven McGann, "Black Studies as an Integral Tradition in African-American Intellectual History," *Issues* (1976), 73–78.

8. W. E. B. Du Bois, "My Evolving Program for Negro Freedom," in *What the Negro Wants,* ed. Rayford W. Logan (Chapel Hill: University of North Carolina Press, 1944), pp. 56–57.

9. For a more in-depth analysis of Du Bois's novels see James B. Stewart, "Psychic Duality of Afro-Americans in the Novels of W. E. B. Du Bois," *Phylon,* 44 (1983), 93–107.

10. W. E. B. Du Bois, *The Philadelphia Negro: A Social Study* (Philadelphia: University of Pennsylvania, 1899).

11. W. E. B. Du Bois, *The Negro* (New York: Henry Holt, 1915).

12. See Clarence Contee, "The Emergence of Du Bois as an African Nationalist," *Journal of Negro History,* LIV (1969), 52–53.

13. W. E. B. Du Bois, *The Ordeal of Mansart* (1957; reprint, Millwood, NY: Kraus-Thomson, 1976), p. 316.

14. Ibid., p. 315.

15. Ibid.

16. W. E. B. Du Bois, *The World and Africa: An Inquiry into the Part Which Africa Has Played in World History* (New York: International Publishers, 1968), p. viii. Originally published in 1946.

17. Herbert Aptheker, "Du Bois as Historian," in *Afro-American History: The Modern Era,* ed. Herbert Aptheker (Secaucus, NJ: The Citadel Press, 1971), p. 50.

18. Ibid., p. 65.

19. W. E. B. Du Bois, "Preface," in *A Documentary History of the Negro People in the United States,* ed. Herbert Aptheker (New York: Citadel Press, 1951).

20. W. E. B. Du Bois, "The Social Origins of Negro Art," *Modern Quarterly,* 3 (1925), 54–55.

21. Rushton Coulburn and W. E. B. Du Bois, "Mr. Sorokin's Systems," *Journal of Modern History,* 14 (1942), 511–512.

22. W. E. B. Du Bois, "The Study of the Negro Problems," *Annals of the American Academy of Political and Social Science* (January 1898), 12.

23. W. E. B. Du Bois, "The Beginning of Slavery," *Voice of the Negro,* 2 (1905), 104.

24. W. E. B. Du Bois, "The Development of a People," *International Journal of Ethics,* 14 (1904), 306–307.

25. W. E. B. Du Bois, "The Talented Tenth Memorial Address," *Boule Journal,* 15 (1948), 5.

26. Ibid., p. 4.

27. Ibid., p. 8.

28. W. E. B. Du Bois, "Education and Work," *Journal of Negro Education,* 1 (1932), reprinted in *The Education of Black People: Ten Critiques 1906–1960,* ed. Herbert Aptheker (Amherst: The University of Massachusetts Press, 1973), p. 68.

29. Ibid., p. 72.

30. Ibid., p. 67.

31. W. E. B. Du Bois, "The Field and Function of the Negro College," Alumni Reunion Address, Fisk University, 1933, reprinted in *The Education of Black People,* ed. Aptheker, pp. 95–96.

32. W. E. B. Du Bois, "*Phylon:* Science or Propaganda?" Phylon, 5 (1944), 7.

33. Paulo Freire, *Pedagogy of the Oppressed,* trans. by Myra Bergman (Ramos) (New York: The Seabury Press, 1970), pp. 76–77.

34. See Jurgen Habermas, *Knowledge and Human Interests* (London: Beacon Press, 1972).

35. W. E. B. Du Bois, "The Field and Function of the Negro College."

36. W. E. B. Du Bois, "The Conservation of Races," American Academy Occasional Papers, No. 2, 1897; reprinted in *W. E. B. Du Bois Speaks: Speeches and Addresses 1890–1919,* ed. Philip Toner (New York: Pathfinder Press, 1979), p. 79.

The Search for an Afrocentric Method

MOLEFI KETE ASANTE

THROUGHOUT THIS BOOK, I HAVE been arguing that all analysis is culturally centered and flows from ideological assumptions; this is the fundamental revelation of modern intellectual history. An Afrocentric method is concerned with establishing a world view about the writing and speaking of oppressed people. Current literary theories—phenomenology, hermeneutics, and structuralism, for example—cannot be applied, whole cloth, to African themes and subjects. Based as they are on Eurocentric philosophy, they fail to come to terms with fundamental cultural differences. Consequently, some authors have mistaken European agitation, manifested as a rhetorical reaction to social, religious, and political repression, with African protest discourse that seeks the removal of oppression. Repression presumes that the persecuted have certain rights; oppression is the denial of these rights and humanity.

The principal crisis with which the Afrocentric writer or speaker is concerned remains the political/cultural crisis with all of its attendant parts, economic and social. Indeed, the same themes spring to life in the revolutionary work of African American musicians, artists, and choreographers who challenge assumptions about the universality of Eurocentric concepts. We are on a pilgrimage to regain freedom; this is the predominant myth of our life.

It is my intention to examine the constituent elements in an Afrocentric discourse, particularly literature; demonstrate how these constituents differ from others; and suggest ways to turn this theory towards a critical method for perfecting African American discourse as a liberating word against all oppressive words. Therefore (as I have been doing) I will treat discourse, both spoken and written, as having essentially the same philosophical problem of perspective.

I recognize that most literary theory, like rhetorical theory, is essentially European. This is not a condemnation; it is rather a basis for understanding the role of an Afrocentric theory. I have argued so far that the rest of the world cannot abandon the theoretical and critical task to European writers who stand on various literary "peaks" as beacons for theory. Almost all of them, moreover, have seen from a male, Eurocentric angle, which, in their estimation, equals "universal," and have therefore negated—and where not negated, ignored—other perspectives. One finds this hostile silence in the writings of Northrop Frye, Ferdinand de Saussere, and de Man, as well as Jacques Derrida.

THE EUROPEAN VISION

What has been the purpose of literary theory in the twentieth century? The aim has been to rescue the depravity of thought, the carnage of ruined dreams, and the death of vision engendered by the first and second great European wars, which were called world wars. Kenneth Burke saw literature in dramatistic terms, but drama for him was essentially a European affair. In the 1930s and 1940s, nothing stood so enormous in European consciousness as their wars and no evil was as threatening as Hitler. He shattered their vision of themselves as morally superior, though they retained his sense of Aryan intellectual superiority, masking it in the myths of German scientific heroics, which also were warped. Hitler dared to enslave twentieth-century white people. Europeans could understand the domination of India and Nigeria, but not of Poland and France. Their idea was to consolidate the basic Western view of the world. They were not concerned about, nor were they under obligation to be concerned about, oppressed peoples.

Thus, out of this concern with Western decline and degradation we see the rise of Husserl's phenomenology and Heidegger's hermeneutics, both inextricably absorbed in European culture, without reservation. Edmund Husserl's *The Crisis of European Sciences* drew from an ideological context where irrationalism flourished, and a bewildering array of sterile positivism appeared to scare

the spirit out of European thought.[1] Although the major advances in European literary theory came during the first real European civil war, it was not to be the last development. This is not a casual point, because the second renaissance of European theory in the twentieth century came during and after the second international European war, when Northrop Frye and Roman Jakobson and Claude Lévi-Strauss were cutting their teeth on structuralist ideologies that hoped either to "totalize" all literary genres or to seize a text as an object in space, synchronically, apart from any polluting social or political facts. Indeed, this "miracle" is still tried, to little avail, in many corners of academic institutions as Eurocentric writers endeavor to "totalize" within a simple Western frame of reference. This becomes, in fact, an imposition, an aggressive attempt to dominate, and is therefore no totalization at all.

Sartre deals with this problem as a problem of analytical reason in his *Critique de la raison dialectique.*[2] He was among the earliest Western writers to understand the complications of traditional Western analysis. He opposes dialectical to analytical reason and claims that the transcendental materialists, those who believe that dialectical reason is merely an extension of analytical reason, do not understand that dialectical reason is "none other than the very movement of totalization."[3] This is almost an African conceptualization as expressed by the Mande in the word *woron,* "to get to the essence" of conversation, art, song, ritual, or music. Thus, the Mande seek to *yere-wolo,* "to give birth to self," by finding the true essence. Sartre says that dialectical knowledge comes in the moment of totalization—not in a reflection of the moment, but in the process itself.[4] He contends that the primary characteristic of the critical experience is that it goes on inside the totalization. While he admits that, in practice, this "should be the reflective experience of anyone," he quickly deepens his position by stating that "when I say that the experience must be *reflective,* I mean that it is no more distinguishable, in the singularity of its moments, from the totalization in process than the reflection is distinguishable from the human *praxis.*"[5]

Of course, Sartre is challenged on this point by Western traditionalists such as Claude Lévi-Strauss. Although they proceed from a Marxist position, they claim that the ultimate goal of human sciences is not to constitute man but "to dissolve man."[6] Such scholars, who believe that studying men is just like studying ants, Sartre called "aesthetes."[7] Small-minded aesthetes represent a considerable influence in Western academic circles. In his attack on Sartre's *Critique,* Lévi-Strauss states the general position of such aesthetes and, in so doing, shows clearly the distinctions between views of reason:

> Sartre in fact becomes the prisoner of his cogito: Descartes made it possible to attain universality, but conditionally on remaining psychological and individual; by sociologizing the cogito, Sartre merely exchanges one prison for another. Each subject's group and period now take the place of timeless consciousness. Moreover, Sartre's view of the world and man has the narrowness which has been traditionally credited to closed societies. His insistence on tracing a distinction between the primitive and civilized with the aid of gratuitous contrasts reflects, in a scarcely more subtle form, the fundamental opposition he postulates between myself and others. Yet there is little difference between the way in which this opposition is formulated in Sartre's work and the way it would have been formulated by a Melanesian savage.[8]

The fact that Sartre tries to escape the confusion he finds in traditional Western conceptual theory is to be applauded by those who seek not merely an extension of a Western way of knowing, but also the peculiar dimensions of other ways of knowing.

OTHER WAYS OF KNOWING

A symbol "revolution" was initiated by the Civil Rights Movement of the '60s and maintained by campaigns against the Viet Nam war. There were, of course, problems of focus. We were articulating a perspective about education that was radical even as we argued that Black Studies was not simply the study of black people but the study of African people from an Afrocentric perspective. This movement was to inaugurate an entire system of thinking about social sciences and criticism, and pointed to the inherent problems of Eurocentric theory when applied to the black literary or rhetorical movements. The intrinsic problems in Western discourse theory were revealed as systemic because even those who were sympathetic to "civil rights" often used a Eurocentric framework to speak of "agitative rhetoric," "protest literature," and so forth, when we should never have forced ourselves to take that position. Thus, even in that situation the European center was assumed and the burden of proof rested with those called dissenters, dissidents, oppressed, the disturbers of myths. What the symbol revolution has attempted to show is that the hallowed concepts of Western thought—rationality, objectivity, progress—are inadequate to explain all of the ways of knowing.

As one of Western culture's chief ideals, objectivity has often protected social and literary theory from the scrutiny that would reveal how theory has often served the interests of the ruling classes. In this respect, it is like other disciplines that have been hewn out of the arts and sciences. Although the 1960s and 1970s brought the Yale deconstructionists—Paul de Man, J. Hillis Miller, Geoffrey Hartman, and others—the whole intellectual enterprise could not be divorced from its internal framework. (In this regard, the deconstructionists are like the Sierra Club in Kenya or the Red Cross in South Africa: their jobs depend on the mistakes of others. An imperial ideology creates the need for missionaries and Red Cross workers.)

More damaging still has been the inability of European thinkers, particularly of the neo-positivist or empiricist traditions, to see that human actions cannot be understood apart from the emotions, attitudes, and cultural definitions of a given context. The Afrocentric thinker understands that the inter-relationship of knowledge with cosmology, society, religion, medicine, and traditions stands alongside the interactive metaphors of discourse as principal means of achieving a measure of knowledge about experience. The Afrocentrists insist on steering the minds of their readers and listeners in the direction of intellectual wholeness.

THE IMPLICATIONS FOR RHETORIC

Rhetoric has its cultural character. Are not speakers and listeners, writers and audiences, separated in the European sense? The separation implies that the speaker seeks "available means" to persuade the listeners. There are therefore speaker and listener societies—a plethora of possibilities to keep the "oppressed" in their places and the oppressors in theirs. Like African American cultural style that seeks to have experience confirmed by the intuition of participants, the objective must be to open the door for intercultural audiences to affirm discourse.

Baraka once understood this necessary insistence. In *Home,* he wrote that the solution to our problems will come from what he calls "Black National Consciousness." "If we feel differently, we have different ideas," he wrote.[9] As science and method combined, Afrocentricity became the rationalization of the alternative consciousness. The protectors of the basest Eurocentric theory, with its racist focus, describe their ethos as the universal ethos, encompassing the only correct view. There are few caveats in their writing; they do not see the narrowness of their own visions. If African American theory follows the same path, what would happen to progressive theory? Would we not be adding to the body

of Eurocentric literature and thereby further isolating ourselves from the rest of humanity? Should not other views claim their rightful places alongside Eurocentric analysis? Further-more, African Americans who participate only in Eurocentric views can easily become anti-black, the logical extension of European cultural imperialism. To be sure, there have been a host of African American critics and theorists who have added to African literature and orature; however, too many still see them-selves as serving some artificial value to European scholarship. They are victims of their own identity crisis, a crisis produced purely by their submission to the roles whites have forced them to play.

How can the oppressed use the same theories as the oppressors? Is it possible that established European theory regards its view as the best way to understand the literature of African Americans? The decline in the number of universities offering courses in African American literary criticism since the 1960s demonstrates the disregard and low esteem the Eurocentric tradition holds for the assertions of change. This is clearly seen in the response of those in rhetoric and oratory.

Eurocentric critics cannot neutralize their cultural "superiority" when they criticize previous white critics or engage in criticism themselves. The deconstructionists come close to redesigning the critical framework, although much of what they do falls squarely within the context of the Eurocentric theoret-ical framework. So the fundamental question of ethnocentrism is never touched. In fact, the Eurocentric writers, both black and white, often try to consolidate their Eurocentric impositions. Their attempts at criticizing ethnocentric rhetoric never go beyond, nor can they go beyond, the limits of Eurocen-tricism. The writer who includes in a discourse the statement that "children act like a bunch of wild Indians" may be criticized by these Eurocentric critics, but for the wrong reasons. They may find logic inconsistent, poor style (according to the norms), semantics imprecise, or other stylistic problems; but they seldom criticize such a speaker or writer for Eurocentric statements as such. They participate in the same Eurocentric thinking as the writer and can only distance themselves in the mechanics of discourse, not the philosophical framework. Let us look at how this is played out in the field of spoken communication, rhetorical discourse.

Rhetoric's problem, and our problem with it, is both historical and systemic. Consider the Egyptian book *The Coming Forth by Day,* called in the West *The Book of the Dead,* which contained the earliest extant examples of public discourse, gave us the forms for salutatory introductions, and became a model for the writers of the Torah, the Koran, and probably the Bhagavad-Gita. From Africa, the seat of the oldest organized civilizations as well as the birthplace of humanity, rhetorical models and interests travelled across the sea to Sicily, Greece, and Rome. The rise of Egypt and Nubia, its mother, is conservatively put at 5,000 years before the rise of Greek civilization. Greek students had studied in Africa even prior to the matriculation of Socrates and Plato at the temples. Only a few writers have acknowledged the African origins, although Africa is the region where spoken and written arts are known to have begun. The neglect of African origins and contributions to the world's intellectual history in effect misrepresents much knowledge and perpetuates a narrow scholarship. I make this point because rhetoric is grounded in the politics and culture of societies. A provincial, ethnocentric, xenophobic view of the world constitutes a serious problem for multicultural realities.

If we examine the flow of rhetoric in Western thought, we will see that even when the rhetorician poses as a critic in the interests of the oppressed, that critic seems incapable of the divestment of Eurocentric views. Criticism becomes criticism within a Eurocentric

context, a sort of ruthless intellectual game in which scores are kept but the oppressed are not even represented. Invariably, rhetoric allies itself with the socio-economic (though not necessarily numerically) dominant culture. Therefore, the dilemma of the scholar who would break out of these restricting chains is fundamentally an ideological one. That is why John Henrik Clarke says that when Europeans colonized the world, they colonized information about it. Ngugi wa Thiong'o, the Kenyan novelist, has argued that the imposition of the European languages on Africans furthers the oppression of the people because their chances for mental liberation become remote. He says that the intended results of this mental colonization is despair, despondency, and a collective death-wish.[10]

Rhetoric must transcend ideologies, whether political or racial, in order to perform the task of continuous reconciliation. Even now, when the demise of the old rhetoric has been proclaimed for at least a quarter of a century, the "white" journals still publish tribe rhetoric, rhetoric that can have meaning in its theoretical content only to one group of people. Thus, many blacks are forced by economic considerations to "go Eurocentric." When all is added up, you get a grand total of pure, whited-out blacks who have fallen into the I-want-whites-to-accept-me trap, and even if they say "Accept me as I am," they mean "as I become whiter."

European cultural referents and Western expansionism are the twin towers of contemporary literary theory—a profound problem that cannot be solved merely by consciousness to themes, for example, black writers, minority communication, Native American, Asian, Mexican, or Puerto Rican creators of discourse. It deserves an architectonic treatment, a total reclamation of philosophical ground. What is needed is a true overarching framework for understanding and practicing literature and rhetoric; not a dictatorial rhetoric but the emergence of parallel frames of reference; the rise of free spirits and the setting straight of a new Ogunic pantheon in America and the world. This would mean the legitimacy of criticism based upon a plurality of cultural views. Universality can only be dreamed about when we have slept on truth based on specific cultural experiences. Isaac Bashevis Singer was asked, after he received the Nobel Prize for Literature, why he had always written about ghosts in Yiddish. He replied, "Are there any other type of ghosts?" This is the posture of a writer who affirms a world view. What can we suggest for ways to approach literature and orature?

DEFINING AFROCENTRIC DISCOURSE

I suggest three fundamental Afrocentric themes of transcendent discourse: (1) human relations, (2) humans' relationship to the supernatural, and (3) humans' relationships to their own being. In any culture and under any conceivable circumstances, these would be the areas of discourse that occur to me. To posit these three general themes is to try to diffuse some of the specific issues that occur as "universals" in contemporary analyses. Almost all knowledge has cultural relevance and must be examined for its particular focus. Cultural differences do exist and must be explained by perspective in any discussion of themes. Take the Ebonics example in language, "Got no money," or the fact that guilt and innocence elicit different responses in whites and blacks. There needs to be more cultural data to give us something like a literary and oratory file.

Again, take oratory as an example. Communicationists, who are as parochial as literary theorists and critics, know British and American speakers, but are generally ignorant of the speeches in other cultures. As we have said, the decline in the number of universities offering courses in African American literary criticism since the 1960s may demonstrate the disregard and low esteem the Eurocentric tradition holds for the assertions of change. This is clearly seen in the response of those in rhetoric and oratory. Increasingly, students obtain degrees without ever looking at an African discourse or conversation analytically. They are, therefore, often ignorant of the discourse cultures of others.

Certain Afrocentric assumptions are necessary when we approach the discussion of African American discourse, both in its theory and its criticism. First, we assume that the objective of such discourse, in the large, is the successful presentation of one of the three principal themes, often within the context of resistance to oppression, liberation from stereotypes, and action in anticipation of reaction. Secondly, we assume that the discourse conforms to certain elementary materials of our corpus of culture; this would suggest stylistic and argumentative features as well. Thirdly, we assume that the discourse is directed principally towards either a black, a non-black, or a mixed audience. Furthermore, we assume that the discourse will have certain adjustment features to various audiences.

Since so much of African American discourse, in the sense of people speaking and writing, occurs within a Eurocentric context, it is necessary to isolate those aspects of a critical theory, derived from the condition, that are applicable to discourse. The assumptions serve as emblematic stools upon which to rest the critical case. You cannot rightly call any African American discourse, merely because it is uttered by a black person, *Afrocentric*. In fact, donning the *agbada* of a critic, I believe that much so-called "black discourse" is essentially white or Eurocentric discourse by black people. A black person's writing does not make the writing Afrocentric, no more than living in Africa makes a person Afrocentric.

Carlton and Barbara Molette's *Black Theatre: Premise and Presentation* is the first genuinely Afrocentric discussion of the black American theater.[11] They establish a method for examining African American theater and, in so doing, demonstrate that space is unified in the Afrocentric ideal. In Eurocentric theater, aesthetic distance is maintained between actor and audience; in Afrocentric theater, there is no attempt to manipulate empathy by separation. It goes without saying that a lot of black theater is not Afrocentric.[12] If a cultural analyst begins with Sophocles rather than African ritual drama, he can only end with the separation of actors and audiences. Afrocentrically, we must say that such a conclusion is only one way to reach success, whether in drama or rhetorical discourse.

Speaking about black issues does not make a discourse Afrocentric. Perhaps there is a cruel hoax being played out in the context of our Western experience. We are often victims of assumptions that support the established value systems and critical theories with little regard to our own profound historical experiences. Among those experiences are the achievements of transcendence against great odds; furthermore, rhythm has been the way to that connection with the cosmic. A truly Afrocentric rhetoric must oppose the negation in Western culture; it is combative, antagonistic, and wholly committed to the propagation of a more humanistic vision of the world. Its foundation is necessarily the slave narrative. Its rhythms are harmonious, discordant only to those who have refused to accept either the truth of themselves or the possibility of other frames of reference. Afrocentric rhetoric, while it is in opposition to the negative in Western culture, allows other cultures to co-exist, and in that particular aspect is substantially different from Western rhetoric. It is neither imperialistic nor oppressive. Therein lies its invigorating power. While beauty is artifactual for the Western world, it is dynamic in the Afrocentric sense. Expression itself can be beautiful to the Afrocentric critic. Thus rhetoric is a transforming power, a mythic discourse in the midst of a plethora of symbols.

Furthermore, it does not secure its efficacy or originality in the same manner as Western discourse, perhaps because it does not force the same separations as Eurocentric lines of argument. Foucault points out that "the reason-madness nexus constitutes for western culture one of the dimensions of its originality."[13] In effect, Foucault says, from Bosch to Shakespeare to Nietzsche and the Western poets and musicians of the nineteenth and twentieth centuries, the threads of madness exist in the cultural fabric.[14] This is not the case with Afrocentric approaches to knowledge and knowing. A more circular system of thought is implied in Afrocentric rhetoric, one with numerous elements united in a grand movement towards freedom of the mind, the irrepressible will to harmony.

Daniel and Smitherman's essay on deep structures within black communication behavior gave currency to the notion of generative, intangible, subjective ideas of a culture.[15] For them, the centrality of religion would constitute a deep structure, revealed through song, worship, and other "surface" features of our communicative behavior. Their emphasis is on the behavioral expressions of people who have shared a common experience. There is validity in this concept.

But his concept alone does not provide us a valid basis for the criticism of orature, except where we listen to the *pathos* of our spirit and comment on the uniqueness of that quality. It is, however, limiting in a pan-African sense, inasmuch as all African peoples have not experienced the same set of oppressive conditions as the Africans of the Americas. I possess all the pathos of the slaveships, the cotton fields, the spit in the face, the segregation, and the multitude of miniviolences in deed, and word-violences found in the Americas, and yet I do not find the same pathos in the voice of my brother from Mali or my sister from Kenya. In the Cuban, the Jamaican, the Brazilian, the Columbian, the Barbadian, the Haitian, the Trinidadian—yes, I recognize what Leon Phillips calls the "cadences and tonal variations that energize, envelop, and stir audiences to communal synthesis."[16] These are people who have had similar oppressive experiences. On the other hand, a critical method should account for more than presentational styles. Delivery is a fundamental constituent of discourse criticism, to be sure, but it is even more difficult than I first realized to generalize beyond certain geo-social and eco-cultural groups.

My intention is more comprehensive: I seek a critical method applicable to Africans, wherever they are, in much the same way Western scholars have set the procedures for criticizing Western discourse. Therefore, although I am interested in the centrality of religion and other "deep structure," I have chosen to concentrate my critical attention on an Afrocentric perspective to the world. How does the speaker view the world? To what end does he speak? Are his symbols discordant or harmonious? Does he demonstrate the currency of his ideas within the context of sanity? These are questions that must be addressed to every African who attempts discourse.

The *etic* and *emic* debate constitutes one way of viewing the challenge I have set. Etic approaches to criticism are those methods that are from *outside* the discourse perspective, whereas the emic approach, which views the perspective from within, is criticism derived from *within* the same culture as the discourse. What is proposed here is an emic criticism, derived from the culture, capable of speaking to the discourse in the language of the culture.

Albert Murray insists that it is necessary to see all statements as counterstatements, inasmuch as blacks in the United States possess a natural, historical, different view of reality than whites.[17] This calls into being the need for emic criticism, an internal understanding without the fault of Eurocentric social sciences, which assures a peculiar universality of European views. Murray contends that "the one place U.S. negroes [sic] have always found

themselves most rigidly segregated is not in the inner sanctum of the is-white family but in the insistent categories of behavioral science surveys, studies, and statistics."[18] Without sensitivity to the intellectual and cultural elements of others, the white social scientist has often proceeded as if what is correct for whites is correct for everybody.

In African philosophy there is a commitment to harmony that some might call spirituality.[19] It is the manifest essence of a search for resolution of cultural and human problems. This essence may be present in poetry, music, or dance. Duke Ellington, Martin Luther King, Jr., and Malcolm X all possessed it. In spoken discourse, it is possible to choose spirituality, word power, and call-and-response as the principal constituents of a culture-sensitive African-base critical method. Yet it seems to me that a proper understanding of spirituality leads us to the conclusion that the discourse of the preacher is of the same genre as that in the good blues musician. The so-called culture-sensitive African-base approach begins to answer these questions better than the neo-Aristotelian, phenomenological, structuralism, or post-structuralism approach to criticism because it admits the possibility of other views. It is one more evidence that African intellectuals question the basis of Western rhetoric as applied to African discourse. We understand the limitations of literary and rhetorical theory in the West. Frye's four narrative categories, *comic, romantic, tragic,* and *ironic,* leave little room for African literature, where romance does not assume such a burden as in the West.

However, Afrocentricity is not merely cultural sensitivity. To be culturally sensitive, one may remain grounded in one's own particular plot of history and mythology. The Eurocentricist may be culturally sensitive to the Wolof custom of leavetaking without ever modifying the central ground. An Afrocentricist may express cultural sensitivity to the Malay greeting behavior. Cultural sensitivity should be valued and practiced, but that does not constitute a cohesive critical direction for a body of discourse. This is why the attempt to define the scope of the concept *Afrocentricity* is important for the development of a more robust theoretical discussion.

THE LINK BETWEEN BLACK STUDIES AND AN AFROCENTRIC PARADIGM

Since the 1960s cultural sensitivity has been confused with the movement to establish Black Studies as an academic pursuit. Black Studies programs (rarely were they privileged with department status) sprouted all over the country, but many traditionalists simply regarded them as places where Black students could build self-esteem and study the achievements of Black writers. The conceptual underpinnings of the movement—the idea that it grew from a unique perspective as well as a coherent culture—were denied. As the key figures in the Black Studies movement, Maulana Karenga, James Turner, and James Stewart have held the front line in the debates about the place of Black Studies in academe.[20]

While recognizing their contributions, I would contend that what Stewart and Karenga view as difficulties in developing a paradigm in African American Studies are not any more significant than problems one encounters in any community or social or human science. Stewart identifies three factors that hinder a Black Studies program: the interdisciplinary nature of Black Studies, the dual nature of scholarship, and *praxis*, and the tendency to assume Black Studies' origins as a discipline in the 1960s, which denies its longer history.[21] These factors represent interesting but not authentic departures for a discussion of the problematics of the discipline of Black Studies. I find Karenga's support of Stewart's concerns troublesome.[22] While both Stewart and Karenga make valuable contributions to the general study of this field, they have not adequately assessed the nature of Afrocentric

theory as the *sine qua non* of Black Studies. Let us examine Stewart's three factors more closely.

First, the fact that Black Studies is interdisciplinary should present no more difficulty for it than such nature presents for sociology, political science, economics, or geography; all are essentially interdisciplinary or multidisciplinary. The creation of a paradigm or the codification of substantive theories and procedures does not depend on singular study of a discipline. In fact, the idea of discipline, inherited from the German School, has little to do with an intellectual enterprise in the twentieth century. The abandonment of this archaic notion has been coming for a long time. Therefore, the fact that Black Studies deals with many subjects is no hindrance to the flowering of an Afrocentric paradigm.[23] Afrocentricity, in recognizing the centrality of a world view based on Africa, "finds its place in the origins of civilization as well as in every compartment of post-modern history."[24] The advancement of the African American Studies paradigm must begin with a codified Afrocentricity, that is, a regularized and orderly arrangement of procedures for inquiry, analysis, and synthesis. Of course, codification must be undertaken on what already exists; once we have the proper grammar, based on what exists, we will be more comfortable with the perspective, now transformed into method and science, regardless of the subject or theme under study.

Stewart's second factor deals with the fact that African American Studies must contain both scholarship and *praxis*. This is a dubious bifurcation. Afrocentric scholarship is itself *praxis*. Afrocentricity as paradigm has propaedeutic value because a myriad of assumptions and basic propositions employed by African American Studies can be examined. Such scholarship as *praxis* reduces the tendency for individuals to make random, non-connected comments, even though those comments might be informative. The logic of procedure provides groundwork for others to follow; this is the value of Afrocentric scholarship as work. I am not convinced that either Stewart or Karenga believes that Afrocentric scholarship is not *praxis*. What Stewart had in mind was, perhaps, a more pedestrian interpretation of *praxis*. Needless to say, this should not be seen as a difficulty in establishing a paradigm.

Finally, Stewart's statement that the tendency to assume Black Studies originated in the 1960s is a problem; in my view, such a tendency does not disconnect the field from its longer history, as he contends. Although African people have been studied prior to the revolutionary paradigmatic changes of the 1960s, I suggest that the origins of African American Studies are in that era. Thus, while stating that Stewart's three factors "were correctly focused and well founded," Karenga challenges this last factor by saying "as an *academic discipline* . . . Black Studies did begin in the 1960s."[25] This position is in keeping with my contention that African American Studies must be defined not by subjects or themes, but by an Afrocentric perspective that is central to the paradigm. Perhaps Karenga was merely attesting to the value of Stewart's conceptualization to a continuing heuristic.

James Turner, the founder of the Africana Research Center at Cornell University, argues in support of James Stewart's thesis that Black Studies originated prior to the 1960s. Citing Carter G. Woodson, the father of African American history, as an early proponent of Black Studies, Turner writes,

> Black Studies as a field of scholarship did not begin with the student turmoil of the late sixties. Men and women have, for many years, studied and written about African American history, literature, and art. A small number of scholars have, for a long time, engaged in critiques of American society from the perspectives of Black Americans. An important fact about these early scholarly endeavors is that they occurred almost entirely at Black colleges or universities or outside the higher

education setting altogether. When the late Carter G. Woodson, a pioneer in African American history, observed that the whole system of education in America conspires to teach Black people to despise themselves, he was referring to the characteristic of the white-dominated education system that almost wholly excluded consideration of Blacks in the history, culture, and economic life of America.[26]

Both Stewart and Turner overstate the case. Woodson, to use Turner's example, was first and foremost a proponent of history, and not of the field of African American Studies; and if he understood history as the sum total of the field, it was a misunderstanding. What we see in the 1960s is the coalescence of Afrocentricity in every compartment of human endeavor; this is the exceptional fact of the creation of the field.

There are several functions that make an Afrocentric paradigm necessary for the advancement of the field of African Studies. The first is the grammar or notational function, which gives a concise base to principal concepts and ideas. Secondly, paradigms make it possible to trace the logical development of arguments because they derive from clear components of the paradigm. Thirdly, paradigms allow us to build upon previous foundations. For example, Afrocentricity becomes a school of thought, a paradigm, based upon work since the 1960s. Fourthly, an Afrocentric paradigm promotes analysis and synthesis rather than mere description. Attention to these functions makes it possible to have a powerful theoretical perspective for examining any branch of human science.

ELEMENTS OF CRITICISM

How do we turn this theoretical perspective towards a critical method? Or should we propose a critical method at all? Is not criticism itself a fundamental category of Western education? Perhaps a more basic question for us is, What function is served by criticism? The aim of criticism is to pass judgment, and judgment is concerned with good and bad, right and wrong; criticism is, therefore, preeminently an ethical act. One may appropriate other qualities to the critical act, but it is essentially a judgment. The Afrocentric critic is also concerned with ethical judgments but finds the aesthetic judgment equally valuable, particularly as the substantial ground upon which to make a decision about the restoration of harmony and balance. Indeed, Afrocentric criticism essentially combines ethics and aesthetics. If we were to examine the aims of oratory according to Western critics, we would typically be drawn to instruction, persuasion, and entertainment. However, these distinctive ends of oratory or literature— as far as that goes—are tied to the goal of influencing people to accept a certain view of reality. The commercialization of the word becomes the chief end of language and what it takes to "get over" the primary driving force.

In an Afrocentric conception of literature and orature, the critical method would be employed to determine to what degree the writer or speaker contributed to the unity of the symbols, the elimination of chaos, the making of peace among disparate views, and the creation of an opportunity for harmony and hence balance. Let me explain further: Harmony, in the sense that I am speaking of it, is an equilibrium among the various factors impinging upon communication.

One sees the difference between an African conception of rhetoric and, say, that of Kenneth Burke. Burke's dramatistic conception is based on a view of human beings as symbol users who often have to be brought together to overcome differences, to persuade. It seems to me that the African pattern as described, for example, in one cultural part of Africa, the Shona, is quite different in that all human beings are a part of an organic whole, and it is not so much the persuasion that implies

estrangement as it is the restoration of balance that matters when one speaks. The critic, therefore, must see to what extent the speaker achieved this purpose.

What are the tools of the critic? Since Afrocentric theory is based upon a cultural and historic perspective, the critic must understand both the cultural and historical bases of the discourse. The critic maintains an empathic engagement with the audience of a writer in order to properly understand how the writer creates or re-creates harmony in audiences. This empathic engagement allows the critic to participate in the event as well as to assess it.

Such a position, of course, is radical empiricism, maintaining that the subjective analysis of data is the most humanistic and correct critical approach to works meant for human audiences. But the critic must ensure that his or her judgment; subjective as it must be, is grounded in the historical and cultural bases of the discourse. One cannot use the Afrocentric critical method if one is ignorant of cultural and historical bases. Attempting to do so would lead to gross errors in judging whether or not a writer has achieved harmony within an audience. To evaluate a piece about Ethiopia, one must know something about Ethiopia; to proceed otherwise would not be Afrocentric. It may be phenomenological. But phenomenological approaches to African culture, based on Eurocentric perspectives, lead to incorrect conclusions.

For example, the writer who wishes to write about African communication, either in the Americas or in Africa, must be familiar with cultural styles. Otherwise the writer will assume that words, even words of a European language, are used in a European manner. We know, of course, that no mere word contains an idea, concept, or thought. The word must first be designated by the verbal expression of a person. Apart from the tonal elements in some African languages, there is immediate meaning to a word, perhaps even several meanings to a word, before one can grasp its meaning. "Bad" may mean evil or good, or something else, depending on the speaker. In this sense, a word may be a tightly contracted sentence, made so by several elisions. I can say "my" as an expression of joy-satisfaction at someone beautiful and express several sentences in that word. I do not imply that such capability is unknown in any other cultures; I simply argue that it is a facility in African culture that must be taken into consideration when making an analysis. Words in this type of context do not become clichés because they are constantly re-energized and re-interpreted.

Harmony has been achieved when the audience says a collective "amen" to a discourse, either through vocal or symbolic acknowledgment. This does not imply that logic has been achieved or that factual information has been presented, though these aspects are most likely present in the discourse when harmony is achieved. However, perceived logic or perceived facts are good enough to achieve harmony. The critic must assess whether the audience experienced harmony or not, to what degree harmony was achieved, and how the speaker handled the major obstacles of harmony. Forensic essays may or may not contribute to harmony, but they should move in that direction. In these cases, the critic wants to analyze what type of problems existed that impeded or facilitated harmony. Could they have been overcome by the writer (or writers) *without* losing integrity? (By "integrity" is meant the attachment to an Afrocentric reality and vision.) If the only way to achieve "harmony" is through divesting a person's cultural and historical bases, then it is an achievement that is without rhetorical merit. It has merit only as demagoguery, because the discourser's aim becomes the achievement of a *product,* regardless of cost. In a sense, it is an exploitation of the readers or audiences.

This critical method, applied to Afrocentric discourse, succeeds in presenting a positive rather than a reactionary posture to discourse. When it is used to assess African American writers, it could be considered a severe method because it would expose in those speakers the lack of an Afrocentric consciousness, much as Marxist method would expose the rhetoric of Abraham Lincoln, Daniel Webster, and Ronald Reagan as reflecting class-interests. This is not to say that black writers could not receive "positive" points on many aspects of their discourse, but it *is* to say that they would not automatically be adjudged great by this method—whereas if one applied any of the critical methods developed in a Eurocentric context, several black writers may be outstanding writers. These are hard questions that will be worked on for years. Is it fair to criticize an Afrocentric writer from a Eurocentric perspective?

I do not castigate any other method, for all methods are valid within their contexts. Initially, I said that analysis is culturally centered; likewise, critical methods flow from some ideological commitment. Truly to understand and appreciate the dilemma of African American and African writers trained in the West, one has to study discourse from an Afrocentric perspective. This, therefore, is a continuation of a literary and rhetorical quest for the theoretical and critical equilibrium necessary for placing African American discourse in its proper place. What is true of discourse is also true of other forms of human activity—transcendence, for example. Transcendence, the quality of exceeding ordinary and literal experience, occurs in the African's response to nature and relationships, when personal and collective harmony is achieved. It is, of course, linked to cultural factors, and any discussion of how people transcend or discuss their transcendence must consider the historical and cultural experiences that constitute their existence.

Notes

1. Edmund Husserl, *The Crisis of European Sciences* (Evanston, Ill.: Northwestern University Press, 1935).

2. Jean-Paul Sartre, *Critique de la raison dialectique* (Paris: Gallimard, 1960).

3. Ibid., p. 138.

4. Ibid., p. 140.

5. Ibid., pp. 140–144.

6. Claude Lévi-Strauss, *The Savage Mind* (Chicago: University of Chicago Press, 1966), p. 247. In this book, Lévi-Strauss tries to distance himself from the conceptions of Malinowski and Levy-Bruhl. Malinowski was quite unabashedly a functionalist. He believed that social institutions could be explained by how people found subsistence, satisfied their sexual drives, and sheltered themselves from the environment. On the other hand, Levy-Bruhl believed that Africans and Asians used intuition and affection as the bases of their thought processes. This "emotional" conceptualization and Malinowski's utilitarian conceptualization were rejected by Lévi-Strauss, who opted for structuralism, which he argued was based on order and rules.

7. Sartre, *Critique*, p. 183.

8. Lévi-Strauss, *Savage Mind*, p. 249.

9. LeRoi Jones (Imamu Amiri Baraka), *Home* (New York: Grove Press, 1969), p. 246.

10. Ngugi wa Thiong'o, *Decolonizing the Mind* (London: Currey, 1981), p. 3.

11. Carlton Molette and Barbara Molette, *Black Theatre: Premise and Presentation* (Bristol, Ind.: Wyndham Hall Press, 1986), p. 91. They have defined African American theater in terms that have been employed by Afrocentricists regarding research and information; that is, they have rejected the notion that the simple treatment of African themes constitutes an Afrocentric theater.

12. Ibid., p. 92.

13. Michel Foucault, *Madness and Civilization* (New York: Random House, 1965), p. 6.

14. Ibid., pp. 23–36. One might look to Foucault's other works, such as *Power/Knowledge: Selected Interviews and Other Writings, 1972–77* (New York: Pantheon, 1981), and *The Archaeology of Knowledge* (New York: Harper and Row, 1976), for elaboration on the intellectual development of the West.

15. Jack Daniel and Geneva Smitherman, "How I Got Ovah: Communication Dynamics in the Black Community," *Quarterly Journal of Speech* 62, no. 1 (February 1976): 26–39.

16. Leon Phillips, "A Comparative Study of Two Approaches for Analyzing Black Discourse" (unpublished dissertation, 1983, Howard University).

17. Murray, *The Omni-Americans*, pp. 1–15.

18. Ibid., p. 82.

19. There are numerous works that emphasize the value of the concept of harmony in African culture. For example, Wade Nobles, *African Psychology* (Oakland, Calif.: Black Family Institute Publications, 1986); Amos Wilson, *The Developmental Psychology of the Black Child* (New York: United Brothers Communication Systems, 1978); Leachim Semaj, *Culture, Africanity, and Male/Female Relationships: Working Papers on Cultural Science* (Ithaca, N.Y.: Cornell University Press, 1980); Jacob Carruthers, *Essays in Ancient Egyptian Studies* (Los Angeles: University of Sankore Press, 1984); and Molefi Asante, "*Ma'at:* The African Way against Injustice and Chaos," paper presented to First World Forum, New York, New York, October 25, 1986. The latter represents a selected part of the corpus of work being done on the concept of harmony as *ma'at*, as *nommo*, as *dja*, and as a relative to Ifa.

20. See Maulana Karenga, "Black Studies and the Problematic of Paradigm: The Philosophical Dimension," *Phylon*, forthcoming: James Turner, "Foreword: Africana Studies and Epistemology: A Discourse in the Sociology of Knowledge," in James E. Turner, ed., *The Next Decade: Theoretical and Research Issues in Africana Studies* (Ithaca, N.Y.: Cornell University African Research Center, 1985), pp. v–xxv; and James B. Stewart, "The Legacy

of W. E. B. Du Bois for Contemporary Black Studies," *Journal of Negro Education* (Summer 1984), pp. 296–311.

21. Stewart, "Legacy of W. E. B. Du Bois," pp. 296–311.

22. Karenga, "Black Studies and the Problematic of Paradigm."

23. See Asante, *Afrocentricity*. Karenga has correctly noted that my definition of Afrocentricity is descriptive, but there is no problem with description in the context of my analysis in *Afrocentricity: The Theory of Social Change,* because that work was itself a kind of *praxis* and was meant to be used as *praxis,* thereby rendering description not only valid but necessary. Nevertheless, I had explained elsewhere that Afrocentricity is a perspective that recognizes the centrality of Africa as a starting point for analysis and synthesis. See, for example, Molefi K. Asante, "Intercultural Communication: An Afrocentric Inquiry into Encounter," in Bruce Williams and Orlando Taylor, eds., *International Conference on Black Communication:* A Bellagio *Conference* (New York: Rockefeller Foundation, 1978).

24. Asante, "Intercultural Communication," p. 16.

25. Karenga, "Black Studies."

26. Turner, *The Next Decade,* p. xxviii.

Part I *Key Terms and Essay/Discussion Questions*

KEY TERMS

Interdisciplinary	*Afrocentric*
Methodology	*Eurocentric*
Talented Tenth	*Culture*
Analyst/activist	*Ideology*
World view	

ESSAY/DISCUSSION QUESTIONS

1. According to Carter G. Woodson, why should we study the experiences of African and African-descended people?

2. We generally conceive of education as an enlightening process that frees the mind. Yet, Woodson seems to argue that conventional educational practices, which insufficiently appreciate and examine African and African American experiences, result in the control of black people's thinking and behavior. Discuss. Can you provide examples of learning as a form of control from your own experiences as a student?

3. According to James Stewart, how is W. E. B. Du Bois a model for contemporary African American Studies scholars and students?

4. On what basis does Molefi Asante challenge the adequacy of the Eurocentric perspective? How persuasive is his criticism?

5. In Asante's view, what is the relationship between the Afrocentric perspective and African American Studies? How adequate is his argument?

Part I *Supplementary Readings*

Adams, Russell L., "Intellectual Questions and Imperatives in the Development of Afro-American Studies," *Journal of Negro Education*, Vol. 53, No. 3 (1984), pp. 201–225.

Alkalimat, Abdul, and Associates, *Introduction to Afro-American Studies: A Peoples College Primer.* Chicago: Twenty-first Century Books and Publications, 1986.

Asante, Molefi K., *The Afrocentric Idea*, Philadelphia: Temple University Press, 1987.

———, *Afrocentricity*, Rev., Trenton: Africa World Press, Inc., 1988.

———, *Kemet, Afrocentricity and Knowledge*, Trenton: Africa World Press, Inc., 1990.

Bailey, Ron, "Why Black Studies?," *The Education Digest,* Vol. 35, No. 9 (1970), pp. 46–48.

Ballard, Allen B., *The Education of Black Folk: The Afro-American Struggle for Knowledge in White America,* New York: Harper & Row, Publishers, 1973.

Ford, Nick Aaron, *Black Studies: Threat or Challenge?,* Port Washington: Kennikat Press, 1973.

Hare, Nathan, "The Battle for Black Studies," *The Black Scholar,* Vol. 3, No. 9 (May 1972), pp. 32–37.

Karenga, Maulana, *Introduction to Black Studies,* Inglewood: Kawaida Publications, 1982.

Ladner, Joyce A., ed., *The Death of White Sociology,* New York: Vintage Books, 1973.

McEvoy, James and Abraham Miller, eds., *Black Power and Student Rebellion,* Belmont: Wadsworth Publishing Company, 1969.

Myers, Linda J., *Understanding the Afrocentric Worldview,* Dubuque: Kendall-Hunt, 1988.

Robinson, Armstead L., Craig C. Foster, and Donald H. Ogilvie, eds., *Black Studies in the University: A Symposium,* New Haven: Yale University Press, 1969.

Turner, James E., ed., *The Next Decade: Theoretical and Research Issues in Africana Studies,* Ithaca: Africana Studies and Research Center, 1984.

Welsing, Frances C. *The Isis Papers: The Keys to the Colors,* Chicago: Third World Press, 1991.

Woodson, Carter G., *The Mis-Education of the Negro,* Washington, D.C.: The Associated Publishers, Inc., 1933.

The African Background

Stories of Africa and its people are still shrouded in mystery and subject to confusion and distortion. Yet if we are to understand the origins and development of the human being, it will be necessary to examine Africa's gift to the world. So far, scientific evidence points to Africa as the birthplace of all humanity. It is logical to think that human beings matured there. Long before Europe emerged, Africa—ancient and medieval Africa—gave to the world its early religion, philosophy, science, mathematics, literature, and art. Indeed, the ancient Greeks paid homage to the antiquity and intellectual greatness of Egypt, often appropriating Egyptian ideas and theories (e.g., the immortality of the human soul) without acknowledgment.

The African past is essential to African American Studies. Retrieving, recapturing, and rehabilitating African history before the coming of the European links African-descended Americans to a human, geographical, temporal, and intellectual context beyond the confines of brutal enslavement and cultural domination in the Americas. African history, then, is part of the collective memory of African-descended Americans, and reclaiming that history has to be one of the vocations of African American Studies. The essays in this section lay a foundation for understanding the meaning of African history and its relationship to African Americans specifically and to world development generally.

John Henrik Clarke's essay, "Africa and World History in Perspective," which introduces John G. Jackson's book, *Introduction to African Civilizations* (1970), places African culture and civilization in the perspective of world history. He thereby debunks the cultural superiority of Western Europe and exposes its denial and misrepresentation of African history; Clarke then resurrects and reconstructs a meaningful interpretation of Africa's heritage from antiquity to the early twentieth century.

The essay by John G. Jackson, "Egypt and the Evolution of Civilization," challenges those who have hypothesized some non-African origin of ancient Egyptian culture and civilization. For him, ancient Egyptian culture was authentically African in its origin and development. Using a plethora of scholarly sources, Jackson recaptures the majesty of early Egyptian civilization: its dynasties and important pharaohs; its contribution to the development of religion, medicine, science, astronomy, astrology, the calendar, and writing; and its later influence upon other ancient world cultures.

In his essay "Lucius Septimius Severus: The Black Emperor of the World," Edward L. Jones explores the life and times of the African emperor of Rome, Lucius Septimius Severus, who ruled from 193 to 211 A.D. Although European writers generally have portrayed Severus as white, Jones's essay reclaims Severus' African heritage. He discusses Severus' social background, his rise to power through the ranks, his shrewd and strategic military genius, his just political administration of Rome, and his death in 211 A.D.

"The Sudanese States and Empires," by Adu Boahen, is a political history of the Ghana, Mali, and Songhai empires, together with the Hausa states and Fulani *jihad* of Usuman dan Fodio, from the sixth to the nineteenth centuries. In discussing the origin, development, and fall of the West African empires of Ghana, Mali, and Songhai, Boahen indicates the strategic importance of geographical factors; the significance of commerce and the trans-Saharan caravan trade; the role and accomplishments of rulers; and the Arab invasions of West Africa and the penetration of Islam. Similarly, Boahen examines the later development of the Hausa states to the east of the Sudanese Empires. Again looking at the significance of Islamic penetration, Boahen describes the factors contributing to Muslim ruler Usuman dan Fodio's *jihad,* or holy war, which resulted in the breakup of the Hausa states and the establishment of a Fulani Empire.

Africa and World History in Perspective

JOHN HENRIK CLARKE

ONE THING SHOULD BE COMPLETELY understood before entering into the main body of this book. Mr. Jackson has not written this volume on African history to tell benevolent stories about so-called savages and how the Europeans came to civilize them. Quite the contrary, in many ways he has reversed the picture and proved his point. Civilization did not start in European countries, and the rest of the world did not wait in darkness for the Europeans to bring the light. In order to understand how this attitude came about, one needs to look at the sad state of what is called "world history." There is not a single book in existence with a title incorporating the words "world history" that is an honest commentary on the history of the world and its people. Most of the history books in the last five hundred years have been written to glorify Europeans at the expense of other peoples. The history of Asia has been as shamefully distorted as the history of Africa.

Most Western historians have not been willing to admit that there is an African history to be written about, and that this history predates the emergence of Europe by thousands of years. It is not possible for the world to have waited in darkness for the Europeans to bring the light because, for most of the early history of man, the Europeans themselves were in darkness. When the light of culture came for the first time to the people who would later call themselves Europeans, it came from Africa and Middle Eastern Asia. Most history books tend to deny or ignore this fact. John G. Jackson has examined this fact and its dimensions with scholarly honesty. He has also examined the origins of racism and its effects on the writing of history.

It is too often forgotten that, when the Europeans emerged and began to extend themselves into the broader world of Africa and Asia during the fifteenth and sixteenth centuries, they went on to colonize most of mankind. Later, they would colonize world scholarship, mainly the writing of history. History was then written or rewritten to show

From *Introduction to African Civilizations* by John G. Jackson. Copyright © 1970 by John G. Jackson. Published by arrangement with Carol Publishing Group. A Citadel Press Book.

**John Henrik Clarke,
eminent historian.**

or imply that Europeans were the only creators of what could be called a civilization. In order to accomplish this, the Europeans had to forget, or pretend to forget, all they previously knew about Africa.

In his booklet *Ancient Greece in African Political Thought* (1966), Professor Ali A. Mazrui of Makerere University in Uganda observes, after reading the book *A History of the Modern World* by R. R. Palmer and Joel Colton, that:

> As Africans begin to be given credit for some of their own civilizations, African cultural defensiveness would gradually wane. Not everyone need have the confidence of Leopold Senghor as he asserts that "Negro blood circulated in the veins of the Egyptians." But it is at any rate time that it was more openly conceded not only that

ancient Egypt made a contribution to the Greek miracle, but also that she in turn had been influenced by the Africa which was to the south of her. To grant all this is, in a sense, to universalise the Greek heritage. It is to break the European monopoly of identification with ancient Greece.

And yet this is by no means the only way of breaking Europe's monopoly. In order to cope with the cultural offensive of the Graeco-Roman Mystique, African cultural defenders have so far emphasized the Africanness of Egypt's civilization. But a possible counter-offensive is to demonstrate that ancient Greece was not European. It is not often remembered how recent the concept of "Europe" is. In a sense, it is easier to prove that ancient Egypt was "African" than to prove that ancient

Greece was "European." In the words of Palmer and Colton:

> There was really no Europe in ancient times. In the Roman Empire we may see a Mediterranean world, or even a West and an East in the Latin and Greek-speaking portions. But the West included parts of Africa as well as of Europe, and Europe as we know it was divided by the Rhine-Danube frontier, south and west of which lay the civilized provinces of the Empire, and north and east the "barbarians" of whom the civilized world knew almost nothing.

The two historians go on to say that the word "Europe," since it meant little, was scarcely used by the Romans at all.

Even as late as the seventeenth century, the notion that the land mass south of the Mediterranean was an entity distinct from the land mass north of it had yet to be fully accepted. Melville Herskovits has pointed out how the Geographer Royal of France, writing in 1656, described Africa as "a peninsula so large that it comprises the third part, and this the most southerly, of our continent."

In the years when the slave trade was getting effectively under way, some Europeans were claiming parts of Africa—especially Egypt—as an extension of their "continent" and their "culture." During this period, most history books were written to justify the slave trade and the colonial system that followed. Therefore, any honest writing of African history today must take this fact into consideration and be, at least in part, a restoration project.

The distinguished Afro-American poet, Countee Cullen, began his poem "Heritage" with the question: "What is Africa to me?" The new writers of African history must extend this question by asking, "What is Africa to Africans and what is Africa to the world?" Asking these questions emphasizes the need for a total reexamination of African history. A new approach to African history must begin with a new frame of reference. We will have to discard a number of words that

have been imposed on African history. There is a need to reject the term "black Africa" because it presupposes that there is a "white Africa." There is an urgent need to discard the term "Negro Africa" and the word "Negro" and all that it implies. This word grew out of the European slavery and colonial systems and it fails to relate the people of African descent to land, history, and culture. There is no "Negroland." When one hears the word "France" or "French," it is easy to visualize the land, history, and culture of a people. The same thing is true of the words "English" or "Englishman." When one hears or reads the word "Negro," the only vision that comes to mind relates to a condition.

There are many physical varieties of African peoples. The complexions of Africans are mainly black and brown. Most of the light-skinned people in Africa today are latecomers or interlopers. They have little or no relationship to Africa's ancient history. The Egyptians are a distinct African people. They did not originally come from Europe or Asia. Their history and their culture started in what is now Ethiopia and the Sudan. It is incorrect to refer to them or any other African people as Hamites. There is no such thing as a Hamite people. This is another term that was imposed upon African history by Europeans who wanted to prove that everything good in African history was brought in from the outside. The Hamites are supposed to be "black white people." Western historians move the so-called Hamites around in Africa as they see fit in order to prove that the rest of Africa has no history worthy of its name.

In a recent speech on "The Significance of African History," the Caribbean-American writer Richard B. Moore has observed:

> The significance of African history is shown, though not overtly, in the very effort to deny anything worthy of the name of history to Africa and the African peoples. This wide-spread, and well nigh successful endeavor, maintained through some five centuries, to

erase African history from the general record, is a fact which of itself should be quite conclusive to thinking and open minds. For it is logical and apparent that no such undertaking would ever have been carried on, and at such length, in order to obscure and to bury what is actually of little or no significance.

The prime significance of African history becomes still more manifest when it is realized that this deliberate denial of African history arose out of the European expansion and invasion of Africa which began in the middle of the fifteenth century. The compulsion was thereby felt to attempt to justify such colonialist conquest, domination, enslavement, and plunder. Hence, this brash denial of history and culture to Africa, and, indeed, even of human qualities and capacity for civilization to the indigenous peoples of Africa.

Mr. Moore is saying, in essence, that African history must be looked at anew and seen in its relationship to world history. First, the distortions must be admitted. The hard fact is that most of what we now call world history is only the history of the first and second rise of Europe. The Europeans are not yet willing to acknowledge that the world did not wait in darkness for them to bring the light. The history of Africa was already old when Europe was born.

In an essay, "The Nations of Black Africa and Their Culture," written in 1955, the Senegalese historian Cheikh Anta Diop makes the following observation:

In our time it is customary to ask ourselves all kinds of questions; so we must ask if it was necessary to study the problems dealt with in this work. Even a superficial examination of the cultural situation in Black Africa justifies such an undertaking. Indeed, if one must believe western works, it is useless to look in the interior of the African forest for a single civilization which, in the last analysis, might be the product of blacks. The civilizations of Ethiopia and Egypt, the express testimony of the ancients notwithstanding, the civilizations of the Ife and Benin, of the Chad Basin, of Ghana, all those referred to as neo-Sudanese (Mali, Gao, etc.) those of Zimbabwe (Monomotapa), of the Congo on the Equator, etc.... according to the coteries of western scholars, were created by mythical whites who then vanished as in a dream, leaving the blacks to perpetuate the forms, organizations, techniques, etc., which they had invented.

The explanation of the origin of an African civilization is only logical and acceptable, serious, objective and scientific if one, by what distortion whatsoever, leads up to this mythical white man. One does not bother to provide proof of his arrival or his settling in these parts. It can be readily understood how scholars could not help being led to the extreme from their reasoning, from their logical and dialectical deductions, to the notion of "whites with black skins," a notion quite widespread in the circles of European specialists. Such modes of thought obviously cannot persist forever since they are completely lacking in any substantial foundation. They are explained only by the passion which consumes those who create them and shows through their appearances of objectivity and calm.

But these "scientific" theories on the African past are highly consistent; they are utilitarian, pragmatic. Truth is what is good for something and, in this instance, good for colonialism: the aim is, under cover of the mantle of science, to make the black man believe that he has never been responsible for anything at all of worth, not even for what is to be found right in his own house and home. In this way, it is made easy to bring about the abandonment and renunciation of all national aspirations on the part of those who are wavering, and the reflexes of subordination are reinforced in those who have already been alienated. It is for this reason that there exist numerous theorizers in the service of colonialism, every one more clever than the other, whose ideas are spread abroad and taught on a popular scale as fast as they are worked out.

The use of cultural alienation as a weapon of domination is as old as the world itself; every time one people in the world have conquered another, they have used it. It is edifying to underline that it is the descendants of the Gauls against whom Caesar used that weapon who, today, are employing it against us.

Many white students of African history are now willing to admit that, according to most of the evidence we now have available, mankind started in Africa. The same students are not also willing to admit that it is logical to assume that human cultures and what we refer to as civilization also started in Africa.

In a lecture on "Early African Civilizations," Professor William Leo Hansberry calls attention to the long search for the origin of man:

> Between the years 1834 and 1908, there occurred a revolution in academic thinking about Africa's place in the outlines of world geography and world history. And in the past 150 years, European explorers and archaeologists have found in the valleys of the Niger, Benwezi, Limpopo and Nile Rivers, in the basin of Lake Chad and the Sahara, extensive remains of hundreds of ruins which bear witness to the existence of former civilizations hundreds and thousands of years ago. This knowledge of the facts about the African past when combined with the known history of other continents reveal that these also are the stories of triumphs and failures of mankind, and form many chapters in the history of the human race.

When and where did living things and human life first appear on earth? Who built the first human civilization? For centuries these questions have been raised in the minds of poets, philosophers, and myth makers among most of the world's peoples. Specifically, the Athenians thought that the first men sprouted from Attic soil; the ancient Hebrews and their spiritual descendants were of the opinion that Adam, the supposed primal parent of mankind, was made in the Garden of Eden six days after the creation of the world. According to Pindar the poet, the ancient Libyans believed that Iarbas, the earliest of men, sprang into existence in the heart of Libya. Ancient Egyptians contended that it was in their country, the oldest in the world, that the gods fashioned the first of all human beings out of a handful of mud moistened by the life-giving water of the "Blessed Nile." Likewise, Creation stories have come from many other parts of Africa (Ethiopia, Tanzania, Rhodesia, Congo, Ghana, Nigeria, etc.).

One of the oldest of such stories told by Africans to account for the origin and early development of man and his culture survives in a Greek version of the thesis first advanced by the ancient Kushites. This remarkable people flourished in olden times in the region called Kush in the Hebrew scriptures and marked on present-day maps as Sudan. The great historian, Diodorus Siculus, wrote that the Kushites were of the opinion that their country was not only the birthplace of the human race and the cradle land of the world's earliest civilization, but, indeed, the primal Eden where living things first appeared on Earth, as reported by the Scriptures. Thus, Diodorus was the first European to focus attention on the Ethiopian claim that tropical Africa was the cradle land of the world's earliest civilization, the original Eden of the human race.

In John G. Jackson's chapter on "Ethiopia and the Origin of Civilization," the reader is literally challenged to reconsider the prevailing definition of civilization and the story of its origin. In the book *Progress and Evolution of Man in Africa,* Dr. L. S. B. Leakey states: "In every country that one visits and where one is drawn into a conversation about Africa, the question is regularly asked by people who should know better 'But what has Africa contributed to world progress?' The critics of Africa forget that men of science today are, with few exceptions, satisfied that Africa was the birthplace of man himself, and that for many hundreds of centuries thereafter, Africa was in the forefront of all world progress."

In his book *Egypt,* Sir E. A. Wallis Budge says: "The prehistoric native of Egypt, both in the old and in the new Stone Ages, was African and there is every reason for saying that the earliest settlers came from the South."

He further states: "There are many things in the manners and customs and religions of the historic Egyptians that suggest that the original home of their prehistoric ancestors was in a country in the neighborhood of Uganda and Punt." (Some historians believe that the Biblical land of Punt was in the area known on modern maps as Somalia.)

European interest in "Ethiopia and the Origin of Civilization" dates from the early part of the nineteenth century and is best reflected in a little-known, though important, paper on "Karl Richard Lepsius' Incomparable Survey of the Monumental Ruins in the Ethiopian Nile Valley in 1843–1844."

The records found by Lepsius tend to show how Ethiopia was once able to sustain an ancient population that was numerous and powerful enough not only to challenge, but on a number of occasions to conquer completely, the populous land of Egypt. Further, these records showed that the antiquity of Ethiopian civilization had a direct link with the civilization of ancient Egypt.

Many of the leading antiquarians of the time, based largely on the strength of what the classical authors, particularly Diodorus Siculus and Stephanus of Byzantium, had to say on the matter, were exponents of the view that the ancient Ethiopians or, at any rate, the black people of remote antiquity were the earliest of all civilized peoples and that the first civilized inhabitants of ancient Egypt were members of what is referred to as the Black Race who had entered the country as emigrants from Ethiopia. A number of Europe's leading writers on the civilizations of remote antiquity have written brilliant defenses of this point of view. Some of these

writers are Bruce, Count Volney, Fabre, d'Olivet, and Heeren. In spite of the fact that these writers defended this thesis with all the learning at their command, and documented their defense, most of the present-day writers of African history continue to ignore their findings.

In 1825, German backwardness in this respect came definitely to an end. In that year, Arnold Hermann Heeren (1760–1842), Professor of History and Politics in the University of Göttingen and one of the ablest of the early exponents of the economic interpretation of history, published, in the fourth and revised edition of his great work *Ideen Über Die Politik, Den Verkehr Und Den Handel Der Vornehmsten Volker Der Alten Weld,* a lengthy essay on the history, culture, and commerce of the ancient Ethiopians, which had a profound influence on contemporary thought respecting such matters, not only in Germany, but throughout the learned world. In 1850, an English translation of Professor Heeren's *Historical Researches into the Politics, Intercourse and Trade of the Carthaginians, Ethiopians and Egyptians* was published. This book gave more support to the concept of the southern African origin of Egyptian civilization. Professor Heeren joined other writers in the conclusion that it was among these ancient black people of Africa and Asia that international trade was first developed, and he thinks that as a by-product of these international contacts there was an exchange of ideas and cultural practices that laid the foundations of the earliest civilizations of the ancient world.

Mr. Jackson's chapter on "Egypt and the Evolution of Civilization" calls to mind the fact that the study of Egyptology developed in concurrence with the development of the slave trade and the colonial system. It was during this period that Egypt was literally taken out of Africa, academically, and made an extension of Europe. In many ways Egypt is the key to ancient African history. African history is out of kilter until ancient Egypt is looked upon as a distinct African nation.

The Nile River played a major role in the relationship of Egypt to the nations in southeast Africa. During the early history of Africa, the Nile was a great cultural highway on which elements of civilization came into and out of inner Africa. Egypt's relationship with the people in the south was both good and bad, depending on the period and the dynasty in power.

Egypt first became an organized nation about 6000 B.C. Medical interest centers upon a period in the Third Dynasty (5345–5307 B.C.) when Egypt had an ambitious pharaoh named Zoser; and Zoser, in turn, had for his chief counselor and minister a brilliant noble named Imhotep (whose name means "he who cometh in peace"). Imhotep constructed the famous step pyramid of Sakkarah near Memphis. The building methods used in the construction of this pyramid revolutionized the architecture of the ancient world.

Egypt gave the world some of the greatest personalities in the history of mankind. In this regard, Imhotep is singularly outstanding. In the ancient history of Egypt, no individual left a deeper impression than the commoner Imhotep. He was probably the world's first multi-genius. He was the real father of medicine. In his book *Evolution of Modern Medicine* (London, 1921, page 10), Sir William Osler refers to Imhotep as "the first figure of a physician to stand out clearly from the mists of antiquity." Imhotep, the Wise, as he was called, was the Grand Vizier and Court Physician to King Zoser and architect of the world's earliest stone building, after which the Pyramids were modeled. He became a deity and later a universal God of Medicine, whose images graced the first Temple of Imhotep, mankind's first hospital. To it came sufferers from all the world for prayer, peace, and healing.

Imhotep lived and established his reputation as a healer at the court of King Zoser of the Third Dynasty about 5345–5307 B.C.,

according to the book *A Scheme of Egyptian Chronology* by Duncan Macnaughton (1932). From a study of the period in which he lived, Imhotep appears to have been one of the most versatile men in history. In addition to being the chief physician to the king, he was sage and scribe, Chief Lector Priest, architect, astronomer, and magician. He was a poet and philosopher. One of his best-known sayings, which is still being quoted, is "Eat, drink and be merry for tomorrow we shall die."

Imhotep's fame increased after his death. He was worshiped as a medical demi-god from 2850 B.C. to 525 B.C., and as a full deity from 525 B.C. to 550 A.D. Kings and queens bowed at his shrine.

When Egyptian civilization crossed the Mediterranean to become the foundation of what we think of as Greek culture, the teachings of Imhotep were absorbed along with the precepts of other great African teachers. When Greek civilization became predominant in the Mediterranean area, the Greeks wanted the world to think they were the originators of everything. They stopped acknowledging their indebtedness to Imhotep and other great Africans. Imhotep was forgotten for thousands of years, and Hippocrates, a legendary figure of two thousand years later, became known as the father of medicine. As regards Imhotep's influence in Rome, Gerald Massey, noted poet, archaeologist, and philologist, says that the early Christians worshiped him as one with Christ.

It should be understood that, while the achievements of Egypt are the best known among African nations, these are not the only achievements that African nations can claim. The nations to the south called Kush, Nubia, and Ethiopia developed many aspects of civilization independent of Egyptian influence. These nations gave as much to Egypt as Egypt gave to them.

Trade was the basis for the earliest contact of Egypt with the rest of Africa. Gold was obtained from Nubia. Trading expeditions were sent to visit the nations along the east coast of Africa, and the city-state of Meroe. These trading expeditions also helped to spread Egyptian ideas. Egypt, in turn, observed and took ideas from other nations within Africa.

Mr. Jackson's chapter on *Africa and the Civilizing of Europe: The Empire of the Moors* challenges two standard myths about Africa: One is that the Africans played no part in introducing civilization into Europe; the other myth is that the "Empire of the Moors" was a white North African achievement and had no relationship to what is referred to as Black Africa. This assumption prevails because most students of the subject, including most so-called African scholars, have no detailed knowledge of the interrelationships of African nations. North Africa did not develop out of context with the rest of Africa, and early Europe did not develop out of context with Africa in general.

There was a considerable African influence on what later became Europe in the period before the Christian era. Africans played a major role in the formulative development of both Christianity and Islam.

Many aspects of the present-day Christian church were developed in Africa during the formative years of Christianity. One of the more notable of African contributions to the early church was monasticism. Monasticism, in essence, is organized life in common, especially for religious purposes. The home of a monastic society is called a monastery or a convent; the inhabitants are monks or nuns. Christian monasticism probably began with the hermits of Egypt and Palestine about the time when Christianity was accepted as a legal religion.

Professor J. C. deGraft-Johnson gives us the following information on the rise of monasticism in Africa:

> It was left to another Egyptian Christian to be the founder of the monastic life. I refer to Pachomius, who established the first Christian monastery on an island in the Nile in the Upper Thebaid. Monastic life became very popular in Egypt and tended to undermine the military and economic life of the country; and in A.D. 365, we find a law of the Valens which decreed that all who left the cities of Egypt for the monastic life of the desert should be compelled either to return to discharge or perform their civic duties, or else to hand over their property to relatives who would be under obligation to perform those duties.

In the Emperor Valens' day the persecution of the African Church had ceased. The persecution of African Christians came to an end with the rise of Constantine as the undisputed master of Rome and the West in A.D. 312.

From the north the church continued to spread southward and eastward. Ethiopia received Christianity at an especially early date. Part of tradition suggests that St. Matthew, who wrote one of the Gospels, preached in Ethiopia.

When an Ethiopian emperor was converted from a "worshiper of Michren" to Christianity in the middle of the fourth century, this transformation marked a turning point in the history of the century. Eventually, the national church that emerged became the strongest supporter of Ethiopian independence.

Hadzrat Bilal ibn Rahab, a tall, gaunt, bushy-haired, black Ethiopian, was the first High Priest and treasurer of the Mohammedan empire. After Mahomet himself, that great religion, which today numbers upwards of 300,000,000 souls, may be said to have begun with Bilal. He was reputed to be the Prophet's first convert. Bilal was one of the many Africans who participated in the establishment of Islam and later made proud names for themselves in the Islamic wars of expansion.

Zaid Bin Harith, another convert of Mahomet, later became one of the Prophet's foremost generals. Mahomet adopted him as his son and made him governor of his tribe, the proud Koreish. He was later married into the Prophet's own family—the highest honor possible. Zaid Bin Harith was killed in battle while leading his men against the armies of the Byzantines. The Encyclopedia of Islam hailed him as one of the first great heroes of that faith.

In writing about the nations on the Mediterranean, Harold Peake, the English scientific writer, has this to say:

> The first light that burst in upon the long night of Europe's Dark Ages and heralded the dawn of a new day was from Moorish Spain, and from their Saracenic comrades who had settled in Sicily and Italy. Light first dawned on Europe from Spain, by means of the foundation by the Moors in the 9th century of a Medical School at Salerno, in Southern Italy. This developed into a university about 1150 A.D. and received a new constitution from Emperor Frederick II in 1231. Thence the new civilization spread up through Italy then to France and soon penetrated all parts of Europe except the north-eastern section.

All over the Arab-Moorish Empire a brisk intellectual life flourished. The Khalifs of both the East and West were, for the most part, enlightened patrons of learning. They maintained immense libraries and offered fortunes for new manuscripts. Khalif Harun-al-Rashid founded the great University of Baghdad, at which the most celebrated professor was Joshua ben Nun, a Jew. Here Greek classics were translated into Arabic. In other fields of science the Arabs and Moors were equally brilliant. Geber, in the eighth century, was an outstanding chemist. He has been called the founder of scientific chemistry. The names of some other savants and their fields of study will further show us the extent of Arab-Moorish erudition.

The outstanding characteristic of the Arab-Moorish rulers was tolerance. Their relations with the most distant nations were most cordial.

The Moslem traveler journeyed with utmost freedom in such widely separated lands as China and the Sudan. When the Mohammedan merchants reached the western Sudan (now West Africa) in the year 1000, or our era, they found well-developed kingdoms flourishing in this region. The commercial relations that they established with these kingdoms lasted for more than five hundred years.

The period covered by the chapter "The Golden Age of West Africa" has a special significance for the whole world. Europe was lingering in her Dark Ages at a time when western Africa was enjoying a Golden Age. In the non-European world beyond Africa, Asians built and enjoyed an age of advancement in technology before a period of internal withdrawal and isolation permitted the Europeans to move ahead of them.

It should be realized that during the Middle Ages oriental technology was far more advanced than European technology, and that until the thirteenth century Europe, technologically, was but an appendage of Asia. While the Greeks and Romans were weaving subtle philosophies, the Chinese were busy inventing gunpowder, paper, alchemy, vaccinations, plastic surgery, paint, and even the pocket handkerchief, which was unknown to the fastidious Greeks.

For more than a thousand years the Africans had been bringing into being empire after empire until the second rise of Europe, internal strife, and the slave trade turned what was an "Age of Grandeur" of the Africans into an age of tragedy and decline. Certain events in Europe and in Africa set this historical period in motion. In this respect no year was more important than 1492.

The fifteenth and the sixteenth centuries were both good and bad for Africa. The great nation states in Africa, especially in western Africa, rose to their height and began to decline. Europe partly recovered from the trouble of the Middle Ages and began to expand into the broader world. Christopher

Columbus opened up the New World for European settlement. The combination of Africans—Moors, Arabs, Berbers, and some Africans who came from south of the Sahara—lost their power in Spain after ruling that country for nearly eight hundred years.

In the great Songhay Empire of West Africa, the Emperor, Sunni Ali, died in 1492. This event brought to power Muhammad Touré, better known in African history as Askia the Great. This man, the last of West Africa's great rulers before the Europeans penetrated the hinterland of Africa, took inner West Africa through the last of its Golden Age after the slave trade had already started.

The story of the African slave trade is essentially the story of the consequences of the second rise of Europe. In the years between the passing of the Roman Empire in the eighth century and the partial unification of Europe through the framework of the Catholic Church in the fifteenth century, Europeans were engaged mainly in the internal matters within their own continent. With the opening up of the New World, after the expulsion of the Moors from Spain during the latter part of the fifteenth century, the Europeans started to expand beyond their homeland. They were searching for new markets and materials, new manpower, and new lands to exploit. The African slave trade was created to accommodate this new expansion.

Had there been no market for the slaves there would have been no slave trade. The market and the motive were the opening up of the New World and the creation of the vast plantation system that followed.

The slave trade had far-reaching repercussions that are acutely apparent today. In fact, there is no way to understand the social, political, and cultural history of black Americans without understanding what happened before and after the slave trade.

Africans were great storytellers long before their first appearance in Jamestown, Virginia, in 1619. The rich and colorful history, art, and folklore of West Africa, the ancestral home of most Afro-Americans, present evidence of this, and more.

Contrary to a misconception which still prevails, the Africans were familiar with literature and art for many years before their contact with the Western world. Before the breaking up of the social structure of the West African states of Ghana, Mali, and Songhay, and the internal strife and chaos that made the slave trade possible, the forefathers of the Africans who eventually became slaves in the United States lived in a society where university life was fairly common and scholars were beheld with reverence.

There were in this ancestry rulers who expanded their kingdoms into empires, great and magnificent armies whose physical dimensions dwarfed entire nations into submission, generals who advanced the technique of military science, scholars whose vision of life showed foresight and wisdom, and priests who told of gods that were strong and kind. To understand fully any aspect of Afro-American life, one must realize that the black American is not without a cultural past, though he was many generations removed from it before his achievements in American literature and art commanded any appreciable attention.

I have been referring to the African origin of Afro-American literature and history. This preface is essential to every meaningful discussion of the role of the Afro-American in every major aspect of American life, past and present. Africans did not come to the United States culturally empty-handed.

I will elaborate very briefly on my statement to the effect that "the forefathers of the Africans who eventually became slaves in the United States once lived in a society where university life was fairly common and scholars were beheld with reverence."

During the period in West African history from the early part of the fourteenth century to the time of the Moorish invasion in 1591, the city of Timbuktu and the University of Sankore in the Songhay Empire were the intellectual center of Africa. Black scholars were enjoying a renaissance that was known and respected throughout most of Africa and in parts of Europe. At this period in African history, the University of Sankore at Timbuktu was the educational capital of the western Sudan. In his book *Timbuctoo the Mysterious,* Felix DuBois gives us the following description of this period: "The scholars of Timbuctoo yielded in nothing, to the saints in their sojourns in the foreign universities of Fez, Tunis and Cairo. They astounded the most learned men of Islam by their erudition. That these Negroes were on a level with the Arabian Savants is proved by the fact that they were installed as professors in Morocco and Egypt. In contrast to this, we find that the Arabs were not always equal to the requirements of Sankore."

I mention here only one of the great black scholars referred to in the book by Felix DuBois.

Ahmed Baba was the last chancellor of the University of Sankore. He was one of the greatest African scholars of the late sixteenth century. His life is a brilliant example of the range and depth of West African intellectual activity before the colonial era. Ahmed Baba was the author of more than forty books; nearly every one of these books had a different theme. He was in Timbuktu when it was invaded by the Moroccans in 1592, and he was one of the first citizens to protest the occupation of his beloved home town. Ahmed Baba, along with other scholars, was imprisoned and eventually exiled to Morocco. During his expatriation from Timbuktu, his collection of 1,600 books, one of the richest libraries of his day, was lost.

Now, West Africa entered a sad period of decline. During the Moorish occupation, wreck and ruin became the order of the day. When the Europeans arrived in this part of Africa and saw these conditions, they assumed that nothing of order and value had ever existed in these countries. This mistaken impression, too often repeated, has influenced the interpretation of African history for over four hundred years.

In order to understand the chapter on "Africa and the Discovery of America," it will be necessary for most students of the subject to suspend all that they think they know about the presence of the Africans in the New World. After reading Mr. Jackson's documented analysis of this little-known aspect of history, it will be difficult for anyone to hold to the old assumption that the Africans just came to the New World as slaves. This assumption will be easier to discard if we look first at the formative development of Africans at the dawn of history. We need to look again and again at this African man and see how he developed and what he contributed to himself and mankind.

In the pamphlet *African Contribution* by John M. Weatherwax (published by the Bryant Foundation of Los Angeles, California, 1964), the following information about early Africa is revealed:

> The languages spoken in Europe and America today have roots in (and may in basic respects be traced to) the languages spoken by Africans ages ago. Those early Africans made hooks to catch fish, spears to hunt with, stone knives to cut with, the bola, with which to catch birds and animals, the blow-gun, the hammer, the stone axe, canoes and paddles, bags and buckets, poles for carrying things, bows and arrows.

> The last few hundred thousand years of the early prehistory of mankind is called the Old Stone Age. It may have lasted half a million years.

> The bola, stone knives, paddles, spears, harpoons, bows and arrows, blow-guns, the hammer and the axe—all of them invented first by Africans—were the start of man's use of power.

> Today's cannon, long-range missiles, ship propellers, automatic hammers, gas engines,

and even meat cleavers and upholstery tack hammers have the roots of their development in the early African uses of power.

Africans gave mankind the first machine. It was the fire stick. With it, man could have fire any time. With it, a camp fire could be set up almost any place. With it, the early Africans could roast food. Every time we light a match, every time we take a bath in water heated by gas, every time we cook a meal in a gas-heated oven, our use of fire simply continues a process started by the early Africans: the control of fire.

Knives and hammers and axes were the first tools. It is the making of tools that sets man apart from and in a sense above all living creatures. Africans started mankind along the toolmaking path.

Of course those early Africans were the first to discover how to make a thatched hut. They had to be the first because for hundreds of thousands of years they were the only people on earth. They discovered coarse basket-making and weaving and how to make a water-tight pot of clay hardened in a fire.

In cold weather, they found that the skins of beasts they had killed would keep them warm. They even made skin wraps for their feet. It was from their first efforts that (much later) clothing and shoes developed. We owe the early Africans much, much more.

They domesticated the dog. They used digging sticks to get at roots that could be eaten. They discovered grain as a food, and how to store and prepare it. They learned about the fermentation of certain foods and liquids left in containers. Thus, all mankind owes to Africans: the *dog* that gives us companionship and protection, the *spade* the farmer uses, the *cereal* we eat at breakfast-time, the *fermented liquids* that many people drink, the woven articles of *clothing* we wear and the *blankets* that keep us warm at night, the *pottery* in which we bake or boil food, and even the very *process* (now so simple) of *boiling water*—a process we use every time we boil an egg, or make spaghetti, or cook corned beef. Canoes made it possible for man to travel farther and farther from his early home. Over many centuries, canoes went down the Nile and the Congo and up many smaller rivers and streams. It was in this way that the early peopling of Africa took place.

From the blow-gun of ancient Africa, there followed, in later ages, many devices based on its principle. Some of these are: the bellows, bamboo air pumps, the rifle, the pistol, the revolver, the automatic, the machine gun—and even those industrial guns that puff grains.

African hunters many times cut up game. There still exist, from the Old Stone Age, drawings of animal bones, hearts and other organs. Those early drawings are a part of man's early beginnings in the field of Anatomy.

The family, the clan, the tribe all developed first in Africa. The family relationships which we have today, they fully understood then. The clan and the tribe gave group unity and strength. It was in these groups that early religious life and beliefs started.

When a great tribal leader died, he became a god to his tribe. Regard for him, appreciation of his services to the tribe, and efforts to communicate with him, became *worship*.

The first formal education was spoken tradition given during African tribal initiation ceremonies. The leaders of these ceremonies were medicine men. From their ranks the priests of following periods came. Ceremonial African ritual dances laid the basis for many later forms of the dance. Music existed in prehistoric Africa. Among instruments used were: reed pipes, single-stringed instruments, drums, gourd rattles, blocks of wood and hollow logs. Many very good prehistoric African artists brought paintings and sculpture into the common culture. The early Africans made a careful study of animal life and plant life. From knowledge of animals, mankind was able to take a long step forward to cattle raising. From the knowledge of plants and how they propagate, it was possible to take a still longer step forward to agriculture.

Today, science has ways of dating events of long ago. The new methods indicate that mankind has lived in Africa over two million years. In that long, long time, Africans and people of African descent migrated to other parts of the earth. Direct descendants of early Africans went to Asia Minor, Arabia, India, China, Japan and the East Indies. All of these areas to this day show an African strain.

Africans and people of African descent went also to Turkey, Palestine, Greece and other countries into Europe. From Gibraltar, they went into Spain, Portugal, France, England, Wales and Ireland.

Considering this information, the pre-Columbian presence of Africans in the New World is highly possible and somewhat logical.

The first Africans to be brought to the New World were not in bondage, contrary to popular belief. Africans participated in some of the earliest explorations by Spanish people into what is now the United States. The best known of these African explorers was Estevanico, sometimes referred to as Little Stephen. He accompanied Cabeza de Vaca during his six years of wandering, 1528–1530, from Florida into Mexico. In 1539, as guide to the Niza expedition, Estevanico set out from Mexico City in the party of Friar Marcos de Niza, in search of the fabled Seven Cities of Cibola. When the others wearied, Estevanico went ahead alone, except for Indian guides, and opened up to European settlers the rich land that is now Arizona and New Mexico.

There were Africans with Christopher Columbus, Balboa, and with Cortez in Mexico.

Most historians writing about the subject have attributed the civilizations of East Africa to every known people except the East Africans. Mr. Jackson's chapter, "Mariners and Merchants of the Eastern Coast," and a recent book by Basil Davidson *A History of East and Central Africa* (Doubleday, Anchor Books) will help to put some of the main historical facts in order.

The early civilizations of this part of Africa are splendid with achievements that most European writers have not been able to accept as evident African accomplishment. The influence of Islam and the Arabs in East Africa has been highly overstated. This influence was not always for the better. In fact, the Arabs, like all of the other invaders of Africa, did more harm than good. They, like the Europeans of a later day, destroyed many African cultures that they did not understand. Their role in the East African slave trade brought wreck and ruin to the nation states in this part of Africa. They were not without achievements, but their achievements are outweighed by the harm they did.

For the last five hundred years of recorded history, East Africa has had one troublesome invader after the other. Following the Arabs, the Portuguese came with a new crew of vandals.

The nations of central and southeast Africa have only recently been given some of the attention by historians that should have been given all along. There was less Arab influence in this area than in the nations of Africa further north. These nations have succeeded in keeping most of their culture intact. This is especially true of Zimbabwe, Monomotapa, and the kingdoms of the interior. The remarkable thing about these African states is that, in most cases, they had a resurgence of development in nation building and in the arts after the slave trade had already started. These were, in the main, landlocked nations that saw fit to avoid the troubles of the coastal African states.

The fall of the western Sudan (West Africa) and the beginning of the slave trade did not mark the end of great state building in Africa. During the slave trade, and in spite of it, great nations and empires continued to be created. One of the most vivid examples is the nations of East and Central Africa.

The people and nations of Central Africa have no records of their ancient and medieval history like the "Tarikh es Sudan" or the "Tarikh el Fettach" of the western Sudan (West Africa). The early travelers to these areas are mostly unknown. In spite of the forest as an obstacle to the formation of empires comparable to those of the western Sudan, notable kingdoms did rise in this part of Africa and some of them did achieve a high degree of civilization.

The Congo Valley became the gathering place of various branches of the people we know now as Bantu. When the history of Central Africa is finally written, it will be a history of invasions and migrations. According to one account, between two and three thousand years ago, a group of tribes began to move out of the region south or southwest of Lake Chad. Sometime during the fourteenth and fifteenth centuries, the center of Africa became crowded with pastoral tribes who needed more land for their large flocks and herds. This condition started another migration that lasted for more than a hundred years. Tribes with the prefix "Ba" to their names spread far to the west into the Congo Basin and southward through the central plains. The Bechuana and Basuto were among these tribes. Tribes with the prefix "Ama"— great warriors like the Ama-Xosa and Ama-Zulu—passed down the eastern side.

In the meantime, some of the more stable tribes in the Congo region were bringing notable kingdoms into being. The Kingdom of Loango extended from Cape Lopez (Libreville) to near the Congo; and the Kongo Empire was mentioned by the Portuguese as early as the fourteenth century. The Chief of Loango, Mani-Congo, extended his kingdom as far as the Kasai and Upper Zambesi Rivers. This kingdom had been in existence for centuries when the Portuguese arrived in the fifteenth century. They spoke admiringly of its capital, Sette-Camo, which they called San Salvador. The Kingdom of Kongo dates back to the fourteenth century. At the height of its power, it extended over modern Angola, as far east as the Kasai and Upper Zambesi Rivers.

Further inland, the Kingdom of Ansika was comprised of the people of the Beteke and Bayoka, whose artistic talents were very remarkable. Near the center of the Congo was the Bakuba Kingdom (or Bushongo), still noted for its unity, the excellence of its administration, its art, its craftsmanship, and the beauty of its fabrics.

South of the Congo Basin the whole Bechuana territory formed a vast state which actually ruled for a long time over the Basutos, the Zulus, the Hottentots, and the Bushmen, including in a single empire the greater part of the black population of southern and central Africa. This was the era of Bushongo grandeur; the people we now know as Bakubas.

Only the Bushongo culture kept its records and transmitted them almost intact to modern research. The Bakubas are an ancient people whose power and influence once extended over most of the Congo. Their history can be traced to the fifth century. For many centuries the Bakubas have had a highly organized social system, an impressive artistic tradition, and a secular form of government that expressed the will of the people through a democratic political system. Today, as for many generations in the past, the court of a Bakuba chief is ruled by a protocol as rigid and complicated as that of Versailles under Louis XIV.

At the top of the Bakuba hierarchy is the royal court composed of six dignitaries responsible for cabinetlike matters such as military affairs, justice, and administration. At one time there were in the royal entourage 143 other functionaries, including a master of the hunt, a master storyteller, and a keeper of oral traditions. In the sixteenth century, the Bakubas ruled over a great African empire. The memory of their glorious past is recalled in the tribe with historical exactitude. They can name the reigns of their kings for the past 235 years. The loyalty of the people to these rulers is expressed in a series of royal portrait-statues dating from the reign of Shamba Bolongongo, the greatest and best known of the Bakuba kings.

Shamba Bolongongo was a peaceful sovereign. He prohibited the use of the shongo, a throwing knife, the traditional weapon of the Bushongo. This wise African king used to say: "Kill neither man, woman, nor child. Are they not the children of Chembe (God), and have they not the right to live?" Shamba likewise brought to his people some of the agreeable pastimes that alleviate the tediousness of life. The reign of Shamba Bolongongo was really the "Golden Age" of the Bushongo people of the southern Congo. After abolishing the cruder aspects of African warfare, Shamba Bolongongo introduced raffia weaving and other arts of peace. According to the legends of the Bushongo people, their history as a state goes back fifteen centuries. Legends notwithstanding, their magnificent sculpture and other artistic accomplishments are unmistakable, the embodiment of a long and fruitful social experience reflecting the life of a people who have been associated with a higher form of culture for more than a thousand years.

In the chapter on "The Destruction of African Culture," Mr. Jackson has dealt with some of the main reasons that African history is so misunderstood and that so many students of the subject get confused while trying to make an assessment of the available information. There has been a deliberate destruction of African culture and the records relating to that culture. This destruction started with the first invaders of Africa. It continued through the period of slavery and the colonial system. It continues today on a much higher and more dangerous level. There are now attempts on the highest academic levels to divide African history and culture within Africa in such a manner that the best of it can be claimed for the Europeans, or at the very least, Asians. That is the main purpose of the Hamitic and the Semitic hypothesis in relationship to African history. It is also one of the main reasons so much attention is being paid to the Berbers and the Arabs in Africa. There is a school of thought supporting the

thesis that, if the main bodies of African history, culture, and achievement have no European origin, they must, at least, have an Asiatic origin. The supporters of this thesis have forgotten several important facts about Africa, if they ever knew them at all: mainly, the evidence of high cultures that the first invaders of Africa found and to what extent these invaders destroyed a great deal of this culture. Every invader of Africa did Africa more harm than good. They destroyed the culture that they would later say never existed at all.

In this chapter, Mr. Jackson documents the events that led to the destruction of some of the great libraries in Africa that had old and priceless manuscripts relating to African history and culture. He further documents the tragedy of the destruction of millions of African men and women in the slave trade and shows the role that the Christian church willingly played in creating the rationale that attempted to justify this event.

His concluding chapter on "Africa Resurgent" recalls the need to look again at the nineteenth-century roots of the twentieth-century African resistance movements and the role that both Africans and Afro-Americans played in bringing this movement into being.

Until near the end of the nineteenth century the African Freedom struggle was a military struggle. This aspect of African history has been shamefully neglected. I do not believe the neglect is an accident. Africa's oppressors and Western historians are not ready to concede the fact that Africa has a fighting heritage. The Africans did fight back and they fought exceptionally well. This fight extended throughout the whole of the nineteenth century. This fight was led, in most cases, by African kings. The Europeans referred to them as chiefs in order to avoid equating them with European kings. They were kings in the truest sense of the word. Most of them could trace their lineage back to more than a thousand years. These revolutionary nationalist African kings are mostly unknown because the white interpreters of Africa still want the world to think that the African waited in darkness for other people to bring the light.

In West Africa the Ashanti Wars started early in the nineteenth century when the British tried to occupy the hinterland of the Gold Coast, now Ghana. There were eleven major wars in this conflict. The Ashanti won all of them except the last one. In these wars, Ashanti generals—and we should call them generals because they were more than equal to the British generals who failed to conquer them—stopped the inland encroachment of the British and commanded respect for the authority of their kings.

In 1844, the Fanti Kings of Ghana signed a Bond of agreement with the English. This Bond brought a short period of peace to the coastal areas of the country. In the 1860's, King Ghartey, the West African reformer, advocated democratic ideas in government at a time when the democratic institutions of Europe were showing signs of deterioration. King Ghartey ruled over the small coastal kingdom of Winnebah in pre-independent Ghana. He was the driving spirit behind the founding of the Fanti Confederation, one of the most important events in the history of West Africa.

There were two freedom struggles in pre-independent Ghana. One was led by the Ashanti in the hinterland and the other was led by the Fanti who lived along the coast. The Ashantis were warriors. The Fantis were petitioners and constitution makers. The Fanti Constitution, drawn up in conferences between 1865 and 1871, is one of the most important documents produced in Africa in the nineteenth century. In addition to being the constitution of the Fanti Confederation, it was a petition to the British for the independence of the Gold Coast.

In 1896 the British exiled the Ashanti king Prempeh and still were not able to completely take over the hinterland of the Gold Coast. Fanti nationalists, led by Casely Hayford, started the agitation for the return of King Prempeh and soon converted this agitation into a movement for the independence of the country.

The stubborn British still did not give up their desire to establish their authority in the interior of the country and avenged the many defeats that they had suffered at the hands of the Ashantis.

In 1900, the British returned to Kumasi, capital of Ashanti, and demanded the right to sit on the Golden Stool. Sir Frederick Hodgson, who made the demand on behalf of the British, displayed his complete ignorance of Ashanti folklore, history, and culture. The Ashanti people cherished the Golden Stool as their most sacred possession. To them it is the Ark of the Covenant. Ashanti kings are not permitted to sit on it. The demand for the Stool was an insult to the pride of the Ashanti people and it started the last Ashanti war. This war is known as the "Yaa Asantewa War," since Yaa Asantewa, the reigning Queen Mother of Ashanti, was the inspiring spirit and one of the leaders of this effort to save the Ashanti kingdom from British rule. After nearly a year of heroic struggle, Queen Yaa Asantewa was captured along with her chief insurgent leaders. At last, the British gained control over the hinterland of the Gold Coast. To accomplish this, they had to fight the Ashanti for nearly a hundred years.

In other parts of West Africa, resistance to European rule was still strong and persistent. While the drama of Ashanti and other tribal nations was unfolding in the Gold Coast, an Ibo slave rose above his humble origin in Nigeria and vied for commercial power in the market places of that nation. In the years before the British forced him into exile in 1885, he was twice a king and was justifiably called "The Merchant Prince of West Africa." His name was Ja Ja. The story of Ja Ja is woven through all of the competently written histories of Nigeria. His strong opposition to British rule in the 1880's makes him the father of Nigerian nationalism.

In the French colonies, the two main leaders of revolts were Behanzin Hossu Bowelle, of Dahomey, and Samory Touré, of Guinea. Behanzin was one of the most colorful and the last of the great kings of Dahomey. He was one of the most powerful of West Africans during the closing years of the nineteenth century. After many years of opposition to French rule in his country, he was defeated by a French mulatto, General Alfred Dodds. He was sent into exile and died in 1906.

Samory Touré, grandfather of Sékou Touré, President of Guinea, was the last of the great Mandingo warriors. Samory is the best known personality to emerge from the Mandingos in the years following the decline of their power and empire in the western Sudan. Samory defied the power of France for eighteen years and was often referred to by the French who opposed him as "The Black Napoleon of the Sudan." He was defeated and captured in 1898 and died on a small island in the Congo River in 1900.

In the Sudan and in East Africa, two men called Dervish Warriors, Mohammed Ahmed, known as the Mahdi, and Mohammed Ben Abdullah Hassen, known as the Mad Mullah of Somaliland, were thorns in the side of the British Empire. Mohammed Ahmed freed the Sudan of British rule before his death in 1885. The country stayed free for eleven years before it was reconquered. Mohammed Ben Abdullah Hassen started his campaign against the British in Somaliland in 1899 and was not defeated until 1921.

Southern Africa has furnished a more splendid array of warrior kings than any other part of Africa. Chaka, the Zulu king and war lord, is the most famous, the most maligned and the most misinterpreted of all South African kings. By any fair measurement, he was one of the greatest natural warriors of all times. He fought to consolidate South Africa and to save it from European rule. When he died in 1828 he was winning that fight.

Chaka's fight was continued with varying degrees of success and failure under the leadership of kings like Moshesh of the Basutos; Khama of the Bamangwato; Dingan, Chaka's half-brother and successor; Cetewayo, nephew and disciple of Chaka; Lobengula, whose father, Maselikatze, built the second Zulu Empire; and Bambata, who led the last Zulu uprising in 1906.

What I have been trying to say is this: For a period of more than a hundred years, African warrior nationalists, mostly kings, who had never worn a store-bought shoe or heard of a military school, outmaneuvered and outgeneraled some of the finest military minds of Europe. They planted the seeds of African independence for another generation to harvest.

At the end of the nineteenth century, some of the personalities in the African and Afro-American Freedom Struggle met and formed an alliance. Out of this meeting of men and ideas the Pan-African concept was born. In Africa, the warrior nationalists gave way to the new nationalists that were now part of the small African educated elite. These men, stimulated by many Africans in the West such as W. E. B. DuBois and Marcus Garvey, laid the basis for the African Freedom Explosion. This was the preface to the "Resurgence of Africa."

This book is about the history of Africa from the origin of man to the present time. This is not just another book on African history. It is, in my opinion, one of the best books that has so far been written on this subject. Mr. Jackson debunks most of the standard approaches and concepts relating to African history. His book will cause many academic feathers to fly. In spite of this, I think this book, because of what it reveals about Africa and its role in history, is of lasting value.

Egypt and the Evolution of Civilization

JOHN G. JACKSON

SEVERAL EGYPTOLOGISTS HAVE theorized that the ancient Egyptians originally came from Asia. But no evidence has been adduced that would validate this opinion; and the only reason this thesis has been entertained is that it was fashionable to believe that no African people were capable of developing a great civilization. Mr. Geoffrey Parsons, in a scholarly historical work, refers to the culture of Egypt as "genuinely African in its origin and development." (*The Stream of History*, p. 154.)

The Edfu Text is an important source document on the early history of the Nile Valley. This famous inscription, found in the Temple of Horus at Edfu, gives an account of the origin of Egyptian civilization. According to this record, civilization was brought from the south by a band of invaders under the leadership of King Horus. This ruler, Horus, was later deified and became ultimately the Egyptian Christ. The followers of Horus were called "the Blacksmiths," because they possessed iron implements. This early culture has been traced back to Somaliland; although it may have originated in the Great Lakes region of Central Africa. In Somaliland there are ruins of buildings constructed with dressed stone, showing a close resemblance to the architecture of early Egypt. Professor Arthur G. Brodeur, in his *The Pageant of Civilization*, has conjectured that the ancestors of the South Egyptians came originally from this region; that they then entered the Nile Valley through Nubia, and brought with them a well-developed civilization. It is estimated that this migration must have occurred long before 5,000 B.C. That these ancient Africans possessed tools and weapons of iron should occasion no surprise; for in the magazine, *Natural History*, Sept.–Oct., 1932, there is an article by the Italian explorer, Nino del Grande, entitled "Prehistoric Iron Smelting in Africa," in which the author tells of his discovery of an iron-smelting furnace in northern Rhodesia of an antiquity of from five thousand to six thousand years.

From *Introduction to African Civilizations* by John G. Jackson. Copyright © 1970 by John G. Jackson. Published by arrangement with Carol Publishing Group. A Citadel Press Book.

The Egyptian culture had attained a high level of development in very ancient times. "When the curtain goes up on the Nile Valley, at the dawn of history," Professor George A. Dorsey notes, "an astounding scene is disclosed, and one as far from primitive as the Café de la Paix. . . . The solid foundations of civilization had been laid; civilization was full-blown, as it were, and in fully working order. Yet what mighty structures were to be erected on those foundations as the next three millenniums were ticked off on time's clock! And to be read in sequence and in detail as nowhere else on earth. Fifty-three centuries of unbroken history!" (*The Story of Civilization: Man's Own Show*, p. 297, by George A. Dorsey.)

Herodotus noticed that the Egyptian women went into the marketplace and engaged in trade, while their husbands stayed at home and sat at the loom; and that sons were not compelled to support their parents, but that daughters were obliged to do so, whether they chose to or not.

Diodorus Siculus, after reference to the matriarchal character of the Egyptian royal family, notes a similar state of affairs among the commoners. "Among private citizens," says that historian, "the husband by the terms of the marriage agreement, appertains to the wife, and it is stipulated between them that the man shall obey the woman in all things." (Cited by Dr. Robert Briffault, in *The Mothers*, 1-volume edition, p. 279.) These customs seemed strange to the Greeks, but they were normal features of African societies. This point is discussed by Briffault, as follows:

> The social features of pre-patriarchal society have sometimes survived under conditions of advanced civilization. This happened notably in Egypt. Down to the time when a dynasty of Greek rulers sought to introduce foreign usages, the conservative society of the great African kingdom, which has contributed so largely to the material and intellectual culture of the Western world, never lost the lineaments of a matriarchal social order. . . .
>
> The functions of royalty in ancient Egypt were regarded as being transmitted in the female line. While every Egyptian princess of the royal house was born a queen and bore the titles and dignities of the office from the day of her birth, a man only acquired them at his coronation, and could do so only by becoming the consort of a royal princess. . . . Those features of the constitution of Egyptian royalty are not singular. They are substantially identical with those obtaining in all other African kingdoms [*The Mothers*, pp. 274–75, by Robert Briffault].

According to Sir Gaston Maspero, the Egyptians made their first appearance on the stage of history about eight thousand to ten thousand years B.C. (See Maspero's *The Dawn of Civilization*, 2nd edition, p. 44.) This estimate should not be considered excessive. The ancient statue known as the Great Sphinx has been estimated by another French Egyptologist, Professor Pierre Hippolyte Boussac, to be at least ten thousand years old. There is an inscription of the Pharaoh Khufu, builder of the Great Pyramid, telling of how a temple adjoining the Sphinx, which had for generations been buried under the desert sands, was discovered by chance in his reign. This inscription, now in the Boulak Museum in Cairo, informs us that the Sphinx was much older than the Great Pyramid, and that the giant statue required repairs during the reign of Khufu. "In addition to the direct evidence for its prehistoric antiquity," Samuel Laing notes, "it is certain that, if such a monument had been erected by any of the historic kings, it would have been inscribed with hieroglyphics, and the fact recorded in Manetho's lists and contemporary records, whereas all tradition of its origin seems to have been lost in the night of ages." (*Human Origins*, p. 20, by Samuel Laing. See also *A Book of the Beginnings*, Vol. I, pp. 9–10, by Gerald Massey.)

The basis of Egyptian chronology is the lost *History of Egypt,* by Manetho. Ptolemy Philadelphus, King of Egypt in the third century B.C., commissioned Manetho, a learned Egyptian priest, of the Temple of Sebennytus, to write a history of Egypt from the earliest times up to his own day. Unfortunately the greater part of this history was lost in the destruction of the Alexandrian Library, but among the surviving fragments are Manetho's list of the kings of Egypt. This list divides the rulers of Egypt into thirty dynasties. Modern Egyptologists have grouped the dynasties into periods as follows: (1) The Old Kingdom (Dynasties I–VI), (2) The Middle Kingdom (Dynasties XI–XIV), (3) The Empire (Dynasties XVIII–XX), and (4) The Saite Age (Dynasty XXVI). In Dynasty XXVII the country was taken over by the Persians. Since that time Egypt has rarely been free from foreign domination. It will be noticed that there were interludes of chaos between the Old and Middle Kingdoms, between the Middle Kingdom and the Empire, and between the Empire and the Saite Age. In studying the history of Egypt we have a choice of two chronological schemes. There is a short chronology, compiled by Meyer and Breasted, and a long one by Petrie. Both lists are given below for comparison:

Dates: – B.C.

Dynasties	Petrie	Meyer and Breasted
I	5500–5300	4186
IV	4780–4500	3430
VI	4275–4075	2920
XII	3580–3370	1995
XVIII	1587–1328	1580
XIX	1328–1202	1315
XX	1202–1102	1200
XXI	1102–952	1090
XXII	952–749	945
XXV	725–664	712
XXVI	664–525	663
XXVII	525–405	525
XXX	378–342	378

The first king of Dynasty I, was Aha Mena, or Menes; but before his time there were many petty kings ruling over small territories in Upper and Lower Egypt. One tribe in Lower Egypt had sixty kings before the reign of Menes. The tribal totem was the "Hornet"; and the king's crown was a low red cap with a high peak at the back. Further south was the "Reed" kingdom, whose regal headdress was a tall white crown. Still more distant to the south were two "Hawk" kingdoms.

All these kingdoms were in time united by marriage and conquest. The father of Menes, as ruler of the United Kingdom of the Reeds and Hawks of Upper Egypt, conquered the Hornets of Lower Egypt. Then Menes, when he ascended the throne, combined the red and white crowns into the famous double crown of United Egypt. Even in predynastic times the Egyptians had reached a high level of civilization. They imported gold, silver, copper, tin, lead, iron, hematite, emery, galena, turquoise, obsidian, serpentine, lapis lazuli, coral, and tortoise shell. With these materials they produced beautiful and useful works of art, which were to call forth the wonder and admiration of later ages.

Egypt's first Golden Age was initiated by an invasion from Ethiopia. According to Petrie: "A conqueror of Sudani features founded the Third Dynasty, and many entirely new ideas entered the country. This new movement culminated in the vast schemes of Khufu, one of history's most dominating personalities. With him the lines of Egyptian growth were established; and the course of events became the subject of the written record." ("Modern Discovery of the Unknown Past," by Sir Flinders Petrie, in *The Encyclopedia of Modern Knowledge*, p. 112, edited by Sir John Hammerton.) The great achievement of the reign of Khufu was the building of the Great Pyramid. The classic account of the building of the Great Pyramid was related by Herodotus, from which we quote the following:

The Pyramid itself was twenty years in the building. It is a square 800 feet each way, . . . built entirely of polished stone, fitted together with the utmost care. The stones of which it is composed are none of them less than 30 feet in length. . . . After laying the stones for the base, they raised the remaining stones to their places by means of machines formed of short wooden planks. . . . There is an inscription in Egyptian characters on the pyramid which records the quantity of radishes, onions and garlic consumed by the laborers who constructed it; and I perfectly well remember that the interpreter who read the writing to me said that the money expended in this way was about 1,600 talents of silver. [A talent in ancient Egypt contained about 56 pounds of silver. So the modern equivalent of 1,600 talents would be the value of 89,000 pounds of silver.] If this then is a true record, what a vast sum must have been spent on the iron tools used in the work, and on the feeding and clothing of the laborers, considering the length of time the work lasted, which has already been stated, and the additional time—no small space, I imagine—which must have been occupied by the quarrying of the stones, their conveyance, and the formation of the underground apartments [*The History of Herodotus,* p. 125].

The French astronomer, Abbé Thomas Moreaux, Director of the Observatory of Bourges, wrote a book entitled *The Mysterious Science of the Pharaohs*. In this work the Abbé argues that the Great Pyramid was used as a vault for the preservation of scientific instruments, and of standard weights and measures, rather than as a tomb. In place of a sarcophagus there is a granite slab, which evidently served as a standard of measure. The length of this slab is one ten-millionth of the distance of either pole from the center of Earth. This invariable distance, only recently determined by modern scientists, is the basis of the metric system. The distance from each of the poles to the center of Earth is 3,949.79 miles. From

this measurement we are enabled to calculate the circumference of Earth through the poles, which is 24,817.32 miles. Abbé Moreaux is convinced that this fact was known to the Egyptian astronomers six thousand years ago. The Chaldeans were able students of astronomy, but their best estimate of the circumference of Earth was twenty-four thousand miles.

It seems that the knowledge of mathematics and astronomy among the ancient Egyptians was considerably more extensive and exact than we had hitherto been led to suspect. The height of the Great Pyramid is one-billionth of the distance from Earth to the sun, a unit of measure not accurately established in modern times until 1874. Abbé Moreaux notes that this pyramid is oriented within one-twelfth of a degree, a remarkably accurate precision; and that the parallel of longitude passing through the pyramid traverses the most land and the least sea of any in the world—a fact which also applies to the parallel of latitude passing through the structure. In the north side of the Great Pyramid is the entrance to an underground tunnel, which is bored through 350 feet of solid rock, at an angle of 26 degrees 17 minutes to the horizon. Alpha Draconis, or Thuban, was the pole-star about 3440 B.C., and for several hundred years before and after that date. At its lower culmination, when 3 degrees 42 minutes from the pole, this star shone down the underground tunnel. The ascending passage runs off from the underground tunnel of the pyramid at the base-line level, and leads into the grand gallery. Both the ascending passage and the grand gallery are inclined to the horizon at an angle of 26 degrees 17 minutes—the same as that of the underground tunnel, but in the opposite direction. These passages seem to have served two purposes; first, they enabled the builders to orient the base and the lower layers of the masonry up to the king's chamber in a true north and south line; and secondly, the passages were so arranged that the grand gallery could serve as the equivalent of the equatorial telescope of a modern astronomical observatory.

The English astronomer, Richard A. Proctor, in his *Problems of the Pyramids,* presents convincing evidence tending to show that the Great Pyramid was used as an astronomical observatory. "The sun's annual course round the celestial sphere," says Proctor, "could be determined much more exactly than by any gnomon by observations made from the great gallery. The moon's monthly path and its changes could have been dealt with in the same effective way. The geometric paths, and thence the true paths of the planets, could be determined very accurately. The place of any visible star along the Zodiac could be most accurately determined." (Cited by Samuel Laing, in *Human Origins,* p. 56.) The triangular area of each of the four sides of the pyramid equals the square of the vertical height, a fact mentioned by Herodotus. The added lengths of the four sides of the square base bear to the vertical height the same proportion as that of the circumference of a circle to its radius. This involves the mathematical constant π (3.1416), so important in modern mathematics. The length of each side of the square base is equal to 365¼ sacred cubits, an equivalence of the length of the year in days. The two diagonals of the base contain 25,824 pyramid inches, a good approximation of the number of years in the precessional cycle. Professor Piazzi Smyth made very careful measurements of the Great Pyramid; and his results were summarized by Dr. Alfred Russel Wallace in an address before the British Association for the Advancement of Science, at Glasgow in 1876, as follows:

1. That the pyramid is truly square, the sides being equal and the angles right angles. 2. That the four sockets on which the first four stones of the corners rested are truly on the same level. 3. That the directions of the sides are accurately to the four cardinal points. 4. That the vertical height of the pyramid bears the same proportion

to its circumference at the base as the radius of a circle does to its circumference.

Now all these measures, angles, and levels are accurate, not as an ordinary surveyor or builder could make them, but to such a degree as requires the best modern instruments and all the refinements of geodetical science to discover any error at all. In addition to this we have the wonderful perfection of the workmanship in the interior of the pyramid, the passages and chambers being lined with huge blocks of stone fitted with the utmost accuracy, while every part of the building exhibits the highest structural science [*British Association Report,* Glasgow Meeting, 1876, Part II, Notices and Abstracts, p. 117].

Sir Flinders Petrie began his archaeological career by journeying to Egypt in 1881. His first major undertaking was a study of the Great Pyramid, which kept him busy for nearly two years. The young scientist was overwhelmed by the amazing craftsmanship displayed by the pyramid builders. "The laying out of the base of the Great Pyramid of Khufu," Petrie asserts, "is a triumph of skill; its errors both in length and angles, could be covered by placing one's thumb on them." But in the inside of the structure he found some odd mistakes. "After having the casing made so finely, the builders made a hundred times the error in levelling of the king's chamber, so that they might have done it far better by just looking at the horizon. After having dressed the casing joints so beautifully, they left the face of the wall in the grand gallery roughly chiselled." (Sir Flinders Petrie, cited by Robert Silverberg in *Empires in the Dust,* p. 30.) Petrie's conclusion was that an architectural genius had planned and commenced the project, but had died before the job was completed; and that he had been succeeded by a man of lesser stature who was both careless and inept.

An unusual feature connected with the orientation of the pyramid has been studied by Colonel Braghine, and we give it in his own words:

A detailed study of the structure will convince any investigator that the wealth of mathematical, geometrical and astronomical data concealed within it is not accidental, but has been produced intentionally after numerous and complex calculations, made by somebody possessing an astounding amount of knowledge. . . . Not the least interesting detail concerning the orientation of the pyramid is the following: the reflection of the sunrays from the sides of the pyramid indicates almost exactly the equinoxes and solstices and therefore, the sowing time. The northern side of the pyramid is lighted at sunrise for some moments during the period from the spring-equinox till the autumn-equinox. During the remainder of the year the southern side is lighted from sunrise till sunset. This phenomenon fixes the moment of the equinoxes within 12 hours. When the stone-facing was intact, this phenomenon of the missing shadows must have been still more pronounced and was noticed by the ancients. The Latin poet Ausonius writes:

"Quadrata cui in fastigio cono
Surgit et ipsa suas consumit puramis umbras."

["The pyramid itself swallows the shadow born on its summit."] This phenomenon has now been explained by Professor Pochan, who discovered that the northern and southern sides of the pyramid are not true planes, but dihedral angles of 179 degrees 50 minutes. Thus in plain speaking, the sides in question have been hollowed out to the extent of 94 centimeters, insuring a rapid disappearance of the shadow of the sunrise at the equinoxes [*The Shadow of Atlantis,* pp. 237–38].

The Pharaoh Khufu has been pictured by certain modern historians as a despot who employed slave labor to erect his colossal pyramid; but this opinion is most certainly erroneous; for slavery was practically unknown in ancient Egypt. "It seems that, on the whole," a modern authority observes, "slavery never attained the serious and infamous proportions that it had in Greece, or in Italy. The serfage, which probably continued throughout the history, prevented the requirements of slave labor on large estates. It was a mild and comparatively harmless obligation, which did not prevent ability from rising, and it saved the land from the ruin which slavery brings." (*Social Life in Ancient Egypt,* p. 25, by W. M. Flinders Petrie.)

The building of the Great Pyramid was a great and well-organized project. One hundred thousand men were employed three months at a time, in transporting the rocks to the construction site. This was during the season of the inundation, when there was no other work to be done. Ten years were needed to make the great causeway, over which the stones were hauled, and in the preparation of the site, and the leveling and hollowing out of the underground tunnel and chamber. The actual construction required an additional twenty years. Sir Flinders Petrie, basing his conclusions on data supplied by Herodotus, gives a vivid picture of how this vast engineering job was accomplished:

This time would imply that a gang of eight men (about as many as could work on one block) could move ten stones from the quarry across the Nile, up the causeways, and raised into place within three months. This would be quite possible with good organization. There are several causeways besides the main one, still visible on the desert, and they must have been closely packed by working gangs to get up the thousand blocks every day during the working season. Of course there were also highly-skilled masons necessary for the thirteen acres of finely jointed casing, and the internal parts; the barracks for these are still visible, and would hold, at the outside, 4,000 men, who would live there continuously. If half of them were engaged on the casing, each man would have to prepare accurately and fit in place one casing block every three weeks, or rather, a gang of three men doing a block in a week. This is also a reasonable result. Of course, the great blocks at the base would take far longer, and the small courses would be done in perhaps half the time for each stone. . . . Much nonsense has been written about the oppression of the people, their tears and groans. With the splendid organization evident in the work, the people must have been well managed, and there was no hardship, whatever, in carrying out the work. Each man might have been levied twice in his lifetime; he would be just as well off there as at home, for he could do nothing during the inundation. All that was necessary was to transport a couple of hundredweight of food with him, which he would eat there instead of home. The immense gain to the people was the education in combined work and technical training [*Social Life in Ancient Egypt*, pp. 25–27, by W. M. Flinders Petrie].

We are told by a well-known archaeologist that: "When the Greeks first began to come to Egypt, awed by its antiquity and overwhelmed by its multiplicity of gods, its castes and its ceremonies, what they really found was a nation of Fellahin ruled with a rod of iron by a society of Antiquaries." (*Progress and Catastrophe*, pp. 108–9, by Stanley Casson.) The priestly caste of Egypt may have been "a society of Antiquaries" in the seventh century B.C., when the first Greeks settled in the country, but that certainly was not the case in the days of the Old Kingdom. The priesthood of early Egypt comprised not only the sacerdotal officialdom, but also the entire learned and professional classes of the nation, including the civil service in its entirety. A colorful and accurate account of the achievements of these African savants is given to us by the brilliant author of *The Martyrdom of Man*, from which work we are pleased to quote the following:

Priests were the royal chroniclers and keepers of the records, the engravers of inscriptions, physicians of the sick and embalmers of the dead, lawyers and law-givers, sculptors and musicians. Most of the skilled labor of the country was under their control. In their hands were the linen manufactories and the quarries between the cataracts. Even those posts in the Army which required a knowledge of arithmetic and penmanship were supplied by them: every general was attended by young priest scribes, with papyrus rolls in their hands and reed pencils behind their ears. The clergy preserved the monopoly of the arts which they had invented; the whole intellectual life of Egypt was in them. It was they who, with their nilometers, took the measure of the waters, and proclaimed good harvests to the people or bade them prepare for hungry days. It was they who studied the diseases of the country, compiled a pharmacopoeia, and invented the signs which are used in our prescriptions at the present day. . . . Their power was immense, but it was exercised with justice and discretion; they issued admirable laws, and taught the people to obey them by the example of their own humble, self-denying lives.

Under the tutelage of these pious and enlightened men, the Egyptians became a prosperous and also a highly moral people. The monumental paintings reveal their whole life, but we read in them no brutal or licentious scenes. . . . The penalty for the murder of a slave was death; this law exists without parallel in the dark slavery annals both of ancient and modern times. . . . It is a sure criterion of the civilization of ancient Egypt that the soldiers did not carry arms except on duty, and that the private citizens did not carry them at all. Women were treated with much regard. . . . When a party was given the guests were received by the host and hostess, seated side by side in a large armchair. In the paintings their mutual affection is portrayed. Their fond manners, their gestures of endearment, the caresses which they lavish on their children, form sweet and touching scenes of domestic life. . . . The civil laws were administered in such a manner that the poor could have recourse to them as well as the rich. The judges received large salaries that they might be placed above the temptation of bribery, and might never disgrace the image of Truth which they wore round their necks suspended on a golden chain [*The Martyrdom of Man,* pp. 12–14, by Winwood Reade].

Before taking leave of the Pyramid Age, we must say something about Imhotep, the architect who designed the first pyramid. This truly great man, besides being an architect, was Vizier (Prime Minister) to King Zoser of the Third Dynasty (5345–5307 B.C.). In addition, he was an astronomer and magician, and held the post of Chief Physician to the Monarch. In later days he was deified and became the God of Medicine. Known to the Greeks as Imouthes, he was recognized as their own Aesculapius. "A temple was erected to him near the Serapeum at Memphis," we are informed by a pioneer American Egyptologist, "and at the present day every museum possesses a bronze statuette or two of this apotheosized wise man, the proverb-maker, physician and architect of Zoser. The priests who conducted the rebuilding of the temple of Edfu under the Ptolemies, claimed to be reproducing the structure formerly erected there after plans of Imhotep; and it may therefore well be that Zoser was the builder of a temple there." (*A History of Egypt,* p. 95, by James Henry Breasted.)

Egypt's first Golden Age ended in 4163 B.C., at the death of King Neterkere, the last ruler of the Sixth Dynasty. From 4163 to 3554 B.C. chaos reigned in the Nile Valley, and this intermediate period covers Dynasties VII through X. Very often several rulers claimed the throne at the same time. This era of confusion was ended by a nobleman from Thebes named Intef, who became the first king of the Eleventh Dynasty, which was the beginning of the Middle Kingdom. Intef I was succeeded by Intef II, who in turn was followed by five Mentuhoteps. Mentuhotep V was such a feeble monarch that he was toppled from his throne by a minister of state named Amenemhet I, who established the

Twelfth Dynasty. This pharaoh was a man of outstanding ability, and we learn from an inscription of his age that "he restored that which he found ruined; that which a city had taken from its neighbor; while he caused city to know its boundary with city, establishing their landmarks like the heavens, distinguishing their waters according to what was in the writings, investigating according to that which was of old, because he so greatly loved justice." (Cited by Robert Silverberg in *Empires in the Dust,* p. 9.)

Under Sesostris I (3373–3327 B.C.) a period of expansion ensued, and the boundaries of Egypt were extended into Nubia. The armies of Amenemhet II invaded the Sinai Peninsula and, under Sesostris III, the conquest was extended into Syria. In the wake of the armies there followed the Egyptian merchants, and the country enjoyed the benefits of foreign commerce. In the year 3184 B.C. Amenemhet IV died, leaving no heirs to the throne. This created a problem, for in Egypt as well as many other African nations the kingship was inherited through the daughter of the monarch. In other words the new queen transmitted the regal prerogatives to her husband, who became the next pharaoh; that is to say that the kingly office passed from father to son-in-law. In order to preserve the royal succession within the family, the custom was adopted of having the oldest son of the king marry his oldest sister, through whom the right of rulership was transmitted. This made the son of the king also his son-in-law and gave him the right of succession to the throne. Now Amenemhet IV had followed the prescribed procedure by marrying his sister Sebeknefrure. Since this pharaoh died childless, the queen was privileged to select the next king, inasmuch as her new husband would by law inherit the throne.

Queen Sebeknefrure was expected to marry a member of the Theban nobility and elevate him to the throne, but she had other ideas. Instead she married a commoner from Lower

Egypt. This action brought on a civil war; for the Theban nobility refused to have a northerner from the Delta as their king. The civil strife that followed dragged on for about one hundred years. Kings of Dynasty XIII ruled from Thebes while a rival ruler of Dynasty XIV sat on the throne at Memphis. Both monarchs claimed the legal succession to Dynasty XII. The armies of both regimes fought each other up and down the Nile Valley, with neither side being able to put down the other. And while this senseless civil war was going on, the country was invaded by nomads from Asia, known as the Hyksos, or "shepherd-kings." They first conquered Lower Egypt, then moved up the river and captured Thebes. These foreign invaders dominated Egypt during the Fifteenth, Sixteenth, and Seventeenth Dynasties; which covered a time span of about 150 years.

While these alien kings sat on the throne, certain Theban nobles traveled southward to Nubia and organized an underground liberation movement. The Hyksos were expelled from Thebes by an army led by Pharaoh Sekenenre, who ended his career on the field of battle. He was followed in the Theban kingship by Ahmose I, who ascended the throne in 1709 B.C. This king led his army northward, liberated Memphis, and drove the "shepherd-kings" out of Egypt into the desert of Sinai. Thus began the Eighteenth Dynasty, which inaugurated the time of the New Kingdom. The new line of pharaohs erected palaces and temples at Thebes which were among the wonders of the world and were the heralds of a new Golden Age in the Nile Valley. Under Thutmose I (1662–1628) Egyptian imperial power reached its zenith. A fine summary of this achievement has been given by Professor Breasted, whom we quote:

Egypt had now become the controlling power in the far reaching group of civilizations clustering in and about the eastern end of the Mediterranean, the center, perhaps the nucleus of the civilized world

of that day. . . . Seated astride both the intercontinental and inter-oceanic highway, Egypt was building up and dominating the world of contiguous Africa and Eurasia. Traditional limits disappeared, the currents of life eddied no longer within the landmarks of tiny kingdoms, but pulsed from end to end of a great empire, embracing many kingdoms and tongues, from the Upper Nile to the Upper Euphrates. The wealth of Asiatic trade circulating through the eastern end of the Mediterranean, which once flowed down the Euphrates to Babylon, was thus diverted to the Nile Delta, long before united by canal with the Red Sea. All the world traded in the Delta Markets ["Zenith of Egyptian Power," by James Henry Breasted, in the *Cambridge Ancient History,* Vol. II, p. 88, edited by J. B. Bury *et al.*].

The true glory of the age emerged in the reign of Amenhotep III (1538–1501 B.C.). From Syria, timber was imported, and large seaworthy ships were built. With this fleet the Egyptians sailed down the East African coast and traded with the peoples of Punt, from whom they imported cargoes of ivory, ebony, ostrich feathers, spices, and gold. To the south they extended their sway over the Kushites of Nubia, and in the north they overcame a confederation of foes in a battle at Har-Megiddo (Armageddon). The domain of Amenhotep III extended from the confines of Nubia to the valley of the two rivers; and all the territories were so well organized and fairly governed as to greatly enhance their productive potential.

Thebes itself expanded into a great metropolis with walls nine miles in circumference. On the outskirts of the city were the elegant mansions of the nobility, some containing fifty or sixty rooms, and halls with the walls covered with colorful paintings, and embellished with costly inlaid furniture, beautiful vases, and attractively carved ornaments and utensils of ebony, bronze, and ivory. Along the great river, temples were built by the order of the king, and were linked together by avenues of sphinxes. Around the mansions

Gold mask from the tomb of Tutankhamen, Valley of the Kings, Egypt. The Pharaoh's features certainly appear to be more African than Asian or Caucasian.

and temples were tree-shaded boulevards and flower gardens; and the environing landscape was enhanced by a series of lakes. Since the vanquished Hyksos had introduced horses into Egypt, an improved system of transport was adopted: Bigger and better roads were constructed and Egyptian gentlemen traveled over the highways in horse-drawn chariots.

In the year 1501 B.C. the death of Amenhotep III brought to an end a brilliant reign of thirty-six years and five months. He was followed by his son, the boy Amenhotep IV. Queen Ti, mother of the youthful king, ruled as regent until her son reached his majority. The new monarch inaugurated a religious revolution which has made his name famous in the annals of history, and at the same time brought an ignominious end to the Golden Age established by his illustrious father. The young pharaoh quitted Thebes and built a new city, Tell el Amarna, for his capital. He disestablished the hundreds of gods of the Egyptian pantheon and worshiped only one god, Aton, whose symbol was the flaming disc of the sun; and he renamed himself Ikhnaton (devoted to Aton). Warnings from the nomarchs (provincial governors) that hostile armies were set to invade the nation were not heeded by the king, and the priests of the disallowed cults rose up in rebellion. So Ikhnaton, the "Heretic-king," died ingloriously, probably poisoned by enemies, and the Aton cult was abolished.

The youthful Tutankhamen, his son-in-law, ascended to the throne, moved back the capital to Thebes, and restored the old cults to their previous positions of power. The career of King Tut was cut short by his untimely death at the age of seventeen years. The throne was taken over by a priest named Eye, whose reign was a disaster to the country; for during his brief rule nearly all the foreign territories annexed by the great kings of Dynasty XVIII were lost. Then a general from the north, Harmhab, seized the throne from the Usurper, Eye, and brought the period of political decline to an end.

Although the monotheistic Aton cult was crushed in Egypt, it did not perish altogether. For there was a young Egyptian priest named Moshe (Moses), who had received his theological education at Heliopolis, and who became a disciple of Ikhnaton. When Atonism was suppressed in Egypt, Moses led a group of "heretics" out of the country and into Palestine. Our authority for the statement that Moses

was an Egyptian priest is the historian Manetho, whom we believe to be a reliable witness. The opinion of Manetho is endorsed by Strabo, who refers to: "Moses, who was one of the Egyptian priests, taught his followers that it was an egregious error to represent the Deity under the form of animals, as the Egyptians did, or in the shape of man, as was the practice of the Greeks and Africans. . . . It is for this reason, that, rejecting every species of images or idols, Moses wished the Deity to be worshipped without emblems, and according to his proper nature; and he accordingly ordered a temple worthy of him to be erected." (Strabo, *Geography, Book 16,* cited by C. F. Volney, in *The Ruins of Empires,* pp. 150–51.) As we know, Moses was not entirely successful, since many of his followers still worshiped the old gods.

> But in vain did he proscribe the worship of the symbols which prevailed in lower Egypt and in Phoenicia [Volney observes] for his god was nevertheless an Egyptian god, invented by those priests of whom Moses had been the disciple. . . . In vain did Moses wish to blot from his religion everything which had relation to the stars; many traits call them to mind in spite of all he has done. The seven planetary luminaries of the great candlestick; the twelve stones, or signs in the Urim of the high priests; the feast of the two equinoxes (entrances and gates of the two hemispheres); the ceremony of the lamb (the celestial ram then in the fifteenth degree); . . . all remain as so many witnesses of the filiation of his ideas, and of their extraction from the common source [*The Ruins of Empires,* pp. 149–51, by C. F. Volney].[1]

The Nineteenth Dynasty began with the reign of Hormhab (1454–1395 B.C.), but the great ruler of this dynasty was Ramses II (1394–1328 B.C.). This pharaoh in a reign of sixty-six years conquered extensive territories in western Asia and built colossal temples in the Nile Valley. In Ethiopia, for example, this Ramses was worshiped as a god; for among the Kushites he erected six new temples, dedicated to Amen, Ra, and Ptah. In discussing these temples, Breasted tells us that "in all of them Rameses was more or less prominently worshipped, and in one his queen, Nefretiri, was the presiding divinity. Of his Nubian sanctuaries, the great rock-temple at Abu Simbel is the finest and deservedly the goal of modern travellers in Egypt." (*A History of Egypt,* pp. 373–75, by James Henry Breasted.) Ramses III (1230–1199 B.C.) of the Twentieth Dynasty was also a great ruler, and he was succeeded by eight kings all bearing the name Ramses, but none of them attained the status of his greatness.

During the years 1075–714 B.C., known as the Third Intermediate period of Egyptian history, there were four dynasties, XXI, XXII, XXIII, and XXIV—some of the rulers being of Libyan and Ethiopian extraction. Sheshonk I (926–905 B.C.), a Libyan, of the Twenty-Second Dynasty led an army into Palestine, captured Jerusalem, and looted King Solomon's temple.

Then in 761 B.C. the Ethiopian king, Piankhi, ascended the throne of Egypt, and rarely after that date was the Nile Valley ruled by Egyptian kings. Piankhi began his career as king of Nubia and, from his palace in the city of Napata, he watched with misgivings the tribute of gold, cattle, and soldiers which his country was obligated to send to King Osorkon III, of Egypt. Finally he decided to end this unsatisfactory state of affairs and, gathering a large fleet and a mighty army, descended the river to lay siege to Hermopolis. The local ruler King Namlot surrendered the city to the Ethiopian conqueror, and turned over to him a great treasure trove; for from an inscription of Piankhi we read that "Hermopolis threw herself upon her belly and pleaded before the king. Messengers came forth and descended bearing everything beautiful to behold; gold, every splendid costly stone, clothing in a chest, and the diadem which was upon his head; the uraeus which inspireth fear of him, without ceasing

during many days." On visiting Namlot's stables, Piankhi was distressed by the malnutrition visited on the horses during the siege of the city. "His majesty proceeded to the stable of the horses, and the quarters of the foals. When he saw that they had suffered hunger, he said: 'I swear as Ra loves me . . . it is more grievous in my heart that my horses have suffered hunger than any evil deed that thou hast done in the prosecution of thy desire.'" (Cited by James Henry Breasted, *A History of Egypt,* pp. 452–53.)

The conquering Kushite king continued down the river, and his next great prize was Memphis. Finally he captured Heliopolis, and was met there by King Osorkon III, of Bubastis, who yielded his regal powers to the Ethiopian monarch. After returning to Nepata, Piankhi had a granite stele erected in the temple of Amen, and on the four sides of this monument he describes his successful campaign in detail. This ancient record possesses intrinsic merit, and has been praised by a modern authority, as follows:

> It displays literary skill, and an appreciation of dramatic situations which is notable, while the vivacious touches wound here and there quite relieve it of the arid tone usual in such hieroglyphic documents. The imagination endues the personages appearing here more easily with life than those of any other similar historical narrative of Egypt; and the humane Piankhi especially, the lover of horses, remains a *man* far removed from the conventional companion and equal of the gods who inevitably occupies the exalted throne of the pharaohs in all other such records. [*A History of Egypt,* p. 456, by James Henry Breasted].

In the inscription referred to above by Breasted, King Piankhi tells of how he washed his face in a spring sacred to the Sun-god, Ra, at the Temple of Heliopolis. Then, to quote from the inscription:

> He brought an offering on the sand-dune in Heliopolis to Ra at his rising, a great

offering of white oxen, milk, incense, balsam, and all sorts of sweet smelling woods. Then he returned to the Temple of Ra; the superintendent of the Temple praised him highly: the speaker of the prayers spoke the prayer for the averting of enemies from the king. The king performed the ceremony in the Chamber of Purification, the putting on of the bands, the purifying with incense and the water of libations, the handing of flowers for the Hat Benben[2] of the god. He took the flowers, he ascended the steps to the great terrace to see Ra in the Hat Benben, he the king himself. When the prince was alone, he undid the bolt, he opened the doors and saw his father Ra in the Hat Benben, he saw the morning boat of Ra and the evening boat of Tum. He closed the doors, he put the seal on, and sealed it with the royal seal. He declared to the priests, "I have put on the seal, no other king shall go in thither." They threw themselves down before His Majesty and said, "May Horus, the darling of Heliopolis, exist, and remain and never pass away." And he went and entered into the Temple of Tum, and they brought the statue of Tum, the Creator, the lord of Heliopolis, and King Osorkon came to see his majesty[3] [extract from the "Inscription of King Piankhi," cited by Sir James George Frazer in *The Worship of Nature,* p. 563].

The Twenty-Fourth Dynasty consisted of only one king, Bocchoris, who according to Manetho reigned only six years (720–714 B.C.). The Twenty-Fifth Dynasty has been called the Kushite or Ethiopian Dynasty. It began in 714 B.C. when, to cite Herodotus: "Egypt was invaded by a vast army of Ethiopians, led by Sabacos, their king." (*History of Herodotus,* p. 129.) This king, better known as Shabaka (714–702 B.C.), successfully undertook the conquest of Lower Egypt and established Ethiopian supremacy in that region. Then he started an Asiatic campaign in which he waged war with the Assyrians. His army escaped defeat only because the Assyrian hordes were afflicted by a plague and were forced to retreat. This king was succeeded by Shabataka, who after a reign of twelve years was slain by Taharka, who seized the crown and set up his capital at Tanis. The reign of this pharaoh was marked by prosperity and cultural advance. The Egyptologist Weigall has referred to this period as "that astonishing epoch of nigger domination."

A temple erected at Karnak was one of the glories of ancient Egypt. "The temple built at Thebes," says Professor DuBois, "had a relief representing the four courts of the four quarters of the Nilotic world: Dedun, the great God of Ethiopia, represents the south; Sopd, the eastern desert; Sebek, the western desert; and Horus, the north." (*The World and Africa,* p. 137, by W. E. Burghardt DuBois.)

There is a tradition that Taharka led expeditions as far as the Strait of Gibraltar. The country was faced with an invasion from Assyria, and Taharka fought the Assyrians until age forced him to turn over the reins of government to Tatutamen; but the new king could not contain the invading foe, and Ashurbanipal's Assyrian armies ascended the Nile and captured and looted the great city of Thebes. But the Assyrians could not hold on to Egypt, so they soon retreated to their own land. The next dynasty, the Twenty-Sixth, lasted from 663 to 527 B.C., and was the last line of native Egyptian kings to rule over the Nilotic dominions.

The last great African pharaoh to reign in Egypt was Ahmose II (569–525 B.C.), of Libyan ancestry. This king, whom the Greeks called Amasis, was a great statesman, but he could not save his country from foreign domination. The best soldiers of the Egyptian army had many years before deserted to the Ethiopian king at Meroe, and Amasis was forced to depend on Libyan and Greek mercenaries for defense against foreign invasion. Being a good diplomat, he managed to maintain peace in his realm, but after his death, early in 525 B.C., the kingship fell to Psamtik III, and after a few months the land of Egypt was overwhelmed by the armies of King Cambyses of Persia. Thus was ushered in Dynasty XXVII. Four puppet dynasties under Persian control followed, lasting until 332 B.C., when the Nile-land succumbed to Alexander the Great. His successors, the Ptolemies, ruled until 30 B.C., when Egypt became a Roman province.

From Menes to Amasis was almost five thousand years, and the record of Egyptian civilization under her native rulers was highly creditable. A summary of the achievements of this African culture has been so interestingly written by a contemporary German scholar that we take the liberty of reproducing it:

The insurgent Amasis stood at the end of Egypt's history, but at its beginnings lay the Nile mud, which came from the interior of Africa, spread itself over the annually-flooded river valley and proved to be an excellent fertilizer. And even in the Neolithic Age men were sowing wheat and barley there. These Neolithic children of the Nile were East Hamitic Africans, related to the present-day Galla, Somali and Massai in East Africa; the later Egyptians were their descendants. The language of the Egyptians was an East Hamitic dialect, as is spoken today by the natives between the Upper Nile and the Masai steppes. Egyptian skeletons, statues and countless pictures of Egyptians in their temples and monuments show the same racial characteristics as the Nubians and the Nilotic tribes, the brown-skinned hunters of the steppes and the savannah husbandmen of the Sudan. Therefore Egypt was a great kingdom created by Africans. . . . Of African inspiration are the pyramids, the golden burial chambers, the statues, plastic arts, temple friezes and other great Egyptian works of art. The Sphinx is an African monument, the hieroglyphs are an African script, and Ammon, Isis and Osiris are African gods. So great was the achievement of the Africans in the Nile Valley that all the great men of ancient Europe journeyed there—the philosophers Thales and Anaximander,

the mathematician Pythagoras, the statesman Solon and an endless stream of historians and geographers whose works are all based on Herodotus' outstanding descriptions of Egypt, to which the second volume of his history is entirely devoted [*It Began in Babel,* p. 58, Herbert Wendt].

Alexander the Great, shortly before his death, planned to build a new city on the Mediterranean coast of Egypt, but he never lived to see this city, which was actually built by one of his generals, named Ptolemy. The new city was named Alexandria, in memory of the Macedonian conqueror. The Alexandrian culture, which stemmed from the building of the city, was under the rule of Greek kings, but the civilization was more Oriental than Hellenic, for the Greeks were inferior to the Orientals, and even to the Romans, in material culture. Much of the lore of ancient Egypt was inherited and diffused by the Hellenistic Alexandrians of the Ptolemaic age. After the split-up of Alexander's empire, Ptolemy got Egypt as his share, and became the first king of the Ptolemaic Dynasty.

The city of Alexandria was built on a strip of land five or six miles long, and about two miles in width, between the Mediterranean Sea and Lake Mareotis. In the harbor of Alexandria was the Island of Pharos, and on this island was erected a lighthouse, one of the Seven Wonders of the World. It was built of marble and reared its pinnacle four hundred feet into the air, and on the summit was a light which could be seen thirty miles out at sea. This grand structure was erected at a cost of about $680,000; and in those days dollars were worth much more than they are at the present time. The walls of Alexandria were about fifteen miles in circumference, and underground cisterns were built to store a supply of fresh water sufficient to meet the needs of an entire population for one year. The city was laid out in modern fashion, with streets running north-south and east-west and crossing at right angles to each other. Canobic

Street ran from one end of the city to the other, from east to west, a distance of five to six miles; it was over one hundred feet wide, and was lined on both sides by a marble colonnade. Another boulevard, equally wide and stately, ran from north to south. These avenues were lined with noble palms and at night were illuminated with lamps.

The mansions, palaces, and public buildings were faced with white marble and polished granite. The glare of the sun was subdued by the use of veils and curtains of green silk, which could be seen everywhere. At the intersection of the two main boulevards was the magnificent tomb of Alexander the Great—in which rested the mummified remains of that monarch—surrounded by gardens, fountains, and obelisks. The glories of Alexandria were the Museum and the Library, institutions which outshone by far the superb palaces, temples, and theaters of the great city. In the establishment of the Museum, and the famous Library, which was an adjunct of the Museum, Ptolemy I had in view three objectives: (1) the perpetuation of extant knowledge, (2) the increase of such knowledge, and (3) the diffusion of knowledge.

On the abdication of Ptolemy I, his son Ptolemy II ascended the throne of Egypt (285 B.C.); and during his reign (285–247 B.C.), Alexandria entered its Golden Age. The coronation of Ptolemy II was an affair of great pomp and ceremony. The following splendid account of it is from the pen of Joseph McCabe:

> From morn to dusk of a mild November day a stupendous procession paraded broad, marble lined avenues. . . . Fourteen lions led a train of panthers, leopards, lynxes, and a rhinoceros. Nubian slaves carried 600 tusks of ivory, 2,000 blocks of ebony, and gold and silver vessels filled with gold dust. A large gold-and-ivory statue of Dionysus rode in a chariot at the head of a vintage pageant which included 24 chariots containing gaily-dressed Hindu ladies and drawn by elephants, and 80 chariots drawn by Asiatic antelopes,

goats and wild asses. Hundreds of slaves carried strange birds in cages or on boughs of trees, and trays of perfume and spices, or led thousands of Indian dogs on the leash. Statues of Gods and kings rode in chariots of ivory and gold. In the royal box were a dozen of the Greek world's most famous scholars and poets; and doubtless they sat close in the specially built banquet hall, with marble columns shaped like palms, the choicest paintings in the world, hangings of Egyptian scarlet and Phoenician purple, and large gold vessels studded with diamonds and rubies. The coronation cost, it is said, 600,000 pounds; and the gold crowns presented to the young king and queen by the cities of the world were worth more than that in value [*The Golden Ages of History,* pp. 66–67, by Joseph McCabe].

The chief librarian of Ptolemy II was a man named Callimachus; and one of his projects was a collection of literature embracing the sacred books of the Ethiopians, Indians, Persians, Elamites, Babylonians, Assyrians, Romans, Phoenicians, Syrians, and Greeks. The chief librarian was ordered by the king to buy whatever books he could at the expense of the government. All books brought into Egypt by foreigners were taken to the Museum; correct copies of such works were made by a corps of transcribers; a copy was given to the owner and the original was placed in the Library. Sometimes large sums of money were paid for books. Ptolemy Euergetes obtained from a citizen of Athens the works of Sophocles, Euripides, and Aeschylus; and to the owner he returned transcripts of the books plus an indemnity of about $15,000. The Library boasted a large and fine collection of books, the total running to over 400,000 volumes.

The Museum was in fact a university, containing Faculties of astronomy, mathematics, literature, and medicine; and connected with the Museum were an astronomical observatory, a chemical laboratory, and an anatomical dissection room. The scientists and scholars of the Museum especially distinguished themselves in the fields of mathematics, astronomy, and geography. One of the shining lights of the Museum was the mathematician, Euclid, author of a "Geometry" still taught in our schools. Ptolemy I asked Euclid to simplify the study of geometry so that he could learn it without too much effort; and to this request Euclid replied: "In geometry there is no special path for kings." Also connected with the Museum was the mathematician Apollonius, author of treatises on conic sections; the famous mathematician and physicist, Archimedes; and Eratosthenes, who was both an astronomer and a geographer. Greatest among the astronomers were Hipparchus and Ptolemy. Another astronomer of note was Sosigenes, who revised the Egyptian calendar at the behest of Julius Caesar, and hence was the true author of the Julian calendar. At the Museum were also engineers and inventors, such as Ctesibius, who invented the single-cylinder fire engine; while his pupil, Hero, improved this engine by constructing it with two cylinders. This same Hero invented the first steam engine, the forerunner of the modern steam turbine. As a center for scientific research the Museum flourished for one hundred years, then went into a decline.

The Library survived until it was burned by a Roman army led by Julius Caesar in 48 B.C. The Library was largely restored by the Romans, by importing books from other libraries, especially that of King Eumenes of Pergamum, whose library was presented to Queen Cleopatra by Mark Antony. This second Alexandrian Library was destroyed by fanatical Christian monks in 389 A.D. and was never rebuilt. The story of the destruction of the Library by the Arab invaders in the seventh century is false, since there was at that time no Library in Alexandria for them to destroy. By the time Alexandria's period of progress had come to an end the Romans had become the new custodians of civilization.

Among the great inventions of the Egyptians were the alphabet, paper, ink, and the pen.

The first paper was made of thin strips of papyrus reeds pasted together; ink was made from vegetable gum and soot mixed with water. By dipping a pointed reed into the ink the Egyptian scribe wrote messages on the papyrus sheet. Writing was a basic invention, and its influence on the evolution of civilization was profound. "The invention of writing and of a convenient system of records on paper," says Breasted, "has had a greater influence in the uplifting of the human race than any other intellectual achievement in the career of man. It was more important than all the battles ever fought and all the constitutions ever devised." (*Ancient Times*, p. 45, by James Henry Breasted.)

Another great Egyptian invention is the calendar. The earliest Egyptians measured time by the moon; for the month, the interval between two new moons, was the unit of time measurement. The moon-month varies in length from 29 to 30 days, and the lunar calendar is cumbersome and inaccurate. The lunar year of 354 days is 11 days shorter than the solar year; and such a calendar can be made to work only by intercalating an extra month at suitable intervals. The Egyptians met this difficulty by devising an accurate calendar. They noticed that the dog star, Sothis (Sirius), rose heliacally (before sunrise) on July 19th, at the beginning of the inundation (the annual overflow of the Nile). This gave them an improved calendar of 365 days in length. The 12 months of the Egyptian year were uniformly of 30 days each in duration, giving a total of 360 days; so 5 feast days were added at the end of the year to make the count come out right. Each 30-day month was divided into 3 weeks of 10 days each; and there were 3 seasons of the year; the Inundation, the Cultivation, and the Harvest, each season consisting of 4 months. The Egyptian astronomers soon discovered that the true length of the year was 365¼ days; hence the calendar could have been improved by adding an extra day every four years, but this was not done. Ptolemy Euergetes issued a decree in 238 B.C., in which it was commanded that every fourth year should be 366 days in length; but the Egyptians were opposed to the institution of leap year so they ignored the royal decree. This calendar, established in Egypt over six thousand years ago, has descended the stream of history to us. It was nearly ruined by certain Roman politicians who made awkward alterations in the length and names of the months, but for these deplorable changes the Egyptians were nowise responsible.

Since the lore of astronomy and the calendar were the basis of much of the mythology, ritual, and religion of ancient Egypt, which in turn has profoundly affected all the great religious systems of later days, we deem it proper to discuss certain aspects of these ancient African cults and creeds, and their effects on other cultures. Sun worship was dominant in the later phases of Egyptian culture, but it was preceded by stellar and lunar cults. The researches of Sir Wallis Budge and Sir Norman Lockyer have shown the priority of star worship in the Nile Valley. The pyramids of northern Egypt are oriented east and west; i.e., to the sun. In southern Egypt, the more ancient step pyramids face southeast; and, as Budge points out: "with such an amplitude that it could not have been a question of the sunlight entering the shrine, we are driven therefore to star-worship." ("On the Orientation of the Pyramids and Temples in the Sudan," by E. A. Wallis Budge, in Vol. 65, *Proceedings of the Royal Society,* London, 1899.) In fact some of the important temples of southern Egypt and Ethiopia were oriented to Alpha Centauri. Lockyer shows in his *The Dawn of Astronomy* that Canopus, a brilliant star in the southern hemisphere, figured prominently in the stellar worship of ancient Egypt. A good summary of Lockyer's data is given by Richard H. Allen, as follows:

Lockyer tells us of a series of temples at Edfu, Philae, Amada, and Semneh, so

oriented at their erection 6400 B.C., as to show Canopus heralding the sunrise at the autumnal equinox, when it was known as the symbol of Khons, or Khonsu,[4] the first southern star-god; and of other similar temples later. At least two of the great structures at Karnak, of 2100 and 1700 B.C., respectively pointed to its setting; as did another at Naga, and the temple of Khons at Thebes, built by Rameses III about 1300 B.C., afterwards restored and enlarged under the Ptolemies. It thus probably was the prominent object in the religion of Southern Egypt, where it represented the god of the waters [*Star Names and Their Meanings,* pp. 70–71, by Richard H. Allen].

In the pantheon of ancient Egypt, the moon-god Thoth held high rank; and on the monuments he is pictured as an ibis, with mingled black and white feathers, representing the dark and bright sides of the moon. The very name "Thoth" means "The Measurer," an appropriate epithet for the moon-god. So he is shown wearing the lunar crescent and disk, and holding a stylus and a notched palm branch; and he is also identified with Hermes Trismegistus, author of the sacred books, and the father of magic.

Egyptian sun-worship was a very complex affair; since the sun was known by several names, and its various attributes were differentiated, and made the objects of divine worship. "The Egyptians in the deification of the Sun," observes Mr. Olcott, "considered the luminary in its different aspects, separating the light from the heat of the Sun, and the orb from the rays. Egyptian sun worship was therefore polytheistic, and several distinct deities were worshipped as sun-gods. Thus, there were sun-gods representing the physical orb, the intellectual Sun, the Sun considered as the source of heat, and the source of light, the power of the Sun, the Sun in the firmament, and the Sun in his resting place." (*Sun Lore of All Ages,* pp. 150–51, by William Tyler Olcott.)

The greatest of the sun-gods of ancient Egypt, it seems, was Ra or Re, who was a personification of the physical sun; indeed Ra was just the ordinary everyday name for the sun. Ra was a member of a solar trinity, the other partners of the trio being Osiris and Horus. The sun-god Ra was usually represented as a man with the head of a hawk holding in one hand the regal scepter, and in the other the crux ansata (cross with a handle). On his head was a globe or disk, around which a uraeus, or asp, was coiled; the serpent being symbolic of the power over life and death. The figure of Ra and the disk on his head were generally painted red, since the god was particularly associated with the heat of the midday sun. Osiris, on the other hand, was emblematic of the setting sun. As a dweller among men, his form was that of the Apis Bull; as Judge of the Dead, he was pictured as a mummy, of sacred blue color, armed with the rod of authority and the crux ansata, and wearing the double crown of upper and lower Egypt. His eldest son, Horus, was the rising sun, who slew the Dragon of Darkness with a spear (ray).

Another Egyptian sun-god, Amen or Ammon, was a personification of the sun after setting, and thus hidden from view. Amen was depicted as a man with the head and horns of a ram; and his figure was painted blue, the sacred color of the source of life. The word "ram" means "concealment" in the Egyptian language, and Amen as the sun-god was called, "the Concealed One," an appropriate title for the solar orb after it had disappeared in the west, and hence descended into the underworld. In Thebes, the cults of Amen and Ra were merged and the sun was there worshiped under the name Amen-Ra. Solarism reached its zenith in the reign of Akhnaton (Amenhotep IV); for this pharaoh forbade the worship of any god save the "great living disk of the Sun"; and he ordered the names of the other gods erased from the monuments and decreed the destruction of their images. This worship of the solar disk, under the name of Aton, came to an end with the death of the monarch, when the old gods again came back into their own. Among the minor Egyptian sun-gods were Ptah; an embodiment of the life-giving power of the sun, and Mandu, the personification of the power of the midday sun of summer. Even the rays of the sun were deified, under the names of Gom, Kons, and Moni; they were regarded as sons of the sun.

So far we have discussed star-gods, moon-gods, and sun-gods, but there were, in the Nilotic pantheon, other gods composite in nature; that is to say, they absorbed the traits and aspects of many other deities. A good example of this type of god is Osiris, the most popular divinity of ancient Egypt. As Professor Alexandre Moret explains:

Of all the gods called into being by the hopes and fears of men who dwelt in times of yore on the banks of the Nile, Osiris was the most popular. His appearance surprises us least of all, when the procession of Egyptian divinities pass before our eyes; this falcon is Horus; this goose Geb or Ammon; that crocodile is Sebek; yonder bull is Hapi, the Nile; and the hippopotamus is Ririt; the pair of lions is Shou and Tafnuit; the vulture and serpent are the goddesses of the South and the North. Stranger still are those divinities whose human bodies are surmounted by the heads of beasts; from the shoulders of Thoth arise the slender neck and the long bill of the ibis; Khnoum wears a ram's head with twisted horns; Sekhit has the terrifying muzzle of a lioness; and Bast carries the head of a cat with ears pricked up and gleaming eyes. By the side of these animals, fetishes and totems of the ancient tribes, raised to the rank of national divinities in more modern times, there appeared from the earliest days of United Egypt, a god whose worship became common to all the cities. Osiris in the beginning a multiform fetish, sometimes a tree, sometimes a bull, detaches himself from his totemic origins and at a very early date assumes a purely

Osiris, the most popular god of ancient Egypt, in his human form, clasping the ox-herd's whip and the shepherd's crook. Several scholars believe that the worship of Osiris passed into Egypt from Ethiopia.

human form. Wherever shone forth the calm beauty of this face whose oval was prolonged by the false beard and tall white mitre, wherever was seen the melancholy outline of this body, draped in a shroud, the two fists crossed upon his breast and clasping the ox-herd's whip and the shepherd's crook, the Egyptians from every province recognized the "chief" of mankind, the "ruler of eternity," a god who by reason of his visible shape was nearly akin to man [*Kings and Gods of Egypt,* pp. 69–70, by Alexandre Moret].

Osiris was the son of the sky-goddess Nut, who was the wife of the sun-god Ra. The father of Osiris, however, was not Ra, but the earth-god Seb. When Ra discovered the unfaithfulness of his wife, he pronounced a curse upon her, predicting that the child would be born in

no month and no year. But Nut had acquired another lover, namely the god Thoth. Thoth in the meantime had been playing a game of draughts with the moon, and had won from the lunar orb one seventy-second part of each day. The fractional parts were compounded into five whole days, and were added by Thoth to the Egyptian year of 360 days. This was a mythological attempt to account for the five supplementary days which were added to the Egyptian year in order to bring the lunar and solar calendars into agreement; and since these extra five days were regarded as entirely outside the year of twelve months, the curse of the sun-god Ra did not rest on them.

Osiris was born on the first of the supplementary days; and at his nativity a mysterious voice rang out announcing the earthly advent of the "Lord of All." But Osiris was not an only child; on the second supplementary day, Nut gave birth to the elder Horus; likewise the sky-goddess became the mother of Set on the third day; of the goddess Isis on the fourth day; and of the goddess Nephthys on the fifth. In due time Set married his sister Nephthys, and Osiris married his sister Isis.

Osiris, it is said, forsook the realm of the gods and became an earthly king; he found the Egyptians savages and conferred on them the blessings of civilization; since the inhabitants of the Nile-land had been cannibals before the earthly pilgrimage of Osiris. Queen Isis found barley and wheat growing wild on the banks of the great river, and King Osiris introduced the cultivation of these grains among the people, who then gave up cannibalism and accommodated themselves to a diet of corn. Osiris was the original gatherer of fruit from trees; he trained the creeping vines to twine themselves around poles, and was the first to tread the grapes. The good king then turned over the government of Egypt to his wife, Isis; while he traveled over the world distributing the blessings of civilization and agriculture to all mankind. In lands where the soil and climate did not permit the culture of the vine, Osiris taught the people to brew beer from barley. On returning to Egypt, the benevolent monarch, on account of the blessings he had diffused among men, was recognized as a god, and thus worshiped by a grateful people.

But Osiris had a wicked and jealous brother named Set; and the evil Set, with seventy-two companions, plotted the death of Osiris. By craft, Set got the measure of his brother's body, and constructed a coffer of attractive design of exactly the same size; then at a banquet, when drinking and revelry were at their height, the wily Set brought in his coffer, and offered to make a present of it to anyone whose body would fit into it exactly. All present tried out the coffer, except Osiris, and none of them fitted into it. Then Osiris lay down in the coffer, which fitted him exactly.

Immediately the conspirators slammed the lid of the coffer, fastened it with nails, and sealed it with molten lead. The coffer was then thrown into the Nile. According to Plutarch, all this occurred on the 17th day of the month of Athyr, when the sun entered the zodiacal sign of Scorpio (The Scorpion), and in the twenty-eighth year of the reign of Osiris.

The widowed Isis soon afterward went into exile in the papyrus swamps of the Delta; and here she gave birth to a son, the younger Horus. Meanwhile, the floating coffin of Osiris had drifted into the Mediterranean Sea, and was finally washed up on the coast of Phoenicia. Here a mysterious tree sprang up, and enclosed the chest in its trunk. The local king saw the tree, and so admired it that he had it cut down and fashioned into a pillar for his palace at Byblos. Isis wandered over the face of the earth seeking the body of her dead husband and eventually arrived at Byblos. After cutting open the tree-pillar and retrieving the coffer, Isis swathed the pillar in linen, poured ointment on it, and gave it to the King of Byblos. The sacred pillar was installed in a Temple of Isis, where it was afterward worshiped by the natives of Byblos. The body of Osiris was taken back to Egypt by Isis and there hidden in a secret place. But one night, while Set was hunting a boar by the light of the full moon, he by chance discovered the hidden chest. Proceeding then to open it, he took the body of Osiris, chopped it into fourteen pieces and scattered them all over the land of Egypt. Isis later searched for and found all of the parts except one, and she buried each fragment where she found it; and that is why so many cities of Egypt claimed possession of the grave of Osiris. The missing part of Osiris was the phallus; so Isis made an image of it for use in the religious festivals of the Egyptians. Such is the myth of Osiris as told by Plutarch in his treatise *On Isis and Osiris*, with some fragmentary data from the ancient Egyptian literature.

The story of Osiris has a happier ending in some of the native Egyptian versions which supplement the account by Plutarch. We are told that, when Isis had discovered the body and collected the fragments, she and her sister Nephthys sat down and wept. This lament was heard by the sun-god Ra who, moved by compassion, sent down from heaven the jackal-headed god Anubis. This divinity, with the help of Horus, Isis, Nephthys, and the ibis-headed Thoth, reassembled the body of Osiris from the numerous fragments; then the gods made a mummy of the corpse. Isis, who by good fortune was fitted out with wings, fanned the mummy with them. The breath of life returned to Osiris, and in consequence occurred his resurrection from the dead. He then betook himself to the other world to reign in perpetuity as the King of the Dead. His son Horus, having grown to manhood, became a king and ruled on Earth; later he became the third person of the great Egyptian trinity of Osiris, Isis, and Horus. The resurrection of Osiris is pictured in a series of bas-reliefs on the walls of that god's temple at Denderah. First we see the dead god as a mummy lying on his bier; then he rises gradually from the bier; and finally we see him standing erect between the guardian wings of Isis, who is stationed behind him. In front of the risen god there is a male figure who holds up before his eyes a crux ansata, the symbol of eternal life.

Another representation of the momentous mystery is depicted in the Temple of Isis at Philae. In this sculpture we see the body of Osiris with stalks of corn growing out of it; and nearby stands a priest pouring water on the cornstalks from a pitcher. Accompanying this scene is an inscription which reads: "This is the form of him whom one may not name, Osiris of the Mysteries, who springs from the returning waters." From the above, we gather that Osiris was a personification of the corn, which sprouts up out of the fields after they have been fertilized by the annual inundation of the Nile. In fact, Osiris was sometimes called the "crop," or the "harvest." So we may reasonably conclude that in one of his aspects this god was a personification of the corn which annually died and came to life again.

Besides being a corn-spirit, Osiris was, among other things, a tree-god. His tree aspect was probably the more primitive of the two, since tree-worship is thought to be an earlier form of religion than the worship of cereals. The church-father Firmicus Maternus wrote a book, *The Errors of the Profane Religions,* where a pagan religious ceremony is described, in which Osiris was featured as a tree-spirit. The worshipers of the god first chopped down a pine tree; then the center of the tree was hollowed out. From the excavated wood an image of Osiris was fashioned; and the image was buried like a corpse in the hollow of the pine. The enclosed image was kept for a year, then burned. In the Hall of Osiris at Denderah, there is a picture of a coffin, within which is shown the hawk-headed mummy of the god, and the coffin is portrayed as enclosed within the trunk of a tree. This scene tends to confirm the accuracy of the account of the ceremony given us by Firmicus Maternus.

Osiris was also a fertility-god. Phallic images of him were displayed in the temples and carried in processions.

> As a god of vegetation [Frazer points out], Osiris was naturally conceived as a god of creative energy in general, since men at a certain stage of evolution fail to distinguish between the reproductive powers of animals and plants. Hence a striking feature of his worship was the coarse but expressive symbolism by which this aspect of his nature was presented to the eye not merely of the initiated but of the multitude. At his festival women used to go about the village singing songs in his praise and carrying obscene images of him which they set in motion by means of strings. The custom was probably a charm to ensure the growth of crops [*The Golden Bough,* abridged edition, p. 381, by James George Frazer].

A familiar role of Osiris was that of a god of the dead; among his titles were Ruler of the Dead, Lord of the Underworld, and Lord of Eternity. On the monuments he is shown occupying the judgment seat, armed with the staff of authority, and holding the crux ansata; while carved on his breast is a St. Andrew's cross; and the throne on which he sits is adorned with a pattern of squares in two colors, like a checkerboard, representing the good and evil which came before him for judgment.

Osiris also shone as a moon-god. He is said to have reigned in Egypt twenty-eight years. This is no doubt an allusion to the twenty-eight days of the lunar month. The rending of the body of Osiris into fourteen parts by Set and his evil companions refers to the waning of the moon, which was imagined to lose a portion of itself on each of the fourteen days of the second half of the lunar month. In the myth, Set finds the body of Osiris at the time of the full moon; the dismemberment of Osiris consequently began with the waning moon. That the god was sometimes identified with the moon we know from fact that he was on occasion depicted as a mummy, wearing on his head a crescent moon in place of the usual crown. Plutarch in his *Isis and Osiris* discusses the theory that Osiris was the moon, and that Set, or Typhon, was the sun; "because the Moon," says he, "with her humid and generative light, is favorable to the propagation of animals and the growth of plants; while the sun with his fierce fire scorches and burns up all growing things, renders the greater part of the earth uninhabitable by reason of his blaze, and often overpowers the Moon herself."

Last, but not least, Osiris was a sun-god; and on this, most authorities on the history and religion of Egypt agree. An outstanding scholar renders the following verdict: "Mythologically, Osiris was the Sun after its disappearance in the west, where he was slain by the envious night, and yet destined to rise again the next morning." (*A Concise History of Religion,* Vol. I,

p. 108, by F. J. Gould.) From this point of view Sir J. G. Frazer vigorously dissents; for he regards Osiris as a vegetation-god, and considers theories identifying that god with the sun as ill-founded. In his own words:

> The ground upon which some modern writers seem chiefly to rely for the identification of Osiris with the Sun, is that the story of his death fits better with the solar phenomena than with any other in nature. It may readily be admitted that the daily appearance and disappearance of the Sun might very naturally be expressed by a myth of his death and resurrection; and writers who regard Osiris as the Sun are careful to indicate that it is the diurnal, and not the annual, course of the Sun to which they understand the myth to apply. Thus Renouf, who identifies Osiris with the Sun, admitted the Egyptian Sun could not with any show of reason be described as dead in winter. But if his daily death was the theme of the legend, why was it celebrated by an annual ceremony? This fact alone seems fatal to the interpretation of the myth as descriptive of sunset and sunrise. Again, though the Sun may be said to die daily, in what sense can he be said to be torn in pieces? [*The Golden Bough,* p. 384, by James George Frazer].

The objections to identifying Osiris with the sun, urged by Frazer, have been ably criticized by the Right Honorable John M. Robertson. According to Robertson:

> Rightly intent on establishing a hitherto ill-developed principle of mythological interpretation, the cult of the vegetation spirit, Dr. Frazer has unduly ignored the conjunction seen deductively to be inevitable and inductively to be normal between the concept of the vegetation-god and that of others, in particular the Sun-god. He becomes for once vigorously polemical in his attack on the thesis that Osiris was a sun-god, as if that were excluded once for all by proving him a vegetation-god. The answer is that he was both; and that such a synthesis was inevitable. . . . Mithra, who, so far as the records go, was primordially

associated with the Sun, and was thereby named to the last, is mythically born on December 25th, clearly because of the winter solstice and the rising of the constellation of the virgin above the horizon. Dionysus and Adonis, Dr. Frazer shows, are vegetation gods. Yet they too are both born on December 25th, as was the Babe-Sun-God Horus, who was, however, exhibited as rising from a lotus plant. Now, why should the vegetation-God be born at the winter solstice save as having been identified with the Sun-god? [*Christianity and Mythology,* 2nd edition, p. 33, by John M. Robertson].

There is a considerable amount of literature on the Osirian cult of ancient Egypt. Among the best is *Adonis, Attis, Osiris: Studies in the History of Oriental Religion* by Sir James George Frazer, third edition, revised and enlarged, in two volumes bound in one; Part IV of *The Golden Bough: A Study in Magic and Religion* published by University Books, New Hyde Park, N. Y., 1961.

A smaller book, well worth reading, is *Osiris: A Study in Myths, Mysteries and Religion* by Harold P. Cooke. After a scholarly analysis of Osirianism, Cooke concludes: "The worship and rites of Osiris may have passed into Egypt, I think, from the neighboring state of Ethiopia." (*Osiris,* p. 154.) Cooke's opinion is quite plausible, for Osiris was indubitably a god of African origin.

This theory is sustained brilliantly by Sir E. A. Wallis Budge in *Osiris: The Egyptian Religion of the Resurrection.* In the introduction of the latest edition of this book we are told by a learned scholar, Dr. Jane Harrison, that: "We may say at once that we believe Dr. Budge triumphantly establishes his main thesis. Osiris is an African, though not necessarily a Nilotic god. Egyptian religion, in . . . its general Negroid coloring, is African through and through." Sir Wallis Budge possessed a profound knowledge of things Egyptian; and speaking of the ancient Egyptian people he declares: "Everything that we know of them

proves that they possessed all the characteristics of the African race, and especially of that portion of it which lived in that great tract of country which extends from ocean to ocean, right across Africa, and is commonly known as the Sudan, i.e., the country *par excellence* of the Blacks." (*Osiris,* Vol. I, p. 174, by E. A. Wallis Budge.) The Osirian mythology and religion are also discussed in *Traits of Divine Kingship in Africa* by the Reverend P. Hadfield.

Another phase of the myths, rites, and religious beliefs of the ancient Egyptians, which we must consider briefly, is that complex of astro-theology exemplified by the symbolism of the zodiac. The zodiac is an imaginary band encircling the celestial sphere; stretching eight degrees on each side of the ecliptic, the apparent path of the sun. The zodiac is divided in twelve sections, each corresponding to one month. The signs and constellations were originally the same but, due to the procession of the equinoxes, each sign moves westward into the next constellation in about 2,155 years. A sign therefore makes a complete circuit of the heavens in about 26,000 years. The constellations of the zodiac have the following names: Aries (the Ram or Lamb), Taurus (the Bull), Gemini (the Twins), Cancer (the Crab), Leo (the Lion), Virgo (the Virgin), Libra (the Balances), Scorpio (the Scorpion), Sagittarius (the Archer), Capricorn (the Goat), Aquarius (the Water-Carrier), and Pisces (the Fishes). These are the signs and constellations of the zodiac as standardized by the ancient Greeks; but there were earlier zodiacs with other signs and symbols, which we shall discuss as we proceed.

The solar zodiac can be traced back to ancient Egypt, where it was known at a remote period of time; but the solar zodiac was preceded by a lunar zodiac, which was divided into twenty-seven or twenty-eight Lunar Mansions instead of twelve signs. "Although the Zodiac is now determined by the course in the heavens apparently pursued by the Sun in his annual journey through the sky," we are told by a noted astronomer, "it is very probable that it was originally determined by the path of the Moon, which follows very closely the path of the Sun, and which can be observed at the same time as the stars. The moon moves eastward among the stars at such a rate that it accomplishes a complete circuit of the sky in about 28 days." (*Astronomy,* p. 250, by Professor Arthur M. Harding.) Since the lunar month is between twenty-seven and twenty-eight days, the Lunar Mansions were sometimes twenty-seven in number, though twenty-eight was the usual figure. The Hindus had a Lunar Zodiac of twenty-seven mansions, whereas the Chinese and Arabs counted twenty-eight.

The symbolism of the zodiac is beautifully displayed in the myth of Hercules. "Of all the ancient divinities," Edward Carpenter observes, "perhaps Hercules is the one whose role as a Sun-god is most generally admitted. The helper of gods and men, a mighty traveller, and invoked everywhere as the Savior, his labors for the good of the world became ultimately defined and systematized as 12, and corresponding in number to the signs of the Zodiac." (*Pagan and Christian Creeds,* p. 48, by Edward Carpenter.) This myth of Hercules was known to the Sumerians, Phoenicians, and Greeks. Herodotus speculated on its origin and traced it back to the Egyptians. (See *The History of Herodotus,* pp. 96–97.) There is no god in the official Egyptian pantheon named Hercules, but there was an ancient Greek tradition that Hercules was identical with the ancient Nilotic deity, Khonsu. Mr. George St. Clair, after considering the principal gods of ancient Egypt, directs our attention to "a little group of divinities standing apart."

These are Amen, Mut and Khonsu, often spoken of as the Triad of Thebes, or the Trinity of Ethiopia. . . . Budge tells us that the Theban triad had nothing whatever to do with the "Book of the Dead," and from this we may suspect that they were either

gods newly come up or gods of foreign derivation. For some good reason the orthodox Egyptian of the old school kept them out of his sacred books. They were divinities of Thebes, and that city was hundreds of miles south of Heliopolis; they were the Trinity of Ethiopia and not of Egypt [*Creation Records Discovered in Egypt: Studies in the Book of the Dead,* p. 404, by George St. Clair].

In the myth of Hercules, the sun (of which Hercules is the personification) begins his zodiacal journey in the constellation Leo, *the Lion.* So the first labor of Hercules was the slaying of the Nemean lion. After killing the lion, the hero flayed the beast and used its skin thereafter as a shield. The skin of the lion has been compared to the tawny clouds which the sun trails behind him as he fights his way through the vapors which he eventually overcomes.

When the sun enters Virgo, the constellation of the *Hydra* sets. The second labor of Hercules was the destruction of the Lernean hydra. This monster had several heads, one of which was immortal. As the hydra raised his heads one by one to attack Hercules, the demi-god burned off the heads in turn. He disposed of the immortal head by burying it beneath a stone. "As the beast was possessed of many heads," writes William Tyler Olcott, "so the storm-wind must continually supply new clouds to vanquish the Sun; but the lighter vapor and mist, the immortal head, is only conquered for a time. The sun easily burns up the heavy clouds, the mortal heads, but only hides temporarily the immortal head which raises again and again to daunt him. In the fight Hercules was attended by his friend Iolus,—this name recalls that of Iole, signifying the violet tinted clouds, the attendants of the Sun in its serene moments." (*Sun Lore of All Ages,* pp. 72–73, by William Tyler Olcott.)

At the beginning of the autumn, the sun enters Libra, and at this time of year the constellation of the *Centaur* rises above the horizon. In his third labor Hercules is entertained by a centaur. Later he slew a group of centaurs, fighting for a cask of wine. When the sun was in Libra, the constellation of the *Boar* rose in the evening sky. So after killing the centaurs, Hercules met the Erymanthian boar and disposed of him in mortal combat.

When the sun enters Scorpio, the constellation Cassiopeia, anciently known as the *Stag*, rises into view. The fourth labor of Hercules was the capture of a stag with golden horns and brazen feet.

As the sun passes into Sagittarius, three constellations, named for birds, rise. These three star-groups are called the *Vulture*, the *Swan*, and the *Eagle*. In his fifth labor Hercules kills three birds with arrows.

The constellation Capricorn is also known as the *Stable of Augeus*. The sixth labor of Hercules was the cleansing of the Augean stable.

When the sun is in Aquarius, the Lyre, or celestial *vulture*, sets. Prometheus also sets, while the *Bull of Europa* is on the meridian. In the seventh labor, Hercules slays the vulture that had preyed on the liver of Prometheus; and also captured the wild bull which had laid waste the island of Crete.

While the sun is in Pisces, *Pegasus, the celestial horse*, rises. In his eighth labor Hercules carried off the horses of Diomede.

As the sun enters Aries, the *Ram* of the Golden Fleece, the *Ship Argos* rises in the evening sky, and Andromeda sets. One of the stars of Andromeda is called her girdle. Hercules in the ninth labor sails in the Ship Argo to search for the Golden Fleece; he fought the Amazons and captured the girdle of Hippolyta, their queen, and rescued Hesione from a sea monster just as Perseus did Andromeda.

The sun passes into the *Bull*, or *ox*, as the *Pleiades* rise and *Orion* sets. The tenth labor of Hercules was to restore the seven kidnapped pleiades to their father, after killing their abductor, King Busiris (Orion); then he went to Spain and stole the oxen of Geryon.

When the sun goes into Gemini, Sirius, the *Dog-Star*, rises. In the eleventh labor Hercules conquered Cerberus, guardian Dog of Hades.

The sun enters Cancer as the constellations of the *River* and the *Centaur* set in the western sky. The constellation *Hercules* descends toward the west, followed by Draco, the *Dragon* of the Pole, guardian of the Golden Apples of the Hesperides. Hercules is represented in star atlases as crushing the head of the dragon with his foot. In his twelfth and last labor Hercules journeyed to the Herperides to seek the Golden Apples; then he put on a robe dipped in the blood of a centaur slain by him at the crossing of a river. The robe mysteriously caught fire and Hercules perished in the flames. "In this death scene of the solar hero," says Olcott, "and in the glories of his funeral pyre, we have the most famous sunset scene that has ever been presented for our contemplation. All the wondrous coloring that adorns the western sky at set of Sun illuminates the canvas, and the reflection of the scene streams afar, lighting the waves of the Aegean and its clustering isles, and painting in enduring hues, a scene that all nations proclaim the sublimest that nature offers to man's vision." (*Sun Lore of All Ages*, p. 74, by William Tyler Olcott.)

In one of his major works Sir Wallis Budge makes the incredible statement that: "The Egyptians borrowed their knowledge of the signs of the Zodiac, together with much else, from the Greeks, who had derived a great deal of their astronomical lore from the Babylonians." (*The Gods of the Egyptians*, Vol. II, p. 312.) This is putting the cart before the horse with a vengeance. A fitting rejoinder was made by Dr. Churchward, as follows:

Why the knowledge of all this was old in Egypt before the Babylonians even existed or knew anything about it. . . . The Egyptians had worked out all the architecture of the heavens, and their priests had carried the same with them to all parts of the world—not only the Northern heavens but the Southern, as well. Probably they worked out the South before the North, and the Druids and the Mayas and the Incas knew it all from the priests of Egypt, the earliest probably thousands of years before the Babylonian nation existed. The Babylonians copied and obtained all their knowledge from the Egyptians, and we are surprised that Dr. Budge should write that they borrowed from the Greeks; they were old and degenerating in decay before the Greek nation was born! Well may he say that "it is a subject of conjecture at what period the Babylonians first divided the heavens into sections, etc.," because they never did; whan they knew they borrowed either *direct from the Egyptians* or Sumerians—the latter obtained it from Egypt. It was the ancient Egyptians who mapped out the heavens into 12 divisions in the North, 12 divisions in the South, and 12 in the center, making 36 in all, and the 12 signs of the Zodiac. . . . It is very well to say that "whether the Babylonians were themselves the inventors of such origins—i.e. (the Zodiac), or whether they are to be attributed to the earlier non-Semitic Sumerian inhabitants of that country, cannot be said"—and when he states that "the Greeks borrowed the Zodiac from the Babylonians, and then the Greeks introduced it into Egypt, probably during the Ptolemaic period," it appears to us that Dr. Budge must have left that part of "the Gods of Egypt" to be written by one of his assistants, who knew nothing about the history of the past [*The Signs and Symbols of Primordial Man,* pp. 212–13, by Dr. Albert Churchward].

Charles F. Dupuis, a French savant of the late eighteenth century, traced the origin of the solar zodiac back to ancient Egypt, and hence anticipated the conclusions of Dr. Albert Churchward by more than a century. And, presently, we shall see that modern research has revealed much evidence tending to support that viewpoint. In the *Open Court* magazine, August, 1906, there appeared a scholarly article entitled "Zodiacs of Different Nations," by Dr. Paul Carus. One illustration displays Egyptian and Greek zodiacs shown side by side in the photograph of a Late Roman Egyptian plaque. A list of the dual set of symbols is given below:

Egyptian	*Greek*
1. Cat	1. Ram
2. Jackal	2. Bull
3. Serpent	3. Twins
4. Scarab	4. Crab
5. Ass	5. Lion
6. Lion	6. Virgin
7. Goat	7. Scales
8. Cow	8. Scorpion
9. Falcon	9. Archer
10. Baboon	10. Goat
11. Ibis	11. Waterman
12. Crocodile	12. Fishes

The Egyptian Sphinx, a colossal statue, sacred to the sun-god Horus, was erected at least six thousand years ago. It has the body of a lion; emblematic, perhaps, of the entrance of the sun into the zodiacal sign of the Lion around 4000 B.C. The Temple of the Sphinx is constructed in the form of a cross, and symbolizes North, South, East, and West, or the cardinal points of the celestial sphere: the two solstices and the two equinoxes. It seems that there were originally only four signs of the zodiac, namely, the quarter signs at the solstices and equinoxes. George St. Clair, an able student of astro-theological mythology has made some illuminating comments concerning the original four zodiacal signs, from which we quote the following:

About 6000 years ago the Spring Sun would be entering Taurus; and the four quarter signs would be the Bull, the Lion, the Scorpion, and the Waterman, though some of these signs might be otherwise named. In memory of that early arrangement—which in many ways left its mark—devices on rings were, for example, a scorpion, a lion, a hawk, and a cynocephalus ape. . . .

From the four quarters we pass to the twelve signs. Between each two quarter signs two other signs were inserted. The planisphere of the Temple of Denderah shows four gods supporting the heavens at the four quarter points, corresponding to the Bull, the Lion, the Scorpion and the Waterman; and shows eight other divinities in pairs, one on either side of each pillar, making up the twelve [*Creation Records Discovered in Egypt,* pp. 136–37, by George St. Clair].

The four gods holding up the heavens were recognized in Egyptian mythology as the four children of the sun-god Horus, and their names were: Amset, Hapi, Tuamutef, and Gebhsennuf. These four amenthes, or Genii of Hades, were depicted as standing at the cardinal points of the celestial sphere and holding up the heavens. Each deity was identifiable by his particular features, as listed below:

AMSET had the head of a MAN.
HAPI possessed the head of an APE.
TUAMUTEF was adorned by the head of a JACKAL.
GEBHSENNUF wore on his shoulders the head of a HAWK.

These same sky gods are referred to in the "Bible" more than once (although the symbols are different), where they are called Cherubim. These celestial creatures were seen by Ezekiel in a vision which he had while in Babylon. "As for the likeness of their faces, they four had the face of a man, and the face of a lion, on the right side; and they four had the face of an ox on the left side; they four had the face of an eagle." (Ezekiel, I, 10).

In the Apocalypse we read about the "Four Beasts." In the "Book of Revelation," Chapter IV, Verse 7, we are told that: "The first beast was like a lion, and the second beast like a calf, and the third beast had a face as man, and the fourth beast was like a flying eagle." These "beasts" were the constellations, situated at the four cardinal points of the zodiac five thousand years ago. They were Taurus the Bull (Vernal Equinox), Leo the Lion (Summer Solstice), Scorpio the Scorpion (Autumnal Equinox), and Aquarius the Waterman (Winter Solstice). In the "Bible" the Eagle has been substituted for the Scorpion. We learn from the erudite Godfrey Higgins that: "The signs of the Zodiac, with the exception of the Scorpion, which was exchanged by Dan for the Eagle, were carried by the different tribes of the Israelites on their standards; and Taurus, Leo, Aquarius and Scorpio or the Eagle, the four signs of Reuben, Judah, Ephraim, and Dan, were placed at the four corners—the four cardinal points—of their encampment, evidently in allusion to the cardinal points of the sphere, the equinoxes and solstices, when the equinox was in Taurus." (*Anacalypsis,* Vol. II, p. 105, by Godfrey Higgins.)

The Egyptians, Chaldeans, and Greeks believed in certain star-gods called Decans. These decans were actually belts of stars extending across the sky, the risings of which followed each other by ten days. Dr. Wilhelm Gundel of Giessen, an authority on ancient astronomy, has produced a monumental work entitled *Dekane und Dekansternbilder (The Decans and Their Stars).* The book was published by J. J. Augustin at Gluckstadt and Hamburg, in Germany, in 1936. It has not been translated into English, but it was reviewed in *Nature,* the scientific journal, by a famous naturalist, and since this review contains information both interesting and important we are pleased to quote from the same, as follows:

When the year (of 360 days) had been divided into its 12 months and put under the zodiacal signs, each of the 12 was again divided into 3 parts, of 10 days each; and these 36 "decans" had their 36 gods, or rulers, or dynasts, watchers of the hours ("horoscopes"), servants or messengers of the greater gods, or of Horus himself in his holy name spelled with 36 letters; each had his own "face," which chanced to be (in Egypt) the face of a bull or an ibis, or of an eagle, or of a man. These were the angels and archangels, the demons and archi-demons, of Hellenistic writers. Each had his own name; in mummy-cases and papyri in obscure and fragmentary works like Hermes Trismegistus, or the Testimonium Salomonis, in Celsus and Firmicus, in the traditional learning of men like Kircher, Salmasius or Scaliger, we find the names of Chont-har, Chont-Chre, Siket, and the 33 others in all kinds of variants and corruptions. Egyptian they were in the beginning, but the true form and meaning of many are long lost ["The Science of Astrology," a book review, by Professor D'Arcy Wentworth Thompson, in *Nature*, Oct. 23, 1937].

After tracing the zodiacal symbols back to ancient Egypt, we might still wonder why these star signs were, in the main, named after animals.

The impression we receive [to cite an authority] is that Sun-worship, and indeed the whole cosmic system of which it is typical was secondary in Egypt, imposing itself on a substratum of Totemism. In any case, . . . one thing is clear, namely, that nine-tenths of the mythology of ancient Egypt is cosmic in origin, and that it was grafted on to a totemic system with which it had originally no connection. Thus to Horus, a Falcon Totem in origin, was attached the whole of the mass of myth which centered around the Sun, while to Thoth, originally an Ibis Totem in the north-eastern Delta, accrued all the legend connected with the Moon [Professor T. Eric Peet, in *The Cambridge Ancient History*, Vol. I, p. 331, edited by Bury *et al.*].

In other words, the stellar symbolism of the zodiac was based on a still more ancient totemic symbolism. When the agriculturists of the Archaic Civilization of Africa were faced with the problem of determining the proper seasons for planting their crops by observing the motions of the stars, they projected the animal symbols of the totemic hunters into the skies, to become the Signs of the Zodiac.

The zodiacal symbolism which we have been discussing is closely connected with the rites and ceremonies of great religious systems, both ancient and modern. For instance in Egypt three thousand years ago, the birthday of the Sun-god was celebrated in the temples on the 25th of December; it was the first day to lengthen obviously after December 21st, the day of the winter solstice. At the midnight hour, on the very first minute of the 25th of December, the birth of the sun was commemorated. At that time the sun was in the zodiacal sign Capricorn, which was known as the Stable of Augeus; so the infant Sun-god was said to have been born in a stable. Shining brightly on the meridian was Sirius (the Star from the East); while rising in the east was Virgo (the Virgin), the line of the horizon passing through her center. To the right of Sirius was Orion, the great hunter, with three stars in his belt. These stars lie in a straight line and point toward Sirius; and in ancient times they were known as the Three Kings. We meet them in the Gospels as the Three Wise Men, or Magi. In the zodiac on the interior of the dome of the Temple of Denderah, the constellation Virgo was pictured as a woman with a spike of corn in one hand; and on the adjacent margin the Virgin is annotated by a figure of Isis with Horus in her arms.

But it is well known as a matter of history [Edward Carpenter observes] that the worship of Isis and Horus descended in the early Christian centuries to Alexandria, where it took the form of the worship of the Virgin Mary and the infant Savior, and so passed into the European ceremonial. We have therefore the Virgin Mary connected by linear succession and descent with that zodiacal cluster in the sky! . . . A curious confirmation of the same astronomical connection is afforded by the Roman Catholic Calendar. For if this be consulted it will be found that the festival of the Assumption of the Virgin is placed on the 15th day of August, while the festival of the Birth of the Virgin is dated the 8th of September. . . . At the present day the zodiacal signs (owing to precession) have shifted some distance from the constellations of the same name. But at the time when the zodiac was constituted and these names were given, the first date obviously would signalize the actual disappearance of the cluster Virgo in the Sun's rays—i.e., the Assumption of the Virgin into the glory of the God—while the second date would signalize the reappearance of the constellation, or the Birth of the Virgin. The Church of Notre Dame of Paris is supposed to be on the original site of a Temple of Isis; and it is said (but I have not been able to verify this myself) that one of the side entrances— that, namely on the left in entering from the north (cloister) side—is figured with the signs of the Zodiac, except that the sign Virgo is replaced by the figure of the Madonna and Child [*Pagan and Christian Creeds*, pp. 32–33, by Edward Carpenter].

At the winter solstice (Christmas), the sun is at its southern-most position in the celestial sphere. After that date it begins to travel northward along the ecliptic; and at the vernal equinox (Easter), it passes over the celestial equator. This passing over of the sun from the south to the north of the equator was the origin of the festival of the Passover. When the sun reached the equinoctial point and crossed, or passed over, the equator three thousand years ago, it was situated in Aries, the Ram or Lamb; so the Lamb became the symbol of god. Here we have a clue to the origin of the passover Lamb, which has been widely regarded as a type of the crucified Christ. If the reader should consult such books as *The World's Sixteen Crucified Saviors* by Kersey Graves, and *Bible Myths and Their Parallels in Other Religions* by T. W. Doane, he would find that several pagan sun-gods were said to have been crucified. The meaning of

this solar crucifixion has been explained in a scholarly manner by L. Gordon Rylands:

> For in an astronomical chart, the Sun is apparently crucified upon the intersecting lines of the equator and the ecliptic at the moment of his descent into the lower hemisphere, the hemisphere of darkness and death; and it is so again at the moment of his resurrection into the hemisphere of light and life; while the period of transit is three days. . . . At the time when the myth of the death of the Sun-god originated, the Sun being in the constellation Aries at the Spring Equinox, was identified with the Ram. That is the Lamb which had been "slain from the foundation of the world." The custom of dressing the paschal lamb in the shape of a cross is referable to the same myth [*The Beginnings of Gnostic Christianity*, p. 217, by L. Gordon Rylands].

Limitations of space preclude a more extensive discussion of the symbols, myths, and rites of the ancient Egyptian religion. For the reader who would like to know more about such subjects, we recommend *The Secret Societies of All Ages and Countries* by Charles William Heckethorn.

The great merchants and mariners of the ancient world were the Phoenicians, who adopted much of the culture of ancient Egypt and were instrumental in the spread of its elements to other nations, various and remote. We first hear of them dwelling on the shores of the Persian Gulf, and we are told that they later colonized the land of Canaan at the eastern end of the Mediterranean. These people called themselves Canaanites; the name Phoenicians was bestowed upon them by the Greeks. These ancient mariners were manufacturers of a famous dye known as "royal purple," which the Greeks called "Phoenix," and as a result they were nicknamed Phoenikes or Phoenicians. We know almost nothing of the early history of these people. "The historical colonization of Africa by Alien peoples," we are told by a modern African scholar, "begins with the exploits of the Phoenicians in Mauretania. . . . The Phoenicians were a Semitic people who, originally, appear to have resembled the Jews in race and language." (*African Glory,* p. 15, by Professor J. C. deGraft-Johnson.)

We think the professor is a bit too dogmatic, for there is a tradition that the ancestors of the Phoenicians originally came from the land of Punt, in East Africa. Though these people adopted a Semitic language, we know that they were considered Ethiopians by the ancient Greeks. Here the opinions of a philosophical American historian are germane: "Who, now, were those Phoenicians . . . whose ships sailed every sea, whose merchants bargained in every port? The historian is abashed before any question of origins; he must confess that he knows next to nothing about either the early or the late history of this ubiquitous, yet elusive, people. We do not know whence they came, nor when, we are not certain that they were Semites." (*Our Oriental Heritage,* pp. 291–92, by Dr. Will Durant.)

On the eastern Mediterranean coast the Phoenicians carried on their industrial and commercial operations from the famous cities of Byblos, Aradus, Sidon, and Tyre. The port of Byblos was exporting timber to Egypt as far back as the 3rd dynasty, when forty ships laden with the famous Cedars of Lebanon sailed up the Nile. We learn from a stone tablet, dating from the reign of the Pharaoh Snefru, that: "We brought 40 ships laden with cedar trunks. We built ships of cedarwood. . . . We made the doors of the king's palace of cedarwood." (Cited by Robert Silverberg in *Empires in the Dust,* p. 112.) In later days when their homeland was overwhelmed by invaders, the Phoenicians established many colonies, among them being Carthage, Utica, and Bizerte on the North African shore, and at Gades (Cadiz) in Spain, and Palermo in Sicily.

Carthage, a city-state, the most celebrated of the Phoenician colonies, was established on

the North African coast in the year 814 B.C. Carthage was one of the great cities of the ancient world, and it is one of the tragedies of history that, after the three Punic Wars, waged by the Romans, Carthage was finally destroyed. After losing Sicily to Rome in 242 B.C., the Carthaginians were faced with a rebellion of their Libyan vassals at home. To forestall Roman aid to the rebels, Carthage had to surrender the island of Sardinia to the Romans.

The Libyans were subdued by Carthaginian arms, under the generalship of Hamilcar Barca in 238 B.C. Hamilcar had a dream of restoring the ancient glories of Carthage, and of recapturing Sicily and Sardinia. So the second Punic War was waged in Europe and Africa, with Hannibal, a son of Hamilcar, leading the Carthaginians, and Cornelius Scipio heading the armies of Rome. A series of blunders on the part of Hannibal brought about the final debacle of the Carthaginians at the Battle of Zama, in 202 B.C. The Roman peace terms were harsh. Carthage was compelled to pay, over a period of fifty years, an indemnity of 10,000 talents of silver, about $20,000,000 in modern currency. All the ships of war and elephants of Carthage were confiscated by the Romans; and the establishment of new colonies or involvement in foreign wars forbidden, unless approved by Rome. The great African city-state, despite all these trials and tribulations, made a good recovery, and might have survived and prospered; but in the year 150 B.C., the armies of King Masinissa of Numidia, an African ally of Rome, invaded Carthaginian territory. The Carthaginians counter-attacked, and a war was on. The Romans, led by the evil-minded Cato, a member of the Roman Senate, who was out to crush Carthage under any pretext, declared war on Carthage. This war, started by Rome in 149 B.C., under the perfidious claim that an old treaty had been violated, raged for three years. In 146 B.C., the city of Carthage was captured by the Romans and was completely destroyed by fire. This wanton destruction of the great African city by the Romans must be regarded as one of the great crimes of history. For the Carthaginians, and their Phoenician forebears, were culturally and intellectually superior to the Romans. We all have heard about the Library at Alexandria, but how many know about the great Library of Carthage? In the words of Professor Hapgood: "They [the Romans] burned the great city of Carthage, their ancient enemy and their incalculable superior in everything relating to science. The library of Carthage is said to have contained about 500,000 volumes, and these no doubt dealt with the history and the sciences of Phoenicia as a whole." (*Maps of the Ancient Sea Kings,* p. 196, by Charles H. Hapgood.)

The ships of the Phoenicians traded with ports on the shores of the Indian Ocean, the Mediterranean, the Black Sea, and the Atlantic Ocean. The Phoenician seafarers and traders worked tin mines in Cornwall and traded with the ancient Britons; and their ships circumnavigated Africa and crossed the Atlantic Ocean to America. The Phoenicians have been credited by certain scholars with the invention of the alphabet, but this claim must be disallowed. It has been shown by the researches of the French Egyptologist, Prisse d'Avennes, that we owe our alphabet to the Egyptians. The Phoenicians adopted the Egyptian alphabet and simplified, and then diffused, it among other nations. "It is sufficiently proved," observes one scholar, "by the papyrus in the Bibliotheque Nationale, Paris, actually the oldest book in the world. It consists of eighteen pages written in black ink with a bold round character, the prototype of the letters copied by the Greeks from the Phoenicians and transmitted through the Latins to us." (*Lost Civilizations,* p. 15, by Charles J. Finger.)

Gerald Massey in his learned work, *A Book of the Beginnings*, argues persuasively that civilization first arose in the interior of the African continent and then, after passing through Egypt, was in due time diffused over the rest of the globe. We have no evidence that the ancient Egyptians ever sent any colonists to the British Isles, yet Mr. Massey shows that there was a definite Egyptian cultural influence among the ancient Britons. In *A Book of the Beginnings* is a long list of English words, still in use today, that seem to be of ancient Egyptian origin. Massey's book is long out of print, but a short selection from his list of Egypto-English words has been reproduced by Lillian Eichler in *The Customs of Mankind*, from which we cite a few examples:

English	*Egyptian*
Abode (habitation)	Abut (abode)
Attack	Atakh
Autumn (the season)	Atum (the red autumnal sun)
Canoe	Khenna (a boat)
Count (a title)	Kannt (a title)
Cow	Kaui (cow)
Foot	Fut (a measure)
Hag (witch)	Hek (magic)
Kick	Khekh (to repulse)
Mamma (the mother)	Mama (to bear)
Married	Mer-T (attached)
Mayor	Mer (he who rules)
Ray (of sunlight)	Ra (the sun)
Suit (to satisfy)	Suta (to please)
Write	Ruit (to engrave)
Youth	Uth (youth)

"Whether this great similarity between English and Egyptian words is coincidence," Miss Eichler comments, "or whether at some remote time there was a pro-Hamitic language which branched off into the Aryan group, is not definitely known. It is a tempting problem for speculation." (*The Customs of Mankind*, p. 133, by Lillian Eichler.)

Many of the problems and puzzles of history could be cleared up if we could only get over the absurd propaganda that Africa for some strange and mysterious reason has for ages been cut off from the rest of the world. If this were so, how is it that the great nation of both ancient and modern times has worshiped black gods, and embraced religious systems of African origin? "At Corinth there was a black Venus," we learn from the extensive researches of Mr. Godfrey Higgins, and that learned author continues:

> In my search into the origin of ancient Druids I continually found at last, that my labors terminated with something black. . . . Osiris and his Bull were black; all the Gods and Goddesses of Greece were black; at least this was the case with Jupiter, Bacchus, Hercules, Apollo, Ammon. The Goddesses Venus, Isis, Hecate, Diana, Juno, Metis, Ceres, Cybele, are black. (*Anacalypsis*, Vol. I, pp. 137–38, by Godfrey Higgins.)

Among the Christian nations of Europe, even into modern times, we notice a similar tendency, and we follow Mr. Higgins in his observations:

> In all the Romish countries of Europe, in France, Germany, Italy, etc., the God Christ, as well as his mother, are described in their old pictures and statues to be black. The infant God in the arms of his black mother, his eyes and drapery white, is himself perfectly black. If the reader doubt my word, he may go to the cathedral at Moulins—to the famous chapel of the Virgin at Loretto—to the church of Annunciata—the church of St. Lazaro, or the Church of St. Stephen at Genoa—to St. Francisco at Pisa—to the Church at Brixen, in the Tyrol, and to that at Padua—to the church of St. Theodore, at Munich . . . to a church and to the Cathedral at Augsburg, where are a black virgin and child as large as life—to Rome, to the Borghese Chapel Maria Maggiore—to the Pantheon—to a small chapel of St. Peter's, on the right hand side on entering, near the door; and, in fact, to almost unnumerable other churches, in countries professing Romish religion. There is scarcely an old church in Italy where some remains of the worship of the BLACK VIRGIN and BLACK CHILD are not to be met with. Very often

the black figures have given way to white ones, and in these cases the black ones, as being held sacred, were put into retired places in the churches, but were not destroyed, but are yet to be found there [*Anacalypsis*, Vol. I, p. 138, by Godfrey Higgins].

We now have evidence of cultural influences from Egypt and other parts of Africa having reached the New World at least three thousand years ago.

APPENDIX TO CHAPTER III

It may be of interest to the reader to know that the ancient Egyptians did not call themselves "Egyptians"; the name was invented by the Greeks. The first Greek visitors to Egypt, in the seventh century B.C., were greatly impressed by the Temple of Ptah, at Memphis. They regarded it as the grandest structure in the Nile Valley and they afterward referred to this ancient land as Hekaptah (The Land of the Temple of Ptah). In the Greek language Hekaptah became Aiguptos; and under the Roman rule the name was Latinized into Aegyptus, from whence we get the name Egypt. The ancient inhabitants of this African land called their country Khem, or Kam, or Ham, which literally meant "the black land"; and they called themselves Khemi, or Kamites, or Hamites, meaning "the black people." (For further information along these lines, see *The Wisdom of the Egyptians* by Brian Brown.)

There is an interesting discourse on this question in Gerald Massey's *A Book of Beginnings;* and since this work is now rare and almost impossible to obtain, we shall quote from it briefly as follows:

"Egypt is often called Kam, the black land, and Kam does signify black; the name probably applied to the earliest inhabitants whose type is the Kam or Ham of the Hebrew writers." (*A Book of the Beginnings*, Vol. I, p. 4, by Gerald Massey.)

"It will be maintained in this book that the oldest mythology, religion, symbols, language had their birthplace in Africa, that the primitive race of Kam came thence, and the civilization attained in Egypt, emanated from that country and spread over the world. The most reasonable view on the evolutionary theory . . . is that the black race is the most ancient, and that Africa is the primordial home." (*Ibid.,* p. 18.)

"The Hebrew scriptures, among their other fragments of ancient lore, are very emphatic in deriving the line of Mizraim from Ham or Kam, the black type coupled with Kush, another form of the black. They give no countenance to the theory of Asiatic origin for the Egyptians. In the Biblical account of the generations of Noah, Mizraim is the son of Ham, i.e., of Kam, the black race." (*Ibid.,* p. 33.)

NOTE: THE ORIGIN OF THE ZODIAC; THE OPINIONS OF COUNT VOLNEY

Should it be asked at what epoch this system [the zodiacal symbolism], took its birth, we shall answer on the testimony of the monuments of astronomy itself, that its principles appear with certainty to have been established about 17,000 years ago. And if it be asked to what people it is to be attributed, we shall answer that the same monuments, supported by unanimous traditions, attribute it to the first tribes of Egypt; and when reason finds in that country all the circumstances which could lead to such a system; when it finds there a zone of sky, bordering on the tropic, equally free from the rains of the equator and the fogs of the north; when it finds there a central point of the sphere of the ancient, a salubrious climate, a great, but manageable river, a soil fertile without art or labor, inundated without morbid exhalations, and placed between two seas which communicate with the richest countries, it conceives that the inhabitant of the Nile, addicted to agriculture, from the nature of his soil, to geometry from the annual necessity of measuring astronomy from the state of his sky, always open to observation, must have been the first to pass from the savage to the social state; and consequently to attain the physical and moral sciences necessary to civilized life.

It was then, on the border of the Upper Nile, among a black race of men, that was organized the complicated system of the worship of the stars, considered in relation to the productions of the earth and the labors of agriculture; and this first worship characterized by their adoration under their own forms and natural attributes, was a simple proceeding of the human mind. . . .

As soon as this agricultural people began to observe the stars with attention, they found it necessary to individualize or group them; and to assign to each a proper name. . . . A great difficulty must have presented itself. . . . First the heavenly bodies, similar in form, offered no distinguishing characteristics by which to denominate them; and secondly, the language in its infancy and poverty had no expression for so many new and metaphysical ideas. Necessity, the usual stimulus of genius, surmounted everything. Having remarked that in annual revolution, the renewal and periodical appearance of terrestrial productions were constantly associated with the rising and setting of certain stars, and to their position as relative to the sun, . . . the mind by a natural operation connected in thought the terrestrial and celestial objects, which were connected in fact; and applying to them a common sign, it gave to the stars and their groups, the names of the terrestrial objects to which they answered.

Thus the Ethiopian of Thebes named the stars of inundation or Aquarius, those stars under which the Nile began to overflow; stars of the ox or bull, those under which they began to plow; stars of the lion, those under which that animal, driven from the desert by thirst, appeared on the banks of the Nile; stars of the sheaf, or of the harvest virgin, those of the reaping season; stars of the lamb, stars of the two kids, those under which these precious animals were brought forth. . . .

Thus the same Ethiopian having observed that the return of the inundation always corresponded with the rising of a beautiful star which appeared towards the source of the Nile, and seemed to warn the husbandman against the coming waters, he compared this action to that of the animal who, by barking, gives notice of danger, and he called this star the dog, the barker (Sirius). In the same manner he named the stars of the crab, those where the sun, having arrived at the tropic, retreated by a slow retrograde motion like the crab or cancer. He named stars of the wild goat or Capricorn, those where the sun, having reached the highest point in his annuary tract . . . imitates the goat, who delights to climb to the summit of the rocks. He named the stars of the balance, or Libra, those where the days and nights being equal, seemed in equilibrium, like that instrument; and stars of the Scorpion, those where certain periodical winds bring vapors, burning like the venom of the scorpion. In the same manner he called by the name of rings and serpents the figured traces of the orbits of the stars and the planets, and such was the general mode of naming all the stars and even the planets, taken by groups or as individuals, according to their relations with husbandry and terrestrial objects, and according to the analogies which each nation found between them and the objects of its particular soil and climate [*The Ruins of Empires,* pp. 120–23, by C. F. Volney].

Notes

1. For a more recent discussion of this question, the reader is referred to *The Signs and Symbols of Primordial Man,* pp. 235–40, by Albert Churchward; and to *Moses and Monotheism* by Sigmund Freud.

2. The Hat Benben referred to in Piankhi's inscription is a title given to the temple of the sun at Heliopolis, and means literally the "House of the Obelisk," for the Benben was a small stone obelisk or pyramid supposed to be an embodiment of the Sun-god Ra himself.

3. Readers who would like to know more about King Piankhi are advised to consult the following: (1) "Sources for the Study of Ethiopian History," p. 32, by Professor William L. Hansberry, Howard University Studies in History, November, 1930; (2) *Personalities of Antiquity,* by Sir Arthur Weigall. This English Egyptologist devotes a chapter of his book to Piankhi and titles it "The Exploits of a Nigger King."

4. The star-god Khonsu later became a moon-god among the Ethiopians and Egyptians.

References

Allen, Richard H. *Star Names and Their Meanings.* G. E. Stechert Co., New York, 1899.

Braghine, Alexandre. *The Shadow of Atlantis.* E. P. Dutton & Co., New York, 1940.

Breasted, James Henry. *Ancient Times.* Ginn and Co., Boston, 1916.

Breasted, James Henry. *A History of Egypt.* Bantam Books, New York, Toronto, London, 1967.

Breasted, James Henry. *Time and Its Mysteries.* Series I. New York University Press, New York, 1936.

Briffault, Robert. *The Mothers.* 1-vol. edition. The Macmillan Co., New York, 1931.

British Association Report, Glasgow Meeting, 1876. London, 1877.

Brodeur, Arther G. *The Pageant of Civilization.* R. M. McBride & Co., New York, 1931.

Brown, Brian. *The Wisdom of the Egyptians.* Brentano's, New York, 1923.

Budge, E. A. Wallis. *The Book of the Dead.* An English translation of *The Papyrus of Ani.* University Books, New Hyde Park, New York, 1960.

Budge, E. A. Wallis. *The Gods of the Egyptians.* 2 vols. Methuen and Co., London, 1904.

Budge, E. A. Wallis. *Osiris: The Egyptian Religion of the Resurrection.* 2 vols., bound in one. University Books, New Hyde Park, New York, 1961.

Bury, J. B.; Cook, S. A.; and Adcock, F. E. (Editors). *The Cambridge Ancient History.* Vols. I and II. Cambridge University Press, Cambridge, Vol. I, 1923, Vol. II, 1926.

Busenbark, Ernest. *Symbols, Sex and the Stars.* The Truth Seeker Co., San Diego, California, 1949.

Carpenter, Edward. *Pagan and Christian Creeds.* Harcourt, Brace and Co., New York, 1920.

Carus, Paul. "Zodiacs of Different Nations," *Open Court,* August, 1906.

Casson, Stanley. *Progress and Catastrophe.* Harper & Bros., New York, 1937.

Churchward, Albert. *The Signs and Symbols of Primordial Man.* Second edition. George Allen & Co., London, 1913. E. P. Dutton & Co., New York, 1913.

Cooke, Harold P. *Osiris: A Study in Myths, Mysteries and Religion.* Bruce Humphries, Inc., Boston, 1931.

DeGraft-Johnson, John Coleman. *African Glory.* Walker & Co., New York, 1966.

Del Grande, Nino. "Prehistoric Iron Smelting in Africa," *Natural History,* Sept.–Oct., 1932.

Doane, T. W. *Bible Myths and Their Parallels in Other Religions.* The Truth Seeker Co., San Diego, California.

Dorsey, George A. *The Story of Civilization: Man's Own Show.* Halcyon House, New York, 1931.

Du Bois, W. E. Burghardt. *The World and Africa.* International Publishers, New York, 1965.

Durant, Will. *Our Oriental Heritage.* Simon and Schuster, New York, 1935.

Eichler, Lillian. *The Customs of Mankind.* Nelson Doubleday, Inc., Garden City, New York, 1924.

Finger, Charles J. *Lost Civilizations.* Haldeman-Julius Co., Girard, Kansas, 1922.

Frazer, James George. *Adonis, Attis, Osiris.* 3rd edition. 2 volumes bound in 1. University Books, New Hyde Park, New York, 1961.

Frazer, James George. *The Golden Bough.* Abridged edition. The Macmillan Co., New York, 1940.

Frazer, James George. *The Worship of Nature.* The Macmillan Co., New York, 1926.

Freud, Sigmund. *Moses and Monotheism.* Alfred A. Knopf, New York, 1939.

Gould F. J. *A Concise History of Religion,* Vol. 1. Watts and Co., London, 1907.

Graves, Kersey. *The World's Sixteen Crucified Saviors.* The Truth Seeker Co., San Diego, California.

Hadfield, P. *Traits of Divine Kingship in Africa.* Watts and Co., London, 1949.

Hammerton, J. A. *The Encyclopedia of Modern Knowledge.* The Amalgamated Press, London, 1936.

Hammerton, J. A. (Editor). *Wonders of the Past.* 2 vols. Wise and Co., New York, 1937.

Hapgood, Charles H. *Maps of the Ancient Sea Kings: Evidence of Advanced Civilization in the Ice Age.* Chilton Book Co., New York and Philadelphia, 1966.

Harding, Arthur M. *Astronomy.* Garden City Publishing Co., Garden City, New York, 1935.

Heckethorn, Charles William, *The Secret Societies of All Ages and Countries.* 2 vols. University Books, New Hyde Park, New York, 1966.

Herodotus. *The History of Herodotus.* Translated by George Rawlinson. Edited by Manuel Komroff. Dial Press, New York, 1928. Tudor Publishing Co., New York, 1939.

Higgins, Godfrey. *Anacalypsis.* 2 Vols. University Books, New Hyde Park, New York, 1965.

Laing, Samuel. *Human Origins.* Chapman and Hall, London, 1892. A revised edition, edited by Edward Godd, published by Watts and Co., London, 1913.

Lockyer, J. Norman. *The Dawn of Astronomy: A Study of the Temple Worship and Mythology of the Ancient Egyptians.* The M.I.T. Press, Cambridge, Mass., 1963.

MacNaughton, Duncan. *A Scheme of Egyptian Chronology.* Luzac and Co., London, 1932.

McCabe, Joseph. *The Golden Ages of History.* Watts and Co., London, 1940.

Maspero, Gaston Camille. *The Dawn of Civilization.* Second edition. Society for the Promotion of Christian Knowledge, London, 1896.

Massey, Gerald. *A Book of the Beginnings.* 2 Vols. Williams and Norgate, London, 1881.

Massey Gerald. *The Natural Genesis.* 2 Vols. Williams and Norgate, London, 1883.

Massey, Gerald. *Ancient Egypt: The Light of the World.* 2 Vols. T. Fisher Unwin, London, 1907.

Moret, Alexandre. *Kings and Gods of Egypt.* G. P. Putnam's Sons, New York and London, 1912.

Olcott, William Tyler. *Sun Lore of All Ages.* G. P. Putnam's Sons, New York and London, 1914.

Parsons, Geoffrey. *The Stream of History.* Charles Scribner's Sons, New York and London, 1932.

Petrie, W. M. Flinders. *Social Life in Ancient Egypt.* Houghton Mifflin Co., Boston and New York, 1923.

Plutarch. "Isis and Osiris." A Treatise in Plutarch's *Moralia,* Vol. V. The Greek text, with an English translation by Frank Cole Babbitt. The Loeb Classical Library, Harvard University Press, Cambridge, Mass., 1962.

Reade, Winwood. *The Martyrdom of Man.* Watts and Co., London, 1934. A new edition published by Pemberton Publishing Co., London, 1968.

Robertson, John M. *Christianity and Mythology.* Second edition. Watts and Co., London, 1936.

Rylands, L. Gordon. *The Beginnings of Gnostic Christianity.* Watts and Co., London, 1940.

St. Clair, George. *Creation Records Discovered in Egypt: Studies in the Book of the Dead.* David Nutt, London, 1898.

Silverberg, Robert. *Empires in the Dust.* Bantam Books, New York, London, Toronto, 1966.

Thompson, D'Arcy Wentworth. "The Science of Astrology," a book review, *Nature,* Oct. 23, 1937.

Volney, C. F. *The Ruins of Empires.* Peter Eckler, New York, 1890. Reissued by the Truth Seeker Co., San Diego, California.

Weigall, Arthur. *Personalities of Antiquity.* Doubleday, Doran & Co., Garden City, New York, 1928.

Wendt, Herbert. *It Began in Babel.* Houghton Mifflin Co., Boston, 1962.

Yarker, John. *The Arcane Schools.* William Tait, Belfast, Ireland, 1909.

"He prevailed over them all by his courage. It is not possible to name another like Severus."[1]

Lucius Septimius Severus: The Black Emperor of the World

EDWARD L. JONES

SEPTIMIUS SEVERUS WAS ONE OF THE first Black African Emperors of Rome, who had successfully fought his way to power and consolidated his position with the strong military backing of the army. Since Severus was born in Africa, many writers have taken the view that his influence was not Roman—"the homeland of Hannibal took a late revenge over Rome." (See Anthony Birley, *The Emperor Septimius Severus* HT, XVII, 1967, p. 668. Also see Gilbert Picard's *Carthage,* translated by Miriam and Lionel Kochan, London, 1964, p. 152). "The Roman song-writers joked about 'Hannibal's revenge' a completely pacific revenge, moreover, which did not prevent Septimius Severus being one of the most energetic defenders of the Empire and a Roman patriot. . . ." The statements about "Hannibal's revenge over Rome" may be interpreted as meaning that both men were Black Africans; and that where Hannibal had not succeeded in conquering Rome, Severus, several centuries later, did as Severus, the Emperor. He built a marble tomb for Hannibal (see chapter on Hannibal) in recognition of

his military genius, and of the fact that he was a fellow countryman, an African.

Speaking of race, there is no need to prove that Severus was of African heritage, that is, Black, because there are numerous pictures and statues of him still in existence (see illustration of the Emperor, his wife and child). Other illustrations of Severus may be found in a book titled *The Portraits of Septimius Severus* (AD 193–211) by Anna Marguerite McCann, published by the American Academy In Rome, vol. XXX, 1968. The purpose of her study of the portraits of Severus was "to present a new corpus of the portraits of the emperor arranged and dated according to portrait types, and secondly, to offer an interpretation of their iconography based on a study of their prototypes." In order to accomplish her purpose, she used numismatic evidence as well as historical and literary sources to determine the date and interpretation of

From *Profiles in African Heritage.* Reprinted by permission of Edward L. Jones, author and publisher.

portrait types. It is of great importance for Black scholars to examine this study so they can be better prepared to define and study their own African past, instead of having to read some white person's interpretation of a Black man who has become white by time, helped along, of course, by a—rock.

Yes, a rock, a piece of white marble or limestone, has successfully transformed this Black Emperor into a white "Roman Emperor," for almost 1800 years. What is being said, is that Africans everywhere have been passing by the statue of Septimius Severus and have been unable to identify with him racially, because the marble is white and his features have been "refined."

The portraits of Severus may be found in the museums of the following countries: Algeria, Austria, Belgium, Canada, Cyprus, Denmark, Egypt, France, Germany, Great Britain, Greece, Italy, Lebanon, Libya, Poland, Spain, Sweden, Tunisia, Turkey and the UNITED STATES. In the U.S., portraits of him may be seen at the following museums: 1) Bloomington, Indiana, Indiana University Art Museum (portraits of Clodius Albinus argues McCann, although the University labels it Septimius Severus); 2) Boston, Museum of Fine Arts; 3) Columbia, Missouri, collection of A. M. McCann, the author; 4) Detroit, Institute of Art; 5) New York, collection of the late Maxime Velay; 6) New York, The Metropolitan Museum of Art; 7) New York, Pier Tozzi Galleries; 8) Los Angeles, private collection; 9) Philadelphia, University Museum; and he is also down south in the 10) Richmond, Virginia Museum of Fine Arts. Finally, if the reader vacations in the USSR, he may see a portrait of Severus in Leningrad, Hermitage. This information comes from Anna M. McCann's Museum Index, pages 213–216 of her book.

Since the majority of the portraits of Severus are represented by white marble, how will Black people be able to identify with one

of their ancient heroes? The answer seems obvious; his portraits must be done in Black marble or limestone. Then Black children everywhere will be able to recognize and read about an outstanding Black African Emperor of Rome.

Many writers have written about Severus as though he had been the *only* Emperor of African descent that became a ruler of Rome. This is not true. There were many and here are some of their names:

DATES (AD)	NAMES
193	P. Helvius Pertinax.
193	M. Didius Julianus.
193–198	L. Septimius Severus.
198–208	L. Septimius Severus.
	M. Aurelius Antoninus (Caracalla).
208–211	L. Septimius Severus.
	M. Aurelius Antoninus (Caracalla).
	L. Septimius Geta.
211–212	M. Aurelius Antoninus (Caracalla).
	L. Septimius Geta.
212–217	M. Aurelius Antoninus (Caracalla).
217–218	M. Opellius Macrinus.
218	M. Opellius Macrinus.

The six Emperors listed are the known African rulers. There may have been many more, and it will be the task of African scholars to search into the past and identity our Black ancestors, as has been done in the case of Severus.

In returning to the comments on Severus, some writers have advanced the idea that Severus, an African, did not show any favoritism towards his homeland. The statement is not true. Birley remarks about Severus' visit to his home town of Leptis Magna, Africa: "At last in 200, he felt able to relax, and began a series of provincial tours, which included a visit to Leptis. He summoned artists and craftsmen from all over the Empire and a massive programme of building began, which was to make the city one of the finest in the Empire." (page 672). H.M.D. Parker also places Severus in Africa in 203. He visited the principal towns of Africa and bestowed the status of colony upon many of them. He raised the status of Numidia from a diocese to a separate, independent imperial province, and placed it under the control of a legion commander. (page 72).

From Severus' attitude towards his native Africa, and his countrymen, it may be justifiably stated that this great African was actively aware of his homeland and the needs of his people. A visit to Leptis Magna today will attest to the proposition that Severus loved his home: there are still many reliefs, statues, and monuments visible to the casual observer.

For those who might visit Rome, the Arch of Septimius Severus was erected in 203. It is located at the northeast corner of the Roman Forum. If it is impossible to visit Rome, then see *The Arch of Septimius Severus In the Roman Forum,* by Richard Brilliant; published by the American Academy In Rome, vol. XXIX, 1967. After reading this commentary and the chapter about this magnificent soldier-emperor, it is hoped that the fires of curiosity and intellectual interests will have been permanently kindled in the mind of the reader.

EARLY LIFE

One of the first Black men to rule the world was Lucius Septimius Severus (his sons later ruled). The world, as the ancients knew it, was divided into three geographical areas: Roman Britain, Roman Asia and Roman Africa.

Septimius Severus, an African, was born in Leptis Magna, Africa, April 11, 146 A.D. There is very little information concerning his childhood. It is known, however, that as a young student he studied Latin, and became highly proficient in Roman literature. Spartianus, a historian, said that despite his achievement of proficiency in literature, he was cursed (or blessed?) all of his life with an African accent.

As a young man, Severus had high hopes of becoming a leader in the Roman government; to this end he devoted himself to the study of law under a famous jurist in Rome for six years (164–170). After acquiring legal training, it seems that his rise to fame was virtually unchecked. In 171, he held a quaestorship (judge or prosecutor); later, he was appointed governor on the staff of the African proconsul, and was given the governorship of one of the three African dioceses.[2]

On December 10, 175, Severus took over the office of Plebeian Tribune. Although most of the powers of the office were vested in the emperor, Severus performed his duties with characteristic vigour and severity. It was during this year that he married his first wife, Marcia, a lady of whom history reveals very little, except a few statues that Severus had erected in her honor after he became emperor. Severus and Marcia had two daughters. In 178, Severus, then 33 years of age, was elected praetor (city magistrate). His province was that of Spain, and he probably controlled one of its three dioceses. In 179, Severus was appointed to the command of the Syrian legion, IV Scythica, but this appointment apparently did not last long, because Severus later retired to a school in Athens to continue his studies.[3]

Severus returned to public life from his schooling in Athens probably in the year 186, when Cleander, the emperor, appointed him Legatus (governor) of Lugdunum (Lyon).[4] It was said that his administration was just and beneficent, and that he was personable, and popular with his subjects. In the year 187, Severus celebrated his second marriage with the famous Julia Domna of Syria. It must be presumed that the widowed governor met her during his command of the Syrian legion in the East. One of the main reasons that

A Roman painting depicting Lucius Septimius Severus, Emperor of Rome from 193 to 211 A.D., with his wife and child.

influenced Severus' decision to marry Julia (as the story goes), was that her horoscope said that someday she would marry a king. So being somewhat superstitious, and possibly harboring a desire to become emperor someday, he married her. In the year 188 a son was born to this marriage; they named him Caracalla.[5]

The next important position that Severus was appointed to was governor of Pannonia, with three Roman legions at his disposal.[6] His effective management of the area and his popularity among the soldiers, which he cultivated over a period of two years or more, certainly helped him when he eventually made his move to take over the Empire.[7]

THE PRAETORIAN GUARDS
In the meantime, back in Rome, the Praetorian Guards, a powerful group of elite soldiers (approximately 16,000) that had been created by the former emperor Augustus to protect his person and put down rebellion, had now

become permanently encamped in Rome. They eventually proved to be a thorn in the side of civil government. The guards were constantly reminded of their own strength and weaknesses by emperors, who rewarded with flattery, and indulged them in their pleasures. The loyalty of the guards could be purchased by liberal donations from the princes and other members of the aristocracy. Later, the guards exacted a donative from every new emperor as a legal claim. Their justification for the use of power, which they enforced with arms, was that the constitution required their consent in the appointment of an emperor.[8] In effect, the guards usurped the rights of the Roman people to elect their own leaders. The guards exercised their illegal power after the death of Emperor Commodus, when the leader of the guards selected Pertinax, who was later killed by the same guards.[9]

THE ARMIES REVOLT

The dealth of Pertinax on March 28, 193, began the War of Accession among the three contenders: Albinus, Niger, and Severus. These generals had their own armies located in different parts of the Roman Empire. The Praetorian Guards started the chain of events that led up to the war by first selling the empire to the highest bidder, as though it were a piece of private real estate. The guards sold the Roman Empire at a public sale to Didius Julianus for 6,250 drachmas to each soldier. It is a staggering thought to comprehend that one man could purchase an Empire, the whole of the known world. However, the same process is still prevalent in Western society today; for example, in the United States, the man with the largest amount of money to spend on his campaign is the one that is most likely to be the winner.

Julianus, realizing what he had done, became fearful when he thought of being an emperor over an Empire that he had purchased with money, and not won by merit. The guards were ashamed of him, and the citizens considered his elevation to emperor an insult to the Roman state.[10]

After Julianus had paid the guards for the Empire, he hastened to the Forum and the senate-house. He was escorted by the Praetorian Guards, who were armed for the purpose of intimidating the senators and citizens alike, in order to secure their allegiance to Julianus. The senate confirmed Julianus and he obtained the imperial power by decrees.

On the following day, the Senate went to pay its respects to the new emperor. Dio, the historian, and also a senator at that time, said the citizens were unhappy and near open revolt against Julianus. Dio described the mood of the people as follows: The populace ". . . went about openly with sullen looks, spoke its mind as much as it pleased, and was getting ready to do anything it could. Finally, when he came to the senate-house and was about to sacrifice Janus before the entrance, all fell to shouting, as if by preconcerted arrangement, calling him stealer of the Empire and parricide."[11] Dio said that Julianus responded to the citizens' taunts at first by offering them money. This attempted bribe infuriated them more, so Julianus, no longer in control of himself, ordered the guards to kill those citizens that were up front. This murderous act exasperated the populace, and, though many were killed, they continued to openly regret the death of Pertinax, and to curse Julianus.[12]

The people of Rome rose up against Julianus and called on the commanders of the three legions on the frontiers to restore the majesty of Rome. The people specifically called on Pescennius Niger in Syria (who was a Black man) to come to their aid.

When the news reached the generals in the field, the armies revolted against Julianus. The army in Britain was headed by Clodius Albinus, the one in Syria, by Pescennius Niger, and the one in Pannonia, by Septimius Severus. All three were anxious to succeed to the position of Emperor. This had been Severus' dream for many years—to become emperor. Gibbon said:

"The Pannonian army was at this time commanded by Septimius Severus, a *native of Africa,* [emphasis mine] who, in the gradual ascent of private honors, had concealed his daring ambition, which was never diverted from its steady course by the allurements of pleasure, the apprehension of danger or the feelings of humanity."[13]

SEVERUS' RISE TO POWER

The African general assembled his troops and addressed them with flaming oratory reminding them of their outrage against the Praetorian Guards in Rome, who are more suited for show and parades than battles. He felt it his sacred duty not to allow Rome to remain in the helpless state, but to restore it to its position of reverence and leadership in the world. Severus recalled how the elder statesman Pertinax was murdered by the guard, and the later sale of the empire by the guards to Julianus, now hated by the people of Rome and no longer trusted by the guard. He told his men that they not only outnumbered the Praetorian Guards, but were also superior in courage to them. His conclusion was that they should immediately occupy Rome, the seat of the Empire. When Severus ended his speech, he received a shouting ovation from his men, praising him as Emperor and calling him "Augustus" and "Pertinax."[14]

Severus, being a shrewd general, understood in advance that, when Julianus was deposed, he would have to fight the other two generals for the right to rule the empire, so he made plans to win over the rival who was nearest to him, Albinus, general of Britain. Severus sent him a letter appointing him "Caesar." As for Niger, general of Syria, Severus had no other plan except to defeat him in battle. Albinus remained in Britain believing that he was going to share in the rule of Rome with Severus.[15]

After winning over Albinus, Severus hastened to Rome, hoping that he could revenge the death of Pertinax, the former emperor, and punish Julianus, the emperor who had purchased the Empire. By so doing, he would receive the blessings of the Senate and the people as their lawful emperor before his two competitors, who were separated from Italy by many miles of land and sea, could become aware of his success. He was only ten days marching time from Italy by forced march. Dio said that not once did any of his soldiers take off their breastplates until they reached Rome.[16] Gibbon also spoke of Severus' determined march:

> During the whole expedition he scarcely allowed himself any moments for sleep or food; marching on foot, and in complete armor, at the head of his columns, he insinuated himself into the confidence and affection of this troops, pressed their diligence, revived their spirits, animated their hopes, and was well satisfied to share the hardships of the meanest soldier, whilst he kept in view the infinite superiority of his reward.[17]

When Julianus heard that Severus was marching on Rome, he became frantic and ordered the Senate to declare Severus a public enemy. He also ordered the Praetorian Guards to erect defenses around the city and to fortify the palace. Then Julianus sent several embassies to either block Severus' advance or to persuade him to turn back. He also sent an embassy to slay Severus; however, most of the men he sent defected to Severus' side. Finally Julianus, realizing that his end was near, made one more desperate move to save himself; he called the Senate together and requested that they appoint Severus emperor to share in his throne.

During the march to Rome, Severus sent letters by his messengers to the Praetorian Guards, promising that no harm would come to them if they would surrender the slayers of Pertinax and then keep the peace until his arrival. The guards arrested the men who had murdered Pertinax and sent word to Severus, informing him that they had the men under arrest.[18]

As Severus drew closer to Rome, the city grew tense, the populace became restless, and many officials began to behave impetuously and irrationally. The Senate decided to act. When the Senators were assembled, they proceeded to sentence Julianus to death, name Severus emperor of Rome, and bestow divine honors upon Pertinax.[19]

There were three important matters Severus dealt with prior to his arrival in Rome: he sent L. Fulvinus Platianus to the capitol, with orders to secure Niger's sons as hostages for their father's loyalty to Severus; next, he appointed Flavinus Juvenalis as prefect of the Praetorian Guards; and, thirdly, he punished the guards for their murder of Pertinax.[20]

Severus used a trick to seize and hold the Praetorian Guards. He sent an open letter to the camp, directing the guards to leave their weapons behind and to assemble at a certain place outside Rome unarmed. He also ordered them to swear an oath of allegiance to him as Emperor, and to present themselves with the thought of continuing to serve as body-guards for the Emperor. The guards believed the orders. They left their arms behind and, dressed in their holiday uniforms, appeared on the assembly ground to hear the Emperor's "welcoming address." Just as Severus was mounting the platform to address the guards, a prearranged signal was given and they were all seized while cheering him.

Severus' soldiers, acting on prior orders, surrounded the guards with a ring of steel. The Emperor bitterly reproached them for their failure to perform their primary duty— to protect and support their former emperor, Pertinax. He recalled their shameful act of selling the Roman Empire to Julianus as though it was their private property. Severus told them that they deserved a thousand deaths as a penalty for such crimes, and that their conduct was in such flagrant violation of their oath that he could no longer allow them to serve as the Emperor's bodyguard. Having spoken thusly, the Emperor ordered his soldiers to strip off the guards' insignia, rank, and uniforms, and take away their horses, leaving them naked and helpless, as war prisoners. Severus banished the guards from Rome, and warned them not to be caught within 100 miles of the city. Those persons who had actually murdered Pertinax were put to death on orders of Severus.[21]

Emperor Severus entered Rome. The Senators and the people met him and honored him as the greatest of men and emperors, who had accomplished great things without bloodshed or difficulty. Severus advanced as far as the gates on horseback in a cavalry uniform, then he changed into civilian clothes and proceeded on foot, with his whole army, the infantry and cavalry, following him in full armor. Dio described the procession as follows:

> The spectacle provided the most brilliant of any that I have witnessed; for the whole city had been decked with garlands of flowers and laurel and adorned with richly colored stuffs, and incense; the citizens, wearing white robes and with radiant countenance uttered many shouts of good omen; the soldiers too, stood out conspicuous in their armour as they moved about like participants in some holiday procession: and finally, we [senators] were walking about in state. The crowd chafed in its eagerness to see him and to hear him say something, as if he had been somehow changed by his good fortune: and some of them held one another aloft, that from a higher position they might catch sight of him.[22]

After being saluted and greeted by the Senators and the people, Severus entered temple of Jupiter and offered sacrifices. Then he entered the palace that he was to occupy as emperor until death. Here is what the historian, Herodian, said of this remarkable African emperor's personality:

> Everything about the man was extraordinary, but especially outstanding were his shrewd judgment, his endurance of toils, and his spirit of bold optimism in everything he did.[23]

On the day following his triumphant march into Rome, Severus went to the Senate to address the Senators. His speech to them was mild and inoffensive. He restated his promise to them, that was, to avenge the death of Pertinax, and he made a new promise that he would return the empire to senatorial rule. No man, promised Severus, would be sentenced to death or have his property confiscated without a fair trial. He said he would bring unlimited prosperity to the citizens of Rome. Most of the Senators believed his promises, but some of the older Senators knew the true character of Severus, and, according to Herodian, these senators privately stated ". . . that he was indeed a man of great cunning, who knew how to manage things shrewdly; they further said that he was very skillful at deceit and at feigning anything and everything; and, moreover, he always did what would benefit and profit his own interests. The truth of these observations was later demonstrated by what the man actually did."[24]

The Emperor had the ability to understand and interpret human nature, especially when his own interests were involved. There were several important facts he had to consider: he needed to secure his shaky position as Emperor of Rome, to defeat Niger in Syria, and to mollify Albinus in the meantime. Obviously, the first plan was to secure his position in Rome and then to prepare for war.

SEVERUS PREPARES FOR WAR

The Emperor spent a short time in Rome, during which he bestowed gifts upon the people, paid his soldiers well and replaced the Praetorian Guards with some of the best men from his army. He then made preparations to march his army to the East. Severus realized the Niger was wasting time living in luxury, so he wanted to surprise him by catching him unprepared for battle.

The Emperor ordered his soldiers to be prepared to march on a date fixed. He then collected young recruits from all the cities in Italy and signed them up in the army. Orders were sent to the rest of his army, left behind in Illyricum, to proceed to Thrace and join him there. He also organized a navy unit with heavily armed troops and dispatched it to the East. Severus organized this large and powerful force with unbelievable speed, knowing that he had to have such force if he was to defeat Niger. Being a thorough and cautious leader, he expressed concern about Clodius Albinus' large and powerful army in Britain. He certainly could not overlook Albinus, a man of senatorial caliber and an aristocrat who had inherited money from his ancestors. Fearing that Albinus, with such a background, would have strong reasons to seek the throne, Severus decided to gain Albinus' friendship in order to deceive him by trick. Severus felt that Albinus might seize the empire and occupy Rome while he was fighting Niger in the East. So Severus deceived Albinus by pretending to bestow an honor upon him, appointing him Caesar, in order to anticipate his hopes and desires for a share in the imperial powers. Severus wrote friendly but deceitful letters to Albinus, in which he asked him to devote his attention to the welfare of the Empire. He wrote that Albinus was young, and that he himself was old, afflicted with gout, and that his sons were too young to rule. Albinus believed Severus and gratefully accepted the honor. Albinus was easily mollified. He thought that he was being given what he had secretly desired, a share of the throne, without having had to fight for it. Severus then made a formal proposal to the Senate to appoint Albinus Caesar. The Senate was impressed by this act, sharing the powers of the throne by Severus. Then, to counteract what he had done, Severus ordered coins struck, bearing his likeness (not Albinus'), erected statues of himself all over Rome, and assumed the rest of the imperial powers. After cunningly arranging his affairs securely in respect to Albinus, and, no longer fearing him, he set out against Niger with his entire army.²⁵

WAR AGAINST NIGER

General Pescennius Niger, commander of the army in Syria, learned that Severus had marched into Rome, had been proclaimed Emperor by the Senate, and was now leading an army supported by naval units against him.

In preparing his defenses against Severus, Niger dispatched orders to his governors of the eastern provinces to keep a close guard on the passes and harbors. He ordered that the narrow passes and cliffs of the Taurus Mountains be defended by strong walls and fortifications as protection for the highways of the West. Niger also sent an army force to occupy Byzantium in Thrace. This city was very rich and strong and he hoped to prevent Severus' army from crossing into Asia through the Propontic Gulf (near the modern Dardanelles).

In the meantime, Severus advanced his army at top speed, seldom halting for rest or food. He had heard that Niger was now occupying Byzantium, which had the strongest walls of defense, so he ordered his army to attack the city of Cyzicus instead.

General Aemilianus, governor of Asia, was in charge of the military preparations and defense of the Cyzicus province. When he received the news that Severus was advancing towards Cyzicus, he marched his army into the province. The two armies met in savage combat, and Severus' army was victorious. Niger's men were routed, put to flight, and slaughtered. It was believed that Aemilianus was forced to betray Niger (and lose the battle) by his own children who begged him to do so for their safety. It may be that Severus had found and seized Aemilianus' children and held them as hostages: when Severus had first come to Rome, he had gathered up most of the children of the governors, and of others who occupied positions of importance in the East, and had held them in custody. He kept these children so that the governors might be influenced to

betray Niger in fear for the safety of their children, and, had they continued to support Niger's cause, their children would have been killed.

After the battle of Cyzicus, Severus swept through several cities, putting them under siege and then burning them. When Niger became aware of his losses, he collected a large army of young recruits from Antioch and marched out to meet Severus. The forces, led by Niger himself, met the troops of Severus in a tremendous battle at Issus near the "Gates," as they are called.

The battle was indecisive for many days; then, suddenly, Niger's forces got the upper hand, because of their superiority in numbers, and the terrain. They would have defeated Severus' army had it not been for the violent rain storm that occurred. The wind blew the driving rain into the faces of advancing troops of Niger, which rendered them helpless and created a state of confusion. Severus' men were not hampered by the storm because it was to their backs. It merely inspired them, but it terrified Niger's men causing them to take flight. Dio, in relating the battle, refers to a priest's dream:

> This proved to be the greatest disaster of the war; for twenty thousand of Niger's followers perished. And this evidently was the meaning of the priest's dream. It seems that while Severus was in Pannonia the Priest of Jupiter in a dream saw a black man force his way into the emperor's camp and come to his death by violence; and by interpreting the name of Niger, people recognized that he was the black man in question.²⁶

A conclusion which may be drawn from Dio's story about the priest's dream is that two black men were fighting each other for the right to rule the world, and one lost. Niger's army was put to rout and Antioch was captured. Niger fled, intending to make his escape back into the friendly areas under his control, but his pursuers overtook him and cut off his head (A.D. 194). Severus caused his head to be sent to Byzantium (the next city he planned to attack) and to be set upon a pale, in order to shock the people into joining and supporting his cause.[27]

Having eliminated Niger, Severus had all of his friends and supporters put to death. He also ordered that the children of Niger and the children of Niger's governors in Syria be put to death. Such was the violent end of the war against Niger. Severus was a master thinker and a master strategist of war. He was thorough in his intent to destroy his adversaries completely.

WAR AGAINST ALBINUS

After settling the affairs of the East by the complete elimination of Niger and his friends, Severus began seriously to consider his other adversary, Albinus, as a menace and the last threat to his bid for complete power as Emperor of Rome.

Severus had heard that Albinus was delighted with the title of Caesar, and that he was beginning to act more and more like the Emperor of Rome. During the time Severus was engaged in the East, some senators and citizens of Rome were writing public and private letters to Albinus, the "Caesar," begging him to return to Rome quickly while Severus was locked in battle with Niger. Severus heard of these developments and decided against challenging Albinus openly, so he devised a trick to eliminate him. He sent his imperial messengers to Britain with secret orders to hand Albinus the dispatches openly; then they were to ask him to meet them privately to receive secret instructions. If Albinus agreed to their request, and if his bodyguards were absent, the messengers were to assault Albinus and murder him. Severus' messengers were also provided with vials containing deadly poisons, in case they had an opportunity to bribe one of Albinus' cooks or waiters to administer a dose in secret.[28]

(It is interesting to note here that when Fidel Castro came to the U.S. after overthrowing Batista, and becoming the leader of Cuba, he brought his own food and cooks to protect himself from the same kind of trick that Severus planned for Albinus.)

Well, the trick, as devised by Severus, did not work because Albinus' advisors became suspicious of Severus' messengers and warned him to be on the alert against the cunning schemer. It was the violent action by Severus against Niger's governors and their children that had seriously damaged his reputation, and had caused Albinus to increase the size of his bodyguard. Albinus ordered that no one was to be admitted into his presence until he had been stripped and searched for hidden weapons. When Severus' messengers delivered the dispatches to Albinus they requested that he retire with them alone to receive Severus' secret orders. Albinus became suspicious and ordered the men seized and tortured. The messengers confessed the plot, and Albinus had them put to death. He then made preparations to resist his now known enemy—Severus.[29]

Severus, through his intelligence network, received information that Albinus was mobilizing his army in Britain to fight him. In order to arouse his men to the fighting spirit and courage needed to defeat a dangerous foe, Severus assembled his army and, in fiery oratory, spoke about Albinus' ingratitude for the many benefits that he had lavished upon him—the rank of Caesar and a share in the throne. Severus exhorted his army to go forth against Albinus with confidence. When he had finished speaking, the entire army called Albinus their enemy, and shouted their praise for Severus, promising to support his leadership until victory was theirs.

The news that "Severus was coming," threw Albinus into a state of panic and confusion. He hastily decided to cross over to the mainland of Gaul (now France) and established his headquarters. It was here that Albinus hoped to direct his troops against the army of Severus.[30]

When Severus arrived with his army in Gaul he met and closed in battle with Albinus' army; the final battle between these two great armies was fought near the large city of Lugdunum (now Lyon). Both leaders were present in this conflict since it was a life and death struggle for the undisputed right to rule the world, that is, to become the one and only Emperor of Rome.

A major battle developed, and for a long time the outcome was unpredictable, because chances for victory were equal on both sides. But Severus was a skillful commander, and superior in warfare to his opponent Albinus. The conflict had many phases and shifts of fortune for each side. Severus' men were defeating Albinus' troops on the left wing, and they retreated. But Albinus' men on the right wing had set a trap of concealed trenches, and started a false retreat. When Severus' men pursued them, they fell into the deep trenches at a great loss of life. Severus personally came to their aid with the Praetorian Guards, but the guards were repulsed, and Severus lost his horse in the melee.

He tore off his imperial cloak and rallied his men by fighting at their side. At that moment, Laetus, one of Severus' generals, appeared with fresh troops, and Severus was able to press the attack. Albinus' men were thrown into a general rout, pursued and slaughtered. Albinus was later caught and his head was cut off and sent to Severus (A.D. 197). The angry emperor had Albinus' head sent to Rome to be displayed so that the people might know the extent of his anger against those who had supported Albinus. He later took vengeance upon Albinus' friends in Rome, just as he had done to Niger's friends— put them to death.[31]

Herodian said of Severus:

The emperor thus won two magnificent victories, one in the East and one in the West. No battles and no victories can be compared to those of Severus, and no army to the size of his army; there are no comparable uprisings among nations, or total number of campaigns, or length and speed of marches.

Herodian refers to other great Roman battles, and then states:

But here is one man who overthrew three emperors after they were already ruling, and got the upper hand over the praetorians by a trick: he succeeded in killing Julianus, the man in the imperial palace; Niger, who had previously governed the people of the East and was saluted emperor by the Roman people; and Albinus who had already been awarded the honor and authority of Caesar. He prevailed over them all by his courage. It is not possible to name another like Severus."[32]

After his defeat of Albinus, Septimius Severus left Gaul for Rome. He made a triumphal march into the city June 2, 197, and was joyfully greeted by the people, who heaped every known honor upon their hero. The Senate, however, was in a state of fear because many senators had collaborated with Clodius Albinus and Pescennius Niger, both defeated as enemies by Severus. Would he seek revenge by wreaking vengence upon this august body? Yes. First, he castigated the Senate in an address to that body, then he brought charges against those who had collaborated with the enemy. He presented as evidence private letters which were sent to Albinus by senators who had supported him for emperor and opposed Severus. Platnauer felt that Severus, who had a legal background, attempted to adhere to some semblance of justice in the trials of the senators: "Of the sixty-four cases which came up for trial thirty-five ended in acquittal, a fact which shows that even if the principles of justice were not strictly observed in all cases the emperor was not beyond the desire of seeming to act in accordance with them."[33] Severus apparently condemned the twenty-nine senators to death and confiscated their property. As emperor, he could have condemned all of them to death, so it is apparent that the rule of law was used to give the senators a fair trial.

THE PARTHIAN WAR

Severus spent the summer months in Rome, but had to leave on short notice. The Parthians, taking advantage of the distraction offered by the civil war in Gaul, crossed the Tigris and invaded Mesopotamia in violation of a former treaty. The Emperor and his praetorian prefect, Plautianus, accompanied by his generals, left in the fall of 197. Besides the Praetorian Guards, several new legions were raised and sent to the East to join the Emperor.

The Parthian king, Vologeses V, upon hearing that Severus had arrived in Syria, raised the seige and withdrew from Nisibis, recrossing the Tigris, from which he had come. Severus immediately advanced on Mesopotamia. Upon reaching Edessa, he received the allegiance of Abgarus, whom he restored to his throne of Osroene, calling him "king of kings." Abgarus, to show his gratefulness, adopted the name Septimius, and later visited Rome upon the invitation of the Emperor. Severus must have developed the political strategy of granting semi-autonomous status or colonial status to the cities and towns within the eastern part of the Empire by recognizing the native princes in these areas, and granting them more power. This was done when he reached Palmyra. He granted colonial status to Palmyra, which was then governed by Prince Odenathus of the famous and influential Odenathii family. Odenathus also took the name Septimius to honor his benefactor. (This town, in the next century, became powerful and wealthy and a rival to Rome.)

After departing from Edessa, Severus advanced on Nisibis, and, finding that the seige had been raised, decided to invade Parthia. He marched his army south along the banks of the Euphrates and sent part of his forces to attack Babylon, which was captured without much resistance; the other part of his forces moved against Seleucia, which had been evacuated by the Parthians. The final assault was against Ctesiphon; resistance was

short and the city fell in March 198. He did not pursue the Parthian King.

While returning from his victory, Severus decided to make a detour with his army and attack a small desert town of Hatra. Its prince, Barsemius, refused to acknowledge the sovereignty of Severus. However, after two attacks, Severus was forced to withdraw in defeat.

To honor his victory in vanquishing Parthia, Severus accepted the title of Parthicus Maximus. He bestowed the rank of Augustus upon the older son, Caracalla, and the title of Caesar upon the younger son, Geta. The Parthian war was over in the summer of 199, and he probably returned to Syria. For the next two years, he visited Palestine and Egypt. He crossed Palestine, not spending much time there, and arrived in Egypt. In Alexandria, he closed Alexander's tomb, so no one else could view the embalmed body. He also made important administrative changes, bestowing the right of self-rule upon Alexandria.

Severus departed from Alexandria and sailed down the Nile, continuing his tour. He visited Memphis and Thebes, where he heard the famous statue of Memnon (the Ethiopian god) "sing" at dawn. Severus was so amazed that he ordered the head and neck restored. As a result of the Emperor's enthusiastic orders to see the statue of Memnon whole again, it was deprived of its "voice," and the statue "sang" no more. Continuing his tour, Severus arrived at the borders of Ethiopia, where he fell ill, and was forced to remain for a time.

The Emperor left Egypt in 201 for Rome. He returned in victory, and the celebration, which combined the triumph with his tenth year of accession, became a festival which lasted for six or seven days.[34]

HOME ADMINISTRATION OF SEVERUS

Severus was not only a distinguished military man, but also an excellent administrator. It appears from his illustrious record that he performed the types of duties and developed the kind of administration which secured his position as emperor. He also provided the people with the necessary goods and services.

To accomplish these ends, he maintained the same form of government, but favored the equestrian knights class over the traditionally favored senatorial class. Severus increased the power of the knights by placing them in charge of the newly established legions and provinces. Although the senators were not removed from any of their positions, they were not given new ones. Thus, their powers were weakened and their class subordinated to that of the knights'. The historians, Couch and Geer, recognized the conflict between Severus and the senators, arising because the senators had sympathized with the other pretenders to the imperial power and were implicated in the defeat of the losers. These authors said: "Septimius filled the vacant places in the Senate with his favorites, chiefly from Africa, his native land, from Syria, the home of his wife, and from the Danube regions, which had first aided him on the road to power. The centurions in the legions were made knights, and from them many of the important positions were filled."[35]

Besides the administrative moves to strengthen his position, Severus increased the authority of the Praetorian Prefect and created a dual post which he filled with two great Africans: the outstanding general, Maecius Laetus, and the famous jurist, Aemilius Papinianus. The prefects' office lost some of its military power, but acquired more judicial and administrative powers. The legal prefect, Papinianus, handled all of the appeals from the sentences of the governors of each province; he also acted as president of the Empire in the absence of the emperor. He was the supreme judge who had criminal jurisdiction in Italy outside the one-hundred-mile radius of Rome. His other duties involved control and distribution of the corn supply, oil, and, possibly, the provision of supplies for the army. The post of Praetorian Prefect was

second only to the Emperor in power and authority. Other great lawyers joined Severus' government. They were Paul and Ulpian, who assisted Papinian in establishing an outstanding system for the administration of justice. It was through his lawyers that Severus gained support for this theory that the Senate had assigned rather than delegated its power to him.

On the legislative side, Severus passed some very humanitarian laws. For instance, laws were enacted to prevent abortion, protect the interests of minors, and laws defining the status of slaves. There were also laws regulating inheritance and fixing advocate's fees.

Severus was a kind and just man to the people. When he took over the government it was practically bankrupt; when he died, the government was solvent and he left his family an immense fortune, commemorated as *"munificentissimus providentissimusque princeps."* (translated: "a bountiful, generous, foresighted and distinguished person, or first man"). During Severus' reign his distribution of money to the people of Rome was extravagant and unbelievable. He financed expensive games during the festival of 202. He had a program of providing free oil and corn, and also free medicine to the sick, under the superintendence of Galen. (Forerunner of Medicare?) He also started the Alimentary system which had been stopped by Commodus.

Many monuments were erected to commemorate Severus, such as the magnificent baths (Baths of Caracalla can still be seen in Rome) and the huge triumphal arch in the Roman forum.[36] These commemorative acts by the people were a tribute to his successful home rule. His problems arose in the provinces.

SEVERUS DIES IN BRITAIN

In 208, the tribes in Britain revolted against Roman leadership. The problem started during the war against Albinus in 197, when most of the Roman legions stationed in Britain were ordered to Gaul by Albinus. This left

Roman Britain unprotected, and the northern tribes took the opportunity to move south and occupy the territory. The successor to Albinus was the legate Virus Lupus, who was forced to compromise with the Maeatae and sue for peace. The leadership of Lupus, and later, Legate Alfenius Senecio, recovered most of the territory lost in an eight-year struggle with the Britons.

Severus decided that he should personally conduct an offensive war against the rebellious tribes, so he made preparations for an expedition in the spring of 208. There was another reason why Severus was anxious to make the trip: his two sons were in constant conflict with one another; they were always attempting to outdo each other by having competitive parties, games, friends, etc. The enmity between them became so intense that Caracalla openly began to threaten to take Geta's life. Severus thought the expedition to Britain would bring about a reconciliation between his sons, since they would have to participate personally in the conduct of the war.

Dio alludes to Severus' wife, Julia, his sons, and the Praetorian Prefect, Papinian, as being some of his family and friends who travelled to Britain with him on the campaign.

The Caledonians and the Maeatae tribes were not easily subdued in the first campaign, fought in 209. Although the Roman army advanced into Scotland in 209–210, they lost heavily because of the terrain, and because of guerilla-type warfare waged by the tribes. Dio claims the Romans lost 50,000 men. Severus had to make peace in 210, and agreed to cede a large portion of the country to the Caledonians. The treaty was a ruse on the part of the tribes to buy time; they attacked again the following year.

Severus, now old and suffering from the gout, rose from his sick bed to fight his last campaign. It was during this time that Caracalla drew his sword and made an attempt on his father's life; he was prevented from accomplishing the foul deed by onlookers who yelled a warning to the Emperor.

Resulting from the combination of grave illness and personal unhappiness with the outrageous conduct of his son, the Emperor died in York, February 4, 211. He was sixty-five at the time of his death, and Dio said of him: "Of his period he ruled for seventeen years, eight months and three days. In fine he showed himself so active that even when expiring he gasped: 'Come give it here, if we have anything to do.'"[37]

Notes

1. Herodian of Antioch, *History of the Roman Empire,* tr. from the Greek, Edward C. Echols, University of California in Berkeley and Los Angeles, 1961, Book III, 7.8.

2. Maurice Platnauer, *The Life and Reign of the Emperor Lucius Septimius Severus,* Oxford University Press, 1918, Chap. III, p. 38.

3. Platnauer, pp. 39–44.

4. Dio, Book LXXIII, 14.4.

5. Platnauer, pp. 46–48.

6. Dio, *Roman History,* Book LXXIV, 14.3.

7. Platnauer, *ibid.*

8. Edward Gibbon, *The History of the Decline and Fall of the Roman Empire,* Harper and Brothers, New York, 1845, Vol. I, p. 348.

9. *ibid.,* p. 349

10. Gibbon, pp. 349–350.

11. Dio, Book LXXIV, 12–13.3.

12. Dio, *ibid.*

13. Gibbon, p. 357

14. Herodian, Book II, Chap. 10.

15. Dio, Book LXXIV, 14.3–15.3.
16. Dio, LXXIV, 15.3.
17. Gibbon, p. 358.
18. Dio, Book LXXIV, 15.3–17.4.
19. Dio, LXXIV, 17.4–5.
20. Platnauer, p. 66.
21. Dio, Book LXXV, 1.1–1.2.
22. Dio, *ibid.*
23. Herodian, Book II, Chap. 14.
24. Herodian, Book II, Chap. XIV; Gibbon, Chap. V, p. 363.
25. Herodian, Book II, Chap. XV.
26. Dio, Book LXXV, 7–8.3; Herodian, Book III, Chap. 2.
27. Dio, Book LXXV, 83; Herodian, Book III, Chap. 3 and 4.
28. Herodian, Book III, Chap. 5.
29. Herodian, *ibid.*
30. Herodian, Book III, Chap. VI.
31. Herodian, Book III, Chap. 7.
32. Herodian, *ibid.*
33. Platnauer, p. 113.
34. H.M.D. Parker, *A History of the Roman World,* pp. 72–75; Platnauer, *ibid.*
35. Herbert N. Couch and Russel M. Geer, *Classical Civilization,* Prentice-Hall, Inc., New York, 1940, p. 266.
36. H.M.D. Parker, *ibid.,* Platnauer, *ibid.;* Couch & Geer, *ibid.*
37. Dio, *ibid;* Platnauer, *ibid;* H.M.D. Parker, *ibid.*

Bibliography

Brilliant, R., *The Arch of Septimius Severus in the Roman Forum,* Rome, American Academy of Rome, 1967.

Couch, H. N., and Geer, R. M., *Classical Civilization,* New York, Prentice-Hall Inc., 1940.

Dio's *Roman History,* vol. IX, New York, E. Cary, G. P. Putnam's Sons, 1927.

Gibbon, E., *The History of the Decline and Fall of the Roman Empire,* vol. I, New York, Harper and Brothers, 1845.

Grant, M., *The Climax of Rome,* London, Weidenfeld and Nicolson, 1968.

Herodian, *History of the Roman Empire,* E. C. Echols, University of California in Berkeley, Los Angeles, 1961.

McCann, A. M., *The Portraits of Septimius Severus,* Rome, American Academy in Rome, 1968.

Millar, F., *The Roman Empire and its Neighbors,* New York, Delacorte Press, 1967.

Milne, G. J., *A History of Egypt Under Roman Rule,* London, Methuen and Co. Ltd., 1924.

Parker, H.M.D., *A History of the Roman World,* London, Methuen and Co. Ltd., 1935.

Platnauer, M., *The Life and Reign of the Emperor Lucius Septimius Severus,* London, Oxford Press, 1918.

Rostovtzeff, M., *The Social and Economic History of the Roman Empire,* Oxford, Clarendon Press, 1926.

The Sudanese States and Empires

ADU BOAHEN

ON THE ATTAINMENT OF INDEPEN-
dence, the Gold Coast was renamed Ghana
after an empire that arose and developed
between A.D. 500 and 1200 in the region
between the bend of the Niger and the middle
reaches of the Senegal. Ghana was of course
not the only state that emerged in that region.
There were also those of Tekrur, Mali and
Songhai and, further to the east, the Hausa
states of Kano, Katsina, Zaria, Gobir and the
Chadic states of Kanem and Bornu. In this
section I will discuss the history of some of
these states beginning with that of the ancient
Ghanaian Empire. I should like to concentrate here on an aspect often neglected by
historians, namely, the cultural aspect, by
answering the question what ancient Ghana
was like at the peak of its glory by about
A.D. 1060.

But before I do that, may I first of all say
a word or two about the origins of the states
I have mentioned. All these early states arose,
significantly enough, in the savannah belt that
stretches from the mouths of the Senegal and
the Gambia to the west and Lake Chad and
the Nile to the east, and from the Sahara to
the north and the forest belt to the south. This
seems to be due to two reasons. In the first
place, about 4000 years ago the savannah belt
was more suitable for human habitation than
the forest regions to the south. That belt,
called *Bilad as-Sudan* by the Arabs, thus saw
a great multiplication of peoples long before
those of the forest, a process which was greatly
accelerated by the increasing desiccation of
the Sahara from about 4000 B.C. onwards, the
independent invention or introduction of
agriculture in the region of the Niger bend
and the introduction of the use of iron. Such
peoples as the Soninke, the Mandinke, the
Serer, the Susu, the Songhai, and probably
some of the present-day forest peoples like
the Akan, the Yoruba and the Temne (in
Sierra Leone) first evolved and multiplied in
this region.

The second factor was the caravan trade
across the Sahara. Though this was begun by
the Berbers as far back as 3000–2000 B.C., it

Reprinted with permission from *Topics in West
African History* by Adu Boahen, published by
Longman Group UK.

did not become important and voluminous until the introduction of the camel into North Africa probably in the first century A.D. As a result of the use of this animal, which is capable of crossing the sandy wastes of the Sahara with relative ease, a complicated network of commercial routes across the Sahara emerged. Along these routes, traders from the Sahara, North Africa, Egypt, and the Middle East exchanged their wares—glass beads, earrings, bangles, items of clothing and later Arabic books—for the gold, ivory and slaves usually obtained from the forest regions. As intermediaries or middlemen for this trade, the people of the Sudan, that is, of the savannah belt, grew wealthy; wealth of course usually generates power and ambition and both give birth to states and kingdoms. It is obvious that the most northerly of the Sudanese people through whose country the trade routes passed would be the first to be enriched, and these were the Soninke or the Sarakole in the west and the Kanembu in the east, and it is significant that it was these two peoples who formed two of the earliest of the Sudanese states, namely Ghana and Kanem. It is interesting to note that it was not until the thirteenth century when the trade routes between the Barbary coast and Hausaland emerged that the Hausa states began to rise. Clearly then, it was not the activities of any white-skinned invaders or the introduction of the use of iron but rather the accessibility and strategic position of the savannah belt or Sudan and the wealth derived from the caravan trade that primarily account for the rise and growth of the early Sudanese states and empires.

1 A PORTRAIT OF ANCIENT GHANA

Ghana was the first of these kingdoms to emerge and to attain the greatest fame and glory. It was probably in existence by A.D. 500 and had attained the peak of its power by about the middle of the eleventh century. By then it extended over an area now occupied by the three independent states of Senegal, Mauretania and Mali. Many Arabic scholars and merchants collected and wrote up accounts from traders who had visited Ghana as well as from Ghanaians visiting the coast. The best known of these scholars were Al-Bakri and Al-Idrisi who wrote their descriptions of Ghana in 1067 just when the empire was at the height of its power, and in 1154, respectively. The portrait of Ghana that I am going to give is based mainly on the accounts of these two Arabic writers.

First, for what was ancient Ghana best known to the outside world? It was best known for its wealth in gold. On this all the Arab writers agree. Al-Fazari, the eminent astronomer, in whose book, written in 772, occurs the first reference to Ghana, called it simply the land of gold. Al-Hamadhani who wrote a century later described Ghana, with some exaggeration, as 'a country where gold grows like plants in the sand in the same way as carrots do, and is plucked at sunset'; Al-Masudi called Ghana the land of gold which is beyond Sijilmasa. Ibn Hawkal, who certainly visited Sijilmasa, the main northern caravan trading centre in Morocco, in 951, though it is doubtful whether he ever crossed the desert to northern Ghana, described the ruler of Ghana as 'the wealthiest of all kings on the face of the earth on account of the riches he owns and the hoards of gold acquired by him and inherited from his predecessors since ancient times'. Al-Bakri and Al-Idrisi also confirm this and even provide further detail. Al-Bakri states that 'all gold nuggets found in the kingdom were reserved for the king, only gold dust being left for the people', and adds that 'the king owns a nugget as large as a big stone'. He also points out that even dogs which guarded he king while he sat in state wore collars of gold and silver. Al-Idrisi, writing in 1154, was also convinced that the king has in his possession 'a nugget of pure gold weighing 30 lb. of absolutely natural formation'. He adds further that a hole had been made through it so that the king's horse could be tethered to it. It appears from these accounts, however, that most of this gold was not mined in Ghana itself but in the region to the south called Wangara by the Arabs. Equally important and lucrative was the trade in salt, which was obtained from Taghaza in the Sahara. So indispensable was this commodity for the peoples of the Sudan and the forest belt that, according to many of the Arab writers, it was exchanged for its weight in gold. Slaves also formed an important export.

How valuable was this trade? An answer to this can be found from the accounts of Ibn Hawkal. He first of all testifies to the state of opulence in which he found Awdaghost and Sijilmasa, both serving respectively as the southern and northern rendezvous and market centres for the caravan trade. Secondly he says that while he was in Sijilmasa, he himself saw a cheque for 42,000 dinars (i.e. about £100,000 today) drawn up by a man of that town on Muhammad b. Ali Sadun. To quote his direct words, 'I have seen a warrant concerning a debt owed by Muhammad b. Ali Sadun in Awdaghost and witnessed by assessors for 42,000 dinas'. He adds that he had never seen anything like that in the East, and that when he told 'people in Faris and Al-Iraq (Syria and Iraq) about it, they queried it'. This trade then must have been exceedingly lucrative and well organized. Since gold, slaves and salt were not obtained from Ghana itself, the wealth that the people of Ghana derived from it must have come mainly from the role which they played as the middlemen between the gold-producers to the south and the merchants from North Africa and Egypt. It is not surprising that Al-Idrisi described Ghana as the country 'with the widest commercial connections', and it was undoubtedly to ensure their grip on the caravan trade and safeguard their intermediary role that in 990 they conquered Awdaghost, the important Berber trading centre in the Sahara.

Next, how was Ghana governed and how was justice administered? Like most states and kingdoms, the Empire was ruled by a king, who was assisted by a Council of Ministers. At the time Al-Bakri was writing, that is about 1067, the King of Ghana was Tunka Manin whom he describes as possessing great authority. His immediate predecessor who was called Basi mounted the throne at the ripe age of 85 and is said to have led 'a praiseworthy life on account of his love of justice and friendship with the Muslims'. However, what amazed most of the Arabic writers is the fact that the system of inheritance was matrilineal and not patrilineal as was the rule in their own states, and Tunka Manin was said to be Basi's nephew. Here I will again quote Al-Bakri: 'This is their custom and habit', he wrote, 'that the kingdom is inherited only by the son of the king's sister.' The reason given for this is, interestingly enough, the very reason given by some Akan of modern Ghana for the same system of inheritance. 'The King', to quote the words of the Arabic scholar written 990 years ago, 'has no doubt that his successor is a son of his sister while he is not certain that his son is in fact his own and he does not rely on the genuineness of this relationship.'

Not only does the system of inheritance in ancient Ghana remind one of the present-day Akan practice, but so also do the kings' palace, the court etiquette, the use of drums, the burial of the king and the system of worship. The king, according to the Arabic authors, lived in a palace which consisted of a number of domed dwellings surrounded by an enclosure like a city wall. When he sat in state, he adorned himself, to quote again, 'like a woman, wearing necklaces round his neck and bracelets on his forearms and put on a high cap decorated with gold wrapped in a turban of fine cloth. Behind the king', the description goes on, 'stand ten pages holding shields and swords decorated with gold.' It is interesting to note that audience was announced by the beating of a drum. Another author also states that a drum, covered with a skin and making 'an awesome sound' when beaten, was used to assemble the people.

The way in which the kings of ancient Ghana were buried has also been described and this also has a familiar ring: 'When their king dies,' writes Al-Bakri, 'they construct over the place where his tomb will be, an enormous dome of saj or (teak) wood. Then they bring him on a bed covered with a few carpets and cushions and place him inside the dome. At his side, they place his ornaments, his weapons and the vessels from which he used to eat and drink, filled with various kinds of food and beverages. They place the men who used to serve his meals. They close the door of the dome and cover it with mats and furnishings. They then assemble the people who heap earth upon it until it becomes like a big hillock and they dig a ditch around it until the mound can be reached at only one place.' 'The people of Ghana', the writer adds, 'sacrifice victims to their dead and make offerings of intoxicating drinks.' All the tombs of the kings were in the same place surrounded by a thicket which was out of bounds to all except those in charge of it. It is further reported that it was in the same thicket that the gods of the state were kept—a sort of Nananom Mpow of the Fante of modern Ghana. Clearly, like most black peoples, the ancient Ghanaians were 'animistic' in their religious beliefs and had state gods.

The administration of justice in ancient Ghana should again sound familiar. For according to Al-Bakri, it was the responsibility of the king. Writing about 100 years later, Al-Idrisi pointed out that the king went out every day on his horse and commanded everyone who had suffered injustice or misfortune to come before him and stay there until the wrong was remedied. Trial by sasswood, or if you like by fetish, was also practised in ancient Ghana. 'When a man is accused of denying a debt or having shed blood or some other crime', testifies Al-Bakri, 'a headman takes a thin piece of wood, which is sour and bitter to taste, and pours upon it some water which he then gives to the defendant to drink. If the man vomits, his innocence is recognized and he is congratulated. If he does not vomit and the drink remains in his stomach, the accusation is accepted as justified.'

Now, how was the kingdom governed and financed? In the first place, it seems that the kingdom of Ghana at the peak of its power consisted of Ghana proper or metropolitan Ghana, and provincial Ghana. The latter consisted of the states that had been conquered and annexed. Central government appeared to have been in the hands of the king and his ministers, the governor of the capital city, and a corps of civil servants who, about the middle of the eleventh century, were Muslims and could keep records and communicate in Arabic.

The government of the provinces was in the hands of the kings of the conquered states. And it appears that in order to ensure their continued allegiance, the kings of Ghana insisted on the son of each vassal king being sent to their court. At least we have the evidence of Al-Bakri that when the king sat in state, he was flanked not only by his ministers but also by the 'sons of the vassal kings of his country wearing garments and their hair plaited with gold'. For the defence of the kingdom, the kings of Ghana could, by 1067, call upon an army of 200,000 of whom 40,000 were archers. To meet the cost of administration, the kings of ancient Ghana resorted to taxation. Vassal kings paid annual tributes. In addition, and here too I may as well quote Al-Bakri: 'for every donkey loaded with salt that enters the country, the king takes a duty of one gold dinar, and two dinars from everyone that leaves. From a load of copper the king's due is five mithqals and from a load of other goods ten mithqals.' Considering the briskness of the caravan trade at the height of Ghana's power, the income from tolls must have been very considerable.

Thus with a civil service, a strong monarchy, a cabinet, an army, an effective system of administering justice and a regular source of income, Ghana certainly presented, in the words of Davidson, 'the familiar picture of a centralized government which has discovered the art and exercise of taxation, another witness of stability and statehood'. Equally fascinating is the fact that the monarchical institution, the system of inheritance, the court etiquette as well as the burial of the kings and the religious beliefs and systems of ancient Ghana are virtually identical with those of the Akan of modern Ghana in particular, and most of the other peoples of the western Sudan and the forest and coastal belts in general. From this one can safely conclude that even if the Akan, like the others, did not migrate from ancient Ghana, they can certainly claim to look upon her as their cultural ancestor.

2 ISLAM AND THE FALL OF GHANA

In spite of her splendour, opulence and wealth in the eleventh century, Ghana was no more by 1240. What then brought about her fall?

The first reason for the fall of Ghana was the way in which the empire was organized. The empire had no political, ethnic or cultural unity; that is, the empire of Ghana was made up of many states and peoples, and the kings of Ghana failed to weld them into a true nation-state. Different peoples such as the Soninke, the Susu, the Serer, the Berber and the Tuculor each with its own distinctive culture and language owed allegiance to the kings of Ghana. States which were conquered such as Tekrur, Silla, Diara and Kaniaga were left under their own traditional rulers and were only expected to pay annual tributes and contribute contingents or levies to the kings of Ghana's army in times of war. As these conquered states and peoples were always anxious to regain their independence, the survival of the empire came to depend, by and large, on the military strength of the central government of Ghana. It follows,

therefore, that if and when that military power became weakened, the empire was bound to break up into its component parts. Unfortunately, this was exactly what happened from the second half of the eleventh century onwards, owing first to the introduction of Islam or Mohammedanism into the Sahara and the western Sudan, and secondly to the rise of two strong new kingdoms to the south, first the Susu kingdom and then the Empire of Mali.

Islam was introduced into North Africa by the Arabs during their meteoric sweep across the whole of North Africa—from Egypt to Morocco—between A.D. 641 and 708. Among the soldiers and freebooters were missionaries who were bent on converting the peoples of the Sahara and the interior of Africa to Islam. Success attended their efforts and by the tenth century the Sanhaja Berbers, the main inhabitants of the western Sahara who had established quite a strong kingdom with Awdaghost as its capital, had been won over. So also had the Berbers of the important Sahara trading centre of Tadmekket. Ibn Hawkal, writing towards the end of the tenth century, described the kings of Tadmekket as 'holders of leadership, learning, and jurisprudence'. And it was these Berbers who, in the course of their normal trading activities in the land of the Negroes, that is the Sudan, began in turn to propagate the religion of Islam. As early as A.D. 985 the ruler of Gao was won over, and by the middle of the eleventh century, the kings of Tekrur, Silla and Kugha, all vassals of the kings of Ghana, had also embraced Islam.

Though the kings of Ghana themselves did not adopt Islam and remained faithful to their traditional gods, they allowed complete freedom of religion and worship and even employed some of the Muslims as civil servants. Al-Bakri tells us that the king of Ghana's interpreter, the official in charge of his treasury and the majority of his Ministers, were Muslims. By 1067 the capital city itself, to quote Al-Bakri again, 'consisted of two towns situated on a plain. One of these towns was inhabited by Muslims. It was large and possessed twelve mosques; in one of these mosques they assembled for the prayers on Fridays. There were Imams and Muezzins as well as jurists and scholars.' This was a sort of Zongo (the name given today in West Africa to the Muslim quarters of the town) and the other town was where the king and his subjects lived. In all the great commercial centres of the empire, similar Muslim sections or 'zongos' were found.

Had this peaceful spread of Mohammedanism continued, all would have been well with Ghana. But unfortunately for Ghana, between 1042 and 1054 a very fanatical religious movement, known as the Almoravid movement arose among the Sanhaja Berbers in the Sahara region to the north of Ghana. This movement was dedicated to the spread of Islam by means of the *jihad* or holy war. Ghana, being a pagan kingdom whose kings had hitherto resisted Islam, naturally attracted the attention of these fanatics. But they had commercial and political motives as well. Commercially the Berbers wanted to regain the control over the caravan trade which they had lost since the conquest of Awdaghost by the Ghanaians. It is no accident that the Almoravids attacked and reconquered this caravan centre as well as Sijilmasa the other caravan centre in the north, in the same year, i.e. 1054. Politically, the Berbers felt that they were being hemmed in by the expanding Zenata kingdom based on Sijilmasa to the north and the Soninke Empire of Ghana to the south, and they naturally wanted to halt these threats to their independence.

This movement attracted the vassal groups of states and peoples who were anxious to regain their independence from Ghana. Most of them, including Tekrur, Silla and Anbara therefore joined forces with the Almoravids. With their forces thus increased, they first wrested Awdaghost from Ghana in 1054 and then attacked and captured the Ghana capital itself twenty-two years later.

Although the people of Ghana reconquered their capital in 1087 and regained their independence, the earlier defeats inflicted on them by the Almoravids weakened their military power, the main force holding the different parts of the Empire together. It therefore began to break up. Tekrur, Silla, Diara and Kaniaga secured their independence. Thus by the beginning of the twelfth century, the ancient Ghana Empire had been reduced to metropolitan Ghana, that is to its original nucleus.

The activities of the Almoravids contributed to the fall of Ghana in two other ways. First, the wars and conquests between 1054 and 1087 diverted attention from the soil. The countryside was laid waste and agriculture was neglected. Ghana must, therefore, have lost part of her fertile land and consequently part of her productivity and wealth. Secondly, as we have seen, the kings of Ghana derived a great part of their revenue from import and export duties while the ordinary Ghanaians earned their livelihood by acting as middlemen in the caravan trade. The wars of the Almoravids, which affected the whole of the western Sahara and Morocco and even extended into the Iberian peninsular, must naturally have disrupted the caravan trade in those regions. The inevitable result was a great decrease in the income of the Ghanaians. Nothing illustrates this decline better than the state of Awdaghost by 1154. Ibn Hawkal described it in the 990's as 'a pleasant town resembling the land of God at Mecca' and estimated its population, obviously with grotesque exaggeration, at as many as 300,000 households or about two million people. By 1054 on the eve of the Almoravid conquest, the town, then under the king of Ghana, was at the peak of its prosperity. It was described as a solidly built town with fine residences and many markets, and its inhabitants were said to include very wealthy Arabs. But according to Al-Bakri, the Almoravids dealt this thriving commercial centre a brutal blow from which it never recovered. Writing in

1154, Al-Idrisi described it as 'a small town in the desert with little water. Its population is not numerous and there is no large trade.' Obviously the other Ghanaian towns that depended on Awdaghost must also have suffered a similar fate.

Metropolitan Ghana, however, seemed to have regained some of its former power and splendour, and it appears the kings founded a new capital on the banks of the Niger which developed about sixty years after the Almoravid occupation into a great commercial metropolis. Al-Idrisi gives the following description of the city: 'Ghana consists of two towns situated on the banks of the river. It is the greatest of all towns of the Bilad as-Sudan, that is, country of the black people, in respect of area, the most populous and with the widest commercial connections. Merchants go there selling commodities from the surrounding countries as well as from all the other regions of al-Magrib-al-Aqsa. The king had a castle on the bank of the Nile [i.e. Niger—the Arab geographers regarded the Niger as an arm of the Nile of Egypt]—'this was strongly built with various sculptures and paintings and provided with glass windows. This palace was built in the years 570 A.H.' (i.e. 1116–17).

However, only fifty years after Al-Idrisi's account, even metropolitan Ghana lost its independence. The city of Ghana had then become but a shadow of its former self and its merchants had emigrated and founded a new commercial centre called Walata to the north-east. This disastrous and decisive change in the affairs of Ghana was caused by another defeat, and this time, a defeat inflicted by one of its own former vassal-states, Kaniaga. On regaining its independence in about 1076, Kaniaga had by 1200 developed into the strong Susu or Soso kingdom, and in 1203, its king, called Sumanguru Kante, conquered Ghana and reduced it, in turn, to a tributary state.

The Susu Empire itself had only a brief spell of life. In 1235, Sumanguru was killed by the ruler of another rising empire, Mali,

and five years later the city of Ghana was razed to the ground by the Mali army. Ibn Khaldun, the famous Arabic philosopher and historian, has described the rather inglorious end of Ghana in the following words: 'The domination of the people of Ghana weakened and their power declined whilst that of the veiled men of the Berberland adjoining them to the north increased. They overcame the Negroes, plundered their territories, imposed upon them the tribute and poll-tax, and forced many of them to join Islam. As a result, Ghana's power declined and the authority of the rulers of Ghana dwindled away and the neighbouring Negro people of Susu conquered and enslaved them and annexed their territory. Next, the people of Mali, increasing in population, gained the ascendancy over the Negro peoples of the region. They conquered the Susu and took over all they possessed, both of their original territory and that of Ghana, as far as the Atlantic in the West.'

Thus, divided by Islam, weakened politically and economically by the Almoravids, defeated first by the Susu and then by Mali, the ancient Empire of Ghana disappeared from the stage of history. Its place had, by the middle of the thirteenth century, been taken by Mali, whose evolution and development we will next consider.

3 THE RISE OF MALI

The Empire of Mali which overthrew first the Susu kingdom and then ancient Ghana, did not of course spring up overnight. It seems to have started life as a small Mandingo or Mande chieftaincy called Kangaba by some historians. Its capital was the town of Jeriba situated near the junction of the river Sankarani and the river Niger—not far from the modern town of Bamako. The evolution of this little principality from nothing but a group of independent families living in small villages appears to have been completed by the tenth century as a result of the work of a Mande chieftain. By the middle of the following century its rulers had been converted to Islam. According to Sheikh Uthman, the Mufti of Ghana, the first of the rulers of Kangaba to be converted to Islam was Barmandana, who is said to have made the pilgrimage to Mecca.

All his successors, we are told, also went on the pilgrimage. So unlike Ghana, Mali started and ended as an Islamic or Mohammedan state, and in her rise to power, she must have benefited from the new statecraft, the system of administering justice and the literacy introduced into the Sudan by Islam.

During the eleventh and twelfth centuries, this small Mandingo principality grew steadily powerful and influential. By the beginning of the thirteenth century, it had become so strong that Sumanguru Kante, the powerful king of Susu, turned his attention to it after he had subdued ancient Ghana, and in 1224 he actually conquered and annexed it. According to oral tradition, Sumanguru must have been a ruthless person because he had eleven of the twelve sons of the king murdered. He only spared the life of the twelfth son because he was a cripple. This cripple was Mari Jata who later became known as Sundiata. Later, he recovered the use of his legs and he became so popular at court as a soldier and hunter that, the king who was reigning at the time exiled him from the state. In 1234, however, Sundiata returned home, seized the throne and during his long reign from 1234 to 1255 he turned this small Mandingo principality and vassal-state of the Susu king into the powerful and rich empire of Mali.

Sundiata was able to accomplish this seemingly impossible feat for three main reasons: namely, the very favourable position of his principality, the existing political conditions at the time, and his own courage, wisdom and ability. If you look at a map of the Western Sudan, you will see that Kangaba occupied an even more advantageous position than ancient Ghana. It was situated right within the savannah belt and not at the junction of the

desert and the savannah as ancient Ghana was. This good position meant that the people of Kangaba could make their living and derive as much wealth from agriculture as from trade. Indeed tradition has it that Sundiata tried to encourage agriculture by introducing the cultivation and weaving of cotton. Furthermore, and this was even more important, Kangaba was just on the edge of the gold-producing regions of Bure and Bambuk, and Sundiata was able to conquer them. Thus, while ancient Ghana never actually controlled the gold-producing regions, Mali had control over them even before the end of Sundiata's reign, and the kings of Mali made good use of this advantage. As she controlled the gold-producing regions, Mali soon attracted all the caravans from the north and by the middle of the fourteenth century, four of her towns, Niani, the then capital, and Jenne, Timbuctu and Gao, had become the main commercial centres of the Western Sudan. In 1353, Ibn Khaldun the famous Arabic historian met the King of Takedda— the copper-producing region—who told him that that year, there passed through his city on its way to Mali, a caravan of merchants from the east containing 12,000 loaded camels.

However, the more immediate causes of Mali's rise were the political conditions at the time of Sundiata's accession to power coupled with his own courage and ability. The political conditions were very favourable to Mali. As we have seen, Sumanguru Kante of Susu was a grasping king. He imposed heavy taxation on the people and one report says that he deprived the Mandingo of 'their most beautiful women as well as their food and gold'. The people, therefore, felt so oppressed that they looked for a deliverer. At the same time, all the vassal or conquered states like Ghana, Bobo and Tabo were ready to revolt and to regain their independence.

In his secret hide-out after he had been driven out of Kangaba, Sundiata decided to exploit the political situation. He raised a

strong standing army and in 1234 triumphantly entered Jeriba, the capital of
Kangaba, and seized the throne. The rulers
of the vassal states hailed him as their
deliverer and joined forces with him. The
king of Bobo in modern Upper Volta for
instance, added a contingent of 1,500 archers
to Sundiata's army. So, with his army
strengthened, Sundiata marched against
Sumanguru. At the famous battle of Kirina
in 1235 Sumanguru was defeated and killed.
Sundiata pressed on and occupied ancient
Ghana in 1240. Next, he turned his attention
to the gold-bearing regions to the south—
Bambuk, Bundu and Wangara—and by the
end of his reign, he had conquered them all,
a feat which neither Susu nor Ghana could
perform. Thus within twenty years Sundiata
had, with the help of his able generals,
extended the frontiers of the small and petty
kingdom of Kangaba to include in the north,
Ghana and the southern regions of the
Sahara, in the west, the Upper Senegal and
in the south the much sought after gold-
producing districts of Wangara, Bambuk and
Bundu and in the east, the Upper Niger. It
was probably with a view to controlling the
trade down the Niger to Timbuctu and Gao
that he built, further north, a new capital,
Niani, which is usually referred to as Mali.

According to certain writers Sundiata was
not just a conqueror but also an able administrator. He is said to have divided his empire
into provinces and to have placed one of his
generals in charge of each. Sundiata died in
1255 after effectively laying the foundations
of the empire and providing it with a capital.
The traditional accounts of his death are conflicting. Some say that he was drowned in the
River Sankarani near Niani, while others
maintain that he was assassinated during a
public demonstration.

There is unfortunately very little information about the successors of Sundiata. His
immediate successor was his own son Mansa
Wali but though he reigned for 15 years—

from 1255 to 1270 and is said to have been
one of the greatest kings of Mali, nothing
much is known about him except that he
made a pilgrimage to Mecca. The next two
rulers after Mansa Wali were also said to have
been sons of Sundiata.

The records are silent on Mansa Wali's
immediate successor, but the second, Mansa
Khalifa, is portrayed as a very wicked king.
He is reported to have been insanely devoted
to archery and to have enjoyed killing people
by shooting arrows at them. It is not surprising, therefore, that a revolt broke out against
him in the very first year of his reign during
which he was killed.

After the death of Mansa Khalifa, there was
a dispute over the succession, and contrary
to the patrilineal system of inheritance practised in Mali, the candidate who was selected
was the son of a daughter of Mari Jata. He
managed to keep the throne for ten years, but
in 1283, there was a revolt during which the
throne was seized by a freed slave of the royal
household called Sabakura or Sakura. It is
evident from Ibn Khaldun's account that
Sakura turned out to be one of the greatest
rulers of Mali. His reign lasted for fifteen
years during which he extended the frontiers
of Mali eastwards to include Takedda, the
copper-producing region, and probably Gao,
although other writers maintain that Gao was
conquered later by a general of Mansa Musa.
Ibn Khaldun writes that during Sakura's reign
the authority and might of Mali were superior
to those of the other Negro peoples. After
his death in 1300, the throne went back to
the legitimate line. First came Mansa Gaw,
Sundiata's grandson, and Gaw was succeeded
by his own son Mansa Mamadu. But they did
not do much to extend the frontiers or increase
the power of Mali during their reigns which
lasted from 1300 to 1307. From 1307 to 1359,
however, the Mali Empire grew to its widest
possible limits and reached the height of its
power, glory and wealth. Mali's great rise to
fame and wealth was mainly the result of the

work of two kings who sat on the throne between 1307 and 1359—Mansa Kankan Musa and Mansa Sulayman.

4 MANSA MUSA OF MALI

There is no doubt that the most famous of the kings of Mali known to the Arabs and the one best known outside the Arab world was Mansa Kankan Musa who is sometimes called simply Mansa Musa. He reigned from 1307 to 1337 and even to this day he is the best remembered of the kings of Mali. Two years after his death, Mali appeared on a European map for the first time, the Mappa Mundi of Angelino Dulcert of 1339. It appeared again on the Catalan map drawn in 1375 by Abraham Crisques for Charles V. To what then are Mansa Musa's fame and glory due? Part of the answer is that we know far more about him from the Arab writers than we do about any of the other kings who came before or after him. The real reason, however, can be found in the work he did during his reign in the fields of politics, commerce and religion.

Let us take first his work in the field of politics. Mansa Musa extended the boundaries of Mali even much further and built up a more effective system of government than any of his predecessors. He also administered justice impartially and established friendly relations with other African states such as Morocco and Egypt. By the time of his accession, the Empire of Mali appeared to have been extended to its possible limits westwards and southwards. Musa and his generals, therefore, concentrated their attention northwards and eastwards. They captured Walata, the famous commercial centre (which, as we have seen, was built by merchants from Ghana after they had been driven out by the King of Susu). Mansa Musa's generals also captured Timbuctu, a small town to the north of Mali which had begun life as a Berber seasonal camp in the eleventh century. Through the work of Mansa Musa and his successors, it soon began its growth into a

great commercial and educational centre of the western Sudan.

Mansa Musa and his successor, Mansa Sulayman, strengthened the administrative machinery of the Empire. There were at least fourteen provinces in the south including the province of Mali, the chief province in which the king's capital Niani was situated. Most of the provinces according to Al-Umari, a contemporary writer, were ruled by governors or emirs (*dya-mana-tigi*) who were usually famous generals. Others, such as the Berber provinces, were governed by their own sheikhs. Some of the important commercial centres also had governors or *farbas* of their own. All these provincial administrators were responsible to the Mansa, and they were all well paid. Some were given fiefs while others received as much as 1,500 mithqals of gold every year, as well as horses and clothes. With a view to obtaining more devoted service, Mansa Musa also instituted national honours, the highest being the National Honour of the Trousers. 'Whenever a hero adds to the list of his exploits,' Al-Dukhari, who had lived in Niani during the reign of Mansa Musa and his successor, told Al-Umari, 'the king gives him a pair of wide trousers, and the greater the number of a knight's exploits, the bigger the size of his trousers. These trousers are characterized by narrowness in the leg and ampleness in the seat.' Besides all this, Mansa Musa is said to have regularly invited and dealt with any complaints and appeals against oppression by the governors. Mansa Musa's impartiality and great sense of justice were remembered and admired long after his death. To help him in his work, the king had judges, scribes and civil servants. All this elaborate machinery must have been expensive to run, and the kings of Mali had the usual sources of income—a tax on crops and livestock, tolls, tribute from vassal states and proceeds from royal estates.

Mansa Musa is noted for the friendly relations he maintained with other African States, especially with the Sultan of Morocco. Ibn

Khaldun recorded that there were diplomatic relations and exchanges of gifts between Mansa Musa and the contemporary king of Morocco, Sultan Abu Al-Hasan, and 'that high-ranking statesmen of the two kingdoms were exchanged as ambassadors'. Mansa Musa's successors maintained these contacts and exchanged gifts.

The empire of Mali enjoyed not only stability and good government under Mansa Musa but also commercial prosperity. As both the salt-producing regions and the gold districts came under her control, Mali naturally attracted traders from the north as well as from the south. Furthermore the king's team of able governors and his strong army, said to be about 100,000 strong, were able to maintain order even among the turbulent Berber tribes of the south-western regions of the Sahara, so that traders and travellers could travel to and fro with ease and a sense of security. Thus commerce became very brisk and traders from as far away as Egypt and Morocco could be found in the commercial towns of Mali.

The main commercial centres of Mali were its capital Niani, Timbuctu, and Gao which later became the capital of Songhai. Ibn Khaldun described Niani as 'an extensive place with cultivated land fed by running water, with an active population, busy markets and at the time, the station for trading caravans from Morocco, Tripoli and Egypt'. However, the markets of Timbuctu and Gao to the north of Niani were even more active.

The medium of exchange for this brisk trade was the white shells known as cowries, though a system of barter was also practised. Al-Umari was told that so scarce was salt in the regions to the south of Mali and beyond that it was exchanged for its own weight in gold. As the controllers of this trade, the people of Mali became wealthy and enjoyed a high standard of living. They lived in good houses—their kings in palaces and the ordinary people in mud houses. Al-Umari has written an interesting description of the style of building in ancient Mali, and as this sounds strikingly and fascinatingly similar to the indigenous style still in vogue on the west coast, I should like to quote the passage:

'Building is by means of clay, like the walls of the gardens of Damascus. They build up clay to the height of two-thirds of a cubit and then leave it till it dries. Then a like amount is added again and so on till the end. Their roofs are built of timber and reeds mostly in the form of circular domes or camel backs like vaults. The floors are earth mixed with sand.'

One of the main things for which Mansa Musa became famous was his work in the religious field. He was not only concerned with the political and material welfare of his people but also with their spiritual well-being. He himself was a very pious man and a great lover of virtue. Indeed he is reported to have told the Egyptian tourist officer who took him round Cairo during his pilgrimage that he would hand over his throne to his son and return to Mecca to live near the sanctuary, and only death prevented him from fulfilling this wish. It is not surprising then that he devoted a great deal of his time to purifying, strengthening and spreading Islam in Mali, especially after his famous pilgrimage to Mecca.

About no other activity of Mansa Musa has so much been written as this pilgrimage through Cairo to Mecca which lasted from 1324 to 1325 and there is no doubt that it was mainly as a result of this pilgrimage that the name of Mansa Musa became known and famous in Egypt, Arabia and even in some parts of Europe. This *hajj* or pilgrimage was undertaken on a scale unheard of before. According to Al-Umari, Mansa Musa left Mali with the fantastic amount of 100 camel-loads of gold (Ibn Khaldun puts the figure at 80) and he also had a huge entourage for his personal service. Five hundred slaves were also said to have gone before the king, each carrying a gold staff weighing 4 lb. But although he took so much money with him, Mansa Musa was so generous in Cairo and Mecca that he ran out of money, and had to borrow at fantastic rates of interest before he could return home. Al-Umari, who visited Cairo twelve years later, wrote that Mansa Musa 'left no emir nor holder of a royal office without a gift of a load of gold. He and his company gave out so much gold that they depressed its value in Egypt and caused its price to fall.'

But the more interesting aspect of this rather extravagant pilgrimage was the effect it had on Mansa Musa himself. He returned to Mali filled with a determination to purify and strengthen Islam, to promote education and to introduce some of the new things he had seen on his journey. To assist him in carrying out his plan, he persuaded a Spanish scholar, poet and architect called Abu Ishaq Ibrahim As-Sahili Tuwajjin to return with him from Mecca to Mali. He began his reforms by ordering that the five pillars of Islam and, in particular Friday prayers in congregation, should be strictly observed. To facilitate worship he commissioned As-Sahili to build a number of mosques as well as some palaces for himself. The palace at either Timbuctu or Gao, built of burnt brick, was described by one of Ibn Khaldun's informers as a 'square building with a dome plastered over and covered with coloured patterns so that it turned out to be the most elegant of buildings'. It is generally admitted that As-Sahili's style of building influenced architecture in the western Sudan. Mansa Musa also started the practice of sending students to Morocco for studies and he laid the foundation of what Timbuctu later became—the commercial and educational centre of the western Sudan.

Clearly then, Mansa Musa was a great ruler who succeeded in establishing peace and order in Mali, in promoting trade and commerce and above all in making the name of Mali known throughout the world. It is not surprising then that after his death in 1337 his name was remembered and cherished for many centuries.

His immediate successor was Mansa Maghan who had a brief and an uneventful reign from 1337 to 1341. Then Mansa Sulayman Mansa Musa's brother, became king and he reigned till 1359. Fortunately for posterity, Ibn Battuta, the celebrated Arabic scholar and one of the greatest travellers of history, was sent by Abu Inan, Sultan of Morocco, to Mali in 1352-3, and he has left an eye-witness account of the Empire. It is absolutely clear from his account as well as those of Al-Umari, whom we have been quoting, that Mansa Sulayman was another extremely competent ruler and a worthy successor of Mansa Musa. Al-Umari wrote 'there accrued to him all the lands of the Negroes which his brother had conquered and brought within the orbit of Islam. He built mosques of worship and convocation and minarets and instituted weekly prayers, gatherings and the call to prayer, and was himself a student of the *fiqh* (i.e. the religious sciences).' Ibn Battuta was also struck by the order and racial tolerance that prevailed, and the care with which the people observed prayers in the Empire. I should also like to quote him here. 'The Negroes (that is the people of Mali) are seldom unjust, and have a greater abhorrence of injustice than any other people. Their Sultan shows no mercy to any one guilty of the least act of it. There is complete security in their country. Neither traveller nor inhabitant in it has anything to fear from robbers or men of violence.' Surely this could be said of only very few contemporary European or Middle Eastern States in the middle of the fourteenth century.

It is clear then that thanks to the ability of Mansa Musa and Sulayman, Mali touched the apogee of her power and glory during the first half of the fourteenth century, a period which can truly be called the golden age of Mali. During the second half of that century, however, decline set in and by the beginning of the following century Mali had shrunk into the tiny principality of Kangaba, back to where it started from. This decline was due internally to the inordinate ambition, frivolity and incompetence of the members of the ruling dynasty, and externally to the attacks of the Mossi and the Tuareg to the north and south respectively, and to the rise of Songhai in the east. There were as many as six kings within a period of forty years from 1360 to 1400 and a spell of civil wars and coups d'état, the outcome of constant rivalry for power at court. Many of the provinces took advantage of this confusion and broke away. The Tuareg of the Sahara conquered the northern parts of the empire whilst the Mossi attacked the southern regions. The final blow was, however, delivered by the new star that arose to the east of Mali. This new star was Songhai and its rise and achievements will form the theme of the next three chapters.

5 THE REIGN OF SUNNI ALI OF SONGHAI

Songhai, like Mali, started life probably in the middle of the ninth century as a small principality referred to in the records as Al-Kawkaw. It was situated on both banks of the Niger from the western boundary of modern Nigeria to the Niger bend and its capital was Gao. Like Mali, this kingdom arose in a fertile area suitable for both agriculture and cattle-rearing. The river also afforded excellent opportunities for fishing. Indeed, the indigenous people of the area, the Songhai, made full use of the natural resources of their region and by the time they entered on the stage of history, they were already divided into two specialized professional groups: the *Sorko* who were the fishermen and *Gow* or *Gabibi* who concentrated on agriculture, cattle-rearing and hunting.

Besides these two occupations, the people of Gao soon became great traders. With the introduction of the camel into North Africa and the Sahara and the subsequent growth of a number of caravan trade routes, the region of Gao became, as early as the end of the ninth century, the terminus of three important routes—the western route from Morocco and Algeria, the central route from Tunis and

Tripoli via Ghat, and above all, the transcontinental route from Egypt through Fezzan, Ghat and Agades. Some of the people of Gao, therefore, took to trading and their capital attracted merchants from Egypt and the other states of North Africa.

Engaged as they were in agriculture, fishing and the caravan trade, the kings and people of this principality became quite wealthy and they attracted the attention of Muslim scholars and traders long before Mali ever did. Two scholars, Al-Yaqubi and Al-Masudi writing as early as 871 and 943, respectively, described not only Ghana but also Al-Kawkaw. Indeed both of them were convinced that Al-Kawkaw was, in their day, as powerful as Ghana. For instance Al-Yaqubi wrote 'There is the kingdom of the Al-Kawkaw which is the greatest of the realms of the as-Sudan, the most important and the most powerful, and all the other kingdoms obey its rulers'. He then referred to Ghana, and described its king too as 'very powerful'. Writing seventy-two years later Al-Masudi also referred to Al-Kawkaw 'as the greatest of all the kingdoms of the as-Sudan (i.e. the Negroes)' and added that many kingdoms were dependent on Al-Kawkaw.

In the eleventh century, however, Gao was completely eclipsed by Ghana and even when the latter collapsed, it was Mali, as we have already seen, that for reasons already outlined, succeeded Ghana in power and wealth. Indeed, in the thirteenth century, Gao was a tributary state of Mali. In 1275, however, according to As-Sadi, two princes of Gao, Ali Kolon and Sulayman, who were employed in the service of the king of Mali as chiefs of military expeditions escaped, 'severed the rope of dominion of the people of Songhai' and founded the Si dynasty. It appears that Gao soon lost its independence to Mali again and when Ibn Battuta visited Gao in 1353, he found it still owing allegiance, even if a nominal one, to Mali. But far from declining, the kingdom of Gao actually prospered during the period it was under Mali, and Ibn Battuta was impressed by its capital. 'Gao', he wrote, 'is a large city on the Nile (i.e. the Niger), and one of the finest towns in the Negroland. It is also one of their biggest and best provisioned towns with rice in plenty, milk, and fish, and there is a species of cucumber there called *inani* which has no equal. The buying and selling of its inhabitants is done with shells and the same is the case at Mali.'

However materially and commercially beneficial the link with Mali was, Gao was always anxious to manage its own affairs and during the last decades of the fourteenth century, probably in 1375, it broke away. The rulers from then on naturally became occupied with maintaining the independence of their little kingdom and so did not embark on any careers of conquest and expansion. Gao thus remained a small but wealthy kingdom until 1464 when Sunni Ali became king. During the twenty-eight years of his reign, he transformed the small kingdom of Gao into the Empire of Songhai.

In many ways the career of Sunni Ali reminds one of that of Sundiata of Mali. Like Sundiata, Sunni Ali came to power at a time when the political conditions were very favourable for a career of conquest. Mali had, as I have pointed out, broken up into tiny principalities, and the northern areas—Walata, Timbuctu and Arawan—had been captured by the Tuareg. As the Tuareg proved tyrannical and extortionate rulers, the people of these regions became anxious for a saviour rather like those of Ghana, Bobo and Tabo when Sundiata seized the throne of Mali. Indeed, the people of Timbuctu, who were feeling the Tuareg rule particularly unbearable, are said to have extended an invitation to Sunni Ali to come to their rescue soon after he became king.

Fortunately, like Sundiata, Sunni Ali had the courage, tact, shrewdness and ambition to turn the political position to his advantage and also to that of Gao. Having consolidated his position at home and built up a strong army consisting of cavalry and infantry wings as well as a powerful fleet of ships for use on the Niger, he embarked on his remarkable career of conquest, from the third year of his reign. He first turned his attention north-west and using the invitation of the people of Timbuctu as an excuse, he marched on that town and captured it without any difficulty. He then turned westwards and attacked Jenne which was then a very prosperous commercial town as well as a great Muslim educational centre. For some time, Jenne was able to keep off the Songhai army because of the network of waterways which acted as a natural defence. However, after a siege said by tradition to have lasted seven years, seven months and seven days, Jenne was captured by Sunni Ali in 1473.

From there, he turned eastwards and conquered all the regions south of Timbuctu as far as the northern borders of Yatenga, the powerful Mossi kingdom. His efforts to reduce the Mossi to subjection failed, and so he pushed on across the Niger and conquered the Hausa state of Kebbi.

Sunni Ali was ruthless to anybody who tried to defy his authority. Thus he is said to have murdered most of the clerics and scholars of Timbuctu who refused to submit to him, while those of Jenne, who readily submitted, he treated with marked generosity. He was said to have been particularly hostile to the Fulani. One chronicle relates that 'he hated no enemy more bitterly than the Fulbe (i.e. the Fulani), he could not see one, whether learned or ignorant, man or woman, without wanting to kill him. He admitted no Fulbe into the administration or judiciary. He so decimated the Sangare tribe (a Fulani tribe) that the remnant which survived could have been gathered under the shade of one tree.' This was most probably due to the fact that not only were the Fulani conducting raids but they would not acknowledge the jurisdiction of the empire into which they were steadily infiltrating.

Besides extending the frontiers of his kingdom, Sunni Ali also realized the need for an effective system of government and attempted to provide one. He divided his conquests into provinces. Over some of these provinces he appointed new governors, but in districts where the rulers readily submitted, he left them in control provided they paid an annual tribute. He also appointed a Commander-in-chief or rather Chief Naval Officer, called the *hi-koy,* for his fleet. For the administration of the turbulent Hombori region, that is the region to the south of Timbuctu and north of the Mossi kingdom, he created a special governor called the *Tondifari,* a Songhai title meaning a governor of the mountains. Sunni Ali was still organizing his conquests into an effective empire when on his way home from one of his wars of conquests in 1492 he was drowned in rather mysterious circumstances.

Thus within a period of twenty-eight years, Sunni Ali converted the little kingdom of Gao into the huge empire of Songhai stretching from Kebbi in the east to Jenne in the west, and from Timbuctu in the north to Hombori in the south. In spite of his achievements, hovever, the Sudanese chroniclers were not particularly complimentary in their tributes to Sunni Ali. One of them called him 'an impious monarch and horrible tyrant'; a second described him as 'a great oppressor and destroyer of towns, with a hard and unjust heart', and a third exclaimed 'A sanguinary despot who slaughtered so many thousands of people that God alone knows their number; he was cruel to the pious and wise, he humiliated them and put them to death'. These comments, however, need not be taken too seriously. It is known that Sunni Ali was so busy about the affairs of this world that he paid little attention to Islam. Indeed it was believed that he was a pagan. Therefore to these fanatical Muslim chroniclers who saw the promotion of Islam as the greatest duty of any ruler, Sunni Ali was bound to appear impious and degenerate. An important reason

for his unpopularity with these chroniclers was his persecution of the clerics and pious men of Timbuctu. But surely, as a builder of a new nation, he could not countenance any insubordination from anybody, pious or otherwise. The very fact that he treated the Muslim scholars and clerics of Jenne with generosity proves that he was not simply anti-clerical or anti-Muslim.

In spite of the testimony of the chroniclers, Sunni Ali was easily the greatest of the rulers who ever mounted the throne of Gao. He laid the solid foundation on which his immediate successor, Mohammed Askia, built. At least one chronicler was pro Sunni Ali. 'He surpassed all the kings, his predecessors, in numbers and valour of his soldiery,' he wrote, 'his conquests were many and his renown extended from the rising to the setting of the sun. If it is the will of God, he will be long spoken of.' Sunni Ali was certainly long spoken of by the Sudanese scholars but, alas, in no complimentary terms. I hope that modern African scholars will be more generous to him for he was a clever politician, a brave soldier and an able administrator.

6 MOHAMMED ASKIA THE GREAT OF SONGHAI

As we saw in the last chapter, Sunni Ali died before he could complete the consolidation of his conquests and the establishment of an effective system of government for his empire. Furthermore his wars had greatly interrupted commerce and Islam had also declined because of the treatment he meted out to some of the devout Muslims and scholars. His successor, Mohammed Askia, then had to complete his administrative work, pacify Timbuctu and exploit its strategic situation, strengthen and purify Islam then at its nadir, and revive trade and commerce dislocated by Ali's wars. Above all, he had to consolidate himself on the throne and win the allegiance of the Songhai. These then were the problems that faced his successor, Mohammed Askia I, and they were made even more complicated by the way in which he succeeded to the throne. Mohammed Askia was in fact Mohammed Ture Ibn Abi Bakr who was Sunni Ali's trusted Soninke general and Prime Minister. He was therefore not a member of the royal family but managed to seize the throne by organizing a coup d'état which resulted in the deposition of his master's son and successor, Abu Bakr Dao. Fortunately not only had he the personal qualifications but his reign was also long enough, from 1493 to 1528, to enable him to tackle all these problems.

As one would expect, the first problem he tackled was that of strengthening his position on the throne and ensuring that his children would rule in Songhai. He solved this in two ways. First of all, he either killed or expelled from the Empire all the surviving members of the two previous Gao dynasties, the Za dynasty that had founded Gao and had ruled till 1275, and the Sonni dynasty that had reigned from 1276 to 1493. Mohammed Askia was so successful in this that the dynasty which he founded and which became known as the Askia dynasty continued to rule in Songhai until the fall of the empire.

Next he tried to win the support and allegiance of his people. This he did by using Islam which, he realized, could be a strong unifying force. Hence, immediately after his accession to the throne, he started courting the friendship of the mallams and devout Muslims whom he and his master Sunni Ali had persecuted. He showered gifts on them and appointed many of them as his advisers and courtiers. Furthermore, as if to remove any doubts about his changed attitude to Islam and the Muslims, he went on the pilgrimage to Mecca in 1497 as soon as he felt that his position at home was secure. This pilgrimage was not improbably deliberately organized on a scale that surpassed that of Musa Mansa. For instance he was said to have been accompanied by 1,000 infantry, and 500 horsemen carrying 300,500 mithkals of gold. He spent this huge amount on alms, presents and on

a hostel which he bought in Cairo for the use of Sudanese pilgrims. Before his return to the Sudan, he cleverly persuaded the Sharif, Al-Abbas, to invest him with the important title of Caliph of the Blacks (*Khalifatu biladi l-Takrur*) which, he knew, could greatly enhance his prestige and position throughout Muslim Africa. This appeal to the devout Muslims proved very successful and throughout his reign the chroniclers and historians of the day hailed him as a great ruler, a devout Muslim and the legitimate ruler of Songhai. For instance one of them described him as 'a brilliant light shining after a great darkness; a saviour who drew the servants of God from idolatry and the country from ruin. The defender of the faithful who scattered joy, gifts and alms around him.'

After Mohammed Askia had secured himself on the throne, won the support of the Muslims and the coveted title *al hajj*, the title which to this day is given to any Muslim who has been on the pilgrimage to Mecca, he tackled the next problem, that of consolidating and extending Sunni Ali's conquests. With a well-trained and fully equipped army, he began his conquests by marching south and attacking the Mossi. Though, like his predecessor, he failed to defeat the Mossi, he was nevertheless able to strengthen the hold of Songhai on the southern regions. From the south, he turned westwards and attacked and conquered what remained of the kingdom of Mali after a war lasting thirteen years. From the west, he marched eastwards and reconquered Agadez and reduced the Hausa states of Kano, Katsina and Zamfara to tributary states of the Songhai Empire. In the north, he also consolidated Ali's conquests and extended Songhai's political sway into the Sahara as far north as the salt-mining centre of Taghaza. Thus, by the end of his reign, the Songhai Empire extended from Takrur in the west to Kano in the east and from Taghaza in the north to the border of the Mossi kingdom in the south.

Mohammed Askia was also an excellent administrator. He first abolished the existing political divisions and redivided his entire empire into four vice-royalties or regions, each under a Regional Commissioner or Viceroy. He then subdivided the regions into provinces each under a governor. He also stationed judges in all the main towns throughout the empire. At the centre, he established a council of Ministers to assist him. These included a commander-in-chief (*balama*), a chief tax-collector or as we might call him today the Minister of Finance (*fari-mundya*), chief of Navy (*hi-koy*), a Minister in charge of foreigners (*korey-farma*), a Minister in charge of property (*warrey-farma*), and the Minister in charge of rivers, lakes and fisheries (*hari-farma*). All these central and provincial posts were filled with people who were either from his own family or had married into it and he could depose of any of them at any time. This was also true of the military chiefs. He left the Hausa states under their rulers but we have the evidence of Leo Africanus who visited Songhai in 1510 as a member of a mission under the leadership of his uncle sent by the Shereef of Fez, Malai Muhammed el-Kaim, that Askia compelled the king of Kano to marry one of his daughters while he stationed officials permanently in all these kingdoms to see that the tributes were regularly paid.

To meet the cost of an administrative machinery of this magnitude and complexity as well as a standing army, Mohammed Askia had reliable sources of income. The most important of these sources were the royal estates established throughout the Empire and worked by slaves. Each had to produce a fixed quantity of a particular commodity per year. For instance, his estate called Abda in the province of Dendi, which had 200 slaves under four *fanfa* or estate-managers, had to produce 1,000 sunhas of rice per year; some had to produce corn and others bales of dried fish. He also had certain groups of slaves who were craftsmen and had to produce a fixed number of say boats, spears, or arrows per year. For example, the Dyam Tene and Dyam Wali tribes had to supply the king with 100 spears and 100 arrows per family per year. All these provisions and equipment were used to maintain the army and the surplus was sold. The second main source of income was tribute from vassal states and regular contributions from the generals who obtained their revenue from taxes on peasants, farmers, and above all from customs duties.

To ensure maximum income from tolls and customs duties, Mohammed Askia and his civil servants did everything to promote trade and commerce. He made the routes safe by rigidly controlling the troublesome Tuareg. Furthermore he unified the system of weights and measures throughout the empire, and appointed inspectors for all the important markets who checked any falsifications. His creation of a professional standing army instead of relying on a feudal array also made it possible for the civilians to participate fully in commercial activities. The result of these measures was that trade boomed. The commercial activities of Songhai were centred on its three main cities. These were Jenne, the centre for the internal commerce, Timbuctu which controlled commercial relations with the west and north-west, and Gao which served the regions to the east and north-east like Kano, Tripoli and Egypt. These towns also became important centres of industry. There were as many as 26 *Tindi* or tailors' shops in Timbuctu alone, each of which had between 50 and 100 apprentices. Leo Africanus has left us eyewitness accounts of both Timbuctu and Gao which should be quoted. Of Timbuctu, he wrote, 'here are many shops of artificers and merchants and especially of such as weave linen and cotton cloth. And thither do the Barbary Merchants bring cloth of Europe. The inhabitants and especially the strangers there residing are exceedingly rich, in so much that the king is now married both his daughters unto two rich merchants.' He also described Gao as a town full of 'exceedingly rich merchants and hither continually resort great store of Negroes which buy cloth brought out of Barbary and Europe. It is wonder to see what plenty merchandise is daily brought thither, and how costly and sumptuous all things be.' The main exports of Songhai remained the traditional ones of gold, ivory and slaves, while her leading imports were salt from Taghaza and horses from North Africa. The medium of exchange was the usual cowries, though Leo Africanus noticed that gold coins without any stamp or superscription were in circulation in Timbuctu.

Mohammed Askia, like Mansa Musa of Mali, cared for the material as well as the spiritual welfare of his subjects. Whether the Askia was on his accession a truly devout Muslim, or whether he merely used Islam to prop up his position, he certainly appears to have become a genuine Muslim, not improbably because of his pilgrimage to Mecca and the great scholars such as Abd-ul Rahman as-Suyuti and Mohammed al-Maghili whom he met and befriended. Hence, from the time of his return from the *hajj* till his death, he did everything in his power to see that Islam was purified and education and learning were promoted. For the purification of Islam, he attacked illiteracy among the mallams, saw to it that the ritual prayers and other duties such as fasting and almsgiving were observed, and insisted that women should go about veiled, making his own family set the example, according to one of the chroniclers. He also ensured that his officials imposed no illegal taxes, and that judges gave judgement according to the laws of the Holy Koran and the *Sharia*. All the chroniclers agree that Islam was greatly strengthened and purified during the reign of Mohammed Askia. To quote one of them, 'he eliminated all the innovations, forbidden practices and blood-shedding characteristic of the Shi (i.e. Sunni Ali) and established Islam upon sure foundations'.

Equally memorable and successful was his encouragement of higher education. Scholars and professors, attracted by the peace and order of the Empire as well as the generosity of Mohammed Askia, flocked into Timbuctu which became, during his reign, not only a commercial but also a great educational metropolis. There were as many as 150 Kuranic schools in that city alone and university education was provided in the mosque of Sankore. The University, consisting, rather, like contemporary Paris and Oxford, of eminent divines and their pupils, attracted many students from far and wide and produced a great number of distinguished jurists, historians and theologians. Among them are the two great historians Mahmoud Kati and Abderahman As-Sadi whose history books, the *Tarikh al-Fattash* and *Tarikh as-Sudan* are still in existence and on which we have been relying for the reconstruction of the history of Songhai. Mahmoud Kati himself had this to say of the intellectual life of his town Timbuctu, 'In those days Timbuctu did not have its equal . . . from the province of Mali to the extreme limits of the region of the Maghrib for the solidity of its institutions, its political liberties, the purity of its morals, the security of persons, its consideration and compassion towards foreigners, its courtesy towards students and men of learning and the financial assistance which it provided for the latter; the scholars of this period were the most respected among the believers for their generosity, force of character and their discretion'. Leo Africanus's eyewitness account of the intellectual life of the city corroborates Mahmoud Kati's. 'Here are great stores of doctors, judges, priests and other learned men that are bountifully maintained at the king's cost and charges,' Leo wrote, 'and hither are brought divers manuscripts or written books out of Barbary, which are sold for more money than any other merchandise.'

This then was the picture of Songhai at the peak of its power in the third decade of the sixteenth century. Peace, order and security reigned, commerce boomed, Islam was purified and intellectual activities and learning, centering on Sankore University, flourished. But alas, by the end of that very century, only about sixty years after the death of Mohammed Askia the Great, this great Empire had faded out of the stage of history. What brought about the fall of Songhai forms the subject of the next chapter.

7 THE FALL OF THE EMPIRE OF SONGHAI

Various reasons have been given for the fall of the vast empire of Songhai whose rise and development we have already discussed. One writer, Mahmoud Kati, attributed the fall of the Empire to the disastrous war between Askia Mohammed Bani who reigned from 1586 to 1588 and his brother Sadiq and to the immoral, irreligious and pagan activities of the successors of Askia the Great, reaching their climax in the reign of Ishak II. To Mahmoud Kati and also some modern historians, then, Songhai collapsed mainly because of internal weakness. This does not appear to be quite true. When the Empire of Songhai did fall, it was essentially due to external rather than to internal factors, that is, to the Moroccan invasion at the end of the sixteenth century, and not to her internal decline.

There is absolutely no doubt that most of the successors of Askia the Great did not have any of his courage, piety, devotion to duty and competence. In 1528, Mohammed Askia had been on the throne for thirty-five years. He was now a grand old man of eighty-five, and for the last ten years he had become increasingly blind and infirm. His children took advantage of this to rise up against him and to depose him. But his son Musa, who succeeded him, was assassinated for his cruelty in 1533, and Askia the Great's nephew, Askia Bankouri, was enthroned. He was no less cruel than Musa and it was he who exiled Askia Mohammed from Gao to the little island of Kankaka on the Niger. He was deposed in 1537 with the help of the viceroy of Dandi. One of Askia the Great's sons, Askia Ismail was then proclaimed King. His reasons

for accepting the crown are rather interesting: 'to rescue my father from his distressful condition, to enable my sisters to resume the veil that Bankouri had obliged them to relinquish, and to pacify Yan Mara, one of the hundred hen ostriches who was wont to throw herself into a frenzy whenever she saw Bankouri.' He proved as good as his words. We do not know whether the ostrich became happy again, but we know that he promptly brought his father Askia the Great from exile to Gao where he died in peace in 1538, and he must also have restored the veil to his sisters. Unfortunately, this able and very promising ruler died only two years after mounting the throne.

It is clear then that the first decade after Askia's deposition was marked by fratricidal struggles. However, these do not appear to have had any serious adverse effects on the peace, prosperity and stability of the Empire. It seems that Askia's administrative machinery was able to absorb all these shocks. It certainly did work with great smoothness during the reign of the next two successors which stretched from 1538 till 1584. The sheer length of these two reigns in itself provides clear evidence of the stability of the government of the Empire. The second of these rulers, Askia Daud, was a particularly able and pious ruler. He succeeded in suppressing all the turbulent peoples, especially the Tuareg in the north, and established further posts in the Sahara to ensure the security of the routes. He tightened Songhai's grip on Mali, Bagu and the Hausa States. Furthermore as a pious Muslim, he embellished Timbuctu, and according to the *Tarikh al-Fattash,* he was the first 'to form treasury storehouses, including libraries, and to have employed scribes to copy manuscripts which he sometimes presented to the Ulamas'. He is also said to have learnt the Koran by heart, and then gone on to read the whole of the *Risala* (the commentaries on the Traditions concerned mainly with jurisprudence).

By 1581 the Songhai Empire had been restored to the position it enjoyed at the time of the deposition of Askia the Great. Peace, order and prosperity were once more established, religion was thriving, and the government was again stable and efficient. The Moroccan invasion occurred only ten years later, during which time succession disputes broke out again and three rulers came to the throne. Though these disputes must have caused some weakness at the court and might well have provided a pretext for Moroccan intervention, and even if the last three Askias were immoral and irreligious, there could not have been any serious damage done to the prosperity and stability of the Songhai Empire as a whole. Towards the end of the sixteenth century, the Songhai Empire could not have been in decline nor tottering to its fall. It was still quite stable and was enjoying considerable prestige and prosperity. If then Songhai fell only ten years after Askia Daud, it fell a victim not so much to its own internal weakness as in the case of Ghana and Mali, but rather to the cupidity of Al-Mansur, the Sultan of Morocco, and, to borrow Trimingham's phrase, 'the barbarian soldiery of the Moroccan army'.

Al-Mansur came to the throne of Morocco in 1578 immediately after the celebrated victory of Morocco over Portugal on the field of Al-Kasr Al-Kebir. Having stabilized his position on the throne and spent all the money which he had obtained from the ransoming of prisoners on the famous palace Al-Bedi which he built in Marrakech, he began to look further afield for more money as well as adventure. The Sudan, from which thousands of camels were bringing in hundreds of pounds worth of gold, ivory and slaves, was the obvious choice. As he told his courtiers, 'I have resolved to attack Sudan. It is an exceedingly rich country and will furnish us with large taxes, and we shall thus be enabled to give greater importance to the Mohammedan armies.' Since the Songhai Empire was then controlling not only the entire western Sahara, with its rich salt mines of Taghaza, but also the gold-producing regions of Wangara and Bambuk, it was the obvious target.

After an unsuccessful attempt in 1584, in which an army of about 20,000 strong is said to have perished in the desert because of inadequate preparations, a more carefully organized military expedition was launched in 1590. The second Moroccan army consisted of 4,000 men carefully selected for their discipline, hardiness and courage; only 1,500 were Moroccans; the rest were all hardened Andalusian or renegade European mercenary fighters and their commander was Judar Pasha, a young Spanish eunuch in the employment of the Sultan.

The army left Morocco in October 1590, successfully crossed the desert at some cost, and hit on the Niger River at Bamba, half-way between Timbuctu and Gao, in February 1591. The then Emperor of Songhai, Askia Ishak II, raised an army composed, according to As-Sadi, of 18,000 cavalry and 9,700 infantry, and courageously marched to meet the invaders. At the battle of Tondibi, thirty-five miles from Gao, in April 1591, the huge army of Ishak was completely defeated and routed. The Moroccans pressed on and seized Gao without a blow and then marched north-westwards and occupied Timbuctu, which they thoroughly sacked in 1593.

Many historians have concluded from the ease with which the Songhai army was defeated that the Empire was in a state of decline and they have, therefore, attributed its fall mainly to internal weakness. But this conclusion is not accurate. The evidence we have shows that the Songhai army was defeated and the Empire readily captured primarily because of the technological superiority that the Moroccans enjoyed over the Songhai. The Moroccan army was a well-trained and well-disciplined army full of hardened professional, renegade and mercenary fighters from Spain, Portugal and

Turkey. Secondly, and this is even more important, of the 4,000 soldiers, 2,000 were armed with arquebus (an early type of portable gun supported on a three-legged stand), 500 were mounted gunmen and there were in addition 70 European musketeers. Their baggage included 31,000 pounds of gunpowder and a similar weight of lead—carried by 800 camels. The Songhai army was armed simply with bows and arrows, spears, swords and clubs. Assuming that even half the number of the Moroccans perished en route, and according to Mahmoud Kati, the Moroccan army was only 1,000 strong at the battle of Tondibi, armed as it was with guns and muskets, it could easily rout any force armed as the Songhai army was. Indeed, so shocked and terrified were the Songhai by the noise which they had never heard before and the smoke they had never seen before that they simply fled in all directions and later gave the name Ruma (meaning shooter) to the Moroccan soldiers, a name by which the descendants of the soldiers in the region of Timbuctu are known to this day.

This superiority in arms which the Moroccan forces enjoyed over the Songhai seems to me to be the main explanation for their easy victory. Indeed Al-Mansur himself realized this, and urged it on his sceptical courtiers and advisers. When his advisers pointed out that it was impossible to conquer the Sudan and reminded him that none of his predecessors had ever embarked on such a dangerous project, this was his reply: 'You forget the defenceless and ill-equipped merchants who, mounted or on foot, regularly cross desert wastes which caravans have never ceased to traverse. I, who am so much better equipped than they, can surely do the same with an army which inspires terror wherever it goes. . . . Moreover, our predecessors would have found great difficulty if they tried to do what I now propose, for their armies were composed only of horsemen armed with spears and of bowmen; gunpowder was unknown to them and

so were fire-arms and their terrifying effect. Today, the Sudanese have only spears and swords, weapons which will be useless against modern arms. It will therefore be easy for us to wage a successful war against these people and prevail over them.' Considering what happened at Tondibi, no one would doubt the prophetic nature of these words, which completely won the courtiers over.

But it should be pointed out that when it had recovered from the first shock and panic, the Songhai army bravely put up some resistance. It deposed the demoralized Ishak II and enthroned Askia Kagho, who bravely took the field and, using guerilla tactics, harassed the Moroccans. Indeed so troublesome did he become that the Moroccans resorted to treachery to get rid of him. They summoned him to what was described as a peace talk and then murdered him and his followers in cold blood. But this did not end the resistance of the Songhai. Askia Nuh succeeded his elder brother and continuing the guerilla tactics in the regions of Dendi and Borgu he kept the struggle going for another three years and is said to have inflicted a number of defeats on the Moroccans. Several reinforcements had indeed to be brought in from Morocco in 1593. However, in 1595 at a battle during which both Nuh and the Commander of the Moroccan forces were killed, the Songhai were decisively beaten. The death of Nuh marked the end of organized resistance and saw the conquest of the great Songhai Empire. By that date, that is, 1595, the Empire from Jenne to Gao had been brought under the domination of the Moroccans and the great Songhai Empire had become a province of the Empire of Al-Mansur, the Sultan of Morocco.

It is obvious then from the above that the Empire of Songhai did not, like her two predecessors Ghana and Mali, decline and then fall. She was literally shot down by the musketeers and gunmen of Morocco at the very peak of her power and in full bloom of her glory and splendour. She was a victim not of her own internal weakness but of the greed of Al-Mansur, the Sultan of Morocco.

The effects of the Moroccan conquest were disastrous not only for the Songhai Empire but also for the entire region of southern Sahara and the Niger Bend. In the first place, the Moroccans failed to establish any system of government in place of the one they had so ruthlessly destroyed. Thus with no effective central government to maintain peace and order, chaos and anarchy set in. The Tuareg of the Sahara, the Fulani and later the Bambara of Segu and the Arma, that is, the Moroccans who had settled permanently in the Sudan, fought against each other for the control of the region and these struggles continued till the nineteenth century. During these wars Timbuctu, Gao and Jenne suffered immensely. Gao declined into an obscure little village and Timbuctu lost most of its scholars. Secondly, as a result of this anarchy and insecurity, trade was greatly disturbed and the caravan trade across the Sahara became an annual affair; the gold and ivory which were sent northwards began to be diverted westwards and southwards to the coast to meet the demand greatly stimulated by the entry of the Dutch and the English into competition with the Portuguese at the very time of the Moroccan victory. Thus by the end of the seventeenth century, although trade from Timbuctu and its regions with the north had not stopped, it had been reduced to only a fraction of its former volume. Thirdly, as the Moroccans paid no attention to religion and learning, Islam declined in these regions and animism, stimulated by the Bambara of Segu, began to flourish. It was not until the first half of the nineteenth century that, as a result of the rise of the Masina Empire of the Fulani, the fortunes of the regions of the Niger Bend began to rise again. But before then, the Hausa States further to the east had begun to flourish and it is to the history of these states that we must now turn.

8 THE HAUSA STATES AND THE FULANI JIHAD

As a result of the rather barbaric and ruthless destruction of the great Songhai empire by the Moroccan army and their failure to establish any effective system of government in its place already discussed, disorder and insecurity set in. Since neither trade nor learning can flourish in an atmosphere of wars and disorder, the merchants as well as scholars began to move eastwards to the relatively peaceful region which was bounded on the west by the Niger and on the east by Lake Chad. This region which is now occupied mainly by the modern state of Nigeria, was then the home of the seven true Hausa states or Hausa *bokwoi* (Daura, Kano, Katsina, Zaria, Rano, Gobir and Biram), the seven bastard Hausa states or *banza bokwoi*, namely Zamfara, Kebbi, Nupe, Gwari, Yauri, Yoruba and Kororofa, and the kingdoms of Bornu and Fumbina. It is the history of these principal Hausa states that I will try to deal with here.

The origins of these Hausa states are, like those of many African states, shrouded in myth and mystery. The Hausa have their own traditional accounts of their origins. The most popular and well known of them is the account known as the Daura legend. According to this Daura was the first of the Hausa states to be founded by one of the daughters, named Daura, of a grandson of a Canaanite named Najib who left Palestine with all his family and settled in Libya. During the reign of one of her successors, the son of the king of Baghdad arrived in Daura with his followers after having first lived in Bornu. He is said to have killed a huge serpent that was preventing the people of Daura from fetching water from their only well except on Fridays, and in appreciation of this service, the Queen agreed to marry him. They had a son called Bawu who succeeded his father. He also had six sons and each of them founded a town which later developed into a state, hence the seven Hausa *bokwoi*.

According to another account, collected in Hausaland in the middle of the nineteenth century by Henry Barth, the famous German scholar and explorer, Bawu was the son of a man named Karbagari who entered Hausaland from the east and captured Biram. Bawu is then said to have married a Berber woman and had six children. These children were Daura, the eldest, Katsina and Zaria or Zegzeg who are represented as twins, Kano and Rano, another pair of twins, and Gobir. And each of these children went out and founded a state to which he gave his own name.

Although neither of these stories can be taken at its face value, it seems clear that the names represent an immigration of various tribes and clans into Hausaland about 1,000 years ago from the Sahara and the east. These groups seem to have settled in some of the then leading villages and towns occupied by the autochthones who were black peoples of the Dalla stock and belonged to the So cycle of civilization. The immigrants soon seized political power and established ruling dynasties. They then began to assimilate the autochthones and to develop their towns and villages into states. In their attempts to extend their power, some of the dynasties were obviously more successful than others, for while some like Rano and Daura, developed into no more than city states, others like Kano, Katsina and Zaria certainly grew into huge kingdoms. It has been suggested recently— and this seems very plausible—that some of the conquered groups withdrew westwards and southwards rather than accept vassalage or assimilation and re-established new kingdoms that developed into the *banza* states.

It is not certain when these city states and kingdoms began to emerge in Hausaland. One thing that is certain is that until the fourteenth century all of them were rather insignificant compared with Ghana and, later, Mali or Songhai in the west, or Kanem in the east. There was up to that century obviously no trade between the Hausa states and the Muslim countries of North Africa nor had Islam entered that region. This view is clearly borne out by the fact that none of the Arabic scholars whom we have been quoting and who wrote before the fourteenth century mentions any of the Hausa states. The first to mention any of them, and even then in a rather casual way, was Ibn Battuta who visited Mali in 1352. He refers to Yufi, which has been identified as Nupe, and describes it as 'one of the largest towns of the Negroes, whose ruler is one of the most considerable of the Negro rulers'. And he also mentions 'Kubar (which has been identified as Gobir) in the regions of the heathens' to which, he says, copper from Takedda was exported. It is not until the beginning of the sixteenth century that we have the first detailed description of four of the seven Hausa *bokwoi* by Leo Africanus. It is clear from his descriptions that all four had developed into full-fledged kingdoms by the end of the fifteenth century, with Gobir and Kano as the most powerful. 'The inhabitants', he writes 'are rich merchants and most civil people.' He also describes the town of Gobir as follows: 'Here are also great stores of artificers and linen weavers: and here are such shoes made as the ancient Romans were wont to wear, the greatest part whereof be carried to Tombuto and Gago.' He noted further that the inhabitants of Zaria were rich and had great traffic with other nations.

The reasons for the growth of these Hausa states during the fourteenth and fifteenth centuries are not difficult to find. The first was the stimulus derived from the reintroduction of Islam from Mali. It has now been established from linguistic evidence that Islam was first introduced into Hausaland from Kanem probably in the twelfth or thirteenth century. But it does not appear to have taken any firm root until fresh bands of Muslim Wangara and Fulani traders and scholars began to enter Hausaland from Mali in the fourteenth century. According to the Kano Chronicle, the first of such bands came into Kano from

Mali during the reign of Yaji (1349–85). It appears that Yaji's successor reverted to animism. However, his successor, Dauda, who was described as a learned man, and those who came after him remained Muslim, and they gave every encouragement to the spread of the religion. More and more missionaries and scholars continued to come from Mali during the fifteenth century. For instance, during the reign of Yakubu from 1452 to 1463, the Chronicle notes that 'the Fulani came to Hausaland from Mali bringing books on Divinity and Etymology. Formerly,' it continues, 'they had in addition to the Koran only the Books of Law and the Traditions.'

The introduction and spread of Islam affected the growth of the Hausa states in a number of ways. In the first place it inspired the kings to embark on the conquest of pagan states. Secondly, it introduced a new legal system, a new system of taxation and above all a new statecraft which most of the Hausa rulers adopted. Thirdly, it introduced literacy and new administrative techniques. Finally, Islam put some of the rulers in touch with the great Muslim scholars and philosophers abroad from whom the Hausa kings could seek advice on political and social problems. The best known of such scholars was Mohammed Al-Maghili with whom Rimfa, the king of Kano from 1463 to 1499, corresponded and from whom he received a treatise on government entitled *The Obligation of Princes* which is still extant.

The second reason was economic. It is clear from the Kano chronicle that it was during the fifteenth century that the Hausa states began to develop commercial contacts not only with Mali, following the entry of the Wangara, the Sahara and North Africa, but also with Gonja and modern northern Ghana. 'At this time' (that is between 1421 and 1438) says the Chronicle, 'Zaria under Queen Amina, conquered all the towns as far as Kwararafa and Nupe. Every town paid tribute to her. The Sarkin Nupe sent forty eunuchs and 1,000 kolas

to her. She first had eunuchs and kolas in Hausaland. In her time, the whole of the products of the west were brought to Hausaland.' This, we may note, is the first reference to the kola nut trade from modern Ghana to Hausaland. From the same source, we also learn that salt was imported from Bilma through Agades into Gobir and Hausaland, and we read of the entry of Arabs and Tuareg in large numbers into Hausaland. The development of this caravan trade must have brought in wealth, an indispensable factor in the rise and expansion of states.

The third reason for the growth of the states was political. Both Zaria and Kano were fortunate in their kings and queens of the fifteenth century. Zaria, under her semi-legendary Queen Amina, who is said to have reigned for thirty-four years from the beginning of that century, extended its frontiers to as far south as Nupe and Kororofa. From the middle of that century, however, thanks to the ability of the two kings, Mohammed Rimfa who reigned from 1463 to 1499, and Abdullahi, from 1499 to 1509, Kano completely eclipsed all the other Hausa states.

Owing then first to the stimulus and unity provided by Islam, secondly, to the wealth generated by the developing caravan trade and thirdly, to the ability of their kings, most of the Hausa states had developed from mere city-states into strong kingdoms by the end of the fifteenth century. During the first three decades of the sixteenth century, however, these Hausa states, like the other states in the regions of the Niger and Senegal, were reduced to tributary states by Mohammed Askia of Songhai or by the kings of Bornu further to the east. Indeed, between about 1450 and 1550, Hausaland became a bone of contention between Bornu and Songhai. But after the death of Mohammed Askia, most of the Hausa states became internally self-governing, and after the Moroccan conquest they became fully independent. Not only did the collapse of Songhai ensure their complete independence but it greatly accelerated the pace of their growth. As has been pointed out already, the disorder and insecurity which resulted in the regions of the Niger diverted the caravan trade into Hausaland via the Tripoli–Ghadames–Ghat–Air route. The scholars and mallams followed in the wake of the traders. The result of all this was that the seventeenth and first half of the eighteenth centuries saw the heyday of the Hausa states.

The first of the Hausa states to gain what the Niger region lost were Katsina and Gobir, because they were the most northwestern of the states. Both traders and scholars flocked into Katsina throughout the seventeenth and in particular the early eighteenth century. Katsina thus became the commercial as well as the educational centre of Hausaland. By the end of the eighteenth century, the capital of the same name, Katsina, was said to have a large population of 100,000 and its king was said to be the most wealthy and most powerful of the rulers of Negroland. In the words of the explorer Barth, 'Katsina during the seventeenth and eighteenth centuries of our era seems to have been the chief city of this part of Negroland, as well in commercial and political importance, as in other respects; for here that state of civilization which had been called forth by contact with the Arabs seems to have reached the highest degree, and as the Hausa language here attained the greatest richness of form and most refined pronunciation so also the manners of Katsina were distinguished by superior politeness from those of the other towns of Hausa.' Gobir, Kano, Kebbi and Zaria also shared in the great economic prosperity and cultural attainments.

However, during the first three decades of the nineteenth century, all the Hausa states were wiped off the political map of the central Sudan, and in their place was established a single Fulani Empire. This almost incredible political change was the outcome of a political revolution organized by the Fulani under the leadership and inspiration of Usuman dan Fodio. Who then were the Fulani, and what were the causes, nature and consequences of their revolt?

The Fulani, whom we have already encountered on a number of occasions, are a people now known to have originated in the lower basins of the Senegal and the Gambia as a result of a mixture between Berber emigrants from the Sahara and the Negroes of the Wolof and Serer stock. It appears that part of them—probably the predominantly Berber portion—stuck to the nomadic mode of life of a section of their ancestors and became known as the *Bororoje* or Cattle Fulani, while part of them remained in the towns, became fanatically Muslim and generally well educated, and are known as the *Fulanin Gidda* or Town Fulani. The two groups began infiltrating eastwards and southwards, into the regions of Ghana, Mali and Songhai between the twelfth and fourteenth centuries, into Hausaland in the fifteenth century and by the sixteenth century they had penetrated as far east as the Cameroons. In all these areas, they maintained their traditional way of life, the *Bororoje* sticking to the rural areas and the *Fulanin Gidda* to the towns. Because of their education, the latter were employed in Hausaland as civil servants, diplomats, and tutors at the courts of the Hausa kings, while some of them established schools of their own where they taught the usual Islamic sciences, namely, Theology, Law, Grammar, Rhetoric and Prosody. One of these *Fulanin Gidda* was Usuman dan Fodio, and the immediate cause of the revolt was a clash between him and the kings of Gobir.

Usuman dan Fodio was born in December 1754 in Gobir to a family of the Toronkawa clan which had migrated from Futa Toro in Senegal some fourteen generations before. He began his education at a very early age which took him to different mallams or teachers in different places including Agades in the oasis of Air in the Sahara desert. At the rather early age of twenty, he began his career as a teacher and preacher at Degel in Gobir. From there, he conducted a number of missionary tours to other parts of Hausaland, especially to Kebbi and Zamfara, advocating the practice of a more orthodox form of Islam and condemning all non-Muslim practices. His increasing fame reached the court of Gobir and in about 1781 he was employed by the King, Bawa, as tutor to the royal family. His continuous insistence on a puritanical form of Islam and his condemnation of illegal taxes and pagan practices implied a criticism of the kings of Gobir, while the steady increase of his following at Degel constituted a threat to their authority. Bawa's successors therefore began to take measures to counter this threat. The first of them, Nafata, for instance, ordered that nobody but dan Fodio was to preach, that there were to be no more conversions to Islam and that those who were not born Muslim were to return to their former religions, and finally that men should not wear turbans nor women veils, customs which, according to one historian, 'gave to the Shehu's party the cohesion and sense of common identity which the Habe kings feared'.

Nafata died shortly after this (1802), but his successor, Yunfa, was even more determined to check the growing power of dan Fodio. According to some sources, Yunfa invited dan Fodio to his court and there attempted to murder him but failed. Yunfa then went on to attack a group of Usuman's followers led by Abdul Salame in December 1803, and when Usuman caused the captives to be released at Degel and repeatedly refused to hand them over, Yunfa threatened to attack Degel itself. This threat led to the flight (*hijra*) of dan Fodio and his followers from Degel to Gudu on 21 February 1804, a date still honoured in Northern Nigeria. At Dugu, he raised the standard of revolt by attacking the near-by towns of Gobir, and then having been proclaimed *Amir al-muminin*, Commander of the Believers, he proclaimed a *jihad* or holy war against the rulers of the Hausa states.

Various Fulani rose up in rebellion in the other states and came to ask for flags from Usuman. Within a decade all the Hausa *bokwoi* had been conquered and in the next two decades Nupe, parts of the Oyo Empire (Ilorin) and Bornu (Katagum and Gombe) were added to the Fulani Empire with its new capital of Sokoto. Before his death in 1817, Usuman divided the Empire into two and gave the western half (Gwandu) to his brother Abdullahi and the eastern half (Sokoto) to his son Bello.

This revolt raises a number of questions which should be answered here. The first is why the Hausa states were so easily defeated. The first answer to this is that all the Hausa states were in a state of weakness by the beginning of the nineteenth century mainly because of the internecine wars among themselves and the attacks of the Kororofa which went on almost continuously during the second half of the eighteenth century. Gobir, which fought with Katsina in the 1750's, and with Zamfara and Kano in the 1760's, bore the brunt of these wars and consequently she became particularly weakened and it is not surprising that the revolt began in that state. Besides weakening the Hausa states, these wars also left behind them a legacy of jealousy and animosity which ruled out any co-operation among these states against a common enemy. When Yunfa appealed to the other kings at the outbreak of the revolt he received no response. Since each Hausa king was thus left to face the Fulani armies, which often received reinforcements from Sokoto or Gwandu, none of them had much chance. Thirdly, while the Hausa kings could not count on each other, they could not count on all their subjects either. Most of them had been alienated by the extortionate taxation and arbitrary nature of the rule of their kings, and therefore looked to Usuman who had been condemning these practices as a deliverer. The fourth and certainly one of the most important reasons was the fanaticism and determination with which Usuman was able to infuse his followers by his preaching, coupled with the ability of Abdullahi and Bello on the battle-field. It is interesting to note that the Fulani failed to conquer Bornu where they encountered a leader in the person of al-Kanami, who was able to provide the same sort of inspiration and leadership.

The second question is what was the real nature and therefore the fundamental causes, of this revolt? What can be stated now in the light of the rapidly accumulating evidence on the subject is that it was of a very complex nature having religious, political as well as social elements in it. The revolt, as we have seen, was touched off by a clash between Usuman dan Fodio and the kings of Gobir, and there is absolutely no doubt that Usuman's main concern was the purification and expansion of Islam, the elimination of all unorthodox practices, and government by god-fearing kings in accordance with the precepts of Islam, all of which were lacking in Hausaland by the end of the eighteenth century. Islam was by then certainly in decline, administration of justice was corrupt, taxes were oppressive, many non-Muslim practices were rampant both at the courts and among the ordinary people, and many areas of Hausaland, such as those which later became known as Bauchi and Adamawa, were still pagan. Moreover, Usuman's generals, his brother Abdullahi, his son Bello, and most of the flag-bearers were all people who shared their leader's zeal for Islam and the enforcement of a Muslim form of government and were also well educated in the Islamic sciences. Indeed, some historians are beginning to call this revolution, rather like the revolution which swept through western Europe in 1848, the revolution of the intellectuals. From all these considerations, it is clear that the revolt had a strong religious element in it and can indeed be regarded as a *jihad* in so far as it aimed at the expansion of Islam and the establishment of Islamic government.

It would be wrong however to regard the revolt simply as a *jihad* or a purely religious movement for a number of reasons. The first is that the revolt was also to some extent an answer to the political as well as the racial question posed by the gradual infiltration of the Fulani, especially the *Fulanin Gidda,* throughout the western Sudan: namely, how long these people, usually highly educated, fanatically Muslim, economically well-to-do and regarding themselves as racially superior, would continue to remain in politically subordinate positions? It is interesting to note that this question was answered not only in Hausaland but indeed throughout the western Sudan by, significantly enough, Fulani-led revolts beginning with the one in Futa Toro in the 1770's, followed by that of Usuman in 1804 in Hausaland, that of Ahmadu Lobbo in Massina in the 1810's, that of al-hajj Umar in the 1840's and that of Samori Toure in the 1870's. As a recent student of Usuman's movement has pointed out, some of the wealthy *Fulanin Gidda* in Hausaland had, by the last decade of the eighteenth century, not only become dissatisfied with the Hausa governmental system, but had also begun 'to manifest and succeed in political ambitions, if only in a limited sense'. The second and an even more significant one is the fact that the leadership of Usuman's revolt was concentrated solely in the hands of the Fulani. Indeed, of the fourteen flag-bearers, only one of them was not a Fulani. What is more, with the exception of two, all the others were in fact, as a recent authority has pointed out, 'primarily the delegates of the influential *Fulanin Gidda* interests', and that the only two who were chosen by Usuman himself were sent out, rather significantly enough, to areas where 'because of the lack of a sizeable Fulani Muslim community, Usuman could have no hope that leadership would arise spontaneously.' Thirdly, the hard core of Usuman's army consisted of the Bororoje, and though they had their own grievances particularly over the cattle-tax or *jangali*, that so many of them joined Usuman's side may have been due 'to their perception of a general threat to all Fulani'. Though it is true that many Fulani remained on the side of the Hausa kings while many Hausa and Tuareg also fought on Usuman's side, in view of the fact that leadership was concentrated in the hand of the Fulani, that Usuman himself and Bello looked to the *Fulanin Gidda* in the other states for leadership and that the Bororoje formed the hard core of the army, the revolt can also be considered to some extent a Fulani national revolt.

Finally, as we have seen, without the support of the Hausa peasants, the *talakawa*, and the Fulani nomads, the revolt would not have succeeded so readily. But these thousands of people were attracted to Degel not simply because of Usuman's magnetic personality and his reformist zeal, but rather because they had their own grievances arising from exorbitant taxation, arbitrary imprisonment, injustice and the oppressive rule that they had been suffering at the hands of the Hausa kings, and which Usuman was condemning in such forthright terms. If it is wrong to consider this revolt simply as a peasant revolt, or the revolt of the down-trodden Hausa peasants and the over-taxed Fulani nomads against the Hausa aristocracy, it is true to say that the movement had a genuine popular basis, at least in the beginning, and could therefore be considered in this sense as a social movement.

Usuman dan Fodio's revolt, then, had strong religious, nationalistic as well as social elements in it. Nor should we be surprised by this, since it was the interaction of all these elements that produced the revolt and ensured its success.

This very complex revolt, needless to say, had very far-reaching and lasting consequences. Politically, as we have seen, it led to the overthrow of all the old Hausa dynasties and the establishment of a single Fulani Empire stretching from the Niger to the Benue, divided into emirates under emirs who were nearly all Fulani. The modern region of Northern Nigeria is more or less co-terminous with the creation of Usuman and his flag-bearers. The Sultan of Sokoto, who was the religious as well as the political head of that region, was a direct descendant of Usuman dan Fodio, and the emirs are also descendants of the flag-bearers—a clear evidence of the lasting nature of the work of Usuman and his colleagues in the political field.

The second consequence was economic. The establishment of a uniform system of government in place of the many competing ones meant a considerable elimination of the internecine wars that had characterized the history of the Hausa states in the eighteenth century. Peace and order therefore reigned in most parts of the Fulani Empire especially between the 1820's and 1850's and both greatly stimulated commercial and industrial activities, as is borne out by the accounts of the European explorers who visited Hausaland during that period. All these explorers—Clapperton, Denham and Barth—were particularly impressed by the commercial and industrial activities of Kano which had by the 1820's regained its former role as the commercial and industrial metropolis of Hausaland and the main entrepôt for the trade with modern Ghana, Dahomey and Western and Eastern Nigeria. To quote Barth's description of Kano in the 1850's, 'The principal commerce of Kano consists in native produce, namely, the cotton cloth woven and dyed here or in the neighbouring towns . . . The great advantage of Kano is that commerce and manufactures go hand in hand, and almost every family has its share in them. There is really something grand in this kind of industry, which spreads to the north as far as Murzuk, Ghat and even Tripoli; to the west, not only to Timbuktu, but in some degree even as far as the shores of the Atlantic, the very inhabitants of Arguin dressing in the cloth woven and dyed in Kano; to the east, all over Bornu . . . and to the south it main-tains a rivalry with the native industry of the Igbira and Igbo, while towards the south-east it invades the whole of Adamawa . . . . The chief articles of native industry, besides cloth, which have a wide market, are principally sandals . . . tanned hides and red sheep skins, dyed with a juice extracted from the stalks of the holcus.' Other towns which benefited from the Fulani *Pax* were Zaria in the emirate of that name, Yola in Adamawa, and Kulfi and Egga in Nupe.

Thirdly, the revolution brought about a great revival and spread of Islam and gave a really great stimulus to education and learn-ing in Hausaland. Areas like Bauchi and Adamawa became converted for the first time.

Furthermore, at least the first generation of emirs led by Bello were sincere religious devotees and saw to the establishment of true Islamic judicial, political and social insti-tutions. Above all, Usuman, Abdullahi and Bello were all very great scholars and wrote a large number of books mainly as textbooks for the guidance of their civil servants, and their literary activities did touch off a veri-table renaissance in Hausaland. If today Islam is a force to reckon with in Nigeria—and indeed in the Sudanese states of Senegal, Mali, Niger and even Guinea—it was because of the revolutionary Islamic movements of the late eighteenth and nineteenth centuries in general, and that of Usuman dan Fodio in particular.

Part II *Key Terms and Essay/Discussion Questions*

KEY TERMS

Imhotep	*Mansa Musa*
Osiris	*Mohammed Askia the Great*
Isis	*Sunni Ali*
Horus	*Jihad*
Great Pyramid	*Usuman dan Fodio*
University of Sankore	*Caravan trade*
Sijilmasa	*Almoravid*
Timbuctu	*Sundiata*
Leptis Magna	*Praetorian guards*
Didius Julianus	*Perscennuis Niger*
Clodius Albinus	*Parthian War*

ESSAY/DISCUSSION QUESTIONS

1. The denial of African history arose out of the European expansion and invasion of Africa that began in the middle of the fifteenth century. What is the significance of African history to world history, according to John Henrik Clarke, and why do we need a new approach for the study of African history?

2. Describe the similarities between the people and customs of the ancient Empire of Ghana and the Akan people of present day Ghana.

3. What forces contributed to the decline and fall of ancient Ghana?

4. How did Lucius Septimius Severus become emperor of Rome? What strategies and tactics did he use to gain and maintain power?

5. How did the political administration of King Mansa Musa contribute to the growth and development of the Mali Empire?

6. Why is Sunni Ali remembered as an important nation builder in fifteenth-century West Africa? What attributes contributed to his success? What are the tasks of leadership?

7. What were the outstanding features of Askia the Great's political administration and what legacy did this ruler leave the Songhai Empire?

8. What was the impact of Islam on the growth and development of the West African Hausa and Fulani states?

Part II *Supplementary Readings*

Ajayi, J. F. Ade, and Ian Espie, eds., *A Thousand Years of West African History: A Handbook for Teachers and Students.* Ibadan: Ibadan University Press, 1965.

Ben-Jochannan, Yosef, *Black Man of the Nile,* New York: Alkebu-Lan Books Associates, 1972.

_____, *Africa: Mother of Western Civilization,* New York: Alkebu-Lan Books Associates, 1971.

_____, *The African Origins of the Major "Western Religions",* New York: Alkebu-Lan Books Associates, 1970.

Birley, Anthony R., *Septimius Severus: The African Emperor,* Rev. Ed., New Haven: Yale University Press, 1988.

Bovill, E. W., *The Golden Trade of the Moors,* New York: Oxford University Press, 1968.

Breasted, James H., *The Dawn of Conscience,* New York: Charles Scribner's Sons, 1933.

_____, *A History of Egypt From the Earliest Times to the Persian Conquest,* New York: Charles Scribner's Sons, 1937.

Clarke, John Henrik, ed., *New Dimensions in African History: The London Lectures of Dr. Yosef ben-Jochannan and Dr. John Henrik Clarke,* Trenton: Africa World Press, Inc., 1991.

Davidson, Basil, *The Lost Cities of Africa,* Boston: Little, Brown and Company, 1959.

Diop, Cheikh Anta, *Civilization or Barbarism: An Authentic Anthropology,* New York: Lawrence Hill Books, 1991.

_____, *Precolonial Black Africa: A Comparative Study of the Political and Social Systems of Europe and Black Africa, from Antiquity to the Formation of Modern States,* Trenton: Africa World Press, 1987.

Drake, St. Clair, *Black Folk Here and There: An Essay in History and Anthropology,* Vol. II, Los Angeles: Center for Afro-American Studies/University of California, 1990.

_____, *Black Folk Here and There: An Essay in History and Anthropology,* Vol. I, Los Angeles: Center for Afro-American Studies/University of California, 1987.

Du Bois, W. E. B., *The World and Africa: An Inquiry into the Part Which Africa Has Played in World History,* New York: International Publishers, 1965.

DeGraft-Johnson, J. C., *African Glory: The Story of Vanished Negro Civilizations,* New York: Walker and Company, 1966.

Felder, Cain H., *Troubling Biblical Waters: Race, Class, and Family,* Maryknoll: Orbis Books, 1990.

Grant, Michael, *History of Rome,* New York: Charles Scribner's Sons, 1978.

Heeren, A. H. L., *Historical Researches into the Politics, Intercourse, and Trade of the Carthaginians, Ethiopians, and Egyptians,* 2 Vols., 1832, New York: Negro Universities Press, 1969.

Jackson, John G., *Man, God, and Civilization*, New Hyde Park: University Books, Inc., 1972.

James, George G. M., *Stolen Legacy*, New York: Philosophical Library, 1954.

Jones, Edward L., *The Black Diaspora: Colonization of Colored People*, Seattle: Edward L. Jones, 1989.

_____, *Tutankhamon: Son of the Sun, King of Upper and Lower Egypt (XVII Dynasty)*, Seattle: Edward L. Jones, 1978.

_____, *Profiles in African Heritage*, Seattle: Edward L. Jones, 1972.

Karenga, Maulana, and Jacob Carruthers, *Kemet and the African Worldview*, Los Angeles: University of Sankore Press, 1986.

Karenga, Maulana, *The Husia*, Los Angeles: University of Sankore Press, 1984.

Lane-Poole, Stanley, *The Story of the Moors in Spain*, New York: Putnam's Sons, 1886.

Massey, Gerald, *A Book of the Beginnings*, 2 Vols., New York: University Books, Inc., 1974.

_____, *Ancient Egypt: The Light of the World*, 2 Vols., New York: Samuel Weiser, Inc., 1970.

Osae, T. A., and S. N. Nwabara, *A Short History of West Africa: A. D. 1000–1800*, London: University of London Press, Ltd., 1968.

Rogers, Joel A., *Nature Knows No Color Line*, New York: J. A. Rogers, 1952.

_____, *Sex and Race*, Vol. I, New York: J. A. Rogers, 1967.

Snowden, Frank M. Jr., *Blacks in Antiquity: Ethiopians in the Greco-Roman Experience*, Cambridge: Harvard University Press, 1970.

Thompson, Lloyd, *Romans and Blacks*, Norman: University of Oklahoma Press, 1989.

_____ and J. Ferguson, eds., *Africa in Classical Antiquity*, Ibadan: Ibadan University Press, 1969.

Tompkins, Peter, *Secrets of the Great Pyramids*, New York: Harper & Row, Publishers, 1971.

Williams, Chancellor, *The Destruction of Black Civilization: Great Issues of a Race from 4500 B. C. to 2000 A. D.*, Dubuque: Kendall/Hunt Publishing Company, 1971.

Western Europe and the Culture of Domination

Western Europe's long march to its modern age—the Renaissance, the rise of capitalism, the Protestant Reformation, and the Enlightenment—culminated in nineteenth- and early twentieth-century imperialism and colonialism. Columbus' voyage to the Americas in 1492, which brought that part of the world to European consciousness, resulted in increased contact between Europeans and non-Europeans, as well as Western territorial and economic expansion on a grand scale. Sixteenth-century Calvinist social ethics and theological absolutism, together with the progressive rise of capitalism and Enlightenment rationalist absolutism of the seventeenth and eighteenth centuries, set in motion the accepted belief in the superiority of Western civilization and the inferiority of non-Western peoples and cultures. Africans and their American descendants were defined by Calvinist Christians as beings without souls and declared by Enlightenment thinkers to be persons unable to reason; thus, they were relegated to a class of subhumanity. This perspective, which assumes European superiority and African inferiority (Eurocentrism), became deeply embedded in the Western culture.

The Eurocentric view assumes that the Western structure of knowledge is true, objective, and politically neutral, applicable to all people and circumstances. Furthermore, European views and values are seen as the human norm. Because of its shortcomings—in particular, its lack of political neutrality—many European writers and thinkers have, wittingly or unwittingly, misrepresented, misinterpreted, or literally omitted the African experience in world history.

A major objective of African American Studies theorists and practitioners has been to unmask and contest the power/knowledge configuration of Eurocentrism and Western cultural domination characteristic of the Academy. The two articles in this section represent attempts to accomplish that task. In "European Mythology: The Idea of 'Progress'," Dona Richards critically analyzes the ideological foundation of the idea of progress as a fundamental element of the Western philosophy of life or ethos. Richards sheds much light on the extent to which the ideology of progress came to buttress European cultural imperialism and Euro-American racism, indicating how destructive this ideology has been with respect to the African self-image. Richards demands that African American Studies expose Western cultural domination and reconstruct a positive image of African-descended people based fundamentally on an African world view.

The essay by Cheikh Anta Diop, "Modern Falsification of History," explores, critiques, and refutes the manner in which many nineteenth-century European Egyptologists, as cultural imperialists, sought to distort and erase the African origin and foundation of ancient Egyptian civilization and culture by suggesting that ancient Egyptians were white Europeans. Utilizing Egyptologists' original documentation, Diop demonstrates the intellectual, linguistic, and textual strategies and tactics they employed to misrepresent and misinterpret the meaning of the Egyptian past. He points out the contradictions and dilemmas that arose in the process. Rejecting this falsification, and relying on ancient and modern documentation, Diop demonstrates persuasively that ancient Egyptians were black and that their culture and civilization were African in origin and content.

European Mythology: The Ideology of "Progress"

DONA RICHARDS

WE, AS PEOPLE OF AFRICAN DESCENT, need to understand the nature of European culture, history, and behavior in order that we might be in a better position to deal with it, reject it, and to comprehend the dimension of its effect on us. Its effect has unfortunately usually been subtle, yet ideologically debilitating. For this reason I have devoted much of my energies to "White Studies," an endeavor which should be an important part of any Black Studies curriculum.

As a black anthropologist looking at white culture, I find the concepts of ethos, ideology, myth, and value to be especially useful in this study. My interest in this concept, the "idea of progress" as it is called, is more than academic; it is ideological. Its relevance to Pan-African self-determination may not appear obvious, and that is precisely the reason for my concern. The study of white culture is complicated by the fact that its ideological or "value" aspects are most often hidden beneath a facade of universalistic, scientistic, and "humanistic" rhetoric. We begin to adopt the values of our oppressors as we assimilate the language of academia from within their institutions of learning. European conceptions must be philosophically and critically analyzed so as to lay bare their value-content. The "idea of progress" in Western thought is just such a phenomenon. It is an essential dynamic of European ideology, misunderstood by us to be a universal statement of human value and motivation. This idea, along with our acceptance of it, has helped tremendously in the destruction of the black self-image.

In order to reveal this ideological theme effectively, I will, in this chapter, first attempt to expose the way in which it operates *within* European society—to look at how the idea works, and the way in which it gains not only philosophical acceptance but ideological force. I will then explore the means by which it helps to determine and to rationalize European behavior *externally*. I hope to demonstrate how the "idea of progress" becomes an ideology of imperialism toward others and of the oppressive technical ordering of the society internally. Perhaps, if these things become clear, we will be able to raise critical ideological questions for ourselves: "Is what we want to achieve simply an uncritical imitation of what the white man has created?" (Edward Wilmot Blyden asked this question in 1881; see Blyden, 1967: 91–92.) In discussing these issues we can create an intellectual atmosphere which demands answers to such ideological questions.

I. FROM "IDEA" TO IDEOLOGY: THE SHAPING OF EUROPEAN SOCIETY

Exposing the Culture-Bound

The "idea of progress" is a fundamental aspect of the Western philosophy of life, providing moral justification for the technical order and giving direction to the strivings of individuals within the society. It has contributed to the formation of Western-European social organization by helping to provide the ideological substratum out of which the oppressive technical order was created. The concept has profound implications. Its effects have been powerful and have spread to other cultures. It has been a potent tool in white hands.

Within the setting of Western culture, however, the relativity and ideological significance of the idea is difficult to discuss. More than a conceptual tool, it has become part of the meaning of existence for white people. In the classroom the attempt to present the idea as being culturally bound is met with blank stares. "What do you mean? *Everyone* wants to make *progress!*" Moreover, because the idea combines Western-European metaphysical assumptions, world view, and values so intricately and is so deeply embedded in them, finding the right way to present it, so that its cultural implications for white behavior, attitudes, and world posture become evident, is not an easy task.

The critical conceptual step is that by which action directed toward a concrete objective

becomes confused with change which is merely reflexive—that is, in which the object is "change" itself. The "progress" toward which Western people perceive themselves to be "moving" is neither concrete nor "reachable"— a spurious goal indeed. Then why does the idea have such attraction for the Western mind—a mind which is at once rationalistic and empirical ("Show *me!*")? The answer lies in the fact that this ingenious invention, "progress," born out of the white ethos, is ideally fashioned to encourage the growth of the technical order while at the same time justifying European cultural and political imperialism. Let us see how this is achieved.

The Western-European ethos is expansionistic. To white people, the universe represents actual physical space into which they can impose themselves. Their movement in this respect is never *from* place *to* place (they are no nomads). It is not displacement, but *increase.* White people expand and extend their possessions, never relinquishing territory they have claimed. They never migrate, but always conquer and consume. By this process white people themselves becomes "bigger." The European idea of progress allows for this same kind of "movement" and "increase." Conceptually, "progressive" motion consumes all of the past within it, and "progress" is not merely "different from," it is "more than." The idea is, in this way, essentially expansionistic. "It contains within itself the germs of indefinite expansion (Beard, 1955: xxviii). What it implies is that there is no fixed limit to change, no boundary limiting the expansionist thrust. Instead, Europeans see themselves as being morally obligated to ceaselessly move/change/expand themselves; *that* is the nature of "progress."

For the Western-European it is the abstractness of the idea which makes it "ideal." Interestingly, this is precisely the nature of Plato's ideal state; it can only be *approximated* by humanity. The commitment to imitate it necessarily entails endless and infinite effort, and therefore assures a certain style of behavior. In opposition, Arthur Lovejoy and J. B. Bury contend that Plato's conception is antithetical to the "idea of progress" in that it involves a commitment to an absolute order already conceived. But what they fail to understand is that it is the absolute order (the "establishment") which itself becomes the *agent* of change (as Theodore Roszak points out in his introduction to *Sources;* see Roszak, 1972). The "establishment" changes in order to remain the same. (One becomes more at home with this seeming paradox the more one studies cultural phenomena. Culture is tenacious, ingeniously using varied techniques to ensure its own survival.)

Admittedly, change is much more the order of the contemporary West than it is of ancient Greece, but Plato's Absolute can still be interpreted to ideologically support *a certain kind of change, in a particular direction,* within a determined and well-defined form. The "idea of progress" does precisely the same thing. What it limits is the *kind* of change which can take place. Ecological sanity, for instance, is not "progress." Prohibiting the building of nuclear reactors is "unprogressive."

It has mistakenly been regarded as a "theory of history." It is not. It does not necessarily imply optimism. It has been misunderstood to refer to a way of interpreting the future. It does not. The "infinite future," once it has been postulated, becomes irrelevant. It is the subtlety of this phenomenon ("idea") which contributes to its distinctiveness. It is a mood—not one of optimism, but of arrogance, superiority, power, and exploitation. These need not be synonymous with optimism. It is common for persons committed to the "Western way" to express concern over where "it" is all leading, and yet to be convinced of their obligation to "take it there" and, what is more, to be convinced of their obligation to bestow the leadership of their culture upon those, less fortunate, who do not know the way.

The idea of progress is a directive of Western behavior, a determinant of attitude, a device whereby Western-Europeans judge and impose their judgments on others. Europeans who "ennoble" the "native" do so from the pinnacle of a state of "progress" which they believe it is incumbent upon "Man" to achieve. It is the Western counterpart of what is meant by tradition when it is said that tradition functions normatively in "traditional" societies. It is the idea of progress which helps to guarantee that Western commitments and values will *not change,* but will always remain *within the same modality.*

The "idea" is more a methodological commitment than a theory of history. It is a process, an operational mode. Its referent is rationalism—not a euphoric or glorious state of perfection in the future (only for Marx does it seem to have this connotation). In fact, its viability contradicts the possibility of such a state. Its mood is much closer to a "survival of the fittest" aura. It is concerned with the evolving, not with the end, product. Progress is always there to be made, because its index is wherever one is at a given time. There is always a "proper" way to attack a problem rationally. Rather than presuming there is perfect state ultimately to be reached, it rests on the presumption of cease-less "problems," constant tension. It presupposes disharmony, disequilibrium, imbalance.

The Republic can be interpreted in this way, as a paramount guide to activity, in an endless approach to unattainable perfection—an ideal which, like Xeno's paradox, allows for an infinite degree of approximation without the possibility of duplication. It is the solving of the problem in the most "rational" way which *is progress.* That is the thrust of the idea within European culture. Its outward thrust, i.e., in relation to other cultures, is to make the "rational" way (the white, European way) best.

E. O. Bassett says that, in Plato's view, "society executes an infinite progression." Furthermore, the end of progress is progress; "the aim is but a directing principle. . . . Since the social as well as the universal aim is maximum orderliness, progress must be perpetual" (Bassett, 1927–1928: 476). But Lovejoy and Boas argue that "the Romantic idea of endless progress for progress' sake is alien to Plato's thought" (Lovejoy and Boas, 1965: 168). Popper (1966: 4–5) agrees:

Plato's sense of drift had expressed itself in his theory that all change, at least in certain cosmic periods, must be for the worse; all change is degeneration. Aristotle's theory admits of changes which are improvements; this change may be progress. Plato had taught that all development starts from the original, the perfect Form or Idea, so that the developing thing must lose its perfection in the degree in which it changes and in which its similarity to the original decreases.

But the trick is that the perfect Form exists only as Idea. If one's interpretation of Plato emphasizes the concrete political, sociocultural implications of his theories for human organization, then it becomes clear that all actual development in the sensate "world of becoming" may properly start from a conceptualized perfection, but certainly not with the "Perfect State." Actual movement is, therefore, not *away from* but *toward* the Ideal. If the Ideal could be actualized, then once this had occurred, all change would, indeed, be for the worse. But such, for Plato, was a contradiction in terms.

Joel Kovel says that the "practical genius" of Protestantism and of the West in general "was to discover that the more remote a desired goal, the more passionately a man would seek it." I would insert "European" before the generic term "man"; and in my view, this is one of the normative functions of the Christ image, insofar as he is a deity conceived as "pure spirit." He is the "human" who is not human, the "more than" human being who only incidentally, and *very* briefly, took "human" form. This image calls for the emulation of that which is superhuman and therefore unrealizable by human beings. (African deities are criticized as being "too

human" in conceptualization; they are therefore "primitive" in European judgment.) As Kovel says of European value, "all that 'counted' was Movement, striving for an endless goal that became ever more remote precisely through the process of striving" (see Kovel, 1971: 125, 128). One never reaches "progress"; one "*makes* progress," and, in the Western view, there is always more of it to be made. This supports the ego which must extend its domain indefinitely, the ethos which manifests an insatiable will-to-power.

The white self-image requires an "inferior" to which it relates as "superior." The idea of progress helps to explain to Western-Europeans in what way they are "superior." They believe, and are able to make others believe, that since they represent the most "progressive" force at any given moment, they are most human and therefore "best." Others in the world represent varying degrees of inferiority. This characteristic of the European ethos is already observable in the archaic West. In comparing the Romans with other peoples, Aristides (1958: 40) claims not only that they are greater than their contemporaries, but that they are greater than anything which preceded them.

Hence the inferiority of those who lived in former times appears because the past is so much surpassed, not only in the element at the head of the empire, but also in cases where identical groups have been ruled by others and by you.

While a particular kind of "improvement" may be essential to the idea of progress— ethnologically, in terms of the European ethos—an equally significant aspect of the idea is the assumption that the present is probably better than and superior to the past. The way the idea is put firmly into the service of European cultural imperialism is that the superior present becomes something more than merely what is occurring (or exists) now. What is "progressive" or "modern" is the proper form or model for what *ought to* exist in the present. Therefore, existent forms which do not conform to the progressive (modern or Western) model are not really part of the present—they are "outdated" or "backward." In this way, European culture, in the vernacular of European cultural chauvinism, is made to be superior not only to what precedes it—as does its own past—but also to coexistent "unprogressive" cultures. In other words, the idea of progress provides a scale on which to weigh and by which to compare people via their cultures (their group creations). The Western-European ethos requires a self-image not merely of superiority but of *supremacy,* and the idea of progress makes white people supreme among human beings. It is superiority placed into the dimension of lineal time, and then the logic of lineal time placed into a timeless dimension. Without the idea and this conceptual sleight of hand, cultures would merely be different; Western culture would merely be intensely and obsessively rational. *With* the assumption of the idea of progress, the West becomes "better." In the ways indicated above, then, the idea of progress supports the expansionism and supremism inherent in the Western-European ethos.

The Inevitability of "Progress"

The idea of progress is a "philosophy of change" and, as such, tends to support any innovation, anything "new." Wherever this force leads is by definition "good"—whereas in the context of other world views what could be defined as "progressive," activity depends on concretized goals. The idea of progress transforms what is merely "change" into "directed movement." Participants in Western culture *perceive* change in this way. Continually influenced by the images of technology, they are provided with directive signposts and the standard which gives order to otherwise directionless motion. Technology provides the model of "efficiency," a model which more perfectly than anything imaginable concurs with the philosophy of change—for, in the European view, there is no end to

efficiency either. No matter how effectively a machine may perform its function, it can always be made more effective and thereby a "new" and "better" machine. Progress is, in this way, "proven," and Western-Europeans can be said to "advance" as technology "advances." It does not matter that there is nothing toward which they advance. Their innovations all seem to contribute to greater order in their society—at least, to a certain *kind* of order. The rationalization (in the Weberian sense) of their culture gives them the impression that they have organized their lives more efficiently. This kind of organization is proof of progress, just as their machines are. All of this taken together means that they are "smart" and getting "smarter," the "best" and getting "better." To the Western self, progress is obviously *more* than an idea. When technology dominates in this way, it is the inexorable drive for power and control characterizing the European ethos that is ideally complemented; but Europeans understand their nature to be the nature of all people, and they project this attitude onto the world, dominating it.

The idea of progress had an irresistible attraction for Europeans; it was, after all, created out of their own sentiment, their ethos. It corresponded to their world view and comprised part of the conquering mood. But it was technological efficiency which "clinched it"—which provided tangible evidence of material gain and accomplishment. Technological success gave Western-Europeans the illusion of an objectively ("universally") valid criterion by which to judge their progress. If power over others is the ultimate and ever-present goal—and clearly technological superiority brings power—then progressive ideology, a philosophy of change, is most certainly "right"; obviously a cyclical (African) as opposed to lineal, view, or, in Charles Beard's (1955) Eurocentric characterization, "the belief in the vicious circle," has certainly led to "powerlessness" (or so the argument goes).

The themes of Western-European culture and ideology complement one another and converge in this way until progress becomes a cultural fact. The more particularized and hardened it becomes in the Western experience, the more housed this fact must be in the language of universalism. White persons are not like other people—their goals and ideals do not seem to work for them unless they can conceive of them as universal goals. The idea of progress is nothing if it is not projected as having universal significance; otherwise it does not work. It must be an implicit statement of value, explicitly stated as a "neutral" fact. As with other aspects of the Western ideological matrix, progress cannot be acknowledged as value-based, because the "scientific" (which to the European connotes the highest value) must be valueless. Statements, dogmas, positions, European "choices" can then be imposed upon the tastes of others. European predilections, tendencies, perspectives become that which is "proper" for all. The idea of progress pervades the European intellect—the European consciousness as well as the European moral sense—and *all* who succumb to it are duped by the sleight of hand by which a chosen way simultaneously becomes "inevitable change" and a Western goal becomes "the human goal."

The idea of progress accomplishes all this, so that when someone who describes himself or herself as a "racialist" or talks about the "importance of race in civilization" (Wayne MacLeod [1968], for instance), he or she is merely making sense of the "facts." Once progress becomes ideology—once it becomes incorporated into the presupposed matter of culture—there is no way out. It is inextricably bound to Western technology, and the technical obsession is the white person's creed, just as is the idea of power over nonwhites. MacLeod is quite right when he points to the weaknesses in Ashley Montagu's arguments. Montagu (1968: 3–4) representing the "enlightened" liberal position, argues that

technical advances are due to "accidental factors." He misses the point. They occur in greater numbers where they are encouraged, even mandated, by a culture which lives for them and by them. The possibility that European-style progress could be rejected does not occur to Montagu any more than it does to MacLeod. To the European mind there is no such possibility. "Enlightened," "liberal" and "racialist" alike, *both* have unconsciously universalized the particular. Both are progressive. For both, progress is a given in experience and assumed to be everywhere. I am saying here that the European idea of progress is inherently racialist ideology. Once it is accepted, the progressive person must always be identified as a white person.

Metaphysic and Ethos

Via the Western-European idea of progress it is possible to see how the metaphysical (ontological and epistemological) definitions of a culture translate into its ideological (value and behavioral) aspects. The assumptions of cause (especially Aristotle's final cause), of lineality, and the sense of telos or "purpose" in the Western metaphysic, as well as a dependence on abstraction, are all necessary conceptual ingredients of progress ideology. Its assimilation depends on the mental habits encouraged by these forms of thought. Its acceptance as a predominant molder of group activity is dependent on a frame of mind already or simultaneously conditioned by "lineal codification" (Dorothy Lee's term) and causalist epistemology. Phenomena must relate to one another within a lineally defined whole, where "causes" precede "effects," and growth implies the incorporation and surpassing of that which has come before in a way that precludes repetition. Progress does not recur; it is triumph over the past. The need for and feeling of triumph is an essential ingredient of the idea of progress. In the European view, life is a continuous struggle, based on competition, and meaning is derived from "winning." Hidden behind the so-called universalism and humanism of the concept are the exigencies of an ethos that feeds on subjugation—surpassing, conquering, winning. Progress means "we are winning; we have triumphed over!" The enemy is vaguely felt, not conceived, to be "everything else out there"— not only nature, but other people, other ways, ideas, forces, beings. The enemy against which the white person competes is everything that he or she is not. The idea involves continual movement, because the enemy is never totally subdued. "He" seeks to close the gap, and we must stay ahead of "him." Progress is *staying ahead*—it is "defeating" the present.

The way in which "history" and "time" are perceived is critical to the European understanding of the meaning of human experience. The idea of progress both creates Western history and simultaneously stands outside that history, becoming an absolute in Western thought. It achieves a unique combination, the illusion of "unchanging change," thereby providing a dynamic principle while at the same time satisfying what Lovejoy (1966: 12) calls the "eternalistic" pathos.

The assumption of lineal time is an ontological prerequisite to the idea of progress. Evolutionary development, an ingredient of the idea, necessitates that points be connected; this is the conceptual function of the line. The written word is the medium of the line, and it provides evidence to the Western mind of progress, because words accumulate. In this way, "more" becomes "better."

Progress is an argument for the discarding of the past. Yet evolutionism, its sibling idea, involves a strange kind of incorporation. Evolution requires the perception of reality as the continual development of a single entity—a single being. Yet, while the form is evolving, its prior essence is being denied. Progress makes "garbage" of the past. The concept of newness (value, in progress ideology) does not mean *new* in the sense that a baby is new. It means *different* from that which

has been seen before, whereas even a newborn baby, in the African conception, is the timeless *re*creation of man. In progress ideology, what precedes on the line is always destroyed and denied.

The European "represent[s] the sequence of time as a line going to the infinite." That is a description of the idea of progress. Uniform and undisturbed flow of time can only be imagined as a line (see Juenger, 1956: 39–40). If other concepts of time are admitted as plausible or operative, the idea of progress does not work. In order for it to work, what must be assumed is a single, infinite, and infinitely divisible time.

In Dorothy Lee's (1959: 110) words, the line "underlies our (western) aesthetic apprehension of the given," and progress is the "meaningful sequence" for Westerners. A people that is not progressive "goes nowhere." The idea of progress "makes sense" because Western-Europeans think in terms of "climatic historical sequence" (Lee, 1959: 91). They are concerned not with events but with their own place within a related series of events (Lee, 1959: 94). As the idea of purpose permeates Western life, so the idea of progress gives the impression of purpose in change.

Progress: "Science" and European Development

A compelling question in this discussion is, "How does the idea of progress relate to European history and development, and what is its relationship to science as it is known in the West?" According to Bury (author of the one major noncritical work devoted to this concept), "it is not till the sixteenth century that the obstacles to its [the idea of progress's] appearance definitely began to be transcended and a favorable atmosphere to be gradually prepared" (Bury, 1955: 7). I would put it differently. In the archaic West, the proper metaphysical atmosphere was already being created in which a subsequent ideological synthesis could take place. The germs of the idea had been planted and some of its ideological functions were already in operation. Sixteenth-century Europe embraced the idea as a fully matured concept because it was also in the process of assimilating an individualistic, accumulative, technocratic ethic in the form of materialistic capitalism. Protestantism supported this tendency and so did the ideology of progress. These aspects of European culture reinforced one another, became identified with one another, and grew together. Their combined momentum in the sixteenth century merely represented the final unbridled commitment to rational forms. The seeds of all of them are to be found at whichever point there are enough uniquely combined traits to be identified as "European culture." The distinguishable periods in Western-European history are ethnologically a matter of difference in emphasis, intensity, and stage of development only. At one point, metaphysical possibilities and tendencies existed; at another, hardened and definitive cultural facts were present, which inescapably began to shape the forms within which people lived.

It was not until the appearance of Francis Bacon and others in the late sixteenth and early seventeenth centuries that "science" triumphed and the idea of progress concomitantly became the unchallenged cultural philosophy of the West. The significance of the Baconian attitude was the formal demise of the tension (albeit ineffective) between Western arrogance and the Western sense of the supernatural. The scientific pursuit became a religion, and Western-Europeans were no longer embarrassed by their own lack of humility.

It is of value to bring attention to the critical relationship between Christian thought in its Western form and the pattern of European ecological behavior. Few are willing to admit or discuss the extent to which European Christianity is predicated on a world view which supports the exploitation of nature. The image with which we are usually presented is that of the life-and-death struggle between religion and science as representing two antithetical frames of mind. Actually, Christian thought provides a view of man, nature, and the universe which supports not only the ascendancy of science, but of the technical order, individualism, and relentless progress. Emphasis within this world view is placed on humanity's dominance over *all* other beings, which become "objects" in an "objectified" universe. There is no emphasis on an awe-inspiring God or cosmos. Being "made in God's image," given the European ethos, translates into "acting *as* God," recreating the universe. Humanity is separated from nature, which becomes "fodder" to be used in whatever way humanity sees fit. It is a concept of control and dominance, not of harmony, equilibrium, and respect. World views such as that of traditional Africa, in which spirit is recognized in all natural beings, are considered to be "superstitious," "ignorant," and are derogatorily labeled "animistic." European-Christian thought sets the tone for a rampant exploitation of nature as well as of people and their cultures.

Lynn White, Jr. (1969: 350), in an impressively perceptive article, remarks:

> The present disruption of the global environment is the product of a dynamic technology and science. . . . Their growth cannot be understood historically apart from distinctive attitudes toward nature which are deeply grounded in Christian dogma.

But this should not surprise us, for ethnologically the relationship between European Christianity and the idea of progress makes sense, since religion in any culture is to be understood as the sacralization of ideology. Hence, Christian thought facilitated the acceptance of a scientific world view, and in the centuries which followed the Baconian era's rationalistic epistemology was totally identified with rationalistic culture. The marriage argued for in Platonism was finally consummated.

By the late nineteenth century, the concept (of progress) had been largely assimilated to the values of a complex and expanding industrial order. Progress could now become a slogan to defend the course of technological innovation and economic rationalization and concentration [Williams, 1970: 469].

As we Africans became more "sold on" (and "sold into") white culture, another sacred cow joined forces with "civilization," "progress," and "Christianity" to convince us of the superiority of the Western-European way: "science." In the contemporary battlefield, in which minds and souls are the objectives and victims, this is still the term which holds us most in awe—*science*. The very word resounds with majesty, like *truth* and *knowledge*. For if nothing else is "neutral," certainly this must be. Like some great almighty and "objective" force, it carries us small humans along, into ever more progressive stages; it is not to be judged or questioned, just worshipped. But again, what is called science in the West has been determined, weighted, and directed by Western value, implicitly stating that value; and we, indeed, have accepted it as "pure." The ideology of progress has helped to make this possible.

Progress determined what was meaningful to the European and what lacked value—what was ethical and what was not. It became a frame of reference, and ideological base out of which other concepts were created and by which they were judged. It was a paramount criterion of suitability. It became linked totally with the scientific-technical and with the power relationships their development suggested. Progress became identified with scientific knowledge. Europeans had to control and use nature to their advantage.

After Bacon, the pursuit of science became morally self-justifying. It became morality itself. The mad scientist of the Western nightmare fantasy is simply acting out zealous loyalty to the Baconian-Western creed. Descartes,

becoming fanatically committed to this creed, took on the task of contributing an "invulnerable method" to the edifice which was being constructed. Notice the intensity with which he worked at severing "mind" from "body" in the *Meditations*. All such metaphysical manipulations contributed to the success of the progress ideology and the scientific world view. Both the Baconian attitude and Cartesian epistemology were intensifications and developments of possibilities already present in the matrix of the culture.

I have said that the idea of progress was created out of the Western ethos, encourages it, and is, therefore, ideally suited to the Western world view. Henryk Skolimowski (1974: 56–57) supports this point and says that "forces which significantly contributed to the formation of our concept of progress" are "the crusading spirit of medieval Christianity," "the white man's mission," "the expansive restlessness of the white man," and his "acquisitive instinct."

All ideologies must state choice in terms of necessity—what has been ideologically created in terms of what is given. The functioning of culture as a synthetic whole requires the commitment of people, and that commitment requires the conviction that one way of life is right for them, as opposed to having been chosen by them—even though they *mean* precisely the same thing. But only in the context of the Western-European ethos does it become necessary to create a category of thought and action ("scientific progress") which is said to be void of ideology and belief. Because only the European ethos makes the *imposition* of that belief on others paramount. By dehumanizing science, the Europeans seek to place themselves above other people who are not "scientific." They have convinced themselves that the character of their life and culture is not a result of ideological choice, but rather of universal human needs met by the principles of "science." In Western culture the phrase, "need for invention," is used normatively to impress others with the inevitability of Western-style development. The fact that *"Different Ideologies define the need for invention in different ways"* (Skolimowski, 1974: 70–71) is ignored. But the ideology of progress is inherently imperialistic and cannot admit of these other possibilities.

How is the concept of "modernity" itself related to the ruling ideology of the West? Progress, in combination with scientism, acts to encourage the use of the term *modern*. *Modern* is, indeed, so much identified with *Western* that it is difficult to see how it can be useful as a tool of analysis or description. Insofar as it means anything other than "that which presently exists," it has been tied to Western technology and the way of life which accompanies it. Even the term *contemporary* connotes for Western people a quality possessed by the most "advanced" evolutionary stage and level of progress. It is the particular kind of tyranny of the ideology of progress (its universalization and unidirectional character) in combination with the overwhelming success of the white man, "the conqueror," which makes the argument that Western forms are universal seem all the more plausible—in spite of that argument's inaccuracy.

In European history, the process of "the mechanization of the cosmos" (Skolimowski, 1974: 75) displayed development along a consistent theme. The Platonic emphasis, while not on the mechanical tool, mandated the use of "objectification" (separation of the "knowing self" from the "known object") as the essential "tool" of conceptual rationalism. The etiological and metaphysical relationship between objectification and "mechanization" is important. Intense objectification is a prerequisite for the despiritualization of the universe, and through it the Western cosmos was made ready for ever-increasing materialization until, indeed, there was no cosmos, no perception of cosmic order. Plato prepared the West for excessive development in a particular direction, paved the way for Bacon's

influence and for an obsessive commitment to the idea of progress in its materialistic emphasis. The Western idea of progress is indeed a part of its "rational" heritage.

As Pan-Africanists, one of our consistent and pressing concerns must be with the nature of Western culture and with its cultural imperialistic expression. The idea of progress is part of that expression. We must devote our energies to a critical discussion of such concepts from an African perspective. The idea of progress must be understood by us to be part of a mythological system used to create and sustain the symbols of whiteness and Westernness as valuable characteristics, and of blackness and Africanness as demeaning ones.

The critique from *within* Western culture is most often tenuous and weak, suffering from the same Eurocentrism it criticizes. Conventionally, the failings to Western-Europeans are universalized and made to be simply the ills of modern humanity. Acceptance of this interpretation is costly for us, for it leads away from, rather than toward, an *African* alternative.[1]

II. AN IDEOLOGY OF IMPERIALISM: CHRISTIANITY, PROGRESS, AND AFRICA

As concerns people of African descent, the ideology of progress has explained to white people why it was their duty to exploit, conquer, and control us and others different from them. It became an ideology of supremacy, a well-constructed mythology of superiority. The point is that the rationale for an oppressive technical order, the rational ordering of the universe, and the endeavor to destroy, dominate, and exploit people of African descent unite in a single ideological concept, the European ideology of progress.

The trappings of religious ideology were used very successfully against a genuinely spiritual people to convince them of their own inferiority,[2] and to rationalize their victimization. These, of course, were related endeavors. From the beginnings of the institutionalization of European Christianity ("Christianism"), the intimate connections between "Christianity", "Progress" and imperialistic behavior becomes visible. Christianity and progress meshed in a consistent ideological statement—"It behooves the 'civilized' to 'Christianize' the world"—one which becomes imperialistic when stated politically. It was Constantine's achievement to fully realize these implications. In 312 "A.D." he needed a new weapon in his struggle for the rule of the Roman Empire. He decided to use a cross, as it had appeared to him in a dream, inscribed "conquer by this":

> He looked upon himself as designated by God to rule the Roman world. And in return for this divine recognition he felt the obligation to promote the cause of Christianity in all possible ways. . . . Constantine saw in Christianity the religion which could and should provide a spiritual bond among his subjects as well as a moral basis for political loyalty to himself as the elect of God [Boak, 1955: 433].

No matter how good they make it sound, we should be able to see through such rationalization. It is an old story for us. The Christians divided the world into "Christians" and "heathens," "Christians" and "pagans." Heathens were (are) godless, irreligious people. By implication, then, Christians had a cornerstone on religion. Pagans were people of the countryside and backward. Christians were associated with the cities, and therefore with progress. In Western value terms, "country" is inferior and "city" is superior. Christianity brought with it the Western-European idea of progress, while at the same time reinforcing the archaic or nascent European self-image.

Christian ideology is teleological, providing a conceptual model peculiar to Western perception, based on a particular image of humanity (that of the white person). The Christian-Western interprets humans as beings who derive meaning from their ability to move toward a universal goal—at once "progressive" and "rational." Reinhold Niebuhr (1946: 24) proudly declares that "the idea of progress is possible only upon the ground of a Christian culture." And in Mbiti's view (1970: 128), African religion is "defeated" because it does not offer a conception of an abstract future and "glorious hope" of redemption and immortality, as is offered by Christianity. Being African, Mbiti should understand that for the African, immortality is achieved through association with the vitality of life.

European Christianity participates in European chauvinism. It emphasizes the "we/they" dichotomy on which Western-European nationalism (culturalism, racialism) depends. It provides images of Westerners and non-Westerners which mandate unlimited expansion of white, Western political control. The essence of the Judeo-Christian tradition is its assumption of theological and moral evolution leading to the superior and humanly proper conception of one God as the ultimate abstraction. The Christian mandate to impose this conception on other peoples represents the epitome of the Western ethos. Essential to this proselytizing mission is an invidious comparison in which non-Westerner in general and Africans in particular not only come out losers but are victimized as well. The "pagan," "heathen," "idolater," "polytheist" *has* no religion in terms of Western value, but is morally inferior, less than human. Whatever is done with the objective of making pagans "more human" (e.g., imposing religion on them) is justifiable.

Christian ideology provides moralistic and universalistic terms of disparagement for the peoples who are objects of Western imperialism, as well as moral justification for their subjugation and exploitation. Progressivism cannot easily be distinguished from Christian ideology. The pagan becomes not only nonreligious, but *pre*religious—backward, ignorant, lacking in the intellectual acumen to develop, reach, attain civilization (white, Western-European culture)—"primitive," "retrogressive," "retarded." The white, Western European at any point in history represents the "highest," "most superior" form of "man."

Here are exposed the mythological conceptions which provide ideological support for European dominance. They rest on a belief system which makes possible and supports imperialistic behavior. The ideology of progress help to form these conceptions. The imperialistic drive becomes "moral" in the context of this mythological system. The concept of the "cultural other" sanctions behavior toward those of us who become symbols of "nonhumanness." The concept of the cultural other is created to satisfy the Western-European ethos and is dialectically related to the white self-concept. The cultural other is black, bad, and nonhuman, the dialectical opposite of the Western self. That self is conceived of as superior—an image "explained" by the idea of progress mythology. This mythology provides a scale by which to judge superiority or inferiority, a criterion for superiority. The superior are the more rational, the smarter ones, the more moral, the ones who invent and discover everything of value. They "own" developed society. They are white. After using the ideology of progress to transform people of other cultures into savages, whites can make themselves responsible for the "welfare" of those savages— e.g. imperial control, dominance.

The ideology of progress allowed white people to speak with impunity of "civilized" and "superior" races in the nineteenth century, and later allowed them to speak of "developed," "advanced," "modern" nations. This part of the mythology helps to explain the "settler syndrome." White people are always justified in taking land from blacks and others who are not white. They, the whites, have the "expertise," the "drive," which allows them to make proper use of it; whereas these cultural others "waste" land, whites "develop" it. Colonialism in Africa, South-African apartheid, white dominance in Zimbabwe, European treatment of native Americans, Jewish settlers on the Gaza strip (to name only a few instances) are all part of *one* culture, *one* movement, *one* ideology exhibiting the attitude, "This place was nothing before *we*

came here." Acceptance of the ideology of progress makes this argument plausible. "Put the nonhumans in reserved, inarable areas, since they do not value the land anyway." This is indeed why white people the world over, no matter how "enlightened," find it difficult to totally condemn the white South-African regime. Clearly and simply, their presence in Africa ensures "progress" (or so says European mythology).

The Western self-image is unique. It requires a negative image of other people in order to be positively reinforced. It is, therefore, we might say, *dependent* on these negative images of others. The thought forms, institutions, ideological constructs which exist within the matrix of the culture must perform the task of creating positive images of the European self, and conversely, negative images of others. The European ethos derives pleasure from and seeks satisfaction in the superior/inferior relationship which translates into "justifiable" European dominance. Both Christian ideology and the ideology of progress perform this function for European culture. The African has long been a whipping boy, fulfilling the negative, devalued, and inferior part of this dichotomy. Africans were "heathens" and therefore fair game for proselytization. For godlike, white superiors to control them was to save them from the sin of "ignorance" and "blackness." It also meant bringing "civilization" to them, and therefore "progress." This was all that was needed to ideologically support a pattern of behavior so consistent, so terrifying, and so successful that it all but destroyed the positive African self-image.

Most Pan-Africanists and African ideologues have failed to effectively reconstruct a positive African self-image because they have either accepted European "Christianism" or the European mythology, and therefore definition of, progress (or, as is usually the case, a combination of both). Quite simply, if civilization represents progress, and civilization is defined by whites in terms of their values and self-image, then to want to progress is to want to be white. Conversely, in white terms, the opposite of civilization is "the primitive," or "that which we want to move away from." It is black, "that which we do not want to be." Any amount of praise bestowed on Africa *within* the conceptual framework stated above, will *only succeed in enhancing the white Western-European self-image, at the expense of a positive African self-image.* That is why it is a mistake to isolate certain aspects of African culture and history as representing the heights of civilization, *using the European definition of that term.* What are we really saying about ourselves when we do that?[3]

To progress, does one have to be white, Western, and European? Does being civilized mean acting like white people? Does being religious mean being Christian? Did the idea of brotherly love originate in the European tradition? Was it nurtured therein? If we reject aspects of our African heritage, let us be very clear about our reasons for doing so. These actions should not be based on our internalization of some abstract concept or mythological structure created by our enemies. Our myths must work for *us.* If we want to *progress,* let us be very specific about what we are progressing toward and why. Let us concretize our goals and not leave them vaguely defined in terms of the rhetoric of Western-European values. If you choose to be a "Christian" you will most certainly have to reject the European conceptualization of what

that means (that is, if you want to embrace your African heritage as well). Our ideals cannot be defined by what whites are. They must be defined in terms of African self-determination and a positive African self-image.

But if we are neither to emulate white behavior nor to adopt European conceptions, what theoretical models shall we use? (Are there any others?) *All cultures* are based on and create ideological constructs and mythological systems which provide the symbols which make them work. African metaphysical conceptions and the African world view are among the most profound. We should be about the business of rediscovery and reevaluation—*not* merely on a rhetorical level, but fundamentally and in relation to concrete and practical political goals. More and more, Europeans are becoming convinced of the limitations of their traditional conceptions. Sadly, we Africans, so anxious to imitate a dying culture, rush to give up breast-feeding because we want to be "civilized" and "sophisticated," while many European physicians are trying to convince mothers that breast-feeding is best for their babies and themselves. What irony! Must we wait until the white tells us that our culture has value in order to appreciate it?

The traditional African view of the universe is as a spiritual whole in which all beings are organically interrelated and interdependent. The cosmos is sacred and cannot be objectified. Nature is spirit, not to be exploited, and there is no obsession with changing the

TABLE 1 EUROPEAN MYTHOLOGY (IMPLICATIONS FOR THE AFRICAN HERITAGE)

Ideology	The Cultural Other		Behavior Dictated		White Self-image
Christianism	heathen: nonreligious, immoral	M U S	saved		Christian Saviour
Idea of Progress	backward	T	developed, advanced	B Y	"modern" man
		B			
Evolutionism	primitive	E	civilized		"civilized" man

natural order for the sake of change. Use without replenishment is sacrilegious because all beings exist in reciprocal relationship to one another; we cannot take without giving, and that is what the ritual of sacrifice symbolizes. Only profane or ordinary time is viewed in terms of simplistic lineal relationships, but within sacred, cyclical time the past, present, and future become one. This conception allows us to draw strength from our origins (and ancestors) in order to build, survive, and create. The mode of harmony (rather than control) which prevails does not preclude the ability to struggle when necessary. Spirit is primary, yet manifested in material being. This world view allows for depth of spirituality, belief, and humanism.

If we are to be developed, let us do the developing. And first we must decide what *development* means. Change and technology are necessary, but the *extent* to which they are needed must be determined in relation to the happiness, well-being, and self-determination of our people, not merely by imitation of the West. We cannot allow an obsessive, technical order to destroy our humanity—our Africanness.

CONCLUSION

Insofar as we continue to accept the rationalization of our victimization by assimilating European chauvinistic ideology and mythology, we have ourselves to blame. The rhetoric and semantics of "science" help to disguise the thrust of that mythology and make it more difficult to reject. It is critical, therefore, that we in Africana Studies devote more of our energies to revealing the mythological, ideological, and value aspects of concepts like the idea of progress, so that they can no longer

be used to enslave African people psychologically and ideologically.

Science and technology as used in European culture have been defined in the context of an "acquisitive, conquering, materialistic" (Skolimowski, 1974: 82) ideology, of which the ideology of white supremacy is a crucial ingredient. Neither science nor technology need be used in this way, so that the rejection of the European idea of progress by no means implies some sort of mystical escapism or retreat from the real problems and contingencies of nation-building which we face.

Progression toward an abstract goal should not become an ideology. It should *not* be an end in itself. *Progress* must be defined in terms of other objectives and goals which are more meaningful in a human and African context. Any commitment to reject European value and to repudiate European historical behavior must necessarily reject the ideology of progress, for its triumph has succeeded in dehumanizing the culture in which it was born. It inherently implies the inferiority of black being, and justifies Pan-African exploitation. When black people uncritically adopt the ideology of progress as it is here defined, they can become overseers on the plantation, tools of the white person used to control other Africans. Let us clearly understand that the syntax of the European idea of progress is the language of white nationalism and Western chauvinism. We have been successfully victimized in part because we have internalized alien concepts which define us negatively. If Black Studies is to be a viable and worthy endeavor, it must be devoted to the task of demystification. Unfortunately this is a long and difficult endeavor, and we have only scratched the surface.

Notes

1. For further theoretical and critical discussions of the progress ideology, see Juenger (1956), Aron (1968), Mumford (1963: especially 182–185), Diamond (1974: Introduction), Roszak (1973, an especially fine work, and 1972: Introduction), and Skolimowski (1974).

2. See Kofi Awoonor's (1975: ch. 2) sensitive discussion of the effects of missionary Christianism on the African self-image.

3. See Cook (1970: 155) for support of this point. Her entire article is relevant to the issues being raised here.

References

Aristides (1958) "To Rome," p. 40 in *History of Western Civilization: Selected Readings, Supplement.* Chicago: University of Chicago Press.

Aron, R. (1968) *Progress and Disillusion.* New York: Praeger.

Awoonor, K. (1975) *The Breast of the Earth.* Garden City, NY: Doubleday.

Bassett, E. O. (1927–1928) "Plato's theory of social progress." *International Journal of Ethics* 28: 476.

Beard, C. A. (1955) "Introduction," p. xxviii in J. B. Bury, *The Idea of Progress.* New York: Dover.

Blyden, E. W. (1967) *Christianity, Islam, and the Negro Race.* Edinburgh: Edinburgh University Press.

Boak, A. E. R. (1955) *A History of Rome to 565 A.D.* New York: Macmillan.

Bury, J. B. (1955) *The Idea of Progress.* New York: Dover.

Cook, A. (1970) "Black pride? some contradictions," in T. Cade (ed.) *The Black Woman.* New York: Signet.

Diamond, S. (1974) *In Search of the Primitive: A Critique of Civilization.* New Brunswick: Transaction Books.

Juenger, F. (1956) *The Failure of Technology.* Chicago: Henry Regnery.

Kovel, J. (1971) *White Racism: A Psychohistory.* New York: Vintage.

Lee, D. (1959) *Freedom and Culture.* Englewood Cliffs, NJ: Prentice-Hall.

Lovejoy, A. O. (1966) *The Great Chain of Being.* Cambridge, MA: Harvard University Press.

Lovejoy, A. O. and BOAS, G. (1965) *Primitivism and Related Ideas in Antiquity.* New York: Octagon.

MacLeod, W. (1968) *The Importance of Race in Civilization.* Los Angeles: Noontide Press.

Mbiti, J. S. (1970) *African Religions and Philosophies.* Garden City, NY: Doubleday.

Montagu, A. (1968) "The fallacy of the primitive," pp. 3–4 in *The Concept of the Primitive.* New York: Free Press.

Mumford, L. (1963) *Technics and Civilization.* New York: Harcourt Brace Jovanovich.

Neibuhr, R. (1946) *The Nature and Destiny of Man, Volume 1.* New York: Scribner.

Popper, K. (1966) *The Open Society and Its Enemies, Volume 1.* Princeton: Princeton University Press.

Roszak, T. [ed.] (1972) *Sources.* New York: Harper & Row.

Roszak, T. (1973) *Where the Wasteland Ends.* Garden City, NY: Doubleday.

Skolimowski, H. (1974) "The scientific world view and the illusions of progress." *Social Research* 41, 1: 56–57.

White, L., Jr. (1969) "The historical roots of our ecological crisis," in P. Shepard and D. McKinley (eds.) *The Subversive Science.* Boston: Houghton Mifflin.

Williams, R. (1970) *American Society: A Sociological Interpretation.* New York: Knopf.

Modern Falsification of History

Cheikh A. Diop

THE PROBLEM OF THE MOST monstrous falsification in the history of humanity by modern historians could not have been posed better than Volney did. No one could have been abler than he to render justice to the black race by recognizing its role as mankind's pioneer guide on the road to civilization. His conclusions should have ruled out the subsequent invention of a hypothetical white Pharaonic race that allegedly imported Egyptian civilization from Asia at the start of the historical period. In fact, that hypothesis is difficult to reconcile with the reality of the Sphinx, which is the image of a Pharaoh having the head of a Black. That image is there for all to see; it can hardly be discounted as an atypical document, nor relegated to the storeroom of a museum to remove it from the dangerous meditation of those susceptible of accepting factual evidence.

After Volney, another traveler, Domeny de Rienzi, early in the nineteenth century, reaches somewhat similar conclusions concerning the Egyptians: "It is true that back in the distant past, the dark red Hindu and Egyptian race dominated culturally the yellow and black races, and even our own white race then inhabiting western Asia. At that time our race was rather savage and sometimes tattooed, as I have seen it depicted on the tomb of Sesostris I in the valley of Biban-el-Moluk at Thebes, the city of the gods."[1]

As far as the dark red race is concerned, we shall see that it is simply a subgroup of the Black race as presented on the monuments of that time. In reality, there is no dark red race; only three well-defined races exist: the white, the black, and the yellow. The so-called intermediate races probably result solely from crossbreeding.[2]

. . . If Rienzi speaks of a dark red race, instead of a black race, this is because he could not possibly rid himself of the prejudices of his day. In any event, his observations on the condition of the white race, then savage and tattooed, while the "dark red" races were already civilized, should have precluded any attempt to explain the origin of Egyptian civilization as due to Whites. Champollion expanded with humiliation on the backward condition of the latter at a time when Egyptian civilization was already several millennia old.

In 1799 Bonaparte undertook his campaign in Egypt. Thanks to the Rosetta stone, hieroglyphics were deciphered in 1822 by Champollion the Younger, who died in 1832. He left as his "calling card" an Egyptian grammar and a series of letters to his brother, Champollion-Figeac, letters written during his visit to Egypt (1828–1829). These were published in 1833 by Champollion-Figeac. From then on the wall of the hieroglyphics was breached, unveiling surprising riches in their most minute details.

Egyptologists were dumbfounded with admiration for the past grandeur and perfection then discovered. They gradually recognized it as the most ancient civilization that had engendered all others. But, imperialism being what it is, it became increasingly "inadmissible" to continue to accept the theory—evident until then—of a Negro Egypt. The birth of Egyptology was thus marked by the need to destroy the memory of a Negro Egypt at any cost and in all minds. Henceforth, the common denominator of all the theses of the Egyptologists, their close relationship and profound affinity, can be characterized as a desperate attempt to refute that opinion. Almost all Egyptologists stress its falsity as a matter of course. Usually these attempted refutations take the following form:

Unable to detect any contradiction in the formal statements of the Ancients after an objective confrontation with total Egyptian reality, and consequently unable to disprove them, they either give them the silent treatment or reject them dogmatically and indignantly. They express regret that people as normal as the ancient Egyptians could have made so grievous an error and thus create so many difficulties and delicate problems for modern specialists. Next they try in vain to find a White origin for Egyptian civilization. They finally become mired down in their own contradictions, sliding over the difficulties of the problem after performing intellectual acrobatics as learned as they are unwarranted. They then repeat the initial dogma, judging that they have demonstrated to all honorable folk the White origin of Egyptian civilization.

It is the whole body of these theses that I propose to expose one after the other. In the interest of objectivity, I feel compelled to examine each point of view thoroughly, so as to be fair to the author involved and to enable the reader to become directly familiar with whatever contradictions and other facts I may point out.

Let us start with the oldest of these theses, that of Champollion the Younger, set forth in the thirteenth letter to his brother. It concerns bas-reliefs on the tomb of Sesostris I, also visited by Rienzi. These date back to the sixteenth century B.C. (Eighteenth Dynasty) and represent the races of man known to the Egyptians. This monument is the oldest complete ethnological document available. Here is what Champollion says about it:

Right in the valley of Biban-el-Moluk, we admired, like all previous visitors, the astonishing freshness of the paintings and the fine sculptures on several tombs. I had a copy made of the *peoples* represented on the bas-reliefs. At first I had thought, from copies of these bas-reliefs published in England, that these peoples of different races led by the god Horus holding his shepherd's staff, were indeed nations subject to the rule of the Pharaohs. A study of the legends informed me that this tableau has a more general meaning. It portrays the third hour of the day, when the sun is beginning to turn on its burning rays, warming all the inhabited countries of our hemisphere. According to the legend itself, they wished to represent the inhabitants of Egypt and those of foreign lands. Thus we have before our eyes the image of the various races of man known to the Egyptians and we learn at the same time the great geographical or ethnographical divisions established during that early epoch. Men led by Horus, the shepherd of the peoples, belong to four distinct families. *The first, the one closest to the god, has a dark red color,* a well-proportioned body, kind face, nose slightly aquiline, long braided hair, and is dressed in white. The legends designate this species as *Rôt-en-ne-Rôme,* the race of men par excellence, i.e., the Egyptians.

There can be no uncertainty about the racial identity of the man who comes next: he belongs to the Black race, designated under the general term *Nahasi.* The third presents a very different aspect; his skin color borders on yellow or tan; he has a strongly aquiline nose, thick, black pointed beard, and wears a short garment of varied colors; these are called *Namou.*

Finally, the last one is what we call flesh-colored, a white skin of the most delicate shade, a nose straight or slightly arched, blue eyes, blond or reddish beard, tall stature and very slender, clad in a hairy ox-skin, a veritable savage tattooed on various parts of his body; he is called *Tamhou.*

I hastened to seek the tableau corresponding to this one in the other royal tombs and, as a matter of fact, I found it in several. The variations I observed fully convinced me that they had tried to represent here the inhabitants of the four corners of the earth, according to the Egyptian system, namely: 1. the inhabitants of Egypt which, by itself, formed one part of the world . . .; 2. the inhabitants of Africa proper: Blacks; 3. Asians; 4. finally (and I am ashamed to say so, since our race is the last and the most savage in the series), Europeans who, in those remote epochs, frankly did not cut too fine a figure in the world. In this category we must include all blonds and white-skinned people living not only in Europe, but Asia as well, their starting point. This manner of viewing the tableau is all the more accurate because, on the other tombs, the same generic names reappear, always in the same order. We find

there *Egyptians and Africans represented in the same way*,* which could not be otherwise; but the Namou (the Asians) and the Tamhou (Europeans) present significant and curious variants. Instead of the Arab or the Jew, dressed simply and represented on one tomb, Asia's representatives on other tombs (those of Ramses II, etc.) are three individuals, tanned complexion, aquiline nose, black eyes, and thick beard, but clad in rare splendor. In one, they are evidently *Assyrians;* their costume, down to the smallest detail, is identical with that of personages engraved on Assyrian cylinders. In the other, are *Medes* or early inhabitants of some part of Persia. Their physiognomy and dress resemble, feature for feature, those found on monuments called *Persepolitan.* Thus, Asia was represented indiscriminately by any one of the peoples who inhabited it. *The same is true of our good old ancestors,* the Tamhou. Their attire is sometimes different; their heads are more or less hairy and adorned with various ornaments; their savage dress varies somewhat in form, but their white complexion, their eyes and beard all preserve the character of a race apart. I had this strange ethnographical series copied and colored. I certainly did not expect, on arriving at Biban-el-Moluk, to find sculptures that could serve as vignettes for the history of the primitive Europeans, if ever one has the courage to attempt it. Nevertheless, there is something flattering and consoling in seeing them, since they make us appreciate the progress we have subsequently achieved.[3]

For a very good reason, I have reproduced this extract as Champollion-Figeac published it, rather than take it from the "new edition" of the *Letters* published in 1867 by the son of Champollion the Younger (Chéronnet-Champollion). The originals were addressed to Champollion-Figeac; therefore his edition is more authentic.

What is the value of this document for information on the Egyptian race? By its antiquity,

---

*Italics Dr. Diop's.

it constitutes a major piece of evidence, which should have rendered all conjecture unnecessary. As early as that very ancient epoch, the Eighteenth Dynasty (between Abraham and Moses), the Egyptians habitually represented, in a manner that could not possibly be confused by the white and yellow races of Europe and Asia, the two groups of their own race: civilized Blacks of the valley, and Blacks from certain areas in the interior. The order in which the four races are consistently arranged in relation to the god Horus, confers upon it the character of a social hierarchy. As Champollion finally recognized, it also brushes aside any idea of a conventional portrayal that might blur the two distinct levels and place Horus on the same plane as the personages, whereas in reality he should rightfully be in front of them all.

It is typical for the Egyptians to be represented in a color officially called "dark red." Scientifically speaking, there really is no dark red race. The term was launched only to create confusion. There is no really black man in the exact sense of the word. The Negro's color in actual fact verges on brown; but it is impossible to apply an exact descriptive term to it, the more so because it varies from region to region. Thus it has been noted that Blacks in limestone areas are lighter than those elsewhere.

Consequently, it is very hard to capture the Negro's color in painting, and one settles for approximations. The color of the two men closest to the god Horus is merely the expression of two Negro shades. If today a Wolof portrayed a Bambara, a Mossi, a Yoruba, a Toucouleur, a Fang, a Mangbetu, or a Baulé, he would need as many if not more hues than there are on the two Blacks of the bas-relief. Would not the Wolof, Bambara, Mossi, Yoruba, Toucouleur, Fang, Mangbetu, and Baulé still be Negroes? This is how the color difference between the first two men on the bas-reliefs should be interpreted. On Egyptian bas-reliefs, it is impossible to find a single

painting which depicts Egyptians in a color different from those of such Negro peoples as the Bambara, Agni, Yoruba, Mossi, Fang, Batutsi, Toucouleur, etc.

If Egyptians were White, then all these forementioned Negro peoples and so many others in Africa are also Whites. Thus we reach the absurd conclusion that Blacks are basically Whites.

On these numerous bas-reliefs, we see that, under the Eighteenth Dynasty, all the specimens of the White race were placed behind the Blacks; in particular, the "blond beast" of Gobineau and the Nazis, a tattooed savage, dressed in animal skin, instead of being at the start of all civilization, was still essentially untouched by it and occupied the last echelon of humanity.

Champollion's conclusion is typical. After stating that these sculptures can serve as vignettes for the history of the early inhabitants of Europe, he adds, "if ever one has the courage to attempt it." Finally, after those comments, he presents his opinion on the Egyptian race:

> The first tribes that inhabited Egypt, that is, the Nile Valley between the Syene cataract and the sea, came from Abyssinia to Sennar. The ancient Egyptians belonged to a race quite similar to the Kennous or Barabras, present inhabitants of Nubia. In the Copts of Egypt, we do not find any of the characteristic features of the ancient Egyptian population. The Copts are the result of crossbreeding with all the nations that have successively dominated Egypt. It is wrong to seek in them the principal features of the old race.[4]

Here we see the first attempts to link the Egyptians with a stock different from that of the Copts, as confirmed by Volney's observations. The new origin that Champollion the Younger thought he discovered was not a happier choice; on both sides the difficulty remains the same. Fleeing from one Negro source (the Copts) only leads to another, equally Negro (Nubians and Abyssinians).

As a matter of fact, the Negro characters of the Ethiopian or Abyssinian race have been sufficiently affirmed by Herodotus and all the Ancients; there is no need to reopen the subject. The Nubians are the accepted ancestors of most African Blacks, to the point that the words Nubian and Negro are synonymous. Ethiopians and Copts are two Negro groups subsequently mixed with different white elements in various regions. Negroes of the Delta interbred gradually with Mediterranean Whites who continually filtered into Egypt. This formed the Coptic branch, composed mostly of stocky individuals inhabiting a rather swampy region. On the Negro Ethiopian substratum a White element was grafted, consisting of emigrants from Western Asia, whom we shall consider shortly. This mixture, in a plateau region, produced a more athletic type.

Despite this constant and very ancient crossbreeding, the Negro characteristics of the early Egyptian race have not yet disappeared; their skin color is still obviously black and quite different from that of a mixed breed with 50 percent white blood. In most cases, the color does not differ from that of other Black Africans. Thus we can understand why the Copts, and especially the Ethiopians, have features slightly deviant from those of Blacks free of any admixture with white races. It often happens that their hair is less frizzy. Although they have remained essentially prognathous, an effort has been made to present them both as pseudo-Whites, on the strength of their relatively fine features. They are pseudo-Whites when they are our contemporaries and when their ethnic reality prevents us from considering them as authentic Whites. But the skeletons of their forebears, found in the tombs, emerge completely whitened by the measurements of the anthropologists. We shall see how, thanks to these so-called scientific measurements, it is no longer possible to distinguish an Ethiopian, that is to say, a Negro skeleton, from that of a German. In

view of the gap separating those two races, we realize how gratuitous and confusing such measurements are.

Champollion's opinion on the Egyptian race was recorded in a memoir prepared for the Pasha of Egypt, to whom he delivered it in 1829.

Now let us see whether the research of the brother of Champollion the Younger, Father of Egyptology, has shed any light on the subject. This is how he introduces the topic:

> The opinion that the ancient population of Egypt belonged to the Negro African race, is an error long accepted as the truth. Since the Renaissance, travelers in the East, barely capable of fully appreciating the ideas provided by Egyptian monuments on this important question, have helped to spread that false notion and geographers have not failed to reproduce it, even in our day. A serious authority declared himself in favor of this view and popularized the error. Such was the effect of what the celebrated Volney published on the various races of men that he had observed in Egypt. In his *Voyage*, which is in all libraries, he reports that the Copts are descended from the ancient Egyptians; that the Copts have a bloated face, puffed up eyes, flat nose, and thick lips, like a mulatto; that they resemble the Sphinx of the Pyramids, a distinctly Negro head. He concludes that the ancient Egyptians were true Negroes of the same species as all indigenous Africans. To support his opinion, Volney invokes that of Herodotus who, apropos the Colchians, recalls that the Egyptians had black skin and woolly hair. Yet these two physical qualities do not suffice to characterize the Negro race and Volney's conclusion as to the Negro origin of the ancient Egyptian civilization is evidently forced and inadmissible.[5]

After indirectly expressing regret that Volney's book is found in all libraries, Champollion-Figeac advances, as a decisive argument to refute the thesis of that scholar and all his predecessors, that black skin and woolly hair "do not suffice to characterize the

Negro race." It is at the price of such alterations in basic definitions that it has been
possible to whiten the Egyptian race. Lo and
behold! It is no longer enough to be black
from head to foot and to have woolly hair to
be a Negro! One would imagine oneself in a
world where physical laws are turned upside
down; in any case, one is certainly far removed
from the analytical Cartesian mind. These,
however, were the definitions and alterations
of the initial data that were to become cornerstones on which "Egyptological science"
would be built.

The advent of Egyptology, through the
interpretation of scientific erudition, is thus
marked by the crude, conscious falsifications
that we have just indicated. That is why Egyptologists so carefully avoided discussing the origin
of the Egyptian race. To treat this question
today, we have been obliged to unearth old
texts by authors once famous, but later almost
anonymous. Champollion's alterations show
how hard it is to prove the contrary of reality
and still remain intelligible. Where we were
expecting a logical, objective refutation, we
meet the typical word, "inadmissible," which is
hardly synonymous with demonstration.

Champollion-Figeac continues:

> It is recognized today that the inhabitants
> of Africa belong to three races, quite dis-
> tinct from each other for all time: 1. Negroes
> proper, in Central and West Africa; 2. Kaffirs
> on the east coast, who have a less obtuse
> facial angle than Blacks and a high nose, but
> thick lips and woolly hair; 3. Moors, similar
> in stature, physiognomy and hair to the
> best-formed nations of Europe and western
> Asia, and differing only in skin color which
> is tanned by the climate. The ancient popu-
> lation of Egypt belonged to this latter race,
> that is, to the white race. To be convinced
> of this, we need only examine the human
> figures representing Egyptians on the
> monuments and above all the great number
> of mummies that have been opened. Except
> for the color of the skin, blackened by the
> hot climate, they are the same men as those

> of Europe and western Asia: frizzy, woolly
> hair is the true characteristic of the Negro
> race; the Egyptians, however, had long hair,
> identical with that of the white race of
> the West.[6]

Let us analyze Champollion-Figeac's statements, point by point. Contrary to his opinion,
the Kaffirs do not constitute a race: the word
Kaffir comes from an Arab word meaning
pagan, the opposite of Moslem. When the
Arabs entered Africa via Zanzibar, this was
the word that designated the populations they
found there who practiced a religion different
from their own. As for the Moors, they
descend directly from post-Islamic invaders
who, starting from Yemen, conquered Egypt,
North Africa, and Spain between the seventh
and fifteenth centuries. From Spain they fell
back on Africa. Thus, the Moors are basically
Arab Moslems whose installation in Africa is
quite recent. Numerous manuscripts preserved
by the principal Moorish families in Mauritania
today, manuscripts in which their genealogy
is minutely traced since their departure from
Yemen, testify to their origin. Moors are therefore a branch of those whom it is customary
to call Semites. What will be said about the
Semites later in this volume will dispel any
possibility of making them the creators of
Egyptian civilization. Like the Berbers, the
Moors are hostile to sculpture, whereas Egyptian culture attaches great importance to that
artistic manifestation. In the same chapter,
the racial admixture of the Semite will be
stressed; to this, rather than to climate, the
color of the Moors should be attributed. Moreover, whether it be a question of mummies
or living persons, there is no possible comparison between the skin color of the Moors,
even tanned by the sun, and the black, Negro
complexion of the Egyptians.

Yet to convince us, Champollion asks us
to examine the human figures representing
Egyptians on the monuments. The whole
reality of Egyptian art contradicts him.
Apparently he paid little attention to Volney's

typical remarks about the Sphinx, although he has just referred to them. On the strength of these same illustrations of which he speaks, we can say that in general, contrary to Champollion-Figeac, as one proceeds from Menes to the end of the Egyptian Empire and from the common people to the Pharaoh, passing in review the dignitaries of the Court and the high officials, it is impossible to find—and still keep a straight face—a single representative of the white race or of the Semitic race. It is impossible to find anyone there except Negroes of the same species as all indigenous Africans. The illustrations in this volume reproduce a series of monuments representing the various social strata of the Egyptian population, including especially the Pharaohs. And they forcibly lead us to note, strangely enough, that Egyptian art is often more Negro than Negro art proper. On examining these pictures, contrasting them one with the other, we wonder how they could possibly inspire the notion of a white Egyptian race.

Finally, after stating that black skin and woolly hair do not suffice to characterize the Negro race, Champollion-Figeac contradicts himself 36 lines later by writing, "frizzy, woolly hair is the true characteristic of the Negro race."[7] He goes so far as to say that the Egyptians had long hair and that, consequently, they belonged to the white race. It would appear from that text that the Egyptians were Whites with black skin and long hair. Though we may be unaware of the existence of such Whites, we can try to see how the author reached that conclusion. What has been said about Ethiopians and Copts shows that their hair may be less frizzy than that of other Negroes. Moreover, a black, completely black, race with long hair exists: the Dravidians, considered Negroes in India and Whites in Africa.

On the monuments the Egyptians are portrayed with artificial coiffures identical with those worn everywhere in Black Africa. We shall return to these in our analysis of Narmer's Tablet. The author concludes by describing the Egyptian's hair as being similar to that of Western Whites. We cannot accept that remark. Even when the hair of the Egyptian is less woolly than that of other Blacks, it is so thick and black as to rule out any possible comparison with the thin, light hair of Westerners. Lastly, it is curious to read about long-haired Egyptians when we know that Herodotus described their hair as woolly. Furthermore, as early as the Eleventh Dynasty, Blacks, Whites, and yellow-skinned men lived in Thebes, just as there are foreigners residing today in Paris.

> When the Theban wants a luxurious coffin for his mummy, a treetrunk is hollowed out and cut into human shape, with the cover representing the front of the corpse. The face is hidden under a yellow, white or black color. The choice of coloring shows that in Thebes, under the Eleventh Dynasty, yellow, white and black men lived, were accepted as fellow-citizens, and admitted into the Egyptian necropolis.[8]

We may wonder then why only long-haired mummies have survived and why the Negro mummies cited by Fontanes are neither shown nor mentioned. What has become of them? Statements by Herodotus leave no doubt about their existence. Were they considered foreign types irrelevant to the history of Egypt? Were they destroyed or hidden in the attics of museums? This is an extremely grave subject. Champollion-Figeac's text continues:

> Dr. Larrey investigated this problem in Egypt; he examined a large number of mummies, studied their skulls, recognized the principal characteristics, tried to identify them in the various races living in Egypt, and succeeded in doing so. The Abyssinians seemed to him to combine them all, except for the Black race. The Abyssinian has large eyes, an agreeable glance, . . . prominent cheekbones; the cheeks form a regular triangle with the prominent angles of the jawbone and mouth; the lips are thick without being everted as in Blacks; the teeth are

fine, just slightly protruding; finally, the complexion is merely copper-colored: such are the Abyssinians observed by Dr. Larrey and generally known as Berbers or Barabras, present-day inhabitants of Nubia.[9]

Champollion adds that Frédéric Cailliaud, who had seen the Barabras, describes them as "industrious, sober, with dry humor . . . their hair is half-frizzy, short and curly, or braided like the Ancient Egyptian's and slightly oiled." This description, once again, sounds familiar. Thick lips, teeth slightly protruding—in clearer terms, prognathism—semi-frizzy hair, copper skin, are basic characteristics of the Negro race.

It is curious to note here that Champollion-Figeac speaks of the Abyssinian complexion as being "merely copper-colored." Yet, two pages later in the same chapter, he refers as follows to the many color nuances of the Negro:

> Lengthy wars had brought Egypt into contact with the African interior; thus, one distinguishes on Egyptian monuments several species of Blacks, differing among themselves in the principal features that modern travelers have listed as dissimilarities either with respect to complexion, which makes Negroes black or copper-colored, or with respect to other features no less typical.[10]

This new contradiction from the same pen confirms what we have said about the two men placed next to the god Horus, namely, the Egyptian and the Negro. These two men belong to the same race; there is no more color difference between them than between a Bambara and a Wolof, who are both Negroes. The so-called "dark red" color of the first, the "merely copper-colored" of the Abyssinian, and the "copper color" of the Negro are one and the same. We note in passing that the author's description tarries over insignificant details, such as an "agreeable glance," and so on.

The confusion over the term Berber must be pointed out. This too is a word improperly applied to populations of the Nile Valley that have nothing in common with those properly called Berber and Tuareg. There are no Berber in Egypt. On the contrary, we know that North Africa was called Barbary, the Barbary States; this area is the only real habitat of the Berber. Subsequently, the term was incorrectly applied to other populations. The root of this word, used during Antiquity, was probably of Negro rather than Indo-European origin. In reality, it is an onomatopoeic repetition of the root *Ber*. This kind of intensification of a root is general in African languages, especially in Egyptian.

Moreover, the root *Bar*, in Wolof, means to speak rapidly, and *Bar-Bar* would designate a people that speaks an unknown language, therefore a foreign people. In Wolof, especially, an adjective indicating nationality is formed by doubling the root: for example, Djoloff-Djoloff, inhabitants of Djoloff.*

Reproducing the bas-relief of Biban-el-Moluk, according to the drawing of Champollion the Younger, Champollion-Figeac did not respect the colors of the original. He completely shaded in the Negro's body, to remind us of his color, but avoided doing the same for the Egyptian, whom he left untinted. This is perhaps one way to whiten the latter, but it is not consistent with the document.

Chérubini, Champollion's travel companion, utilizes the same Biban-el-Moluk document to characterize the Egyptian race. He insists beforehand on the anteriority of Ethiopia to Egypt and cites the unanimous opinion of the Ancients that Egypt is merely a colony of Ethiopia, that is, Sudanese Meroitic. Throughout Antiquity, the Meroitic Sudan was even believed to be the birthplace of humanity:

> The human race must have been considered there as spontaneous, having been born in the upper areas of Ethiopia where the two sources of life—heat and humidity—are ever present. It is also in this region that the

---

*Djoloff: one of the seven regions of Senegal.

first glimmerings of history reveal the origin of societies and the primitive home of civilization. In the earliest Antiquity, before the ordinary calculations of history, a social organization appears, fully structured, with its religion, laws and institutions. The Ethiopians boasted of having been the first to establish worship of the divinity and the use of sacrifices. There, too, the torch of science and the arts was probably first lighted. To this people we must attribute the origin of sculpture, the use of written symbols, in short, the start of all the developments that make up an advanced civilization.[11]

. . . They boasted of having preceded the other peoples on earth and about the real or relative superiority of their civilization while most societies were still in their infancy, and they seemed to justify their claims. No evidence attributed to any other source the beginnings of the Ethiopian family. On the contrary, a combination of very important facts tended to assign it a purely local origin at an early date.[12]

Ethiopia was considered as a country apart. From this more or less paradisiacal source, the beginnings of life, the origin of living beings, seemed to emanate. . . .

Except for some particulars furnished by the Father of History on those Ethiopians known as Macrobians, there was a rather hazy idea that Ethiopia produced men who surpassed the rest of humanity in height, beauty and longevity. One nevertheless recognized two great indigenous nations in Africa: the Libyans and the Ethiopians. The latter included the southernmost peoples of the Black race; they were thus distinguished from the Libyans who, occupying the north of Africa, were less tanned by the sun. Such is the information that the Ancients have provided. . . .[13]

It is reasonable to assume that nowhere else on earth could we find a civilization whose progress would seem more certain and present such unquestionable evidences of priority . . .

Consistent with the original monuments, the writings of scholarly philosophical Antiquity authentically testify to this anteriority.

In the history of primitive societies, perhaps no fact is supported by more complete and more decisive unanimity.[14]

Once again a modern reminds us that the Ancients, the very scientists and philosophers who have transmitted present-day civilization to us, from Herodotus to Diodorus, from Greece to Rome, unanimously recognized that they borrowed that civilization from Blacks on the banks of the Nile: Ethiopians or Egyptians. This text clearly indicates that the Ancients never questioned the Negro's role as an initiator of civilization.

Yet Chérubini nonetheless interprets the facts as he wishes. On the strength of the Biban-el-Moluk bas-relief, after Champollion the Younger and Champollion-Figeac, he supplies no new element concerning the Egyptian race, except a wrong interpretation of its complexion. He reports that if the *Rôt-en-ne-Rôme* (man par excellence) is depicted in a reddish-brown color (!), it is in order that he may be distinguished from the rest of mankind; thus it is a purely conventional choice:

In this classification of men of Antiquity that they themselves have bequeathed to us, we see the African population of the Nile Valley constituting by itself alone one of the four divisions of humanity and invariably occupying the first rank next to the god. This order is observed in several other places and does not appear to be due to chance. . . .

To make the distance separating them from other men more readily discernible, they attributed to themselves, as well as to the god incarnate in human form, a reddish-brown color perhaps a bit exaggerated or even somewhat conventional, which left no doubt about the originality of their race. They characterized it, moreover, on the monuments of their ancient civilization, by special features which would disclose an unquestionable African origin.[15]

The "reddish-brown" color that Champollion called "dark red" and which is quite simply "Negro colored," could not be a conventional color as Chérubini suggests. If it were, it would be the only conventional color on that bas-relief, whereas all the others are natural. There is no doubt about the reality of the white clothes worn by the first man, or the "flesh-colored bordering on yellow" complexion or tanned tint of the third, or the "white skin of the most delicate shade," the blond beard, and eyes of the fourth. Among so many natural colors, why should only one be conventional? Even less understandable is that it should be a Negro color rather than any other. According to Chérubini:

> The Egyptians carried their classification, or more precisely, their racial pride so far as to establish the most clear-cut distinction between themselves and their native African neighbors, such as the Negro populations with whom they were loath to be confused, and whom they placed in a separate category.[16]

The Egyptians went even further and represented their god in a Negro color, i.e., in their own image: coal black. The idea of anything conventional is thus to be rejected purely and simply. So, after Champollion-Figeac, it is Chérubini who sees the same Biban-el-Moluk document through blinkers. In this connection, we may appropriately repeat what was said earlier: By running away from the evidence of a Negro origin, the specialists fall into improbabilities and dead-end contradictions. Only such blindness can explain how Chérubini found it reasonable to resort to a conventional representation which contradicts his own opinion on the Egyptians and which they, too, would have found inadmissible. The author invokes the bas-reliefs of the Abu Simbel Temple (Lower Nubia), where prisoners captured by Sesostris after an expedition toward the south are portrayed. Chérubini reproduces these in an attempt to demonstrate that Egyptians and Blacks belonged to two different races:

> We see King Sesostris returning from an expedition against these Southerners; several captives precede his chariot. Farther on, the monarch offers the local gods two groups of prisoners evidently belonging to these savage tribes, an offering consecrated to the powerful protectors of civilization, who have smiled on the punishment of its enemies . . . these men, roped together, almost stark naked except for a panther skin about their loins, are distinguished by their color, some entirely black, others dark brown. The long facial angle, the top of the head quite flat, the combination of coarse features and a generally frail body, characterize a special type, a race on the lowest rung of the human ladder. . . . The hideous grimaces and contortions that contract the faces and limbs of these men reveal savage habits; the strangeness of that race, in which the moral sense seems almost nonexistent, would tend to place it on a plane more or less intermediate between man and brute. These facts are all the more striking when compared with the noble, serious attitude of their Egyptian captors.

> This impressive contrast demonstrates sufficiently that the ancient population on the banks of the Nile was as far removed from the species of southern Africans as from that of Asian peoples. It refutes the theories which, until now, had tried to establish a purely Negro origin for it.[17]

Disregarding Chérubini's pejorative epithets, let us try to see how the prisoners he describes differ ethnically from the Egyptian. His account does not contain a single scientific term likely to attract our attention. On the contrary, the excessive nature of the insults that form the greater part of this description—written by a representative of a people whose sense of proportion is reputed to be a national virtue—indicates the irritation of a person unable to establish what he would like to prove. He goes so far as to forget the objective order followed on the Biban-el-Moluk bas-relief, on which he dwells at length. In reality, if the Black race is "on the lowest rung of the human ladder," even so it stands ahead of Gobineau's "blond beast" on that bas-relief, in an order consistently observed on all the monuments. . . .

The color of these Abu Simbel prisoners refutes the claim that the Egyptians did not encounter Negroes until the Eighteenth Dynasty and depicted them in a color different from their own; this claim stems from the imagination, not from documentary evidence. . . . The facial "contortions" and "contractions" of the persons in the forefront, the disdainful resignation of those in back, suggest a high conception of dignity, rather than moral degradation, to the viewer strong enough to interpret them objectively. It has also been insinuated that if Sesostris—and Pharaohs in general—fought the Black populations of southern Ethiopia, it was because they did not belong to the same race. This is tantamount to saying that since Caesar undertook expeditions in Gaul, the Gauls and Romans did not belong to the same white race or that, if the Romans were white, the Gauls must have been yellow or black. The Negroes who lived in the African interior were at times very warlike and often raided Egyptian territory. . . . Sesostris' intervention, which the Abu Simbel bas-relief commemorates, fits into the context of these repressions. Furthermore, this expedition occurred during the later period of the Egyptian Empire (Eighteenth Dynasty). Thus it was that Shem's sons came to call their southern brothers: "wicked sons of Kush."[18]

But those most detested by the Egyptians were the Asian shepherds of all kinds, from the Semites to the Indo-Europeans. For these, no epithets were insulting enough. According to Manetho, they called them: "ignoble Asians." From *Hyk* = king, in the sacred language, and *Sos* = shepherd, in the popular tongue, came the name *Hyksos* to designate the invaders. The Egyptians also called them "accursed" and "pestiferous," "pillagers," "thieves . . ."[19] They also called the Scythians "Scheto's plague" (cf. Chérubini, p. 34).

The bas-reliefs left by the Egyptians and commemorating Pharaonic expeditions against those mobile plagues from Asia portray

personages whose ethnic contrast with the Egyptians is visible at first glance and without any possible doubt. . . .

Despite his efforts, Chérubini clearly failed dismally to destroy the thesis "which, until now, had tried to establish" the purely Negro origin of the Egyptians. By the incoherence and weakness of arguments he deems overwhelming, he confirmed that Negro origin better than anyone.

In *Les Egyptes,* a volume published around 1880, Marius Fontanes attacks the same problem:

Since the Egyptians always painted themselves red on their monuments, partisans of the "southern origin" had to point out a great number of interesting peculiarities likely to help solve the ethnographical problem. Near the Upper Nile today, among the Fulbe, whose skin is quite yellow, those whom contemporaries consider as belonging to a pure race, are rather red; the Bisharin are exactly of the same brick-red shade used on Egyptian monuments. To other ethnographers, these "red men" would probably be Ethiopians modified by time and climate, or perhaps Negroes who have reached the halfway mark in the evolution from blackness to whiteness. It has been noted that, in limestone areas, the Negro is less black than in granitic and plutonic regions. It has even been thought that the hue changed with the season. Thus, Nubians were former Blacks, but only in skin color, while their osteology has remained absolutely Negritic.

The Negroes represented on Pharaonic paintings, so clearly delineated by engravers and named Nahasou or Nahasiou in the hieroglyphics, are not related to the Ethiopians, the first people to come down into Egypt. Were the latter then attenuated Negroes, Nubians? Lepsius's canon* gives . . .

---

*Richard Lepsius, nineteenth-century German Egyptologist. For an explanation of his "canon of proportions", see p. 117 of his *Discoveries in Egypt, Ethiopia and the Peninsula of Sinai in the years 1842–1848*. London, 1852.

the proportions of the perfect Egyptian body; it has short arms and is Negroid or Negritian. From the anthropological point of view, the Egyptian comes after the Polynesians, Samoyeds, Europeans, and is immediately followed by African Negroes and Tasmanians. Besides, there is a scientific tendency to find in Africa, after excluding foreign influences, from the Mediterranean to the Cape, from the Atlantic to the Indian Ocean, nothing but Negroes or Negroids of various colors. The ancient Egyptians were Negroes, but Negroes to the last degree.[20]

Fontanes's view, which needs no comment, confirms once again the impossibility of escaping the reality of a Negro Egypt, however little one is willing to accept the facts. Limiting himself to objective measurements, Lepsius reaches the formal, major conclusion that the perfect Egyptian is Negritian. In other words, his bone structure is Negritic and that is why anthropologists say little about the osteology of the Egyptian.

Fontanes next considers the claim that Egypt was probably civilized by Berbers or Libyans coming from Europe, via the west:

If it is shown that civilization moved from north to south, from the Mediterranean to Ethiopia, it does not necessarily follow that this civilization is Asiatic; it can still be African, but coming from the west instead of the south. In that case, North African Berbers could have "civilized" Egypt.

A goodly number of present-day Berbers have an essentially Egyptian osteology. The ancient Berber was probably brown. It is to the influence of the European race, to the immigration of the "men of the north," that we should attribute this description of the Tamhou, Libyans of the Nineteenth Dynasty, "with pale face, white or russet, and blue eyes"! These Whites, hired as mercenaries by the Pharaohs, strongly hybridized the Egyptian and also the Libyan. It is therefore necessary to disregard this and go back to the brown Libyan, the true Berber, to find the people who probably civilized Ancient Egypt. This is a difficult task, for the African Berber has become increasingly rare in Algeria. In Egypt the Berber type is too mixed. According to this theory, the African Berber from the west, the brown Libyan, settled in the valley of the new Nile; but almost immediately, or shortly afterwards, an invasion of Europeans hybridized the North African Libyan. This Libyan mixed-blood "with white skin and blue eyes" may have modified the early Egyptian. By his European blood, this Egyptian could be related to the Indo-European race and to the Aryan.[21]

This thesis is the masterpiece of explanations based on pure imagination; it rests solely on emotion. I have cited it only for its ingenuity and determination to succeed at any cost in demonstrating that somehow or other the Egyptians had something Aryan about them. Aryan was the key word he had to reach. I have quoted the passage because, contrary to the previous theories, it is explicit. It is the fruit of unwarranted suppositions by specialists convinced that everything valuable in life can come only from their race and that, if we look carefully, we are sure to be able to prove it. An explanation is not complete until it attains that objective. From then on it matters little whether the demonstration is supported by facts. It is self-sufficient; its valid criterion merges with its aim.

We have already referred to the confused ideas about the Berber, so there is no need to return to that subject. The brown Libyan, the true Berber, prototype of the white race, is as real as the Sirens. Moreover, if one sticks to the archeological documents, North Africa has never been the starting point of a civilization. It began to count in history only with the Phoenician colony of Carthage, when Egyptian civilization was already several millennia old. If the Egyptian civilization had come from the south of Europe, as Maspero assumes, and if it had "slipped into the valley via the west or southwest,"[22] to introduce elements of civilization, we cannot understand why it should not have left traces in its birthplace or along its route. It is difficult to perceive how this white race, propagator of culture, could have left Europe, a milieu so conducive to the development of civilization, without having created it, how it crossed the rich plains of Tell and the enormous expanse that separates North Africa from Egypt—before that expanse became a desert—or why it would have crossed the swampy, unhealthy region of Lower Egypt, spanned the Nubian desert, climbed to the high plateaus of Ethiopia, traversed thousands and thousands of miles to create civilization on some caprice in so remote an area, so that this civilization might later return slowly down the Nile. Assuming this to be the case, how can we explain that a fraction of that race, which stayed at home, in an environment so favorable to the flowering of a civilization, remained unpolished until the centuries just preceding the Christian era?

Opposing the hypothesis that North Africa was inhabited from early Antiquity by a white race, we can invoke archeological and historical documents unanimously attesting that this region was always inhabited by Negroes. Furon tells us that, at the end of the Paleolithic, in the province of Constantine, Algeria, five layers of fossilized men were found. Among these, "several Negroids presenting affinities with the Nubians of Upper Egypt are mentioned."[23]

During the historical epoch, Latin documents testify to the existence of Blacks throughout North Africa: "Latin historians have given us information on the population, mostly names which mean little to us. We should remember that at least a sizable Negro population existed, Herodotus' Ethiopians, whose descendants were probably the Haratins of the Moroccan Upper Atlas."[24] This last quotation proves that, even now, there are Blacks in the area. The only prehistoric civilization which radiated from there, even in Egypt, was probably due to Blacks.

During that time, in Africa and the Orient, which are untouched by the Solutrean and Magdalenian, Aurignacian Negroids are directly continued by a civilization called Capsian, the center of which seems to have been Tunisia. From there it probably reached the rest of North Africa, Spain, Sicily, and southern Italy, on the one hand, competing with Caucasians and Mongoloids for the Mediterranean basin. On the other hand, Libya, Egypt, and Palestine. In short, its influence was felt to some extent in the Sahara, Central Africa, and even South Africa. This Capsian civilization leads to an artistic flowering comparable in its cave drawing to what the Magdalenian attained in Europe. But Capsian art tends to abstraction, to that schematic stylization of figures which was perhaps to become the origin of writing. True enough, everyone does not agree on the date of those drawings found in numerous places in the Sahara and even in Hoggar (Algeria). Some view them as the expression of a Capsian civilization, while others attribute them to a later period, in the Neolithic. . . .[25]

The appearance of the ram holding a disc or a sphere between his horns would link this Saharan civilization to predynastic Egyptian cults. This is Amon, the ram-god, whom we see created in the Sahara, then inhabited by shepherds leading their sheep and oxen to pasture where today there is only a desert.[26]

The examination of the documents therefore testifies, as early as prehistoric times, to the presence of a Negro civilization on the very spot claimed as the starting point of Egyptian civilization.

Previously, in the Capsian and Magdalenian, the facts noted would reveal instead an invasion of Eurasia by Blacks who supposedly conquered the world. So it is that Dumoulin de Laplante writes, referring to the beginning of the Pleistocene:

A migration of Hottentot-type Negroes, then leaving South and Central Africa, probably submerged North Africa, Algeria,

Tunisia, Egypt, and forcibly brought a new civilization—the Aurignacian—to Mediterranean Europe. These Bushmen were the first to engrave rough drawings on rocks and to carve limestone figurines representing monstrously fat pregnant women. Was it to these Africans that the inner Mediterranean basin owed the cult of fertility and of the Maternity Goddess? . . .

This hypothesis of an invasion by Negro Africans on both shores of the Mediterranean clashes, however, with several objections. Why, fleeing the sun, would these men have come to seek the cold? If we accept the assumption of a migration from Africa, it is not surprising to find Aurignacian tools in France, Italy, and Spain. But the presence of these tools in Bohemia, Germany, and Poland, makes the hypothesis more fragile. Finally, Aurignacian tools exist in Java, Siberia, and China. Either the Blacks had conquered the world or we would have to assume that there were "cultural exchanges" between the different peoples on the planet.[27]

Facing the same archeological evidence, Furon adopts the idea of a fertility cult, to avoid reaching the same conclusions.[28] To accept that theory is to favor the hypothesis of a Negro invasion, which, indeed, is supported by the Aurignacian skulls, the Grimaldi skeletons.

Africa's civilizing role, even in prehistoric times, is increasingly affirmed by the most distinguished scholars: "Moreover," writes Abbé Breuil, "it seems more and more probable that, even in the age-old days of ancient pebble tools, Africa not only knew stages of primitive civilization comparable to those of Europe and Asia Minor, but was perhaps the source of several such civilizations, whose swarms conquered those classic lands toward the North."[29] The opinion of that great scholar goes even further. It seems increasingly evident that humanity was born in Africa. In fact, the most important stock of human bones found up to now has been in South Africa. Although not the most extensively excavated location, it is the only place

in the world where the bones found allow us to reconstitute the genealogical tree of mankind uninterruptedly from its beginnings until today.

Although it is not in the field of archeology, I shall first speak about the problem of the origin of the human type. Thanks to the finds of Dr. Raymond Dart in Taung and Makapan, and to those of Dr. Robert Broom in Sterkfontein, Kromdraai, and Swartkrans, great progress has been made in that country. Before man, two-legged anthropoids of many forms were there, but increasingly developing hominian traits, so much so that we can begin to believe that the human type was created there. The attention of all the specialists is more and more attracted to these magnificent discoveries which multiply almost every month.[30]

Practically everyone agrees that until the fourth glacial epoch, flat-nosed Negroids were the only humans. A South African scientist has recently declared that the first men were black, strongly pigmented, according to the proofs at his disposal. It was probably not until the fourth glaciation, which lasted 100,000 years, that the differentiation of the Negroid race into distinct races occurred, following a long period of adaptation by the fraction isolated and imprisoned by the ice: narrowing of the nostrils, depigmentation of the skin and of the pupils of the eyes.

A single fact then remains vouched for by the documents in the "Libyan" thesis (Aryan, cited by Fontanes): that is the utilization of Whites, blue-eyed, tattooed blonds, as mercenaries by the Negro Pharaohs. Those tribes, called Libyans, were savage hordes in the western part of the Delta, where their presence, historically, is not recognized until the Eighteenth Dynasty. The Egyptians, who always considered them as veritable savages, took care not to be confused with them. At most, they condescended to use them as mercenaries. They never stopped holding them in check outside their borders by constant expeditions. Not until the low epoch was Egypt gradually permeated by domesticated Libyans who settled in the Delta area.

Herodotus' description shows that, until the end of Egyptian history, the Libyans remained on the lowest rung of civilization. The word "civilized," however broadly defined, could not be applied to them. Concerning the Libyan tribe of the Adrymachidae, the Father of History wrote: "Their women wear on each leg a ring made of bronze; they let their hair grow long and when they catch vermin on their person, bite it and throw it away."[31] Consequently, we may well be puzzled by the attempts to attribute Egyptian civilization to the Libyans.

As a result of this hypothesis, efforts have been made to relate the Berber and Egyptian languages by claiming that the Berber is the descendant of the Libyan. But Berber is a strange tongue that can be related to all kinds of languages:

> On the one hand, similarities have been noted between Berber, Gaelic, Celtic, and Cymric. But the Berber use as many Egyptian as African words and, depending on one's point of view, the basis of their language becomes Indo-European, Asian, or African. The Libyan languages are, in fact, African. Through these languages the Ligurians and Siculans, on arriving in Europe from North Africa, probably imported an African tongue, of which Basque could be one example.[32]

The same applies to Berber grammar. Specialists in Berber are careful not to insist on the relationship between Berber and Egyptian. Professor André Basset, for example, felt that more convincing facts should be presented before he could accept the Hamitic-Semitic hypothesis (Berber-Egyptian kinship, in particular). Both form the feminine by adding *t* to the noun, but the same is true of Arabic. Given what is known about the Arab and Berber peoples, we can wonder with Amélineau (*Prolégomènes*) why the influence should not be assumed to come from the opposite direction,

which would conform to the historical relationship between those two peoples.

That is not the whole story. Careful search reveals that German feminine nouns also end in *t* and *st*. Should we consider that Berbers were influenced by Germans or the reverse? This hypothesis could not be rejected *a priori,* for German tribes in the fifth century overran North Africa via Spain, and established an empire that they ruled for 400 years.[33] After that conquest, the Vandals who remained there mixed with the population. Only one segment, led by Genseric, tried unsuccessfully to conquer Rome by crossing through Sicily, and probably returned to North Africa. Furthermore, the plural of 50 percent of Berber nouns is formed by adding *en,* as is the case with feminine nouns in German, while 40 percent form their plural in *a,* like neuter nouns in Latin.[34]

Since we know that the Vandals conquered the country from the Romans, why should we not be more inclined to seek explanations for the Berbers in that direction, both linguistically and in physical appearance: blond hair, blue eyes, etc.? But no! Disregarding all these facts, historians decree that there was no Vandal influence and that it would be impossible to attribute anything in Barbary to their occupation.

However barbarous they were, however imperfect their administration, we cannot believe, in view of their number and their position as conquerors, that they spontaneously abandoned their language to adopt that of the Berbers; no Latin text indicates this. Usually, social relations are much more complex and that complexity is reflected in linguistics. Even when a language disappears, it reacts on the victorious tongue by transforming it and the latter no longer remains exactly what it was before. Thus, it is hard to understand how modern Berber can be free from any Vandal influence. Even harder to understand is that the modern Berber is not a descendant of the Vandals, especially when he has blue eyes and blond hair.

Ibn Khaldun's treatise on the Berber is merely a series of undocumented quotations.[35] The fact that there are no Berber in Egypt, except imaginary ones, that there are scarcely any in Tunisia, and that their number increases from east to west to reach its maximum in Morocco, seems to confirm the hypothesis of a Vandal origin. Historians pay little attention to these facts because it is absolutely necessary to make the Berber ancient enough to justify Egyptian civilization. Yet the 20 Berber sentences found in Arab texts scarcely date back to the twelfth century, whereas "Tifinagh" writing and the still undeciphered symbols called "Libyan" seem due to the influence of the indigenous element of the Negroid Phoenician colony of Carthage, prior to the arrival of the Vandals.

To recapitulate, the stratification of the North African population, from prehistoric times to our day, would be as follows:

Negroes and Cro-Magnons (a race
  extinct for 10,000 years);
Negroes in the Capsian;
Negroes during the Phoenician epoch;
Indo-Europeans, starting in 1500 B.C.
  and probably mixed with Negroes;
Negroes at the time of the Romans, with
  a large percentage of mixed-bloods;
Vandals; and
Arabs.

What then is more natural than that the basis of Berber vocabulary should be in turn Indo-European, Semitic, or African, depending on one's point of view?

Continuing with the development of Egyptology, we reach Maspero who, in the first chapter of his *Histoire ancienne des peuples de l'Orient*, describes the origins of the Egyptians:

The Egyptians seem quite early to have lost the memory of their beginnings. Did they come from Central Africa or from the interior of Asia? According to the almost unanimous testimony of the ancient

historians, they belonged to an African race which, first established in Ethiopia on the Middle Nile, gradually came down toward the sea, following the course of the river. To demonstrate this, one relied on the evident analogies between the customs and religion of the kingdom of Meroë and the customs and religion of the Egyptians proper. Today we know beyond the shadow of a doubt that Ethiopia, at least the Ethiopia known by the Greeks, far from having colonized Egypt, was itself colonized by Egypt, starting with the Twelfth Dynasty, and was for centuries included in the kingdom of the Pharaohs.[36]

Before continuing with Maspero's thesis, we should note what seems already to have been altered in those few introductory sentences. It is unlikely that the Egyptians ever forgot their origin. Maspero apparently confuses two distinct notions: the primitive birthplace from which a people started and the ethnic origin responsible for the color of the race. The Egyptians never forgot the latter, any more than they forgot the former.[37] It is expressed in all their art, throughout all their literature, in all their cultural manifestations, in their traditions and language. So much so that even their country was designated—by analogy with their own color, not by analogy with the color of the soil—by the name *Kemit,* which coincides with Ham (Cham), Biblical ancestor of Blacks. To say that *Kemit* refers to the color of the Egyptian earth, rather than designating the country through the color of the race, could inspire similar reasoning to explain the present-day expressions: "Black Africa" and "White Africa."

Maspero refers to the unanimous testimony of ancient historians on the Egyptian race, but he intentionally omits their precision. What we already know about the testimony of the Ancients proves that they did not use the vague term "African race." From Herodotus to Diodorus, whom Maspero quotes, whenever they mentioned the Egyptian people, they specified that a Negro race was involved.

Here we can trace the evolution of the gradual alteration of facts in textbooks that will mold the opinion of high school and university students. This is all the more serious because the great mass of knowledge to be acquired, in the modern world, leaves the younger generation, with the exception of professionals, no time to consult original sources and to appreciate the gap between the truth and what they have been taught. On the contrary, a certain tendency to laziness encourages them to be satisfied with the textbooks and to accept stereotyped notions of "infallible authority" from them, as if from a catechism. If we applied Maspero's reasoning to refute the ideas of Diodorus on Ethiopia's Antiquity, we would be able to conclude that, since Napoleon conquered and annexed Italy in the nineteenth century, Rome never civilized Gaul—which would be an obvious historical error.

"Moreover, the Bible states that Mesraim, son of Ham, brother of Kush and of Canaan, came from Mesopotamia to settle, along with his children, on the banks of the Nile."[38] Maspero fails to add that Ham, Canaan, and Kush are Negroes, according to that same Bible he is quoting. This means once again that Egypt (Ham, Mesraim), Ethiopia (Kush), Palestine and Phoenicia before the Jews and Syrians (Canaan), Arabia Felix before the Arabs (Pout, Hevila, Saba), were all occupied by Negroes who had created civilizations thousands of years old in those regions and had maintained family relationships. But then he continues:

Loudim, the eldest among them, personifies the Egyptian proper, the Rotou or Romitou of the hieroglyphic inscriptions. Anamim represents the great tribe of the Anu, who founded On of the north (Heliopolis) and On of the south (Hermonthis) in prehistoric times.

Lehabim is the Libyan people living west of the Nile, Naphtouhim settled in the Delta, south of Memphis; finally, Pathrousim (Patorosi, land of the south)

inhabits present-day Said, between Memphis and the first cataract.

This tradition which brings the Egyptians from Asia, through the Isthmus of Suez was not unknown to classical authors. Pliny the Elder attributes the founding of Heliopolis to Arabs; but it was never so popular as the opinion that they came from the high plateaus of Ethiopia.[39]

This identification* is more or less unfounded. It becomes contradictory when it links Libyans, said to have blue eyes and blond hair, with Lehabim, son of Mesraim, both of them Negroes. Another contradiction: Maspero seems at times to accept the theory of an Asiatic origin for the Egyptians and recalls the opinion of Pliny the Elder, who attributes the founding of Heliopolis to Arabs. In the same text, Maspero credits the settlement of that city to the Anu, whom he identifies with Anamim, son of Mesraim, a Negro. Our comments on the Arabs in a later chapter will eliminate any possibility of placing them at the founding of Heliopolis, especially if it occurred in "prehistoric" times, as the author affirms. We can see why Pliny's opinion did not enjoy the popularity among the Ancients that Maspero would have wished. To return to Maspero's account:

In our day the origin and ethnographic affinities of the population have inspired lengthy debate. First, the seventeenth- and eighteenth-century travelers, misled by the appearance of certain mongrelized Copts, certified that their predecessors in the Pharaonic age had a puffed up face, bug eyes, flat nose, fleshy lips. And that they presented certain characteristic features of the Negro race. This error, common at the start of the century, vanished once and for all as soon as the French Commission had published its great work.[40]

---

*Borrowed by Maspero from Rougé's *Recherches sur les monuments qu'on peut attribuer aux six premières dynasties de Manéthon.*

Anyone reading that statement without first consulting Volney's testimony and explanatory note on climatic effects on racial appearance . . . might easily be persuaded that those travelers in centuries past could have let themselves be easily deceived by appearances. Bearing in mind what has been said about the gradual infiltration of Whites into Egypt—especially during the low epoch—in the Delta, if there was mongrelization, it could only have resulted in whitening the population, not in any Negrification that would make former Whites unrecognizable by unprejudiced observers. Let us see how, if we are to believe Maspero, that "common error" vanished once and for all after the publication of the "great work" by the French Commission:

On examining innumerable reproductions of statues and bas-reliefs, we recognized that the people represented on the monuments, instead of presenting peculiarities and the general appearance of the Negro, really resembled the fine white races of Europe and Western Asia. Today, after a century of research and excavation, we no longer find it difficult to imagine, I shall not say Psammetichus and Sesostris, but Cheops, who helped to build the Pyramids. It suffices to enter a museum and examine the old-style statues assembled there. At first glance, we feel that the artist has sought to reproduce an exact likeness, in the accurate portrayal of head and limbs. Then, brushing aside the nuances proper to each individual, we easily detect the general character and principal types of the race. One of them, thick-set and heavy, corresponds quite well to one of the prevalent types among the modern fellahs. Another, depicting members of the upper class, shows us a man tall and slender, with broad, muscular shoulders, well-developed chest, sinewy arms, small hands, slim hips, thin legs. The anatomical details of his knee and calf muscle stand out, as is the case with most people who walk a lot. His feet are long, narrow, flattened at the end by habitually walking without shoes. His head, often too heavy for his body,

expresses kindness and instinctive sadness. His brow is square, perhaps somewhat low; his nose short and fleshy; his eyes are large and opened wide; his cheeks round; his lips thick but not everted; his mouth, stretched a bit too far, retains a resigned and almost painful smile. These features, common to most of the statues of the Old and Middle Empire, persist through all the epochs. The monuments of the Eighteenth Dynasty, so inferior in artistic beauty to those of the old dynasties, transmit the primitive type without appreciable alteration. Today, although the upper classes have been disfigured by repeated miscegenation with the foreigner, ordinary peasants almost everywhere have retained the appearance of their ancestors. Any fellah can contemplate with astonishment the statues of Chephren or the colossi of Sanuasrit transporting across Cairo, after more than 4,000 years of existence, the physiognomy of those old Pharaohs.[41]

Such is the hub of Maspero's demonstration. We have not omitted a single word. What does it prove? What does the "great work" teach us? The author informs us that Egyptology is already a very old science; for a century specialists have excavated and searched; now we know the prototype of the ancient Egyptian down to the most minor ethnic detail. The artist has depicted his "exact likeness." Thanks to this realistic art, we can reconstitute ethnically the members of the upper class. According to Maspero's observations, they had a "nose short and fleshy," a "mouth stretched a bit too far," "thick lips," "large eyes opened wide," "round cheeks," a brow "perhaps somewhat low," "broad, muscular shoulders," "small hands," "slim hips," "thin legs." These common features, perpetuated throughout the Old and Middle Kingdoms, "instead of presenting peculiarities and the general appearance of the Negro, really resembled the fine white races of Europe and Western Asia." That conclusion needs no commentary.

After so solemn a confirmation of the Negro origin by an author whose intent was to destroy it, we see once again the impossibility of proving the opposite of the truth. Gaston Maspero, who became in 1889 the Director of the Cairo Museum, was a scholar to whom we are indebted for several translations of Egyptian texts. He had the technical preparation necessary for establishing all that was demonstrable. His failure, despite that knowledge, like the failure of scholars who tackled this problem before or after him, constitutes, as it were, the most solid, if unintentional, proof of the Negro origin.

Next we come to the thesis of Abbé Emile Amélineau (1850–1916), a great Egyptologist seldom mentioned. He excavated at Om El'Gaab, near Abydos, and discovered a royal necropolis where he was able to identify the names of 16 kings more ancient perhaps than Menes. He found tombs of four kings: Ka, Den, the Serpent King Djet (whose stela is at the Louvre), and another whose name has not been deciphered. As Amélineau reports, attempts have been made to include these monarchs in the historical period: "At the meeting of the Academy of Inscriptions and Belles-Lettres, Mr. Maspero tried to place these kings in the Twelfth Dynasty . . . then . . . he attributed them to the Eighteenth . . . next to the Fifth . . . then to the Fourth. . . ."[42] After refuting his detractors, Amélineau concludes: "Those are reasons which seem to me not to deserve scorn, but rather to merit serious consideration by scholars of good will, for the others do not count in my opinion."[43]

To Amélineau we owe the discovery of Osiris' tomb at Abydos, thanks to which Osiris could no longer be considered a mythical hero but an historic personage, an initial ancestor of the Pharaohs, a Black ancestor, as was his sister, Isis. Thus we can understand why the Egyptians always painted their gods black as coal, in the image of their race, from the beginning to the end of their history. It would be paradoxical and quite incomprehensible for a white people never to have painted its gods white, but to choose, on the

contrary, to depict its most sacred beings in the black color of Isis and Osiris on Egyptian monuments. This fact reveals one of the contradictions of the moderns who assert dogmatically that the White race created Egyptian civilization with an enslaved Black race living by its side. The choice of the slaves' color, rather than that of the masters and civilizers, to represent the deities, is, to say the least, inadmissible and should shock a logical, objective mind. . . .

So it is that Amélineau, after his tremendous finds and his in-depth study of Egyptian society, reaches the following conclusion of major importance for the history of mankind:

> From various Egyptian legends, I have been able to conclude that the populations settled in the Nile Valley were Negroes, since the goddess Isis was said to have been a reddish-black woman. In other words, as I have explained, her complexion is *café au lait* (coffee with milk), the same as that of certain other Blacks whose skin seems to cast metallic reflections of copper.[44]

Amélineau designates the first Black race to occupy Egypt by the name *Anu*. He shows that it came slowly down the Nile and founded the cities of Esneh, Erment, Qouch, and Heliopolis, for, as he says:

> All those cities have the characteristic symbol which serves to denote the name *Anu*.[45]
> It is also in an ethnic sense that we must read the term *Anu* applied to Osiris. As a matter of fact, in a chapter introducing hymns in honor of Ra and containing Chapter XV of *The Book of the Dead*, we read: "Hail to thee, O God Ani in the mountainous land of Antem! O great God, falcon of the double solar mountain!"

If Osiris was of Nubian origin, although born at Thebes, it would be easy to understand why the struggle between Set and Horus took place in Nubia. In any case, it is striking that the goddess Isis, according to the legend, has precisely the same skin color that Nubians always have, and that the god Osiris has what seems to me an ethnic epithet indicating his Nubian origin. Apparently this observation has never before been made.[46]

If we accept the evidence of their own creations, *The Book of The Dead* among others, these Anu, whom Maspero tried to transform into Arabs . . . appear essentially as Blacks. In support of Amélineau's theory, it may be pointed out that *An* means man (in Diola). Thus *Anu* originally may have meant men. . . .

According to Amélineau, this Black race, the Anu, probably created in prehistoric times all the elements of Egyptian civilization which persist without significant change throughout its long existence. These Blacks were probably the first to practice agriculture, to irrigate the valley of the Nile, build dams, invent sciences, arts, writing, the calendar. They created the cosmogony contained in *The Book of the Dead,* texts which leave no doubt about the Negroness of the race that conceived the ideas.

> These Anu . . . were an agricultural people, raising cattle on a large scale along the Nile, shutting themselves up in walled cities for defensive purposes. To this people we can attribute, without fear of error, the most ancient Egyptian books, *The Book of the Dead* and the *Texts of the Pyramids,* consequently, all the myths or religious teachings. I would add almost all the philosophical systems then known and still called Egyptian. They evidently knew the crafts necessary for any civilization and were familiar with the tools those trades required. They knew how to use metals, at least elementary metals. They made the earliest attempts at writing, for the whole Egyptian tradition attributes this art to Thoth, the great Hermes, an Anu like Osiris, who is called the Onian in Chapter XV of *The Book of the Dead* and in the *Texts of the Pyramids.* Certainly the people already knew the principal arts; it left proof of this in the architecture of the tombs at Abydos, especially the tomb of Osiris, and in those sepulchers objects have been found bearing the unmistakable stamp of their origin— such as carved ivory, or the little head of a

Nubian girl found in a tomb near that of Osiris, or the small wooden or ivory receptacles in the form of a feline head—all documents published in the first volume of my *Fouilles d'Abydos.*[47]

Formulating his theory, Amélineau continues:

> The conclusion to be drawn from these considerations is that the conquered Anu people guided its conquerors at least along some of the paths to civilization and the arts. This conclusion, as can readily be seen, is most important for the history of human civilization and the history of religion. It clearly follows from what has been stated earlier: Egyptian civilization is not of Asiatic, but of African origin, of Negroid origin, however paradoxical this may seem. We are not accustomed, in fact, to endow the Black or related races with too much intelligence, or even with enough intelligence to make the first discoveries necessary for civilization. Yet, there is not a single tribe inhabiting the African interior that has not possessed and does not still possess at least one of those first discoveries.[48]

Amélineau supposes that a Negro Egypt, already civilized by the Anu, may have been invaded by a coarse white race from the African interior. Gradually conquering the valley as far as Lower Egypt, this uncultivated white race was probably civilized by the Black Anu, large numbers of whom it nonetheless destroyed. The author bases this theory on an analysis of scenes depicted on Narmer's Tablet, discovered at Hierakonpolis by James Edward Quibbell (1867–1935). Current opinion unanimously recognizes that the prisoners portrayed on that tablet, with their aquiline noses, represent Asian invaders conquered and punished by the Pharaoh who, in that remote epoch, had his capital in Upper Egypt.

This interpretation is confirmed by the fact that the persons walking ahead of the Pharaoh and belonging to his victorious army are Nubians, wearing Nubian insignia, such as the symbol of the Jackal and that of the Sparrow-hawk, which we would call Nubian totems. Besides, archeological data do not support the hypothesis of a white race originating in the heart of Africa.

The ox-tail carried by the Pharaoh on this tablet, and that Egyptian Pharaohs and priests always carried, is still borne at ceremonies and official functions by Nigerian religious leaders. The same is true of the garment worn by the Pharaoh; the amulet-filled sachet on his chest is always present throughout Egyptian history. It is found on the chest of any Negro chief who holds a responsible position; in Wolof, it is called *dakk*.

The servant is holding the Pharaoh's sandals, identical with the Negroes' *voganti*. Walking behind the king and carrying a kettle, he has the typical attitude of the modern Negro servant, or *bek-neg* (compare with *bak*, which means servant in Egyptian). The fact that the king has taken off his sandals suggests that he is about to perform a sacrifice in a holy place, and that he must first purify his limbs with the water in the kettle. The Egyptians are known to have practiced ablutions thousands of years before the advent of Islam. Thus, Narmer's Tablet probably portrays a ritual sacrificial scene after a victory. Similar human sacrifices were still practiced in Black Africa until very recent times; in Dahomey, for example.

Above the victim, the scene depicting Horus holding what seems to be a cord passing through the nostrils of an amputated head, perhaps symbolizes these very lives sacrificed to the god, escaping through the nose of the victims and being accepted by Horus. This idea conforms to the Negro belief that life escapes through the nostrils. *Life* and *nose* are synonyms in Wolof and often used interchangeably.

What is the racial identity of the persons represented on this side of the tablet, which I consider the front rather than the back, as is generally thought? I contend that they all belong to the same Black race. The king has thick lips, even everted. His profile cannot conceal the fact that his nose is fleshy. This is also true of all the persons on this side, even the captives in the scene underneath, who are running away. The latter, like the victims about to be immolated, have artificial hair, arranged in layers or tiers, a style still seen in Black Africa. A similar hair-do, worn by girls, is called *djimbi;* slightly modified and worn by married women, it is called the *djéré,* which disappeared from the Senegalese scene some 15 years ago. Quite recently, Islam has caused the men to discontinue the custom. Such hair-dos are no longer seen except among the non-Islamic Serer prior to circumcision, and among the Peul. A special form of these coiffures is called *Ndjumbal*. The king's hair and that of his servant is hidden by their bonnets; in Egypt, the use of such wigs was popular with all social classes. The king's bonnet is still worn in Senegal by those about to be circumcized, although this usage tends to disappear under the influence of Islam. It is made by sewing together two elliptical pieces of white cloth, with one end left open for the head to pass through. A bamboo frame gives it the form of the crown worn by the Pharaoh of Upper Egypt. When this bonnet is worn by mature men, the bamboo frame is omitted and the oblong part is generally smaller. This produces what has been called the form of the Phrygian bonnet that the Greeks were to transmit to the Western world. In *Dieu d'eau*, Marcel Griaule has published photographs of these bonnets worn by the Dogon.

It can be noted here that the king carries only a mace in his right hand; his left hand, weaponless, holds the head of the victim. The mace may thus be considered as an attribute of Upper Egypt, as was the white crown. The king was probably beginning the conquest of the Nile Valley in this first scene. This was perhaps the moment when he was subjecting men of his own race to his domination.

The back of the tablet begins with a typical scene: the conquered victim belongs to the city of the "abominables," as indicated by the hieroglyph pointed out by Amélineau. The fortified city was probably a town in Lower Egypt, inhabited by a race clearly different from the Black race on the other side: a white Asiatic race. The hair of the captives is long and natural, without layers; the noses exceptionally long and aquiline; the lips quite indistinct. In short, all the ethnic features of the race on the back are diametrically opposite to those of the race on the front. We cannot overemphasize the fact that only the race on the back has Semitic features.

After this second victory, the unification of Upper and Lower Egypt was probably achieved. It was symbolized by the scene in the middle of the reverse side: the symmetry of the two felines with menacing leonine heads, indicating that they would be fighting if they were free. But they will henceforth be held in check and unable to injure each other, thanks to the ropes tied around their necks and held by the two symmetrical personages. This would symbolize unification, in line with a characteristic representation common to Egyptians and Blacks in general.

In the scene at the top, the king is wearing the crown of Lower Egypt, which shows that he has just conquered it. The second stage of the conquest of the Nile Valley is thus ended by the Pharaoh. He now holds in both hands what can be considered as the attributes of Lower and Upper Egypt. Here, once again, the king has removed his sandals. These are held by his servant who, carrying the same receptacle, walks behind him as in the scene on the front side. We may therefore assume that the site is sacred and that the victims were immolated ritually, not massacred.

Before the king stand five persons, four of them hold banners bearing totems. The first two—Hawk and Jackal—are clearly from Upper Egypt. The last one represents not an animal, but an unidentified object which may well be the emblem of Lower Egypt just conquered.

For all these reasons, Amélineau's interpretation seems unacceptable. The opinion that all the captives depicted are Asiatics is apparently a generalization that overlooks the detail of the tablet. To the same extent, Amélineau's explanation, which considers all the conquered people as Nubians, seems erroneous. The fact that the captives on the obverse are really Nubians may have led him to miss the ethnic difference between the latter and the victim crushed by the bull on the reverse. According to Amélineau's own reproduction, the latter does not wear his hair in layers as do the Nubians on the other side. Furthermore, he does not have their other ethnic features. Only by disregarding these details, in good faith, could he have reached the conclusion that an uncultivated white race from Central Africa probably conquered the valley from the Negro Anu population.

As a matter of fact, even if there were infiltration by Asians or early Europeans during that prehistoric period, the Egyptian Negroes had never lost control of the situation. This is also indicated by the numerous Amratian statuettes portraying a conquered race of foreigners. In his *Les Débuts de l'art en Égypte,* the Belgian Egyptologist Jean Capart reproduces a statuette of a white captive kneeling, hands bound behind his back, hair in a long braid hanging down his back.[49]

From the same period proto-caryatids are also found, in the form of furniture pedestals, depicting the type of the conquered white race.[50] By contrast, we see Blacks shown as citizens freely strolling around in their own country:

Here we see four women in long skirts, quite similar to Black women represented on Eighteenth Dynasty tombs, including the tomb of Rekhmara*. Although indistinct, the object they seem to he carrying has been

---

*Vizier of Pharaohs Tuthmosis III and Amenhotep II (circa 1471–1448 B.C.)

assumed to be a cow's ear! I should be inclined to view it as the earliest appearance of the ansate cross, a symbol that soon thereafter entered Egyptian semeiology and never left it. This indicates that Negro women were quite at home in the midst of animals from their own land. The question again arises: How could the Egyptians of that epoch know animals from Central Africa, as well as the inhabitants of Central Africa, if these people were Asians or Semites entering the Nile Valley through the Isthmus of Suez? Is not the recorded presence of the aforementioned animals and Blacks on the ivory pieces just described conclusive evidence that Egypt's conquerors came from Central Africa? (*Prolégomènes,* pp. 425–426.)

Contrary to generally accepted notions, it is clear that the most ancient documents available on Egyptian and world history portray Blacks as free citizens, masters of the country and of nature. Near them, the several white prototypes then known, the result of early European or Asian infiltration, are depicted as captives, with hands tied behind their backs, or else crushed by the load of a piece of furniture. (This, incidentally, could be the origin of the caryatids of the fifth-century Erechtheum, imitated by the Greeks thousands of years later.)

Notes

1. *L'Océanie.* Paris: Collection l'Univers, 1836, vol. I.

2. The yellow race as well was probably the result of crossbreeding between Blacks and Whites at a very ancient time in the history of mankind. In fact, the yellow peoples have the pigmentation of mixed breeds, so much so that comparative biochemical analysis would be unable to reveal any great difference in the quantity of melanin. No systematic study of blood groups in mixed breeds has been made to date. It would have permitted an interesting comparison with those of the yellow race.

   The ethnic features of yellow peoples, lips, nose, prognathism, are those of the mixed breed. Their facies (high cheekbones, puffed eyelids, Mongolian pucker, slant eyes, depression at the bridge of the nose) could merely result from the effect of thousands of years in a climate that blows cold winds on the face. The crispation of the face as a result of the wind would suffice to explain the prominent cheekbones and puffed eyelids, which form two correlative ethnic traits.

   Beating against the face in cold weather, the wind can escape through the corner of the eye only by following an oblique upward movement, after the molecules of air have been warmed. In the long run, this mechanical force could produce a deformation of the eye in the same direction. Such an action by the climate could be even stronger on a young organism like that of a child. This explanation obviously assumes the heredity of acquired characteristics.

   It is known, moreover, that these features, called Mongolian, change from northern to southern Asia, following to some extent a climatic curve. And it has been observed that, wherever there are yellow-skinned peoples, one still finds small pockets of Blacks and Whites who seem to be the residual elements of the race. This is the case throughout southeast Asia: the Mois in the mountains of Viet-Nam where, in addition, it is curious to encounter such names as Kha, Thai, and Cham; the Negritos and Ainus in Japan, etc. According to a Japanese proverb: "For a Samurai to be brave, he must have a bit of Black blood." Chinese chroniclers report that a Negro empire existed in the south of China at the dawn of that country's history.

   Proto-Aryan + Proto-Dravidian + cold climate = Yellow?

3. Champollion-Figeac, *Egypte ancienne.* Paris: Collection l'Univers, 1839, pp. 30–31.

The oldest Egyptian monuments which depict all the races of the earth—the bas-reliefs of Biban-el-Moluk, for example—show that during those early epochs only the so-called Nordic race was tattooed. Neither Negro Egyptians nor other African Blacks practiced tattooing, according to all known Egyptian documents. Originally, tattooing made no sense except on a white skin where it produced a difference of tint. With the white Libyans, it was introduced into Africa, but would not be imitated by Negroes until much later. Since the blue-white or any other contrast cannot possibly be realized on a black skin, they resorted to scarification. Unfortunately, we have been unable to publish a reproduction of Champollion's bas-reliefs.

4. Champollion-Figeac, *ibid.,* p. 27.

5. *Ibid.,* pp. 26–27.

6. *Ibid.,* p. 27.

7. Figeac was unaware that all frizzy hair is woolly. Keratin, a chemical substance basic to wool, makes hair curly. Thus, his argument is worthless.

8. Marius Fontanes, *Les Egyptes (de 5000 à 715).* Paris: Ed. Lemerre, n.d., p. 169.

9. Champollion-Figeac, *ibid.,* p. 27.

10. *Ibid.*

11. Chérubini, *La Nubie.* Paris: Collection l'Univers, 1847, pp. 2–3.

12. Chérubini alludes to this passage from Diodorus of Sicily:
"The Ethiopians call themselves the first of all men and cite proofs they consider evident. It is generally agreed that, born in a country and not having come from elsewhere, they must be judged indigenous. It is likely that located directly under the course of the sun, they sprang from the earth before other men. For, if the heat of the sun, combining with the humidity of the soil, produces life, those sites nearest the Equator must have produced living beings earlier than any others. The Ethiopians also say that they instituted the cult of the gods, festivals, solemn assemblies, sacrifices, in short, all the practices by which we honor the gods. For that reason they are deemed the most religious of all men and they believe their sacrifices to be the most pleasing to the gods. One of the most ancient and the most respected poet in Greece renders them this homage when he introduces Jupiter and other gods en route to Ethiopia (in the *Iliad*) to attend the feast and annual sacrifices prepared for them all by the Ethiopians:
Jupiter today, followed by all the gods,
Receives the sacrifices of the Ethiopians.
(*Iliad,* I, 422)
They claim that the gods have rewarded their piety by important blessings, such as never having been dominated by any foreign prince. In fact, thanks to the great unity that has always existed among them, they have always kept their freedom. Several very powerful princes, who tried to subjugate them, have failed in that endeavor. Cambyses came to attack them with numerous troops; his army perished and he ran the risk of losing his own life. Semiramis, the queen, known for her cleverness and exploits, had scarcely entered Ethiopia when she realized that her plan could not succeed. Bacchus and Hercules, after crossing the whole earth, abstained from fighting the Ethiopians, either through fear of their power or respect for their piety. . . ."
(*Histoire universelle,* Bk. I, 337–341.)

13. Chérubini, *ibid.,* pp. 28–29.

14. *Ibid.,* p. 73.

15. *Ibid.,* p. 30.

16. *Ibid.*

17. *Ibid.,* p. 32.

18. Nahas: "good-for-nothing," in Wolof.

19. According to Marius Fontanes, *ibid.,* p. 219.

20. Fontanes, *ibid.,* pp. 44–45.

21. *Ibid.,* pp. 47–48.

22. Maspero, *ibid.,* p. 19. Maspero observes that this is also the thesis of naturalists and anthropologists such as Hartmann, Morton, Hamy, and Sergi.

23. Raymond Furon, *Manuel d'archéologie préhistorique.* Paris, 1943, p. 178.

24. *Ibid.,* p. 371.

25. *Ibid.,* pp. 14–15.

26. *Ibid.,* p. 15.

27. Dumoulin de Laplante, *Histoire générale synchronique.* Paris, 1947, p. 13

28. Cf. the passage from Furon which we quote in note 26.

29. Abbé Henri Breuil, "L'Afrique du Sud", *Les Nouvelles littéraires,* April 5, 1951.

30. Abbé Breuil, *ibid.*

31. *History of Herodotus,* p. 256.

32. Fontanes, *ibid.,* pp. 60–61.

33. Cf. Hardy, *Histoire d'Afrique,* pp. 28–29.

34. These two plural forms in *n* and *a* also existed in old High German.

35. Abderrahman es-Sa'di, *Tarikh es-Sudan.*

36. Maspero, *ibid.,* p. 15.

37. According to Amélineau, the Egyptians designated the heart of Africa by the word *Amami:* land of the ancestors; *Mamyi:* ancestors, in Wolof.

38. Maspero, *ibid.,* p. 16.

39. *Ibid.*

40. *Ibid.,* pp. 16–17.

41. *Ibid.,* pp. 17–18.

42. Abbé Emile Amélineau, *Nouvelles Fouilles d'Abydos.* Paris: Ed. Leroux, 1899, p. 248.

43. *Ibid.,* p. 271.

44. Amélineau, *Prolégomènes à l'étude de la religion égyptienne.* Paris: Ed. Leroux, 1916, part 2, 124.

45. Hieroglyph: an arrow with two feathers or reeds.

46. Amélineau, *Prolégomènes,* pp. 124–125.

47. *Ibid.,* pp. 257–258.

48. *Ibid.,* p. 330.

49. Jean Capart, *Les Débuts de l'art en Egypte.* Brussels: Ed. Vromant, 1904, fig. 14, p. 37.

50. Cf. Amélineau, *Prolégomènes,* p. 413.

Part III *Key Terms and Essay/Discussion Questions*

KEY TERMS

European ethos   Abbé Emile Amélineau

Cultural imperialism   Modernity

Rationalism   Chauvinism

Universalism   Colonialism

Humanism   White supremacy

Ontology   Egyptology

Epistemology   Champollion the younger

Metaphysics   Champollion-Figéac

Individualism

ESSAY/DISCUSSION QUESTIONS

1. Dona Richards suggests that "White Studies," or the critical examination of European culture and civilization, should be included in any African American Studies curriculum. Why?

2. According to Richards, the "idea of progress" derived from the Western European cultural ethos. Discuss five dimensions of this ethos.

3. Richards argues that the European idea of progress is essentially a racist ideology that has been used to justify the oppression and exploitation of African and African-descended people. Discuss her argument.

4. What alternative to the effects of the "idea of progress" on African and African-descended people does Richards propose? Evaluate her proposal.

5. According to Cheikh A. Diop, how and why did Europeans falsify African history, particularly the image of ancient Egypt and its people?

6. What interests are served by the European falsification of African history, and how does this endeavor contribute to the cultural domination of African and African-descended people?

7. Why is it important for us to investigate and to expose European attempts to distort the African past?

Part III *Supplementary Readings*

Abu-Lughod, Janet L., *Before European Hegemony: The World System, A. D. 1250–1350*, New York: Oxford University Press, 1989.

Adas, Michael, *Machines as the Measure of Men: Science, Technology, and Ideologies of Western Domination,* Ithaca: Cornell University Press, 1989.

Amin, Samir, *Eurocentrism,* New York: Monthly Review Press, 1989.

Blumenberg, Hans, *The Legitimacy of the Modern Age,* Cambridge: The MIT Press, 1983.

Cox, Oliver C., *Caste, Class & Race: A Study in Social Dynamics,* New York: Monthly Review Press, 1948.

Doyle, Michael W., *Empires,* Ithaca: Cornell University Press, 1986.

Gay, Peter, *The Enlightenment: An Interpretation,* Vol. II, *The Science of Freedom,* New York: Alfred A. Knopf, Inc., 1969.

———, *The Enlightenment: An Interpretation,* Vol. I, *The Rise of Modern Paganism,* New York: Alfred A. Knopf, Inc., 1966.

Gossett, Thomas F., *Race: The History of an Idea in America,* New York: Schoken Books, 1965.

Hobsbawm, Eric, *The Age of Empire, 1875–1914,* New York: Pantheon Books, 1987.

———, *The Age of Capital, 1848–1875,* New York: A Mentor Book/New American Library, 1979.

———, *The Age of Revolution, 1789–1848,* New York: A Mentor Book/New American Library, 1962.

Hodge, John L., Donald K. Struckmann, and Lynn D. Trost, *Cultural Bases of Racism and Group Oppression: An Examination of Traditional "Western" Concepts, Values and Institutional Structures Which Support Racism, Sexism and Elitism,* Berkeley: Two Riders Press, 1975.

Horsman, Reginald, *Race and Manifest Destiny: The Origins of American Racial Anglo-Saxonism,* Cambridge: Harvard University Press, 1981.

Jefferson, Thomas, "Notes on the State of Virginia," in Merrill D. Peterson, ed., *The Portable Thomas Jefferson,* New York: Penguin Books, 1977, pp. 23–232.

Jordan, Winthrop D., *White Over Black: American Attitudes Toward the Negro, 1550–1812.* Chapel Hill: The University of North Carolina Press, 1968.

Marx, Karl, *Capital: A Critique of Political Economy,* Vol. I, New York: Vintage Books, 1977.

———, *Grundrisse: Foundations of the Critique of Political Economy,* New York: Vintage Books, 1973.

Mendelssohn, Kurt, *The Secret of Western Domination.* New York: Praeger Publishers, 1976.

Mosse, George L., *Toward the Final Solution: A History of European Racism,* Madison: The University of Wisconsin Press, 1985.

———, *The Culture of Western Europe: The Nineteenth and Twentieth Centuries,* Chicago: Rand McNally & Company, 1961.

Mudimbe, V. Y., *The Invention of Africa; Gnosis, Philosophy, and the Order of Knowledge,* Bloomington: Indiana University Press, 1988.

Nandy, Ashis, ed., *Science, Hegemony & Violence: A Requiem for Modernity,* Delhi: Oxford University Press, 1988.

Nesbit, Robert, *History of the Idea of Progress,* New York: Basic Books, Inc., Publishers, 1980.

Poggi, Gianfranco, *Calvinism and the Capitalist Spirit: Max Weber's "Protestant Ethic,"* Amherst: The University of Massachusetts Press, 1983.

Said, Edward W., *Orientalism,* New York: Vintage Books, 1978.

Schama, Simon, *The Embarrassment of Riches: An Interpretation of Dutch Culture in the Golden Age,* New York: Alfred A. Knopf, 1987.

Spadafora, David, *The Idea of Progress in Eighteenth-Century Britain,* New Haven: Yale University Press, 1990.

Tawney, Robert H., *Religion and Rise of Capitalism: A Historical Study,* New York: Harcourt, Brace, and Company, Inc., 1926.

Von Laue, Theodore H., *The World Revolution of Westernization,* New York: Oxford University Press, 1987.

Weber, Max, *The Protestant Ethic and the Spirit of Capitalism,* London: Unwin Hyman Ltd., 1985.

Wuthnow, Robert, *Communities of Discourse: Ideology and Social Structure in the Reformation, the Enlightenment, and European Socialism,* Cambridge: Harvard University Press, 1989.

IV

Africa and the Americas: Pre-Columbian Contact, Enslavement, and Resistance

The historical forces and events that gave rise to the populations of African-descended Americans constitute one of the most dramatic and complex developments in human history. That contact between Africa and the Americas has resulted in the emergence of a people, particularly in the United States of America, whose legacy has been a historic struggle for human rights, social development, and collective survival. It was through the Atlantic slave trade and chattel slavery that the histories of Africa, Europe, and the Americas converged.

Although the mid-fifteenth century exchange between Western Europe and West Africa began with the trade in goods, European greed, lust for power, and the drive for global expansion rapidly transformed that exchange into the capture and trade of African flesh. As a result, massive depopulation, social dislocation, and political disruption weakened the African continent and prepared the way for Western European imperialism and colonialism during the nineteenth and early twentieth centuries. The turbulent voyage of the "middle passage" from Africa to the Americas, which included the genocide of millions of Africans, resulted in one of the most dramatic population transplantations in human history. Possessing different names, cultures, and languages, Africans from numerous nations were crammed into slave ships and forced upon American shores. They were Bambara, Malinka, Fon, Dinka, Ewe, Bakongo, Igbo, Yoruba,

Ashanti, Wolof, and hundreds more. The Colonial American institution of chattel slavery was the dehumanizing context in which the members of this pan-African assembly fought back, improvised, and refashioned themselves into a new, yet very old, people—African-Americans.

Although it is generally thought that the initial connection between Africa and the Americas was set in motion by Christopher Columbus' voyage, the Atlantic slave trade, and chattel slavery, there is substantial evidence of an ancient, pre-Columbian African presence in the Americas that dates back at least 2,000 years. The possibility that Africans could have visited the Americas long before Columbus should call for no stretch of the imagination, for Africa is less than 2,000 miles from South America. The articles in this section explore early African contact with the Americas; the slave trade and chattel slavery; and the African-American resistance to chattel slavery.

In his article, "The Black Origins of 'American' Civilization: A Bicentennial Revelation," Legrand Clegg investigates an ancient Meso-American civilization that arose between 1000 and 2000 B.C. in the southern region of Mexico. Clegg points out that the evidence—skeletal and sculptural remains—indicates that the inhabitants of ancient Meso-America, a people known as the Olmecs, were the descendants of African immigrants. Modern European investigators, Clegg says, ignored the skeletal evidence that bore African characteristics and that earlier had been classified as African in origin; they merely reclassified these remains as Mongoloid. Clegg also discusses the discovery of the massive stone head sculptures in southern Mexico. These colossal heads, some as tall as nine feet and as heavy as fifteen tons, possess facial features that unmistakably are African. Finally, Clegg discusses Olmec culture—including agriculture, architecture, urban organization, religion, a computational system, and calendar development—and its influence on Meso-American civilization.

The impact of the trans-Atlantic slave trade and chattel slavery on European and American civilizations is the subject of C. L. R. James's article, "The Atlantic Slave Trade and Slavery: Some Interpretations of Their Significance in the Development of the United States and the Western World." Noting that every human society has experienced slavery, James writes that in ancient times, although they were harshly treated, slaves were still considered human beings who could be educated and could hold governmental office. According to James, the introduction of mechanical power into military conflict and the expansion of capitalism made the slave trade and chattel slavery devastating. Moreover, James argues that the trade of African flesh and the dehumanizing institution of chattel slavery set in motion Western Europe's Industrial Revolution. James shows that the enslavement of Africans was systematically cruel, which meant that slavers lived in constant fear of slave revolts. The late-eighteenth-century Haitian Revolution and the overthrow of French slavocracy in the Western Hemisphere sent shock waves throughout the planter classes in the Americas. James goes on to examine the suppression of the slave trade, the movement to abolish chattel slavery, the Underground Railroad, and the emancipation of the slaves. Finally, he argues persuasively that the impact of chattel slavery became deeply embedded in the American personality, political culture, social vision, and institutional practices.

The essay by Vincent Harding, "Symptoms of Liberty and Blackhead Signposts: David Walker and Nat Turner," examines the African American struggle to overturn chattel slavery in the first quarter of the nineteenth century. Harding focuses on the lives and times of David Walker, a free African American who strongly protested chattel slavery, and Nat Turner, a minister and a leader of one of the most significant slave rebellions in the American South. Born into a slave community in 1800, Nat Turner apparently possessed special gifts, which his family and the surrounding slave community recognized and encouraged. Harding notes that as a youth, Turner's religious development was nurtured by his grandmother; his father, who became a fugitive slave, taught Turner that chattel slavery must be resisted. Hence, Nat Turner grew into adulthood with a powerful religious zeal and an anti-slavery passion.

Slavery's violent oppression brought into existence its opposite, as slaves revolted and struggled for freedom throughout the Western Hemisphere. In an atmosphere of repression and rebellion, Nat Turner stepped forward on August 22, 1831, to lead a group of avengers in the slaughter of whites in Southhampton County, Virginia. Turner was later captured, tried in court, imprisoned, and put to death. Turner's insurrection, however, sent waves of fear throughout the slaveholding South. In reaction, frightened whites indiscriminately massacred hundreds of African Americans.

If Turner represented the radical tradition of slave revolt, David Walker exemplified the radical tradition of critical analysis and anti-slavery protest among free African Americans. Born legally free in 1785 in Wilmington, North Carolina, Walker later traveled throughout the South and witnessed the violent, degrading, and dehumanizing effects of chattel slavery. In 1826, he moved to Boston, Massachusetts, where he joined forces with other African American abolitionists as an organizer, lecturer, and writer. In 1827, *Freedom's Journal*, the first African American newspaper, was published in Boston; Walker became its agent. Harding observes that the almost simultaneous emergence of "David Walker and *Freedom's Journal* represented one of the earliest institutional manifestations of . . . the Great Tradition of Black Protest."

A fiercely religious and outspoken person, Walker denounced the twin evils of chattel slavery in the South and racist discrimination in the North. Harding thus demonstrates that Walker recognized and advocated, as did many other black abolitionists, a commonality of interest and struggle between the chattel slave and "free" African Americans. In 1829, Walker published a pamphlet, *Appeal*, which set in motion an African American tradition of radical analysis and criticism of white greed and racism and advocacy of black solidarity and liberation. Clearly energized by Walker's religious zeal and sense of social justice, the *Appeal* combined the two major belief systems in early nineteenth-century America—Protestant Evangelical Christianity and natural rights philosophy. As Harding shows, Walker linked the struggle for African American freedom to God's justice: the fight for African American liberation was a holy crusade, and resistance to slavery was obedience to God.

Walker's thoroughgoing criticism of chattel slavery, white racism, and the American white supremacist government electrified and inspired African Americans but terrified and angered white Americans. Even though whites condemned and tried to suppress the *Appeal*, copies circulated through African American communities in the North and South. As copies reached the South, it was reported not only that some whites intended to kill Walker but also that a monetary reward had been offered for his death. Undaunted, Walker stood his ground, holding the view that in the struggle for African American freedom and justice, some would perish. On June 28, 1830, Walker became suddenly and mysteriously ill; he died on that day in his Boston store. It was believed throughout Boston's African American community that Walker had been poisoned.

For Vincent Harding, Nat Turner and David Walker represent an early tradition of African American radicalism and collective struggle against the structures of racial and cultural domination in America. One a slave and the other "free," both persons and their comrades fought for liberation and justice, providing a beacon of light in America's racially troubled waters for the generations of African Americans who would follow.

The Black Origin of "American" Civilization: A Bicentennial Revelation

LEGRAND H. CLEGG, II

INETEEN HUNDRED AND seventy-six represents the two hundredth anniversary of the European takeover of that part of North America now known as the United States. While the entire continent had not been snatched from its black and red occupants by 1776, within one hundred years thereafter well over half of North America had been seized and today the entire Western Hemisphere, all of the Americas, is either directly or indirectly under European (white) dominion and control.

The bicentennial celebration in the United States should be a time of grave soul-searching for historians. Rather than resurrecting banal myths about pious pilgrims and "fearless" pioneers who cleared the wilderness for "freedom of religion", scholars would do well to ponder and explain the paradoxes of European expansion: the Christian slaveholder; missionaries who sanctioned the annihilation of "natives" and theft of their land; the rise and triumph of Jim Crow in the "Land of the Free"; the spread of democracy and its imperious sway over the First World, etc.[1]

These and other significant issues respecting the American past must be dragged out of the national closet, swept from under the rug of democratic pretense, analyzed and served to a public starving for academic integrity. To anticipate that white scholars will yield to this appeal, however, would reflect incredible naiveté and contradict over six thousand years of colonial hypocrisy [1]. Therefore, in view of current realities, we as black students of history, must move from ingenuous expectations rooted in moral imperatives to the courageous heights of consciousness-raising and independent thinking. No greater moment than now stands before us beckoning that we seize the time, for the American Bicentennial occasions more than opportunity for frolic and political bombast; it is a time for liberating western academia and its chief servant, the white historian.

In our move toward demythologizing western culture and thereby freeing academic

Reprinted, with permission, from *A Current Bibliography on African Affairs*, Vol. 9, No. 1, 1976–1977. Copyright © 1976, African Bibliographic Center, Inc.

slaves, we are here defying all tradition and, by an act doubtless to be labeled heresy, not simply citing the ills of white America, "Negroes who made America great" or even the massive, oft-ignored slave rebellions, but exposing the naked truth to a hostile and thankless Western World: that black people laid the foundation of "American" civilization; that it was they who pioneered in an attempt to settle certain problems of living together—of government, defense, religion, family, property, science and art; and it was from these folk that the torch of civilization passed—first to red men and finally, following brutal aggression, religious hypocrisy and theft—into the hands of Europe by the close of the sixteenth century.

Of what "America" do we speak owing its origin to the Black race? While we are not restricting ourselves to that area of the world now labeled the "United States," we shall certainly include a part of its territory in our discussion. By and large, however, we are focusing on the true "America"—Mesoamerica; the "America" that knew a better way, whose body and soul rejected the quest for profit while seeking the maximal development of youths and the ultimate enrichment of all.

The first "America" lay far to the south of the current United States, having as its seeming origin the northeastern region of Yucatan. "The archaeological sites and monuments too large to be moved which have been found up to the present time are limited by the Gulf of Mexico to the north and the first slopes of the mountains to the south; by the Papaloapan River to the west and the basin of the Blassillo-Tonala' to the east . . . Perhaps at a given moment it extended eastward as far as the basin of the Zanapa River and the Laguna del Carem or somewhat farther, to the Grijalva River" [2]. This, then, was the seat of early "America," Mesoamerica, the land to which Caso, an esteemed scholar, refers as the "Mesopotamia of the Americas" [3].

It was in this region of what is now southern Mexico, covering about 7000 square miles, that certain village cultures began appearing around the third millennium before Christ, and that Mesoamerican civilization emerged sometime between 1000 and 2000 B.C. [2, p. 4, 4].[2]

The name Olmec, now assigned this civilization, has been the subject of much discussion and remains an issue among some scholars. It is derived, according to Luis Aveleyra Arroyo de Anda, the eminent archaeologist, from a Nahautl word for rubber, a product which—based on the opinions of early Spanish chroniclers—was one of the major sources of this society's wealth [5]. This name, moreover, has been said to mean, "Dweller of the Land of Rubber", and would therefore apply as much to the occupants of Olmec territory as to the culture itself [2, p. 11].

Who were these early folk nestled at the outskirts of the Western Hemisphere, hidden by impenetrable swamps, jungle thickets, a mountainous mass and the northern gulf? Whence did they come and when? The answers are not absolute; but those few clues that have emerged leave western science mute with embarrassment and in ceaseless pursuit of counter evidence. This paper, then, will center on a revelation of the true Olmec physical type and its probable origin, followed by a synopsis of Olmec contributions to and widespread influence on the ancient New World.

SKELETAL REMAINS

"Because of the humid climate and the acidity of the soil where Olmec burials have been found," laments Ignacio Bernal, an authority on the early Olmec people, "not one skeleton has been preserved to reveal the physical types of these people. We can reconstruct a type only on the basis of representations in clay, stone or jade which the Olmecs themselves left, or (if the present-day inhabitants of the area are their direct physical descendants) by observing some of the ancient racial characteristics they might have preserved" [2, p. 25].

Unlike Bernal, we do not believe that revelation of the Olmec physical type need depend, even in part, on skeletons exhumed directly from Olmec burial sites; and, while we shall soon consider Olmec sculptural remains (as he suggests), we do not feel that, in seeking the ancient type, one need examine the current population of southern Mexico that represents an extraordinary conglomeration of foreign and native peoples whose very heterogeneity obscures traceable links to the early Olmecs.

Obviously, human fossils from Olmec burial sites would be most desirable in that they could provide significant clues to the race and origin of the people in question. Until such discoveries are made, however, if we are to rely, at least in part, on skeletal remains, we should direct our attention to existent evidence, exhumed from sites throughout ancient Mesoamerica, and attempt to extract therefrom possible theories respecting the origin and race of the Olmec people.

The earliest human crania that have been discovered in Mesoamerica date back to prehistoric times [6]. Although these finds clearly pre-date Mexico's early pre-classic era, c. 2000 B.C.–1000 B.C., during which the Olmecs are believed to have appeared in the Western Hemisphere, an analysis of the crania may cast light upon the Olmec physical type, particularly since the Olmec people are generally said to have derived from indigenous Mesoamericans.

Scientists are generally agreed as to the age of the crania in question and their locations of discovery, but a dispute, first thought to be a sincere schism between legitimate academic forces, but now exposed as a struggle between science and race prejudice, has arisen concerning the racial characteristics of the most ancient skulls of Mesoamerica.

Modernly, following a long and bitter struggle, anti-diffusionist dogma has emerged triumphant across academia. Therefore, science has made a simple but dangerous deduction regarding the peopling of the early New World that rejects or ignores all dissenting opinion: *since early European explorers met "Indians" in the New World and anthropologists have proven that these Indians came from Asia via the Bering Strait, no counterevidence, despite its weight and merit, will survive the conclusion that the early New World was exclusively Mongoloid.* To this position have rushed most current anthropologists, paleontologists, ethnologists and historians and around this dogma has gathered a great body of scientific literature. Typical of authorities who have legitimized the foregoing view is Carlton S. Coon, an oft-cited western anthropologist:

> Both the American Indian and the Eskimo, which inhabit North and South America, are Mongoloid. All the skulls and bones of their ancestors which have been unearthed to date are also Mongoloid. There is not a real Australoid, Melanesian, Negroid or Caucasoid piece of bone in the lot [7].

Against this opinion stands a strong body of skeletal evidence, once widely discussed by a number of distinguished men of science, many of whose opinions fed the diffusionist movement and spawned theories regarding the probable black origin of "American" civilization.

For example, Carlos Cuervo Marquez, an early Mexican investigator, spoke of "the youthful America [as] also a black continent" and based his opinion largely on Africoid skeletons exhumed from "Bolivia to Mexico." So convinced was Marquez of the validity of his opinion that he classified the Otomies of Mexico, the Caracoles of Haiti, the Arguaos of Cutara, the Aravos of the Orinico, the Porcijis and the Matayas of Brazil, the Manabis of Quito, the Chuanas of Darien and the Albinos of Panama as remnants "of the aboriginal black race out of which later developed what is known as the Red or American race" [8].

Perhaps the most widely known anthropologists to consider the presence of black people in ancient America were Earnest A. Hooton and Roland B. Dixon. Hooton was one of the first, if not indeed the first scientist, to examine crania exhumed from "lower archaeological strata" in the Pecos River Valley in and around Southern Texas and Mexico. He described several of the skulls as near-"Negroid," with "flat, broad nasal bones, platyrrhiny, pronounced alveolar prognathism, and bulbous frontal regions" [9]. These remain among the oldest, if not absolutely the oldest, human crania ever exhumed from Mesoamerican soil, "became rarer in later periods," and were virtually nonexistent in higher strata [9].

In the same vein, Dixon speaks of an Africoid type found in the burial caves of Coahuila in northern Mexico, associates these folk with the ancient Basket-makers of Arizona and adds that "there was an early stratum of Proto-Negroid and Proto-Australoid types in the Mexican region, driven back into the arid areas of the northeast in prehistoric times, but surviving as a minority still among the Otomi, the Tarahumare, and the Pima."

Other early anthropologists and historians, such as Griffith Taylor, Louis Sullivan, Milo Hellman, Rene Verneau, Paul Rivet, A. H. Keene, A. C. Haddon, Juan de Dios Carresquilla and Frederick A. Peterson also cite ancient Africoid skulls throughout Mesoamerica and even South America, and advance persuasive arguments to the effect that these remains represent the first human inhabitants of the Western Hemisphere [8, pp. 179–180; 11–17].

Modern authorities are not unaware of the foregoing evidence, but have conspired to ignore it lest the narrow boundaries of accepted black achievement and distribution broaden beyond traditional limits. Harold S. Gladwin, a brilliant but "heretical" anthropologist, exposed this conspiracy nearly thirty years ago:

It has been this negative attitude of mind, for instance, which has consistently refused to recognize the definite implications of the many references by physical anthropologists to such types as Australoid or Negroid in the make-up of various Indian tribes—even though veiled by such qualifications as Proto-Negroid or pseudo-Australoid. Terms such as these will be found only in technical papers on physical anthropology, but never in orthodox reconstructions of native American history. We have included them here because we think they cannot fairly be ignored, and, once you accept them as facts to be reckoned with, they turn out to be essential to an understanding of the problems since they show that Mongoloid people could not have reached North America before the time of Christ [18].

There is, then, no real dispute here. We have instead ancient skeletal remains, once classified as "black," now falling victim to the racist whims of modern "authority." Current scientists, just as their predecessors, realize that the most ancient crania thus far discovered in Mesoamerica bear Africoid characteristics,[3] but proceed, as if by instinct, to label them Mongoloid.

W. E. B. Du Bois probably provides the best definition of the black race that is currently available:

It is reasonable, according to fact and historical usage, to include under the word "Negro" the darker peoples of Africa characterized by a brown skin, curled hair, some tendency to a development of the maxillary parts of the face, and a dolichocephalic head. This type is not fixed nor definite. The color varies widely; it is never black as some say, and it becomes often light brown or yellow. The hair varies from curly to a crisp mass, and the facial angle and crania form show wide variation.

The color of this variety of man, as the color of other varieties, is due to climate. Conditions of heat, cold, and moisture, working for thousands of years through the skin and other organs, have given men their differences of color. This color pigment is a protection against sunlight and consequently varies with the intensity of the sunlight. Thus in Africa we find the blackest of men in the fierce sunlight of the desert, red Pygmies in the forest, and yellow Bushmen on the cooler southern plateau.

Next to the color, the hair is the most distinguishing characteristic of the Negro, but the two characteristics do not vary with each other. Some of the blackest of the Negroes have curly rather than woolly hair, while the crispest, most closely curled hair is found among the yellow Hottentots and the Bushmen. The difference between the hair of the lighter and darker races is mainly one of degree, not of kind, and can easily be measured. The elliptical cross section of the Negro's hair causes it to curl more or less tightly.

It is impossible in Africa as elsewhere to fix with any certainty the limits of racial variation due to heredity, to climate and to intermingling. In the past, when scientists assumed one distinct Negro type, every variation from that type was interpreted as meaning mixture of blood. Today we recognize a broader normal African type which, as Palgrave says, may best be studied "among the statues of the Egyptian rooms of the British museum; the large gentle eye, the full but not over-protruding lips, the rounded contour, and the good-natured, easy, sensuous expression. This is the genuine African model". To this race Africa in the main and parts of Asia have belonged since prehistoric times.

It does not matter that crania of similar type, exhumed from prehistoric and historic graves in Australia, Africa and the South Pacific, are, without the slightest hesitation, respectively classified as "Australoid" and "Negroid" by these same decision-makers. What is important, however, is that the racist posture assumed by modern science survive at all cost and that black history and culture be sacrificed to keep it alive. Hence, it is not the character of the Mesoamerican crania in question that forces them out of the black race, but the age and locality. In other words, anthropologists are now free to alter their definitions of specific racial types to conform to "scientific" guidelines pre-ordained for fossil remains of certain antiquity discovered in a given region. In the present case, then, had the crania been traceable to post-slavery Mesoamerica and no further back in time, there would be no conflict of opinion. Modern thinkers would have routinely labeled the skulls "Negroid" and explained their presence by the African slave-trade.

In view of the above, we are compelled to ignore the verdict of modern anthropology and thereby apply the reasoning here that was advanced by a number of early scientists: since the most ancient crania thus far discovered in Mesoamerica bear characteristics traditionally associated with the Africoid type, such remains doubtlessly represent the early presence of black people in this region. Furthermore, it is quite possible, particularly in view of the sculptural remains to which we shall now turn, that these ancient Mesoamerican crania, while not exhumed from Olmec burial cites, represent the race to which the later Olmec people also belonged.

SCULPTURAL REMAINS

To our skeletal finds must certainly be added the growing testimony of Olmec sculptural remains discovered throughout Mesoamerica and reproduced today in many museums throughout the Western World. While some investigators, conscious of what observers refer to as the "strange" and "foreign" characteristics of Olmec sculptures of the human face and form, rush forth to explain that these reproductions are merely "stylizations" and "idealizations" of the Mongoloid type and that no other postulates need be advanced [19], most present thinkers concede that Olmec sculptured forms, whether figurines or colossal heads, often "look Negroid" and are possible clues to the Olmec physical type.

Respecting the most frequent physical type surviving among Olmec figurines, Bernal has written: "The commonest one has a snub nose and thick lips, fat cheeks with bloated and slanting eyes, a jutting chin, and mouths with sunken sutures" [20]. Andre Emmerich, an art historian, adds that Olmec figurines often represent "relatively short, squat and fleshly men with clean-shaven, elongated, almost pear-shaped heads, a deformation deliberately affected by binding the head in infancy. Their short noses have perforations in the septum indicating the wearing of nose ornaments" [21]. Furthermore, in his book, *The Art of Terracotta Pottery in Pre-Columbian Central and South America,* Alexander von Wuthenau has presented innumerable photographs of Olmec figurines, dating from circa 2000 B.C. to 300 A.D., that invariably represent black racial types; and the author adds that "it is precisely the Negroid representations which often indicate personalities of high position, who can unhesitatingly be compared to the outstanding Negroes who served as models for great works of art in Egypt and in Nigeria" [4, p. 187].

While the Olmec figurines are intriguing and clearly buttress our position, the most significant and artistically acclaimed Olmec sculptural remains thus far discovered are the ancient colossal heads about which so many observers have written.

"As early as the middle of the nineteenth century," states Jonathan Leonard, a specialist on early Mesoamerica, "reports had come from this coastal region [the Mexican Gulf Coast] of gigantic heads with negroid features" [22]. The first of these Olmec heads to be exhumed from Mesoamerican soil was the *cabeza colosal.* Found in the wilds of Veracruz, the head was observed by J. M. Melgar, who first published a report on it in 1869 [23]. Not until 1938, however, did archaeologists renew their exploration of the forests of Veracruz. At that time, an archaeologist, Dr. Matthew W. Sterling, discovered an enormous stone head,

6.5 feet tall and ten tons [23, pp. 237–238]. John G. Jackson, a contemporary historian, has described it:

> The head turned out to be a solid block of basalt, six feet in height and eighteen feet in circumference, with its base attached to a platform of crudely hewn stones. A member of Dr. Sterling's staff noted the African features of the stone face and thought that the headdress resembled the training of a pugilist, and then gave the *cabeza colosal* the name of Joe Louis [23, p. 238].

A number of colossal heads, ranging from 4.70 to 9.85 in height and weighing from ten to twenty tons, have thus far been discovered. All are bodiless and bear "the thick drooping lips and flat nose that are the hallmarks of Olmec sculpture" [22, p. 32].

So advanced is this Olmec artwork that many observers of various persuasions have felt impelled to describe it, and the words of these writers provide significant clues to the Olmec racial type:

André Emmerich has written:

> The massive stone heads portray men with characteristic Olmec features; thick heavy lips, full cheeks, broad nostrils, almost swollen eyelids and a peculiar type of close-fitting head-dress or helmet [24, p. 69].

Charles Wicke, an art historian, adds:

> The Colossal Heads . . . do conform to the Olmec aesthetic ideal, however, in that all are plump, snub-nosed, thick-lipped and helmeted. They very well might be memorial portraits of rulers [24, p. 69].

Selden Rodman, who has engaged in considerable study respecting Latin American history and culture, has provided this description:

> The earliest of the great "horizon" cultures of Mexico, and the most recently identified, is known as Olmec. It flourished along the Gulf Coast from Tres Zapotes to La Venta and here were discovered some of the colossal "Negroid" heads up to nine feet and weighing as much as fifteen tons . . . [25].

Walter Hanf, a European journalist who has lived in Mexico for several years and studied Olmec sculptures, confirms the "Negroid" features of the colossal heads:

> The Olmecs worked in jade, basalt, rock crystal, and quartz. From these materials they carved colossal heads with Negroid features, deformed and close-shaven skulls, blunt noses and protruding lips [26].

Sharon McKern, a freelance writer and anthropologist, sheds further light on the race depicted by the colossal heads:

> (T)here appears also in Mesoamerica a face strongly Negroid in character—at a time in a land where the presence of African peoples cannot be explained. At numerous sites in Mexico, archaeologists have excavated dozens of colossal heads carved from single blocks of stone. Most are at least 6 feet tall in circumference and weigh more than ten tons; several specimens loom even larger . . . The faces on these immense stone heads seem inescapably Negroid [27].

Historian Nicholas Cheetham appears to believe that the colossal heads represent a foreign element in ancient America:

> The principal sites in the Olmec homeland are called LaVenta, Tres Zapotes and San Lorenzo. Here were found the finest examples of the colossal and sometimes grotesque sculpture which is the hallmark of Olmec art . . . (T)heir exaggeratedly Negroid features seem to have no kinship with the clearly marked traits of the American Indian [28].

Robert Quirk of Indiana University is of similar opinion:

> The origin and even the identity of the Olmecs are unknown today . . . They possessed artistic skills so advanced and sophisticated as to indicate a long period of development in Mexico or elsewhere. (There are intriguing hints of extra-American influence, however, in their portrayal of what appear to be Negroid or Caucasoid faces.) [29].

Finally, Floyd Hayes, a budding young historian at the University of Maryland, has provided a thought-provoking assessment of the racial significance of these immense reproductions:

> One might merely ask himself: if Africans were not present in the Americas before Columbus, why the typically African physiognomy on the monuments? It is in contradiction to the most elementary logic and to all artistic experience to suggest that these ancient Olmec artists could have depicted, with such detail, African facial features they had never seen [30].

As if anticipating the hypocrisy of modern anthropology and the mockery that would be made of its chief victim, the black race, the foregoing skulls, figurines and colossal heads stand as veritable monuments to the physical type of the Olmec people, and to the world declare: "The ancient Olmecs were black"! Given the present posture of academia, however, this revelation, though virtually unimpeachable, is indeed revolutionary and compels inquiry into the origin of these black folk who laid the foundation of "American" civilization.

OLMEC ORIGINS

Very little evidence is currently available concerning the possible origins of the Olmec people. Yet, in view of our contention that the Olmecs were probably black, we are fortunate in that several scholars have advanced theories as to the origin of America's ancient blacks; and it is to such theories, then, that we must turn in seeking Olmec origins.

As was pointed out to some extent above, a number of thinkers have grappled with the question of whether America's indigenous population was black.

Riva Palacio, a distinguished Mexican historian, has given the question considerable attention:

> But who is that aboriginal man, inhabitant of the Valley of Mexico since the most ancient epoch? No doubt in answering, it was the Olmec people.

Drawing of one of the ancient Olmec heads found in Mexico. Some of the carvings are over six feet high.

Nevertheless, the existence of the Black man on our territory gives us material to hesitate. Did he precede the Otomi people or was he the first invader? On the continent that was united to our westside the man was Black and after the separation of the continents this Black man remained in New Zealand, Australia and Southern Africa. The Black man also existed in Asia: in India, invaded by other peoples, the remainder of the Black race sought refuge in the mountains in the central region called Vindhya. Even today these Black men exist: the Glondos, the Kolas, the Bhillas, the Meras of Aravali mountain, the Chitasy, the Minas and the Pahorias whose conquest has given rise to the name Pariahs.

With regard to our continent, scarcely traces of the Black man remain. Proof of his existence was in a very distant epoch. Was he the first in the world and was this the race that spread everywhere by virtue of the union of the continents, or when he arrived in our region, were the Otomies already present? His disappearance suggests to us it being the exiled race therefore the former; but there are indications opposing the indigenous character of the Otomi race and a traditional fact that in our view is very important: until recent times the priests painted themselves Black as if it was a remembrance of the introducers of the first cult [31].

In support of this early black presence in the Western Hemisphere, Palacio then refers to widespread Olmec sculptures, some of which were considered above, and finally concludes:

> But the peremptory test of the ancient existence of the Black race on our continent are the still-encountered remains of him, and the other primitive story-tellers that speak of him. They are: the Caracoles of Haiti, the Califurnams of the Caribe Islands, the Arquahos of Cutara, the Aroras or Yaruras of Orinoco, the Chaymans of Guyana, the Maujipas, Porcigas and Matayas of Brazil, the Nigritas, Chuanas or Gaunas of the Isthmus of Darien, the Manabis of Popayan, the Guavas and Jaras or Zambos of Honduras, the Esteros of New California, the Black Indians encountered by the Spaniards in Louisiana and the Ojos de Luna and albinos, some of which were discovered in Panama and others destroyed by the Iroquois.
>
> All of this demonstrates that in a very ancient epoch or before the existence of the Otomies or better yet invading them, the Black race occupied our territory when the continents were joined. This race brought its religious ideas and its own cult. Later they were dislodged and forced to the coasts by the Otomies or perhaps they were obliged to look for warm places to which they were more appropriately accustomed by their nature, and fled the freezing temperatures and other cataclysms that occurred after this continent was separated [31, p. 64].

Another Mexican scholar, Nicholas Leon, is of similar opinion:

> The oldest inhabitants of Mexico, according to some, were Negroes, and according to others, the Otomies. The existence of Negroes and giants is commonly believed by nearly all the races of our soil and in their various languages they had words to designate them. Several archaeological objects found in various localities demonstrate their existence, the most notable of which is the colossal granite head of Hueyapan, Vera Cruz, and an axe of the same located near the city. In Teotihuacan abound little heads of the Ethiopian type and paintings of Negroes. In Michoacan and Oaxaca the same have also been found . . . Memories of them in most ancient traditions induce us to believe that the Negroes were the first inhabitants of Mexico [32].

Marquez adds that "(s)everal isolated but concordant facts permit the conjecture that before the formation and development of the three great ethnographic groups . . . a great part of America was occupied by (the) Negroid type" [8, p. 23; 33–36]; and historian Alexandre Braghine concludes that "(h)itherto, ethnologists imagined that Negroes appeared in the New World only during our own epoch, when they were imported as slaves; but the most recent researches demonstrate that they came to America in a period very remote . . . [37].

"The autochthonous black races in America were either gradually mixed with the Indian ones, or became extinct, but in a very remote time Negroes, or Negroids, were numerous in the New World . . ." [37, p. 41].

While the foregoing scholars consider the black race to have been either indigenous to the Americas or to have spread there and elsewhere during a period of world-wide continental connections in the remote past, these theories appear to be unsatisfactory. Even if Africoids were the first of our modern racial types to occupy the Western Hemisphere, it would appear that man did not evolve there as in Africa, for no anthropoid apes or ancient species of man have thus far been exhumed from "American" soil [38]. It is for this reason, in fact, that the Western Hemisphere has been labeled the "New World" and is thereby distinguished from the "Old" in which man evolved and over which his most ancient treks were made. The black man, therefore, could not have been "indigenous" to early America.

That the Old and New Worlds were once joined appears likely. Improbable, however, is the theory that remote continental connections account for the ancient Africoid presence in the Americas. "Certainly the Americas may have been connected at some point distant in time to other of the great land masses," argues McKern; "science is gradually proving it so. But such direct land links disappeared long before man diverged from his ancestral stock" [38].

More likely explanations for this ancient black presence in the Americas may be found in the investigations of other distinguished scholars:

Jose M. Melgar, the first writer to embark on an in-depth study of blacks in early America, began his work while visiting San Andres Tuxtla in the State of Veracruz, Mexico in 1862. Upon learning of the existence of a huge Olmec stone head in this region, Melgar insisted on visiting the hacienda at which the stone carving was located:

> We went, and I was struck with surprise; as a work of art it is without exaggeration a magnificent sculpture as it is possible to judge by the photo which is along with this article, but what astonished me was the Ethiopic type which it represents. I reflected that there had undoubtedly been Blacks in this country and this had been in the first epoch of the world; that head was not only important for Mexican archaeology but also would be for the world in general . . . [39,⁴ 40].

So impressed was Melgar with this Olmec sculptured head that he wrote two articles concerning the early "Ethiopian" migrants whom he insists the sculpture represents.

In both studies, Melgar liberally cites Lorenzo Boturini Benaducci's *Idea de una*

nueva historia general de la America Septentrional [41]. The latter gives considerable attention to the work of Don Francisco Nuñez de la Vega, former Bishop of the Royal City of Chiapa and Soconusco, who, while visiting his diocese in 1691, came upon a set of "very old" Indian calendars and an early history book. The contents of both, which are far too extensive to summarize here, were astounding to Melgar, Boturini and Nuñez, especially where mention of black folk was made. At page 116, for example, Boturini states:

> . . . I'm not surprised that the same bishop (Francisco Nuñez de la Vega), in no. 32, chap. 28 of the same preamble, writes that they [the Indian people] have painted in their repertoire or calendars seven *negritos* for divinations and prognostications, corresponding to the seven days of the week, beginning to count as the gentiles do, with the seven planets [39, p. 293].

Boturini further quotes Nuñez as stating that the Indian people were very much afraid of "the blacks" for the Indians recalled an historic figure of "Ethiopian" color who was a great warrior and so "cruel" that the Indians of Ochuc and other settlements of the Mexican plains greatly revered him and called him Yalahau, meaning "Lord of the Blacks" [39, p. 294].

Finally, after debating the merits of the works of a few other scholars as to the probable presence of early blacks in the Western Hemisphere, Melgar speculates that, in view of ancient Olmec sculptures, Indian customs and traditions and philological similarities between Old and New World peoples, it is entirely possible that at one time black people were the sole occupants of Mesoamerica and that during this period it is likely that the climate of this region was only suitable to their habitation [39, pp. 295–296].

As to the origin of these Africoids, Melgar looks first to Asia and Africa, but, in both articles, concludes with the oft-cited passage of Plato—wherein the latter refers to the Egyptian tradition of conquerors from beyond the "Pillars of Hercules"—and suggests that the early American blacks may have had as their homeland the "lost continent" of Atlantis, and thereby traveled from Atlantis to the Western Hemisphere and other parts of the world [39, p. 296].

Paul Rivet, a noted anthropologist, is also impressed by the early presence of black people in the Americas and theorizes that it was from neither Atlantis, continental Asia nor Africa that these Africoids migrated to the New World, but Melanesia [14]. Rivet contends that black seamen scoured the South Seas [and perhaps even the Indian Ocean—precisely where tradition places the prehistoric continent of Lemuria] [42] and reached the Americas in very ancient times.

In support of his theory, Rivet states that the Melanesians discovered all of the South Pacific islands, and even today, at the lowest point of their culture, undertake voyages of 4,500 miles. Furthermore, certain American people and Melanesians used similar boats, implements, dwellings and weapons; made bark cloth, played on panpipes, and hunted with blowguns. Moreover, the Hokan languages of California, Mexico and Central America are quite similar to Melanesian; and, Rivet insists, as do some of the other scientists cited in our discussion of "skeletal remains," that the skulls of the extinct Pericu "Indians" of lower California and the Punin crania of South America are almost identical to those of Melanesians [14].

Perhaps the most "scientific" theory thus far advanced to explain the prehistoric and ancient presence of Africoids in the New World and from which may be derived clues as to the derivation of the black Olmecs, is that of H. S. Gladwin.

Recognizing that India [43–49], China [43, 50–52], Japan [10, pp. 287–292; 32, pp. 72–78; 53, 54], and the South Sea islands [55] were once occupied by at least two distinctly non-Mongoloid peoples, and acknowledging that

"America's" first occupants probably came from Asia via the Bering Strait, Gladwin, in a considerable part of his work, focuses on one central issue: who were the early occupants of Asia who pioneered the trek over the Bering Strait and into the New World? To which he answers: "Australoids" and "Negroids"—two of several black variants to which we assign the name Africoid.

Relying on skeletal and cultural evidence, Gladwin states that by 25,000 B. C., "Australoids" filtered up the northeastern coast of Asia, crossed over the Bering Strait, moved into North America, and thereby became the first *homo sapiens* to enter the New World. From Alaska, Gladwin traces these folk down the Pacific coast to southern California, then turns eastward and moves into the American South. From there he again moves southward, following the "Australoid" skeletons through Mexico and Central America, and finally reaches Punin and Paltacalo in Ecuador and the Lagoa Santa caves of eastern Brazil [18, pp. 49–75].

On the heels of the "Australoids," according to Gladwin's theory, came successive waves of "Negroids" between 15,000 B.C. and 2500 B.C. The "Negroid" immigrants were expert hunters whom Gladwin identifies with Folsom man, maker of fine flint spear points. These black folk settled much of the southern half of the United States where, in certain regions, they mixed with their "Australoid" kinsmen [18, pp. 87–122].

Into the Americas came later Algonquins, Eskimos, Mongoloids, Melanesians and Polynesians respectively [18, pp. 137–323]. Gladwin theorizes, then, that it was from these varied peoples that a number of the "American Indians" inherited their "mixed" morphology.

To Africa some scholars have turned in search of the origin of the early Afro-Americans, and the average thinker would doubtless believe that, of all places, the "Mother Continent" would be the most logical to which to look for supportive evidence. While there is now little question that Africans reached the New World long before Columbus, most of these African-American contacts appear to have been made after the birth of Christ and therefore follow not only the rise, but perhaps even the decline of Olmec civilization. The only African civilization that has thus far been widely investigated as to its possibly having influenced ancient American culture is that of the early Nile Valley.

Although the pyramids of Egypt and Kush antedate those of Mesoamerica, and the former were constructed as tombs while the latter were erected bases for temples, the fact of their existence on both sides of the Atlantic has intrigued many and encouraged the belief that here lie similarities that are inexplicable but for the intercontinental transmission of ideas. This argument was strengthened in 1949, following the discovery of an underground funeral chamber concealed deep within the Pyramid of the Inscriptions at Palenque in Mesoamerica—proving that early "Americans" also constructed pyramids that served, at least in part, as depositories for sepulchres [27, p. 102].

Other Afro-American cultural similarities include spindle whorls which, "unearthed in Palestine and Egypt," are "scarcely distinguished, even by experts, from those found in Mexico and Peru"; and Peruvial looms that, whether horizontal or vertical, "duplicate those of Egyptian origin from 1900 B.C.— down to the identical number and arrangement of working parts" [27, pp. 108–109]; moreover, although Peru, mentioned above, is not in Mesoamerica, we should also note the following:

> The overwhelming majority of recovered mummies from the earliest times come from Peru—and from Egypt. In both regions, the brain and viscera are surgically removed from the body cavities, cleansed and preserved with herbs and spices and stored in canopic jars. In both Egypt and Peru, the body is dried and wrapped in the finest fabrics available—

fabrics woven on identical looms, as we have seen [38, p. 85].

Both the Egyptians and Kushites were extraordinary seamen and may well account for the early "Indian" tradition of an ancient people who, preceding the Toltecs, came "from the east in ships in order to settle in the New World"; a possibility to which Augustus Le Plongeon makes reference in his book *Maya Archaeology* [23, p. 241]. Furthermore, Jackson appears to believe that this tradition relates specifically to the ancient Kushites:

> If ancient civilizations in Africa, Asia and America show certain traits pointing to a common origin in times remote in the past, then civilization is much older than many modern authorities are willing to admit. It is our opinion, and we have presented some of the data in . . . this work, that all the early civilizations were of African Ethiopian origin. If these ancient Kushites could found such cultures as those of Egypt and Sumer, there is no reason that they could not have sailed across the Atlantic and planted the seeds of the first civilization in the New World [23, p. 260].

A few other diffusionists have given attention to additional peoples, especially the Phoenicians and Carthaginians, who were of "Negroid" ancestry and probably reached early America [56]. While the evidence supporting the presence of these folk in ancient America remains sparse and fragmented, a thorough and objective investigation of all available clues might well yield surprising results.

To which continent, now, in view of our analysis, must we turn for Olmec origins? It would seem relatively certain that Europe should be excluded, for the Olmecs appear to have been black and, while Africoid Grimaldis occupied prehistoric Europe, no blacks of appreciable numbers have settled this continent since ancient times. We are therefore limited to a consideration of Africa, Asia and Australia, with blacks having occupied all, or nearly all, of Africa and much of Asia until sometime around the birth of Christ, and having occupied all of Australia until well into modern times. Ironically, however, even narrowing our focus to these three continents hardly simplifies matters. Were the Olmecs descendants of "Australoids" and "Negroids" who first peopled the Western Hemisphere via the Bering Strait? Did they come instead from Melanesia by way of the Pacific islands? Or was it the Atlantic over which the Olmecs came—sailing from Egypt, Sumer or India. All that appears evident is that the Olmecs were a black people who had similar cultural traits to other black peoples in various parts of the Old World. In view of this, the real clue to the origin of the Olmec people may only be found following a prolonged and thorough analysis of the cultural similarities between these ancient Mesoamericans and certain early black civilizations of the Old World—a task that is beyond the scope of this article. Even this task, however, must be approached with caution, for if, indeed, the Olmecs were descendants of prehistoric Afro-Asian immigrants, who came over the Bering Strait, it is entirely possible that their civilization may well have evolved independently—as did the most ancient civilization of the Old World. In such cases, cultural similarities between the Old and New Worlds would be coincidental.

OLMEC CULTURE AND INFLUENCE

The Olmec contribution to the Americas was profound and unmistakable and its imprint still survives in Mesoamerica where first it was known and from whose borders it sprang forth and quickly spread abroad.

At an early period, the Olmecs became masters of agriculture in the tradition of their racial counterparts throughout the southern spheres of the Old World—in Egypt, Sumer, India and Arabia [57]. This is of special interest to historians in view of that fact that, just as in the first three of the above lands, Mesoamerica was a "civilization and not a village culture, which developed along the rivers

which with their flooding renew the agricultural land . . ." [3, pp. 1–52].

So significant was the Olmec agricultural contribution to early Mesoamerica that corn, beans and squash, which served as the basis of the Olmec diet, remain the central staples of Mesoamericans today [58]. It is also possible that the early Olmecs cultivated cotton, cocoa and tobacco [2, p. 21].

The Olmec way of life, while based on agriculture, complemented by the products of fishing, hunting and food gathering, appears to have owed much of its wealth and stability to highly developed commercial trading:

> In explorations of the Metropolitan area—within the Olmec period—no discoveries have been made of *manufactured* objects from outside: on the contrary, everything seems to have been made at the site. On the other hand, we do find objects which are without any doubt Olmec—not Olmecoid—in such faraway places as Monte Alban, Tlatilco and even Central America. These objects, small and precious, occasionally of jade, almost surely were made in the Olmec zone and exported (Emphasis added) [2, p. 87].

Archaeologists are further proving that Olmec trading was not confined to the exportation of manufactured objects but entailed massive importation of natural products to be worked in the region itself. For example, the great stones, from which the monoliths were carved, appear to have been brought in from outside the metropolitan area of the Olmecs.

What appears most interesting is that natural roads and waterways were used in this trade, with the latter being especially beneficial, since the main waterways flow from outside the Olmec area inward, thereby facilitating transportation of imported products of incredible size [2, pp. 87–88].

As a settled people, who practiced agriculture and trading, it is not surprising then that the Olmecs also became the first urbanized Americans and leaped ahead of their neighbors in architecture and city planning.

Little is known of the dwelling places of the common man or in fact of the more sumptuous adobes of the chieftains—if we are privileged to make such an assumption. It is speculated, however, that the early houses were of wood with palm-thatched roofs, their walls covered with hardened mud, made with the wattle and daub system so common in Mesoamerica today. Rectangular house plans of this kind have been discovered sitting on low mounds arranged around "courts" [2, pp. 48–49].

To be sure, highly sophisticated structures have also been discovered. For example, in La Venta, one of the main centers of Olmec life, has been found a pyramid erected over 2000 years ago. Built of piled-up clays, it is 420 feet in diameter, 103 feet high and has a general mass of 3,500,000 cubic feet. Other pyramids have also been found in this region [2, p. 36].

Additional structures exhumed from Olmec burial sites include mounds. In Rio Chiquito, for example, "The mounds are important, constructed around ample quadrangular plazas. A long rectangular courtyard is bordered on its eastern and western sides by parallel mounds; to the north can be seen an edifice 60 feet high, and another limits the courtyard at the south. The whole is obviously planned and possesses a definite orientation" [59].

The Olmecs, therefore, appear to have been an urban people who established well-planned, architecturally sophisticated metropolises and ceremonial centers, characterized by thatch-roofed houses, pyramids and mounds that were surrounded by sprawling rural zones. In summary, Caso draws a picture of the political and religious centers of ancient Olmec society that appear to have been nourished by:

> . . . wards which were later to be called barrios and which still exist today as such in our indigenous communities and are not integral parts of a city as they are in Europe but small settlements where are found the authorities, the local place of worship, and

a division of labor which permits specialization in production . . . In its structure each barrio reproduces the organization of the ceremonial and political center . . . and at times is an ethnic division, representing a clan or *calpulli* whose provenance is to be found outside . . . . We suggest that this urban organization be called a *dispersed city*, since its manner of functioning is that of a city—a very large one—because it embraces within its limits the tilled fields, such as are found today in our modern villages [3, pp. 34–35].

It would appear then that the Olmec urban organization followed a settlement pattern wherein houses with their lands were centered between large groups of buildings. Such a pattern of living would place the Olmecs between the small, virtually neolithic village and the sophisticated sites which were later found at Teotihuacan and Mayapan [2, p. 52].

Of countless Olmec inventions, two of the greatest were the Long Count system and the calendar. While there is certainly no complete catalog available of the glyphs found at Olmec excavation sites, Michael Coe, an American specialist on early Mesoamerica, has discussed some of them [60]. He points out that various peoples during the Olmec period inscribed not only hieroglyphs but dates on their monuments. Some of these writing techniques appear to have been in the relatively simple system employed by the later Aztecs, in which dates could only be indicated within a span of fifty-two years, after which the system was repeated. Other Olmec inscriptions reflect the most complete and nearly perfect system of calculating time conceived in the Americas, the Long Count system, heretofore believed to have been invented by the Maya.

Of the Olmec calendar and its significance to Olmec society, Bernal has written:

> . . . (A) calendar of this kind would be impossible without the study of the movements of the sun, the moon, and of certain heavenly bodies. We can assume that the knowledge of the latter might have been a

later acquisition, but it is undeniable that the Olmecs had discovered at least the length of the year and of the lunar month, and that they also computed time with the system of days that is characteristic of Meso-america. This calendar, which was probably intimately related to the agricultural cycle and to various types of ceremonies (as it undoubtedly was later) was one of the most powerful elements in the hands of the priests since it gave them the possibility of directing agricultural life and perhaps, as occurred later, served as the basis of an astrology which determined the name given to the newborn.

It was only through a knowledge of astron-omy that the Olmecs could orient their cities and monuments correctly. The rigorous orientation of Olmec cities, that obsession for order, the style of the great sculptures, the splendid tomb of La Venta, and the burial offerings of extremely valuable jade, the attire of the priests officiating in ceremonial acts represented on the monuments . . . all of these indicate the existence of the most characteristic trait of Mesoamerican civiliza-tion: ceremonialism, the vast importance given to rites and to religion in general [2, pp. 96–97].

Mesoamerican religion appears to have been polytheistic; and Heizer, who has engaged in considerable study respecting the characteristics of what he calls the Olmec "theocratic state," feels that the Olmecs created a pantheon of cosmological deities [16]. Despite Heizer's position and the opinions of other Olmec specialists, however, only a few archaeologists have identified evidence from Olmec sites that shed light on Olmec gods or religious practices. Stirling, for example, speaks of a figure sculptured on the popular Tres Zapotes box as a sun god [62]; Flores Guerrero, a Mexican scholar, cites the oft depicted jaguar as an animal that was widely feared and worshipped as a god [63]; Alfonso Medellin, an historian, identifies what may be the god of fire from Laguna de los Cerros [64]; and, in this writer's view, the giant colossal heads

may certainly represent ancient Mesoamerican deities. Little more is known, however, concern-ing the religion of the early Olmec people.

Sophisticated urban centers supported by extensive trading encourage the belief that the Olmec people built a fairly elaborate society with class stratifications and distinc-tions, that might well be called a state or indeed a nation—the first "America."

Were there, to steer this huge, ancient con-glomerate, high priests or kings, under whom stood workers, professionals and warriors, all appointed his special task for maintenance of the nation? Western science shudders: "A nation? A black nation in ancient 'America'?" Modern authorities may grudgingly concede the existence of urban clusters of people— even black people—in ancient Mesoamerica, but to assert that the early Olmecs were not only black, but a nation of blacks passes all legitimacy and cuts off even liberal white support. Therefore, to the foregoing inquiry the answer remains "unavailable," but we suspect that science knows. Despite our sus-picions, we shall not assert that the Olmecs actually planted a *state* or *nation,* headed by kings or priests, with attendant class stratifica-tions, on early Mesoamerican soil. We do hold, however, that the existence of state systems among the Teotihuacan, Mayan and Zapotec, direct heirs of the Olmecs, is powerful evidence in support of the belief that the Olmec pre-cursors comprised a state or nation—the first civilization of the Western Hemisphere.

Whether a nation, state or "sphere of influ-ence", Olmec culture, dawning near the tip of Yucatan sometime following the close of the second millennium B.C., spread through Guatemala, Central America, Chiapas, Oaxaca, Morelos, the Central Highlands, and Veracruz [2, pp. 15–21, 123–185], filtered across the Gulf of Mexico, reached the northwest coast of Florida, penetrated and then influenced what is now called the American South [23, p. 244].

The widespread presence and influence of the early Olmecs are not only borne out by their religious, artistic and scientific traits that were absorbed by later, highly civilized peoples, such as the Maya, Zapotec and Teotihuacan [2]; but Olmec inscriptions, ornaments, implements, figurines, masks and ceramic pieces are dispersed throughout pre-classic, classic and post-classic Central and Mesoamerica [2, pp. 209–268]; early mounds, possibly traceable to the Olmecs, are spread across southern and central North America [23, p. 244]; and, historically, by legend and science, the Olmec "nation" has been labeled the "Mother Culture" of the Western Hemisphere [5, p. 725].

We therefore conclude that, despite perverted tradition, academic deception, scientific shuffling and ethnocentricism, a black folk, presently called Olmec, laid the foundation of "American" civilization: than this position there is none more rational in view of the evidence presently accessible to scientists and researchers. We assert, furthermore, that perhaps more profound than the conclusion reached herein is the inverted posture assumed by present "authorities" who, rather than advancing some of the hypotheses encouraged by the evidence—if solely for the sake of scientific discussion—ignore every clue that would extinguish the myths upon which their crumbling academic towers were so cleverly built.

Finally, it is our hope that white celebrants of the American Bicentennial will pause to explore, in greater depth, the black origins of the Western Hemisphere, over which they currently wield extensive influence and control, and thereby demand that the lords of science, on whom we all depend for learning, replace widespread fraud and concealment with historical truth.

Notes

1. The expression "First World," coined by Shirley Graham Du Bois, widow of the great scientist and scholar, W. E. B. Du Bois, appears a more appropriate description of the so-called underdeveloped "Third World," since it was in Africa that man and civilization first emerged and it was to adjacent Asia that man then spread. Furthermore, the majority of the present occupants of Latin America are of African and Asian ancestry and therefore traceable to man's first habitats.

2. While Bernal, a modern Olmec authority, only traces the origin of Olmec civilization back to 1100 B.C., certain sculptural evidence indicates that this civilization began as early as 2000 B.C. [2, p. 4, 4].

3. By "Africoid" is meant every variant of the black race: Grimaldi, Bushmen-Hottentot, Negroid, Pygmoid, Congoid, Dravidian, Hamitic, Australoid, Melanesoid, Negritoid, Polynesoid, etc.

4. Jose Melgar's, "Notable escultural antigua, antiguedades mexicanos", *Boletin de Geografia y Estadistica*, was translated by Saul Solache, Professor of Sociology at UCLA, architect and artist of some eminence; and Joseph Beaver, retired Foreign Service Consular Officer, presently writer and independent publisher.

References

1. C. Williams, *The Destruction of Black Civilization: Great Issues of a Race From 4500 B.C. to 2000 A.D.*, Third World Press, Chicago, revised edition, 1974.

2. I. Bernal, *The Olmec World*, Berkeley University of California Press, p. 15, 1969.

3. A. Caso, Existio un Imperio Olmeca?, *Memorias del Colegio Nacional, 3,* p. 12.

4. A. von Wuthenau, *The Art of Terracotta Pottery in Pre-Columbian Central and South America,* Crown Publishers, Inc., New York, pp. 70–71, 1969.

5. P. R. Vasques, et al., *The National Museum of Anthropology; Mexico: Art, Architecture, Archaeology, Anthropology,* Abrams, New York, p. 125, 1968.

6. C.S. Coon, *The Living Races of Man,* Alfred A. Knopf, New York, pp. 136–138, 1965.

7. _____, *The Origin of Races,* Alfred A. Knopf, New York, p. 477, 1969.

8. C. C. Marquez, *Estudios Arqueologicas y Etnograficos,* D. E. E. Kelly, Bogota, Mexico, translated by M. Lumumba, linguist, scientist and scholar, Los Angeles, California, pp. 179–180, 1956.

9. E. A. Hooton, *Apes, Men and Morons,* G. P. Putnam's Sons, New York, p. 183, 1937.

10. R. B. Dixon, *The Racial History of Man,* Scribner's Sons, New York, p. 441, 1923.

11. G. Taylor, *Environment, Race and Migration,* The University of Chicago Press, Chicago, p. 246, 1937.

12. L. R. Sullivan and M. Hellman, *The Punin Calvarium,* American Museum of Natural History, New York, 1925.

13. R. Verneau, Cranes d'Indienes de la Colombia, *Anthropologie,* 1924.

14. P. Rivet, *Los Origens Hombre Americano Mexico,* 1943.

15. A. H. Keene, *Man: Past and Present,* The University Press, Cambridge, p. 340, 1920.

16. A. C. Haddon, *The Races of Man and Their Distribution,* The University Press, Cambridge, p. 133, 1924.

17. F. A. Peterson, *Ancient Mexico,* Capricorn Books, New York, pp. 39–40, 1962.

18. H. S. Gladwin, *Men Out of Asia,* McGraw-Hill Book Co., New York, pp. 184–185, 1947.

19. M. D. Coe, *America's First Civilization,* American Heritage Publishing Co., New York, p. 55, 1968.

20. I. Bernal, *Mexico Before Cortez,* Doubleday & Co., Garden City, New York, p. 29, 1963.

21. A. Emmerich, *Art Before Columbus,* Simon and Schuster, New York, p. 54, 1963.

22. J. N. Leonard, *Ancient America,* Time Incorporated, New York, p. 32, 1967.

23. J. G. Jackson, *Introduction to African Civilization,* University Books, New York, p. 237, 1970.

24. C. Wicke, *Olmec: An Early Art Style of Pre-Columbian Mexico,* The University of Arizona Press, Tuscon, p. 69, 1971.

25. S. Rodman, *The Mexico Traveler,* Meredith Press, New York, p. 6, 1969.

26. W. Hanf, *Mexico,* Rand McNally & Company, Chicago, p. 19, 1967.

27. S. S. McKern, *Exploring the Unknown: Mysteries in American Archaeology,* Praeger Publishers, New York, p. 104, 1972.

28. N. Cheetham, *Mexico: A Short History,* Thomas Y. Crowell, New York, p. 19, 1970.

29. R. E. Quirk, *Mexico,* Prentice-Hall, Inc., Englewood, New Jersey, p. 10, 1971.

30. F. W. Hayes, III, The African Presence in America Before Columbus, *The Black World,* p. 13, July 1973.

31. R. Palacio, *México a Través de los Siglos,* translated by M. Lumumba, Ballesca y Comp, Editores, Mexico, p. 63, 1889.

32. J. A. Rogers, *Sex and Race,* published by the author, New York, *1,* p. 270.

33. Gomara, Historia General de las Indias, Part 1, Calpe, Madrid, 1922.

34. F. J. Vergara y Velasco, Nueva Georgrafia de Colombia, *1,* p. 878.

35. E. Restrepo, Un Viajex el Darien.

36. C. C. Marquez, Prehistoria y Viajes, San Agustin, pp. 137–138, 1893.

37. A. Braghine, *The Shadow of Atlantis,* E. P. Dutton & Co., New York, pp. 40–43, 1940.

38. T. McKern and S. McKern, Odyssey: The Peopling of the New Work, *Mankind,* 2:6, p. 66, April 1970.

39. J. Melgar, Notable Escultural Antigua, Antiguedades Mexicanos, *Boletin de Geografia*

y Estadistica, Secunda Epoca., translated by S. Solache, *1,* pp. 292–297, 1869.

40. _____, Estudio Sobre la Antiguedad y el Origen de la Cabeza Colosal de Tipo Etiopico que Esiste en Hueyapan, *Boletin de la Sociedad Mexicana,* Secunda Epoca., translated by M. Lumumba, *3,* pp. 104–109, 1871.

41. L. B. Benaducci, Idea de una Nueva Historia General de la America Septemtrional, Madrid, Impr. de J. de Zuniga, 1746.

42. W. E. B. DuBois, *Black Folk: Then and Now,* Henry Holt and Company, New York, p. 4, 1939.

43. W. E. B. DuBois, *The World and Africa,* International Publishers, New York, pp. 176–177, 1961; N. K. Dutt, *The Aryanisation of India,* published by the author, Calcutta, pp. 76–101, 1925.

44. R. C. Dutt, *Ancient India,* Longmans, Green and Co., New York, pp. 12–19, 1893.

45. G. Higgins, *Amcalypsis, 1,* pp. 51–59, 1965.

46. E. A. Hooton, *Up From the Ape,* Macmillan, New York, p. 592, 1931.

47. W. W. Hunter, *The Indian Empire,* Trubner and Co., London, pp. 69–70, 1882.

48. L. Thorndike, *A Short History of Civilization,* F. S. Cofts, New York, p. 227, 1936.

49. W. Durant, *Our Oriental Heritage,* New York, p. 396, 1935.

50. L. C. Goodrich, *A Short History of the Chinese People,* Routledge and Kegan Paul, London, p. 7, 1950.

51. C. Lan-po and W. Ja-kang, Fossil Human Skull Base of Late Paleolithic State from Chilihshan Leipin District, Kwangsi, China, VP 3, 1, 1959.

52. K. Latourette, The Chinese, Their History and Culture, 4th Edition, p. 438, 1967.

53. H. Johnston, *The Negro in the New World,* Methuen and Co., London, pp. 24–27, 1910.

54. N. G. Munro, Prehistoric Japan, Yokohama, pp. 676–678, 1911.

55. J. P. Widney, *Race Life of the Aryan Peoples,* Funk and Wagnalls, New York, *2,* pp. 238–239, 1907.

56. C. H. Hapgood, *Maps of the Ancient Sea Kings: Evidence of Advanced Civilizations in the Ice Age,* Chilton Book Co., New York and Philadelphia, pp. 193–194, 1966.

57. C. A. Diop, *The African Origin of Civilization: Myth or Reality,* Lawrence Hill & Co., New York, 1974.

58. M. W. Stirling, Discovering the New World's Oldest Dated Work of Man, *National Geographic Magazine, LXXVI,* pp. 183–218, 1939.

59. M. W. Stirling, Stone Monuments of the Rio Chiquito, Veracruz, Mexico, *Bureau of American Ethnology,* Bulletin, Washington, *164,* pp. 213–240, 1955.

60. M. D. Coe, The Olmec Style and Its Distribution, *Handbook of Middle American Indians, 3,* pp. 739–775, 1965.

61. R. F. Heizer, Agriculture and the Theocratic State in Lowland Southeastern Mexico, *American Antiquity, XXVI,* pp. 215–222, 313, 1960.

62. M. W. Stirling, Stone Monuments of Southern Mexico, *Bureau of American Ethnology,* Bulletin, Washington, *138,* p. 18, 1943.

63. R. F. Guerrero, *Historia General del Arte Mexicano,* Epoca Prehispanica, Mexico and Buenos Aires, 1962.

64. A. M. Zenil, Monolitos Ineditos Olmecas, *La Palabra y el Hombre Revista de la Universidad Veracruzana, XVI,* p. 91, 1960.

The Atlantic Slave Trade and Slavery: Some Interpretations of Their Significance in the Development of the United States and the Western World

C. L. R. JAMES

EVERY PEOPLE, EVERY RACE, has passed through a stage of slavery. That which ought to be a commonplace of history has been obscured, corrupted and ignored by the injection of slavery into a modern and advanced society like the United States. It would be not only inextricably confusing but impossible to attempt any summary of the infinite varieties of slavery in past ages. However, it is useful to bear in mind two of these varieties. The first is the systematic breeding and selling of their own children into slavery by the backward peoples of Northern Europe. They traded with the highly developed civilization of Rome, even when Rome was ruled by the papacy. The second is the oft-repeated sneer that the magnificent civilization of ancient Greece was based on slavery. Slavery did not help to build the social order of Greece that laid the foundations of Western civilization in so many spheres. Rather, it was the growth of slavery which ruined ancient Greece. Furthermore, the term "slave" did not then have the meaning it has had since the African slave-trade to the Americas. The slaves in the mines of Greece were cruelly exploited, but in Athens itself slaves could become educated and officials in the city administration, and could attend the ritual performances of the dramatic festivals. As late as the fourth century B.C., when the democracy was on the decline, Plato complained that the concept and practices of democracy were so deeply ingrained in Athenian society that not only the slaves, but the very horses and dogs walked about in the streets of Athens in a manner that proclaimed their democratic rights.

Today it would be impossible to examine the most important of all phases of slavery, African slavery in the American continents, without having some view of the slavery in Africa itself before the Europeans established the Atlantic slave-trade, and the African slavery which was the result of that trade. African slavery before the European slave-trade was internal. For the most part it was also patriarchal. Thirty years ago, I summarized

Reprinted, with permission, from John A. Williams and Charles F. Harris, eds., *Amistad: Writings in Black History and Culture,* Vintage Books, 1970.

African civilization and the effects of the European slave-trade as follows:

> . . . In the sixteenth century, Central Africa was a territory of peace and happy civilization. Traders travelled thousands of miles from one side of the continent to another without molestation. The tribal wars from which the European pirates claimed to deliver the people were mere sham fights; it was a great battle when half-a-dozen men were killed. It was on a peasantry in many respects superior to the serfs in large areas of Europe, that the slave-trade fell. Tribal life was broken up and millions of detribalised Africans were let loose upon each other. The unceasing destruction of crops led to cannibalism; the captive women became concubines and degraded the status of the wife. Tribes had to supply slaves or be sold as slaves themselves. Violence and ferocity became the necessities for survival. The stockades of grinning skulls, the human sacrifices, the selling of their own children as slaves, these horrors were the product of an intolerable pressure on the African peoples, which became fiercer through the centuries as the demands of industry increased and the methods of coercion were perfected . . .

Within recent decades an immense amount of research has been done on pre-European Africa. Not only does that analysis still hold its ground, but there has been added to it a conception of pre-European African history which stresses the intellectual achievements of the postwar world. In a study done for UNESCO on *Race and History,* Claude Lévi-Strauss, after a recognition of the "richness and audacity of the aesthetic invention" of primitive peoples turns to Africa:

> The contribution of Africa is more complex, but also more obscure, for it is only at a recent period that we have begun to suspect the importance of its role as a cultural melting pot of the ancient world: a place where all influences have merged to take new forms or to remain in reserve, but always transformed into new shapes. The Egyptian civilization, of which one knows the importance for humanity, is intelligible only as a common product of Asia and of Africa and the great political systems of ancient Africa, its juridical creations, its philosophical doctrines for a long time hidden from the West, its plastic arts and its music which explored methodically all possibilities offered by each means of expression are equally indications of an extraordinarily fertile past. The latter besides is directly attested to by the perfection of the ancient techniques of bronze and of ivory which surpass by far all that the West was practicing in those spheres in the same period.

Neolithic man tilled the soil, domesticated animals, invented and used tools, and lived a family life subject to certain social regulations. Claude Lévi-Strauss believed that this was the decisive moment in the history of human civilization. However, he is prepared to admit that there has been one other fundamental change in the life of civilized man. The Industrial Revolution, bringing mechanical power into use, altered the conditions of life and created a new type of society.

We can see this most dramatically in the two most important concerns of civilized man, war and revolution. Alexander the Great, Hannibal, Julius Caesar, and Napoleon each would have understood what the others were trying to accomplish on the field of battle; their strategy and tactics would have been much the same. But the moment we examine the American Civil War, military conflict breaks entirely out of the limits in which it had remained for thousands of years. The reason was the introduction of mechanical power—in the form of the railway—into war. Armies could now be five times as large as before. This larger army, with its rapidity of movement, upset the industrial and the social structure of the nation. Today, a little more than a hundred years later, the development of industrial power imperils the very continuation of civilized life.

It is the move to large-scale industry and the accumulation of great numbers of men in factories which is the starting point and the basis of Marx's theory of socialist revolution, and the contemporary nightmare of social destruction. There is no question today that the resources which initiated and established this epoch-making change in human life resulted from the Atlantic slave-trade and the enslavement of Africans in the Americas. Jean Léon Jaurès, in his history of the French Revolution, a work which is a landmark not only in the history of the Revolution, but in the writing of modern history, comments wistfully: "Sad irony of human history . . . The fortunes created at Bordeaux, at Nantes, by the slave-trade, gave the bourgeoisie that pride which needed liberty and contributed to human emancipation." But Jaurès, whose thought represented the quintessence of Social Democracy, was here limited by his preoccupation with parliamentary politics. Gaston-Martin, in his *L'Ere des Négriers*, makes it clear that nearly all the industries which developed in France during the eighteenth century had their origin in goods or commodities destined either for the Coast of Guinea or for America. It was the capital gained from the slave trade which fertilized what became the Industrial Revolution. Though the bourgeoisie traded in many things, everything depended on the success or failure of the traffic in slaves. In *Capitalism and Slavery*, Eric Williams has demonstrated that it was in slavery and the slave trade that the power originated which created modern industry in England, making it the workshop of the world.

The overwhelming majority of historians show a curious disinclination to deal with the seminal role played by the slave trade and slavery in the creation of what distinguished Western civilization from all other civilizations. As far back as 1847, Karl Marx stated in very aggressive terms what modern civilization, and in particular the United States, owed to the enslavement of black people from Africa. Karl Marx, in 1846 in his polemical work *The Poverty of Philosophy*, made slavery in the United States the center of his comprehensive uncovering of the fires which stoked Western civilization.

> Direct slavery is just as much the pivot of bourgeois industry as machinery, credits, etc. Without slavery you have not cotton; without cotton you have no modern industry. It is slavery . . . and it is world trade that is the pre-condition of large-scale industry. Thus slavery is an economic category of the greatest importance.
>
> Without slavery North America, the most progressive of countries, would be transformed into a patriarchal country. Wipe North America off the map of the world, and you will have anarchy—the complete decay of modern commerce and civilization. Cause slavery to disappear and you will have wiped America off the map of nations.
>
> Thus slavery, because it is an economic category, has always existed among the institutions of the peoples. Modern nations have been able only to disguise slavery in their own countries, but they have imposed it without disguise upon the New World.

Fifty years after Marx's statement, an American historian, a young man twenty-four years of age, tackled the question. In 1954, looking again at his doctoral dissertation written for Harvard University in 1896, *The Suppression of the African Slave Trade to the United States of America, 1638–1870*, Dr. W. E. B. Du Bois, in an apologia of two and a half pages, three times expressed his regret that when he was doing the work he had not had the benefit of any acquaintance with the works or theories of Karl Marx. Yet with his own independent, if youthful, judgment Dr. Du Bois here showed himself as far in advance of American historiography as he was to show himself in other spheres of American life.

First of all, the title of the book could be misleading. The actual attempt at suppression (1807–1825) is treated as late as Chapter Eight. What we have here is a history of the slave trade and slavery in the United States. It is true that the very first sentence of the monograph, as he calls it (197 pages of text and 98 pages of appendices), declares that he proposes to set forth the efforts from early colonial times until the present to limit and suppress the trade in slaves between Africa and America.

He first separates the Planting Colonies (the South) from the Farming Colonies (New Jersey), and then moves into the period of the Revolution. He notes that from about 1760 to 1787, there is a "pronounced effort to regulate, limit, or totally prohibit the traffic." Chapter Six deals with the Federal Convention and the spirit of compromise leading each state (i.e., in the South) to deal with the question of slavery as it pleased. Then comes a most interesting chapter where we see at work the same mind which in *Black Reconstruction in America* linked the emancipation of the slaves in 1865 to the Paris Commune in 1871, and the black struggle for freedom in 1935 to the world-wide struggle against fascism and for colonial emancipation. Young Du Bois heads the chapter "Toussaint L'Ouverture and Anti-Slavery Effort, 1787–1807." The Haitian Revolt sharpens the debate for and against slavery in the U.S.A. It is "the main cause of two laws" and soon was "the direct instigation to a third." But despite the combined efforts of

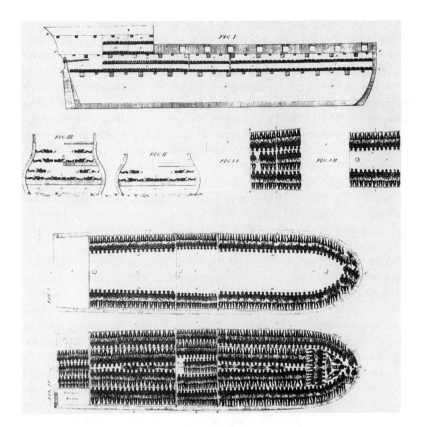

Detailed drawing of a
slave ship, showing
traders how to make
the most efficient use
of space in carrying
their cargo.

fear and philanthropy, the profits of trade won in the end.

Du Bois is pretty certain that it was the Haitian Revolution and its influence which was one of the main causes of the suppression of the slave trade by national law. But to the apathy of the federal government is now added "The Rise of the Cotton Kingdom, 1820–1850." He concludes with a chapter on "The Lesson for Americans." The Constitutional Convention had avoided the issue when it had been possible to do something about it. "No American can study the connection of slavery with United States history and not devoutly pray that his country will never have a similar social problem to solve, until it shows more capacity for such work than it has shown in the past." The last sentence of the text is even more clearly a product of

moralistic thought. "From this we may conclude that it behooves nations, as well as men, to do things at the very moment when they ought to be done."

We can only estimate the numbers involved, but it is certain that the slave trade shifted many millions of Africans from their homeland. A conservative estimate is that 15,000,000 Africans landed after crossing the Atlantic; but some estimates give 50,000,000 and some go even higher. Further, the mortality rate on the voyage to the Americas was often high, and in addition some were killed in Africa in the raids and wars conducted to get slaves, and some died while waiting to be sold or shipped.

Effectively (and officially) the slave trade lasted three centuries, from about 1550 to

1850. Its period of greatest activity began after the middle of the seventeenth century. There have been many arguments about the effects of the trade on the African economy and population. We know it led directly to nineteenth-century colonialism in Africa and the accompanying degradation of the Africans. But an important area of research remains uninvestigated, which we can only mention here. What were the social and moral effects of slaving on the Africans who bought and sold slaves—what did they think of it themselves? What have been the long-term effects on the African peoples who remained on the continent? Our sources and scholarship are almost entirely Western, and Western thinking has governed our assessment, regardless of whether our standards have been overtly racist or antipathetic to slavery. But surely one of the most important areas of study is what Africans themselves thought of the trade, and what effect it had and perhaps lingeringly continues to have on Africa itself.

Scholars continue to argue about the effects on those taken into slavery. A plateau was reached in 1959, when Stanley Elkin examined the basis for what he called the "Sambo" stereotype of North American slave character. One of the most important bases of his argument is that the capture, voyage, sale, and adjustment to the new environment of the Africans may have created a "shock" that stripped them of their former personalities and rendered their cultural background meaningless.

Most revolts came either at the point of embarkation or between that time and actual sailing. Gaston-Martin catalogues several slave revolts on board ships, and says that he discovered fifty references to revolts, or about one every fifteen trips, in his studies of Nantes slaving. (Nantes is a French seaport.) He adds that there were almost certainly many revolts which were never recorded, and he comments that they were very likely accepted as a normal hazard of the trade. Some revolts even took place at sea, where the slaves would perish even if they overcame the crew, for they had no idea of how to steer the ships. Ships' logs record the ferocity of these revolts. Usually they failed, with only a few slaves and crew members dead; sometimes the death toll went as high as forty or fifty. Rather than be taken again some blacks drowned themselves. Many crew members died. A few revolts did succeed, in which case the crew was usually massacred, sometimes merely taken captive.

In these revolts, captains accessed the most Europeanized slaves as the leaders—for some slaves had been to Europe at one time or another. Informers among the slaves existed from time to time; but when they were discovered by their fellows, they were killed.

One writer quotes a 1788 account saying the blacks were always on the lookout to rebel or escape. "Insurrections are frequently the consequence, which are seldom suppressed without much bloodshed. Sometimes these are successful and the whole ship's company is cut off." Basil Davidson himself adds, "When they failed to revolt before they reached the Americas, they revolted there." Of the slaves, he writes, "The best and strongest took the first or second chance to resist or revolt; the rest endured. But endurance did not mean acceptance."

Revolts might also take place in coordination with attacks by Africans on the ship or shore "warehouse." Around 1760, the *Diane* was attacked by Africans while the captives revolted. The French crew was captured and ransomed by Europeans who later handed them over to a French ship. The *Diane* was lost. The *Concorde* underwent two revolts. During the first, forty-five blacks disappeared; in the second a coordinated attack between revolting slaves and a party from land destroyed the ship and killed all the crew but one.

Once the ship had sailed, the danger of revolt was greatly diminished. Suicides were frequent among slaves who could not bear their misery or stand the idea of enslavement. Some slaves threw themselves overboard during the voyage, and there are many reports

Death of Capt. Ferrer, the Captain of the Amistad, July, 1839.

Don Jose Ruiz and Don Pedro Montez, of the Island of Cuba, having purchased fifty-three slaves at Havana, recently imported from Africa, put them on board the Amistad, Capt. Ferrer, in order to transport them to Principe, another port on the Island of Cuba. After being out from Havana about four days, the African captives on board, in order to obtain their freedom, and return to Africa, armed themselves with cane knives, and rose upon the Captain and crew of the vessel. Capt. Ferrer and the cook of the vessel were killed; two of the crew escaped; Ruiz and Montez were made prisoners.

of slaves dying of nostalgia either en route or in the Americas. To combat nostalgia and simultaneously give the slaves an early recovery period from the first stage of the voyage, which was invariably the worst stretch for them, about one fifth of the Nantes slavers out of Guinea would stop off for four to six weeks at islands in the eastern Atlantic. Here the slaves could rest, get fresh food, and rebuild the strength they had lost during the first stage of the voyage. Sometimes a high rate of sickness would prompt a ship to make a stopover. "Already isolated from the continent, the Negroes, in spite of a few examples of revolts, seem less antagonistic than on land, returned to good physical condition, they better endure the two or three months at sea separating them from the American islands."

Epidemics were frequent and could kill up to half to two thirds of the cargo. The most common illnesses were scurvy, diarrhea, and various skin diseases. Insurrections, as we have seen, were still an occasional threat, and if the attempt failed masses of slaves might commit suicide together rather than submit to recapture. The mortality rate varied considerably from voyage to voyage and year to year. This is reflected in a list of mortality rates among slaves traded by Nantes shippers between 1715 and 1775. The rate ranged from 5 to 9 percent in sixteen years; from 10 to 19 percent in twenty-two years; 20 to 29 percent in fourteen years; and was 34 percent in 1733. In 1751, the year of the greatest slaving activity on the records, 10,003 Negroes were traded and 2,597 died, giving a mortality rate of 26 percent. For the total period from 1715 to 1775, 237,025 slaves were shipped and 35,727 died, giving a mortality rate of 15.1 percent.

After leaving the African coast and any stopovers, the "middle passage" began, lasting normally two or three months, though large ships might occasionally make the trip in forty days. The slaves could still die or commit suicide, though if there had been a stopover for "refreshment," the number of these deaths declined. But other dangers and the length of the middle passage eclipsed the earlier problems. Storms and calms were equally dangerous—the former because it could sink a ship, the latter because it could extend a voyage beyond the range of provisions. Pirates were a constant threat, and the frequent European wars put many enemy ships on the main sea lanes. As with the gathering of captives, a slaver's life, from his point of view, was not an easy one, and expenses could be disastrous. The degree of profit had to be calculated after several voyages, averaging out likely single losses against long-term gains. Whatever the problems, the trade was so extensive that it surely must have been profitable overall.

Treatment of the slaves on board depended a great deal on the captain. But if slavers were not systematically cruel, they were not at all benevolent.

A few writers emphasize that captains were normally not excessively cruel, for it was in their own interest to bring into port as large a live shipment as possible. but when we say "excessively," we are certainly speaking in relative terms. The slaves were never well treated; they were crowded into pens too small to stand up in. The slavers' basic doctrine was that the blacks would obey only in the face of force and terror. Fear of the slaves was the permanent psychological feature of slaver, slave trader, and slave owner. The captives were kept in irons throughout the voyages; the whips would be used for the most trivial purposes. And revolts were brutally punished. Normally only a few suspected ringleaders and examples were executed; but the manner of execution involved torture.

Upon arrival at his destination, the slaver first had to be cleared with health authorities. The inspectors were often bribable—indeed, they often refused clearance unless bribed. Sometimes they would demand that the captain disinfect his ship—buying the disinfectant in the colony, of course. A local governor who feared the captives might be dangerous could quarantine the ship under pretext of fearing a health problem. And genuine epidemics existed often enough to make genuine quarantine a necessity.

Next came port taxes. In the French colonies, Louis XV decreed that the island governors should receive a 2 percent ad valorem gratuity, half for themselves, half to be split by the two lieutenant governors. In fact this gratuity system was often used as the basis for extortion of much higher amounts. Captains who protested too much could find themselves in jail.

Official cheating of slaving captains was common, even when forbidden by royal edict. Large fees could be extorted for such things as anchorage, legal costs, registration of documents, and so on. And of course if the captain had to make calls at several ports, these expenses all were multiplied.

Captains normally tried to give their slaves refreshment to prepare them for sale. When they did not have time, they doped the slaves to give them as healthy an appearance as possible. Slavers would first get rid of their worst-looking slaves at a low price. Many speculators were prepared to take a chance on buying such slaves and hoping they would survive, reckoning a one-third survival rate as satisfactory. The slaver would receive about what he had originally paid for them.

Sometimes the sale might be held up until a propitious moment, especially if there was a glut on the slave market. Either the captain or the company's agent would handle the sale, sending out leaflets to announce the time and place, and the time when the "merchandise" could be inspected. The seller would divide his slaves up into lots of about three or four, grouping them in a way that would bring the highest bidding. The auction would either be done in the usual way—taking competing bids until the highest was reached; or else bidders would be allowed each to make one bid for an entire lot.

If the sales were transacted on board, there was a reasonable chance of suicide by some of the slaves; if on land, there was a reasonable chance of escape. Here, again, we have evidence that at least some of the slaves were not so shattered at this point that they had lost all sense of personality.

Payment was rarely in cash. Often it was on credit, and defaulted payments were frequent. Apparently noncash payments accounted for

Slaves captured in raids were examined for fitness and hardiness (above). Depletion of Africans by slavers destroyed customs, cultures and mores to such an extent that Africa still has not recovered from its effects. This drawing (below) reveals the parting of mother and daughter, and a child at the breast of its mother. When the slave trade was drawing to a close, slave breeding became the method by which more slaves were propagated.

over half of the sales for Nantes slavers. At the start of the French and Indian War, they were owed 15,000,000 pounds. In order to stay on in the islands and collect their money, captains would frequently send their ships home under command of their first mates.

A second method of payment was either in merchandise or by deposit transfer at home.

Most French planters kept bank accounts in France, and captains seem to have been good judges of which ones to trust. The most common method, certainly, was exchange of commodities. Either the buyer would give his goods to the seller directly, or else the buyer would write out I.O.U.'s which the captain would quickly spend on the island, buying up goods to bring home. The captains suffered some loss on the merchandise in this way—but presumably they more than made up for it when the commodities came to be sold in Europe, where they commanded very high prices.

This, then, was the slave trade. It was not easy on the slavers or on the slaves. It is notable that probably as many crew members as slaves died during the voyages. African leaders, if not ordinary free Africans, often willingly collaborated in the trade; and if they and the Europeans were out to get what they could from each other, and prepared to cheat each other where possible, it remains those who were actually enslaved who suffered the greatest miseries and hardships, and who died in vast numbers.

Who were the slaves? They came for the most part from West Africa, these slaves who had been stolen and taken from their homes and brought virtually nothing with them, except themselves. The slaves not only could not bring material objects with them, they could not easily bring over their older social institutions, their languages, and cultures. Coming from a large area of West Africa in which dozens upon dozens of distinct peoples lived, with their own languages, social relations, cultures, and religions, these Africans were jumbled together on board the slave ships, "seasoned" by the middle passage and then seasoned again in their first years in the New World.

For the slave brought himself; he brought with him the content of his mind, his memory. He thought in the logic and language of his people. He recognized as socially significant that which he had been taught to see and comprehend; he gestured and laughed, cried, and held his facial muscles in ways that had been taught him from childhood. He valued that which his previous life had taught him to value; he feared that which he had feared

in Africa; his very motions were those of his people and he passed all of this on to his children. He faced this contradictory situation in a context into which he was thrown among people of different African backgrounds. All Africans were slaves, slaves were supposed to act in a specific way. But what was this way? There was no model to follow, only one to build.

The slave from Africa was denied the right to act out the contents of his mind and memory—and yet he *had* to do this. How was this contradiction resolved? What were the new forms created in the context of slavery?

A new community was formed; it took its form in the slave quarters of the plantations and the black sections of the cities. In the United States, this community developed its own Christian church, one designed to meet the needs of slaves and Afro-American freedmen in the New World. It had its own system of communication based on the reality of the plantation. It had its own value system, reflective of the attitudes of African peasants, but at the same time owing its allegiance to dominant American modes. It had its own language patterns, because of the isolation of the plantation system from steady European linguistic influences. West African words and speech patterns were combined with the speech of the eighteenth-century Scotch-Irish.

This black community was the center of life for the slaves; it gave them an independent basis for life. The slaves did not suffer from rootlessness—they belonged to the slave community, and even if they were sold down the river they would find themselves on new plantations. Here, people who shared a common destiny would help them find a life in the new environment.

Each plantation was a self-sufficient unit. The slaves worked at all the skills necessary to maintain the plantation in working order and keep at a minimum the expense of importing necessary items from England. Slave blacksmiths manufactured everything from nails to plowshares. Coopers made the hoops around the tobacco barrels. The clothing they wore was turned out by slave shoemakers, dyers, tanners, and weavers. The slave artisan moved from one task to another as the need arose.

Skilled labor also took the slave off the plantation. Black pilots poled the rafts laden with tobacco from the tributaries of the river to its mouth, where the ship was anchored; black seamen conducted the ferries across Virginia's rivers to transport new settlers. Many planters found it more profitable to hire out their skilled black workmen for seventy-five to two hundred dollars a year. This black crafts- man living away from the plantation was allowed seventy-five cents a week as his allow- ance for food and board. When the colonies engaged in their war with England for inde- pendence, all imports from the mother country ceased. Crude factories were started and slaves were used to work them; also, out of the mines they dug lead, a necessary ingredient in the manufacture of bullets.

The tedium of tobacco cultivation was worse than the exhaustion of simple physical labor. Cotton, which succeeded tobacco as the planta- tion's output, had to be chopped with great care when the young plant had no more than three or four leaves.

Overworked field hands would take off to the nearby weeds or swamps where they would lay out for a time. At night they would steal back to the slave quarters for food and information about what the master intended to do about their absence. In the swamps of the eastern section of North Carolina, runaways were employed by black lumbermen or the poor whites and could raise their own children for a time. The master, who didn't know the hideouts as well as the slaves did, let it be known through a word passed on to the slave quarters that he was prepared to negotiate for less work and no whippings if only his precious laborers would return.

The slaves fought to set their own tempo and rhythm of work. Says Frederick Douglass:

There is much rivalry among slaves, at times, as to which can do the most work and masters generally seek to promote such rivalry. But some of them were too wise to race each other very long. Such racing, we had the sagacity to see, was not likely to pay. We had times out for measuring each others strength, but we knew too much to keep up the competition so long as to produce an extra-ordinary days work. We knew that if by extra-ordinary exertion, a large quantity of work was done in one day, the face becom- ing known to the master, the same would be expected of us every day. This though was enough to bring us to a dead halt whenever so much excited for the race.

There was very little of the slave's life that he could call his own. In the slave quarters at night there was a lowering of the mask that covered the day's labors. Bantering and mimicry, gossiping and laughter could be unrestrained. House servants regaled other members of the "row"—some of whom had never set foot in the big house—with tales of "master" and "missus," would "take them off" in speech and gesture so faithful that the less privileged would shake with laughter.

Besides the oppression of the master him- self, his laws and his overseers, the slaves were oppressed by their limited knowledge of the world outside the plantation. Masters felt that a slave who learned how to read and write would lose his proficiency at picking worms off tobacco leaves or at chopping cotton, so thoroughly had slavery separated thought and feeling from work. But the capacities of men were always leaping out of the confinements of the system. Always with one eye cocked toward the door, the slaves learned how to read and write, thus they attained that standard—besides the accumulation of money, tobacco, cotton, and lands—by which society judged the stand- ing of its members. The Bible was the most readily available book; its wide and varied use by the slave would have made the founders of Christianity proud. It was a course in the alphabet, a first reader, and a series of lessons in the history of mankind.

The capacities of men were always leaping out of the confinements of the system. Written passes, which slaves were required to carry on their person when away from the plantation, could be made up by those who had learned how to read and write. Deciphering the alphabet opened new avenues to the world. A primary achievement of the slaves as a class is that they fashioned a system of communication—an illegal, underground, grapevine telegraph which would stand the test of an emergency.

When hostilities broke out between the thirteen colonies and the King of England, the British field commander in the South offered freedom to every slave who would enter his army. In Virginia alone, thirty thousand fled their labors; the bitter comment of a slaveholder points up this situation: "Negroes have a wonderful art of communicating intelligence among themselves; it will run several hundred miles in a fortnight." There was such a large proportion of slaves in the state, that South Carolina did not even dare enter the War of Independence for fear of what its laboring force would do. It lost twenty-five thousand nevertheless. Across the South every fifth slave fled toward the British army.

An independent national state was being set up by an American Congress. The very air became filled with expressed passions of human rights, liberties, dignity, equality, and the pursuit of happiness. One of its effects on the slaves was seen on the night of August 30, 1800. Over one thousand slave rebels gathered some six miles from Richmond, capital city of Virginia, the state which was to produce four of the first five American Presidents. All through the spring of that year the slaves prepared their own arms, including five hundred bullets, manufactured in secret. Each Sunday for months, Gabriel Prosser entered the city, noting its strategic points and possible sources of arms and ammunition. Their plan was to

proclaim Virginia a Negro state. If the merchants of Richmond would yield their fortunes to the rebels their lives would be spared and they would be feted at a public dinner.

On the night appointed for the march a heavy rain had fallen, making the road into Richmond impassable. The delay gave the stunned authorities an opportunity to mobilize themselves. Some forty slaves were arrested and put on trial. They revealed no names of other participants. Some estimates placed the extent of the rebellion at ten thousand slaves, others put the figure as high as sixty thousand. The demeanor and remarks of the prisoners on trial—Gabriel: "I have nothing more to offer than what General Washington would have had to offer, had he been taken and put on trial by them. I have adventured my life to obtain the liberty of my countrymen . . ."

In this early period the slave who ran away was most often a skilled craftsman, a man with confidence of making his way in the world. As described by a newspaper advertisement of the day:

Run away from the subscriber's farm, about seven miles from Anapolis, on the 8th instant; two slaves Will and Tom; they are brothers. Will, a straight tall well-made fellow, upwards of six feet high, he is generally called black, but has a rather yellowish complexion, by trade a carpenter and a cooper, and in general capable of the use of tools in almost any work; saws well at the whip saw, about thirty years of age. When he speaks quick he stammers a little in his speech. Tom, a stout well-made fellow, a bright mulatto, twenty-four years of age, and about five feet nine or ten inches high; he is a complete hand at plantation work and can handle tools pretty well . . . they have a variety of clothing, and it is supposed they will not appear abroad in what they wear at home. Will writes pretty well, and if he and his brother are not furnished with passes from others they will not be lost for them, but upon proper examination may be discovered to be forged. These people it is imagined are gone for Baltimore as Tom has a wife there . . .

Except in a general way he could not be sure of the direction of his travels, guiding himself by the stars and by the moss which grew on the shady side of the trees. In earlier days the safest places of concealment were the nearby swamps, the neighboring Indian tribes and Spanish Florida. The long military arm of the slavocracy eventually reached into all these temporary outposts of freedom and incorporated them into slavery. Then soldiers returning from the War of 1812 brought the news that slavery was outlawed in Canada. The route of flight began to cut across the Kentucky mountain ranges and the Atlantic seacoast.

John Parker, a free black man from Ripley, Ohio, considered it below his dignity to ask any white man how to conduct slaves to freedom; he was responsible for the successful passage of one thousand runaways, but left no memoirs as to how he carried out his work.

In later years the work of the scout took him into the Deep South rather than await the knock on the door. On her expeditions, Harriet Tubman would take the precaution of starting on Saturday night so that they would be well along their journey before they were advertised. Harriet often paid another black person to follow the man who posted the descriptions of her companions and to tear them down. The risks of taking along different types of people in one group had to be considered. Babies were sometimes drugged with paregoric. She sometimes strengthened the fainthearted by threatening to use her revolver and declaring, ". . . you go on you die . . . dead (N)egroes tell no tales . . ."

As with practical people everywhere, everything was done with the materials at hand. An iron manikin in front of the home of Judge Piatt marked an interrupted station; the judge was hostile to the activity, but his wife was an enthusiastic undergrounder. A flag in the hand of the manikin signaled that the judge was not home and that his house had become a temporary station on the road. For disguise one runaway was provided simply with a gardening tool placed on his shoulder. He marched through town in a leisurely way like a man going to work somebody's garden, left the tool in a selected thicket at the edge of town, and proceeded on his way.

The Underground Railroad in the period of the 1840's grew so saucy that it advertised itself publicly as the only railroad guaranteed not to break down. Multiple routes were the key to the practical success of the railroad. It all came into being after the period of the Founding Fathers had definitively come to an end. The men of education, the leading figures of the Revolution, Washington, Jefferson, Adams, Hancock, Hamilton, Lafayette, and Kosciusko, all expressed opposition to slavery in their private conversations and correspondence. But their chief fear was that pushing antislavery to the fore might permanently divide the country into antagonistic sections.

Washington accurately described the sentiment in certain parts of the country after he himself had lost a slave in New England. "The gentleman in whose care I sent him has promised every endeavor to apprehend him; but it is not easy to do this when there are numbers who would rather facilitate the escape of slaves than apprehend them when they run away."

In the early formation of the Underground Railroad, another group whom the runaway touched with his fire was the Quakers. When they arrived in America to escape persecution, the prosperous trade in slaves corrupted even the most tender of consciences. Not being interested in politics, and prohibited by religious belief from being diverted by the theater, sports, or drink, the Quakers became highly successful businessmen and farmers. The Quakers were prominent and influential people and could afford to rely on the letter of the law which in Northern states had declared slavery illegal.

Having established the principle, effective organization for antislavery work came naturally to a group whose life had been drawn tightly together for hundreds of years as a religious sect. By 1820 there were some four thousand fugitive slaves in the Quaker stronghold of Philadelphia and all advertisements for runaways disappeared from Pennsylvania newspapers.

Free blacks, Quakers, and New Englanders, linked up to each other, conducted the Atlantic coast route of Underground Railroad operations. Men of a different stamp initiated a section of the western route. At the turn of the century the back-country farmer of Virginia and the Carolinas suffered much from the poverty of his land. The state legislatures were in the control of coastal planters and their lawyers; new government taxes and old debts magnified his poverty. He freed himself of all these burdens by migrating westward into the wilderness.

The slaves who accompanied this first great tide of migration, which depopulated Virginia of two hundred thousand people, were as scattered as their masters. On the early frontier there was less consciousness of their slave status. They helped in the household chores, building cabins and protecting them from Indian attack. Often they were the boatmen, whose arrival was as welcome in the settlement as the ringing of a postman in a modern apartment house.

The runaway slave heightened the powers of the popular imagination. Here was a figure who not only fled oppressive institutions, but successfully outwitted and defied them. And his flight was to the heart of civilization, not away from it; he was a universal figure whose life was in turn adventurous, tragic, and humorous.

The runaway, freed from the disabilities of slavery, was in the second and third decades of the nineteenth century coming into close contact with another highly specialized group of people—the intellectuals. The thinking of intellectuals is characterized by the fact that they view matters whole and in general, however one-sidedly and abstractly. This jamming up of two diverse elements—the black man who supposedly had no civilization in the range of his existence, and the white intellectual in whom society had placed the whole heritage of civilization—produced those works that reminded people who gave thought to the slave held in bondage that they were themselves intimately bound with him for life.

The antislavery movement was produced by the specific relation of blacks and whites during the first third of the nineteenth century. It is a fantastic phenomenon climaxed by the central phenomenon of all American history, the Civil War. Writers offer various explanations, but after a certain amount of reflection it becomes clear that abolition must be seen as an absolutely necessary stage in making America a distinct civilization, rather than just one more piece of boundaried territory in the mosaic of the world's geography.

Abolition is the great indicator of parallel movements before the Civil War and after. History really moves when the traditionally most civilized section of the population—in this case New Englanders representing the longest American line of continuity with the English tradition of lawful sovereignty—joins as coequals with those without whose labor society could not exist for a day—in this case the plantation chattel. Otherwise, history stays pretty much the same, or worse yet, repeats itself. Such was the case of the independent lay preachers in the Great English Revolution, who joined with the apprentices and day laborers; the French intelligentsia in conjunction with peasants and slum proletarians of royalist France; the Russian intellectuals meeting on certain grounds with factory workers under a Czar. In all these instances history moved forward with lasting impress.

Abolition, itself an important instance of democracy, took upon itself the extension of a certain practice and mode of national behavior. Much of the mode of national behavior was based upon regional considerations—the great potential for abolition was the Southern slave in flight to freedom from plantation labor. Then there was the firmest base of abolition extant, the free black communities of Northern city and town. New York City, for a time, provided heavy financing. Garrison's Massachusetts was becoming an antislavery fortress and the rest of New England followed, in various degrees. Children of New England had settled in the fine agricultural flatlands of Ohio and upstate New York; a momentous development as "free soil" was prepared to clash with slave expansion appetites. Pennsylvania housed an antislavery diffused with Quakerized quietist feelings.

Without the self-expressive presence of the free blacks in the cities, embodying in their persons the nationally traumatic experience of bondage and freedom, antislavery would have been a sentiment only, a movement remote and genteel in a country known as impetuous and volatile. The bulk of subscribers to Garrison's *The Liberator* were blacks in New York, Boston, and Philadelphia. It was the publicity surrounding the revolt of Nat Turner which guaranteed that Garrison, the white advocate of immediate abolition, would become a household word. The independent conventions of free blacks were anterior to the rise of Garrison and his friends. The succession of slave personalities delivered by the Underground Railroad would eventually lead to black political independence from Garrison himself.

Ohio was the scene in the 1840's of the "Hundred Convention"—political life as daily fare, with regional figures turning into nationally representative ones. Douglass, the self-emancipated slave by way of Baltimore; Garrison, who hardly had left New England before except to visit neighboring New York

or far-off merrie old England; these two together spoke themselves hoarse and into general exhaustion. This now-settled middle frontier, this venerable Old Northwest, was clamoring to hear about the state of the nation from true figures of national stature, since nothing more was heard from the doughfaces in Congress sitting on the hundreds of thousands of petitions pleading for justice to the slave, and discussing the role of free settlers in a democracy.

Impending war with Mexico was a spur to far-reaching conclusions. The revived National Negro Conventions listened to a proposal for a general strike by the slave laborers of the South, who would act as a human wall barring the United States Army from invading Mexican territory and turning it into a slave planting domain. The proposal lost by one vote.

Sophisticated prejudice tells us that *Uncle Tom's Cabin* by Harriet Beecher Stowe is another vast mistake! In impact and implications marking off the hour and the decade of its arrival it rang true; in universal aspect, clear. The average worker competing with the free black man for a job and a place to live, and wrestling with his prejudices all the while, went to see the play and wept upon his identification with the slave runaway. Where formal government failed on the slavery question, people reached for a government which the Greeks had introduced so very many years earlier: that of popular drama—which the city-state then made sure everyone could see for free—so that whatever they thought of politics they could see, through the form of dramatic representation, principles, conditions, and resolutions, and sense from that emotional experience where a whole society was going. Mere political representation was succeeded by a more intense social reproduction, a more popular accurate representation; in book form, *Uncle Tom's Cabin* circulated more widely through the whole of the nineteenth century than any other, with the sole exception of that book of books, the Bible.

And if it was the running debates with Stephen A. Douglas which elevated Abraham Lincoln from the legislator's semiobscurity to national star-fire, who or what besides abolition had initiated the debate, fixing free discussion of nearly obscured cruelties on a Mississippi cotton field as the nation's prime business; set forth the concrete choices, which no mere election could decide, on the future of mid-nineteenth-century America? And if the abolitionists' method had so elevated Lincoln, what shall we say of their achievement in turning each runaway slave, now threatened with kidnapping under a new and permanent sectional compromise, into a monument either to the American's love of liberty or acquiescence to captivity? Before abolition enabled Lincoln to hallow his name, it inscribed Shadrach and Anthony Burns and Dred Scott onto the heavens for the whole world to read the American future through them.

The leading charge against abolition in the 1850's was aimed at its nearly absolute trust in the uninterrupted processes of civilization. The main critique centered upon Garrison and Phillips' endorsing—before civil war broke out—the secession of the South, confident that slavery, separated from federal protection, must die.

The Civil War was a corrective of the notorious nineteenth-century optimism which trusted free speech and free press and the industriousness of unchatteled labor to push authoritarianism of every familiar type over that same cliff where the vestiges of feudal relations had been shattered or left to hang for dear life. Confronted by preslavery compromises which were a source of infinite corruption, abolition gave obeisance to certain eternal principles: themselves corollaries of the civilizing process at a certain stage. Growing transcending morality titled "the higher law" would overwhelm all momentary deviousness, nullify all expedients and prearrangements disguising themselves as pillars of the Federal Union.

Belief in the morality of "the higher law" was hardly an empty absolute, devoid of content and barren of result. It was a driving impetus separating democracy in politics from a growing "hunkerism," mere hankering after public office and governmental seat-warmings which dulled the very sense of social accountability and paled before the historical momentousness of American existence.

The years of Civil War show what might have been done much earlier during the War for Independence itself when this nation was first born, and egalitarian feelings were at a zenith. But then there had been no antislavery organization. The unity of the young nation, monarchies all, had taken a certain turn at the Constitutional Convention and elsewhere, indicating that the semblance of national solidity could be maintained only if the slave kept his back bent to his labor; the North and South, East and West would not divide, and foreign enemies would wait in vain for internal weakness as the signal to spring upon their prey, the New World as distinguished from the old. But national unity excluded the black from independence; national prosperity was guaranteed by subordinating the laborer to his labor. The very existence of abolitionists during the next climactic phase of this very same question—Civil War—simply insured that the slave would not be lost sight of no matter how much the government tried to lose sight of him.

The destruction of the Colonizationists earlier was the main factor staying the hand of the government which wanted to colonize blacks, freed men, even in the midst of, and because of, the tensions of Civil War to avoid disputations as to their American destiny.

On the universal effect of American abolition: it helped free the Russian serf on the other side of the world—but not directly. Indirectly, it is clear enough if we go by stepping-stone geography. Harriet Beecher Stowe's book was banned in Italy as an incitement to the peasantry. But the leading Russian

publication of the intellectual exiles translated the whole work as a free supplement for
all subscribers. Keep in mind, too, that from
the time of Peter the Great, Russia had been
trying to make its way through the front door
of world civilization. Add to this a fact of
international power politics: When England
and France threatened to join the South,
Russia shifted its weight to the North. In the
middle of the Civil War the Russian fleet
showed up in New York harbor, a great ball
was thrown and a festive time was had by all.
Abolition of serfdom there and of slavery
here occurred almost simultaneously.

Something should be said about the white
American worker in regard to abolition. Some
were antislavery, some were not. Skilled
workers, proud of their craft which brought
them a measure of independence, were by
and large antislavery. The unskilled, fearing
possible competition from the blacks, inclined
toward neutrality or gave in to caste prejudice.
However, skilled or unskilled, the worker in
America was an ardent democrat. No matter
how much he suspected another man might
take his job, he could not develop a great
affection for plantation life as the prototype
of American life as a whole.

Abolitionists were not only concerned with
the rights of blacks, free and slave, they were
concerned with their education. The abolitionist created the first integrated education
in the United States—including higher education. And when they did not create integrated
education they conducted classes and schools
for the ex-slaves, schools partially staffed by
black teachers. The abolitionists were at the
center of the educational reforms and changes
of this period in the United States. In schools
for Negro children they experimented with
improved methods of education.

But more. They fought not only for the
emancipation of Negroes and the improvement of the lives of freedmen. They fought
for the emancipation of women, their education, and their own self-development. Oberlin

College, the first college to accept Negroes
in the United States, was also the first college
to accept women in the United States, becoming the first co-educational institution of
higher learning.

In their struggle for women's rights, a
struggle that went on inside and outside of
the movement, abolitionists set in motion the
liberation of women—and consequently of
men. What Margaret Fuller and other great
female abolitionists were trying to establish
was their right to create relations with men
in which they were not in effect the chattel
of their husbands through the marriage contract, as slaves were chattel in the grip of
property holders.

The abolitionists were involved in a crucial
way in the most significant struggles for human
emancipation that were going on in the United
States: the abolition of capital punishment,
prison reform, attacks on established religion
in the name of purified religion, work for the
rights of new waves of immigrants and better
treatment of American Indians, and the
movement to abolish war. Though they often
differed among themselves, and were very
often confused in the way that people are who
are going forward, there is a very direct development from the Declaration of Independence
to the abolitionists' efforts to Lincoln's understanding that the Civil War was about whether
government of the people, by the people, and
for the people would perish from the earth.

It must be said that the slave community
itself was the heart of the abolitionist movement. This is a claim that must seem most
extraordinarily outrageous to those who think
of abolitionism as a movement which "was
unique, in the sense that, for symmetry and
precision of outline, nothing like it had ever
previously been seen." The element of order
in the barbarism was this: the rationalization
of a labor force upon which the whole process
of colonization depended had the African at
its most essential point. If he had not been
able to work or sustain himself or learn the

language or maintain cooperation in his social life, the whole question of America as a distinct civilization could never have arisen. We might be then talking about a sort of New Zealand or perhaps Canada.

The native American Indian was migratory in his habits and a hunter in his relation with nature. But the slave had to be an African laborer, a man accustomed to social life, before he could ever become a profitable grower of cotton or tobacco—the vital element required before America could claim that it had salvaged something from the wilderness. Something which could be extended to the point where it would win recognition as a landmark in man's emergence from subservience to any laws of nature.

The man who made it possible, and we do not know if he knew he was making it possible, was the transported African. Rationalization of the labor supply was tied in with rationalization of production itself. Planters in Louisiana would weigh the pros and cons of working slaves to death in the hazardous work of the rice paddies as against protecting the slave from excessive labor in order to maintain the interest in him as property. The long letters George Washington wrote on the organization of labor on his plantation represent merely one side. The exchange of letters between Thomas Jefferson and Benjamin Banneker, the surveyor of what was to become Washington, D.C., about the propensities and capacities of black people enslaved and otherwise is the other side of the same phenomenon: the recognition that for reasons both clear and obscure the fate of America had depended upon the blacks as laborers. This was to be argued out in the antislavery movement at a higher level, and in the midst of the Civil War and Reconstruction. It is also a seemingly inescapable fact to everybody, but historians have managed to escape it. That is not altogether a surprise. The writing of history comes about at a period when men think about their activity so as to record it in a more permanent form. To give the slave his actual historical due is to alter one's notion about the course of civilization itself. If, for example, each plantation had to strive to be self-sufficient as a unit, it was the skilled and semi-skilled black who would make it so.

The runaway slave fled to the North without compass or definite point of destination, without being blessed like Columbus by Queen Isabella selling her jewels for the voyage, or like the pilgrims to Plymouth Rock—members of a church soon to make a revolution affecting all of England and Ireland; or like pioneers into the wilderness, trying to set a distance between themselves and civilization. If, as can be later demonstrated, the flight of the runaway slave from the South is seen as setting in motion a whole series of forces, which no other class of people, no mere party or political sect, no church or newspaper could succeed in animating, then the whole configuration of America as a civilization automatically changes before our eyes. The distinguishing feature of the slave was not his race but the concentrated impact of his work on the extensive cultivation of the soil, which eventually made possible the transition to an industrial and urban society.

The triumph of slavery, the negative recognition that the slave received in every work sphere shows how little the South or skilled workers themselves sometimes could tolerate the black as an artisan. In prebellum America he had to be driven out of trade after trade before the assertion could be demonstrated that the black man is fit for nothing more than brutish labor with its inevitable consequence.

Historically one can now begin almost anywhere to show what civilization meant to the slave as a preliminary to showing what the slaves meant to civilization. The natural form of organization was the work gang during the day and the slave quarters at night. The large scale of cultivation required for a profitable export crop guaranteed social connections for the slave even if he was isolated from the centers of "civilization" by the rural surroundings.

But the first specific form of slave organization was the fraternal association which was organized to accompany to their permanent resting place those caught up in life's mortal coils. Small coins were saved for accomplishing that occasion in at least minimal style. The slave was no more afraid to die than is or was any other mortal; he was fearful of dying unaccompanied by those with whom he had associated in the fullness of his life.

Given a holiday, that is, an occasion, the slave was, like most working humans up to this day, his own person. It was for naught that the defenders of the planter's way of life feared the effect of Fourth of July oratory. They might just as well have feared the Christianity in Christmas. It was not only intellectually that everything universal in sentiment panicked the "peculiar institution." It was the concentration of people all experiencing the unbridgeable gap between their arduous daily toll and the exceptional holiday from work—with the to-ing and the fro-ing from plantation to plantation, the arrival of guests and the spreading of news—which brought about the system of slave patrollers and written passes across the South.

We are dealing with matters of individual skill and social impulse. Small equivalents of the strike action took place at work. Flight to the neighboring woods, followed by messages trailed back to the work area showed that the blacks knew above all that, even if despised for race, they were necessary—vital to a labor process geared to the agricultural season. Feigning of illness was a commonplace; indeed, one simple definition of the abolition of slavery is that a man or woman need not go to work when incapacitated. This absenteeism may seem of no great import by itself, but the diaries and records of the slavemasters show it to be a matter of grave concern. Everybody knew what was involved in the work process.

And the blacks knew what was involved in their day of rest. The growth of an autonomous black church draws up a balance sheet on historical Christianity. It is not finished yet, but if Christianity, as some assert, brought the principle of personality into a world that knew no such thing, and in the person of a simple carpenter who later recruited an equally simple fisherman and so on, the climax of that primitive church was the mass joining together of a population considered as so much flesh to be traded and hands to be worked and backs to be bent or broken under the lash. To the whites religion may have meant a buttress to conscience. To the blacks it meant a social experience out of which would come the active principle of personality: the black preacher.

In the more practical workings of the plantation, the slave owners themselves discovered that the position of foreman or driver was one which fewer and fewer whites measured up to in personal stature. So that in the decade before the Civil War there was a wholesale increase in the number of black overseers. Though it did not mean that race prejudice on the part of the slave owners had changed one whit, this problem of supervision was proof of the demoralizing effect black laborers had upon those who not only considered themselves superior to the slave's lot but had the weapons and the authority to put their superiority into momentary practice. Most white overseers went even before the slave system fell into the dust of Civil War. And by a healthy process of circularity, the fictional summations of the type, the Simon Legrees of the world, were portrayed with such effectiveness that it stimulated the movement toward that system which produced such monsters wholesale. The important point of the slave's contribution to civilization is that he recognized and did battle with the slavery system every day before, long before, white audiences would stare with horror at the representation on stage or in a book.

There is also the matter of the link-ups of the plantation to the outside world. Blacks were the boatmen and teamsters of that day in the South. They would have been the long-shoremen as well, but were driven out. Simply by driving the master's coach around they learned of the outside world and brought back information to the slave community. It was known in some of the deepest haunts of the South that there was some kind of underground which would transport a runaway from one hiding place to another if he would but risk the trip.

Indeed, if by virtue of the brutishness and isolation of his situation the slave were himself a brute, how then could he make contact with such varying and even opposing sections of the population as he did? Harriet Tubman had a rapt listener in the philosopher Ralph Waldo Emerson, and Frederick Douglass in governor—and later Presidential candidate—William Seward. William Wells Brown could speak to all size groups, from two hundred to two hundred thousand people across Europe. It was not a matter of dispute about the capacity of the Negro; it was not even the great political debates about the future of America—slave or free. It was something so concrete, so easy to overlook and yet so broad in its consequences: The black man was a social being, in some senses the most highly social product of the United States. This was not necessarily due to skin color, but to the close relation between labor and society that he experienced more than did planters, ethnic immigrants, religious societies, pioneering settlements and their human products, political parties and their candidates.

That link of labor and society took on national and even international proportions. Starting from obscure places which nobody ever heard of or even wanted to hear, it became writ large as the experience of slavery intertwined with everything else—politics, diplomacy, commerce, migration, popular culture, the relation between the sexes, the question of labor and civilization in the future of America as a whole. The black man was not in any popularity contest as to who most

represented this new man—this undefined American—who so intrigued the Europeans. He was something more: a self-appointed minister with nothing but experience, social experience, to guide him toward those qualities most universally recognizable in the ordinary people—some of whom are still tied to the land in Europe; some recently incorporated into proliferating industry; some hearkening to the American experience; some settling matters with crowns and courts in their Old World countries. The black man was the supreme example not just of how to rise in the world but of how to raise the world toward his own level. He inherited the Declaration of Independence which the plantation plutocracy mocked. In politics, Frederick Douglass took the Constitution as an antislavery document when his own abolition colleagues, Wendell Phillips and William Lloyd Garrison, set the match to it. The runaway slave, Dred Scott, threw the Chief Justice of the Supreme Court (and the country as a whole) into confusion on whether slavery was a national or regional issue. The black man was not afraid to declare war on war, for instance the conflict with Mexico over Texas in 1846. He could link himself to movements for temperance in drink or for the right of women to divorce or to the nonpayment of rents by upper New York State farmers.

It was training in social labor which gave blacks the opportunity to increasingly affect all social questions of their day. It was their concrete ability to turn from the faculties used in physical work to the powers of speech and other forms of self-expression which made certain of the ex-slaves the astonishing figures they were. After he drew two hundred thousand people to hear him in Europe, William Wells Brown then returned to a port near the Great Lakes, between America and Canada, to help fugitive slaves across the water, unite families, violating the mere boundaries of national existence. In addition he printed a paper announcing the uniting of families, the successes and sometimes failures of the underground travelers, their adventures and misadventures; and denouncing the "peculiar institution" and all those who would compromise with it, thinking they could thereby escape compromising themselves.

The startling challenge to current notions about civilization was presented by the slaves, as soon as they won the public's ear, on the familiar matter of conscience. The contribution of the blacks was that type of social experience—whether it was lyceum, church, or Underground Railroad—which challenged one set of social institutions with a social impact of a most original kind. Doomed by slavery to impersonality, the ex-slave responded with a personality and personal force that had the most obvious social implications and conclusions. Condemned to seasonal labor, and the rhythm and routine determined thereby, the blacks carried on agitation in and out of season until the body politic came to recognize that the country could no longer survive as it was; could survive only by embarking on an uncharted course of slave confiscation and Southern reconstruction. After having been isolated by slavery in provincial fixity, the runaway traversed national boundaries and oceanic waters. Graded by the abolition movement itself as fit only to tell slavery as an atrocity tale, Frederick Douglass and others insisted on publishing their own political policies. This is a long way from the reflex response to slavery by a disturbed conscience. It is a social impact on all media that distinguishes civilization from barbarism. The impact of the slave labor system upon the South as a distinct region has a number of aspects clearly visible to this day.

The plantation was an organized community that was part of a larger regional configuration, but given the isolation concomitant with the rural character of slave society, the social stamp upon the individual, particularly the slave himself, guaranteed certain results. The internal economic principle of the plantation was self-sufficiency. To the slavemaster this meant insularity: foreign immigration mainly excluded; missionary society activity suspect (including the riding preachers who would as likely as not be antislavery); no lyceum or lecture circuit on any extensive scale; no compulsory elementary or secondary education; little exercise of the faculty of logical speculation. For a break in the routine of plantation life there were visits to the North, often no further than the river port city of Cincinnati; or politics in the state capital or in Washington, D.C., actually a Southern city.

To a large extent, certain of the above characteristics were true of America as a whole, or at least of its western part. Especially the smaller Southern planters had certain characteristics in common with the yeomanry of the American Northwest: the need to create isolated pockets of white habitation in a land belonging to the Indians, the establishment of paths into the wilderness, the harsh life for the women of the family, the back-breaking toil in wresting some socially productive result from the natural surroundings, and the independence of habit and speech that is the inevitable result in people living under these conditions.

The dialectical set of connections of the South to the old Northwest is both genuinely subtle and profound. Both were agrarian areas, with the Mississippi and other rivers serving as the turnstiles to ports and citified places. Other similarities were the suspiciousness toward all those outside the isolated region where one's house and cultivated areas and perhaps hunting grounds were located; the tightness of the family and usually its patriarchal basis; the shortage of monies and credit, such that life frequently remained, generally according to the season, on a subsistence level, with only the holiday season to punctuate with some enjoyment above the everyday standard.

Further, there is the historical connection. All of American settlement, at its origins, proceeded in the same manner for both inland planters and Northern yeomanry, and their pioneering ways continued right up to the Civil War. In that sense Southern rural inhabitants were "these new men," the Americans who so intrigued the European observer often skeptical of America as (1) a civilization and (2) a viable nationality. Thus if the black man has been left out of so many history books, if the controversy over the significance of slavery to the South seemed until very recently a matter of no great moment, it is because a certain aspect of American historical continuity seemed to justify itself and no mere racist conspiracy of silence could accomplish what seems to have been imbedded within that historical aspect. To which must be added the fundamental matter of political organization and the effect of the South on certain basic institutions by which an organized society emerged out of the natural wilderness. The individual planter was conditioned not only by pioneering inland to new territories; he had to become an individualist with a social authority larger than the boundaries of his plantation. The reasons are as follows: The South had been originally colonized by British trading companies licensed by the Crown. The Northern settlements were more likely to be religious colonies or fur-trading outposts. So that from the very start the planter, who had to be in charge of the practical and hazardous work of founding some lasting economic basis in the New World, was thrown into conflict with the concentrated mercantile capitalism of the metropolitan colonizing land. To put it succinctly, the anticapitalist bias of the Southerner was there from the day of his birth. It was no small thing. The former slave—the supposedly emancipated black—became, for lack of credit, a sharecropper. This happened because all of Southern history had prepared somebody for that role, and the people at the bottom of the social ladder fell into it and remained there, some unto this day. To make up for their embattlement as regards the

shortage of capital, the Southerners would compensate with (a) their geography, strategically considered, (b) the fixed position of the main section of the laboring force—the slaves, and (c) a type of politics which would guarantee the viability of (a) and (b).

All these things add up to a "nativist" outlook that is not that of country bumpkins, but one characterized by a sophistication that was constantly changing by the very reason of its taking place in a nineteenth- and late eighteenth-century setting that was becoming rapidly modernized. Slavery is a peculiar institution not only because of its horrors but because it was something-unto-itself. The Southern attitude seems so often a matter of temperament—unformed character expressing itself against a general trend in worldly affairs which opposed the fixed investment of wealth in land and human chattel. In other words, the South produced "personality" rather than minds of singular or original power. But the personalities are of a similar and sustaining force: Patrick Henry, Jefferson, Jackson, Calhoun, Clay, Stonewall Jackson, Tom Watson, Huey Long are personage who will interest the public imagination until possibly they are surpassed by the characterization of the lives of the obscure slaves and indigent blacks. This tends to be the ongoing matter of interest in our own day.

There is a material basis for the Southern production of men and women of outstanding temperamental force. (The fictional Scarlett O'Hara or Blanche DuBois convey that the matter is not limited to the male gender.) Despite all geographical rationalizations, the commodity crops—tobacco, rice, sugar, cotton, and hemp—were not limited to the South by climate. The planters were a class capable of taking over matters of national interest: they had warred against nature, against the Indian; they had warred against the blacks on the plantation, against the British, the French, and the Spaniards. Their experience had a certain cast by virtue of the international nature of their products—human flesh and large-scale commodity crops. Such large-scale experiences do not lead to the production of small-minded men. So they participated in the formation of an original American nationality. The historical claim can be substantiated that they produced more figures of national distinction than did, say, by comparison, the robber barons. All this combines to make the controversy about the impact of slavery on American civilization such a pregnant and vital intellectual confrontation.

Certain mundane matters have to be mentioned at least in a preliminary way. It was the boredom and harshness of plantation life that ensured that not general activity, but politics was the only matter of universal interest and appeal. If the rural character of their life induced in the planters, or at least in some of them, a certain respect for plebeian democracy in other sections of the population, it had to be by the nature of the planter's own setting, an abridged version of popular participation in decision-making. The father of the political party of any mass status in American life was the planter-political philosopher, Thomas Jefferson. The father of popular participation in political office, apart from mere suffrage, was the planter Andrew Jackson. The head of an army having the popular militia as a section of its base was the planter George Washington. Yet the halfway houses to genuine democracy which each of these figures created remain America's bones of contention unto this day.

What of social vision? The early accomplishments of these men corresponded to the formative period of American nationality. They could not go beyond. The results were imbedded in the American mentality but not anywhere in self-generating institutions. The popular militia is now the not-very-progressive National Guard. The political parties resting on mass suffrage are now in a state alternating between paralysis and crisis. The spoils of office distributed to members of the population are now a source of perpetual scandal and parasitism.

The Southern figures of the mid-nineteenth century vacillated between accommodation and hopeless fanaticism. Clay was a genius of the first order. He could never win actual leadership of the country as a whole, though he was persistent and colorful enough to engage the political attentions of his countrymen. Calhoun was a different sort. He sought to make the American Constitution a protector of the South's position in national life, invulnerable to changing national majorities. And of Jefferson Davis it can perhaps best be said that though he failed in the Southern rebellion, he was saved from hanging by the long tradition of Northern-Southern accommodation—a tradition punctured only by the actualities of the Civil War.

Some of the bobbling of the minds of the planters was due to the very fact that they stood on a tripod of vital revolutions in the then-known Western world: the Puritans in 1642, the War for Independence in 1776, and volatile France of 1789. The Clays and Calhouns lived to consider the realities of the continental-wide European Revolution of 1848. Their situation was one of Anglo-Saxon nativism turning against itself. Immigrant New York might celebrate 1848, Puritan New England might relate revolutionary antislavery sentiments to the wars between Cavaliers and Roundheads, the democratic yeomanry of the western territories might enjoy the sight of crowns falling all over Europe. The Southern planters had no comparable frame of reference. They stuck by Constitution and Compromise.

And when that did not last they went to war to protect geography. It was not all that simple. The border states which did not produce commodity crops but which had domestic slaves were the geniuses of accommodation right up to the last moment and beyond. The idyllic notion of domestic servitude, patriarchal chatteldom, originates from those Kentucky, Tennessee, upper Virginia, Maryland, and even

Delaware manors. If American politics became entwined with a style of life rather than a manner of thought, we have no difficulties discovering why. In short, the Southern position was that of a provincialism entwined with American nationality as a whole, but defenseless against the universal trends of revolutionary democracy of the nineteenth century.

Nevertheless the effects of the planters were immense: The location of the nation's capital in the borderline South; the creation and manipulation of national political parties; the fielding of armies and the tradition of militant armed conflict; the specialization of the South in politics as maneuver and divagation; the bias in favor of the notion that agricultural wealth was real, and commercial wealth always fraudulent; the sense of the manor not as parasitic but as a center of human community; the assertion that the concreteness of the manorial community was superior to the impersonality of the large Northern city; the impulsiveness of the Southern personality as more appealing than the social discipline seemingly inherent in industry and commerce; the general link-up with the rural-romantic character of America's past—all of this seems irrevocable and untouchable by general intellectual argument.

The only way to deal with it is by taking up its foundations. The Southern planter could engage in politics on a much larger scale than many Northerners or Westerners because he was of a leisure class, born and bred—a commander of the fate of men, women, and children of a different color with a more permanently fixed status. Suckled by a black nurse, attended by black servants, often encouraged to sexual experiments in the slave quarters, accustomed to the sight of blacks caring for all business involving manual labor; encouraged, even inspired, by the succession of Southern Presidents, the ambitious Southerner could see politics, even statesmanship, as destiny's decision, and cast himself in the role of fortune's darling. Furthermore, for the isolated manorial communities, politics was the prime form of social communion, whereas in the North religious revivals swept all before them in periods in between political excitement. In today's parlance, the prebellum white planter gives the impression of having found an early answer to the problems of the "lonely crowd" in the solidity of his native tradition, the fixity of his social status and the values of an inherent and irrevocable individualism.

The availability and accessibility of having things always at hand extended itself to the vast virgin lands and the supply of slaves. If capital and credit were in short supply, then the curse was on the head of the mercantilists—be they tyrannical Englishmen or grasping Boston Yankees. Social status had taken on an overweening importance; but even greater was the display of public personality—elections as jousting contests, a codified individualism rather than the self-expansive effluvia of the Northern Transcendentalists.

The rationalizations for the Atlantic slave trade and American slavery, whether borrowed from the Bible or the instances of Greece and Rome, raise a compelling challenge to the whole matter of what indeed constitutes a civilization. It is safe to say that the majority of Western scholars seem to have placed a gloss on the manner and the matter of this case.

I speak Americans for your good. We must and shall be free . . . in spite of you. You may do your best to keep us in wretchedness and misery, to enrich you and your children, but God will deliver us from under you. And wo, wo, will be to you if we have to obtain our freedom by fighting.
DAVID WALKER, 1829

I heard a loud voice in the heavens, and the Spirit instantly appeared to me and said . . . I should arise and prepare myself, and slay my enemies with their own weapons . . . for the time was fast approaching when the first should be last and the last should be first.
NAT TURNER, 1831

Symptoms of Liberty and Blackhead Signposts: David Walker and Nat Turner

VINCENT HARDING

THERE WAS MUCH ABOUT AMERICA IN the 1820s that made it possible for white men and women, especially in the North, to live as if no river of struggle were slowly, steadily developing its black power beneath the rough surfaces of the new nation. Indeed, the newness itself, the busyness, the almost frenetic sense of movement and building which seized America, were all part of the comfortable cloud of unknowing that helped preserve a white sense of unreality. Nor was the incessant movement of the majority simply imagined. Every day hundreds of families were actually uprooting themselves from the more settled areas of the East and seeking their fortunes beyond the Appalachians, even beyond the Mississippi River. Other whites from Europe and the British Isles were landing regularly at the Eastern ports, making their way into the seaboard cities and across the country to the new West, providing an intimation of the waves of immigrants soon to come. Thus the sense of movement in America was based on a concrete, physical reality.[1]

Naturally, much attention and energy were invested in the political, economic, and social institutions being developed and refined to serve the new American society. The national government was defining its own sense of purpose and power. Courts, banks, corporations, systems of transportation, and religion—all were being molded, reshaped, and re-examined, set in motion to serve a nation of settlers intent on dominating a continent. Because of that goal, the natives of the land were receiving their share of attention, too—much to their regret. Relentlessly, the collective white behemoth pushed them from river to river, back into the wilderness, smashing the cultures of centuries as if the Anglo-Americans and their cousins were agents of some divine judgment in the land.[2]

As a matter of fact, major segments of white America were possessed by just such visions of divine action in their midst, saw America as a Promised Land, as a staging ground for the earthly manifestations of the coming (white) Kingdom of God. Such godly visions, built strangely on the deaths of significant portions of the nonwhite children of this Father, contributed their own peculiar busyness to the blurring of American vision. For from the stately church buildings of New England (many built on profits from the Trade), to the roughhewn meeting houses of the Northwest and the sprawling campgrounds of the South, men who considered themselves agents of God proclaimed the need of the people to prepare the way for His Coming. Whatever the differences in their theology or lack of it, from Unitarians to Hard-Shell Baptists, they were united in their sense that the God of Israel was among them in a special way, and busily announced the various implications of that presence among the (mostly white) people. Partly as a result of such holy activism and fervent conviction, various sections of the nation were periodically swept by paroxysms of religious ardor, and the enthusiastic style of evangelical Protestant revivalism set its mark on large sectors of American life.

It was a time for building, whether canals or corporations or Kingdoms of the Saints, a hectic time of new buildings when busy men and overworked women might understandably ignore certain dark and troubling movements among them. It was a time that some called the "Era of Good Feelings," when party strife among whites seemed less pronounced than during the earlier founding periods. But the harsh and bitter debate which was then being carried on in Congress and across the country over the expansion of slavery's territory spoke to a different reality, one which often seemed to break out and threaten all the white kingdoms.[3]

Meanwhile, down in the kingdom that cotton was building, there was just as much movement, building, and expansion, but of a somewhat different quality. Louisiana had become a state in 1812. Alabama entered the Union in 1817, and Mississippi two years later. Within the decade from 1810 to 1820,

the population of the Alabama-Mississippi area alone had increased from 40,000 to 200,000 persons, including more than 70,000 enslaved Africans. Since the official closing of the Atlantic slave trade to America, the internal traffic in human bondage had burgeoned; Virginia served as its capital, while the nearby slave markets of Washington, D.C., provided an appropriate commentary on the state of American democracy. With the rise of this domestic trade, which eventually took hundreds of thousands of black people from the seaboard breeding and trading grounds into the interior of the developing South, new sectional bonds were established across that entire area, helping to create a self-conscious South which was tied together in many ways by the chain of black lives.[4]

The nation had committed itself to slavery, and the South was the keeper. In the 1820s the Southern black population grew from 1.6 million to more than 2 million persons, comprising some 40 percent of the section's total population, and ranging as high as 70 to 90 percent in some plantation counties and parishes. In this kingdom that cotton was building, enslaved black people were everywhere, and it was at once harder and easier for white men and women to deceive themselves. But there was no escape from the realities represented by the radical black presence in America. Thus private and public writings from the South continually referred to deep levels of fear—fear of insurrection, fear of death at black hands, fear of black life, fear of blackness, fear of repressed and frightening white desires. Usually it came out in references to "an internal foe," or "the dangerous internal population," or "the enemy in our very bosom," perhaps revealing more than the writers ever knew.[5]

Yet even in the South, even there where all the busyness of America could not shield white men and women from the stark black reality, it was still possible not to see where the objective enemy really was. In the 1820s, in Virginia's Southhampton County, who would have chosen Nat Turner for the role?

On the surface, Nat Turner appeared to represent much of that development which allowed men who called themselves masters to rest in the rightness of their ways. The ascetic Turner seemed to have imbibed deeply all the best elements of evangelical Southern white religion, all the proper anesthesia against the knowledge of who he had been, what he had lost, and what there was to regain. He did not use tobacco or liquor, he seemed to live a perfectly disciplined life among men as well as women (though not all owners would think well of *that* fruit of the Spirit); by and large, he caused no real trouble for the keepers of the status quo. Indeed, around 1821 the young black man had vividly demonstrated to whites the exemplary advantage of his high standing among the other Africans by returning voluntarily to Samuel Turner after having run away for about thirty days. Such a faithful black exhorter and singer of spiritual songs was of great value in the eyes of the white world. Of course the eyes of the white world did not see into the deepest level of Nat's real relationship to the black community, or into his real relationship to his God. Therefore whites could never have predicted that Nat, once harshened and honed in the burning river, would be possessed by a driving messianic mission to become God's avenging scourge against the slaveholders and their world.[6]

After his birth in 1800, the first community Nat Turner knew was that of his mother, father, and grandmother, a family not far removed from Africa but held in slavery by one Samuel Turner. Had they considered themselves or young Nat simply to be "slaves," he would never have become a Messenger. Rather, from the outset they taught him that he was meant for some special purpose (and therefore so were they), and they led him in that path. For instance, the immediate family and the surrounding black community were evidently convinced—as was Nat—that he had learned to read without instruction. Soon they were fascinated by his experiments in the ancient crafts of Africa and Asia: pottery, papermaking, and the making of gunpowder. Perhaps this was seen as another manifestation of the esoteric knowledge the community was convinced that he possessed—knowledge that included events and times before his own birth. Meanwhile his grandmother Bridget, a "very religious" woman, instructed him in what she knew from the Scriptures and other sources, nurtured him in the songs of nighttime and sleep.[7]

We are not sure of all that Nat learned from his immediate family, but his father taught him at least one thing: slavery was not to be endured. While Nat was still a child his father had joined the ranks of the fugitives. (Who can imagine the conversation in that family before his father ran away into the shadows of history? How much of their substance did Nat carry to his own grave?) From the rest of the community of captives Nat learned the same lesson, which was often taught in the captives' own flight from slavery, in spite of the high costs involved. He knew of the injustices suffered by his community. He learned its ritual songs and prayers, and the stories of heroes like Gabriel. But Nat claimed that his most profound lessons came in his own lonely, personal struggles with the spirit, whom he identified as "the Spirit that spoke to the prophets."[8]

By the time he was twenty-five, Nat had wrestled many times in the night with the Spirit of his God, the God of his Fathers. He had been pressed especially hard by the words: "Seek ye first the Kingdom of God and all things shall be added unto you." As he attempted to plumb the meaning and mystery of that promise, he had been driven into his own month-long experience of the wilderness, but then had returned to the Turner farm. Steadily he became more convinced that the Kingdom he sought was not the one preached by most of the white men he had heard. Instead, he saw the promised Kingdom of righteousness as one which would somehow be realized on the very farms and fields of Virginia, a Kingdom in which the power of the slavemasters would be broken. What made the vision chilling and exhilarating was his vivid awareness of being a chosen instrument for the bringing in of this Kingdom.[9]

Still, the way forward was not yet really clear, and Nat Turner went about his life and work, waiting. By this time Turner was a familiar figure in Southhampton County and the surrounding areas. Of about average height, muscular in build, coffee-tan in complexion, with a wide nose and large eyes, he walked with a brisk and active movement among his people, marked within himself and among them as a special man. On Sundays and at midweek meetings he exhorted and sang in black Baptist gatherings. At one point, word spread that Nat Turner had cured a white man of some serious disease, and then had baptized the white believer and himself in a river. Such a story only added to his renown.[10]

None of these developments, none of this high regard, moved Turner from his central purpose and passionate search. He waited and worked and married, but knew that all these things were only a prelude. Then in 1825 a clearer vision came: "I saw white spirits and black spirits engaged in battle, and the sun was darkened—the thunder rolled in the Heavens, and blood flowed in streams—and I heard a voice saying, 'Such is your luck, such you are called to see, and let it come rough or smooth, you must surely bear it.'" Again, one day as he worked in the fields Nat claimed to have "discovered drops of blood on the corn as though it were dew from heaven." On the leaves of the trees he said he found "hieroglyphic characters, and numbers, with the forms of men . . . portrayed in blood." Through this African imagery the white and black fighters had appeared again, but this time the meaning was even clearer in his mind.

What it signified to Nat was that "the blood of Christ had been shed on this earth . . . and was now returning to earth." Therefore, he said, "it was plain to me that the Saviour was about to lay down the yoke he had borne for the sins of men, and the great day of judgement was at hand."[11]

On one level, Turner was obviously living within the popular nineteenth-century Euro-American millenarian religious tradition, marked by a belief in the imminent return of Christ to rule his earth. Often, for persons thus convinced, a terrible and sometimes beautiful urgency caught fire and burned within them, annealing and transforming their being.[12]

But the burning within Nat Turner came from an at once similar and very different fire. That became evident in the spring of 1828, when the fullest description of the Kingdom he sought, and of his own role in its coming, were spoken to Nat's third ear. With very rare exceptions, white American evangelical religion could not contain such a Word, had no ear for it. On May 12, 1828, Nat said, "I heard a loud voice in the heavens, and the Spirit instantly appeared to me and said the Serpent was loosened, and Christ had laid down the yoke he had borne for the sins of men, and that I should take it and fight against the serpent, for the time was fast approaching when the first should be last and the last should be first." As if to clear away any lingering doubt he might have had, Nat heard the spirit's clear instructions, that at the appearance of the proper sign "I should arise and prepare myself, and slay my enemies with their own weapons." After that he waited, he bided his time.[13]

> Oh praised my honer, harshener
> till a sleep came over me,
> a sleep heavy as death. And when
> I awoke at last free
>
> And purified, I rose and prayed
> and returned after a time
> to the blazing fields, to the humbleness.
> And bided my time.[14]

For twenty-eight years Nat Turner had been nurtured by the black community, instructed by signs on the leaves and in the skies. Now he was clear about who the enemy of righteousness was, and who were the servants of the devil; he had only to wait for the sign. But it may have been difficult to wait: about this time, it seems, Turner was whipped by Thomas Moore, his present owner, "for saying that the blacks ought to be free, and that they would be free one day or another."[15]

A bustling, growing, building white nation could miss the sign that such a man carried in his own flesh, but for persons who were willing to see, more obvious signs were available. These were the years of black insurrections in Martinique, Cuba, Antigua, Tortola, Jamaica, and elsewhere in the Western Hemisphere, and black people in the States were not oblivious of them or of their promise. This was demonstrated in the fall of 1826, when twenty-nine black people were being taken by sea from Maryland to Georgia on the *Decatur,* a vessel owned by one of the nation's largest slave traders. The black captives rebelled, killed two members of the crew, then ordered another crew member "to take them to Haiti" because they knew of the black struggle there. The boat was captured before they could reach their destination, but when the *Decatur* was taken to New York City, all but one of the captives escaped.[16]

Two years later a group of four black slave artisans were on a similar journey by ship from Charleston to New Orleans. Before leaving South Carolina, they vowed that they would never be slaves in New Orleans. By the time the boat docked, they all had committed suicide. At about the same time, fragmentary reports of rebellions and death on island plantations seeped out of other parts of Louisiana.[17]

There was no surcease. While Nat Turner saw visions and waited for signs, others continued to fight. In Mobile County, Alabama, a black man named Hal had led a group of outlyers for several years. By the spring of 1827 the fugitives were organized to the point where they were building a fort in the swamps. One day while the construction was still going on, they were surprised, attacked, and defeated by a large group of whites. Later one of the white men reported: "This much I can say that old Hal . . . and his men fought like spartans, not one gave an inch of ground, but stood, was shot dead or wounded fell on the spot."[18]

While Nat Turner waited for the sign, and black people fought on ships, in forests, and on plantations, there were still other options and other signs, especially for those who could no longer bide their time. David Walker was one such man. He had been born legally free in 1785 in Wilmington, North Carolina, the child of a free mother, but he knew that he was not free, that his status ultimately depended upon the good will of white men. By the 1820s, while Nat waited for signs and saw visions, Walker had traveled across the South and into the trans-Appalachian West, had seen what America was doing to black people in slavery, and had become concerned about what slavery might yet do to him. Later, two scenes from those journeys stood out especially in his mind. He claimed to have watched the degradation of two black men: a son who was forced to strip his mother naked and whip her until she died; and a black husband forced to lash his pregnant wife until she aborted her child. Walker knew that, if faced with such savage choices, he would kill white men—and most likely be killed. "If I remain in this bloody land," he told himself, "I will not live long." By 1826, led by his own signs and visions, David Walker had moved to Boston.[19]

By then he was forty-one years old. A tall, slender, handsome man of dark complexion, Walker was a bachelor when he arrived. Perhaps he had thought it unwise to give too many hostages to white fortune while living and traveling in the South and West. Perhaps he wanted to be untrammeled in his passionate work on behalf of black freedom, a task he took up in very concrete ways soon after arriving in Boston. Almost immediately, the North Carolinian's house became a refuge for all black people in need of aid, especially the fugitives from slavery who came regularly into Boston. Walker was also an organizer and lecturer for the General Colored Association of Massachusetts, a black abolitionist organization, and when *Freedom's Journal*, the first black newspaper in America, began publication in 1827, Walker became an agent for the paper in Boston.[20]

The meeting of David Walker and *Freedom's Journal* in the Northern phase of the struggle raised a question of great moment: what is the role of the word—the spoken word, the preached word, the whispered-in-the-nighttime word, the written word, the published word—in the fight for black freedom?

In the slave castles and by the riversides of Africa, where our ancestors had gathered for the long journey into American captivity, the spoken word had many functions. It provided a bridge between and among them, to draw them together for the unity those first efforts demanded. On the ships the word was used to strengthen men and women and urge them toward the dangers of participation. It was often on the ships that the word, for the first sustained length of time, was directed toward the white captors. Early, in such a setting, the word was used in protest, in statements of black rights and white wrongs, of black people's determination to be men and women in spite of European attempts to dehumanize them. There, too, the word publicly spoken to white men often served as a rallying point for the Africans. For in many cases the word was openly uttered in spite of the rules and laws of the whites, spoken in the face of threats and punishment and even death. Such courageous speakers of the word understandably evoked strength and courage and hope in other captives.

Similar situations often prevailed when the black-white struggle moved from the prison ships into the fields and forests of the New World prison state. In the South, the word was used as an organizing tool for the flight into the outlyers' camps or toward the North. In many such situations it spoke the truth about white oppression, black suffering, and the potential power of organized black will. Such a word strengthened and encouraged friends to continue to struggle to survive, to bide their time toward the struggle to overcome. And on many occasions, the prison states exacted the same cruel penalties as the prison ships for the honest, defiant, encouraging black word. For such words were radical acts.[21]

No less dangerous to white power in the South were the words spoken honestly from the Bible, the Word, telling men and women of a humanity no one could deny them, reminding a people that God opposed injustice and the oppression of the weak, encouraging believers to seek for messianic signs in the heavens, for blood on the leaves. On the tongues of black people—and in their hands—the Word might indeed become a sword.

On the other hand, in the antebellum North the role of the word developed somewhat differently, progressing less starkly but in the same essential direction. There, in situations where black men and women brought that word to bear against their oppressors, they usually addressed two intersecting realities: the bondage forced upon their brothers and sisters in the South, and the racist discrimination practiced against their own immediate community in the North. When they spoke or wrote against slavery, the fate of their word often depended upon where it was spoken and to what audience it was directed. Put forth among black people or white sympathizers, words from black speakers and writers denouncing slavery and its defenders usually did not present the same outright, abrasive challenge as in the South. However, such words could never be confined to those circles. They carried their own resonance and therefore their own dangers. No black critics, whatever their audiences, were suffered gladly, and it was not unusual—especially as the nation's argument over slavery grew more heated—for white mobs to break in on abolitionist meetings and especially attack the black men and women who dared stand as public judges of white law and order.[22]

As the debate over slavery intensified, the black word from the north became more provocative, more slashing in its condemnation, more daring in its encouragement to resistance. Then, when attempts were made to publish and distribute those words among the Afro-American captives of the South, radical words and deeds were clearly joined, and the challenge was explosive. In the same way, as black men and women pressed their fierce arguments against the conditions of Northern racism, they found increasing hostility in that section, too. For the word often called upon their brothers and sisters to struggle for changes in their status there, to resist, to fight back. Ultimately, the words against slavery in the South and discrimination in the North were joined, for the black community of the North was finally called upon to resist the laws which endangered the fugitive slaves who came among them. From pulpit, platform, and press the black word would urge them to take up the struggle of the enslaved on free ground, thereby proclaiming all American soil to be contaminated, unfree, and in need of the rushing, cleansing movement of the river.

So the word had many roles and many places in the Northern struggle. In 1827 the almost simultaneous appearance of David Walker and *Freedom's Journal* represented one of the earliest institutional manifestations of what we have called the Great Tradition of Black Protest. As such, it was in the mainstream of the river, closer to the surface than the churning depths. In its first issue this pioneer black periodical announced: "The civil rights of a people being of the greatest value, it shall ever be our duty to vindicate our brethren when oppressed, and to lay the cure before the public. We also urge upon

our brethren (who are qualified by the laws of the different states) the expediency of using their elective franchise; and of making an independent use of the same. We wish them not to become the tools of party." For the *Journal,* the word meant quiet, sound advocacy of the black cause, an encouragement to acceptable black social and political development, and a source of information and advice for any whites who might be concerned about black needs. In 1827 the word of the Great Tradition was less strident than it had been on the slave ships, but it was the same tradition, and the time for its renewed stridency would come.[23]

By the following year, David Walker began his brief career as a goad to moderate voices like that of *Freedom's Journal.* For even as he moved within the Great Tradition, Walker's history, temperament, and commitments urged him toward deeper and more radical levels of struggle. In the fall of 1828 he delivered an address before the General Colored Association of his adopted state, calling on blacks to organize and act on their own behalf. In the address Walker first spoke of the need for political and social organization within the black community, identifying such structured, inner cohesion as a prerequisite to any effective struggle for freedom. "Ought we not to form ourselves into a general body to protect, aid, and assist each other to the utmost of our power?" Proceeding beyond this, he also said that "it is indispensably our duty to try every scheme we think will have a tendency to facilitate our salvation, and leave the final result to . . . God."

This last sentiment was not escapist. Rather, it suggested a certain affinity between Walker and the waiting Nat Turner. For David Walker was a staunch and faithful member of a black Methodist church in Boston, and he firmly believed that people—especially oppressed people—were called upon to act as well as pray, always placing their ultimate confidence in God. It was that context of active faith which illuminated the final words of Walker's speech to the Colored Association: "I verily believe that God has something in reserve for us, which when he shall have poured it out upon us, will repay us for all our suffering and misery."[24]

In February 1829, two months after the publication of Walker's December speech, a document which seemed to express certain elements of his thought more explicitly appeared in print. One Robert Young, a black New Yorker, published a pamphlet called *The Ethiopian Manifesto,* evidently intending to put forward a longer version later. It appears now that the larger statement never came, but the *Manifesto* picked up the themes from Walker's work and carried them forward. For Young, as for many Biblically oriented blacks of the time, the word Ethiopian was synonymous with African: where Walker had spoken generally of the need for political and social organization, Young seemed to advocate the establishment of a theocracy of Ethiopian people in America. Calling for the "convocation of ourselves into a body politic," Young said that "for the promotion of welfare of our order," it was necessary "to establish to ourselves a people framed into the likeness of that order, which from our mind's eye we do evidently discern governs the universal creation. Beholding but one sole power, supremacy, or head, we do of that head . . . look forward for succor in the accomplishment of the great design which he hath, in his wisdom, promoted us to its undertaking."[25]

Equally important, perhaps more so, was the *Manifesto*'s announcement to the black people of America and elsewhere that "the time is at hand, when, with but the power of words, and the divine will of our God, the vile shackles of slavery shall be broken asunder from you, and no man known shall dare to own or proclaim you as his bondsmen." This was a deliverance rather different from the kind Nat Turner pondered in Virginia, or that David Walker would soon propose. It depended solely on "the power of words" and

the will of God. But according to Young, it would be manifested through a mulatto Messiah chosen by God from "Grenada's Island" in the West Indies. This Messiah would be the means whereby God would "call together the black people as a nation in themselves." Thus Young could say to white people: "Of the degraded of this earth, shall be exalted, one who shall draw from thee as though gifted of power divine, all attachment and regard of thy slave towards thee."[26]

Here was true messianic promise: divine intervention on behalf of the Ethiopian nation in America, to provide a savior to draw black people together as a nation, and somehow miraculously break the shackles of slavery. Its pan-Africanism, its sense of nationhood, its radical hope all marked this rather mysterious announcement as part of the stream of radical ideas in the struggle. But by then both David Walker and Nat Turner had heard other voices.

Not long after his arrival in Boston, David Walker had set up a new and used clothing shop on Brattle Street. That provided his living: but the freedom struggle of black people in America was his life. Not only did he regularly attend the abolitionist meetings and assist all the fugitives he could, but those who knew him noted that Walker was devoting very long, hard hours to reading and study. Driven by an urgency that he attributed to the spirit of God, his special role was taking shape, only faintly suggested by the speech near the end of 1828.

Sometime during this period Walker took time to get married, but there was no release of the internal pressure, no relaxation in the harsh schedule of reading and writing which he had set himself. Finally, having developed a series of notes and drafts, in September 1829 Walker supervised the printing of his explosive seventy-six-page pamphlet, *Walker's Appeal . . . to the Colored Citizens of the World But in Particular and very Expressly to those of the United States of America.* It read as if all the

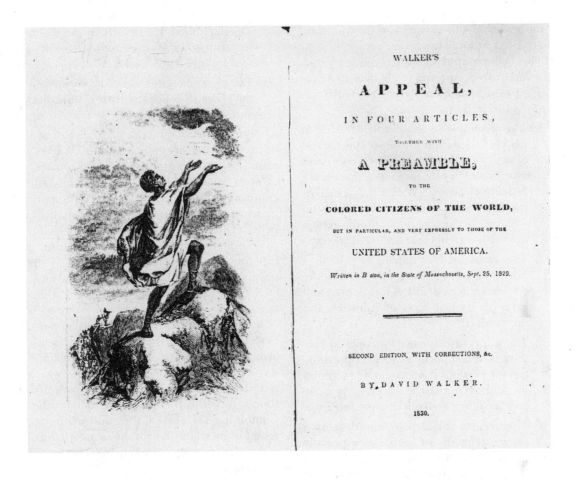

WALKER'S

APPEAL,

IN FOUR ARTICLES,

TOGETHER WITH

A PREAMBLE,

TO THE

COLORED CITIZENS OF THE WORLD,

BUT IN PARTICULAR, AND VERY EXPRESSLY TO THOSE OF THE

UNITED STATES OF AMERICA.

Written in B ston, in the State of Massachusetts, Sept. 28, 1829.

SECOND EDITION, WITH CORRECTIONS, &c.

BY DAVID WALKER.

1830.

passion and commitment of his life had been poured into the document. In its pages, filled with exclamations and pleas, with warnings and exhortations, one could almost hear the seething, roaring sounds of the black river, from the wailings of the African baracoons to the thundering declarations of Dessalines, and the quiet signals of the outlyers in Wilmington's swamps.[27]

Near the beginning of the work, Walker proclaimed it one of his major purposes "to awaken in the breasts of my afflicted, degraded and slumbering brethren, a spirit of inquiry and investigation respecting our miseries and wretchednesses in this REPUBLICAN LAND OF LIBERTY!!!!!" Essentially, he was demonstrating several of the major functions of radical

teaching among dominated African peoples: to raise questions about the reasons for their oppression, to speak the truth concerning both oppressed and oppressor, to clarify as fully as possible the contradictions inherent in both communities, and to indicate the possible uses of these contradictions in the struggle for freedom. Actually, he accomplished even more than he set out to: for over a century, Walker's *Appeal* remained a touchstone for one crucial genre of black radical analysis and agitation. As such, its primary strength lay in the breadth and honesty of its analysis, in the all-consuming passion of its commitment to black liberation, and in the radical hope which lifted it beyond the familiar temptations to bitter despair. Understandably, then, David

Walker's heirs, both conscious and unconscious, have been legion.[28]

In the pamphlet, which quickly went through three editions (with new material added to the later ones), ten major themes were addressed:

1. The profound degradation of African peoples, especially those in the United States, as a result of the racism and avarice which supported and shaped the system of slavery. (Walker was perhaps the first writer to combine an attack on white racism and white economic exploitation in a deliberate and critical way.)

2. The unavoidable judgment which a just God would bring upon the white American nation, unless it repented and gave up its evil ways of injustice and oppression.

3. The imperative for black people to face their own complicity in their oppression, and the need for them to end that complicity through resistance in every possible way, including the path of armed struggle.

4. The need for black people to develop a far greater sense of solidarity, especially between the "free" and captive populations within the United States, and between the children of Africa here and Africans in the rest of the world. (This was the first clear, widely publicized call for pan-African solidarity.)

5. The need to resist the attempts of the American Colonization Society to rid the country of its free black population.

6. The need to gain as much education as possible as a weapon in the struggle.

7. The possibility that a new society of peace and justice could come into being if white America were able to give up its malevolent ways, especially its racism and avarice.

8. The need for an essentially Protestant Christian religious undergirding for the black struggle for justice.

9. The likelihood that he, Walker, would be imprisoned or assassinated as a result of the *Appeal*.

10. The repeated statement of his own essential sense of solidarity with his brothers and sisters in slavery.

Actually, this last-mentioned sense of solidarity was the deepest source of Walker's radicalism. He was impelled not by a hatred of white America, but by a profound love and compassion for his people. It was this commitment to black people, and his unshakable belief in a God of justice, which led inevitably to an urgent statement of black radicalism, a call for uprooting and overturning of the system of life and death that was America.

Because of the nature and preoccupations of American society, the *Appeal*, in spite of its other urgent concerns, gained its greatest notoriety through advocacy of black messianic armed resistance to white oppression and slavery. Of course it was this advocacy which posed the most obvious, if not the most profound, threat to the American social order. Combining social, political, and economic religious messianism with the secular natural rights doctrine then current, Walker urged black people:

> Let your enemies go with their butcheries, and at once fill up their cup. Never make an attempt to gain our freedom or *natural right*, from under our cruel oppressors and murderers, until you see your way clear—when that hour arrives and you move, be not afraid or dismayed; for be you assured that Jesus Christ the king of heaven and of earth who is the God of justice and of armies, will surely go before you. And those enemies who have for hundreds of years stolen our *rights*, and kept us ignorant of him and his divine worship, he will remove.[29]

A black man had again taken products of white civilization and transmuted them for purposes of black freedom. In the *Appeal*, the two major systems of belief in early nineteenth-century

America—Protestant evangelical Christianity and natural rights philosophy—were lifted up and bound in blood as a weapon in the struggle of black people toward justice. For Walker, the cause of freedom was the cause of God, and the cause of black justice was the cause of Jesus Christ; he readily promised the divine presence to all black people who would stand up and fight in that "glorious and heavenly cause" of black liberation.

Obviously such conclusions had never been dreamed of on the campgrounds of the South, in the churches of the North, or in the town halls, universities, and legislatures of the white nation. But whatever those white assumptions, Walker knew his own purposes, and his urging of a divinely justified armed struggle against oppression was relentless. Calling upon black people to fight openly against all who sought to maintain them in slavery, he wrote: "If you commence, make sure work—do not trifle, for they will not trifle with you—they want us for their slaves, and think nothing of murdering us in order to subject us to that wretched condition—therefore, if there is an *attempt* made by us, kill or be killed." He also added: "It is no more harm for you to kill a man who is trying to kill you, than it is for you to take a drink of water when thirsty; in fact the man who will stand still and let another man murder him is worse than an infidel."[30]

As he saw it, the fight for black freedom was in reality a holy crusade. Black resistance to slavery was sacred obedience to God; continued submission was sinful and risked God's judgment. Nor was Walker reticent about his own views on the need for such judgment: "The man who would not fight under our Lord and Master Jesus Christ, in the glorious and heavenly cause of freedom and of God . . . ought to be kept with all of his children or family, in slavery, or in chains, to be butchered by his cruel enemies."[31]

(Had Walker read the words of Dessalines? A quarter of a century before, calling for the blood of the white oppressors, the Avenger had asked: "Where is that Haytian so vile, Haytian so unworthy of his regeneration, who thinks he has not fulfilled the decrees of the Eternal by exterminating these blood-thirsty tyggers? If there be one, let him fly; indignant nature discards him from our bosom . . . the air we breathe is not suited to his gross organs; it is the air of liberty, pure, august, and triumphant.")[32]

For those who needed a different kind of encouragement, Walker offered the promised Messiah, a figure first raised up by Robert Young and now militarized by Walker. Thus the passionate Boston radical promised the black nation that "the Lord our God . . . will send you a Hannibal," and urged black people to fight valiantly under his leadership, since "God will indeed deliver you through him from your deplorable and wretched condition under the Christians of America." There was no doubt about the warlike intentions of *this* Messiah, for under him, Walker said, "my colour will root some of the whites out of the very face of the earth." Indeed, David Walker was so certain of his God's judgment upon the evil of white American society that he foresaw the possibility of another route of judgment in case black people and their Hannibal-Messiah did not prove adequate. Here, his prediction was eventually and vividly confirmed: "Although the destruction of the oppressors God may not effect by the oppressed, yet the Lord our God will surely bring other destructions upon them—for not infrequently will he cause them to rise up against one another, to be split and divided, and to oppress each other, and sometimes to open hostilities with sword in hand."[33]

Did David Walker see signs and visions, as the waiting Nat Turner had seen them? Did such revelations explain the accuracy of his prophecies regarding the nation? Although he did not claim this sort of inspiration as explicitly as Nat Turner, Walker did reply to

247

some of his critics by saying: "Do they believe that I would be so foolish as to put out a book of this kind without strict—ah! very strict commandments of the Lord? . . . He will soon show you and the world, in due time, whether this book is for his glory." So perhaps there really were visions; but there was something less esoteric as well. For it was obvious that Walker was driven to many of his conclusions not by kaleidoscopic images and voices whirring in the wind, but by a profound, unshakable belief in the justice of God, an element of faith which remained consistently present in the radical streams of black struggle. Confidence in that divine justice led to an assurance of divine retribution against America, which in turn encouraged black struggle in the cause of that justice and retribution. At one point in the *Appeal*, Walker asked: "Can the Americans escape God Almighty? If they do, can he be to us a God of justice?" To Walker the central answer was unmistakably clear: "God is just, and I know it—for he has convinced me to my satisfaction—I cannot doubt him."[34]

But even more than this lay behind Walker's fiercely accurate conclusions. Not for nothing had he spent years of travel, reading, and research examining white oppression in America, seeking to clarify his people's situation. For instance, his observations across the land led him to refer again and again to the economic motives behind white oppression. Early in the *Appeal* he said that, after years of observation and reading, "I have come to the immovable conclusion that [the Americans] have, and do continue to punish us for nothing else, but for enriching them and their country." This he called "avarice." Pursuing the theme of white avarice and greed, Walker moved to conclusions which would appear repeatedly in radical black analysis. Thus he continually referred to whites as "our *natural enemies*." He conceded that "from the beginning [of international contacts between blacks and whites], I do not think that we were

natural enemies to each other." But he quickly added that since the opening of the slave trade, the whites by their avarice and cruel treatment had made themselves the natural enemies of blacks. It was therefore logical for him not only to call for relentless struggle, but also to explore the possibility of emigration: he suggested Canada or Haiti.[35]

The use of such a term as "natural enemies" raised questions which continued to arise: precisely who were the enemies of black freedom, of black humanity, natural or otherwise? Were they all white Americans, thereby positing a struggle of white against black? Were some white Americans not the enemy? What was the role of the federal government in this conflict? Was it also the enemy? These were crucial questions, profoundly affecting the ways in which black people looked at whites as well as themselves, and the ways in which they organized themselves for struggle toward freedom.

In the *Appeal* it was not always clear where Walker was focusing his attack, and who was included among the "natural enemies." At times he mentioned "slave-holders and their advocates," but he also included Northern white racists, perhaps classifying them also as "advocates." On one occasion he pressed the issue to the critical point, saying, "Is this not the most tyrannical unmerciful and cruel government under Heaven?" Generally, the primary enemies that he identified—with sometimes more, sometimes less clarity—were these: the system of slavery and its advocates in North and South alike; the American government, which supported that system and other aspects of white supremacy; and the white citizens of the country at large who co-operated in any way in the degradation of black people. To identify the government, the system of slavery, and most of the people of white America as the enemies of black freedom, was to put forward a radical analysis in keeping with the slave-ship experience.[36]

His sound and basic analysis of the American situation and of the human condition led

Walker also to explore further the matter of black self-government which he had originally raised in 1828, and which Robert Young had put forward in a more spiritualized form in February 1829. Now, in the fall of 1829, Walker found no inconsistency in advocating implacable struggle on these shores, and at the same time preparing for self-government here or elsewhere. In the course of the *Appeal*'s powerful attack on the racism of Thomas Jefferson's *Notes on Virginia*, Walker wrote: "Our sufferings will come to an end, in spite of all the Americans this side of eternity. Then we will want all the learning and talents among ourselves, and perhaps more, to govern ourselves."[37]

Whatever the future of black people in America, by 1829 Walker had also developed a mature and fascinating sense of pan-African identity, tying together past, present, and future. He not only identified black people with the past greatness of Egypt and the rest of Africa, but went on to identify the bonds of future struggle. He spoke to all black people in America, especially those who "have the hardihood to say that you are free and happy." For him there was no true freedom or happiness apart from his brothers and sisters in slavery; moreover, he insisted to black people that it was "an unshakable and forever immovable *fact* that your full glory and happiness, as well as that of all other coloured people under Heaven, shall never be fully consummated [without] the entire emancipation of your enslaved brethren all over the world. . . . I believe it is the will of the Lord that our greatest happiness shall consist in working for the salvation of our whole body." For those who doubted and said such pan-African liberation could never be accomplished, Walker spoke out of his profound faith in the God of our ancestors: "I assure you that God will accomplish it—if nothing else will answer he will hurl tyrants and devils into *atoms* [!] and make way for his people. But O my brethren! I say unto you again, you must go to work and prepare the way of the Lord."[38]

Everything in Walker's mind led back to "the way of the Lord," the way of justice for the Lord's oppressed African peoples. This way demanded harsh judgment upon white America. Or did it? In spite of Walker's passionate commitment to black freedom and God's justice, the *Appeal* shows a certain ambivalence toward white America and its future, as in this ambiguous warning: "I tell you Americans! that unless you speedily alter your course, *you* and your *Country are gone*!!!! For God Almighty will tear up the very face of the earth!!!!" In his mind, then, there seemed to be some alternative: America might "speedily alter" its course. But was it really possible? He doubted it: "I hope that the Americans may hear, but I am afraid that they have done us so much injury, and are so firm in the belief that our Creator made us to be an inheritance to them for ever, that their hearts will be hardened, so that their destruction may be sure."[39] Nevertheless, in a tradition soon to be firmly set, Walker continued to speak to the hopeless white "Americans," continued to call them to new possibilities. Perhaps there was no other choice, since black people jointly occupied with the "Americans" the territory which was to be torn up by God's judgment. Who could be eager for a judgment on America, when its land was filled with Africa's children?

Thus he spoke as a kind of angry black pastor to white America: "I speak Americans for your good. We must and shall be free . . . in spite of you. You may do your best to keep us in wretchedness and misery, to enrich you and your children, but God will deliver us from under you. And wo, wo, will be to you if we have to obtain our freedom by fighting." And what if the miracle occurred, and America decided that it wanted to change its ways, to seek justice and love misery, to let the oppressed go free? What would repentance require where black men and women (to say nothing of the natives of the land) were concerned?[40]

Here, as in the case of many of his later heirs, Walker was vague: "Treat us like men, and . . . we will live in peace and happiness together." What did that mean? What did justice and manhood require? Ending slavery was, of course, one obvious requirement, and Walker cited it. But beyond that, his answer was less clear: "The Americans . . . have to raise us from the condition of brutes to that of respectable men, and to make a national acknowledgment to us for the wrongs they have inflicted upon us." Perhaps that statement implied compensation to the African captives for the generations of unpaid labor. Perhaps it meant reparations in other forms. Perhaps it suggested some special role of honor in the society for those who had been so long humiliated by its racism and greed.[41]

At this point, we cannot be certain what David Walker saw as the proper acts of white repentance and restitution. Whatever he meant, his "Americans" did not care. As the three editions of the *Appeal* came rushing off the presses between October 1829 and June 1830, white men were in no way drawn to Walker's pastoral/prophetic calls to penance for the oppression of black people. What they reacted to in the *Appeal* were the sanguinary calls to black men, the ringing summonses to armed struggle against the white keepers of the status quo. For the "Americans," *that* was Walker's *Appeal,* and it constituted sedition.

Of course it was precisely because they were not interested in Walker's invitations to repentance that white people were forced to be frantically concerned with his summonses to divinely ordained rebellion. They were right to be concerned. In the months following publication there is some evidence that David Walker, in addition to distributing it among Northern blacks, made distinct attempts to see that his *Appeal* reached black captives of the South, sometimes sewing copies into the inner linings of coats he traded to Southern-bound black seamen, sometimes using other clandestine methods—including at least one white courier—to circulate it. Word came back from Georgia and Louisiana, from the Carolinas and Virginia (did it reach Southhampton County?) that the message was breaking through.[42]

Meanwhile white condemnation erupted from many sources. The governor of North Carolina, most likely mindful of the swamps around Walker's native Wilmington, denounced (and praised) the *Appeal.* He called it "an open appeal to [the black's] natural love of liberty . . . and . . . totally subversive of all subordination in our slaves." He was, of course, totally correct. More unusual was the response from Benjamin Lundy, the best-known white antislavery publicist of the time: "A more bold, daring, inflammatory publication, perhaps, ever issued from the press of any country. . . . I can do no less than set the broadest seal of condemnation on it." Thus conservatives who placed the preservation of their way of life before black freedom, and liberals who placed the validity of their own solutions before black-defined struggle, were equally dismayed.[43]

Some of Walker's "Americans" were more than dismayed. Shortly after whites in the South first gained access to the *Appeal,* it is said that "a company of Georgia men" not only vowed that they would kill David Walker, but offered a thousand-dollar reward for his death. When Walker's wife and friends heard of this, they frantically urged him to go to Canada at least for a time. It was useless advice to David Walker. He replied: "I will stand my ground. *Somebody must die in this cause.* I may be doomed to the stake and the fire, or to the scaffold tree, but it is not in me to falter if I can promote the work of emancipation."[44]

Nor was he alone in this determination. Walker's message electrified the black community of the North and provided new sources of courage for those among them who saw no ultimate solution apart from the sword of the Lord. Even more important, perhaps, scores of now anonymous black people throughout the South risked their lives to distribute the *Appeal.* In Savannah an unidentified "negro preacher" distributed it after it had reached the city by boat. In February 1830 four black men were arrested in New Orleans on charges of circulating the *Appeal*. That same winter, thirty copies of it were found on a free black man in Richmond, Virginia. Meanwhile black seamen carried it along the coast at similar peril.[45]

If he was able to follow the progress of the *Appeal* into the South, it is possible that David Walker may have been most moved by its appearance in his home town of Wilmington, North Carolina. As a result of it, much "unrest and plotting" were noted in the black community. But there was also a great cost to pay. Early in 1830, a report from Wilmington announced that "there has been much shooting of negroes in Wilmington recently, in consequence of symptoms of liberty having been discovered among them."[46]

Walker had said it: "I will stand my ground. *Somebody must die in this cause.*" On the morning of June 28, 1830, in Boston's fair precincts of liberty, David Walker became suddenly and mysteriously afflicted, and fell dead in a doorway near his shop. Almost all of black Boston was convinced that the dauntless crusader had been poisoned.[47]

And what of Nat Turner? Did Walker's *Appeal* ever reach him as he waited for the proper sign in Southhampton County? No record exists of that contact, if it ever occurred. But the contact was not necessary, for Nat Turner had long been convinced that the God of Walker's *Appeal* had always been in Southhampton.

By the time of Walker's death, Turner had moved to a new home in the country, on the farm of Joseph Travis near Barrow Road. Legally, as such madness went, Nat was now owned by Putnam Moore, an infant. The child's father, Thomas Moore, Nat's last owner of record, had recently died, and in 1830 Moore's widow—Putnam's mother—married Joseph Travis. At that point she and the child moved with Nat to the Travis home and land. But wherever he was, working for whichever

white person currently claimed to be his owner, Nat Turner knew that he had only one Master, who spoke in thunder and lightning and through the swaying, leafy trees. This was the Master who possessed his life, who had honed and harshened him in the wilderness, in the midst of the black community, in the movement of black struggle. This was the leader of the black angels who would scourge the white oppressors and pour judgment like a red bloodtide over the land. So Nat did his temporary work and bided his time, watching for the sign.[48]

> *Green trees a bending*
> *Poor sinner stands a tremblin'*
> *The trumpet sounds within-a my soul*
> *I ain't got long to stay here.*

The sign came in February 1831, with an eclipse of the sun. White men seeking a sign may have thought it marked an end to their bleak season of economic suffering in Virginia and North Carolina, but Nat found a different message: the movement of the last into their proper place had begun. And so, soon after the eclipse, he told his closest comrades that the time of battle and blood was approaching. With him in the initial leadership cadre were four men: Henry Porter, Hark Travis, Nelson Williams, and Samuel Francis. Evidently there was a group of some twenty-five who would form the core of the fighting force at first, convinced that others would be recruited as the struggle was openly joined.[49]

The Fourth of July, that prime symbol of white American contradictions, was chosen as the date for the uprising. But as the time approached, Nat became ill (were there fears or premonitions?) and the date was abandoned. Another sign had to be sought. On August 13, 1831, there was "a day-long atmospheric phenomenon, during which the sun appeared bluish green," and Nat knew that he had found the way again. One week later he met with Hark and Henry to agree on a final plan. The next night they met again, this time with several others; they agreed on their work, and ate a final meal together. In the dark hours of the morning of August 22, Nat Turner's God pressed him forward at the head of his band of black avenging angels, drove him in search of what seemed the ultimate justice: that "the first should be last and the last should be first." According to a black tradition, Nat's final words to his followers were: "Remember, we do not go forth for the sake of blood and carnage; but it is necessary that, in the commencement of this revolution, all the whites we meet should die, until we have an army strong enough to carry out the war on a Christian basis. Remember that ours is not a war for robbery, nor to satisfy our passions; it is a *struggle for freedom*." Whatever the words, this was the goal, and the river now was churning.[50]

They began at the Travis household with hatchets and axes, and no life was spared. At that point, with very few exceptions, all whites were the enemy. It was not a matter of "good" and "bad" masters; all were involved in slavery. And the children—even Putnam Moore— were the heirs. Temporarily filled with such resolve, organized into rudimentary cavalry and infantry sections, Nat's men continued down the Barrow Road, storming house after house, destroying family after family: Francis, Reese, Turner, Peeples, Whitehead, each in its turn experienced the terrible slaughter, not alien to the children of Africa.

At the height of the advance, there were apparently some sixty men in Nat Turner's company, including several described as "free." Together, in a breathlessly brief period of solidarity, they were marching to Jerusalem, Virginia, and their leader was now "General Nat." Once again a captive black prophet, wresting the religion of white America out of its hands, had transformed it and had in turn been utterly changed. Now, as an insurrectionary commander carrying out the sanguinary vengeance of a just God, Nat Turner took up the spirit of David Walker's *Appeal* and

burned its message into the dark and bloody ground of Virginia, streaking the black river with blood.[51]

Apparently, he had hoped to move so quickly and kill so thoroughly that no alarm would be given before his marchers reached Jerusalem, and had captured the cache of arms stored there. As in the case of Gabriel and Vesey, the steps beyond that action were not certain. Perhaps they planned to head toward the swamps. There were even rumors that they expected somehow to find their way to Africa. But in the brutal light of August, it was still Virginia, U.S.A. The skies had not broken open, the earth had not erupted in divine power and judgment—and they were not fully angels of light. Indeed, as time wore on that Monday there was a growing sense of confusion, disarray, and sometimes drunkenness among some of Nat's men. Often the prophet himself seemed distracted, and rode at the rear of his troops rather than at the front. Added to these internal problems was the tragic fact that General Nat's men "had few arms among them—and scarcely one, if one, that was fit for use." So it was still Virginia. They had not moved as rapidly, mobilized as effectively, transformed themselves as fully, nor destroyed as efficiently as Nat had expected. Before they reached the road to Jerusalem, the alarm had been spread, leaping like fire from one blanched and trembling set of lips to another, echoing in the clashing sound of church bells across the countryside. The alarm struck fear in the heart of some of Turner's band and they deserted. Others, still on plantations, decided that the struggle was now hopeless, and decided to remain with their masters, biding their time.[52]

Nevertheless, Nat had already challenged Virginia, the government of the United States, and all the fierce and chilling fears which raged within the depths of the white community everywhere. So vigilante groups, militia companies, and the ever-present military arm of the federal government were soon on their way to the battleground. By noon on Monday, in the blazing heat of a cornfield, Turner's insurrectionaries had their first encounter with the white militia and the the volunteer companies which had rushed to organize. The blacks were heavily outgunned and, after suffering significant casualties among some of their best men, were forced to retreat. Still, with less than a third of his army remaining, General Nat maintained his resolve to reach Jerusalem. But the path was blocked each way he moved, fear was rising among his decimated command, and night was now upon them. So they hid and prayed and hoped, while isolated members of their company were being trapped, captured, and sometimes murdered in the woods.

By the next day, Tuesday, August 23, it was hard to see how hopes or prayers would prevail. The countryside was swarming with hundreds of armed white men from surrounding counties, cities, and military bases in Virginia and North Carolina, and Turner had fewer than twenty rebels remaining. Even in the face of these odds, Nat and his men were determined to fight on, if only they could draw more blacks to their side. Before daybreak they moved to attack a large plantation near their encampment, daring to hope they would attract fresh recruits out of the slave quarters there. Instead, Turner's fighters were repulsed by a defending force made up of the owners and their enslaved blacks. At least one of the rebels was killed there and several were severely wounded, including Nat's close friend, Hark. That may have been the decisive experience of defeat. Soon after, in one last skirmish with the militia, three more of Nat's little band were killed; others were wounded and captured, becoming offerings to a fearful spirit of vengeance which raged through the white community. Only Prophet Nat and four followers managed to escape. Finally, before Tuesday was over, as the beleaguered black remnant force separated in desperate search for other

possibly surviving companies, all save Nat were killed or captured.

The march to Jerusalem was over. The band of black avenging angels was crushed. Still, Nat Turner was not captured and was not defeated. That night he hid and hoped. As hundreds of men and animals searched him out he dug a hole in the ground and lay there, daring to nurture the dream that he might yet regroup his forces, refusing to believe that the promised time of judgment for Virginia's slaveholders had not come (or had arrived in some form unrecognizable to him).[53]

In spite of Turner's desperate hope, there was no regrouping for his troops. Rather, while the residue of the black men hid or were rounded up, the outraged, terrified white forces struck back in overwhelming fury. Estimates range from scores to hundreds of black people slaughtered, most of whom evidently had no intimate connection with the uprising. Meanwhile, the prophet-turned-general was alone in the woods again, hiding, biding his time, most likely wondering if there would ever be another sign. He remained in hiding, avoiding capture for six weeks after the attempted revolution. But the signs were not propitious. His wife was found and lashed until she gave up those papers of his in her possession, papers "filled with hieroglyphical characters," characters which "appear to have been traced with blood."[54]

"The blood of Christ . . . was now returning to earth."

His friends were being captured and killed. Perhaps, though, there may have been some comfort afforded him if Turner learned that many of them manifested an amazing spirit of courage and commitment, even in the face of death. Of some it was said that "in the agonies of Death [they] declared that they was going happy for that God had a hand in what they had been doing."[55]

While Nat was still hiding, another black preacher—this time one named David—

attempted to enter the radical stream. In Duplin County, in southeastern North Carolina, far from Nat's place in the woods, David planned rebellion. With other enslaved Africans he plotted an insurrection for October 4, 1931, to culminate in a march on Wilmington. Were these some of David Walker's heirs, readers of the *Appeal,* marching on his native city in his honor? Or were they, as the authorities feared, part of Nat Turner's band of avengers? No one was certain, and the insurrection was blocked before it could demonstrate the direction of its flow. So even in Duplin County signs were not good, though the river was clearly in ferment.[56]

Out of that ferment, while Nat was still hiding, a fiery letter reached the town of Jerusalem, sounding almost as if the most stunning visions of Turner, Walker, and every other black insurrectionary leader had been put on paper and thrust into the Southern furnaces. Arriving from Boston, signed simply by "Nero," the missive proudly and provocatively announced to the white authorities that a paramilitary organization of black men was forming which would eventually lead hundreds of thousands of black people to take up arms in revenge for all the oppression of their people. According to Nero, their leader was even then traveling throughout the South, visiting "almost every Negro hut and quarters there." Key cadre members were training in Haiti, learning from the surviving leaders of that celebrated revolution. Everywhere in America they were recruiting, telling blacks "that if they are killed in this crusade that heaven will be their reward, and that every person they kill, who countenances slavery, shall procure for them an additional jewel in their heavenly crown." Had David Walker finally arrived in Southhampton County, vindicating the hidden Turner and his scores of dead companions? Or was this simply another of those radical, bloody visions which must soar wildly out of the river of a people's freedom struggle, expressing all the yearnings buried in the spirits of the mute sufferers?[57]

The silence which followed the letter offered no answers for the future and no concrete hope in the present, least of all for the fugitive insurrectionary. Then on October 30, 1831, Nat Turner was captured. His sign had not come; Nero's army had not appeared. Charged with "conspiring to rebel and making insurrection," he told his counsel that he wished to plead not guilty, because he "did not feel" that he was a guilty person. Guilt was not a relevant category for an instrument of divine judgment—even if the last sign had not come.[58]

Perhaps he was sign in himself. Thomas Gray, a local slaveholding attorney who produced his own widely read version of Turner's confession, described Nat in prison as "clothed with rags and covered with chains, yet, daring to raise his manacled hand to heaven, with a spirit soaring above the attributes of man." Then Gray added, "I looked on him and my blood curdled in my veins." Turner's presence provoked similar terror and awe in other white observers, as well as deep levels of rage. Clearly some of that rage—and terror—had been spent in the postrebellion bloodletting, but lynching was still a possibility, so during the trial the court ordered the normal detachment of guards increased "to repel any attempt that may be made to remove Nat alias Nat Turner from the custody of the Sheriff." Nevertheless, when whites faced the reality of Nat Turner, other feelings and emotions seemed to overwhelm their rage. Indeed, there was something approaching fascination in the words of one contemporary: "During the examination, he evinced great intelligence and much shrewdness of intellect, answering every question clearly and distinctly, and without confusion or prevarication." Nat had no reason to be confused or to lie. Indeed, he did not hesitate to say that if he had another chance he would take the same bloody path to God again.[59]

It was on November 11, 1831, that Nat Turner went to the gallows, refusing to speak any final word to the crowd gathered to see him die, knowing that it was his living which had been his last, best testimony. Then, in its quiet, secret ways, the black community of Virginia and of the nation took his life into its own bosom and pondered it, just as some had done at the outset of his life. They continued to see signs, beginning with the day of his execution, for on that day, according to black tradition, "the sun was hidden behind angry clouds, the thunder rolled, the lightning flashed, and the most terrific storm visited that county ever known."[60]

> *My Lord He calls me, He calls me by*
> *the thunder*
> *The trumpet sounds within-a my soul*
> *I ain't got long to stay here.*

Perhaps, though, in keeping with all the irony of the history of our struggle, it was the terrified and ruthlessly driven white community which provided the ultimate sign of meaning for Nat Turner's movement. In the course of the massacre of blacks following the insurrection, the severed head of a black man had been impaled on a stake just where the Barrow Road, Nat's way of judgment, intersected the road to Jerusalem. The juncture became known as Blackhead Signpost and was meant, as usual, to be a warning against all future hope of black freedom.[61]

In spite of the white world's intentions, that macabre roadmark, with its recollections of similar slave-ship rituals and other bloody American roads, may have been the awaited black sign, fraught with many meanings: the suffering and death continually interwoven with the black march toward the freedom of Jerusalem; the white force of arms forever placed in the way of the life-affirming black movement. But even that terrible sign may have been transmuted to mean much more, just as Nat Turner meant more. Perhaps above all else it was a statement of the way in which all black people were a collective Blackhead Signpost for America. By the time of Nat Turner, that possibility was clearer than ever before. For white America's response to the black struggle for freedom might well determine the ultimate destination of its own people, moving them toward greater, truer human freedom, or eventually closing all pathways into a dead end of tragic, brutish varieties of death. So black struggle and black radicalism had no choice but to continue as an active, moving, relentless sign, forcing the issue of the nation's future, never allowing any of our God-driven, freedom-seeking, Jerusalem-marching fathers to have died in vain, pointing the way.

Notes

1. The following overview of America in the late 1820s is based on many sources, including: Robert Baird, *Religion in America* (New York, 1844); Charles I Foster, *An Errand of Mercy: The Evangelical United Front, 1790–1837* (Chapel Hill: University of North Carolina Press, 1960); Sidney E. Ahlstrom, *A Religious History of the American People* (New Haven: Yale University Press, 1972); John B. McMaster, *A History of the People of the United States,* 8 vols. (New York: D. Appleton and Company, 1918–24), IV, V; Perry Miller, *The Life of the Mind in America* (New York: Harcourt, Brace & World, 1965); Alice Felt Tyler, *Freedom's Ferment: Phases of American Social History to 1860* (Minneapolis: University of Minnesota Press, 1944); George Dangerfield, *The Era of Good Feelings* (New York: Harcourt, Brace & World, 1963). Of course the interpretation is largely my own.

2. See for instance Helen Hunt Jackson, *A Century of Dishonor* (1885; rpt. Minneapolis: Scholarly Press, 1964), *passim;* Grant Foreman, *Indian Removal* (Norman: University of Oklahoma Press, 1953), *passim.* See also the excellent

collection of documents on the dispossession in Virgil J. Vogel, ed., *This Country Was Ours: A Documentary History of the American Indian* (New York: Harper and Row, 1972).

3. On the Missouri Compromise debates, see Dangerfield, *The Era*, pp. 95–245; and Glover Moore, *The Missouri Controversy, 1819–1821* (Lexington: University of Kentucky Press, 1953), *passim.*

4. *Negro Population*, pp. 24–57. The internal slave trade is discussed fully in Frederic Bancroft, *Slave Trading in the Old South* (1931, rpt. New York: Frederic Ungar, 1959), pp. 19–66; also Robinson, *Slavery*, pp. 427–66.

5. *Negro Population*, pp. 24–57. Examples of the references are to be found, for instance, in Aptheker, *Slave Results*, pp. 18–45, and Tragle, *Southampton*, p. 17.

6. In dealing with the local attorney, Thomas Gray, and his version of Turner's *Confession* (Tragle, pp. 300–21), we are faced with many problems. Tragle offers a helpful analysis of the document and its authenticity in the course of his sharp and telling criticism of the novelist William Styron, pp. 401–09. I suspect that there is much truth in the *Confession*, that Gray inserts himself more than is helpful, and that Nat Turner conceals a good deal. Oates's biography, *The Fires of Jubilee*, is competent but flat, missing the mystery inherent in a man like Turner.

7. Tragle, *Southampton*, pp. 306–07.

8. *Ibid.*, p. 308.

9. *Ibid.*

10. Indeed, there soon developed a belief among many blacks that Nat was endowed with the gift of healing; others said he had power to control the clouds. Such stories, clearly drawing on the lively traditions of Africa, only added to the young man's renown. See Tragle, *Southampton*, pp. 222, 420–21, 100, 309–10; Oates, *Fires*, pp. 35–41; Aptheker, *Slave Revolts*, pp. 294–95.

11. On Nat Turner's marital status, the documents and suggestions provided by Tragle (*Southampton*, pp. 90, 281, 327) are valuable; also Oates, *Fires*, pp. 29, 162–63, 308–09.

12. The millenarian setting of early nineteenth-century Christianity is discussed in H. Shelton Smith, Robert T. Handy, Lefferts A. Loetscher, eds., *American Christianity*, 2 vols. (New York: Charles Scribner's Sons, 1960), II, 12, 16, 18; Nelson Burr, *A Critical Bibliography of Religion in America*, Vol. IV of James W. Smith and A. Leland Jamison, eds., *Religion in American Life*, 4 vols. (Princeton: Princeton University Press, 1961), I, 326–27; Ahlstrom, *Religious History*, pp. 474–78.

13. Tragle, *Southampton*, p. 310; Herbert Aptheker, *Nat Turner's Slave Rebellion* (New York: Humanities Press, 1966), pp. 137–38; Oates, *Fires*, p. 41.

14. Robert Hayden, "Ballad of Nat Turner," *Selected Poems* (New York: October House, 1966), pp. 72–74.

15. Tragle, *Southampton*, p. 92; Oates, *Fires*, p. 42.

16. Aptheker, *Slave Revolts*, p. 265. On the subject of these other uprisings, there is a helpful bibliography in Eugene D. Genovese, *Roll, Jordan, Roll: The World the Slaves Made* (New York: Pantheon, 1974), pp. 709–11; an important, expanded version of his treatment and of his bibliography on the subject is available in *From Rebellion to Revolution: Afro-American Slave Revolts in the Making of the Modern World* (Baton Rouge: Louisiana State University Press, 1979). See also Aptheker, *Slave Revolts*, p. 278.

17. The story of the shipboard suicides is found in Austin Bearse, *Reminiscences of Fugitive-Slave Law Days in Boston* (1880; rpt. New York: Arno Press, 1969), p. 9.

18. Aptheker, *Slave Revolts*, pp. 279–80; a continued movement of rebellion and resistance by Alabama outlyers in this period is confirmed by James B. Sellers, *Slavery in Alabama* (University: University of Alabama Press, 1950), pp. 282–83. Also see Franklin, *From Slavery*, pp. 210–11.

19. Unfortunately, we still have nothing more comprehensive on David Walker's life than Henry Highland Garnet's "A Brief Sketch on the Life and Character of David Walker," first published in 1848 and reprinted in Herbert Aptheker, ed., *One Continual Cry: David Walker's*

Appeal to the Colored Citizens of the World (New York: Humanities Press, 1965), pp. 40–44. A modern essay focusing especially on Walker's Boston years indicates a number of the pertinent questions about him: Donald M. Jacobs, "David Walker: Boston Race Leader, 1825–1830," *Essex Institute Historical Collections*, 107 (Jan. 1971), 94–107.

20. Garnet, "Brief Sketch," p. 41; *Freedom's Journal*, Mar. 16, 1827; Jacobs, "David Walker," pp. 95–97.

21. For examples of such words and their costliness, see Ira Berlin, *Slaves Without Masters* (New York: Pantheon, 1975), pp. 89–97, 336–38; Samuel Ringgold Ward, *Autobiography of a Fugitive Negro* (1855; rpt. Chicago: Johnson Publishing, 1970), p. 12; Robert S. Starobin, ed., *Blacks in Bondage: Letters of American Slaves* (New York: Franklin Watts, 1974), pp. 107–10. Moreover, persons like Nat Turner (above, p. 80) and Frederick Douglass (below, p. 103) could also testify to these realities.

22. For the dangers faced by black abolitionists in the North, see Aptheker, *Documentary*, I, 220; Dorothy Sterling, ed., *Speak Out in Thunder Tones* (New York: Doubleday, 1973), pp. 132–36; Ward, *Autobiography*, pp. 35–37.

23. Quoted in Bracey et al., *Black Nationalism*, p. 25.

24. The text of the speech appeared in *Freedom's Journal*, Dec. 19, 1828.

25. [Robert Alexander Young], *The Ethiopian Manifesto* (New York, 1829). The most readily available source of the full text is Sterling Stuckey, ed., *The Ideological Origins of Black Nationalism* (Boston: Beacon Press, 1972), pp. 30–38.

26. Stuckey, *Ideological Origins*, p. 30. In the light of Young's reference to Grenada as the source of the mulatto Messiah, a few alert twentieth-century black nationalists have noted that the mother of Malcolm X came to the United States from Grenada. However, internal evidence in the *Manifesto* suggests that Young was really pointing to himself as the promised deliverer. It is also important to note that, like so many similar manifestoes in the later black struggle, this one was addressed at least as fully to whites as to "Ethiopians."

27. There are several modern editions of the complete text of the *Appeal*. Among the most accessible are Charles M. Wiltse, *David Walker's Appeal* (New York: Hill and Wang, 1965), and Aptheker's *One Continual Cry*. Aptheker's introduction and footnotes are by far the most helpful; his text is used in this study.

28. Walker/Aptheker, pp. 64–65. Certainly the line of spiritual heirs reaches at least from Henry Highland Garnet (below, pp. 133–35, 140–43) to Malcolm X.

29. Walker/Aptheker, pp. 73–74.

30. *Ibid.*, p. 89.

31. *Ibid.*, p. 75. It is fascinating to note how directly Walker is related to the traditions of religious/political revolution. For instance, very similar sentiments were expressed by the Anabaptist revolutionary Thomas Muntzer during the German Peasants' War of the sixteenth century; see Guenther Lewy, *Religion and Revolution* (New York: Oxford University Press, 1974), p. vii. Also, many concepts and even certain stylistic aspects of the *Appeal* suggest that Walker had had access to the April 1804 proclamation by Jacques Dessalines, the Haitian liberator. See the Dessalines document in Drake, "Black Nationalism," pp. 28–35.

32. Drake, "Black Nationalism," p. 30; above, pp. 58–59.

33. Walker/Aptheker, pp. 83–85, 65–66.

34. Confidence in God's retributive justice is a constant in the literature of black struggle. Many of its modern manifestations were most deeply lodged in the teachings of the Nation of Islam and their foremost heretic, Malcolm X. Compare Malcolm X, *The Autobiography of Malcolm X* (New York: Grove Press, 1964), pp. 246, 370; Elijah Muhammad, *The Fall of America* (Chicago: Muhammad's Temple of Islam No. 2, 1973), pp. 52–55, 108–11; and Louis E. Lomax, *When the Word Is Given* (New York: New American Library, 1964), pp. 175–76.

35. Walker/Aptheker, pp. 76, 126–28. Again, Walker seems very close to Dessalines. Indeed, his description of whites as the "natural enemies" of black people is precisely the same as

Dessalines's in the 1804 proclamation: Drake, "Black Nationalism," p. 29.

36. Walker/Aptheker, pp. 139, 140, n.

37. *Ibid.,* pp. 77–78.

38. *Ibid.,* pp. 93–94. Consciously or not, Walker, the church member, introduced here a pan-African parallel to the New Testament concept of the Christian Church as the indivisible "body of Christ."

39. *Ibid.,* p. 104.

40. *Ibid.,* pp. 137–38.

41. *Ibid.* In our own post–Montgomery Boycott generation, we have seen leaders and institutions as varied as Martin Luther King, Jr., Malcolm X, James Forman, the Nation of Islam, and the Urban League, struggle mightily with the issue of what *would* be the appropriate restitution and reparations due to the black community.

42. Walker/Aptheker, pp. 45–50; William H. Pease and Jane H. Pease, "Document: Walker's *Appeal* Comes to Charleston: A Note and Documents," *JNH*, 59 (July 1974), 287–92; H. E. Sterkx, *The Free Negro in Ante-Bellum Louisiana* (Rutherford, N.J.: Fairleigh Dickinson University Press, 1972), p. 98.

43. Quoted in Litwack, *North,* p. 234.

44. Walker/Aptheker, p. 43. Eventually the bounty on Walker was raised to $3,000.

45. *Ibid.,* pp. 45–50.

46. Aptheker, *Slave Revolts,* p. 290.

47. Walker/Aptheker, pp. 43–44. Jacobs, "David Walker," pp. 106–07, does not accept the poisoning theory, and raises an interesting question about Walker's age when he died.

48. Tragle, *Southampton,* p. xv. Oates, *Fires,* p. 51, identifies the marriage year as late 1829.

49. According to his *Confessions* (Tragle, p. 310), the four men named comprised the first group to whom Nat revealed his plans. By the time of the actual event, two more persons,

50. Tragle, *Southampton,* p. 310. The final words are quoted in G. Williams, *History of Negro Race,* II, 88. Williams knew and appreciated the oral traditions of the black community. This quotation may well have been reconstructed from such a source.

51. Tragle, *Southampton,* pp. 310–13. In addition, for all their lack of precision and accuracy, several contemporary newspaper reports suggest the impact of the event on the surrounding population. They are quoted in Tragle, pp. 31–72. See Oates, *Fires,* pp. 66–91.

52. On the poor supply of arms, see a contemporary statement quoted in Aptheker, *Nat Turner's Slave Rebellion,* p. 55.

53. On the involvement of the U.S. military, two different emphases appear in Aptheker, *Slave Revolts,* p. 300, and Tragle, *Southampton,* pp. 16–17. Also, note Oates, *Fires,* p. 97.

54. Tragle, pp. 34, 69, 74–75, 92; Aptheker, *Nat Turner's Slave Rebellion,* pp. 60–62.

55. Aptheker, *Nat Turner's Slave Rebellion,* pp. 37–38.

56. [Samuel Warner], *Authentic and Impartial Narrative of the Tragical Scene . . . in Southampton County* (New York, 1831), p. 23. The Warner document is also reproduced in Tragle, *Southampton,* pp. 279–300.

57. Ira Berlin, "Documents: After Nat Turner, A Letter from the North," *JNH,* 55 (Apr. 1970), 144–51.

58. The wording of the formal charge against Nat Turner is found in the Minute Book of the Court of Southampton County. The more familiar formulation: ". . . making insurrection, and plotting to take away the lives of divers free white persons," is evidently Gray's own version: Tragle, *Southampton,* pp. 221, 318.

59. Tragle, pp. 221, 132, 317; Oates, *Fires,* p. 119.

60. G. Williams, *History of Negro Race,* II, 90.

61. Tragle, p. 7

Part IV *Key Terms and Essay/Discussion Questions*

KEY TERMS

Olmecs

Meso-America

Yucatan

Africoid

Cabeza colosal

La Venta

Atlantic slave trade

Middle passage

Industrial Revolution

Haitian Revolution

Slave revolt

Gabriel Prosser

David Walker

Nat Turner

Underground railroad

Harriet Tubman

Abolitionist movement

Planter class

Civil War

Fugitive slave

ESSAY/DISCUSSION QUESTIONS

1. What two types of evidence does Legrand Clegg use to support his argument that Africans laid the foundation for ancient American civilization?

2. Why is it important to investigate the African presence in the ancient world in general and in the Americas before the arrival of Christopher Columbus in particular?

3. Describe the cultural contributions of the Olmecs to the development of ancient American civilization.

4. What was the impact of enslavement in America on captured Africans, and how did they respond?

5. In reference to the system of chattel slavery, C. L. R. James states: "The capacities of men were always leaping out of the confinements of the system." What does he mean?

6. Discuss the ways in which African slaves resisted the dehumanizing process of chattel slavery.

7. James argues that white historians largely ignored the contributions that African slaves made to the development of American civilization. In what ways did chattel slaves shape this process?

8. Vincent Harding notes that David Walker's 1829 *Appeal* was one of the earliest radical statements in the great tradition of African American protest thought. It indicted white America, challenged the dehumanizing system of chattel slavery, and called for black solidarity and resistance. What impact did the *Appeal* have on black and white America?

9. It is often stated that Christianity was used to pacify African slaves in America. Yet Nat Turner and David Walker were highly religious men, strongly influenced by Christian theology, who played leadership roles in the struggle for African American liberation in the nineteenth century. Explain.

10. It can be argued that as a result of the Atlantic slave trade and chattel slavery, white American attitudes and practices directed toward African Americans became deeply embedded in the American personality, culture, and institutional arrangements. Discuss.

Part IV *Supplementary Readings*

Aptheker, Herbert, *One Continual Cry: David Walker's Appeal to the Colored Citizens of the World (1829–1930)*, New York: Humanities Press, 1965.

———, *Negro Slave Revolts*, New York: International Publishers, 1963.

Bernal, Martin G., *Black Athena: The Afro-Asiatic Roots of Classical Civilization, Vol. II: The Archaeological and Documentary Evidence*, New Brunswick: Rutgers University Press, 1991.

———, *Black Athena: The Afro-Asiatic Roots of Classical Civilization, Vol. I: The Fabrication of Ancient Greece*, New Brunswick: Rutgers University Press, 1987.

Blackburn, Robin, *The Overthrow of Colonial Slavery, 1776–1848*, New York: Verso, 1988.

Blassingame, John W., ed., *Slave Testimony: Two Centuries of Letters, Speeches, Interviews, and Autobiographies*, Baton Rouge: Louisiana State University Press, 1977.

———, *The Slave Community: Plantation Life in the Ante-Bellum South*, New York: Oxford University Press, 1972.

Bradley, Keith R., *Slavery and Rebellion in the Roman World, 140 B. C.–70 B. C.* Bloomington: Indiana University Press, 1989.

Cheek, William and Aimee L. Cheek, *John Mercer Langston and the Fight for Black Freedom, 1829–1865*, Urbana: University of Illinois Press, 1989.

Davidson, Basil, *The African Slave Trade: Precolonial History, 1450–1850*, Boston: Little, Brown and Company, 1961.

Davis, David B., *Slavery and Human Progress*, New York: Oxford University Press, 1984.

———, *The Problem of Slavery in the Age of Revolution*, Ithaca: Cornell University Press, 1975.

———, *The Problem of Slavery in Western Culture*, Ithaca: Cornell University Press, 1966.

Davis, Ronald W., "Negro Contributions to the Exploration of the Globe," in Roucek, Joseph S. and Thomas Kiernan, eds., *The Negro Impact on Western Civilization*, New York: Philosophical Library Inc., 1970, pp. 33–50.

Douglass, Frederick, *My Bondage and My Freedom,* New York: Arno Press, and the New York Times, 1969.

_____, *Life and Times of Frederick Douglass,* New York: Collier Books, 1962.

Duberman, Martin, ed., *The Antislavery Vanguard: New Essays on the Abolitionists,* Princeton: Princeton University Press, 1965.

DuBois, W. E. B., *The Suppression of the African Slave Trade to the United States of America, 1638–1870,* New York: Russell & Russell, Inc., 1965.

_____, *Black Reconstruction in America, 1860–1880,* Cleveland: A Meridian Book/The World Publishing Company, 1964.

Edwards, Paul, ed., *Equiano's Travels: The Interesting Narrative of the Life of Olaudah Equiano or Gustavus Vassa, the African,* New York: Frederick A. Praeger, Publishers, 1967.

Foner, Eric, *Reconstruction: America's Unfinished Revolution, 1863–1877,* New York: Harper & Row, Publishers, 1988.

Forbes, Jack D., *Black Africans & Native Americans: Color, Race and Caste in the Evolution of Red-Black Peoples,* New York: Basil Blackwell Inc., 1988.

Frederickson, George M., *The Arrogance of Race: Historical Perspectives on Slavery, Racism, and Social Inequality,* Middletown: Wesleyan University Press, 1988.

Freyre, Gilberto, *The Masters and the Slaves: A Study in the Development of Brazilian Civilization,* New York: Alfred A. Knopf, 1956.

Greene, Lorenzo J., *The Negro in Colonial New England,* New York: Atheneum, 1968.

Harding, Vincent, *There is a River: The Black Struggle for Freedom in America,* New York: Harcourt Brace Jovanovich, Publishers, 1981.

_____, *The Other American Revolution,* Los Angeles: Center for Afro-American Studies/University of California and Institute of the Black World, 1980.

Harris, Joseph E., *The African Presence in Asia: Consequences of the East African Slave Trade,* Evanston: Northwestern University Press, 1971.

Hayes, Floyd W. III, "The African Presence in America Before Columbus: A Bibliographical Essay," *Black World,* Vol. 22, No. 9 (July 1973), pp. 4–22.

Irwin, Graham W., *Africans Abroad: A Documentary History of the Black Diaspora in Asia, Latin America, and the Caribbean During the Age of Slavery,* New York: Columbia University Press, 1977.

Jacobs, Harriet, *Incidents in the Life of a Slave Girl,* New York: Harcourt, Brace, Jovanovich, 1973.

James, C. L. R., *The Black Jacobins: Toussaint L'Ouverture and the San Domingo Revolution,* New York: Vintage Books, 1963.

Lawrence, Harold G., "African Explorers of the New World," *The Crisis,* (June–July 1962), pp. 321-332.

Littlefield, David F., Jr., *Africans and Seminoles: From Removal to Emancipation,* Westport: Greenwood Press, 1977.

McPherson, James, *Battle Cry of Freedom: The Civil War Era,* New York: Oxford University Press, 1988.

Montejo, Esteban, *The Autobiography of a Runaway Slave,* ed., Miguel Barnet, New York: The World Publishing Company, 1969.

Mullin, Gerald W., *Flight and Rebellion: Slave Resistance in Eighteenth-Century Virginia,* New York: Oxford University Press, 1972.

Nichols, Charles H., *Many Thousand Gone: The Ex-Slaves' Account of their Bondage and Freedom,* Bloomington: Indiana University Press, 193.

Patterson, Orlando, *Slavery and Social Death: A Comparative Study,* Cambridge: Harvard University Press, 1982.

Perdue, Theda, *Slavery and the Evolution of Cherokee Society, 1540–1866,* Knoxville: The University of Tennessee Press, 1979.

Phillips, William D., Jr., *Slavery from Romans Times to the Early Transatlantic Trade,* Minneapolis: University of Minnesota Press, 1985.

Postma, Johannes M., *The Dutch in the Atlantic Slave Trade, 1600–1815,* New York: Cambridge University Press, 1990.

Quarles, Benjamin, *Black Abolitionists,* New York: Oxford University Press, 1969.

Rodney, Walter, *How Europe Underdeveloped Africa,* London: Bogle-L'Ouverture Publications, 1972.

——, "African Slavery and Other Forms of Social Oppression on the Upper Guinea Coast in the Context of the Atlantic Slave Trade," *Journal of African History,* Vol. 7 (1966), pp. 431–443.

Rogers, Joel A., *Africa's Gift to America,* New York: Futuro Press, 1961.

Schama, Simon, *The Embarrassment of Riches: An Interpretation of Dutch Culture in the Golden Age,* New York: Alfred A. Knopf, 1987.

Stampp, Kenneth M., *The Peculiar Institution: Slavery in the Ante-Bellum South,* New York: Vintage Books, 1956.

Tannenbaum, Frank, *Slave and Citizen: The Negro in the Americas,* New York: Vintage Books, 1946.

Thompson, Vincent B., *The Making of the African Diaspora in the Americas, 1441–1900,* New York: Longman Inc., 1987.

Van Sertima, Ivan, *They Came Before Columbus,* New York: Random House, 1976.

Von Wuthenau, Alexander, *The Art of Terracotta Pottery in Pre-Columbian Central and South America,* New York: Crown Publishers, Inc., 1970.

Weiner, Leo, *Africa and the Discovery of America,* Vol. I, Philadelphia: Innes & Sons, 1920.

——, *Africa and the Discovery of America,* Vols. II & III, Philadelphia: Innes & Sons, 1922.

Welch, Galbraith, *Africa Before They Came: The Continent, North, South, East and West, Preceding the Colonial Powers,* New York: William Morrow and Company, 1965.

Williams, Eric, *Capitalism and Slavery,* Chapel Hill: The University of North Carolina Press, 1944.

Wiltse, Charles M., ed., *David Walker's Appeal,* New York: Hill and Wang, 1965.

V

African American Expressive Culture: Music and Literature

Although the oppressive and dehumanizing system of chattel slavery sought to destroy (and post-Emancipation America sought to deny) any remnants of African culture and to impose white European culture in its place, Africans and their American descendants preserved and transformed their own resilient culture. Significantly, it has been this African-based creative impulse that has largely energized and shaped what has emerged as American popular culture.

In the historic struggle to survive and resist Euro-American cultural domination—from the shock and chaos of chattel slavery to the contemporary period—African-descended Americans have refashioned themselves by transforming aspects of African culture. Through a tradition that included sacred and secular music, folktales, and autobiography, African American slaves were able to salvage a degree of self-esteem, dignity, and hope; in the process, they left a legacy that twentieth-century African American writers, singers, poets, and producers have taken and transformed.

The articles in this part depict aspects of African American expressive culture, particularly in the areas of music and literature. The purpose is not to ignore other areas of cultural expression, such as drama, dance, sculpture, painting, photography, film-making, but to limit coverage to what is manageable.

Portia K. Maultsby's work "Africanisms in African American Music" skillfully examines the historic interaction between African and African American musical traditions. She points out that this African/African American culture connection is not the retention of particular African songs but a conceptual framework that links these two dynamic traditions and clearly distinguishes them from Western European cultural forms. According to Maultsby, Africanisms were preserved in culture and music because African-descended Americans maintained ties to their African past, adapting to a hostile and changing environment by relying on familiar traditions and cultural practices.

Showing the development from the earliest African American sacred and secular musical forms to the most contemporary musical expressions, the author delineates the elements that characterize African and African American expressive culture. African and African American music-making, she says, is above all else communal and participatory.

The article by Sterling Brown, "Negro Folk Expression: Spirituals, Seculars, Ballads and Work Songs," carefully probes the development, character, structure, and meaning of African American folk culture—its oral and musical tradition. Refuting the interpretation of scholars who denied any African influence on African American spirituals and who said they were the same as white spirituals, Brown points out the uniqueness of African-descended religious folk songs. As are all African American musical forms, Brown says, African American spirituals are characterized by a great degree of improvisation. He argues that although these religious folk songs referred to the spiritual world and used Biblical imagery, spirituals also emphasized the everyday life of the slaves who created them. Hence, where freedom meant religious salvation to white singers, African American singers meant physical liberation from the conditions of chattel slavery.

According to Brown, secular folk songs and ballads were sometimes called "devil-tunes" because they often irreverently challenged Biblical songs and stories. African American secular folk singers satirized chattel slavery, poked fun at slaveowners, and laughed at poor whites. Their music became more outrageous near the end of the nineteenth century as folk-seculars joined with the vaudeville stage. Finally, with the transition from rural to urbanized/industrialized/commercialized life, Brown notes, the African American folk culture was progressively displaced by working class culture. That is, the spirituals and secular music of folk culture increasingly gave way to the gospels and blues of working class culture.

Nelson George in the essay "Black Beauty, Black Confusion (1965–70)" examines critically the interaction between the rise of soul music (an elaboration of rhythm and blues) and the political economy of the music world when the Civil Rights movement was declining and the Black Power movement was emerging. George explores the musical and business life and times of James Brown ("the hardest working man in show business") and Aretha Franklin ("the Queen of Soul"), who represent a period of volatile and creative African American cultural politics. In a moment when political activists were calling for African American self-determination and self-reliance, George shows that James Brown clearly exemplified a cultural and economic response. Hard working, audacious, innovative, versatile, and powerful on stage, Brown displayed these qualities on the business end as well; he controlled every aspect of his organization. George shows that during the late 1960s Brown was an important musical, and to some degree social, leader in the African American community because he exemplified African American pride and self-reliant development. Pointing out Brown's success, George also critically assesses Brown's ideological conservatism and the contradictions in his music's messages.

If James Brown was the godfather of rhythm and blues-soul, Aretha Franklin certainly was/is its undisputed queen. Emerging from the urban African American church, she integrated a sacred (gospel) ethos into her secular music-making with a unique and versatile style, a deeply emotional and meaningful message, and a hard-driving vocal power. This rendered Aretha heir to a long tradition of African American female blues, jazz, and rhythm-and-blues singers, which includes Dinah Washington, Ella Fitzgerald, Sarah Vaughn, Billie Holiday, Bessie Smith, and Ma Rainey. George traces Aretha's musical evolution from the restraining conditions at Columbia Records to her expressive freedom and blossoming at Atlantic Records. He reviews the wide range of her songs, showing how her uncompromising African American sound and musical versatility made her music accessible and acceptable to a broad spectrum of Americans— African American and white. Nelson George also talks about other developments in the music world during the late 1960s.

It is ironic that the African and African American literary tradition (that is, literary production in European languages) emerged during the eighteenth century largely so authors could contest Europeans' negative or distorted portrayal of African-descended people. From Phillis Wheatley's poetic efforts in the early 1770s to the present, African Americans active in the literary culture (including folklorists, essayists, novelists, poets, autobiographers, critics, playwriters, comedians, and screen-writers) have sought to tell their own stories about the African and African American experience. In the process, they have had to reject, refute, refashion, or improvise upon the literary conventions of the dominant Euro-American cultural establishment at particular historical moments.

The two remaining articles in this section focus on some of the trends and developments in twentieth-century African American literature, particularly literary theory and the novel. In his 1937 essay, "Blueprint for Negro Writing," Richard Wright theorizes about the role, perspective, culture, purpose, and necessary unity of African American writers. [Considered by some to be one of the greatest African American writers of all time, Wright authored an assortment of works, including *Uncle Tom's Children* (1938), *Native Son* (1940), *Twelve Million Black Voices* (1941), *Black Boy* (1945), *The Outsider* (1953), *Black Power* (1954), *The Color Curtain* (1956), *Pagan Spain* (1957), *White Man, Listen!* (1957), *Eight Men* (1961), *Lawd Today* (1963), and *American Hunger* (1977).] Wright argues that African American writers must speak to the needs, sufferings, hopes, and aspirations of the great multitude of working-class African Americans. Drawing on its church and folk cultural traditions, African American writing should develop among the people an attitude of critical self-consciousness in the struggle for African American human rights. Wright sees the importance and significance of culture and a progressive nationalist outlook; the writer must begin with a Marxist conception of reality and society but must also be capable of transcending its absolutism in order to deal with the complex simplicity of African American life. Wright challenges African American writers to develop a greater discipline, sense of social responsibility, and unity with all progressive ideas in order to work collectively to produce a higher level of social consciousness among the masses of African Americans.

The essay by Bernard W. Bell, "The Contemporary Afro-American Novel, 1: Neorealism," investigates the character of African American novels influenced by the Black Power/Black Arts Movements and the Women's Liberation Movement of the 1960s and 1970s. Bell shows that the Black Arts Movement was the cultural expression of the politically aggressive Black Power Movement. An emerging Afrocentric perspective, largely influenced by pan-African ideas and grounded in cultural nationalism, increasingly contested the artistic and literary conventions of the dominant Eurocentric cultural establishment. During this period of the African American liberation movement, a rebirth—a "New Renaissance"—occurred in African American cultural expression, including drama, poetry, fiction, literary criticism, and music.

Equally significant was the reemergence of women's struggle for justice and equal rights and the concomitant sexual revolution, largely energized by the African American liberation struggle. Feelings of being excluded because of race from a basically white feminist movement and from a mainly male-headed black power movement because of gender created the conditions necessary for resurrecting the nineteenth-century tradition of African American women's organizations to struggle against class, race, and gender discrimination and domination. The task of recuperating and reclaiming an African American female-centered (or after Alice Walker, womanist) literary tradition represented the expressive cultural turn of the African American women's social and political struggle in the 1970s.

Bell employs the general term neorealism to categorize the African American novels of this period. He points out that what characterizes neorealism is the assumption that humans are social beings who should not be dislocated from their social and historical context, no matter how despairing and chaotic. Neorealist novels portray characters who are alienated from the old social order of race, class, and gender exploitation and who struggle for a new society. Bell further divides the neorealism of contemporary African American novels into two types: critical realism and poetic realism.

Bell indicates that critical realism is related to social realism, and both are Marxist literary concepts. Socialist realism is developmental and thoroughgoing in its analysis of society as a whole, and intends to specify the human qualities required to establish a new, progressive society. Alternatively, critical realism is not so much an endorsement of socialism as it is a radical critique of capitalism and an openness to a socialist order. Bell then examines the life and novels of exemplars of this category: John O. Killens, John A. Williams, and Alice Walker.

Poetic realism and the Gothic fable constitute Bell's second dimension of African American literary neorealism. In the Gothic outlook of African American poetic realists, the interest in truth is interwoven with a focus on the supernatural links between the past and the present and on psychological and sociological terms for their images of moral behavior in a world of mystery and unnatural happenings. In poetic realism, figurative expressions stand for literal expressions. Bell analyzes the life and work of Toni Morrison as representative of this literary class.

Africanisms in African-American Music

PORTIA K. MAULTSBY

Since the first quarter of the twentieth century scholars have examined African-American history and culture in the context of an African past.[1] Their studies support the premise that the institution of slavery did not destroy the cultural legacy of slaves nor erase the memories of an African past. The survival of slaves in the New World depended on their ability to retain the ideals fundamental to African cultures. Although slaves were exposed to various European-derived traditions, they resisted cultural imprisonment by the larger society. Slaves adapted to life in the Americas by retaining a perspective on the past. They survived an oppressive existence by creating new expressive forms out of African traditions, and they brought relevance to European-American customs by reshaping them to conform to African aesthetic ideals.

The transformation of African traditions in the New World supports the position of Lawrence Levine that culture is a process rather than a fixed condition. Levine argues that culture is

the product of interaction between the past and present. Its toughness and resiliency are determined not by a culture's ability to withstand change, which indeed may be a sign of stagnation not life, but by its ability to react creatively and responsively to the realities of a new situation.[2]

The continuum of an African consciousness in America manifests itself in the evolution of an African-American culture. The music, dance, folklore, religion, language, and other expressive forms associated with the culture of slaves were transmitted orally to subsequent generations of American blacks. Consequently, Levine adds, many aspects of African culture continue "to exist not as mere vestiges but as dynamic, living, creative parts of group life in the United States." This position contradicts that of earlier scholars who interpreted the fundamentals of African-American culture as distorted imitations of European-American culture.[3]

Reprinted, with permission, from Joseph E. Holloway, ed., *Africanisms in American Culture*, Indiana University Press, 1990.

The music tradition established by slaves evolved over centuries in response to varying circumstances and environmental factors. Each generation of slaves and freeborn blacks created new musical genres and performance styles (see figure). These forms are unique by-products of specific contexts and historical periods. The purpose of this essay is to show that an identifiable conceptual framework links these traditions to each other and to African music traditions.

THE AFRICAN MUSICAL DIMENSION

The first scholars to examine customs and practices among blacks in the New World described the existence of African retentions in quantitative terms.[4] Although this practice of trait listing is valid, it does not account for changes that took place within the American context. Over the centuries specific African elements either have been altered or have disappeared from the cultures of New World blacks altogether. Yet the concepts that embody and identify the cultural heritage of black Americans have never been lost. The African dimension of African-American music is far-reaching and can be understood best when examined within this conceptual framework.

Early accounts of African performance in the New World, for example, document the existence of instruments clearly of African origin.[5] Eventually Western European musical instruments began to infiltrate and dominate African-American musical practice. Because the tempered tuning of these Western instruments differed from that of African instruments, black musicians were forced to deviate from certain African principles of melodic structure. Challenged to explore new means of melodic expression, blacks unconsciously created new ideas founded on existing African musical concepts. The result was the emergence of "blue notes" (flatted third and seventh degrees) and the production of pitches uncommon to Western scale structures.

Africanisms in African-American music extend beyond trait lists and, as African ethnomusicologist J. H. Kwabena Nketia observes, "must be viewed in terms of creative processes which allow for continuity and change."[6] This point of view is shared by Olly Wilson, who concludes that African retentions in African-American music are defined by the sharing of conceptual approaches to the music-making process and hence are "not basically quantitative but qualitative." Moreover, Wilson argues that the African dimension of African-American music does not exist as

> a static body of something which can be depleted, but rather [as] a conceptual approach, the manifestations of which are infinite. The common core of this African-ness consists of the way of doing something, not simply something that is done.[7]

Music is integral to all aspects of black community life.[8] It serves many functions and is performed by individuals and groups in both formal and informal settings. The fundamental concept that governs music performance in African and African-derived cultures is that music-making is a participatory group activity that serves to unite black people into a cohesive group for a common purpose. This use of music in African-American communities continues a tradition found in African societies where, as Nketia observes,

> music making is generally organized as a social event. Public performances, therefore, take place on social occasions—that is, on occasions when members of a group or a community come together for the enjoyment of leisure, for recreational activities, or for the performance of a rite, ceremony, festival, or any kind of collective activity.[9]

The conceptualization of music-making as a participatory group activity is evident in the processes by which black Americans prepare for a performance. Since the 1950s, for example, black music promoters have advertised concerts as social gatherings where active

African-American Music: Its Development

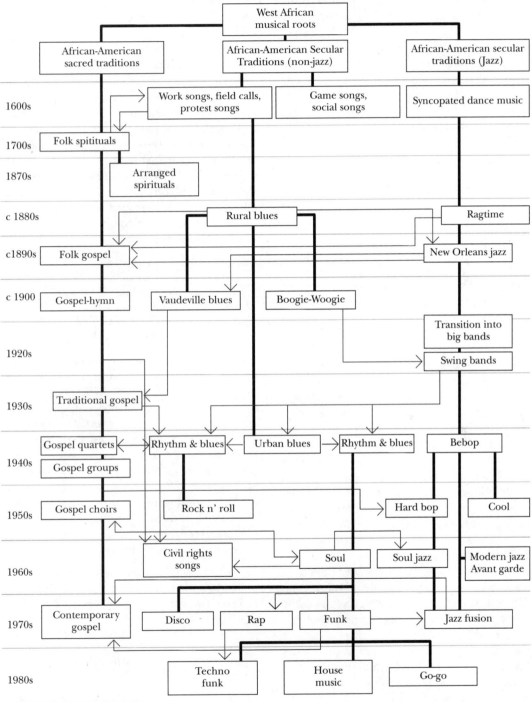

© 1980, 1988, 1989, Portia K. Maultsby
Revised 1986, 1987, 1988 and 1989

audience involvement is expected. Promotional materials encourage potential concert-goers to "Come and be moved by" a gospel music concert or to "Come and jam with," "Come and get down with," or "Come and party with" a secular music concert. As Nketia notes, regardless of context—church, club, dance hall, or concert hall—public performance of black music serves

> a multiple role in relation to the community: it provides at once an opportunity for sharing in creative experience, for participating in music as a form of community experience, and for using music as an avenue for the expression of group sentiments.[10]

This communal approach to music-making is further demonstrated in the way contemporary performers adapt recorded versions of their songs for performance on the concert stage. Many begin their songs with ad lib "rapping" (secular) or "sermonettes" (sacred) to establish rapport with the audience. When the singing actually begins, the style of the performance complements the "we are here to jam" or "we are here to be moved" attitude of the audience/congregation. The audience/congregation is encouraged to participate in any way, sometimes even to join performers on stage. Soul singer Sam Moore of the duo Sam and Dave recalls how he "would stop the band and get hand-clapping going in the audience [and] make them stand up."[11] Many black performers use this technique to ensure the active participation of audience members in the music event.

Music-making in Africa requires the active involvement of all present at the musical event. This approach to performance generates many of the cultural and aesthetic components that uniquely characterize music-making throughout the African diaspora. In a study of gospel music, ethnomusicologist Mellonee Burnim defines three areas of aesthetic significance in the black music tradition: delivery style, sound quality, and mechanics of delivery.[12]

These categories are useful in examining qualities common to both African and African-derived music.

Style of Delivery

Style of delivery refers to the physical mode of presentation—how performers employ body movements, facial expressions, and clothing within the performance context. Burnim accurately asserts that music-making "in Black culture symbolizes vitality, a sense of aliveness."[13] This "aliveness" is expressed through visual, physical, and musical modes, all of which are interrelated in African musical performances. Olly Wilson defines the African musical experience as a

> multi-media one in which many kinds of collective human output are inextricably linked. Hence, a typical traditional [African] ceremony will include music, dance, the plastic arts (in the form of elaborate masks and/or costumes) and perhaps ritualistic drama.[14]

In African-American culture, the element of dress in musical performance is as important as the musical sound itself. When performers appear on stage, even before a musical sound is heard, audience members verbally and physically respond if costumes meet their aesthetic expectations. Performers establish an image, communicate a philosophy, and create an atmosphere of "aliveness" through the colorful and flamboyant costumes they wear. In the gospel tradition, Burnim observed that performers dress in "robes of bold, vivid colors and design." She also noted:

> At the 1979 James Cleveland Gospel Music Workshop of America in New Orleans, Louisiana, one evening's activities included a competition to select the best dressed male and female in gospel choir attire. The fashions ranged from brightly colored gowns and tuxedos to matching hooded capes lined in red.[15]

Ethnomusicologist Joyce Jackson, in her study of black gospel quartets, also observed that

**Early photograph of
a young entertainer,
in a splendidly
rich gown and head
covering.**

costumes are judged as part of the overall performance in gospel quartet competitions.[16]

The importance of dress in black music performances is demonstrated further in the popular tradition. In the film *That Rhythm . . . Those Blues,* vocalist Ruth Brown recalled how audiences expected performers to dress in the latest fashions. Responding to this expectation, Brown labeled herself as one of the first female singers

> that became known for the crinoline and multi-petticoats and the shoes that matched the dresses. All of the singing groups [of the

1950s and 1960s] were impeccably dressed [in coordinated outfits] when they went on stage. If they wore white shoes . . . they were *white* shoes. Griffin shoe polish made all the money in the world.

The array of colors and fashions seen in concert halls, black churches, and other black performance sites is a vital part of the total visual experience. It is such a fundamental part of black cultural expression that these same principles of dress are observed by the audience. For example, audiences at Harlem's Apollo theater always wore the latest fashions.

During the 1930s, the men "appeared in tight-belted, high-waisted coats" and the women "gracefully glided through the lobby in tight slinky dresses, high heels, and veils."[17]

The visual dimension of performance, according to Burnim's model, extends beyond dress to the physical behavior of musicians and their audiences. In communicating with their audiences, musicians display an intensity of emotion and total physical involvement through use of the entire body. Nketia points out that physical expression is part and parcel of music-making in African cultures:

> The values of African societies do not inhibit this. . . . it is encouraged, for through it, individuals relate to musical events or performing groups, and interact socially with others in a musical situation. Moreover, motor response intensifies one's enjoyment of music through the feelings of increased involvement and the propulsion that articulating the beat by physical movement generates.[18]

Accounts of religious services conducted by slaves illustrate the retention of these cultural values and attitudes in the New World. During the worship, slaves became active participants, freely responding verbally and physically to the sermon, the prayer, the music, and each other. This behavior prompted missionary Charles Colcock Jones to describe a revival meeting of slaves as a "confusion of sights and sounds!"

> Some were standing, others sitting, others moving from one seat to another, several exhorting along the aisles. The whole congregation kept up one loud monotonous strain, interrupted by various sounds: groans and screams and clapping hands. One woman specially under the influence of the excitement went across the church in a quick succession of leaps; now down on her knees with a sharp crack that smote upon my ear the full length of the church, then up again; now with her arms about some brother or sister, and again tossing them

wildly in the air and clapping her hands together and accompanying the whole by a series of short, sharp shrieks. . . . Considering the mere excitement manifested in these disorderly ways, I could but ask: What religion is there in this?[19]

Observers of other religious gatherings of slaves noted that "there is much melody in their voices; and when they enjoy a hymn, there is a raised expression of the face. . . ." And "they sang so that it was a pleasure to hear, with all their souls and with all their bodies in unison; for their bodies wagged, their heads nodded, their feet stamped, their knees shook, their elbows and their hands beat time to the tunes and the words which they sing. . . ."[20]

The style of delivery that characterized musical performance during the seventeenth, eighteenth, and nineteenth centuries continues to be operative in both sacred and secular spheres of contemporary black America: black people consciously use their entire bodies in musical expression, and music and movement are conceived as a single unit. These concepts clearly are demonstrated in the presentation style of performers of popular music. Soul singer Al Braggs, for example, concluded his shows

> by pulling out all the vocal and choreographic stops . . . in the general manner of James Brown or Little Richard. He screams; he groans; he crawls rhythmically across the stage on his stomach dragging the microphone behind him; he leaps over, under, and around the microphone behind him; he lies on his back and kicks his feet in the air; he does some syncopated push-ups; he falls halfway over the edge of the stage and grabs the nearest hands; initiating a few unfinished dance steps, he does the limbo; he bumps and grinds; and gradually maneuvers himself off stage with a flying split or two, still twitching and shouting.[21]

This "unification of song and dance," as Burnim describes it, characterizes contemporary performances of black music. In the gospel tradition, choirs "march" in synchronized movements through the church during the processional and "step," "clap," and "shout" (religious dance) to the music performed during the worship.[22] This intrinsic relationship between music and movement is also seen during performances by popular music groups. Sam Moore commented that he and his partner, Dave Prater, "danced and moved around so much" during their performances that they lost "at least four or five pounds a night in sweat."[23] The accompanying musicians also danced in synchronized steps while playing their instruments, a concept patterned after black marching bands.

Sound Quality

The participatory dimension of music performance is only one aspect of the conceptual approach to music-making. Descriptions of black music performances over several centuries reveal that timbre is a primary feature that distinguishes this tradition from all others. The concept of sound that governs African-American music is unmistakably grounded in the African past. As Francis Bebey suggests,

> The objective of African music is not necessarily to produce sounds agreeable to the ear, but to translate everyday experiences into living sound. In a musical environment whose constant purpose is to depict life, nature, or the supernatural, the musician wisely avoids using beauty as his criterion because no criterion could be more arbitrary.
>
> Consequently, African voices adapt themselves to their musical contexts—a mellow tone to welcome a new bride; a husky voice to recount an indiscreet adventure; a satirical inflection for a teasing tone, with laughter bubbling up to compensate for the mockery—they may be soft or harsh as circumstances demand.[24]

In Africa and throughout the diaspora, black musicians produce an array of unique sounds, many of which imitate those of nature, animals, spirits, and speech. They reproduce these sounds using a variety of techniques, including striking the chest and maneuvering the tongue, mouth, cheek, and throat.[25] When arranged in an order and bound together by continuity of time, these sounds form the basis for musical composition.

The unique sound associated with black music results from the manipulation of timbre, texture, and shading in ways uncommon to Western practice. Musicians bring intensity to their performance by alternating lyrical, percussive, and raspy timbres; juxtaposing vocal and instrumental textures; changing pitch and dynamic levels; alternating straight with vibrato tones; and weaving moans, shouts, grunts, hollers, and screams into the melody. The arbitrary notion of beauty has resulted in descriptions of black music as "weird," "strange," "noise," "yelling," "hollering," "hooting," "screaming." The use of these words clearly indicates that the black music tradition does not adhere to European-American aesthetic values.

Instrumental sounds in African and African-derived music imitate timbres produced by the voice. Bebey observes that

> Western distinctions between instrumental and vocal music are evidently unthinkable in Africa where the human voice and musical instruments "speak" the same language, express the same feelings, and unanimously recreate the universe each time that thought is transformed into sound.[26]

Black instrumentalists produce a wide range of vocally derived sounds—"hollers," "cries," "grunts," "screams," "moans," and "whines," among others—by varying timbre, range, texture, and shading. They create these sounds by altering traditional embouchures, playing techniques, and fingerings and by adding distorting devices.[27] The vocal dimension of instrumental sounds is reflected in such phrases as "make it talk," "talk to me," and "I hear ya talkin'" used by black people to communicate that their aesthetic expectations have been met.

Mechanics of Delivery

The distinct sounds produced by black performers are combined with other aesthetic components to generate a pool of resources for song interpretation. Black audiences demand variety in music performances, and they expect musicians to bring a unique interpretation to each performance and to each song. Black performers meet these expectations in demonstrating their knowledge about technical aspects of performance. Within the African context, Bebey observes that "there is always plenty of scope for improvisation and ornamentation so that individual musicians can reveal their own particular talents and aptitudes. Thus, no two performances of any one piece will be exactly alike."[28] Improvisation is central to the category mechanics of delivery, which forms the third part of Burnim's aesthetic model.

Burnim convincingly argues that time, text, and pitch are the three basic components that form the structural network for song interpretation in black music. The element of time in black music is manipulated in both structural and rhythmic aspects of the performance. Time can be expanded by extending the length of notes at climactic points, by repeating words, phrases, and entire sections of songs, and by adding vocal or instrumental cadenzas. The density of textures can be increased "by gradually adding layers of handclaps, instrumental accompaniment, and/or solo voices."[29] This latter device, referred to as staggered entrances, characterized the improvised singing of slaves:

> With the first note of the hymn, began a tapping of feet by the whole congregation, gradually increasing to a stamp as the exercises proceeded, until the noise was deafening. . . . Then in strange contrast to this came the most beautiful melody the negroes have—a chant, carried by full bass voices; the liquid soprano of the melody wandering through and above it, now rising in triumphant swell, now falling in softened cadence. . . .[30]

The call-response structure is the key mechanism that allows for the manipulation of time, text, and pitch. The response or repetitive chorus provides a stable foundation for the improvised lines of the soloist. The use of call-response structures to generate musical change has been described many times in black music literature.

> These ditties [work songs sung by slaves], though nearly meaningless, have much music in them, and as all join in the perpetually recurring chorus, a rough harmony is produced. . . . I think the leader improvises the words . . . he singing one line alone, and the whole then giving the chorus, which is repeated without change at every line, till the general chorus concludes the stanza. . . .[31]

The call-response structure also is used by jazz musicians to establish a base for musical change and rhythmic tension.

> [Count] Basie's men played short, fierce riffs. Their riff patterns were not even melodic elements, they were just repetitive rhythmic figures set against each other in the sections of the band. Against this sharp, pulsing background, Basie set his soloists, and they had free rein.[32]

Perhaps the most noticeable African feature in African-American music is its rhythmic complexity. Early descriptions of this tradition reveal that

> Syncopations . . . are characteristic of negro music. I have heard negroes change a well-known melody by adroitly syncopating it. . . . nothing illustrates the negro's natural gifts in the way of keeping a difficult tempo more clearly than his perfect execution of airs thus transformed from simple to complex accentuations.[33]

In both African and African-American music, rhythm is organized in multilinear forms. Different patterns, which are repeated with slight, if any, variation, are assigned to various instruments. The combination of these patterns produces polyrhythms.[34] Polyrhythmic structures increase the overall intensity of musical performances because each repetition produces added rhythmic tension. At the same time the repetition of patterns in one part allows for textual and melodic variation in another.

Many accounts of black music have described its repetitious form while noting the creative ways in which performers achieve variety. An example is this 1862 notice:

> Each stanza [of a song sung by slaves] contains but a single thought, set in perhaps two or three bars of music; and yet as they sing it, in alternate recitatives and choruses, with varying inflections and dramatic effect. . . .[35]

Under the mechanics of delivery category, the element of pitch is manipulated by "juxtaposing voices of different ranges or by highlighting the polar extremes of a single voice." Pitch is also varied through the use of "bends, slides, melismas, and passing tones" and other forms of melodic embellishment "in order to achieve the continuous changes, extreme latitude, and personalization"—an identifying trait of black musical expression.[36] "Playing" with pitch—or "worrying the line," as Stephen Henderson calls it[37]—is a technique integral to the solo style of many black performers, including blues singer Bobby Blue Bland.

> All the distinctive features of Bland's vocal style are in evidence, notably the hoarse cry and his use of melisma on key words. Bland's cry usually consists of a twisted vowel at the beginning of a phrase—going from a given note, reaching up to another higher one, and coming back to the starting point. . . . Almost without exception Bobby uses more than one note per syllable on the concluding word of each phrase. . . . In slower tempos he will stretch out syllables with even more melisma, using as many as ten or eleven notes over a two-syllable word.[38]

Time, text, and pitch are manipulated by black performers to display their creative abilities and technical skills and to generate an overall intensity within their performance.

When performers create and interpret songs within the aesthetic boundaries framed by black people, audiences respond immediately. Their verbal comments and physical gestures express approval of both the song being performed and the way it is performed. For example, performances by musicians in the popular idiom often are based on principles that govern black worship services. These principles are recognized and valued by black audiences who respond in the same manner as they do to the presentations of black preachers and church choirs. Sam Moore recalled:

> When we performed, we had church. On Sundays the minister would preach and the people in the pews would holler and talk back to him. This is what we started doing. I arranged the parts between Dave and me so that one of us became the preacher and would say "Come on Dave" or "Come on Sam." The audience would automatically shout "Come on Sam" or "Sing Dave" or "Yes Sir." That was our style.[39]

Vocalist Deniece Williams believes that an audience actively participates in her performances because they identify with the gospel roots of her delivery style:

> You hear that [Church of God in Christ] in my music even though it is not the same deliverance of Aretha Franklin. But you feel it. A lot of people say to me "when you sing I feel it." I think that feeling comes from those experiences of church, gospel music and spirituality, which play a big part in my life.[40]

Audiences of Bobby Bland also respond in the character of the Sunday morning service:

> women sprinkled throughout the audience yell back at him, shaking their heads and waving their hands [in response to Bland's melisma]. . . . Suddenly the guitarist doubles the tempo and repeats a particularly funky phrase a few times accompanied by "oohs," "aahs," and "yeahs" from the audience.[41]

When performers demonstrate their knowledge of the black musical aesthetic, the responses of audiences can become so audible that they momentarily drown out the performer. The verbal responses of audiences are accompanied by hand-clapping; foot-stomping; head, shoulder, hand, and arm movement; and spontaneous dance. This type of audience participation is important to performers; it encourages them to explore the full range of aesthetic possibilities, and it is the single criterion by which black artists determine whether they are meeting the aesthetic expectations of the audience. Songwriter-vocalist Smokey Robinson judges his concerts as unsuccessful if the audience is "not involved in what's happening on the stage."[42]

The concept of "performer-audience" as a single unit is even apparent in the way black people respond to music in nonpublic settings. Twentieth-century technological advances make music accessible twenty-four hours a day, every day. African-Americans often use recorded music as a substitute for live performances. While listening to recordings they become involved as active participants, singing along on familiar refrain lines and choruses, snapping their fingers, clapping their hands, moving to the beat, and verbally responding to especially meaningful words or phrases and sounds with "sing it baby," "tell the truth," "play your horn," "tickle them keys," and "get on down." This level of involvement, which replicates interaction at live performances, preserves an African approach to music-making in contemporary society.

Music-making throughout the African diaspora is an expression of life where verbal and physical expression is intrinsic to the process. This conceptual framework links all black music traditions together in the African diaspora while distinguishing these traditions from those of Western and Western-derived cultures. A salient feature of black music is the conceptualization of music-making as a communal/participatory activity. In addition, variation in timbre, song interpretation, and presentation style mirrors the aesthetic priorities of black people.

An African approach to music-making has been translated from one genre to the next throughout African-American musical history. Although these genres (see figure) are by-products of specific contexts and time frames, each genre is distinctly African-American because it is governed by the conceptual framework already discussed. The remainder of this essay provides a chronology of African-American musical forms from slavery to the present.[43] The discussion presents evidence of how this conceptual unity has been transmitted from one African-American genre to the next since the first musics were created in the New World.

MUSIC IN THE SLAVE COMMUNITY

For more than 150 years slave traders and slaveholders unwittingly helped preserve an African identity in the African-American music tradition. Slave traders brought African instruments on board ships and encouraged slaves to sing and dance for exercise during the long voyage to the New World. These artifacts and creative expressions were among the cultural baggage slaves brought with them to the Americas.[44]

Studies of the institution of slavery point out that slave systems varied throughout the Americas and among colonies in the United States.[45] In situations where slaves had some measure of personal freedom they engaged in leisure activities that clearly reflected their African heritage.[46] In the United States, for example, slaves celebrated holidays for more than two centuries in African style. Two of the most spectacular and festive holidays, 'Lection Day and Pinkster Day celebrations, were observed from the mid-eighteenth through the mid-nineteenth centuries. On 'Lection Day slaves in the New England colonies elected a black governor or king and staged a big parade. Dressed in elaborate outfits, slaves celebrated by playing African games, singing, dancing, and playing African and European instruments in a distinctly African style. Pinkster Day was of Dutch origin, but slaves and free blacks in the North and South transformed it into an African-style festival.[47]

The unique character of the Pinkster Day celebration prompted James Fenimore Cooper to record his impressions:

Nine tenths of the blacks of the city [New York], and of the whole country within thirty or forty miles, indeed, were collected in thousands in those fields, beating banjos [and African drums], singing African songs [accompanied by dancing]. The features that distinguish a Pinkster frolic from the usual scenes at fairs . . . however, were of African origin. It is true, there are not now [1845], nor were there then [1757] many blacks among us of African birth; but the traditions and usages of their original country were so far preserved as to produce a marked difference between the festival, and one of European origin.[48]

The diaries of missionaries, travelers, and slaveholders and the accounts of slaves themselves further document that slaves continued to keep African traditions alive in the United States. In 1680 a missionary observed that slaves spent Sundays singing and dancing "as a means to procure Rain." An army general heard his slaves sing a war song in an African language during a visit to his plantation after the Revolutionary War. In another instance, a slave born in 1849 reported that African-born slaves sang their own songs and told stories about African customs during Christmas celebrations. And many observers noted the African flavor of the songs slaves sang while working.[49]

Slaveholders generally did not object to these and other African-derived activities provided they did not interfere with the work routine of slaves. Missionaries, on the other hand, objected to the singing and dancing,

which they described as pagan and contrary to the teachings of Christianity. Committed to eliminating these activities, they mounted a campaign to proselytize slaves. Missionaries experienced success in the New England colonies but met resistance among slaveholders in the South, who feared that a change in religious status would alter the social status of slaves as chattel property.[50]

By the nineteenth century southern slaveholders had begun to support the activities of missionaries. Faced with the growing number of slaves who ran away, sabotaged plantation operations, and organized revolts, they believed that tighter control over slaves could be exercised through religion. Many slaveholders allowed their slaves to receive religious instruction, and some even facilitated the process by building "praise houses" on the farms and plantations.[51] Despite these and other efforts, the slaves' acceptance of Christianity was at best superficial. They interpreted Christian concepts and practices through the filter of an African past, transforming the liturgy into an African ritual.

When slaves were allowed to conduct their own religious services, they defied all rules, standards, and structures established by the various denominations and sects. Their services were characterized by an unorthodox sermonizing style, unconventional behavior, and spontaneous musical expressions.[52] Missionaries frequently expressed disapproval of these services:

The public worship of God should be conducted *with reverence and stillness on the part of the congregation;* nor should the minister— whatever may have been the previous habits and training of the people—encourage demonstrations of approbation or disapprobation, or exclamations, or response, or noises, or outcries of any kind during the progress of divine worship; nor boisterous singing immediately at its close. These practices prevail over large portions of the southern country, and are not confined to one denomination, but appear to some extent in all. I cannot think them beneficial.[53]

Missionaries were especially critical of the music they described as "short scraps of disjointed affirmations . . . lengthened out with long repetitious choruses."[54] The call-response structure and improvisatory style unique to musical performances of slaves did not adhere to European-American aesthetic values. These aesthetic differences prompted missionaries to include psalm and hymn singing in the religious instruction of slaves so that they would

> lay aside the extravagant and nonsensical chants, and catches and hallelujah songs of their own composing; and when they sing, which is very often while about their business of an evening in their houses [and in church], they will have something profitable to sing.[55]

In spite of these efforts, slaves continued to sing "songs of their own composing" while adapting psalms and hymns to conform to African aesthetic principles. Henry Russell, an English musician who toured the United States from 1833 to 1841, described this process:

> When the minister gave out his own version of the Psalm, the choir commenced singing so rapidly that the original tune absolutely ceased to exist—in fact, the fine old psalm tune became thoroughly transformed into a kind of negro melody; and so sudden was the transformation, by accelerating the time, that, for a moment, I fancied that not only the choir but the little congregation intended to get up a dance as part of the service.[56]

One observer who witnessed the changing of a hymn into a "Negro song" commented that "Watts and Newton would never recognize their productions through the transformation they have undergone at the hands of their colored admirers."[57]

Other descriptions of religious services conducted by slaves confirm that they frequently fashioned Protestant psalms, hymns, and spiritual songs into new compositions by altering the structure, text, melody, and rhythm. They transformed the verse structure of the original song into a call-response or repetitive chorus structure; replaced the original English verse with an improvised text of African and English words and phrases; wove shouts, moans, groans, and cries into the melody of the improvised solo; substituted a faster tempo for the original one; and produced polyrhythmic structures by adding syncopated foot-stomped and hand-clapped patterns.[58] The body of religious music created or adapted by slaves and performed in a distinctly African style became known as "folk spirituals."

The religious tradition of slaves dominated the eighteenth- and nineteenth-century literature on African-American music. The scarcity of information on the secular tradition results in part from the reluctance of slaves to sing secular songs in the presence of whites. Missionaries discouraged slaves from singing secular songs, and slaves responded by going underground with these songs. The few accounts of secular music performances nevertheless confirm that this tradition shares the aesthetic qualities characteristic of folk spirituals:

> The negroes [a dozen stout rowers] struck up a song to which they kept time with their oars; and our speed increased as they went on, and become warmed with their singing. . . . A line was sung by a leader, then all joined in a short chorus; then came another [improvised] solo line, and another short chorus, followed by a longer chorus. . . . Little regard was paid to rhyme, and hardly any to the number of syllables in a line; they condensed four or five into one foot, or stretched out one to occupy the space that should have been filled with four or five; yet they never spoiled the tune.[59]

As in the folk spiritual tradition, the call-response structure allowed for improvised solos and recurring refrain lines.

MUSIC IN THE FREE COMMUNITY

The northern states began to abolish slavery during the first half of the nineteenth century. Yet freed slaves were faced with discriminatory state legislation that once again placed restrictions on their mobility. The small percentage of freed slaves who lived in the South were in precarious positions because their "color suggested servitude, but [their] status secured a portion of freedom." Only a "portion of freedom" was theirs because legislation barred southern free blacks from participating in mainstream society.[60] Determined to create a meaningful life, freed blacks in the North and South established communities and institutions where they defined their own mode of existence and cultural frame of reference.[61] The black church became the center of community life, serving an array of functions—religious, cultural, social, educational, and political. Within this context, many blacks kept alive the cultural traditions and musical practices associated with the praise houses of the South.[62]

The abolition of slavery in the South temporarily disrupted the communal solidarity of the slave community. Individually and in small groups, African-Americans attempted to establish new lives within the larger society. Some migrated from rural areas to cities and from South to North in search of social, political, and economic viability. Discriminatory practices, however, restricted their employment possibilities to such menial roles as domestic servants, janitors, chauffeurs, and delivery boys. Many could not find even menial jobs and, as a last resort, worked as sharecroppers on the land they had farmed as slaves. Others attempted to take advantage of educational opportunities to upgrade their social status. Despite these efforts toward "self-improvement," the broader society continued to control the mobility of blacks, forcing the masses to remain economically dependent on whites.[63]

The Fourteenth Amendment to the U.S. Constitution, ratified in 1868, guaranteed citizenship to freed slaves, and the Fifteenth Amendment of 1870 gave black men voting rights. Yet African-Americans became victims of discriminatory state legislation.[64] Many blacks survived as free persons in America because they relied on their traditional past for direction. They created a meaningful existence by preserving old values, fashioning new ones when necessary, and reestablishing the group solidarity they had known as slaves.

For many decades following the Civil War, blacks continued to make music from an African frame of reference. White northerners who migrated south to assist blacks in their transition into mainstream society were especially critical of this practice among children at school:

> In the infant schoolroom, the benches were first put aside, and the children ranged along the wall. Then began a wild droning chant in a minor key, marked with clapping of hands and stamping of feet. A dozen or twenty rose, formed a ring in the centre of the room, and began an odd shuffling dance. Keeping time to this weird chant they circled round, one following the other, changing their step to quicker and wilder motion, with louder clapping of the hands as the fervor of the singers reached a climax. The words of their hymns are simple and touching. The verses consist of two lines, the first being repeated twice. . . . As I looked upon the faces of these little barbarians and watched them circling round in this fetish dance, doubtless the relic of some African rite, I felt discouraged. . . . However, the recollection of the mental arithmetic seemed a more cheerful view of the matter.[65]

Another observer concluded that common aesthetic features link the secular and religious traditions:

> Whatever they sing is of a religious character, and in both cases [performances of

secular and religious music] they have a leader . . . who starts a line, the rest answering antiphonally as a sort of chorus. They always keep exquisite time and tune, and no words seem too hard for them to adapt to their tunes. . . . Their voices have a peculiar quality, and their intonations and delicate variations cannot be reproduced on paper.[66]

These descriptions confirm that African aesthetic concepts—of music and movement as a single unit, the varying timbres, the shadings, and the use of call-response structures to manipulate time, text, and pitch—remained vital to black musical expression in postbellum African-American culture.

Other accounts of postbellum black music reveal that both children and adults continued to sing songs from the past while creating new musical forms out of existing traditions.[67] As I wrote in an earlier essay, "The old form persisted alongside the new and remained a vital form of expression within specific contexts."[68] The new idioms, including blues, jazz, gospel, and popular music, became a unifying and sustaining force in the free black community. These and the older forms reaffirmed the values of an African past and simultaneously expressed a sense of inner strength and optimism about the future.

The secular music tradition became increasingly important. Even though missionaries had attempted to discourage slaves from singing secular songs, many free blacks asserted their independence by responding to the daily events in their lives through secular song. The secular form that became and remains particularly important to African-American culture is the blues.

The blues form shares general features and aesthetic qualities with past music traditions. It combines the musical structure and poetic forms of spirituals, work songs, and field cries with new musical and textual ideas. The improvisatory performance style emphasizes call-response (between the voice and accompanying instruments). Integral to the melody are slides, slurs, bends, and dips, and the timbres vary from moans, groans, and shouts to song-speech utterances.[69] The accompanying instruments—guitar, fiddle, piano, harmonica, and sometimes tub basses, washboards, jugs, a wire nailed to the side of a house, and other ad hoc instruments—are played in an African-derived percussive style.[70]

For more than a hundred years the essence of the blues tradition has remained the same. Amplified instruments added in the 1940s, rhythm sections in the 1950s, and horns in the 1960s are perhaps the only significant—yet in a sense only superficial—changes that have taken place in this tradition. In the twentieth century the "blues sound" crossed into the sacred world, giving life to an original body of sacred music called gospel.

Gospel music is a by-product of the late nineteenth- and early twentieth-century black "folk church." This church, associated with the Holiness and Pentecostal sects, is a contemporary version of plantation praise houses. Its character, as Pearl Williams-Jones has stated, "reflects the traditional cultural values of Black folk life as it has evolved since slave days, and is a cumulative expression of the Black experience."[71] The black folk church is distinguished from black denominational churches by the structure and nature of its service, religious practices, and philosophical concepts and the socioeconomic background of its members. The official doctrine of the folk church encourages spontaneous expressions through improvised song, testimonies, prayers, and praises from individuals.[72] Unlike other black churches, the folk church did not evolve from white Protestant denominations. Its musical repertoire, therefore, is distinctly different from that of mainline Protestant churches.

The music of the folk church, known as "church songs," has as its basic repertoire the folk spirituals and modified hymns sung by slaves in plantation praise houses. The new songs that became standards in the folk church were created spontaneously during the service by the preacher and congregation members, and they were performed in the style of folk spirituals. The only substantive change made in this tradition was the addition of musical instruments to the established accompaniment of hand-clapping and foot-stomping.[73] These instruments included tambourines, drums, piano, guitar, various horns and ad hoc instruments, and later the organ. The "bluesy," "jazzy," and "rockin'" sounds from these instruments brought a secular dimension to black religious music. The instrumental accompaniment, which became an integral part of religious music in the folk church, defined new directions for black religious music in the twentieth century.

During the first two decades of this century, the prototype for gospel music was established in the folk church. Horace Boyer noted, however, that members of this church "were not the first to receive recognition as gospel singers. Until the forties, Holiness churches did not allow their members to sing their songs before non-Holiness persons."[74] This policy did not confine the emerging gospel sound to the Holiness church. Members of the black community whose homes surrounded these churches were well aware of their existence.

Gospel music first reached the black masses as a "composed" form through the compositions of ministers and members of black Methodist and Baptist churches. Charles Albert Tindley, a Methodist minister in Philadelphia, created the prototype for a composed body of black religious music between 1900 and 1906. Some of these songs were hymnlike verses set to the melodies and rhythms of folk church songs; others were adaptations of spirituals and revival hymns.[75]

In the 1920s the Baptist songwriter Thomas Dorsey used Tindley's model to compose an identifiable and distinct body of black religious music called gospel. The former blues-jazz pianist organized his compositions around the verse-chorus form in which is embedded the call-response structure. Drawing from his blues background, he fashioned his melodies and harmonies using blues scale structures and developed a "rockin'" piano accompaniment in the boogie-woogie and ragtime traditions.

Unlike other black music genres, gospel songs often are disseminated as printed music. Yet the score provides only a framework from which performers interpret and improvise. Gospel music performances are governed by the same aesthetic concepts associated with the folk spiritual tradition. In interpreting the score, performers must demonstrate their knowledge of the improvisatory devices that characterize black music performances.

For more than eighty years the gospel tradition has preserved and transmitted the aesthetic concepts fundamental to music-making in Africa and African-derived cultures. Since its birth in the Holiness and Pentecostal churches it has found a home in storefront churches of various denominations and in many black middle-class Baptist, Methodist, Episcopal, and Catholic churches. The impact of gospel has been so great that its colorful African-derived kaleidoscope of oratory, poetry, drama, and dance and its musical style established a reservoir of cultural resources that contributed to the development of black popular music.

New secular forms of black musical expression were created in response to changes in society following World War II. The war years stimulated growth in the American economy, which in turn led to changes in the lives of black Americans. As I recounted in an earlier monograph, almost two million southern rural blacks abandoned "their low-paying domestic, sharecropping and tenant-farming jobs for work in factories located throughout the country. In cities, both Blacks and whites earned the highest wages in American history. So Americans, especially Black Americans, had much to celebrate during the postwar years."[76] The music to which they celebrated was termed rhythm and blues—a hybrid form rooted in the blues, gospel, and swing band traditions.

Blacks left the rural South with expectations of improving their economic, social, and political status. They soon discovered that opportunities for advancement in society were limited and that the segregated structure of cities restricted their mobility. Discriminatory housing laws, for example, forced many blacks to live and socialize in designated sections of cities—ghettos. These and other patterns of discrimination led to the reestablishment of familiar institutions, thereby continuing southern traditions and practices in the urban metropolis.

The ambiance of southern jukejoints was transferred to blues bars, lounges, and clubs, which became the center of social gatherings in urban cities. Southern music traditions—blues and jazz—were central to the activity in these establishments. The segregated environment, the faster pace, the factory sounds, the street noises, and the technology of the metropolis gave a different type of luster, cadence, and sophistication to existing black musical forms. In response to new surroundings, the familiar sounds of the past soon were transformed into an urban black music tradition.

Blues, jazz, and gospel performers were among the millions of blacks who moved to the cities. They joined forces to create an urban-sounding dance music, rhythm and blues. This music is characterized by a boogie bass line, "riffing" jazz-derived horn arrangements, blues-gospel piano, "honking" and "screaming" tenor sax, "whining" blues guitar, and syncopated drum patterns. The intensity of this sound was increased by the addition of blues and former gospel singers who "moaned" and "shouted" about life in the city. The rhythmic complexity and the performance style of rhythm and blues music preserved traditional values in the music of the city dwellers.

The spirit that captured the excitement of postwar city living began to fade in the mid-1950s. Conditions deteriorated, and life continued to be harsh for many African-Americans, especially the inner-city dwellers. They responded by organizing a series of grass-roots protest activities that quickly gained momentum and attracted national attention. The spread of these political activities throughout the country was the impetus behind the civil rights and black power movements of the 1950s and 1960s. "Soul music" was a by-product of the 1960s movements.[77]

Leaders of the black power movement encouraged the rejection of standards and values of the broader society and a return to values of an African past. Many soul music performers became ambassadors for this movement. Through song they communicated its philosophy, advocating an awareness of an African heritage, encouraging the practice of African traditions, and promoting the concept of black pride. Their "soul message" was communicated in a style that captured the climate of the times and the spirit of a people. This style embraces all the aesthetic qualities that define the essence of the gospel tradition.[78]

The interrelatedness of soul and gospel music is illustrated through the interchangeability of the genres. For example, many gospel songs have been recorded under the label "soul" and vice versa. In some instances the text is the only feature that distinguishes one style from another. In others, genre identification may be determined only by the musical identity of the artist who first recorded the song. Performances of soul and gospel music further illustrate that an aesthetic conceptual framework links the secular and sacred traditions to each other.

The era of soul music reawakened the consciousness of an African past. It sanctioned the new thrust for African exploration and simultaneously gave credence to an obscured heritage. This profound era also established new directions in black popular music that would continue to merge African expressions into new forms. The decade of the 1970s heralded this new music.

The 1960s ended with the anticipation of new opportunities for economic independence and full participation in mainstream life. Affirmative action, school desegregation, and other legislation was passed, and the early 1970s implied future changes in the structure of society. Such legislation cultivated a renewed sense of optimism among blacks, and many began to explore new economic, political, and social opportunities outside the black community.

By the mid-1970s this optimism had begun to fade with increased opposition to affirmative action legislation. The economic recession and the "reverse discrimination" concept of the 1970s led to a retrenchment of civil rights and economic opportunities designed to effect equality for blacks. Whites protested against busing and affirmative action policies. In response, the federal government retreated on earlier commitments to rights for blacks. The "gains" made in the early 1970s gave way to fiscal and social conservatism in the late 1970s and the 1980s. The general opposition to any social advantages for blacks fostered a return to the status quo where racism shaped the American ethos.[79]

Blacks responded to the realities of the 1970s and 1980s in diverse ways and with mixed feelings. Many assessed progress toward social, economic, and political equality as illusory at best. Some felt conditions had worsened, though a few privileged blacks believed the situation had improved.[80] The ambivalent feelings about social progress for blacks found its expression in new and diverse forms of black popular music—funk, disco, rap music, and personalized or trademark forms.

The song lyrics and music styles of funk, disco, and rap music epitomize the changing and sometimes conflicting viewpoints about progress. Although many performers continued to express optimism about the future,

some introduced lyric themes of frustration, disillusionment, and distress. The "soul sound" dominated during the first half of the 1970s, but by the mid-1970s it had been transformed. Whereas soul carries the trademark of "message music," funk, disco, and rap music bore the stamp of "party" music.[81] It injected a new spirit of life into black communities and became a major unifying force for a core of African-Americans. This spirit is reflected in the lyric themes: "party," "have a good time," "let yourself go," and "dance, dance, dance." These themes suggest that the music had a therapeutic function. Rather than communicate political or intellectual messages, it encouraged blacks to release tension by simply being themselves. At the same time, the infectious beat of this music created an atmosphere that allowed for self-expression and unrestricted social interactions.

Funk, disco, and rap music are grounded in the same aesthetic concepts that define the soul music tradition. Yet the sound is distinguished from soul because emphasis is given to different musical components. These forms of the late 1970s are conceived primarily as dance music where melody plays a secondary role to rhythm. The African-derived polyrhythmic structures, the call-response patterns, and the quasi-spoken group vocals generate audience participation. The percussive sounds and timbrel qualities of synthesizers and other electronic devices add another dimension to the black sound. The musical and cultural features in 1970s and 1980s popular traditions continue to give credence to the vitality of an African past in contemporary forms of black music.

CONCLUSIONS

A study of African-American music from the seventeenth through the twentieth centuries reveals that African retentions in African-American music can be defined as a core of conceptual approaches. Fundamental to these approaches is the axiom that music-making is conceived as a communal/participatory group activity. Black people create, interpret, and experience music out of an African frame of reference—one that shapes musical sound, interpretation, and behavior and makes black music traditions throughout the world a unified whole.

The New World experiences of black people encouraged them to maintain ties to their African past. This unspoken association enabled them to survive and create a meaningful existence in a world where they were not welcomed. They adapted to environmental changes and social upheavals by relying on familiar traditions and practices. Music played an important role in this process. Although

specific African songs and genres eventually disappeared from the culture of African-Americans, Nketia points out that new ones were "created in the style of the tradition, using its vocabulary and idiom, or in an alternative style which combined African and non-African resources."[82] In essence, new ideas were recycled through age-old concepts to produce new music styles. The fundamentals of culture established by slaves persist in the twentieth century; they are reinterpreted as social times demand. African retentions in African-American culture, therefore, exist as conceptual approaches—as unique ways of doing things and making things happen—rather than as specific cultural elements.

Notes

1. Historical studies include Ira Berlin, *Slaves without Masters: The Free Negro in the Antebellum South* (New York: Vintage, 1974); Eugene D. Genovese, *Roll Jordan Roll: The World the Slaves Made* (New York: Pantheon, 1974); John Blassingame, *The Slave Community* (New York: Oxford University Press, rev. ed., 1979); Gerald W. Mullin, *Flight and Rebellion* (New York: Oxford University Press, 1972); and Robert Haynes, *Blacks in White America before 1865* (New York: David McKay, 1972).

For cultural studies, see John W. Work, *Folk Song of the American Negro* (Nashville, Tenn.: Fisk University Press, 1915; reprinted by Negro Universities Press, New York, 1969); James Weldon and J. Rosamond Johnson, *American Negro Spirituals*, 2 vols. (New York: Viking Press, 1925 and 1926; reprinted in one volume by Da Capo Press, New York, 1969); Zora Neale Hurston, "Spirituals and Neo-Spirituals" [1935], in *Voices from the Harlem Renaissance*, Nathan Huggins, ed. (New York: Oxford University Press, 1976), 344–47; Hall Johnson, "Notes on the Negro Spiritual" [1965], in *Readings in Black American Music*, Eileen Southern, ed. (New York: Norton, 2d ed., 1983), 273–80; Henry Krehbiel, *Afro-*

American Folksongs (New York: Ungar, 1914); Melville J. Herskovits, *The Myth of the Negro Past* (Boston: Beacon Press, 1958); Lawrence Levine, *Black Culture and Black Consciousness* (New York: Oxford University Press, 1977); Dena Epstein, *Sinful Tunes and Spirituals* (Chicago: University of Chicago Press, 1977); Alan Dundes, ed., *Mother Wit from the Laughing Barrel* (Englewood Cliffs, N.J.: Prentice-Hall, 1973); Norman E. Whitten and John F. Szwed, eds., *Afro-American Anthropology* (New York: Free Press, 1970); Paul Oliver, *Savannah Syncopators: African Retentions in the Blues* (New York: Stein and Day, 1970); Albert J. Raboteau, *Slave Religion* (New York: Oxford University Press, 1978); Frederick Kaufman and John Guckin, *The African Roots of Jazz* (Alfred Publishing Company, 1979); Olly Wilson, "The Significance of the Relationship between Afro-American Music and West African Music," *Black Perspective in Music* (Spring 1974) 2:3–22; and J. H. Kwabena Nketia, "African Roots of Music in the Americas: An African View," 82–88, Olly Wilson, "The Association of Movement and Music as a Manifestation of a Black Conceptual Approach to Music," 98–105, and David Evans, "African Elements in Twentieth-Century United States Black Folk Music," 54–66, in Report of the 12th Congress, London, American Musicological Society. 1981.

2. Levine, *Black Culture,* 5.

3. For a summary of theories advanced by these writers, see Herskovits, *Myth,* 262–69; Guy B. Johnson, *Folk Culture in St. Helena Island* (Chapel Hill: University of North Carolina Press, 1930); Lawrence Levine, "Slave Songs and Slave Consciousness." in *American Negro Slavery.* Allen Weinstein and Frank Otto Catell, eds. (New York: Oxford University Press, 2d ed., 1973), 153–82; and Dena Epstein, "A White Origin for the Black Spiritual? An Invalid Theory and How It Grew," *American Music* (Summer 1983) 1:53–59.

4. Richard Waterman, "African Patterns in Trinidad Negro Music," Ph.D. dissertation. Northwestern University, 1943, 26, 41–42; "Hot Rhythm in Negro Music," *Journal of the American Musicological Society* (1948) 1:24–37; and "On Flogging a Dead Horse: Lessons Learned from the Africanisms Controversy," *Ethnomusicology* (1963) 7:83–87. Alan Lornax, *Folk Song Style and Culture* (Washington, D.C.: American Association for the Advancement of Science, 1968). Herskovits, *Myth,* 261–69. Krehbiel, *Afro-American Folksong.*

5. For a summary of these accounts, see Epstein, *Sinful Tunes.* 19–99.

6. Nketia, "African Roots," 88.

7. Wilson, "Significance," 20.

8. For a discussion of the way music functions in African societies, see J. H. Kwabena Nketia, *The Music of Africa* (New York: Norton, 1974), 21–50, and Francis Bebey, *African Music: A People's Art,* Josephine Bennett, trans. (New York: Lawrence Hill, 1975), 1–38.

9. Nketia, *Music of Africa,* 21.

10. Ibid., 22.

11. Sam Moore, interview with author, 25 February 1983.

12. Mellonee Burnim, "The Black Gospel Music Tradition: A Complex of Ideology, Aesthetic, and Behavior," in *More than Dancing,* Irene V. Jackson, ed. (Westport, Conn.: Greenwood Press, 1985), 154.

13. Ibid., 159.

14. Wilson, "Association of Movement," 99.

15. Mellonee Burnim, "Functional Dimensions of Gospel Music Performance," *Western Journal of Black Studies* (Summer 1988) 12:115.

16. Joyce Jackson, "The Performing Black Sacred Quartet: An Expression of Cultural Values and Aesthetics," Ph.D. dissertation, Indiana University, 1988, 161–90.

17. Ted Fox, *Showtime at the Apollo* (New York: Holt, Rinehart and Winston, 1983), 69.

18. Nketia, *Music of Africa,* 206–7.

19. Letter from Rev. R. Q. Mallard to Mrs. Mary S. Mallard, Chattanooga, May 18, 1859, in *The Children of Pride,* Robert Manson Myers, ed. (New Haven, Conn.: Yale University Press, 1972), 483.

20. Andrew Reed and James Matheson, *A Narrative of the Visit to the American Churches* (London: Jackson and Walford, 1835), 219. Frederika Bremer, *Homes of the New World,* 1, trans. Mary Howitt (New York: Harper, 1854), 393.

21. Charles Kell, *Urban Blues* (Chicago: University of Chicago Press, 1966), 122.

22. Burnim, "Black Gospel Music Tradition," 160.

23. Sam Moore, interview with author, 25 February 1983.

24. Bebey, *African Music,* 115.

25. See Ruth M. Stone, "African Music Performed," in *Africa,* Phyllis M. Martin and Patrick O'Meara, eds. (Bloomington: Indiana University Press, 2d ed., 1986), 236–39, and Bebey, *African Music,* 119–24, for more in-depth discussions of musical sound in African cultures.

26. Bebey, *African Music,* 122.

27. Instrumental playing techniques of black musicians are discussed in Thomas J. Anderson et al., "Black Composers and the Avant-Garde," in *Black Music in Our Culture,* Dominique-Rene de Lerma, ed. (Kent, Ohio: Kent State University Press, 1970), 66, 68; David Evans, "African Elements," 61; Oliver, *Savannah Syncopators;* and Wilson, "Significance of the Relationship," 15–21.

28. Bebey, *African Music,* 30.

29. Burnim, "Black Gospel," 163.

30. [Elizabeth Kilham], "Sketches in Color," *Putnam's,* March 1870, 306.

31. Philip Henry Goose, *Letters from Alabama* (London: Morgan and Chase, 1859), 305.

32. Samuel B. Charters and Leonard Kunstadt, *Jazz: A History of the New York Scene* (New York: Da Capo Press, 1981), 288.

33. Quoted in Epstein, *Sinful Tunes,* 294–95.

34. For discussions of rhythmic structures in black music, see Wilson, "Significance of the Relationship," 3–15; Nketia, *Music of Africa,* 38; Evans, "African Elements," 17–18; Portia K. Maultsby, "Contemporary Pop: A Healthy Diversity Evolves from Creative Freedom," *Billboard,* June 9, 1979, BM-22; and Pearl Williams-Jones, "Afro-American Gospel Music in Development of Materials for a One Year Course," in *African Music for the General Undergraduate Student,* Vada Butcher, ed. (Washington, D.C.: Howard University Press, 1970), 211.

35. J[ames Miller] McKim, "Negro Songs," *Dwight's Journal of Music,* August 9, 1862, 148–49.

36. Burnim, "Black Gospel Music Tradition," 165.

37. Stephen Henderson, *Understanding the New Black Poetry* (New York: Morrow, 1973), 41.

38. Keil, *Urban Blues,* 124.

39. Sam Moore, interview with author, 25 February 1983.

40. Deniece Williams, interview with author, 22 April 1983.

41. Keil, *Urban Blues,* 124, 139.

42. Smokey Robinson, radio interview, WBLS, New York City, 16 January 1983.

43. My discussion in this limited space necessarily centers on selected genres, but a review of black music literature will show that the principles discussed are applicable to all genres of African-American music.

44. See Epstein, *Sinful Tunes,* 8–17.

45. See Laura Foner and Eugene D. Genovese, eds., *Slavery in the New World* (Englewood Cliffs, N.J.: Prentice-Hall, 1969), and Blassingame, *Slave Community.*

46. See Epstein, *Sinful Tunes.*

47. See Eileen Southern, *The Music of Black Americans* (New York: Norton, 2d ed., 1983), 53–59, and Epstein, *Sinful Tunes,* 66–68.

48. J[ames] Fenimore Cooper, *Satanstoe,* I (London: S.&L. Bentley, Wilson, and Fley, 1845), 122–23.

49. Descriptions are found in Morgan Godwyn, *The Negro's and Indian's Advocate, Suing for Their Admission into the Church* (London: F. D., 1680), 33; Jeanette Robinson Murphy, "The Survival of African Music in America," *Popular Science* (1899) 55:660–72; Epstein, *Sinful Tunes,* 41, 127–38, 161–83; and Southern, ed., *Readings,* 71–121.

50. See Epstein, *Sinful Tunes,* 63–76, and Charles C. Jones, *Religious Instruction of the Negroes in the United States* (New York: Negro Universities Press, 1969; reprint of 1842 edition), 21, for information on the proselytizing activities of missionaries.

51. Praise houses were places designated for the slaves' worship. For detailed information about the conversion of slaves, see Raboteau, *Slave Religion;* Milton Sernett, *Black Religion and American Evangelicalism* (Metuchen, N.J.: Scarecrow Press, 1975); John Lovell, *Black Song: The Forge and the Flame* (New York: Macmillan, 1972), 71–374; and Epstein, *Sinful Tunes,* 100–111, 191–216.

52. See Raboteau, *Slave Religion;* Sernett, *Black Religion;* Epstein, *Sinful Tunes,* 191–237; and Levine, *Black Culture,* 3–80.

53. Quoted in Epstein, *Sinful Tunes,* 201.

54. Southern, *Readings,* 63.

55. Jones, *Religious Instruction,* 266.

56. Henry Russell, *Cheer! Boys, Cheer!: Memories of Men and Music* (London: John Macqueen, Hastings House, 1895), 85.

57. [Kilham], "Sketches," 309.

58. See Portia K. Maultsby, "Afro-American Religious Music 1619–1861," Ph.D. dissertation, University of Wisconsin–Madison, 1974, 182; Epstein, *Sinful Tunes,* 217–358; and Murphy, "Survival of African Music," 660–62. These aesthetic concepts may be heard on recordings: *Been in the Storm So Long,* recorded by Guy Carawan on Johns Island, South Carolina

(Folkways Records FS 3842); *Afro-American Spirituals, Work Songs, and Ballads,* ed. by Alan Lomax, Library of Congress Music Division (AAPS L3); *Negro Religious Songs and Services,* ed. by B. A. Botkin, Library of Congress Music Division (AAFS L10).

59. Epstein, *Sinful Tunes,* 169–70. The secular musical tradition of slaves is discussed in Levine, *Black Culture,* 15; Harold Courlander, *Negro Folk Music U.S.A.* (New York: Columbia University Press, 1963), 80–88, 89–122, 146–61; and Epstein, 161–90.

60. Richard C. Wade, *Slavery in the Cities: The South 1820–1860* (New York: Oxford University Press, 1964), 249.

61. Leon F. Litwack, *North of Slavery* (Chicago: University of Chicago Press, 1961), 14, 64.

62. For descriptions of services associated with independent black churches, see Berlin, *Slaves without Masters,* 284–303; Wade, *Slavery in the Cities,* 160–76; Epstein, *Sinful Tunes.* 197, 223; Portia K. Maultsby, "Music of Northern Independent Black Churches during the Ante-Bellum Period," *Ethnomusicology,* September 1975, 407–18; Avrahm Yarmolinsky, ed., *Picturesque United States of America: 1811, 1812, 1813* (New York: William Edwin Rudge, 1930), 20; and Southern, *Readings,* 52–70.

63. Information about the status of blacks after the Civil War may be found in E. Franklin Frazier, *The Negro in the United States* (New York: Macmillan, 1949), 171–272; Levine, *Black Culture,* 136–70; C. Vann Woodward, *The Strange Career of Jim Crow* (New York: Oxford University Press, 2d rev. ed., 1966), 11–65; and Jeff Todd Titon, *Early Downhome Blues: A Musical and Cultural Analysis* (Urbana: University of Illinois Press, 1977), 3–15.

64. See Frazier, *Negro in the United States,* 123–68; Woodward, *Strange Career,* 11–65; and Michael Haralambos, *Right on: From Blues to Soul in Black America* (New York: Drake, 1975), 50–51.

65. Quoted in Epstein, *Sinful Tunes,* 281–82.

66. J[ames] W[entworth] Leigh, *Other Days* (New York: Macmillan, 1921), 156.

67. Ibid., 274–81, and Levine, *Black Culture,* 191–217, 239–70.

68. Portia K. Maultsby, "The Role of Scholars in Creating Space and Validity for Ongoing Changes in Black American Culture," in *Black American Culture and Scholarship* (Washington, D.C.: Smithsonian Institution, 1985), 11.

69. See Samuel Charters, *The Bluesmen* (New York: Oak Publications, 1967); Haralambos, *Right On,* 76–82; Titon, *Early Downhome Blues;* Levine, *Black Culture,* 217–24; Keil, *Urban Blues,* 50–68; Oliver, *Savannah Syncopators,* 36–66; and Evans, "African Elements," 57–62.

70. See William Ferris, *Blues from the Delta* (New York: Anchor Press, 1978), 37–38; David Evans, "Afro-American One-Stringed Instruments," *Western Folklore* (October 1970) 29:229–45; Oliver, *Savannah Syncopators,* 37–38; and Evans, "African Elements," 59–60.

71. Pearl Williams-Jones, "The Musical Quality of Black Religious Folk Ritual," *Spirit* (1977) 1:21.

72. See ibid., 23, 25, and Melvin D. Williams, *Community in a Black Pentecostal Church* (Pittsburgh: University of Pittsburgh Press, 1974), for religious practices associated with this church.

73. See Pearl Williams-Jones, "Afro-American Gospel Music: A Crystallization of the Black Aesthetic," *Ethnomusicology* (September 1975) 19:374, 381, 383; Levine, *Black Culture,* 179–80; and Mellonee Burnim, "The Black Gospel Music Tradition: A Symbol of Ethnicity," Ph.D. dissertation, Indiana University, 1980. A variety of instruments used to accompany early gospel music may be heard on *An Introduction to Gospel Song,* compiled and edited by Samuel B. Charters (RBF Records RF5).

74. Horace Boyer, "Gospel Music," *Music Education Journal* (May 1978) 64:37.

75. Arna Bontemps, "Rock, Church, Rock!" *Ground* (Autumn 1942) 3:35–39. Bontemps gives the years 1901–6 as the period when Tindley wrote his first songs, whereas Boyer believes the period to be between 1900 and 1905.

76. Portia K. Maultsby, *Rhythm and Blues (1945–1955): A Survey of Styles* (Washington, D.C.: Smithsonian Institution, 1986), 6.

77. For a history of these movements, see Martin Luther King, Jr., *Why We Can't Wait* (New

York: Signet, 1964), and Stokely Carmichael and Charles V. Hamilton, *Black Power: The Politics of Liberation in America* (New York: Vintage, 1967).

78. Portia K. Maultsby, "Soul Music: Its Sociological and Political Significance in American Popular Culture," *Journal of Popular Culture* (Fall 1983) 17:51–52. Many James Brown recordings released between 1969 and 1974 illustrated the black pride concept in soul music; also see Cliff White, "After 21 Years, Still Refusing to Lose," *Black World,* April 1977, 36. Other performers whose music reflected the social climate of the 1960s and early 1970s include the Impressions, "We're a Winner" and "This Is My Country"; Marvin Gaye, "Inner City Blues"; Staple Singers, "Respect Yourself" and "Be What You Are"; Gladys Knight and the Pips, "Friendship Train"; O'Jays, "Back Stabbers" and "Love Train"; Sly and the Family Stone, "Thank You for Talkin' to Me Africa," "Africa Talks to You," and "The Asphalt Jungle"; Temptations, "Cloud Nine"; and Diana Ross and the Supremes, "Love Child."

79. See Gerald R. Gill, *Meanness Mania: The Changed Mood* (Washington, D.C.: Howard University Press, 1980); Faustine Childress Jones, *The Changing Mood: Eroding Commitment?* (Washington, D.C.: Howard University Press, 1977); Harry C. Triandis, *Variations in Black and White Perceptions of the Social Environment* (Urbana: University of Illinois Press, 1976); Angus Campbell, *White Attitudes toward Black People* (Ann Arbor: Institute for Social Research, University of Michigan, 1971); Charles Murray, *Losing Ground: American Social Policy 1950–1980* (New York: Basic Books, 1984); George Davis and Glenn Watson, *Black Life in Corporate America* (New York: Anchor, 1982); William Moore, Jr., and Lonnie H. Wagstaff, *Black Educators in White Colleges* (San Francisco: Jossey-Bass, 1974); Marvin W. Peterson, Robert T. Blackburn, et al., *Black Students on White Campuses: The Impact of Increased Black Enrollments* (Ann Arbor: Institute for Social Research, University of Michigan, 1978); and Janet Dewart, ed., *State of Black America* (New York: National Urban League, 1987).

80. See Gill, *Meanness Mania;* Jones, *Changing Mood;* and Dewart, ed., *State of Black America.*

81. Maultsby, "Role of Scholars." 19–21

82. Nketia, "African Roots," 83–84.

Negro Folk Expression: Spirituals, Seculars, Ballads and Work Songs

STERLING BROWN

THOMAS WENTWORTH HIGGINSON, ONE of the very first to pay respectful attention to Negro spiritual, called it a startling flower growing in dark soil. Using his figure, we might think of this flower as a hybrid, as the American Negro is a hybrid. And though flowers of its family grew in Africa, Europe, and other parts of America, this hybrid bloom is uniquely beautiful.

THE SPIRITUALS

A large amount of recent scholarship has proved that the spirituals are not African, either in music or meaning (a claim made once with partisan zeal), that the American Negro was influenced by the religious music of rural America from the Great Awakening on, that at the frontier camp meetings he found to his liking many tunes both doleful and brisk, and that he took over both tunes and texts and refashioned them more to his taste. But careful musicologists, from studying phonograph records of folk singing rather than, as earlier, inadequate, conventional notations of "art" spirituals, are coming around to the verdict of Alan Lomax that "no amount of scholarly analysis and discussion can ever make a Negro spiritual sound like a white spiritual."

A new music, yes. But what of the poetry? Scholars have discovered that many phrases, lines, couplets, and even whole stanzas and songs, once thought to be Negro spirituals, were popular in white camp meetings. A full comparison of the words of white and Negro spirituals is out of the question here. It might be said that some of the parallels turn out to be tangents. Thus, "At his table we'll sit down, Christ will gird himself and serve us with sweet manna all around" is supposed to be the white source of "Gwine to sit down at the welcome table, gwine to feast off milk and honey," and "To hide yourself in the mountain top, to hide yourself from God" is supposed to have become "Went down to the rocks to hide my face, the rocks cried out no hiding place." Even when single lines were identical, the Negro made telling changes in

This article originally appeared in *Phylon, the Atlanta University Review of Race & Culture,* First Quarter, 1953.

the stanza. Briefly, the differences seem to result from a looser line, less tyrannized over by meter and rhyme, with the accent shifted unpredictably, from a more liberal use of refrains, and from imagery that is terser and starker. The improvising imagination seems freer. Some of the changes of words arose from confusion: "Paul and Silas bound in jail" has been sung: "bounded Cyrus born in jail," and "I want to cross over into camp-ground" has been sung as "I want to cross over in a calm time." Some of the changes, however, result from the truly poetic imagination at work on material deeply felt and pondered: "Tone de bell easy, Jesus gonna make up my dying bed." "I'll lie in de grave and stretch out my arms, when I lay dis body down." "Steal away, steal away, steal away to Jesus. Steal away, steal away home; I ain't got long to stay here."

Many spirituals tell of the joys of Christian fellowship. "Ain't you glad you got out de wilderness?" "I been bawn of God, no condemnation; no condemnation in my soul." "I been down in the valley; Never turn back no mo.'"

I went down in the valley to pray
My soul got happy and I stayed all day.

"Just like a tree, planted by the waters, I shall not be moved." Belonging to the glorious company, the slaves found comfort, protection. Sinners would find no hole in the ground, but those of the true faith had "a hiding place, around the throne of God." "I got a home in that rock, don't you see?" "In God's bosom gonna be my pillow." Their souls were witnesses for their Lord. "Done done my duty; Got on my travelin' shoes." "I done crossed the separatin' line; I done left the world behind."

The world could be left behind in visions.

I've got two wings for to veil my face
I've got two wings for to fly away. . . .

Gabriel and his trumpet caught the imagination. "Where will you be when the first trumpet sounds; sounds so loud its gonna wake up the dead?" "O My Lord, what a morning, when the stars begin to fall!" "When the sun refuse to shine, when the moon goes down in blood!" In that great getting up morning, "you see the stars a falling, the forked lightning, the coffins bursting, the righteous marching." "The blind will see, the dumb will talk; the deaf will hear; the lame will walk." This apocalyptic imagery, clear to the initiated, is a release, a flight, a message in code, frequently used by oppressed people.

Then they'll cry out for cold water
While the Christians shout in glory
Saying Amen to their damnation
Fare you well, fare you well.

It was not only to the far-off future of Revelations that the dreams turned. Heaven was a refuge too. In contrast to the shacks of slave row and the slums of the cities, to the work clothes and the unsavory victuals, would be the throne of God, the streets of gold, the harps, the robes, the milk and honey.

A-settin' down with Jesus
Eatin' honey and drinkin' wine
Marchin' round de throne
Wid Peter, James, and John. . . .

But the dream was not always so extravagant. Heaven promised simple satisfactions, but they were of great import to the slaves. Shoes for instance, as well as a harp. Heaven meant home: "I'm gonna feast at de welcome table." Heaven meant rest: just sitting down was one of the high privileges often mentioned. And acceptance as a person: "I'm going to walk and talk with Jesus." Moreover, the Heaven of escape is not a Heaven bringing forgetfulness of the past. The River Jordan is not Lethe.

I'm gonna tell God all my troubles,
When I get home . . .
I'm gonna tell him the road was rocky
When I get home.

The makers of the spirituals, looking toward heaven, found their triumphs there.

But they did not blink their eyes to the troubles here. As the best expression of the slaves' deepest thoughts and yearnings, they speak with convincing finality against the legend of contented slavery. This world was not their home. "Swing low, sweet chariot, coming for to carry me home." They never tell of joy in the "good old days." The only joy in the spirituals is in dreams of escape.

That the spirituals were otherworldly, then, is less than half-truth. In more exact truth, they tell of this life, of "rollin' through an unfriendly world." "Oh, bye and bye, bye and bye, I'm going to lay down this heavy load." "My way is cloudy." "Oh, stand the storm, it won't be long, we'll anchor by and by." "Lord keep me from sinking down." And there is that couplet of tragic intensity:

> *Dont know what my mother wants to*
> *stay here fuh,*
> *Dis ole world ain't been no friend to huh.*

Out of the workaday life came figures of speech: "Keep a-inchin' along lak a po' inchworm"; such a couplet as:

> *Better mind that sun and see how she run*
> *And mind! Don't let her catch you wid yo'*
> *work undone.*

And such an allegory: "You hear de lambs a-crying; oh, shepherd, feed-a my sheep." Out of folk wisdom came: "Oh de ole sheep, they know de road; young lambs gotta find de way," and "Ole Satan is like a snake in the grass."

> *Sister, you better watch how you walk*
> *on the cross*
> *Yo' foot might slip, and yo' soul git lost.*

The spirituals make an anthology of Biblical heroes and tales, from Genesis where Adam and Eve are in the Garden, picking up leaves, to John's calling the roll in Revelations. There are numerous gaps, of course, and many repetitions. Certain figures are seen in an unusual light; Paul, for instance, is generally bound in jail with Silas, to the exclusion of the rest

of his busy career. Favored heroes are Noah, chosen of God to ride down the flood; Samson, who tore those buildings down; Joshua, who caused the walls of Jericho to fall (when the rams' lambs' sheephorns began to blow); Jonah, symbol of hard luck changed at last; and Job, the man of tribulation who still would not curse his God. These are victors over odds. But losers, the wretched and despised, also serve as symbols. There is Lazarus, "poor as I, don't you see?" who went to heaven, in contrast to "Rich man Dives, who lived so well; when he died he found a home in hell." And finally there is Blind Barnabas, whose tormented cry found echoes in slave cabins down through the long, dark years:

> *Oh de blind man stood on de road an'*
> *cried*
> *Cried, "Lord, oh, Lord, save-a po' me!"*

In telling the story of Jesus, spirituals range from the tender "Mary had a little baby" and "Little Boy, how old are you" to the awe-inspiring "Were You There" and "He Never Said A Mumbalin' Word." Jesus is friend and brother, loving counselor, redeemer, Lord and King. The Negro slave's picturing of Calvary in such lines as

> *Dey whupped him up de hill . . .*
> *Dey crowned his head with thorns . . .*
> *Dey pierced him in de side,*
> *An' de blood come a-twinklin' down;*
> *But he never said a mumbalin' word;*
> *Not a word; not a word.*

belongs with the greatest Christian poetry. It fused belief and experience; it surged up from most passionate sympathy and understanding.

Some scholars who have found parallels between the words of Negro and white spirituals would have us believe that when the Negro sang of freedom, he meant only what the whites meant, namely freedom from sin. Free, individualistic whites on the make in a prospering civilization, nursing the American dream, could well have felt their only bondage to be that of sin, and freedom to be religious salvation. But with the drudgery, the hardships, the auction-block, the slave-mart, the shackles, and the lash so literally present in the Negro's experience, it is hard to imagine why for the Negro they would remain figurative. The scholars certainly do not make it clear, but rather take refuge in such dicta as: "The slave did not contemplate his low condition." Are we to believe that the slave singing "I been rebuked, I been scorned; done had a hard time sho's you bawn," referred to his being outside of the true religion? Ex-slaves, of course, inform us differently. The spirituals speak up strongly for freedom not only from sin (dear as that freedom was to the true believer) but from physical bondage. Those attacking slavery as such had to be as rare as anti-Hitler marching songs in occupied France. But there were oblique references. Frederick Douglass has told us of the double-talk of the spirituals: Canaan, for instance, stood for Canada; and over and beyond hidden satire the songs also were grapevines for communications. Harriet Tubman, herself called the Moses of her people, has told us that *Go Down, Moses* was tabu in the slave states, but the people sang it nonetheless.

Fairly easy allegories identified Egypt-land with the South, Pharaoh with the masters, the Israelites with themselves and Moses with their leader. "So Moses smote de water and the children all passed over; Children, ain't you glad that they drowned that sinful army?"

> *Oh, Mary don't you weep, don't you*
>   *moan;*
> *Pharaoh's army got drownded,*
> *Oh, Mary, don't you weep.*

Some of the references were more direct:

> *Didn't my Lord deliver Daniel,*
> *And why not every man?*

In the wake of the Union army and in the contraband camps spirituals of freedom sprang up suddenly. The dry grass was ready for the quickening flame. Some celebrated the days of Jubilo: "O Freedom; O Freedom!, And

before I'll be a slave, I'll be buried in my grave! And go home to my Lord and be free." Some summed up slavery starkly: "No more driver's lash for me, no more, no more . . . . No more peck of corn for me; many thousand go." "Slavery's chain done broke at last; gonna praise God till I die." And in all likelihood old spirituals got new meanings: "Ain't you glad you got out the wilderness?" "In That Great Gittin' Up Morning!" "And the moon went down in blood."

The best of the spirituals are, in W. E. B. Du Bois's phrase, "the sorrow-songs of slavery." In spite of indifference and resentment from many educated and middle-class Negroes, the spirituals are still sung, circulated, altered and created by folk Negroes. Some of the new ones, started in the backwoods, have a crude charm; for instance Joseph and Mary in Jerusalem "to pay their poll-taxes," find the little boy Jesus in the temple confounding with his questions the county doctor, lawyer, and judge. Some of them mix in more recent imagery: "Death's little black train is coming!" "If I have my ticket, Lord, can I ride?" and a chant of death in which the refrain "Same train. Same train" is repeated with vivid effect:

> *Same train took my mother.*
> *Same train. Same train.*

Some use modern inventions with strained incongruity: "Jus' call up Central in Heaven, tell Jesus to come to the phone," and "Jesus is my aeroplane, He holds the whole world in his hands"; and "Standing in the Safety Zone." But there is power in some of the new phrasing:

> *God's got your number; He knows*
>   *where you live;*
> *Death's got a warrant for you.*

Instead of college choirs, as earlier, today it is groups closer to the folk like the Golden Gates, the Silver Echoes, the Mitchell Christian Singers, the Coleman Brothers, the Thrasher Wonders and the Original Harmony Kings, who carry the spirituals over the land. These groups and soloists like the Georgia Peach, Mahalia Jackson, Marie Knight and Sister Rosetta Tharpe, once churched for worldly ways but now redeemed, are extremely popular in churches, concert halls, and on record. They swing the spirituals, using a more pronounced rhythm and jazz voicing (some show-groups, alas, imitate even the Mills Brothers and the Ink Spots). Even the more sincere singers, however, fight the devil by using what have been considered the devil's weapons. Tambourines, cymbals, trumpets and even trombones and bass fiddles are now accepted in some churches. The devil has no right to all that fine rhythm, so a joyful noise is made unto the Lord with bounce and swing.

The Gospel Songs, sung "out of the book" as signs of "progress," are displacing the spirituals among the people. These are even more heavily influenced by jazz and the blues. One of the most popular composers of Gospel Songs is Thomas Dorsey, who once played barrelhouse piano under the alias of Georgia Tom. Many lovers of the older spirituals disdain the Gospel Songs as cheap and obvious. But this new urban religious folk music should not be dismissed too lightly. It is vigorously alive with its own musical values, and America turns no unwilling ear to it. And to hear some fervent congregations sing "Just a Closer Walk With Thee," "He Knows How Much You Can Bear," and "We Sure Do Need Him Now" can be unforgettable musical experiences. In sincerity, musical manner, and spirit, they are probably not so remote from the old prayer songs in the brush arbors.

SECULARS AND BALLADS

The slaves had many other moods and concerns than the religious; indeed some of these ran counter to the spirituals. Irreverent parodies of religious songs, whether coming from the black-face minstrelsy or from tough-minded cynical slaves passed current in the quarters. Other-worldliness was mocked: "I don't want to ride no golden chariot; I don't want no golden crown; I want to stay down here and be, Just as I am without one plea." "Live a humble to the Lord" was changed to "Live a humbug." Bible stories, especially the creation, the fall of Man, and the flood, were spoofed. "Reign, Master Jesus, reign" became "Rain, Mosser, rain hard! Rain flour and lard and a big hog head, Down in my back yard." After couplets of nonsense and ribaldry, slaves sang with their fingers crossed, or hopeless in defeat: "Po' mourner, you shall be free, when de good Lord set you free."

Even without the sacrilege, many secular songs were considered "devil-tunes." Especially so were the briskly syncopated lines which, with the clapping of hands and the patting of feet, set the beat for swift, gay dancing. "Juba dis, Juba dat; Juba skin a yeller cat; Juba, Juba!" Remnants of this syncopation are today in such children's play songs as

> *"Did you feed my cow?" "Yes, Maam."*
> *"Will you tell-a me how?" "Yes, Maam."*
> *"Oh, what did you give her?" "Cawn*
>   *and hay."*
> *"Oh, what did you give her?" "Cawn*
>   *and hay."*

Verses for reels made use of the favorite animals of the fables. "Brer Rabbit Brer Rabbit, yo' eare mighty long; Yes, My Lord, they're put on wrong; Every little soul gonna shine; every little soul gonna shine!" Often power and pomp in the guise of the bullfrog and bulldog have the tables turned on them by the sassy blue-jay and crow:

> *A bullfrog dressed in soldier's clothes*
> *Went in de field to shoot some crows,*
> *De crows smell powder and fly away,*
> *De bullfrog mighty mad dat day.*

Even the easy going ox or sheep or hog acquired characteristics:

> *De ole sow say to de boar*
> *I'll tell you what let's do,*
> *Let's go and git dat broad-axe*
> *And die in de pig-pen too.*

Die in de pig-pen fighting,
Die wid a bitin' jaw!

Unlike Stephen Foster's sweet and sad[1] songs such as "Massa's in the Cold, Cold Ground," the folk seculars looked at slavery ironically. And where Foster saw comic nonsense, they added satiric point. Short comments flash us back to social reality: "Ole Master bought a yaller gal, He bought her from the South"; "My name's Ran, I wuks in de sand, I'd rather be a nigger dan a po' white man." Frederick Douglass remembers his fellow slaves singing "We raise de wheat, dey gib us de corn; We sift de meal, dey gib us de huss; We peel de meat, dey gib us de skin; An dat's de way dey take us in."[2] Grousing about food is common: "Milk in the dairy getting mighty old, Skippers and the mice working mighty bold. . . . A long-tailed rat an' a bowl of souse, Jes' come down from de white folk's house." With robust humor, they laughed even at the dread patrollers:

Run, nigger, run, de patterollers will
ketch you
Run, nigger, run; its almost day.
Dat nigger run, dat nigger flew;
Dat nigger tore his shirt in two.

The bitterest secular begins:

My ole Mistis promise me
Fo' she died, she'd set me free;
She lived so long dat her head got bald,
And she give out de notion dyin' at all.

Ole master also failed his promise. Then, with the sharp surprise of the best balladry: "A dose of poison helped him along, May de devil preach his funeral song!"

Under a certain kind of protection the new freedmen took to heart the songs of such an abolitionist as Henry C. Work, and sang exultantly of jubilo. They sang his lines lampooning ole master, and turned out their own:

Missus and mosser a-walkin' de street,
Deir hands in deir pockets and nothin'
to eat.

She'd better be home a-washin' up de
dishes,
An' a-cleanin' up de ole man's raggitty
britches. . . .[3]

But when the protection ran out, the freedmen found the following parody too true:

Our father, who is in heaven,
White man owe me eleven and pay me
seven,
Thy kingdom come, thy will be done,
And if I hadn't took that, I wouldn't
had none.

Toward the end of the century, there was interplay between the folk-seculars and the vaudeville stage, and the accepted stereotypes appeared. "Ain't no use my working so hard, I got a gal in the white folks yard." From tent shows and roving guitar players, the folks accepted such hits as the "Bully Song" and the "coon-songs." "Bill Bailey, Won't You Please Come Home," and "Alabama Bound" shuttled back and forth between the folk and vaudeville. In the honky-tonks ribald songs grew up to become standbys of the early jazz: "Make Me a Pallet on The Floor," "Bucket Got A Hole In It," "Don't you leave me here; if you must go, baby, leave me a dime for beer." "Jelly Roll" Morton's autobiography, now released from the Library of Congress Archives, proves this close connection between the rising jazz and the old folk seculars. In the honky-tonks, songs handled sex freely, even licentiously; and obscenity and vituperation ran rampant in songs called the "dirty dozens."

One of the heroes of secular balladry is Uncle Bud, who was noted for his sexual prowess, a combination Don Juan and John Henry. His song is perhaps as uncollected as it is unprintable. Appreciative tales are told of railroading, of crack trains like The Cannon Ball and The Dixie Flyer, and The Rock Island Line, which is praised in rattling good verses. Such folk delights as hunting with the yipping and baying of the hounds and the yells and cheering of the hunters are vividly recreated.

"Old Dog Blue" has been memorialized over all of his lop-eared kindred. The greatest trailer on earth, Old Blue keeps his unerring sense in heaven; there he treed a possum in Noah's ark. When Old Dog Blue died,

> *I dug his grave wid a silver spade*
> *I let him down wid a golden chain*
> *And every link I called his name;*
> *Go on Blue, you good dog, you!*

The above lines illustrate a feature of Negro folksong worth remarking. Coming from an old sea-chantey "Stormalong," their presence in a song about a hunting dog show the folk habit of lifting what they want and using it how they will. Like southern white groups, the Negro has retained many of the old Scotch-English ballads. Still to be found are Negroes singing "In London town where I was born" and going on to tell of hard-hearted Barbara Allen. John Lomax found a Negro mixing up "Bobby Allen" with the cowboy song "The Streets of Laredo," burying "Miss Allen in a desert of New Mexico with six pretty maidens all dressed in white for her pallbearers."[4] But Negroes hand down fairly straight versions of "Lord Lovel," "Pretty Polly," and "The Hangman's Tree," which has special point for them with its repetend: "Hangman, hangman, slack on the line." The Elizabethan broadside "The Frog Went A-Courtin'" has long been a favorite Negro lullaby. From "The Lass of Roch Royal" two stanzas beginning "Who's gonna shoe yo' little feet" have found their way into the ballad of John Henry. The famous Irish racehorse Stewball reappears in Negro balladry as Skewball and Kimball. English nonsense refrains appear in songs like "Keemo-Kimo" and "Old Bangum." Even the Gaelic "Schule Aroon" has been found among Negroes, though the collector unwarily surmises it to be Guinea or Ebo. Similarly the Negro folk singer lends to and borrows from American balladry. "Casey Jones," though about an engineer, is part of the repertory; it has been

established that a Negro engine-wiper was the first author of it. "Frankie and Johnnie," the most widely known tragedy in America, is attributed to both white and Negro authorship. It could come from either; it probably comes from both; the tenderloin cuts across both sections. Current singers continue the trading of songs: Leadbelly sings cowboy songs, yelling "Ki-yi-yippy-yippy-yay" with his own zest; and Josh White sings "Molly Malone" and "Randall, My Son" with telling power. But it is in narratives of their own heroes that Negro ballad makers have done best.

Prominent among such heroes are fugitives who outtrick and outspeed the law. "Travelin' Man" is more of a coon-song than authentically folk, but the hero whom the cops chased from six in the morning till seven the next afternoon has been warmly adopted by the people. Aboard the Titanic he spied the iceberg and dove off, and "When the old Titanic ship went down, he was shooting crap in Liverpool." More genuine is "Long Gone, Lost John" in which the hero outmatches the sheriff, the police, and the bloodhounds: "The hounds ain't caught me and they never will." Fast enough to hop the Dixie Flyer—"he missed the cowcatcher but he caught the blind"—Lost John can even dally briefly with a girl friend, like Brer Rabbit waiting for Brer Tortoise. But when he travels, he goes far: "the funniest thing I ever seen, was Lost John comin' through Bowlin' Green," but "the last time I seed him he was jumping into Mexico."

When Lost John "doubled up his fist and knocked the police down" his deed wins approval from the audience as much as his winged heels do. With bitter memories and suspicion of the law, many Negroes admire outlaws. Some are just tough killers; one is "a bad, bad man from bad, bad land"; another is going to start "a graveyard all of his own"; another, Roscoe Bill, who sleeps with one ear out because of the rounders about, reports to the judge blandly that

*I didn't quite kill him, but I fixed him
    so dis mornin'
He won't bodder wid me no mo'
Dis mornin', dis evenin', so soon.*

But the favorites, like such western despera-
does as Jesse James, Billy the Kid, and Sam
Bass, stand up against the law. Railroad Bill
(an actual outlaw of southern Alabama) "shot
all the buttons off the sheriff's coat." On the
manhunt, "the policemen dressed in blue,
come down the street two by two." It took a
posse to bring him in dead. Po' Lazarus also
told the deputy to his face that he had never
been arrested "by no one man, Lawd, Lawd,
by no one man." Unlike his Biblical namesake
in nature, Po' Lazarus broke into the commissary. The high sheriff sent the deputy to
bring him back, dead or alive. They found
him "way out between two mountains" and
they "blowed him down."

*They shot Po' Lazarus, shot him with
    a great big number
Number 45, Lawd, Lawd, number 45.*

They laid Po' Lazarus on the commissary
counter, and walked away. His mother, always
worrying over the trouble she had with
Lazarus, sees the body and cries.

*Dat's my only son, Lawd, Lawd, dat's
    my only son.*

In contrast "Stackolee" ends on a hard
note. At Stack's murder trial, his lawyer pleads
for mercy because his aged mother is lying
very low. The prosecutor states that

*Stackolee's aged mammy
Has been dead these 'leven years.*

Starting from a murder in Memphis in a dice
game (some say over a Stetson Hat), Stackolee's
saga has travelled from the Ohio River to the
Brazos; in a Texas version, Stack goes to hell,
challenges the devil to a duel—pitchfork versus
forty-one revolver—and then takes over the
lower world.

One of America's greatest ballads tells of
John Henry. Based on the strength and courage
of an actual hammer-swinging giant, though
in spite of what folk-singers say, his hammer
cannot be seen decorating the Big Bend
Tunnel on the C. & O. Road, John Henry
reflects the struggle of manual labor against
the displacing machine. The ballad starts with
ill omens. Even as a boy John Henry prophe-
sies his death at the Big Bend Tunnel. But he
stays to face it out. Pitting his brawn and
stamina against the new-fangled steam drill,
John Henry says to his captain:

*A man ain't nothing but a man.
But before I'll let that steam driver
    beat me down
I'll die with my hammer in my hand.*

The heat of the contest makes him call for
water (in one variant for tom-cat gin). When
John Henry is momentarily overcome, his
woman, Polly Ann, spelled him, hammering
"like a natural man." At one crucial point,
John Henry gave "a loud and lonesome cry,"
saying, "A hammer'll be the death of me."
But the general tone is self-confidence. John
Henry throws the hammer from his hips on
down, "Great gawd amighty how she rings!"
He warns his shaker (the holder of the drill)
that if ever he misses that piece of steel,
"tomorrow'll be yo' burial day." His captain,
hearing the mighty rumbling, thinks the
mountain must be caving in. John Henry
says to the captain: "It's my hammer swinging
in the wind." Finally he defeats the drill,
but the strain kills him. The people gather
round, but all he asks is "a cool drink of
water 'fo I die." Polly Ann swears to be true
to the memory (although in another version
she turns out to be as fickle as Mrs. Casey
Jones). John Henry was buried near the railroad where

*Every locomotive come a-roarin' by
Says, "There lies a steel-drivin' man,
    Lawd, Lawd;
There lies a steel-drivin' man."*

The topical nature of American balladry
is seen in "Boll Weevil," a ballad that grew

up almost as soon as the swarm of pests descended. "Come up from Mexico, they say."

> *The first time I seed the boll weevil*
> *He was sitting on the square—*

(The folk poet puns on the "square" of the cotton boll, and the familiar southern town square.) A tough little rascal is celebrated who, when buried in the hot sand, says "I can stand it like a man"; when put into ice, says: "This is mighty cool and nice," and thrives and breeds right on, until finally he can take over:

> *You better leave me alone*
> *I done et up all your cotton,*
> *And now I'll start on your corn.*

The ballad has grim side glances; the boll weevil didn't leave "the farmer's wife but one old cotton dress"; made his nest in the farmer's "best Sunday hat"; and closed the church doors since the farmer couldn't pay the preacher.

> *Oh, de Farmer say to de Merchant*
> *I ain't made but only one bale*
> *An' befo' I bring you dat one*
> *I'll fight an' go to jail*
> *I'll have a home*
> *I'll have a home.*

The stanzaic forms and general structure of "John Henry" and "The Boll Weevil" are fairly developed. One of the best folk ballads, however, is in the simpler, unrhymed African leader-chorus design. This is "The Grey Goose," a ballad about a seemingly ordinary fowl who becomes a symbol of ability to take it. It is a song done with the highest spirits: the "Lord, Lord, Lord" of the responding chorus expressing amazement, flattery, and good-humored respect for the tough bird:

> *Well, last Monday mornin'*
> *Lord, Lord, Lord!*
> *Well, last Monday mornin'*
> *Lord, Lord, Lord!*

They went hunting for the grey goose. When shot "Boo-loom!" the grey goose was six weeks a-falling. Then it was six weeks a-finding, and once in the white house, was six weeks a-picking. Even after the great feather-picking he was six months parboiling. And then on the table, the forks couldn't stick him; the knife couldn't cut him. So they threw him in the hog-pen where he broke the sow's jaw-bone. Even in the sawmill, he broke the saw's teeth out. He was indestructible. Last seen the grey goose was flying across the ocean, with a long string of goslings, all going "Quank-quink-quank." Yessir, it was one hell of a gray goose. Lord, Lord, Lord!

WORK SONGS AND SOCIAL PROTEST

More work songs come from the Negro than from any other American folk group. Rowing the cypress dug-outs in Carolina low-country, slaves timed their singing to the long sweep of the oars. The leader, a sort of cox-swain, chanted verse after verse; the rowers rumbled a refrain. On the docks Negroes sang sailors' chanteys as metronomes to their heaving and hauling. Some chanteys, like "Old Stormy," they took over from the white seamen; others they improvised. Along the Ohio and Mississippi waterfronts Negro roustabouts created "coonjine" songs, so-called after the shuffling dance over bucking gang-planks in and out of steamboat holds. Unless the rhythm was just right a roustabout and his bale or sack of cottonseed might be jolted into the brown waters. The singers cheered the speed of the highballing paddlewheelers: "left Baton Rouge at half pas' one, and got to Vicksburg at settin of de sun." But they griped over the tough captains "workin' hell out of me" and sang

> *Ole Roustabout ain't got no home*
> *Makes his livin' on his shoulder bone.*

For release from the timber and the heavy sacks there was always some city around the bend—Paducah, Cairo, Memphis, Natchez, and then

> *Alberta let yo' hair hang low . . .*
> *I'll give you mo' gold*
> *Than yo' apron can hold . . .*
> *Alberta let yo' hair hang low.*

These songs flourished in the hey-day of the packets; today they are nearly lost.

Another type of work song was chanted as a gang unloaded steel rails. Since these rails weighed over a ton apiece and were over ten yards long, any break in the rhythm of lifting them from the flat cars to the ground was a good way to get ruptured, maimed, or killed. So a chanter was employed to time the hoisting, lowering, and the getting away from it. He was a coach, directing the teamwork, and in self-protection the men had to learn his rhythmic tricks. In track-lining, a similar chanter functioned to keep the track straight in line. As he called, the men jammed their bars under the rails and braced in unison:

> *Shove it over! Hey, hey, can't you line it!*
> *Ah shack-a-lack-a-lack-a-lack-a-lack-a-*
> *lack-alack (Grunt)*
> *Can't you move it? Hey, hey, can't you*
> *try.*[5]

As they caught their breath and got a new purchase, he turned off a couplet. Then came the shouted refrain as the men strained together.

More widely spread and known are the Negro work songs whose rhythm is timed with the swing back and down and the blow of broad-axe, pick, hammer, or tamper. The short lines are punctuated by a grunt as the axe bites into the wood, or the hammer finds the spike-head.

> *Dis ole hammer—hunh*
> *Ring like silver—hunh (3)*
> *Shine like gold, baby—hunh*
> *Shine like gold—hunh.*

The leader rings countless changes in his words and melody over the unchanging rhythm. When he grows dull or forgets, another singer takes over. The song is consecutive, fluid; it is doubtful if any one version is ever exactly repeated. Ballads, blues, even church-songs are levied on for lines, a simple matter since the stanzas are unrhymed. Some lines tell of the satisfaction of doing a man's work well:

> *I got a rainbow—hunh*
> *Tied 'round my shoulder—hunh—(3)*
> *Tain't gonna rain, baby—hunh*
> *Tain't gonna rain.*

(The rainbow is the arc of the hammer as the sunlight glints on the moving metal.) Sometimes a singer boasts of being a "sun-down man," who can work the sun down without breaking down himself. Lines quite as popular, however, oppose any speed-up stretch-out system:

> *Dis ole hammer—hunh*
> *Killt John Henry—hunh—(3)*
> *Twon't kill me, baby—hunh*
> *Twon't kill me.*

Some lines get close to the blues: "Every mail day / Gits a letter / Son, come home, baby / Son, come home." Sometimes they tell of a hard captain (boss)

> *Told my captain—hunh*
> *Hands are cold—hunh—(3)*
> *Damn yo' hands—hunh*
> *Let de wheelin' roll.*

The new-fangled machine killed John Henry; its numerous offspring have killed the work songs of his buddies. No hammer song could compete now with the staccato roaring drill even if the will to sing were there. The steamboat is coming back to the Mississippi but the winches and cranes do not call forth the old gang choruses. A few songs connected with work survive such as the hollers of the lonely worker in the fields and woods, or the call boy's chant to the glory-hole.

> *Sleeping good, sleeping good,*
> *Give me them covers, I wish you would.*

At ease from their work in their bunkhouses, the men may sing, but their fancies ramble from the job oftener than they stay with it. Song as a rhythmic accompaniment to work is declining. John and Alan Lomax, whose bag of Negro work songs is the fullest, had to go to the penitentiaries, where labor-saving devices were not yet numerous, in order to find the art thriving. They found lively cotton-picking songs:

> A-pick a bale, a-pick a bale
> Pick a bale of cotton
> A-pick a bale, a-pick a bale
> Pick a bale a day.[6]

Slower songs came from gangs that were cutting cane or chopping weeds or hewing timber. Prison work is of course mean and tough: "You oughta come on de Brazo in nineteen-fo'; you could find a dead man on every turn-row." So the convicts cry out to the taskmaster sun:

> Go down, Ol' Hannah, doncha rise no
> mo'
> Ef you rise any mo' bring judgment day.

They grouse about the food: ever "the same damn thing," and at that the cook isn't clean. An old evangelical stand-by, "Let the Light of the Lighthouse Shine On Me," becomes a hymn of hope that the Midnight Special, a fast train, will some day bring a pardon from the governor. They sing of their long sentences:

> Ninety-nine years so jumpin' long
> To be here rollin' an' cain' go home.

If women aren't to be blamed for it all, they are still to be blamed for a great deal:

> Ain't but de one thing worries my min'
> My cheating woman and my great
> long time.

One song, like the best balladry, throws a searchlight into the darkness:

> "Little boy, what'd you do for to get so
> long?"
> Said, "I killed my rider in the high
> sheriff's arms."

From these men—long-termers, lifers, three-time losers—come songs brewed in bitterness. This is not the double-talk of the slave seculars, but the naked truth of desperate men telling what is on their brooding minds. Only to collectors who have won their trust—such as the Lomaxes, Lawrence Gellert and Josh White—

and only when the white captain is far enough away, do the prisoners confide these songs. Then they sing not loudly but deeply their hatred of the brutality of the chain-gang:

> If I'd a had my weight in lime
> I'd a whupped dat captain, till he
> went stone blind.
>
> If you don't believe my buddy's dead
> Just look at that hole in my buddy's
> head.[7]

A prisoner is told: "Don't you go worryin' about forty [the years of your sentence], Cause in five years you'll be dead."

They glorify the man who makes a crazy dare for freedom; Jimbo, for instance, who escapes almost under the nose of his captain, described as "a big Goliath," who walks like Samson and "totes his talker." They boast: "Ef ah git de drop / Ah'm goin' on / Dat same good way / Dat Jimbo's gone / Lawd, Lawd, Lawd."[8] They reenact with graphic realism the lashing of a fellow-prisoner; the man-hunting of Ol' Rattler, "fastest and smellingest bloodhound in the South"; and the power of Black Betty, the ugly bull-whip. They make stark drama out of the pain, and hopelessness, and shame.

> All I wants is dese cold iron shackles
> off my leg.

It is not only in the prison songs that there is social protest. Where there is some protection or guaranteed secrecy other *verboten* songs come to light. Coal miners, fortified by a strong, truculent union, sing grimly of the exorbitant company stores:

> What's de use of me working any
> more, my baby? (2)
> What's de use of me working any
> more,
> When I have to take it up at de
> company store,
> My baby?[9]

Or they use the blues idiom with a new twist:

> Operator will forsake you, he'll drive
> you from his do' . . .

> No matter what you do, dis union
>   gwine to stand by you
> While de union growing strong in dis
>   land.[10]

And the sharecroppers sharply phrase their plight:

> Go in the store and the merchant
>   would say,
> 'Your mortgage is due and I'm looking
>   for my pay.'
> Down in his pocket with a tremblin'
>   hand
> 'Can't pay you all but I'll pay what I
>   can,'
> Then to the telephone the merchant
>   made a call,
> They'll put you on the chain-gang, an'
>   you don't pay at all.[11]

Big Bill Broonzy is best known as a blues singer, but in the cotton belt of Arkansas he learned a great deal that sank deep. His sharp "Black, Brown, and White Blues" has the new militancy built up on the sills of the old folksong. In an employment office, Big Bill sings. "They called everybody's number / But they never did call mine." Then working side by side with a white man:

> He was getting a dollar an hour
> When I was making fifty cents.

Onto this new protest he ties an old vaudeville chorus, deepening the irony:

> If you's black, ah brother,
> Git back, git back, git back.[12]

Such songs, together with the blues composed by Waring Cuney and Josh White on poverty, hardship, poor housing and jim crow military service, come from conscious propagandists, not truly folk. They make use of the folk idiom in both text and music, however, and the folk listen and applaud. They know very well what Josh White is talking about in such lines as:

> Great gawdamighty, folks feelin' bad
> Lost everything they ever had.

PROSPECT

It is evident that Negro folk culture is breaking up. Where Negro met only with Negro in the black belt the old beliefs strengthened. But when mud traps give way to gravel roads, and black tops and even concrete highways with buses and jalopies and trucks lumbering over them, the world comes closer. The churches and schools, such as they are, struggle against some of the results of isolation, and the radio plays a part. Even in the backwoods, aerials are mounted on shanties that seem ready to collapse from the extra weight on the roof, or from a good burst of static against the walls. The phonograph is common, the television set is by no means unknown, and down at the four corners store, a jukebox gives out the latest jive. Rural folk closer to towns and cities may on Saturday jaunts even see an occasional movie, where a rootin'-tootin' Western gangster film introduces them to the advancements of civilization. Newspapers, especially the Negro press, give the people a sense of belonging to a larger world. Letters from their boys in the army, located in all corners of the world, and the tales of the returning veterans, true Marco Polos, also prod the inert into curiosity. Brer Rabbit and Old Jack no longer are enough. Increasingly in the churches the spirituals lose favor to singing out of the books or from broadsides, and city-born blues and jive take over the jook-joints.

The migration of the folk Negro to the cities, started by the hope for better living and schooling, and greater self-respect, quickened by the industrial demands of two world wars is sure to be increased by the new cotton picker and other man-displacing machines. In the city the folk become a submerged proletariat. Leisurely yarn-spinning, slow-paced aphoristic conversation become lost arts; jazzed-up gospel hymns provide a different sort of release from the old spirituals; the blues reflect the distortions of the new way of life. Folk arts are no longer by the folk for the folk; smart businessmen now put them up for sale. Gospel songs often become show-pieces for radio slummers, and the blues become the double-talk of the dives. And yet, in spite of the commercializing, the folk roots often show a stubborn vitality. Just as the transplanted folk may show the old credulity, though the sophisticated impulse sends them to an American Indian for nostrums, or for fortune-telling to an East Indian "madame" with a turban around her head rather than to a mammy with a bandanna around her's; so the folk for all their disorganization may keep something of the fine quality of their old tales and songs. Assuredly even in the new gospel songs and blues much is retained of the phrasing and the distinctive musical manner. Finally, it should be pointed out that even in the transplanting, a certain kind of isolation—class and racial—remains. What may come of it, if anything, is unpredictable, but so far the vigor of the creative impulse has not been snapped, even in the slums.

Whatever may be the future of the folk Negro, American literature as well as American music is the richer because of his expression. Just as Huckleberry Finn and Tom Sawyer were fascinated by the immense lore of their friend Jim, American authors have been drawn to Negro folk life and character. With varying authenticity and understanding, Joel Chandler Harris, Du Bose Heyward, Julia Peterkin, Roark Bradford, Marc Connelly, E. C. L. Adams, Zora Neale Hurston and Langston Hughes have all made rewarding use of this material. Folk Negroes have them-selves bequeathed a wealth of moving song, both religious and secular, of pithy folk-say and entertaining and wise folk-tales. They have settled characters in the gallery of American heroes; resourceful Brer Rabbit and Old Jack, and indomitable John Henry. They have told their own story so well that all men should be able to hear it and understand.

Notes

1. Thomas Talley, *Negro Folk Rhymes* (New York, 1922), p. 39.

2. Frederick Douglass, *Life and Times* (Hartford, Conn., 1882), p. 39

3. Talley. *op. cit.,* p. 97.

4. John Lomax, *Adventure of A Ballad Hunter* (New York, 1947), p. 179.

5. Zora Neale Hurston, *Mules and Men* (Philadelphia, 1935), p. 322.

6. The Library of Congress, Music Division. Archive of American Folk Song for this and the following quotations.

7. Josh White, *Chain Gang Songs* (Bridgeport, Conn., Columbia Recording Corporation), Set C-22.

8. Willis James, "Hyah Come De Cap'n," from Brown, Davis, and Lee, *The Negro Caravan* (New York, 1948), p. 469.

9. John and Alan Lomax, *Our Singing Country* (New York, 1941), pp. 278–288.

10. *Ibid.*

11. *Ibid.*

12. *People's Songs*, Vol. I, No. 10 (Nov. 1940), p. 9.

Black Beauty, Black Confusion (1965–70)

NELSON GEORGE

SPEAKING AT HOWARD UNIVERSITY'S 1965 commencement, Lyndon Baines Johnson pledged his total effort to bring blacks into the mainstream. His rhetoric was met with the cheers of the students and faculty of the prestigious black university in Washington, D.C. For, unlike so many speech-makers of the sixties, Johnson could, as president of the United States, back up what he promised. The legislative landmarks—the 1964 Civil Rights Act prohibiting racial segregation in public accommodations and the 1965 Voting Rights Act barring all forms of racial and religious discrimination in voting procedures—passed because Johnson, a white rural Southerner, believed in them enough to push them through. Johnson moved blacks into the heart of his government, naming five black ambassadors, the first black to a Cabinet-level position (Robert Weaver, director of the Department of Housing and Urban Development), and placed Thurgood Marshall on the Supreme Court.

Marshall's ascension to the nation's highest court was his just reward for successfully pursuing case after case for the NAACP—and black America—over his long career. Throughout the 1960s and into the 1980s Marshall would as a jurist, just as he had as a lawyer, fulfill the integrationist agenda of the "new Negro."

While Judge Marshall prospered and pressed on, two of his most important contemporaries stumbled. In 1965 Adam Clayton Powell, Jr., was one of Congress's most influential legislators. He'd been in the House of Representatives twenty years and, considering how loved he was in Harlem, it appeared he'd be there another twenty. In Chicago on March 28, 1965, he introduced a seventeen-point program, "My Black Position Paper for America's 20 Million Negroes," which was far from the assimilationist rhetoric of his peers. Powell spoke of blacks seeking "audacious power—the kind of power which cradles your head amongst the stars"—and fused the ideas of Washington and Du Bois by demanding that the civil-rights movement "shift its emphasis to the two-pronged thrust of the Black

From *The Death of Rhythm and Blues* by Nelson George. Copyright © 1988 by Nelson George. Reprinted by permission of Pantheon Books, a division of Random House, Inc.

Revolution: economic self-sufficiency and political power." He felt the legislation of Johnson, particularly the 1964 Civil Rights Act, meant nothing in the North without the economic component of "black power" to support it. More than any other leader of his generation, Powell articulated the dissatisfaction of young blacks with the traditional integrationist views of the civil-rights movement and the rising currents of black nationalism it fueled among activists.

Unfortunately, Powell never had a chance to pursue the vision put forward in his position paper. As reckless in his personal life as he was charismatic on the podium, Powell was a poor manager and had messy personal entanglements with women. Both made him vulnerable to attack. A lawsuit by a female constituent charging him with abuse led Powell, in 1967, to be stripped of his committee chairmanship and then his seat. Later that year Harlem would vote him back into Congress, but his colleagues refused to seat him. Finally, in 1969, after a suit to regain his seat was won in the Supreme Court, Powell was returned to Congress, but without his seniority. And by then, he was a broken man. He lost the 1970 congressional election and died two years later.

Martin Luther King, Jr., confronted a different barrier, but one that was almost as damaging to his effectiveness. In the fall of 1965 he announced that his Southern Christian Leadership Conference would begin an offensive in Chicago, hoping to use Southern civil-rights techniques in what King called the most "ghettoized" city of the North. He said, "The nonviolent movement must be as much directed against the violence of segregation. . . . Egypt still exists in Chicago but the Pharaohs are more sophisticated and subtle."

Alas, King was right. Mayor Richard Daley, last of the big-city Irish power brokers of the North and a man as willful as any Pharaoh, was ready for Dr. King. So were a raft of complications he hadn't confronted during civil-rights triumphs in Birmingham and Selma. In Chicago, many local black leaders had intimate financial ties to Daley's white power structure. As a result, King never enjoyed the undivided support of Chicago's strong black establishment. Also, in contrast to their attitude during the Southern struggle, the national media weren't as supportive of the Chicago campaign and often suggested that the Nobel Peace Prize winner was now misguided. Daley outflanked King by shrewdly offering him a role in an existing antipoverty program. This offer allowed Daley to portray King as a disruptive force in the city. It didn't help that King had come out against the Vietnam War when that was still a radical stance, particularly for a civil-rights leader dependent on the good will of government officials. Many Chicago whites who'd applauded King's victories in the South were uncomfortable when blamed for the economic disparities in their city. While the Southern Jim Crow barriers had presented easily identifiable (and distant) targets for reform, in Chicago it was difficult to convince whites that they had a responsibility to participate in rectifying economic discrimination. For white Chicagoans it was one thing to abolish racist laws. It was quite another to establish government policies ensuring blacks a chance at a life-style equivalent to whites.

Ultimately, after over a year of struggle and the threat of a potentially violent mass demonstration in nearby Cicero—the same city where that black family was almost lynched in the 1950s—King and Daley signed an open-housing agreement. It was a nice piece of writing, full of the right words and positions. But the bottom line was that King's energies had been wasted. Nothing had changed. Chicago was the same divided city the day he left as it had been before he arrived. King's only legacy to Chicago was an organization called Operation Breadbasket he left in the hands of an ambitious young minister named Jesse Jackson.

As King returned to the South, a leader clearly wounded by the lost Chicago struggle, black America bled into the streets. Watts and Chicago experienced black riots in 1965. Within two years, Tampa, Cincinnati, Atlanta, Newark, and Detroit all had similar explosions in the heart of their black communities, and would suffer even more unrest in 1968 when King was assassinated in Memphis. Because of the riots, "Black Main Street, U.S.A." became a series of before-and-after photographs, filled with businesses that in a blaze of anger became burnt-out shells. In place of stores came short-lived antipoverty programs. Once primarily the bane of jazzmen, heroin flooded the streets of black neighborhoods, infecting the children of the 1960s with a horrifying disease which eventually led them to crimes that debased their community and themselves. Civil rights, self-sufficiency, protest, politics . . . all of it faded for those trapped in the shooting galleries of the body and the mind.

The civil-rights struggle was not dead, but its energy was increasingly scattered. The Black Panthers embraced communism. Ron Karenga's U.S. organization advocated an Afrocentric cultural nationalism that saw African tradition as the cure for American ills. Powell's Black Power came to mean whatever its user needed it to. Of course, the assimilationists pressed on, encouraged by government support and anti-discrimination laws, though the leadership vacuum left by King's murder was immense.

But in the R&B world—known by then as "the world of soul"—there was no such leadership gap, no energy scattered, no philosophical conflict. The most powerful individual on the scene had arrogance, black appeal, and a cultural integrity that was the envy of the young-blood political activists of the civil-rights center and the nationalist left. His name was James Brown.

THE GODFATHER

During the 1960s James Brown singlehandedly demonstrated the possibilities for artistic and economic freedom that black music could provide if one constantly struggled against its limitations. Brown was more than R&B's most dynamic performer. "J.B." used his prestige as a weapon to push through innovations in the sound and the marketing of black music. Though Berry Gordy's name tops the list of black music's great entrepreneurs, Brown's efforts—despite being directed in a single-minded celebration of self—are in some ways just as impressive. He was driven by an enormous ambition and unrelenting ego, making him a living symbol of black self-determination. White managers may have made all the business decisions for most black stars, but Brown maneuvered his white manager, Jack Bart, and later his son, Ben, into a comanaging situation, where no crucial decisions (and few minor ones) could be made without the singer's input. In the early sixties, when Brown's contemporaries (and rivals) Jackie Wilson and Sam Cooke traveled with, at best, a guitar and a bass player, Brown built a raucous revue backed by the preeminent big band of its era, one that performed with the flair of Louis Jordan's Tympany Five and the discipline of the Count Basie orchestra. Where booking agents and arena managers often dictated appearances to even the biggest R&B acts, Brown's organization used their clout to demand the best dates and biggest dollars. Eschewing national promoters, Brown handled the chore himself, cutting out the middlemen, which allowed him to offer black retailers and deejays a piece of the action in exchange for special promotional "consideration." Motown may have been the sound of young America, but Brown was clearly the king of black America. How he managed his kingdom illustrates his impact and remains his enduring legacy.

Brown was rightfully dubbed "the hardest-working man in show business" because of a work load of five to six one-nighters a week from the mid-sixties through the early seventies. Until 1973 he worked anywhere from nine to eleven months a year. The only breaks in his

**James Brown,
godfather of "soul."**

nonstop touring came when he played a lengthy stand at the Apollo, Howard, Uptown, or elsewhere. What isn't generally known is that this rigorous schedule was very much of Brown's own making. Every two months or so Brown and his road managers (in the late 1960s it was Bob Patton and Alan Leeds) would pull out the Rand-McNally maps and decide the show's routing. A key city, "a money town" they called it, would be picked for the crucial Friday and Saturday night dates. Brown and company would then study the map and judge the next town they could reach comfortably by the next night. If they played

Philadelphia's Uptown on Friday, maybe they'd hit Richmond, Virginia, Saturday, and Fayetteville, Arkansas, on Sunday. An ideal schedule would be laid out and then Brown's employees would call around the country to see if the show could be booked according to their plan. More often than not it was, since Brown was much loved by arena managers. For all the grit and earthiness of his music, Brown put on a clean show—no cursing, no gross sexuality—that brought in the entire family. Since arenas dealt directly with Brown's organization, instead of going through a local promoter, they never worried that Brown wouldn't show up or would be late—all conse-quences for such unprofessional conduct would fall directly on Brown. Brown's team was very sensitive to not overbooking a lucra-tive market and squeezing it dry. They tried to space dates in a "money town" between six to nine months apart and played slow mar-kets once every year and a half.

Since Brown controlled his always lucrative shows, he was able to use them to reward and penalize deejays or retailers who had or had not cooperated in promoting his material. In smaller cities, Brown often awarded deejays, notoriously underpaid as we've seen, a piece of the date, ensuring both their loyalty and the play of Brown's current release in the weeks prior to his appearance. In many cases these deejays became known in the market as "Mr. Brown's representatives"—a prestigious title in the black community—and were expected to provide Brown's organization with firsthand feedback on his records and supervise distribution of posters promoting the show.

The local deejays, in conjunction with Brown's national office, coordinated radio time buys and the purchase of advertising space in the black press beginning two months before Brown came to town. Usually two weeks before the appearance, Brown's office would monitor ticket sales to see if additional promotional efforts (radio spots, ticket give-aways, etc.) were needed.

Unlike today's tours, where tons of equip-ment are carried from city to city by a convoy of trucks, the entire James Brown Revue— forty to fifty people and all the gear—traveled in one truck and one bus. In the mid- to late 1960s the show's equipment consisted of two Supertrooper spotlights, one microphone, and an amplifier for the saxophones. The drum and rhythm section (bass, guitars) weren't mixed at all except for their own onstage amplifiers. Road manager Leeds remem-bers that in 1966, when Brown introduced

a flickering strobe light into the act while dancing "the mashed potato, people in the audience were awestruck."

In 1985 it took the recording of "We Are the World" and the Live Aid concert to bring top stars and musicians together. In the R&B world twenty years before, it was customary for any other musicians in town to come around and say hello to the touring star. Backstage at a James Brown concert was a party, networking conference, and rehearsal studio all in one. Part of this was just profes-sional camaraderie, though for many musi-cians these gatherings allowed them to bid for a spot in Brown's band. In the late 1960s, with Brown's low man making $400 a week and veteran players around $900, he was paying among the most generous rates in R&B.

Moreover, critics, deejays, and even other players generally acknowledged the band to be the best of its kind. Some thought Otis Redding's Bar-Kays were tough. So were the guys Sam and Dave used. Same for Joe Tex's band. But the JBs, as they came to be called, earned their reputation because they were as strong-willed and intense about their music as their boss. Under the guidance of Brown and superb mid-sixties bandleader Alfred (Pee Wee) Ellis, the JBs took the rhythm & blues basics laid down by Louis Jordan and his disciples and created a style, now known as funk, that inspired Sly Stone, George Clinton, and so many others to come.

Funk evolved while the JBs were on the road, on the tour bus, in hotels, backstage, and in hastily called recording sessions. A great many of Brown's pioneering dance jams were cut following concerts, including the early funk experiment from 1967, "Cold Sweat," and the landmark 1970 single "Sex Machine." Often a rare off-day would sud-denly become a work day when the musical mood struck Brown. He liked to record his music as soon as he got an idea. The spark often came on the road, as Ellis and the players strove to keep the show fresh. With these rearrangements, new songs emerged from old.

For example, in January 1967, Brown's "Let Yourself Go," a two-and-a-half minute dance track now little recalled, reached number five on *Billboard's* soul chart. One reason it has faded from memory is that it was eventually overshadowed by a better song created from its chords. On the road that winter, "Let Yourself Go" became a ten-minute jam during which Brown displayed his mastery of several dances, including the camel walk and the mashed potato. While he was performing at the Apollo, someone pointed out that the jam was virtually a new tune. As a result, "There Was a Time," a song marked by one of the JBs' best horn lines, was recorded live and went on to become one of Brown's funkiest hits. As the melodies of Brown's songs became more rudimentary, and the interlocking rhythmic patterns grew more complex, the JBs began to use horns, guitar, and keyboards—usually melodic instruments—as tools of percussion. Short, bitter blasts of brass and reeds now punctuated the grooves and complemented Brown's harsh, declamatory vocals. Listening to recordings of the JBs from 1967 to 1969, the band's most innovative period, it is hard at times to distinguish the guitars from the congas because the band is so focused on rhythmic interplay.

As Robert Palmer wrote in the *Rolling Stone Illustrated History,* "Brown, his musicians, and his arrangers began to treat every instrument and voice in the group as if it were a drum. The horns played single-note bursts that were often sprung against downbeats. The bass lines were broken up into choppy two- and three-note patterns, a procedure common in Latin music since the forties but unusual in R&B." "Sheer energy" is what writer Al Young felt when he first heard Brown's classic "Cold Sweat." "James Brown was pushing and pulling

and radiating in ultra-violent concentric circles of thermo-radiant funk," Young said. By the time of Brown's last great recording, "The Big Payback" in 1973, the JBs sounded as tense and sparse as a Hemingway short story, though admittedly a lot easier to dance to.

Brown's relentless flow of singles, many released in two parts, were products of an uncontrollable creative ferment. The grooves simply couldn't be contained by the three-minute 45 RPM format of the day. Unfortunately, the twelve-inch single was not yet in vogue; it would have been the perfect format for Brown's propulsive music. But today Brown's output would be constrained by other marketing strategies and corporate-release patterns—the conventional wisdom that only so much product can be put out in any twelve-month period. At King Records, however, his recording home during his greatest years, Brown had carte blanche. It was a power he had fought for and won.

The sales of his 1962 *Live at the Apollo* were phenomenal. Even without wide white support, the record went gold at a time when most black studio albums sold only 200,000 copies; it stayed on *Billboard's* album chart for sixty-six weeks, and reached number two. Despite this success, Brown felt his singles weren't being marketed properly. So in an ambitious stab at gaining more control of his career, in 1964 Brown formed Fair Deal Productions, and, instead of delivering his next set of recordings to King, he sent them to Smash, a subsidiary of Chicago's Mercury Records. One of the records was "Out of Sight," a brilliant cut that in its use of breaks—sections where voices, horns, or guitars are heard unaccompanied—anticipated the work of disco deejays of the next decade. With Mercury's greater clout, the song became one of Brown's first records to reach whites.

Syd Nathan, King's feisty president and a charter member of the R&B indie old school, didn't hesitate to sue, and for almost a year,

Brown, Nathan, and Mercury battled. The outcome: Brown stayed with King, but Nathan promised more aggressive promotion and gave Brown broader artistic control—similar to what Ray Charles enjoyed at Atlantic and ABC and Sam Cooke had with SAR and later at RCA. It was this control that would allow Brown to make the most controversial and important records of his career.

Dr. Martin Luther King, Jr., was assassinated in Memphis on April 4, 1968. Brown was booked for that night at the Boston Garden. Initially city officials were going to cancel the show, in light of the riots shaking Boston's black neighborhoods. Then the idea of broadcasting the show live on public television stations was suggested as a way to keep angry blacks off the streets. And so it was. Today, tapes of that performance are bootlegged and still treasured by black-music fans. At the time, it served its purpose, keeping the historically tense relations between whites and blacks in that "liberal" city cool, at least for the evening.

For Brown, never one lacking in self-esteem, this confirmed his power in black America, a power that the previous summer had led vice-president and presidential candidate Hubert Humphrey to give him an award for helping quell riots with public statements. A capitalist and a patriot (he played for troops in Vietnam and Korea), Brown was also genuinely moved by the black-pride movement. Seeking to fulfill his role as a leader, he cut "America Is My Home," and was branded an Uncle Tom by radical blacks. (His "Living in America" is the 1986 counterpart.) But he saw no contradiction, and shouldn't have, when he released "Say It Loud, I'm Black and I'm Proud" in the summer of 1968. Supported by the JBs' usual rhythmic intensity, Brown shouted out a testimonial to black pride that, like the phrase "Black Power," was viewed as a call to arms by many whites. For a time Brown's "safe" reputation with whites in the entertainment business suffered. In interviews,

Brown has blamed resentful whites for his failure to enjoy another top-ten pop single until the 1980s. (In 1969 "Mother Popcorn" reached number eleven and "Give It Up or Turn It Loose" number fifteen.) Still, it didn't deter Brown from his newfound leadership role, and he went on to cut the message-oriented "I Don't Want Nobody to Give Me Nothing," the motivational "Get Up, Get Into It, Get Involved," the prideful "Soul Power," the cynical "Talking Loud and Saying Nothing," and the nondance rap record "King Heroin," a black jail-house rhyme put to music. The irony of Brown's musical statements and public posturing as "Soul Brother #1" was that he became an embarrassingly vocal supporter of that notoriously antiblack politician, Richard Milhous Nixon.

Much of Nixon's appeal for Brown was the president's advocacy of "black capitalism," a seemingly fine philosophy that saw an increase in black-owned businesses as the key to black advancement. At the time, Brown owned several radio stations, much property, and a growing organization. He identified with black capitalism's self-reliant tone. Nixon, who understood the desire for power, made Brown feel he was a key example of black capitalism at work, which appealed to the singer's gigantic ego. Brown didn't understand the nuances of Nixon's plan—reach out to showcase some black business efforts while dismantling Johnson's Great Society programs, which for all their reputed mismanagement had helped a generation of blacks begin the process of upward mobility.

But naive though he might have been about Nixon, Brown did choose this juncture in his long career to assume some kind of leadership role in black America. It wasn't enough for him to be an artist anymore; he saw himself as a spokesman with as much right to articulate his world view as H. Rap Brown, Stokely Carmichael, Eldridge Cleaver, or any of the other more obviously political figures who professed authority. The "Godfather of Soul" had decided that he, too, could aggressively project his vision.

Looking back I find it is simply impossible to resolve all the contradictions in James Brown. As a businessman with a long and lucrative career based on astute self-management, he was a sterling example, and advocate, of black self-sufficiency. He was also as happy as he could be within the white-dominated system, buying diamond rings for his fingers with the profits from his white fans. A stone-cold assimilationist in the general political realm, he carried himself with an arrogant, superconfident demeanor that in fact wasn't far removed from the street-corner polemical style of other, far more radical sixties black spokesmen. In a way, it is these very contradictions—and Brown's own unbothered attitude about them—that make him a consummate American.

There is another aspect of Brown, though, that causes some unease if we try to hold him up as a kind of model. Given the unbridled machismo that was part and parcel of the energy driving him (as well as Carmichael, Cleaver, and others), black women were simply attached as a postscript to a male-directed message. As Michelle Wallace, with some overstatement but a lot of truth, observed in *Black Macho and the Myth of the Superwoman,* these men thought of women as mothers, cooks, and servants of the revolution, not as its leaders. It didn't have to be that way. Black women were, of course, as capable of leadership as any male. Fallout from this political patriarchy would be felt in black literature in the future, but in the late 1960s, feminist issues weren't overtly part of the agendas of the nationalist or even civil-rights movements.

THE QUEEN

Yet the one voice that spoke most directly to the aroused black psyche of the 1960s, though apolitical and preoccupied with struggles of the heart, was a woman's. If anyone wondered what "soul" was, all they had to do was play any of Aretha Franklin's Atlantic albums.

From 1967, when she joined Atlantic after six frustrating years at Columbia—when she recorded pop standards and traditional blues that didn't highlight her fiery gospel style—until about 1971, Aretha Franklin was not just indisputedly the best singer in the R&B-soul world but the focus for, to use a sixties cliché, the positive spiritual energy of her listeners. As daughter of Detroit's flamboyant and strong-voiced Reverend C. L. Franklin, Aretha was an heir to a legacy of redemption through music. At the same time, her widely publicized marital problems—*Time* made them an essential part of a June 1968 cover story—and her unmistakable voice made her the epitome of soul music, just as Ray Charles had been a decade before. Ah, that voice. One of the more cogent passages from the *Time* piece describes Franklin's approach as a "direct natural style of delivery that ranges over a full four octaves, and the breath control to spin out long phrases that curl sensuously around the beat and dangle tantalizingly from blue notes. But what really accounts for her impact goes beyond technique: it is her fierce, gritty conviction."

Jerry Wexler, in the wisest move of his long career, recorded Franklin at Fame Studio, in Muscle Shoals, Alabama, and at Criteria Studio in Miami, with Southern session men—white and black—who gave her voice the kind of complementary musical backing that had eluded her at Columbia. The songs were written by Aretha, or specifically written for her and chosen by her, with the rhythm arrangements usually built around her gospel-style piano. In a time when popular black, and then white, slang ("Do your thing!" "Sock it to me!") were admonitions to be loose, uninhibited, and natural, few things communicated these values better than Franklin's vocals. Despite singing love songs, many of them quite melancholy, Franklin's voice communicated so wide a range of emotion as to truly defy description.

"Intangible" is a word that music critics overuse daily, but listen to Franklin on "Dr. Feelgood" or "Ain't No Way" or "Say A Little Prayer" or "Think." One discovers not one Aretha Franklin but a cast of hundreds of women: some sweet, some mad, some cool, some sad, some angry, and a great many playful and sexy. Franklin expressed all a black woman could be, while her contemporaries (Diana Ross, Tina Turner, Dionne Warwick, Martha Reeves, even the underrated Gladys Knight) seemed trapped in one persona by the artistic decisions of male producers as well as by their own vocal limitations. Given her talent and the tenor of the times, it wasn't surprising that Franklin became a prime example of "natural crossover." Compared to Motown, Franklin's music made few concessions to "white" sensibilities. She and Atlantic found that white America was, at this point, more willing to accept "real" black music by blacks than at anytime since World War II. Why?

The Western world, politically and culturally, was undergoing a profound upheaval. With the civil-rights movement and the Vietnam War as catalysts, traditional values of every kind— machismo, monogamy, patriotism—were being rejected, or at least questioned. The white teen market Alan Freed once cultivated had matured into a dynamic force for change; its interest in politics, drugs, and free love altered its music. "Rock & roll," that straightforward, unambitious consumer product, was now evolving into something more experimental, less categorizable, roughly dubbed "rock." White musicians were more explicitly articulating their cultural experience in pop music. And in 1967 the broader perspective rock represented was crytallized by the Beatles' *Sgt. Pepper's Lonely Hearts Club Band.* This music had plain old rock & roll drumming, playing, and singing—the adaptation of black R&B—plus instrumentation and melodies from European classical music and English music halls This was more ambitious than mere rock & roll. It was electronic. It was experimental. It sold albums instead of just 45s (and so got major labels interested). It was art. It was rock. It was white.

It was also liberal—probrotherhood and all that. The civil-rights movement's evolution into various forms of black nationalism and self-assertion had, in music as well as in Democratic politics, caused a breach. Into the late sixties, Motown was still selling itself as "The Sound of Young America," but it wasn't without critics, black and white, who now saw the label's aggressive upward mobility as an unnecessary attempt to escape blackness and sell out to the Establishment. So soul, with the uncompromising Aretha as its star, was enjoyed and purchased by whites and blacks. One of the most intense album-length explorations of soul ever recorded, *Aretha Live At the Fillmore,* with a guest appearance by Ray Charles, was cut at one of white promoter Bill Graham's temples of rock, San Francisco's Fillmore West.

In the 1950s rock & roll overshadowed R&B; in the sixties white musicians had difficulty synthesizing their own version of soul. This was primarily because white singers just couldn't match the intense vocal style of soul, though at the time the gap between white and black music was perceived differently, as less a musical than a political distinction. For example, in his introduction to the 1969 book *The Age of Rock,* Jonathan Eisen explained why only three of thirty-four essays dealt with black music by saying, "I have not placed as much emphasis on the music of the black community as I have on that of the white. The reasons, I trust, are evident. In recent years, young black musicians on the whole have been involved within an entirely different milieu, both social and musical, most of them concentrating on developing greater nationalistic self-consciousness."

In the late 1960s, with soul integral to the lives of black America, the white rock audience revived 1950s electric blues, a music

Aretha Franklin, queen of "soul."

which had been part of the R&B world but which, like rock & roll and straight doo wop, had been forsaken for soul. B. B. King, whose career had been in decline since the early sixties, was suddenly discovered in 1966 by the rock audience through the praise of white guitar heroes like the Electric Flag's Mike Bloomfield and Cream's Eric Clapton, and bookings at Graham's Fillmores East and West.

Muddy Waters, Howlin' Wolf, and Bobby (Blue) Bland were among the grand old electric bluesmen who found themselves getting paid better than at any time in their lengthy careers because they had suddenly started reaching that elusive white audience. Few blacks showed up at rock festivals and concert halls. Older black fans, who'd loved Muddy and company at the neighborhood bar, rarely came to these temples of youth culture partly because they didn't feel comfortable among middle-class white teens and college students, and partly because they didn't know about the gigs: advertising, in the underground press and progressive rock radio (the key media of ascendant rock culture), never reached them. To blacks who still valued the blues, it seemed these cultural heroes had been kidnapped by the younger brothers and sisters of the folks who'd led Chuck Berry astray. And to younger blacks—the soul children of the sixties—the blues just wasn't (remember this one?) "relevant" in a world of dashikis, Afro picks, and bell-bottoms. To paraphrase Ahmet Ertegun, black music is in constant flight from the status quo. Young blacks at the time abandoned the blues because it was "depressing," backward," or "accommodating" to white values. This argument is crap—"relevancy" irrelevant itself—but then as now a lot of blacks believed it. In fact, blues was only suffering the same fate that, surprisingly, would soon befall soul.

CULTURE SHOCK

The black audience's consumerism and restlessness burns out and abandons musical styles, whereas white Americans, in the European tradition of supporting forms and style for the sake of tradition, seem to hold styles dear long after they have ceased to evolve.

The most fanatical students of blues history have all been white. These well-intentioned scholars pick through old recordings, interview obscure guitarists, and tramp through the Mississippi Delta with the determination of Egyptologists. Yet with the exception of Eric Clapton and maybe Johnny Winter, no white blues guitarist has produced a body of work in any way comparable to that of the black giants. Blacks create and then move on. Whites document and then recycle. In the history of popular music, these truths are self-evident.

But—and here's the paradox—all the great black musicians working in a pop idiom—be it rock & roll, R&B, or funk—become cultural curators or historical critics. By taking established black forms, preserving their essence but filtering these textures through an ambitious creative consciousness, they made astounding music that is in the tradition yet singular from

it. For example, Jimi Hendrix used blues and R&B as his building blocks, and Sly Stone worked from gospel and soul. Yet black America's reaction to each was different: Hendrix was rejected, while Sly was viewed, before drug days, as a hero.

The difference was that Hendrix drew from a style blacks had already disposed of; Sly shrewdly stayed just a few steps ahead of the crowd. Both were children of the R&B world. Hendrix had been a sideman for numerous R&B bands after leaving Seattle in his teens, including the Isley Brothers. Sly, baptized as Sylvester Stewart, was reared in a roof-raising, sanctified church and worked as a popular deejay on several Bay Area stations. And both Sly and Jimi rebelled against the narrow-mindedness in which they grew up. It is not coincidental that they blossomed in environments removed from the traditions of black America, Hendrix in London and Sly in "free-love" San Francisco, where they each plunged into the hippie life-styles of those two countercultural centers, emerging with a black-based sound drenched in flower-power rhetoric that had little in common with the soul consciousness of James Brown or Aretha.

Unfortunately, Hendrix fatally damaged his connection with black audiences because of his innovative brilliance on the electric guitar, an instrument that, with the declining black interest in blues, fell into disfavor. At Motown, electric guitars, sometimes as many as four, were locked in intricate patterns. At Stax, Steve Cropper's lead lines were short, concise statements. But in rock, lead guitar extravagance was crucial to the music and the supporting culture. It was the perfect accompaniment to LSD and other chemicals of choice. Hendrix, once frustrated by R&B background work, greedily hogged every available space for his Stratocaster. In essence, Hendrix was the revenge of the R&B sideman, one with the ability to turn the voices inside his head into music—problem was, you just couldn't dance to it. Maybe if you were stoned at a light show the Jimi Hendrix Experience could be boogie fodder. Maybe if the grass was flowing at a local love-in you'd dance. However, to the audiences of Stax and Motown and James Brown, "Purple Haze" and "Hey Joe" just didn't do the do. Jimi's music was, if not from another planet, definitely from another country. In a weird symmetry, Hendrix, with his young white-teen audience, was a sixties equivalent of Chuck Berry. Like Berry, his success with guitar-based music made him an outcast on Black Main Street.

Sly was, alas, just as drug-crazed as Hendrix and just as enamored of "rock culture." He had an integrated band, not just racially but sexually, that looked as if the members had just wandered off the corner of Haight and Ashbury. No slick choreography around the Family Stone. It was organized chaos or, as Dave Marsh wrote, "The women played, the men sang: the blacks freaked out, the whites got funky; everyone did something unexpected." Sly never worked the chitlin circuit. Like Hendrix, he played gigs with rock acts at rock revues almost from the beginning, working through contacts in the West Coast music scene.

But Sly always gave up the funk. His rhythm section, with bassist Larry Graham, drummer Greg Errico, and guitarist Freddie Stone, mirrored James Brown's jagged polyrhythms. On "I Want to Take You Higher," "Thank You (Falettinme Be Mice Elf Agin)," and "Sing A Simple Song," Sly brought Brown's funk to the rock masses almost uncut. Almost, because it would be inaccurate to say that Sly's music just allowed the mass dissemination of Brownish bottom. His memorable melodies and knack for sloganeering ("Hot Fun in the Summertime," "Stand!," "Everyday People," "Everybody Is a Star," "You Can Make It If You Try") were as infectious as the chant-vocal approach he pioneered. In addition, and this is a crucial point, Sly was the first great R&B innovator raised to stardom on a corporate label.

Two years before the release of Sly's 1968 debut, "Dance to the Music," on Epic Records, its CBS corporate sister of the Columbia label had let Aretha's contract lapse and ended its affiliation with Carl Davis and the "Chicago sound." CBS was virtually out of the black music business. Things turned around at CBS, and the credit goes to its young president, Clive Davis. In 1965, CBS Records (Columbia, Epic, and its subsidiaries) had 11 percent of the overall market. By the end of 1968, CBS commanded 17 percent, and the figure was climbing due to Davis's aggressive signing of rock artists such as "white Negro" Janis Joplin; Chicago; Blood, Sweat and Tears; Simon and Garfunkel; and Sly and the Family Stone. Davis at first wasn't convinced that, in the age of Aquarius, Sly's glittery costumes could reach whites, which at the time was the only market that concerned CBS. In his autobiography, Davis recalls a soul-searching meeting with Sly about his direction. According to Davis, the bandleader contended, "They will know what to make of it soon," he said. "I have a definite idea of what I am trying to do and I want to stay with it. Maybe the kids will be put off at first, but they'll get into it." Davis admitted he underestimated Sly's vision. But Sly's play worked; CBS backed the group all the way. This didn't mean, however, that Columbia had a fully developed strategy for exploiting black music. At the time, while Columbia was becoming a dominant force in rock music, a new entity was emerging as its chief foe in the youth market—the conglomerate Warner Bros., Elektra-Asylum, and (with its stellar black catalogue) Atlantic Records. Eventually, this combination, known today as WEA, would become CBS's chief rival in the industry.

Atlantic's absorption set Ahmet Ertegun and Jerry Wexler financially for life. The influx of dollars also solidified an ongoing sea change in the label's direction. In 1967, Atlantic's ATCO subsidiary signed one of rock's first supergroups, Cream (with guitarist Eric Clapton, bassist Jack Bruce, and drummer Ginger Baker), and the Beatlesque Australian vocal trio, the Bee Gees. In 1969, Led Zeppelin delivered two albums to Atlantic that laid the foundation for a new genre, heavy metal, while Ertegun personally wined and dined the Rolling Stones into a deal. Atlantic was now as closely identified with British rock as it had been with black music. After the late sixties, the balance at Atlantic would be tipped permanently to rock. It began with the death of Otis Redding in a plane crash on December 10, 1967. Then, during a bitter negotiation between Wexler and Stax's Jim Stewart, it was revealed that Atlantic, back in 1962 when the original distribution deal was made, had gained control of all the Stax masters. Taking advantage of a technicality in the contract, Atlantic held on to them. Apparently Wexler first mentioned them merely as a negotiating ploy. Embarrassed and stung, Stewart and Al Bell made a deal with Paramount Pictures Music Division, a subsidiary of Gulf + Western, for almost $3 million plus G + W stock. As part of this transaction, Bell was appointed executive vice-president of Stax and given a piece of the label's growing East Memphis catalogue.

So, unexpectedly, Stax became, just like Atlantic, a part of corporate America—though it was a relatively small acquisition for a huge oil company. Few observers at the time foresaw the negative impact these distribution shifts would have on the music and the institutions that made up the R&B world. It was simply assumed that the sudden influx of corporate dollars would allow everyone to do a better job at making, promoting, and distributing black music than ever before.

NARA

Sly's success at Columbia, and the Atlantic and Stax deals, signaled a significant realignment of power in the R&B world. At the same time, black radio was undergoing an internal political struggle and a stylistic evolution

that brought revolutionary changes in how it sounded and was perceived.

The genesis of this change, according to Del Shields, then a jazz deejay at New York's WLIB, was the assassination of King. While James Brown was being broadcast on public TV in Boston, deejays across the country were on all night, sometimes against their owner's wishes, to stifle black backlash against this latest instance of American racism. Shields says, "Black radio came of age the night Dr. King was killed. Up until that time, black radio had never been tested nationally. No one ever knew its power. You knew the popularity of black disc jockeys, the power to sell various products. But on the night Dr. King was killed, all across America every black station was tested and everybody who was on the air at that time, including myself, told people to cool it. We tried to do everything possible to keep the black people from just exploding even more than what they were.

"We were on WLIB, a daytime station that was supposed to go off at sunset. We stayed on till twelve, one o'clock at night. We went beyond the FCC ruling and, of course, had to answer to the FCC later with reports about why we stayed on. The oddity was that we, the black disc jockeys, made the decision to stay on. As a result, the station got the Peabody Award. The owner himself had called and told me I had no right to do that, but I told him I didn't have time to talk to him. When America looked at black radio in that particular period, it suddenly hit them that this was a potent force. If, in every major city, a black disc jockey had said, 'Rise up,' there would have been pandemonium. And that night was also the beginning of the end of black radio. It was never allowed to rise up again."

In the sixties, Shields was a highly politicized man who, before and after his jazz broadcast from Harlem's Lenox Avenue, hung out with a wide range of people, from Black Power advocate H. Rap Brown to his cousin, Bill Cosby, a rising comedian and costar of TV's first integrated action-adventure show, *I Spy*. Shields saw in the energy of both—a spokesman for radical black America and a mass-market symbol of upward mobility—the kind of mix that would fulfill black radio's potential. But for Shields's vision to become reality, several things had to happen: there had to be more black ownership (in the late sixties, fewer than ten stations had black owners); better trained disc jockeys who could demand higher salaries (Shields, a top deejay in New York, made only $250 a week; white counterparts earned $800); and black deejays needed some form of protection from abuse by station-managers and manipulation by record-label executives. Because of the differences in job description and salary for deejays around the country, unionization was ruled out. An organization of some kind, with the committed leadership and membership of a civil-rights organization, was needed, and the framework for one existed.

The National Association for Radio Announcers (NARA) was an outgrowth of an old-boy network of black deejays that Jack Gibson had helped establish in the fifties. In 1955, Gibson formally dubbed it an organization, though social club might have been a more apt description. NARA's parties were legendary. The deejays, many from small Southern stations, used the organization's annual gatherings to show off as flamboyantly as any recording star or pimp. Gibson recalls one gathering in St. Louis where NARA took over a hotel "and partied until it was time to go to church," which was typical of the organization. Well before the excesses of rock stars became common, NARA had a reputation for leaving an enduring impression on hotel managers. Much of this had to do with ego. Gather together four hundred men who make their living with glib tongues and jive, and you've got a hotel full of one-upmanship. Everyone wanted to know, who drank more? Who fucked more and longer? Who played the slyest poker? Who got the most payola?

That competitiveness is of some importance to NARA's history since the biggest deejays controlled the organization and set the tone for its hell-raising. NARA and its members weren't oblivious of the civil-rights movement and the changes it brought to the fabric of black life. They gave money; they gave lip service. But their internal will for collective effort was weak. Business as usual was good for many; others feared reprisals from white bosses if they got too political.

In 1965, three years before King's assassination, Shields, then at Philadelphia's WDAS, had a fateful talk with Clarence Avante. Avante, the manager of jazz organist Jimmy Smith and soundtrack composer Lalo Schriffen, was viewed by whites and blacks as one of the most able deal-makers around, and he cultivated close ties with white record and TV executives at ABC, and within the CBS corporate structure. He told Shields it was time to upgrade NARA and asked him to prepare an outline with ideas. Together with Ed Wright, program director of Cleveland's WABQ, and Jimmy Bishop, a deejay at WDAS, Avante and Shields began networking with other jocks around the country to prepare a coup d'etat. At that year's convention in Houston, the group, known affectionately and pejoratively as the "new breed," surprised everyone by winning an election for control of NARA.

Suggestive of this new breed's perspective, they changed the organization's name from NARA to NATRA (National Association of Television and Radio Announcers), feeling that they needed to reach out beyond radio and records to all parts of the communications industry. An awards banquet, the first ever specifically for blacks in the broadcast industry, was held at the Waldorf-Astoria. The choices were intriguing and revealing: Lena Horne, not a popular figure in black America at the time, and Sheldon Leonard, the white producer of *I Spy*, were respectively NATRA's woman and man of the year. Horne was chosen in a generous attempt to refurbish an image unfairly tarnished in black America by what many viewed as her career-long accommodation to whites; and Leonard, to emphasize to NATRA's membership that the world of communications encompassed more than hit records.

More ambitiously, political and social issues were introduced into the organization. Representatives of NATRA visited the Center for Study of Democratic Institutions in Santa Barbara, a liberal think tank, where they discussed strategies to politicize its membership. In 1968 a relationship was nurtured with Vice-President Hubert Humphrey resulting in NATRA's appointment to two presidential commissions on youth. If Humphrey was elected president, Shields thought he would help blacks acquire more broadcast outlets. At the same time, as executive vice-president, Shields began to lobby for increased advertising by Madison Avenue on black radio, meeting with advertising agencies and speaking to trade presses.

Through Shields, H. Rap Brown made an unscheduled speech at a NATRA meeting in Atlanta. The next year, after King's death and the unexpected power it revealed in black radio, meetings were organized by NATRA in New York between the white owners of these stations and their black deejays to discuss their differences for the first time ever. The owners were reluctant participants since they had the same respect for the jocks as the jocks had for them—none. It was testimony to NATRA's growing importance that any showed up at all.

Shields and Avante's boldest move was to propose that NATRA start its own school of broadcast science. In 1968 they found a failing college in Delaware and began negotiations to make it the site. Through Avante's contacts, CBS's and ABC's broadcast divisions promised equipment. Ten record companies at NATRA's 1968 convention said they would donate $25,000 each.

Shields recalls wistfully, "We were going to walk out of the Miami convention with a quarter of a million dollars [in donations] to build the NATRA School of Broadcast Science, and we blew it." He speculates that there were "certain people in the broadcast and TV industry who did not want to see black deejays gain the kind of responsibility and power we were talking about." It sounds like Shields thought some kind of Big Brother was watching—and he may not have been wrong. Someone was certainly on the prowl, jealous of the power NATRA was accumulating and looking for a way to get in on it, and they weren't afraid to use force. A series of violent events over the next few months involving both blacks and whites left the ambitious NATRA plan in shreds.

There was a lot of talk among people in the industry about "pressure" being applied—black activists were strong-arming white record-company owners for "reparations for past exploitation" (which many blacks applauded), but according to Shields, reprisals against black deejays too weren't unknown. For months before the 1968 convention, Shields recalls being the target of a series of threats from individuals who were after a cut of the new breed's action. "I'll never forget," says Shields, "Clarence Avante saying to me, 'Whatever you do, don't sell out.'" Just before the convention, the rumors in Harlem heated up—some dudes were out to hurt Shields—and one night, just after Shields left WLIB's offices on Lenox Avenue near 125th Street, three men beat him to the ground. The perpetrators were never caught.

It was only a prelude. At Miami, between August 14 and 18, white record men and black radio men were threatened, and some were beaten. Marshall Sehorn, Bobby Robinson's old New Orleans contact, was beaten. Phil Walden, Otis Redding's white manager, was threatened. So was Jerry Wexler. Shields spent only one day in Miami. When he arrived at the airport, members of NATRA warned him not to stay: "they" were after him. Meanwhile, members of NATRA's Southern branch complained in sessions that the organization wasn't responsive to the needs of the underpaid Southern jocks because its leadership was too busy politicking.

Once back in New York, Shields was visited by FCC head Nicholas Johnson, and the city's district attorney tapped his phone and put him under twenty-four-hour surveillance for two months—after the events at the Miami convention. After the violence and dissension of that gathering, the commitments to the school evaporated and the enthusiasm for the new breed waned. At the 1969 convention in Washington, D.C., Shields paid $10,000 to hire guards to protect himself and convention attenders. In fact, one of Shields's antagonists chided him for "stooping so low" as to hire his own thugs.

After 1969, the new breed pulled out of NATRA. Shields and Avante moved to Los Angeles in 1971 to fulfill one of their dreams by buying radio station KACE. NATRA's offices moved to Chicago and the organization quickly returned to its historic role as a movable feast for black deejays. Four years of attempted "relevance" proved to be a little too much for the brothers on the microphone. Instead of becoming a unified political force dedicated to raising professional standards, black deejays remained unorganized and unfocused. And even while they tried just to maintain their status quo, the radio industry was evolving in ways that would alter the role of black deejays forever.

GARY BYRD

Gary Byrd, a Buffalo native who grew up listening to Hound Dog Lorenz and Eddie O'Jay on WUFO, can be seen as a transitional figure in black radio. His career began in the era of the personality jock, continued into its period of decline, and then saw the birth of a new style of black radio that emphasized a rigidly defined professionalism.

Byrd's story begins in 1965 when, as a fifteen-year-old actor, he appeared in a "hip" school play called "The In Crowd," based on

Dobie Gray's hit record. Hank Cameron, a schoolteacher and part-time WUFO jock, was impressed enough with Byrd's voice to ask the youngster if he had ever considered a career in radio. Byrd, who had aspirations to act and do comedy, thought radio announcing was close enough and said that he had. So Cameron arranged for Byrd to be trained at the station. He was given his own weekend air shift, where he initially concentrated on jazz, but quickly discovered that R&B was the people's choice. Moreover, the audience wanted the music presented with flair. Byrd had a lot to learn, but, as he explains, he developed ways to help himself catch up: "I was writing all this stuff down. I had a little notebook that I kept and I would write things down that seemed to be what you had to do as a personality deejay. Basically, when I came in, I was into jazz. I remember a guy cutting my hair and he said there was a lot of arguing about who could sing higher, Smokey Robinson or Eddie Kendricks. I was like, 'Who's Smokey and Eddie?' I was into John Coltrane. That was what I was into because I had grown up in that side of Buffalo where there was always jazz around me. So when they started talking about these guys Smokey and Eddie, it was a year or so before I realized who they were talking about.

"When those records would come in, I made a little note that said, 'Pick your favorite records and present them big,' and I underlined 'big' to indicate you gotta do something. So I'd take 'Baby Do the Philly Dog' and some of those other records I really liked and I tried to work and build them up in my little primitive way as a teenage jock. And it worked for me, and stuff happened. And it was definitely part of a concept of personality radio which I came in on the last edges of."

By 1966, Byrd's on-air experience had made him a radio junkie, and he vowed one day to visit his favorite station, New York's WWRL. On junior day, a day set aside in Buffalo for juniors to celebrate their ascension to the senior class (students even saved money for it), Byrd informed his grandmother, who raised him, "I didn't really care about junior day. What I wanted to do was go to New York City." His grandmother asked, "New York City for what?" Byrd told her, "I want to hear this radio station, WWRL. I want to try to visit the station." His grandmother said he could stay with an aunt in the city, so Byrd, who'd never flown before, went to New York. "The first thing I did was turn RL on," he recalls. "The second was to call the station and tell them I wanted to visit." It's inconceivable today that at fifteen Byrd could land an on-air job at a station like WUFO, much less gain entry to an important New York radio station on the strength of a phone call. But not long after his call, Byrd was sitting in the WWRL studio with Rocky (G.) Groce. "I went and sat in and he asked me whether I was interested in radio. I said, 'I'm a jock.' Groce said, 'How you going to be a jock at seventeen?' I said, 'I'm a jock. I jock everyday and I do a show on the weekends.' He said, 'Get outta here. You from Frankie Crocker's hometown Buffalo?' I said, 'Yeah.' He said, 'Well, what if I open this microphone and put you on. What will happen?' I said, 'What are you asking me to do?' He said, 'Introduce the record.' So the record was 'Shake, Rattle and Roll' by Arthur Cobbs. He opened the mike, and when he turned on the mike, it tuned off the cuing system, because you can't hear the speakers and I didn't have a headset on. But I hit the cue anyway. I just hit it blind. You hear the first two beats of a record and you kind of get a sense of it. I hit the cue and, of course, when it closed out, he was really surprised. So was Fred Barr, who was the big gospel jock, a white guy, who was there. The general manager came in and offered me a job at seventeen to come on RL. I was real blown out."

Byrd's grandmother, however, was perfectly willing to stand in the way of progress. She called him home to Buffalo where, not prepared to be your average kid, Byrd landed a spot on WYSL, a top-forty station in upstate New York utilizing a format that refined pop radio into a synthetic consistency that station owners loved and old-line deejays hated. Developed by Bill Drake, the format was initiated in 1965 at Los Angeles's KHJ, where Drake turned a money-losing outlet into the number-one station in the second-largest U.S. market. Drake did it by "tightening" the playlist, which meant playing the most popular records with frequency, limiting and shortening station identification, and holding commercials to below fourteen minutes per hour, four minutes under the FCC maximum. Playing two songs back to back, and beginning records under the deejay's introduction or as the news ended were Drake innovations that became American radio staples because they accelerated the pace of the broadcast. It also gave the deejays very little time to talk, for Drake believed that a uniform station sound was more important than cultivating star deejays. From KHJ, Drake went on to consult on the formats of all RKO-owned stations and rose to a vice-presidency at the chain before forming his own very lucrative consulting firm. Byrd describes the Drake format as, "Time, temperature, artist, title of the record. 'It's 4:07 on CKLW. I'm Gary Byrd. Here are the Temptations.' On comes 'Ain't Too Proud to Beg.'"

In Byrd's analysis, the Drake format "started to take over the country because it shut up jocks who basically may have had nothing to say in an entertaining way. And white jocks at the time were more into wacky humor. I'm not saying all the black jocks were doing something great, but it was a different sense of relationship. It wasn't like the craziness kind of stuff. That was the basic thing it did. It equalized the formats. It meant that if a guy didn't have talent, he could still come in and do the format if he had a nice voice and could control himself. He could give the station a uniform sound. If he blows, take him out, put another jock on. It was that simple. Because it was no longer the jock, it was the station."

And this philosophy, to Byrd's chagrin, was being brought into black radio. Looking back, Byrd cites two reasons the R&B world embraced Drake's format. Like Shields, Byrd puts much of the blame for the demise of the black personality deejay on white management's fear of their power. "It was a plantation mentality we're talking about," he says. "What black radio had along this time was powerful personalities who were built through rapping and an ability to relate to the community and then became very popular. Well, again, the station managers were white. They didn't want to see a black jock become bigger than the station."

The other reason was the changing psychology of black America. To a wide cross section of the community—from those who identified with Dr. King's uplifting cadences to those who pursued Ron Karenga's nationalism, from those who embraced the Panther's socialism to the many seeking to prove they were as all-American as any white—the rapid ramblings of the black deejays were embarrassments. At a time when Sidney Poitier was America's number-one box-office star, black folks of every description had no patience with the Eddie (Rochester) Andersons of the airwaves. Drake's format was the leash that reined them in.

As Byrd remembers ruefully, "What I'll say about integration is it was a kind of period where you learn to put on your suit, put on this shirt, and get a job, now. Suddenly management is saying, 'We have white people listening. Let's be careful. Don't talk too ethnically. Talk proper. Pronounce your *-ings.*' It was this sort of thing. What it did was take jocks who were doing that and made them symbolic of all jocks. So even the jock who was doing a very hip personality thing in a hip way got wiped out. He was lumped with the rest."

In the view of Byrd and others, the era of the black personality jock ended in 1967, when the Drake format seeped into black radio. That seems premature. As we know from NATRA, many of the best-known R&B deejays retained their power to move audiences and influence record companies past that point. In addition, there were many stations, including WWRL from 1969 to 1971, that, while adopting a modified top-forty format, didn't sound radically different to the untrained ear from a few years before. Byrd was on the air there in the evening in 1970 when WWRL went to number five in New York City, the highest Arbitron rating in its history.

What finally ended the old era and ushered in a new one was FM radio, a technological development that wouldn't take hold in black America until the 1970s. When it hit, tradition went out the window, taking with it a great many careers.

Notes

Between talking at length with Alan Leeds, now a member of Prince's organization, and reading James Brown's autobiography, *The Godfather of Soul* (Macmillan, 1986), I found out more about the hardest-working man in show business than I wanted to know. Clive Davis's *Clive* (Morrow, 1974), Jonathan Eisen's *The Age of Rock* (Vintage, 1969), and Guralnick's *Sweet Soul Music* (Harper & Row, 1986) talk not just about the mechanics of selling music but about the attitudes toward that side of the business. *Time* magazine's 1968 cover story on Aretha Franklin is a collector's item.

Gary Byrd, when not broadcasting or songwriting, gives great interviews. Del Shields, now a reverend, though still a radio broadcaster, gave me access not just to his memories but many of his papers and articles outlining the changes NARA-NATRA underwent. Stephen Oates's biography of Dr. King, *Let the Trumpet Sound* (Harper & Row, 1982), Landess and Quinn's antagonistic look at the head of the Rainbow, *Jesse Jackson and the Politics of Race* (Jamerson Books, 1985), and E. Curtis Alexander's self-published Adam Clayton Powell celebration (1983) helped with the politics.

Blueprint for Negro Writing

RICHARD WRIGHT

ENERALLY SPEAKING, NEGRO writing in the past has been confined to humble novels, poems, and plays, prim and decorous ambassadors who went a-begging to white America. They entered the Court of American Public Opinion dressed in the knee-pants of servility, curtsying to show that the Negro was not inferior, that he was human, and that he had a life comparable to that of other people. For the most part these artistic ambassadors were received as though they were French poodles who do clever tricks.

White America never offered these Negro writers any serious criticism. The mere fact that a Negro could write was astonishing. Nor was there any deep concern on the part of white America with the role Negro writing should play in American culture; and the role it did play grew out of accident rather than intent or design. Either it crept in through the kitchen in the form of jokes; or it was the fruits of that foul soil which was the result of a liaison between inferiority-complexed Negro "geniuses" and burnt-out white Bohemians with money.

On the other hand, these often technically brilliant performances by Negro writers were looked upon by the majority of literate Negroes as something to be proud of. At best, Negro writing has been something eternal to the lives of educated Negroes themselves. That the productions of their writers should have been something of a guide in their daily living is a matter which seems never to have been raised seriously.

1) THE ROLE OF NEGRO WRITING: TWO DEFINITIONS

Under these conditions Negro writing assumed two general aspects: 1) It became a sort of conspicuous ornamentation, the hallmark of "achievement." 2) It became the voice of the educated Negro pleading with white America for justice.

Rarely was the best of this writing addressed to the Negro himself, his needs, his sufferings, his aspirations. Through misdirection, Negro writers have been far better to others than they have been to themselves. And the mere

Reprinted from *The Black Aesthetic*, Addison Gayle, Jr., ed., Doubleday & Company, Inc., 1971.

recognition of this places the whole question of Negro writing in a new light and raises a doubt as to the validity of its present direction.

2) THE MINORITY OUTLOOK

Somewhere in his writings Lenin makes the observation that oppressed minorities often reflect the techniques of the bourgeoisie more brilliantly than some sections of the bourgeoisie themselves. The psychological importance of this becomes meaningful when it is recalled that oppressed minorities, and especially the petty bourgeois sections of oppressed minorities, strive to assimilate the virtues of the bourgeoisie in the assumption that by doing so they can lift themselves into a higher social sphere. But not only among the oppressed petty bourgeoisie does this occur. The workers of a minority people, chafing under exploitation, forge organizational forms of struggle to better their lot. Lacking the handicaps of false ambition and property, they have access to a wide social vision and a deep social consciousness. They display a greater freedom and initiative in pushing their claims upon civilization than even do the petty bourgeoisie. Their organizations show greater strength, adaptability, and efficiency than any other group or class in society.

That Negro workers, propelled by the harsh conditions of their lives, have demonstrated this consciousness and mobility for economic and political action there can be no doubt. But has this consciousness been reflected in the work of Negro writers to the same degree as it has in the Negro workers' struggle to free Herndon and the Scottsboro Boys, in the drive toward unionism, in the fight against lynching? Have they as creative writers taken advantage of their unique minority position?

The answer decidedly is *no*. Negro writers have lagged sadly, and as time passes the gap widens between them and their people.

How can this hiatus be bridged? How can the enervating effects of this longstanding split be eliminated?

In presenting questions of this sort an attitude of self-consciousness and self-criticism is far more likely to be a fruitful point of departure than a mere recounting of past achievements. An emphasis upon tendency and experiment, a view of society as something becoming rather than as something fixed and admired is the one which points the way for Negro writers to stand shoulder to shoulder with Negro workers in mood and outlook.

3) A WHOLE CULTURE

There is, however, a culture of the Negro which is his and has been addressed to him; a culture which has, for good or ill, helped to clarify his consciousness and create emotional attitudes which are conducive to action. This culture has stemmed mainly from two sources: 1) the Negro church; and 2) the folklore of the Negro people.

It was through the portals of the church that the American Negro first entered the shrine of western culture. Living under slave conditions of life, bereft of his African heritage, the Negroes' struggle for religion on the plantations between 1820–60 assumed the form of a struggle for human rights. It remained a relatively revolutionary struggle until religion began to serve as an antidote for suffering and denial. But even today there are millions of American Negroes whose only sense of a whole universe, whose only relation to society and man, and whose only guide to personal dignity comes through the archaic morphology of Christian salvation.

It was, however, in a folklore moulded out of rigorous and inhuman conditions of life that the Negro achieved his most indigenous and complete expression. Blues, spirituals, and folk tales recounted from mouth to mouth; the whispered words of a black mother to her black daughter on the ways of men, to confidential wisdom of a black father to his black son; the swapping of sex experiences on street corners from boy to boy in the deepest

Richard Wright, one of America's finest novelists.

vernacular; work songs sung under blazing suns—all these formed the channels through which the racial wisdom flowed.

One would have thought that Negro writers in the last century of striving at expression would have continued and deepened this folk tradition, would have tried to create a more intimate and yet a more profoundly social system of artistic communication between them and their people. But the illusion that they could escape through individual achievement

the harsh lot of their race swung Negro writers away from any such path. Two separate cultures sprang up: one for the Negro masses, unwritten and unrecognized; and the other for the sons and daughters of a rising Negro bourgeoisie, parasitic and mannered.

Today the question is: Shall Negro writing be for the Negro masses, moulding the lives and consciousness of those masses toward new goals, or shall it continue begging the question of the Negroes' humanity?

4) THE PROBLEM OF NATIONALISM IN NEGRO WRITING

In stressing the difference between the role Negro writing failed to play in the lives of the Negro people, and the role it should play in the future if it is to serve its historic function; in pointing out the fact that Negro writing has been addressed in the main to a small white audience rather than to a Negro one, it should be stated that no attempt is being made here to propagate a specious and blatant nationalism. Yet the nationalist character of the Negro people is unmistakable. Psychologically this nationalism is reflected in the whole of Negro culture, and especially in folklore.

In the absence of fixed and nourishing forms of culture, the Negro has a folklore which embodies the memories and hopes of his stuggle for freedom. Not yet caught in paint or stone, and as yet but feebly depicted in the poem and novel, the Negroes' most powerful images of hope and despair still remain in the fluid state of daily speech. How many John Henrys have lived and died on the lips of these black people? How many mythical heroes in embryo have been allowed to perish for lack of husbanding by alert intelligence?

Negro folklore contains, in a measure that puts to shame more deliberate forms of Negro expression, the collective sense of Negro life in America. Let those who shy at the nationalist implications of Negro life look at this body of folklore, living and powerful, which rose out of a unified sense of a common life and a common fate. Here are those vital beginnings of a recognition of value in life as it is *lived*, a recognition that marks the emergence of a new culture in the shell of the old. And at the moment this process starts, at the moment when a people begin to realize a *meaning* in their suffering, the civilization that engenders that suffering is doomed.

The nationalist aspects of Negro life are as sharply manifest in the social institutions of Negro people as in folklore. There is a Negro church, a Negro press, a Negro social world, a Negro sporting world, a Negro business world, a Negro school system, Negro professions; in short, a Negro way of life in America. The Negro people did not ask for this, and deep down, though they express themselves through their institutions and adhere to this special way of life, they do not want it now. This special existence was forced upon them from without by lynch rope, bayonet and mob rule. They accepted these negative conditions with the inevitability of a tree which must live or perish in whatever soil it finds itself.

The few crumbs of American civilization which the Negro has got from the tables of capitalism have been through these segregated channels. Many Negro institutions are cowardly and incompetent; but they are all that the Negro has. And, in the main, any move, whether for progress or reaction, must come through these institutions for the simple reason that all other channels are closed. Negro writers who seek to mould or influence the consciousness of the Negro people must address their messages to them through the ideologies and attitudes fostered in this warping way of life.

5) THE BASIS AND MEANING OF NATIONALISM IN NEGRO WRITING

The social institutions of the Negro are imprisoned in the Jim Crow political system of the South, and this Jim Crow political system is in turn built upon a plantation-feudal economy. Hence, it can be seen that the emotional expression of group-feeling which puzzles so many whites and leads them to deplore what they call "black chauvinism" is not a morbidly inherent trait of the Negro, but rather the reflex expression of a life whose roots are imbedded deeply in Southern soil.

Negro writers must accept the nationalist implications of their lives, not in order to encourage them, but in order to change and transcend them. They must accept the concept of nationalism because, in order to transcend it, they must *possess* and *understand* it. And a nationalist spirit in Negro writing means a nationalism carrying the highest possible pitch of social consciousness. It means a nationalism that knows its origins, its limitations; that is aware of the dangers of its position; that knows its ultimate aims are unrealizable within the framework of capitalist America; a nationalism whose reason for being lies in the simple fact of self-possession and in the consciousness of the interdependence of people in modern society.

For purposes of creative expression it means that the Negro writer must realize within the area of his own personal experience those impulses which, when prefigured in terms of broad social movements, constitute the stuff of nationalism.

For Negro writers even more so than for Negro politicians, nationalism is a bewildering and vexing question, the full ramifications of which cannot be dealt with here. But among Negro workers and the Negro middle class the spirit of nationalism is rife in a hundred devious forms; and a simple literary realism which seeks to depict the lives of these people devoid of wider social connotations, devoid of the revolutionary significance of these nationalist tendencies, must of necessity do a rank injustice to the Negro people and alienate their possible allies in the struggle for freedom.

6) SOCIAL CONSCIOUSNESS AND RESPONSIBILITY

The Negro writer who seeks to function within his race as a purposeful agent has a serious responsibility. In order to do justice to his subject matter, in order to depict Negro life in all of its manifold and intricate relationships, a deep, informed, and complex consciousness is necessary; a consciousness which draws for its strength upon the fluid lore of a great people, and moulds this lore with the concepts that move and direct the forces of history today.

With the gradual decline of the moral authority of the Negro church, and with the increasing irresolution which is paralyzing Negro middle-class leadership, a new role is devolving upon the Negro writer. He is being called upon to do no less than create values by which his race is to struggle, live and die.

By his ability to fuse and make articulate the experiences of men, because his writing possesses the potential cunning to steal into the inmost recesses of the human heart, because he can create the myths and symbols that inspire a faith in life, he may expect either to be consigned to oblivion, or to be recognized for the valued agent he is.

This raises the question of the personality of the writer. It means that in the lives of Negro writers must be found those materials and experiences which will create a meaningful picture of the world today. Many young writers have grown to believe that a Marxist analysis of society presents such a picture. It creates a picture which, when placed before the eyes of the writer, should unify his personality, organize his emotions, buttress him with a tense and obdurate will to change the world.

And, in turn, this changed world will dialectically change the writer. Hence, it is through a Marxist conception of reality and society that the maximum degree of freedom in thought and feeling can be gained for the Negro writer. Further, this dramatic Marxist vision, when consciously grasped, endows the writer with a sense of dignity which no other vision can give. Ultimately, it restores to the writer his lost heritage, that is, his role as a creator of the world in which he lives, and as a creator of himself.

Yet, for the Negro writer, Marxism is but the starting point. No theory of life can take the place of life. After Marxism has laid bare the skeleton of society, there remains the task of the writer to plant flesh upon those bones out of his will to live. He may, with disgust and revulsion, say *no* and depict the horrors of capitalism encroaching upon the human being. Or he may, with hope and passion, say *yes* and depict the faint stirrings of a new and emerging life. But in whatever social voice he chooses to speak, whether positive or negative, there should always be heard or *over*-heard his faith, his necessity, his judgement.

His vision need not be simple or rendered in primer-like terms; for the life of the Negro people is not simple. The presentation of their lives should be simple, yes; but all the complexity, the strangeness, the magic wonder of life that plays like a bright sheen over the most sordid existence, should be there. To borrow a phrase from the Russians, it should have a *complex simplicity*. Eliot, Stein, Joyce, Proust, Hemingway, and Anderson; Gorky, Barbusse, Nexo, and Jack London no less than the folklore of the Negro himself should form the heritage of the Negro writer. Every iota of gain in human thought and sensibility should be ready grist for his mill, no matter how far-fetched they may seem in their immediate implications.

7) THE PROBLEM OF PERSPECTIVE

What vision must Negro writers have before their eyes in order to feel the impelling necessity for an about face? What angle of vision can show them all the forces of modern society in process, all the lines of economic development converging toward a distant point of hope? Must they believe in some "ism"?

They may feel that only dupes believe in "isms"; they feel with some measure of justification that another commitment means only another disillusionment. But anyone destitute of a theory about the meaning, structure and direction of modern society is a lost victim in a world he cannot understand or control.

But even if Negro writers found themselves through some "ism," how would that influence their writing? Are they being called upon to "preach"? To be "salesmen"? To "prostitute" their writing? Must they "sully" themselves? Must they write "propaganda"?

No; it is a question of awareness, of consciousness; it is, above all, a question of perspective.

Perspective is that part of a poem, novel, or play which a writer never puts directly upon paper. It is that fixed point in intellectual space where a writer stands to view the struggles, hopes, and sufferings of his people. There are times when he may stand too close and the result is a blurred vision. Or he may stand too far away and the result is a neglect of important things.

Of all the problems faced by writers who as a whole have never allied themselves with world movements, perspective is the most difficult of achievement. At its best, perspective is a pre-conscious assumption, something which a writer takes for granted, something which he wins through his living.

A Spanish writer recently spoke of living in the heights of one's time. Surely, perspective means just *that*.

It means that a Negro writer must learn to view the life of a Negro living in New York's Harlem or Chicago's South Side with the consciousness that one-sixth of the earth surface belongs to the working class. It means that a Negro writer must create in his readers' minds a relationship between a Negro woman hoeing cotton in the South and the men who loll in swivel chairs in Wall Street and take the fruits of her toil.

Perspective for Negro writers will come when they have looked and brooded so hard and long upon the harsh lot of their race and compared it with the hopes and struggles of minority peoples everywhere that the cold facts have begun to tell them something.

8) THE PROBLEM OF THEME

This does not mean that a Negro writer's sole concern must be with rendering the social scene; but if his conception of the life of his people is broad and deep enough, if the sense of the whole life he is seeking is vivid and strong in him, then his writing will embrace all those social, political, and economic forms under which the life of his people is manifest.

In speaking of theme one must necessarily be general and abstract; the temperament of each writer moulds and colors the world he sees. Negro life may be approached from a thousand angles, with no limit to technical and stylistic freedom.

Negro writers spring from a family, a clan, a class, and a nation; and the social units in which they are bound have a story, a record. Sense of theme will emerge in Negro writing when Negro writers try to fix this story about some pole of meaning, remembering as they do so that in the creative process meaning proceeds *equally* as much from the contemplation of the subject matter as from the hopes and apprehensions that rage in the heart of the writer.

Reduced to its simplest and most general terms, theme for Negro writers will rise from understanding the meaning of their being transplanted from a "savage" to a "civilized" culture in all of its social, political, economic, and emotional implications. It means that Negro writers must have in their consciousness the foreshortened picture of the *whole,* nourishing culture from which they were torn in Africa, and of the long, complex (and for the most part, unconscious) struggle to regain in some form and under alien conditions of life a *whole* culture again.

It is not only this picture they must have, but also a knowledge of the social and emotional milieu that gives it tone and solidity of detail. Theme for Negro writers will emerge when they have begun to feel the meaning of the history of their race as though they in one life time had lived it themselves throughout all the long centuries.

9) AUTONOMY OF CRAFT

For the Negro writer to depict this new reality requires a greater discipline and consciousness than was necessary for the so-called Harlem school of expression. Not only is the subject matter dealt with far more meaningful and complex, but the new role of the writer is qualitatively different. The Negro writers' new position demands a sharper definition of the status of his craft, and a sharper emphasis upon its functional autonomy.

Negro writers should seek through the medium of their craft to play as meaningful a role in the affairs of men as do other professionals. But if their writing is demanded to perform the social office of other professions, then the autonomy of craft is lost and writing detrimentally fused with other interests. The limitations of the craft constitute some of its greatest virtues. If the sensory vehicle of imaginative writing is required to carry too great a load of didactic material, the artistic sense is submerged.

The relationship between reality and the artistic image is not always direct and simple. The imaginative conception of a historical period will not be a carbon copy of reality. Image and emotion possess a logic of their own. A vulgarized simplicity constitutes the greatest danger in tracing the reciprocal interplay between the writer and his environment.

Writing has its professional autonomy; it should complement other professions but it should not supplant them or be swamped by them.

10) THE NECESSITY FOR COLLECTIVE WORK

It goes without saying that these things cannot be gained by Negro writers if their present mode of isolated writing and living continues. This isolation exists *among* Negro writers as well as *between* Negro and white writers. The Negro writers' lack of thorough integration with the American scene, their lack of a clear realization among themselves of their possible role, have bred generation after generation of embittered and defeated literati.

Barred for decades from the theater and publishing houses, Negro writers have been *made* to feel a sense of difference. So deep has this white-hot iron of exclusion been burnt into their hearts that thousands have all but lost the desire to become identified with American civilization. The Negro writers' acceptance of this enforced isolation and their attempt to justify it is but a defense-reflex of the whole special way of life which has been rammed down their throats.

This problem, by its very nature, is one which must be approached contemporaneously from *two* points of view. The ideological unity of Negro writers and the alliance of that unity with all the progressive ideas of our day is the primary prerequisite for collective work. On the shoulders of white writers and Negro writers alike rest the responsibility of ending this mistrust and isolation.

By placing cultural health above narrow sectional prejudices, liberal writers of all races can help to break the stony soil of aggrandizement out of which the stunted plants of Negro nationalism grow. And, simultaneously, Negro writers can help to weed out these choking growths of reactionary nationalism and replace them with hardier and sturdier types.

These tasks are imperative in light of the fact that we live in a time when the majority of the most basic assumptions of life can no longer be taken for granted. Tradition is no longer a guide. The world has grown huge and cold. Surely this is the moment to ask questions, to theorize, to speculate, to wonder out of what materials can a human world be built.

Each step along this unknown path should be taken with thought, care, self-consciousness, and deliberation. When Negro writers think they have arrived at something which smacks of truth, humanity, they should want to test it with others, feel it with a degree of passion and strength that will enable them to communicate it to millions who are groping like themselves.

Writers faced with such tasks can have no possible time for malice or jealousy. The conditions for the growth of each writer depend too much upon the good work of other writers. Every first rate novel, poem, or play lifts the level of consciousness higher.

When Black women's books are dealt with at all, it is usually in the context of Black literature, which largely ignores the implications of sexual politics. When white women look at Black women's words they are of course ill-equipped to deal with the subtleties of racial politics. A Black feminist approach to literature that embodies the realization that the politics of sex as well as the politics of race and class are crucially interlocking factors in the works of Black women writers is an absolute necessity.

BARBARA SMITH—*"Toward a Black Feminist Criticism"*

The Contemporary Afro-American Novel, 1: Neorealism

BERNARD W. BELL

REBELLION OR REVOLUtion—that was the burning question of the 1960s. Whether the cry was "We Shall Overcome" or "Burn, baby, burn!" black and white voices were raised in protest against racism, poverty, war, corruption, and sexism. Americans were deeply disillusioned by the moral bankruptcy of their political and economic system and took radical action to correct or to escape the social injustice of the decade in myriad forms of movements and cults. These radical movements and cults ranged from the bombing of buildings identified as part of the military-industrial complex by the Weathermen, a white revolutionary splinter group of Students for a Democratic Society (SDS), and the burying of cars as menaces to the ecology by college students, to the emergence of the drop-out and turn-on followers of Timothy Leary, the guru of the drug culture and former Harvard professor, and the ritual murders by the Charles Manson cult. Eclipsing the first manned United States landing on the moon in 1969, a revolution in moral conscience and social consciousness was underway. Spearheading these radical

changes and most significant for their impact on the Afro-American novel from 1963 to 1983 were the black power movement and, toward the end of the 1960s, the women's rights movement.

THE BLACK POWER AND BLACK ARTS MOVEMENTS

The slogan *Black Power* was popularized by Stokely Carmichael and Willie Ricks during SNCC'S continuation of James Meredith's protest march through the South in 1966. But the phrase is more than a slogan and has a meaning as large as the history of the struggle of black people against racism in the United States. As a concept *black power* expresses the determination of black people to define and liberate themselves. The concept rests on the fundamental premise "that group solidarity is necessary before a group can operate effectively from a bargaining position of strength

Reprinted from *The Afro-American Novel and Its Tradition,* by Bernard W. Bell (Amherst: University of Massachusetts Press, 1987), copyright © by The University of Massachusetts Press.

in a pluralistic society." As Stokely Carmichael and Charles V. Hamilton explain:

> The adoption of the concept of Black Power is one of the most legitimate and healthy developments in American politics and race relations in our time. . . . It is a call for black people in this country to unite, to recognize their heritage, to build a sense of community. It is a call for black people to begin to define their own goals, to lead their own organizations and to support those organizations. It is a call to reject the racist institutions and values of this society.[1]

Black power thus has a wide range of meanings, from the development of ecomonic and political solidarity and the attainment of full equality as American citizens to the radical reform or, if necessary, revolutionary overthrow of old political and economic structures.

The concept also has a long history. In 1954 Richard Wright titled his book about Ghana *Black Power,* but as the essays in Floyd Barbour's *Black Power Revolt* reveal, the concept can be traced back to Benjamin Banneker's letter to Thomas Jefferson in 1791. The most passionate early statement on black power is David Walker's "Appeal to the Colored Citizens of the World" in 1829. On the international level the concept was promoted by the six Pan-African meetings convened between 1900 and 1945. "From the end of World War II through the early 1960s," historian John H. Bracey, Jr., writes, "integration was the dominant ideology among Negro protest movements. A few nationalist groups, such as the UNIA splinter groups and the Nation of Islam, persisted but could arouse little mass support."[2] Among the many legal actions, sit-ins, marches, freedom rides, boycotts, demonstrations, and voter registration drives, the most salient civil rights events of the period were the 1954 Supreme Court school desegregation decision, the 1963 March on Washington, and the 1964 Civil Rights Act. The two dominant yet vastly different black leaders of the period were Malcolm X, the charismatic, militant Minister of the

Nation of Islam and its chief spokesman until 1964, when Malcolm broke with his leader Elijah Muhammad over irreconcilable doctrinal differences; and Martin Luther King, Jr., the equally charismatic, nonviolent Southern Baptist preacher who rose to national prominence as the moving spirit of the Montgomery bus boycott in 1955, of the passive resistance tactics of the Southern Christian Leadership Conference (SCLC), a major civil rights organization, and the March on Washington in 1963. Assassinated for their activism, Malcolm in 1965 and King in 1968, both men became martyrs of the black power movement and paradigms of heroism in the black arts movement, most compellingly re-created in the tradition of the Afro-American novel in John A. Williams's *Man Who Cried I Am.*

In the early 1960s the example of the emerging free African nations and the Cuban Revolution kindled the latent revolutionary nationalism of many black Americans and spurred the development of black studies programs in colleges across the nation. Black power advocates redefined the liberation struggle of black Americans as part of the larger struggle of oppressed peoples against Western imperialism. Frustrated by the snail's pace of integration efforts and the tactics of passive resistance, they revived indigenous theories of the colonial relationship of blacks to the dominant culture of the United States. In a cogent explanation of the theory of black Americans as subjects of domestic colonialism, social critic Harold Cruse writes:

> The American Negro shares with colonial peoples many of the socioeconomic factors which form the material basis for present day revolutionary nationalism. Like the peoples of the underdeveloped countries, the Negro suffers in varying degree from hunger, illiteracy, disease, ties to the land, urban and semi-urban slums, cultural starvation, and the psychological reactions to being ruled over by others not of his kind. He experiences the tyranny imposed upon

the lives of those who inhabit underdeveloped countries. . . . From the beginning, the American Negro has existed as a colonial being. His enslavement coincided with the colonial expansion of European powers and was nothing more or less than a condition of domestic colonialism. Instead of the United States establishing a colonial empire in Africa, it brought the colonial system home and installed it in the Southern states. When the Civil War broke up the slave system and the Negro was emancipated, he gained only partial freedom. Emancipation elevated him only to the position of a semi-independent man, not to that of an equal or independent being. . . . As a wage laborer or tenant farmer, the Negro is discriminated against and exploited. Those in the educated, professional, and intellectual classes suffer a similar fate. Except for a very small percentage of the Negro intelligentsia, the Negro functions in a subcultural world made up, usually of necessity, of his own race only. . . . The factor which differentiates the Negro's status from that of a pure colonial status is that his position is maintained in the "home" country in close proximity to the dominant racial group. It is not at all remarkable then that the semi-colonial status of the Negro has given rise to nationalist movements. It would be surprising if it had not.[3]

In the revolt against historical exploitation and the many beatings, jailings, and killings of civil rights activists, blacks in the communities across the nation began striking out in rage: in Harlem in 1964, Watts in 1965, Newark and Detroit in 1967, and nearly every city in the nation in 1968 after the assassination of Martin Luther King, Jr. Responding to the needs of the black lower class, some groups, such as US, promoted the development of an indigenous African-based cultural value system, ritualized in the ceremony of Kwanzaa, a holiday celebrated from December 26 through January 1 to reinforce the spiritual ties of black Americans to Africa. Others, such as the Black Panther Party, the Revolutionary Action

Movement (RAM), the Republic of New Africa, and the League of Revolutionary Black Workers, adopted the idealogy and strategy of achieving black self-determination by any means necessary, including armed struggle.

"Black Art is the aesthetic and spiritual sister of the Black Power concept," writes Larry Neal, a major proponent of the black arts movement. "As such, it envisions an art that speaks directly to the needs and aspirations of Black America. In order to perform this task, the Black Arts Movement proposes a radical reordering of the western cultural aesthetic. It proposes a separate symbolism, mythology, critique and iconology."[4] It was launched in the spring of 1964 when LeRoi Jones, whose play *Dutchman* had stunned the theater world, and other black artists opened the Black Arts Repertory Theatre-School in Harlem and took their plays, poetry readings, and concerts into the streets of the black community. Before the end of the summer the Harlem school was forced to close because of internal problems, but black art groups soon sprang up on campuses and in cities across the nation. At the same time, black musicians like Little Richard, Chuck Berry, B. B. King, Muddy Waters, Otis Redding, Aretha Franklin, John Coltrane, Stevie Wonder, Jimi Hendrix, Isaac Hayes, and the Supremes became national and international style setters. Black actors and actresses such as Sidney Poitier, James Earl Jones, Cicely Tyson, Ossie Davis, Ruby Dee, Harry Belafonte, Clarence Williams, and Bill Cosby became more highly visible in major roles in the movies and on television. And mass periodicals such as *Essence, Encore, Black Collegian, Black Enterprise,* and *Black World;* small presses like Broadside and Third World; and journals like *Umbra, Black Dialogue, Liberator, Journal of Black Poetry,* and *Black Scholar* were born and, in some cases, died early, untimely deaths due to financial difficulties.

Because the black arts and black power concepts both relate broadly to the Afro-American's desire for self-determination and nationhood, both are nationalistic. "One is concerned with the relationship between art and politics; and other with the art of politics."[5] Nevertheless, most black writing of the 1960s, Neal contends, was aimed at the destruction of the double-consciousness described by Du Bois in *The Souls of Black Folk*. "It has been aimed at consolidating the African-American personality. And it has not been essentially a literature of protest. It has, instead, turned its attention inward to the internal problems of the group. . . . It is a literature primarily directed at the conscience of black people."[6]

THE WOMEN'S RIGHTS MOVEMENT

Just as the nineteenth-century struggle for equal rights for women was fired by the struggle to free the slaves, the women's rights movements of the 1960s were fired by the civil rights and black power movements. "The call to that first Woman's Rights Convention came about," as feminist Betty Friedan explains, "because an educated woman, who had already participated in shaping society as an abolitionist, came face to face with the realities of a housewife's drudgery and isolation in a small town."[7] Similarly, participation in the civil rights movement, ambivalence about the black power movement, especially its male chauvinism, and boredom with their actual or expected lives as suburban housewives spurred many American women more than a century later to renewed activism for women's rights. Most of the leading feminists, of course, were and are middle-class white women. Consequently, the question arises: How relevant are the experiences, truths, and priorities of white women to black women? Subject to all the restrictions against blacks as well as those against women, the black woman is for many people, as black folk wisdom teaches, "de mule uh de world." Her experience and truths are generally glossed over or ignored when references are made to women and blacks. Even so, as Gerda Lerner documents in *Black Women in White America*, "black women, speaking with

many voices and expressing many individual opinions, have been nearly unanimous in their insistence that their own emancipation cannot be separated from the emancipation of their men. Their liberation depends on the liberation of the race and the improvement of the life of the black community."[8] Thus, as the public interest began to shift in the late 1960s from the rights of blacks to the rights of women, publishers became more receptive and the voices of black women writers, and novels by Margaret Walker, Rosa Guy, Mary Vroman, Louise Meriwether, Paule Marshall, Kristin Hunter, Caroline Polite, Sarah Wright, Alice Walker, Alice Childress, Ellease Southerland, Gloria Naylor, Toni Morrison, Gayl Jones, and Toni Cade Bambara, among the better known, were all published before the end of 1983.

Facile generalizations about the parallels between the struggle of blacks and women for status ignore the complexity and distinctiveness of the history of black women, a history that reaches from the legacy of their African past and slave experience to their experience with industrialization and modern corporate America. "There is nothing to indicate," as political analyst Toni Cade astutely reminds us, "that the African woman, who ran the marketplace, who built dams, who engaged in international commerce and diplomacy, who sat on thrones, who donned armor to wage battle against the European invaders and the corrupt chieftains who engaged in the slave trade, who were consulted as equals in the affairs of state—nothing to indicate that they were turning their men into faggots, were victims of penis envy, or any such nonsense. There is nothing to indicate that the Sioux, Seminole, Iroquois or other 'Indian' nations felt oppressed or threatened by their women, who had mobility, privileges, a voice in governing of the commune. There is evidence, however, that the European white was confused and alarmed by the egalitarian system of these societies and did much to wreck it, creating wedges between the men and women."[9] In the late sixties, therefore, many Afro-Americans were encouraged by historical circumstances to continue resisting or rejecting Eurocentric models and interpretations of manhood and womanhood. They turned instead to non-Western, nonwhite communities and Afrocentric models to discover or create possibilities for autonomous selves and communities through a commitment to the development of a more just, egalitarian social order.

This means, then, that the reality of black womanhood is not dependent on black males first defining their manhood. "Above all else," stresses "The Black Feminist Statement" of the Combahee River Collective, "our politics initially sprang from the shared belief that Black women are inherently valuable, that our liberation is a necessity not as an adjunct to somebody else's but because of our need as human persons for autonomy."[10] Although drafted in 1977 by a radical group of primarily New York black feminists and lesbians, this statement nevertheless crystallizes the alienation of many black women from the Euro-American feminist movement:

> We believe that sexual politics under patriarchy is as pervasive in Black women's lives as are the politics of class and race. We also often find it difficult to separate race from class from sex oppression because in our lives they are most often experienced simultaneously. We know that there is such a thing as racial-sexual oppression which is neither solely racial nor solely sexual, e.g., the history of rape of Black women by white men as a weapon of political repression.
>
> Although we are feminists and lesbians, we feel solidarity with progressive Black men and do not advocate the fractionalization that white women who are separatists demand. Our situation as Black people necessitates that we have solidarity around the fact of race, which white women of course do not need to have with white men, unless it is their negative solidarity as racial oppressors. We struggle together with Black

men against racism, while we also struggle with Black men about sexism.[11]

In *Black Women Writers at Work* Bambara in 1983 told an interviewer:

> What has changed about the women's movement is the way we perceive it, the way black women define the term, the phenomena and our participation in it. White bourgeois feminist organizations captured the arena, media attention, and the country's imagination. . . . Black women and other women of color have come around to recognizing that the movement is much more than a few organizations. The movement is exactly what the word suggests, a motion of the mind. . . . We're more inclined now, women of color, to speak of black midwives and the medicine women of the various communities when we talk of health care rather than assume we have to set up women's health collectives on the same order as non-colored women have. In organizing, collectivizing, researching, strategizing, we're much less antsy than we were a decade ago. We are more inclined to trust our own traditions, whatever name we gave and now give those impulses, those groups, those agendas, and are less inclined to think we have to sound like, build like, non-colored groups that identify themselves as feminist or as women's rights groups, or so it seems to me.[12]

This not only gets to the heart of the differences that many black women have about the priorities and objectives of the women's rights movement, but also explains in part why Alice Walker adapted the term *womanist* from black folk expression to signify a black feminist or feminist of color, a woman who, among other things, is audaciously committed to the survival and wholeness of entire people, male and female. More to the point of my readings of contemporary Afro-American novels by black women, the comments above provide the necessary context or subtext for a better understanding of why black women are primarily concerned with how racism, sexism, and classism have influenced the development of love, power, autonomy, creativity, manhood, and womanhood in the black family and community.

In pursuing these themes black women novelists provide a much neglected perspective and chorus of voices on the human experience, but, contrary to the assumptions of some critics, this does not necessarily mean that their works constitute a distinctive literary tradition. The absence, silence, or misrepresentation of black women in literary and nonliterary texts or contexts by black men as well as white men and women is now commonplace knowledge. "Except for Gwendolyn Brooks, and perhaps Margaret Walker," as Calvin Hernton reminds us in an extremely rare and perceptive black feminist essay by a black male, "the name of not one black women writer and not one female protagonist was accorded a worthy status in the black literary world prior to the 1970's."[13] Black feminist critics, such as Mary Helen Washington in her introduction to *Black-Eyed Susans* and Barbara Christian in *Black Women Novelists,* applaud the displacement of stereotypic with realistic images by black women writers like Morrison, Meriwether, Marshall, and Bambara. In her essays Andrea Benton Rushing convincingly illustrates that Eurocentric qualities and categories of stereotypic white women such as passivity, compliancy, the submissive wife, and the woman on a pedestal are inappropriately applied in analyses of black women characters, whose historical experiences and cultural imperatives are different from white women.[14] As illustrated in their fiction, interviews in *Black Women Writers at Work,* and the pioneer essays on black feminist criticism by Barbara Smith and Deborah E. McDowell, many black women novelists employ to a greater or lesser degree the following signs and structures: (1) motifs of interlocking racist, sexist, and classist oppression; (2) black female protagonists;

(3) spiritual journeys from victimization to the realization of personal autonomy or creativity; (4) a centrality of female bonding or networking; (5) a sharp focus on personal relationships in the family and community; (6) deeper, more detailed exploration and validation of the epistemological power of the emotions; (7) iconography of women's clothing; and (8) black female language.[15] While agreeing with Smith that feminist criticism is "a valid and necessary cultural and political enterprise," McDowell questions the impreciseness of current definitions of lesbianism by black feminists, the possible reductiveness of a lesbian aesthetic, and the vagueness of Smith's analysis in "Toward a Black Feminist Criticism." McDowell advocates that black feminist critics combine a contextual approach with rigorous textual analysis, including a concern for the issue of gender-specific uses of language.[16]

But many black women writers, including feminists, who acknowledge the influence of male as well as female literary foreparents, underscore the problematics of a separate black female literary tradition. Bambara, for example, says:

> Women are less likely to skirt the feeling place, to finesse with language, to camouflage emotions. But a lot of male writers knock that argument out . . . one of the crucial differences that strikes me immediately among poets, dramatists, novelists, storytellers is in the handling of children. I can't nail it down, but the attachment to children and to two-plus-two reality is simply stronger in women's writings; but there are exceptions. And finally, there isn't nearly as large a bulk of gynocentric writing as there is phallic-obsessive writings. I'd love to read/hear a really good discussion of just this issue by someone who's at home with close textual reading—cups, bowls and other motifs in women's writings. We've only just begun . . . to fashion a woman's vocabulary to deal with the "silences" of our lives.[17]

Mary Helen Washington agrees, as she argues for a black female literary tradition in her introduction to *Midnight Birds:* "Black women are searching for a specific language, specific symbols, specific images with which to record their lives, and, even though they can claim a rightful place in the Afro-American tradition and the feminist tradition of women writers, it is also clear that, for purposes of liberation, black women writers will first insist on their own name, their own space."[18] Because there are many intertextual parallels between black male and female novelists, readers should examine these parallels to determine the distinctiveness, consistency, and frequency of their appearance and use in narratives by black women in deciding for themselves whether a separate black female literary tradition exists.

TOWARD MODERNISM

Because the novel is a synthetic literary form, the product of a complex blend of the social and cultural forces that shape the novelist's attitude toward life and language, especially the imaginative use of narrative conventions, it is not surprising that from 1962 to 1983 the Afro-American novel has been characterized by continuity and change. During this period, black novelists sought structures and styles appropriate for the imaginative reconstruction of their sense of the double-consciousness of black people as refracted through their particular vision of a rapidly changing experience of social reality and art. The eruption of the Vietnam and Arab-Israel wars, the assassinations of major political leaders and civil rights workers, the profiteering of multinational corporations, the launching of the first manned flight to the moon, the emergence of the black power movement, the exposure of the Watergate scandal involving "high crimes and misdemeanors" by President Nixon, and the influence of the pill in radicalizing the women's rights movement swept away most of the vestiges of the traditional grounds for

confidence in a stable universe, a democratic society, and a mimetic approach to art. Ambivalence toward authority (father, president, God, family, nation, Kingdom of God) with its conflicting attitudes of acceptance and rejection, deepened and spread to all aspects of life and to all fields, resulting often in a crisis of belief for many novelists and readers.

In the past, fact was often stranger than fiction, but in the modern and contemporary worlds the line between fantasy and reality is nearly invisible. To protect the rights of the Vietnamese people the American military machine destroys their villages, crops, and countryside with thousands of tons of bombs and deadly toxic chemicals. To preserve law and order the police use clubs, water hoses, electric cattle prods, and snarling dogs on praying, singing civil rights demonstrators. To save the souls of his flock of followers, a contemporary shepherd, the Reverend James Jones, encouraged hundreds to drink poison Kool-Aid. Challenging the authority and purpose of literature, cultural theorists and literary critics celebrate it as a nondiscursive, nonconceptual mode of discourse that has no authority or purpose beyond its symbols, signs, and structure. How do contemporary novelists respond to this moral breakdown, social absurdity, and discrediting of the moral authority of art? More in despair than in hope, more concerned with problems of language than with problems of life, postmodernist Euro-American novelists such as John Barth, William Gass, Donald Barthelme, Kurt Vonnegut, Jr., Ronald Sukenick, and Richard Brautigan turn to fantasy and black or gallows humor. Other contemporary novelists such as Bernard Malamud, Saul Bellow, and Flannery O'Connor use more traditional techniques to portray more conventional visions and values. In contrast, as contemporary Afro-American novelists attempt to displace personal ambivalence and social absurdity with a new order of thinking, feeling, and sharing based on self-determination, a sense of community, and a respect for human rights, most, like John O. Killens, John A. Williams, and Alice Walker continue the tradition of realism; while some, like Toni Morrison, explore poetic realism. Others, like Margaret Walker, Ernest Gaines, William Melvin Kelley, Ronald Fair, Hal Bennett, Charles Wright, Clarence Major, John Wideman, and Ishmael Reed, experiment with modern forms of slave narrative, romance, fable, and satire.

LITERARY NEOREALISM: CRITICAL AND POETIC

Despite the modern formalist view that separates the literary work from objective reality, the appeal of several types of traditional realism is seen in first novels by the majority of black novelists of the sixties. Many of these, such as Gordon Park's *Learning Tree* (1963), Kristin Hunter's *God Bless the Child* (1967), Rosa Guy's *Bird at My Window* (1966), Barry Beckham's *My Main Mother* (1969), Louise Meriwether's *Daddy Was a Number Runner* (1970), and Al Young's *Snakes* (1970), and *bildungsromans*, stories about growing up black in Kansas, Harlem, Maine, and Detroit. Some, such as Nathan A. Heard's *Howard Street* (1968), Robert Dean Pharr's *Book of Numbers* (1969), and George Cain's *Blueschild Baby* (1970), are graphic, naturalistic accounts of the sporting life of hustlers, whores, and addicts. Others, like Cecil Brown's *Life and Loves of Mr. Jiveass Nigger* (1969) and Clarence Major's *All Night Visitors* (1969) are clinically detailed studies of black expatriate and domestic existential stud types. All are essentially mimetic in their tacit common-sense assumption of an intelligible though problematic reality and in their efforts to achieve a close correspondence between their symbolic act of representation and aspects of objective reality. As realists the authors, with Major the most striking exception, are generally more pragmatic than idealistic in their quest for truth and their concern for the effect of their work on the reader. Because limitations of space preclude

discussing all of these by no means mutually exclusive types of neorealism, I will focus on two that represent the polarities of the continuing tradition of realism—critical and poetic—and ambivalence of Afro-American novelists toward their dual cultural heritage.

But first we should be clear about the meaning of neorealism. Like earlier types of realism in the Afro-American novel, which used the conventional linear, closed plot and combined elements of the slave narratives, historical romance, and genteel realism, and which attacked racial discrimination while embracing middle-class values, neorealism is not only a literary method, but also a philosophical and political attitude toward the human condition. It is in sharp contrast to the implicit nihilism and explicit antimimesis of Alain Robbe-Grillet and Ronald Sukenick, who reject conventional approaches to plot and characterization as inadequate for expressing their perceptions of cultural disintegration and the indeterminacy of language. They prefer to experiment with fantasy and self-reflexional linguistic signs in reconstituting both the novel and reality as fictions. But Afro-American neorealists, like earlier black realists, assume that man is a social being who ought not to be separated from the social and historical context, no matter how alienating and discontinuous, in which he finds his significance and develops his potential as an individual. In short, there is more hope for humanity and the world expressed in Afro-American neorealism and, as the next chapter will illustrate, modernism and postmodernism than in European and Euro-American postmodernism. However, in contrast to traditional social realism such as Frank Webb's *The Garies and Their Friends* and Jessie Fauset's *Chinaberry Tree*, which are essentially bourgeois in the truth they express in a documentary, linear manner, neorealism, as John O. Killen's *Youngblood* illustrates, is generally alienated from the old racist, sexist, socioeconomic order and seeks to displace it with new terms of order. Aside from the neoslave narratives of Margaret Walker and Ernest Gaines, which will be examined more appropriately in the next chapter, the most fascinating types of neorealism in the contemporary Afro-American novel are critical realism, which is related to socialist realism, and poetic realism, which uses regional and racial matter in a poetic manner.

CRITICAL REALISM

Influenced by the radical struggles of the age for social change, especially the black power, black arts, and women's rights movements, some contemporary Afro-American novelists explored the flexibility and appropriateness of critical realism for their color, sex, and class approach to reality. Unlike social realism, a non-Marxist term referring to the generally middle-class life, manners, and truth treated in nineteenth-century realism, critical realism is a Marxist literary concept that is illustrated in the work of Balzac and Flaubert as well as Turgenev and Tolstoy. It is most meaningfully explained by its relationship to socialist realism, which is the antithesis of modernism. The perspective of "socialist realism differs from critical realism," writes Hungarian critic Georg Lukács, "not only in being based on a concrete socialist perspective, but also in using this perspective to describe the forces working towards socialism *from the inside.*" Concreteness involves an awareness of the class and ideological development, structure, and goal of society as a whole. Socialist realism, then, is historical and comprehensive in its description of the totality of society, and seeks to identify the human qualities essential for the creation of a new, progressive social order. In contrast, critical realism is not an outright affirmation of socialism so much as it is a negative attitude toward capitalism and a readiness to respect the perspective of socialism and not condemn it out of hand. Whenever such an affirmation is evident though, it will be somewhat abstract, "for even where a critical realist attempts to describe socialism, his is bound to

be a description from the outside." The writer using the "outside" method derives exemplary character types from the individual and his personal conflicts; and from this base he works toward wider social significance. But the writer using "the 'inside' method," Lukács explains, "seeks to discover an Archimedian point in the midst of social contradictions, and then bases its typology on an analysis of these contradictions."[19] Although none of the black neorealists is politically committed to Marxist doctrines, Killens, Williams, and Alice Walker, as I will illustrate, use the indirect, outside method of critical realism as well as other conventions to develop their negative attitude toward capitalism and their positive typologies for a new social order. Aesthetically, they all seem to believe with Georg Lukács that perspective is of major importance, with Henry James that character is the essence of everything, and with Ralph Ellison that contemporary fiction, despite its technical experimentation, is an ethical as well as a linguistic sign system. Because of their historical ambivalence, contemporary Afro-American novelists, have, in short, tailored critical realism and traditional social realism to fit their consciousness of the interrelated dynamics of racism, capitalism, and sexism.

John Oliver Killens (1916–)

If Richard Wright is the spiritual father of critical realism, John O. Killens is its contemporary moving force. Born on January 14, 1916, in Macon, Georgia, he was raised and educated primarily in the South. He also attended Howard, Columbia, and New York universities. A major figure in the Harlem left-wing literary movement of the 1950s, Killens was a founder of the Harlem Writer's Guild and contributor to Paul Robeson's *Freedom* newspaper. In the June 1952 issue of *Freedom* he reveals his belief in a rather inflexible theory of socialist realism by denouncing Ralph Ellison's *Invisible Man* as a "vicious distortion of Negro life."[20] His commitment to the tradition of realism was expressed not only in his writings but also in the creative writing workshops he taught in the 1960s at the New School for Social Research and at Fisk, Howard, and Columbia universities, where he encouraged the creative efforts of black women writers like Sarah Wright.

Although he has written a couple of screen-scripts and plays, a collection of essays, and numerous uncollected pieces, Killens is best known for his four novels: *Youngblood* (1954), *And Then We Heard the Thunder* (1963), *'Sippi* (1967), and *The Cotillion* (1971). His declared intention in all his writing is "to change the world, to capture reality, to melt it down and forge it into something entirely different." Politically, the envisioned something different is socialism, and the method is critical realism. The emphasis in his novels is on telling "as much of the truth as he knows the painful truth to be, and let the flak fall where it may."[21] Believing with Du Bois and Wright that the truth will set us free, he focuses on past and present socioeconomic forces and racial prejudices in America that inhibit and distort the development of dignity and unity among black and working-class people. More important, for him and some other black neorealists the concept of "the hero" is still viable. "At a time when the novel throughout the world celebrates the emergence of the anti-hero," writes Addison Gayle, "Killens reasserts the value of the hero, argues, that is, that heroism lay in the attempt to produce a better world for oneself and his people, and that the telling mark of the hero is his love for people."[22]

Youngblood and *The Cotillion* are the best examples of Killens's preoccupation with color and class, for in them he affirms the potential of black people and celebrates their development of black consciousness. In *Youngblood* Killens portrays the life of a black family in a small Southern town during the Depression when thousands of blacks were fleeing the South in search of a better life and vicariously triumphing over the power of whites with Joe Louis. The novel primarily delineates the character of Robert Youngblood, but it also bares the tough roots of the Youngblood family tree. The accounts of Robert's parents, Laurie Lee and Joseph Youngblood, for example, foreshadow the heroic spirit of their son, whose experiences, like those of his parents, convince him that the only way for blacks to live with dignity in America is to unite and fight for their human and civil rights.

The title of the novel, the biblical subtitles, and the verses from black spirituals which introduce its four major divisions, together with its episodic structure and realistically drawn characters, all reinforce the theme that a dynamic, assertive new generation of black Americans is coming of age and continuing the struggle against racial, economic, and sexual exploitation. In documentary fashion, Killens moves from one episode to the next, invariably selecting episodes that reveal the heroic spirit of the Youngbloods while, at the same time, vividly—sometimes melodramat-ically—depicting the fear, hate, and violence that characterized race relations in the Deep South at the turn of the twentieth century. Laurie's earliest and most indelible impres-sion of white people, for instance, is the terri-fying, debasing experience she had at eleven years old with a white man who not only tried to rape her, but also "upped her skirt and peed on her thigh" in utter contempt for her as a black person.

More important than the structure and style of *Youngblood,* however, are its characters, who dramatize the moral and political idea that blacks ought to stay in the South and fight for their rights. As idealized "new Negroes" of the twentieth century, the Youngbloods repre-sent the generation of proud, enlightened people whose sacrifices, unity, and militancy are essential qualities for the progressive society of tomorrow. Laurie, symbolically born in Tipkin, Georgia, at precisely 12:01 AM

January 1, 1900, is a heroic Southern black mother who passes on the lessons of her grandmother and teaches her children to "fight em every inch of the way, especially the big rich ones."[23] Her husband, Joe, stands as a strong, fiercely proud working-class black who resolves to die a man rather than live a coward. For his determination to end the practice of short-changing his pay, Joe is shot and killed by the white paymaster. Although the narrator is a disembodied omniscient presence, there is little moral, political, or emotional distance between him and the Youngbloods. He completely embraces their values and encourages our identification with them.

In addition to the parents, there are the Youngblood children, Jenny and Robert, who, in their proud spirit and firm belief in the power of black unity and militancy to achieve economic and social freedom, continue the tradition of their parents. Richard Myles, a black college-educated New Yorker whose tragic love affair motivated him to rebel against his middle-class background and plunge into civil rights work in Georgia, also helps to shape the protagonist's growing black consciousness. More traditional and negative in character are Leroy Jackson and Benjamin Blake, twentieth-century "handkerchief heads": black people who betray their race to the white community for personal gain.

On the other side are such stock white characters as George Cross, Jr., a die-hard conservative Southerner who is irrevocably committed to the exploitative way of life on which his power and privilege are based; Dr. Riley, a Southern liberal who does not live up to his expressed commitment to social equality when a dying black man needs his help; the ministers Culpepper and Poultry, traditional Southern fundamentalist leaders who pervert the Scriptures to terrorize and control their guilt-ridden followers; and Oscar Jefferson, the obligatory "good" poor white Southerner whose gnawing conscience impels

him to volunteer his blood in a futile effort to save Joe Youngblood's life.

At the end of the novel, the progressive color and class consciousness of the Youngblood family prevails. Although Joe Youngblood is killed for his courageous refusal to be cheated by the white paymaster, the success of his son Robert in organizing fellow workers into a union and the silent display of unity and militancy at Joe's funeral at the close of the book imply victory for the family and a new social order. Predictably, Killens's answer to the thematic question of the book—"How do you live in a white man's world?"—is dramatically answered by the indomitable fighting spirit of the Youngbloods themselves.

Revealing an increasing use of the black oral tradition, *And Then We Heard the Thunder* and *'Sippi* also focus on the themes of black awareness and unity. The message in *And Then We Heard the Thunder* is that blacks should neither sacrifice their manhood nor compromise their dignity at any time, place, or cost. The Southern setting and dialogue, which sparkles with signifying, folksayings, and ethnic humor, estalish the ironic situation and define the characters. The irony of the plot is that black Americans had to wage a double war for freedom during World War II: one overseas against foreign fascism and the other at home against domestic fascism. The third-person narrator traces the evolving black consciousness of Solomon "Solly" Saunders, an ambitious middle-class soldier who attempts to ignore his color in order to achieve success in the white world only to discover in an apocalyptic racial war that "all of his individual solutions and his personal assets—Looks, Personality, Education, Success, Acceptance, Security, the whole damn shooting match, was one great grand illusion, without dignity."[24] Through Solly, Killens predicts the transformation of many Negroes into blacks during the 1960s. "If I'm proud of me," Solly says after reading Wright's *Twelve Million Black Voices*, "I don't need to hate Mister Charlie's people. I don't want to. I don't need to. If I love me, I can also love the whole damn human race. Black, brown, yellow, white" (p. 372). But love is an ideal state derived from social reality. "Perhaps the New World *would* come raging out of Africa and Asia with a new and different dialogue that was people-oriented. What other hope was there?" (p. 499). Meanwhile, the reality was the racial war that ends the novel and the conviction of the black soldiers who died in that war that it was necessary to beat some sense into the heads of white folks to get their respect. The class struggle does not therefore dominate the struggle for racial justice in Killens's consciousness but, as Solly illustrates, it is intertwined with it.

In *'Sippi* Killens explores the human story behind the impact of the Supreme Court school desegregation decision of 1954. With Mississippi and New York as the backdrop of his huge canvas, he outlines the radical changes in attitude and strategy that characterize the increasingly bitter conflict between white power and black power during the 1960s. For the most part, however, the idea that black people must unite and organize their economic and political strength so that they can seize the constitutional rights that whites will not grant them is passionately but less credibly and excitingly rendered in *'Sippi*. At the center of Killens's third novel is the growth of the protagonist into black manhood and an Afro-American version of the tale of two star-crossed lovers of the mid-twentieth century: Carrie Wakefield, the daughter of a wealthy plantation owner and the apotheosis of Southern white womanhood, and Charlie Chaney, the son of Wakefield's faithful black field hand and the prototype of the contemporary militant black prince. A fusion of critical realism and historical romance, the novel opens with a stylized prologue that explains the folkloristic and thematic significance of the book's title. The chain of reactions set off by the Supreme Court school

desegregation decision of 1954—beginning with Jesse Chaney's wry announcement that there "'ain' no more Mississippi. Ain' no more Mississippi. It's jes' 'Sippi from now on'"[25] and concluding the book with the assassination of the leader of the black revolution and the protagonist's grim decision to join the Elders for Protection and Defense of Wakefield County—ushered in a new age of black militancy and self-determination.

In *Youngblood* Killens comes closest to portraying the role that the revolutionary working class plays in the new society; in *The Cotillion*, despite the working-class status of the Lovejoys, this perspective is underdeveloped. In Killens's alienation from the old order, melodramatically illustrated in the apocalyptic battle between white and black American soldiers at the end of *And Then We Heard the Thunder*, class, color, and culture were inextricably linked. But class, for him, becomes a subordinate element in his writing during the black power and black arts movements of the late 1960s when the struggle for racial and cultural identity was at its peak, and the intended primary audience was the black underclass. This is particularly true in the satirical typology of *The Cotillion*, which is self-consciously neither comprehensive in its description of society nor objective in its historical vision.

Set in New York, *The Cotillion* is a "Black black comedy," written in "Afro-Americanese" to satirize debutante balls and "other Bourgeois bullshit . . . pulling Black folks in the opposite direction of peoplehood."[26] The characters, with the exception of the narrator, are flat and one dimensional, the language idiomatic and hyperbolic, the events melodramatic and ironic, the structure loose and freewheeling, and the style vibrant and witty. "White folks invented these debitramp balls," the heroine's father explains, "so that their darling little heifers could git a good shot at the prize bull in the pasture. . . . But colored folks just do these things cause they see white folks doing them" (p. 158). In her quest for identity Yoruba Evelyn Lovejoy, the heroine, is torn between the urge to whiteness of Daphne, her pretentious, Barbadian mother, and the call to black consciousness of her Georgia-born father, Matthew, and her black prince, Ben Ali Lumumba, the jive-talking narrator-writer who turns the Grand Cotillion into a black and beautiful occasion.

Using conventional techniques, Killens is less concerned in his novels with the forces breaking up our society than with those leading toward a new nation, a new social order. Because of his faith in the future and in people, he continues the tradition of conventional plots and of the outsider as hero. But the essential values of the new social order he envisions are found in his love and respect for the dignity, unity, and potential of black people, his primary audience. Because the journey of his characters to self-esteem and social awareness is predictable, and because the characters themselves are more often types than individuals, his novels lack the suspense, complexity, and, except for *The Cotillion,* vibrancy, ambiguity, and ambivalence of contemporary life and major contemporary Afro-American novels. What they provide in the tradition of the Afro-American novel is a simple, clear moral and political reaffirmation of the revolutionary potential of black history, culture, and youth in creating a better tomorrow for all people.

John Alfred Williams (1925–)

His parents met and married in Syracuse, New York, but John A. Williams was born on December 5, 1925, in Jackson, Mississippi, his mother's hometown. While he was an infant, the family returned to Syracuse, where he grew up, joined the navy, married, and attended Syracuse University. A childhood interest in reading and early efforts at poetry while in the navy were subsequently cultivated by the discipline acquired in creative writing classes at Syracuse University in 1951. After writing

for the *Progressive Herald, Chicago Defender,* and the National Negro Press Association, Williams began his first novel in 1954. "When I began the process of becoming a writer," he says, "it wasn't for the money and it wasn't for fame; it was to keep my sanity and to find some purpose in my life."[27] Although completed in 1956, this first novel, *The Angry Ones,* was not published until 1960. Since then Williams has published more than a dozen books, including several novels.

Clearly in the tradition of realism, Williams's novels nevertheless reveal a growing radical consciousness and preoccupation with form. "I suppose I am a realistic writer," he explains. "I've been called a melodramatic writer, but I think that's only because I think the ending of a novel should be at the ending of the book. . . . In terms of experimenting, I think that I've done some very radical things with form in *The Man Who Cried I Am* and in *Captain Blackman,* which had to be an experimental novel in order to hold the theme of the novel. What I try to do with novels is deal in forms that are not standard, to improvise as jazz musicians do with their music, so that a standard theme comes out looking brand new."[28] Thematically and structurally, Williams, unlike Killens, is primarily concerned with the struggle of the individual black American to reconcile his present marginal middle-class status with the past experience of his race.

This and an increasing bitterness at capitalism and racism are dramatically evident in the early novels. In *The Angry Ones,* his first and weakest novel, Steve Hill, the protagonist, triumphs over the anger and frustration of economic and sexual exploitation by white liberal friends, renouncing violence and finding a tenuous, unconvincing security in a new job and marriage to his brother's widow. *Night Song* (1961) is the bitter-sweet story of the creative yet self-destructive rage of Eagle, a black jazz musician, and the impotent rage of Keel Robinson, his friend, a "black white man." Because it is a more experimental and successful novel than *The Angry Ones,* it will be discussed more fully, along with *The Man Who Cried I Am,* later in this chapter. *Sissie* (1963) is an exploration of the psychic damage suffered by the modern black family and a demythicizing of black matriarchy. In his fourth novel, *The Man Who Cried I Am* (1967), Williams's radical consciousness culminates in the theme of racial genocide and an experiment with time structure.

The later novels continue to explore the themes of armed violence and love as alternatives to American racism and to experiment with time structure, but, except for *Captain Blackman* (1972), they are less original and effective in their fusion of form and content. In *Sons of Darkness, Sons of Light* (1969) Eugene Browning, a political moderate, triggers a racial Armaggedon with his plan to have a white detective killed for his merciless shooting of a black youth. *Captain Blackman*—Williams's most self-conscious experiment with multiple time shifts, flashbacks, dream sequences, and interior monologues—retraces through Abraham Blackman the heroic exploits of black soldiers back down the corridors of American history, from Vietnam to the Revolutionary War. In *Mothersill and the Foxes* (1975), Odell Mothersill, a black social worker, is a modern-day Priapus or Legba and sower of seeds who discovers that love and selfhood involve more than sex. And through the reminiscences of the multiple narrators in *The Junior Bachelor Society* (1976), we discover along with Richard "Bubbles" Wiggins, a frustrated high school third-string halfback and president of the Junior Bachelor Society, that the nostalgia of thirty-year-old boyhood friendships disappears in the face of the harsh truths and painful memories that surface in their reunion.

Looking more closely at *Night Song,* we discover that it is a blues story in the jazz mode. Set in "a world of cool, of arrogant musicians and worrying night club owners . . . a world in which the days were really nights because you lived in the dark and sang your song of life then,"[29] the novel is antiphonal in structure, stressing the call-and-response relationship between Keel and Eagle with a sharp counterpoint provided by David Hillary. The traditional blues theme that life and one's humanity should be affirmed in the face of disappointment, defeat, and even death is the melodic base for improvisation by the disembodied third-person omniscient narrator.

Basically, *Night Song* is the tragic story of Richie "Eagle" Stokes, a romantic takeoff on the legendary saxophonist Charles "Bird" Parker, and those whose lives he touches and renews through the sacrifice of his own: Keel Robinson, a black Harvard Divinity School graduate and converted Muslim (Sadik Jamal) whose moral outrage at the hollowness of bourgeois values, especially institutionalized religion, and at racial prejudice leaves him incapable of consummating his love for his white girl friend; and David Hillary, a morally impotent white liberal college instructor, "the kind who do nothing when it counts for everyone" (p. 140), who is guilt ridden over killing his wife in a car accident. The source of Eagle's blues is that everyone uses him, especially the white world. "'You white,'" he tells Hillary after taking him in off the street. "'It's your world. You won't let me make it in it and you can't. Now ain't that a bitch?'" (p. 67). More viable as a mythic and legendary culture hero than as a conventional realistic character, Eagle is driven by his love-hate feelings and embodies the paradoxes of Afro-American character and culture, its possibilities and limitations. "'Some people preserve statues and old drawings on cave walls,'" Keel explains to Hillary, "'but we have to have Eagle. He's us. He's fire and brain; he's stubborn and shabby; proud and without pride; kind and evil. His music is our record: blues. . . . Eagle is our aggressiveness, our sickness, our self-hate, but also our will to live in spite of everything. He symbolizes the rebel in us'" (p. 93).

In addition to his significance as an ethnic cultural symbol, Eagle, his music, and the bohemian world are the agents for spiritual redemption for Keel and Hillary. For both, the experience is "like an immersion . . . a baptism" (p. 90). Keel, supported by the patience, understanding, and love of Della, his girlfriend, responds by publicly and frequently reciprocating Eagle's humanitarianism, an act that enables him to rise gradually above the impotence of racial hatred to a renewed faith in himself and life. In contrast, Hillary, who thinks that he has risen above cowardice and bigotry to become "a new man, changed by the people he'd been living with," betrays his "new-found humanitarianism" and Eagle when he fails to come to Eagle's aid as a cop brutally billy-clubs him senseless. "'How could we be unworthy of your love yet worthy of your confession?'" Keel asks him after discovering the betrayal. "'It's not only that you don't know where you are, you don't know where we are. Are you at the top looking down or at the bottom looking up?'" (pp. 142–43).

In the ambiguity and ambivalence of this passage as well as in the thematic structure of the novel, the author-narrator's close philosophical and political identification with Keel Robinson is apparent. Because Keel cannot politically and economically "understand why a white man can't make it in his society" (p. 15), he immediately distrusts and hates Hillary as another white exploiter. The author-narrator's delineation of Hillary as an outsider who knows the surface but not the deeper, ritualistic meaning of jazz foreshadows Hillary's betrayal of Eagle and confirms Keel's suspicion that his friendship for blacks is self-serving and unreliable. Only in "Bohemia, that isolation in time and space which impelled one to act basically" (p. 119), does the author-narrator reveal Hillary cautiously responding to Eagle's charity and acknowledging his potential for moral salvation. For John Williams, then, it was in the apolitical diversity and individualism of

Greenwich Village, not the black community, where "people were more like people." It is also in the Village that Keel, like many alienated and talented blacks and whites of the late 1950s, sought salvation from socialized ambivalence. His problem was "resisting reality" and affirming his love for the white woman who loved him. Middle-class family, money, Protestantism, and Islam did not sustain his faith in himself as a black man, so he turned to the interracial world of the Village where Eagle and Della helped him to reconcile the tensions of this double-consciousness. "Della had come, he always said to himself, when he needed her most, almost immediately after he had left the church, and at a time when he felt his obligations to his parents had been paid" (p. 41). But Keel was confused, torn between love and hate, because Della was white, and it is only after Hillary's climactic betrayal of Eagle that Keel is able to express fully and publicly his love for her. Thus racial integration and interracial love, still a radical solution for American racism in 1961, are the cornerstones of Williams's early vision in this underrated novel of a new social and ethical system. But how new, how progressive, is the social system that Williams projects? Actually, the class and color struggles are presented within an apolitical, bourgeois framework with their effects on society being demonstrated indirectly by their personal moral and psychological consequences. Williams explored this vision more deeply and politically in an international historical context in *The Man Who Cried I Am*.

The Man Who Cried I Am, like *Night Song*, is in the realistic tradition, but its plot, which culminates in the discovery of a bold plan of racial genocide and closes ambiguously on an apocalyptic note, is complicated by a shifting temporal and spatial frame and a sardonic use of symbolism. It is the story of the political radicalization and death of Max Reddick, a successful black novelist and former presidential speechwriter, whose faith in the American

Dream is betrayed at every level and whose rectal cancer symbolizes the pain and danger that constantly threaten the lives of American blacks. Realizing that he is dying of advanced carcinoma, Max flies to the Paris funeral of his friend and rival literary lion, Harry Ames, and then takes a train to Amsterdam for a final visit with his estranged Dutch wife, Margrit Reddick. He discovers in Leiden the reason for his friend's death in a letter that Harry leaves which contains the details about King Alfred, an elaborate government plan to "terminate, once and for all, the Minority threat to the whole of the American society, and, indeed, the Free World."[30]

Divided into three major parts, *The Man Who Cried I Am* is Williams's most thematically provocative and technically innovative novel. Because of institutionalized racism, the novel intriguingly reveals, the assertion of individuality and independence by black Americans, especially writers, is painful and dangerous. As in the tradition of critical realism, Williams emphasizes the internal contradictions of the characters in an exploitative social system rather than the forces working toward reconciliation and coexistence in a new system. The existential theme suggested by the title is that the survival of mankind depends on the moral commitment of the individual to self and society in the face of irrationality and death. The actual time and place of the action is twenty-four hours in May 1964, in the Netherlands, but Williams skillfully manipulates the time through multiple flashbacks, recollections, dreams, and interior monologues to cover nineteen years, 1945–1964, and three continents: Europe, Africa, and the United States. Part 1 introduces the cannibalistic theme of white against black and black against black as the white publishing establishment pits black writers against each other in a dog fight for the status of king of the black literary mountain; Part 2 explores the problems of black writers and interracial couples in America and Europe; and Part 3 reveals

the ultimate treachery of the American government as black CIA agents, who have infiltrated the black American colony of expatriate artists in Paris, systematically assassinate everyone suspected of having knowledge of King Alfred. Max's decision to marry Margrit Westover is the climactic episode of the existential theme of moral courage implicit in the novel's title. The personal commitment of taking a white wife is a prelude to the political commitment to race that he affirms by arming himself for racial war and by calling Minister Q to inform him of King Alfred.

The spirits of the two major black leaders of the sixties and a few of the celebrated modern black male expatriate writers walk the pages of the novel. Minister Q reminds us of Malcolm X; the Reverend Paul Durrell, of the Reverend Martin Luther King, Jr.; and Harry Ames, of Richard Wright. "Where Durrell employed fanciful imagery and rhetoric, Minister Q preached the history, economics and religion of race relations; he preached a message so harsh that it hurt to listen to it" (pp. 209–10). Minister Q and Durrell are one-dimensional characters, but Harry Ames has many of the frailties of the flesh, much of the socialized ambivalence and the dread of conspiracy, of his historical model, who died mysteriously in Paris. In a dialogue with Max about being a writer, Harry rejects the idea of a "tradition of colored writers" and expresses the view that by writing and publishing a book Max, like himself, is a very special person. This is a cause for pride in producing more books, but it "'also makes you dangerous because they don't burn people anymore, they burn books, and they don't always have bonfires'" (p. 45). In literary achievement and life style Max Reddick embodies the individualistic spirit of Chester Himes and Williams himself.

The undramatized third-person omniscient narrator enhances the compelling force of the major characters and events in the novel. We move from an intimate view of an estranged interracial couple to a broad view of racial and political conspiracy. The tone is tragic, ambivalent, and sensational. We get sympathetic internal views of Margrit and Harry, but it is Max's double-consciousness that predominates and represents the norms of the work. By extensive use of the flashback techique to telescope the past into the present and to reenact Max's memories, Williams minimizes the effects of authorial intrusions and dramatizes his hero's double-consciousness and many of the crucial events, both public and private, that led to his radicalization and death. Harry's posthumous letter to Max containing information about King Alfred is a short-fused time bomb that enables Max to reflect on his ambivalent relationship with Harry and that serves as an effective device for Williams to shift between internal and external views of the characters and events. "The one alternative left for Negroes," we read with Max at the end of the novel, "would be not only to seek that democracy withheld from them as quickly and as violently as possible, but to fight for their very survival. King Alfred . . . leaves no choice" (p. 304). The intimate view we get of Margrit and Max overshadows the intense but brief view we get of Lillian Patch, Max's middle-class black fiancée who dies from a botched abortion. "If there had been no Lillian would there be a Margrit?" Max wonders after his momentous decision to marry Margrit (p. 281). Because the story is told predominantly through Max's consciousness, there is little moral, philosophical, and political distance between the omniscient author-narrator and his hero. Williams thus closely identifies with the values of his central character, and encourages the reader to do so as well.

Because of his experiment with technique and form, Williams is a critical realist in only the broadest sense of our definition. His critical attitude toward capitalism and its system of privilege emphasizes the exploitation and exclusion of blacks, which may be interpreted as an implicit respect for the socialist perspective. But his title, theme, and central character

are romantically individualistic. Borrowing from Malcolm Lowry's telescoping of time in *Under the Volcano* and from Richard Wright, Chester Himes, and Ralph Ellison, among others, in technique, Williams develops the wider social significance of his critical attitude toward America from the personal conflicts and alienation of members of the black middle class, especially male artists. He therefore combines Eurocentric and Afrocentric techniques in continuing the tradition of realism while simultaneously expanding the form of the novel through a reaffirmation of the symbolic importance of the legends and rituals of black music in Afro-American life and literature. "What I try to do with novels," he tells an interviewer, "is to deal in forms that are not standard, to improvise as jazz musicians do with their music, so that a standard theme comes out looking brand new. This is all I try to do with a novel and, like those musicians, I am trying to do things with form that are not always immediately perceptible to most people."[31]

Alice Walker (1944–)

Born on February 9, 1944, to sharecroppers in Eatonton, Georgia, Alice Walker was the youngest of eight children. She was a lonely, solitary child as a result of a disfiguring scar she suffered at eight years of age. Educated in local schools and reacting to the cruel insults of her peers and relatives, she "retreated into solitude," she told an interviewer, "and read stories and began to write poems."[32] In 1961 she entered Spelman College, and in her sophomore year was spiritually reborn as an activist in the Georgia voter registration movement of SNCC. She transferred to Sarah Lawrence in 1963 and received her B.A. in 1965. In the summer of 1965 she traveled to East Africa, returning to college pregnant, sick, alone, and suicidal. It was during this crisis in the winter of 1965 that she completed in one week most of the poems in *Once,* her first book of poetry, which was not published until 1968 when the women's movement began displacing the black power movement in the social arena. Walker has taught at several East Coast colleges and has worked with Head Start in Mississippi and the Department of Welfare in New York City. Her numerous honors and awards include Bread Loaf Writers' Conference Scholar in 1966, Merrill Writing Fellow in 1966–1967, McDowell Colony Fellow in 1967, the Rosenthal Award in 1974 for *In Love and Trouble,* the Lillian Smith Award in 1973 for *Revolutionary Petunias,* and the Pulitzer Prize in 1982 for *The Color Purple.* Walker's publications through 1983 include three volumes of poetry; *Once* (1968), *Revolutionary Petunias* (1973), and *Good Night, Willie Lee, I'll See You in the Morning* (1979); two collections of short stories: *In Love and Trouble* (1973) and *You Can't Keep a Good Woman Down* (1981); and three novels: *The Third Life of Grange Copeland* (1970), *Meridian* (1977), and *The Color Purple* (1982).

"I am preoccupied with the spiritual survival, the survival *whole* of my people," she explains her thematic concerns to an interviewer. "But beyond that, I am committed to exploring the oppressions, the insanities, the loyalties, and the triumphs of black women. . . . For me, black women are the most fascinating creations in the world. Next to them, I place the old people— male and female—who persist in their beauty in spite of everything." Consistent with this professed concern for the wholeness of both males and females and celebration of "outrageous, audacious, courageous or willful" black women, Walker calls herself a womanist rather than feminist. In her fiction as in her life she has an openness to mystery, animism, which she believes is both the one thing that Afro-Americans have retained of their African heritage and the thing that is "deeper than any politics, race, or geographical locations." She therefore admires women writers who are responsive to mystery: Chopin, the Brontës, Simone de Beauvoir, and Doris Lessing. She admires these writers also because they are "well aware of their own oppression," and

"their characters can always envision a solution, an evolution to higher consciousness on the part of society even when society itself cannot."[33] In other words, the class and political struggle explored in Walker's novels is primarily sexual. And the higher consciousness she seeks for society is based on her insider's view of the working-class history of blacks in general and the socialized ambivalence of black women in particular as well as her outsider's view of the conflict of white women with capitalism. Among the many writers who influenced her, she lists Russians, Greeks, Africans, Asians, and such Americans, black and white, as Jean Toomer, Zora Neale Hurston, Arna Bontemps, Emily Dickinson, Robert Graves, William Carlos Williams, e. e. cummings, and Flannery O'Connor. Of these, Hurston is the literary precursor, foremother, and spirit-guide that inspires the audacious autonomy that she expresses in her womanist vision.

The Third Life of Grange Copeland, her first novel, is structured like a crazy quilt in that it is disproportionately divided into eleven parts with forty-eight minichapters that outline the three lives of the patriarch of the Copeland clan. Ostensibly about Grange Copeland's rebirth of self-respect after a youth and manhood of dissolution, the novel actually details the social pathology that he passes on to his son, Brownfield. Part 1 briefly outlines the weekly cycles of sweat, fear, and hatred broken on Saturday by the rituals of song, dance, drink, and fighting that characterized the sharecropping life of Grange, and, after years of violent abuse, his wife Margaret. When Grange finally deserts the family, Margaret poisons herself and Brownfield's baby brother, whose "father might have been every one of its mother's many lovers." The pace of the narrative picks up in Parts 2 and 3 as Brownfield follows in his father's footsteps from sharecropper to wife beater. Grange also abruptly and inexplicably reappears to marry Josie, the whore he abandoned but now shares with his son. The eight pages of Part 4 are exclusively reserved for the birth of Ruth, Grange's granddaughter and the agent of his miraculous redemption. Parts 5, 6, and 7 detail Brownfield's malicious treatment of his wife and three daughters with only a brief interlude when his wife, Mem, asserts herself with a shotgun. The novel reaches its violent climax with Brownfield killing Mem and with Ruth going to live on the farm with her grandfather and Josie. In Part 8 Brownfield plots with Josie to take Ruth after his release from prison. Parts 9 and 10 reveal Grange passing on the lessons of his life to Ruth, briefly summarizing his life of hatred in the North. In Part 11 Grange kills Brownfield after he succeeds in getting custody of Ruth, and Grange in turn is killed by the police after returning to Ruth's cottage on their farm.

With more compassion for her female than male characters, with the exception of Grange as an old man, the omniscient author-narrator catalogs episodes in the Copeland family life, especially Brownfield's, to arouse the reader's indignation at the price black women pay as the victims of economic, racial, and sexual exploitation. Margaret Copeland, Brownfield's mother, was like the family dog in some ways. "She didn't have a thing to say that did not in some way show her submission to his father."[34] Grange drives her to drink, degradation, and death. His dreams of escaping the sharecropping system gone, his pride crushed, Brownfield makes his wife quit her teaching job—"Her knowledge reflected badly on a husband who could scarcely read and write," says the editorializing narrator—and begins beating her regularly "because it made him feel, briefly, good. Every Saturday night he beat her, trying to pin the blame for his failure on her by imprinting it on her face. . . . The tender woman he married he set out to destroy" (p. 63). Through violent abuse and forcing the family to move from one sharecropper's shack to another, Brownfield destroys his wife spiritually and physically. Only Ruth's

birth is viewed as a miraculous event. "'Out of all kinds of shit,'" says Grange, "'comes something clean, soft and sweet smellin'" (p. 79). But Brownfield felt that his three daughters "were not really human children" and gave them only the dregs of his attention when he was half drunk. "'You nothing but a sonnabit,'" four-year-old Ruth tells her father after he moves them back into sharecropping. Walker's weaving of character, event, and point of view indicates that she fully agrees with this sentiment. Through Ruth's innocence, Grange learns to love and to accept the responsibility of his life before he dies, but his own son Brownfield goes to his grave blaming white folks and others for the failure of his life. "He felt an indescribable worthlessness," says the author-narrator, "a certain ineffectual *smallness,* a pygmy's frustration in a world of giants" (p. 231).

Although more middle class and less physically violent, the black men of the 1960s in Walker's second novel, *Meridian,* are, with the exception of the father, similarly disloyal and despicable in their abuse of women. Meridian's father was a "dreamy, unambitious" history teacher who grieves over crimes committed against native Americans and, who gives as restitution the family's sixty acres containing one of their ancient cemeteries to a local native American. He also "cried as he broke into" his wife's body ". . . as she was to cry later when their children broke out of it."[35] In contrast, Eddie, Meridian's teenaged husband, was "good" because he kept his promise to marry her if she got pregnant and, even though he "cheated" on her and later deserted her and his child, he did not beat her. Truman, her conquering prince, the French-speaking civil rights organizer and painter, impregnated her but betrayed her to marry and then desert a white exchange student and his child. Tommy, a bitter civil rights activist, rapes Truman's wife, Lynne, in revenge for the arm he lost to a white sniper. And Alonzo, the apolitical scrap-yard worker, was so grateful for Lynne's invitation to sleep with her that he "licked her from her earlobes to her toes" (p. 167). Like the omniscient narrator, the implied author thus encourages the reader to see most of her black male characters in the limited moral category of the "low-down dirty dog" in the novel who impregnated the thirteen-year-old tragic Wild Child.

Towering over the low-down dirty dogs and moving like a soul possessed through the thirty-four titled brief chapters of the three-part narrative is the protagonist, Meridian Hill. She shares with her father the legendary peculiar madness of her eccentric paternal great-grandmother, Feather Mae, and is haunted by guilt at her inability to embrace a nurturing role as daughter, wife, and mother. Frail and hallucinatory, Meridian agonizes "for shattering her mother's emerging self," gives away her first child in order to go to college, aborts her second in disillusionment with its unfaithful father, and then, at the suggestion of a callous male gynecologist, has her tubes tied to avoid being further trapped by sex and motherhood while pursuing her commitment in the rural South to community organizing, teaching, and poetry (pp. 40–41). Unlike her mother and grandmother, we learn from the narrator, Meridian "lived in an age of choice" (p. 123). Despite her unorthodoxy, however, a black Baptist church memorial service for a young civil rights martyr in 1968 lifts her burden of guilt and shame. Affirming the respect she owed her life and the dedication she owed her people, she promises to kill for freedom if necessary, a revolutionary commitment that she had rejected earlier in the novel and that Walker's language implicitly endorses. But the social context and symbolic conclusion resound with personal self-indulgence, for Walker does not describe the revolutionary role of the working class in contemporary society. Nor does the novel end apocalyptically. Instead, Meridian forgives Truman, leaves him in her small religious house, and "returns to the world cleansed of sickness." Wearing her cap

and snuggled in her sleeping bag, he wonders if she "knew that the sentence of bearing the conflict in her own soul which she had imposed on herself—and lived through— must now be borne in terror by all the rest of them" (pp. 227–28). The civil rights movement, in short, provided a means of spiritual and moral redemption from a guilty past for individuals like Meridian, not a radical new social order in which all could realize their full potential.

The best but most problematic of Walker's novels is the Pulitzer Prize–winning *The Color Purple*. Less compelling as critical realism than as folk romance, it is more concerned with the politics of sex and self than with the politics of class and race. Whereas its epistolary form continues the tradition of Samuel Richardson's *Clarissa Harlowe* (1748) and William H. Brown's *Power of Sympathy* (1789) (the sentimental, sensational tales of seduction that initiated the British and Euro-American traditions of the novel), its unrelenting, severe attacks on male hegemony, especially the violent abuse of black women by black men, is offered as a revolutionary leap forward into a new social order based on sexual egalitarianism. Like Hurston's *Their Eyes Were Watching God*, the style of *The Color Purple* is grounded in black folk speech, music, and religion; and its theme is a contemporary rewriting of Janie Crawford's dreams of what a black woman ought to be and do. But rather than heterosexual love, lesbianism is the rite of passage to selfhood, sisterhood, and brotherhood for Celie, Walker's protagonist.

Although rooted in the particularity of the folk experience of some Southern black women, the awakening of the protagonist's consciousness to love, independence, and sisterhood is more romantic than realistic. Rather than portray the growth into womanhood of an average Southern black woman of the 1920s and 1930s, Walker has created a contemporary paradigm of the liberated woman. Covering more than thirty years between the two world wars, the ninety-four letters in which Celie emerges from the brutal domination and abuse of men to a liberated, autonomous self include twenty-three letters to her from Nettie, her younger sister, fourteen from her to Nettie, which came back unopened, and one from Shug Avery, the blues singer who is the moral center of the novel, to Celie. Most of the confusingly undated, often arbitrarily arranged letters are a dramatic monologue to a white, patriarchal God, symbolizing the complexity of metaphysical as well as social oppression for black women in their quest for freedom, literacy, and wholeness. Focused on psychological rather than historical realism, they begin when Celie is fourteen, and they tell more than show her realization of womanist consciousness: from her repeated rape and impregnation by her stepfather; brokered violent marriage to Albert; and rejection of God as a "trifling, forgitful and lowdown" man; to her transforming love for Shug; economic and artistic independence as a seamstress and merchant; and reunion on July 4th with family, friends, and an animistic God that Shug teaches her "ain't a he or she, but a It."[36]

By her handling of the symbolic significance of Shug as a blues singer, of Afro-American religion, and of the black vernacular to develop Celie's long black song of suffering and womanist consciousness, Walker effectively weaves a magic spell that conjures up the socialized ambivalence and double-consciousness of Afro-American culture and character between 1914 and 1945. In the tradition of such blues "bad" women as Bessie Smith, Shug embodies and evokes the moral ambivalence of many black Americans toward music and behavior that they feel make the best of a bad situation by being as raw, mean, and wild as human existence itself frequently is. Worldly black folk flock to concerts and jukejoints to see Shug and hear the devil's music, while less worldly and otherworldly folk scorn her as a sinner and sing the Lord's music. Like her "wild sister" in

Memphis and the legendary Bessie, Shug, called the Queen Honeybee of the blues, drinks, fights, and "love mens to death" (p. 104). Telling Celie about her earlier love for Albert and how the black community, including her parents and his, condemned her because she moved beyond liberty to license in "taking other women mens" and having three children out of wedlock, Shug says: "I was so mean, and so wild, Lord. I used to go round saying, I don't care who he married to, I'm gonna fuck him. . . . And I did, too. Us fuck so much in the open us give fucking a bad name" (p. 104). Only Albert, the father of her three children, and Celie, who fantasizes about her, honestly and completely love Shug. This socially forbidden love inspires her to create a "low down dirty" blues that she calls Miss Celie's song, which, of course, is Walker's text, and culminates in their bisexual affair. By living the liberated life she sings about without compromising her integrity, Shug, like Bessie, romantically challenges Albert, Celie, and readers to live with boldness and style in the face of adversity, absurdity, and conventional morality.

Shug teaches Celie not only about the sexual importance of her "little button" and "finger and tongue work," but also about the spiritual necessity of conversion to an animistic idea of God. "Just because I don't harass it like some peoples us know," says Shug, "don't mean I ain't got religion" (p. 164). By sympathetically delineating Shug as a blues heroine with religion, who is estranged from the orthodoxy of the Christian tradition, Walker offers her as a contemporary symbol of the ideal pattern of sexual and spiritual liberation and rebuke of traditional Afro-American values and institutions.

Walker, in other words, is morally and politically unsympathetic toward what she considers anachronistic, chauvinistic conventions in the black family and the black church. She ascribes Celie's abject shame and passivity to the dominance of patriarchy, hypocrisy, and otherworldliness in the black church and family. By contrasting the stepfather's incest and the daughter-in-law Sofia's temerity with Celie's timidity, she clearly distances herself from Celie's belief in the biblical injunction to "Honor father and mother no matter what" and to suffering in this world, for "This life soon be over. . . . Heaven last for all ways" (p. 39). In the only church scene that is dramatized, however, the implied author is morally and politically close to both Celie and Shug as "even the preacher got his mouth on Shug, now she down. He take her condition for his text. . . . Talk about slut, hussy, heifer and streetcleaner" (p. 40). Intertextually, Walker's text—a rewrite and conflation of the legendary lives of her great-grandmother, "who was raped at twelve by her slaveholding master,"[37] and Bessie Smith, the literary life of Janie Crawford, and both the legendary and literary lives of Zora Neale Hurston—parallels Shug's embedded text of Celie's song and contrasts with the preacher's embedded text. Finally, in Celie's second letter to Nettie in which she renounces God, Walker implicitly supports Shug's belief that people "come to church to *share* God, not find God" and that because "Man corrupt everything," Celie ought to "conjure up flowers, wind, water, a big rock" (pp. 165, 168). Morally and politically, both Celie and Shug are reliable narrators for the womanist norms of the novel. The sign of these norms is the color purple. "I think it pisses God off if you walk by the color purple in a field somewhere and don't notice it," Shug tells Celie and us (p. 167). The color purple signifies a metaphysical, social, and personal rebirth and a celebration of lesbianism as a natural, beautiful experience of love.

Like her treatment of religion and blues, Walker's encoding of black speech and male characters signifies her sexual, moral, and political closeness to the outrageously audacious black women in the narrative. The values and vitality of black American communities, including the socialized ambivalence and quest for wholeness from cradle to grave

of its members, are encoded in the sounds, semantics, and syntax of their speech: from "It be more than a notion taking care of children ain't even yourn" (p. 6) to "She look like she ain't long for this world but dressed well for the next" (p. 42). In contrast to the truth of this double vision, the letters in standard Euro-American English from Nettie that tell how the Reverend Samuel and Corrine, the black couple who adopt Celie's kidnapped children and homeless sister, and practice their sanctified religion among the Olinka people as token members of a largely white missionary association, conjure up neither the texture, the tone, nor the truth of the traditional lives of African peoples.

Equally problematic is the implied author and protagonist's hostility toward black men, who are humanized only upon adopting womanist principles of sexual egalitarianism. Except for Odessa's Jack, the black men are depicted as dogs or frogs—a rewriting of feminist fictions of male sexuality in general and Hurston's deadly signifying on Jody Starks in particular—with no hope of becoming princes. Gender role reversal or sharing, however, does foster some redemption for them. For example, Harpo not only acquires a love for housekeeping, especially cooking, but also becomes a househusband while his wife works as a storekeeper. Adam, Celie's son, endures the traditional facial scarification initiation rite of Olinka females to prove his love for Tashi. And Albert, whom Celie calls Mr. ———, learns not only to make quilts, Walker's symbol for the repressed creativity of women, with Celie, but also to acknowledge her independence and integrity as a person. Guided by the spirit and achievement of Hurston, Walker has Shug to express this theme of the book more poetically in the vernacular when she tells Celie: "You have to git man off your eyeball, before you can see anything a'tall" (p. 168).

In her novels, then, Alice Walker provides a contemporary black feminist's vision of the lives of black Southerners. Although she does not promote socialism as the panacea for the ills of capitalist America, she does stress in *The Third Life of Grange Copeland* the need to change a patriarchal economic system that breeds alienation, exploitation, and the destruction of people's lives, especially black women's. Her characters are uneducated, ignoble young working-class types like Grange and Brownfield Copeland who, except for Grange as an old man, lack the "inner sovereignty" and "embedded strength" of educated, heroic women like Mem and Ruth. In *Meridian* she focuses more sharply on the making of a revolutionary and on living up to what is required by history and economic change, the second novel answers the basic question: "Is there no place in a revolution for a person who *cannot* kill?" (p. 193; Walker's emphasis). Most strikingly, her protagonist is a naive, guilt-ridden visionary for whom the civil rights movement is the rite of passage to liberation from guilt and rebirth as a committed community organizer and candidate for political sainthood. Even more revolutionary, the sexual politics of *The Color Purple* also reduces the scale of the struggle for social change to the task of creating a new autonomous self: an androgynous self and society. Walker's hope for change in the future rests, then, with the young, old, and outrageously bold black woman. By exploring the oppressions and celebrating the triumphs of Southern black wives, mothers, and daughters as they relate more to each other than to working-class black men, she tailors the tradition of critical realism to fit into folk romance and reinforces the theme of black feminism in the Afro-American novel.

Before comparing Walker to the other critical realists discussed in this chapter, it is important to note in passing that the theme of black feminism is explored by Gayl Jones in *Corregidora* (1975) and *Eva's Man* (1976) with even more mystery and horror, and by Toni Cade Bambara in *The Salt Eaters* (1980)

with more political insightfulness and technical brilliance.

Because of a hysterectomy following an accident caused by her domineering, drunk husband, blues singer Ursa Corregidora cannot live up to the legacy of three generations of Corregidora women to procreate and perpetuate the incestuous line of tragic witnesses begun by her slavebreeding, Portuguese ancestor, who fathered his own slaves and prostitutes. To avenge the abuse that she and other black women have suffered, she kills her husband with kindness as the novel closes ambiguously with the act of fellatio. *Eva's Man* continues less ambiguously this castration motif in women's resistance to historical sexual abuse by opening with Eva Medina, the forty-three-year-old, college-educated protagonist, undergoing psychiatric treatment in prison for poisoning and biting off the penis of her weekend lover. The chilling terror of both novels is evoked through flashbacks, reveries, and interior monologues that effectively modulate the tempo, suspense, and horror of these first-person Gothic narratives.

Less sensational but more dialectical in its understanding of the historical forces of progress and reaction, Bambara's *Salt Eaters* affirms the viability of traditional divinatory practices that celebrate the mystery and sacredness of life in the post–civil rights activist period of the 1970s, teaching those in search of personal wholeness "the difference between eating salt as an antidote to snakebit and turning into salt, succumbing to the serpent."[38] After a suicide attempt, Velma Henry—mother, wife, sister, computer analyst, community organizer, civil rights activist, antinuclear activist, women's rights activist, and protagonist—learns through the legendary faith healer of Claiborne, Georgia, Minnie Ransom, and the community healing circle that personal and social wholeness and health are "no trifling matter." Philosophically, the implied author and omniscient narrator share the protagonist's conviction "that the truth was in one's own people, and the key was to be centered in the best of one's own traditions" (p. 169). The retrospective, discontinuous narrative therefore focuses primarily on Velma in the healing session but constantly shifts and probes with clinical precision into the internal and external lives of other characters. Like the ritual of the healing session, the double-edged wit of the black vernacular—e.g., the faith healer was "dressed for days," looking "like a farmer in a Halston, a snuff dipper in a Givenchy" (pp. 4, 8)—brilliantly plumbs the depths of Afro-American double-consciousness and fosters a sympathetic understanding of Velma. At the same time, the banter between Minnie and her spirit-guide Old Wife and among the Seven Sisters of the Grain singing troupe dramatizes the interrelated roles of ancestral intelligence and political activism in attaining and sustaining unity of self and society.

Continuity and change, then, are the chief characteristics of these novels I have loosely grouped here under the rubric *critical realism*. Killens, Williams, and Alice Walker, like William Attaway, employ both an insider's and outsider's view in their use of critical realism, responding in different ways to the problems of the past and the modern winds of social and cultural change. Their novels, except for *The Color Purple*, are generally more historical and mimetic than romantic and didactic. Fidelity to the truth of the actual past and to the truth of the psychology of the present are their common objectives. They also attempt to develop from the inside the psychology and morality of individuals in search of a better future. Killens, however, is more direct in style and characterization than Walker, and is more concerned with historical types than individuals. Killens's creation of members of the working class and their middle-class allies heralds the emergence of a bold new world of proud, heroic types like the Youngbloods, Charlie Chaney, and Ben Ali Lumumba, and illustrates his anticapitalist position and strong, sometimes polemical,

support for the perspective of socialism. Alice Walker's men, on the other hand, are traditional black male chauvinists of both the lower and middle class who stereotypically vent their hatred of exploitation by whites on their families, especially the women, and whose only redemptive act is, like Grange Copeland's, to turn hatred to love and to faith in a new social order based on sexual, economic, and racial equality. In contrast, the struggle—sometimes violent, usually sensational and tragic—by her women characters to reject traditional roles of motherhood, nurturing, and dependence heralds the emergence of a new generation of radical black heroines in search of selfhood, security, and power.

Perhaps the most experimental in technique and structure in this group, excluding Jones and Bambara as well as Walker's use of quilting and epistles, is John A. Williams, whose underrated *Night Song* and *The Man Who Cried I Am* occupy the outer boundaries of social and critical realism. They probe the socialized ambivalence of the black artist, musician, and writer rather than the proletariat or the social forces responsible for their alienation and exploitation; and *Night Song* experiments with the modalities of black music. By their talented, usually compelling, occasionally brilliant, use of black folklore, especially music, religion, and speech, Killens, Williams, and Walker deepen our understanding of the limitations and possibilities of the lives of black Americans, and the vitality of the tradition of the Afro-American novel, including its poetic and Gothic qualities.

POETIC REALISM AND THE GOTHIC FABLE
By combining a concern for the truth of the lives of men and women in actual situations with a concern for the imaginative power, compression, and lyricism of language, poetic realism calls attention to the problematics of reality and language while simultaneously insisting that reality is shaped more by consciousness than consciousness is by reality.

Like Toomer, contemporary black poetic realists strive more for truth of sensation and environment than for truth of fact, focusing on the supernatural ties of the present to the past and on psychological and sociological concepts for their images of ethical conduct in a world of mystery and unnatural events. In other words, the mystery and terror of atmosphere, events, and character are exploited in the Gothic vision of Afro-American poetic realists. In poetic realism the metaphoric and metonymic qualities of the language—the substitution of figurative for literal expressions—as well as deft, bold strokes of color, distilled experiences, and fleeting but sharp and frequently recurring images of the dominant, often eccentric, traits of the characters and their environment are also usually more meaningful to the author than the photographic representation of external reality. Although occasionally such characters are one dimensional, static, and grotesque, they are more frequently, as in Toomer's *Cane*, impressionistic and dynamic, with the poetic sensibility of the author-narrator distilling characters and events. Lyrical passages, of course, appear in the narratives of many black novelists, and many others, including Walker, Jones, and Bambara, explore the Gothic aspects of contemporary Afro-American experience, but Morrison has published two of the best recent examples of this tradition in what I call the Gothic fable: generally short poetic narratives whose celebration of the beauty, truth, and possibilities of life is derived from the exploitation of its magic, mystery, and terror.

Chloe Anthony "Toni" Morrison (1931–)

Born to a shipyard worker and choir singer on February 18, 1931, in Lorain, Ohio, Chloe Anthony Wofford changed her name to Toni after finishing school in Lorain and going East to Howard in 1949. At Howard she majored in English, taking her B.A. in 1953 and an M.A. from Cornell University in 1955.

Having traveled to the Deep South with the Howard University Players, she returned there after college to teach at Texas Southern University from 1955 to 1957 and then moved on to a similar post at Howard University from 1957 to 1964. While teaching at Howard, she married a Jamaican and had two sons. She went on to become an editor in 1964, first at a textbook company in Syracuse and then in 1965 at Random House. By the end of 1983, she had published four novels: *The Bluest Eye* (1970), *Sula* (1973), *Song of Solomon* (1977), and *Tar Baby* (1981).

All four novels continue the poetic and Gothic branches of the Afro-American narrative tradition. Despite its primarily Caribbean setting, occasional Faulknerian sentences, and extended metaphors like the female soldier ant conceit in chapter 10 that reinforces the thematic ambiguity of ensnaring, autonomous black females symbolized in the title, *Tar Baby* is the least poetic and Gothic of the four.

The most ambitious and Gothic is *Song of Solomon*. The two-part novel opens in 1931 in a town near Lake Superior with the mysterious, bizarre suicide flight from a hospital roof of Mr. Robert Smith, a black insurance agent dressed in a blue costume with wide silk wings. On one hand, the symbolic and thematic significance of this leap to death by a commonly named minor character is apparent: it causes the early birth of the uncommonly named black protagonist, Macon "Milkman" Dead, in the historically for-whites-only Mercy Hospital, which blacks sardonically call No Mercy Hospital. On the other hand, the mystery and horror of this event and the fact "that Mr. Smith didn't draw as big a crowd as Lindberg had four years earlier,"[39] despite having announced his suicide plans two days before, are even more richly exploited metaphorically and metonymically by Morrison. The densely woven, arabesque texture of this opening scene includes the trivia of the daily lives of the absent poor ("most of the women were fastening their corsets and getting ready to see what tails or entrails the butcher might be giving away" [pp. 3–4]; the anecdotal humor of black names (Not Doctor Street, No Mercy Hospital, and Lincoln's Heaven) that wryly reveal cultural and social differences between white and black townspeople; and the mysterious song of the strange black woman wrapped in an old quilt and wearing a knitted cap pulled down over her forehead. We are immediately alerted to the theme that life is precious and that many dead lives and faded memories are buried in the names of places and people in this country: Not Doctor Street, Lincoln's Heaven, Solomon's Leap, Macon Dead, Milkman Dead, Magdalene called Lena Dead, First Corinthians Dead, Pilate Dead and Sing Dead. But we do not discover until chapter 6 that Robert Smith's suicide is the result of pressures he can no longer endure as a member of the Seven Days, a secret black vigilante society that avenges the deaths of black victims of white terror. And it is not until chapter 12 of the fifteen-chapter novel that we learn the legendary meaning of the Song of Solomon that Pilate sings as Smith plunges to his death and that the protagonist sings at the end of the novel before plunging to his. Setting, story, and characters thus create a haunting mood of unknown terror.

We move with Milkman through the compressed thirty-two years of his haunted, self-absorbed life up North in Part 1 and his trip South to his buried family legacy in Part 2. The melodramatic flashbacks and reveries of the characters as well as the digressions of the editorializing omniscient narrator enable us to discover with Milkman the hidden truth about himself and his strange family, with which he must deal in order to become a whole person. With shifting degrees of delight and disgust, we learn with the protagonist that his mother Ruth continued breast feeding him in a small green room long after he began school; that she was caught by her husband making love to her dead father, whose grave she still secretly visited; that

his maternal "grandfather was a high-yellow nigger who loved ether and hated black skin" (pp. 76–77); that his father Macon sold his soul to own things and compelled Ruth to attempt repeatedly to abort Milkman's birth; and that his paternal great-grandfather Solomon was an African slave who fathered twenty-one children in Virginia, where legend and a children's song tell of him flying back home to Africa. We also learn that his Aunt Pilate, who wore a brass box earring containing her name, was an unkempt, bootlegging mystic who was miraculously born without a navel after her mother's death. Pilate spoke with the dead—especially her father—and used her supernatural powers to save Milkman's life before he was born. Our moral sympathies are further manipulated by flashbacks revealing that the top of Milkman's paternal grandfather's head was shot off from the back by white Pennsylvanians who wanted his farm, Lincoln's Heaven; and that his friend Guitar became a vigilante because of his conviction that "white people are unnatural" and his fear that "every one of them is a potential nigger-killer, if not an actual one" (pp. 155–56). Because her supernatural birth and powers mark her as a bridge between the living and the dead, Pilate, who has "acquired a deep concern for and about human relationships" (p. 149), is the moral center of the novel. Her death at the end of the novel while she and Milkman are reburying her father Jake's bones on Solomon's Leap moves Milkman to embrace the whole truth of his life in a suicidal leap down on her assassin, Guitar.

"What is curious to me," Morrison says in her lecture, "is that bestial treatment of human beings never produces a race of beasts." Since her childhood in Lorain, she was fascinated by the uncommon efforts of common black people to cope with socialized ambivalence. How do they deal with the sexist rules and racist absurdities of life in a small town? Drawing on her family's tradition of telling ghost stories and her long-standing commitment to literature, Morrison began attempting to answer this question and expanding her commitment in 1962 by joining a writers' workshop at Howard. The short story she began in this workshop became the nucleus of *The Bluest Eye*.

Less ambitious in scope and length than *Song of Solomon*, both *The Bluest Eye* and *Sula* are novels of poetic realism and Gothic fables about growing up poor, black, and female in a male-dominated, white middle-class society. In *The Bluest Eye* Morrison contrasts the experience and values of two black families, the poor yet proud MacTeers and the poor, ashamed Breedloves, with those of the Shirley Temple of the white Fisher family. The major focus is on eleven-year-old Pecola Breedlove and the MacTeer sisters, ten-year-old Frieda and nine-year-old Claudia, the narrator. The novel is cleverly structured around an opening story from the standard elementary school Dick-and-Jane readers of the 1940s (the time of the action), which insidiously inculcated an inferiority complex in black children of the inner city by promoting the values of the homogenized white suburban middle-class family. The brief children's story, which Morrison repeats in three different styles—from standard to nonstandard English—provides an ironic contrast to the plot, which is further reinforced by the narrator with a marigold-planting analogy that ingeniously and immediately establishes the lyrical style and tragic mood of the narrative. The novel proper is then divided into the four seasons (autumn, winter, spring, and summer) with the Dick-and-Jane story also broken down into seven headnotes for the minichapters, sharpening the contrast between the ideal experience of the white world and the actual experience of blacks portrayed in the minichapters. After being raped by her drunk father, deceived into believing God had miraculously given her the blue eyes she prayed for, suffering a miscarriage, and being ridiculed by other children, Pecola loses her sanity, and the marigold seeds planted by the MacTeer sisters

do not grow. Metaphor and metonomy thus complement each other in their significance: it is painfully difficult for little black girls to grow into healthy womanhood with a positive self-image when "all the world had agreed that a blue-eyed, yellow-haired, pink-skinned doll was what every girl child treasures."[40]

Progressing from girlhood to womanhood, *Sula*, the most poetic of Morrison's four novels, focuses on the friendship of two black women and moves into retrospection over a period of forty-six years. Part 1 with six chapters that chronicle the years from 1919 to 1927 distills the legendary qualities of the Bottom, a hilltop black neighborhood in Ohio, of Shadrack, the shell-shocked World War I veteran and founder of National Suicide Day; of Sula Peace, the tough, adventuresome main character and of her girlhood friendship with Nel Wright, whose wedding ruptures the special relationship they shared. The five chapters of Part 2 (1937, 1939, 1940, 1941, and 1965) continue the chronicle with a worldly-wise, independent Sula returning to the Bottom after a ten-year absence, becoming both a pariah and redeemer of her time and place and people.

Morrison's language throughout Sula is even more charged with the beauty, wonder, and pain of the poetry of the black experience than it is in *The Bluest Eye*. Our feelings are stirred and our awareness of the characters' ambivalence about people and events deepened by the irony of such place names as the Bottom (a name derived from the legend or "nigger joke" about the white farmer who kept his promise of freedom and a piece of bottom land to his slave by convincing him to accept infertile land up in the hills as the bottom of heaven), Irene's Palace of Cosmetology, Edna Finch's Mellow House, and the Time and a Half Pool Hall. Equally striking are such metaphorical images as "Grass stood blade by blade, shocked into separateness by an ice that held for days"; and "As Reverend Deal moved into his sermon, the hands of the women unfolded like pairs of ravens and flew high above their hats in the air."[41] But the most clever is Sula's use of a spider conceit to express her disappointment with Nel:

Now Nel was one of *them*. One of the spiders whose only thought was the next rung of the web, who dangled in dark dry places suspended by their own spittle, more terrified of the free fall than the snake's breath below. Their eyes so intent on the wayward stranger who trips into their net, they were blind to the cobalt on their own backs, the moonshine fighting to pierce their corners. If they were touched by the snake's breath, however fatal, they were merely victims and knew how to behave in that role (just as Nel knew how to behave as the wronged wife). But the free fall, oh no, that required—demanded—invention: a thing to do with the wings, a way of holding the legs and most of all a full surrender to the downward flight if they wished to taste their tongues or stay alive. But alive was what they, and now Nel, did not want to be. Too dangerous. Now Nel belonged to the town and all of its ways. She had given herself over to them, and the flick of their tongues would drive her back into her little dry corner where she would cling to her spittle high above the breath of the snake and the fall. (P. 120)

Insensitive to Nel's pain at finding her husband, Jude, in bed with her, Sula, as this elaborate analogy reveals, is disappointed at the possessiveness and jealousy of the one person to whom she felt close. No longer, she thinks, is Nel willing to affirm the possibilities of life, to risk rebellion against social conventions and traditional sex roles in order to define herself and assert her independence and vitality.

When they met in 1922, Sula and Nel's friendship was as intense as it was sudden. "Because each had discovered years before that they were neither white nor male, and that all freedom and triumph was forbidden to them, they had set about creating something else to be" (p. 52). Solitary and lonely, they were the only children of distant mothers and incomprehensible fathers—Sula's was dead

and Nel's a seaman. Nel's mother, Helene Wright, was attractive, vain, and oppressively class conscious in an effort to escape her Creole mother's wild blood. Resisting her mother's attempts to impose distorted middle-class values on her, Nel declares: "'I'm me. I'm not their daughter. I'm not Nel. I'm me. Me'" (p. 28). Sula's mother, Hannah Peace, was "a kind and generous woman" with "extraordinary beauty and funky elegance," who, like her own mother, Eva Peace, loved all men. Unlike Eva, however, Hannah was promiscuous. Neither Eva nor Hannah showered her daughter with motherly affection. Eva had little time or energy to provide more than the basic necessities for her children's survival, yet she fiercely and ironically demonstrates the depth of her maternal love by burning her drug-addict son to death and throwing herself out of a two-story window in a futile attempt to save Hannah from burning to death. Receiving no sustaining affection from Eva, Hannah is unable or unwilling to show affection to Sula. "'You love her,'" she tells a friend, "'like I love Sula. I just don't like her. That's the difference'" (p. 57). Feeling unloved and revealing the evil she embodies, Sula emotionlessly watched Hannah burn to death. Although at twelve years old both were "wishbone thin and easy-assed," Nel "seemed stronger and more consistent than Sula, who could hardly be counted on to sustain any emotion for more than three minutes" (p. 53). Thus, Nel and Sula found in each other the intimacy they needed, and they are equally responsible for the drowning of a small boy, Chicken Little, a secret guilt that seals the bond between them and with Shadrack, whom they suspect saw their wicked act.

Morrison intentionally makes Sula an ambitious character who evokes ambivalence from all quarters, including the undramatized author-narrator. On one hand, Sula represents a liberated modern black woman, who, in rejected marriage, declares: "'I don't want to be somebody else. I want to make myself,'" and defiantly tells her grandmother: "'Whatever's burning in me is mine. . . . And I'll split this town in two and everything in it before I'll let you put it out'" (pp. 92–93). But Ajax, the handsome, sinister street poet who stirred Sula's girlhood sexual fantasies, becomes her nemesis and the agent for her discovery of the meaning of possessiveness after he responds to her brain as well as her body. On the other hand, Sula represents the actual and imagined force of evil in the black community. When she put her grandmother in a home, they called her a roach; and when she took Jude from Nel and slept with white men, they called her a bitch. The folks of the Bottom, true to their culture, also remembered the "weighty evidence" of Gothic events that proved that Sula was evil: the talk about her watching her mother burn, the plague of robins that announced her return to Medallion, the accidental injury of Teapot and death of Mr. Finley, and the ominous birthmark over her eye.

The voice of the omniscient author-narrator is at once sympathetic toward and critical of the black people of the Bottom. She explains their "full recognition of the legitimacy of forces other than good ones" with the awareness and compassion of an insider, affirming their resolve to survive in the face of hard times and evil. But she is critical of the tradition of inferiority implicit in black women's shame of dark complexion, of broad, flat noses, and of coarse, short hair. Ambivalent about Sula, Morrison ascribes her dangerous behavior to her limited opportunities and alternatives for personal growth as a black woman:

In a way, her strangeness, her naivete, her craving for the other half of her equation was the consequence of an idle imagination. Had she paints, or clay, or knew the discipline of the dance, or strings; had she anything to engage her tremendous curiosity and her gift for metaphor, she might have exchanged the restlessness and preoccupation with whim for an activity that provided

her with all she yearned for. And like any artist with no art form, she became dangerous. (P. 121)

Most important, the author-narrator, like the blacks of the Bottom, sees Sula as both a pariah and a redeemer:

Their conviction of Sula's evil changed them in accountable yet mysterious ways. Once the source of their personal misfortune was identified, they had leave to protect and love one another. They began to cherish their husbands and wives, protect their children, repair their homes and in general band together against the devil in their midst. In their world, aberrations were as much a part of nature as grace. It was not for them to expel or annihilate it. . . . The presence of evil was something to be first recognized, then dealt with, survived, outwitted, triumphed over. (P. 118)

At the end of the novel, Eva, with a tough-minded understanding of life despite her senility, compels Nel to realize that she and Sula were just alike.

In theme and style Toni Morrison's novels are a fine example of vintage wine in new bottles. Her exploration of the impact of sexism and racism on the lives of black women in her Gothic fables provides a more complex and, perhaps, controversial vision of the personalities and bonding of fiercely alive modern black women than the idealized images of most writers in the 1960s. Particularly in *The Bluest Eye* and *Sula* she distills history and fact with the poetic freedom and Gothic vision of modernist and postmodernist writers. Her sharp eye for the concrete details and telltale gestures that evoke a sense of place and character in the fables and *Song of Solomon* are complemented by a wonderful gift for metaphor and metonymy that are as penetrating in their insightfulness as they are arresting in their freshness and suggestiveness. Her characters are eccentric and maimed as a result of their experience as black men and women in an environment that rigidly defines their humanity by economic, sexual, and racial myths, but still they persevere in their efforts to cope with or triumph over the obstacles in their path to self-esteem, freedom, and wholeness. Thus Pecola is destroyed psychologically, Sula dies an outcast among her own, and Milkman follows the path of his African ancestor, but both Claudia and Nel survive the terror and tragedy of their friends' lives, achieving in the process a precarious adjustment to the worlds of Shirley Temple and the Bottom. Pilate's moral victory is even more Pyrrhic. Because Morrison probes the awesome will to live of her characters in order to suggest the truth of their psychic experience and the complexity of their humanity, her Gothic fables, reminiscent of Toomer's *Cane,* are a quintessential blend of realism and poetry, bizarreness and beauty, revelation and lyricism.

CONTINUITY IN THE NOVEL OF THE SIXTIES AND SEVENTIES

Of the more than one hundred novels by fifty black American novelists published between 1962 and 1983 that I have examined for this and the following chapter, most continue the synthesis of traditional forms of realism and romance that characterized the beginning of the Afro-American novel in 1853. In this chapter I have focused on twenty-one novels by six authors that reveal two intriguing trends in realism of the 1960s and 1970s: critical realism and poetic realism. Of the six authors selected on the basis of their contributions both to these trends in the Afro-American novel and to stimulating readers' awareness of the possibilities of life, all are first-generation college-educated individuals who, except for Bambara, have published two or more novels. Bambara's extraordinarily insightful synthesis of traditional and modern conventions in her first novel compelled its brief examination. In general, the six authors are representative of the educational background, literary

productivity, and preferred narrative conventions of contemporary Afro-American novelists. The classifications, it should be remembered, indicate narrative conventions that the authors have employed with distinction in one or more novels, and are intended as neither arbitrary nor immutable labels to confine the authors or their novels. Rather, the classifications are intended to foster clarity and coherence in understanding the ambivalence of the authors toward all traditions and the contributions they have made to continuity and change in the tradition of the Afro-American novel.

These authors' conflicting emotions and various literary contributions were influenced in part by the radical political and cultural developments of the 1960s—beginning with the March on Washington in 1963, the black arts movement in 1964, the accelerated use of paperback books in college classrooms in 1965, and with cultural democratization, the cashing-in on the new vogue in black studies and feminism by publishers and reprint houses in 1969. These developments generated a new, often heated debate in academic circles over the purpose of art, the function of the artist, and the death of the novel. There was, of course, less discussion about black American fiction in the media than about Euro-American and African fiction, and, except for *Negro Digest* (*Black World*), both the black and white media were more interested in promoting black poetry and drama. Nevertheless, there was more than enough ferment in the literary marketplace and writers' workshops for writers like John O. Killens, John A. Williams, Alice Walker, Gayl Jones, Toni Cade Bambara, and Toni Morrison to fulfill their roles as black artists in defining the complexity of Afro-American life and, to paraphrase Ralph Ellison, to realize that in spite of all its technical experimentation, the autonomy of the novel as a system of artificial signs is qualified by its interrelationships with other cultural systems, especially linguistic and ethical.

In their definition of Afro-American life, these writers therefore continue to tap the roots of Afro-American culture and institutions—black music, speech, religion, and the family—repudiating those codes and conventions that impede individual and collective growth and self-determination, and celebrating those that enhance these humanistic objectives. Consistent with recent social developments, there is more emphasis on the importance of music, speech, and religion as the foundations of contemporary Afro-American culture and the principal modalities for expressing the complex double vision of Afro-American character than on institutionalized Christianity, which is increasingly criticized and even displaced in importance in the works of some novelists by politics, ancestralism, or other Afrocentric beliefs and rituals. Bambara's *Salt Eaters* is exceptional in its quest for a balance of the spiritual and political, of the traditional and modern. In Williams's *Sissie*, Alice Walker's *Third Life of Grange Copeland* and *The Color Purple,* and Morrison's *Bluest Eye* and *Sula,* we see a critical exploration of the strengths and weaknesses of the institutions of the black family and church as well as of the continuing racial and sexual exploitation of black people, especially women. Influenced by the sexual revolution as well as by the continuing color and class struggle in the American social arena, contemporary Afro-American neorealists are still basically inclined toward a redemptive, paradoxically progressive and apocalyptic view of history even when the surface patterns are dialectical, cyclical, and spiral. Ambivalent in their narrative allegiances to a black aesthetic, they have increased the range of their thematic concerns from the religious and political to the economic, psychological, and philosophical aspects of contemporary life.

Because most contemporary black American novelists are college educated, it is not surprising that the literary and nonliterary influences on their use of narrative conventions have been wide-ranging and varied. Many acknowledge the importance of Western and Euro-American writers, some mention Russians, Asians, and Africans, and others include such Afro-Americans as Toomer, Hurston, Wright, Himes, and Ellison. In a national poll of thirty-eight black writers in 1965, more than half named Richard Wright as the most important black American writer of all time; and John A. Williams's *Man Who Cried I Am* and John O. Killens's *And Then We Heard the Thunder* were ranked equally high as the most important novels written by a black American since *Invisible Man.* According to the managing editor of *Negro Digest,* "The writers were asked no questions dealing with style and technique, partly because these considerations—the editors believe—are more the concern of English teachers and creative writing courses than of readers interested in knowing which writers and which ideas the writers think are important. Style and technique are problems for the individual writer to work out for himself, and his attitude toward style and technique will be reflected in his own work and in the work he admires."[42] Viewed from the historical, anthropological, and formalistic perspectives of this study, however, *The Man Who Cried I Am* is the more successful of the two novels. There are, of course, several novels written since 1965 that are better or equally well written, including Ernest Gaines's *Autobiography of Miss Jane Pittman,* Morrison's *Sula,* and Bambara's *Salt Eaters.* In the 1970s Zora Neale Hurston was rediscovered and reassessed as a major voice in the tradition of the Afro-American novel, inspiring the search of many black women writers beyond their mothers' gardens for other literary mothers. Because of the diverse influences, interests, and talents of contemporary black American novelists, we find a corresponding diversity in their attitudes toward and use of realism and modernism. Even among the neorealists examined in this chapter, we find that some—especially Williams, Morrison, and Bambara—are inclined on occasions to move beyond realism. This is not to imply that modernism and postmodernism are more viable modes for constructing the vision of contemporary Afro-American novelists. Nor does it imply that the neoslave narratives of Margaret Walker and Ernest Gaines . . . are necessarily superior on all levels to novels by other neorealists. Readers, like novelists, in short, should be as open minded and responsive to the imperatives of change and the revitalization of earlier forms in the narrative tradition as they are in affirming their identification with historical continuity and enduring ethical values that underlie the distortions and discontinuities of our contemporary culture of narcissism.

Notes

1. Stokeley Carmichael and Charles V. Hamilton, *Black Power: The Politics of Liberation in America* (New York: Vintage, 1967), p. 44.

2. John H. Bracey, Jr., "Black Nationalism Since Garvey," in Huggins, Kilson, and Fox, *Key Issues in the Afro-American Experience*, 2: 266–67.

3. Harold Cruse, *Rebellion or Revolution?* (New York: William Morrow, 1969), pp. 75–77.

4. Larry Neal, "The Black Arts Movement," in *The Black Aesthetic*, ed. Addison Gayle, Jr. (1971; rpt. Garden City: Anchor, 1972), p. 257.

5. Ibid.

6. Larry Neal, "And Shine Swam On," in *Black Fire: An Anthology of Afro-American Writing*, ed. LeRoi Jones and Larry Neal (New York: William Morrow, 1968), pp. 643–48.

7. Betty Friedan, *The Feminine Mystique* (New York: Dell, 1975), p. 85.

8. Gerda Lerner, ed., *Black Women in White America: A Documentary History* (New York: Vintage, 1973), p. xxv. See also Bell Hooks, *Ain't I A Woman: Black Women and Feminism* (Boston: South End Press, 1981), pp. 119–96.

9. Toni Cade, "On the Issue of Roles," in *The Black Woman: An Anthology*, ed. Toni Cade (New York: Signet, 1970), pp. 103–4.

10. Combahee River Collective, "Black Feminist Statement," in *All the Women Are White, All the Blacks Are Men, But Some of Us Are Brave*, ed. Gloria T. Hull, Patricia Bell Scott, and Barbara Smith (Old Westbury: Feminist Press, 1982), p. 15.

11. Ibid.

12. Toni Cade Bambara, cited in *Black Women Writers at Work*, ed. Claudia Tate (New York: Continuum, 1983), p. 34.

13. Calvin Hernton, "The Sexual Mountain and Black Women Writers," *Black American Literature Forum* 18 (Winter 1984): 139.

14. Andrea Benton Rushing, "Images of Black Women in Afro-American Poetry," in *The Afro-American Woman: Struggles and Images*, ed. Sharon Harley and Rosalyn Terborg-Penn (Port Washington: Kennikat, 1978), pp. 74–84; "Images of Black Women in Modern African Poetry: An Overview," in *Sturdy Black Bridges: Visions of Black Women in Literature*, ed. Roseann P. Bell, Bettye J. Parker, and Beverly Guy-Sheftall (Garden City, N.Y.: Anchor, 1979), pp. 18–24; and "Family Resemblances: A Comparative Study of Women Protagonists in Contemporary African-American and Anglophone-African Novels" (Ph.D. diss., University of Massachusetts, Amherst, 1983).

15. Barbara Smith, "Toward a Black Feminist Criticism," in *The New Feminist Criticism: Essays on Women, Literature, and Theory*, ed. Elaine Showalter (New York: Pantheon, 1985), pp. 168–85; and Deborah E. McDowell, "New Directions for Black Feminist Criticism," ibid., pp. 186–99.

16. McDowell, "New Directions for Black Feminist Criticism," pp. 190–95.

17. Bambara cited in Tate, *Black Women Writers at Work*, pp. 19–20.

18. Mary Helen Washington, ed., *Midnight Birds: Stories of Contemporary Black Women Writers* (Garden City, N.Y.: Anchor, 1980), p. 43.

19. George Lukács, *Realism in Our Time*, pp. 93, 94. Lukacs's emphasis.

20. John Killens, quoted in Harold Cruse, *The Crisis of the Negro Intellectual* (1967; rpt. New York: Apollo, 1968), p. 235. Cruse's critique of the failure of the Harlem Left is highly informative despite his personal attacks on individuals. On Killens, see pp. 206–52.

21. John O. Killens, "The Black Writer Vis-à-Vis His Country," *Black Man's Burden* (New York: Trident, 1965), pp. 34, 31.

22. Gayle, *Way of the New World*, p. 276.

23. John O. Killens, *Youngblood* (1954; rpt. New York: Pocket Books, 1955), p. 9.

24. John O. Killens, *And Then We Heard the Thunder* (1963; rpt. New York: Pocket Books, 1964), p. 496. Subsequent references to this novel will be in the text.

25. John O. Killens, *'Sippi* (New York: Trident, 1967), p. xiii. For an informative discussion on Killens's use of folklore, see William H. Wiggins, Jr., "Black Folktales in the Novels of John O. Killens," *Black Scholar: Journal of Black Studies and Research*, November 1971, pp. 50–58.

26. John O. Killens, *The Cotillion; or One Good Bull Is Half the Herd* (New York: Pocket Books, 1972), p. 171. Subsequent references to this novel will be in the text.

27. John A. Williams, "Career by Accident," *Flashbacks: A Twenty-Year Diary of Article Writing* (Garden City, N.Y.: Doubleday, 1973), p. 394.

28. John Williams quoted in O'Brien, *Interviews with Black Writers*, p. 230.

29. John A. Williams, *Night Song* (1961, *Sweet Love Bitter*; rpt. New York: Pocket Books, 1970), p. 41. Subsequent references to this novel will be in the text.

30. John A. Williams, *The Man Who Cried I Am* (1967; rpt. New York: Signet, 1968), p. 308.

31. "Nobody has really influenced me," Williams tells the interviewer. "This is because I read without discrimination when I was a great deal younger. In terms of form, my single influence has been Malcolm Lowry in *Under the Volcano*. I tried to emulate him in *Sissie* and improve on what he did with the telescoping of time. But I think I did it much better in *The Man Who Cried I Am*" (O'Brien, *Interviews*, pp. 233, 230).

32. Ibid., p. 187.

33. Ibid., pp. 192, 193.

34. Alice Walker, *The Third Life of Grange Copeland* (1970; rpt. New York: Avon, 1971), p. 12. Subsequent references to this novel will be in the text.

35. Alice Walker, *Meridian* (New York: Harcourt Brace Jonanovich, 1976), pp. 40–47. Subsequent references to this novel will be in the text.

36. Alice Walker, *The Color Purple* (New York: Harcourt Brace Jovanovich, 1982), p. 167. Subsequent references to this novel will be in the text.

37. Trudier Harris, "On *The Color Purple*, Stereotypes, and Silence," *Black American Literature Forum* 18 (Winter 1984): 157.

38. Toni Cade Bambara, *The Salt Eaters* (New York: Random House, 1980), p. 8. Subsequent references to this novel will be in the text.

39. Toni Morrison, *Song of Solomon* (New York: Knopf, 1977), p. 3. Subsequent references to this novel will be in the text.

40. Toni Morrison, *The Bluest Eye* (1970; rpt. New York: Pocket Books, 1972), p. 20.

41. Toni Morrison, *Sula* (New York: Knopf, 1973), pp. 152, 65. Subsequent references to this novel will be in the text.

42. Hoyt W. Fuller, "A Survey: Black Writers' Views on Literary Lions and Values," *Negro Digest*, January 1968, p. 21.

Part V *Key Terms and Essay/Discussion Questions*

KEY TERMS

Africanism	*Black Power*
Folk songs	*Black Arts Movement*
Work songs	*Neorealism*
Spirituals	*Alice Walker*
Gospels	*John A. Williams*
Improvisation	*Toni Morrison*
Blues	*Womanist*
NARA	*Toni Cade Bambara*
Gary Byrd	*John O. Killens*

ESSAY/DISCUSSION QUESTIONS

1. It has been argued persuasively that the slave trade and chattel slavery did not destroy all aspects of African culture among African-descended Americans. Rather, slave populations retained Africanisms of various kinds. How does Portia Maultsby demonstrate this thesis in regard to African American music?

2. Describe the characteristics of African and African-derived music as discussed by Maultsby. What role did Africanisms play in the growth and development of African American expressive culture?

3. How have music and religion intersected in slave and free African American communities?

4. What is the importance of studying African American folk culture?

5. According to Sterling Brown, what distinguishes African American folk music from its white American counterpart?

6. Nelson George argues that in the 1960s, the black-pride movement and black capitalism strongly influenced rhythm and blues performer James Brown's artistic and economic practices. Discuss.

7. According to George, Queen of Soul music Aretha Franklin delivered uncompromisingly a powerful musical sound and social message that emerged from the life experiences of the African American woman, yet she was able to transcend the boundaries of race, class, and gender and to appeal to a broad public. Explain.

8. In a critical statement, George declares: "Blacks create and then move on. Whites document and then recycle. In the

history of popular music, these truths are self-evident." What does he mean? Do you agree or disagree with this observation?

9. According to Richard Wright, what should be the black writer's role and perspective.

10. How did the Black Arts Movement of the 1960s and the Women's Rights Movement of the 1970s provide a political and cultural context for the emergence of black feminist critics and the increasing development of and public attention to African American women's literature?

11. According to black feminist critics Barbara Smith and Deborah McDowell, many African American female novelists use similar themes. First, delineate these themes. Second, select a novel by a contemporary African American female writer and examine the extent to which the themes appear.

12. To what extent do the novels by John O. Killens and John A. Williams reflect the critical realism of Richard Wright?

Part V *Supplementary Readings*

Abrahams, Roger D., *Deep Down in the Jungle: Negro Narrative Folklore from the Streets of Philadelphia*, Chicago: Aldine Publishing Company, 1970.

Awkard, Michael, *Inspiriting Influences: Tradition, Revision, and Afro-American Women's Novels*, New York: Columbia University Press, 1989.

Baker, Houston A. Jr., *Workings of the Spirit: The Poetics of Afro-American Women's Writing*, Chicago: The University of Chicago Press, 1991.

_____, *Afro-American Poetics: Revisions of Harlem and the Black Aesthetic*, Chicago: The University of Chicago Press, 1988.

_____, *Modernism and the Harlem Renaissance*, Chicago: The University of Chicago Press, 1987.

_____, *Blues, Ideology, and Afro-American Literature: A Vernacular Theory*, Chicago: The University of Chicago Press, 1984.

_____, *The Journey Back: Issues in Black Literature and Criticism*, Chicago: The University of Chicago Press, 1980.

_____, and Patricia Redmond, ed., *Afro-American Literary Study in the 1990s*, Chicago: The University of Chicago Press, 1989.

Baldwin, James, *The Price of the Ticket: Collected Nonfiction, 1948–1985*, New York: St. Martin's Press, 1985.

_____, *The Devil Finds Work*, New York: The Dial Press, 1976.

_____, *The Fire Next Time*, New York: Dell Publishing Company, 1962.

_____, *Nobody Knows My Name: More Notes of a Native Son*, New York: Dell Publishing Company, 1961.

_____, *Notes of a Native Son*, Boston: Beacon Press, 1955.

Baraka, Amiri, *Selected Plays and Prose of Amiri Baraka/LeRoi Jones,* New York: William Morrow and Company, Inc., 1979.

_____ and Fundi, *In Our Terribleness,* Indianapolis: The Bobbs-Merrill Company, Inc., 1970.

Barksdale, Richard and Kenneth Kinnamon, eds., *Black Writers of America: A Comprehensive Anthology,* New York: The Macmillan Company, 1972.

Bell, Roseann P., Bettye J. Parker, and Beverly Guy-Sheftall, eds., *Sturdy Black Bridges: Visions of Black Women in Literature,* Garden City: Anchor Books/Doubleday, 1979.

Braxton, Joanne M. and Andree N. McLaughlin, eds., *Wild Women in the Whirlwind: Afra-American Culture and the Contemporary Literary Renaissance,* New Brunswick: Rutgers University Press, 1990.

Brown, Sterling A., *The Collected Poems of Sterling A. Brown,* New York: Harper & Row, Publishers, 1980.

Cain, George, *Blueschild Baby,* New York: McGraw-Hill Book Company, 1970.

Carby, Hazel V., *Reconstructing Womanhood: The Emergence of the Afro-American Woman Novelist,* New York: Oxford University Press, 1987.

Charters, Samuel B. and Leonard Kunstadt, *Jazz: A History of the New York Scene,* New York: Da Capo Press, 1981.

Chinweizu, Onwuchekwa Jemie, and Ichechukwu Madubuike, *Toward the Decolonization of African Literature,* Washington, D.C.: Howard University Press, 1983.

Christian, Barbara, *Black Women Novelists: The Development of a Tradition, 1892–1976,* Westport: Greenwood Press, 1980.

Cole, Bill, *John Coltrane,* New York: Schirmer Books, 1976.

Collier, James L., *The Making of Jazz: A Comprehensive History,* Boston: Houghton Mifflin Company, 1978.

Corbin, Steven, *No Easy Place to Be,* New York: Simon and Schuster, 1989.

Dance, Stanley, *The World of Count Basie,* New York: Charles Scribner's Sons, 1980.

Davis, Miles, *Miles: The Autobiography,* New York: Simon and Schuster, 1989.

Dillard, Joey L., *Black English: Its History and Usage in the United States,* New York: Vintage Books, 1973.

Ellison, Ralph W., *Going to the Territory,* New York: Random House, 1986.

_____, *Shadow and Act,* New York: A Signet Book/The New American Library, 1966.

_____, *Invisible Man,* New York: Random House, Inc., 1952.

Evans, Mari, ed., *Black Women Writers (1950–1980): A Critical Evaluation,* Garden City: Anchor Books/Doubleday, 1994.

_____, *I am a Black Woman,* New York: William Morrow and Company, Inc., 1970.

Fisher, Miles M., *Negro Slave Songs in the United States,* New York: The Citadel Press, 1963.

Garland, Phyl, *The Sound of Soul,* Chicago: Henry Regnery Company, 1969.

Gayle, Addison Jr., *Richard Wright: Ordeal of a Native Son,* Garden City: Anchor Press/Doubleday, 1980.

_____, *The Way of the New World: The Black Novel in America,* Garden City: Anchor Press/Doubleday, 1975.

Gates, Henry L. Jr., *The Signifying Monkey: A Theory of Afro-American Literary Criticism,* New York: Oxford University Press, 1988.

_____, *Figures in Black: Words, Signs, and the "Racial" Self,* New York: Oxford University Press, 1987.

_____, ed., *The Black Aesthetic,* Garden City: Anchor Books/Doubleday and Company, Inc., 1972.

Goss, Linda and Marian E. Barnes, eds., *Talk That Talk: An Anthology of African-American Storytelling,* New York: Simon & Schuster Inc., 1989.

Gwaltney, John L., *Drylongso: A Self-Portrait of Black America,* New York: Random House, 1980.

Harrison, Daphne D., *Black Pearls: Blues Queens of the 1920s,* New Brunswick: Rutgers University Press, 1988.

Henderson, Stephen, *Understanding the New Black Poetry: Black Speech and Black Music as Poetic References,* New York: William Morrow and Company, Inc., 1973.

Herskovits, Melville J., *The Myth of the Negro Past,* Boston: Beacon Press, 1958.

Himes, Chester, *The Third Generation,* New York: Thunder's Mouth Press, 1989.

_____, *Black on Black,* Garden City: Doubleday & Company, Inc., 1973.

Holloway, Joseph E., ed., *Africanisms in American Culture,* Bloomington: Indiana University Press, 1990.

Hughes, Langston, ed., *The Book of Negro Humor,* New York: Dodd, Mead & Company, 1966.

Hughes, Langston and Arna Bontemps, eds., *The Book of Negro Folklore,* New York: Dodd, Mead & Company, 1958.

Huggins, Nathan I., *Harlem Renaissance,* New York: Oxford University Press, 1971.

Hurston, Zora Neale, *Their Eyes Were Watching God,* Urbana: University of Illinois Press, 1978.

Jackson, Blyden, *A History of Afro-American Literature, Vol. I, The Long Beginning, 1746–1895,* Baton Rouge: Louisiana State University Press, 1989.

Jones, LeRoi, *Black Music,* New York: William Morrow and Company, 1968.

_____, *Blues People,* New York: William Morrow and Company, 1963.

_____ and Larry Neal, eds., *Black Fire: An Anthology of Afro-American Writing,* New York: William Morrow & Company, 1968.

Levine, Lawrence W., *Black Culture and Black Consciousness: Afro-American Folk Thought from Slavery to Freedom,* New York: Oxford University Press, 1977.

Lewis, David L., *When Harlem was in Vogue,* New York: Alred A. Knopf, Inc., 1981.

Locke, Alain, *The New Negro,* New York: Atheneum, 1969.

———, *The Negro and His Music,* Port Washington: Kennikat Press, Inc., 1968.

Long, Richard A. and Eugenia W. Collier, eds., *Afro-American Writing: An Anthology of Prose and Poetry,* 2 Vols., Washington Square: New York University Press, 1972.

Keil, Charles, *Urban Blues,* Chicago: The University of Chicago Press, 1966.

Kofsky, Frank, *Black Nationalism and the Revolution in Music,* New York: Pathfinder Press, 1970.

McDowell, Deborah E. and Arnold Rampersad, eds., *Slavery and the Literary Imagination,* Baltimore: The Johns Hopkins University Press, 1989.

McMillan, Terry, ed., *Breaking Ice: An Anthology of Contemporary African-American Fiction,* New York: Penguin Books, 1990.

———, *Disappearing Acts,* New York: Viking, 1989.

Miller, Eugene, *Voice of a Native Son: The Poetics of Richard Wright,* Jackson: University Press of Mississippi, 1990.

Miller, R. Baxter, *The Art and Imagination of Langston Hughes,* Lexington: The University Press of Kentucky, 1989.

Naylor, Gloria, *Mama Day,* New York: Ticknor & Fields, 1988.

———, *Linden Hills,* New York: Ticknor & Fields, 1985.

———, *The Women of Brewster Place,* New York: Viking Books, 1982.

Neal, Larry, *Visions of a Liberated Future: Black Arts Movement Writings,* New York: Thunder's Mouth Press, 1989.

Reed, Ishmael, *Terrible Threes,* New York: Atheneum, 1989.

———, *Writin' is Fightin': Thirty-Seven Years of Boxing on Paper,* New York: Atheneum, 1988.

———, *Reckless Eyeballing,* New York: St. Martin's Press, 1986.

———, *Terrible Twos,* New York: Atheneum, 1982.

———, *Mumbo Jumbo,* New York: Avon Books, 1972.

Roberts, John W., *From Trickster to Badman: The Black Folk Hero in Slavery and Freedom,* Philadelphia: University of Pennsylvania Press, 1989.

Rose, Phyllis, *Jazz Cleopatra: Josephine Baker in Her Time,* New York: Doubleday, 1989.

Sernett, Milton C., ed., *Afro-American Religious History: A Documentary Witness,* Durham: Duke University Press, 1985.

Simpkins, Cuthbert O., *Coltrane: A Bibliography,* New York: Herndon House Publishers, 1975.

Smith, Valerie, *Self-Discovery and Authority in Afro-American Narrative,* Cambridge: Harvard University Press, 1987.

Smitherman, Geneva, *Talkin and Testifyin: The Language of Black America,* Boston: Houghton Mifflin Company, 1972.

Sollors, Werner, *Amiri Baraka/LeRoi Jones: The Quest for a "Populist Modernism",* New York: Columbia University Press, 1978.

Southern, Eileen, *The Music of Black Americans: A History,* New York: W. W. Norton & Company, Inc., 1971.

Stuckey, Sterling, "Through the Prism of Folklore: The Black Ethos in Slavery," *The Massachusetts Review,* Vol. 3 (Summer 1968), pp. 416–437.

Tate, Claudia, ed., *Black Women Writers at Work,* New York: The Continuum Publishing Corporation, 1988.

Thomas, J. C., *Chasin' the Trane: The Music and Mystique of John Coltrane,* New York: Da Capo Press, 1976.

Tirro, Frank, *Jazz: A History,* New York: W. W. Norton & Company, 1977.

Turner, Lorenzo, *Africanisms in the Gullah Dialect,* Chicago: The University of Chicago Press, 1949.

Walker, Margaret, *Richard Wright: Daemonic Genius,* New York: Warner Books, 1988.

————, *Jubilee,* Boston: Houghton Mifflin, 1966.

Wall, Cheryl A., ed., *Changing Our Own Words: Essays on Criticism, Theory, and Writing by Black Women,* New Brunswick: Rutgers University Press, 1989.

Washington, Helen M., ed., *Memory of Kin: Stories about Family by Black Writers,* New York: Anchor Books/Doubleday, 1991.

————, ed., *Black-Eyed Susans/Midnight Birds: Stories by and about Black Women,* New York: Anchor Books/Doubleday, 1990.

————, *Invented Lives: Narratives of Black Women, 1860–1960,* New York: Anchor Books/Doubleday, 1987.

Whitten, Norman E. Jr., and John F. Szwed., eds., *Afro-American Anthropology: Contemporary Perspectives,* New York: The Free Press, 1970.

Wideman, John E., *Philadelphia Fire,* New York: Henry Holt and Company, 1990.

————, *The Lynchers,* New York: Henry Holt and Company, 1973.

Williams, Sherley A., *Dessa Rose,* New York: William Morrow and Company, Inc., 1986.

Willis, Susan, *Specifying: Black Women Writing the American Experience,* Madison: The University of Wisconsin Press, 1987.

Wilmore, Gayraud S., ed., *African American Religious Studies: An Interdisciplinary Anthology,* Durham: Duke University Press, 1989.

Wood, Forrest G., *The Arrogance of Faith: Christianity and Race in America from the Colonial Era to the Twentieth Century,* New York: Alfred A. Knopf, 1990.

Wright, Ellen and Michel Fabre, eds., *Richard Wright Reader,* New York: Harper & Row, Publishers, 1978.

VI

The African American Family: Historical and Policy Issues

Shaken by the chaos, dislocation, and dehumanization of enslavement, the African American family has nevertheless played a major role in the collective survival and social development of African-descended Americans. Drawing from their disrupted but not destroyed cultural traditions, African slaves from diverse ethnic backgrounds (for example, Wolof, Bambara, Igbo, Yoruba, Akan, Fon) who were transported to America had to re-create family and community life in the crucible of economic exploitation and racial oppression. These harsh and changing circumstances set in motion a historical process that required the refashioning of African American family dynamics. Today, race and class discrimination continue to dictate the conditions under which the contemporary African American family will survive.

The articles collected in this section provide both information about some trends in the historical development of the African American family and a debate about the cultural and socio-economic conditions that are influencing the contemporary African American family. Among observers and analysts of the African American situation, there is much agreement on the facts of African American family instability: rising rates of broken marriages, out-of-wedlock births, female-headed households, teenage pregnancies, and welfare dependency among economically impoverished urban African Americans. Where there is considerable disagreement is about the causes of and alternatives to the mounting African American family predicament.

The essay by Andrew Billingsley, "Historical Backgrounds of the Negro Family," examines structures and processes of traditional West African family and communal culture and the effects of chattel slavery on the development of African American family and community life in the United States. By comparing and contrasting the cultural patterns of different and highly complex West African societies, Billingsley illustrates the central importance of the family. He surveys different kinship relations, patterns of residence, and family organization, and he points out the roles of fathers, mothers, and other significant adults in the love and care of children. However, the slave trade and slavery massively disrupted these regularities of social life both among West African societies and among the West Africans who were involuntarily and brutally transported to the Americas.

Billingsley then turns to the impact of chattel slavery on the emergence of the African American family and its life in the community. Transforming free human beings into unfree commodities, the dynamic process of enslavement forcefully reshaped and deformed the development of the African American personality, culture, and family and community life. It is the dehumanizing experience of enslavement, according to Billingsley, that distinguishes African Americans from those groups of people who voluntarily immigrated to America.

Billingsley contrasts patterns of slavery in the United States with those in Latin America, particularly Brazil. Although noting that both institutions of enslavement were cruel and inhuman, he suggests that the "closed" system of slavery in the United States was more brutal and its negative consequences more enduring than was the "open" system of slavery in Latin America. Billingsley finds that the institution of chattel slavery in the United States denied to the enslaved the most fundamental rights, even the recognition of the slave's humanity. In contrast, the influence of the Catholic Church and other Spanish and Portuguese cultural and legal traditions resulted in a Latin American system of enslavement that generally protected the physical and personal integrity of slaves, encouraged their manumission, and allowed more stable marriages between slaves and free people of color.

In the American South, however, slave families were denied the protection of the law; slaveowners generally held supreme power over all aspects of their slaves' family and community life.

Significantly, male slaves and husbands were relatively powerless to protect their wives, children, and other family members from the violent and/or sexual aggression of slaveowners. Billingsley employs slave narratives to depict the difficulty slaves experienced in their efforts to establish and maintain family ties. The narratives show that when slaves escaped, even the so-called favorite and trusted ones expressed anger toward their former slaveowners about the exploitation, cruelty, and the indignity of being enslaved. The narratives also illustrate the intense love between members of enslaved families and their determination to sustain some form of family life, even as slaveowners sought to destabilize and break up this institution.

Billingsley charges that when the slaves were freed following the Civil War, America never compensated them or their descendants for the more than two centuries of cultural, economic, and political exploitation under chattel slavery. Therefore, during the years immediately after Emancipation, freedom from chattel slavery for thousands of African Americans meant freedom to die of starvation or illness. Indeed, Reconstruction and its aftermath proved to be a monumental disaster for the great mass of African Americans, as the white South reconstituted its regime of violent domination and reinstated the disenfranchisement of former slaves and their descendants. Therefore, African Americans and their families continued a virtual struggle for survival long after chattel slavery had ended.

In his article "The Negro Family," sociologist E. Franklin Frazier skillfully examines the social and economic forces that helped to shape the structure and dynamic of African American families from slavery to freedom. Like Billingsley, Frazier points out that the plantation organization had a major impact on the development of the African American family during the period of chattel slavery. The enslaved family was subject to the changing conditions of the slave system. Since the father might be sold away, the African American mother came to represent the most dependable and important member of the enslaved family. Additionally, the enslaved family was shaped by the practice of slaveowners, some of whom sexually violated their female slaves, producing racially mixed children. Some white men acknowledged and cared for these children, but many did not.

Frazier goes on to analyze the social forces affecting the internal structure and composition of African American families in rural and urban areas. He points out that by the 1940s, economic and social conditions contributed to an increasing tendency toward female heads of household among African Americans in the rural South. The tendency was greater among sharecroppers than among homeowners, resulting from women being widowed, divorced, or unmarried. Out of this development, which had its ultimate origin in chattel slavery, emerged a pattern of maternal family organization in which the grandmother came to play a dominant role. Frazier observes that the "matriarchal" pattern of family life actually developed in the form of an extended family structure, including several generations of biologically related and adopted children. Additionally, in upper-class African American communities in the rural South, semipatriarchal and extended family patterns developed. In Southern cities, emerging class and geographical differentiation among African Americans also shaped family organization: increasingly, stable and semipatriarchal family patterns characterized middle- and upper-class homeowners, while the opposite was the case for lower-class families.

Frazier indicates that the migration from Southern rural to Northern urban areas, beginning at the turn of the century, dislodged many African American families. Yet, he notes, by the 1940s the impact of urban living and emerging socioeconomic class distinctions gave rise to different patterns of African American family and community organization. Frazier observes that the tendency toward family instability was greater in the less well-off center of African American communities, while patterns of family stability and homeownership were greater among middle- and upper-class families who resided on the periphery of these communities.

In recent years, it has become increasingly evident that the African American family is facing a major crisis. Of course, there seems to be a general American trend toward increased divorce, and the increase in out-of-wedlock births among whites just twenty years ago was popularized by the use of such terms as "love child" to refer to the newborn babies. Moreover, Americans seem to be marrying at a later age, and more couples are living together without having gone through a marriage ceremony. Hence, the growing crisis of African American family destabilization needs to be seen in the context of a general alteration of American family arrangements. But that is not the complete story.

The last two articles in this section represent the kind of ideological debate underway among African American policy analysts about the character of the catastrophe confronting the African

American family and the future challenge to the African American community posed by a rapidly changing American society. Conservative and Marxian perspectives appear here; a third perspective, the liberal approach, is not represented. The conservative perspective tends to find the problem within the individual; it is a matter of moral and value development or change. Because the conservative tends to be critical of government's role, even calling government the cause of many social problems, the conservative advocates a minimal or limited role for government in handling social difficulties. The liberal perspective tends to place the problem within the structural impediments of the existing society. Hence, liberals tend to advocate a more active role for government in managing social problems within existing societal arrangements. The Marxian perspective tends to locate problems at the level of the social order, or its changing character, and in the social relations of power and domination between ruling and subordinate classes. Hence, Marxists tend to view social problems as coming out of the ruling class's exploitation of subordinate classes in a particular social order. In the view of Marxists, problems can be either better handled or exacerbated by a fundamental change in the existing social order.

In his article, "The Black Family: A Critical Challenge," conservative Glenn C. Loury argues that the catastrophic problem of African American family dislocation (i.e., the rise in rates of teenage pregnancy and out-of-wedlock births) is largely a result of the prevailing and confused values, attitudes, and behavior of young African American women and men. He says that many poor inner-city African American youngsters lack self-esteem and produce children for whom they cannot care in a desperate effort to gain social status. He charges that government welfare policy reinforces and even rewards this behavior by making public assistance easily available and free of stigma. Declaring that government cannot solve the African American family crisis, Loury challenges the African American middle class and its social and religious institutions to take the initiative and provide the leadership necessary to promote more positive moral values and virtuous behavior among impoverished inner-city African American youth.

William Darity, Jr., and Samuel L. Myers, Jr., offer a neo-Marxian analysis of the African American family predicament in their article, "Public Policy Trends and the Fate of the Black Family." They suggest that the declining condition of the African American family is related to a contemporary social transformation of major proportions—the winding down of capitalism and the coming of managerialism. The traditional Marxist outlook states that capitalist society is to be overtaken not by a managerialist but by a socialist society. According to Darity and Myers, the declining capitalist society has been energized by money and manufacturing; in contrast, the rising managerial society increasingly is driven by mental capacity and managerial skill. In the emerging social order, a new class of intellectuals and technical intelligentsia is struggling to claim political and cultural dominance from its initial benefactor, the old business class.

Although the managerial class's struggle with the capitalist class for power and dominance is not completed, Darity and Myers suggest that the outlook for impoverished African Americans is bleak under either alternative. Since many inner-city impoverished African Americans, who are at the lower end of the working class, are attracted to public assistance because low wages provide insufficient family income, business elites are advocating public policies that require recipients of public welfare to meet more stringent standards, be employed, and receive reduced levels of benefits. On the other hand, efficiency-driven and technocratically oriented social managers ultimately may design population control strategies for racially targeted groups. For Darity and Myers, policy strategies emanating from business class interests may tend to increase the numbers of female-headed families and marginalize the status of many already impoverished African American men. On the other hand managerial family policy may very well result in the control and reduction of the numbers of impoverished African American and other undesirable populations through such measures as reproductive regulation or the redefinition of African American female-headed family arrangements as an acceptable option among many, representing a kind of cultural pluralism within managerial society.

To know the possibilities of a race
An appraisal of its past is necessary.
CARTER G. WOODSON

Historical Backgrounds of the Negro Family

ANDREW BILLINGSLEY

IN THEIR STUDY OF THE major ethnic groups in New York, Glazer and Moynihan concluded their discussion of the Negro family with the observation that: "The Negro is only an American, and nothing else. He has no values and culture to guard and protect."[1] This statement could not possibly be true. And yet, it represents the prevailing view among liberal intellectuals who study the Negro experience from the outside. Nat Hentoff, who holds a different view, has pointed out that not one of the critical reviewers of Glazer and Moynihan's book took them to task for this generalization.[2] The implications of the Glazer-Moynihan view of the Negro experience are far-reaching. To say that a people have no culture is to say that they have no common history which has shaped them and taught them. And to deny the history of a people is to deny their humanity.

If, on the other hand, the Negro people constitute in some important respects an ethnic subsociety with a distinct history, what are the essential elements of this history? Three facts stand out above all others. The first is that the Negro people came to this country from Africa and not from Europe. The second

is that they came in chains and were consequently uprooted from their cultural and family moorings. The third is that they have been subjected to systematic exclusion from participation and influence in the major institutions of this society even to the present time. Because of these three factors, "the Jews, Irish, Italians, Poles or Scandinavians who see no difference between their former plight and that of Negroes today are either grossly uninformed or are enjoying an unforgiveable false pride."[3]

At the same time, it needs saying that the Negro experience has not been uniform. It has varied according to time, place, and other conditions. The consequences of these experiences have also been varied and complex. Furthermore, not all the history of the Negro people has been negative. There is much in the historical backgrounds of the Negro people which has helped them survive in the face of

From the book: *Black Families in White America* by Andrew Billingsley. © 1968. Used by permission of the publisher: Prentice Hall/A Division of Simon & Schuster, Englewood Cliffs, N.J.

impossible conditions. This history has produced a most resilient and adaptive people with a strong appreciation for the realities of existence, as reflected in the ability of Negroes to "tell it like it is," and to "get down to the nitty-gritty" in talking about their life circumstances, at least among their friends, if not always when among their enemies. (Perhaps the increasing ability of Negroes of all social classes to speak out to the wider society about their conditions and "tell it like it is" also indicates a feeling, or at least a precarious hope, that we are indeed among friends.)

In this chapter, we will set forth some highlights of the historical backgrounds of the Negro people which have helped to shape both the structure and the functioning of Negro families. The family is at once the most sensitive, important, and enduring element in the culture of any people. Whatever its structure, its most important function is everywhere the same—namely, to insure the survival of its people.

Two aspects of Negro history will be considered, their African backgrounds and the impact of slavery. Each of these topics could and should be the subject of full-length books. We can only sketch some of the highlights to show their relevance for a more general understanding of Negro families, and a more comprehensive strategy for the reconstruction of Negro family and community life.

AFRICAN BACKGROUNDS

Negroes, under the tutelage of white Americans, have long viewed their African background with a sense of shame. To be called an African when I was growing up in Alabama was much worse than being called a "nigger." And, to be called a "black African" was a sign of extreme derision.

Later, when I was a student in a Negro college, we were more sophisticated, but we were no less ambivalent about our heritage. The two or three African students on campus were isolated. They were viewed and treated

with great disdain, while the two or three white students were the objects of adulation. The African students represented the deep, dark past, while the Caucasians represented to great white hope of the future. In spite of vast changes which have occurred in the world since World War II, with respect to Africa and its place in the world, large numbers of Negroes still feel just a twinge of inferiority associated with their African heritage. How could it be otherwise, considering the sources of our knowledge about ourselves and our past? Yet the image is changing radically and rapidly. Negroes are taking seriously the questions posed by Lincoln Lynch, formerly of the Congress on Racial Equality: "It is a question of who are we, and where do we come from, and where do we going?"

A careful reading of history and ethnographic studies reveals a pattern of African backgrounds which are ancient, varied, complex, and highly civilized. The evidence suggests that far from being rescued from a primitive savagery by the slave system, Negroes were forcibly uprooted from a long history of strong family and community life every bit as viable as that of their captors. It was a very different type of society from the European-oriented society in the new world.

Several general features of African family life showed great viability. First, family life was not primarily—or even essentially—the affair of two people who happened to be married to each other. It united not simply two people, but two families with a network of extended kin who had considerable influence on the family, and considerable responsibility for its development and well-being. Marriage could neither be entered into nor abandoned without substantial community support. Secondly, marriage and family life in pre-European Africa, as among most tribal people, was enmeshed in centuries of tradition, ritual, custom, and law. "When the Arabs swept into North and West Africa in the Seventh Century," writes John Hope Franklin, "they found a civilization that was already thousands of years old."[4] Thirdly, family life was highly articulated with the rest of the society. The family was an economic and a religious unit which, through its ties with wider kinship circles, was also a political unit. Family life, then, was strong and viable, and was the center of the African civilization. "At the basis even of economic and political life in Africa was the family, with its inestimable influence over its individual members."[5]

Patterns of Family Life

The most striking feature of African family and community life was the strong and dominant place in family and society assigned to and assumed by the men. This strong, masculine dominance, however, far from being capricious authoritarianism, was supported, guided, and limited by custom and tradition, which also provided a substantial role for the women. The children were provided a quality of care and protection not common in modern societies, for they belonged not alone to their father and mother, but also, and principally, to the wider kinship group.

Family life in West Africa was patterned along several dimensions, including descent, type of marriage, type of family (nuclear, extended), residential pattern, and patterns of child care and protection.

There were three basic patterns of descent or kinship in Africa. The most common was patrilineal descent, in which kinship ties are ascribed only through the father's side of the family. The next most common pattern was matrilineal, in which kinship was reckoned through the mother's side of the family. A third pattern present in only a small part of Africa, mostly in the southern portion of the continent, was double descent, in which kinship was reckoned through both the male and female. This pattern, the only one recognized in America, was virtually unknown in the part of West Africa from which American Negroes came.

The Ibo of Eastern Nigeria, the Yoruba of Western Nigeria, and their neighbors the Dahomeans were patrilineal societies.[6] The Ashanti of Ghana were matrilineal.[7] The Yako people (of Nigeria) practiced double descent.[8]

Lineage carried with it distinct rights and obligations. Certain responsibilities of relatives for the care of the family, and especially the children followed the ascription of lineage, as did legal rights and inheritance. In the patrilineal societies, only one's father's relatives were legally and socially responsible for one's welfare. Inheritance was confined to the father's line. Even in patrilineal situations, however, certain informal courtesies were extended to the mother's relatives. Marriage among mother's relatives was generally forbidden, and other relatives often took on major responsibilities in helping with the care of children even though not legally required to do so.

Even in double descent societies there were norms providing for orderly functioning. According to Daryll Forde, the Yako managed rather well.

> The rights and obligations which derive from matrilineal kinship do not formally conflict with those derived patrilineally. . . . Matrilineal kinship should take precedence over patrilineal in the inheritance of transferable wealth, especially livestock and currency . . . and payments made to a wife's kin at the time of her marriage. . . . On the other hand, patrilineal rights and obligations . . . largely relate to the use of land and houses and to the provision of cooperative labor.[9]

Marriage in Africa was rarely an informal matter between two consenting partners and their relatives. Ceremony and exchange of property were important aspects of an elaborate process which consisted of two basic types: those marriages based on the initiation of the two consenting partners and those based on the initiative of their parents and kin.[10] In either case, both the relevant partners and their parents had to give their consent. While there were more than a dozen specific forms which mating and marriage took in one West African tribe alone, they nevertheless followed these two basic patterns. Those initiated by the principals were less elaborate than those initiated by their parents.

A central feature of marriage in West Africa, as among other non-Western peoples, was the bride price, the requirement of some property or material consideration on the part of the bride to legitimize the marriage contract. The bride price might be paid in goods, money such as native beverages, foodstuffs, livestock, and the like. Or it might be paid in the form of services, such as the bridegroom agreeing to help his prospective father-in-law in the fields, or bringing firewood for his mother-in-law. Thirdly, the bride price might be a payment in kind, in which the bridegroom delivers to his bride's relatives a sister, daughter, or other female relative in exchange for the one he is taking away from them.

The bride price not only was a symbol of the serious and communal nature of marriage, but also served to compensate the parents for a real loss.

Once a couple was married, there were several possible patterns of residence they might follow. The pattern most common in Europe and America is referred to by anthropologists as "neolocal" residence. This pattern involves both partners leaving their homes and taking up residence together in a household not determined by parental ties. This pattern was present, but not common, in Africa. It was almost nonexistent in that portion of West Africa from which American Negroes came.

Another pattern which also had restricted use in Africa was "duolocal" residence, in which neither partner left his parental home after marriage; both partners continued to live among their relatives while visiting each other for brief periods and perhaps working together in the fields. This was a rare custom in Africa, but in Ghana a few tribes practiced this arrangement for the first few years of marriage. Duolocal residence had certain economic advantages for newlyweds who had not had time to establish their economic viability.

Much more common in Africa was a third residential pattern referred to as "unilocal," in which one partner left his or her home and kin to live with the other, who remained in or near the household of his or her parents. There were three varieties of unilocal residence. One pattern was of matrilocal residence, which involved the man leaving his home and taking up residence with his wife in her family home. This pattern, while common in other parts of the world where matrilineal societies predominate, had very limited currency in West African societies. Common in West Africa was another pattern of unilocal residence referred to as "avunculocal" residence, in which the wife left her home to live with her husband who lived, not in the household of his parents, but in that of his maternal uncle. This happened most often in those matrilineal societies where the man had already left home at the time of adolescence and gone to live with or near his maternal uncle, who was primarily responsible for him. A third pattern was patrilocal, in which the wife went to live in the home and compound of her husband and his relatives. This patrilocal residential pattern corresponds with the patrilineal rule of descent, and was the most common residential pattern for families in all of West Africa.

Of the three basic forms of marriage, monogamy, which unites one man with one woman, was the most common throughout West Africa. Polyandry, which unites one woman with two or more husbands, was almost unknown in this part of the world. But polygyny, which unites one man with two or more wives, was common, though not dominant, throughout that portion of Africa from which slaves were brought to America. Murdock found, as late as 1957, that polygyny was still practiced and sanctioned in 88 per cent of the 154 African societies he studied.

Household organization followed two basic patterns, the nuclear family and the extended family. These two forms of residence existed side by side. Under the nuclear residential pattern, a man and his wife or wives and their children lived together in his house or compound. Often, each woman, along with her small children, occupied a small hut within the husband's compound. Either the man visited them in turn or they took turns coming to spend two or three nights in his hut while doing the cooking and housekeeping. In the extended family household, two or more families, related to each other, lived in the house or compound of a single head. In a typical patrilocal, polygamous extended family, the household might include a patriarchal head, his several wives, and their children, his older sons and their wives and children, plus his younger brothers and their wives and children.

Among the Dahomeans, for example, a senior man in the community may preside over a compound in which live himself and his wives, his younger brothers and their wives, his grown sons and their wives, and the children of all these women.

There were many instances where a first wife welcomed her second, and where both joined to make a place for the third. Indeed, a woman who, caring for her husband, wishes to further his position in society will . . . make it possible with her own savings for him to obtain another wife. Similarly, when the four day week assigned to a given wife to cohabit with a common husband comes while she is menstruating, her co-wives arrange their time so that this conflict does not deprive her of her opportunity to be with him. And it is far from unusual for a woman to be kind to her husband's children by other women, and for a man to be as close to his children as to their mother. In essence, the great mass of Dahomean matings, either because of complacency or of human ability to make the best of a situation, are permanent ventures

which, in terms of human adjustment, cannot be called failures.[11]

The Care and Protection of Children

The father played a very important role in the care and protection of the children in all these West African societies. The strong bonds that bind both fathers and mothers to their children are suggested by the experience of the Ashanti:

In terms of personal behavior and attitudes, there is often no apparent difference between the relations of mother and children and those of father and children. The warmth, trust, and affection frequently found uniting parents and offspring go harmoniously with the respect shown to both.[12]

Legally, however, an Ashanti father had no authority over his children. In this matrilineal society, the children belonged to the mother's family. Her oldest brother, therefore, carried out the legal responsibilities assigned, in other societies, to the father. Nevertheless, by custom, the children grow up in their father's house, and it was both his obligation and privilege to "feed, clothe, and educate them, and later to set them up in life."[13] The father was responsible for their moral and civic, as well as their economic training. "If anything, Ashanti fathers (unlike mothers) tend to be overly strict in exacting obedience, deference, and good behavior from their children."[14] The following excerpt from Fortes shows the nature of this relationship:

Ashanti say that a man has no hold over his children, except through their love for him and their conscience. A father wins his children's affection by caring for them. They cannot inherit his property, but he can and often does provide for them by making them gifts of property, land, or money during his lifetime or on his deathbed.[15]

The children reciprocate the affection and respect of their father. Fortes continues:

To insult, abuse, or assault one's father is an irreparable wrong, one which is bound to bring ill luck. While there is no legal obligation on a son or daughter to support a father in his old age, it would be regarded as a shame and an evil if he or she did not do so.[16]

A father was responsible for the moral behavior of his sons. He, as well as the mother, must give the consent for his son to marry. He is responsible to find his son a wife and to make sure that the suitor of his daughter is able to support her.

Among the Ibo, who were patrilineal, the father's authority was so strong that it was felt his curse would render a child useless for life.[17] Even among the Yako, who recognized double descent, the father was the paramount authority unless the mother and her small children left the compound. Then, as in the case of the matrilineal groups, the mother's brother took up the father's authority.

In all of West African society, whether patrilineal or matrilineal, the relationship between mother and child was primary and paramount. Until he was weaned at the age of one or two, a child was almost never without his mother. "The Ashanti regard the bond between mother and child as the keystone of all social relations."[18] Among the Dahomeans, in spite of their patrilineal descent, the relationship between mother and child was especially strong.

Fortes has described the role of the Ashanti mother:

An Ashanti woman stints no labour or self-sacrifice for the good of her children. It is mainly to provide them with food, clothing and shelter that she works so hard, importunes her husband, and jealously watches her brother to make sure that he discharges the duties of legal guardian faithfully. No demands upon her are too extreme for a mother. Though she is loathe to punish, and never disowns a child, an Ashanti mother expects obedience and affectionate respect from her children.[19]

The stong attachment to the mother carries over into adulthood for both men and women:

Ashanti say that throughout her life, a woman's foremost attachment is to her mother, who will always protect and help her. A woman grows up in daily and unbroken intimacy with her mother, learns all feminine skills from her, and above all, derives her character from her. . . . For a man, his mother is his most trusted confidante, especially in intimate personal matters. A man's first ambition is to gain enough money to be able to build a house for his mother if she does not own one. To be mistress of her own home, with her children and daughters' children around her, is the highest dignity an ordinary woman aspires to.[20]

Herskovitz has observed that among the Dahomeans, children are much more relaxed with their mother than in their father's presence. He continues, "An outstanding instance of the closeness of the relationship between mother and child in this patrilineal society was had in connection with the recording of songs." On one such occasion, he observed of a chief that "though when he commanded his wives and subordinates, he was imperious and his slightest desire was promptly gratified, he was both gentle and affectionate with his mother."[21]

In a matrilineal society, sole legal authority over a child was vested in his mother's oldest living brother. A man's sister's children, and not his own children, were his legal heirs. The rights and obligations associated with this relationship were especially likely to be brought into play in the case of divorce. The mother's brother then assumed the duties and obligations of a father to the children, in addition to his duties to his own children. In general, however, this relationship was more legal than actual, except in regard to inheritance. In this respect, it was sometimes said that the nephew was the enemy of the mother's brother, waiting for him to die.

The father's sister also assisted in the care and protection of his children. She received respect and affection similar to that offered the father, but the attachment was not so deep as to the father and his brothers. She referred to her brother's children as her own, and would discipline and scold them if necessary. His children felt at home in her house and often ate and slept there. This relationship, while not legally binding, was functional and reciprocal. The father's sister could count on her brother's kindness and helpfulness with her own children. They were, after all, his potential heirs.

> Men say that it is to his sister that a man entrusts weighty matters, never to his wife. He will discuss confidential matters, such as those that concern property, money, public office, legal suits, and even the future of his children, or his matrimonial difficulties with his sister, secure in the knowledge that she will tell nobody else.[22]

In the matrilineal society, the strongest bond, next to that between mother and child, was that between siblings by the same mother.

> An older sibling is entitled to punish and reprimand a younger sibling and must be treated with deference. He is, conversely, obliged to help his younger sisters and brothers if they get into trouble. In all other matters, however, equality and fraternity are the governing norms of siblings. It is often said among the Ashanti, for example, "Your brother or your sister, you can deny them nothing."[23]

Among the Ashanti, the relationship between sisters was particularly close.

> Sisters try to live together all their lives. A woman treats her sister's children so much like her own that orphan children often do not know whether their apparent mother is their true mother or their mother's sister. This holds, though to a lesser degree, for the brother's.

Siblings borrowed from each other freely, as if their property were joint. "Borrowing between siblings cannot create debts." The strong relationship between siblings was supported by law and custom.

> The pivot of the Ashanti kinship system in its function as a system of legal relationship is the tie between brother and sister. A brother has legal power over his sister's children because he is her nearest male equivalent and legal power is vested in males (even in a matrilineal society). A sister has claims on her brother because she is his female equivalent and the only source of the continuity of his descent line (in a matrilineal society).[24]

It is sometimes said that "men find it difficult to decide what is more important to them—to have children or for their sisters to have children." If there is a conflict between the need to care for one's sister's children or producing one's own, men generally concluded, according to Fortes, that "sad as it may be to die childless, a good citizen's first anxiety is for his lineage to survive."

If the position of mother and child was the closest, and that of brother and sister the most fraternal, that between a person and his grandparents was the most revered in all of West African society. In Ashanti, for example, "The grandparents on both sides are the most honored of all one's kinfolk." Their position and status were of the greatest importance for the whole social system, in part because they stood between ordinary citizens and the ancestors. If the ancestors got their status because they stood between man and god, the grandparents got theirs because they stood only a little lower on the ladder of infinity. Among the Yoruba, it was the duty and privilege of grandparents to name newborn children. Among the Ashanti, grandmothers—both maternal and paternal—exercised great influence and responsibility in the care and protection of children. "It is from the grandparents of both sexes that children learn family history, folklore, proverbs, and other traditional lore. The grandparents are felt to be the living links with the past."[25]

Family life in the West Africa of our forebears was heavily influenced by geographic, historical, and cultural conditions in that part of the world. A preliterate people, the West Africans nevertheless had a highly complex civilization. Their patterns of family life were closely knit, well organized, highly articulated with kin and community, and highly functional for the economic, social, and psychological life of the people.

Thus the men and women who were taken as slaves to the New World came from societies every bit as civilized and "respectable" as those of the Old World settlers who mastered them. But the two were very different types of society, for the African family was much more closely integrated with the wider levels of kinship and society. The simple transition of millions of persons from Africa to America would in itself have been a major disruption in the lives of the people, even if it had proceeded on a voluntary and humane basis. As we shall see presently, however, this transition was far from simple, voluntary, and humane.

THE IMPACT OF SLAVERY ON NEGRO FAMILY LIFE

The Negro family in the United States began with Anthony and Isabella, who were among the original twenty Negroes landed at Jamestown in 1619, one year before the Mayflower. Later Anthony and Isabella were married, and in 1624 their son William became "the first Negro child born in English America."[26] These first Negroes were treated essentially as indentured servants. However, after 1690 the bulk of Negroes were brought into the country and sold as slaves.

We have shown that the Negroes brought to the United States were the descendants of an ancient and honorable tradition of African family life. While scholars are still in considerable dispute about the relative influence of this heritage on Negro family life today, particularly in the United States, there is no doubt that the breaking up of that tradition

by the slave trade has had a major impact on both the form and substance of the Negro family. African slavery, stretching over a period of four centuries and involving the capture of more than 40 million Africans, was, for the European countries, a colossal economic enterprise with effects not unlike those of the discovery of gold. But for the African Negroes, it was a colossal social and psychological disruption.

The transportation of slaves from Africa to the New World completely disrupted the cultural life of the Africans and the historical development of the Negro people. This total discontinuity had a particular impact on the Negro family, because the family is the primary unit of social organization. Some of the ways in which this culture was disrupted may be briefly stated.

First, moving as they did from Africa to the New World, the Negroes were confronted with an alien culture of European genesis. Thus, unlike some of the later migrants, including the Germans, Irish, and Italians, they were not moving into a society in which the historical norms and values and ways of life were familiar and acceptable. Secondly, they came from many different tribes with different languages, cultures, and traditions. Thirdly, they came without their families and often without females at all. In the fourth place, they came in chains. These are all major distinctions between the Negro people and all the other immigrants to this country. Therefore, whatever the nature of the two cultural systems from which they came and to which they arrived, and whatever their capacity for adaptation, they were not free to engage in the ordinary process of acculturation. They were not only cut off from their previous culture, but they were not permitted to develop and assimilate to the new culture in ways that were unfettered and similar to the opportunities available to other immigrant groups.

The Negro slaves in the United States were converted from the free, independent human

**Early photograph
of a slave couple
outside their cabin.**

beings they had been in Africa, to property. They became chattel. This process of dehumanization started at the beginning of the slave-gathering process and was intensified with each stage along the way. It should not be difficult to discern that people who, having been told for 200 years—in ways more effective than words—that they are subhuman, should begin to believe this themselves and internalize these values and pass them on to their children and their children's children. Nor is it difficult to imagine how the history and current status of the Negro people might be different if, for all those 200 years, our ancestors had been paid a decent wage for their labor, taught how to invest it, and provided all the supports, privileges, and responsibilities which the New World offered its immigrants of Caucasian ancestry. Conversely, the process of Negro dehumanization provided superior opportunities, privileges, and status to the white majority at the expense of the black minority, and deeply ingrained within white people a crippling sense of superiority.

These are the dynamics of the slave system which must have been in the mind of

President Lyndon Johnson when he spoke so eloquently of the need of our society to "heal our history." But the dehumanizing experience of slavery did not come all at once; it came in stages. "Slavery," says Lerone Bennett,

> was a black man who stepped out of his hut [in Africa] for a breath of fresh air and ended up ten months later in Georgia with bruises on his back and a brand on his chest.[27]

It was that and more. At every stage of this process, the Negroes became progressively more disengaged from their cultures, their families, and their humanity. This transition from freedom to slavery has been captured graphically in personal accounts of the experience.

One such account comes directly from the pen of an African who was captured and sold into slavery. Olaudah Equiano, who was later known as Gustavus Vassa, was born in Africa in 1745. When he was eleven years old, he was kidnapped, sold into slavery, and transported to the New World. After being sold and resold several times, he finally was given an opportunity by a Philadelphia merchant to work and buy his freedom. He became educated and in 1791 wrote his autobiography. He tells of his early experience with slavery.

> The first object which saluted my eyes when I arrived on the coast was the sea, and a slave ship, which was then riding at anchor, and waiting for its cargo. These filled me with astonishment, which was soon connected with terror, when I was carried on board. I was immediately handled, and tossed up to see if I were sound, by some of the crew; and I was now persuaded that I had gotten into a world of bad spirits, and that they were going to kill me. Their complexions too differing so much from ours, their long hair, and the language they spoke (which was very different from any I had ever heard), united to confirm me in this belief.
>
> . . . When I looked round the ship too and saw a large furnace or copper boiling, and a multitude of black people of every description chained together, every one of their countenances expressing dejection and sorrow, I no longer doubted of my fate; and, quite overpowered with horror and anguish, I fell motionless on the deck and fainted.
>
> . . . I was soon put down under the decks, and there I received such a salutation in my nostrils as I had never experienced in my life: so that with the loathsomeness of the stench and crying together, I became so sick and low that I was not able to eat, nor had I the least desire to taste anything.
>
> I now wished for the last friend, death, to relieve me; but soon, to my grief, two of the white men offered me eatables; and, on my refusing to eat, one of them held me fast by the hands, and laid me across, I think, the windlass, and tied my feet, while the other flogged me severely.
>
> . . . I would have jumped over the side, but I could not; and, besides, the crew used to watch us very closely who were not chained down to the decks, lest we should leap into the water; and I have seen some of these poor African prisoners most severely cut for attempting to do so, and hourly whipped for not eating. This indeed was often the case with myself.
>
> In a little time after, amongst the poor chained men, I found some of my own nation, which in a small degree gave ease to my mind. I inquired of these what was to be done with us? They gave me to understand we were to be carried to these white people's country to work for them. I then was a little revived, and thought, if it were no worse than working, my situation was not so desperate.[28]

These episodes capture the essence of the several stages of the slave trade. These consisted first of gathering slaves in Africa, principally as a result of intertribal warfare, but sometimes by simple barter with the chiefs. Premium was placed on young males. The disruptive elements in this practice to family life are apparent. The preponderance of men was so great until, in later years, it was necessary for the European government to require that at least a third of the slaves sold in the New World should be female. In spite of this practice, on many of the plantations, men outnumbered women by nine to one. After capture the slaves were marched to the seaports, a walk often requiring weeks or months of travel. While most of the slaves were gathered on the West Coast of Africa, sometimes they were gathered as many as one thousand miles inland. These slave marches were essentially human caravans, guarded by armed men "with the leaders of the expedition carried in hammocks." The situation has been described by Tannenbaum as follows:

> Little Negro villages in the interior of Africa were frequently attacked in the middle of the night, the people were either killed or captured by Europeans themselves or . . . by Africans acting [for profit] and the victims left alive were shackled with a collar about the neck, men, women and children, and driven for hundreds of miles to the coast.[29]

The rate of sickness and death of the Africans along the slave march was very high. Du Bois has said, "Probably every slave imported represented on the average 5 corpses in Africa or on the high seas."[30] On reaching the coast, the Africans were there sold to the European traders, branded, and put aboard ship for the next phase, which consisted of the celebrated "middle passage." During this passage across the ocean, the slaves were kept in holds like cattle, with a minimum of room and sanitation facilities. When they died, which was frequent, or became seriously ill, which was more frequent, they were cast overboard. The fourth stage consisted of the seasoning of the slaves on the plantations of the West Indies, where they were taught the rudiments of New World agriculture. They were also taught the rudiments of communication in English so as to be able to carry out the instructions of the slave owners and overseers on the plantations. The next stage consisted of the transportation of the slaves to the ports on the mainland, where they were sold to

local slave traders, who in turn auctioned them off to the highest bidder, without special regard to their families or tribal connections. The final stage consisted of their disbursal to the plantations in North and South America. The whole process, from the time of a person's capture in Africa until he was settled on a plantation in the New World, sometimes took six months to a year.

Slavery, then, was a massive disruption of the former cultural life of the Africans, which at the same time, by its very nature, prevented the adequate assimilation of the slaves into the New World culture. The crass commercialism of the slave system dominated every phase of this process.

In summary, the Africans came from a vastly different cultural and social system than was known in Europe and the New World. They came in chains under brutal conditions. Whatever their capacity for adaptation, they were not permitted to adapt. They were often sold to plantations and scattered without regard for their former tribal or family connections. The difficulty of reestablishing and maintaining their cultural systems was as apparent in this process as it was appalling. The small number of slaves distributed on each plantation prevented their developing a reliable set of new cultural forms. And finally, the absence of powerful institutions for the protection of the slaves and their humanity accounted for both the destruction of the previous cultural forms and the prevention of the emergence of new ones as a free and open human development. No other immigrant group can make these statements.

Dominant Patterns of Slavery

While slavery everywhere was cruel and inhuman, it did not everywhere take the same pattern. There were important variations and degrees of cruelty, with differing consequences for the family life of the slaves. Slavery was very different in the United States from what it was in the Latin American countries.

All the major historians who have treated slavery in the New World agree that it was a vastly different and much more oppressive institution in the United States than in Latin America. The essential distinction was that in Latin America slavery was an "open" institution, whereas in the United States it was "closed." These are relative rather than absolute distinctions, but the evidence supporting these general differences is striking.

If historians are agreed on the nature of slavery on the two New World continents, they are not completely agreed on the causes. The major distinction seemed to lie in the structure of the societies and economies of the United States and Brazil, with their different historical and cultural approaches to slavery. Stanley Elkins has pointed to the institutional nature of some of these social forces:

> In Latin America, the very tension and balance among three kinds of organizational concerns—the church, crown, and plantation agriculture—prevented slavery from being carried by its planting class to its ultimate logic. For the slave, this allowed for the development of men and women as moral beings, the result was an "open system"; a system of contacts with free society through which ultimate absorption into that society could and did occur with great frequency.[31]

Tannenbaum has laid heavy stress on the role of the church as an institution and on the Portuguese and Spanish slave laws, which helped to make the slave system in Brazil more humane. The legal system protecting the slaves in this area, and the strong intervention of the church on behalf of the slaves were absent in the United States, which accounts, in part, for the severity of the slave system here. The French slaveholding systems had the active interest of the Catholic church, but not the slave legal tradition.[32]

While not discounting completely the influence of the Catholic church and of the legal traditions protecting slaves, Marvin Harris lays much more stress on the third factor—the types of plantation agriculture involved.[33] In addition, he introduces a fourth factor, the demographic distribution of the population. The Negro slaves in Latin America significantly outnumbered the white settlers, in part because Spain, and probably also Portugal, had a permanent manpower shortage. Since England had a population surplus, the English colonies had many more white settlers. Still a fifth social factor which helps to explain the differences in the two systems of slavery is that the Spanish and the Portuguese both had a history of racial assimilation, while the English and other Northern European people had a history and tradition of racial homogeneity and exclusion of other peoples. A sixth factor is that the Spanish and Portuguese men came to the New World alone in large proportions, while the English brought their wives and families.

In our view, all these forces operated together in the Latin American countries to produce a kind of slave system which helped to generate the social, economic, and political climate for three basic conditions which were absent in the United States: (1) the protection of the physical and personal integrity of slaves; (2) the open, sanctioned, and actual encouragement of manumission; (3) the open, sanctioned, and actual encouragement of stable marriages among slaves and free Negroes.

Physical and Personal Integrity

Slavery in Latin America was a matter of a contract between the bondsman and his master, focused essentially on the master's ownership of the bondsman's labor under certain restricted conditions, with protections of the slave built into the law. In the United States, on the contrary, without such history of legal protections, slavery was allowed to reach its logical extreme of complete ownership of the slave by the master, who was free, depending on his needs, resources, and conscience, to do with his slave as he wished.

The Brazilian law provided for the physical protection and integrity of the slaves as it did for free citizens. For example, in Spanish and Portuguese colonies, it was illegal to kill a slave. In the United States, to kill or not to kill a slave was up to the conscience of the master, and he could beat, injure, or abuse a slave without just cause. In Brazil, if the owner did any of these things, the slave had access to the court, and the judge, if he found the owner guilty, required him to sell the slave to another and kinder owner, pay the original owner a fair price, and forbade the resale of the slave to that owner. This protection for the life and limb of the slave, so crucial to the maintenance and development of both physical and mental health, was completely absent from the legal system of the United States. In the United States, this legacy of the white man's prerogatives to mistreat the Negro man has myriad ramifications in the behavior and the personality structures of both white and Negro men today. For white men, even among liberals and radicals, there is a pervasive sense of condescension toward Negroes which is sometimes reflected in paternalism, sometimes in arrogant disregard, and often in both. Rarely does the sense of true fraternity exist. For the Negro, the chronic sense of inferiority, vulnerability, and submission is sometimes expressed in hostility and, at other times, in dependence. The dominance-submission pattern of white-Negro interrelationships, which often pervades interracial efforts, is a legacy of this slave tradition, in which the Negro slave in the United States was so completely at the mercy of the white man for his very life and physical safety. Elkins has likened the absolute authority of slavery to that of the Nazi concentration camps, in which Jews became dehumanized in a few years.

> The new adjustment, to absolute power in a closed system, involved infantilization, and the detachment was so complete that little trace of prior (and thus alternative) cultural sanctions for behavior and personality remained for the descendants of the first generation. . . . We do not know how generally a full adjustment was made by the first generation of fresh slaves from Africa. But we do know—from a modern experience—that such an adjustment is possible, not only within the same generation, but within two or three years. This proved possible for people in a full state of complex civilization, for men and women who were not black and not savages.[34]

Legal protections for slaves were not systematic; rather, they were sporadic and unevenly enforced. Every slave state had slave codes, but they differed according to time, place, and manner of enforcement.[35] A slave rebellion could set off a new pattern of enforcement. The essential feature of all the codes was, of course, the same. They were not designed to protect the slaves, but to protect the master in the exercise or use of his property.

The very essence of the slave codes was the requirement that slaves submit to their masters and other white men at all times.[36] They controlled his movements and communications with others and they forbade all persons, including the master, to teach a slave to read and write.

In the United States slaves accused of committing some act of misbehavior were dealt with, for the most part, directly and swiftly by the master or his overseers. If they were brought into court, it was most likely to be one of the informal slave courts with one Justice of the Peace or three to five slave owners sitting as judge and jury. Occasionally, for serious felonies, slaves might be tried in a regular court. The consequences for the slaves were pretty much the same whatever the form of adjudication. Only rarely, for example, did courts enforce laws against the killing of a slave.[37] Neither slaves nor free Negroes could testify against white people. White prosecutors, juries, and judges were not predisposed to provide justice for the slaves. This orientation, fortified by the legal system, was designed to protect the master and other white persons from the slaves and other Negroes.

In a chapter of his book entitled, "To Make Them Stand in Fear," Kenneth Stampp has described the six processes slavemasters used and recommended to each other in their common goal of reducing the slave to sub-human status and perpetuating that status.

> Here, then, was the way to produce a perfect slave: accustom him to rigid discipline, demand from him unconditional submission, impress upon him his innate inferiority, develop in him a paralyzing fear of white men, train him to adopt the master's code of good behavior, and instill in him a sense of complete dependence.[38]

All these efforts at suppression and submission of the slaves worked most of the time and exacted their heavy toll on the personality and behavior of the slaves and their descendants. It was not all smooth sailing for the masters, however. Numerous efforts on the part of the Negroes to fight back included runaways, fights with and murders of cruel masters, and actual insurrections. For all these acts of outrage, the penalties were as swift as they were harsh.

The most notable rebellion was led by Nat Turner on August 22 and 23, 1831. It lasted only forty-eight hours, killed only sixty whites, actively involved only seventy slaves. But it has been described as the most fateful of the slave revolts. It sent fear through the hearts of both whites and Negroes, and its multiple consequences were reflected in the loss of white lives, the retaliation of the whites, and the fear it engendered, in part, because Nat Turner had been such a model slave, deeply religious and obedient. He was sheltered by slaves for two months before he was caught, tried, and hanged.[39]

Manumission

A second respect in which the political, legal, religious, economic, and demographic forces combined to produce a different slave system in Latin America involved manumission. Not only were slaves treated with certain limited, though specified, degrees of humanity, but the very system of slavery in Latin America encouraged the freeing of slaves. There were hundreds of ways in which slaves could earn their freedom, and slave owners were often rewarded for freeing their slaves.

Slaves could purchase their own freedom or the freedom of a wife or of a child at birth for money which they could earn from work performed on Sundays or any of the other numerous holidays in these Catholic countries. In Brazil, the Negroes had altogether 84 days a year in which they could work for themselves, save their money, and do with it as they wished. They could even purchase their own freedom on the installment plan. Each installment provided certain liberties. On paying the first installment, for example, a slave was free to move out of his master's house, provided that he continued working for him. The practice was so widespread that slaves often paid all but the final installment, so that they remained technically a slave while in most respects free, and thus avoided the taxes and military service imposed on citizens. Freedom societies sprang up; these were savings associations for the purchase of the freedom of their fellow members. A man would often purchase the freedom of his wife while he remained a slave, and thus their children would be free because their status followed their mother's. For the most part, the original purchasing price of the slave was the price a slave had to pay for himself, though he might actually be worth more on the open market.

In addition to purchasing his freedom, there were a myriad of other ways in which a slave in Latin America could become free. His master could simply free him of his own accord, provided that he did it in the church or before a judge or by some solemn and explicit procedure, such as making a statement to that effect in writing. If a slave was owned by two people—say husband and wife—and one wanted to free him, the other was bound to accept a just price fixed by a local judge and accede to the freedom. A slave could become free against his master's will for doing heroic deeds for the community, such as reporting disloyalty against the king, or by denouncing a forced rape or murder in the community. Under some circumstances, a slave could become free even against his master's will by becoming a minister. If a slave became heir to his master, or was appointed guardian of his master's children, he was automatically freed. A parent having ten children could automatically claim freedom. In addition, freeing of one's slaves became an honorable tradition. Masters often would free a slave or two on the occasion of their daughter's wedding or the birth of the first son in the family. Favorite house slaves were often freed on the occasion of their birthdays or weddings.

These measures, in which the law itself facilitated manumission, had far-reaching consequences in the whole social structure of Latin America, setting up social expectations and values favorable to the freeing of slaves, but totally absent in the system of laws, norms, and social values of the plantation South in the United States. A man wanting to free his slave in Latin America was encouraged by the system. A man wanting to free his slave in the United States had to go against prevailing norms. For the Negro slaves, slavery in Latin America was a burning caldron with a ladder and an open top. In the United States, there was no ladder, and though people sometimes found their way out by the aid of kindly masters, their own daring escapes, or the aid of abolitionists, including especially the underground railroad, the top of the caldron was not to any significant extent open. There merely were holes in it which served as "screens of opportunity," through which only a few were allowed to escape.

In Brazil, fully two-thirds of the Negroes had already been freed through various procedures

by the time of general emancipation in 1888. In the United States, on the other hand, never more than 10 per cent of the Negroes were free. In Brazil, once the slave had been freed, he enjoyed all the ordinary civil rights of other citizens; in fact, if a Negro was not known to be a slave in Brazil, he was presumed to be a free man. A completely different culture existed in the United States. Freed Negroes had only limited and circumscribed privileges and almost no legal rights. And a Negro in the United States South, prior to emancipation, was presumed to be a slave unless he could prove his free status.

Among the most far-reaching consequences of the two different slave systems were the manner of their dissolution and the status of the masses of freed men after emancipation. Brazil managed to escape the bloody holocaust which ended slavery in this country and produced a crisis in the social order which has not yet been healed. Slavery was actually abolished gradually and in stages in Brazil. In 1871, the Portuguese government promulgated the "doctrine of the free womb." This doctrine held that since slavery in Brazil was ownership of a person's labor and not of his innermost parts, the womb of a slave woman was free, and consequently any issue from that womb was also free. In view of this practice of freeing all newborn babies, it was only a matter of time till slavery would have died a natural death in Brazil. In 1885, a law was passed declaring that all slaves should become free on reaching the age of sixty. And finally, on May 13, 1888, "The Golden Law" was passed, abolishing slavery and freeing all slaves in Brazil.[40]

There were, of course, exceptional men in the United States who violated the slave codes because of self-interest, paternalism, humanitarianism, or a combination of all three. Slaves were sometimes freed for such "meritorious" service as reporting a planned slave insurrection. Among the very rare instances of outright manumission for apparently humanitarian reasons, a man in the upper South who willed that his slaves be freed on his death gave four reasons for such unusual, if still cowardly behavior:

> Reason the first. Agreeably to the rights of man, every human being, be his or her color what it may, is entitled to freedom. . . . Reason the second. My conscience, the great criterion, condemns me for keeping them in slavery. Reason the third. The golden rule directs us to do unto every human creature as we would wish to be done unto. . . . Reason the fourth and last. I wish to die with a clear conscience.[41]

Another major distinction between the United States and Latin America is that while the emancipated Negroes in the United States were "freedmen," in Brazil they were for the most part simply "free men." They were accepted into the free society, not only of the other ex-slaves, but of the whites as well. The closed system of slavery in the United States had produced a caste-like set of relations between white and Negro unknown in Brazil, where a person was considered to be inferior only if he was a slave—a condition that could be remedied. In the United States, on the other hand, it was considered that a person was a slave because he was innately inferior, and both conditions were associated with his blackness. Consequently, it has proved, even after emancipation, much more difficult for our society to shake off the badge of inferiority associated with color and the caste-like qualities which confound the socioeconomic distinctions between the races. In Latin America, the distinction is primarily socioeconomic.

The Family

A third respect in which the Latin American legal system protected the slaves was by providing for the creation and preservation of the family.

In Latin America, the law and the Church provided certain protections for the family

life of the Negro slaves. Slaves were free to marry, even against the will of their masters, provided only that they keep serving him as before. They were free to intermarry with free persons, provided only that their slave status not be concealed. Slaves who were married could not be sold apart from each other unless it was guaranteed that they could continue to live together as man and wife. None of these minimum protections of the family were built into the system of slavery in the United States, where slaves were often permitted to marry, but only at the discretion of the master. In the United States, the slave husband was not the head of his household; the white owner was the head. The family had no rights that the slave owner was bound to respect. The wholesale disregard for family integrity among the slaves may be suggested by the following quotation from an actual advertisement in a New Orleans newspaper: "A Negro woman, 24 years of age, and her two children, one eight and the other three years old. Said Negroes will be sold separately or together as desired."[42] Another, in South Carolina in 1838, offered 120 slaves for sale of both sexes and every description, including "several women with children, small girls suitable for nurses, and several small boys without their mothers."[43]

The official records of shipping companies also reflected this family disruption. "Of four cargoes, making a total of 646 slaves, 396 were apparently owned by Franklen and Armfield. Among these there were only two full families. . . . There were 20 husbandless mothers with 33 children."[44]

Perhaps the cruelest of all the forms of emasculation of the Negro family was the very widespread practice, perhaps in all the slave states, of breeding slaves for sale as if they were cattle. An enterprising slave master, then, could enjoy not only the emotional advantages accrued from sex relations with his female slaves, but also the economic advantage which accrued from selling his offspring in the open market. Such decadence was much too common to have been confined to a few undesirable or emotionally disturbed white citizens. It was widespread and normative, though of course not all planters engaged in such practices. More common, perhaps, was the practice of breeding slaves among each other. One advertisement of a shipment of slaves claimed that

> they are not Negroes selected out of a larger gang for the purpose of a sale, but are prime. Their present owner, with great trouble and expense, selected them out of many for several years past. They were purchased for stock and breeding Negroes and to any planter who particularly wants them for that purpose, they are a very choice and desirable gang.[45]

In the United States, then, contrary to Latin America, the legal system made no provision for, and took no special recognition of, marriage and family life among the Negro slaves. In addition, the slave owners and other whites took frequent sexual advantage of the slave women. Even if she were the wife of a slave, her husband could not protect her. The Attorney General of Maryland observed in one of his reports that "a slave never has maintained an action against the violator of his bed."[46] This statement apparently would apply in other states as well, regardless of whether the violator was slave or citizen. The powerlessness of the Negro man to protect his family for two and a half centuries under slavery has had crippling consequences for the relations of Negro men and women to this very day.

Slavery and Family Life in the United States

Marriage among slaves was not altogether absent in the United States, and was probably more common than has been generally recognized. It was, however, a far different institution with much less structural and institutional support in this country than in Latin America.

The strong hand of the slave owner dominated the Negro family, which existed only at his mercy and often at his own personal instigation. An ex-slave has told of getting married on one plantation:

> When you married, you had to jump over a broom three times. Dat was de license. If master seen two slaves together too much he would tell 'em dey was married. Hit didn't make no difference if you wanted to or not; he would put you in de same cabin an' make you live together. . . . Marsa used to sometimes pick our wives fo' us. If he didn't have on his place enough women for the men, he would wait on de side of de road till a big wagon loaded with slaves come by. Den Marsa would stop de ole nigger-trader and buy you a woman. Wasn't no use tryin' to pick one, cause Marsa wasn't gonna pay but so much for her. All he wanted was a young healthy one who looked like she could have children, whether she was purty or ugly as sin.[47]

The difficulties Negro men had in establishing, protecting, and maintaining family ties, together with the strong values they placed on family life and responsibilities, are graphically depicted in the correspondence between ex-slaves and their ex-masters. It often happened that the slaves who escaped into freedom by the underground railroad were those who had been treated relatively well by their owners, and who even had been taught to read and write. Often they were the "favorite" slaves of the owners, highly trusted and considered dependable and grateful. Thus, it was not uncommon that when a slave holder found out the whereabouts of an ex-slave, he would write to him, imploring him to return. Three letters by ex-slaves written in response to such appeals will illustrate the damaging consequences slavery had for Negro family life. The first was written by Henry Bibb in 1844, after he had escaped into Canada by way of the underground railroad.

**Early photograph
of a slave family,
posing outside their
dwelling.**

Dear Sir:—I am happy to inform you that you are not mistaken in the man whom you sold as property, and received pay for as such. But I thank God that I am not property now, but am regarded as a man like yourself, and although I live far north, I am enjoying a comfortable living by my own industry. If you should ever chance to be traveling this way, and will call on me, I will use you better than you did me while you held me as a slave. Think not that I have any malice against you, for the cruel treatment which you inflicted on me while I was in your power. As it was the custom of your country, to treat your fellow men as you did me and my little family, I can freely forgive you.

I wish to be remembered in love to my aged mother, and friends; please tell her that if we should never meet again in this life, my prayer shall be to God that we may meet in Heaven, where parting shall be no more.

You wish to be remembered to King and Jack. I am pleased, sir, to inform you that they are both here, well, and doing well. They are both living in Canada West. They are now the owners of better farms than the men are who once owned them.

You may perhaps think hard of us for running away from slavery, but as to myself, I have but one apology to make for it, which is this: I have only to regret that I did not start at an earlier period. I might have been free long before I was. But you had it in your power to have kept me there much longer than you did. I think it is very probable that I should have been a toiling slave on your property today, if you had treated me differently.

To be compelled to stand by and see you whip and slash my wife without mercy, when I could afford her no protection, not even by offering myself to suffer the lash in her place, was more than I felt it to be the duty of a slave husband to endure, while the way was open to Canada. My infant child was also frequently flogged by Mrs. Gatewood, for crying, until its skin was bruised literally purple. This kind of treatment was what drove me from home and family, to seek a better home for them. But I am willing to forget the past. I should be pleased to hear from you again, on the reception of this, and should also be very happy to correspond with you often, if it should be agreeable to yourself. I subscribe myself a friend to the oppressed, and Liberty forever.[48]

Another letter was written in 1860 by J. W. Loguen who escaped to New England:

Mrs. Sarah Logue: Yours of the 20th of February is duly received, and I thank you for it. It is a long time since I heard from my poor old mother, and I am glad to know that she is yet alive, and, as you say, "as well as common." What that means, I don't know. I wish you had said more about her.

You are a woman; but had you a woman's heart, you never could have insulted a brother by telling him you sold his only remaining brother and sister, because he put himself beyond your power to convert him into money.

You sold my brother and sister, Abe and Ann, and twelve acres of land, you say, because I ran away. Now you have the unutterable meanness to ask me to return and be your miserable chattel, or, in lieu thereof, send you $1000 to enable you to redeem the land, but not to redeem my poor brother and sister! If I were to send you the money, it would be to get my brother and sister, and not that you should get land. You say you are a cripple, and doubtless you say it to stir my pity, for you knew I was susceptible in that direction. I do pity you from the bottom of my heart. Nevertheless, I am indignant beyond the power of words to express, that you should be so sunken and cruel as to tear the hearts I love so much all to pieces; that you should be willing to impale and crucify us all, out of compassion for your foot or leg. Wretched woman! Be it known to you that I value my freedom, to say nothing of my mother, brothers, and sisters, more than your whole body; more, indeed, than my own life; more than all the lives of all the slave-holders and tyrants under heaven.

You say you have offers to buy me, and that you shall sell me if I do not send you $1000, and in the same breath and almost in the same sentence, you say, "You know we raised you as we did our own children." Woman, did you raise your own children for the market? . . .

. . . But you say I am a thief, because I took the old mare along with me. Have you got to learn that I had a better right to the old mare, as you call her, than Manasseth Logue had to me? Is it a greater sin for me to steal his horse, than it was for him to rob my mother's cradle, and steal me? If he and you infer that I forfeit all my rights to you, shall not I infer that you forfeit all your rights to me? Have you got to learn that human rights are mutual and reciprocal, and if you take my liberty and life, you forfeit your own liberty and life? Before God and high heaven, is there a law for one man which is not a law for every other man?

If you or any other speculator on my body and rights, wish to know how I regard my rights, they need but come here, and lay their hands on me to enslave me. Did you think to terrify me by presenting the alternative to give my money to you, or give my body to slavery? Then let me say to you, that I meet the proposition with unutterable scorn and contempt. The proposition is an outrage and an insult. I will not budge one hair's breadth. I will not breathe a shorter breath, even to save me from your persecutions. I stand among a free people, who, I thank God, sympathize with my rights, and the rights of mankind; and if your emissaries and venders come here to re-enslave me, and escape the unshrinking vigor of my own right arm, I trust my strong and brave friends, in this city and State, will be my rescuers and avengers.[49]

A third letter is from Jourdon Anderson, who was freed by the Union Army Forces during the Civil War.

Sir: I got your letter, and was glad to find that you had not forgotten Jourdon, and that you wanted me to come back and live with you again, promising to do better for me than anybody else can. . . .

. . . I want to know particularly what the good chance is you propose to give me. I am doing tolerably well here. I get twenty-five dollars a month, with victuals and clothing; have a comfortable home for Mandy,— the folks call her Mrs. Anderson—and the children—Milly, Jane, and Grundy—go to school and are learning well. The teacher says Grundy has a head for a preacher. They go to Sunday School, and Mandy and me attend church regularly. We are kindly treated. Sometimes we overhear others saying, "Them colored people were slaves" down in Tennessee. The children feel hurt when they hear such remarks; but I tell them it was no disgrace in Tennessee to belong to Colonel Anderson. Many darkeys would have been proud, as I used to be, to call you master. Now if you will write and say what wages you will give me, I will be better able to decide whether it would be to my advantage to move back again.

. . . Mandy says she would be afraid to go back without some proof that you were disposed to treat us justly and kindly; and

we have concluded to test your sincerity by asking you to send us our wages for the time we served you. This will make us forget and forgive old scores, and rely on your justice and friendship in the future. I served you faithfully for thirty-two years, and Mandy twenty years. At twenty-five dollars a month for me, and two dollars a week for Mandy, our earnings would amount to eleven thousand six hundred and eighty dollars. Add to this the interest for the time our wages have been kept back, and deduct what you paid for our clothing, and three doctor's visits to me, and pulling a tooth for Mandy, and the balance will show what we are in justice entitled to.

. . . In answering this letter, please state if there would be any safety for my Milly and Jane, who are now grown up, and both goodlooking girls. You know how it was with poor Matilda and Catherine. I would rather stay here and starve—and die, if it come to that—than have my girls brought to shame by the violence and wickedness of their young masters. You will also please state if there has been any schools opened for the colored children in your neighborhood. The great desire of my life is to give my children an education, and have them form virtuous habits.

Say howdy to George Carter, and thank him for taking the pistol from you when you were shooting at me.[50]

The Negro family existed during slavery in the United States, but it was a most precarious existence, dependent wholly on the economic and personal interests of the white man, and the grim determination and bravery of the black man.

Interracial Marriage

A fourth respect in which the slave system in the United States differed markedly from that in Latin America relative to family life was in the area of interracial marriage. Marriage between white persons and black persons, particularly between European men and African women, was common, sanctioned, and encouraged in Latin America even under slavery. It was forbidden by law in the United States, not only during slavery, but in modern times as well. Not until 1967 were the last legal supports for such bans struck down by the U. S. Supreme Court. Even now, however, despite the lack of legal support for such bans on interracial marriage, the customs and norms of the white majority in the country, and to some extent the black minority, make interracial marriage a rare and deviant sort of behavior.

Marriage among peoples of different cultural backgrounds is considered, by many students of assimilation, to be the ultimate test of the process of integration, as well as of whether a caste system exists, separating two peoples into superior and inferior beings. In these respects, then, the question of interracial marriage is more than a matter of personal choice; it is an index of the view and place of different peoples in the national life.

It is not, of course, that miscegenation and other forms of interracial contact have been absent in the United States. In fact, they have been persistent. But they have been more or less illicit, unsanctioned by the wider society. Consequently, the white men who have been the chief exploiters of Negro women in such relationships have escaped the responsibilities associated with these relationships. The manner in which Negro women were exploited by white men during slavery, and the damage these relationships caused to the stability of Negro family life can be seen from two personal accounts provided us by two remarkable Negro women writers, Pauli Murray and Margaret Walker. Both accounts are taken from actual family histories.

Pauli Murray tells of her own great-grandmother, Harriet, who was born a slave in 1819. She was the product of miscegenation and described as mulatto. When she was fifteen, she was sold to a medical doctor in North Carolina who bought her as a house-maid for his own eighteen-year-old daughter.

These two women, the slave and the mistress, grew into the most intricate of relationships filled with all the human drama of love, envy, and hate imaginable.[51]

When Harriet was twenty years old, she asked her owner for permission to marry a young mulatto man who was born free, and who lived and worked in the town. It is said that Dr. Smith, her owner, readily agreed. "It was good business. He had no obligation to the husband, and every child by the marriage would be his slave and worth several hundred dollars at birth." Harriet and her husband were not permitted to live together permanently, but he was permitted to visit her in the evenings after she had finished her work in the "big house." After three years, in about 1842, they had a child. Of course, this son became a slave like his mother, and was the property of Dr. Smith.

Sometime after this, Dr. Smith's two grown sons came home from college, and both took a special interest in Harriet. "Before long," Miss Murray tells us, "everybody in the house knew that a storm was brewing between the brothers, and that Harriet was the cause of it." The author then describes an encounter between Sydney, one of the Smith sons, and Reuben, Harriet's free Negro husband.

Sydney Smith informed Reuben that he could not be legally married to a slave, and that if he were ever caught visiting Harriet again he would be whipped and thrown in jail. The author continues: "Reuben had to leave without a word to Harriet. That was the last she ever saw of him." It is not, however, that Reuben abandoned his wife, his child, and his rights so easily; he came back to see them one time, but the two Smith brothers saw him.

> The brothers beat Reuben with the butt end of a carriage whip and when they finally let him go, they told him if he ever came back on the Smith lot, they'd shoot him on sight. He disappeared from the county and nothing was heard of him again.

Shortly after Reuben was banished from his wife's cabin, Sydney Smith "had his way with her" in the presence of her little boy.

> He raped her again, again, and again in the weeks that followed. Night after night he would force open her cabin door and nail it up again on the inside so that she could not get out. Then he would beat her into submission.

Sydney's brother Frank was furious at the turn of events. One night he accosted Sydney on his way from Harriet's cabin.

> The brothers had it out once and for all, and there was a terrible fight. Early the next morning, one of the slaves found Sydney lying unconscious in the yard, his clothes soaked with blood and an ugly hole in his head. . . . He learned his lesson. He never touched Harriet again.

But already Harriet was pregnant with Sydney's child. This child, born on the Smith lot in February 1844, was Pauli Murray's grandmother.

After the baby was born, Sydney's brother Frank "had his way" with Harriet. This time she did not fight back.

This relationship was long and enduring. Over the course of five years, Harriet bore to Francis Smith three daughters. Harriet was now the mother of five children by three different fathers, all growing up on the same plantation but treated according to their father's positions. Julius, the oldest, was almost ignored by the Big House, and his mother was almost a stranger to him. When he was around thirteen, he got lost in the woods during a heavy snowstorm. They found him almost frozen to death. He was severely crippled for the rest of his life.

The girls lived lives of crippling ambivalence.

> The Smiths were as incapable of treating the little girls wholly as servants as they were of recognizing them openly as kin. At times the Smiths' involuntary gestures of kinship were so pronounced, the children could not help thinking of themselves as Smith

grandchildren. At other times, their innocent overtures of affection were rebuffed without explanation and they were driven away with cruel epithets.

In *Jubilee* Margaret Walker tells a similar story[52] of her own grandmother Vyry, and her great-grandmother Hetta. Several generations before the Civil War, Hetta, a slave girl, had borne fifteen children by the time she was twenty-nine. She died in childbirth with the sixteenth. Many of them, including Vyry, were by the son of her owner. Vyry is the center of a most fascinating account of the pre-Civil War period in the life of the slaves, freedmen, and masters. Randall Ware, a young freedman, who loved, courted, married, and lost her, is a most remarkable example of black manhood, who, despite the efforts of the system to crush him, managed to survive. There was a man, if only for one brief season! He insisted on exercising his freedom in the plantation South, which conspired to make slaves of all black people. He almost rescued his wife and family from slavery. He escaped to the North by way of the underground railroad and returned to fight in the Civil War. This is not, however, a story of essential triumph. It is a vivid illustration of the tragedy of slavery and the crippling consequences it had for Negro family life.

In summary, it may be said that the slave system had a crippling effect on the establishment, maintenance, and growth of normal patterns of family life among the Negro people. This impact was cruel in all the Americas. It was exceedingly vicious in the United States. There were several facets of this process of personal, family, and social emasculation. First, the family was broken up at the very beginning of the slave trade in the manner in which the slaves were gathered, the disregard the captors showed to family and kinship ties, the preference they showed for selecting young men in the prime of their life, and the consequent underrepresentation of females for hundreds of years, and the inhumane

conditions under which the slaves were quar-
tered, worked, and treated.

All these conditions were found everywhere
in the slave system, although some evidence
suggests that the living conditions were worse
in the United States. The particular factors
which characterize the impact of slavery on
the Negro family in the United States include,
in addition to the above, the absence of
legal foundation, sanction, and protection of
marriage as an institution among the slaves,
the exploitation of slave women by white
owners and overseers for both pleasure and
profit; the systematic denial of a role for the
man as husband and father; the willful separation of related men, women, and children
and selling them to different plantations. In
short, there was the absence, in the United
States, of societal support and protection for
the Negro family as a physical, psychological,
social, or economic unit. This crippled the
development, not only of individual slaves,

but of families, and hence of the whole society of Negro people. The consequences these conditions wrought for generations of Negroes under the slave system were direct and insidious. The consequences for succeeding and even modern generations of Negroes are, perhaps, less direct, but no less insidious. At no time in the history of this country have Negroes experienced, systematically and generally, the kind of social supports from the society which would even approach the intensity of the negative impact of slavery. Not only has the society not made any massive efforts to undo the damages of slavery and actively integrate the Negro people into the society on the basis of equality, but many of the explicit conditions of slavery still exist at the present time.

The Failures of Reconstruction after the Civil War

It is often said that slavery was a long time ago; that surely the freedom and opportunity granted to the Negro people by emancipation has been sufficient to overcome the ravages of slavery; and that, surely, contemporary white people and institutions bear no responsibility for slavery and reap no benefit from this dark chapter in human history.

But the historical facts are otherwise. The Negro people have never been indemnified, either economically, or politically, or socially, or psychologically for two centuries of bondage. And furthermore, the wider society has not reconstructed itself to any substantial degree in any of these areas of life.

The end of slavery with the Civil War in the United States brought a certain freedom to the slave and the free Negro alike, but it was also a crisis of major proportions. For tens of thousands of Negroes, émancipation meant the freedom to die of starvation and illness. In some communities, one out of every four Negroes died. The destitution and disease among the Negroes, who were now uncared for and had no facilities to care for themselves, was so great that the editor of a famous newspaper observed with considerable glee that "The child is already born who will behold the last Negro in the State of Mississippi."[53] And Mississippi had more Negro slaves than any other state. Nor were such dire straits and predictions confined to one state. The eminent southern scholar, Dr. C. K. Marchall, expressed a similar and more general hypothesis: "In all probability New Year's Day on the morning of the 1st of January, 1920, the colored population in the South will scarcely be counted."[54]

The survival of the Negro people after such a holocaust can be attributed primarily to the resiliency of the human spirit. It most certainly cannot be attributed in large measure to the efforts of his society to help him survive. For the ingredient most absent to make freedom meaningful was the ingredient which has been most useful to other depressed people, namely opportunity.

There were no national, regional, or other large-scale plans for dealing with the ex-slaves. How could they be integrated into the life of the embattered republic as free men? Uncertainty abounded. There were enlightened voices who put forward suggestions. The most rational package suggested that the nation should give each ex-slave forty acres of land, a mule, the ballot, and leave him alone. Charles Sumner of Massachusetts plugged hard for the ballot, Thaddeus Stevens of Pennsylvania plugged even harder for the forty acres. And several generations before Justice Louis D. Brandeis was to expound his famous doctrine of the freedom to be let alone, Frederick Douglass, the ex-slave, echoed the same sentiment.

> The Negro should have been let alone in Africa. . . . If you see him plowing in the open field, leveling the forest, at work with a spade, a rake, a hoe, a pick-axe, or a bill, let him alone; . . . If he has a ballot in his hand, let him alone.[55]

But the nation's response was to be much more limited and temporary. The Freedman's

Bureau, probably the first national social welfare administration, during six short years with severely limited funds, administrative imagination and courage, and in the face of apathy in the North and hostility in the South, strove to feed and clothe ex-slaves and poor whites, and to establish hospitals and schools. It did a commendable job under the circumstances, but much too little and over too short a time. President Andrew Johnson's heart was not in the efforts of the Freedman's Bureau, and despite certain efforts of Congress he crushed this program.

John Hope Franklin has summed up the period of reconstruction as follows:

> Counter reconstruction was everywhere an overwhelming success. In the face of violence the 14th and 15th Amendments provided no protection for the Negro citizen and his friends. The federal enforcement laws of 1870 and 1871 proved wholly inadequate, especially when enforcement was left to the meager forces that remained in the South at the time of their enactment. Negroes could hardly be expected to continue to vote when it cost them not only their jobs but their lives. In one state after another, the Negro electorate declined steadily as the full force of the Klan came forward to supervise the elections that federal troops failed to supervise. . . . The federal government was, more and more, leaving the South to its own devices. Even more important was the enormous prestige

that the former Confederates enjoyed. In time they were able to assume leadership in their communities without firing a shot or hanging a single Negro. What they lacked in political strength they made up in economic power. By discharging or threatening to discharge Negro employees who persisted in participating in politics, they could reduce the Negro electorate to a minimum. By refusing to pay taxes to support the expanded and inflated functions of the new governments, they could destroy Radical Reconstruction in a season. But the former Confederates relied on no one method. By political pressure, economic sanctions, *and* violence they brought Radical Reconstruction crashing down almost before it began.[56]

Of course, Emancipation had some advantages for the Negro family. Although family members could be whipped, run out of town, or murdered, they could not be sold away from their families. Marriages were legalized and recorded. The hard work of farming, even sharecropping, required all possible hands—husband, wife, and children.

Emancipation, then, was a catastrophic social crisis for the ex-slave, and Reconstruction was a colossal failure. At the same time, thre were some "screens of opportunity" which did enable large numbers of families to survive, some to achieve amazingly stable and viable forms of family life, and a few to achieve a high degree of social distinction.

Notes

1. Nathan Glazer and Daniel P. Moynihan, *Beyond the Melting Pot* (Cambridge, Mass.: The M.I.T. Press and The Harvard University Press, 1963), p. 51.

2. Nat Hentoff, "The Other Side of the Blues," in *Anger and Beyond: The Negro Writer in the United States,* ed. Herbert Hill (New York: Harper & Row, Publishers, 1966), p. 76.

3. Harold L. Sheppard and Herbert E. Striver, *Civil Rights, Employment, and the Social Status of American Negroes* (Kalamazoo, Mich.: The W. E. Upjohn Institute for Employment Research, June, 1966), p. 47.

4. John Hope Franklin, *From Slavery to Freedom* (New York: Alfred A. Knopf, Inc., 1956), p. 11.

5. *Ibid.*, p. 28.

6. Melville J. Herskovits, *Dahomey: An Ancient West African Kingdom* (New York: J. J. Augustin, 1938), I; and Francis I. Nzimiro, "Family and Kinship in Ibo Land: A Study in Acculturation Process" (Ph. D. dissertation, University of Cologne, 1962).

7. Melville J. Herskovits, *The Myth of the Negro Past* (Boston: Beacon Press, 1958), Robert A. Lystad, *The Ashanti: A Proud People* (New Brunswick, N. J.: Rutgers University Press, 1958); and Meyer Fortes, "Kinship and Marriage Among the Ashanti," in *African Systems of Kinship and Marriage*, eds. A. R. Radcliffe-Brown and Daryll Forde (New York: Oxford University Press, Inc., 1950), pp. 207–51. Future quotations from this source reprinted by permission of Oxford University Press, Inc.

8. Daryll Forde, "The Yako of Nigeria," in A. R. Radcliffe-Brown, *op. cit.*

9. *Ibid.*, p. 306.

10. George P. Murdock, *Africa: Its People and Their Culture History* (New York: McGraw-Hill Book Company, 1959).

11. Herskovits, *Dahomey*, p. 341.

12. Meyer Fortes, "Kinship and Marriage Among the Ashanti," *op. cit.*, p. 270.

13. *Ibid.*, p. 268.

14. *Ibid.*, p. 268.

15. *Ibid.*, p. 268.

16. *Ibid.*, p. 268.

17. Nzimiro, *op. cit.*

18. Fortes, p. 262.

19. *Ibid.*, p. 263.

20. *Ibid.*, p. 263.

21. Herskovits, *Dahomey*, p. 155.

22. Fortes, p. 275.

23. *Ibid.*, p. 273.

24. *Ibid.*, p. 274.

25. *Ibid.*, p. 276.

26. Lerone Bennett, Jr., *Before the Mayflower: A History of the Negro in America* (Chicago: Johnson Publishing Co., 1964), p. 30.

27. *Ibid.*, pp. 30–31.

28. Milton Meltzer, ed., *In Their Own Words: A History of the American Negro 1619–1865*, copyright © 1964 by Milton Meltzer (New York: Thomas Y. Crowell Company, 1954; Apollo Edition, 1967), pp. 3–5. Reprinted by permission of Thomas Y. Crowell Company, and Harold Ober Associates, Inc.

29. Frank Tannenbaum, *Slave and Citizen: The Negro in the Americas* (New York: Random House, Inc., 1946), p. 21.

30. W. E. B. Du Bois, *The Negro* (New York: Holt, Rinehart & Winston, Inc., 1915), pp. 155–56.

31. Stanley Elkins, *Slavery: A Problem in American Institutional and Intellectual Life* (New York: Grosset & Dunlap, Inc., 1963), p. 81.

32. Tannenbaum, p. 65.

33. Marvin Harris, *Patterns of Race in the Americas* (New York: Walker and Co., 1964), p. 81.

34. Elkins, pp. 88–89.

35. Kenneth M. Stampp, *The Peculiar Institution: Slavery in the Ante-Bellum South* (New York: Vintage Books, 1956), p. 206.

36. *Ibid.*, p. 207.

37. *Ibid.*, p. 222.

38. *Ibid.*, p. 148.

39. Meltzer, pp. 33–34.

40. E. Bradford Burns, *A Documentary History of Brazil* (New York: Alfred A. Knopf, Inc., 1966), p. 278.

41. Stampp, pp. 235–36.

42. Tannenbaum, p. 77.

43. *Ibid.*, pp. 77–78.

44. *Ibid.*, p. 78.

45. *Ibid.*, p. 80.

46. *Ibid.*, pp. 76–77.

47. Meltzer, pp. 46–47.

48. *Ibid.*, pp. 100–101.

49. *Ibid.*, pp. 120–22.

50. *Ibid.*, pp. 170–72.

51. Pauli Murray, *Proud Shoes: The Story of an American Family* (New York: Harper & Row, Publishers, 1956), quotes from pp. 38–48.

52. Margaret Walker, *Jubilee* (Boston: Houghton Mifflin Company, 1966).

53. Bennett, p. 188.

54. *Ibid.*, p. 188.

55. *Ibid.*, pp. 186–87.

56. John Hope Franklin, *Reconstruction After the Civil War* (Chicago: University of Chicago Press, 1961), pp. 172–73.

The Negro Family

E. FRANKLIN FRAZIER

THROUGHOUT ITS DEVELOPMENT, THE Negro family has been influenced in its internal social and psychological organization as well as in its formal structure by the economic and social forces which have determined the character of Negro communities.

THE NEGRO FAMILY DURING SLAVERY

In a previous chapter we have seen how difficult it is to establish upon a factual basis any connection between the development of the Negro family in the United States and the African family system.[1] The attempts to explain the sex behavior and familial life of American Negroes by reference to African culture traits rest upon speculation and specious analogies. Among some isolated groups of Negroes in the New World, as for example in Haiti and Jamaica, it appears that elements of African culture have been retained in the Negro family.[2] But even in Brazil, where conditions were more favorable for the survival of the African family system, one can scarcely find traces of the African family system today.[3] Therefore, in tracing the development of the Negro family we shall simply analyze the

known economic and social factors in the American environment which offer a sufficient explanation of the past development and present character of the Negro family.[4]

During the early development of the plantation system the excess of males in the Negro population resulted in casual associations for satisfaction of sexual hunger.[5] But soon there was no lack of women and mating ranged from purely physical contacts, sometimes enforced by the masters, to permanent associations in which deep sentiment between spouses and parental affection toward children created a stable family group. At the same time the character of the sexual contacts and family life of the slaves was determined to some extent by the master's attitudes toward his slaves. Some masters with no regard for the preference of their slaves mated them as they did their stock. There were instances where Negro males were

Reprinted with the permission of Macmillan Publishing Company from *The Negro in the United States* by E. Franklin Frazier. Copyright © 1957 by Macmillan Publishing Company; copyright renewed © 1985 by Marie Brown Frazier.

used as stallions.[6] In a world where patriarchal traditions were firmly established, even less consideration was shown for the wishes of the female slaves. But this was not the whole story, for the majority of masters either through necessity or because of their humanity showed some regard for the wishes of the slaves in their mating.

Since African mores and traditions ceased to control the sexual impulses and determine the forms of mating, their behavior in this regard was subject to individual impulse and sexual attraction. It appears that from the beginning spontaneous attraction played an important part in mating. Moreover, there was rivalry among the males for the sexual favors of the females. This rivalry was kept under control by the master in the interest of order on the plantation. But rivalry did not manifest itself solely in the display of brute force. There came into existence a form of courtship in which tender feelings and attention to the wishes of the woman played an important part in winning her favors. In addition to these psychological factors there were social forces within the plantation organization that tended to humanize the sexual impulses of the slaves and place moral restraints upon their mating. The plantation, as we have seen, was a social as well as an industrial institution in which there was a division of labor and an opportunity for the expression of the individual talents.[7] Within the social world of the plantation, there were social distinctions, involving obligations and expectations in regard to behavior. Consequently the sexual conduct and mating of the slaves were not without moral restraints.

Where slavery became a settled way of life and the plantation organization acquired a patriarchal character, the slave family achieved some degree of permanence. The master's concern for the moral welfare of the slaves included a close supervision of their sex behavior and marital relations. On some plantations there were slave families including three generations that had "married" according to slave customs under the close supervision of their mistresses. Such family groups generally included the father and husband as well as the mother and her children. This was especially true where the father was, for example, a skilled mechanic and had acquired a responsible position in the plantation organization.[8] The solidarity and permanence of such families were due to a number of factors. Habitual association in the same household played some part. But, in addition, genuine affection often developed between the spouses and between the parents and children. Where the family was permitted privacy and permitted to cultivate its own gardens and engage in other common activities, family unity was given substantial basis in common interests. Thus under the most favorable conditions of slavery the Negro family did among certain elements of the slave population acquire considerable stability. But very often the exigencies of the slave system, such as the settlement of an estate, might destroy the toughest bonds of conjugal affection and parental love.

Because of the conditions imposed by the slave system, the mother was the most dependable and the most important member of the Negro family. The idealized picture of the Negro mother during slavery has represented her as a devoted nurse of the master's children.[9] But there is also plenty of evidence of the devotion of the slave mother to her own offspring. Despite the hardships and suffering which pregnancy and childbirth often involved, the slave mother often exhibited a fierce devotion to her children. In the case of young children, masters were compelled in their own interest to recognize the biological dependence of the child upon the mother. But, in addition, they were forced to recognize the affectional and sentimental ties between the Negro mother and her offspring. A Negro father might be sold and separated from his family, but when the Negro mother was sold the master was forced to take into account her relation to her children. The bonds of affection between mother and offspring were generally developed in the slave cabin where the Negro mother nurtured her brood and was mistress. Even if she were separated from her children she often visited them at night to care for them and find affection and solace from her cares. On the other hand, the father was often a visitor to the cabin two or three times a week, while his interest in his children might only be adventitious. He was compelled not only to recognize the mother's more fundamental interest in the children but her authority in the household. Thus there developed among the slaves a type of family that was held together principally by the bonds of blood and feeling existing between the mother and her offspring and the sentimental ties that often developed between the children in the same household.

Although it is difficult to estimate the extent to which members of the slaveholding class had sexual relations with the slaves, there is sufficient evidence of widespread concubinage and even polygyny on the part of the white masters. The maternal family organization, i.e., the family in which the mother was the head and main source of support, was fostered partly by the sexual association between the males of the white race and the slave women on the plantation. In the cities where the slaves were released from the plantation discipline and there were free Negroes, the associations between white men and Negro and mulatto women were generally casual.[10] Mulatto children resulting from these relationships were often neglected and became public charges. The sexual relations between the white men and colored women, slave and free, were undoubtedly due at times to physical compulsion on the part of white men. Moreover, mutual attraction also played some part in securing the compliance of the colored woman. But, it appears from available evidence, that the prestige of the white race and the advantages resulting from these

associations were generally sufficient to secure the acquiescence of the colored woman. The character of the family groups resulting from the association of the men of the master race and the women of the subordinate race varied considerably.

At the bottom of the scale was the Negro woman who was raped and became separated from her mulatto child without any violence to her maternal feelings; or the slave woman who submitted dumbly or out of animal feeling to sexual relations that spawned a nameless and unloved half-white breed over the South. . . . Sexual attraction gave birth at times to genuine affection; and prolonged association created between white master and colored mistress enduring sentiment. There were instances where white fathers sold their mulatto children; but more often they became ensnared by their affection for their colored offspring.[11]

There were white men who acknowledged their offspring and gave them an education and a start in the world. There were white slaveholders who neglected their wives and gave their affection and their worldly goods to their colored mistress and their mulatto offspring.[12] In some cases the white masters even separated themselves from white society and lived entirely with their colored mistresses and mulatto offspring. But since such unions were rare and without the legal and moral support of the communities, the black or mulatto woman was generally the head of the household.

FAMILY LIFE AMONG THE FREE NEGROES

The family life of many of the Negroes who were free before the Civil War was less stable than that of the better-situated slaves. This was especially true of the impoverished Negroes who crowded the slums of the cities of the North as well as the South. Among these elements in the free Negro population there was much sexual promiscuity and family relationships were loose and uncertain. Though there was less moral degradation in the rural areas, nevertheless, the family life of the free Negroes in the poorer regions of the South rested upon a precarious basis. On the other hand, there was emerging among the free Negro workers a class of skilled artisans whose family life conformed to the family pattern of the white laboring class. In some cases the tradition of stable family life had been built up during several generations of freedom and economic security. Or the tradition of stable family life might even have its roots in slavery. Very often the male head of the family had bought his freedom and that of his wife and some of his children. This class continued to increase in areas where slavery was becoming less profitable up to the Civil War.

However, it was chiefly in Charleston, South Carolina, New Orleans, and a few other areas that the free Negro families acquired to a marked degree an institutional character. Marriage as a legal relationship became a part of the mores of this group as they took over the familial behavior of the whites and the stability and continuity of their family life became rooted in property as well as traditions. Moreover, members of these families were accorded a superior social status by the community. In Charleston as well as in New Orleans a number of the free colored families were descended from the mulatto refugees who fled from San Domingo during the revolution in the latter part of the eighteenth century. The community of free mulattoes in New Orleans was much larger and had a longer history than the free colored people of Charleston. When thousands of well-to-do and cultured mulatto refugees from Haiti poured into New Orleans in the latter part of the eighteenth century the government found it necessary to relax the laws restricting the freedom of this class in regard to dress or to move about at will. At the time of the Louisiana Purchase this class had become an important element in the population and formed an intermediate social stratum between the whites and the slaves. Since these families were of mulatto origin they had taken over the culture of the whites. Moreover, their white forebears had frequently given them educational advantages as well as property. The imprint of this cultural heritage was apparent in the personalities of the members of these free families. They were dignified and undertook to support a literary and artistic culture. They took pride in their white ancestry, which included many whites of distinction. They were intensely conscious of their superior status in a society where Negro blood was the badge of slavery. In New Orleans the traditions of a large number of the free mulatto families went back to the role of the mulattoes in the defense of the city against the British in 1814. Many of them sent their children to France to be educated, thus preserving a mode of life that was similar to that of their French neighbors but alien to their Anglo-Saxon neighbors as well as the mass of black slaves.

The patterns of family life developed in this group were as different from that of the great mass of the Negro population as the type of family life which developed among those isolated communities of Negro, Indian, and white descent scattered in various parts of the country.[13] In some cases these communities originated in the eighteenth century.[14] In such communities patriarchal family traditions were firmly established during the pioneer days. These families generally cherished their white and Indian ancestry. But sometimes the Indian character of these communities has been completely effaced and they are classified as Negro communities.[15] Therefore, in tracing the roots of the Negro family in the United States it is necessary to take account of the role of these families in the development of Negro family life.

DISORGANIZATION AND REORGANIZATION OF NEGRO FAMILY LIFE AFTER EMANCIPATION

The immediate effect of the Civil War and Emancipation upon the family life of the slaves was to disrupt the customary relationships and destroy whatever control the master exercised over the sex and family life of the slaves. When the invading armies disrupted the plantation organization, thousands of Negroes were set adrift and began to wander footloose about the country. Not only were the sentimental and habitual ties between spouses severed but even Negro women often abandoned their children. Among the demoralized elements in the newly emancipated Negroes promiscuous sexual relationships and frequent changing of spouses became the rule. The northern missionaries who came South during and following the Civil war were often perplexed by the confusion in marital relations. On the the other hand, the disorders arising from the Civil War and Emancipation often provided a proof of the strength of marital and family ties that had developed during slavery. Many mothers kept their children with them and cared for them at a tremendous sacrifice. Describing the fleeing refugees, Higginson wrote, "Women brought children on their shoulders; small black boys carried on their backs little brothers equally inky, and gravely depositing them, shook hands."[16] Moreover, it was noted by the missionaries and others who were in a position to observe the newly emancipated blacks that there was a general disposition on the part of the Negroes to search for their kinfolk.

The development of the Negro family following the confusion which ensued as the result of Emancipation was influenced by a number of social and economic factors. The heroic efforts of the northern missionaries, who attempted to place marriage on a legal and institutional basis, bore fruits wherever they labored. They were supported in their efforts by the Negro church organizations with intelligent ministers and a core of stable families. Moreover, the schools in which the missionaries labored became centers in which sexual mores were taught and enforced and institutionalized family relations were

cultivated. Despite the important contributions which the missionaries made to stabilizing family relations, the operation of more fundamental social and economic forces in the life of the Negro were to determine the character of his family life.

The family life of the emancipated Negro was influenced to a large extent by his social development under slavery. Even during slavery some of the freedmen had engaged in semi-free economic activities in order to support their families. Among the better situated slaves, the family had acquired considerable stability and the transition to freedom did not result in disorganization. The father had developed a deep and permanent attachment to his wife and an interest in his children. As a freedman he remained on the plantation as a tenant and assumed responsibility for his family.[17] The more ambitious freedmen were not willing to continue as tenants but began to acquire land.

In acquiring land the Negro husband and father laid foundation for patriarchal authority in the family. His interest in his wife and children no longer rested upon a purely sentimental or habitual basis but on an economic tie. In some cases the interest of the father in his wife and children began when he bought them from their owners before Emancipation. But it was only after the Emancipation when the former slave established himself as a freedman that this phase of the development of masculine authority in family relations became important. Even among the freedmen who were tenants, it was customary for the father and husband to make contracts with the landowners and assume responsibility for their families.

This development of the family was associated with the development of other phases of the institutional life of the Negroes. The churches were under the control of men and the control which it exercised tended to confirm the man's interest and authority in the family. Moreover, in the Bible, which for the freedmen was the highest authority in such matters, they found a sanction for masculine authority. The families that had been free before the Civil War played an important role in consolidating masculine authority in the Negro family. Although in some localities the prejudice of this group toward the newly emancipated blacks prevented intermarriage at first, gradually the more successful freedmen married into the families that had been free before Emancipation.

During the latter part of the nineteenth century and the first decade of the present century, two general tendencies were apparent in the development of the Negro family. First, there was an ever increasing number of stable families with a pattern of family organization similar to the American pattern. These families, which were to be found in both rural and urban communities throughout the country, were sharply differentiated from the Negro masses. The emergence of this group of stable families is roughly indicated in the growth of homeownership up to 1910. By 1910 a fourth of the Negroes in rural areas and 22 per cent of the Negroes in cities were homeowners.[18] A part of the homeowning families formed an upper class in Negro communities, while the remaining homeowning families represented the slow emergence of a middle class. The second general tendency is represented in the development of family life on a habitual and sentimental basis among the Negro masses in the rural South. The migration of Negroes to cities, especially the mass migrations to northern cities during and following World War I, has affected both of these developments. In the discussion which follows, we shall consider the changes which have occurred between the two World Wars and the present status of the Negro family.

HIGH PROPORTION OF FAMILIES WITH FEMALE HEADS

As we have seen there has been an excess of females in the Negro population since 1840.[19]

However, the excess of females has been characteristic of the cities rather than the rural areas. In fact, the excess of males in the rural-farm Negro population has been increasing during the past two decades.[20] At the same time, there has been a decrease in the ratio of males to females in the rural-nonfarm Negro population to the point that there was a slight excess of females in 1940. It is not possible to determine the effect of these changes in the sex ratio on the marital status of the rural Negro population over the past fifty years. As has been shown in a number of studies, there is considerable uncertainty concerning the real marital status of the Negroes in the rural South.[21]

In Table XIX, we have the proportion of nonwhite (Negro) families in the rural and farm areas of the South with female heads and the marital status of the female heads of families.[21a] Women are heads of more than a fifth of the Negro families in the South. In the rural-nonfarm areas the proportion of Negro families with female heads is about the same as that for the South as a whole. But in the rural-farm areas the proportion of families with female heads is only one-half as great as that for the entire region, and one-third as great as the proportion in urban areas. The larger proportion of families with female heads among owners than among tenants in rural areas is most likely due to the fact that landlords prefer to have tenant families with male heads or in the absence of legal marriage, families with a male who plays the role of husband. In view of the uncertainty concerning the real marital status of Negroes in rural regions, several facts should be noted in regard to the marital status of female heads of families. First, the husband is absent in a fifth of the families of tenants as compared with a tenth of the families of owners. Secondly, a much larger percentage of the female heads of owner families than of tenant families are described as widowed. Widowhood is the real marital status of a

TABLE XIX PERCENTAGE OF NONWHITE FAMILIES WITH FEMALE HEADS AND
MARITAL STATUS OF FEMALE HEADS OF FAMILIES BY TENURE FOR URBAN AND
RURAL SOUTH: 1940*

| Tenure | Percentage of Families with Female Heads | Families with Female Heads | | | | |
		Total	Husband Absent	Widowed	Divorced	Single
Total	21.7	100.0	21.6	62.2	4.9	11.3
Owner	24.5	100.0	11.5	77.4	3.4	7.7
Tenant	20.9	100.0	25.4	56.5	5.4	12.7
Urban	31.0	100.0	24.6	57.9	5.1	12.4
Owner	29.5	100.0	12.4	76.0	3.2	8.4
Tenant	31.5	100.0	27.9	53.0	5.6	13.5
Rural-Nonfarm	22.7	100.0	18.2	65.6	5.1	11.1
Owner	27.5	100.0	11.7	76.7	3.7	7.9
Tenant	20.1	100.0	22.8	57.6	6.1	13.5
Rural-Farm	11.6	100.0	16.7	70.9	3.9	8.5
Owner	16.4	100.0	16.7	70.9	3.9	8.5
Tenant	10.3	100.0	19.7	66.5	4.2	9.6

*Based on *Sixteenth Census of the United States: 1940. Population and Housing Families.* "General Characteristics," p. 31.

larger proportion of owners than of tenant women who are returned in the federal census as widows. Then, the greater proportion of divorced women among the tenant families with female heads is indicative of the greater instability of the tenants. Finally, the larger proportion of single women who are head of tenant families undoubtedly reflects the large amount of illegitimacy in these rural communities.

THE NEGRO FAMILY ON THE PLANTATION

Among a large proportion of the Negroes in the plantation South, courtship begins at an early age through mutual attraction and often involves sexual relations. Where sex relations result in pregnancy, the young people may or may not marry.[22] The birth of a child imposes certain obligations upon the mother because the mores of the Negro community make the relation between mother and child the most sacred of human relations. In fact, a certain distinction attaches to being fruitful or the fulfillment of one's function as a woman. On the other hand, marriage has not become a part of the mores. The father of the child may suggest "marriage" because he wants a woman to provide a home for him and he in turn is willing to provide subsistence for his family. The woman's response to his offer of "marriage" depends upon the attitude of her parents or her desire to start a new family. In the isolated rural communities where this type of so-called "sexual freedom" is permitted there are, nevertheless, certain restraints placed upon sex relations. During a period of courtship a girl is supposed to have one man only. Since in becoming pregnant she imposes economic burdens upon her family, she is obligated out of consideration for her parents to keep this in mind. The father of her child is likewise under obligation to help take care of the child. But in such communities the moral restraints of the larger community are absent. The women generally do not have a sense of guilt in regard to having children outside of marriage. When the couple decide upon marriage, which is generally of the common-law type, they enter into a cooperative relationship. The permanence of the "marriage" depends not only upon affection and sentiment but often upon the extent to which they can "work together" on the farm. Moreover, even after the men and women have entered "marriage," they may not have a sense of guilt when they have outside affairs. They seem to have fulfilled their obligation to their mates by giving him or her preference in their affections.

In the isolated rural communities, especially among the lower classes, these courtships and forms of marriage do not result in personality conflicts or in social disorganization. In the less isolated communities there are personality conflicts because of the influence of the dominant mores and the control exercised by those conventional family groups that attempt to enforce American family mores. Moreover, outside of the plantation region where there are communities of rural Negroes who have assimilated American standards of family behavior and there are schools and other agencies of communication, the family behavior described is confined largely to the lower classes. In the upper-class families there is supervision of the behavior of young people and legal marriage is a prerequisite to the founding of a family. Throughout the rural South these upper-class families

place great value upon morality in sex and family relations and the father is recognized as the head.[23]

As the result of the sex and marital practices which we have described, the Negro family in the rural areas assumes certain peculiar forms of organization. It is not possible to secure a measure of the extent of the various forms in the Negro rural population. However, for the South as a whole, we have statistics on the distribution of the population in private households with relation to the head of the household (See Table XX). Since there is a much higher percentage of families with female heads among nonwhites (Negroes) than among whites, a smaller proportion of Negro women than of white women is in the relationship of wife to the head of the family. There are, however, other differences which reflect divergences in family organization and practices, such as the larger proportion of "grandchildren," "other relatives," and "lodgers" in Negro families. The larger proportion of "servants or hired hands" is also indicative of certain features of the Negro family rather than of the greater employment of servants in the household. The significance of these statistical differences will become clear as we study the organization of the Negro family.

TABLE XX PERCENTAGE DISTRIBUTION OF POPULATION IN PRIVATE HOUSEHOLDS BY HEADS AND RELATION TO HEAD AND BY COLOR AND SEX FOR THE SOUTH: 1940*

Head	Nonwhite		White	
	Male	*Female*	*Male*	*Female*
	39.5	10.3	44.4	6.5
Relationship to Head				
Wife	——	31.9	——	40.9
Child	41.5	38.2	45.2	40.8
Grandchild	5.4	4.8	2.1	1.9
Parent	0.6	2.4	0.9	2.5
Other Relative	6.3	6.7	4.1	4.3
Lodger	6.2	4.8	3.1	2.3
Servant or Hired Hand	0.5	0.9	0.2	0.5

*Sixteenth Census of the United States: 1940. Population. Vol. IV. "Characteristics by Age." Part I, p. 114.

The maternal Negro family, or the family in which the mother is the head, functions in its most primitive form as a natural organization in the rural areas of the South.[24] Historically, it had its origin as we have seen during the slavery period when the mother was the most dependable element in the family. Since Emancipation the maternal family has been supported by the folkways and mores of the rural communities. The matricentric family grows into a type of matriarchate in which the grandmother is the dominant figure. The mother acquires the status of a grandmother when her daughters become mothers and bring their children into the household.[25] Because of her age and experience the grandmother exercises authority over the members of the family and assumes responsibility for their welfare. The grandmother is a repository of folk wisdom and is called upon during the major crises of life. She attends the sick and the dead; but her superior wisdom and authority are recognized chiefly in matters concerning childbirth. She is often the "granny" or midwife who supplies young mothers with knowledge concerning babies and attends them during the crisis of childbirth. In 1940 four-fifths of the live births of Negroes in Mississippi and South Carolina were attended by midwives as compared with a fourteenth of white live births in these states.[26] In Virginia and Tennessee the percentage of live births of Negroes attended by midwives was 58.6 and 26.1 respectively.

The "matriarchal" type of family among rural Negroes in the South is an extended family in that it includes several generations and nephews and nieces and adopted children. This is indicated to some extent by the statistics in Table XX in the larger percentage of grandchildren and "other" relatives in Negro private households than in white households. There is not, however, a larger percentage of "parents" in Negro private households because the persons who would normally be in the relationship of "parent" to the head of the household are themselves the grandparents, who are often the heads of the household.

The extended Negro families are not all matriarchal in organization. Among the upper-class families in the rural South there are semipatriarchal families of the extended type. The development of the semipatriarchal type of family has been related to the acquisition of land. Moreover, the extent of homeownership in the rural-farm area of the South is related to the socioeconomic status of the inhabitants of the rural area. More than a fifth (Table XXI)

TABLE XXI PERCENTAGE OF NONWHITE FAMILIES WITH EMPLOYED HEAD THAT WERE HOMEOWNERS IN EACH OCCUPATION GROUP IN THE SOUTH: 1940*

Occupation Group	Total	Urban	Rural-Nonfarm	Rural-Farm
Professional and Semiprofessional	49.3	49.6	45.1	56.7
Farmers and Farm Managers	23.1	54.7	45.9	22.4
Proprietors, Managers, etc.	48.0	42.5	62.2	75.0
Clerical, Sales, etc.	41.4	37.3	62.4	68.8
Craftsmen, Foremen, etc.	34.7	29.7	46.2	41.5
Operatives	21.6	20.7	21.9	29.6
Domestic Service	17.3	13.9	28.5	15.6
Service Workers	27.9	25.0	43.6	37.9
Farm Laborers	10.2	20.0	25.6	5.0
Laborers	20.5	16.1	25.8	29.1
Total	21.9	21.3	29.6	19.3

*Based upon *Sixteenth Census of the United States: 1940. Population and Housing Families.* "General Characteristics," p. 43.

of the farm families, including farmowners and renters owned their homes, while among the farm laborers only one family in twenty was a homeowner. Landowners and homeowners often exercise authority over their married sons as well as their unmarried daughters. But generally their sons are "emancipated" upon reaching maturity and establish their own families on an independent basis.

THE NEGRO FAMILY IN SOUTHERN TOWNS AND CITIES

In the towns and smaller cities of the South, these various forms of family organization tend to persist with certain modifications. The maternal family plays a larger role because of the opportunities for the employment of women in domestic service and the grandmother continues to be the head of a large proportion of Negro families. On the other hand, the extended family tends to disintegrate and the growth of the semipatriarchal type of family is encouraged as the chance for homeownership is increased. It is, however, in the larger cities of the South that the effects of urbanization and the occupational differentiation of the Negro population are manifested in the organization of family life. There is, first, a decline in the size of the family or the number of children to women of

childbearing age. For example, the number of children under five years of age to 1,000 Negro women 15 to 49 years of age in Atlanta, Birmingham, and Memphis was 170, 177, and 163 respectively as compared with 472 for Negro women in the rural-farm South.[27] In the cities of the South a much larger proportion—nearly a third as compared with a tenth for rural areas—of Negro families have female heads. As one may observe in Table XIX the proportion of families with female heads is slightly higher among tenants in urban areas than among owners. There are even more striking differences between female heads of families who are owners and tenants in regard to marital status. In the tenant families with female heads over a fourth of the husbands are absent as compared with an eighth of the owner families; and three-fourths of the owners are widowed as compared with a little more than half of the renter families.

There is a tendency for the upper- and middle-class families to become segregated into the better areas of the Negro community. These families are distinguished from the lower-class families in regard to the extent of homeownership. In Table XXII, we have the amount of homeownership among the different occupational groups in four southern cities with Negro communities numbering

TABLE XXII PERCENTAGE OF NONWHITE FAMILIES WITH EMPLOYED HEAD THAT WERE HOMEOWNERS IN EACH OCCUPATION GROUP IN FOUR SOUTHERN CITIES: 1940*

Occupation Group	Atlanta	Birmingham	Memphis	New Orleans
Professional and Semi-professional	46.4	35.7	53.3	32.3
Proprietors, Managers, etc.	29.0	36.4	33.3	36.4
Clerical, Sales, etc.	33.3	19.0	50.0	23.9
Craftsmen, Foremen, etc.	10.1	17.9	30.2	17.8
Operatives	9.6	20.1	19.1	7.1
Domestic Service	8.0	8.5	14.9	3.2
Service Workers	14.5	7.9	22.0	8.4
Laborers	9.1	10.5	16.9	7.7
Total	12.7	14.0	21.1	9.4

*Based upon *Sixteenth Census of the United States: 1940. Population and Housing Families*, p. 290.

over 100,000. In New Orleans where home-ownership is comparatively low, the difference in pattern of homeownership among the various occupational classes is most pronounced. Homeownership is lowest for the domestic workers with low incomes and considerable family disorganization. It is higher for laborers and unskilled workers in industry and even higher for service workers among whom there are many stable and ambitious families. Among the skilled workers or craftsmen, homeownership is twice as high as among the service workers. It is among the white-collar workers—professional and clerical workers and proprietors—that homeownership assumes considerable importance and that the most stable families with a semipatriarchal organization are found.

THE NEGRO FAMILY IN BORDER CITIES

In the border cities, as in the cities of the South, the various types of family organization described above tend to persist. There has been, however, in the border cities a comparatively large group of stable families with a semipatriarchal organization over a long period. Many of these families have their roots among the Negroes who were free in these cities before the Civil War. Moreover,

the constant migration of Negroes from the South has brought to the border cities many stable families. There is a tendency for the various patterns of family life to correspond to the class structure of the Negro communities in border cities.[28] Although among the lower class there is considerable family disorganization and many families have only a mother or grandmother as head, there is a core of stable families even in this class. It is, however, among the middle class, embracing about a fourth of the Negro community, that one finds the largest group of stable families of a semipatriarchal type. In border cities as in southern cities the extent of homeownership in the various occupational groups provides a rough indication of family stability in the different classes (See Table XXIII). In the District of Columbia, where Negro women of this class have an opportunity for desirable employment, some of these families tend to become equalitarian in their organization, that is, the husband and wife have equal status in the family.

However, it is among the upper-class families that the equalitarian type of family is most pronounced. Unlike the wives in upper-class Negro families in the South, many of the wives in the upper-class families in the border cities are

TABLE **XXIII** PERCENTAGE OF NONWHITE FAMILIES WITH EMPLOYED HEAD THAT WERE HOMEOWNERS IN EACH OCCUPATIONAL GROUP IN THREE BORDER CITIES: 1940*

Occupational Group	Baltimore	Washington, D.C.	St. Louis, Mo.
Professional and Semi-professional	53.1	59.6	35.1
Proprietors, Managers, etc.	18.2	23.1	9.3
Clerical, Sales, etc.	30.0	37.0	19.4
Craftsmen, Foremen	9.0	19.5	10.4
Operatives	12.2	20.6	4.2
Domestic Service	8.0	7.4	6.5
Service Workers	11.9	18.5	8.1
Laborers	5.3	14.6	7.1
Total	11.1	20.4	8.8

*Based upon *Sixteenth Census of the United States: 1940. Population and Housing,* "General Characteristics," pp. 290–91.

employed in professional and clerical occupations. This not only gives the wives a certain degree of independence but enables the family to maintain certain standards of consumption. Because of their standards of consumption and their values upper-class families have few children and there are many childless couples. A study in 1937 of 114 colored faculty members of Howard University revealed that those who had been married ten years or more had an average of 1.1 children per family. Of the entire group studied, 60 per cent indicated that they had voluntarily restricted their families.[29] Likewise, in a study of 65 families among the Washington colored elite it was found that 36 of the 65 families had no children and that in the remaining 29 families there were only 43 children or an average of less than 0.7 of a child per family for the entire group.

THE NEGRO FAMILY IN NORTHERN CITIES

The effects of urban living upon the character and organization of Negro family life are most pronounced in the large cities of the North.[30] The mass migration of Negroes to the cities of the North resulted in considerable family disorganization. In a later chapter this phase of Negro family life will be considered among the problems of the adjustment of the Negro to American civilization. Here we are concerned primarily with the forms of family organization which have evolved in the urban areas of the North. In the Negro community in the northern city, as we have seen, there is a selection and segregation of various elements in the Negro population.[31] There is a selection and segregation on the basis of age and sex, a process which is related to the marital and family status of the population. The proportion of females and children in the population increases in the successive zones of the cities as one moves from the center outward, marking the expansion of the Negro community.[32] There is a selection and segregation of the population on the basis of marital status. This can be seen in the case of the Harlem Negro community in New York City (See Table XXIV). The decrease in the percentage of men and women single from the first to the fifth zone is associated with a progressive increase in the proportion of men and women married. The progressive increase in the proportion married is correlated with a decrease in the proportion widowed. This reflects not so much a difference in the death rates of men and women as a difference in the institutional character of the family. Because of the increasing importance of legal marriage, there are proportionately fewer deserted women and unmarried mothers who call themselves widows and there is an increase in the percentage of women divorced. The

TABLE XXIV PERCENTAGE OF NEGRO MALES AND FEMALES FIFTEEN YEARS OF AGE AND OVER, SINGLE, MARRIED, WIDOWED, AND DIVORCED, IN THE FIVE ZONES OF THE HARLEM NEGRO COMMUNITY, NEW YORK CITY, 1930*

Marital Status	Sex	Zone I	Zone II	Zone III	Zone IV	Zone V
Single	M	42.6	38.5	35.3	34.0	31.1
	F	30.9	27.6	26.3	25.6	23.5
Married	M	49.8	56.0	60.3	62.3	64.2
	F	50.5	54.8	57.6	59.8	60.1
Widowed	M	7.3	4.7	3.6	2.9	3.8
	F	17.6	16.4	15.0	13.0	14.4
Divorced	M	0.2	0.5	0.4	0.6	0.5
	F	0.6	0.8	0.7	1.1	1.6

*Reproduced with the permission of The University of Chicago Press, from *The Negro Family in the United States*, p. 318.

small percentage of divorced persons in the zones in and near the center of the community does not mean greater stability of family life in these areas but rather that separations are irregular and without legal sanctions as probably were also the unions in the first place.

The differences in marital status in the successive zones of expansion of the Negro community are indicative of the selective effects of urban life on the Negro family. In Zone I, which is the business and recreational center of the Negro community, family life tends to disappear as in the center of American cities.[33] Although the concentric zones marking the expansion of the Negro population are not homogeneous in culture, they nevertheless reflect the growing influence of family life in the successive zones. Not only is this indicated in the increase in the proportion married but in the birth rates and in the number of children (See Table XXV). In the first zone only 66 children were born in 1930 to each 1,000 Negro women of childbearing age and there were only 115 children under five to each 1,000 women 20 to 44 years of age. The birth rates and the ratio of children to women of childbearing age increase regularly in the successive zones. In the fifth zone on the periphery of the Harlem community the ratio of children to women of childbearing age is almost equal to the ratio in the rural-farm South.

The progressive stabilization of family life in the zones marking the expansion of the Negro is indicated in some cities by the regular increase of the rate of homeownership in the successive zones. In the District of Columbia the rates of homeownership among Negroes for the five zones in 1940 were: 2.5, 9.3, 17.3, 27.9, and 51.2.[34] The same phenomenon was observable in Chicago in 1930, where the rates for the seven zones were: 0.0, 1.2, 6.2, 7.2, 8.3, 11.4, and 29.8.[35] These increases in the rate of homeownership are related to the tendency for the higher occupational classes to become concentrated in the areas on the periphery of the Negro community. This is seen in Table XXVI, where the percentage of homeownership for the different occupational classes is given. Higher rates of homeownership for the higher occupational groups are most marked in Chicago, Detroit, and Philadelphia. Although it is not so pronounced in New York City with its numerous apartment houses, homeownership there too is higher among the higher occupational classes.

TABLE XXV NUMBER OF CHILDREN UNDER FIVE BORN TO 1,000 NEGRO WOMEN, 20 TO 44 YEARS OF AGE, AND NUMBER OF CHILDREN BORN TO 1,000 NEGRO MARRIED WOMEN, 15 TO 44 YEARS OF AGE, IN THE NEGRO HARLEM COMMUNITY, NEW YORK CITY: 1930*

Zone	Women 20–44	Children Under 5	Ratio of Children to Women	Married Women, 15–44 (Estimated)	Number of Births	Births per 1,000 Married Women 15–44
I	4,141	476	115	2,495	165	66.1
II	23,612	4,160	176	15,087	1,230	81.5
III	21,107	4,749	225	13,883	1,276	91.9
IV	12,498	3,940	315	8,552	1,211	141.6
V	3,872	1,790	462	2,833	477	168.4

*Reproduced with permission from *The Negro Family in the United States* by E. Franklin Frazier, pp. 321 and 322. Copyright 1939 by The University of Chicago Press.

TABLE XXVI PERCENTAGE OF NONWHITE FAMILIES WITH EMPLOYED
HEAD THAT WERE HOMEOWNERS IN EACH OCCUPATION GROUP IN
FOUR NORTHERN CITIES: 1940*

Occupation Group	New York	Chicago	Philadelphia	Detroit
Professional and Semi-professional	6.5	20.6	32.4	30.8
Proprietors, Managers, etc.	7.1	22.9	10.3	26.7
Clerical, Sales, etc.	8.6	18.1	33.3	50.0
Craftsmen, Foremen	9.6	6.8	6.8	21.1
Operatives	3.3	3.7	10.2	17.9
Domestic Service	2.6	4.0	14.3	5.6
Service Workers	4.1	7.1	12.9	19.1
Laborers	5.0	5.5	5.9	11.1
Total	4.9	7.9	20.4	19.2

*Based upon the *Sixteenth Census of the United States: 1940. Population and Housing.* "General Characteristics," pp. 290–291.

FAMILY LIFE AMONG THE VARIOUS CLASSES

Because of the extent to which class differentiation has evolved in the large northern cities, the organizaiton of Negro family life must be studied in relation to the class structure in these communities. It may be well to begin at the bottom of the class structure, since as one considers the higher levels the effects of urban living from the standpoint of reorganization of the family in the urban environment become more pronounced. The lower-class families are physically segregated to a large extent in the deteriorated areas where Negroes first secure a foothold in the community. It is among this class that one finds the large proportion of families with female heads. This is the result of the economic insecurity of the men and illegitimacy. Because of the precarious hold which women of this class have on men, their attitudes alternate between one of subordination to secure affection and one of domination because of their greater economic security than their spouses.[36] But there is in the lower class a "church centered" core of families that endeavor to maintain stable family relations despite their economic insecurity and other

exigencies which make family life unstable. Even during periods of comparative prosperity the employment of women may prove a disintegrating factor since these families lack a deeply rooted tradition.

The occupational differentiation of the Negro population in the northern city, as we have seen, has made possible the emergence of a substantial middle class.[37] The middle class is comprised largely of clerical workers and persons in the service occupations, though there are professional workers and some business persons in this class.[38] But, perhaps, the most important accession to the middle class in the northern cities has been the families of industrial workers, especially the skilled workers. It is among this occupational class that the male head of the family has sufficient economic security to play the conventional role of provider for his family without the aid of the wife. This was indicated in a study of the industrial employment of Negro men and the employment of Negro married women in 75 northern and southern cities with a total population of 100,000 or more in 1930. It was found that the proportion of married women employed declined as the proportion of employed Negro males in industry increased.[39]

Although the husband or father in the middle-class Negro family is generally recognized as the head of the family, the wife or mother is not completely subordinated. There is often a division of labor in the management of the household and a spirit of democracy in the family. The dignified and respected position of the wife and mother is due partly to the tradition of independence among Negro women. The spirit of democracy often springs from the fact that there is considerable cooperation in order that the family may purchase a home or that the children may obtain an education. The education of children means that the family is "getting up" in the world. To be respectable and to "get up" in the world are two of the main ambitions of middle-class families. Therefore, it is not unusual that parents in middle-class families make tremendous sacrifices to enable their children to get a college education.[40] At the same time the children of the middle class are not as a rule spoiled as are often the children in the upper class. They are generally subjected to strict discipline but they are not treated with the harshness which is often found in the case of children in lower-class families. The boys who begin at any early age to earn money in such jobs as running errands and selling newspapers generally develop a sense of responsibility and habits of industry. Consequently, the ambitious and thrifty middle-class families are the mainstay of the Baptist and Methodist churches and other institutions in the Negro community.

We come finally to the upper-class families in the large cities of the North. The upper-class Negro families do not derive their support from invested wealth but rather from professional and other kinds of services. Yet because of their class position, their outlook is often that of a wealthy leisure class. Many heads of upper-class families can tell success stories of their rise in the world, but these stories are very seldom concerned with becoming heads of business enterprises. As a rule the stories tell

of their struggle to achieve a professional education. Moreover, the wives of these upper-class men like upper-class wives in the border cities are sometimes employed in professional occupations.

Where the wife is employed the upper-class family is generally equalitarian in its organization. But even where the wife is not employed, the wife in the upper-class family enjoys considerable equality in the family and freedom in her activities and contacts in the community. In some upper-class families, where the wife is economically dependent, she nevertheless determines to a large extent the manner in which the family income is spent. She herself may be the object of much conspicuous consumption since she becomes the symbol of her husband's economic position. Whether engaging in "social life" or aiding in "civic" activities, she behaves according to the expectations of her class position. Since respectability is taken for granted in this class, the unconventional behavior of husband or wife is not allowed to become a matter of public knowledge. When unconventional behavior of husband or wife becomes public, it generally means the divorce court. An important feature of the expectations of her class is that while respectability is taken for granted, the wife is supposed to appear as "refined" and "cultured."[41]

Among the upper class in the northern city there are many childless couples and relatively few children in families with children. Men and women who have struggled to achieve a high position in the Negro community are not inclined to have the standards which they attempt to maintain lowered by the burden of children. Moreover, since these men have often experienced many privations to achieve an education, they want to spare their children similar hardships. As a consequence the children of the upper class are often spoiled. The parents attempt to satisfy their children's wishes and try often to maintain them in the manner of the children of the rich. Upper-class parents in border and southern cities often send their children to the colleges in the North that represent, in their opinion at least, a certain exclusiveness. There is some evidence to support the rumors which have often circulated in Negro communities that mulatto women sometimes have refused to have children by their black husbands. A sampling of Negro families in three southern cities, secured from the unpublished data of the 1910 federal census, revealed that couples in which the husband was black and the wife was a mulatto had fewer children on the average than either the couples in which both husband and wife were black or both husband and wife were mulatto.[42] In contemplating marriage, upper-class Negroes in the North as well as in the South take into consideration the color of their prospective mates, especially its effect upon the color of their children.

Among upper-class families there is much individualism. Husbands, wives, and children insist as a rule upon the right to follow their own interests. This individualism becomes very conspicuous among the so-called "emancipated" and "sophisticated" elements in the upper class. Many of these "families" are really childless couples. Their outlook on life is not only individualistic but secular. They represent a new type of intelligentsia in the Negro group. They are acquainted with the latest and best literature; they are concerned with movements within and without the Negro group. They associate freely with white middle-class intellectuals. Among this group may be

found many of the "interracial" couples, since the intelligentsia does not exhibit the same hostility to intermarriage as the more conservative and isolated elements in the upper class. Thus they provide a bridge for the complete integration of the Negro in the northern city.

In this chapter we have traced the development of the Negro family and its organization in relation to the emerging class structure of rural and urban communities. It was shown how the family acquired a stable character during slavery as the result of the social and economic organization of the plantation. Then, it was shown how the family first became established on an institutional basis among the Negroes that were free before the Civil War. The analysis revealed the disorganizing effects of the Civil War and Emancipation and the subsequent reorganization in the rural South. Then we saw how the migrations to cities, especially the mass migrations to northern cities, produced a new crisis in the family life of the Negro. The experience with city life, it was seen, has not resulted simply in the disorganization of the family, held together chiefly by habit and sentiment, but in the reorganization according to middle-class patterns, thus reflecting the new class structure in urban communities. The family has been, thus, not only the most important form of organized social life among Negroes, but it has been the means by which the new forms of adjustment have been mediated to succeeding generations. . . .

Notes

1. See Chapter I, pp. 10–14.

2. See Melville J. Herskovits, *Life in a Haitian Valley* (New York, 1937), pp. 81–121; and Martha W. Beckwith, *Black Roadways: A Study of Jamaican Folk Life* (Chapel Hill, 1929), p. 54.

3. E. Franklin Frazier, "The Negro Family in Bahia, Brazil," *The American Sociological Review*, Vol. VII, pp. 465–78.

4. The discussion which follows is based almost entirely upon E. Franklin Frazier, *The Negro*

Family in the United States (Chicago, 1939), which contains a detailed analysis, supported by documents and statistics, of the points presented in this chapter.

5. A visitor to America made the following observations: "Those [slaves] who cannot obtain women (for there is a great disproportion between the number of the two sexes) traverse the woods in search of adventures, and often encounter those of an unpleasant nature. They often meet a patrol of whites, who tie them up and flog them, and then send them home." Berguin Duvallon, "Travels in Louisiana and the Floridas, in the Year 1802," pp. 79–94, in *Journal of Negro History*, II, 172.

6. See, for example, Edward Kimber, *Itinerant Observations in America*. Reprinted from the *London Magazine*, 1745–46 (Savannah, Ga., 1878), pp. 37–38.

7. See Chapter III above.

8. See for example J. W. C. Pennington, *The Fugitive Blacksmith: or Events in the History of J. W. C. Pennington* (London, 1850).

9. Writers on Negro slavery, especially apologists for the system, have represented the Negro mother or "Mammy" as a devoted nurse of the children of the master and as indifferent to her own children. The attitude of the Negro woman toward the children of the master was conditioned by her association with the white children and the rewards which her role as substitute mother brought her. Likewise, her attitude toward her own children was determined by what pregnancy and childbearing meant to her. See Frazier, *The Negro Family in the United States*, pp. 42–57, for a full discussion of this point.

10. In Charleston and more especially in New Orleans associations between white men and mulatto women often developed into stable alliances.

11. *The Negro Family in the United States* by E. Franklin Frazier, p. 85. Copyright 1939 by The University of Chicago Press.

12. Although many white women in the South, accepting masculine prerogatives in a patriarchal system, resigned themselves to the situation, others gave vent to their jealousy

and displeasure by acts of cruelty to the slave women and their mulatto offspring. The same reaction on the part of white women occurred in Brazil. See Gilberto Frevre, *Casa Grande & Senzala* (Rio de Janeiro, 1943), Vol. 2, pp. 539–40.

13. See Frazier, *The Negro Family in the United States*, Chapter XI, "Racial Islands."

14. See, for example, William and Theophilus G. Steward, *Gouldtown: A Very Remarkable Settlement of Ancient Date* (Philadelphia, 1913).

15. For the origin of some of these communities we have historical evidence; but for others one must depend upon the traditions which have been preserved concerning the pioneers. See *Legislative Petitions, Archives of Virginia, King William County, 1843*. Quoted in J. H. Johnston, "Documentary Evidence of the Relations of Negroes and Indians," *Journal of Negro History*, XIV, pp. 29–30.

16. Thomas Wentworth Higginson, *Army Life in a Black Regiment* (New York, 1900), p. 235.

17. As a rule the freedmen were unwilling to continue to work in gangs as during slavery; but insisted upon having the land divided so that each family could work as an independent unit.

18. See Frazier, *The Negro Family in the United States*, pp. 246–47.

19. See pp. 180–81.

20. See *Sixteenth Census of the United States, 1940. Population* "Characteristics of the Population," 2, Part I, pp. 19–20.

21. See Frazier, *The Negro Family in the United States*, pp. 108 ff; Hortense Powdermaker, *After Freedom* (New York, 1939), pp. 152 ff; Charles S. Johnson, *Shadow of the Plantation* (Chicago, 1934), pp. 40–44.

21a. A female head of a family is a woman—single, widowed, divorced, or if married her husband is not living with the family—who is regarded as head of the family.

22. Early sex relations account for the high birth rates among young Negro families. For the age group, 10 to 14, the birth rate for Negro women is 3.1 as compared with 0.2 for white women; and for the age group, 15 to 19, 102.7 for Negro

women as compared with 42.1 for white women. Bureau of the Census. *Vital Statistics of the United States: 1940.* Part I, p. 9.

23. See Frazier, *The Negro Family in the United States,* Chapter XII, "The Black Puritans."

24. Ernest W. Burgess and Harvey J. Locke, *The Family. From Institution to Companionship* (New York, 1945), p. 161, use the term "matricentric" to designate the type of family organization described here.

25. See Frazier, *op. cit.,* Chapter VIII.

26. Burgess and Locke, *op. cit.,* p. 165.

27. *Sixteenth Census of the United States: 1940. Population* "Differential Fertility 1940 and 1910," pp. 78, 231, 233.

28. See pp. 285–89 above.

29. See Frazier, *The Negro Family in the United States,* p. 442.

30. It appears, however, that increases in the sex ratio among Negroes in southern cities has a greater influence on marriage rates than in northern cities. See Oliver C. Cox, "Sex Ratio and Marital Status Among Negroes," *American Sociological Review,* Vol. 5, p. 942.

31. See pp. 257 ff. above.

32. See E. Franklin Frazier, *The Negro Family in Chicago* (Chicago, 1932), pp. 117–18; and Frazier, *The Negro Family in the United States,* pp. 315–16.

33. See Burgess and Locke, *op. cit.,* pp. 118–19.

34. An interesting aspect of this process is that the rates for white homeownership closely paralleled the rates for Negroes. They were for the five zones; 2.2, 9.7, 20.7, 31.9, and 53.9.

35. Frazier, *The Negro Family in Chicago,* p. 127.

36. St. Clair Drake and Horace R. Cayton, *Black Metropolis, A Study of Negro Life in a Northern City* (New York, 1945), pp. 583–84.

37. See pp. 300–02 above.

38. Cf. Drake and Cayton, *op. cit.,* p. 661. See also pp. 300–01 above.

39. The coefficient of correlation was − 0.67. See Frazier *The Negro Family in the United States,* pp. 461 and 616–18.

40. *Ibid.,* pp. 473–74.

41. Cf. Drake and Cayton, *op. cit.,* p. 531.

42. The samples were taken from Birmingham, Alabama, Charleston, South Carolina, and Nashville, Tennessee. See Frazier, *The Negro Family in the United States,* Appendix B, Table 26, p. 603.

The Black Family: A Critical Challenge

GLENN C. LOURY

HE NUCLEAR FAMILY, WHETHER EURO-pean or Oriental, socialist or bourgeois, modern or traditional is the center of social life in all cultures. Societies rely on the family, in one form or another, to accomplish the essential tasks of producing and socializing children. The continued prosperity—indeed the survival—of any society depends on how adequately families discharge this responsibility.

TRENDS IN AMERICAN FAMILY LIFE

There is now enormous concern in many quarters that the American family has weakened, and that this weakening is implicated in an array of social problems from criminal participation to declining academic achievement. Measures to strengthen the family have been proposed and enacted in the Congress and the need to restore family values is widely discussed. Private foundations and government agencies are spending millions of dollars annually on research and demonstration projects that seek to understand how changes now occurring in family life can be dealt with best.

The basis for this concern is reflected in recent demographic trends. Compared to a generation ago, the American family of today has changed dramatically: Older and younger single adults are more likely to live alone (Fuch, 1983). Marriage seems to have become less popular. Divorce is a much more prevalent phenomenon today than it was thirty years ago (Cherlin, 1981). The age at which women first marry has been rising, the fraction of first children conceived prior to marriage has been increasing and the proportion of these women who marry by the time their child is born has been falling. O'Connell and Moore (1980) estimate that among white teens (15–19) who had a first birth between 1959 and 1962, less than one-third of the births were premaritally conceived, though slightly more than two-thirds of these were legitimated by marriage. Whereas among white teens who experienced first births between 1975 and 1978, nearly two-thirds had conceived prior to marriage and slightly more than half of these births were subsequently legitimated.

The traditional relationship between childbearing and marriage is also undergoing dramatic change. The fertility of married women is falling, and that of most groups of unmarried women is rising (see the tables below). The incidence of teenage sexuality and childbearing has risen sharply in recent years. Between 1971 and 1979 the fraction of American teenage girls who were sexually active rose from 30% to 50% (Zelnick and Kanter, 1980). A recent Planned Parenthood report comparing teenage fertility rates in the U.S. with those in other industrialized countries shows that in 1980 the number of pregnancies per 1,000 women aged 15–19 was nearly twice as high in the U.S. as in the closest Western European country. (Elise Jones, et al., "Teenage Pregnancy in Developed Countries: . . .")

As a result of these trends, there has been an increase in family instability—i.e., a growing number of families which break up or never form, leaving children to be raised by one of the parents, almost always the mother. This is a phenomenon affecting whites, blacks and Hispanics alike, though it is by far most significant among blacks (Wilson and Neckerman, 1984). Divorce, separation and widowhood are the principal means by which single-parent families arise among whites (Cherlin, 1981; Bane and Ellwood, 1984), but the most important source of such families among blacks is the high rate of out-of-wedlock births. Among black women aged 15–24 the fraction of births which occurred outside of marriage rose from 41% in 1955 to 68% in 1980. Out-of-wedlock births have also risen to unprecedented levels for white women. This has occurred in part because of the growing fertility of unmarried women, but an even more important reason is the recent, sharp decline in marital fertility.

It is clear from Tables 1 & 2 that, while the fertility of unmarried women (with the exception of white teens) held steady or declined between 1970 and 1980 (note the decline by more than 50% in fertility of unmarried nonwhite women ages 25–29 from 1960–1980), birth rates among married women fell sufficiently faster than the fraction of births occurring to unmarried women of all ages and races rose notably over this period. Indeed between 1960 and 1979 fertility among both white and nonwhite married women fell by roughly one-third (*Vital Statistics of the United States, 1979*). In addition, the fraction of women who are unmarried has been rising dramatically in recent years. Among white women 20–24 years of age, the percent single rose from 32.2% to 47.2% between 1965 and

TABLE 1 BIRTHS TO UNMARRIED WOMEN PER THOUSAND WOMEN, BY RACE AND AGE OF MOTHER, SELECTED YEARS

	Whites			Nonwhites		
	15–19	*20–24*	*25–29*	*15–19*	*20–24*	*25–29*
1940	3.3	5.7	4.0	42.5	46.1	32.5
1950	5.1	10.0	8.7	68.5	105.4	94.2
1955	6.0	15.0	13.3	77.6	133.0	125.2
1960	6.6	18.2	18.2	76.5	166.5	171.8
1965	7.9	22.1	24.3	75.8	152.6	164.7
1970	10.9	22.5	21.1	90.8	120.9	93.7
1975	12.0	15.5	14.8	86.3	102.1	73.2
1980	16.0	22.6	17.3	83.0	109.2	79.1

Source: Adapted from Wilson and Neckerman, 1984, Tables 3 & 4.

TABLE 2 PERCENT OF BIRTHS WHICH OCCUR OUT-OF-WEDLOCK, BY RACE AND AGE OF MOTHER, SELECTED YEARS

	Whites			Nonwhites		
	15–19	*20–24*	*25–29*	*15–19*	*20–24*	*25–29*
1955	6.4	1.9	0.9	40.1	18.9	13.3
1960	7.1	2.2	1.1	42.1	20.0	14.1
1965	11.4	3.8	1.9	49.2	23.0	16.3
1970	17.1	5.2	2.1	61.3	29.5	18.1
1975	23.0	6.1	2.6	74.7	39.9	22.7
1979	30.3	9.5	3.7	82.5	50.1	28.7

Source: Adapted from Wilson and Neckerman, 1984, Tables 3 & 4.

1980, while the rise for comparable black women was from 34.3% to 68.7%! For women 25–29 the fraction unmarried more than doubled among white (8.0% to 18.3%) and more than tripled among blacks (11.6% to 37.2%) between 1965 and 1980 (Wilson and Neckerman, 1984).

Also important for the rise of out-of-wedlock births among young and black women has been the trend in the fraction of women who never marry, which, according to Census data, rose from 9% to 23% of black women aged 25–44 between 1950 and 1979, while staying constant at roughly 10% over this period for whites (Cherlin, 1981). This racial difference in the increased fraction of never married women has also been observed in the Panel Study of Income Dynamics by Bane and Ellwood, who report a widening black-white difference in the fraction never married, and claim that ". . . in 1982 four times as large a proportion of black as white women were never married,

separated, divorced or widowed mothers (Bane and Ellwood, 1984:33)."

Thus, female family heads have become both more numerous and younger among blacks and whites, but especially among blacks. The increasing prevalence of female-headed families is illustrated by the experience of the last decade.

These trends have significant implications for the living arrangements of children, and therefore for the incidence of childhood poverty, as has been emphasized by recent observers (Moynihan, 1985; Wilson and Neckerman, 1984; Bane and Ellwood, 1984). For obvious reasons the incidence of poverty is substantially greater among female-headed households; the poverty rate of female-headed families was 36.3% in 1982, compared to a rate for married couple families of 7.6%. Female-headed families made up 45.7% of the poverty population in 1982, and 71% of the black poor (U.S. Bureau of the Census, 1983).

TABLE 3 PERCENT OF FAMILIES WITH FEMALE HEADS BY RACE 1974–1983

	White	Black	Hispanic		White	Black	Hispanic
1974	9.9	34.0	17.4	1979	11.6	40.5	19.8
1975	10.5	35.3	18.8	1980	11.6	40.2	19.2
1976	10.8	35.9	20.9	1981	11.9	41.7	21.8
1977	10.9	37.1	20.0	1982	12.4	40.6	22.7
1978	11.5	39.2	20.3	1983	12.2	41.9	22.8

Source: Adapted from Wilson and Neckerman, 1984, Table 2.

Young, never married mothers, though likely to be living at home when they have their children, are also likely to change households before their child reaches the age of six. Bane and Ellwood estimate (using the PSID) that two-thirds of black and white unwed mothers who give birth while living at home will move into different living arrangements prior to their child's sixth birthday. Among blacks, though, two-thirds of these moves are into independent female-headed families, while for whites two-thirds of the moves are into two parent families. They further estimate that, independent of the original living arrangements of the mother, among children born out-of-wedlock, less than 10% of whites but more than 50% of blacks will remain in female-headed families for their entire childhood (Bane and Ellwood, 1984).

The consequences of early pregnancy for both mother and child can be quite severe. Teenage motherhood has been shown to be associated with prolonged poverty and welfare dependency (Wilson and Neckerman, 1984; Bane and Ellwood, 1983; Hofferth and Moore, 1979), low achievement in education by the mother (Hofferth and Moore, 1979), and increased subsequent fertility and the closer spacing of births (Trussel and Menken, 1978). A careful longitudinal study of inner-city black children in Chicago raised under alternative family circumstances has found that the children growing up in households where their mother is the only adult are significantly more likely to exhibit difficulty adapting to the social environment of the classroom, as measured by their first and third grade teachers' descriptions of the child's behavior in school (Kellam, et al., 1977).

CONCERN FOR THE BLACK FAMILY

Thus, these trends in adolescent and out-of-wedlock child-bearing should occasion the most serious public concern. This is especially so for the black population, in which the extent of the problem is vastly greater than

for whites, for the decay of black family life is an awesome barrier to economic and social progress for blacks. It is directly implicated in the continued extent of poverty among black children. In 1980, nearly three of every five female-headed black families lived below the poverty line, compared to only about one of every six two-parent black families (U.S. Bureau of the Census, Current Population Reports, Series P-60, 1981). Even though the poverty rate fell during the 1970s for both male and female-headed black families, the fraction of black families below the poverty line increased, due to the higher rate of poverty among female-headed families, together with their growing number. This is a circumstance which deserves serious public attention.

A discussion of this sort can hardly avoid recalling the experience surrounding the controversial "Moynihan Report" (U.S. Dept. of Labor, 1965). There Moynihan had made two arguments: one regarding the causes of the (then only recently noticed) trend in family instability among blacks, and the other concerning the policy implications of this trend for the pursuit of equality of opportunity. His causal argument derived from the earlier work of E. Franklin Frazier (Frazier, 1939) and held that the black population was plagued by a "matri-focal family structure" deriving from the experience of slavery, during which the role of black men within the family had been severely circumscribed. His policy argument was that, in light of the deleterious economic consequences of this family instability, a national policy of racial equality should attempt to directly promote alternative family behaviors among blacks. He concluded that "The Negro family in the urban ghettos is crumbling. . . . So long as this situation persists, the cycle of poverty and disadvantage will continue to repeat itself."

The last two decades of history has shown that Moynihan had been remarkably accurate in his forecast. Today, the fraction of black children in single-parent homes is twice that of when his report was released. Moreover, there is now a consensus, among blacks and whites, liberals and conservatives alike, that the birth of children to young, unwed teens is a critical element of the cycle of ghetto poverty. But at the time of its release, his report occasioned a firestorm of political protest, making it impossible that his policy recommendations be adopted. Prominent black intellectuals and politicians attacked Moynihan as a racist, and dismissed his report as an attempt to impose white, middle-class values on poor blacks whose behavior was simply different from, not inferior to, the norm. (For a discussion of the reactions to the "Moynihan Report" see Rainwater and Yancy, 1967.) As a result, plans by the Johnson Administration to develop a national initiative to assist the black family were abandoned, and many years passed before public officials dared to broach the subject again.

This tragic error must not be repeated. Never again should we refuse to acknowledge grave social problems facing any segment of our society. Still, there is the need to maintain a delicate balance when discussing these issues. It is not the proper role of government to mandate the morals of its citizens. Nor should public officials label specific groups of citizens as exhibiting "deviant" or "pathological" behavior. But this does not mean that social norms and community values have no role to play in restraining individuals' antisocial and dysfunctional behavior. Nor does it rule out the possibility that the problems are sometimes more severe for some groups than for others.

Though correct in his emphasis on the problem and his recommendation that public action was necessary, recent historical research has demonstrated that Moynihan's explanation of family problems among blacks as having derived from the slave experience is almost certainly wrong. Racial differences of the extent discussed above are a post-World War II phenomenon, and are not to be found

in the earlier historical record; they therefore cannot be explained by reference to the experience of black slavery. Although national information on family structure first became available only with the 1940 decennial census, examination of early manuscript census forms for individual cities and counties clearly demonstrates that most women heading families in the late nineteenth and early twentieth centuries were widows; that even among the very poor, a substantial majority of the families were intact; and that, for the most part, the positive association between intact family structure and social class was due to the higher rate of mortality among poor men (Furstenberg et al., 1975).

The evidence also demonstrates that among northern, urban black migrant communities in the early twentieth century, the intact family was also the norm. Approximately 85% of black families living in Harlem in 1925 were intact, and the teenage mother raising her children alone was virtually unknown; comparable findings were noted for blacks in Buffalo in 1910 (Gutman, 1976). In 1940 10.1% of white families and 14.9% of black families were female-headed; and though single-parent families were more common among city dwellers, census data from that year indicate that fully 72% of urban black families with children were headed by men (Wilson and Neckerman, 1984). By 1960 the proportion of single-parent families had begun to increase sharply for blacks, rising from 21.7% in 1960, to 28.3% by 1970, and reaching 41.9% in 1983. Among whites the proportion also rose, from 8.1% in 1960 to 12.2% in 1983.

BLACK TEENAGE PREGNANCY: TRENDS AND RESPONSES

We may ask then, if Moynihan's (and Frazier's) sociology was wrong, what accounts for the current group disparity in family instability? Given the higher rate of teenage childbearing among urban blacks, investigators have explored a number of hypotheses to explain this phenomenon. Beginning in the mid-1960s, a series of ethnographic studies involving close observation of specific communities have been undertaken (Clark, 1965; Rainwater, 1970; Stack, 1974; Gilder, 1978). These studies have called attention to cultural and normative factors operative in poor urban communities, deriving from the severe economic hardship of inner-city life, but interacting with governmental income support systems (Gilder, 1978; Murray, 1984) and evolving in such a way as to feed back onto individual behavior and exacerbate this hardship.

Wilson and Neckerman (1984), citing evidence from a survey of black female teens undertaken in 1979 by the Urban League of Chicago and compiled by Dennis Hogan of the University of Chicago, argue that there is an insufficient aversion to unwed pregnancy in this population. The aforementioned data are said to show that black teen mothers reported far fewer pregnancies to be unwanted than their white counterparts (among whom Zelnick and Kanter, 1980, report finding 82% of premarital pregnancies to 15–19 year olds to have been unwanted). Stack, 1974, observing an unnamed midwestern inner-city community, notes "People show pride in all their kin, and particularly new babies born into their kinship networks. Mothers encourage sons to have babies, and even more important, men coax their 'old ladies' to have their baby (p. 121)."

Observation of participants in Project Redirection, a two-year planned intervention with teenagers who had already borne one child out-of-wedlock, which had the objective of preventing the additional pregnancy, confirms that prevailing values and attitudes among these young women and their boyfriends constitute a critical part of the teen pregnancy story (Branch et al., 1984). There it was observed that "Participants who lack self-esteem often find it difficult to resist pressure from boyfriends. . . . Participants tolerate (being beaten by their boyfriends, or exploited economically) believing that,

because of their children, other men will not want them (p. 39)." Moreover, concern at the Harlem site of this project regarding the issue of welfare dependency led to the following observation:

> Staff initially took an activist stance in their efforts to intercede with the welfare system on behalf of participants . . . This pattern changed, however when . . . (certain) behavior patterns were beginning to emerge . . . It seemed that many were beginning to view getting their own welfare grants as the next stage in their careers . . . (I)t became apparent that some participants' requests for separate grants and independent households were too often a sign of manipulation by boyfriends, in whose interest it was to have a girlfriend on welfare with an apartment of her own . . . (S)taff realized that these attitudes and behaviors were . . . counterproductive to the goal of promoting self-sufficiency (Branch et al., p. 60).

Project Redirection involved the use of "community women," older women who befriended and advised the teen mothers over the course of the first year of the study. It is noteworthy that these community women ". . . have come out strongly against emancipated minor status for participants (which allows 15 and 16 year old mothers to obtain public aid, including housing, independently of their parents), feeling that it is better that teens remain under family guidance, no matter how difficult the family situation or conflict may be (Branch et al., 1984:60)." This project had a very limited impact on the sexual behavior and subsequent additional pregnancies of the young women enrolled. Commenting on this outcome Branch et al. (1984) observed: "The major finding is that members of this target group . . . hold a constellation of attitudes and values about boyfriends, sexual relationships, pregnancy and childbearing that are extremely resistant to change. Against the tenacity of these values, the presentation of factual information alone is inadequate to bring about substantial behavioral improvement (p. 103)." These findings lend credence to the view that peer group and community behavioral norms in the inner-city play a substantial role in the explosion of young single parents.

In seeking an appropriate response to these developments we must understand two things: (1) the forces that have caused the teen pregnancy and illegitimate birth rates to be so high in poor black communities; and (2) the manner in which governmental policies and private actions within black communities can combine to counteract these forces. What was missing in 1965, and what remains scarce now, is *combined* public and private actions that can effectively attack the problem. The confusion of values, attitudes and beliefs of black youngsters who produce children for whom they cannot provide must be addressed; and, those aspects of government policy which reinforce, or reward such values must be publicly questioned. It is the job of black civic, political and religious leaders to do the former, and the task of public leadership at the local, state and federal levels to undertake the latter.

It should be stated at the outset that some of the factors influencing the behavior of young people do not lie within anyone's control. Our youth are engaging in sexual activity outside of marriage at a higher rate, and at a younger age than did their parents. Social taboos that exercised some restraint on extramarital sexuality a generation ago have become passé. Yet, though yesterday's moral climate cannot be restored, teaching our young people to behave responsibly in the face of today's social pressures and temptations should be within our grasp. It has traditionally been the role of the family and of religious institutions to instill this sense of responsibility, and so it remains. For blacks, this issue is especially critical.

The National Urban League has taken the lead with its Male Responsibility Campaign.

The program objective is to reach young black males through a national advertising effort of print ads, posters and a radio commercial. Its theme: "Don't make a baby if you can't be a father." With the voluntary cooperation of black newspapers, music associations, and broadcasters it is geared to reach a mass audience. Several aspects of the program deserve special emphasis. First, it illustrates the opportunity for traditional civil rights organizations to provide leadership for the black community on important social issues too sensitive for public agencies. Second, it focuses on the male. Too often intervention is directed exclusively at the teen mother—helping her to return to school and trying to prevent further pregnancies. Third, it harnesses the creative talents and notoriety of prominent blacks to improve the quality of life for ordinary black people.

One often hears the argument that nothing significant can be done about "children having children" until something is done about the lack of economic options for poor ghetto youngsters. Some commentators have suggested that the unemployment of black men is mainly responsible for the family problems observed in this population (Norton, 1985; Wilson and Neckerman, 1984). In their interesting and valuable paper, Wilson and Neckerman note that the numbers of employed black men relative to the numbers of black women of comparable age has declined sharply for every age group of blacks since 1960, with the decline being particularly precipitate for younger men. The low employment of black men is presumed to reduce their propensity to marry, without having a comparable negative effect on the propensity to reproduce. The result is an increasing out-of-wedlock birth rate, with comparable increases in the percentage of families headed by women.

There is, to be sure, a great need to expand employment among poor young people, but more is involved here than limited economic opportunity. The foregoing argument is far from satisfactory, because it presumes what in part needs to be explained—that young men will continue to father children though they know they cannot support them. The link between employment and family responsibilities for men is very complex, and the direction of causality is far from clear. It is arguable, for example, that a man's effort to find and keep work would be greater to the extent that he feels himself primarily responsible for the maintenance of his family.

The fact that so many young black men are fathers but not husbands, and that they do not incur the financial obligations of fatherhood, might then be taken as an explanation of their low levels of employment. A more serious kind of unemployment plagues young men in poor black communities. There many women struggle to raise their children without financial or emotional support from fathers who have jobs, but make no effort to see their children. These men are unemployed with respect to their most important adult responsibility. Yet unlike the hardship caused by a lost job and income, this kind of unemployment can be cured by an act of will. Every means of persuasion should be used to see that both parents take full responsibility for their children.

Unfortunately, some of the crippling social problems evident in poor black communities have been exacerbated by the way public programs and agencies have chosen to treat those problems. Easy and stigma-free availability of public assistance, and the financial penalty imposed when a welfare family takes a job and thereby loses its public housing and medical benefits along with its welfare payments, may discourage responsible behavior by young men and women who bring children into the world without the means to support them. This concern, expressed by Charles Murray in his recent, much debated book *Losing Ground* (Murray, 1984), is of particular significance to blacks, because such a large fraction of our community depends on state and federal assistance.

It is clear from statistical evidence that, while conditions have worsened for the low-income central city black population since the 1960s, the status of blacks with good educations and marketable skills has improved significantly. Increasingly, the black community is becoming divided into a relatively prosperous middle-class and a desperately poor underclass. Though problems of discrimination continue to exist for middle-class blacks, they are minor when compared to the life-threatening conditions and dwindling opportunities poor blacks face. It has become evident that the problems of poor black communities are greater than simply a lack of resources—that the norms and behaviors of residents in these communities contribute to their difficulty. Thus, the question becomes whether government efforts to help have, in any way, served to undermine the normative base of poor black communities.

Murray believes that they have, and his argument deserves the most serious attention. He charges that aspects of the conventional wisdom which has dominated thinking about public policy in the social sciences and allied helping professions since the sixties have contributed to the decline in living standards among inner-city blacks, one aspect of which is the growth of female-headed families. He holds that a complex and delicately balanced system of values and norms regulates the behavior of individuals in poor (and all other) communities, that adverse change in these behavioral norms has occurred in recent decades, and that ideological precepts particular to the liberal wisdom on social policy (e.g., that those in need of public assistance were in no way to be held accountable for the behavior which may have led to their dependency) may have played a key role in abetting this change.

Yet, in our effort to avoid the sin of "blaming the victim," we sacrificed the ability to reward those persons who, though perhaps of modest financial means, conducted themselves in such a way as to avoid falling into the trap of dependency. The status and dignity that people derive from conducting their lives honorably—working to support themselves and their children, raising their sons to stay out of trouble with the law, and their daughters to avoid early unwed pregnancy—was undermined by the idea that poverty is everywhere and always the result of a failure in the system, not the individual. For if those who fail are seldom at fault, those who succeed can only have done so by their good fortune, not their virtue.

This points to what I consider to be the most critical element of any strategy to confront the current black family crisis—the need to promote virtuous behavior among the inner-city poor. This is inevitably a sensitive, controversial matter, one which public officials will often seek to avoid. But it is a crucial aspect of the problem which concerned private leaders in the black community must confront head-on. Among those many black families who have attained middle-class status in the last two decades, there is a keen sense of the importance of instilling in *their* children values and norms consistent with success. It would seem then that there is a responsibility for successful blacks, through religious and civic organizations and personal contacts internal to the black community, to transmit the norms that have proved so useful in shaping their own lives to the black poor who have fallen behind the rest of society (Loury, 1985). One might refer to such an activity as supplying "moral leadership." No one else can do it; the matter is urgent.

Community organizations, public housing resident management associations, churches and the rest must deal with this matter. Mutually concerned people who trust one another enough to be able to exchange criticism must seek to establish and enforce norms of behavior that lie beyond the capacity of the state to promulgate. Government has, after all, limited coercive resources (incarceration, or the denial of financial benefits being the main ones). Communities can invoke more subtle and powerful influences over the behavior of their members. The expectations of people about whom we care constitutes an important source of such influence. Yet to employ these means requires that people be willing to come forward and say: "This is what we believe in; this is what we stand for; yet, look at where we now are."

References

Bane, Mary Jo and David Ellwood (1984), "Single Mothers and their Living Arrangements," unpublished paper, Harvard University.

Branch, Alvia, James Riccio and Janet Quint (1984), *Building Self-Sufficiency in Pregnant and Parenting Teens*, Final Implementation Report of Project Redirection, New York: Manpower Demonstration Research Corporation (April).

Cherlin, Andrew (1981), *Marriage, Divorce and Remarriage*, Cambridge, Ma.: Harvard Univ. Press.

Clark, Kenneth B. (1965), *Dark Ghetto*, New York: Harper & Row.

Frazier, E. Franklin (1939), *The Negro Family in the United States*, Chicago; University of Chicago Press.

Fuch, Victor (1983), *How We Live: An Economic Perspective on Life and Death*, New York: Basic Books.

Furstenberg, Frank (1976), *Unplanned Parenthood: The Social Consequences of Teenage Childbearing*, New York, Free Press.

Gilder, George (1978), *Visible Man: A True Story of Post-Racist America*, New York: Basic Books.

Gutman, Herbert G. (1976), *The Black Family in Slavery and Freedom, 1750–1925*, New York: Pantheon Books.

Hofferth, Sandra L. and Kristin A. Moore (1979), "Early Childbearing and Later Economic Well-Being," *American Sociological* Review, 44:784–815 (October).

Kellam, Sheppard, Margaret Ensminger and R. Jay Turner (1977), "Family Structure and the Mental Health of Children," *Archives of General Psychiatry* 34:1012–22.

Loury, Glenn C. (1985), "The Moral Quandary of the Black Community," *The Public Interest,* No. 79 (Spring).

Moynihan, Daniel P. (1985), "Family and Nation," *The Godkin Lectures,* Harvard University (forthcoming from Harvard University Press).

Murray, Charles (1984), *Losing Ground: American Social Policy 1950–1980,* New York: Basic Books.

O'Connell, Martin and Maurice J. Moore (1980), "The Legitimacy Status of First Births to U.S. Women Aged 15–24, 1939–1978," *Family Planning Perspectives* 12(1): 16–25.

Rainwater, Lee (1970), *Behind Ghetto Walls: Black Families in a Federal Slum,* Chicago: Adeline Publishing Co.

Rainwater, Lee, and William Yancey (1967), *The Moynihan Report and the Politics of Controversy,* Cambridge, Mass.: MIT Press.

Stack, Carol (1974), *All Our Kin: Strategies for Survival in a Black Community,* New York: Harper and Row.

Trussel, J. and J. Menken (1978), "Early Childbearing and Subsequent Fertility," *Family Planning Perspectives* 10(4):209–218.

U.S. Bureau of the Census (1983), "Characteristics of the Population Below Poverty Level: 1982," *Current Population Reports,* P-60, No. 144, Washington, D.C.: Government Printing Office.

U.S. Department of Labor (1965), *The Negro Family: The Case for National Action,* Washington, DC: Government Printing Office.

Wilson, William J. and Katherine M. Neckerman (1984), "Poverty and Family Structure; The Widening Gap Between Evidence and Public Policy Issues," University of Wisconsin-Madison, Institute for Research on Poverty Conference Paper, December 1984.

Zelnick, Melvin and John Kanter (1980), "Sexual Activity, Contraceptive Use and Pregnancy Among Metropolitan-Area Teenagers: 1971–1979," *Family Planning Perspectives* 12:230–237 (September/October).

Public Policy Trends and the Fate of the Black Family*

WILLIAM DARITY, JR., AND
SAMUEL L. MYERS, JR.

HE LOVE, GROWTH, AND NURTURE OF the family is the central hope of unity for the Afro-American. The family, or rather, the extended family, has historically included not only blood relatives, but also neighbors and friends. The family will become more essential to everyday life as government programs are cut back or eliminated. The family will once again have the premier responsibility to come to the aid of the elderly, the poor, the single parent, the unemployed, the ill, the disabled, the homeless, and the jailed. The safety net of concern for the unfortunate and downtrodden is being shifted from the state to the community.

In prehistoric times, the family was the core mechanism for human survival which provided food, care and education of children, and protection from enemies. Later, tribes or clans formed and eventually government was instituted. In Africa, historically, sharing with and caring for one's family had preeminent importance. In the United States, the infamous Dred and Harriet Scott case of 1856–57 was not a personal appeal for Dred Scott's individual freedom from chattel slavery, but a pleading for their recognition as human beings, the right to a family, and to determine the destiny of their two daughters.

Why has the cohesiveness of the Black family been threatened, particularly at a time when unity and solidarity is so important? Among other influences, the cultural shockwave of the 1960's which emphasized the "me" generation has had its impact on Black families, as well as the populace at large. We see the heralding of the rights of children against their parents, women against their men, and sisters against their brothers.

Although individual freedom has its merit, it has been sought to the extent that the burning desire for individual attainment has led to chaos: the chaos of divorce, runaways, castaways, and neighbors who don't know and don't care about one another or one another's property. The "I got mine, now you get yours" philosophy has gone from bedroom to boardroom and cannot lead to optimal outcomes.

*This paper was prepared for presentation at a symposium titled "The Current Economic Revolution and Black America" sponsored by the Center for African and Afro-American Studies and Research at the University of Texas at Austin held April 3–4, 1985. We are grateful to Jewell Mazique for keeping us closer to the path of truth with this effort. Originally published in the *Humboldt Journal of Social Relations*, Vol. 14, Nos. 1 & 2, pages 134–164.

Narcissism has so permeated this society, that we have come to a point where fantasies of unlimited success, power or beauty have replaced concern for the family, the neighbor, and the Afro-American condition.

Further, Afro-American family ties, in particular, were destroyed historically in this country as a key component of chattel slavery, colonialism and imperialism. Diffusion of the Afro-American family was a condition for domestication/dehumanization of captured Africans, and continued post-slavery as a legacy of discrimination and segregation.

In the 1980s Black self-help is essential, although not mutually exclusive of other aid, and must be incorporated socially with the family being one's starting point. Development of secure family ties is a process that takes generations to reach its zenith. The reunification of the family has a great deal of potential in almost all areas of life such as education of our young, development of values conducive to a better society, assistance to those in need, and development of self-confidence and security in all human beings.—*Donna Blackshear, 1985*

PROLOGUE: THE MANAGERIAL AGE

There is a revolution in social relations underway in the United States today. We are witnesses to the rise to dominance of a relatively new social class comprised of intellectuals and the intelligentsia—a managerial class separate from both labor and capital. This "new class" is engaged comprehensively in social control and social management, ultimately, on its own behalf, rather than on behalf of another class.

Many observers have viewed Marx's famous conclusion that capitalist society would come to an end under the weight of its own contradictions—like all previous historical epochs eventually came to an end—as false.[1] The working class has not come to power in the United States nor, arguably, has it come to power anywhere else. But these observers have not understood that the demise of

capitalism need not usher in a "dictatorship of the proleteriat." Instead the winding down of capitalism could bring forth an entirely new elite extending new patterns of domination that replace the previous cultural domination of the business interests. The decline of capitalism and the rise of the managerial estate represents precisely such an overturning and the fulfillment of Marx's conclusion about capitalism's inevitable death—*without* empowerment of the masses.[2]

The newly ascendant managerial class finds its basis for power in its control over knowledge, information, and technique. Its avenue to power lies in its access to the decision-influencing and decision-making positions within the nexus of institutions that coalesce under the labels of government, the universities, and the nonprofit foundations.

Its functional role—the role that provides its class identity—is to identify and design solutions to social problems. Accompanying this role is its ability to direct cultural and ideological development. The essence of its class activity is the production of images and ideas. What delineates the members of this class from all others are professional credentials, however obtained.

The contrast with the once dominant capitalist class could not be sharper.[3] The older class finds its basis for power in its control over money and finance. Its avenue to power lies in its access to the decision-influencing and decision-making positions within the business enterprise. Its functional role is mobilization of labor and introduction of new productivity-enhancing methods. Its motive force is the pursuit of profit. What distinguishes the members of this class from all others is wealth, however obtained.

The rise of the managerial class is not being gained without struggle. Older dominant classes always die hard, and the business and corporate interests are not brushed aside easily in a world where money and finance still exercise great effect. But the presumption here is that in the battle that has been joined between those who produce ideas and those who produce profits, the former are likely victors.

A major indicator of the direction in which the battle has turned is the growing identification of status in modern America with acquisition of degrees and having studied and worked at the "best" institutions or with the "right" persons. Status is linked more closely today with the accumulation of credentials than the accumulation of wealth.[4] In fact, in the eyes of most members of the rising managerial class, the active and open pursuit of fortune-building "has no class."[5] This change in expressed values is only the tip of the iceberg of the underlying change in the balance of power between the managerial and the capitalist classes.

The rising managerial class, as do all rising classes, cloaks itself in altruism.[6] Its members' own descriptions of their actions sound the themes of "enhancement of the commonwealth" or "improvement of the general social welfare." In fact, its professional positions are intimately tied to the provision of collective social services.

But professionalism itself means exclusivity—an exclusivity preserved by erection of standards of entry. This is not to argue that such standards are not legitimate from the standpoint of the tasks to be performed— although at times they are not—but the meeting of such standards separates the members of this class from the rest of the population. Positions are to be obtained on "merit" in the managerial age; the meritocratic ideal is the ideological capstone of the managerial class.[7]

This new class also is unproductive in the sense meant by the Classical economists. Its members do not contribute directly—and in many instances not even indirectly—to the production of profit. In fact, the class's more left-leaning members actively resist the notion that the production of profit should be the center around which to organize civilization. Their views represent the most extensive and self-conscious vision of the destiny of the managerial class.

Paradoxically, the activities of the managerial class are supported out of the social surplus—out of profit.[8] Over the course of this century, growth in productivity has led to an immense rise in the social surplus, facilitating the expansion of a well-educated, unproductive stratum. It is through the appropriation of the social surplus generated under capitalism that a vast development has come about in arenas for planning, research, program administration, and the general "ministering" to the population at large. Companion organizational settings—public sector bureaucracies, think tanks, social service agencies—all require, for their continued existence and operation, diversion of the social surplus in their direction. This diversion has been accomplished primarily through a structure of redistributive policies that have evolved from the New Deal to the present, policies that have *de facto* nurtured the expansion of these managerial institutions.

The continued dependence of the managerial class on profit generated by the traditional, capitalistic sector has led to the great ideological breach within the class. The right-leaning element feels inclined to accommodate and even support a continued significant role for corporate capital while the left-leaning element would prefer to see social production placed directly under the control of their class. Whether the right-leaning element is sincere or merely engaged in a strategic retreat in the face of the political resurgence of the business interests is unimportant. What is important is the fact that this intraclass dispute has shaped the terms of debate during the course of this entire century over the nature of proper economic policy in the United States. It is especially pertinent today in the dispute between proponents of "supply-side economics" and proponents of "industrial policy." But the key point is it is a dispute between the social managers themselves.[9]

It is perhaps ironic that the "new" class is now in a position to openly assess how much space should remain for the corporate interests. Historically, the managerial class was nurtured by corporate capital to perform a supervisory function over the working class both inside and outside the factory.[10] The managerial class's initial appearance in the United States coincided with late 19th century and early 20th century Progressivism and the creation of a cadre of workers ("social" workers) whose purpose was to work with the working class. These new workers were soon to become third party advocates on behalf of the working class laying bare, in hindsight, the difficulty from the beginning: can third party advocates ever genuinely speak on behalf of anyone but themselves?

The newly anointed professionals of the early 20th century—the antecedents of today's managerial class—were, in a direct sense, corporate progeny. They were, however, quite unruly progeny. Their capacity to utilize the crisis of the 1930s to inaugurate a host of reforms—to protect themselves at least as much as to protect the working class from the Great Depression—provided the springboard for managerial independence from immediate control and direction by corporate capital. The New Deal did not unleash the working class; instead it unleashed the managerial class. Additional post-New Deal policy interventions—in particular the Great Society of the 1960s—further extended managerial prerogatives and prerequisites. Unlike the business interests' preferences for limited government within a "structure of natural rights,"[11] the managerial class's impulse always has been toward unlimited government and, hence, unlimited terrain for managerial planning.

This thrust of managerialism has created greater and greater environment difficulties for capital since the New Deal. These difficulties have been articulated by spokespersons for the corporate elite—often recruits from the managerial class—in the form of complaints over a rising wage floor attributed to social transfer programs, an overreaching regulatory apparatus, and excessive wage demands by trade unions. The environment was deemed so unhealthy in the 1970s that corporate capital undertook a pronounced withdrawal from productive investment. The accompanying growth slowdown posed a crisis; for the managerial class had to address how to get growth going again, bringing to the surface the central ideological division among its members. The crisis also provided a political opportunity for corporate capital to attempt to restore the old order and to return their restless progeny back to their "proper place" as capitalist functionaries.

Ronald Reagan's political revolution thus can be seen properly as a counterrevolution against the managerial class's growing power. The Reagan counterrevolution seeks to recreate the labor market conditions of the 1920s—a climate that ostensibly would produce an old-fashioned capitalist boom. To the extent that the retrenchments on New Deal/Great Society programs have taken hold, any current evidence of economic recovery can be taken as signalling the "success" of the effort. But, of course, to restore fully the general market conditions of the 1920s is to subject the economy once more to the boom and bust cycle so characteristic of relatively unregulated industrial economies. The concurrent deregulation of financial institutions plainly points toward restoration of credit market conditions that existed prior to the 1929 crash of the New York Stock Exchange.

In sum, there is a class struggle taking place in America today. One protagonist is corporate capital. The other is the class that increasingly colors the nation's cultural fabric, the managerial class. The working class seems to have been relegated to the sidelines as each of the engaged classes solicits its support in their battle. The business elite mobilizes finance; the managerial elite mobilizes expertise. There are momentary truces in the struggle and occasional alliances—but invariably there is struggle over which class will shape the nation's future.

It is through the lens of this struggle that the status of black Americans and the black American family can be best understood. For, as we have observed elsewhere, "The Black family is caught in a maelstrom of cultural crosscurrents that have evolved in the struggle between the older capitalist elite and the new managerial elite."[12] The deepening crisis in black family life can be traced to the progressive marginalization of black Americans in the unfolding managerial age. The rise in the incidence of impoverished, female-headed families among black Americans is an index of the declining importance attributed to the social presence of black people in modern America. What is occurring with the black family also can be viewed as foreshadowing the fate of other elements of the population that may be deemed superfluous.

BLACK AMERICA IN THE MANAGERIAL AGE

Although both the capitalist and managerial classes seek political support from the working class, dominance by each has quite different implications for the working class. For corporate capital the working class is necessary, since its labor is the source of profit. Even the extraneous element of the working class—those workers not actually employed nor perceived as employable—serve at least two functions. The existence of such an unemployed reserve of labor provides capital with a pool of workers to draw upon freely during periods of rapid industrial expansion and generally serves as a lever to restrain the demands of workers with employment.[13] The only truly useless worker to the capitalist is the one physically unable to work or obstinate enough not to work at any wage rate the capitalist perceives as remunerative.

But for the managerial class the necessity of the working class is merely attributable to the pragmatic recognition that even the current advanced state of machine technology does not yet permit production to be conducted strictly on a machine basis. But the secular momentum of technical change renders more and more labor superfluous from the standpoint of social production. More and more of the working class is rendered redundant with the passage of time—and especially redundant is the fraction of the working class least likely to be put to useful work. From a managerial perspective the "excess" population that carries over from the capitalist era is genuinely unnecessary.[14]

These observations have an important bearing on the position of black Americans as the managerial age unfolds. Black Americans overwhelmingly are part of the working class, but they also are disproportionately part of the *inactive portion* of the working class. For among their numbers are a large percentage of persons rarely employed, deeply entrenched in poverty, most likely to be imprisoned, most likely to be the military's foot soldiers, and least likely to have a sense of optimism about the opportunities offered to them by American society. This extremely deprived fraction of the black working class sociologists now customarily refer to as "the black underclass."[15]

From the standpoint of corporate capital there still may be a place for the black underclass if its members will be productive laborers. The strategists for the business elite express the opinion that members of the black underclass have chosen to avoid work for wages because they have no incentive to do so, given the structure of social transfer programs. From this viewpoint since the black underclass only is expected to be eligible for low wage labor, the availability of a comparable income from social transfers leads to the rational decision to stay out of the regular labor market altogether. So the appropriate policy is to alter or eliminate such transfer programs to create stronger inducements to work. Thus, the business interests press for workfare, more stringent eligibility requirements for transfer programs, and lower levels of benefits.

The managerial class, on the other hand, will find less and less reason to retain such an excess population at all. For its rational view of production—unvarnished by anything but pure efficiency considerations—leads it to see no major reason to maintain a reserve of the unemployed. Over the shorter term the social work bureaucrats will uphold maintenance of the welfare apparatus and resist reforms that eliminate their administrative and supervisory positions. But in the longer term the managerial class will restructure itself, reducing class dependence on positions within the welfare bureaucracy and increasing class reliance on more purely technocratic positions. The sheer "planning" impulse will overwhelm the "helping" impulse. The current assault on the welfare system by capital could prove fortuitous for the technocratic core of the managerial elite, insofar as it creates a pretext to pare away relatively weaker and less indispensable fractions of their class. In the meantime, however, the fraction of the managerial class that is ensconced within the welfare bureaucracy will fight to maintain the welfare system regardless of whether or not the system uplifts the poor.[16] Moreover, the "helping" element of the managerial class provides the help of the paternalist.

Over the long term the managerial class is likely to move to eradicate "useless" layers of the working class. Since those layers most likely to be deemed superfluous are disproportionately black, then the fates have grim times in store for the black underclass. The managerial class in its more humanitarian guise will advocate programs to change members of the black underclass into people more like members of the managerial class (manpower training, educational programs, etc.). As frustration accelerates with such a project, the managers will push for racially targeted population control measures.

The superfluity of the black underclass—from the perspectives of both elites—is reinforced not only by technological developments that reduce the social necessity of all labor, inclusive of black labor, but it is aggravated further by the new immigrants. The latter stand as replacements. They are less jaded, more enthusiastic, less rebellious, and cheaper workers, unaccustomed to the "cushion" provided by the American social transfer scheme.

In the short term the managerial class may promise and even deliver a renewed expansion of social programs to garner black political support—in part because of the interests of the social welfare bureaucracy. But the longer term tendency is for the broader managerial class to prune away superfluous elements of other classes as well as their own. Once power is consolidated the voting power of blacks no longer will be required and the nonaccommodative black poor may be viewed as simply *too* expensive. Steps will be taken to prune away the black underclass and, subsequently, an equally superfluous, weaker fraction of its own class, the black social managers.

Why will the black social managers be deemed unnecessary? The black social managers—largely equivalent to the black middle class—hold positions in the public sector that involve administration of the same social programs in which the black poor are overrepresented as clientele. The recent growth and "progress" of black professionals can be traced directly to the expansion of social welfare programs under the rubric of the Great Society.[17] If the black underclass is deemed altogether unnecessary, then the segment of the black population that "ministers" to the underclass will have no social function either. What purpose is there for service providers if there are no longer service recipients? The black members of the managerial class are far more deeply tied to administration of social welfare programs than white members of the class.

While capitalist society seeks to make every black a worker, managerial society calls into question the existence of the race. Corporate capital threatens the class position of blacks whose affluence and status hinge on the perpetuation of social welfare program administration, but managerialism threatens the existence of black America as a cultural entity. Managerial society, more than any before, is liable to declare "the Negro" obsolete.

This is the context in which we find the typical black family today, buffeted between the punitive policies of the business elite and the exterminative policies of the managerial elite. Both sets of policies aim at reducing the black dependent population—the first by dint of the coercion of starvation and the latter by dint of the "voluntarism" of reproductive choice.

THE BLACK FAMILY AND THE FAMILY POLICY OF THE BUSINESS ELITE

One of the major instruments of government policy regulating the lives of a large segment of the black population in the United States is public welfare. A currently perceived emergency in the public welfare system justifiably can be identified with the emergency conditions in black family life. More than half of the long-term recipients (8 or more years) of welfare between 1969 and 1978 were black. Sixty percent of all black females who were heads of households or wives in 1970 received welfare at some point between 1969 and 1978. Among these women, 40 percent received welfare for five years or more and 30 percent received welfare for eight years or more.[18]

Dependence of the black poor on welfare payments is only one of many ways the black underclass relies on a variety of federal transfer programs as a major or primary source of income:

> One out of every four blacks in America is now enrolled in Medicaid . . . One of four gets stamps . . . One out of every five receives aid to families with dependent children [AFDC] . . . One of every seven lives in federally subsidized housing.[19]

Such statistics display the magnitude of black dependence on the overall structure of social transfer programs that move revenues from those above to those below on the income ladder. Numerous social planners, including many affiliated with both major political parties but especially those within the Reagan camp, now argue that perverse outcomes result from such dependency. They contend that public assistance saps the initiative to work and robs individuals of the desire even to seek gainful employment. More dramatically they argue that AFDC or welfare has anti-family consequences, contending that it induces women to leave their husbands or to have babies out-of-wedlock in order to qualify for the public largesse.

These effects often are alleged to reach full confirmation in the case of the black family where both female headship and welfare dependency have grown at astonishing rates over the past two decades alone. The Reagan administration policy circle wears the hats of conventionally-minded economists, contending that the structure of transfer payments to the poor creates incentives for women to form families without a male partner as well as incentives for both them and the males to stay out of the labor market.

But such starkly economistic explanations do not provide a sufficiently rich basis for understanding the key transitions in the pattern of black dependency in the United States. In slavery times the dependent condition of blacks generally was viewed as desirable by nonblack elements of the society; today black dependency on the so-called social "safety net" is viewed as an albatross by much of the rest of American society. Nor does the individualistic, materialistic model of childbearing and marital behavior provide an adequate foundation for understanding the growth in female headship among black families.

Furthermore, the motives of the Reagan planners are by no means pure. The pro-family veneer of their argument merely masks the consistency of their thrust toward eradication of the New Deal, for the New Deal laid the building blocks for the managerial class's revolution. The assault on the structure of transfer payments for the poor is intended less as an attack on the poor as it is intended as an attack on the managerial class's independence from capital. Moreover, the rhetoric of restoration of the two-parent family with the woman in the home performing the traditional nurturing function is incompatible with the administration's policy initiatives that seek to discharge welfare mothers from the dole and into the workforce.

In a recent study we asked "Does Welfare Dependency Cause Female Headship?"[20] We concluded that statistical evidence for the post–World War II period throws up a negative answer with respect to the black family. If anything, the statistical evidence may be mounted more readily to support a reverse causal relationship. Administrative and legislative mechanisms for determining welfare eligibility and benefit levels probably make increased female headship among blacks the statistical driving force behind increased welfare dependency. The 1970s, a period that witnessed a spectacular increase in female headship among black families, also was a decade when real benefit levels actually declined for welfare recipients.

The Reagan administration's proposed work requirements for mothers and new age limitations on eligibility of children in welfare families have their prelude in the workfare experiments now underway at the state level.[21] This sort of welfare reform may be desirable on other scores, but when it is offered ostensibly to "save the family" the case is unpersuasive. Even if the existence of the American welfare system facilitated development of female-headed families over a long period of time, more stringent eligibility requirements

or lower benefit levels today will not have the reverse effect. The forces perpetuating female headship among black families now go far beyond the scheme of social transfer payments. Welfare cutbacks will do no more than what such steps are administratively capable of doing—reduce the numbers of welfare recipients and reduce the expense of the system. Rejuvenative effects on the family, however, are unlikely to materialize. A more austere welfare system or a workfare reform is not liable to reduce out-of-wedlock births, reduce the number of female-headed families, or, for that matter, increase the earned income of these families, even if mothers can find suitable day care when they go to work at whatever low paid jobs they can find.

Our research suggests that the most salient correlate with the growth in female headship among black American families is the sex ratio. This signals, in our estimation, the more profound problem of the general vulnerability of blacks in the evolving era. The matter can be highlighted by reviewing in detail current trends in black family structure.

The fraction of black families headed by females grew from a customary 25 percent in the 1950's to the startling proportion of more than 45 percent in recent years. This has occurred during a period when family incomes have improved slightly. In 1969 the median black family income was $10,783 in 1978 dollars. By 1978 the median black family income had increased 1 percent to $10,879. Simultaneously, the median income of female-headed families actually declined. In 1969 it was $5,946; by 1978 it had fallen to $5,888. This illustrates an important pattern. Black families are increasingly headed by females, and female-headed families have been sinking deeper into poverty.

Less than a fifth of all black families receiving total money incomes of $5,000 or less now are intact, married couple families. In contrast, almost 90 percent of black families with money incomes in excess of $20,000 are married couple families. Moreover, poverty strikes hardest among those female-headed families with young children. While one-half of the persons in black female-headed families fell below the official poverty level in 1978, more than two-thirds of the children living in female-headed families fell below the poverty line. As a symptom of this, median income was lowest among female heads under 24 among all female-headed families in 1978. What is worse is that the real incomes in these families headed by young women have seen the sharpest drop between 1969 and 1978. In 1969 incomes for these young families averaged $4,114 in constant 1978 dollars. By 1978, these young families averaged only $3,584.

Although increasing numbers of female heads of families are entering the labor force—perhaps under the pressure of the workfare regulations—fewer are finding jobs. Among blacks the labor force participation rate for female family heads rose from 50 percent in 1970 to 54 percent in 1979. But their unemployment rate rose to 13 percent in 1979, nearly twice as high as at the start of the decade. Those who could find jobs were employed as service workers (36 percent) and as clerical workers (28 percent).[22] Thus the trend toward the formation of households among black women is met with an increasingly bleak employment outlook. While service and clerical jobs are certain to remain in abundant supply, the incomes that they can expect to generate are unlikely to reverse the continued plunge into poverty of their recipients.

This finding is of great importance in understanding the consequences of welfare reforms that purport to increase work incentives by reducing benefits and instituting more rigid job search or employment requirements. Workfare may help to increase labor force participation among women with children, it may reduce the number of mothers and their children who are eligible for welfare, and it may reduce the costs

of the welfare system, but will it increase the incomes of female-headed families? If the employment experience of welfare recipients in the late 1970's is any guide, the answer may be no. In 1977, for example, the large majority of mothers in AFDC recipient families were not employed. Although 10.6 percent were actively seeking work, only 8.4 percent were employed full time, with another 5.4 percent employed part-time. By 1979, the distribution of those seeking work and those working remained about the same. In that year 10 percent of the AFDC mothers were actively seeking work, 8.8 percent were employed full-time and 5.4 percent were employed part-time. But a shift in those short two years occurred in the composition of the welfare population: it was becoming younger and less experienced in the labor market. Job tenure fell and the fraction of mothers with no known prior work experience rose. While in 1977 almost 280,000 of the more than 3.2 million mothers of AFDC recipient children had been on a current job for more than one half of a year, in 1979 of the reduced welfare population of 3.1 million mothers only 234,000 had such job tenure. Moreover, most had no prior work experience at all. In 1977 the percent who had never worked was 43; it rose to 44.1 percent two years later.[23]

The explicit move toward welfare reforms that attempt to increase work incentives by lowering the fraction of basic needs covered by the AFDC benefit or by incorporating work requirements runs counter to the trend among black female-headed and largely welfare dependent families.[24] These families are increasingly being headed by younger and more inexperienced workers.

And while the new female-headed families among blacks that are being formed are increasingly ones with younger, never married heads, the outlook for their becoming married—presumably losing their welfare eligibility—is bleak. Age at first marriage has been rising steadily among blacks and the fraction of black women who were ever married by the age of 44 has been declining. Historically more than 90 percent of black women have been married by the age of 44; in the 1970's this fraction fell to 75 percent. Fully one third of black women had never been married by the age of 44 in 1980.[25]

Poverty and female headship intertwine among black families. The phenomenon can be linked directly to a declining pool of eligible male partners for black women.

Mortality rates among blacks have been falling. In 1950 the age-adjusted mortality rate for black females of all ages was 1,107 per 100,000.[26] In 1960 it was 917 and in 1970 it was 814. By 1979, moreover, the number of deaths per 100,000 resident population fell to 636. Black women are experiencing lower death rates and the trend seems to be toward further declines.

Mortality rates have been falling for black men also. In 1950 the age-adjusted number of deaths per 100,000 resident population for all ages of black men was 1,373. In 1960 this rate was 1,246, but in 1970, at the height of the Vietnam War, it rose again to 1,317.[27] Thus black males are experiencing lower death rates, although the decline has not occurred steadily over the past three decades.

At least in the decade of the seventies the impact of declining death rates among *both* black men and black women has been to leave

relatively unchanged the historically high ratio of black women to black men. Just among those over 18, for example, the ratio crept up almost imperceptibly from 1.18 in 1970 to 1.19 in 1979, as seen in Table 1 (for every 100 black men in 1970 there were 118 black women). Among 20 to 24 year olds, by illustration, one finds that the ratio of black women to black men actually fell from 1.15 to 1.09 over the decade despite the astonishingly high mortality rates among young black males during the Vietnam War and the aforementioned fall in black female mortality rates in the early 1970s. But even in the older age group of 34 to 39 year olds the female-male ratio dropped slightly for blacks in the last decade.

These short-run patterns, apparently deviating from the quarter century old decline in the relative supply of black men, at best obscure what we view as a significant marginalization of black men in America. This marginalization is manifest in their declining role as providers and leaders of their own families. In particular, the reduction in the supply of potential husbands for black women is real and, even in the most recent years, has reached alarming proportions.

Table 2 provides a different perspective on the sex-ratio phenomenon among blacks. Instead of calculating the ratio of females to males in identical age groups we examined the

TABLE 1 BLACK FEMALE-MALE RATIOS 1970–1979

	Over 18	**18–65**	**20–24**	**25–29**	**30–34**	**34–39**
1970	1.18439	1.16816	1.15439	1.17018	1.20419	1.21296
1971	1.18263	1.16473	1.13127	1.16667	1.20034	1.21402
1972	1.18081	1.15994	1.11235	1.15950	1.19386	1.21350
1973	1.18268	1.15991	1.10884	1.15415	1.18731	1.21416
1974	1.18386	1.15906	1.10541	1.15080	1.18182	1.21544
1975	1.18576	1.15921	1.10394	1.14884	1.18156	1.21809
1976	1.18560	1.15761	1.09741	1.14532	1.17847	1.21515
1977	1.18768	1.15867	1.09331	1.14611	1.17560	1.20930
1978	1.18968	1.15956	1.09440	1.14257	1.17092	1.20607
1979	1.19148	1.16041	1.09402	1.14245	1.16927	1.20216

five-year age cohorts where men are two years older. For example, we compared women in the 10 to 24 year old group with men in the 22 to 26 year old group. This more nearly captures an "availability" ratio because among men and women who do marry, the age differential is on average two years.

Whereas Table 1 revealed that when we calculate the sex ratio with comparable age groups there were 9 percent more black women than black men in 1980 in the 20 to 24 year old group, Table 2 shows that the excess of women 20 to 24 over men who are 22 to 26 is 16 percent. As women age, moreover, the excess increases. For women over 25 there are more than one and a quarter as many females as there are men two years

older. Since 1970 this excess of women over men has risen fairly steadily.

The plight of marriageable women over 25 is further underscored by the figures in Table 3 which provides a third way to look at the sex ratio. Here we consider the ratio of women to men five years older. Not only is the excess even larger—approaching fifty percent in 1980—but it shows even more clearly the creeping trend upward in the ratio of women to men. The marriage prospects of women are not improving in part because those men who do marry, marry younger women, and the supply of relatively older men declines more rapidly than that of relatively older women.

A further slice of evidence on the worsening of the sex ratios among blacks is found

TABLE 2 BLACK FEMALE-MALE RATIOS 1970–1979

Females Males	20–24 22–26	25–29 27–31	30–34 32–36	35–39 37–41
1970	1.22457	1.20840	1.27778	1.22659
1971	1.22970	1.16607	1.29401	1.22761
1972	1.28538	1.25904	1.28970	1.23148
1973	1.21772	1.29204	1.29125	1.23432
1974	1.19939	1.29126	1.28110	1.23450
1975	1.19728	1.30171	1.26935	1.24682
1976	1.18750	1.31520	1.23994	1.26750
1977	1.18638	1.28605	1.26369	1.29078
1978	1.17931	1.24220	1.30028	1.29948
1979	1.16268	1.24663	1.30563	1.29402

TABLE 3 BLACK FEMALE-MALE RATIOS 1970–1979

Females Males	20–24 22–29	25–29 30–34	30–34 35–39
1970	1.48645	1.35602	1.27778
1971	1.56342	1.33165	1.31550
1972	1.52427	1.35057	1.34854
1973	1.50329	1.35604	1.39201
1974	1.46477	1.38748	1.42370
1975	1.43256	1.42363	1.45390
1976	1.37029	1.50708	1.43201
1977	1.37202	1.48257	1.45681
1978	1.35446	1.47194	1.46645
1979	1.33713	1.44418	1.50309

in Table 4. Here we consider the female-male ratio in identical five-year cohorts from birth until age thirty for five year intervals from 1960 to 1980. Under age 15, the ratio is very nearly equal to one in the entire twenty year span. Parity exists during the late teens as well. When one includes the total population, including incarcerated males and those in the armed forces overseas, one sees that since the mid-1960's there has been a major jump in the black female-male ratio between the teen years and the young adult years. In 1970, for example, there were about as many 15 to 19 year old black females as there were black males in that age group. There were seven percent more females than males in the 20 to 24 year old group, however. By including the young males in the armed forces we discover many of the missing men hidden in Table 1. Similarly in 1975, there was near parity in the teens but an excess of females over males by seven percent in the early twenties. The situation worsens by 1980; there is still parity in the teens, but the excess grows to nine percent in the early twenties.

Is the sex ratio problem a transitory one, one that is a purely demographic phenomenon linked perhaps to the high death rates resulting from the Vietnam War, one that provides pessimism for older women but will not affect the next generation of mothers? Recognizing that the twenty year olds of today were the fifteen year olds of five years ago, we computed a value that addresses this question. In Table 5 we calculated the ratio of the sex ratio in a given birth cohort in a given year to the corresponding sex ratio for the same cohort in a given year to the corresponding sex ratio for the same cohort five years later. For example, the entry in the transition matrix

TABLE 4 BLACK FEMALE-MALE RATIOS FOR FIVE YEAR COHORTS AND FIVE YEAR INTERVALS (TOTAL POPULATION INCLUDING ARMED FORCES OVERSEAS)

Year	Age Cohort						
	Under 5	*5–9*	*10–14*	*15–19*	*20–24*	*25–29*	*30–34*
1960	1.0027	1.0025	1.0030	1.0203	1.1056	1.1337	1.1588
1965	.9874	1.004	1.0041	1.0050	1.0269	1.1128	1.1408
1970	.9951	.9942	.9979	1.0082	1.0741	1.1462	1.1856
1975	.9810	.9890	1.0000	1.0724	1.1418	1.1801	
1980	.9838	.9842	.9889	1.0040	1.0947	1.1402	1.1678

Source: Current Population Reports, *Population Estimates and Projections*, Series P-25, Nos. 385, 721, 800 and 917.

TABLE 5[a] AGE COHORT SHIFTS IN BLACK FEMALE-MALE RATIOS (TOTAL POPULATION INCLUDING ARMED SERVICES)

Year	Ratio of Female-Male Ratio in Cohort i and Year t to Female-Male Ratio in Cohort i + 5, Year t + 5						
	Under 5	*5–9*	*10–14*	*15–19*	*20–24*	*25–29*	*30–34*
1960	—	—	—	—	—	—	—
1965	—	1.00	1.00	1.00	.99	.99	.99
1970	—	.99	1.01	1.00	.94	.90	.94
1975	—	1.00	1.01	1.00	.94	.94	.97
1980	—	1.00	1.01	.99	.91	.94	.98

a. Computed from Table 4.

under 20–24 for 1965 is .99. This is the ratio of the sex ratio in 1960 for 15 to 19 year olds to the sex ratio in 1965 for 20 to 24 year olds.

From the previous Table 4 we find that the numerator and denominator are 1.0203 and 1.0269 respectively, yielding a value of .99. The obvious interpretation of this statistic is the ratio of the percent of men who "survive" as compared to women who "survive." It also is equal to the ratio of the relative change in the number of women, over the five year span. So, in the case of blacks who were 20 to 24 year olds in 1965, 1 percent fewer males than females survived the transition from teenage to young adulthood.

What Table 5 reveals starkly is that fewer and fewer young black males are making the transition since the 1960's. In 1970, .94 times as many 20 to 24 year old black males from the previous five years' cohort of 15 to 19 year olds survived as did females. That is, 6 percent fewer male teenagers than female teenagers made the transition. By 1980, 9 percent fewer males than females were making the transition. Indeed, in 1980, the transition from the 10 to 14 year old age group to the 15 to 19 year old age group showed a slipping of the grasp of young males as they move into late adolescence. Only .99 times as many boys made the transition as did girls. This does not bode well for the future generation of black women for whom fatherless families have become, even at an early age, an unwelcomed reality.

The three most important sources of death among black males in recent years have been heart disease, cancer and accidents. Of the 1090 deaths per 10,000 black men of all ages in 1979, 319 were due to heart disease, 224 were due to various cancers, and 82 came about as a result of accidents and their adverse effects.

Young black men do not have the highest death rates among black men; infants and men over 55 share this distinction. But the transition from youth to young adulthood is a very uncertain event for many. Whereas 50 out of every 100,000 5 to 14 year olds died

in 1979, 204 out of 100,000 15–24 year olds died in that year. The death rate for young black men in the 15 to 25 year old group was actually lower in 1979 than it was in 1970 and has been declining steadily over the decade, but the transition from youth to adulthood has become no more stable. The jump in death rates between the childhood years and the young adult years has remained staggering in recent years. In 1970, the death rate among black males 5 to 14 years old was 67 per 100,000. In 1979 it was 50 per 100,000. Thus even though the death rates have fallen the chances of a 15 to 24 year old black male dying are still four or more times that of a 5 to 14 year old.

How does the death rate in 1970 among 15 to 24 year olds break down? Fifteen of those are due to suicide, far more deaths among black males than the 5 per 100,000 in 1950 or the 10 per 100,000 in 1970. Another 36 of the deaths per 100,000 are accounted for by motor vehicle accidents, a rate which is almost the same as the average death rate for black males *of all ages.* By far the largest killer of young black men, however, is homicide. Seventy-nine of the 203 deaths per 100,000 black males aged 15 to 24 were classified as murders. Nearly forty percent of all of the deaths in this age group among black males can be attributed to homicides. Violent death, unfortunately, has become increasingly the fate of these young men. In 1950, 20 percent of deaths in the 15 to 24 year old group of black males were due to homicides. In 1960 this percent rose to 22. By 1970, the rate was 32 percent.

Death by violence is a recent, post-1960 dominating cause of the depletion of the supply of black men in the young adult and late adolescence stages. Marginalization can lead to self-destruction. As of now we only can speculate at the relationship with gang and police violence. The business elite's policies—aimed at altering the structure of social welfare payments—does not address the outcast status of the young black underclass male. Therefore, it affords no genuine hope of "saving" the black family.

THE BLACK FAMILY AND THE FAMILY POLICIES OF THE MANAGERIAL ELITE

As the helping face of the managerial class increasingly gives way to the purely planning face, its anti-populationist and anti-natalist inclinations will become more and more apparent. The managerial class's extermi- native disposition towards the underclass emerges most plainly already in the embrace of the premises of the "women's agenda" by large numbers of its members. The specific aspect of the women's agenda that is perti- nent to attempts to cope with the welfare system emergency is the emergence of an anti- natalist reproductive policy in the United States, under the cloak of freedom of choice for women.

Groups like the Planned Parenthood Federation (PPF) have advocated reduction of the numbers of children born-out-of-wedlock via effective family planning measures, includ- ing abortion. Such reductions PPF spokes- persons argue would be a crucial step in reducing the supply of welfare eligible persons. It is now conventional for family planning advocates to suggest that expanded legal avail- ability of abortion to welfare eligible women will lower the costs of the welfare system.

As early as 1967 J. William Leasure attempted to construct a case for the pecu- niary advantages of birth control using North Carolina data, based in part upon the preven- tion of births of children who would subse- quently require support from public health and welfare programs.[28]

A more recent case has been made for preserving the availability of federal funds to finance abortions by low-income women to reduce the long-term costs of social transfer programs. Paul Sommers and Laura Thomas have analyzed what they call "the fiscal impact" of the Hyde Amendment by inquiring about

"the average cost to the taxpayer of rearing a child from birth to 18 years of age . . ."[29] They argue that children who are "unwanted" and "from low-income high-fertility homes experience difficulty entering the labor force and finding gainful employment."[30] They do not address whether "unwantedness" and "low-income" status are the fundamental causes of these youth's employment problems. They proceed instead to contend that ". . . it seems likely that the tax revenue provided by such individuals would be less than the cost to all levels of government of providing them with necessary social services."[31]

Sommers and Thomas conclude that the expected behavior of the offspring that were "unwanted births" of low-income women imposes a greater cost on society in a fiscal sense than their contribution. Using an earlier study by Willard Cates,[32] they observe that "restrictions on Medicaid funding of abortions probably compelled 14,000–30,000 women to have unintended births in 1978—births they would otherwise have terminated by abortion. If costs are discounted at 5 percent, we estimate the public cost in 1978 to be $342–732 million compared to the $86 million actually spent on publicly funded abortions a year before enforcement of the Hyde Amendment."[33]

Aside from the troublesome notion of "unwantedness" which they accept without question, the social costs of restricting abor- tion are identified exclusively with the fertility of low-income women. Sommers and Thomas do not even bother to ask about the "costs" and "benefits" of ending the women's low- income status. Sommers and Thomas are fatalistic not only about the lives to be lived by the offspring of poorer women who, at some state in their pregnancy did not want to carry it to term, but they also are fatalistic about prospects for the women themselves.

Sommers and Thomas thus express the height of managerial impulses toward the underclass—a doctrine of *preemptive extermina- tion* of the unborn.[34] Such elimination will

occur silently through the "voluntary decisions" of the mothers. These 14,000 to 30,000
"unintended births" constitute in their view
an excess fertility or an expendable stratum of
the population. One wonders, are the criteria
of "low-income" and "unwantedness" any
more valid than any other criteria advanced
by eugenicists early in the 20th century?

Even more striking in this regard is an
important new national Bureau of Economic
Research study on neonatal mortality in the
United States.[35] Hope Corman and Michael
Grossman find that there has been a narrowing in the gap between black and white infant
mortality rates. Both rates declined between
1964 and 1977, but the still higher black rate
fell more than the white rate.

But what is disturbing about the Corman
and Grossman study is the conclusion they
draw from one of their central findings.
Corman and Grossman discover that the
major factor contributing to the decline in the
black infant mortality was the greater availability of abortion substantially outweighing
the availability of prenatal care. This leads them
to conclude that political successes for the anti-
abortion movement are inimical to the goal of
reducing black neonatal mortality.[36]

Presumably Corman and Grossman are
assuming that the mechanism whereby abortion exercises salutory effects on black neonatal
mortality is by preventing the births of a good
proportion of infants with a low probability of
surviving the first month of life. Of course, the
availability of abortion does not neatly select
out only those infants who are "weakest." And,
again, should the "weakest" infants not be given
the opportunity to survive past birth? When the
doctrine of preemptive extermination becomes
operative such questions are not raised or, if
raised, they are swept aside.[37]

Managerial family policy thus points directly
toward curbing the numbers of the black
underclass and, concomitantly, curbing the
numbers of those on the welfare rolls. The
managerial class and the underclass both are

supported by a redistribution of the social
surplus, but the less visible transfers to the
class in power are not to be given the negative
attention devoted to the transfers to the
surplus population.

Of course managerial family policy is not
limited to reproductive policy. It extends to
a vision of the "new family," which need have
no specific characteristics or structure. There
is no presumed form families *must* take in the
managerial age.[38] Female headship need not
be an index of familial decline, simply one
of an infinity of options, reflecting an openness to diversity under managerialism.

But again, as we have observed earlier,
"Despite a professed agnosticism over the
'correct' family form, the managerial elite
endorses policies that operate against maintenance of the two-parent, male-headed family."[39]
These policies, largely consonant with the
premises of feminist ideology, promote independence of women from men as familial
partners, embodied, for example, in the
Economic Equity Act, parts of which passed
in the last session of Congress.

More telling still, those women most likely
to be without male partners in a family—
black women—can find little concrete assistance from such policy initiatives. Although
black women's support has been enlisted
by organizations such as NOW on behalf of
such proposals, the proposals are meant for
women of a different social class from most
black female family heads.

As Julianne Malveaux has observed, aside
from provisions concerning child care, there
is "little of interest" to black poor women in
the Economic Equity Act:

> The tax retirement reforms proposed
> would affect few black women, since so
> many black women head families and since
> so many black women's spouses do not
> participate in the labor force. The treatment
> of pensions as a property right, though
> important for [white] woman, may mean
> little to minority women.

Provisions to enforce child support judg-ments were part of the Economic Equity Act. Because the earnings of many black men are so low, black women will gain little from "mandatory wage assignments" for child support benefits. In fact, where black men earn marginal wages, the mandatory reduction of wages to pay child support may make it difficult for men to afford to participate in the legal labor force.

While no one would argue that black men should be exempt from paying child support, high poverty rates in the black community suggest that job creation might save more black children from poverty than will mandatory enforcement of child support awards, especially when men are unable to pay.[40]

Malveaux's central point is that, despite the best efforts of the proponents of the notion of the "feminization of poverty," the poverty of black Americans is not separable into male and female components.

EPILOGUE: THE FUTURE?

Consider the vise confronting many black women contemplating motherhood. Potential income from the labor market does not appear grand. Income from social transfer programs is being eroded in the face of the resurgence of the business interests. Under such conditions many black women may accept the managerial class's "offer" to forgo motherhood altogether—"voluntarily" choos-ing to terminate a pregnancy when there really is no other choice. Caught in the cross-fire the most vulnerable are the most prone toward genocide.

Is there a way out? The only conceivable route must be an alliance of all the dispos-sessed that resists the impulses of *both* elites. For as we noted above blacks are not the only segment of the population whose family life and very existence are threatened by the effects of the current struggle for class power in the United States. There is a generalized sense across wide segments of America's working class that the family is in danger and that, correspondingly, social cohesion is in danger as well. Such angst may be the cornerstone for the joining of hands of all those who are victims of social experimentation conducted from above.

Notes

1. See Marx's development of the "law of the tendency of the rate of profit to fall." In Karl Marx, *Capital: Volume 3*. New York: Vintage Books 1981, pp. 317–75.

2. For a fuller development of the view that the end of capitalism need not mean a successful proletarian revolution see William Darity Jr., Ronald Johnson, and Edward Thompson "The Political Economy of U.S. Energy and Equity Policy." In Hans Landsberg (ed.). *High Energy Costs: Assessing the Burden.* Washington D.C.: Resources for the Future 1982 and Erik Olin Wright "Capitalism's Futures." *Socialist Review,* March/April 1983, pp. 77–126.

3. For a thorough, penetrating and debunking analysis of the era in which the power of the 'captains of industry' had attained its greatest height see Thorstein Veblen, *The Theory of Business Enterprise.* New York: Charles Scribners & Sons 1904.

4. In the academic context the attention and interpretation contemporary economists devote to Adam Smith's concept of "human capital" is a reflection of this societal shift in emphasis from acquisition of financial wealth to acquisition of educational or work experi-ence credentials. Economists, nevertheless, tend to conflate the two.

5. See David Lebedoff "The Dangerous Arrogance of the New Elite." *Esquire* August 29, 1978, pp. 10–27 and Jean-Christophe Agnew "A Touch of Class." *Democracy,* Spring 1983, pp. 59–72.

6. James Burnham wrote in *The Managerial Revolution: What Is Happening In the World Today.* New York: John Day 1941, p. 193: "Managers tend to identify the welfare of mankind as a whole with their own interests and the salvation of mankind with their assuming control of society."

7. A second, related ideological principle that resonates well with the managerial class is equal opportunity—the notion that there should be a "fair" environment that permits any individual with ability and motivation to cross the barrier set by entire standards. Thus, the managerial class pictures itself as a group toward which there is open access for all who display sufficient "merit" to be admitted as members.

8. See, e.g., Paul Zarembka (ed.) "The Capitalist Mode of Production: Economic Structure." *Research in Political Economy* Vol. 1. Greenwich: JAI Press, 1977, pp. 19–22.

9. For an interesting discussion of intra-managerial disputes over macro-stabilization policy see Kathryn E. Allen "The Phillips Curve Controversy and Orthodox Visions of the Labor Market." In William Darity Jr. (ed.). *Labor Economics: Modern Views.* Hingham: Kluwer-Nijhoff 1984.

10. See Barbara and John Ehrenreich "The Professional-Managerial Class." In Pat Walker (ed.) *Between Labor and Capital,* Boston: South End Press 1979.

11. Veblen, op. cit., p. 376.

12. William Darity Jr. and Samuel Myers Jr. "Public Policy and the Condition of Black Family Life." *The Review of Black Political Economy* Vol. 13: Nos. 1–2, Summer-Fall 1984, p. 180.

13. Karl Marx. *Capital: Volume 1.* New York: Vintage Books pp. 784–794.

14. See William Darity Jr. "The Managerial Class and Surplus Population. *Society,* November-December 1983, pp. 54–62.

15. See William J. Wilson. *The Declining Significance of Race.* Chicago: The University of Chicago Press, 1980.

16. Evidence of the impact of the capitalist counter-revolution has been pronounced lately in the social work profession. In 1972 only 3.3 percent of all social workers were employed in the private sector, whereas by 1983 the proportion had risen to 12 percent. See Jacqueline Trescott "The New Breed of People Who Help." *The Washington Post.* November 27, 1983 p. K1. The rise in the proportion was attributed to "reductions in public funding as well as expanding opportunities." A similar push is evident in the medical and health services field with the development and implementation of various proposals to "privatize" the delivery of such services. See Judith Feder, John Holahan, Randall R. Bonbjerg, and Jack Hadley "Health." In Isabel Sawhill and John Palmer (eds.). *The Reagan Experiment.* Washington D.C.: The Urban Institute 1982. This pattern suggests that the "helping" fraction of the managerial elite finds it easier to land on their feet than their clients.

17. Michael K. Brown and Steven P. Erie. "Blacks and the Legacy of the Great Society: The Economic and Political Impact of Federal Social Policy." *Public Policy,* Summer 1981, pp. 308–309.

18. Richard Coe. "Welfare Dependency: Fact or Myth?" *Challenge,* September/October 1982, pp. 43–49.

19. Milton Coleman. "More Reliant on Aid Than Whites, Blacks Hit Hard by Cuts." *The Washington Post,* December 4, 1983, p. A1.

20. William Darity Jr. and Samuel L. Myers Jr. "Does Welfare Dependency Cause Female Headship? The Case of the Black Family." *Journal of Marriage and the Family,* November 1984.

21. See, e.g., *Workfare: The Impact of Ihe Reagan Program on Employment and Training.* From a conference sponsored by the National Council on Employment Policy, June 17, 1983.

22. U.S. Bureau of the Census, Current Population Reports, "Families Headed By Female Householders 1970–1979." No. 107, Tables 21, 19, 15, 16, p. 23.

23. U.S. Department of Health and Human Services, "AFDC Recipient Characteristics Study," 1977, 1979, Tables 25–28.

24. For more on how work requirements are being used to reduce welfare rolls, see Mildred Rein,

"Work in Welfare." *Social Service Review,* June 1982, pp. 211–29. Southern states in particular have employed this tactic of reducing welfare participation. Moreover, the Southern states all have maximum benefits that are lower than the need level established in those states. For example, the percent of need paid in Mississippi is 37 percent for a family of four; in Alabama it is 31 percent; in Louisiana it is 35 percent; and in the District of Columbia it is 55 percent. "Background Material on Poverty, " Ways and Means Committee, Subcommittee on Public Assistance and Unemployment 1983.

25. Willard L. Rodgers and Arlene Thornton, "Changing Patterns of First Marriage in the United States." A paper read at the Annual Meetings of the American Sociological Association, San Francisco, September, 1982. See especially, Table 5.

26. U.S. Department of Health and Human Services, Health: United States, 1982 Table 9, p. 52. Mortality statistics cited in following paragraphs also refer to this table.

27. The period of the 1970's has seen a gradual decline in the black male mortality rate with much of the decline accounted for by the drop in the infant mortality rate (from 4299 in 1970 to 2830 per 100,000 in 1979 and the drop in the death rate among black men over 85 years (from 14,415 in 1970 to 10,745 per 100,000 in 1979).

28. J. William Leasure. "Some Economic Benefits of Birth Prevention." *Milbank Memorial Fund Quarterly* Vol. 45, October 1967, pp. 417–425.

29. Paul M. Sommers and Laura S. Thomas. "Restricting Federal Funds For Abortion: Another Look." *Social Science Quarterly* Vol. 64(1) March 1984 p. 342.

30. Ibid., p. 343.

31. Ibid., p. 343.

32. Willard Cates Jr. "The Hyde Amendment in Action: How Did the Restriction of Federal Funds for Abortion Affect Low-Income Women?" *Journal of the American Medical Association* Vol. 246(10) September 4, 1981, pp. 1109–1112.

33. Sommers and Thomas, op. cit., p. 344.

34. It should be noted in this context that rape and incest is not the authentic social policy issue with regard to the availability of abortion. Cates, op. cit., p. 1110 finds that after the Hyde Amendment was implemented the 6,000 abortions that took place over the 2 1/2 year period that were reimbursable by federal funds could be split in the following way: "82% were for life-endangering situations, 16% for long-lasting physical health damage, and only 2% for rape or incest." Obviously, for the woman experiencing rape or incest, whether or not it results in pregnancy, there is severe trauma which may never be reversed during the course of her life. But these cases of pregnancy are not numerically significant with respect to the abortion question. The social issue involves the choice to have an abortion because of the inconvenience associated with child-bearing and child-rearing.

35. Hope Corman and Michael Grossman. "Determinants of Neonatal Mortality Rates in the U.S.: A Reduced Form Model." NBER Working Paper No. 1387, June 1984.

36. Ibid., p. 39.

37. For the Right-to-Life movement, of course, an abortion is an infant death.

38. Representative of managerial agnosticism over the appropriate form of the family is Daniel Moynihan's recent refusal to say which type of family should be the object of public support in a major address on family policy at the Kennedy School of Government on April 8, 1985. Lisa Schiffren "The Key to Family Policy: Families." *The Detroit News,* April 21, 1985 has made the following report:

> "Significantly, after a cumulative six hours of lecturing, Mr. Moynihan was not able to define the very "family" that he wishes to save. . . . Glenn Loury . . . noted that the senator was not willing to specify any particular family structure, or to defend the two-parent nuclear family, then asked, 'What is the minimum family definition that you would defend without looking at poll data first?' Despite some laughter Moynihan was steadfast in his

refusal to advocate one set of household arrangements over another.

"This is revealing because Mr. Moynihan's argument was predicated on the fact that children who live in female-headed households are usually much worse off materially than children who live in two-parent nuclear families . . ."

39. Darity and Myers. "Public Policy and the Condition of Black Family Life," op. cit., p. 180.

40. Julianne Malveaux. "Similarities and Differences In the Economic Interests of Black and White Women." Paper presented at the American Economic Association Meetings, Dallas, Texas, December 27–30, 1984, p. 22, forthcoming in *The Review of Black Political Economy.*

Part VI *Key Terms and Essay/Discussion Questions*

KEY TERMS

Kinship system
Matrilineal descent
Patrilineal descent
Double descent
Monogamy
Polygamy
Extended family
Nuclear family
Slave code
Miscegenation

Freedman's Bureau
Female-headed family
Fertility rate
Marital status
Aid to Families with Dependent Children
Persistently poor
Poverty spell
Social structural factors
Managerial class

ESSAY/DISCUSSION QUESTIONS

1. According to Andrew Billingsley, the slave trade and chattel slavery disrupted patterns of traditional African family and community life. Even so, slaves retained aspects of traditional African culture and values and then refashioned them within the context of American chattel slavery. Discuss some dimensions of traditional African family and community life; then indicate some aspects of that tradition retained and refashioned by African slaves.

2. Slaveowners and the dehumanizing system of chattel slavery powerfully influenced the development of slave families and communities; yet, African slaves were able to create families and communities of their own even under conditions of cultural domination, political oppression, and economic exploitation. First, discuss the character of the slaveowner's power over slaves. Second, probe those conditions of culture and of limited autonomy that enabled slaves to develop their own patterns of family and community life.

3. E. Franklin Frazier seems to argue that African American family and community life experienced cycles of instability and stability as a result of changing social and economic forces. Discuss.

4. To what extent do regional (urban and rural or southern and northern) and socioeconomic class differences affect patterns of African American family and community life?

5. Public policy analysts with differing ideological persuasions agree that the problems associated with the instability within the contemporary African American family have reached crisis

proportions. Describe at least three indicators of current black family instability that analysts specify.

6. William Darity, Jr., and Samuel Myers, Jr., argue that the destabilization of the African American family is related to the changing character of American society. According to them, what is the nature of the social transformation now underway and what may be its consequences for the African American family?

Part VI *Supplementary Readings*

Billingsley, Andrew, "Black Families and White Social Science," in Joyce A. Ladner, ed., *The Death of White Sociology,* New York: Vintage Books, 1973, pp. 431–450.

————, *Black Families in White America,* Englewood Cliffs: Prentice-Hall, Inc., 1968.

Blassingame, John, *The Slave Community: Plantation Life in the Ante-Bellum South,* New York: Oxford University Press, 1972.

Clark, Reginald M., *Family Life and School Achievement: Why Poor Black Children Succeed or Fail,* Chicago: The University of Chicago Press, 1983.

Darity, William A., Jr., "The Class Character of the Black Community: Polarization Between the Black Managerial Elite and the Black Underclass," *Black Law Journal,* Vol. 7, No. 1 (1981), pp. 21–31.

DuBois, W. E. B., ed., *The Negro America Family,* Cambridge: MIT Press, 1970.

Frazier, E. Franklin, *The Negro Family in the United States,* Chicago: The University of Chicago Press, 1939.

————, "The Negro Slave Family," *Journal of Negro History,* Vol. 15 (April 1930), pp. 198–259.

Gary, Lawrence, E., *Black Men,* Beverly Hills: Sage Publications, 1981.

Gutman, Herbert G., *The Black Family in Slavery and Freedom, 1750–1925,* New York: Pantheon Books, 1976.

Gwaltney, John L., *Drylongso: A Self-Portrait of Black America,* New York: Random House, 1971.

Hill, Robert B., *The Strength of Black Families,* New York: The National Urban League, 1971.

Johnson, Charles S., *Growing Up in the Black Belt: Negro Youth in the Rural South,* Washington, D.C.: The American Council on Education, 1941.

————, *Shadow of the Plantation,* Chicago: The University of Chicago Press, 1934.

Ladner, Joyce A., *Tomorrow's Tomorrow: The Black Woman,* Garden City: Doubleday and Company, Inc., 1971.

Lightfoot, Sara, *Worlds Apart: Relationships Between Family and Schools,* New York: Basic Books, 1978.

McAdoo, Harriet P., ed., *Black Families,* Beverly Hills: Sage Publications, 1981.

Madhubuti, Haki R., *Black Men: Obsolete, Single, Dangerous?—The Afrikan American Family in Transition,* Chicago: Third World Press, 1990.

Malson, Micheline R., Elisabeth Mudimbe-Boyi, and Jean F. O'Barr, eds., *Black Women in America: Social Science Perspectives,* Chicago: The University of Chicago Press, 1988.

Moynihan, Daniel P., *Family and The Nation,* New York: Harcourt Brace Jovanovich, 1986.

———, *The Negro Family: The Case for National Action,* Washington, D.C.: Office of Planning and Research, U.S. Department of Labor, 1965.

Nobles, Wade, "Africanity and Black Families," *The Black Scholar,* Vol. 5 (1974), pp. 10–17.

Powdermaker, Hortense, *After Freedom: A Cultural Study in the Deep South,* New York: The Viking Press, 1939.

Rainwater, Lee, *Behind Ghetto Walls: Black Life in a Federal Slum,* Chicago, Aldine, 1970.

Rainwater, Lee and William L. Yancey, *The Moynihan Report and the Politics of Controversy,* Cambridge: The MIT Press, 1967.

Rodgers-Rose, La Frances, ed., *The Black Woman,* Beverly Hills: Sage Publications, 1980.

Scanzoni, John H., *The Black Family in Modern Society,* Chicago: The University of Chicago Press, 1971.

Scott v. Sandford, 60 U.S. (19 How.) 393 (1856).

Stack, Carol, *All Our Kin: Strategies for Survival in a Black Community,* New York: Harper and Row, Publishers, 1974.

Staples, Robert, *The World of Black Singles: Changing Patterns of Male Female Relations,* Westport: Greenwood Press, 1981.

———, *Introduction to Black Sociology,* New York: McGraw-Hill Book Company, 1976.

———, *The Black Woman in America: Sex, Marriage, and the Family,* Chicago: Nelson-Hall Publishers, 1973.

———, ed., *The Black Family: Essays and Studies,* Belmont: Wadsworth Publishing Company, 1971.

Watkins, Mel and Jay David, ed., *To Be a Black Woman: Portraits in Fact and Fiction,* New York: William Morrow and Company, Inc., 1970.

Wilkinson, Doris Y. and Ronald L. Taylor, eds., *The Black Male in America: Perspectives on His Status in Contemporary Society,* Chicago: Nelson-Hall Inc., 1977.

Willie, Charles V., *The Family Life of Black People,* Columbus: Charles E. Merrill, 1970.

Wilson, William J., *The Truly Disadvantaged: The Inner City, The Underclass and Public Policy,* Chicago: The University of Chicago Press, 1987.

VII

The African American Struggle for Literacy and Quality Education

The struggle for literacy and quality education has been a major dimension of the historic battle for African American human rights and social development. It is a struggle that began with the slave trade and continues into the 1990s. Chattel slaves were denied literacy and formal education because whites feared that literate slaves would become enlightened, communicate with each other, and plan slave rebellions. The tradition of denying formal education to African-descended Americans became deeply embedded in the nation's culture, thought, and institutions.

Yet within the slave quarters Africans and their American descendants came to believe in the power of knowledge as a tool for liberation. The body might be shackled but the mind could be free; a free mind often could struggle to free the body. As early as the 1830s, slaves and free African Americans established secret schools in homes and churches, even under threats of legal punishment and white terrorism. Indeed, Union soldiers during the Civil War were surprised to find many literate slaves, their literacy carefully kept from the slaveowner's knowledge. As early as the eve of Emancipation, then, education as a pathway to freedom had emerged as a strong tradition among African Americans. It was this tradition that motivated southern African American legislators during Reconstruction to advocate public education; it was this tradition that encouraged African Americans to establish their own schools and colleges during the nineteenth and early twentieth centuries; and it was this same tradition that galvanized the African American struggle to overthrow segregated educational institutions and practices in the Old South during the mid-1950s.

Segregation, which rested on the ideological foundation of chattel slavery, was the post-emancipation theory and practice of white American oppression of African-descended Americans. Based on assumptions of white supremacy and black inferiority, segregation denied African Americans full citizenship rights and privileges, deprived them of equal protection of the laws, and excluded them from using first-class public accommodations. The 1896 *Plessy v. Ferguson* Supreme Court decision had established the "separate but equal" doctrine, which resulted in the effective legalization of separate public schools for black and white Americans throughout the South. Educational segregation in practice also continued outside the South even though it was not legally sanctioned. Although separate, the two sets of schools were hardly equal; educational apartheid in America generally denied effective schooling to former slaves and their descendants.

The landmark 1954 Supreme Court decision of *Brown v. Board of Education* outlawed dual public school systems throughout the South. The decision raised the hopes of African Americans across the country, for they interpreted *Brown* as providing the means to achieve equal educational opportunity and excellence in education. But the 1955 Supreme Court *Brown* decision, which directed the implementation of the earlier ruling, was a disappointment to African Americans and a joy to white segregationists. It provided no precise time frame for instituting desegregated school systems; rather, the justices allowed the South to move "with all deliberate speed."

Even with the Supreme Court's moderation, many public school systems sought to evade the Court's ruling. In some southern communities white parents flatly refused to send their children to schools with African American children, choosing instead to enroll them in white private academies, which sprouted overnight. Other public school systems developed policies and programs, such as tracking, that channeled large numbers of African American youngsters into educational dead-ends. Many African American spokespersons labelled these strategies "programmed retardation" and charged that they were worse than segregation in the Old South.

The *Brown* ruling resuscitated the Civil Rights movement, whose main thrust was racial desegregation. In the mid-1960s, the interests of the Civil Rights elite and educational experts converged. Unfortunately, their emphasis on racial integration seemed to overshadow a concern for good education. It was the 1966 Coleman Report, an example of educational expertise, that contributed significantly to the transition from desegregation to integration by encouraging busing to achieve racial balance in public schools. This approach was given effective legitimacy by the courts and supported strongly by the Civil Rights establishment. Although many educators, lay persons, and some experts initially opposed the Coleman Report—James Coleman himself later repudiated the report's major findings—busing for racial balance was proclaimed the dominant solution to the problem of public school segregation. The fact that the *Brown* decision was intended to foster education seemed to be forgotten.

By the late 1970s and early 1980s, it was becoming increasingly clear that many of nation's public schools were failing to educate their students. In many cases, the limitations of such integration strategies as busing for racial balance were becoming evident as urban demographic changes transformed big city school districts into enclaves of African American and Hispanic American students. To bus African American or Hispanic American students from one school where they are the majority population across town to another school where they also are a majority population is redundant and meaningless. Another strategy, the magnet school, was instituted to attract white students into predominantly African American or Hispanic American schools. To the consternation of African American and Hispanic American parents and students, magnet schools became two schools within a school. White youngsters are enrolled in the magnet curriculum, but resident African American or Hispanic American students attending the school because it is in their district generally are excluded from this curriculum. Therefore, the 1980s witnessed growing tensions in America's politics of urban education.

The educational dilemmas emerging in the last three decades have caused many African American observers to ask how well current educational theory and practice serve the interests of most African American children. Many have become skeptical about the existing system's ability to meet the scholastic needs of African American children.

The articles in this section provide an examination of major historical trends in the development of African American education, some contemporary contradictions and dilemmas in the provision of equal educational opportunity and quality education to African Americans, and an examination of the impact of desegregation policies on historically black colleges and universities.

"Learning to Read" and "Growing in Knowledge" come from Frederick Douglass' autobiography, *Life and Times of Frederick Douglass,* published in 1892, three years before his death. Douglass, born into slavery, escaped and later became an abolitionist, a renowned orator, an advisor to President Abraham Lincoln, a diplomatic representative of the United States to Haiti and the Dominican Republic, and a newspaper publisher. He was one of the major African American leaders of the nineteenth century. His autobiography is considered a classic work within the slave narrative genre.

In the two chapters included here, Douglass recalls his childhood experiences in learning to read and write. In the first, Douglass describes a brief moment when his new mistress in Baltimore, Mrs. Auld, unwittingly and in her husband's absence began to teach him to read. He notes that her constant reading aloud from the Bible prompted him to ask for her assistance. Informed by his wife of young Douglass' developing success at learning the alphabet, Mr. Auld apparently chastised her and forbade her educating Douglass further. The slaveowner pointed out to his wife how the slave management system depended upon keeping slaves illiterate. This episode made Douglass even more determined to learn how to read and write.

In the second chapter included here, Douglass recounts the shrewd and ingenious strategies he employed to become literate and gain information. The acquisition of knowledge allowed him to grasp the underlying character of the slave management system and its dehumanizing process. He asserted: "Slaveholders . . . are only a band of successful robbers, who, leaving their own homes, went into Africa for the purpose of stealing and reducing my people to slavery." Douglass' autobiography indicates his hatred of chattel slavery and its attempt to keep him ignorant. His narrative also presents Douglass' absolute determination to learn.

In the late 1960s, community activist Jewell R. C. Mazique, wrote an impassioned attack on public school systems' increasing inability to provide educational excellence. In her essay, "Betrayal in the Schools: As Seen by an Advocate of Black Power," Mazique argues that the growing problem of public school decline resulted from the ideas, policies, and programs of a liberal coalition of educational experts, behavioral specialists, political policy makers, business elites, and black civil rights elites. She asserts that because black and white liberals insisted on imposing busing and other integrationist policies before all else, public schools abandoned educational fundamentals (reading, writing, and computational skills), subverted academic motivation, and perverted positive character development. Educational professionals increasingly excluded black and working class white parents from the policymaking process, which resulted in growing parental frustration and anger. Whites continued their massive migration to the suburbs, and urban public school systems were being transformed into failure factories. According to Mazique, the alternative to an emerging educational disaster, for both black and white youngsters, would be the incorporation of quality education into public schools: educational basics, academic motivation, and positive character development. The collapse of effective public schooling in the 1990s and its dire consequences for the nation make Mazique's analysis foresighted. However, the necessary educational redevelopment entails a struggle for power. As Mazique concludes: "The constant in all of this is power. Power determines the denial of the fundamental tools of knowledge, and power can determine the nature and extent of the education meted out."

The general problem of communities facing a powerful political force bent on integration is particularized by Floyd Hayes, as he recounts the struggle of citizens in Washington, D. C., to have a say in their school policies. His article, "Race, Urban Politics, and Educational Policy-Making in Washington, D. C.: A Community's Struggle for Quality Education," examines the politics of public school desegregation in the nation's capital during the late 1950s and 1960s. Using an in-depth interview with one of the key community participants in the city's early educational politics, as well as official reports and documents of the District of Columbia public school system, Hayes chronicles the community's struggle against the central administration's tracking policy, one that many community participants viewed as racially discriminatory and more damaging to African American children than was school segregation in the Old South. Hayes focuses on the community's challenge to educational professionals and their expertise. Although the tracking system ultimately was terminated by U. S. Court of Appeals Judge J. Skelly Wright in the *Hobson v. Hansen* (1967) case, the local community lost the battle to establish quality education in the public school system as local and national policymakers and professional experts advanced busing and other integration strategies as alternative policy solutions.

The legal effort to manage public school change has been accompanied by a similar process in relation to higher education, resulting in similar problems for African American educational advancement. John Matlock in his essay, "The Effect of Desegregation Policies on Historically Black Colleges and Universities," examines the role of the courts in desegregating state dual systems of higher education and concludes that this litigation may hurt, more than help, historically black colleges and universities. He reviews the *Adams* decision of 1973, along with the contradictions and dilemmas arising from that ruling, governmental policies, and the desegregation planning processes of state higher-education systems. Although the court declared that historically black colleges and universities were not to bear the brunt of the desegregation process, Matlock suggests that the *Adams* case may ultimately transform these institutions. In this regard, he examines the 1977 court-ordered merger of the historically black Tennessee State University with the traditionally white University of Tennessee at Nashville. Matlock states that while there were some changes, full racial integration has not been achieved. In assessing the effect of desegregation on historically black institutions of higher learning, Matlock suggests that these institutions may lose the authority to define their mission. They are being forced to attract substantially more white students, while traditionally white institutions are less pressured to attract African American students. Moreover, historically black institutions may lose black faculty members as a result of "raids" by white institutions. Matlock concludes with a series of recommendations directed toward sustaining and improving historically black institutions of higher education, from which the great majority of African American students graduate.

Learning to Read and Growing in Knowledge

FREDERICK DOUGLASS

ESTABLISHED IN MY NEW HOME in Baltimore, I was not very long in perceiving that in picturing to myself what was to be my life there, my imagination had painted only the bright side, and that the reality had its dark shades as well as its light ones. The open country which had been so much to me was all shut out. Walled in on every side by towering brick buildings, the heat of the summer was intolerable to me, and the hard brick pavements almost blistered my feet. If I ventured out on to the streets, new and strange objects glared upon me at every step, and startling sounds greeted my ears from all directions. My country eyes and ears were confused and bewildered. Troops of hostile boys pounced upon me at every corner. They chased me, and called me "eastern-shore man," till really I almost wished myself back on the Eastern Shore. My new mistress happily proved to be all she had seemed, and in her presence I easily forgot all outside annoyances. Mrs. Sophia was naturally of an excellent disposition—kind, gentle, and cheerful. The supercilious contempt for the rights and feelings of others, and the petulance and bad humor which generally characterized slave-holding ladies, were all quite absent from her manner and bearing toward me.

She had never been a slaveholder—a thing then quite unusual at the South—but had depended almost entirely upon her own industry for a living. To this fact the dear lady no doubt owed the excellent preservation of her natural goodness of heart, for slavery could change a saint into a sinner, and an angel into a demon. I hardly knew how to behave towards "Miss Sopha," as I used to call Mrs. Hugh Auld. I could not approach her even as I had formerly approached Mrs. Thomas Auld. Why should I hang down my head, and speak with bated breath, when there was no pride to scorn me, no coldness to repel me, and no hatred to inspire me with fear? I therefore soon came to regard her as something more akin to a mother than a slaveholding mistress. So far from deeming it impudent in a slave to look her straight in the face, she seemed ever

Reprinted from *Life and Times of Frederick Douglass*, written by himself. Collier Books, 1962.

to say, "Look up, child; don't be afraid." The sailors belonging to the sloop esteemed it a great privilege to be the bearers of parcels or messages for her, for whenever they came, they were sure of a most kind and pleasant reception. If little Thomas was her son, and her most dearly loved child, she made me something like his half-brother in her affections. If dear Tommy was exalted to a place on his mother's knee, "Freddy" was honored by a place at the mother's side. Nor did the slave-boy lack the caressing strokes of her gentle hand, soothing him into the consciousness that, though motherless, he was not friendless. Mrs. Auld was not only kind-hearted, but remarkably pious, frequent in her attendance at public worship and much given to reading the Bible and to chanting hymns of praise when alone.

Mr. Hugh was altogether a different character. He cared very little about religion, knew more of the world and was more a part of the world, than his wife. He doubtless set out to be, as the world goes, a respectable man and to get on by becoming a successful ship-builder, in that city of shipbuilding. This was his ambition, and it fully occupied him. I was of course of very little consequence to him, and when he smiled upon me, as he sometimes did, the smile was borrowed from his lovely wife, and like borrowed light, was transient, and vanished with the source whence it was derived. Though I must in truth characterize Master Hugh as a sour man of forbidding appearance, it is due to him to acknowledge that he was never cruel to me, according to the notion of cruelty in Maryland. During the first year or two, he left me almost exclusively to the management of his wife. She was my lawgiver. In hands so tender as hers, and in the absence of the cruelties of the plantation, I became both physically and mentally much more sensitive, and a frown from my mistress caused me far more suffering than had Aunt Katy's hardest cuffs. Instead of the cold, damp floor of my old master's kitchen, I was on carpets; for the corn

bag in winter, I had a good straw bed, well furnished with covers; for the course corn meal in the morning, I had good bread and mush occasionally; for my old tow-linen shirt, I had good clean clothes. I was really well off. My employment was to run of errands, and to take care of Tommy, to prevent his getting in the way of carriages, and to keep him out of harm's way generally.

So for a time everything went well. I say for a time, because the fatal poison of irresponsible power, and the natural influence of slave customs, were not very long in making their impression on the gentle and loving disposition of my excellent mistress. She at first regarded me as a child, like any other. This was the natural and spontaneous thought; afterwards, when she came to consider me property, our relations to each other were changed, but a nature so noble as hers could not instantly become perverted, and it took several years before the sweetness of her temper was wholly lost.

The frequent hearing of my mistress reading the Bible aloud, for she often read aloud when her husband was absent, awakened my curiosity in respect to this *mystery* of reading, and roused in me the desire to learn. Up to this time I had known nothing whatever of this wonderful art, and my ignorance and inexperience of what it could do for me, as well as my confidence in my mistress, emboldened me to ask her to teach me to read. With an unconscious and inexperience equal to my own, she readily consented, and in an incredibly short time, by her kind assistance, I had mastered the alphabet and could spell words of three or four letters. My mistress seemed almost as proud of my progress as if I had been her own child, and supposing that her husband would be as well pleased, she made no secret of what she was doing for me. Indeed, she exultingly told him of the aptness of her pupil and of her intention to persevere, as she felt it her duty to do, in teaching me, at least, to read the Bible. And here arose

the first dark cloud over my Baltimore prospects, the precursor of chilling blasts and
drenching storms. Master Hugh was astounded
beyond measure and, probably for the first
time, proceeded to unfold to his wife the true
philosophy of the slave system, and the peculiar
rules necessary in the nature of the case to
be observed in the management of human
chattels. Of course he forbade her to give me
any further instruction, telling her in the first
place that to do so was unlawful, as it was also
unsafe, "for," said he, "if you give a nigger an
inch he will take an ell. Learning will spoil the
best nigger in the world. If he learns to read
the Bible it will forever unfit him to be a slave.
He should know nothing but the will of his
master, and learn to obey it. As to himself,
learning will do him no good, but a great
deal of harm, making him disconsolate and
unhappy. If you teach him how to read, he'll
want to know how to write, and this accomplished, he'll be running away with himself."
Such was the tenor of Master Hugh's oracular
exposition, and it must be confessed that he
very clearly comprehended the nature and
the requirements of the relation of master
and slave. His discourse was the first decidedly
anti-slavery lecture to which it had been my
lot to listen. Mrs. Auld evidently felt the force
of what he said, and, like an obedient wife,
began to shape her course in the direction
indicated by him. The effect of his words *on
me* was neither slight nor transitory. His iron
sentences, cold and harsh, sunk like heavy
weights deep into my heart, and stirred up
within me a rebellion not soon to be allayed.

This was a new and special revelation,
dispelling a painful mystery against which my
youthful understanding had struggled, and
struggled in vain, to wit, the white man's
power to perpetuate the enslavement of the
black man. "Very well," thought I. "Knowledge unfits a child to be a slave." I instinc-
tively assented to the proposition, and from
that moment I understood the direct pathway
from slavery to freedom. It was just what I
needed, and it came to me at a time and from
a source whence I least expected it. Of course
I was greatly saddened at the thought of losing the assistance of my kind mistress, but the
information so instantly derived, to some
extent compensated me for the loss I had
sustained in this direction. Wise as Mr. Auld
was, he underrated my comprehension, and
had little idea of the use to which I was capable of putting the impressive lesson he was
giving to his wife. He wanted me to be a slave;
I had already voted against that on the home
plantation of Col. Lloyd. That which he most
loved I most hated, and the very determination which he expressed to keep me in
ignorance only rendered me the more reso-
lute to seek intelligence. In learning to read,
therefore, I am not sure that I do not owe
quite as much to the opposition of my master
as to the kindly assistance of my amiable
mistress. I acknowledge the benefit rendered
me by the one, and by the other, believing
that but for my mistress I might have grown
up in ignorance.

* * *

I lived in the family of Mr. Auld, at Baltimore, seven years, during which time, as the
almanac makers say of the weather, my condition was variable. The most interesting feature of my history here was my learning,
under somewhat marked disadvantages, to
read and write. In attaining this knowledge
I was compelled to resort to indirections by
no means congenial to my nature, and which
were really humiliating to my sense of candor
and uprightness. My mistress, checked in her
benevolent designs toward me, not only
ceased instructing me herself, but set her
face as a flint against my learning to read by
any means. It is due to her to say, however,
that she did not adopt this course in all its
stringency at first. She either thought it unnecessary, or she lacked the depravity needed to
make herself forget at once my human nature.
She was, as I have said, naturally a kind and

tender-hearted woman, and in the humanity of her heart and the simplicity of her mind, she set out, when I first went to live with her, to treat me as she supposed one human being ought to treat another.

Nature never intended that men and women should be either slaves or slaveholders, and nothing but rigid training long persisted in, can perfect the character of the one or the other.

Mrs. Auld was singularly deficient in the qualities of a slaveholder. It was no easy matter for her to think or to feel that the curly-headed boy, who stood by her side, and even leaned on her lap, who was loved by little Tommy, and who loved Tommy in turn, sustained to her only the relation of a chattel. I was more than that; she felt me to be more than that. I could talk and sing; I could laugh and weep; I could reason and remember; I could love and hate. I was human, and she, dear lady, knew and felt me to be so. How could she then treat me as a brute, without a mighty struggle with all the noblest powers of her soul? That struggle came, and the will and power of the husband were victorious. Her noble soul was overcome, and he who wrought the wrong was injured in the fall no less than the rest of the household. When I went into that household, it was the abode of happiness and contentment. The wife and mistress there was a model of affection and tenderness. Her fervent piety and watchful uprightness made it impossible to see her without thinking and feeling that "that woman is a Christian." There was no sorrow nor suffering for which she had not a smile. She had bread for the hungry, clothes for the naked, and comfort for every mourner who came within her reach.

But slavery soon proved its ability to divest her of these excellent qualities, and her home of its early happiness. Conscience cannot stand much violence. Once thoroughly injured, who is he who can repair the damage? If it be broken toward the slave on Sunday, it will be toward the master on Monday. It cannot long endure such shocks. It must stand unharmed, or it does not stand at all. As my condition in the family waxed bad, that of the family waxed no better. The first step in the wrong direction was the violence done to nature and to conscience in arresting the benevolence that would have enlightened my young mind. In ceasing to instruct me, my mistress had to seek to justify herself *to* herself, and once consenting to take sides in such a debate, she was compelled to hold her position. One needs little knowledge of moral philosophy to see where she inevitably landed. She finally became even more violent in her opposition to my learning to read than was Mr. Auld himself. Nothing now appeared to make her more angry than seeing me, seated in some nook or corner, quietly reading a book or newspaper. She would rush at me with the utmost fury, and snatch the book or paper from my hand, with something of the wrath and consternation which a traitor might be supposed to feel on being discovered in a plot by some dangerous spy. The conviction once thoroughly established in her mind, that education and slavery were incompatible with each other, I was most narrowly watched in all my movements. If I remained in a separate room from the family for any considerable length of time, I was sure to be suspected of having a book, and was at once called to give an account of myself. But this was too late— the first and never-to-be-retraced step had been taken. Teaching me the alphabet had been the "inch" given, I was now waiting only for the opportunity to "take the ell."

Filled with the determination to learn to read at any cost, I hit upon many expedients to accomplish that much desired end. The plan which I mainly adopted, and the one which was the most successful, was that of using as teachers my young white playmates, with whom I met on the streets. I used almost constantly to carry a copy of *Webster's Spelling-Book* in my pocket, and when sent on errands, or when playtime was allowed me, I would step aside with my young friends and take a lesson in spelling. I am greatly indebted to these boys—Gustavus Dorgan, Joseph Bailey, Charles Farity, and William Cosdry.

Although slavery was a delicate subject and, in Maryland, very cautiously talked about among grown-up people, I frequently talked with the white boys about it, and that very freely. I would sometimes say to them, while seated on a curbstone or a cellar door, "I wish I could be free, as you will be when you get to be men." "You will be free, you know, as soon as you are twenty-one, and can go where you like, but I am a slave for life. Have I not as good a right to be free as you have?" Words like these, I observed, always troubled them, and I had no small satisfaction in drawing out from them, as I occasionally did, that fresh and bitter condemnation of slavery which ever springs from natures unseared and unperverted. Of all consciences, let me have those to deal with, which have not been seared and bewildered with the cares and perplexities of life. I do not remember ever while I was in slavery, to have met with a *boy* who defended the system, but I do remember many times, when I was consoled by them, and by them encouraged to hope that something would yet occur by which I would be made free. Over and over again, they have told me that "they believed I had as good a right to be free as *they* had," and that "they did not believe God ever made any one to be a slave." It is easily seen that such little conversation with my playfellows had no tendency to weaken my love of liberty, nor to render me contented as a slave.

When I was about thirteen years old, and had succeeded in learning to read, every increase of knowledge, especially anything respecting the free states, was an additional weight to the almost intolerable burden of my thought—"*I am a slave for life.*" To my bondage I could see no end. It was a terrible reality, and I shall never be able to tell how sadly that thought chafed my young spirit. Fortunately or unfortunately, I had, by blacking boots for some gentlemen, earned a little money with which I purchased of Mr. Knight, on Thames street, what was then a very popular school book, viz., *The Columbian Orator,* for which I paid fifty cents. I was led to buy this book by hearing some little boys say that they were going to learn some pieces out of it for the exhibition. This volume was indeed a rich treasure, and, for a time, every opportunity afforded me was spent in diligently perusing it. Among much other interesting matter, that which I read again and again with unflagging satisfaction was a short dialogue between a master and his slave. The slave is represented as having been recaptured in a second attempt to run away, and the master opens the dialogue with an upbraiding speech, charging the slave with ingratitude, and demanding to know what he has to say in his own defense. Thus upbraided and thus called upon to reply, the slave rejoins that he knows how little anything that he can say will avail, seeing that he is completely in the hands of his owner, and with noble resolution, calmly says, "I submit to my fate." Touched by the slave's answer, the master insists upon his further speaking, and recapitulates the many acts of kindness which he has performed toward the slave, and tells him he is permitted to speak for himself. Thus invited, the quondam slave made a spirited defense of himself, and thereafter the whole argument for and against slavery is brought out. The master was vanquished at every turn in the argument, and, appreciating the fact, he generously and meekly emancipates the slave, with his best wishes for his prosperity.

It is unnecessary to say that a dialogue with such an origin and such an end, read by me when every nerve of my being was in revolt at my own condition as a slave, affected me most powerfully. I could not help feeling that the day might yet come when the well-directed answers made by the slave to the master, in this instance, would find a counterpart in my own experience. This, however, was not all the fanaticism which I found in *The Columbian Orator.* I met here one of Sheridan's mighty speeches on the subject of Catholic Emancipation, Lord Chatham's speech on the American War, and speeches by the great William Pitt, and by Fox. These were all choice documents to me, and I read them over and over again, with an interest ever increasing, because it was ever gaining in intelligence, for the more I read them the better I understood them. The reading of these speeches added much to my limited stock of language, and enabled me to give tongue to many interesting thoughts which had often flashed through my mind and died away for want of words in which to give them utterance. The mighty power and heart-searching directness of truth, penetrating the heart of a slaveholder and compelling him to yield up his earthly interests to the claims of eternal justice, were finely illustrated in the dialogue, and from the speeches of Sheridan I got a bold and powerful denunciation of oppression and a most brilliant vindication of the rights of man.

Here was indeed a noble acquisition. If I had ever wavered under the consideration that the Almighty, in some way, had ordained slavery and willed my enslavement for His own glory, I wavered no longer. I had now penetrated to the secret of all slavery and of all oppression, and had ascertained their true foundation to be in the pride, the power, and the avarice of man. With a book in my hand so redolent of the principles of liberty, and with a perception of my own human nature and of the facts of my past and present experience, I was equal to a contest with the religious advocates of slavery, whether white or black, for blindness in this matter was not confined to the white people. I have met, at the South, many good, religious colored people who were under the delusion that God required them to submit to slavery and to wear their chains with meekness and humility. I could entertain no such nonsense as this,

and I quite lost my patience when I found a colored man weak enough to believe such stuff. Nevertheless, eager as I was to partake of the tree of knowledge, its fruits were bitter as well as sweet. "Slaveholders," thought I, "are only a band of successful robbers, who, leaving their own homes, went into Africa for the purpose of stealing and reducing my people to slavery." I loathed them as the meanest and the most wicked of men. And as I read, behold! the very discontent so graphically predicted by Master Hugh had already come upon me. I was no longer the light-hearted, gleesome boy, full of mirth and play, that I was when I landed in Baltimore. Light had penetrated the moral dungeon where I had lain, and I saw the bloody whip for my back and the iron chain for my feet, and my good, kind master was the author of my situation. The revelation haunted me, stung me, and made me gloomy and miserable. As I writhed under the sting and torment of this knowledge I almost envied my fellow slaves their stupid indifference. It opened my eyes to the horrible pit, and revealed the teeth of the frightful dragon that was ready to pounce upon me, but alas, it opened no way for my escape. I wished myself a beast, a bird, anything rather than a slave. I was wretched and gloomy beyond my ability to describe. This everlasting thinking distressed and tormented me, and yet there was no getting rid of this subject of my thoughts. Liberty, as the inestimable birthright of every man, converted every object into an asserter of this right. I heard it in every sound, and saw it in every object. It was ever present to torment me with a sense of my wretchedness. The more beautiful and charming were the smiles of nature, the more horrible and desolate was my condition. I saw nothing without seeing it, and I heard nothing without hearing it. I do not exaggerate when I say that it looked at me in every star, smiled in every calm, breathed in every wind and moved in every storm.

I have no doubt that my state of mind had something to do with the change in treatment which my mistress adopted towards me. I can easily believe that my leaden, downcast, and disconsolate look was very offensive to her. Poor lady! She did not understand my trouble, and I could not tell her. Could I have made her acquainted with the real state of my mind and given her the reasons therefor, it might have been well for both of us. As it was, her abuse fell upon me like the blows of the false prophet upon his ass; she did not know that an angel stood in the way. Nature made us friends, but slavery had made us enemies. My interests were in a direction opposite to hers, and we both had our private thoughts and plans. She aimed to keep me ignorant, and I resolved to *know,* although knowledge only increased my misery. My feelings were not the result of any marked cruelty in the treatment I received; they sprung from the consideration of my being a slave at all. It was *slavery,* not its mere *incidents* that I hated. I had been cheated. I saw that slaveholders would have gladly made me believe that, in making a slave of me and in making slaves of others, they were merely acting under the authority of God, and I felt to them as to robbers and deceivers. The feeding and clothing me well could not atone for taking my liberty from me. The smiles of my mistress could not remove the deep sorrow that dwelt in my young bosom. Indeed, this came, in time, but to deepen the sorrow. She had changed, and the reader will see that I too, had changed. We were both victims to the same overshadowing evil, she as mistress, I as slave. I will not censure her harshly.

Betrayal in the Schools

JEWELL R. C. MAZIQUE

THE PROBLEM IN THE PUBLIC schools is not exclusively racial anymore, if indeed it ever was. Rather, the shutdown in New York City and the predictions of more to come in Philadelphia, Washington, Detroit, Chicago and other cities represent a clash of cultures, a conflict of interests, a struggle for power. While the discord is clearly evident in the area of education, the coming community breakdown will not be limited to school shutdowns. Rather, as is already occurring in New York, there will be a chain reaction spilling over into other areas of the community, black and white, igniting everything touched. In the meantime, the white masses will come to identify with struggling blacks— for white children, too, have gradually become victims of a system which destroys rather than builds. This is why the New York situation is being watched nationally by questioning parents and community leaders who face similar problems.

The children of the masses, black and white, in the United States are not learning to read, write, spell and figure because these indisputable fundamentals have been getting less and less attention while budgets, school plants, cafeterias, projectors and other academic paraphernalia, to say nothing of administrative staff (including psychologists, counselors, paraprofessionals and drivers for "balancing and bussing") have been accepted as standard equipment for educating the young. The fashionable and passionate emphasis on fads, frills and fun is such that the profound significance and proficient art of teaching have been lost on many younger teachers, themselves more and more the product of the modern system of education without literacy. It is not unusual to hear a "liberal" instructor assure a parent disturbed by her child's lack of reading progress that poor spelling is no deterrent to learning and should not be a source of worry— after all, the teacher herself never could spell. Besides, "What do we have dictionaries for?"

But the further along in school such pupils advance, the harder it becomes to "guess" words, and harder still to stop every minute

Reprinted from the January 1969 issue of *Triumph*. Copyright © 1969, Triumph Magazine, Inc.

Jewell Mazique at work in the Library of Congress early in her career.

of an assignment to seek out proper spelling from a dictionary. Disgust, loss of interest, declining motivation soon follow, and eventually a turning away from school entirely. The personality of the student is thus subverted, the character of the community changes as radical deterioration of the learning institution takes place, and the school, as a learning institution, finally dies.

Consequently, legislation and judicial decisions directing programs against "de facto" segregation and racial discrimination are outdated and self-defeating not alone for the masses of blacks, but for the masses of whites

as well. Like Alice in Wonderland, the faster the blacks have run in the last several years (since the Supreme Court's momentous school desegregation decision) the "behinder" they have gotten in education; while the faster the white masses have run to stay ahead, the more they have locked themselves, with their children, into a well-fashioned but ill-conceived trap.

The subversion of the public school system is as tragic for the white masses as it is for the blacks; but neither the subversion nor its significance has been recognized by whites, for several reasons. The rapid decline in the mastery of basic skills by the offspring of whites has

unfortunately been attributed to "the revolution" in education and the advent of blacks in
their midst—a necessary evil, in other words,
if the world's leading democracy is to be truly
democratic. Second, the importance of literacy
and computation, traditionally recognized by
slaves and ex-slaves as essential for securing freedom against re-enslavement, is not so fresh in
the minds of whites as it is in the consciousness
of blacks. To the latter, therefore, any school
that fails to distribute the "tools of knowledge"
"ain't no school at all," it is an institution preparing our offspring for slavery again in this technological age or, worse still, perhaps preparing
them for more advanced, more implacable institutions—incarceration in mental institutions or
criminal penitentiaries, for example. Once the
trick is recognized for what it is—the imposition of a handicap on youngsters in the name
of education—no amount or variety of foods
to substitute for a deficient mental diet served
at two hour intervals, coupled with programs of
entertainment and "sustained excitement," will
placate black parents.

THE ELECT AND THE UNELECT

Our forebears were enslaved for 250 years not
because they were "savages" and "uncivilized"
as claimed, but rather, because there was born
in those days in the Western World a new
form of government founded largely on the
Judaeo-Calvinist concept of "the elect and the
unelect"—a pre-Christian doctrine based on
the premise that some men are born outside
salvation. Actually this form of government
arose in response to a desire on the part of
a select minority to dominate the majority.
Later, that minority of whites could reenforce
its position with the profits, power and
pleasure to be derived from enslaved blacks.
Since no man, black or white, willingly sub-
mits to slavery, it became necessary, in order
to institutionalize the system, to break up
the family, tribe and clan as fast as blacks
debarked from the slave ship. The second
essential for guaranteed control over blacks

was to deny them literacy while educating
them for service on the plantation lands and
in the "Big House." Thus, in the larger sense,
it cannot be asserted honestly that Africans
were denied education, for they were taught
weaving and sewing, cooking and housekeeping, carpentry and numberless skills, but
teaching the alphabet and numbers was immediately frowned upon, then finally barred completely. (Literate slaves would have been able
to pick up knowledge of their heritage and the
outside world; they could also communicate
in writing, plot up-risings and plan escape
through the underground railroad, as Frederick
Douglass did following his "boot-leg" instruction in reading, writing and arithmetic.)

Since World War I, when we fought "to
make the world safe for democracy," emphasis on that political ideal steadily rose. But
strangely, as the ideal came closer and closer
to realization in other areas, the development
of youth through mass education to fulfill the
objective shifted into reverse—exactly in
proportion to the vast outlay of money, the
expanding school staff and startling development of educational "innovations." For ours
is a heritage that adheres, in spite of it all, to
the Judaeo-Calvinist concept or an "elect-
elite"—a concept that was applied to our
educational system through the philosophy of
John Dewey. That philosophy, unfortunately,
provides a means of keeping the disadvantaged in a disadvantaged position.

Beginning in the twenties the revolution in
public education spread rapidly from Columbia
University and New York City to the smallest
hamlet in the United States. This was so effectively accomplished through teacher's colleges,
workshops and seminars on teaching methods,
the mass media and public relations channels,
that functional illiteracy soon became widespread among the American masses.

Just as blacks began questioning the American system of "education without literacy"
two things happened. With the introduction
of TV, "looking at the idiot's box" became the

"thing" (as possession of the television set as a piece of furniture conferred status), offering hope to youth for effortless development. Secondly, educational theorists introduced a proliferation of new interpretations, assumptions, and evaluations of pupils and parents necessitating radical changes in "groupings," eating habits, transportation, parent-child relations, etc. which had little or no bearing on the quality of education. In fact, black parents could eventually protest that as the budget went up, educational achievement went down, that as "innovations" were introduced, youngsters became frustrated, until finally the new techniques became so suspect among black parents that they would charge the school system with *programmed retardation.*

Silence on the effects of modern mass education was broken in 1955 with the publication of Rudolph Flesch's enlightening work, *Why Johnny Can't Read,* suggesting a kind of conspiracy at work, cataloguing the ravages of Dewey's revolution.

What Flesch had noted about the effect of education on children in general was more true of blacks. Many southern black fathers and mothers, who had never got beyond eighth grade, managed to send their children to college even during the Depression. Although these young students' experiences were limited and the books and libraries available were in short supply, most became quite literate in English and many went on to master other languages. Moreover, the dialect handicaps and speech difficulties of black children, so often complained about by educational theorists and teachers in northern cities and "integrated" schools, were readily overcome in the Ole South as fast as pupils learned to read, spell and master grammar and sentence structure. These same blacks, parents now, residing in big cities, cannot understand the reason for today's pervasive functional illiteracy and its accompanying loss of motivation, but they do know that it is a terrible thing which is undermining

their most precious dreams and aspirations. More and more they have become suspicious of the various forces at work—politically astute and financially well-equipped—and always blaming them for little Johnny's inability to read, write, spell and compute, and consequently his restlessness in the classroom and trouble-making.

How to Grow Criminals

In the early fifties, Flesch pleaded with the educational theorists and school administrators to mend their ways so that the 33 million babies born between 1945 and 1953 might fare better than the immediately preceding generation of children. But where are these black and white children today, now ranging in ages from twenty-three to fifteen, who were never taught to read, never developed the responsibility to carry out an assignment, to follow directions, never learned to respect knowledge or the purveyors of knowledge, never became masters of their own souls with the self-discipline that separates the civilized from the savage, the criminal from the contained? They are the drop-outs, juvenile delinquents and dope addicts of our time using their energies toward destructive ends and applying their talents to bank robberies and con games—to bringing down the nation which allowed them to be betrayed.

Why did Mr. Flesch's brilliant work, which hit the academic terrain like a thunderstorm on the desert sands, die aborning? Why did he lose so soon the ear of questioning, anxious parents? Because overnight the Supreme Court's *Brown* decision had deflected the full energies of the nation to ending school segregation and racial discrimination. For the small businessman or would-be businessman, block-busting became the most profitable of the early community innovations following "desegregation" of schools. It was to become a source of quick profits for these speculators both in terms of housing turnover and of "mechanizing" the classroom. White parents leap-frogged over "integrated" communities to suburbia, seeking new schools for their own children. At the same time black parents were running so fast in search of acceptance and better education for their children, that few stopped long enough to observe what was happening to these children. It was too late when blacks discovered that schools were being "integrated" but that education was being taken out of them. The whites were running so fast to suburbia to escape it all that they did not notice that they had left education behind and that once in suburbia they had to start from scratch, building a whole new system of education from plant to curriculum. By the time they questioned the new arrangement, the issue of "balancing and bussing" broke.

Balancing and bussing now became the thing in public school education, based on the premise that homogeneous neighborhood schools limit education, especially when their charges are "culturally deprived" low-income blacks. Liberals explained to doubting black parents that school district boundary changes and zigzag zoning were necessary to eliminate "tracking," or "ability grouping," an earlier desegregation scheme.

Soon, black parents in the big cities were complaining that the new district boundaries removed their children further from their local communities and a normal school atmosphere, alienating them from their natural environment. Moreover, it made parental participation in the educational process more difficult both because of geographical distance, and because of their strange and strained relations with other parents in far-away communities with whom they had nothing in common.

Interestingly, far-out innovations like balancing and bussing were the exclusive creation of white liberals, although black Anglo-Saxons often executed the plans. Regardless of the declining situation in public schools—in education itself—the white masses have continued running to suburbia wilh their children, while

blacks, under the direction of white liberal educational theorists, opportunistic politicians, engaging psychologists and enterprising businessmen, push them out. Seldom has it occurred to anxious black and white parents that such issues as interracial mixing, seating arrangements, ability grouping, balancing and bussing, or even "blackfaces" in history books, are really issues of organization, mobility, transportation, individual comfort and such like, and have little bearing on the acquisition of literacy. Moreover, these non-academic issues affected many black pupils more adversely than segregation had, while paralyzing public education for the masses of whites. But the dust had to settle before black and white masses were to comprehend the direction of a social revolution which consisted of one step forward and two steps backward.

THE FREUDIAN ETHIC

Education theorists, with their quackish prescriptions based on misleading misdiagnosis of pupil problems, would have been exposed in the fifties in spite of all the confusions accompanying the "civil rights movement" and "race-mixing," if the "mental health movement" and related idiocies had not been flourishing at the same time. Mythological tradition, now representing itself as a science (in the form of the "Freudian Ethic") demanded the abandonment of allegiance to God, and consequently to man as the center of things, making of all men mere objects subject to political manipulation.

Thus, when pupils could not read after not being taught how, it was explained that "non-reading" was a condition due to Oedipus complexes, lack-love mothers, parental anxieties, family conflicts, poverty, hunger, cultural deprivation, nervous stomachs, heredity, parental interferences, matriarchal homes, unwed or broken homes, sibling rivalries, "bookless homes." The school thus became, in fact, a failure clinic to which anxious parents, black and while, periodically reported to receive futility reports on their children. The school system of Washington, D.C. could report to the House Committee on Education and Labor in 1965 that in some of the District's public schools as many as 85 percent of the pupils were reading below normal, if reading at all. Today, the heart of the New York struggle over decentralization is the fact that last year's Regents' test revealed that 85 percent of black and Puerto Rican pupils were reading below grade level. The District of Columbia senior high school teachers have reported being assigned twelfth grade students reading on the first grade level. One high school teacher has reported a section of senior nonreaders rated minus one—that is, they did not know even the alphabet.

Flesch had protested the instruction of children by "guessing or gambling" reading techniques. These techniques, I believe, became the persistent habit pattern of the young as the way to approach the problems of the world. Rather than digging in for mastery and understanding of the complexities of life and human development, which requires hard work, group action and collective concern, a generation of black youth has been sacrificed in the battle for "civil rights." However talented and worthy a student may be, if he cannot read, write or spell in his native longue, how can he major in languages, history or philosophy? If he has never learned the multiplication tables and how to calculate square roots, how can he enter engineering and physics?

Flesch had predicted it all: "I say, therefore, that the word method is gradually destroying democracy in this country; it returns to the upper middle class the privileges that public education was supposed to distribute evenly among the people. The American Dream is, essentially, equal opportunity through free education for all. This dream is beginning to vanish in a country where the public schools are falling down on the job."

In the breeze we can still hear Martin Luther King romanticize "I had a dream" for the benefit of black children. But it will remain a dream unfulfilled as long as the fundamental tools of knowledge are denied to inquiring tender black minds when they come to the first grade searching for it. As long as the manipulators, masquerading as psychologists, counselors, educational philosophers and theoreticians, are allowed to function as an "elect-elite," the masses they are dehumanizing will be left intellectually and spiritually naked in an age of automation and cybernation.

Tragically, the gates of the highest academic citadels, sealed tight for centuries against blacks, now swing open; but the "comers" from the ranks of blacks are few and far between, for the public schools are such that their products never qualify. The liberal educator-class, which controls these schools, financed, marched and otherwise participated in the "civil rights movement"; but what they gave with one hand—desegregation of schools and "decovenanting" of housing—they took with the other, all the while being regarded as the greatest, most charitable and philanthropic liberals the world has ever known.

In this connection, Patrick J. Moynihan argues that racism is destined to overcome the handicaps imposed by liberals, and that blacks will eventually qualify for places in first-rate universities and colleges. This movement would certainly be getting under way right now, as the calls go out from Yale, MIT, Brown and other universities, had black youth been taught the fundamentals in the public schools where their poor parents were forced to enroll them while they struggled to make ends meet.

THE CULTURAL CLASH

For some of the black masses, at least until recently, the parochial schools have provided a sort of "hot-house" situation where the indigenous strain of black worth, creativity and individual dignity could survive, while other blacks were being victimized by the

Protestant-Freudian ethic and the drive for "civil rights" and "mental health." In these Catholic schools many children who had been written off as uneducable before transfer from the public schools learned to read, write, spell and compute in spite of race and economic circumstances. And recently black children who transferred from public to Muslim schools in New York, Chicago, Washington and elsewhere have achieved similar gains.

Some may argue the motives of the desegregation theoreticians and politicians, but none can dispute results: hundreds of thousands of blacks have lost hope for the first time since Emancipation. The struggle in New York is one result—and there will be others. But if the real issues underlying declining literacy and undermining achievement had been aired, the tragic New York debacle, which threatens a cultural conflict such as was never experienced in the South or for that matter in the whole history of the United States, might have been avoided.

The lines of democracy, the rights and wrongs, the good and the bad have gotten so tangled that the country, at least a significant segment of it, may find itself re-examining its whole historical role in servicing the masses, especially the education of their children. It may also find itself thinking seriously about the charges by John F. Hatchett, a black nationalist teacher in New York, who maintains that Jewish teachers were poisoning the minds of black children, even while Albert Shanker, in the name of the teachers' union which he heads, blasted blacks in general as anti-Semites and even "Nazis."

Had the trouble in New York merely reflected issues related to the race problem, we might look forward to a relatively prompt and happy solution. But the cultural clash, accompanied by a conflict of interest and a struggle for power in New York City and elsewhere in the nation is cutting sharply across lines of religion and race, polarizing the United States in a most unexpected fashion.

Behind the facade of school desegregation and the emphasis on racial discrimination and civil rights, serious trouble has been brewing for some time. But many black intellectuals who wish "to tell it as it is" have not been able to be heard. They could have warned—and the nation would have been the better for it—that by providing the public schools with ever-increasing federal funds (Title I, Title II and so on) the government was literally planting the seeds of its own destruction. Programs turning the school into a service station providing amply for everything from food to "sustained excitement," everything except a steady diet of fundamental education, drills and homework, were destined to do for the growing child what food and entertainment does for an untrained animal: make him big and strong, the better to turn on his keeper.

But St. Luke says "I tell you, if these are silent [or silenced] the rocks will cry out." The rocks have not cried out in recent years without reason. Young people of the District of Columbia did not turn out and turn on the community without cause last April 5. Vandalism of school buildings in recent years by betrayed and disappointed young people represents the logical development of a cold war directed against a system which has betrayed and alienated youth, and which is steadily becoming worse.

THE "INNOVATION" RACKET

Failure factories supported and fed by a system of programmed retardation, and promoted by the change racketeers, is what has stirred blacks to revolt. The schemes, the machines, the tests on materials untaught, the change agents—these are the persons and forces serving to make blacks and growing numbers of the white masses feel more and more estranged from their institutions and their culture. We cannot alienate black youth, deculturize, and dehumanize them, and simultaneously develop them for positive citizenship.

While disappointed youngsters are smashing display cases and breaking school windows, looting and burning in disgust within the exploited areas, change agents are locked up in "innovation" shops cooking up other schemes, tactics and excuses for failing to distribute the tools of knowledge which have been promised to all the children of the black and white masses in this democracy of ours.

Blacks, as do whites wherever they reside, want their children to enjoy the advantages of effective education. These advantages are rooted in the basic fundamentals of knowledge—reading, writing and arithmetic. Education begins with a mastery of the lingua franca—literacy—in any country for any people. The constant in all of this is power. Power determines the denial of the fundamental tools of knowledge and power can determine the nature and extent of the education meted out.

Race, Urban Politics, and Educational Policy-Making in Washington, D.C.: A Community's Struggle for Quality Education

FLOYD W. HAYES, III

IN THE 1950S AND 1960S, the movement for public school desegregation came to a head in the context of a convergence of a budding challenge to educational progressivism's theory and practice of societal guidance and the emerging struggle for African-American civil rights. Both efforts challenged the administrative authority of education professionals, experts, and theorists. At the turn of the century, a coalition of educational reformers, local business elites, and the educated middle class succeeded in establishing urban school bureaucracies headed by professional educational managers. The Progressive Era of educational reform is best distinguished by its enthusiasm for a "science" of education, which emphasized expertise, efficiency, and a growing organizational complexity of urban school systems. Since administrative progressives believed that people could manage their own destiny through the conscious application of science to social difficulties, applied educational research—expert knowledge rather than common sense—came to be viewed as a foundation for social engineering (Tyack and Hansot 1982). These arrangements, however,

severely restricted popular participation in the urban educational policy-making process.

By the 1950s, public discontent mounted with educational professionals and theorists who were accused of lowering educational standards and introducing into the public school curriculum courses that many parents and citizen groups interpreted as replacing reading, writing, and arithmetic with fun, fads, and frolicking (Washington 1969). Many concerned parents were encouraged and sustained by such widely read and discussed books as *Why Johnny Can't Read,* by Rudolf Flesch (1955), and *Education and Freedom,* by Hyman Rickover (1959). The authors of these texts harshly criticized the limitations of educational progressivism and school professionals and experts.

The Supreme Court's epic 1954 *Brown* decision, outlawing public school segregation, and the intensifying civil rights movement of

Reprinted from *Urban Education,* Vol. 25, No. 3, October 1990, pp. 237–257. Copyright © 1990 Sage Publications, Inc. Reprinted by permission of Sage Publications, Inc.

the 1950s and 1960s, helped to set in motion forces in many urban African-American communities that, in turn, came to challenge fundamentally the prerogatives and intent of educational professionals and the exclusionary bureaucratic policy-making process of urban public school systems. For example, in Washington, D.C., African-American community organizations and activists clashed with educational professionals over the implementation of the school system's desegregation policy of tracking. In opposition to this policy strategy, citizen groups and participants demanded traditional quality education: the distribution and mastery of the fundamental tools of knowledge, academic motivation, and good character building.

The broad goal of this article is to examine the politics of educational policy-making in Washington, D.C., during the 1950s and 1960s. More specifically, the aim is to chronicle the community struggle against the central administration's tracking-policy strategy, a policy strategy that many community participants saw as more damaging to African-American children than school segregation in the Old South was. Until 1968, when Washington's first elected school board took office, the city's public schools were the only major federally controlled educational system in the nation. Hence the politics of school desegregation in Washington are significant because, as the nation's capital, the city generally was considered a bellwether for the rest of the country (LaNoue and Smith 1973). Moreover, the specific events recounted in this article have been largely overlooked in the scholarly literature on educational politics in Washington, D.C.

Primary data sources for the research presented here include official reports and documents of the District of Columbia public school system. A further step in the process includes an in-depth interview with a key participant in the city's early educational politics examined in this study.[1]

DEMOGRAPHIC TRANSFORMATION

Changing demographic trends in the nation's capital help to explain the politicization of educational policy-making as the desegregation process unfolded. From 1930 to 1950, while the proportion of the African-American population in the Washington metropolitan area as a whole decreased slightly (from 24.9 percent to 23.6 percent), the proportion of African-Americans in the District of Columbia itself increased from 27.1 percent to 35.7 percent. However, percentages can be deceiving. In actual numbers, the African-American population for the Washington metropolitan area increased from 167,409 to 345,954 persons, and the actual numbers of African-American District residents rose from 132,068 to 289,600 persons during that twenty-year period. A more dramatic population change occurred over the next decade. By 1960, although the proportion of African-Americans for the Washington metropolitan area only increased 25.0 percent, this represented an increase in actual numbers to 502,546 persons. Significantly, the proportion of the District's African-American population rose to 55.2 percent, or to 427,100 persons (Passow 1967). Over the next two decades, the proportion and number of Washington's African-American residents would continue to mount as increasing numbers of whites relocated to surrounding suburban areas.

The transformation of Washington's racial composition, begun twenty years before the schools were desegregated, set in motion changes in the racial makeup of the city's public school enrollment. A more dramatic transformation took place following school desegregation. Between 1949 and 1953, white enrollment had declined by about 4,000 students; between 1954 and 1958, that enrollment fell by nearly 12,000 students. Overwhelmingly members of a rising middle class of professionals and managers employed chiefly in the burgeoning federal bureaucracy, many whites left Washington to enroll their children in predominantly white public schools in the nearby affluent suburbs of Maryland and Virginia.

The growth of African-American enrollment in the District's public schools also was striking. As Table 1 portrays, from 1951 to 1956, African-American enrollment rose from 52.4 percent to 68.0 percent, or from 50,250 to 72,954 students. Five years later, African-American students constituted 81.6 percent of the public school enrollment. There were then 103,804 African-American students in a total public school enrollment of 127,268.

DESEGREGATION AND THE STRUGGLE AGAINST TRACKING

In the aftermath of the Supreme Court's decisions on 17 May 1954 in *Brown* and *Bolling* v. *Sharpe* (which terminated the dual-school system in Washington, D.C.), and along with some pressure from the White House, the District government moved to desegregate its public schools. Because of the city's unique political history, its schools were the only major federally controlled public educational system in the nation, and the Eisenhower administration expected Washington to serve as a "showcase" to the nation in making an orderly and prompt transition to a desegregated school system (LaNoue and Smith 1973).

In 1957, following the departure of Superintendent Hobart Corning, the Washington school board appointed Associate Superintendent Carl Hansen as the new superintendent to lead the school desegregation campaign. Hansen was a Nebraska native who had graduated from the state's university in Lincoln; he had obtained an education doctorate at the University of Southern California and had been a high school teacher and later a high school principal in Omaha before coming to Washington. Thus Hansen was an experienced educator who blended managerial expertise with a strong commitment to desegregated schooling. Indeed, he became one of the nation's foremost spokespersons for school desegregation (Wolters 1984).

At the commencement of the 1956 school year, the district's educational administration instituted a new program of tracking high school students. Hansen, then associate superintendent responsible for high schools, played a major role in the new policy's implementation. The stated objective of the tracking policy was to allow students with similar academic ability to work together regardless of racial or economic background. Based upon motivation, teachers' evaluation of students' past classroom performance, and scores on achievement

TABLE 1 ENROLLMENTS BY RACE, WASHINGTON, D.C., PUBLIC SCHOOLS, 1951–1981

Year	Total Enrollment	Afro-American Enrollment	White Enrollment	Percentage Afro-American	Percentage White
1951	95,932	50,250	45,682	52.4	47.6
1956	107,312	72,954	34,358	6,0	32.0
1961	127,268	103,804	23,464	81.6	18.4
1966	146,644	133,275	13,369	90.9	9.1
1971	142,899	136,256	6,643	95.4	4.6
1976*	125,908	119,814	4,406	95.2	3.5
1981	94,425	89,160	3,321	94.4	3.5

Source: Adapted from Wolters (1984, 16).
*Percentages do not add up to 100 after 1973 because Indians, Asians, and Hispanics are counted separately.

and aptitude tests given by educational researchers in the school system's pupil appraisal department, students were steered into one of four separate curriculum tracks: honors, college preparatory, general, and basic (remedial). High-performing students with IQ scores above 120 were to be placed in a special honors course of study; students with IQ scores between 120 and 75 were assigned either to the college preparatory or the general track if they were performing near grade level; students with IQ scores below 75 were put in the remedial or basic track. This latter track included mentally retarded students and those performing three years below grade level with IQ scores between 85 and 75 (U.S. Congress 1966; Wolters 1984).

While the tracking system did result in a modicum of racial and social class mixture in the honors and college preparatory categories, the general and basic tracks, which at the outset consisted overwhelmingly of African-American pupils from economically poor families, came increasingly to include African-American youngsters from professional classes as well. From the beginning, the tracking system was the target of numerous critics who expressed the view that students were being labeled and channeled by educational professionals and researchers into a narrow groove from which they would never exit (Mazique 1986; LaNoue and Smith 1973; Wolters 1984).

Starting with the 1959 school year, upon Superintendent Hansen's recommendation the Washington school board extended the tracking system by including elementary and junior high schools. The new policy established three tracks. Beginning with the fourth grade, youngsters with low IQ scores and a significant level of mental retardation were channeled into the basic track. Students ranking normal on aptitude tests and classroom performance were steered into the general track. Students with IQ scores above 125 and high classroom performance were directed to the honors track (Wolters 1984).

From its inception, the administratively driven policy of tracking elementary and junior high school students caused conflict. And, as the negative consequences of the tracking strategy became more and more apparent, broad community opposition increased precipitously into the 1960s. Three school board members expressed the apprehension that categorizing youngsters in the basic and general tracks at the beginning of their educational careers was premature and might retard normal and later academic growth and development (Wolters 1984). Community groups protested that the tracking system was a new tactic for labeling students and for reinstating a structure of dominance and African-American subordination more harmful than racial segregation in the Old South. Many charged that when educational managers, experts, and researchers applied to African-American students such terms as *culturally deprived, economically disadvantaged, victims of developmental disability,* or *permanently handicapped by degenerative evolution,* the implication of inherent racial inferiority would result. Moreover, community participants held the view that these characterizations helped to legitimize a theory and practice of withholding basic education from African-American students labeled *uneducable.* Critics charged, then, that the tracking system early excluded African-American youngsters from academic preparation and the educational specialists and managers then tested these students on what they had not been taught. This process allowed educational professionals to achieve a self-fulfilling prophecy (Mazique 1986).

In the early 1960s, community discontent continued to mount as citizen groups and activists charged that tracking denied African-American children a quality education or even a basic one. Community spokespersons intensified their criticism of the tracking system, arguing that steering children into low and middle tracks during elementary school would thwart subsequent educational growth. Additionally, it was reported that in some cases African-American children were summarily defined as mentally retarded without being examined and then automatically channeled into the low track (U.S. Congress 1966; Mazique 1986). Finally, angry African-American District residents demanded that all elementary school students, regardless of racial and class backgrounds, be given a basic education.

In the fall of 1960, the central administration responded to community concerns by establishing the Amidon School, an experiment in integrated quality education (Hansen 1960). The Amidon Plan proved to be a controversial undertaking. Superintendent Hansen announced that the new school, located in the extensively redeveloped quadrant of southwest Washington, was to be an integrated school that provided a program of educational fundamentals. Students from all over the District were admitted on a first-come, first-served basis. Superintendent Hansen stated bluntly the guiding assumptions of the Amidon Plan:

> If you teach children directly and in a highly organized way, they will learn better and faster and will, if teaching is consistent with what is known about the nature of learning, grow wholesomely, developing confidence as they acquire competence and gaining in self-respect as they accomplish difficult objectives. (Hansen 1960, 6)

Starting with the first grade, Amidon's curriculum stressed basic subjects—spelling, penmanship, arithmetic, and reading (taught by the traditional phonic method). Grammar, normally taught in the sixth grade, was introduced in the third grade, together with French and Spanish. History and geography were taught individually and not included in "social studies." While students were grouped together on the basis of similar academic achievement, tracking was not implemented in the Amidon Plan. There were no school parties, no orchestra, and no student government;

field excursions also were minimized. In this academically demanding program, homework was the rule (Hansen 1960).

Controversy, however, could not be avoided. Many liberal educational reformers and theorists condemned the Amidon School as a capitulation to conservatism. Some charged that the new school might succeed only as a result of selecting students from middle-class families who prized quality education and were willing to transport their children personally to and from the school. Other liberal educational reformers attacked the Amidon School's subject-centered curriculum and the institution's emphasis on structured student activity. However, when Hansen later announced that a staggering 94 percent of Amidon's students—a substantial number of whom came from low-income and working-class families—scored above the national average in both reading and mathematics, many educational experts were put on the defensive (U.S. Congress 1966). A growing number of parents and community groups argued that the Amidon model of quality education should be implemented throughout the Washington public school system.

By the mid-1960s, the issue of public school integration polarized the District and the nation. Many angry African-American parents and community organizations charged that as public school integration was pushed forward at all costs as the primary goal of education by educational professionals and even civil rights proponents, good classroom teaching, academic motivation, and positive character development in the public schools increasingly were set aside. Since the federal government controlled the Washington public school system, many African-American and white community groups and civic activists lobbied various congressional committees, appealing for improvement in the quality of education for all students in the District's schools.

The League for Universal Justice and Goodwill was one of the community organizations most critical of the tracking system. A grass-roots organization headed by the Reverend Walter A. Gray, the League consisted mainly of Baptist and Methodist ministers, African-American parents, and an assortment of African-American civic groups, including the National Capital Voters Association and the University Neighborhoods Council. The League's primary goal was not particularly racial integration but rather enhancement of the quality of education in Washington's schools. From its founding in 1960 to 1965, the League continually lobbied local and national policymakers to institute effective measures to stem the tide of educational decline and decay in the District's public schools (Mazique 1986).

In 1965, the League petitioned the U.S. House of Representatives Committee on Education and Labor, then chaired by Congress-man Adam Clayton Powell, to investigate racial discrimination and the tracking sys-tem in the Washington public schools. One hundred twenty-five leaders of civic, religious, professional, and fraternal organizations signed the 13 September 1965 petition. As a direct result of the League's petition, the House Committee on Education and Labor's Task Force on Antipoverty in the District of Columbia held a series of public hearings in October 1965 and January 1966, to look into the condition of the Washington public schools. Significantly, the League's important petition (a formal request by a local commu-nity organization) cannot be found in the early pages of the congressional report of the hearings; rather, it is deeply embedded in the more than 850-page document (U.S. Congress 1966, 260–261).

The petitioners leveled a general accusa-tion of racial discrimination against the District's public school system. Additionally, the petitioners made four specific charges: (1) the tracking system denied equal educa-tional opportunity; (2) school funds were allocated inversely proportional to needs;

(3) there was a growing trend toward estab-lishing an all-white administration in the areas of curriculum development and educa-tional policy-making; and (4) the District school system flagrantly attacked the personal dignity of African-American students, which resulted in rising community hostility and increasing dropouts and delinquency. In addi-tion to urging that the congressional committee undertake a fuller study of the petitioners' complaints, the petition contained a detailed description and elaboration of the petitioners' four major charges against the school system (U.S. Congress 1966).

The Reverend Gray appeared before the congressional task force and submitted a lengthy written statement, which contained a powerful indictment of the tracking system and Superintendent Hansen. The Reverend Gray labeled the tracking system "programmed retardation" and called Hansen a "promoter of educational colonialism and cultural suprem-acy, the manager of the unfair distribution of funds, violator of public trust and inaugurator of the mass destruction of [the] self-image" of Washington's African-American students (U.S. Congress 1966, 266). Gray denounced the tracking system and predicted the progressive deterioration of the District's schools if authori-tative measures were not taken to reverse trends he considered disastrous.

The Reverend Gray concluded his state-ment with a strong recommendation for the immediate abolition of the tracking system and the dismissal of Superintendent Hansen. In addition, he called for a prime emphasis on quality education; a uniform curriculum; annual performance ratings for teachers; the encouragement and promotion of qualified African-American teachers; a system of public financial accountability to ensure against discriminatory school-funding policies favor-ing more affluent schools; the termination of the policy of assigning staff personnel and other professionals to nonteaching services (e.g., testers and counselors), resulting in a spiraling school budget; and the end of the school system's theories and practice of racial and cultural supremacy and attacks on the personal dignity of African-American students (U.S. Congress 1966).

Other League members also spoke during the hearings and directly challenged the administrative hegemony of the District's public schools. Significantly, Mrs. Jewell Mazique, a parent and consultant to the League, expressed the views of many ordinary citizens when she exposed the limits of professional expertise and stated the lay public's role in educational policymaking. She asserted:

> Mr. Chairman and members of this committee, we believe that conditions in our local schools, where moral development has declined, and where the quality of education obtained has deteriorated (in spite of rising budgets and federal aid), command a public airing and an honest investigation of what is wrong. *If the administrators, educational theorists and other professionals cannot supply the answer, then it becomes the public's duty to assist* [italics in original]. We cannot continue indefinitely the downward trend toward imminent collapse of public education and expect our country to maintain its place in the sun [emphasis added]. (U.S. Congress 1966, 266).

In her lengthy statement, Mrs. Mazique provided a critical analysis of the tracking system. She, too, referred to tracking as a system of "programmed retardation," exposing the fact that through a kind of unwritten law, children were placed in tracks at the end of kindergarten following the administration of "readiness" tests and evaluation by the school principal, teachers, and counselors. Mrs. Mazique attacked the practice of using the terms *ability grouping* and *tracking* interchangeably, pointing out that the former term allowed for parental choice while the latter concept denied parental decision making in children's educational development. Charging that the tracking system was grounded in

theories of "cultural deprivation," which assumed that African-American children were uneducable or lacked sufficient motivation to learn, Mrs. Mazique pointed out that the African-American traditional yearning for knowledge dated back to the emancipation of the slaves. If something had occurred in recent years to interrupt that motivation, Mrs. Mazique observed, the problem should be placed at the door of the tracking-policy makers who systematically retarded the educational development of African-American and poor white children in Washington, D.C. Mrs. Mazique concluded with a demand for the end of the tracking system and the institutionalization of an educational program of excellence throughout the District's schools (U.S. Congress 1966).

Some educational experts also condemned Washington's public school tracking system, observing that the policy discriminated against students on the basis of race and class. For example, Howard University education professor Elias Blake presented a statistical analysis that showed that low track assignment correlated with low family income. Marvin Cline, a Howard University psychology professor, attacked the tracking system as racially discriminatory. He advocated a policy strategy of racial balance in the schools to improve educational quality. For Cline, desegregation was merely a step in the direction of complete racial integration (U.S. Congress 1966).

Significantly, neither Blake nor Cline had plugged into the network of community groups and concerns set in motion earlier by the Reverend Gray and the League for Universal Justice and Goodwill. When they eventually learned of Blake and Cline and their presentations before the Education and Labor Committee task force, many community participants felt sabotaged. As many community leaders later asserted, Blake's charge that the tracking system targeted low-income families and Cline's emphasis on racial integration and busing subtly shifted the issues away from community hopes and aspirations for enhancing quality education (Mazique 1986).

Following an extensive set of hearings, the House Committee on Education and Labor's task force recommended the termination of the District's tracking system. However, nothing resulted from the recommendation, as most congressmen considered it advisable to leave educational matters in the hands of local school officials. Since the majority of the District's judicially appointed school board members were loyal to Superintendent Hansen, the tracking system remained unchanged, for a time (Wolters 1984).

What led ultimately to the abolition of tracking in the District's public schools was a lawsuit filed by Julius Hobson, Sr. Hobson, a civil rights activist and government employee, was also one of the District's most vocal critics of the tracking system and Superintendent Hansen. Hobson, too, had testified before the Education and Labor Committee's task force, where he assailed the tracking system for racial and class bias. In the aftermath of the hearings, Hobson took legal action against the District's school officials, challenging the constitutionality of their educational policies, including tracking. However, the resulting legal policy decisions contrasted sharply with the hopes and aspirations of the District's African-American community for the institutionalization of quality education throughout the schools. In effect, traditional community leaders and organizations lost control of the issues as new persons like Hobson emerged to play major roles and put forward alternative issues. A discussion of these issues follows.

HOBSON V. HANSEN AND THE ABOLITION OF TRACKING: CONTRADICTIONS AND DILEMMAS

In July 1966, Hobson filed a class action suit in federal district court against Superintendent Hansen, the school board, and the Washington judges who appointed the board.

He complained that Washington's public schools unconstitutionally denied African-American and impoverished students equal educational opportunities provided to more well-off and white students. Additionally, Hobson charged that these educational disparities were the consequences of the tracking system, the principle of neighborhood schools, unfair teacher appointments to schools, and optional school zones for some students. Hobson questioned the constitutionality of the congressional act giving federal district court judges the power to appoint school board members. The last complaint was separated from the others, and a three-judge district court heard it. The nature of Hobson's challenge required that the three-judge panel be composed of circuit judges unrelated to the appointment process. In a decision from which Judge J. Skelly Wright dissented, the panel upheld the constitutionality of the statute, ruling that Congress could delegate appointive authority to federal judges in Washington, D.C. However, a request of the Judicial Conference of the District of Columbia Circuit resulted in a subsequent congressional amendment of the statute to allow for an elected school board (Horowitz 1977; LaNoue and Smith 1973).

Judge J. Skelly Wright of the U.S. Court of Appeals heard Hobson's remaining charges. Judge Wright sustained Hobson in *Hobson* v. *Hansen* (1967). The judge held a lengthy hearing and wrote a far-reaching opinion and decree, ordering the school board to: abolish the tracking system, develop a student assignment policy in harmony with the court's order and not based completely on the neighborhood-school principle, provide transportation to African-American students wishing to transfer to white schools, terminate optional school zones, and design a program of "color-conscious" faculty assignments to effect teacher integration (Horowitz 1977; LaNoue and Smith 1973).

The *Hobson* v. *Hansen* ruling did not put an end to controversy surrounding the assortment of major educational issues in Washington. Indeed, some dilemmas emerged as a result of the decision. However, the case is important to Washington's public school history because it set in motion future challenges to educational policy-making by accentuating the major issues. The leading actors in the District's educational politics from 1967 to 1971 also emerged as a result of the case and its late effect on the school system (LaNoue and Smith 1973). These new issues and leaders effectively supplanted goals and struggles of traditional community leaders and organizations, like the Reverend Gray and the League for Universal Justice and Goodwill, which had fought for quality education since the late 1950s and early 1960s.

Stated in brief, it might be suggested that the *Hobson* v. *Hansen* decision sought to achieve three objectives: integration, quality education, and equality of educational opportunity. Three prominent actors in Washington's educational politics became publicly associated with each of these objectives. Judge Wright came to represent an ongoing allegiance to integration; Hobson came to represent equal educational opportunity; and Mrs. Anita Allen, recently appointed to the school board, came to represent the quest for quality education. Allen, as a member of Washington's first predominantly African-American school board, helped carry the vote to effectuate Judge Wright's decision and to direct Superintendent Hansen not to challenge the ruling. This occurred on 1 July 1967—the day Allen took office. Hansen promptly resigned and joined a dissenting board member in an unsuccessful suit to appeal the *Hobson* decision. Several ineffective superintendents followed Hansen, resulting in the school system's lack of strong executive authority. Moreover, the school board could not provide vigorous leadership because it was embroiled in internal squabbles and faced with community discontent (LaNoue and Smith 1973).

Although Hobson became Washington's first elected official in more than a century when he was a member of the school board for one year in 1968, he generally played the role of an agitator and outside critic of the school system. Similar to many middle-class reformers, however, Hobson failed to establish strong linkages with the community he was supposed to represent. In his reelection bid in 1969, Hobson lost to Exie Mae Washington, a former domestic worker who was promoted to community leadership status through the poverty program. Hobson also had been damaged in his attempt to encourage educational change because of a weakened school bureaucracy and the lack of strong administrative leadership to respond to his demands (LaNoue and Smith 1973).

In the final analysis, the three major objectives of the Wright decision in the *Hobson* case could not be accomplished all at once. Judge Wright had strongly emphasized racial integration and set in motion policies and practices that contradicted the Washington African-American community's original goal of quality education. As a result of the judge's decree, coupled with the research findings of educational policy entrepreneurs (particularly, the Coleman report of 1966), the goal shifted from quality education to racial balancing and busing. This was not the policy strategy desired by Washington's African-American community, although racial balancing and busing fit well within the social management policy agenda of educational reform's liberal professional-managerial elites and many civil rights advocates. The African-American community had demanded quality education: the distribution and mastery of the fundamental tools of knowledge (reading, writing, and computational skills), academic motivation, and good character building. For many African-American community participants, emphasis on racial balancing and busing set aside the concern for achieving quality education. One community observer flatly characterized the result as a "betrayal in the schools" (Washington 1969).

Judge Wright's decision in the *Hobson* case also contributed to the continuation of white flight from Washington and its public schools. By the time the decree was handed down, the city's public schools were 92 percent African-American, and with the continued growth in the proportion of African-American students, integration became impossible. Even the school board seemed to realize the declining possibility and importance of integration when it released the findings of the Passow report, an exhaustive study and analysis of Washington's schools. One section of the report stated bluntly that it was pointless to speak of racial integration or racial balance in a school system with a student enrollment of more than 90 percent African-American (Passow 1967).

CONCLUSION

Prior to the 1950s, American educational politics and policy were largely dominated by the legacy of the turn-of-the-century Progressive Era of school reform. That earlier reform movement sought to remove politics from urban education by centralizing executive power in the person of professional educational managers; establishing bureaucratically organized school systems; and using the rhetoric of "science," expertise, and efficiency as the guiding principles of the educational enterprise. Indeed, both lay officials on urban school boards and the lay public largely were deferential to educational professionals, managers, and their expert knowledge.

However, a managerial style, organizational form, and educational ideology operative in one period can frequently become impediments in the next. An inherent problem with the managerial decision-making process, organizational complexity, and scientistic rhetoric of the educational reform period was that they severely restricted public participation in

the urban educational policy-making process. Thus, in the 1950s and 1960s, these arrangements gave rise to a popular challenge to the prerogatives of educational professionals and their exclusive bureaucratic policy-making process. Moreover, ordinary citizens began to confront the hegemonic role of expert knowledge in educational decision making.

In the case of Washington, the introduction of the tracking system into the public schools is an example of managerial-bureaucratic policy-making that effectively excluded popular participation. Moreover, the strategy of channeling children into different curricular tracks—based upon "scientific" IQ test scores as interpreted by educational experts and classroom performance evaluations by principals and teachers—exemplified educational reformers' rhetoric and practice of social management. In addition, the policy had racial overtones, as it directed a large proportion of African-American children to the low track. As a result of being constrained from influencing decisions affecting their interest in protecting their children's future educational development, parental and community groups became increasingly angry and directly challenged the District's educational professionals and specialists. The efforts of the League for Universal Justice and Goodwill and other grass-roots organizations to attack politically the formulators and implementors of the tracking system represented a shift from the past era of public school politics when educational professionals largely commanded popular deference to an emerging politics of education distinguished by increased community challenge to public school professionals. This new brand of open and aggressive community politics would come to characterize the politics of urban educational policy-making in the 1970s and 1980s (Hayes 1985).

The present study of the historical trends and developments in the politics of public schooling in the District of Columbia exposes a transition from segregation with parental and community concern for quality education to integration with official emphasis on tracking and later racial busing and balancing, ultimately newer forms of racial discrimination that denied quality education to African-American youngsters. The District's public school officials advocated the tracking system as a means of complying with the *Brown* and *Bolling* Supreme Court decisions. In contrast, the African-American community attacked this policy, seeking the institutionalization of quality education throughout the public school system. The League and its members defined quality education as the distribution and mastery of the basic tools of knowledge, academic motivation, and positive character development. They characterized the tracking system as "programmed retardation," charging that this policy strategy was worse than segregation in the Old South. Community spokespersons argued forcefully that tracking would result in the eventual deterioration of public education in Washington.

Asserting that tracking early on retarded a child's later academic growth and development, legitimized a practice of withholding educational fundamentals from African-American students, and denied African-American children a quality education or even a basic one, the District's African-American residents demanded a basic education in all of the city's schools. Indeed, the success of the District's Amidon Plan and its subject-centered curriculum served as proof then and now that a return to the basics in public schools would lead to quality education for all students regardless of race or class background. Recognizing the value of Amidon's curriculum, Washington's community leaders called in vain for similar plans to be implemented throughout the District.

Because of the District's unique political history as the nation's capital, the city public schools were controlled by Congress. Therefore, as community frustration and discontent

with public school officials grew, the League petitioned the House Committee on Education and Labor to investigate charges of racial and class discrimination in the District's schools. The hope was that Congress would abolish the tracking system.

Congress did not abolish the tracking policy, maintaining the collective opinion that educational matters should remain in the hands of local officials. The community was defeated in its struggle for quality education, even though community leaders had initiated an effective challenge to Washington's public school professionals and the tracking system. Judge J. Skelly Wright's ruling in the *Hobson* case did terminate tracking in the District's schools; however, he ignored the community's cry for quality education as a priority for Washington 's schools. Thus, with Wright's decision, the issues shifted from the community's concern for enhancing quality education to the educational professionals' and experts' policy agenda and debate (at the national and local levels) regarding racial balancing and busing. This was the "great betrayal" and represented a regrouping and continuation of educational reform's goal of social management into the 1960s and 1970s. While racial balancing and busing could not be achieved in Washington's schools, whose students were more than 90 percent African-American, racial balancing and busing did command the attention of educational professionals and community participants in the surrounding suburban jurisdictions of the greater Washington metropolitan area (see Hayes 1985). Moreover, in the 1970s, an increasingly active judiciary came to sanction and enforce various forms of racial balancing and busing in metropolitan areas across the nation (Kirp 1982; Willie and Greenblatt 1981). Such judicial activism may have been the single most significant factor in the ultimate decline of public education.

Although the District's African-American community lost its struggle for quality education, its leaders' earlier predictions of the dire consequences of the tracking system's "programmed retardation" cannot be ignored today (see Oakes 1985). Moreover, Mrs. Mazique's warning before the 1966 congressional task force regarding "the downward trend toward imminent collapse of public education" is confirmed by the contemporary national anxiety and debate about America's current educational predicament (for example, see Altbach, Kelly, and Weis 1985; National Commission on Excellence in Education 1983). As in many other urban school systems, the number of National Merit scholars graduating from Washington's high schools is minuscule, and a substantially large proportion of them require remedial assistance upon entering college. Washington's public schools are faced with an assortment of educational and social difficulties: dropouts and continued enrollment decline since 1970, drug-related activities, teenage pregnancies, school closings, and growing parental discontent (Sanchez 1990; Vassell 1990). There are recent indications that many African-American parents are withdrawing their children from the public schools and enrolling them in private and parochial schools. Commenting on the progressive deterioration of public trust in the District's schools, one researcher has observed that "a permanent lack of confidence has now replaced the 'crisis of confidence'" (Diner 1990). For the Washington, D.C. public school system, and for urban public school systems throughout America, the great challenge of the future will be to reinstate quality education and thereby rebuild confidence in public education.

Note

1. This study benefited from in-depth interviews with Mrs. Jewell R. Mazique conducted in 1986. She is one of the few, if not the only, remaining key community participants in the events chronicled in this article. I am grateful to her for sharing with me her wealth of historical knowledge and personal experience regarding educational politics in Washingtion, D.C., since the 1950s.

References

Altbach, P. G., G. P. Kelly, and L. Weis, eds. 1985. *Excellence in education. Perspectives on policy and practice.* Buffalo NY: Prometheus.

Bolling v. *Sharpe*, 347 U.S. 497 (1954).

Brown v. *Board of Education*, 347 U.S. 483 (1954).

Coleman, J., E. Campbell, C. J. Hobson, J. McPartland, A. M. Mood, F. D. Weinfeld, and R. L. York. 1966. Equality of educational opportunity. 2 vols. (Report no. OE-38001, Office of Education.) Washington, DC: GPO.

Diner, S. J. 1990. Crisis of confidence: Public confidence in the schools of the Nation's capital in the twentieth century. *Urban Education* 25:112–37.

Flesch, R. 1955. *Why Johnny can't read.* New York: Harper & Row.

Hansen, C. F. 1960. *The Amidon Plan: For education in the sixties in the D.C. Public Schools. Washington, DC: D.C. Government.*

Hayes. F. W., III. 1985. Division and conflict in postindustrial politics: Social change and educational policymaking in Montgomery County, Maryland. Ph.D. diss., University of Maryland.

Hobson v. *Hansen*, 265 F. Supp. 902 (1967).

Horowitz, D. F. 1977. *The courts and social policy.* Washington, DC: Brookings Institute.

Kirp, D. L.. 1982. *Just schools: The idea of racial equality in American education.* Berkeley: University of California Press.

LaNoue, G. R., and B. L. R. Smilh. 1973. *The politics of school decentralization.* Lexington: Lexington Books.

Mazique, J. R. 1986. Interview. 5 March.

National Commission on Excellence in Education. 1983. *A nation at risk: The imperative for educational reform.* Washington, DC: GPO.

Oakes, J. 1985. *Keeping track: How schools structure inequality.* New Haven, CT: Yale University Press.

Passow, A. H. 1967. *Toward creating a model urban school system: A study of the Washingon D.C. public schools.* New York: Teachers College, Columbia University.

Rickover, H. C. 1959. *Education and freedom.* New York: E. P. Dutton.

Sanchez, R. 1990. New D.C. school figures show large declines. *Washington Post* (7 March): A1, A12.

Tyack, D. B., and E. Hansot. 1982. *Managers of virtue: Public school leadership in America 1820–1980.* New York: Basic Books.

U.S. Congress. House. Commitee on Education and Labor. *Investigation of the schools and poverty in the District of Columbia: Hearings before the Task Force on Antipoverty in the District of Columbia.* 89th Cong., 1st and 2d sess., 1965–1966. Y4.

Vassell, O. 1990. Parents group wants board booted. *Washington Post* (14 April): A1, A2.

Washington, M. W. 1969. Betrayal in the schools: As seen by an advocate of African-American power. *Triumph Magazine* (January): 16–19.

Willie, C. V., and S. L. Greenblatt, eds. 1981. *Community politics and educational change: Ten school systems under court order.* New York: Longman.

Wolters, R. 1984. *The burden of Brown: Thirty years of school desegregation.* Knoxville: University of Tennessee Press.

The Effect of Desegregation Policies on Historically Black Public Colleges and Universities

JOHN MATLOCK

FROM THE U.S. SUPREME COURT'S land-mark *Brown* v. *Board of Education* decisions in 1954 and 1955 up to the present, considerable attention has been directed to desegregation of elementary and secondary schools in the United States. Declaring "the fundamental principle that discrimination in public higher education is unconstitutional" (*Brown* 1955), the Court made no distinction between various levels of public education—elementary, secondary, and higher education. Yet, public institutions of higher education managed to escape the impact of the *Brown* mandates, and continued to exclude blacks legally, leaving them no choice but to attend historically black institutions. Prior to *Brown*, the Supreme Court had dealt narrowly with several issues associated with segregation in public higher education: *Gaines* v. *Canada* 1938; *Sipuel* v. *Board of Regents* 1948; *McLaurin* v. *Oklahoma* 1950.

OVERVIEW OF THE *ADAMS* CASE

In 1969, the Office for Civil Rights (OCR) in the Department of Health, Education and Welfare (HEW) concluded that ten states (Louisiana, Mississippi, Oklahoma, Arkansas, Pennsylvania, Georgia, Virginia, Maryland, Florida, and North Carolina) were operating racially segregated higher education systems in violation of the 1964 Civil Rights Act. OCR used enrollment data in establishing these violations. Racial enrollment at historically black and historically white institutions were basically the same as they had been when higher education institutions were legally segregated in these states. In other words, historically black schools were still nearly all black, and historically white schools were still virtually all white.

Based on OCR's conclusions, HEW requested the ten states to develop and submit plans designed to desegregate their dual higher education systems. Arkansas, Pennsylvania, Georgia, Maryland, and Virginia developed and submitted plans, but Louisiana, Mississippi, Oklahoma, North Carolina, and Florida

Reprinted from *Black Colleges and Universities: Challenges for the Future,* edited by Antoine Garibaldi, 1984. Reprinted with permission of Praeger Publishers, New York, an imprint of Greenwood Publishing Group, Inc.

refused. Furthermore, the five plans submitted to HEW were deemed unacceptable.

In 1970, the NAACP Legal Defense and Educational Fund, Inc. (LDF) filed a class action suit against HEW stating that the agency had been derelict in its duty to enforce the Civil Rights Act because it had not taken steps to compel states to desegregate their racially segregated systems of higher education. The suit requested that HEW take action to cut off federal funds to these states. HEW countered by asking that the suit be dismissed because it had the authority to decide what actions, if any, should be taken against the ten states.

In 1973, over three years after the suit was filed, the U.S. District Court in Washington, D.C. ruled that the states were in violation of the Civil Rights Act and that HEW had a duty to begin enforcement proceedings (*Adams* v. *Richardson*). The court ordered HEW to initiate enforcement proceedings within 60 days.

Black Colleges' Arguments

Various civil rights groups and educators were elated with the court's mandate, but other groups, particularly those representing black colleges and universities, viewed the mandate skeptically. Their concerns were that the desegregation mandate would be utilized by states to diminish the role of public black colleges and universities; the mandate potentially endangered the future existence of these institutions.

HEW appealed the ruling to a circuit court which upheld the lower court's ruling, but gave HEW additional time to obtain desegregation plans from the affected states. During the appeal, the National Association for Equal Opportunity in Higher Education (NAFEO), an organization of presidents of historically black institutions, intervened as *amicus curiae*. NAFEO argued that the historically black public institutions had not practiced segregation and discrimination, and stressed that these institutions had a unique role in higher

education. NAFEO also stated that these colleges had provided compensatory and reparative educational services to black students, who historically suffered from segregated school systems as well as discrimination in employment.

Obviously swayed by NAFEO's argument, the court ruled that it was important that desegregation of public higher education be resolved on a state system-wide basis, rather than on an individual institutional basis. The court noted:

> The problem of integrating higher education must be dealt with on a statewide rather than a school-by-school basis. Perhaps the most serious problem in this area is the lack of statewide planning to provide more and better trained minority group doctors, lawyers and other professionals. A predicate for minority access to quality post-graduate programs is a viable, coordinated, statewide higher education policy that takes into account the special problems of minority students and of black colleges. As *amicus* points out, these black institutions currently fulfill a crucial need and will continue to play an important role in black higher education (*Adams* v. *Richardson,* D.C. Cir. 1973).

With the exception of Louisiana, which refused to submit a plan, and Mississippi, which had its plan rejected because it did not include community colleges, the states submitted desegregation plans to the Office of Civil Rights and they were accepted. OCR evaluated the plans and later said they were not specific in delineating how the delineated goals and programs would desegregate the states' higher education systems. The NAACP Legal Defense Fund filed a "Motion for Further Relief" on the basis that HEW, by accepting inadequate plans, had not lived up to its court-imposed obligations.

Again, NAFEO filed an *amicus curiae* brief in opposition to the "Motion for Further Relief" request. NAFEO contended that the roles and missions of traditionally black institutions were valid, and that they provided

Howard University. (Left) Frederick Douglass Memorial Hall. (Below) In 1968, during a protest, students demand that the university be renamed.

equal education to black students. According to NAFEO, without the historically black public institutions there would be no mechanism for providing education to blacks who had received inadequate training from public elementary and secondary schools as the result of segregation.

In early 1977, the court granted the Legal Defense Fund's request for relief noting that the plans accepted by HEW were inadequate, and that HEW had not fulfilled its obligation under the court order. The court ordered the plaintiffs and defendants to draft an order that HEW could utilize in negotiating acceptable plans from the six states, Arkansas, Georgia, Virginia, Oklahoma, North Carolina, and Florida, which, by law, had operated racially segregated public higher education systems. A federal court in Maryland enjoined HEW from initiating enforcement proceedings against Maryland, and Pennsylvania intervened as a defendant in the *Adams* case and agreed to a separate negotiation with the plaintiffs and HEW.

HEW and the plaintiffs could not reach an agreement and HEW requested an extension of time in late March 1977. On April 1, however, the court, while granting HEW an additional two months, issued a supplemental order requiring the agency to develop and issue specific criteria for the states to utilize in developing their desegregation plans. The result was a document entitled *Amended Criteria Specifying the Ingredients of Acceptable Plans to Desegregate State Systems of Public Higher Education,* which was accepted by the court.

The criteria developed by HEW were to apply to the six states listed above. Desegregation was to be accomplished on a statewide basis and the states were required to take affirmative steps to overcome the causes and effects of prior discrimination in public higher education. Specific goals and timetables were to be developed for desegregating faculty, administrators, nonacademic staffs, and governing boards of state public higher education

systems. The states were cautioned to consider the characteristics of higher education systems which would make desegregating them different from public elementary and secondary schools. Finally, the states were instructed to recognize the unique role of the historically black colleges.

The Special Mission of Black Colleges

On this final criterion, the court in its Second Supplemental Order (*Adams* v. *Califano* 1977), specifically stated:

> The process of desegregation must not place a greater burden on black institutions or black students' opportunity to receive a quality public higher education. The desegregation process should take into account the unequal status of the black colleges and the real danger that desegregation will diminish higher education opportunities for blacks. Without suggesting the answer to this complex problem, it is the responsibility of HEW to devise criteria for higher education desegregation plans which will take into account the unique importance of black colleges and at the same time comply with the Congressional mandate.

Despite the court's caution concerning HEW's criteria for developing desegregation plans, supporters of black colleges and universities wondered if states that previously perpetuated segregated public higher education systems, and for many years neglected and underfunded black institutions, could now do an about-face. Would these states provide the resources and leadership necessary to expand and enhance the historically black institutions? And are predominantly white institutions, which in the past excluded blacks, now committed to advancing educational opportunities for blacks, or are they more interested in filling the empty chairs that demographic data show will exist in the future?

It was the court's premise in *Adams* that long-range planning offered the best and most realistic promise for desegregating within a reasonable time, since instant desegregation probably could not be achieved. As a result of court mandates, governmental policies, and the desegregation planning processes of state higher-education systems, the current and future roles of historically black colleges and universities most certainly will change. This chapter focuses on the impact desegregation planning is having on these colleges and will have on their future roles in higher education.

PROGRESS OF DESEGREGATION PLANS
In late 1983, desegregation of higher educa-tion was still unresolved in a number of *Adams* states. In others, progress was being made toward a plan, but all were in different stages of development. The original court order required that the NAACP Legal Defense Fund approve the plans submitted by the Depart-ment of Education (DOE), but the LDF has not approved all plans accepted by the DOE. The DOE's Office for Civil Rights has approved plans in Alabama, Delaware, Kentucky, Louisiana, North Carolina (university system only), South Carolina, Missouri, Texas, Virginia, and West Virginia. Plans submitted by Arkansas, Florida, Georgia, North Carolina (community-college system), and Oklahoma had been rejected as of July 1983; Pennsylvania had just submitted its plans. Arkansas and Florida were told to add to their plans "measures designed to increase the recruit-ment of black students at traditionally white institutions and to increase the number of blacks employed in academic positions"; North Carolina and Oklahoma were told to submit supplemental information on how they planned to increase black enrollment at certain institutions; and Georgia officials were advised to provide specific steps to increase the amount of black faculty and staff members, as well as "to further enhance and desegregate the state's traditionally black public institutions" (McDonald 1983). All revised plans were due to DOE on August 15, 1983 and, if they were rejected, the affected states could face the loss of federal educa-tion support.

A UNIQUE MERGER: TENNESSEE STATE UNIVERSITY AND THE UNIVERSITY OF TENNESSEE AT NASHVILLE
On July 1, 1979, after a ten-year court battle, the traditionally white University of Tennessee at Nashville (UTN) was merged into historically black Tennessee State University (TSU) (Matlock and Humphries 1979). The merger was the result of a court order upheld by the U.S. Supreme Court when it declined to review the case. While Tennessee is a non-*Adams* state, the desegregation principles the court advanced are similar to those in the *Adams* case. It was the first merger of two institutions— one traditionally black and the other tradi-tionally white—where the black institution emerged as the surviving institution.

Historical Overview
In 1968, a class action suit was filed by Rita Sanders (now Rita Geier) in the U.S. District Court in Nashville, Tennessee, on behalf of all blacks living in Tennessee, as well as all white residents, students, and faculty at Tennessee State A & I University (now TSU), and students attending Tennessee public high schools. The governor of Tennessee, the UTN's board of trustees, the Tennessee Higher Education Commission (the coordinating agency for Tennessee higher education), the U.S. Depart-ment of Health, Education and Welfare (HEW), and the State Board of Education (the govern-ing body for TSU) were named as defendants in the suit.

The suit sought an injunction to prohibit UTN from expanding its downtown Nashville campus by constructing a new building. The basis of the suit was that expansion of UTN's Nashville campus would perpetuate segregation at TSU and a dual public higher-education system based on race in Tennessee. HEW was named in the suit because it was providing some of the funds for the construction of the downtown building. HEW was eventually excused as a defendant in the suit and then joined with the plaintiffs. It asserted that the maintenance of several white institutions and one black institution in Tennessee violated the Fourteenth Amendment's Equal Protection Clause on the premise that students at TSU received inferior education opportunities. HEW requested a court order requiring that the state dismantle the dual system and that the defendants submit to the court a statewide plan for desegregating public higher education in Tennessee.

Tennessee's public higher-education system previously was segregated by law under the state constitution of 1870, and no blacks were permitted to attend any of the numerous white public institutions until 1960. Tennessee State, founded in 1912 as a land-grant institution for Negroes, was the only choice for black students prior to this time. In 1947, UTN was established in downtown Nashville, the state capital, as a two-year extension center, to provide evening instruction for part-time students employed by business and governmental agencies. UTN was accredited in 1971 to award external degrees.

After holding hearings, the court denied the plaintiff's injunction request that would have prevented the construction of UTN's building, but mandated that the defendants submit to the court a plan for desegregating higher education in Tennessee. The court said that UTN did not show intentions of becoming a degree-granting institution and was not in direct competition for students with TSU since the two schools served vastly different clienteles. The court concluded that expansion of UTN would not contribute to the perpetuation of a dual higher-education system in the state.

The defendants submitted a plan that offered recommendations rather than specific plans of action. These recommendations included recruiting black high-school students to attend white colleges and universities, increasing black faculty at white campuses, recruiting white students and faculty to go to TSU, and providing joint TSU and UTN academic programs. The court was neutral on the plan and directed the defendants to report on their recommendations and to develop a more specific plan.

The defendants submitted numerous reports over a period of years. The court continued to maintain that, while progress was being made in breaking up the state's dual education system, the recommendations aimed at resolving the problems associated with white UTN and black TSU were not satisfactory. The court finally indicated that the plan submitted by the defendants would not work and ordered that a new plan which would involve developing programs at TSU to attract white students and to desegregate its faculty. The defendants were also asked to consider the possibility of merging TSU and UTN.

A second plan was submitted which the court accepted as minimal. This plan included selecting white faculty at TSU over black applicants, special TSU scholarships for white students, constructing a business building and a library, and transferring UTN's social work program to TSU's campus but maintaining it under UTN's control.

Several subsequent reports reflected little progress on the plan. TSU had attracted few white students. Additionally, UTN was given degree-granting status in 1971. UTN now offered undergraduate degrees in approximately 22 areas including a master's degree in business administration. Furthermore, the Tennessee Higher Education Commission (THEC) recommended that merger was the only way to eliminate the segregated public higher-education system in Tennessee.

Finally, in 1977, while accepting the statewide desegregation plan, the court ordered the merger of TSU and UTN and stipulated that the merger be completed within three years from July 1, 1977. The court noted the failure of the various previous plans in desegregating TSU and UTN. In 1977, enrollment at TSU was 84 percent black, 15 percent nonblack, and 1 percent foreign students; 23 percent of the 284 faculty members were white. The court indicated that, while most of the white institutions had made significant progress in desegregating their institutions, TSU had had little success in attracting white students.

At the time of the merger order, TSU was under the direction of the Tennessee State Board of Regents (SBR), which was formed in 1972 as the governing board for six regional universities and ten community colleges in Tennessee. The UTN system comprises four campuses and has a separate governing body. One of TSU's major concerns was that the SBR, not TSU, was given authority by the court to plan and implement the merger. In many cases, TSU could only make recommendations to the SBR for their consideration.

TSU was in the position of being ordered by a court to have another institution merge with it, without retaining control of selection of personnel or organizational structure. Additionally, the chancellor of the SBR at the time of the merger had been UTN's chancellor prior to his appointment in 1975.

The defendants appealed the decision; but, on April 13, 1979, the U.S. Sixth Circuit Court of Appeals in Cincinnati, Ohio, upheld the decision. The appeals court supported the lower court's findings that, although the state's plan for desegregating public higher education in Tennessee was acceptable, TSU "required special attention because it was the heart of the dual system," and that previous plans and the expansion of UTN "impeded the required dismantling of the dual system." The appeals court decreed that the district court did not exceed its power in ordering the merger. The defendants appealed the case to the U.S. Supreme Court, which declined to hear it.

Impact of the Merger and Desegregation Policies

As the result of the merger, TSU's enrollment rose from 5,358 students in fall 1978 to 8,438 in fall 1979. In fall 1978 the enrollment of UTN at Nashville was 5,419; 805 or 15 percent were black students. So the combined enrollment could have been close to 11,000 students, but many white students from UTN did not enroll in TSU after the merger.

TSU's enrollment declined from 83.1 percent black in 1978 to 60.5 percent black in 1979 after the merger. In 1978, 63.3 percent (219 of 346) of TSU's faculty was black. After the merger only 44.5 perent were black (216 out of 406). The percentage of black administrators dropped from 90.8 (59 of 65) in 1978 to 68.8 (64 of 93) after the merger.

The merger created an interesting mix of students, exclusive of race. Formerly UTN was a commuter school attracting part-time, older, working students compared to TSU's residential, younger, full-time student body. After the merger, TSU acquired the UTN facility on a lease arrangement. The campuses, four miles apart, remain much the way they were prior to the merger, causing some concern that there are still a predominantly white and a predominantly black campus. This will probably change in the future as TSU administrators shift programs and activities between the two campuses. To reduce the shock of the merger, full integration of the two campuses did not occur during the first year.

From 1977 to 1979 throughout the state college system, excluding TSU, desegregation efforts have resulted in only small percentage increases in black student enrollment—from 11.6 percent to 18.8 percent (15,137 to 15,495). The percentage of black undergraduates increased from 12.5 to 12.6 of total undergraduate enrollment (13,748 to 13,892). Black graduate enrollment rose from 7.2 percent (1,305) of total graduate enrollment to 8.5 percent (1,603). There were only slight increases in the percentage of black faculty (3.1 to 3.4 percent) and of black administrators (3.7 to 4.2 percent).

IMPACT OF DESEGREGATION ON BLACK INSTITUTIONS

One major criticism of desegregation plans by officials at historically black institutions was that black administrators had little input into the planning process (Haynes 1979, 1980). In some cases, they were asked to submit data, but institutional self-studies and other plans were disregarded.

Desegregation planning has resulted in a closer scrutiny of historically black institutions in various states. Not only were these institutions underfunded in the past, but they were given far less political, technical, and management support than other institutions. In other words, as long as the institutions educated only black students, they received little assistance or attention. Now, as states attempt to desegregate these institutions, the management and fiscal abilities of the administrators are being called into question. Numerous historically black schools are undergoing management reviews that are resulting in administrative changes from presidents on down. For example, the University of North Carolina system has begun a study to assess the administrator of its five traditionally black schools; and the Tennessee Board of Regents conducted a yearlong evaluation of the president of TSU and his administration almost a year prior to the merger of UTN into TSU.

Role Changes for Black Colleges

In some cases, the states' new activities recommended for historically black institutions appear to alter the roles and missions of these institutions. For example, one state has selected its black university to become an urban institution, despite its being a land-grant institution. This could drastically alter its status and role. Furthermore, some states propose activities and programs for their historically black institutions that disregard the existing roles and missions of the institutions, instead of enhancing and expanding those roles.

Few states, in their desegregation plans, acknowledge having any prior responsibility for the problems of their public black institutions, despite years of underfunding, neglect, and the building of neighboring, competing higher-education institutions. In fact, one gets the impression from several plans that the states almost blame the black institutions for their problems.

Administrators at historically black institutions see these efforts as a ploy to discredit the black institutions. One administrator noted that most fiscal problems at black schools are the result of underfunding. He states that all state colleges and universities are audited each year and are not permitted to have a deficit budget. He wondered why these fiscal problems and deficits were not identified by state auditors years ago, and why the states did nothing to help the traditionally black schools to resolve them.

Emphasis on Attracting White Students

As Haynes (1979, 1980) noted, some desegregation plans show little evidence of any sound rationale or logic for determining the academic requirements of the historically black institutions. Programs are proposed for these institutions without the benefit of analysis of employment needs and opportunities in the state. The concern appears to be to develop academic activities at the black institutions to attract white students, rather than to address the needs of the institutions and the state and local communities.

Black institutions generally have not been successful in attracting white students, despite the statewide implementation of desegregation plans. Yet there has been a significant increase in the number of black students attending predominantly white institutions. Enrollment at historically black institutions continues to drop as black students have greater access to other educational settings including community colleges, proprietary schools, as well as the white institutions. The desegregation plans do not adequately address this problem, nor that of the decreasing numbers of blacks who are entering colleges and universities.

Goals to increase the number of black students at historically white institutions tend to be low and are easily obtained in some of the desegregation plans. For example, a 150 percent increase of black students in a discipline that enrolls an abnormally low number of black students will still result in small numbers, although the percentage goal may have been reached.

Faculty Changes

On the other hand, white schools have not been successful in attracting black faculty and administrators, despite the desegregation and affirmative action plans. In some states, they have done so by "raiding" historically black colleges. The result is little overall change in the number of black faculty in a particular system. Most of the desegregation plans compare faculty salaries among institutions but do not make it possible to reach conclusions regarding their equity; important variables such as years in rank, discipline, highest degree awarded, and sex are not controlled.

How Will Desegregation Be Funded?

While the intent of the court was to eliminate public higher-education segregation through systemwide planning in the *Adams* states, some plans show considerable evidence of individual institutional planning rather than systemwide planning. The quality and consistency of statistical data included in the desegregation plans vary considerably. It is apparent that states that lacked an adequate data base relied more on data submitted by individual institutions.

The funding mechanisms of the desegregation plans reviewed seem very unrealistic. For example, one plan suggested that it would take approximately $90 million to bring the state's traditionally black institutions up to par with their counterparts, but the plan did not indicate the source of the additional funds. Furthermore, several states suggested that funds to assist the historically black schools would come from higher education allocations, thus inviting a competitive environment among institutions that see little chance of obtaining the necessary resources to adequately operate their campuses.

A key omission in all the desegregation plans, primarily because it was not required, is a description of the legislative process relative to higher education in each state. For example, what involvement do the governor and the legislature have in the budget development and approval process?

Monitoring and Evaluation

Some plans leave the monitoring of the desegregation process to the agency that develops the plan. In one state, no provisions were made for a citizen's advisory board to monitor the progress of the desegregation process. Some plans also fail to establish an adequate process for evaluating the impact of proposed changes on various institutions. Yet, careful evaluation is a requisite of any ongoing desegregation plan.

RECOMMENDATIONS

More detailed research is needed on the potential effects that desegregation has had and will have on the historically black institutions. Without this information, it will be difficult to develop and evaluate plans for the inevitable changes that will come. Considerable analytic research has been conducted on the impacts of desegregation in elementary and secondary schools but there is a paucity of research that examines the actual impact of desegregation on public higher education, especially at the institutional level. The following recommendations for change (which are directed to black institutions, states, and students), therefore, depend on impact analysis or must incorporate research and evaluation in the planning and execution of programs.

Before various academic programs and policies are implemented, historically black public institutions should conduct impact analyses to determine potential effects of the programs and policies on their campuses, as well as on how the programs meet the needs of the community and the state. Such analyses will help to identify needed institutional support and resources to sustain new programs and the effect these new initiatives will have on current and future enrollments.

Research is needed on the economic and social impacts that black institutions have on their communities, and whether a new and different clientele will alter their historic roles and missions.

Historically black public institutions will need to determine what impact their state's proposed changes and desegregation planning efforts will have on them, review and revise their missions, develop long-range plans and strategies, and collect and analyze longitudinal data. Moreover, they should take an active role in the desegregation process, primarily to assure that proposed plans concur with their self-studies.

Black institutions, as a group, should develop and implement improved recruiting and marketing strategies, in order to effectively compete with other institutions.

Black institutions should conduct analyses of their management and resource allocation/utilization processes, to determine how effectively and efficiently they operate, how programs and staff are evaluated, and how limited funds are distributed and utilized.

State desegregation plans should be consistent with educational and other master plans, rather than treating them separte from other statewide long-range plans.

The states must define clearly what factors constitute a desegregated public higher-education system, and collect data on attrition, graduation, and transfer rates of minority students. They should also expand the roles of historically black institutions in the areas of research, graduate studies, and public service activities. Too much attention has thus far been placed on processes rather than significant outcomes.

States should analyze salary inequities between black and white institutions, develop strategies for increasing the graduation rates of black high-school students, and increase the number of black students in undergraduate and graduate programs. This will not only influence future student enrollments but will also have an impact on the future available pool of black faculty.

Additional research is needed on the high attrition rates of black students, particularly at white institutions, and why a higher percentage of black students complete their studies at black institutions. Finally, some data to determine why there are large numbers of black students attending community colleges would be useful. Would these students attend historically black public and private four-year institutions if they had the opportunity or do they represent a unique group that would not attend any other type of institution?

This chapter revealed that some historically black public institutions have benefited from the desegregation process, while others have not. As a result of desegregation planning, changes are now being implemented that might alter and diminish their roles and missions in the future, rather than enhance and expand them. Officials at many black public institutions feel that desegregation will be used to eliminate or merge them into neighboring historically white institutions. Only the future will show whether the *Adams* principle will enable all citizens to attend a higher-education institution of their choice, and whether current desegregation planning will strengthen and expand the long-standing and viable roles of historically black public institutions in U.S. higher education.

References

Adams v. *Richardson.* 356 F. Supp. 92 (D.D.C. 1973).

———. 480 F 2nd 1159 (D.D.Cir. 1973).

Adams v. *Califano.* Civil Action No. 3095-70, United States District of Columbia, Second Supplemental Order, April 1, 1977.

Bell, Derrick. "The politics of desegregation." *Change,* October 1979.

"Black colleges show black percentage drops." *Memphis Commercial Appeal,* April 13, 1980.

Braddock, Jomills. *The perpetuation of segregation across levels of education: A behavioral assessment of the contract-hypothesis.* Baltimore, MD; Center for Social Organization of Schools, Johns Hopkins University, October 12, 1979.

Braddock, Jomills, and James McPartland. *The perpetuation of segregation from elementary-secondary schools to higher education.* Unpublished study. Baltimore, MD: Center for Social Organization of Schools, Johns Hopkins University, 1980.

Brown v. *Board of Education.* 347 U.S. 483 (1954).

———. 349 U.S. 294 (1955).

Carter-Williams, Mary. *Profile of enrollments in the historically black colleges.* Washington, D.C.: Institute for Services to Education, 1978.

Change magazine. "Report: Faith, hope and parity." October 1979.

Coalition for the Concerns of Blacks in Postsecondary Education. *Report Number 3.* Columbia, SC: Coalition for the Concerns of Blacks in Postsecondary Education, March 1, 1980.

Commercial Appeal (Memphis, TN). "Iranians lament tuition measure." June 30, 1980.

———. "Tuition hike for Iranians is temporarily prohibited." July 4, 1980.

Crain, Robert, and Rita Mahard. *High school racial composition, composition, achievement and college attendance.* Santa Monica, CA: Rand Corp., 1977.

Crossland, F. E. *Minority access to college: A Ford foundation report.* New York: Schocken Books, 1971.

Davis, J. A., C. Burkheimer, and A. Borders-Patterson. *The impact of special services programs in higher education for "disadvantaged" students.* Princeton, NJ: Educational Testing Service, June 1975.

Fields, Cheryl M. "U.S. accepts 5-year, $19.8 million plan to desegregate South Carolina's colleges." *The Chronicle of Higher Education* (July 27, 1981).

Florida State Department of Education. *Florida's commitment to equal access and equal opportunity in public higher education.* Tallahassee, FL: State University System of Florida, Revised Plans for Equalizing Educational Opportunity in Public Higher Education, February 1978.

Geier v. *Dunn.* 337, F. Supp. 573, 1972, U.S. District Court for the Middle District of Tennessee.

Georgia State Board of Regents. *Fourth segment of a plan for the further desegregation of the university system of Georgia.* Submitted to the Office for Civil Rights, HEW. Atlanta, GA: Georgia State Board of Regents, October 19, 1978.

Goodrick, Welch. "Minorities in two year colleges." *Community and Junior College Journal* (December–January 1972–73).

Haynes, Leonard L., III. *A critical analysis of the Adams case: A sourcebook.* Washington, D.C.: Institute for Services to Education, 1978.

_____. *The Adams mandate: A blueprint for realizing equal educational opportunity and attainment.* Washington, D.C.: Institute for Services to Education, 1979.

_____. *An updating of desegregation planning and its effect upon historically black public colleges and universities.* Paper presented at the American Association for Higher Education, Washington, D.C., March 7, 1980.

Haynes, Leonard L., III, Henry Cobb, and Robert T. Homes. *An analysis of the Arkansas-Georgia statewide desegregation plans.* Washington, D.C.: Institute for Services to Education, 1979.

"Hearings for University of North Carolina system on ending federal funding begin July 22nd." *Minority Higher Education Reports* 1 (July 4, 1980).

"Improved access found at two-year colleges, but other problems cited in report." *Minority Higher Education Reports* 1 (June 20, 1980).

Institute for the Study of Educational Policy. *Minorities in two-year colleges: A report and recommendations for change.* Washington, D.C.: Howard University, 1980.

Kolstad, A. *Attrition from college: The class of 1972 two and one-half years after high school graduation.* Washington, D.C.: Department of Health, Education and Welfare, National Center for Education Statistics, 1977.

Lloyd, Crystal. *Adams vs. Califano: A case study in the politics of regulations.* Cambridge, MA: Sloan Commission on Government and Higher Education, Revised 1978.

Maryland State Board for Higher Education. *Fourth mid-year desegregation status report for public postsecondary education institutions in the state of Maryland.* Annapolis, MD: Maryland State Board for Higher Education, July 1978.

_____. *Summary of the fifth annual desegregation status report for public postsecondary education institutions in the state of Maryland.* Annapolis, MD: Maryland State Board for Higher Education, 1979.

Matlock, John, and Frederick Humphries. *The planning of the merger of two public higher education institutions: A case study of Tennessee State University and the University of Tennessee at Nashville.* Paper presented at the Association for Institutional Research Nineteenth Annual Forum. San Diego, CA, May 13–17, 1979.

McDonald, Kim. "U.S. rejects college desegregation plans of 5 states, threatens to cut off funds." *Chronicle of Higher Education* (July 13, 1983).

McLaurin v. *Oklahoma.* 339, U.S. 637 (1950).

McPartland, James R. *Desegregation and equity in higher education and employment: Is progress related to the desegregation of elementary and secondary schools?* Baltimore, MD: Johns Hopkins University's Center for Social Organization of Schools, May 1978.

Middleton, Lorenzo. "A black university in Oklahoma is given a new urban mission." *The Chronicle of Higher Education* (August 7, 1978).

_____. "Desegregation in 5 states slowed by decrease in black enrollment." *The Chronicle of Higher Education* (January 21, 1980).

_____. "Louisiana proposes compromise on higher education desegregation." *The Chronicle of Higher Education* (June 23, 1980).

_____. "Desegregation Plan for N.C. colleges labeled 'sellout' by NAACP lawyer." *The Chronicle of Higher Education* (July 15, 1981).

Mingle, James. *Black enrollment in higher education: Trends in the nation and the South.* Atlanta, GA: Southern Regional Education Board, 1979.

_____. *Black and Hispanic enrollment in higher education, 1978: Trends in the nation and the South.* Draft document. Atlanta, GA: Southern Regional Education Board, 1980.

Missouri, ex rel. Gaines v. *Canada.* 305, U.S. 337 (1938).

Morris, Lorenzo. *The role of testing in institutional selectivity and black access to higher education.* Paper presented at the annual meeting of the American Educational Research Association. San Francisco, CA, April 1979.

National Advisory Committee on Black Higher Education and Black Colleges and Universities. *Access of black Americans to higher education: How open is the door?* Washington, D.C.: U.S. Government Printing Office, January 1979.

"N.C. to assess 5 black colleges." *The Chronicle of Higher Education* (June 16, 1980).

New Orleans Times Picayune. "The States-Item. Accord gives millions to La. black colleges." August 22, 1981.

North Carolina University Board of Governors. *The revised North Carolina state plan for the future elimination of racial inequality in public higher education systems, phase II: 1978–83.* Chapel Hill, NC: North Carolina University Board of Governors, May 1978.

Payne, Ethel. *Black colleges: Can they survive? Challenges and changes.* The Ford Fellow in Education Journalism Report. Washington, D.C.: George Washington University's Institute for Educational Leadership, January 1979.

Peterson, Marvin, R. T. Blackburn, Z. F. Gamson, C. H. Arce, R. W. Davenport, and J. R. Mingle. *Black students on white campuses: The impact of increased black enrollments.* Ann Arbor, MI: University of Michigan Press, 1978.

Pettigrew, Thomas. "Continuing barriers to desegregated education in the South." *Sociology of Education* 38 (Winter 1965).

Savannah State College Desegregation Committee. *A plan for the desegregation of Savannah State College.* Savannah, GA: Savannah State College Desegregation Committee, June 26, 1978.

Sipuel v. *Board of Regents.* 332 U.S. G31 (1948).

Southern Regional Educational Board. *Fact book on higher education in the South: 1975 and 1976.* 1977.

———. *Racial composition of faculties in public colleges and universities in the South.* 1979.

Sweatt v. *Painter.* 339, U.S. 628 (1950).

Tennessee Higher Education Commission, State Board of Regents, University of Tennessee Board of Trustees. *1979 desegregation progress report.* Nashville, TN: Tennessee Higher Education Commission, January 17, 1980.

U.S. Commission on Civil Rights. *Social indicators of equality for minorities and women.* Washington, D.C.: Government Printing Office, August 1978.

United States Court of Appeals for the Sixth Circuit. Case Number 77-1621 and 77-1623; 77-1625; *Geier, et al.* vs. *University of Tennessee, et al.* Cincinnati, Ohio. Decided and filed April 13, 1979.

———. Case Number 77-1622 and 77-1624; *Richardson, et al.* vs. *Blanton, et al.* Cincinnati, Ohio. Decided and filed on April 13, 1979.

U.S. Department of Health, Education and Welfare. *Criteria specifying the ingredients of acceptable plans to desegregate state systems of public higher education.* Prepared by the Department of Health, Education and Welfare pursuant to the Secondary Supplemental Order of the U.S. District Court of the District of Columbia entered on April 1, 1977, Washington, D.C., July 5, 1977.

———. National Center for Education Statistics. *Traditionally black institutions of higher education: Their identification and selected characteristics.* Washington, D.C.: HEW, 1978.

Watson, Bernard. "Through the academic gateway." *Change,* October 1979.

Weinberg, Meyer, Charles Grigg, David Sly, and Louis Pol. *Three myths: An exposure of popular misconceptions about school desegregation.* Atlanta: GA: Southern Regional Council, 1976.

Part VII *Key Terms and Essay/Discussion Questions*

KEY TERMS

Programmed retardation	Adams *case*
Brown *v.* Board of Education	*Cultural clash*
Segregation	*Basic skills*
Desegregation	*Literacy*
Integration	*Tracking*
Quality education	*League for Universal Justice and Goodwill*
Hobson *v.* Hansen	

ESSAY/DISCUSSION QUESTIONS

1. Why did slaveowners deny literacy and formal education to their slaves?

2. Why was formal education of great importance to slaves?

3. Jewell Mazique argues that the great educational betrayal in the late 1960s was the denial of quality education to public school students. According to her, what were the causes and consequences of this problem?

4. In the aftermath of the Supreme Court's 1954 and 1955 *Brown* rulings, many public school systems employed an assortment of strategies to avoid racial desegregation. What major policy did the Washington, D. C., school system implement, and how did the local community leaders and organizations respond? Why were they ultimately defeated, and what have been the consequences for public schooling in Washington, D. C.?

5. Racial desegregation in higher education continues to be a complex policy problem. What are the consequences of desegregation for historically black colleges and universities?

Part VII *Supplementary Readings*

Anderson, James D., *The Education of Blacks in the South, 1860–1935,* Chapel Hill: The University of North Carolina Press, 1988.

Arons, Stephen, and Charles Lawrence, III, "The Manipulation of Consciousness: A First Amendment Critique of Schooling," in Robert B. Everhart, ed., *The Public School Monopoly: A Critical Analysis of Education and the State in American Society,* Cambridge: Ballinger Publishing Company, 1982, pp. 255–268.

Bell, Derrick, "Brown v. Board of Education and the Interest-Convergence Dilemma," *Harvard Law Review,* Vol. 93 (January 1980), pp. 518–532.

Bond, Horace M., *The Education of the Negro in the American Social Order,* New York: Prentice-Hall, 1934.

Brazziel, William F., *Quality Education for All Americans,* Washington, D. C., Howard University Press, 1974.

Bullock, Henry A., *A History of Negro Education in the South, From 1619 to the Present,* New York: Praeger Publishers, 1967.

Clark, Kenneth B., *Dark Ghetto: Dilemmas of Social Power,* New York: Harper and Row, Publishers, 1965.

Clark, Reginald M., *Family Life and School Achievement: Why Poor Black Children Succeed or Fail,* Chicago: The University of Chicago Press, 1983.

Coleman, James S., Ernest Q. Campbell, Carol J. Hobson, James McPartland, Alexander Mood, Ferderic D. Weinfeld, Robert L. York, *Equality of Educational Opportunity,* 2 Vols., Washington, D. C.: U.S. Government Printing Office, 1966.

Corson, William R., *Promise or Peril: The Black College Student in America,* New York: W. W. Norton and Company, Inc., 1970.

Dreyfuss, Joel, and Charles Lawrence III, *The Bakke Case: The Politics of Inequality,* New York: Harcourt Brace Jovanovich, 1979.

Du Bois, W. E. B., *The Education of Black People: Ten Critiques, 1906–1960,* ed. Herbert Aptheker, New York: Monthly Review Press, 1973.

————, "The Field and Function of the American Negro College," in Andrew G. Paschal, ed., *A W. E. B. Du Bois Reader,* New York: Macmillan Publishing Co., Inc., 1971, pp. 51–69.

————, "Does the Negro Need Separate Schools?," *Journal of Negro Education,* Vol. 4 (July 1935), pp. 328–335.

Edmonds, Ronald R., "Improving the Effectiveness of New York City Public Schools," in *The Minority Student in Public Schools: Fostering Academic Excellence,* Princeton: Educational Testing Service, Office for Minority Education, 1981, pp. 23–30.

Edwards, Harry, *Black Students,* New York: The Free Press, 1970.

Fleming, John E., Gerald R. Gill, and David H. Swinton, *The Case for Affirmative Action for Blacks in Higher Education,* Washington, D. C., Howard University Press, 1978.

The 14th Amendment and School Busing, Hearings Before the Subcommittee on the Constitution of the Committee on the Judiciary, United States Senate, Washington, D. C.: U. S. Government Printing Office, 1972.

Franklin, Vincent P., *The Education of Black Philadelphia: The Social and Educational History of a Minority Community, 1900–1950,* Philadelphia: University of Pennsylvania Press, 1979.

————, and James D. Anderson, eds., *New Perspectives on Black Educational History,* Boston: G. K. Hall and Company, 1978.

Freire, Paulo, *Pedagogy of the Oppressed,* New York: Herder and Herder, 1972.

Garibaldi, Antoine, ed., *Black Colleges and Universities: Challenges for the Future,* New York: Praeger Publishers, 1984.

Gurin, Patricia and Edgar Epps, *Black Consciousness, Identity, and Achievement: A Study of Students at Historically Black Colleges,* New York: John Wiley and Sons, Inc., 1975.

Hale-Benson, Janice, *Black Children: Their Roots, Culture, and Learning Styles,* Baltimore: The John Hopkins University Press, 1982.

Hayes, Floyd W. III, "Politics and Education in America's Multicultural Society: An African American Studies' Response to Allan Bloom," *The Journal of Ethnic Studies,* Vol. 17, No. 2 (Summer 1989), pp. 71–88.

_____, *Retreat from Quality: Policy Intellectuals, Education Policymaking and Politics in a Changing Society,* Washington, D. C.: Institute for Independent Education, Inc., 1989.

_____, *Structures of Domination and the Political Economy of Black Higher Education in a Technocratic Era: A Theoretical Framework,* Occasional Papers, No. 3, Washington, D. C.: Institute for the Study of Educational Policy, 1981.

Hochschild, Jennifer L., *Thirty Years After Brown,* Washington, D. C.: Joint Center for Political Studies, 1985.

_____, *The New American Dilemma: Liberal Democracy and School Desegregation,* New Haven: Yale University Press, 1984.

Investigation of the Schools and Poverty in the District of Columbia, Hearings Before the Task Force on Antipoverty in the District of Columbia of the Committee on Education and Labor, House of Representatives, Washington, D. C.: U. S. Government Printing Office, 1966.

Jones, Faustine C., *A Traditional Model of Educational Excellence: Dunbar High School of Little Rock, Arkansas,* Washington, D. C.: Howard University Press, 1981.

Kirp, David L., *Just Schools: The Idea of Racial Equality in American Education,* Berkeley: University of California Press, 1982.

Kluger, Richard, *Simple Justice: The History of Brown v. Board of Education and Black America's Struggle for Equality,* New York: Alfred A. Knopf, 1975.

Kozol, Jonathan, *Savage Inequalities: Children in America's Schools,* New York: Crown Publishers, Inc., 1991.

Lightfoot, Sara, *The Good School: Portraits of Character and Culture,* New York: Basic Books, Inc., Publishers, 1983.

Lomotey, Kofi, ed., *Going to School: The African-American Experience,* Albany: State University of New York Press, 1990.

Lukas, J. Anthony, *Common Ground: A Turbulent Decade in the Lives of Three American Families,* New York: Alfred A. Knopf, 1985.

McNeil, Linda M., *Contradictions of Control: School Structure and School Knowledge,* New York: Routledge and Kegan Paul, 1986.

Meier, Kenneth J., Joseph Stewart Jr., and Robert E. England, *Race, Class, and Education: The Politics of Second-Generation Discrimination,* Madison: The University of Wisconsin Press, 1989.

Misgeld, Dieter, "Education and Cultural Invasion: Critical Social Theory, Education as Instruction, and the 'Pedagogy of the Oppressed'," in John

Forester, ed., *Critical Theory and Public Life*, Cambridge: The MIT Press, 1985, pp. 77–118.

Moore, William Jr., and Lonnie H. Wagstaff, *Black Educators in White Colleges*, San Francisco: Jossey-Bass Publishers, 1974.

Mosteller, Frederick and Daniel P. Moynihan, eds., *On Equality of Educational Opportunity*, New York: Vintage Books, 1972.

National Commission of Excellence in Education, *A Nation at Risk: The Imperative for Educational Reform*, Washington, D. C.: U. S. Department of Education, 1983.

Nkomo, Mokubung, ed., *Pedagogy of Domination: Toward a Democratic Education in South Africa*, Trenton: Africa World Press, Inc., 1990.

Oakes, Jeanne, *Keeping Track: How Schools Structure Inequality*, New Haven: Yale University Press, 1985.

Orfield, Gary, *School Desegregation Patterns in the United States, Large Cities and Metropolitan Areas, 1968–1980*, Washington, D. C.: Joint Center for Political Studies, 1983.

_____, *Desegregation of Black and Hispanic Students from 1968 to 1980*, Washington, D. C.: Joint Center for Political Studies, 1982.

Persell, Caroline H., *Education and Inequality: The Roots of Stratification in America's School*, New York: The Free Press, 1977.

Peterson, Marvin W., Robert T. Blackburn, Zelda F. Gamson, Carlos H. Arce, Roselle W. Davenport, James R. Mingle, *Black Students on White Campuses: The Impacts of Increased Black Enrollments*, Ann Arbor: Institute for Social Research/The University of Michigan, 1978.

Pride, Richard A. and J. David Woodard, *The Burden of Busing: The Politics of Desegregation in Nashville, Tennessee*, Knoxville: The University of Tennessee Press, 1985.

Rist, Ray C., *The Invisible Children: School Integration in American Society*, Cambridge: Harvard University Press, 1978.

_____, *The Urban School: A Factory for Failure—A Study of Education in American Society*, Cambridge: The MIT Press, 1973.

Rubin, Lillian B., *Busing and Backlash: White Against White in an Urban School District*, Berkeley: University of California Press, 1972.

School Desegregation, Hearings Before the Subcommittee on Civil and Constitutional Rights of the Committee on the Judiciary, House of Representatives, Washington, D. C.: U. S. Government Printing Office, 1982.

Schere, Robert G., *Subordination or Liberation?: The Development and Conflicting Theories of Black Education in Nineteenth-Century Alabama*, University: The University of Alabama Press, 1977.

Scott, Hugh J., *The Black School Superintendent: Messiah or Scapegoat?*, Washington, D. C.: Howard University Press, 1980.

Sowell, Thomas, *Black Education: Myths and Tragedies*, New York: David McKay Company, Inc., 1972.

Thomas, Gail E., ed., *Black Students in Higher Education: Conditions and Experiences in the 1970s*, Westport: Greenwood Press, 1981.

Thompson, Daniel C., *Private Black Colleges at the Crossroads,* Westport: Greenwood Press, Inc., 1973.

U. S. Commission on Civil Rights, *Racial Isolation in the Public Schools,* Vol. I, Washington, D. C.: U. S. Government Printing Office, 1967.

Webber, Thomas L., *Deep Like the Rivers: Education in the Slave Quarter Community, 1831–1865,* New York: W. W. Norton and Company, Inc., 1978.

Willie, Charles V., ed., *The Sociology of Urban Education: Desegregation and Integration,* Lexington: Lexington Books, 1978.

_____, and Susan L. Greenblatt, eds., *Community Politics and Educational Change: Ten School Systems Under Court Order,* New York: Longman, 1981.

_____, and Ronald R. Edmonds, eds., *Black Colleges in America: Challenge, Development, Survival,* New York: Teachers College Press/Columbia University, 1978.

Wolters, Raymond, *The Burden of Brown: Thirty Years of School Desegregation,* Knoxville: The University of Tennessee Press, 1984.

_____, *The New Negro on Campus: Black College Rebellions of the 1920s,* Princeton: Princeton University Press, 1975.

VIII

Political Economy of the African American Situation

In colonial America, the African American struggle for collective survival and secular and spiritual salvation began under the most extreme conditions of economic exploitation—chattel slavery. Concomitantly, the governing white financial elite accumulated enormous wealth by means of the slave trade and from chattel slaves' free and exploited labor; this capital served as the basis of a rapidly growing American economy.

After slavery's abolition, the former bondspeople had to fight a continuous battle against geographical, socioeconomic, cultural, and political obstacles to improve their economic situation. At the dawn of the twentieth century, African Americans embarked on a historic journey from rural to urban and from southern to northern regions, seeking better life chances. In the process, they gradually refashioned themselves from mainly rural agricultural laborers to largely urban industrial workers. In the last quarter of the twentieth century, which is witnessing the decline of America's industrial manufacturing economy and the rise of a postindustrial-managerial economy, the trajectory of the African American economic predicament appears increasingly ambivalent. Impoverished inner-city enclaves are growing rapidly, yet there is also an emerging class of college-educated and professional suburbanites and urban gentry.

The two articles in this part profile the African American participation in the changing American political economy from chattel slavery to the contemporary period. In "The Demand for Black Labor: Historical Notes on the Political Economy of Racism," Harold M. Baron analyzes critically the manner in which America's capitalist economic exploitation and racist political oppression constrained African American economic development from the colonial period to the mid-1960s. Baron argues that African slave labor in colonial America contributed to the large-scale accumulation of wealth during the early stages of American capitalist development. But he reveals that the enslavement and exploitation of African labor could not have existed if it had depended on a market-oriented system alone. Baron suggests that white Europeans subordinated Africans and their American descendants by means of an elaborate culture of racial control, which became woven deeply into the fabric of American ideology, culture, and social and political institutional practices. Hence, the ideologies of profit maximization and white European supremacy, together with the institutional practices of the slave trade and chattel slavery, resulted in a veritable culture of domination that uniquely characterized the new American nation-state.

Baron points out that after slavery was abolished, the economic condition of the former bondspeople did not change substantially. Although international war and the rise of a new European middle class undercut chattel slavery in the Americas, the culture of racial control continued to operate in the American South. In the years from 1860 to World War I, Baron points out, African Americans shifted to sharecropping and other forms of agrarian labor, which brought in barely subsistence wages. Slavery may have ended but the great mass of African Americans remained economically and politically powerless.

After the nation's transition from agrarian to industrial capitalism, Baron shows, skilled factory work initially went to white workers, while African American workers were either excluded or given unskilled menial jobs. Hence, white workers were not required to compete with African American workers for employment in the emerging industrial manufacturing sector of the economy. World War I set in motion the African American penetration into America's industrial labor force. Migrating to northern urban areas, African Americans initially entered such industries as steel, meat packing, and automobile manufacturing as strike breakers. Even then, there were particular jobs, usually the hardest and most dangerous, designated for African American workers. Especially during the Great

Depression of the 1930s, white labor unions fought hard to maintain preferential employment practices for white workers and to institute racially discriminatory and exclusionary practices directed at African American industrial workers.

Baron shows that from World War II to the mid-1960s, African Americans made the transition to a largely urban working class population. African American organizations and leadership—for example, Marcus Garvey's black nationalist mass movement, the liberal National Association for the Advancement of Colored People, and A. Phillip Randolph's socialist Brotherhood of Sleeping Car Porters labor union—represented in various ways a new stage in the self-conscious, collective struggle of African American working masses to confront racially based political and economic oppression in America. Although economic conditions for the northern urban African American working class improved over those of their southern peasant counterparts, Baron argues that in America's metropolitan centers there arose a dual labor-market system—a primary market into which white workers were recruited and hired and a secondary one in which African American workers were recruited and hired. These conditions resulted in lower wages, higher job turnover, and higher unemployment for blue-collar urban African American workers. It was within this context that African American frustration with economic and racial subordination exploded into urban rebellions across America in the mid-1960s.

The work by Daniel R. Fusfeld and Timothy Bates, "Black Economic Well-Being Since the 1950s," investigates closely the African American economic situation since World War II. The authors describe areas of improvement and decline, suggesting that trends indicate a growing economic polarization within the African American community: younger and better-educated persons show improved income and occupational status; those persons with less education but with average skills experience the ups and downs associated with fluctuating economic conditions; and those at the bottom of the economic ladder are getting worse off, even experiencing conditions of semipermanent impoverishment. These changing employment trends coincide with shifts in regional patterns of industrial employment. The authors also suggest a pessimistic future for many urban African American industrial workers.

Fusfeld and Bates argue that indicators of African American economic progress since World War II are complicated. On the one hand, and in comparison to whites, there was general improvement in individual income, education, white-collar employment, high visibility occupations (e.g., entertainment and professional sports), and professional-managerial positions in private enterprise. On the other hand, the authors show that conditions for many non-southern urban African Americans worsened, particularly among teenagers and adult males. These trends also have contributed to other patterns of social dislocation and represent a progressive deterioration of urban African American communities: increased female-headed households, out-of-wedlock births, teenage pregnancy, violent death among African American males, and imprisonment.

The authors closely analyze economic trends and developments during the 1950s, 1960s, 1970s, and 1980s. In the decade of the 1950s, the continuing northern and urban migration, together with ongoing racial discrimination in the industrial labor market, resulted in rising unemployment and underemployment for African Americans. This pattern was somewhat offset by some African American penetration into the white-collar occupational force. During the 1960s, improvements in African American economic and employment conditions resulted from better economic conditions generally, more opportunities in white-collar occupations, and anti-discriminatory civil rights activism. In the 1970s, a general deterioration of industrial manufacturing cities (snowbelt) and a decline in the number of blue-collar jobs generally hurt African American employment. In the 1980s, shifting economic conditions were apparent as economic growth and development continued in cities and regions whose economies were based on human services and government (sunbelt). Under these conditions, young and well-educated African Americans experienced gains in professional, technical, and managerial occupations. Fusfeld and Bates suggest that in the new economy, the employment future for professionals is brighter than that for less-educated industrial workers; however, employment prospects for the uneducated are bleak.

Finally, Fusfeld and Bates comment on the emergence of big-city African American political executives and administrators. This is generally taking place in older, larger cities that are experiencing economic trauma and decline. The authors point out that election or appointment of African American political executives and administrators does not necessarily translate into general economic advancements for the great multitude of African American city residents.

The Demand for Black Labor: Historical Notes on the Political Economy of Racism

HAROLD M. BARON

HE ECONOMIC BASE OF RACISM would have to be subjected to intensive analysis in order to get at the heart of the oppression of black people in modern America. If we employ the language of Nineteenth Century science, we can state that the economic deployment of black people has been conditioned by the operation of two sets of historical laws: the laws of capitalist development, and the laws of national liberation. These laws were operative in the slave era as well as at present. Today the characteristic forms of economic control and exploitation of black people take place within the institutional structure of a mature state capitalist system and within the demographic frame of the metropolitan centers. The economic activities of blacks are essentially those of wage (or salary) workers for the large corporate and bureaucratic structures that dominate a mature capitalist society. Thus today racial dynamics can be particularized as the working out of the laws of the maintenance of mature state capitalism and the laws of black liberation with the metropolitan enclaves (rather than a consolidated territorial area) as a base.

This essay places major emphasis on capitalist development. While attention will be paid to aspects of national liberation, it would be a very-different essay if that were the main point of concentration. Further, in order to make the inquiry manageable, it concentrates on the key relationship of the demand for black labor.

A backward glance at certain factors in the evolution of racism will help establish the cogency of the major categories that we employ in the analysis of the present day. Historically, the great press for black labor as the work force for plantation slavery simultaneously supplied the momentum for the formation of institutional racism and set the framework for the creation of the black community in the United States. The strength of this demand for black slaves, in regard to both the vast numbers of persons involved and its duration over centuries, was based on the dialectics of the relationship between slavery in the New World and the development of capitalism in Europe: Each provided necessary conditions for the other's growth.

A large-scale accumulation of capital was a prerequisite for the emergence of capitalism as the dominant system in Europe. Otherwise capitalism was doomed to remain basically a mercantile operation in the interstices of a primarily manorial economy. From the Sixteenth Century on, the strength of developing nation-states and their ability to extend their tentacles of power beyond the limits of Europe greatly accelerated the process that Marx called "the primitive accumulation of capital".

> The discovery of gold and silver in America, the extirpation, enslavement, and entombment in the mines of the aboriginal population, the beginning of the conquest and looting of the East Indies, the turning of Africa into a warren for the hunting of black skins, signalized the rosy dawn of the era of capitalist production. These idyllic proceedings are the chief momenta of primitive accumulation. This phase of the accumulation process was accomplished not only by domestic exploitation, but also by the looting of traditional stores of non-European peoples and the fostering of a new system of slavery to exploit their labor.[1]

In a sense European capitalism created, as one of the pre-conditions for its flourishing, a set of productive relations that was antithetical to the free-market, wage-labor system which characterized capitalist production in the metropolitan countries. English capitalism at home was nurturing itself on a proletariat created through the dispossession of the peasantry from the land, while at the same time accumulating much of the capital necessary to command the labor of this proletariat through the fixing of African deportees into a servile status in the colonies. "In fact, the veiled slavery of the wage-earners of Europe needed for its pedestal slavery pure and simple in the New World."[2]

Slaves from Africa, at first in the mines and then on the plantations of the New World, produced goods that enlarged the magnitude of the circulation of commodities in international trade—a process that was essential to the mercantilist phase of capitalist history.[3] Although this slavery was not capitalist in the form of production itself, that is was not based on the purchase of alienated wage labor[4], the plantation system of the New World composed an integral part of the international market relations of the growing capitalist system. The demand for slaves was subject to mercantile calculations regarding production costs and market prices:

> Long before the trans-Atlantic trade began, both the Spanish and the Portuguese were well aware that Africa could be made to yield up its human treasure. But in the early part of the Sixteenth Century the cost of transporting large numbers of slaves across the Atlantic was excessive in relation to the profits that could be extracted from their labor. This situation changed radically when, toward the middle of the century . . . sugar plantings were begun in Brazil . . . and by the end of the Sixteenth Century sugar had become the most valuable of the agricultural commodities in international trade. Importation of Negroes from Africa now became economically feasible.[5]

Once in the world market, a commodity lost all the markings of its origin. No distinction could be made as to whether it was produced by free or slave labor. It became just a good to be bought and sold.

Production from the slave plantations greatly increased the volume of commodities in circulation through trade, but the social relations of slavery and racism rendered the black producers so distinctly apart that it was possible to appropriate a greater proportion of their product as surplus than it was through any other established mechanism that defined lowly social status. Two sets of conditions combined to make the exploitation of the New World slaves particularly harsh. First, the production of plantation goods for the impersonal needs of the rapidly expanding international market removed many of the restraints and reciprocities that had inhered in patriarchal forms of slavery in which production was essentially for home use. Second, since West Africa was outside of Christendom or Mediterranean civilization, there were few existing European cultural or political limitations that applied to the treatment of black chattels.

The economics of slavery could not have existed over an extended period as just a set of shrewd market-oriented operations. Elaboration of a whole culture of control—with political, social, and ideological formulations—was necessary to hold dominance over the black slaves and to keep the non-slave-holding whites in line. Given that the white Europeans were subjugating the black Africans, the culture of control became largely structured around a color-oriented racialism. "Slavery could survive only if the Negro were a man set apart; he simply had to be different if slavery were to exist at all."[6] The development of a rationale regarding the degradation of all blacks and the formation of conforming institutional practices were necessary to maintain a social order based on enslavement of some blacks. Accordingly, this culture of racial control rapidly diffused throughout the whole of North Atlantic civilization and all the American colonies of its various nations. In the United States, racism—that is, subjugation based on blackness rather than on servitude alone—was more sharply defined than in most other places in the Americas.

When the European powers extended their influence down the African coast, they did not have sufficient military and economic advantage to establish sovereignty over the lands. They could only set up trading outposts. However first on islands off the coast of Africa and then on the islands and coastal lowlands of the Americas, the Europeans were able to gain control of the land, often exterminating the indigenous population. In such distant territories black workers from Africa could be driven in the mines and plantations free from any constraints that could be imposed by the states, tribes, and traditions of Africa. Set apart by their servitude and their blackness, they were also removed from any rights that low-status groups within the metropolitan country might have had. Laboring on the American plantations came to embody the worst features of ancient slavery and the cash nexus.

Black chattel slavery, with the concomitant elaboration of institutional and ideological racism as its socio-political corollary, became a new type of societal formation. True, as David Brion Davis has pointed out, the institutions of New World slavery grew out of the forms of the late Middle Ages' Mediterranean slavery.[7] Regarding racism, Winthrop Jordan has shown that the pre-existing derogatory imagery of darkness, barbarism, and heathenism was adapted to formulate the psychology and doctrines of modern racism.[8] While the adaptation of these available institutional and ideological materials provided the original forms for New World slavery, as a whole the system was something distinctly novel. This novelty was chiefly conditioned by the developing capitalist relations that provided the seemingly insatiable demand for plantation products. Accordingly, the demand for black labor under circumstances like these had to be different from any slavery that was indigenous to West Africa or had operated earlier in Europe.

Capitalism's stamp on New World slavery was sharply revealed via the slave trade that supplied the demand for black labor. Alongside the marketing of the output of slave labor, the trade in the bodies which produced these goods became a major form of merchant capitalistic enterprise in itself. Down into the Nineteenth Century the purchase of black slaves frequently was a constant cost of production. This held in extreme for parts of Brazil where it was considered more economical to work slaves to death within five to ten years and replace them with fresh purchases than to allow enough sustenance and opportunity for family living so that the slave force could be maintained by natural reproduction.[9] The latest and most careful estimate of the total deportation of black slaves to the Americas is between 9,000,000 and 10,000,000. Up to 1810 about 7,500,000 Africans were imported—or about three times the number of Europeans immigrating in the same period.[10]

Slave trade and slave production brought wealth and power to the bourgeois merchants of Western Europe. As C.L.R. James has summed up the situation for France: "Nearly all the industries which developed in France during the Eighteenth Century had their origin in goods or commodities destined for either the coast of Guinea or America. The capital from the slave trade fertilized them. Though the bourgeois traded in other things than slaves, upon the success or failure of the (slave) traffic everything else depends."[11] In the case of England, Eric Williams, in *Capitalism and Slavery*, has detailed in terms of manufacturing, shipping, and capital accumulation how the economic development of the mother land was rooted in New World Slavery.[12] But it is more dramatic to let a contemporary Eighteenth Century economist speak for himself:

The most-approved judges of the commercial interest of these kingdoms have ever been of the opinion that our West Indian and African trades are the most nationally-beneficial of any carried on. It is also allowed on all hands that the trade to Africa is the branch which renders our American colonies and plantations so advantageous to Great Britain; that traffic only affording our planters a constant supply of Negro servants for the culture of their lands in the produce of sugar, tobacco, rice, rum, cotton, pimento, and all plantation produce; so that

the extensive employment of our shipping into and from our American colonies, the great brook of seamen consequent thereupon, and the daily bread of the most-considerable part of our British manufacturers, are owing primarily to the labor of Negroes....[13]

WITHIN THE BOUNDARIES OF THE UNITED STATES

In the colonial period of the United States the commercial basis of all the colonies rested largely on the Atlantic trade in slave-produced commodities. The Southern colonies directly used a slave population to raise tobacco and rice for export. While the Northern colonies all had slave populations, their major links were auxiliaries to the Atlantic trade—growing provisions for the Caribbean plantations, developing a merchant marine to carry slaves to the islands and sugar to Europe. After Independence the slave production of cotton provided the base for the pre-Civil War economic take-off and industrial revolution:

It was cotton which was the most important influence in the growth in the market size and the consequent expansion of the economy: . . . In this period of rapid growth, it was cotton that initiated the concomitant expansion in income, in the size of the domestic markets, and in the creation of social overhead investment (in the course of its role in marketing cotton) in the Northeast which were to facilitate the subsequent rapid growth of manufactures. In addition, cotton accounted for the accelerated pace of westward migration, as well as for the movement of people out of self-sufficiency into the market economy.[14]

In the territory of the United States, the elaboration of plantation slavery had some distinctive features that are worthy of attention for the light that they shed on the present. For one thing the slave system here tended to become a self-contained operation in which the demand for new slaves was met by natural increase, with the slave deficit areas of the

Lower South importing black bondsmen from the Upper South. Self-containment was also defined in that there were few possibilities that a black man could achieve any other status than that of slave—involuntary servitude and blackness were almost congruent. Plantations operating under conditions of high prices for manufactured goods and easy access to their own land holdings for whites had been forced to train black slaves as artisans and craftsmen. As one scholar concluded:

> Indeed, it is hard to see how the Eighteenth Century plantation could ever have survived if the Negro slave had not made his important contribution as an artisan in the building and other trades calling for skill in transforming raw materials into manufactured articles. The self-sufficiency of the Southern colonies necessitated by the Revolution was more successful than it could have been if the Negro slave artisan had not been developing for generations before.[15]

But skills only exceptionally led to freedom. Even the relatively small number of what John Hope Franklin calls "quasi-free Negroes" tended to lose rights, both in the North and in the South, after the adoption of the Constitution. By way of contrast, in Latin America an extensive free black population existed alongside a large number of freshly imported slaves.

The position of the "quasi-free Negro" is one of the most important keys to understanding later developments. Sheer economic conditions operated to prevent him from developing a secure social status. The flourishing of the cotton culture sustained a high demand for slaves at the same time that state and federal illegalization of the slave trade reduced the importation of Africans. Therefore limitations on both the numbers and prerogatives of non-slave blacks functioned to maintain the size of the slave labor force.

The completeness with which race and slavery became merged in the United States is revealed by a review of the status of blacks on the eve of the Civil War. About 89% of the national black population was slave, while in the Southern states the slave proportion was 94%.[16] The status of the small number of quasi-free Negroes was ascribed from that of the mass of their brothers in bondage. Nowhere did this group gain a secure economic position; only a few of them acquired enough property to be well off. In the countryside, by dint of hard work, a few acquired adequate farms. Most, however, survived on patches of poor soil or as rural laborers. Free blacks fared the best in Southern cities, many of them being employed as skilled artisans or tradesmen. The ability of free blacks to maintain a position in the skilled trades was dependent on the deployment of a larger number of slaves in these crafts and industrial jobs. Slave-owners provided a defense against a color bar as they protected their investment in urban slaves. However the rivalry from a growing urban white population between 1830 and 1860 forced blacks out of many of the better jobs, and in some cases out of the cities altogether. "As the black population dropped, white newcomers moved in and took over craft after craft. Occasionally to the accompaniment of violence and usually with official sanction, slave and free colored workers were shunted into the most menial and routine chores."[17]

Basic racial definitions of the slave system also gained recognition in the North, through the development of a special servile status for blacks. During the colonial era, Northern colonies imported slaves as one means of coping with a chronic labor shortage. While most blacks were employed in menial work, many were trained in skilled trades. "So long as the pecuniary interests of a slave-holding class stood back of these artisans, the protests of white mechanics had little effect. . . ." With emancipation in the North, matters changed. As Du Bois further noted concerning Philadelphia, during the first third of the Nineteenth Century, the blacks, who had composed a major portion of all artisans, were excluded from most of the skilled trades.[18] Immigrants from Europe soon found out that, although greatly exploited themselves, they could still turn racism to their advantage. The badge of whiteness permitted even the lowly to use prejudice, violence, and local political influence to push blacks down into the lowest occupations. In 1850, 75% of the black workers in New York were employed in menial or unskilled positions. Within five years the situation had deteriorated to the point at which 87.5% were in these categories.[19] Northern states did not compete with slave states for black workers, even when labor shortages forced them to encourage the immigration of millions of Europeans. Through enforcement of fugitive slave laws and discouragement of free black immigration, through both legal and informal means, the North reinforced slavery's practical monopoly over blacks.

For the pre-Civil War period, then, we can conclude that there was no significant demand for black labor outside the slave system. The great demand for black workers came from the slave plantations. No effective counterweight to plantation slavery was presented by urban and industrial employment. As a matter of fact, in both North and South the position of the urban skilled black worker deteriorated during the generation prior to the Civil War. In the South the magnitude of cities and industries was limited by the political and cultural imperatives inherent in hegemony of the planter class. Whatever demand there was for black labor in Southern cities and industries was met essentially by adapting the forms of slavery to these conditions, not by creating an independent pressure for free blacks to work in these positions.

To a large extent the more-heightened form of racism in the United States grew out of the very fact that the USA was such a thoroughgoing bourgeois society, with more bourgeois equalitarianism than any other nation around. Aside from temporary indenture, which was

important only through the Revolutionary era, there were no well-institutionalized formal or legal mechanisms for fixing of status among whites. Up to the Civil War the ideal of an equalitarian-yeoman society was a major sociopolitical factor in shaping political conditions. Therefore if the manumitted slave were not marked off by derogation of his blackness, there was no alternative but to admit him to the status of a free-born enfranchised citizen (depending on property qualifications prior to the 1830s).[20]

Under these circumstances the planter class made race as well as slavery a designation of condition. A large free black population that had full citizens' rights would have been a threat to their system. They therefore legislated limitations on the procedures for manumission and placed severe restrictions on the rights of free blacks. Low-status whites who did have citizens' rights were encouraged by the plantocracy to identify as whites and to emphasize racial distinctions so as to mark themselves off from both slave and free blacks precisely because this white group did have a legitimate place in the political process. Fear of competition from blacks, either directly or indirectly through the power of large planters, also gave the large class of non-slave-holding whites a real stake in protecting racial distinctions. In Latin America, by contrast, the remnants of feudal traditions regarding the gradations of social ranks already provided well-established lowly positions into which free Negroes or half-castes could step without posing a threat to the functional hegemony of the slave-master class. Further, given the small number of Europeans and the great labor shortage, ex-slaves provided ancillary functions, such as clearing the frontier or raising food crops, that were necessary for the overall operation of the slave system.[21]

This absoluteness of racial designation, so intimately related to the character of bourgeois order in this nation, meant that racism became intertwined in the entire state system of rule. That is to say that not only were the procedures of slave control and racial derogation of the blacks embodied in the Constitution and other fundamental features of state action, but these mechanisms soon interpenetrated the general state operations for the control of certain classes of whites over other whites. Therefore, while racism was as American as apple pie, and was subscribed to in some form even by most white abolitionists, it also became a special weapon in the regional arsenal of the Southern plantocracy in their contention for a dominant position in determination of national policy. The planters' employment of racist appeals proved effective on a national basis, especially in the generation prior to the Civil War, only because an underlying acceptance of their assumptions existed in all regions. Domestically within the South, racism operated to cement the solidarity of all whites under the hegemony of the planter class— even though slavery provided the power base from which the plantocracy were able to subordinate the white yeomanry. This strategy met with success, for the intensification of racist propaganda during the ante-bellum period was accompanied by a slackening of attacks on the plantation system. In return for the security granted to the base of their power, the planters had to make some concessions to the poor whites regarding formal rights of citizenship such as extension of the franchise and legislative reapportionment; but alterations in form did not change the fundamental power relations. The racialist culture of control merged into both the political apparatus and the social forms of hegemony by which white class rule was sustained. White rule was not identical with, but did mediate, the rule of the plantocracy over all of Southern society.

THE TRANSITION ERA, FIRST PHASE: 1860 TO WORLD WAR I

So far we have been establishing a comprehension of some of the underlying contradictions

that frame the control of black labor by examining their origins in the slave era. Before we turn to the present period there is another set of relationships that will provide further conceptual illumination: the conditions that underlay the abolition of slavery. One set of factors lay in the world development of capitalism itself. The bourgeoisie's seizure of power in the French Revolution destabilized that nation's colonial regime and undermined the slave system by promulgating the doctrine of the rights of man as a universal dictum. In England, the expansion of its capitalist might into Asia gave rise to a powerful political interest counter to that of the West Indian planters; plus, the success of the industrial revolution created the material base for envisioning a liberal bourgeois order with thorough formal equality. In the United States, the demise of slavery occurred in the midst of a war that established the further course of capitalist development—whether it would proceed on a "Prussian model", with the planters playing the role of the Junkers, or the industrialists and little men on the make would independently establish their hegemony through an entrepreneurially oriented state.

The other source of abolition lay in the role of the black people in the Americas. Denied the right to reconstruct their African societies, they strove to survive and reconstitute themselves as a people. Amidst the plantations and the black quarters of the cities, a new community was formed.[22] At crucial points these black communities transcended the need for survival and struck out for liberation. While sabotage, escapes, and uprisings were consistent themes of New World slavery, the key move was the successful revolt of the black Jacobins in Haiti under the leadership of Toussaint L'Ouverture, which set an example for black and other oppressed people from that time on. By winning their freedom and defeating the most powerful armies in the world, these revolutionaries not only forced changes in the relative relations of the forces in Europe, but also undermined much essential confidence in the continuing viability of the slave system as a whole. It was little accident that both the British and the US abolition of the slave trade followed shortly on the heels of the Haitian revolution.

In the United States, where a large white population was always close at hand, there were few important slave revolts, and even those were invariably put down before they could become well established. Black self-determination took the form of day-to-day slave resistance, and the development of an independent political line within the abolitionist movement. Most important, the role of black people in the Civil War converted it into a struggle for their own freedom. As Du Bois cogently summarizes:

> Freedom for the slave was a logical result of a crazy attempt to wage war in the midst of four million black slaves, trying the while sublimely to ignore the interests of those slaves in the outcome of the fighting. Yet these slaves had enormous power in their hands. Simply by stopping work, they could threaten the Confederacy with starvation. By walking into the Federal camps, they showed to doubting Northerners the easy possibility of using them as workers and as servants, as spies, as farmers, and finally as fighting soldiers. And not only using them thus, but by the same gesture depriving their enemies of their use in just these fields. It was the fugitive slave who made the slave-holders face the alternative of surrendering to the North or to the Negroes.[23]

The Civil War destroyed the Southern plantocracy as a major contender for the control of national power. For a decade during Reconstruction, the freedmen struggled to establish themselves as an independent yeomanry on the lands they had worked for generations. However both South and North agreed that blacks were to be subservient workers—held in that role now by the workings of "natural" economic and social laws rather than the laws

of slavery. The Compromise of 1877 was the final political blow to black Reconstruction, remanding to the dominant white Southerners the regulation of the black labor force.[24]

Abolition of slavery did not mean substantive freedom to the black worker. He was basically confined to a racially-defined agrarian labor status in which he was more exploited than any class of whites, even the landless poor. White land-owners extracted an economic surplus from the labor of blacks through a variety of arrangements, including peonage, wage labor, sharecropping, and rent tenancy. Even the black owners of land were often dependent on white patronage for access to the small plots of inferior soil to which they usually held title. Profits predicated on low wages or onerous share arrangements were often augmented by long-term indebtedness at usurious rates of interest for advances of provisions and supplies. Many a sharecropper and laborer would not realize any appreciable money income for years on end.

The methods of labor control over the black peasantry did not greatly raise net labor costs over those of the slavery era. In both eras the black masses received only enough to survive and reproduce. Pressure on profits came from falling commodity prices rather than from rising labor costs. "The keynote of the Black Belt is debt. . . ." wrote W. E. B. Du Bois at the turn of the century. "Not commercial credit, but debt in the sense of continued inability of the mass of the population to make income cover expenses." Of conditions in Dougherty County, Georgia he wrote:

> In the year of low-priced cotton, 1898, of 300 tenant families 175 ended their year's work in debt to the extent of $14,000; 50 cleared nothing; and the remaining 75 made a total profit of $1600. . . . In more prosperous years the situation is far better—but on the average the majority of tenants end the year even or in debt, which means they work for board and clothes.[25]

From the obverse side white planters in racist language gave their supporting testimony to this extra economic exploitation of the black peasants. One Alabama landlord declared: "White labor is totally unsuited to our methods, our manners, and our accommodations. No other laborers (than the Negro) of whom I have any knowledge would be so cheerful or so contented on four pounds of meat and a peck of meal a week, in a little log cabin 14 by 16 feet, with cracks in it large enough to afford free passage to a large-size cat." From Mississippi a planter spoke to the same theme: "Give me the nigger every time. The nigger will never 'strike' as long as you give him plenty to eat and half clothe him: He will live on less and do more hard work, when properly managed, than any other class or race of people."[26]

Black agriculturists were important to the economic development of the South and the nation. Raw cotton production tripled between 1870 and 1910. Consumption of cotton by domestic manufacturers increased six-fold from 800,000 bales in 1870 to 4,800,000 bales in 1910. Cotton continued to be the United States' leading export commodity in global trade, still accounting for a quarter of the value of all merchandise exports on the eve of World War I—in spite of the fact that prices had decreased greatly through international competition as the European powers encouraged cotton production in the overseas areas in which they were augmenting their imperial power. Such rapid growth of cotton production (and that of other farm commodities) implied a great demand for black workers in the fields. Characteristically blacks were engaged on the cotton plantations, especially those with richer lands. The form of engagement was roughly divided between sharecropping, wage labor, and rental tenancy. Between 1890 and 1910 the number of black men in agriculture increased by over half a million, or 31%. During this entire period three out of five black men were employed in agriculture.

Maintaining the semi-servile status of the black labor force required the augmentation of colorcaste distinctions. Southern slavery, after all, had been more than just an economic arrangement: it was a cultural system that provided a wide range of norms congruent with plantation discipline. Slave status had served as a line of demarcation throughout the society. Therefore emancipation not only changed the economic form of planter control, but also left gaps in the social superstructure that reinforced it. Under these conditions the strengthening of racialism per se in all cultural arrangements became an imperative for any hope of continuance of the planters' hegemony over Southern society. Since racism had pervaded all major facets of social and political control, much of the further elaboration of colorcaste distinctions arose in the course of the Southern ruling class's struggles to keep the rest of the whites in line.

The road to the establishment of this new system of order in the South was by no means a smooth one. Abrogation of the slave system had made possible some new types of mobility among both blacks and whites, bringing about changes in the forms of inter-racial conflict and class conflict. Blacks were now able to move geographically, even in the face of continued legal and extralegal restraints. The migration that took place was mainly a westerly one within the South. Inside the black community class mobility developed through the emergence of a small middle class. At the same time, there now opened up to poorer whites areas that had formerly been the preserve of slavery. During the pre-Civil War era no white would compete with a slave for his position on the plantation. Albeit when planters and slaveless small farmers did contend for land, as frequently occurred, the black slave was indirectly involved. With emancipation, racial rivalry for the soil became overt. Freedmen struggled to gain land, sometimes as owners but more frequently as indebted tenants. At the same time, many white smallholders, forced out from infertile and worn soil, sought many of the same lands. After the Civil War the white farmers increased in numbers at a greater rate than the blacks. By 1900, even as tenants, the whites were in the majority. Blacks moved from a non-competitive status in slavery (or perhaps better "concealed competition between the bond and the free"), as Rupert Vance has pointed out, to a condition of overt inter-racial competition." As slaves Negroes were objects of race prejudice; as a new competitive group stuggling for status and a place on the land Negroes found themselves potential objects of mass pressure and group conflict."[27]

Transformations also took place within the Southern ruling class. Ownership of land tended to shift out of the hands of the old planter class into those of merchants, lawyers, and in some cases Northern interests, removing many of the impediments to land-owners' making their decisions more markedly, on the basis of pure entrepreneurial calculations. This partial unfreezing of labor and capital resources provided some important pre-conditions for the industrialization of the South. Nevertheless, the ideal for black labor in the eyes of dominant white groups was that of a contented agrarian peasantry. Paternal-istic members of the Southern elite spoke of satisfied workers controlled by fair but rigidly-enforced rules. "Let the Negro become iden-tified with and attached to the soil upon which he lives, and he himself, the land-owner, and the country alike will be advanced by his labor."[28]

In the social and politial realms the con-flicts inherent in the black peasantry's subju-gation became intertwined with the conflicts inherent in the subordination of any poten-tial political power in the hands of the white smallholders and landless. As things turned out, blacks were to suffer both from the control of the propertied and from the competition of the poor. The political process provided a

major means by which this was carried out. "It is one of the paradoxes of Southern his-tory," writes C. Vann Woodward, "that polit-ical democracy for the white man and racial discrimination for the black were often products of the same dynamics." The impera-tives of preserving class rule supplied the basis of the paradox: "It took a lot of ritual and Jim Crow to bolster the rule of white supremacy in the bosom of a white man working for a black man's wage."[29] Function-ally the poorer whites were permitted to influ-ence the formal political process only under conditions that would not undermine the essential power and economic control of the ruling class. The execution of this strategy was completed during the defeat of the Populist movement in the 1890s by excluding the black people from politics and by heightening the color-caste distinctions through an extension of Jim Crow laws and customs. Since the black people had already been defeated through Redemption 20 years before, the moves to disfranchise black people at the turn of the century had as "the real question . . . which whites would be supreme". Ruling circles channeled disfranchisement to their own ends "as they saw in it an opportunity to establish in power 'the intelligence and wealth of the South' which could of course 'goven in the interests of all classes'".[30] Many whites as well as blacks were denied the ballot, and the substantive differences expressed in the political process were delimited to a narrower range. Inter-class conflicts among whites were much displaced by inter-racial conflicts, and the hegemony of larger property interests was secured.

The agrarian designation of the black masses was reinforced by the lack of competi-tion for their labor from other sectors of the economy. The Southern demand for factory help, except for unskilled work, was essen-tially a demand for white labor. The textile industry, the primary industry of the New South, was marked off as a preserve of the white worker. The mythology that black workers were incapable of measuring up to the conditions in the textile mills was reinforced by the rationale that the domestic peace required that white poor have some kind of economic preserve, free from competition.[31]

> Thus when the industrialization of the South began about 1880 and attained remarkable proportions by the outbreak of the (First) World War, it had comparatively little significance for the Negro agricultural workers.... The poor whites took the cotton mills as their own; and with the exception of sweeping, scrubbing, and the like in cotton factories, there was virtually no work for the Negroes in the plants. They were, therefore, compelled to labor on the farms, the only other work that was available.[32]

The rather-considerable increase in industrial employment of blacks between 1890 and 1910 was concentrated in railroading, lumbering, and coal mining—that is, in non-factory-type operations with these three industries often located in rural areas. Lumbering and allied industries could almost have been considered an extension of agriculture, as the workers shifted back and forth from one to the other.

Outside of agriculture the vast bulk of black workers were to be found either in domestic and personal service or in unskilled menial fields that were known in the South as "Negro jobs". In the cities the growth occupations were chiefly porters, draymen, laundresses, seamstresses. However non-propertied whites did begin to crowd into many skilled positions that had been the black man's preserve under slavery. Black mechanics and artisans, who had vastly outnumbered Southern whites as late as 1865, fought a losing battle for these jobs down to 1890, when they were able to stabilize a precarious minority position in some of the construction trades.[33]

Exclusion of black workers from industry was not based on rational calculation regarding the characteristics of the labor supply. Contrary to all the racist rationales about incapacity and lack of training, most industrial firms considered blacks good workers. When the employers were questioned specifically about the comparative quality of black and white workers in their plants, the majority held that they were equally satisfactory. The Chattanooga Tradesman in 1889 and 1891, on its own, and again in 1901 in co-operation with the Atlanta University Sociology Department, made surveys of firms employing skilled and semi-skilled blacks. The Tradesman's editor concluded from the results that "the Negro, as a free laborer, as a medium skilled and common worker, is by no means a 'failure' . . . he is a remarkable success." In the 1901 survey over 60% of the employers held that their black workers were as good as or better than their white workers.[34]

Northern ruling classes were quick to accept those conditions in the South that stabilized the national political system and provided the raw commodities for their mills and markets. Therefore they supported the establishment of a subservient black peasantry, the regional rule of the Southern propertied interests, and the racial oppression that made both of these things possible. The dominant Northern interests shared the ideal of the smooth kind of racial subjugation projected by the paternalistic Southern elite, but they went along with what proved necessary. "Cotton brokers of New York and Philadelphia, and cotton manufacturers of New England . . . knew full well the importance of bringing discipline to the Southern labor force. When theories of Negro equality resulted in race conflict, and conflict in higher prices of raw cotton, manufacturers were inclined to accept the point of view of the Southern planter rather than that of the New England zealot."[35] Northern businessmen who supported black education in the South had in mind a system that would encourage the students to stay in rural areas and would train them for hard work and menial positions.[36]

Thus, through a process that Harvard's Paul Buck approvingly called *The Road to*

Reunion and Howard's Rayford Logan scathingly labeled *The Betrayal of the Negro,* national political, business, and intellectual elites came to define race as a Southern question for which they would not assume any leadership. By 1900 Southern sympathizer and Northern anti-slavery man alike agreed on the rightfulness of the subjugation of the black man. It was accepted as a necessary condition for order in the American state. And order was most essential to the extraordinary expansion of the industrial system. Beyond that point the black man was ignored and considered a "nothing", especially on Northern ground. Reasons of state and racism had combined to legitimize the new form of agrarian thralldom.

In the North itself during this period there was minimal work for blacks, even though the Northern economy was labor-starved to the extent that it promoted and absorbed a European immigration of over 15,000,000 persons. Blacks were not only shut off from the new jobs, but lost many of the jobs they had traditionally held. The Irish largely displaced them in street paving, the Slavs displaced them in brickyards, and all groups moved in on the once-black stronghold of dining-room waiting. Study the chapters on economic life in Leon Litwack's *North of Slavery: The Negro in the Free States, 1790–1860* and Leslie Fishel's unfortunately unpublished dissertation "The North and the Negro, 1865–1900: A Study in Race Discrimination".[37] They both read as if they are describing the same situation. If there is a difference, it is that Fishel describes a greater decline in status.

The reasons for this displacement of black workers in the North are complex. Northern capital engaged Southern workers, both black and white, by exporting capital to the South rather than by encouraging any great migration, thus enabling itself to exploit the low wage structure of the economically backward South while avoiding any disturbance in its precarious political or economic balance. Sometimes racism would operate directly, as

when the National Cash Register Company (Dayton, Ohio) laid off 300 black janitors because the management wanted to have white farm boys start at the bottom and work their way up.[38] In addition, job competition often led white workers to see blacks, rather than employers, as the enemy. At least 50 strikes, North and South, in which white workers protested the employment of blacks have been recorded for the years 1881 to 1900.[39] There was a minor counter-theme of class solidarity which existed to a certain extent in the Knights of Labor and was reaffirmed by the Industrial Workers of the World, but as the job-conscious American Federation of Labor gained dominance over the union movement, racial exclusion became the operative practice, with the only major exception occurring among the United Mine Workers.[40] (It was actually more common in the South than in the North for black workers to hold a position so strong in particular industries that unions had to take them into account; in these instances they were generally organized in separate locals.) Episodes in which blacks were used as strikebreakers contributed to the unions' hostility toward blacks, but it should be added that racism seriously distorted the perceptions of white workers. Whites were used as scabs more frequently and in larger numbers, but the saliency of racial categories was able to make the minority role of blacks stand out more sharply, so that in many white workers' minds the terms "scab" and "Negro" were synonymous.[41]

The course of national development of black people was set within the framework of their concentration in the Southern countryside. During Reconstruction a truly heroic effort was made by the black masses to establish a self-sufficient yeomanry on the land. Smashing of this movement set back the progression of independent black militancy more than a generation. New forms of embryonic nationalism emerged or re-emerged. Exodus groups tried with a certain success to establish themselves on the land in Kansas, Oklahoma, and Indiana. Pan-Africanism appeared once again with interest in colonization. But the major expression took place in a muted form through the role of Booker T. Washington, who, as August Meier has shown so well[42], had his base in the black people's desire for racial solidarity, their struggle for land and for the preservation of crafts, and the aspirations of a rising bourgeoisie in the cities which derived its livelihood from the black masses. Washington's social and political accommodations allowed the movement to exist and even gain support from Northern and Southern ruling circles. At the same time Washington's withdrawal from socio-political struggle reflected the weak post-Reconstruction position of black people in the agrarian South. Militant forms of black national liberation would not re-emerge until a black proletariat had developed in the urban centers.

THE TRANSITION ERA, SECOND PHASE: WORLD WAR I TO WORLD WAR II

The new equilibrium of racial regulation that had stabilized around tenancy agriculture as the dominant force of black exploitation received its first major disturbance from the impact of World War I. A certain irony inheres in the condition that imperialism's cataclysm should begin the break-up of agrarian thralldom within the United States. The War's effect on black people took place through the mediation of the market-place, rather than through any shake-up of political relations. Hostilities in Europe placed limitations on American industry's usual labor supply by shutting off the flow of immigration at the very time the demand for labor was increasing sharply due to a war boom and military mobilization. Competition with the Southern plantation system for black labor became one of the major means of resolving this crisis of labor demand.

The black labor reserve in the countryside that had existed essentially as a *potential* source of the industrial proletariat now became a very

active source. Whereas in the past this industrial reserve had not been tapped in any important way except by rural-based operations such as lumbering, with the advent of the War the industrial system as a whole began drawing on it. This new demand for black workers was to set in motion three key developments: first, the dispersion of black people out of the South into Northern urban centers; second, the formation of a distinct black proletariat in the urban centers at the very heart of the corporate-capitalist process of production; third, the break-up of tenancy agriculture in the South. World War II was to repeat the process in a magnified form and to place the stamp of irreversibility upon it.

Migration out of the countryside started in 1915 and swept up to a human tide by 1917. The major movement was to Northern cities, so that between 1910 and 1920 the black population increased in Chicago from 44,000 to 109,000; in New York from 92,000 to 152,000; in Detroit from 6,000 to 41,000; and in Philadelphia from 84,000 to 134,000. That decade there was a net increase of 322,000 in the number of Southern born blacks living in the North, exceeding the aggregate increase of the preceding 40 years. A secondary movement took place to Southern cities, especially those with shipbuilding and heavy industry.

Labor demand in such industries as steel, meat-packing, and autos was the key stimulant to black migration. The total number of wage-earners in manufacturing went from 7,000,000 in 1914 to around 9,000,000 in 1919—an increase twice that of any preceding five-year period. A survey of the experience of the major employers of black labor in Chicago reported that "Inability to obtain competent white workers was the reason given in practically every instance for the large number of Negroes employed since 1914."[43] A contemporary US Government report stated:

All of these employment managers and the higher executives of Northern industry are sadly worried by their labor problem. They feel that things are going from bad to worse; that even wage increases can avail little; they hope for national labor conscription for the period of the War as the only adequate solution to their problem, and are eager for Federal aid. . . . The majority of executives interviewed were favorable to the experiment with Negro employment in the North, and were sympathetic to suggestions concerning selection, training, housing, and recreation for the newcomer.[44]

The profit-maximization imperatives of Northern capitalist firms for the first time outweighed the socio-political reasons for leaving the Southern planters' control over black labor undisturbed and without any serious competition.

Labor agents sent South by railroad and steel companies initiated the migration by telling of high wages and offering transportation subsidy. In some cases whole trainloads of workers were shipped North. Though American firms had employed labor recruiters for work among the European peasantries for decades, this was the first time they went forth in any strength to bring black peasants to the city. Many Southern localities tried to protect their labor stocks by legislating proscriptions on labor agents and charging them prohibitive license fees, but on the whole recruiters played only a secondary role.[45] A more important impetus to migration came from the Northern-based black press, most notably the *Chicago Defender,* and above all from the letters and the reports of blacks who had already moved north. Successful employment served as its own advertisement, and better wages outside the South proved very attractive. During the summer of 1917 male wage-earners in the North were making $2.00 to $2.50 a day while the money wages on Mississippi farms ranged from 75¢ to $1.25.[46] Early migrations to Northern cities had been from the Upper South. Now blacks came in from all over, with the Deep South having the heaviest representation. In many

cotton areas boll-weevil invasions destroyed the crop, acting as a push off the land at the same time Northern industry was providing a pull.

There was a temporary slackening of the demand for black labor when post-war demobilization caused heavy unemployment. In Chicago, where as many as 10,000 black laborers were out of work, the local Association of Commerce wired to Southern chambers of commerce: "Are you in need of Negro labor? Large surplus here, both returned soldiers and civilian Negroes ready to go to work."[47] In Detroit in 1921, black unemployment rates were five times as great as those of native white workers, and twice as great as those of the foreign-born.[48] But a strong economic recovery at the very time that restrictive immigration laws went into effect brought a second great migration out of the South in the years 1922 to 1924. The magnitude of this second movement has been estimated at slightly under a half-million persons, and may have been greater than that of the wartime movement.[49] The employers who already had a black sector in their work force were able to tap this supply with much less trouble and cost than had been incurred a few years before. As William Graves, personal assistant to Julius Rosenwald, told the Chicago Union League Club: "The Negro permanency in industry was no longer debatable."[50]

The tremendous social dislocations created by the mobilization and the wartime economic boom heightened inter-racial tensions and laid the groundwork for over 20 race riots that occurred on both sides of the Mason-Dixon Line. Careful studies of the two major race riots in Northern industrial centers (East Saint Louis in 1917 and Chicago in 1919) reveal the tremendous friction that had developed between white and black workers.[51] These hostilities were not simply an outgrowth of race prejudice, for in both cases employers had fostered competition for jobs, especially by employing blacks as strikebreakers. Conflict between working-class whites and working-class blacks was analogous in a way to the previously-discussed racial competition among tenants and smallholders for land in the South. When the conflict erupted into mass violence, the dominant whites sat back and resolved the crises in a manner that assured their continued control over both groups.

The first feature of the program that Northern industry developed in relation to the inter-racial conflicts that the riots evidenced was that the permanency of black workers in the North was conclusively established. Management accepted its interest in guaranteeing minimal survival conditions of housing, education, et cetera to perpetuate this labor force. Even during slack times business had to maintain a certain continuity of employment, especially in those jobs that functionally became Negro jobs. Economically, even in a recession, long-run costs are reduced if something of a permanent work force is retained, for when good times return the recruitment and training of an entirely new labor force can require a great monetary outlay.[52] Thus, as the 1920s wore on, while there was a virtual cessation of articles regarding the employment of blacks in business-oriented and welfare publications, the fact that blacks *would* be employed was now accepted. The shifting of racial stereotypes to fit the new situation was indicated by a business spokesman who reported that the black man "has lost his slovenliness, lazy habits, gambling, and liquor-drinking propensities". He noted that plant superintendents in heavy industry had come to consider black workers especially tractable. "They found Negroes on the whole far more adjustable than the foreign-born. They used a common language, were loyal in times of stress, and were more co-operative in matters such as stock purchases, buying insurance, et cetera."[53]

At the same time, it has to be understood that black workers were employed on management's own terms. Sometimes these terms would involve the deliberate use of blacks to divide the work force. As a case in point, International Harvester integrated the hiring of blacks into its open-shop policies. Part of its strategy was to keep any nationality group from becoming too numerous in any one plant lest they become cohesive in labor conflicts. The decision on hiring was left up to the individual plant superintendents, some keeping their shops lily-white, others hiring large numbers of black workers. Harvester's management was caught up in a contradiction between its need for black workers, especially in the disagreeable twine mill and foundry, and its desire to keep them below 20% at any one plant.[54]

A somewhat different approach was taken by Ford Motor Company. In the 1921 depression Henry Ford decided to maintain the black work force at the gigantic River Rouge plant in the same proportion as blacks in the total population of the Detroit area. The great majority of blacks at the River Rouge plant were employed in hot, heavy jobs in the rolling mills and foundry, but it was company policy to place a few in every major production unit and even allow a certain amount of upgrading to skilled positions. At the other Ford plants, as at the other major auto companies, black workers were confined to hard unskilled jobs. But the job concessions at Rouge became a mechanism by which Ford was able to gain considerable influence over Detroit's black community. Hiring was channeled through some preferred black ministers who agreed with Henry Ford on politics and industrial relations. Company black personnel officials were active in Republican politics and in anti-union campaigns. Ford had learned early a racial tactic that is widely employed today—that of trading concessions, relaxing economic subordination in order to increase political subordination.[55]

In industry generally the black worker was almost always deployed in job categories that effectively became designated as "Negro jobs". This classification, openly avowed in the South, was often claimed in the North to be merely the way things worked out through application of uniform standards. The superintendent of a Kentucky plough factory expressed the Southern view:

> Negroes do work white men won't do, such as common labor; heavy, hot, and dirty work; pouring crucibles; work in the grinding room; and so on. Negroes are employed because they are cheaper. . . . The Negro does a different grade of work and makes about 10¢ an hour less.[56]

There was not a lot of contrast in the words of coke works foremen at a Pennsylvania steel mill: "They are well fitted for this hot work, and we keep them because we appreciate this ability in them." "The door machines and the jam cutting are the most undesirable; it is hard to get white men to do this kind of work."[57] The placement of workers in separate job categories along racial lines was so marked in Detroit that in response to a survey many employers stated that they could not make a comparison between the wages of whites and blacks because they were not working on the same jobs.[58] In the North there was some blurring of racial distinctions, but they remained strong enough to set the black labor force off quite clearly. While the pay for the same job in the same plant was usually equivalent, when blacks came to predominate in a specific job classification, the rate on it would tend to lag. White and black workers were often hired in at the same low job classification; however for the whites advancement was often possible, while the blacks soon bumped into a job ceiling. In terms of day-to-day work, white labor was given a systematic advantage over black labor and a stake in the racist practices.

Northern management's public equal-opportunity posture to preserve their black work force was expressed with clarity at a 1920 conference of officials from five Chicago firms, employing over 6,000 workers, and an official of the Chicago Urban League:

All of these labor managers expressed the opinion that there would be no reduction in the force of Negro employees. They cited the shortage of men for heavy labor, due to the lack of immigration from abroad, and all said that their companies were eager to employ more Negroes. Equal pay for the same work to whites and to Negroes was given as general practice. General satisfaction with Negro labor was expressed, and the ability of their Negro workers is equal, they said, to that of white workers of corresponding education. All mentioned the advantage, as compared with various immigrant groups, of a common language, enabling all foremen and officers to speak directly with the men. No discrimination in use of restaurants, sanitary facilities, et cetera was reported. All testified that Negroes were given the same opportunities as white workers for advancement to higher positions. The fact that a smaller percentage of Negroes are to be found in the higher positions is due, they said, to the fact that a smaller proportion are as well educated.[59]

The amazing thing about this meeting is that if the references to the immigrants are deleted it has the sound of similar sessions that are held today—half a century later.[60]

In the South, where four-fifths of the nation's black population still lived at the end of the 1920s, the situation of black labor was to all appearances essentially unchanged. The number of black men engaged in Southern industry grew during this decade only 45% as fast as the number of whites. Black workers were concentrated in stagnant or declining plants, such as sawmills, coal mines, and cigar and tobacco factories. The increased hiring of blacks in such places was chiefly a reflection of the fact that the jobs had no future and the employers were not able to attract white workers. Black employment in textiles was severely limited, as in South Carolina, where state law forbade blacks to work in the same room, use the same stairway, or even share the same factory window as white textile workers.[61] Industry in the South, as far as black workers were concerned, still offered little competition to the dominance of agrarian tenancy.

Beneath the surface, however, significant changes were taking place in the rural South. While as late as the mid-1930s Charles S. Johnson could write of a cotton county in Alabama that "The plantation technique on the side of administration was most effective in respect to discipline and policing, and this technique has survived more or less despite the formal abolition of slavery"[62], this state of affairs was then being undermined. Cotton cultivation was moving westward, leaving many blacks in the Southeast without a market crop. Out in the new cotton lands in Texas and Oklahoma whites provided a much larger proportion of the tenants and sharecroppers. By 1930 a slight decrease was seen in the number of black farm operators and laborers. Later, the great depression of the 1930s accelerated this trend as the primary market for agricultural commodities collapsed and the acreage in cotton was halved. Black tenants were pushed off land in far greater proportions than whites. New Deal agricultural programs were very important in displacing sharecroppers and tenants, since they subsidized reductions in acreage. In the early government-support programs landlords tended to monopolize subsidy payments, diverting much of them out of tenants' pockets. When the regulations were changed in the tenants' favor, the landowner had an incentive to convert the tenants to wage laborers or dismiss them altogether so as to get the whole subsidy.[63] The great depression marked the first drastic decline in the demand for black peasants since their status had been established after the Civil War.

In 1940 there were 650,000 fewer black farm operators and laborers than there had been a decade earlier—representing a one-third drop in the total. The push out of the countryside helped maintain a small net rate of migration to the North. More significantly, however, during the depression decade a high rate of black movement to the city kept on while the rate of white urbanization slackened greatly.

Although the great majority of black people remained in the rural South, we have dealt primarily with the character of the demand for black workers in the course of their becoming established directly in the urban industrial economy. This initial process was to form the matrix into which the ever-increasing numbers of black workers were to be fitted.[64] As the size of the black population in big cities grew, "Negro jobs" became roughly institutionalized into an identifiable black sub-labor market within the larger metropolitan labor market. The culture of control that was embodied in the regulative systems which managed the black ghettos, moreover, provided an effective, although less-rigid, variation of the Jim Crow segregation that continued with hardly any change in the South. Although the economic base of black tenancy was collapsing, its reciprocal superstructure of political and social controls remained the most powerful force shaping the place of blacks in society. The propertied and other groups that had a vested interest in the special exploitation of the black peasantry were still strong enough to maintain their hegemony over matters concerning race. At the same time, the variation of Jim Crow that existed in the North was more than simply a carry-over from the agrarian South. These ghetto controls served the class function for industrial society of politically and socially setting off that section of the proletariat that was consigned to the least-desirable employment. This racial walling off not only was accomplished by direct ruling-class actions, but also was mediated through an escalating reciprocal process in which the hostility and competition of the white working class was stimulated by the growth of the black proletariat and in return operated as an agent in shaping the new racial controls.

The prolonged depression of the 1930s that threw millions out of work severely tested

(Upper left) A tenant farmer and his wife, photographed in 1941. (Upper right) The son of a family of migrant strawberry pickers sits in the doorway of the family's quarters, 1939. (Bottom left) A family of share-croppers is forced to move from their farm in Missouri during the depth of the Great Depression, 1939.

the position of blacks in the industrial economy. Two somewhat contradictory results stood out for this period. First, whites were accorded racial preference as a greatly disproportionate share of unemployment was placed on black workers. Second, despite erosion due to the unemployment differential, the black sub-sectors of the urban labor markets remained intact.

In the first years of the slump, black unemployment rates ran about two-thirds greater than white unemployment rates. As the depression wore on, the relative position of the black labor force declined so that by the end of the decade it had proportionately twice as many on relief or unemployed in the Mid-Atlantic States, and two and a half times as many in the North Central States. In the Northern cities

only half the black men had regular full-time employment. In the larger cities, for every four black men in full-time regular employment there was one engaged in government-sponsored emergency relief. The differential in the South was not as great, for much of the unemployment there was disguised by marginal occupations on the farms.

The rationing out of unemployment operated in such a way as to reinforce the demarcation of "Negro jobs". Blacks were dismissed in higher proportions from the better positions. In Chicago they were displaced from professional and managerial occupations at a rate five times that of whites. The displacement rate from clerical, skilled, and semi-skilled jobs was three times larger, while from unskilled and service jobs it was down to twice

Sleeping car porter on trains was a job exclusively given over to blacks. The porters joined together in a union, the Brotherhood of Sleeping Car Porters, and were able to mount effective labor actions.

that of whites. As a result the total percentage of skilled and white-collar workers in the black labor force declined to half its former proportion, and the servant and personal service sector expanded again. Nationally, blacks lost a third of the jobs they had held in industry, declining from 7.3% to 5.1% of the total manufacturing employment. In the South the continuous unemployment even made white workers bid for those jobs in the tobacco industry that for generations had been recognized as "Negro jobs". An example from Northern industry: International Harvester no longer had a dire need for black workers, and the company let them slip off from 28% to 19% in the twine mill, and 18% to 10% at the McCormick Works.[65]

The limited openings available to black job-seekers were in precisely those fields that were defined as "Negro jobs". Therefore, in the urban areas, young white workers with less than a seventh-grade education had a higher rate of unemployment than blacks. With grade-school and high-school diplomas, however, the whites' chances for jobs increased markedly while blacks' chances actually declined. In general increased age and experience did not improve the black worker's position in the labor market.

On the eve of World War II, when defense production really began to stimulate the economy, the number of jobs increased rapidly. At first, however, it was almost as if the black unemployed had to stand aside while the whites went to work. In April 1940, 22% of the blacks (about 1,250,000 persons) were unemployed, as were 17.7% of the white labor force. By October, employment had increased by 2,000,000 jobs, and white unemployment had declined to 13%, while black unemployment remained at the same level. Firms with tremendous labor shortages still abided by their racial definitions of jobs and refused to take on available black workers. In September 1941 a US Government survey found that of almost 300,000 job openings,

over half were restricted to whites. In Indiana, Ohio, and Illinois, 80% of the openings were thus restricted.[66]

Military mobilization of much of the existing labor force and an almost 20% growth in non-farm employment from 32,000,000 in 1940 to 40,000,000 in 1942 were the preconditions necessary to enlarge the demand for black labor. While the President's creation of the Fair Employment Practice Committee (FEPC) under pressure from black organizations helped open up some doors, it was the logic of the labor market that shook the racial status quo. By 1942, management-oriented publications were dealing with the question of employing black workers—a topic they had not considered since the mid-1920s.

The American Management Association told its members: "As some shortages develop for which there is no adequate supply of labor from the usual sources, management is forced to look elsewhere. It is then that the Negro looms large as a reservoir of motive power—a source which management has hitherto given only a few furtive, experimental pokes with a long pole." Once more surveys were conducted which showed that most employers consider black workers as efficient as whites. Management reiterated statements about non-discrimination when production conditions forced them to change their racial hiring practices. *Fortune* magazine consoled its executive readers that their personal racism need not be violated: "Theoretically, management should have fewer objections to hiring colored labor than any other part of the industrial team. The employer seldom has social contact with his workers anyway, and his primary concern is production efficiency and satisfactory investment return."[67]

Nationally, the demand for black labor was tremendous. In the spring of 1942 it composed 2.5% to 3% of the war-production work force, and by the fall of 1944 this proportion had risen to 8.3%. These million and a half black war workers were concentrated in the areas of the most stringent labor shortage. Fourteen industrial centers accounted for almost half of these war workers, and of these centers only one was located in the South and only two were border cities. In areas of acute labor shortage, the absence of any white reserve of labor gave blacks much greater access to war work than in labor surplus areas. Black migration was a necessary condition for this employment, and the movement of the families out of the Southern countryside and small towns was accelerated.

The vast demand for labor in general, that had to turn itself into a demand for black labor, could only be accomplished by way of a great expansion of the black sectors of metropolitan labor markets. Training programs for upgrading to skilled and semi-skilled jobs were opened up, at first in the North and later in the South. By 1943–1944, 35% of pre-employment trainees in shipbuilding courses and 29% in aircraft were blacks. World War I had established a space for black laborers as unskilled workers in heavy industry. During World War II this space was enlarged to include a number of semi-skilled and single-skilled jobs in many industries.[68]

World War II marked the most dramatic improvement in economic status of black people that has ever taken place in the urban industrial economy. The income of black workers increased twice as fast as that of whites. Occupationally, blacks bettered their positions in all of the preferred occupations. The biggest improvement was brought about by the migration from South to North (a net migration of 1,600,000 blacks between 1940 and 1950). However within both sections the relative proportion of blacks within skilled and semi-skilled occupations grew. In clerical and lower-level professional work, labor shortages in the government bureaucracies created a necessity for a tremendous black upgrading into posts hitherto lily-white.

During the era between the two World Wars the national aspirations of blacks worked themselves out on the base of their new material conditions—that is, those of their becoming an urban people whose masses were proletarians. Conflicting tendencies beset this movement at every stage. The dominant white society usually followed the strategy of denying the very existence of its peoplehood. The black community was considered a pathological form rather than something valid in itself. Whenever the black community did thrust itself forward, the tactics of management shifted to a balance of naked repression with co-optive channeling. Within the community there was a constant contention as to which of the class forces would dominate—the black bourgeoisie, that sector of the black working class operating under the dominance of white trade-union organizations, or a nationally-based black working class.

The greatest organized expression of black nationalism occurred in the Garvey Back-to-Africa Movement after 1920. As Harry Haywood has so trenchantly characterized this broad mass development, it was conditioned by the convergence of two class developments:

> On the one hand it was the trend of the recent migrants from the peasant South. . . . The membership of these organizations by and large was composed of the new, as yet non-integrated Negro proletarians; recent migrants from the cotton fields, who had not yet shaken the dust of the plantation from their heels and remained largely peasants in outlook. Embittered and disillusioned by post-war terror and unemployment, they saw in the Garvey scheme of a Negro nation in Africa a way out to the realization of their deep-grounded yearnings for land and freedom. . . . On the other hand, Garveyism reflected the ideology of the Negro petty bourgeoisie, their abortive attempt at hegemony in the Negro movement. It was the trend of the small property-holder: the shopkeepers, pushed to the wall, ruined or threatened with ruin by the ravages of the crisis; the frustrated and unemployed Negro professionals—doctors and lawyers with

impoverished clientele, storefront preachers, poverty-stricken students—in sum those elements of the middle class closest to the Negro laboring people and hence affected most keenly by deterioration of their conditions.[69]

When the migration of black peasants to the Northern cities dropped off in the mid-1920s, the Garvey movement began to lose out, and the US Government was able to move in with prosecutions to break it up.

The more-successful entrepreneurial types, such as the bankers, insurance executives, and newspaper publishers, were able now to seize the lead in the cities. They generated an optimism about the future of black capitalism that has never been recaptured. This group, which provided services chiefly to a black clientele, lost out when the depression brought wholesale bankruptcy, and this experience smashed illusions about the future of black business.[70]

Proletarian leadership now re-emerged on a firmer foundation of having assimilated its new conditions of existence. From the masses themselves there was a surge of battles in the cities for emergency relief and against housing evictions. This intervention of the working class and unemployed inserted a new vigor into the "Don't Buy Where You Can't Work" campaigns that bourgeois leadership had initiated to win jobs from white firms operating in the ghetto. In 1935 a riot broke out in Harlem, and for the first time blacks moved from a defensive posture in such a situation and employed violence on a retaliatory basis against the white store-owners. As concessions were gained, part of the energy was channeled into the New Deal relief bureaucracy and Democratic Party politics, where patronage and paternalism took the edge off much independent thrust. Nevertheless, important struggles for jobs, government-supported housing, and more territory for living space helped consolidate an institutional infrastructure for the black community and gave an urban definition to its national consciousness, or race pride, as it was called in those days.

The trade-union organizing drives of the CIO which actively sought out black workers in heavy and mass-production industry provided a new focus. From 1937 to World War II the CIO conducted the most massive working-class campaign that has ever taken place in America. Its dynamism was so great that it reset the direction of the political activity of the working class, the black community, and the Left. Even the bourgeois-led organizations, like the NAACP, came to accept the decisive leadership role of the CIO. While black workers played an integral part in this organizing campaign, with over 200,000 members in the CIO ranks by 1940, the black working class did not develop an independent program or organization that dealt with the national oppression of their people.[71]

Only after the outbreak of World War II, when blacks were still being excluded from much of the rapidly expanding economy, did a black movement set out independently from the New Deal-labor coalition and take the initiative in defining a race position on the national level. In January 1941 A. Philip Randolph, President of the Brotherhood of Sleeping Car Porters, an all-black AFL union, issued a call for a massive march on Washington to demand of the Government a greater share in the defense effort. The March on Washington Movement expressed the mood of the black community and received an upswelling of support sufficient to force President Roosevelt to establish a Fair Employment Practice Committee in return for the calling off of the projected march. Although this movement was not able to establish a firmly organized working-class base or sustain itself for long, it foreshadowed a new stage of development for a self-conscious black working class with the appeal that "An oppressed people must accept the responsibility and take the initiative to free themselves."[72]

CURRENT CONDITIONS OF DEMAND— AN OUTLINE

(A full examination of the present-day political economic conditions regarding the demand for black labor requires a whole separate essay. We are limited here to indicating some of the most essential features.)

The changes that took place in the economic deployment of black labor in World War II were clearly an acceleration of developments that had been under way since World War I. In a process of transition, at a certain point the quantity of change becomes so great that the whole set of relationships assume an entirely-different character. Such a nodal point took place during World War II, and there resulted a transformation in the characteristic relations of institutional racism from agrarian thralldom to a metropolitan ghetto system.

Within a generation, few of the concrete economic or demographic forms of the old base remained. In 1940, over three-fourths of all blacks lived in the South, close to two-thirds lived in rural areas there, and just under half were still engaged in agriculture. By 1969, almost as many blacks lived outside the South as still resided in that region, and only 4% of the black laborers remained in agriculture, as they had left the farms at a much more rapid rate than whites. Today, only about a fifth of the total black population live in the rural areas and small towns of the South.

The United States, during the Twentieth Century, has become a distinctively urban nation—or, more accurately, a metropolitan nation with its population centered in the large cities and their surrounding configurations. The first three decades of this century witnessed the rapid urbanization of whites; the next three decades saw an even more rapid urbanization of blacks. In 1940 the proportion of the country's black population living in urban areas (49%) was the same as that proportion of whites had been in 1910. Within 20 years, almost three fourths of all blacks were urban dwellers, a higher proportion than the corresponding one for whites. More specifically, the black population has

been relocated into the central cities of the metropolitan areas— in 1940, 34% of all blacks resided in central cities; in 1969, 55%. The larger cities were the points of greatest growth. In 1950 black people constituted one out of every eight persons in the central cities of the metropolitan areas of every size classification, and one out of every twenty in the suburbs. By 1969, black people constituted one out of every four in the central city populations of the large metropolitan areas (1,000,000 plus), and about one out of six in the medium-size metropolitan areas (250,000 to 1,000,000), while in the smaller-size metropolitan areas (below 250,000) and the suburbs the proportions remained constant. Today black communities form major cities in themselves, two with populations over 1,000,000, four between 500,000 and 1,000,000, and eight between 200,000 and 500,000.[73] Newark and Washington DC already have black majorities, and several other major cities will most likely join their ranks in the next 10 years.

The displacement of blacks from Southern agriculture was only partially due to the pull of labor demand in wartime. Technological innovation, being a necessary condition of production, acted as an independent force to drive the tenants out of the cotton fields. The push off the land occurred in two phases. Initially, right after the war, the introduction of tractors and herbicides displaced the cotton hands from full-time to seasonal work at summer weeding and harvest. The now part-time workers moved from the farms to hamlets and small towns. During the 1950s mechanization of the harvest eliminated most of the black peasantry from agricultural employment and forced them to move to the larger cities for economic survival.[74]

Elimination of the Southern black peasantry was decisive in changing the forms of racism throughout the entire region, for it meant the disappearance of the economic foundation on which the elaborate superstructure of legal Jim Crow and segregation had originally been erected. Not only did this exploited agrarian group almost vanish, but the power of the large landholders who expropriated the surplus it had produced diminished in relation to the growing urban and industrial interests. While the civil-rights movement and the heroic efforts associated with it were necessary to break the official legality of segregation, it should be recognized that in a sense this particular form of racism was already obsolete, as its base in an exploitative system of production had drastically changed. The nature of the concessions made both by the ruling class nationally and by the newer power groups of the South can be understood only in terms of this fuller view of history.[75]

For the United States as a whole, the most important domestic development was the further elaboration and deepening of monopoly state capitalism. As the political economy has matured, technological and management innovation have become capital-saving as well as labor-saving. Capital accumulation declines as a proportion of the gross national product, and a mature capitalist economy enters into a post-accumulation phase of development. Under these conditions the disposal of the economic surplus becomes almost as great a problem as the accumulation of it. Corporations promote consumerism through increased sales effort, planned obsolescence, and advertising. The State meets the problem by increasing its own expenditures, especially in non-consumable military items, by providing monetary support to consumption through subsidies to the well-off, and by spending a certain amount on welfare for the working class and the poor. Markedly lower incomes would add to the surplus disposal problems and would create economic stagnation as well as risking the most-disruptive forms of class struggle.

Working-class incomes have two basic minimum levels, or floors. One is that which can be considered the level of the good trade-union contract which has to be met even by non-union firms that bid in this section of the labor market. State intervention is usually indirect in the setting of these incomes, but has grown noticeable in the last few years. The other income floor is set by direct government action via minimum-wage and welfare legislation. In the Northern industrial states where trade unions are stronger, both these income floors tend to be higher than in rural and Southern states.

Although in the mature capitalist society both economic and political imperatives exist for a certain limiting of the exploitation of the working class as a whole, each corporation still has to operate on the basis of maximizing its profits. The fostering of a section of the working class that will have to work at the jobs that are paid at rates between those of the two income floors works to meet the needs of profit maximization. Other jobs that fall into this category are those that might pay at the collective bargaining contract level but are subject to considerable seasonal and cyclical unemployment, and those from which a high rate of production is squeezed under hard or hazardous conditions. In all the developed Western capitalist states, there exists a group of workers to fill the jobs that the more politically established sectors of the working class shun. These marginal workers generally are set apart in some way so that they lack the social or the political means of defending their interests. In Western Europe usually they are non-citizens coming from either Southern Europe or Northern Africa. In England they are colored peoples coming from various parts of the Empire.[76] In the urban centers of the United States race serves to mark black and brown workers for filling in the undesirable slots.

Further, in the distribution of government transfer payments each class and status group strives to maximize its receipts. Therefore the powerless tend to receive a smaller proportion of these funds, and those that are delivered to them come in a manner which stigmatizes and bolsters political controls.

Specifically, in the metropolitan centers in America, there is a racial dual labor-market structure.[77] Side by side with the primary metropolitan job market in which firms recruit white workers and white workers seek employment, there exists a smaller secondary market in which firms recruit black workers and black workers seek jobs. In the largest metropolitan areas this secondary black market ranges from one-tenth to one-quarter of the size of the white market. For both the white and black sectors there are distinct demand and supply forces determining earnings and occupational distribution, as well as separate institutions and procedures for recruitment, hiring, training, and promotion of workers.

The distinctiveness of these two labor forces is manifested by many dimensions— by industry, by firm, by departments within firms, by occupation, and by geographical area. Within all industries, including government service, there are occupational ceilings for blacks. In a labor market like that of the Chicago metropolitan area, there are a number of small and medium-size firms in which the majority of the workers are black. However about two-thirds of the small firms and one-fifth of the medium ones hire no blacks at all. In larger firms a dual structure in the internal labor market marks off the position of the black worker along the same lines that exist in the metropolitan labor market.

A review of black employment in Chicago in 1966 finds that blacks tend to work in industries with lower wages, higher turnover, and higher unemployment. Further, they are also over-represented in the industries which exhibit sluggish growth and obviously less chance for advancement. Black men provide a third of the blue-collar workers in such industries as textiles, retail stores, primary metals, and local transportation, while in utilities, advertising, and communication they constitute less than 6%. Black women are even more concentrated in furnishing over

half the blue-collar women workers in five industries—personal services, education, retail stores, hotels, and railroads.

In terms of internal labor market segregation, one of the Chicago firms best known as a fair-practice employer has a major installation located in the black community in which blacks constitute 20% of the blue-collar workers and less than 5% of the craftsmen and white-collar workers. A General Motors plant with 7500 workers is reported to have 40% black semi-skilled operatives, but only between 1% and 2% black craftsmen. A foundry firm will have one black clerk out of nearly 100 white-collar workers, while 80% of its blue-collar operators will be black.

The most-detailed information we have on racial dualism for an internal labor market is for the Lackawanna plant of Bethlehem Steel Company near Buffalo.[78] The Lackawanna plant is a major employer of black workers in the Buffalo labor market. In 1968 it employed 2600 out of a total black labor force of about 30,000 for the area. Within the plant blacks constituted about 14% of the work force, which runs in the neighborhood of 19,000. The majority of black employees were assigned to only five of the plant's departments, while only 15% of the whites were in the same units. Within the individual units, blacks were given either the hardest or the lowest-paying jobs. In the plant's Coke Oven Department blacks held 252 out of 343 of the labor jobs, while whites held 118 out of 119 craft jobs. Blacks predominated in the battery and coal-handling units, where the top job paid $3.12 an hour. Whites made up the bulk of the work force in the better-paying by-products and heating units, which had hourly pay rates ranging up to $3.42 and $3.65.

Basic Steel is a high-labor-turnover industry. From April 1, 1966 to December 31, 1967 the Lackawanna plant hired about 7000 workers. Black job-seekers obviously identified the firm as being active in this labor market. Although 30% to 50% of the job applicants were black, the initial screening ended up with only 20% blacks among those newly hired. Prospects were screened by a general-aptitude test the passing score for which was not validated by any measure of performance. As the labor market tightened, the passing score lowered. About an eighth of those hired were hired without taking a test, and 96% of this category were whites. The Supervisor of Employment also gave clear preference to residents of Angola, a nearly all-white suburb. Once on the payroll, a majority of the newly-hired blacks were assigned to one of the five departments in which most of the black workers already were placed. Only 20% of newly-hired whites were assigned to these departments, all of which were among the hotter and dirtier locations in the plant.

The dual labor market operates to create an urban-based industrial labor reserve that provides a ready supply of workers in a period of labor shortage and can be politically isolated in times of relatively high unemployment. In a tight labor market the undesirable jobs that whites leave are filled out of this labor reserve so that in time more job categories are added to the black sector of the labor market. If the various forms of disguised unemployment and sub-employment are all taken into account, black unemployment rates can run as high as three or four times those of whites in specific labor markets in recession periods. The welfare and police costs of maintaining this labor reserve are high, but they are borne by the State as a whole and therefore do not enter into the profit calculations of individual firms.

This special exploitation of the black labor force also leads to direct economic gains for the various employers. Methodologically it is very difficult to measure exactly the extra surplus extracted due to wage discrimination, although in Chicago it has been estimated that unskilled black workers earn about 17% less on similar jobs than unskilled white workers of comparable quality.[79] While in a historical sense the entire differential of wage income between blacks and whites can be attributed to discrimination, the employer realizes only that which takes place in the present in terms of either lesser wage payments or greater work output. Estimates of this realized special exploitation range on the order of 10% to 20% of the total black wage and salary income.[80]

The subordinate status of the black labor market does not exist in isolation, but rather is a major part of a whole complex of institutional controls that constitute the web of urban racism.[81] This distinctive modern form of racism conforms to the 300-year-old traditions of the culture of control for the oppression of black people, but now most of the controls are located within the major metropolitan institutional networks—such as the labor market, the housing market, the political system. As the black population grew in the urban centers a distinctive new formation developed in each of these institutional areas. A black ghetto and housing market, a black labor market, a black school system, a black political system, and a black welfare system came into being—not as parts of a self-determining community, but as institutions to be controlled, manipulated, and exploited. When the black population did not serve the needs of dominant institutions by providing a wartime labor reserve, they were isolated so that they could be regulated and incapacitated.

This model of urban racism has had three major components with regard to institutional structures: (1) Within the major institutional networks that operate in the city there have developed definable black subsectors which operated on a subordinated basis, subject to the advantage, control, and priorities of the dominant system. (2) A pattern of mutual reinforcement takes place between the barriers that define the various black subsectors. (3) The controls over the lives of black men are so pervasive that they form a system analogous to colonial forms of rule.

The history of the demand for black labor in the post-war period showed the continued importance of wartime labor scarcities. The new job categories gained during World War II essentially were transferred into the black sectors of the labor market. Some war industries, like shipbuilding, of course, dropped off considerably. In reconversion and the brief 1948–1949 recession blacks lost out disproportionately on the better jobs. However the Korean War again created an intense labor shortage, making black workers once more in demand, at least until the fighting stopped. The period of slow economic growth from 1955 to the early 1960s saw a deterioration in the relative position of blacks as they experienced very high rates of unemployment and their incomes grew at a slower rate than those of whites. The civil-rights protests had generated little in the way of new demand. Only the coincidence of the rebellions of Watts, Newark, and Detroit with the escalation of the Vietnam War brought about a sharp growth in demand for black labor.

All the available evidence indicates that there has been no structural change of any significance in the deployment of black workers, most especially in private industry. Certain absolute standards of exclusion in professional, management, and sales occupations have now been removed, but the total growth in these areas has been slight except where a black clientele is serviced, as in the education and health fields. The one significant new demand in the North has been that for women clerical workers. This arises from a shortage of this particular kind of labor in the central business districts, which, being surrounded by the black community, are increasingly geographically removed from white supplies of these workers. About 90% of Chicago's black female white-collar workers work either in their own communities or in the central business districts, and are not employed in the rapidly growing outlying offices. In the South the whole pattern of

racial regulation in the major cities is shifting over to a Northern model, so that the basic situation of black workers in Atlanta or Memphis is approaching that of the North about a decade ago.

Until the uprisings in the mid-60s, management of racial affairs was carried out either by the unvarnished maintenance of the status quo (except when black workers were needed) or by an elaborate ritual of fair practices and equal employment opportunity. The latter strategy operated as a sort of sophisticated social Darwinism to make the rules of competition for the survival of the fittest more equitable. Actually it blurred institutional realities, channeling energies and perceptions into individualized findings of fact. The black protest movement finally forced a switch to a policy of affirmative action that is supported by legal encouragement. In either case no basic structures have actually been transformed. As a review of studies on the current racial status in several industries finds: "Over the long haul, however, it is apparent that the laws of supply and demand have exercised a greater influence on the quantitative employment patterns of blacks than have the laws of the land."[82]

In the Cold War era the trade-union movement lost its innovative dynamism and became narrowly wage-oriented. Overwhelmingly, the net racial effect of the collective-bargaining agreements was to accept the given conditions in a plant. Only a very few unions, usually from the CIO, conducted any fights for the upgrading of black workers. More usual was the practice of neglecting shop grievances. Within union life itself the black officials who arose as representatives of their race were converted into justifiers of the union administration to the black workers.[83] On the legislative and judicial fronts—that is, away from their day-to-day base of operations—national unions supported the programs of civil-rights organizations and the fair-employment symbolism. In fact by the early 1960s the racial strategies of national trade unions and those of the most sophisticated corporate leadership had converged.

The actions of the black community itself were destined to become the decisive political initiator, not only in its own liberation struggles but on the domestic scene in general. From World War II through the Korean War the urban black communities were engaged in digesting the improvements brought about by the end of the depression and by the wartime job gains. Both bourgeois and trade-union leadership followed the forms of the New Deal-labor coalition, but the original substance of mass struggle was no longer present.

The destabilization of the whole agrarian society in the South created the conditions for new initiatives. The Montgomery bus boycott was to re-introduce mass political action into the Cold War era. The boldness of the civil-rights movement, plus the success of national liberation movements in the Third World, galvanized the black communities in the major cities. At first the forms of the Southern struggle were to predominate in pro-integration civil-rights actions. Then youth and workers were swept into the movement and re-defined its direction toward black self-determination. The mass spontaneity in the ghetto rebellions revealed the tremendous potential of this orientation.

The ghetto systems and the dual labor markets had organized a mass black proletariat, and had concentrated it in certain key industries and plants. In the decade after World War II the most important strategic concentration of black workers was in the Chicago packing houses, where they became the majority group. United Packinghouse Workers District I was bold in battles over conditions in the plants and supplied the basic leadership for militant protest on the South Side. Even though the UPW was the most advanced of all big national unions on the race question, a coalition of black officials and shop stewards had to wage a struggle against the leadership for substantive black control. This incipient nationalist faction was defeated in the union, and the big meat packers moved out of the city, but before it disappeared the movement indicated the potential of black-oriented working-class leadership. The Packinghouse Workers' concrete struggles contrasted sharply with the strategy of A. Philip Randolph, who set up the form of an all-black Negro American Labor Council and then subordinated its mass support to maneuvers at the top level of the AFL-CIO.[84]

After the ghetto uprisings workers were to re-assert themselves at the point of production. Black caucuses and Concerned Workers' Committees sprang up across the country in plants and installations with large numbers of blacks.[85] By this time the auto industry had created the largest concentration of black workers in the nation on its back-breaking production lines in Detroit. Driven by the peculiarities of the black labor market, the "big three" auto companies had developed the preconditions for the organization of the Dodge Revolutionary Union Movement (DRUM) and the League of Revolutionary Black Workers. The insertion onto this scene of a cadre that was both black-conscious and class-conscious, with a program of revolutionary struggle, forged an instrument for the militant working-class leadership of the Black Liberation Movement. The League also provides an exemplary model for proletarians among other oppressed groups, and might even be able to stimulate sections of the white working class to emerge from their narrow economistic orientation.

The ruling class is caught in its own contradictions. It needs black workers, yet the conditions of satisfying this need compel it to bring together the potential forces for the most effective opposition to its policies, and even for a threat to its very existence. Amelioration of once-absolute exclusionary barriers does not eliminate the black work force that the whole web of urban racism defines. Even if the capitalists were willing to forgo their economic and status gains from racial oppression, they could not do so without shaking up all of the intricate concessions and consensual arrangements through which the State now exercises legitimate authority. Since the ghetto institutions are deeply intertwined with the major urban systems, the American

Government does not even have the option of decolonializing by ceding nominal sovereignty that the British and French empires have both exercised. The racist structures cannot be abolished without an earthquake in the heartland. Indeed, for that sophisticated gentleman, the American capitalist, the demand for black labor has become a veritable devil in the flesh.

Notes

1. Karl Marx: *Capital* (Kerr Edition), Volume 1, Page 823.

2. Ibid., Page 833.

3. "As is well known, commodity production preceded (capitalist) commodity production, and constitutes one of the conditions (but not the sole condition) of the rise of the latter." V. I. Lenin: *Development of Capitalism in Russia* (Moscow, Foreign Languages Publishing House, 1956), Page 606.

4. Eugene D. Genovese: *The Political Economy of Slavery* (New York, 1967) contends that the plantation slave system was the base of a social order in the American South that essentially was pre-capitalist and quasi-aristocrat.

5. Marvin Harris: *Patterns of Race in the Americas* (New York, 1964), Page 13.

6. Winthrop Jordan: *White Over Black* (Chapel Hill, 1968), Page 184.

7. *The Problem of Slavery in Western Culture* (Ithaca, 1966), Pages 41–46.

8. *White Over Black*, Pages 3–43.

9. Carl N. Degler: "Slavery in the United States and Brazil: An Essay in Comparative History", *American Historical Review* (April 1970), Pages 1019–1021; Davis: *The Problem of Slavery*, Pages 232–233.

10. Philip Curtin: *The Atlantic Slave Trade* (Madison, 1969), Page 269; A. M. Carr Saunders, *World Population* (Oxford, 1936), Page 47.

11. *The Black Jacobins* (Second Edition, New York, 1963), Page 48. See also Gaston Martin: *Nantes au XVIII Siecle: L'Ere des Negriers* (Paris, 1931), Pages 422–433.

12. *Capitalism and Slavery* (Chapel Hill, 1944), Pages 50–84.

13. Malachi Postlethwayt: *The Advantage of the African Trade* (1772), quoted in Abram L. Harris: *The Negro as Capitalist* (Philadelphia, 1936), Pages 2–3.

14. Douglas North: *The Economic Growth of the United States, 1790–1860* (Englewood Cliffs, New Jersey, 1961), Pages 68–69.

15. Marcus Wilson Jernegan: *Laboring and Dependent Classes in Colonial America, 1607–1763* (Chicago, 1931), Page 23.

16. By this time free blacks constituted between 40% and 60% of the black population in Brazil and 35% in Cuba: Herbert S. Klein: "The Colored Freedmen in Brazil", *Journal of Social History* (Fall 1969), Pages 30–54.

17. Richard Wade: *Slavery in the Cities* (New York, 1964), Page 275.

18. W. E. B. Du Bois: *The Philadelphia Negro* (1967 Edition, New York), Page 33. See also Herman Bloch: *The Circle of Discrimination* (New York, 1969), Pages 21–26.

19. Robert Ernst: "The Economic Status of New York Negroes, 1850–1863", reprinted in August Meier and Elliot Rudwick (editors): *The Making of Black America* (New York, 1969), Volume 1, Pages 250–261.

20. This statement is not meant to imply that there were not some important class distinctions or

inequalities in income or wealth, but it does claim that the social and political means of defining status along these lines were not as clear-cut as they were in Europe or in Latin America.

21. Harris: *Patterns of Race,* Chapter 7. A modern analogy to the Latin American status situation is evidenced in the US Army's ability to be one of the very first major American institutions to desegregate. "Placement of white adult males in a subordinate position within a rigidly-stratified system, that is, appears to produce behavior not all that different from the so-called personality traits commonly held to be an outcome of cultural or psychological patterns unique to Negro life. Indeed, it might be argued that relatively little adjustment on the part of the command structure was required when the infusion of the Negroes into the enlisted ranks occurred as the military establishment was desegregated. It is suggested, in other words, that one factor that contributed to the generally-smooth racial integration of the military might be the standard treatment—like 'Negroes' in a sense—that was accorded to all lower-ranking enlisted personnel." Charles C. Moskos Junior: "Racial Integration in the Armed Forces", *American Journal of Sociology* (September 1966), reprinted in Raymond Mack: *Race, Class, and Power* (Second Edition, New York, 1968), Pages 436–455.

22. CLR James: "The Atlantic Slave Trade and Slavery", *Amistad I* (New York, 1970), Pages 133–134. The possibility of a bourgeois mode of development of the black community in the US was cut off, although valiant efforts were made in this direction by black professional men, entrepreneurs, and craftsmen. Nineteenth Century Pan-Africanism and black nationalism most likely had significant roots in this phenomenon.

23. W. E. B. DuBois: *Black Reconstruction in America,* 1860–1880 (1962 Edition, Cleveland), Page 121.

24. "The Compromise of 1877 did not restore the old order in the South, nor did it restore the South to parity with other sections. It did assure the dominant whites political autonomy and non-intervention in matters of race policy, and promised them a share in the blessings of the new economic order. In return the South became . . . a satellite of the dominant region. . . . Under the regime of the Redeemers the South became a bulwark instead of a menace to the new order." C. Vann Woodward: *Reunion and Reaction* (Second Edition, New York, 1956), Pages 266–267.

25. *The Souls of Black Folk,* Chapter 8.

26. Quoted in Woodward: *Origins of the New South,* Page 208.

27. Rupert Vance: "Racial Competition for Land", in Edgar T. Thompson (editor): *Race Relations and the Race Problem* (Durham, 1939), Pages 100–104.

28. J. B. Killebrew: *Southern States Farm Magazine* (1898), Pages 490–491, cited in Nolen (previously cited), Page 170. For a concrete explication of this approach, see Alfred Holt Stone: *Studies in the American Race Problem* (New York, 1909), Chapter 4.

29. Woodward: *Origins of the New South,* Page 211.

30. Ibid., Pages 328–330.

31. Charles H. Wesley: *Negro Labor in the United States, 1850–1925* (New York, 1927), Pages 238–239; Claude H. Nolen: *The Negro's Image in the South* (Lexington, Kentucky, 1968), Page 190.

32. Lorenzo J. Greene and Carter G. Woodson: *The Negro Wage Earner* (Washington, 1930), Pages 49–50.

33. Wesley: *Negro Labor,* Page 142; W. E. B. DuBois: *The Negro Artisan* (Atlanta, 1902), Pages 115–120.

34. DuBois: *The Negro Artisan,* Pages 180–185. However, when the *Manufacturer's Record of Baltimore* conducted its own survey in 1893, the majority of manufacturers held that blacks were unfitted for most employment, but admitted that with training they could be used—an opinion they also held of the "primitive white man". One big difference in this latter survey was the inclusion of the cotton mills, a line that had already been declared a "white man's industry". Cited in Wesley: *Negro Labor,* Pages 244–248.

35. Paul H. Buck: *The Road to Reunion* (Boston, 1937), Pages 154–155.

36. Carter G. Woodson: "Story of the Fund", Chapter 2, typescript, Julius Rosenwald Papers, University of Chicago Library; Louis Harland: *Separate and Unequal* (Chapel Hill, 1958), Page 77.

37. Department of History, Harvard University, 1953.

38. Frank U. Quillan: *The Color Line in Ohio* (Ann Arbor, 1913), Page 138.

39. W. E. B. DuBois: *The Negro Artisan*, Pages 173–175.

40. Spero and Harris: *The Black Worker* is still essential on this. Also see: Bernard Mandel: "Samuel Gompers and the Negro Workers, 1886–1914", *Journal of Negro History* (January 1955), Pages 34–60; Herbert G. Gutman: The Negro and the United Mine Workers of America", in Julius Jacobson (editor): *The Negro and the American Labor Movement* (New York, 1968, Pages 49–127; and the entire issue of *Labor History* (Summer 1969).

41. William M. Tuttle Junior: "Labor Conflict and Racial Violence: The Black Worker in Chicago, 1894–1919", *Labor History* (Summer 1969), Pages 406–432; Spero and Harris: *The Black Worker*, Pages 131–134. For a national survey on strikebreaking see Fishel: *The North and the Negro*, Pages 454–471.

42. August Meier: *Negro Thought in America, 1880–1915* (Ann Arbor, 1963).

43. Chicago Commission on Race Relations: *The Negro in Chicago* (Chicago, 1922), Pages 362–363.

44. US Labor Department: *Negro Migration in 1916–17* (Washington 1919), Page 124.

45. Ibid., Pages 22–23, 27–33, 118–122; Spear: *Black Chicago*, Pages 33–38.

46. Wesley: *Negro Labor,* Pages 293–294; US Labor Department: *Negro Migration*, Pages 125–126.

47. William M. Tuttle Junior: *Race Riot: Chicago in the Red Summer of 1919* (New York, 1970), Pages 130–132.

48. Herman Feldman: *Racial Factors in American Industry* (New York and London, 1931), Pages 42–43.

49. Louise V. Kennedy: *The Negro Peasant Moves Cityward* (New York, 1930), Pages 35–36.

50. William C. Graves: "Memorandum of Address Made June 17th Before the Inter-racial Committee of the Union League Club", Julius Rosenwald Papers, University of Chicago Library.

51. Elliot M. Rudwick: *Race Riot at East Saint Louis, July 2, 1917* (Carbondale, 1964); Tuttle: *Race Riot.*

52. Spero and Harris: *The Black Worker*, Pages 167–168.

53. Graves: "Memorandum of Speech Made June 17th".

54. Robert Ozanne: *A Century of Labor-Management Relations at McCormick and International Harvester* (Madison, 1967), Pages 183–187.

55. Bailer: "The Negro Automobile Worker", Pages 416–419; Herbert Northrup: *Organized Labor and the Negro* (New York, 1944), Pages 189–195.

56. Spero and Harris: *The Black Worker,* Page 169.

57. Cayton and Mitchell: *The Black Worker,* Page 31.

58. Kennedy: *The Negro Peasant Moves Cityward,* Page 98; Feldman: *Racial Factors in American Industry,* Pages 57–58.

59. "Conference on the Negro in Industry Held by the Committee on Industry, Chicago Commission on Race Relations, April 23, 1920", typescript, Julius Rosenwald Papers, University of Chicago Library.

60. This writer gave such a reading to several hundred management officials at a session sponsored by the Graduate School of Management of the University of Chicago in 1969. It was an ironic success.

61. Erwin D. Hoffman: "The Genesis of the Modern Movement for Equal Rights in South Carolina, 1930–1939", *Journal of Negro History* (October 1959), Page 347.

62. Charles S. Johnson: *The Shadow of the Plantation* (Chicago, 1934), Page 210. For a good review of the situation of blacks in the rural South during this period, see E. Franklin Frazier: *The Negro in the United States* (New York, 1949), Chapter 10.

63. Gunnar Myrdal: *An American Dilemma* (1964 Edition, New York, two volumes), Volume 1, Pages 256–269.

64. One indication that the current pattern was established by 1930 is given by Herman Feldman's *Racial Factors in American Industry,* published the following year. Feldman was able to prescribe and to concretely illustrate a set of industrial-relations practices that sound amazingly similar to what today are called equal-opportunity programs. The major difference is that in 1930 the firms did not have to take into account the political strength of the black community.

65. Drake and Cayton: *Black Metropolis,* Volume 1, Pages 215–217 and 226–227; Richard Sterner: *The Negro's Share* (New York, 1934), Pages 39–46 and 219–291, providing a useful compilation of material used in this and the following paragraph; Ozanne: *A Century of Labor Management Relations,* Page 187; Charles S. Johnson: "The Conflict of Caste and Class in an American Industry", *American Journal of Sociology* (July 1936), Pages 55–65.

66. "The Negro's War", *Fortune* (June 1942), Pages 76–80.

67. Ibid.; American Management Association: *The Negro Worker* (Research Report Number 1, 1942), Pages 3–4 and 27–28; Nicholas S. Falcone: *The Negro Integrated* (New York, 1945).

68. Robert Weaver: *Negro Labor, A National Problem* (New York, 1946), Pages 78–93.

69. Harry Haywood: *Negro Liberation* (New York, 1948), Pages 198–199.

70. A few years after the collapse of 1929 Abram Harris surveyed this flourishing of black capitalism and concluded: The limits of a separate economy are precariously narrow within the confines of the present industrial system. How the independent black economy is to develop and function in the face of persistent industrial integration, business combinations, the centralization of capital control, and the concentration of wealth none of the advocates of the plan can explain. . . . As long as capitalism remains, however, it is reasonably certain that the main arteries of commerce, industry, credit, and finance will be controlled by white capitalists. Under the circumstances, the great mass of black and white men will continue to be dependent on these capitalists for their livelihood, and the small white capitalist in turn will continue to be subordinate to these larger financial and industrial interests. Thus it is obvious that the independent black economy—whether it develops on the basis of private profit or on the basis of co-operation—cannot be the means of achieving the Negro's economic salvation. (*The Negro as Capitalist,* Page x)

71. Cayton and Mitchell: *Black Workers and the New Unions;* Drake and Cayton: *Black Metropolis,* Volume 1, Pages 312–341; James Olsen: "Organized Black Leadership and Industrial Unionism: The Racial Response, 1939–1945", *Labor History* (Summer 1969), Pages 475–486.

72. The standard work on the MOW movement is Herbert Garfinkel: *When Negroes March* (Glencoe, 1959). The MOW movement actually presaged two forms of future tactics. In its appeal to the masses for a black-defined program of struggle it summarized all of the decade's action for jobs on a local level and impelled them forward on a national basis. On the other hand, in that the movement failed to develop an organized working-class constituency, it foretold tactics of maneuver without mass struggle—of legislative lobbying, judicial procedures, and jockeying within the Democratic Party—which were to be pursued by the bourgeois and trade-union organizations until demonstrations and civil disobedience finally arose from below out of the civil-rights movement.

73. These estimates are as of 1969. Data from the 1970 census were not available at the time of writing.

74. Richard H. Day: "The Economics of Technological Change and the Demise of the Sharecropper", *American Economic Review* (June 1967), Pages 427–449; Seymour Melman: "An Industrial Revolution in the Cotton South", *Economic History Review,* Second Series (1949), Pages 59–72.

75. Analysis of the relation of economic and class shifts in the South to the civil-rights movement and the nature of its limited victories from 1954 to 1965 has been seriously neglected. Anyone undertaking such a study should keep

in mind V. I. Lenin's fundamental law of revolution: "It is not enough for revolution that the exploited and oppressed masses should understand the impossibility of living in the old way and demand changes, it is essential for revolution that the exploiters should not be able to live and rule in the same way." (Left Wing Communism)

76. David J. Smyth and Peter D. Lowe: "The Vestibule to the Occupational Ladder and Unemployment: Some Econometric Evidence on United Kingdom Structural Unemployment", *Industrial and Labor Relations Review* (July 1970), Pages 561–565.

77. This and following paragraphs on the dual labor market are basically a summary of Harold M. Baron and Bennett Hymer: "The Negro Worker in the Chicago Labor Market", in Julius Jacobson (editor): *The Negro and the American Labor Movement* (New York, 1968), Pages 232–285.

78. The following facts come from the *United States of America Versus Bethlehem Steel Company and Associates*, US District Court, Western District of New York, Civ-1967-436, Stipulation of Facts, July 1, 1968 and Second Stipulation of Facts, September 20, 1968.

79. D. Taylor: "Discrimination and Occupational Wage Differences in the Market for Unskilled Labor", *Industrial and Labor Relations Review* (April 1968), Pages 375–390.

80. For a recent estimate see Lester Thurow: *The Economy of Poverty and Discrimination* (Washington 1969). He finds the gains to wage discrimination were $4,600,000,000 in 1960. Advantages to white workers due to higher employment rates were $6,500,000,000.

81. For an extended treatment of the institutionalization of racism in the metropolis see Harold Baron: "The Web of Urban Racism", in Louis Knowles and Kenneth Prewitt (editors): *Institutional Racism in America* (New York, 1969), Pages 134–176.

82. Vernon M. Briggs Junior: "The Negro in American Industry: A Review of Seven Studies", *Journal of Human Resources* (Summer 1970), Pages 371–381.

83. William Kornhauser: "The Negro Union Official: A Study of Sponsorship and Control", *American Journal of Sociology* (March 1952), Pages 443–452; Scott Greer: "Situational Pressures and Functional Role of the Ethnic Labor Leader", *Social Forces* (October 1953), Pages 41–45.

84. The writer has the records of the Chicago chapter of the NALC in his possession.

85. For a description of some of these organizations see Herbert Hill: "Black Protest and Struggle for Union Democracy", *Issues in Industrial Society* (1969), Pages 19–24 and 48.

Black Economic Well-Being Since the 1950s

DANIEL R. FUSFELD AND TIMOTHY BATES

*H*AS BLACK ECONOMIC well-being improved since World War II? There are no simple answers. This chapter will document areas of improvement as well as deterioration, and we will explore the causes of these diverse trends. Overall, the evidence points to polarization within the black community: the younger and better-educated are registering strong and sustained gains in income and occupational status; those who are not highly educated—yet not below average in skills and years of schooling—continue to ride the cyclical roller coaster, prospering in periods of labor shortage and suffering during prolonged recessions; those on the bottom appear to be positively worse off, perhaps representing a semipermanent lumpenproletariat facing very uncertain prospects for future job market upgrading. Regional trends, interacting with major shifts in industry employment patterns— the decline of automobile industry employment for example—complicate all generalizations about trends in black well-being.

Future income and employment prospects for black workers are assessed rather pessimistically in this chapter. Particularly among black male workers the future may bring about an affluent elite of white-collar workers, a greatly diminished number of middle-income blue-collar workers, and a large and growing number of low-income unemployed and underemployed workers whose labor force attachment is quite marginal.

THE EVIDENCE FOR MAJOR ECONOMIC PROGRESS

Black progress in education and occupational status has been quite pronounced in recent decades. Income trends are less clearcut, but evidence that incomes of blacks have been rising relative to incomes of whites, summarized in table 9.1, has been widely cited to demonstrate long-term, sustained improvements in the well-being of blacks. Although black family incomes have fallen relative to white incomes in the 1970s (table 9.1), long-term improvement is still apparent. Furthermore,

Reprinted, with permission, from *The Political Economy of the Urban Ghetto,* by Daniel R. Fusfeld and Timothy Bates, Southern Illinois University Press, 1984.

there are a number of valid reasons for using incomes of individuals, as opposed to families, as the "more accurate" measure of trends in relative black income position.[1] For example,

much of the decline in black family incomes since 1970 is directly related to the rise of single-parent families rather than changes in labor market status. Table 9.1 clearly shows that

TABLE 9.1 INCOMES OF BLACK INDIVIDUALS AND FAMILIES, STATES AS PERCENTAGES OF WHITE INDIVIDUAL AND FAMILY INCOMES

Year	Black Families*	Black Males†	Black Females†
1947	51	—	—
1948	53	54	43
1949	51	48	46
1950	54	54	45
1951	53	55	42
1952	57	55	39
1953	56	55	59
1954	56	50	54
1955	55	53	52
1956	51	52	57
1957	53	53	58
1958	51	50	59
1959	52	47	62
1960	55	53	62
1961	53	52	67
1962	53	49	67
1963	53	52	67
1964	56	57	70
1965	55	61	73
1966	60	59	79
1967	59	57	80
1968	60	61	81
1969	61	59	85
1970	61	60	92
1971	60	60	90
1972	59	62	96
1973	58	63	93
1974	60	64	92
1975	61	63	92
1976	60	63	95
1977	57	61	88
1978	59	64	92
1979	57	65	93
1980	58	63	96
1981	56	63	92

Sources: U.S. Bureau of the Census, *Current Population Reports*, ser. P-60, no. 137, table 15 (Washington, D.C.: Government Printing Office, Mar. 1983), pp. 39–42. Ibid., table 16, pp. 43–46.

*Figures prior to 1967 include blacks and other races; figures since 1967 include blacks only.
†Figures for blacks refer to blacks and other races.

black male incomes improved dramatically during the prosperous 1960s (the relevant black-white income ratio rose from .47 in 1959 to .59 in 1969); furthermore, some additional improvement occurred during the recessionary 1970s—black male incomes rose from 59 percent of white incomes in 1969 to 65 percent in 1979. An even more clearcut improvement in relative incomes is apparent in data describing relative black female incomes in table 9.1. In each of the last three decades, black female incomes (expressed as a percentage of white female incomes) have increased dramatically. Whereas black females received only 46.3 percent as much as their white female counterparts in 1949, their 1979 relative incomes were 93.1 percent of white incomes. By 1979, black females actually exceeded white cohort incomes in every area of the United States except the South. Now that's progress. Or is it? We will argue that nationwide black relative income comparisons (or black-white income ratios) are severely flawed measures of black economic well-being. Essentially, data such as those summarized in table 9.1 obscure more than they reveal, actually setting back our understanding of complex issues by relying upon overly simplistic measures of black income position.

The issue of black educational gains since World War II is much more straightforward than a comparison of relative incomes. Progress in the education realm has been widespread, as shown in table 9.2. Among black adults, median years of school completed in 1980 was 12.0 years, only slightly behind the 12.5 years reported by the white adult population. The incidence of teenagers (16 through 19 years of age) out of school with no high school diploma in 1981 was 13.6 percent for blacks, 11.7 percent for whites.[2] The incidence of black college enrollment for those eighteen to twenty-four years old rose from 10.3 percent in 1965 to 19.4 percent in 1981; the corresponding enrollment rate for whites was roughly 26 percent throughout this period. Although college enrollment of black students peaked at 1,103,000 in 1977, 1,080,000 were enrolled in 1981 which suggests approximate stability rather than enrollment declines. Available evidence indicates black educational gains throughout the 1960s and 1970s, with no trend towards backsliding emerging to date in the 1980s.

Educational achievements have translated into occupational gains for many black workers, especially among young college graduates. Black male college graduates twenty-five to

TABLE 9.2 TRENDS IN BLACK EDUCATIONAL ATTAINMENT

A. Median Years of School Completed by Persons 25 and Older

	Nonwhite	*Black*	*White*	*Difference*
1940	5.8	—	8.7	2.9
1960	8.2	—	10.9	2.7
1980	—	12.0	12.5	0.5

B. Number of Blacks Enrolled in Colleges and Universities

1965	274,000
1970	522,000
1975	948,000
1980	1,007,000

Sources: Census of population data, cited in John Reid, "Black America in the 1980s," *Population Bulletin* 37, no. 5 (1982):25; U.S. Bureau of the Census, *Current Population Reports,* ser. P-20, no. 373, table 3 (Washington, D.C.: Government Printing Office, Feb. 1983), p. 5

thirty-four years old earned in 1959 only 59 percent as much as their white college graduate cohorts; by 1979 this figure had jumped to 84 percent. In the case of students holding MBA degrees, black-white parity has apparently been achieved. The Association of MBA Executives reports MBA degree holders hired in 1980 started out with average salaries of $24,259, with blacks and whites receiving approximately equal pay.[3]

Penetration into white-collar occupations has been prevalent among younger black women. In 1980, 49.4 percent of the black females who worked during the year were employed in white-collar jobs. The incidence of white-collar employment for black males was 23.9 percent; over 17 percent were employed as skilled craftsmen, however, while another 25.2 percent worked as operatives—which is commonly well-paid factory work. These occupational figures must be interpreted with one important qualification in mind: those not working are excluded.[4] Similarly, income figures such as those summarized in table 9.1 include *only* those persons having income. Of course, the incidence of blacks working in any given time period is lower than the incidence of employed whites; the same pattern applies to income recipients. Nonetheless, real occupational gains have been realized by black workers since the 1950s, and this is especially true for females.

One final piece of evidence indicating black progress in recent decades is the increase of blacks in highly visible, prestigious positions. The traditional areas of high visibility—entertainment and professional sports—are now overshadowed by blacks serving in top elected offices. Since the 1960s, blacks have also served at very high levels in government bureaucracies: the presidential cabinet, the Supreme Court, major state government positions. In fact, increased representation of blacks is apparent at all levels of government (table 9.3).

In the private sector, blacks account for rapidly growing numbers of younger executives at major corporations. In the media, black stereotypes of thirty years ago have been largely relegated to the dustbin of history; blacks now appear in authoritative roles such as newscasters.

In light of all the above—relative income gains, narrowing the educational gap, upward occupational mobility, including penetration of society's most prestigious positions—it is not surprising that most respondents to a 1980 Gallup poll felt that the quality of life for blacks had improved during the 1970s.[5]

THE EVIDENCE SUGGESTING THAT BLACK ECONOMIC WELL-BEING IS DECLINING

Most of the respondents to the Gallup poll mentioned above were whites. Among black respondents, the majority felt that their quality

TABLE 9.3 GROWTH IN THE NUMBER OF BLACK ELECTED OFFICIALS

	1970	1982
Federal	10	18
State, Regional	169	397
County	92	465
City	623	2,451
Judicial, Law Enforcement	213	563
Education	362	1,266
Total number of elected black officials	1,469	5,160

Source: E.R. Shipp, "'63 Marcher sees gains but a 'Long Way to Travel,'" *New York Times* 28 Aug 1983, p. 30.

of life had stayed the same or gotten worse during the 1970s. The broad generality of the question—How have blacks fared over time?—is apt to produce oversimplified answers supported by simplistic evidence. Some are better off; others are worse off. While widespread economic and social progress was clearly the norm during the 1960s, much evidence indicates regression in black economic status in the 1970s. According to Vernon Jordan, former president of the Urban League, "For Black Americans the decade of the 1970s was a time in which many of their hopes, raised by the civil rights victories of the 1960s, withered away."[6]

The economic well-being of black Americans has traditionally improved during periods of labor scarcity: World War I, the 1920s, World War II, and the Vietnam War. Relative income gain has also accompanied the twentieth-century residential shift from the rural South to northern and southern urban areas. But aside from boom periods that have drawn black workers into better-paying jobs, how widespread and enduring are the black income and occupational gains of recent decades? Has the change from a predominantly southern rural to a predominantly urban America drastically lessened racial discrimination, or have new forms of racial inequality arisen in the cities? Long-term occupational gains appear to endure, particularly for black females, but other labor force trends are ominous. Abstracting from the cyclical ups and downs, blacks since World War II have experienced rising unemployment rates and falling labor force participation rates; the labor force status of urban black males shows signs of long-run deterioration. By 1980, 15 percent of all black males twenty-five to sixty-four years of age were telling the Census Bureau that they had earned absolutely nothing during 1979. In 1969, median black family incomes in the north central states were $19,182 (in 1981 dollars); by 1981 the comparable median figure had plummeted to $15,474.[7]

Relative incomes of urban blacks have not risen dramatically in the post–World War II era. Incomes of blacks in the cities still ride the cyclical roller coaster: up in the 1940s, down in the 1950s, up in the 1960s, down in the 1970s. Numerous studies that argue otherwise invariably fail to sort out the one-time-only income gains accompanying urbanization, labor market cyclical swings, and the income gains of the highly educated.[8] Gains of migration, of boom periods, and of a fortunate few are incorrectly interpreted as evidence of overall black economic uplifting.

The simplest way to clarify trends in black economic status is to segment blacks geographically into those residing in southern states, and northern and western states.[9] Blacks residing in the nonsouthern states are overwhelmingly urban, and table 9.4 shows that their relative incomes—for both males and females—fell between 1959 and 1979. The drop was particularly pronounced for black males, whose incomes, stated as a percentage of median white male incomes, fell from 78 percent in 1969 to 66 percent in 1981. Recall that this *excludes* all zero income earners, thereby understating the extent of relative black income decline for the entire population.[10] The picture in the South was entirely different. Agricultural transformation . . . increased the impoverishment of many southern blacks during the 1950s. This is reflected in table 9.4: the ratio of black to white incomes fell from .46 to a rock bottom .33 for males between 1953 and 1959, and the female ratio fell from .45 to .42. Starting from a position of widespread southern poverty and deprivation in 1959, steady and sustained improvement took place in the next two decades. During this period of transition, blacks residing in the South shifted from being predominantly rural to largely urban in residence.[11] Their shift from agriculture to the urban job market was facilitated by strong southern urban economic expansion, . . . which continued in the 1970s despite recessionary national conditions. In other words, the large relative income gains of southern blacks (table 9.4) reflect the one-time-only gains accompanying urbanization and integration into nonagricultural lines of work.

Rural to urban migration was, of course, part of a nationwide redistribution of black population. Table 9.5 shows that, in addition to rural to urban migration within the South, the net migration out of the South was nearly 4.5 million for blacks from 1940 to 1970. This,

too, reflected a movement that was predominantly rural to urban. Nationwide gains in relative black incomes (table 9.1) that accompanied this population shift, however, did *not* produce proportionate increases in black economic well-being. Rural areas of the South have the lowest cost of living of any region of the United States, much lower than comparable living costs in urban areas.[12] In fact, black migrants of this era disproportionately moved to large cities where living costs are

TABLE 9.4 INCOME OF BLACKS* BY REGION AND SEX STATED AS PERCENTAGES OF WHITE INCOMES (*CALCULATIONS BASED ON MEDIANS*)

A. North, West	Black Males	Black Females
1953	74	85
1959	73	106
1964	75	110
1969	78	120
1974	75	113
1979	70	105
1981	66	103
B. South	Black Males	Black Females
1953	46	45
1959	33	42
1964	46	53
1969	54	62
1974	54	74
1979	60	81
1981	58	74

Sources: U.S. Bureau of the Census, *Current Population Reports,* ser. P-23, no. 80, table 30 (Washington, D.C..: Government Printing Office, 1979) p. 46. Ibid., ser. P-60, no. 129, table 47 (Nov. 1981), pp. 183–193. Ibid., ser. P-60, no. 137, table 43 (Mar. 1983), pp. 133–40.

*Data for 1964 and earlier refer to black and other races; post-1964 data refer to blacks only.

TABLE 9.5 NET MIGRATION OF BLACKS BY REGION (*IN THOUSANDS*)

	South	Northeast	North Central	West
1940–1950	− 1,599	+ 463	+ 618	+ 339
1950–1960	− 1,473	+ 496	+ 541	+ 293
1960–1970	− 1,380	+ 612	+ 382	+ 301
1970–1980	+ 209	− 239	− 103	+ 132
Total	− 4,243	+ 1,332	+ 1,438	+ 1,065

Sources: U.S. Bureau of the Census, *Current Population Reports,* ser. P-23, no. 80, Tables 8 and 9 (Washington, D.C.: Government Printing Office, 1979), pp. 15–16. Ibid., ser. P-20, no. 368, table 42 (Dec, 1981), p. 130.

among the highest in the nation. The 1980 census reported that 34 percent of all blacks resided in just seven urban centers: New York, Chicago, Los Angeles, Philadelphia, Detroit, Baltimore, and Washington, D.C. A rural South Carolina family subsisting on $2,500 a year may or may not be better off subsisting on $7,500 a year in Harlem. Rural South Carolina housing rental rates are certainly dwarfed by the cost of comparable housing in big city ghettos. Higher living costs obviously consume a share of the gains realized by rural to urban migrants, significantly offsetting relative black-white median income gains.

The validity of black-white income ratio comparisons over time is suspect for many reasons. Forms of noncash compensation, for example, have augmented white real incomes faster than that of blacks in recent decades. Especially in the professional and managerial occupations (disproportionately white), compensation in such forms as educational stipends, pensions, insurance premiums, and expense account living has increased more rapidly than actual wages and salaries. One study showed that black employees were much less likely than whites to participate in private pension plans, and those who did participate were eligible for or receiving pensions that were far smaller than those of white recipients.[13]

Another severe conceptual problem for black-white income comparisons concerns exclusion of some forms of income—such as capital gains and undistributed profits—from the census income definition. Nor are the wealthy the only ones receiving such uncounted income; families at the other end of the spectrum are often recipients of food stamps, Medicaid, and other forms of uncounted income. The list of biases goes on and on. The rich, for example, disproportionately receive property income, and income from property is systematically underreported to the government on a much larger scale than wage income.

Do the corporate elite, with their company cars, country club memberships, dining and entertainment expense allowances, generous pensions, etc. bias the reported income statistics more or less than poor blacks who receive free school lunches and subsidized housing? We really have no idea. Black-white income comparisons lose their validity increasingly as such forms of uncounted income expand over time. Reported income is a crude measure of actual income, and long-term comparisons of black-white income ratios should be viewed as even cruder measures of relative black well-being.

In summary, the evidence cited in table 9.1 does not show that blacks as a group are relatively better off than they were in the early 1950s.

1. A large share of reported income gains is negated by the shift from low cost of living areas in the rural South to high cost of living urban areas.

2. Income figures include only those earning income; the proportion of black males with zero income rose absolutely from 1953 to 1981 and it rose relative to whites. In contrast, the proportion of black women with zero income fell in absolute terms, but rose relative to whites.

3. Black-white income ratios obscure trends in income distribution within the black community. Black incomes could, for example, be a constant percentage of white incomes during a time period when rapid gains by the well-educated are forcing up this percentage, and income losses by the less-educated are pulling down relative black incomes. When one abstracts from the rural to urban shift (which produced major gains for low-income blacks), it turns out that the post–World War II period is indeed characterized by rising income inequality within the black community.

4. Differences in reported versus actual income are present due to income concealment, income measurement peculiarities, as well as

conceptual problems as to what is and is not income. These problems tend to make the precision of black-white income comparisons highly uncertain.

Among less-educated and less-skilled black Americans, absolute improvement in economic well-being may indeed be absent. Our inability to adjust accurately for cost of living differences between rural southern and urban areas alone makes it impossible to compare the well-being of less-skilled blacks in the 1950s with that of the 1980s. Measures of unemployment and labor force participation, however, suggest deterioration among less-skilled male workers.[14] The proportion of black males employed full-time for the entire year of 1955 was 56.6 percent. During the prosperous year of 1969 this percentage had fallen to 51.7 percent, and by 1980 only 45.0 percent of those who worked were employed full-time year-round.

Black teenagers face employment problems that dwarf those of older black workers.[15] Black teenagers have closed most of the education gap with their white cohorts, suggesting that their labor force status should begin to resemble more closely that of white teenagers. The opposite has in fact occurred (table 9.6). Indeed, education advances may be having a perverse effect on the labor force status of young blacks. Stronger educational credentials often create an unwillingness to accept jobs to which particularly low status is attached.[16]

The most disturbing statistics on black well-being are not directly related to the labor market. Signs of breakdown in the social fabric of low-income urban black communities, although poorly understood, are undoubtedly exacerbated by labor market problems. In 1979, for example, 15 percent of all deaths among black men were attributable to accidents, homicide, and suicide. Black males twenty-five to

TABLE 9.6 CIVILIAN LABOR FORCE PARTICIPATION RATE *(PERCENTAGE)*

	Male		Female	
	Black*	White	Black*	White
A. Participation Rate for Persons Age 16 or older				
1969	75.0	78.7	48.0	40.5
1971	75.5	79.7	47.4	42.7
1973	71.3	78.7	47.6	42.8
1975	72.1	78.7	48.2	45.7
1977	70.9	77.8	49.3	47.0
1979	71.7	78.5	52.3	49.9
1981	70.4	77.8	52.7	51.4
1983	69.5	76.2	53.6	52.2
B. Participation Rate for Persons 18–19 Years Old				
1969	62.3	59.6	41.8	48.1
1971	54.0	65.5	33.5	52.6
1973	59.7	69.3	41.0	53.9
1975	54.2	71.8	38.4	58.5
1977	55.5	71.4	40.6	58.7
1979	58.6	73.8	42.3	63.7
1981	59.0	72.8	43.0	61.6
1983	49.1	65.6	41.0	60.8

*Includes all nonwhites

Sources: U.S. Bureau of Labor Statistics, "Employment and Earnings" (Washington, D.C. Government Printing Office), various issues.

thirty-four years of age experienced death rates two and one-half times higher than whites in the same age group. The age-adjusted black death rate from homicide was over six times higher than the corresponding white rate.[17] Throughout the 1970s, the incidence of imprisonment of young black males rose dramatically. On an entirely different matter, black families of the form "single-parent female with her own children" increased in number 91.6 percent from 1970 to 1980. During the same time period, married couple families with their own children decreased in number by 5.9 percent.[18]

The proportion of black families living in poverty has increased since 1970, from 9.5 percent to 30.8 percent in 1981. This development is related to the increasing incidence of households headed by females; 52.9 percent of all such black families were below the poverty level in 1981. High rates of out-of-wedlock births exacerbate the trend of more black children being raised in households whose income is sub-poverty level. Rates of out-of-wedlock childbearing are particularly high among black teenagers.[19] Childbearing typically terminates the education of young mothers, resulting in limited job access. Young single women with small children, little education, and few skills often end up on welfare. A recent study found that approximately 40 percent of all black families with children under 18 are getting AFDC (Aid to Families with Dependent Children) benefits, compared to 6.8 percent for white families.

Causes of all the above, from violent death to the rising incidence of female-headed households living in poverty, are only dimly understood, but they do not suggest a pattern of widespread, across the board increases in black well-being. Rather, they suggest the sort of deterioration in community cohesion that would accompany declining labor market opportunities. High and rising unemployment rates among the young, falling labor force participation rates, a rising incidence

of violent death and of incarceration in prisons—these are traits of an emerging class of disaffected young urban blacks. They are the emerging lumpenproletariat.

THE UNANSWERED QUESTIONS

The progress portrayed in the first section, "The Evidence For Major Economic Progress," is the picture that dominates existing social science literature. It is so filled with overgeneralizations and so reliant upon one analytical tool—the black-white income ratio—that its message is largely wrong. And yet, very real educational gains do exist and it is important to understand why they have not resulted in more enduring and widespread income gains. Racial discrimination in the labor market along with more sophisticated forms of statistical discrimination . . . account for part of the problem. Many of the mysteries about trends in black economic welfare, though, can be clarified by putting them in the context of events described in previous chapters. Changing patterns in the demand for labor (chap. 8) have simultaneously improved female labor force status and undermined male prospects. The role of organized labor has shaped black occupational access, as has civil rights activism (chap. 7). Trends in major industries that employ blacks disproportionately—manufacturing, government, services—determine the value of educational credentials and thus shape black occupational access and earnings. These factors have varied greatly from decade to decade, producing diverse trends in black earnings. Furthermore, these are the factors that will shape black economic status in the years ahead.

THE 1950S

In several important ways, the 1950s reflected the beginnings of trends that were to become dominant determinants of urban black well-being in the 1980s—gains in white-collar occupations for the more educated and an increasingly tenuous employment situation for the less-educated. During the decade, rural to urban migration continued at a brisk pace and the largest black population gains were registered by major industrial cities. Most of the employed black males worked in the major blue-collar occupations—operative, general laborer, craftsmen, and foremen—and the majority of these were employed in manufacturing. Black females were concentrated primarily in low-wage service occupations and secondly, in the operative category. The frequency of white city residents in the white-collar occupations—professional, manager, clerical, and sales—was three to four times greater proportionally than the incidence of blacks in white-collar jobs.

Factory jobs were the highest paying type of employment that was widely available to urban blacks. They provided the route to upward mobility for the less-skilled, and the early 1950s, spurred by the Korean War, brought sustained gains in manufacturing employment. Nationwide unemployment rates for nonwhites stood at 4.1 percent in 1953, and the teenage unemployment incidence was 7.3 percent. In this era of 20 percent plus unemployment rates (early 1983 figures) for prime working age black males, it is useful to recall that 30 years ago, blacks with fewer skills and much less education experienced full employment in urban America.

The 1950s decade was not, however, a period of uninterrupted black economic gain. While blacks were being ejected en masse from southern agriculture, their economic fortunes in the cities ebbed and flowed along with the uneven demands for their labor services.

There were two very distinct sides to the coin of black economic prospects in northern and western cities: opportunities were more diverse and the pay was generally higher, but black unemployment in the North was much higher than it had been traditionally in the rural South. After the Korean War, an ominous new trend developed: 1953 was the last year of relatively low black unemployment— 4.4 percent for males and 3.7 percent for females. The corresponding rates for prosperous years in the 1960s were typically more than double the 1953 black unemployment rates. These were years of retrogression rather than progress. Whereas nonwhite unemployment rates as a percentage of white rates averaged around 170 percent during the late 1940s and early 1950s, in 1955 the nonwhite unemployment rate was more than double the corresponding white rate.[20] After 1955, black unemployment rates were consistently more than twice as high as white unemployment rates. During the 1950s, the relative income of black males declined significantly in every major region of the country. For the entire United States, though, the black-white income ratio for males declined only moderately, attributable solely to black migration from low-income rural southern areas to higher-income northern states.[21]

Black migration in the 1950s was heavily responsible for the decline in relative black economic well-being experienced in northern and western states. As machinery displaced men on a large scale in the most backward areas of the rural South, a northward stream of black migrants engulfed inner cities in the North and West. The migrants of the 1950s found a different situation in the cities than did their counterparts of earlier periods. There were few jobs available for them in the northern cities. The reasons were chiefly to be found in labor market structural difficulties as well as national economic trends. Briefly, the migrants were moving to the big city at the wrong point in history.

First, the southern refugees of the 1950s were among the least-skilled and the worst-educated of all Americans. The skills that they had were largely agricultural; the little education that they had was obtained in rural southern schools of poor quality. Their few skills and talents were not widely demanded by urban employers.

Second, the mass production industries in northern cities were hiring few blue-collar workers. Many large employers of earlier black migrants—automobile, steel, and electrical equipment—were actually reducing their unskilled and semiskilled labor forces. Job availability in manufacturing was greatest for white-collar workers such as engineers and technicians, but blacks generally lacked the skills required for entry into these jobs. Manufacturing growth no longer required vast numbers of unskilled workers.[22]

Third, black migrants from the South faced competition in the labor market from whites displaced from farms, particularly in the Midwest. Technological transformation of agriculture was a national phenomenon. When the decline in farm employment began in 1920, some 11.5 million persons were employed in agriculture. By 1940, the figure had fallen to 9.5 million, but by 1964 it had dropped to 4.7 million.[23] The white workers displaced from agriculture also moved into urban areas. Since they were better educated and more highly skilled than the southern black migrants (and were not black), they tended to get the more desirable jobs.

Fourth, national economic growth had slowed down. The nation's gross national product increased at a rate of only 2.4 percent annually between 1953 and 1960, as compared to 4 percent per year from 1946 to 1953. Unemployment rose throughout the economy, and a substantial amount of economic slack developed. Under these conditions, the uneducated black migrant was not only the last hired, but in many instances he or she was not hired at all.

Fifth, what economic expansion there was took place on the fringes of metropolitan areas. Jobs created in suburban locations were often not easily accessible to the poorest of the black migrants who settled mainly in the central cities.[24]

The economic experience of black migrants after the Korean War was often one of unemployment and underemployment. By 1958,

nonwhite unemployment had reached 12.6 percent nationwide, and it stayed between 10 and 13 percent until the escalation of the Vietnam War in 1964. The unemployment rates do not include those involuntarily restricted to part-time work or those employed at very low wages—the subemployed. The ranks of the subemployed typically exceeded the ghetto unemployed, often by wide margins.[25] Ghetto joblessness had always been widespread during recessions and depressions. Since the 1950s, however, high rates of black unemployment have been a permanent feature of ghetto life—in boom times as well as during recessionary periods. This is entirely a post–Korean War phenomenon.

The decade of the 1950s was not entirely bleak for urban blacks. The brunt of increased unemployment and underemployment was absorbed by recent migrants and young people. The more educated, long-term ghetto dwellers made occupational gains in the white-collar fields, particularly in clerical work (table 9.7). Increased penetration into clerical occupations was particularly beneficial to black females in the 1950s, and it helped to boost black female incomes relative to their white female counterparts. Many of the older industrial cities that had experienced heavy black in-migration were, during the 1950s, experiencing CBD expansion; a number of large-scale employers of clerical labor—corporate headquarters, banks, insurance companies, and government agencies—were expanding their central-city operations.

Aside from gains in certain white-collar areas, though, the dominant features of black labor market involvement in the 1950s were rising unemployment and underemployment, restricted opportunities in manufacturing after 1953 (the traditional route of upward mobility for unskilled blacks), and deteriorating incomes of black males relative to their white counterparts.

Problems in manufacturing employment were exacerbated by discriminatory policies concerning layoff and job upgrading.

TABLE 9.7 OCCUPATION OF EMPLOYED BLACKS BY SEX, FOR
CENTRAL-CITY RESIDENTS OF CHICAGO, BALTIMORE, CLEVELAND,
DETROIT, AND PHILADELPHIA (*PERCENTAGE*)

	1950	1960	1970
A. *Male*			
Professional, Technical	2.3	4.0	5.8
Manager, Proprietor	2.7	2.4	3.0
Sales	1.9	2.4	2.6
Clerical	6.4	9.7	10.0
Craftsmen, Foremen, and Kindred	11.4	13.0	16.0
Operative	30.9	33.9	34.4
Laborer	26.3	18.5	12.5
Service	16.5	15.6	15.2
Private Household	1.0	0.5	0.4
(% White Collar)	(13.3)	(18.5)	(21.4)
B. *Female*			
Professional, Technical	4.8	8.4	11.1
Manager, Proprietor	1.4	1.3	1.6
Sales	2.3	2.9	3.4
Clerical	7.5	16.9	30.8
Craftsmen, Foreman, and Kindred	1.2	1.2	1.7
Operative	27.6	22.9	18.3
Laborer	2.5	1.3	1.8
Service	21.1	23.6	22.9
Private Household	32.6	21.5	8.4
(% White Collar)	(16.0)	(29.5)	(46.9)

Source: U.S. Census of Population.

. . . [U]nion concern for black worker rights fell rather dramatically during the 1950s, and unions were often supportive of unfair treatment of black employees. The seniority system was a particular irritant. There are a number of seniority system designs, each with its own set of problems for black workers. During full employment periods, blacks benefit from the widest possible seniority base (one that is commonly plant-wide in scope). Seniority may then be a basis for maximum upgrading and promotion opportunities *if* the system is applied in an impartial manner. But, during periods of employment contraction, blacks benefit most from a narrow-based seniority system (departmental or occupational) since their high concentration in several occupations and departments provides protection from being bumped by whites who have greater seniority. In fact, plants often used departmental seniority for job upgrading and plant-wide seniority for layoffs. This arrangement clearly favored white workers over blacks, and it directly reflected the balance of racial power in the unions.[26] While the job upgrading opportunities went mainly to white workers, black workers were most likely to be laid off during recessions. These discriminatory practices were widespread in such supposedly progressive unions as the United Auto Workers. Although blacks accounted for 8 to 9 percent of all auto workers in the 1950s, they never accounted for as much as one-half of 1 percent of skilled craftsmen. General Motors had over 11,000 skilled workers in the Detroit area; fewer than 100 were black.[27]

THE 1960S

During periods of labor shortage, the swollen ranks of unemployed and underemployed urban blacks are drawn off to staff more stable and remunerative jobs. Black workers often find it possible to move from low-wage competitive sector jobs into higher-wage work with large corporations or the government. Second, job upgrading invariably becomes an issue during boom periods, and barriers to black occupational advancement are challenged. It is no coincidence that concern about racially discriminatory employment practices always appears to be most prevalent during periods of rapid economic expansion and job creation. This was the situation in the 1960s: jobs were available in areas where black penetration had traditionally been minimal, and discriminatory hiring practices were reduced, allowing black employment gains in skilled and white-collar lines of work.

In important ways the World War II era provided the model for1960s black employment gains. . . . [T]he federal government led the way to expanded job access in the early 1940s. Executive Order 8802, signed by President Roosevelt in 1941, required that all defense contractors adopt nondiscriminatory employment practices. The federal government reformed its own hiring practices during World War II and employed hundreds of thousands of black workers in white-collar jobs. Hiring black females as clerical workers on a large scale thus began in the 1940s. One important difference between World War II and the 1960s, however, was the role of organized labor as a champion of black rights. While the CIO unions played this role in the early 1940s, blacks themselves—via the civil rights movement—won many victories in the struggles of the 1960s for improved job access.

Two major themes dominate the improvement in black economic well-being during the 1960s. First, this long period of sustained economic growth created strong labor demands that translated into widespread income and occupational gains for black workers (tables 9.4 and 9.7). Second, civil rights activism produced an outpouring of legislation designed to curb racial discrimination as well as an avalanche of court rulings that advanced the cause of equal rights. All of this produced a reshaping of public attitudes about the roles of minority groups in U.S. society: black willingness to assume subservient economic, social, and political roles fell, and whites increasingly accepted the notion that equality of opportunity should apply to blacks as well as to themselves.

Trends in the Demand for Labor

In the urban labor markets (particularly the big city job markets) where most black workers compete for jobs, long-run trends toward expanding white-collar employment accelerated, while trends toward stagnant or declining manufacturing employment were reversed during the 1960s. Even in the older northeastern and midwestern cities, the long-term loss of manufacturing jobs was actually halted. Cleveland, for example, is an old industrial city that has lost well over 50 percent of its manufacturing production jobs since 1947. Between 1963 and 1967, Cleveland manufacturing employment actually grew slightly— from 168,900 to 171,300 jobs.[28] Baltimore typified the employment trends of many snowbelt cities. This city experienced a net increase of nearly 9,000 manufacturing jobs between 1962 and 1967. Bennett Harrison and Edward Hill estimated that, in those lines of Baltimore manufacturing offering high-wage blue-collar work, employment had declined by 19 percent between 1953 and 1959, stabilized from 1959 to 1962, and then increased by 5 percent between 1962 and 1970.[29] In the suburban areas of snowbelt cities, manufacturing production jobs were typically growing in availability, inducing the more mobile elements of the ghetto labor force to commute to suburban jobs. Black males in Detroit made particularly large gains in numbers of jobs held in high-wage manufacturing employment. By 1970, over 33 percent of the employed central-city black male Detroit residents were commuting to suburban jobs.

Declining manufacturing employment after the Korean War severely reduced black employment prospects during the mid- to late 1950s. Rapidly increasing unemployment was the result. The long 1960s boom partially reversed this situation, predictably bringing falling black male unemployment rates and rising real incomes. For the snowbelt cities, however, the prosperous 1960s were merely an interlude; manufacturing production work had already resumed its long-term decline by 1970, and the trend has been straight downhill ever since. Furthermore, the suburban periphery is no longer a source of growing manufacturing employment for blue-collar workers. This long-term decline is one of the key factors behind the sharp drop since 1969 (table 9.4) in the relative incomes of black males who reside in northern and western states.

. . . [L]ong-term growth patterns in major urban areas favor the white-collar worker over his blue-collar counterpart. During the prosperous 1960s, both blue- and white-collar job holders progressed, but opportunities were greatest in the white-collar occupations. Ghettos are usually located near central-city CBDs, where white-collar employment is most heavily concentrated. For those black urban residents having the educational background necessary to compete for these jobs, expanding CBDs in the 1960s offered numerous possibilities. Younger, better-educated black females benefited most from this situation, moving heavily into clerical occupations while also registering some gains in the professions. In 1950, "cleaning lady" had been the most common job title among urban black females. By 1970, private household employment was a distant fourth, and clerical work was in first place. In cities such as Chicago during the 1960s, it was commonplace to observe tripling and

even quadrupling of black female clerical employment in industries like banking.

Rapidly expanding government employment probably provided the greatest opportunities for black female gains.[30] Over half of all government jobs are clerical or professional and these are the two occupations that black females have penetrated most rapidly since 1950. Indeed, most of the employed black women who work as professionals are employed by the government; among them, teaching is the most common profession. In many northern cities such as Baltimore and Chicago, over 25 percent of all employed black females in 1970 worked for the government.

The shift in black female occupational structure has been profound since 1950. While black males were still overwhelmingly employed in blue-collar and service occupations, black women were in the 1960s rapidly narrowing differences in occupational structure with white females by moving into white-collar jobs. Like whites, black females have been steadily shifting away from the operative occupational category but black male operative employment grew in both absolute and relative terms after 1950, following a trend that dates back to World War I. Black men remain heavily employed in manufacturing, which is a highly cyclical sector of the economy that is shrinking in significance, while black women rely increasingly on administrative and professional work that is both less cyclical and growing. Although blue-collar manufacturing jobs for men and white-collar clerical work for women provided important gains for blacks in the 1960s, low-wage work continued to be a major employer of ghetto labor. Services and retail trade are major low-wage employers. Even in manufacturing, certain sectors such as apparel offer poor-paying, dead-end, unstable work of the least desirable sort. Employment growth in these low-wage sectors during the 1960s was particularly prevalent in the sunbelt cities.[31]

Civil Rights Activism

Comprehensive treatment of the civil rights movement would require more than a chapter; it requires a separate volume. Here we simply highlight those aspects that are most directly relevant to the employment status of blacks. The Civil Rights Act of 1964 is one obvious landmark. Title VII of that act outlawed discrimination based on race, sex, or national origin by private employers, unions, and employment agencies; the Equal Employment Opportunity Commission (EEOC) was set up to investigate charges of discrimination. In 1972, the Commission's powers were expanded, allowing it to file suits on behalf of those injured by employment discrimination. Another major piece of the fair employment infrastructure grew out of Executive Order 11246, issued in 1965, which prohibits employment discrimination by recipients of federal contracts. The Office of Federal Contract Compliance (OFCC) was created to monitor compliance with the order. Given the subjective nature of much employment discrimination, actual government policy in this realm has varied from year to year, and numerous court cases have been necessary to define boundaries between discrimination, nondiscrimination, and affirmative action.

The EEOC and OFCC lack the personnel necessary to enforce adequately their legislative mandates, but the effectiveness of anti-discrimination efforts in the employment realm is not totally dependent upon these two agencies. Quite aside from the EEOC and the OFCC, the law permits injured parties to seek redress through the courts. Nonetheless, the EEOC's record has been disappointing. In 1973, for example, nearly fifty thousand individuals filed complaints with the EEOC alleging discrimination, many more than the approximately one thousand EEOC professional staff could handle. By 1977, the backlog of cases had grown to 130,000.[32] The OFCC has the power to cancel or suspend government contracts and it sometimes exerts strong pressure on government contractors. In 1969, for example, the OFCC issued the Philadelphia Plan for affirmative action by federal construction contractors in that city: contractors were ordered to increase their employment of minority craftsmen from the current 2 percent to goals of 4 to 9 percent within one year, and 19 to 26 percent within four years.[33] Thus affirmative action plans became part of civil rights law.

Aggressive use of EEOC and OFCC powers is rare. The OFCC debarred no contractors between 1965 and 1970 and debarred an average of two per year between 1971 and 1977. All EEOC litigation through 1977 resulted in estimated back pay settlements of only $65 million. Nonetheless, a few well-publicized settlements have induced many employers to hire at least a few blacks for better-paying jobs. In 1973, American Telephone and Telegraph signed a consent decree that included a multi-million dollar package providing back pay and future promotions for women and minorities. Large firms in general have established minority hiring plans and, at a minimum, pay lip service to minority hiring and promotion.

Estimating the exact impact of anti-discrimination laws on black employment and earnings is quite impossible, but several conclusions are warranted. First, blatant discrimination as formerly practiced by such unions as the AFL building trades has been sharply curtailed. Second, it is now the norm for large companies to employ at least a few blacks in both skilled blue-collar ranks and managerial white-collar jobs. Third, fair employment laws depend upon active enforcement for much of their effectiveness. Proponents of these laws face a constant battle to insure that the enforcement agencies possess the resources and the willingness to combat employment discrimination. The record to date suggests that comprehensive enforcement has never been attempted. Fourth, employers are most likely to adhere to the spirit of anti-discriminatory laws during periods of economic expansion. Tough questions such as racial implications of various seniority systems need not arise when black employees are being hired and upgraded. During economic downturns, however, the last hired are most apt to be the first fired; these are black workers disproportionately.

One difficulty in assessing the impact of measures as controversial and subjective as anti-discrimination laws is the fact that they are inseparable from overall attitudes on the status of minorities. One major impact of civil rights activism is that black workers themselves are less likely to tolerate discrimination on the job in a milieu where equal rights concerns are paramount. In the 1920s, blacks were grateful for access to any kind of position in better-paying industries. In contrast, the charged environment in the 1960s encouraged black workers to speak out against discrimination in the work place, in unions, and in society in general. Most employers, especially those large enough to attract the attention of the EEOC or OFCC, wanted to avoid the publicity that was apt to accompany allegations of discrimination in hiring and promotion. Firms hiring numerous blacks for several occupations (such as clerical or operative) often improved promotion opportunities and upgraded at least a few blacks. Creating the perception of better job opportunities helped to legitimize employment practices, thus perhaps lessening black disenchantment in all ranks. Less discriminatory hiring practices were widely adapted as pragmatic business practices: an expanding economy generated the need to hire additional workers, and greater access to job openings for blacks not only helped to avoid government scrutiny, it was also a wise public relations gesture.

THE 1970S

The three major industry groups employing black workers are manufacturing, services, and government. Job growth in manufacturing was moderate during the 1960s, while employment creation in government and services was quite rapid and widespread. Black employees benefited from these strong labor demands. But the 1960s also created job gains in traditionally discriminatory industries such as construction, which lessened racial barriers because of government scrutiny and declining public acceptance of racist hiring and training policies. Similar pressure, plus growing clerical worker needs, caused industries traditionally employing few blacks—finance, communications, utilities—to recruit black workers actively during the 1960s. Rapid educational gains also helped to deepen the industry-occupational mix open to black job seekers. In the more rapidly growing sunbelt regions of the United States, this 1960s pattern of improved job access continued well into the 1970s. Declining labor demands in the slower growing, more recession-prone snowbelt economy set the stage for losses in black economic well-being during the 1970s. Job losses in manufacturing were heavily concentrated in several high-paying, unionized industries where black male employment gains of the 1960s had been particularly strong. Job losses in government were much less widespread, but they were concentrated heavily in areas such as New York City and Cleveland, where black employment in government had risen substantially in the 1960s.[34]

The impact of manufacturing sector decline upon black workers is shown clearly by the situation in motor vehicles. Blacks prospered disproportionately from auto industry prosperity in the 1960s. The proportion of all motor vehicle industry employees who were black rose from 9.1 percent in 1960 to 13.4 percent in 1970; 138,609 blacks worked in this one industry at the end of the 1960s.[35] The rule of thumb that the auto companies employ at least one million workers during a good year—valid as late as 1978 when employment reached 977,000—is no longer applicable. The industry in the 1980s is investing heavily in labor-saving equipment and use of foreign-made parts is increasing. Researchers for the United Auto

Workers Union estimate that 1985 auto industry employment may be as low as 527,000, only 54 percent of the 1978 total.[36] Future industry employment, of course, depends upon the market share of imported autos: the 527,000 job estimate assumes a 30.9 percent import share of the U.S. car market. The U.S. Chamber of Commerce estimates that communities lose, on average, two service jobs for every three manufacturing jobs that disappear.[37]

A study of workers displaced from manufacturing industries in the early 1970s found that average annual percentage earnings losses, during the first two years after job loss, were: autos, 43.4%; steel, 46.6%; aerospace, 23.6%; electronic components, 8.3%; shoes, 11.3%; and women's clothes, 13.3%.[38]

Re-employment was the norm for workers displaced in the early 1970s, and the severity of earnings loss is associated with two obvious factors: wages before displacement, and alternative opportunities for employment. Since autos and steel are both high-wage industries heavily concentrated in slow-growth snowbelt states, their displaced workers predictably experienced high earnings losses. Displacement from lower-wage manufacturing industries produced the smallest earnings losses, especially in instances such as electronic components where employment is concentrated in the healthier sunbelt states. These patterns of earnings losses may actually be accentuated in the 1980s, due to the severity of regional employment declines in the Midwest, where steelmaking and auto manufacturing and assembly are so heavily concentrated.

Industrial cities like Cleveland, Chicago, and Pittsburgh no longer provide the route to upward mobility via manufacturing employment for less-skilled workers. The massive losses of blue-collar manufacturing jobs in the 1970s and 1980s, interacting with local government fiscal difficulties, are effectively reversing many of the employment gains captured by blacks in the 1960s. Yet these are the same cities in which highly educated blacks continued in the 1970s to gain jobs in the expanding management and administrative sectors. It is precisely in these older industrial cities where the contrast between the haves and the have nots is sharpening most rapidly: a portion of the smaller white-collar group prospers while the larger blue-collar urban black workforce is undermined. In the aggregate regional statistics (table 9.8), the misfortune of the many swamps the progress of the few, and the income gains of the 1960s are decisively erased. The severity of the losses recorded in table 9.8 undoubtedly reflects, too, weakening local government employment, which reduced the ranks of the more affluent white-collar group. The fact that Michigan is the only state registering a gain since 1959 in relative black family incomes partially reflects the superior unemployment compensation benefits received by auto workers.

The situation in the South was altogether different in the 1970s. A stronger regional economy has created blue-collar as well as white-collar jobs, and local government fiscal difficulties were less severe than in the snowbelt cities. Relative black incomes continued their 1960s trajectory. Regional differences are particularly apparent in the unemployment data. In March 1980, black male unemployment rates in Illinois and Ohio exceeded 16 percent; the corresponding rates in Georgia and North Carolina were 8.7 and 8.3 percent. The differential in female unemployment rates for blacks was less pronounced: 13.6 and 13.2 percent in Illinois and Ohio, versus 11.2 and 11.1 percent in Georgia and North Carolina.[39] The female differential pattern reflects the fact that sunbelt black women workers have penetrated white-collar jobs to a much lesser degree than their snowbelt counterparts. Continued black economic gains in the South were brought to a halt, however, by the severe recession of the early 1980s, as shown in table 9.4.

TABLE 9.8 RATIO OF NONWHITE TO WHITE FAMILY MEDIAN INCOMES IN
SELECTED STATES, 1959–1979

	1959	1969	1979	Change: 1959–1979
A. Snowbelt Industrial States				
Illinois	.68	.70	.60	− .08
Ohio	.70	.74	.67	− .03
Michigan	.68	.75	.69	+ .01
Pennsylvania	.71	.74	.62	− .09
B. Sunbelt Southeastern States				
Alabama	.42	.49	.55	+ .13
Georgia	.44	.52	.56	+ .12
North Carolina	.43	.57	.63	+ .20
Virginia	.50	.59	.62	+ .12

Sources: U.S. Bureau of the Census, *Advance Estimates of Social, Economic, and Housing Characteristics—
Supplementary Report: Counties and Selected Places* (by State) Alabama ser. PHC80-S2-2 (Washington,
D.C.: Government Printing Office, 1983), p. 39; ibid., Georgia S2-12, p. 79; ibid., Illinois S2-15,
p. 75; ibid., Michigan S2-24, p. 67; ibid., North Carolina S2-35, p. 55; ibid., Ohio S2-37, p. 67;
ibid., Pennsylvania S2-40, p. 63; ibid., Virginia S2-48, p. 75. U.S. Bureau of the Census, *Census
of Population: 1970, General Social and Economic Characteristics, Final Report PC (1)-C2*, Alabama
(Washington, D.C.: Government Printing Office, 1972), pp. 2–164; ibid., *Georgia*, pp. 12–238; ibid.,
Illinois, pp. 15–336; ibid., *Michigan*, pp. 24–246; ibid., *North Carolina*, pp. 35–201; ibid., *Ohio*,
pp. 37–327; ibid., *Pennsylvania*, pp. 40–308; ibid., *Virginia*, pp. 48–209.

THE 1980S

Has the twentieth-century transition of blacks
from a predominantly southern rural to a
predominantly urban America drastically
lessened racial discrimination, or have new
forms of racial inequality arisen in the cities?
Black economic progress in the sunbelt cities
sheds the most light on this question. Table 9.8
shows a trend toward convergence in snowbelt and sunbelt black-white income ratios.
Relative black incomes were still slightly
higher in most of the northern states in 1979,
but the continued 1980s decline of blue-collar
jobs in high-wage manufacturing industries
pulled the regional wage ratios into closer
alignment. Briefly, the labor market in northern cities is increasingly resembling the
southern job scene: blacks in both regions
face most rapid job growth at the higher and
lower ends of the market, and least opportunity in the middle occupational echelons.

Harrison's study of sunbelt cities shows
that blacks there have traditionally had a
much higher proportion of low-wage and

part-time jobs than their snowbelt counterparts.[40] . . . [S]outhern and southwestern
cities were more service and trade oriented,
while snowbelt cities and SMSAs were more
manufacturing oriented. Declining snowbelt
manufacturing along with growth in services
is lessening these differences in industrial
composition as well as wage structure; service
work is very low in pay relative to manufacturing. Furthermore, the sunbelt manufacturing production jobs, relatively low paying, are
frequently in those fields that are most likely
to be growing nationwide in coming years.
Electronics, for example, is expected to expand
in snowbelt as well as sunbelt regions, but it
rarely offers blue-collar workers the wages
paid by such traditional employers as the
metal shaping and manufacturing industries.
. . . [T]he expanding lines of manufacturing
tend to produce jobs for highly trained, technical, scientific, and professional personnel,
and production jobs staffed by low-wage
workers. Rapidly rising productivity per worker
also characterizes this sector, minimizing high

tech industry's ability to create new jobs (fig. 9.1) Data Resources Incorporate (DRI) estimates that output per high tech worker will rise by 46 percent between 1983 and 1993, double the projected increase for services (23 percent) and manufacturing (24 percent).[41] The manufacturing sector lost roughly three million jobs between 1980 and 1982. Neither a cyclical upswing in manufacturing industries nor continued growth in high tech areas is predicted to replace, by 1990, the production jobs lost during the early 1980s.[42]

Those industries where job growth is most rapid, services and trade (fig. 9.1), are primarily low-wage industries; high-wage sectors—construction, transportation, public utilities, government, and manufacturing—have been stagnant since the 1960s, with available job openings concentrated in white-collar, skilled fields. Aside from the 1960s, these trends in job growth have actually been apparent since the end of the Korean war. In Baltimore, for example, 31 percent of all private sector jobs in 1953 were found in the low-wage nonmanufacturing industries; by 1974, 43 percent of the jobs were found in this sector. During this same time period, high-wage manufacturing work fell from 32 percent to 25 percent of Baltimore's private sector employment. While high-wage sectors tend to offer full-time year-round work predominantly, low-wage industries such as services and retail trade more frequently offer only part-time work to their employees.[43]

Sources of future income gains for black workers in urban America are not readily apparent. Even in the best paying occupations the outlook for gains is not altogether bright. In the professional and technical occupations for example, most blacks are employed as teachers, nurses, health care technicians, social workers, and counselors.[44] These represent the lowest paying types of jobs available in this heterogeneous occupational grouping,

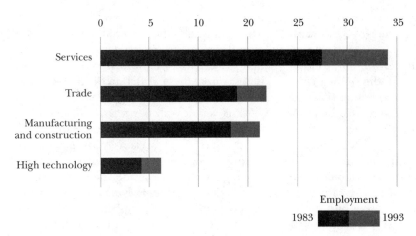

Assumptions:
1983–88 3.4 percent average annual increase in GNP, 2.1 percent average annual increase in nonfarm employment.
1988–93 2.7 percent average annual increase in GNP, 1.2 percent average annual increase in nonfarm employment.
Source: Data Resources, Inc.

Figure 9.1. Employment by Industry: 1983 and 1993 *(in millions of workers).*

and they are largely lines of work where career opportunities for upgrading in pay and responsibilities are minimal. Furthermore, black professionals rely heavily on government, particularly city government, for employment and they are concentrated in older, larger cities where fiscal problems are most severe. Not only are future employment gains unlikely, but outright employee reductions are the norm in cities such as Chicago and Detroit.

The situation in the clerical occupations is brighter, since long-term employment growth in this line of work is expected to continue into the foreseeable future. While government workforce reductions have a negative impact on clerical job opportunities, this has been offset by growing private sector demand for workers in this field. Jobs in computer-related fields, such as data entry, should continue to grow rapidly. Clerical work, however, offers few opportunities for occupational advancement, and pay is below average relative to wage and salary levels in the overall economy. While the large-scale shift of black workers into clerical occupations does represent a long-term upgrading in labor force status, it certainly does not represent a move towards long-term equality in labor force status. In fact, the social status and remuneration associated with clerical work have been steadily declining, relative to the other occupations, throughout the twentieth century.[45]

Nonetheless, prospects in clerical and professional occupations are brighter than those facing blue-collar workers. Advances in education and training can lead to further gains in growth areas such as the managerial and non-government professional occupations, and younger black workers are increasing their penetration in these lines of employment. Yet it is among the young that polarization appears to be most pronounced: rapid income gains for the best educated coexist with very high unemployment rates and falling labor force

participation rates for the majority of young blacks. Long-term economic trends suggest that the latter group is most likely to find work in low-paying but growing industries, particularly services. Night-watchman, dishwasher, janitor—these are the types of low-wage, unstable work that will increasingly typify job opportunities for ghetto residents.

High unemployment and low labor force participation rates among black teenagers are often cited as evidence of declining job prospects. The unemployment problems of this group are indeed staggering—the unemployment rate for blacks sixteen to nineteen years of age actually topped 50 percent in August 1981—but we feel that teenagers are not an appropriate group for illustrating labor market trends. Part of the black teenage employment problem reflects improved education and training opportunities. These opportunities have induced many young blacks to substitute schooling or military service for work. Because those with better than average employment prospects are most likely to pursue advanced education and training, the attractiveness to employers of the remaining out-of-school civilian black youth population is reduced.[46] This process partially explains both the rising incidence of black youth unemployment and the occupational and income gains realized by educated young blacks.

To illustrate the polarization process we focus not upon black teenagers but upon those twenty to twenty-four years of age. Trends in their labor market status are documented utilizing data from the Census of Population Public Use Samples for Illinois and Ohio. Similar data for North Carolina and Georgia are used below to explain differences in snowbelt/sunbelt employment situations facing young black males. The labor force participation rate of black males twenty to twenty-four years old in Ohio and Illinois resembles that of all adult black males in those states—70.3 percent for the former versus 70.7 percent for the latter—but the similarities end there. These younger blacks are better educated than the overall black workforce and they have entered the labor force during the time when all of the forces promoting polarization discussed above were fully operative. Census data yield the following information: (1) the labor force participation rate of black males twenty to twenty-four years of age fell from 76.5 percent in 1970 to 70.3 percent in 1980; (2) their unemployment rate rose from 12.5 percent in 1970 to 29.3 percent in 1980; (3) they were heavily concentrated in manufacturing employment in both 1970 and 1980, and the majority of those in manufacturing worked in three high-wage sectors: metal (predominantly steel mills), machinery, and transportation equipment; (4) 43.8 percent of this group worked in manufacturing in 1970, versus 31.1 percent in 1980; (5) their incidence of white-collar employment rose from 23.6 percent in 1970 to 28.1 percent in 1980; (6) their incidence of employment in service occupations rose from 10.4 percent in 1970 to 20.1 percent in 1980.

Overall, the proportion of black males twenty to twenty-four years of age in Ohio and Illinois who held jobs fell precipitously between 1970 and 1980. Whereas 63 percent were working in 1970 on the date when they filled out their census forms, only 41 percent were employed in 1980. Job loss in the traditional manufacturing sector was partially offset by growth of white-collar employment, but it was in the low-wage service sector where job expansion was most pronounced. Table 9.9 compares earnings and employment stability in the manufacturing and service areas. Relative to manufacturing, service work is low paying. In 1979, mean wage and salary incomes for black male service workers in Ohio and Illinois reached only $8,137; mean wage incomes of their cohorts employed in manufacturing stood 75.3 percent higher, at $14,263. The service workers receive low hourly wages, but they are also handicapped by their higher incidence of part-time work. According to table 9.9, average weeks worked in 1979 was 37.2 for service workers and 44.4 for manufacturing employees. Similarly, the average number of hours worked per week was a lower 35.8 hours in services, versus 40.0 hours in manufacturing. Finally the typical service worker portrayed in table 9.9 spent 5.6 weeks unemployed in 1979 (versus 3.6 in manufacturing) and he spent 9.2 weeks as a nonparticipant in the labor force (versus

TABLE 9.9 SELECTED DATA ON BLACK MALE EMPLOYEES IN OHIO AND ILLINOIS IN 1979 (*MEANS ONLY*)*

	Manufacturing	**Services**	**All Employees**
Total wage and salary income	$14,263	$8,137	$12,346
Total income from all sources	$14,742	$8,609	$12,882
Weeks worked in 1979	44.4	37.2	42.0
Average number of hours worked per week	40.0	35.8	38.4
Weeks unemployed in 1979	3.6	5.6	4.2
Total number of observations	4,723	2,282	13,285

Source: Sample A of the 1980 Census of Population and Housing: Public Use Microdata Sample.

*This table represents a 2.5 percent random sample of the population of Ohio and Illinois. According to the data source, 2.5 percent of the universe of black male employees 16 years of age or older in 1980 in these two states constituted 15,079 observations. In performing the mean calculations, 1,794 of the observations were excluded because they had not worked as employees during 1979. Unpaid workers in family businesses were excluded from the sample of 13,285 observations.

4.0 weeks in manufacturing). The educational credentials of black workers employed in manufacturing and services were quite similar overall: 23.0 percent of those in services had attended school beyond the high school level, as had 22.8 percent of those in manufacturing. Both groups, however, lagged behind the average educational credentials of black males employed outside of the service and manufacturing areas.

Rising unemployment rates and declining labor participation of blacks twenty to twenty-four years of age are partially caused by the nature of the service jobs that increasingly typify their employment alternatives. Many service industries do not offer full-time, year-around work. Employment in services frequently entails enduring bouts of unemployment and labor force nonparticipation. Seven specific types of industries employed nearly 81 percent of the black male service workers summarized in table 9.9. In order of importance they were: restaurant (employing 20.3 percent of the service workers), public administration, hospital, education, service to building firms, real estate, and hotel. Restaurants and hotels that cater to tourists are normally seasonal employers, and educational institutions often have reduced needs for service workers in the summertime. Other major service employers such as hospitals often provide stable work, but wage rates for their service employees are typically very low. Employment in hospitals has grown quite rapidly for all blacks in Ohio and Illinois in the last two decades. It was the largest single industry in which black females in these two states worked in 1980; over 16 percent of all black working women listed hospitals as their industry of employment in 1980, and while most were service workers, 27.2 percent worked as professionals, primarily nurses.

While younger snowbelt black males shifted rapidly out of high-wage manufacturing work in the 1970s and toward unemployment as well as low-wage service jobs (and white-collar employment), their sunbelt cohorts experienced no such tumultuous changes in labor force status. Southern blacks are protected from the trauma of losing high-wage manufacturing jobs because they had few of them in the first place. Among the black males working in manufacturing in North Carolina and Georgia, three lines—textiles, wood products, and food processing—provide over one-half of the jobs. These three low-wage industries employed 54.2 percent of the Georgia and North Carolina black males working in manufacturing in 1970, versus 55.2 percent of those in manufacturing in 1980. Among those twenty to twenty-four years of age, black males in these two states relied on manufacturing for 38.6 percent of their jobs in 1970, and 36.7 percent of them in 1980. White-collar and service work did increase in incidence over the 1970s decade, but the changes were minor ones. Black males twenty to twenty-four years old saw the incidence of service employment rise from 13.4 percent to 15.7 percent while the percentage of those in white-collar jobs rose from 15.7 percent in 1970 to 17.1 percent in 1980. Their incidence of unemployment did rise slightly over the decade, but the 2.4 percent rise from 12.6 to 15.0 percent in the unemployment rate was dwarfed in magnitude by the 16.8 percentage points (from 12.5 to 29.3 percent) that were tacked on to the unemployment rate of their northern cohorts.

The changes in labor force status among twenty- to twenty-four-year-old black males of course reflect changes that in varying degrees shape the economic well-being, of all black male workers. Thus, the declining incidence of employment in manufacturing is undercutting the job status of all snowbelt black workers. Among all employed Ohio and Illinois black male employees, 40.1 percent worked in manufacturing in 1970 versus 34.4 percent in 1980. Rising unemployment and falling rates of labor force participation typify black male workers from twenty-five to fifty-four years of age. For those in Illinois and Ohio, the incidence of unemployment rose from 4.4 to 13.5 percent between 1970 and 1980, while their labor force participation rate fell from 87.4 to 82.7 percent. In contrast, their cohorts in Georgia and North Carolina experienced stable labor force participation rates and an increase in the incidence of unemployment from 3.1 to 6.8 percent. During the recessionary early 1980s, snowbelt black workers fell further behind their sunbelt counterparts because of their greater dependence upon the most cyclical segments of manufacturing—steel, autos, and related durables. Indeed, in 1982, the North Central region actually surpassed the South for the first time in history as the region having the highest rate of black poverty (39.8 percent).[47] It would be incorrect, however, to conclude that southern black economic well-being is surpassing that of northern blacks precisely because of the highly cyclical nature of much northern durable goods manufacturing. Although the long-term outlook for employment in snowbelt heavy industry is dim, upturn phases in the business cycle are still capable of alleviating (partially) the large cyclical component of black unemployment.

INCREASING GOVERNMENT REPRESENTATION MAY NOT IMPROVE BLACK ECONOMIC WELL-BEING

History suggests that strong and sustained economic growth periods improve black labor force status in both absolute and relative terms. Overall health of the economy will continue to be a vital determinant of black economic well-being in the future. A strong political voice, typified by 1960s civil rights activism, may also produce economic dividends for the black community. Gains in local government, though, may offer little potential unless the fiscal crises of the older, larger cities are alleviated.

Black political goals in central cities have been city hall power, improved city services for black neighborhoods, and a larger proportion of city government jobs.[48] Winning city hall, though, is increasingly a hollow political prize. Facing constant job loss, disinvestment, and tax base deterioration, black leaders in cities like Detroit, Gary, and Newark are increasingly dependent upon state and federal funds. The early 1980s has produced a rising indifference to the fiscal problems of declining central cities by state and particularly national government bodies. Black mayors can thus do little to alter the well-being of their constituents because they lack control over the economic resources needed to do the job.

Private capital can be induced to invest in America's aging cities if the terms are right: enter CBD renovation, convention centers, "favorable" tax climates, and the like. Leveraged by federal dollars, multibillion dollar urban renewal programs have transformed or are transforming downtown areas in cities as diverse as Boston and Pittsburgh. Urban renewal often removes "blight" from the periphery of the CBD, freeing potentially valuable property for use as infrastructure that complements CBD interests, and sites for private sector expansion, ranging from high-rise apartments to corporate office buildings. Blight typically consists of low-cost housing for blacks; it is replaced by parking facilities, sports stadiums, convention centers, freeway interchanges, and high-cost apartments. Urban renewal thus becomes urban removal, with the displaced minority population squeezed into a diminished stock of rental housing.[49]

Although urban renewal policies do indeed seem to be renovating downtown areas in many large cities, their political feasibility is increasingly being undermined by an obvious contradiction. How can black politicians be elected when they espouse CBD renovation projects, especially when these projects have traditionally destroyed black neighborhoods? How can scarce local government services be concentrated on downtown areas when the social needs of ghettos are so astoundingly high? Some ghetto blacks, of course, expect to benefit from the jobs generated by downtown expansion. Because these jobs are largely administrative, however, the highly educated segment of the labor force, managers and the professionals, are likely to benefit disproportionately from CBD job growth. Successful downtown renovation increasingly attracts young white professionals into inner-city neighborhoods, and a process of gentrification often results. Rents are invariably driven up in black neighborhoods adjacent to gentrified districts, further reducing the accessible housing supply for low-income blacks.

The resultant political unpopularity of urban renewal programs in black communities makes it difficult for black mayors to pursue the types of policies most apt to attract private capital to the central city. Equitable redistribution of city services and property tax burdens is similarly fraught with political dangers. Envision a mayor who successfully reallocates city services from the haves to the have-nots: educational resources are assigned to ghetto schools to bring them up to par with the city's best schools; police are transferred from the CBD to high-crime, inner-city neighborhoods, and so forth. Does the quality of life subsequently improve for the lower-income residents of this equitably governed metropolis? The answer is unclear. A city government that offers higher taxes and fewer services to the resident wealthy and local business interests is perceived as a threat to their well-being. If this threat appears to be more than transitory, the powerful and the prosperous will react in ways that may destroy much of the city's economic base. If local government does not cater to the interests of the business community, firms will cut back drastically on their local investment plans. Financial institutions, fearing a contraction in business activity, tighten up on their local lending activities. Firms that had contemplated moving job-generating activities into this locality will be inclined to locate in "friendlier" environs. Many higher-income residents will respond to service cuts and tax increases by moving to suburbia. Outward migration of both residents and economic activity, combined with tight local money markets, will generate declining property values. Declining property values create a need for higher local taxes and/or cuts in services. The city economy spirals downward; local employment opportunities diminish. Thus, even in cities where blacks have achieved political power, improvement programs become hostages to the economic interests of the corporate elite.

Notes

1. The increasing incidence of two-earner families among whites is partially responsible for the downward trend in relative black family incomes. See Charles Brown, "The Federal Attack on Labor Market Discrimination: The Mouse That Roared?" National Bureau of Economic Research Working Paper no. 669 (Cambridge, Mass., Apr. 1981) pp. 2–14, for a discussion of this question.

2. John Reid, "Black America in the 1980s," *Population Bulletin* 37, no. 5:24–25.

3. Cited in Christopher Jencks, "Discrimination and Thomas Sowell," *New York Review of Books* 3 Mar. 1983, p. 36.

4. Occupational figures were taken from U.S. Bureau of the Census, *Current Population Reports,* ser. P-60, 132, table 55 (Washington, D.C.: Government Printing Office, July 192), pp. 192–99. These figures refer to persons eighteen years of age and older as of Mar. 1981; occupation was recorded for all who worked during the 1980 calendar year.

5. Results of this Gallup poll were cited in "Black Statistics: A Look at the Figures on Social Change," *Focus* (Spring 1981):1. A good overview of the employment gains of better-educated blacks appears in Richard Freeman, *Black Elite: The New Market for Qualified Black Americans* (New York: McGraw, 1976), chaps. 6 and 9.

6. National Urban League report, *The State of Black America 1980,* cited in ibid., p. 4.

7. U.S. Bureau of the Census, *Current Population Reports,* ser. P-60, no. 137, table 16 (Washington, D.C.: Government Printing Office, Mar. 1983), pp. 43–46.

8. See, for example, Richard Freeman, "Black Economic Progress Since 1964: Who Has Gained and Why" in *Studies in Labor Markets* ed. Sherwin Rosen (Cambridge, Mass.: National Bureau of Economic Research, 1981), pp. 247–94.

9. Regional breakdowns of relative income trends over time must be done with caution because of incomparability problems between the two groupings, "nonwhite" and "black." Nonwhite and black are often used interchangeably as groupings for describing black income trends; this procedure is invalid when applied to the western United States because trends in nonwhite incomes differ sharply from black income trends. This bias rises due to rapid income gains realized by the sizeable Oriental population that resides in the West. Smaller Oriental populations in other regions of the United States decrease this bias substantially.

10. Studies showing substantial progress in black economic well-being typically focus upon wage and salary earnings only. This approach further distorts trends in *overall* black status, particularly among males, because it neglects the high and rising incidence of zero-wage and salary earners which is much higher than the incidence of black zero-income earners. See, for example, James Smith and Finis Welch, "Race Differences in Earnings: A Survey and New Evidence," in *Current Issues in Urban Economics,* ed. Peter Mieszkowski and Mahlon Straszheim (Baltimore: Johns Hopkins Univ. Pr., 1979), pp. 40–69.

Severe biases arising in relative income studies that exclude the zero-income (or wage) individuals are analyzed in William Darity "Illusions of Black Economic Progress," *Review of Black Political Economy* 10, no. 4 (1980):153–67, and Charles Brown, "Black-White Earnings Ratios Since the Civil Rights Act of 1964: The Importance of Labor Market Drop-outs," National Bureau of Economic Research Working Paper no. 617 (Cambridge, Mass.: National Bureau of Economic Research, Jan. 1981).

11. Michael Reich, *Racial Inequality* (Princeton, N.J.: Princeton Univ. Pr., 1981), p. 65. By 1970, the proportion of southern blacks residing in urban areas had risen to 67.4 percent.

12. Sar Levitan, William Johnson, and Robert Taggert, *Still A Dream. The Changing Status of Blacks Since 1960* (Cambridge, Mass: Harvard Univ. Pr., 1975), p. 24.

13. Ibid., p.26.

14. Improved social security disability benefits have contributed to falling labor force participation rates among black males 45 and older. Older people who have not yet reached retirement age opt for these benefits, because they are poor and unhealthy—not because they are black—according to a study by Donald Parsons, "Racial Trends in Male Labor Force Participation," *American Economic Review* 70, no. 5 (1980):912–14. Blacks disproportionately are recipients of disability benefits. Parsons found, however, that black-white differences in the incidence of benefit recipients were eliminated when health and economic circumstances were controlled for.

15. Before 1970, black teenage labor force participation rates were falling nationally but this was caused largely by the shift out of southern, agricultural work. In nonsouthern areas, participation rates were stable between 1950 and 1970, although unemployment rates were rising. See John Cogan, "The Decline in Black Teenage Employment: 1950–1970," *American Economic Review* 72, no. 4 (1982):621–35.

16. Michael J. Piore, *Birds of Passage* (Cambridge: Cambridge Univ. Pr., 1979), pp. 79–80, 162–63.

17. Reid, "Black America in the 1980s," p. 16.

18. Ibid., p. 21.

19. Ibid., pp. 11–12.

20. Arthur Ross, "The Negro in the American Economy," in *Employment, Race, and Poverty,* ed. Arthur Ross and Herbert Hill (New York: Harcourt, 1967), p. 30.

21. Alan Batchelder, "Decline in the Relative Income of Negro Men," *Quarterly Journal of Economics* 78, no. 4, (1964):525–48.

22. In the Chicago SMSA, for example, white-collar jobs in manufacturing increased from 1950 to 1960, while production jobs decreased in number; on balance, total manufacturing employment declined by approximately three thousand. Black employment in manufacturing declined by about two thousand between 1950 and 1960 in the Chicago: SMSA. See John Kain and John Quigley, *Housing Markets and Racial Discrimination: A Microeconomic Analysis* (New York: National Bureau of Economic Research, 1975), p. 89.

23. See Walter Butcher, "Productivity, Technology and Employment in U.S. Agriculture," in *The Employment Impact of Technology Change, Appendix, Vol. II, Technology and the American Economy,* Report of the National Commission on Technology, Automation, and Economic Progress (Washington, D.C. Government Printing Office, 1966), pp. 135–52.

24. Evidence on this issue is highly conflicting but it points, on balance, to limited suburban job access for the younger and poorer (least mobile) ghetto residents. See Mahlon Straszheim, "Discrimination and Transportation Accessibility in Urban Labor Markets for Black Workers," University of Maryland Project on the Economics of Discrimination (College Park, Md.: Mimeograph, 1979), pp. 10–15, for a good summary of the controversy surrounding this issue.

25. See Batchelder, "Decline in Relative Income," p. 544. A more comprehensive survey known as the "Wirtz Survey" revealed shockingly high rates of ghetto subemployment in 1966. This survey is discussed in Francis Fox Piven and Richard A. Cloward, *Regulating the Poor: The Functions of Public Welfare* (New York: Pantheon, 1971), pp. 215–17.

26. James Geschwender, *Class, Race, and Worker Insurgency* (Cambridge: Cambridge Univ. Pr., 1977), pp. 32–34.

27. Ibid., pp. 41–42.

28. U.S. Bureau of the Census, *Census of Manufacturers 1967,* vol. 3, *Area Statistics* Part 2, Nebraska-Wyoming, (Washington, D.C.: Government Printing Office, 1971), pp. 36–37.

29. Bennett Harrison and Edward Hill, "The Changing Structure of Jobs in Older and Younger Cities," Joint Center for Urban Studies of MIT and Harvard University Working Paper no. 58 (Cambridge, Mass.: Joint Center for Urban Studies of MIT and Harvard University, Mar. 1979), p. 21.

30. Occupation data cited in this section have been calculated from the public use samples of the U.S. Census of Population.

31. Harrison, "Changing Structure," pp. 12–19.

32. Brown, "Federal Attack," p. 9.

33. Levitan, Johnson, and Taggert, "Still a Dream," p. 272.

34. Peter Eisinger, "The Economic Conditions of Black Employment in Municipal Bureaucracies," Institute for Research on Poverty Discussion Paper no. 661–81 (Madison, Wis.: Institute for Research on Poverty, 1981), p. 16.

35. Geschwender, *Class, Race, and Worker Insurgency,* p. 43.

36. Mark Dodosh, "Auto Industry's Moves Jolt Many in Midwest and More Jolts Loom," *Wall Sreet Journal,* 26 May 1981, p. 1.

37. Barry Bluestone and Bennett Harrison, *The Deindustrializaion of America* (New York: Basic Books, 1982), pp. 69–71.

38. Ibid., p. 57.

39. U.S. Bureau of the Census, *Advance Estimates of Social, Economic, and Housing Characteristics—Supplementary Report: Counties and Selected Places* (by state), ser. PHC80-S2 (Washington, D.C.: Government Printing Office, 1983).

40. Harrison and Hill, "Changing Structure," pp. 16–32.

41. "America Rushes to High Tech for Growth," *Business Week* 28 Mar. 1983, p. 86.

42. Total manufacturing employment declined from 26,382,000 in Jan. 1979 to 23,133,000 in Jan. 1983. The emerging consensus on this decline is summarized by Audrey Freeman, senior research associate at the Conference Board: "Employment is going to recover somewhat among production workers, simply because output is going to rise again, but I don't think it will ever reach its former level," in Henry Myers, "Recession Ripples: Economists Say Slump Hastened Some Trends but Spawned Very Few," *Wall Street Journal,* 25 May 1983, p. 1

43. Harrison and Hill, "Changing Structure," pp. 20–26.

44. Reich, *Racial Inequality,* p. 30.

45. Harry Braverman, *Labor and Monopoly Capital* (New York: Monthly Review Pr., 1974), chap. 15.

46. This is documented in Robert Mare and Christopher Winship, "Racial Socioeconomic Convergence and the Paradox of Black Youth Joblessness: Enrollment, Enlistment, and Employment, 1964–1981," University of Chicago Economics Research Center Discussion Paper 83–14, (Chicago, July 1983).

47. Timothy Schellhardt, "North Central U.S. Surpasses South in Black Poverty Rate," *Wall Street Journal* 9 Aug. 1983, p. 35.

48. Richard Child Hill, "Fiscal Collapse and Political Struggle in Decaying Central cities in the United States," in *Marxism and the Metropolis,* ed. William Tabb and Larry Sawers (New York: Oxford Univ. Pr., 1978) pp. 226–28.

49. For an excellent case study of this phenomenon, see Chester Hartman and Rob Kessler, "The Illusion and Reality of Urban Renewal: San Francisco's Yerba Buena Center," in *Marxism and the Metropolis,* ed. William Tabb and Larry Sawers (New York: Oxford Univ. Pr., 1978), pp. 153–78.

Part VIII *Key Terms and Essay/Discussion Questions*

KEY TERMS

Economic exploitation

Racism

Capitalism

Culture of control

Planter class

Poor whites

Sharecropping

A. Phillip Randolph

Brotherhood of Sleeping Car Porters

Fair Employment Practice Committee

"Negro jobs"

Working class

Equal Employment Opportunity Commission

Urban migration

ESSAY/DISCUSSION QUESTIONS

1. How did the demand for African labor as the unpaid workforce for plantation slavery simultaneously provide the motivation for the development of institutional racism and set in motion the formation of the black community in the United States?

2. How did the Atlantic slave trade contribute to the rise of industrial capitalism in Western Europe?

3. How did the slave trade and chattel slavery provide the foundation for the development of colonial America's political economy?

4. How did the white planter class control poor and non-slave-holding whites in the South?

5. Baron argues that chattel slavery was more than an economic arrangement; it was a system of cultural domination and control. Discuss.

6. As black people migrated from the agrarian South to the industrial North around the turn of the century, they were confronted with the racism, fear, and terrorism of urban working-class whites. Discuss the causes and consequences of racial antagonism within America's emerging urban industrial economy. How was this racism an extension of America's slave past, and how did both of these conditions help to shape an emerging black working class and economic instability within urban black communities?

7. Daniel Fusfeld and Timothy Bates suggest that a major trend in the last few decades has been the economic polarization of the African American community. What is the nature of this polarization, and what are some of its causes and possible consequences?

8. What factors seem to be contributing to a growing discontent among many young urban African Americans? What role should

government play to improve the life chances of low-income urban African Americans? What are some of the historical and contemporary societal forces that hinder large-scale black entrepreneurial efforts?

9. The American economy seems to be experiencing a transition from an industrial-manufacturing base in the first half of the twentieth century to a service-knowledge base in the second half. What are possible implications of this economic transformation for African Americans? What is the significance of education in the emerging economy?

Part VIII *Supplementary Readings*

Anderson, Elijah, "Race and Neighborhood Transition," in Paul E. Peterson, ed., *The New Urban Reality,* Washington, D. C.: The Brookings Institution, 1985, pp. 99–127.

Braddock, Jomillis H. II, and James M. McPartland, "How Minorities Continue to Be Excluded from Equal Employment Opportunities: Research on Labor Market and Institutional Barriers," *Journal of Social Issues,* Vol. 43, No. 1 (1987), pp. 5–39.

Brown, Michael K., and Stephen P. Erie, "Blacks and the Legacy of the Great Society: The Economic and Political Impact of Federal Social Policy," *Public Policy,* Vol. 29 (Summer 1981), pp. 299–330.

Bunche, Ralph J., "A Critique of New Deal Social Planning As It Affects Negroes," *Journal of Negro Education,* Vol. 5 (January 1936), pp. 59–65.

Clark, Kenneth B., *Dark Ghetto: Dilemmas of Social Power,* New York: Harper and Row, Publishers, 1965.

Danziger, Sheldon H., and Daniel H. Weinberg, eds., *Fighting Poverty: What Works and What Doesn't,* Cambridge: Harvard University Press, 1986.

Darity, William A., Jr., ed., *Labor Economics: Modern Views,* Boston: Kluwer-Nijhoff, 1984.

———, "Reaganomics and the Black Community," in Sidney Weintraub and Marvin Goodstein, eds., *Reaganomics in the Stagflation Economy,* Philadelphia: University of Pennsylvania Press, 1983, pp. 59–77.

———, and Samuel Myers, Jr., "Does Welfare Dependency Cause Female Headship?: The Case of the Black Family," *Journal of Marriage and the Family,* Vol. 46 (November 1984), pp. 765–780.

Du Bois, W. E. B., *The Philadelphia Negro: A Social Study,* New York: Benjamin Blom, 1967.

Erie, Steven P., "Public Policy and Black Economic Polarization," *Policy Analysis,* Vol. 6 (Summer 1980), pp. 305–318.

Farley, Reynolds, *Blacks and Whites: Narrowing the Gap?* Cambridge: Harvard University Press, 1984.

Foner, Philip S., *Organized Labor and the Black Worker, 1619–1973,* New York: International Publishers, 1974.

Franklin, Raymond, and Solomon Resnik, *The Political Economy of Racism,* New York: Holt, Rinehart and Winston, Inc., 1973.

Gill, Gerald, *Meanness Mania: The Changed Mood,* Washington, D. C.: Howard University Press, 1980.

Glasgow, Douglas G., *The Black Underclass: Poverty, Unemployment, and Entrapment of Ghetto Youth,* San Francisco: Jossey-Bass Publishers, 1980.

Gould, William B., *Black Workers in White Unions: Job Discrimination in the United States,* Ithaca: Cornell University Press, 1977.

Greene, Lorenzo, and Carter G. Woodson, *The Negro Wage Earner,* Washington, D. C.: Associated Publishers, 1930.

Grossman, James R., *Land Of Hope: Chicago, Black Southerners, and the Great Migration,* Chicago: The University of Chicago Press, 1989.

Hayes, Floyd W. III, "The Political Economy, Reaganomics, and Blacks," *The Western Journal of Black Studies,* Vol. 6, No. 2 (Summer 1982), pp. 89–97.

Hill, Robert B., "The Illusion of Black Economic Progress," *Social Policy,* Vol. 9, No. 3 (November-December 1978), pp. 14–25.

Jones, Barbara A., "Black Women and Labor Force Participation: An Analysis of Sluggish Growth Rates," *Review of Black Political Economy,* Vol. 14, No. 2-3 (Fall–Winter, 1985–1986), pp. 11–31.

Jones, Faustine C., *The Changing Mood in America: Eroding Commitment?,* Washington, D. C.: Howard University Press, 1977.

Jones, Jacqueline, *The Dispossessed: America's Underclasses from the Civil War to the Present,* New York: Basic Books, 1992.

Kasarda, John D., "Urban Change and Minority Opportunities," in Paul E. Peterson, ed., *The New Urban Reality,* Washington, D. C.: The Brookings Institution, 1985, pp. 33–67.

Kerner, Otto, *Report of the National Advisory Commission on Civil Disorders,* Washington, D. C.: U. S. Government Printing Office, 1968.

Kotlowitz, Alex, *There Are No Children Here,* New York: Doubleday, 1991.

Landry, Bart, *The New Black Middle Class,* Berkeley: University of California Press, 1987.

Lemann, Nicholas, *The Promised Land: The Great Migration and How It Changed America,* New York: Alfred A. Knopf, 1991.

Marable, Manning, *How Capitalism Underdeveloped Black America: Problems in Race, Political Economy and Society,* Boston: South End Press, 1983.

Maxwell, Joan P., *No Easy Answers: Persistent Poverty in the Metropolitan Washington Area,* Washington, D. C.: Greater Washington Research Center, 1985.

Mead, Lawrence M., *The New Politics of Poverty: The Nonworking Poor in America,* New York: Basic Books, 1992.

_____, *Beyond Entitlement: The Social Obligations of Citizenship,* New York: The Free Press, 1986.

Meier, August, and Elliot M. Rudwick, *From Plantation to Ghetto: An Interpretive History of American Negroes,* New York: Hill and Wan, 1966.

Murray, Charles, *Losing Ground: American Social Policy 1950–1980,* New York: Basic Books, 1984.

Ofari, Earl, *The Myth of Black Capitalism,* New York: Monthly Review Press, 1970.

Perlo, Victor, *Economics of Racism: Roots of Black Inequality,* New York: International Publishers, 1975.

Pinkney, Alphonso, *The Myth of Black Progress,* New York: Cambridge University Press, 1984.

Quincey, Richard, *Class, State, and Crime,* New York: Longman Inc., 1977.

Ransom, Roger L., and Richard Sutch, *One Kind of Freedom: The Economic Consequences of Emancipation,* New York: Cambridge University Press, 1977.

Reich, Michael, *Racial Inequality: A Political-Economic Analysis,* Princeton: Princeton University Press, 1981.

Reich, Robert, *The Work of Nations: Preparing Ourselves for 21st-Century Capitalism,* New York: Alfred A. Knopf, 1991.

Reiman, Jeffrey, *The Rich Get Richer and the Poor Get Prison: Ideology, Class, and Criminal Justice,* New York: John Wiley and Sons, 1979.

Shulman, Steven, and William Darity, Jr., eds., *The Question of Discrimination: Racial Inequality in the U. S. Labor Market,* Middletown: Wesleyan University Press, 1989.

Smith, James P., and Finis R. Welch, *Closing the Gap: Forty Years of Economic Progress for Blacks,* Santa Monica: The RAND Corporation, 1986.

Sowell, Thomas, *Knowledge and Decisions,* New York: Basic Books, 1980.

Spero, Sterling D., and Abram L. Harris, *The Black Worker: The Negro and the Labor Movement,* New York: Columbia University Press, 1931.

Starobin, Robert S., *Industrial Slavery in the Old South,* New York: Oxford University Press, 1970.

Steidlmeier, Paul, *The Paradox of Poverty: A Reappraisal of Economic Development Policy,* Cambridge: Ballinger Publishing Company, 1987.

Tidwell, Billy J., *Playing to Win: A Marshall Plan for America,* New York: National Urban League, Inc., 1991.

Valentine, Charles A., *Culture and Poverty: Critique and Counter-Proposals,* Chicago: The University of Chicago Press, 1968.

Westcott, Diane N., "Blacks in the 1970s: Did They Scale the Job Ladder?," *Monthly Labor Review,* Vol. 105, No. 6 (June 1982), pp. 29–38.

Wilhelm, Sidney, *Who Needs the Negro?,* Cambridge: Schenkman Publishing Company, Inc., 1970.

Williams, Eric, *Capitalism and Slavery,* Chapel Hill: University of North Carolina Press, 1944.

Willie, Charles V., ed., *The Caste and Class Controversy,* New York: General Hall Inc., 1979.

Wilson, William J., *The Truly Disadvantaged: The Inner City, the Underclass, and Public Policy,* Chicago: The University of Chicago Press, 1987.

_____, *The Declining Significance of Race: Blacks and Changing American Institutions,* Chicago: The University of Chicago Press, 1978.

Yette, Samuel, *The Choice: The Issue of Black Survival,* New York: G. P. Putnam's Sons, 1971.

Politics and the African American Experience

The political history of African America can be characterized as the long-standing struggle for human rights, social development, and collective survival. The historic battle has been to dislodge and dismantle the Euro-American system of cultural domination that has constrained and controlled the life experiences of African Americans. Initially set in motion during colonial American development, the dehumanizing system of domination was institutionalized in the forms of the trans-Atlantic slave trade, chattel slavery, segregation, and racism. From the outset, Euro-American slave traders and slaveowners defined Africans and their American descendants as a class of sub-humanity to make them ashamed of their cultural heritage; destabilized and destroyed African families and social structures in the scramble for slaves; made literacy and the formal education of slaves a criminal offense; exploited slave labor to achieve enormous economic profits and wealth; and denied chattel slaves all political rights and protection of the law. Even the relatively small proportion of pre-Civil War "free" African Americans possessed few rights, and so were often the victims of dehumanizing and ambivalent circumstances.

Each generation of African Americans has fought against the impact of the dehumanization process. However, because the negative image of African Americans is so deeply embedded in American culture, thought, and institutional practices, the

African American struggle for human rights, social development, and collective survival has experienced contradictions
and dilemmas.

The essays in this section explore the relationship between
the American system of power and politics and the African
American effort to engage that system.

In his essay, "Democratic Politics and Black Subordination,"
Milton D. Morris argues that four factors help explain the
persistence of African American subordination. First, the establishment of the American nation-state was flawed because the
American revolution actually was extremely superficial, leaving
the colonial society fundamentally unchanged, and because
the founders of the American political system and the U.S.
Constitution protected the slave trade and chattel slavery.
Second, because of fear, economic necessity, and imperialist
desires, white Americans developed and used racist ideologies
to justify the subordination of African Americans. Third,
Jacksonian or mass democracy served not to expand African
American political participation but to further limit it. Finally,
federalism and the traditional view of the minimalist role to
be played by the federal government enhanced the power of
state governments to control and constrain African American
political and social development.

"Blacks and the Politics of Redemption," by Mary F. Berry and
John W. Blassingame, describes the historic African American
struggle to gain political rights and to participate in the American
political process from the pre-Civil War period to the end of the
1970s. Chattel slaves, of course, were denied all political rights,
but, the authors show, "free" African Americans also were for the
most part politically powerless, even when they had the right to
vote for a short period prior to the Civil War. When, in 1863
during the Civil War, President Lincoln issued the Emancipation
Proclamation, African Americans began to support the Republican
party. The presidential administration following Lincoln's, that
of Andrew Johnson, attempted to reject policies and programs
designed to improve the conditions of former slaves. A decade
of radical Reconstruction followed, during which time Congress
passed the thirteenth, fourteenth, and fifteenth amendments to
the Constitution, freeing former slaves and giving them citizenship
and voting rights. Berry and Blassingame indicate that African
Americans gained a measure of political authority in some southern state legislatures. However, with the collapse of Reconstruction,
the white South reconsolidated its power and, until well into the

twentieth century, terrorized and disenfranchised African Americans. While the 1896 Supreme Court ruling in *Plessy* v. *Ferguson* legalized racial segregation in the South, regions outside the South also customarily practiced the racial exclusion of African Americans.

As African Americans migrated to the urban north and mid-west during the early twentieth century, they gradually shifted political allegiance from the Republican to the Democratic party. President Franklin D. Roosevelt, who had been elected in 1932, was the major catalyst for this shift. Throughout the 1930s, various African American leaders, including black nationalist Marcus Garvey and educator Mary McCleod Bethune, supported the Roosevelt administration, which resulted in growing African American support for the Democratic party. African Americans also gained some political strength in big city politics, but, as Berry and Blassingame point out, Democratic party allegiance did not prevent racial discrimination against African American workers and soldiers. Moreover, southern Democrats continued to constrain African American political participation.

From the 1940s to the 1960s, African Americans engaged in an assortment of legal and political strategies and tactics calcu-lated to terminate America's system of apartheid. Berry and Blassingame show that organizational protests and legal battles began to chip away at segregation policies and practices. The monumental 1954 *Brown* v. *Board of Education* Supreme Court decision, followed by new civil rights legislation in the late 1950s and 1960s, helped to galvanize civil rights organizations and activities in the early 1960s. In the South, hostile white citizens and even law enforcement personnel terrorized and murdered African American and white civil rights workers, who were engaged in nonviolent demonstrations and voter registration campaigns. The Johnson administration brought out the military to protect civil rights workers. Also, Johnson began to appoint a growing number of African Americans to federal govern-ment positions.

However, as Barry and Blassingame indicate, the South's continued terrorism of nonviolent civil rights demonstrations and the murder of civil rights leader Martin Luther King, Jr., in 1968, angered northern African Americans, many of whom were living in increasingly impoverished urban communities. As the civil rights movement reached its limits in the mid-1960s, African Americans revolted in northern cities across the nation. Moreover, some organizations embraced black nationalist ideology and rejected the integrationist orientation of civil rights organizations and leaders. Berry and Blassingame show that African American participation in electoral politics rose dramatically, which increased the numbers of elected and appointed African American officials in city and national government. However, the emergence of these politicians and administrators did not appear to increase their policymaking influence or to empower the African American masses.

Democratic Politics and Black Subordination

MILTON D. MORRIS

HEN AMERICANS CELEBRATE THE Fourth of July they commemorate much more than the birth of another sovereign state. Firmly rooted in the lore of America is the conviction that they celebrate the birth of "modern democratic government." Precisely what democracy meant in this context was not entirely clear to the founders of the nation and even now remains somewhat murky. Motivated by the views of European political philosophers like John Locke, these early Americans attempted to fashion a system of government based upon two fundamental tenets: (1) The equality of individuals in the society as far as rights and obligations were concerned; and (2) the limited character of governmental power with respect to the individual. To a considerable extent these themes—equality and liberty—inspired and justified rebellion from Britain and have remained the central elements of the American political culture.

If, as Donald Devine suggests, political culture "is a historical system of widespread, fundamental, behavioral, political values actually held by system members,"[1] it is one of the profound ironies of history that a society

deeply committed to these "democratic values" created and maintained the subordinate-superordinate structure [seen in relations between blacks and whites]. Such a pattern of social organization is obviously in sharp conflict with these democratic values, or what Gunnar Myrdal labelled the "democratic creed." Examination of the black political experience requires that we consider this peculiarity in American culture and try to determine what factors contributed to the development and persistence of this pattern of subordinate-superordinate relations between blacks and whites in the society.

This inquiry inevitably begins with the observation that "racism" also has been an important part of the American political culture. In this context, racism is not being used merely as another odious epithet, but as a concept denoting a set of attitudes and beliefs that affect virtually all aspects of social relations. Pierre van den Berghe defines it as

> . . . any set of beliefs that organic, genetically transmitted differences (whether real or imagined) between human groups are intrinsically associated with the presence or absence of certain socially relevant abilities or characteristics, hence that such differences are a legitimate basis for invidious distinctions between groups socially defined as races.[2]

This racism is a pervasive and deep-rooted attitude that is at least as old as the first meetings of blacks and whites on the continent. To an extent it goes beyond the purely black-white encounter in America and can be viewed as part of a larger "disease" of cultural chauvinism which the colonists brought with them from Europe. Contempt by the colonists for the native Americans, and their early desire to Christianize them, and failing in that to exterminate them, reflects this larger cultural chauvinism. Racism can be viewed as the most visible and persistent manifestation of white America's cultural chauvinism. The extent to which it permeates American society is suggested by Joel Kovel's observation that "racism, far from being the simple delusion of a bigoted and ignorant minority, is a set of beliefs whose structure arises from the deepest levels of our lives—from the fabric of assumptions we make about the world, ourselves and others and from patterns of our fundamental social actions."[3]

Racism prompted creation and maintenance of the subordinate-superordinate structure of the society. It has had important and continuing consequences for the place accorded blacks in the political system, the distribution of goods and services by the system and, in some respects, the very structure of the political system itself. The extent of this impact is reflected throughout this survey of the black political experience but the distinction suggested by Carmichael and Hamilton between "individual" and "institutional"

racism helps to clarify its total impact.[4] One involves overt acts of hostility by individual whites against blacks and their property, while the other involves the operation of established and respected institutions in society. Knowles and Prewitt further illustrate the two types by observing that

> The murder by Ku Klux Klan members and law enforcement officials of three civil rights workers in Mississippi was an act of individual racism. That the sovereign state of Mississippi refused to indict the killers was institutional racism. The individual act by racist bigots went unpunished in Mississippi because of policies, precedents, and practices that are an integral part of that state's legal institutions.[5]

Instances of institutional racism, of course, are not confined to a few states or to legal institutions but embrace virtually every level and area of political life in the society.

THE ORIGINS OF BLACK SUBORDINATION

The Kerner Commission reported in 1968 that American society was "rapidly moving toward two societies—one black, one white, separate and unequal."[6] This characterization of American society was appropriate then except for one important flaw. America is not in the process of *becoming* two societies; it has always been two separate and unequal societies. The structure of black subordination took shape with the gradual emergence of the institution of slavery within a relatively short time after the first European settlers appeared. Students of American slavery have identified several factors that encouraged its growth, the most prominent of them being economics. In addition to its economic aspect, slavery clearly served as an effective instrument of social control, providing a permanent, highly visible, legally supported mechanism for black subordination.

Not all blacks in America were slaves. In 1790 there were about 60,000 blacks in the country who were not slaves, and by 1860 this

It was on just such a segregated bus that Rosa Parks took a seat up front, refused to move, and took her place in the history books.

number had grown to over 485,000.[7] All blacks, however, both slaves and nonslaves, became victims of the status ordering provided by slavery. Nonslaves shared the subordinate status of the slave, thus these people, often called "free Negroes," were never really free but were trapped by their color in an offensive and humiliating form of subordination. This fact about American slavery was emphasized by John Woolman, an early Quaker opponent of the institution, who pointed out that the system of racial slavery was unique and particularly sinister because slavery had come to be associated with black color and liberty with white.[8]

Black subordination through the institution of slavery was legitimized by a complex array of laws and customs designed to ensure the dehumanization of all blacks or at least establish their inferiority to whites. The laws of the land defined slaves as "chattel" rather than "persons" and imposed severe constraints on every area of the lives of all blacks, notably marriage and family relations, movement and assembly, education, religious practice and interpersonal relations within and across racial lines. This form of institutionalized subordination persisted unimpeded until 1863, when the exigencies of civil strife forced its termination.

Societal attitudes and values are persistent. They are not swept away by hasty and half-hearted decrees; thus while the Civil War destroyed the formal institution of slavery, it left largely untouched the basic status-ordering of the society. Slavery was an efficient means of maintaining black subordination but it was not indispensable to the preservation of this condition. In fact, in the Northern states where slavery hardly existed, blacks remained thoroughly and effectively subordinated by law and custom as both slaveholders and non-slaveholders shared a common perception of them. Abraham Lincoln, later the president whose executive order freed the slaves and who often has been lauded as the liberator of black people, apparently reflected the general consensus with his commitment to preservation of the subordinate status of blacks as this assertion in 1858 suggests:

> I will say, then, that I am not, nor ever have been, in favor of bringing about in any way the social and political equality of the white and black races . . . and while they [blacks and whites] do remain together there must be the position of superior and inferior, and I as much as any other man am in favor of having the superior position assigned to the white race.[9]

Much has been written about the continuing consequences of slavery, such as its destruction of the social and cultural values of the black population and the deep psychological scars it has left on them,[10] but its most far-reaching impact on black political life may be the permanent relegation of blacks to a lower status than whites. So profound was its impact that many blacks for a long time perceived themselves as inferiors, and white Americans accepted as natural and desirable this subordinate status for blacks.

After the total abolition of slavery by the Thirteenth Amendment in 1865, new devices were utilized to maintain the subordinate status of blacks. The "Black Codes," a harsh series of laws passed immediately after the Civil War, virtually reimposed total slavery and were employed to maintain full control over the black population. Partly as a result of these laws, Congress intervened to restrain white Southerners in these excesses and to alleviate the hardship on blacks. Later terroristic activities by whites, a series of laws and constitutional changes, and the economic vulnerability of blacks combined to ensure their continued subordination. Over the years since the Civil War substantial changes have occurred in the techniques by which black subordination is maintained. Although the more visibly offensive aspects of this subordination have been gradually removed, the basic subordinate-superordinate structure remains.

The perception of blacks as belonging to a lower status than whites is so deeply a part of the cultural heritage of Americans that it continues to operate even though many whites appear to have intellectually rejected the old thesis of "Negro inferiority." A 1963 opinion survey by William Brink and Louis Harris revealed the deep continuing prejudice toward blacks among white Americans. Sixty-six percent of them still thought blacks were less ambitious than whites, 60 percent thought they smelled different, 55 percent thought they had looser morals, and 41 percent thought they wanted to live by handouts.[11] A more recent empirical study by Angus Campbell further documents this pattern of white attitudes and clarifies for us the character of these attitudes. He reports that

> White Americans are racist in degree. Some would like to keep the black man in his place, send him back to Africa if necessary. Most would not go that far but many would oppose legislation that would bring Negroes closer, especially into their neighborhoods. Some white people give verbal approval to equalitarian principles as they apply to race but they are disturbed by the pace of change in race relations which they see going on around them. Finally, there is a minority of the white population who seem to have no

apparent racist orientation, who are sympathetic to the various aspects of the black protest, and in some cases contribute support to it.[12]

Black subordination in American society long has been viewed as inconsistent with the ringing assertion of the Declaration of Independence that "we hold these truths to be self-evident, that all men are created equal, that they are endowed by their Creator with certain unalienable Rights, that among these are Life, Liberty, and the Pursuit of Happiness." Well before the doctrines of liberty and equality fueled the sparks of rebellion among the American colonists, opponents of slavery like the Quakers emphasized the contradiction between the institution of slavery and the Christian beliefs of the European settlers.[13] By the time of the break with Britain in 1776, a group of philosophers, the environmentalists, went beyond the religious and moral arguments of the Quakers to stress the flagrant discrepancy between the stated commitment of Americans to liberty and equality and the realities of human bondage in the form of slavery.[14] With even greater passion, the "black abolitionists" utilized all of these arguments against the subordination of the race and urged not only an end to slavery but the granting of the full rights of free people to blacks. Frederick Douglass' celebrated Fourth of July oration succinctly expressed the abolitionist feeling:

> Americans! your republican politics, not less than your republican religion, are flagrantly inconsistent. You boast of your love of liberty, your superior civilization and your pure christianity, while the whole political power of the nation as embodied in the two great political parties, is solemnly pledged to support and perpetuate the enslavement of three million of your countrymen.[15]

These are essentially the same themes that have dominated the twentieth-century struggle for change in the subordinate status of black Americans. They were invoked by revolutionaries like Monroe Trotter at the turn of the century;[16] they were articulately formulated by Myrdal in 1945 in his description of white America's "moral dilemma." These themes were again echoed by Martin Luther King and the hosts of activists in the civil rights movement of the 1950s–1960s. The discrepancy between the bold commitments to liberty and equality and the subordination of blacks has been central to the black political experience, and has been a persistent theme in the struggle for change. This anomaly has been described more often than it has been explained. While we cannot here attempt to unravel the complex array of factors that have contributed to the persistence of black subordination in American society despite apparently conflicting beliefs, it is necessary and appropriate that we examine some of these factors. Among those that are of particular significance are (1) the peculiar circumstances surrounding the birth of the nation, (2) emergence of an ideology of racism, (3) the impact of democratic ideology and the democratization process, (4) the consequences of a federal system.

THE BIRTH OF THE NATION AND BLACK SUBORDINATION

The American revolution which resulted in the birth of an American nation is now one of the most celebrated revolutionary episodes of all time. The event is so thoroughly shrouded in myth and sentiment that it is rarely critically evaluated, and then hardly ever in terms of its implications for black people. However, some of the more careful students of the event provide important insights into why it left untouched the elaborate institution of black subordination, slavery. They suggest that (1) in contrast to the gigantic social upheavals accompanying other revolutions, the American revolution was an extremely superficial one that did not fundamentally alter the society, and (2) the revolution was not guided by a potent and far-reaching set of new values but by limited economic self-interest. In a brief but insightful analysis, Pierre van den Berghe suggests that the break with Britain and the establishment of a republic were not the bold revolutionary steps most historians suggest. On the contrary, the much romanticized revolution "was in fact a movement of political emancipation by a section of the white settlers against England."[17] The eminent American historian Daniel Boorstin also concludes that the American revolution was hardly a revolution, "it was one of the few conservative colonial rebellions of modern time."[18]

These analyses do not ignore the existence of genuinely revolutionary sentiment among the colonists; rather they suggest that those revolutionary sentiments did not give primary impetus to the revolution. This impetus came from the economic interests of a group of wealthy settlers. The revolutionaries such as Sam Adams and Tom Paine were vital instruments but were never the decisive influences on the revolution. The implications of these observations are significant. Because of the conservative and superficial character of the revolution, there was no major social upheaval that substantially altered the patterns of thought and practice that developed during the colonial era. In fact, the revolution left most Americans untouched and even indifferent to the event, and their values and institutions remained intact.

One basic reason for the conservative character of the revolution and the superficiality of its impact is that the American colonies were not oppressed, "colonial societies." In sharp contrast to the experience of the nonwhite peoples of Asia, Africa and the Caribbean, they were not subjected to systematic exploitation by a "foreign power." The government holding final authority was distant, but not alien and was generally protective and benevolent rather than oppressive. The principal sources of discontent in the colonies were a few radical intellectuals

and the Eastern merchants and traders. The genuinely oppressed, the slaves, were only peripheral to the revolt.

Instead of introducing a genuinely new equalitarian set of values, the much celebrated Declaration of Independence presented primarily a rationale for rebellion. Boorstin notes the sharp contrast between the United States Declaration of Independence and the French Declaration of the Rights of Man and the Citizen. The American document, he suggests, was "situation-specific" and drew heavily upon the Whig theory of the British revolution of 1688, in sharp contrast to the broad sweep of the French document and its exposition of new and fundamental principles.[19] It is not surprising, therefore, that such a revolution left a culture of religious bigotry and racism intact, and that its principal instrument served as a document to which people referred vaguely, without a need to fully implement its principles. Whatever freedom or liberty was achieved by the American revolution was confined to whites only. In one of the many ironies of black political life in America, a black man, Crispus Attucks, was the first casualty in the struggle for independence—for freedom that excluded black people. Minor outcroppings of rage notwithstanding, slaves retained their shackles and other blacks continued in their awkward state of limbo, neither slave nor free.

In what became a pattern in the development of the American political system, the birth of the nation involved a compromise perpetuating slavery. Thomas Jefferson's first draft of a Declaration of Independence contained a strong indictment of slavery as an immoral institution inflicted on Americans because of Britain's greed. Some other delegates also shared Jefferson's discomfort with slavery, but before the document could be approved, denunciation of slavery had to be deleted. So fervent was the commitment to the enslavement of blacks in some colonies that the issue threatened to obstruct agreement on a declaration of independence. As Jefferson wrote later, "Southern states wanted to continue slavery," and "[our] Northern brethren, though their people had very few slaves themselves, yet they had been pretty considerable carriers of them themselves."[20] With this compromise the ground was laid for the strange coexistence between a dedication to freedom and equality on the one hand and a commitment to racial oppression and subordination on the other.

The founders of the Federal Republic in 1789 gave further strength to this contradiction. In drafting what often has been hailed as a great charter of modern democratic government, they took care specifically to protect the institution of slavery. Although they refused to sully the document with use of the word "slave," their deliberations included the issue of slavery. The learned men, perhaps the most august gathering of Americans up to that time, debated the nature of the slave—whether he is a "person" or "property." None other than James Madison concluded of the slave that "they partake of both these qualities, being considered by our laws, in some respects as persons, and in other respects as property. . . . The Federal Constitution, therefore, decides with great propriety on the case of our slaves, when it views them in the mixed character of persons and of property."[21] By tacit agreement they refused to examine the implications of slavery for the principles they so fervently embraced. Instead the slave, dealt with in the context of representation and taxation for the Southern states, became the subject of one of the great compromises of the Constitutional Convention.

Because slaves were considered "property" and not "persons," the Northern states refused to have them included in the "population" of the South when computing representation among the states. On the other hand they insisted that they all be counted in computing the taxes for these states. The South took

the opposite position whereupon both sides agreed, after a long stalemate, that five slaves would be counted as three persons for both representation and taxation. This agreement, known as the "Three-fifths Compromise," resolved one of the major controversies of the Constitutional Convention and at the same time represented an endorsement of "a less than human" status of blacks.

Treatment of the issue of slavery by the Constitutional Convention further illustrates the limited extent to which concepts such as liberty and equality influenced creation of the political system. Aside from the Three-fifths Compromise, the Constitution went on to explicitly protect the slave trade for at least twenty years, protected the traders from import taxes of more than $10, and by requiring a two-thirds majority in the Senate to ratify treaties, protected slavery from the President's treaty-making powers. The Constitution, van den Berghe points out, was essentially a compact between a Northern bourgeoisie and a Southern slave-owning aristocracy, and more than anything else it was designed to protect the interests of these two groups.[22] This interpretation is consistent with Charles Beard's classic economic interpretation of the Constitution. Beard concludes that the Founding Fathers were motivated more by their own economic interests and a desire to ensure economic prosperity than by a desire to protect democratic and humanitarian values.[23] Richard Hofstadter's analysis goes even further, pointing out that while the Founding Fathers were advocates of liberty, they were not committed to the modern conception of democracy, but to property.[24] Thus their principal objective was to protect property rights rather than extend liberty to those most in need of it. Furthermore, since any change in the status of blacks threatened the economic well-being of the wealthy, political values were formulated and articulated in such a manner as to ensure continued black subordination.

THE IDEOLOGY OF RACISM AS A SOURCE OF BLACK SUBORDINATION

We have suggested that black subordination which began prior to the Declaration of Independence continued undisturbed afterward because of the superficiality of the revolution and the essentially limited economic aims of the national leaders. Even among those who perceived an uncomfortable inconsistency between the values espoused by the Declaration of Independence and the new Constitution, an array of circumstances compelled a rationalization of the inconsistency and eventually a repudiation of some of those values. Eventually black subordination ceased to be something which white Americans apologetically supported. It became a positive good justified by an ideology of racism. The forces contributing to this shift are several, but three were particularly prominent: (1) economic necessity, (2) fear, and (3) the imperialist impulse.

For a long time the economic benefits of slavery were modest. In fact it even appeared unprofitable in some slave states and declining in value. Eli Whitney's invention of the cotton gin in 1794 dramatically altered this by sharply increasing the demand for cotton and in turn the need for slave labor on cotton plantations throughout the South. This major industrial innovation suddenly made any thought of changing the status of blacks grossly inconsistent with the economic interests of the society. Slavery became so inextricably related to the new economic prosperity that to an increasing number of people the abolitionist arguments became almost irresponsible. Once-timid apologists of slavery quickly began to find arguments asserting its necessity, desirability, and even its righteousness.

The link between slavery and "unopposed capitalism" has been frequently emphasized, perhaps most effectively so by Stanley Elkins, who argues persuasively that the institution of slavery and its uniquely brutal and totally dehumanizing practice in the United States were direct consequences of unbridled capitalism.[25] Looking back at this period, W. E. B. Du Bois asserts that "once slavery began to be the source of vast income for men and nations, there followed a frantic search for moral and racial justifications. Such excuses were found and men did not inquire too carefully into either their logic or truth."[26]

A second and equally potent factor in seeking new rationalizations for the oppression and enslavement of blacks was fear. White Americans had always been fearful of the seething black slave population and the prospect that it might one day rise up and destroy its oppressor. This fear lay behind many of the stringent rules affecting the slave as well as the black nonslave populations of many states. By the early 1800s there was new cause for even more widespread fear among whites. Throughout the Caribbean and in the several slave states, slaves resorted to violence to liberate themselves. The first and most dramatic fruit of these revolts was the birth of the Republic of Haiti. In 1804 the black slave population of that French colony, led by Pierre Dominique Toussaint L'Ouverture, erupted in revolutionary violence to overthrow French rule and establish a black Republic. Gruesome accounts of this and several less dramatic but equally significant uprisings throughout the Caribbean were widely reported in the American press.

These events had an enormous impact on white Americans. As Winthrop Jordan observes, "To trace the spread of Negro rebellion in the New World and to examine American responses to what they saw as a mounting tide of danger is to watch the drastic erosion of the ideology of the American Revolution."[27] Several states responded by attempting to isolate their slave population from the infectious urge for liberty and the revolutionary impulse it produced. They enacted severe restrictions on the importation of "Negroes" and prohibited entry to "West Indian Negroes" over 15 years of age. Most significantly, they came increasingly to view the association of liberty with the black population as dangerous. White society would be safer if there were no "careless talk" about the rights of black people.

The recognition that the desire for liberty was contagious, and among the black population represented a threat to the domestic tranquility, became a crucial issue in white attitudes toward blacks. It was heightened by relatively small outbreaks within the United States. The uprisings led by Gabriel Prosser in 1800, by Denmark Vesey in 1822, and by Nat Turner in 1831 seemed to confirm these fears and to prolong them. It did not really matter that the revolts were relatively minor or that the Haitian situation had no parallel in the United States. The fear that blacks would seek their liberty at all costs became a major justification for maintaining their bondage. Although slaves were perceived as the principal threats, all black people, including freedmen, came to constitute a danger. They were increasingly subjected to rigid controls, and denied freedom of movement and freedom to participate in political life.

White fear of blacks is not confined to these early years; over time it has been a strong force in shaping white attitudes toward blacks, and in influencing the style and content of white politics. Even now it constitutes one of the principal bases of white hostility to black efforts at changing their lot in society. It played a large part in the development of one-party politics in the South and was almost the only issue in Southern politics for generations. Its impact is equally pervasive outside the South, as indicated by the pattern of responses to the varied expressions of black discontent during the 1960s—such as the burning of decayed ghettos—or the black power concept and demands for economic and social changes. Only an overpowering or what Holden terms "pathological" fear explains such bizarre twists in American politics as the enormous popularity achieved

by George Wallace as a candidate for President in 1972 and which he retains even at this writing. Although a relatively successful governor in his state, Wallace's national popularity rests primarily on a flagrant defiance of the law in his effort to prevent a black student from registering at the University of Alabama and his skill in capitalizing on white fears by resurrecting racism as a "respectable" theme in American national politics. These contemporary manifestations of fear by whites make it easy to grasp the nineteenth-century passion to suppress and control the black population both slave and free.

Important changes were also occurring at that time in national attitudes toward the entire question of slavery when it emerged as a major national controversy in 1819 with debate over the Missouri territory. Northerners, for practical and political reasons, resisted further expansion of slavery into new territory while the South championed such expansion. The Missouri Compromise temporarily resolved this national crisis but it further contributed to a militant, proslavery attitude among Southerners and hastened widespread indulgence in the elaborate ideology of racism that developed to justify not only slavery but the subordination of all black people. Slavery was justified as humane and consistent with the "inferiority of the Negro race." Biblical arguments were adduced showing that the black race was cursed or was ordained to serve whites. Pseudoscientific arguments sprang up to buttress the claim of "Negro inferiority" by providing evidence of their lower intelligence and suitability only for supervised manual labor. Before long what had been felt and institutionalized in somewhat guilty fashion had a plausible argument in its favor. "Negro inferiority" quickly became an almost universally accepted belief.

The rise of a racist ideology in America coincided with a similar trend in Western Europe. A dramatic outpouring of racist literature set the stage for a century of intensely racist thought and actions by Europeans. According to van den Berghe, this development became very prominent by the 1830s.[28] Michael Banton argues that it reached its peak between 1850 and 1854 as the most influential racist publications clustered around this period.[29] Robert Know, *The Races of Men: A Fragment;* J. A. De Gobineau, *Essai sur l'inégalité des races humaines* (trans. as *The Inequality of the Human Races*), and J. C. Nott and G. R. Glidden, *Types of Mankind,* are representative of this genre. The scholarship of this era concentrated on finding "scientific explanations" of racial differences and at the same time establishing unequivocally the superiority of the white Anglo-Saxon races over the nonwhite races. Several prominent American scholars contributed significantly to the effort. Their findings, not surprisingly, coincided with the domestic need to rationalize or explain away the treatment of the black population.

Formulation of this ideology of racism was enormously aided by the appearance of Charles Darwin's *On the Origin of Species by Means of Natural Selection* in 1859. The work was not concerned with the origins of races, but its findings were soon applied to the area of race relations. Darwin suggested that existence was a competitive process in which the strong survived and the weak perished. Social Darwinists soon equated the principle of the survival of the fittest with the right of this element to rule. With this reasoning it became possible to justify subordination of black people within the United States and colonization and exploitation of other "inferior," i.e., nonwhite peoples.

This rise of racist thinking coincided with the renewed efforts in Europe and later in the United States to colonize and plunder the non-Western world. Colonialism seemed somewhat more tolerable, less grating on the conscience of a "civilized people" when they could point to their unquestioned superiority over the oppressed "native." Oppression itself came to be justified as a benevolent and humane effort by "superior peoples" to civilize and Christianize the heathen savages who occupied colonial areas and who Rudyard Kipling matter-of-factly referred to as "lesser breeds without the law." The convergence of the imperialist impulse and racist doctrines is clearly demonstrated in the expansionist activities of the United States during the nineteenth century and in the domestic debate on this activity. Expansionism on the American continent and later in the Pacific was supported in primarily racist terms, and domestic racial attitudes were quickly transferred to these areas. For example, in commenting on the Supreme Court's decision in a Mississippi case permitting disfranchisement of blacks, the *Nation* observed that it is "an interesting coincidence that this important decision is rendered at a time when we are considering the idea of taking in a varied assortment of inferior races in different parts of the world which of course could not be allowed to vote."[30] Some prominent academicians concluded approvingly that in the process of colonizing millions of Asiatics the Republican Party had changed its views on race relations and accepted those of the South.[31] The colonialist argument was that colonized people were inferior and incapable of self-government and thus needed the protection and guidance that the benevolent white race was willing and eager to bestow. Essentially the same view of blacks in the South prevailed.

DEMOCRACY AND THE BLACK EXPERIENCE

We observed earlier that the drafters of the Constitution had a very limited conception of democracy, one more oriented to the protection of their property interests than recognition of the equality of individuals in the political arena. But early in the nineteenth century the then Western world experienced a dramatic upsurge in the mass impulse to participate in the political process. This process of democratization, or as Lucian Pye and others characterize it, "the crisis of participation" in

America opened the political arena to the masses, introducing what we now know as popular democracy. The many virtues attributed to this essentially modern form of democracy ordinarily would lead one to expect that with it came considerable improvement in the position of blacks in the society. Indications are, however, that the process of democratization in America brought with it no immediate benefits for blacks. In some important respects it served as a formidable obstacle to change in their status, and even intensified their subordinate status.

In the United States, as in South Africa, Rhodesia, and the United Kingdom, black subordination has persisted alongside commitment to "mass participation" in politics. Noting that in societies of this kind democratic procedures or principles usually are applicable to the superordinate group only, van den Berghe characterizes them as *Herrenvolk democracies.*[32] Carl Degler observes that in the United States blacks were not only excluded from participation but in at least two basic ways this form of democracy operated to their disadvantage. He points out that in societies like Brazil where there was no commitment to democratic values blacks, during and after slavery, fared better than they did in the United States. In this country assertion of the equality of individuals imposed on whites the need to justify black subordination by destroying his humanity, by stressing in every way possible that he was less than human.[33] This need contributed to the harshness of black life and to the seemingly ridiculous extent to which white Americans often went in affirming black inferiority.

Degler's second observation about the impact of democracy on blacks relates to its overt use as an instrument for maintaining black subordination. He observes that periods of rapid democratization and extension of the franchise to large segments of the masses coincided with vigorous new efforts to reinforce black subordination. In the minds of lower-class or poor whites, blacks—slave or free—were competitors, and these whites fought against every move that seemed to threaten their own status and economic well-being. As these masses entered the political arena as voters under the banner of Jacksonian democracy, Degler concludes, "new cognizance was given in both society and politics to the wishes and prejudices of the common man."[34] Thus as the removal of property qualification to suffrage brought the poor into the electorate, the condition of blacks deteriorated. In those states where nonslave blacks held the right to vote, such as the New England states, New York, Pennsylvania, New Jersey, North Carolina, Tennessee and Maryland, this right was quickly withdrawn or severely circumscribed. In several other states the upsurge of this mass democracy was accompanied by the imposition of stringent new controls on the black population. In the same vein C. Vann Woodward concluded that in the post-Civil War South, "political democracy for the white man and racial discrimination for the black were often products of the same dynamics." As black and white workers were thrown together in the new industrial towns and had to compete for work, poor whites became more insistent on discriminatory laws. He concluded that "the barriers of racial discrimination mounted in direct ratio with the tide of political democracy among whites."[35]

With uncanny insightfulness, Alexis de Tocqueville recognized and commented on the sinister consequences of American democracy for the black population:

> I do not believe that the white and black races will live in any country on an equal footing. But I believe the difficulty to be still greater in the United States than elsewhere. An isolated individual may surmount the prejudices of religion, of his country, or of his race; and if this individual is a king, he may effect surprising changes in society; but a whole people cannot rise, as it were, above itself. A despot who should subject

Americans and their former slaves to the same yoke might perhaps succeed in commingling the races; but as long as the American democracy remains at the head of affairs, no one will undertake so difficult a task; and it may be foreseen that the freer [that is, more democratic] the white population of the United States becomes, the more isolated it will remain.[36]

The vote in the hands of the masses has continually provided the impetus for discriminatory laws and practices and has served to restrain political leaders from pursuing policies likely to be beneficial to blacks. The presidential elections of 1972 provided new evidence of the power of the democratic process in matters of race relations. Traditional champions of equal opportunities for blacks were forced to retreat by embracing the convenient bogey of opposition to "quotas" as a new threat to America. Long-standing supporters of school integration clung to the straw man of "forced busing" in beating a quick retreat before the aroused masses of voters who insist on largely segregated school systems.

The role of democracy as a device for perpetuating black subordination is considerably enhanced by the peculiarly political character of virtually every facet of public life. Not only are traditionally "political" roles filled by popular election, but law-enforcement, judicial, and some administrative or bureaucratic roles as well. This means that few significant roles are free from the direct pressures of the popular vote. Popular racial attitudes thus influence virtually every area of public life.

These observations are not intended to blame the entire ordeal of black Americans on the democratic process or to suggest that democracy is itself sinister. They emphasize that democratic values held by Americans have not been a significant hindrance to the institutionalization of racism. Rather these values have been easily adapted to the task of maintaining black subordination. To protect everyone in the society, the democratic process as it exists in America requires the existence of an overarching set of values that includes everyone on equal terms. "Popular democracy" has been the hand-maiden of racism in the United States because of the absence of such values.

FEDERALISM AND THE BLACK EXPERIENCE

Federalism may be more readily viewed as a structural characteristic of the American polity rather than a cultural or attitudinal one. It is considered here, however, because values and attitudes basic to the cultural tradition of America are reflected in federalism and because these values along with the federal structure have been crucial in perpetuating black subordination. Racism and attitudes toward federalism have been so intimately linked that it is hardly possible to study one without reference to the other. Even a cursory review of the federal relationship quickly reveals that the black presence was one important factor in its adoption, and that this black presence and the many problems of race relations have been continuing and highly potent forces in shaping the existing pattern of federalism.

Federalism was one of the genuine innovations introduced by the American Constitution in 1789. Several factors contributed to the adoption of this form of political organization. These included (1) the practical problems resulting from development of thirteen distinct colonial societies each with its separate interests and over a decade of experience with virtually complete independence within the fatally flawed Confederacy; (2) some of the more thoughtful members of the Constitutional Convention saw federalism as a device for ensuring free and limited government by decentralizing power. It is clear, however, that different interests and customs which the separate units wanted to preserve weighed heavily in favor of the adoption of federalism, and that the black presence constituted the most notable of these different interests and customs. In fact, James Madison conceded that the basic division among the states represented at the Constitutional Convention was not between large and small states, as is often suggested, but between those states that permitted slavery and those that did not.[37]

Those colonies in which slavery was a valued institution felt threatened by antislavery sentiments elsewhere and federalism, along with other specific constitutional guarantees, afforded protection for the institution. On the other hand, federalism provided an escape for the national government from direct responsibility for slavery. As Mark De Wolfe Howe suggests, "the decision of the framers of the Constitution that the domestic destiny of slavery was to be in the hands of the states and not in those of the Nation meant, of course, that Congress should not by positive law sustain slavery or by negative law end it."[38] With abolition of slavery federalism became even more important in ensuring the continued subordination of blacks. Their status remained largely within state jurisdiction, and the states—especially the Southern states—spared no effort in legislating black subordination. During the decade immediately following the Civil War the national government intervened briefly and halfheartedly in efforts to define the status of blacks and to protect them from the atrocities of Southern state governments, but the effort soon ended and blacks again became helpless victims of the state governments under whose jurisdiction they found themselves.

In evaluating American federalism, William Riker concludes that it is difficult to find any evidence that federalism has in fact operated to protect individual freedom. On the contrary he suggests, "it is impossible to interpret federalism as other than a device for minority tyranny."[39] The history of black America's efforts to alter their subordinate status has, in fact, been largely that of overcoming the roadblocks imposed by federalism. Duane

Lockard asserts in this regard that "in retrospect it is clear that the independence of the Southern states helped greatly to assure their complete discretion in handling not only the institution of slavery but also the social and economic condition of the "freedmen."[40] Burke Marshall points to the use of federalism in obstructing efforts for significant change, noting that in the South "state police power and Criminal processes have been used in retaliaion against efforts to encourage Negroes to exercise their right to the vote and to protect the caste system. They have also been used to defy federal court orders."[41]

Throughout the nation's history the national government has been more sympathetic than the Southern states to the plight of blacks. On those occasions when the national government attempted to respond to vital needs of blacks either by legislative or judicial action, the rights and prerogatives of the states have been invoked to obstruct national effort. The first major Civil Rights Act passed by the national government in 1873 was invalidated by the Supreme Court on the basis of a distinction between federal and state jurisdictions. Ever since that time, arguments based on "states' rights" principles have been utilized in efforts to prevent implementation of national norms in the area of race relations. It is one of the chilling facts of American history that decades of efforts to enact a federal antilynching law were frustrated by arguments about possible usurpation of state authority by the national government. The shrill appeals to states' rights reached their peak after the Supreme Court's decision in *Brown vs. Board of Education* in 1954. Alabama, followed shortly afterward by Georgia, Mississippi, South Carolina and Virginia, all adopted resolutions of "nullification," declaring the Court's decision null and void in their states. The nullification acts proved to be mere symbols of defiance, since their major premise—the claim that states possess final authority to decide what is constitutional—was discredited long before that time. It is significant, however, that when Governor George Wallace of Alabama made his infamous stand "in the schoolhouse door" to prevent black students from entering the University of Alabama in 1962, he was defending a long-standing symbol of black subordination by invoking "the sovereign right of states" against the federal system.

Against this background the following assessment of American Federalism by Riker appears beyond serious challenge.

> The main beneficiary (of federalism) throughout American history has been Southern whites, who have been given the freedom to oppress Negroes, first as slaves and later as a depressed caste. Other minorities have from time to time also managed to obtain some of these benefits; e.g., special business interests have been allowed to regulate themselves, especially in the era from about 1890 to 1936, by means of the judicial doctrine of dual federalism, which eliminated both state and national regulation of such matters as wage rates and hours of labor. But the significance of federal benefits to economic interests pales beside the significance of benefits to the Southern segregationist whites. The judgment to be passed on federalism in the United States is therefore a judgment on the values of segregation and racial oppression.[42]

One weakness of Riker's analysis is that it makes the Southern states the sole villains in utilizing federalism as a means of perpetuating black subordination. This is clearly not the case, for federalism served the rest of the nation as a convenient excuse for not really trying to bring about significant change. Federalism as an obstacle to change in the condition of blacks was thus all the more formidable because it shielded whites outside the South from blame for some of the excesses of the South, and by contrast made forms of racial subordination outside the South seem insignificant.

The role of federalism in perpetuating black subordination is not confined to the formal constitutional protection it provides to the "legally" established symbols and rituals of subordination. Even where the states'-rights argument has given way to the imposition of national norms, federalism continues to facilitate delays in the full implementation of these national norms. The federal structure, Lockard notes, provides "a special set of weapons for resistance in the form of countless legal, constitutional and administrative devices that can long delay and sometimes defeat a detested national decision."[43] Nowhere have these special weapons been more widely displayed than in the areas of voting rights, school desegregation and the administration of justice.

American federalism has changed drastically in recent years as the role of the national government increased substantially vis-à-vis state government. Several powerful forces have contributed to this change, among them an increasing trend toward urbanization and technological development, and increase in the financial power of the national government (and hence its larger role in education, medical care, welfare and other social services for the society). One of the most potent forces for change, however, has been the efforts of blacks to alter their position in the society. Federalism has been affected by the black struggle in at least three ways: (1) The national government has been forced to play a larger role in protecting citizens in the exercise of constitutionally guaranteed rights as a result of the civil rights struggle and the consequent atrocities by local law enforcement officials. (2) A series of Supreme Court decisions highlighted by *Brown vs. Board of Education* (1954) considerably reduced the freedom of states to enact discriminatory laws and required compliance with nationally stated policies of nondiscrimination. (3) Legislative responses to black demands, particularly the 1964 Civil Rights Act and the Voting Rights Act of 1965 have extended the powers of the federal government into areas once reserved almost exclusively to the states. Under the pressures of black political activism, the Fourteenth Amendment and other portions of the Constitution like the Commerce Clause have been extensively developed and broadened to enhance national governmental powers vis-à-vis the states.

SUMMARY

The persistence of black subordination in a society which from the outset claimed a strong commitment to democratic values and belief in the equality of individuals is not, upon examination, a paradox as is often suggested. We have observed that the subordinate-superordinate pattern of relationship emerged with the beginning of American colonial societies and persisted unchanged after independence because of the very limited and superficial character of the American revolution. Thereafter a variety of factors contributed to the development of an ideology of racism—a set of rationalizations for black subordination—which relied upon self-serving interpretations of the Bible, pseudoscientific jargon, and the distortion of genuine scientific research. This racist ideology was not a product of Americans alone but was a Western European undertaking and functioned to justify pursuit of imperialist policies in which virtually all nonwhite peoples were victims.

Democracy has been often invested with virtues it does not merit. It has not been an obstacle to racism or to black subordination. On the contrary, this chapter suggests that it served as an instrument for black subordination. In the United States democracy had a limited meaning, one that protected the interests of wealthy upper classes rather than those of the entire society and even when the concept was extended to embrace mass participation in politics, subordinate groups were excluded from the democratic process. Of even greater consequence for the black experience, however, is the extent to which it became a weapon utilized by the masses to ensure and reinforce the subordinate status of blacks. This in spite of the fact that for almost 200 years black spokesmen pursued their struggle for change by appealing to the democratic and humanitarian values of America. In recent years further development of conceptions of democracy, the many external pressures on the United States as a "champion of democratic values" and the highly competitive character of politics has increased the extent to which the democratic process has contributed to black advancement. Finally, the federal structure of the political system took shape primarily under the impetus of the black presence, and over time has had its most significant impact on the society by preserving black subordination.

Notes

1. Donald Devine, *The Political Culture of the United States* (Boston: Little Brown, 1972), p. 17.

2. Pierre L. van den Berghe, *Race and Racism* (New York: Wiley, 1967), p. 5.

3. Joel Kovel, *White Racism: A Psychohistory* (New York: Pantheon, 1970), p. 3.

4. Stokely Carmichael and Charles Hamilton, *Black Power: The Politics of Liberation in America* (New York: Random House, 1967), pp. 4–5.

5. Louis Knowles and Kenneth Prewitt, *Institutional Racism in America* (Englewood Cliffs, NJ.: Prentice-Hall, 1969), p. 4.

6. *Report of the National Advisory Commission on Civil Disorders* (New York: Bantam, 1968), p. 1.

7. Karl Taeuber and Alma Taeuber, "The Negro Population in the United States," in John P. Davis, ed., *The American Negro Reference Book*

(Englewood Cliffs, N.J.: Prentice-Hall, 1966), pp. 98–100.

8. Winthrop Jordan, *White over Black, American Attitudes Toward the Negro 1550–1812* (Baltimore, Md.: Penguin, 1968), p. 274.

9. Quoted in Richard Hofstadter, *The American Political Tradition* (New York: Knopf, 1951), p. 116.

10. Stanley Elkins, *Slavery* (Chicago: University of Chicago Press, 1968), pp. 81–139.

11. William Brink and Louis Harris, *Negro Revolution in America* (New York: Simon & Schuster, 1963), pp. 140–141.

12. Angus Campbell, *White Attitudes Toward Black People* (Ann Arbor, Mich.: Institute for Social Research, 1971), p. 156.

13. Jordan, *op. cit.*, pp. 290–292.

14. *Ibid.*, pp. 294–296.

15. Frederick Douglass, "Fourth of July Oration," in Herbert J. Storing, ed., *What Country Have I? Political Writings by Black Americans* (New York: St. Martin, 1970), p. 35.

16. In this regard see John Brisbane, *The Black Vanguard* (Valley Forge, Pa.: Judson Press, 1970), pp. 35–44.

17. Van den Berghe, *op. cit.*, p. 17.

18. Daniel J. Boorstin, "The American Revolution: Revolution Without Dogma," in Edward Keynes and David Adamany, *The Borzoi Reader in American Politics* (New York: Knopf, 1971), p. 40.

19. *Ibid.*, pp. 44–45.

20. Quoted in Eli Ginzberg and Alfred Eichner, *The Troublesome Presence, American Democracy and the Negro* (New York: Mentor, 1964), p. 50.

21. In Alexander Hamilton, *The Federalist* (New York: Putnam, 1923), pp. 340–341.

22. Van den Berghe, *op. cit.*

23. Charles Beard, *An Economic Interpretation of the Constitution* (New York: Macmillan, 1913), pp. 152–188.

24. Hofstadter, *op. cit.*, pp. 10–12.

25. Elkins, *op. cit.*, pp. 37–52

26. Quoted in Carey McWilliams, *Brothers Under the Skin* (Boston: Little, Brown, 1964), p. 252.

27. Jordan, *op. cit.*, p. 375.

28. Van den Berghe, *op. cit.*, p. 16.

29. Michael Banton, *Race Relations* (New York: Basic Books, 1967), pp. 28–33.

30. Quoted in C. Vann Woodward, *The Strange Career of Jim Crow* (New York: Oxford University Press, 1955), p. 54.

31. *Ibid.*

32. Van den Berghe, *op. cit.*

33. Carl Degler, *Neither Black Nor White* (New York: Macmillan, 1971), pp. 356–357.

34. *Ibid.*, pp. 358–360

35. Woodward, *op. cit.*

36. Alexis de Tocqueville, *Democracy in America* (New York: Knopf, 1945), pp. 373–374.

37. Farrand, *op. cit.*, 110.

38. Mark De Wolfe Howe, "Federalism and Civil Rights," in Archibald Cox, Mark De Wolfe Howe, and J. R. Wiggins, eds., *Civil Rights, The Constitution and the Courts* (Cambridge, Mass.: Harvard University Press, 1967), p. 38.

39. William H. Riker, *Federalism: Origin, Operation and Significance* (Boston: Little, Brown, 1964), p. 142.

40. Duane Lockard, *The Perverted Priorities of American Politics* (New York: Macmillan, 1971), p. 90.

41. Burke Marshall, *Federalism and Civil Rights* (New York: Columbia University Press, 1964), p. 9.

42. Riker, *op. cit.*, pp. 152–153.

43. Lockard, *op. cit.*, p. 91.

We
worship
different heroes
now.
We stop
bowing to Uncle Tom
baseball players
and phony politicians
who drive long shiny cars
and attend 25 dollar a plate
luncheons for the United Appeal.
We now listen

to our bushy head
brother
standing on the corner
rapping out the side of his mouth
about the man.
2 . . .
We
worship different heroes
now.
Since we
stop reading the newspaper.
NORMAN JORDAN

Blacks and the Politics of Redemption

MARY F. BERRY AND JOHN W. BLASSINGAME

JEFFERSONIAN DEMOCRACY, JACKSONIAN Democracy, Progressivism, and many of the other labels frequently used in describing American politics had virtually no meaning for blacks. For long periods of time, white men excluded Afro-Americans from the body politic. Throughout most of their sojourn in America, blacks confronted the unshakeable white belief that Chief Justice Roger B. Taney expressed succinctly in his 1857 decision in the Dred Scott case. According to Taney, American blacks "had for more than a century been regarded as beings of an inferior order . . . so far inferior that they had no rights which the white man was bound to respect."

Confronting such white supremacists as Taney, blacks argued that both the Declaration of Independence and the Constitution had been perverted. Until white men lived up to the ideals embodied in these documents, they would be cursed by the prophecy of Isaiah:

Wherefore hear the word of the Lord, ye scornful men, that rule this people which is in Jerusalem. Because ye have said, we have made a covenant with death, and with

hell are we at agreement. Your covenant with death shall be disannulled, and your agreement with hell shall not stand; when the overflowing scourge shall pass through, then ye shall be trodden down by it.

Outside of abolitionists, there were few whites who placed any stock in the prophecy until expediency and moral concerns led to the formation of the nation's first antislavery political parties.

With a passion born of denial, blacks struggled consistently to obtain the right to hold office as a means of gaining freedom and equality in American society. Whites just as consistently denied blacks the right to vote or to hold office in order to guarantee the economic and social subordination of Afro-Americans. Free Negroes before the Civil War and blacks after emancipation believed, however, that the franchise held the key to gaining true citizenship. Blacks wanted political power because they believed it would end racial discrimination and ultimately result in improved economic and social conditions in the black community. Beyond the usual rewards of political action in a democratic system—patronage, influence on domestic and foreign policy, and access to decision makers—they expected better jobs, better education, and ultimately equal status with whites in the society. They believed political participation would free white Americans from bondage to the practices of racism and inequality and would liberate blacks from their oppression.

Throughout most of American history the efforts to gain some of the traditional rewards from political participation failed, with some major exceptions—Reconstruction after the Civil War, machine politics in Chicago in the twentieth century, the post-1965 period in the South, and the election of Jimmy Carter to the presidency in 1976. But when the exceptions arose, blacks saw that the rewards of political participation had limits. They saw that voting and holding office alone could lead to the end of overt racial discrimination but did not solve the social and economic problems facing the black community. The legacy of slavery and racism required more radical solutions than the normal business of politics. Protest was perceived as an essential element. But before this truth became evident, blacks had to win the battle to participate in politics.

POLITICAL PARTICIPATION BEFORE THE CIVIL WAR

The masses of black people were slaves who were not permitted to participate in American politics in the period before slavery's abolition, the enactment of the Reconstruction Act of March, 1867, and the Fifteenth Amendment. Free Negroes before the Civil War believed political participation would provide the leverage for ending their unequal status. But by 1830, free Negroes had been excluded from voting state by state. They had little political influence.

The political powerlessness of the free blacks led to numerous systematic attempts to win or regain the franchise. Despite overwhelming and repeated rejections of their claims by white voters, judges, and legislators, the free blacks persisted. Elaborating their political philosophy in petitions, periodicals, and state and national conventions, the free Negroes demonstrated their deeply held belief in the redemptive power of the ballot. In Rhode Island, free Negroes petitioned in 1831 for full voting rights or an exemption from taxes, and the 1834 Negro National Convention proposed a committee to investigate voting rights in the various states. In August, 1840, the New York State Convention of Colored Men met in Albany and resolved that the absence of respect for Negroes stemmed "from the want of the elective franchise." The New York *Colored American* of October 10 that same year insisted that the "possession of political rights," was the essential power needed to destroy caste. "The reason the colored population of this country are not socially and morally elevated is because they are almost universally, as they ever have been, disarmed of this power for their own, and the good of others. . . ."

The Pennsylvania decision to disfranchise blacks in 1838 stirred new efforts on the part of free Negroes to gain the vote. In the fall elections of 1837, Bucks County Democrats had been defeated, they claimed, by black votes. The Democrats obtained a county court decision that blacks were not "freemen" as defined by the 1790 Constitution and therefore could no longer vote. The second session of the state constitutional convention incorporated this ruling into the state constitution. Blacks responded by campaigning unsuccessfully against ratification of the new constitution through "an appeal of forty thousand citizens threatened with disfranchisement to the people of Pennsylvania." The Pennsylvania developments alarmed New York blacks, who expanded the suffrage campaign started earlier by Henry Highland Garnet and Charles Reason. The target of the campaign was the provision in New York's constitution permitting blacks to vote only if they could prove they held at least $250 worth of property. Since white voters did not have to meet a property requirement, blacks appealed to the legislature to repeal the discriminatory constitutional provisions. In county and state meetings blacks passed condemnatory resolutions, wrote addresses to white voters and state officials, and drafted petitions demanding an unrestricted ballot.

After the Albany convention, Garnet and others repeatedly pressed their petitions for suffrage before the New York legislature. They failed each time. The repeated defeats when the issue was put to a vote, according to Frederick Douglass, resulted from "unmitigated pride and prejudice"; whites intended to continue to "depress and degrade" blacks. In Pennsylvania and Connecticut repeated efforts to obtain the vote could not overcome white prejudice. Rhode Island blacks, however, took advantage of the revolt by Thomas Dorr and his followers in 1841 to gain the vote. The Dorrites demanded universal manhood suffrage, but for whites only. Blacks openly supported the conservative government and volunteered to fight when violence was threatened. The anti-Dorrite constitutional convention eliminated all restrictions on the franchise in 1842.

Blacks lost the right to vote in most northern states in the years prior to the Civil War. In New Jersey they were disfranchised in 1844. In the Northwest Territory states, black laws denied them the vote. As new western states came into the Union, black suffrage was prohibited. By the time of the Civil War, except in five New England states, blacks either could not vote or, as in New York, had to meet special qualifications. Despite their struggles, nowhere had blacks gained the vote,

except in Rhode Island. In New York and northern and central New England, where some blacks could vote, their numbers were too small to be politically significant.

Although their small numbers reduced the political influence they had at the polls, free Negroes clearly recognized that they had to establish their right to vote if they were ever to improve their unequal status. They were left out of a political process which was of enormous interest to the general public. Unlike the twentieth century, mass participation in politics was pronounced in the antebellum period. Voter turnouts ran as high as 84 percent for the North in 1860, for example. Local political rallies in 1856 easily mobilized from 20,000 to 50,000 persons. Politics was, in part, mass entertainment, and leading politicians served as a focus for popular interests, aspirations, and values. Politics was both fun and a serious business from which blacks were largely excluded.

In pressing for suffrage in the 1840s, blacks were caught up in the general debate in abolitionist circles over whether slavery should be attacked by organizing an antislavery party, by moral suasion, or by noninvolvement in politics. Most blacks supported the political action group among the abolitionists.

Denied their natural, God-given rights, and perceiving themselves as descendants of men who had fought and died in the American Revolution, blacks held firmly to the view that the Declaration of Independence and the Constitution guaranteed their citizenship. Any laws denying them the right to vote were negated by God's laws. Disfranchisement, blacks contended, was immoral, undemocratic, and tyrannical. It subjected blacks to taxation without representation. Believing with the abolitionists that "politics rightly conducted are properly a branch of morals," blacks tried to convince American whites to vote for men of principles, free the slaves, enfranchise blacks, and to see clearly the distinction between political and social equality.

White politicians and voters were not convinced by the appeals of blacks. When, for example, the Liberty Party ran on a platform calling for the abolition of slavery in 1840, its presidential candidate James G. Birney only received a total of 7,000 votes out of the 2,500,000 cast. Running on the Free Soil ticket in 1848, former President Martin Van Buren received only 14 percent of the votes cast in the North. Given a choice between an antislavery or a proslavery presidential candidate, whites consistently voted for the proslavery one. In fact, between 1789 and 1852, southern slaveholders held a virtual monopoly on the White House.

The bleakness of the antebellum political horizon was relieved for blacks with the rise of the Republican party, the nomination of John C. Frémont as its first presidential candidate in 1856, and the adoption of its heavily symbolic slogan, "Free Speech, Free Press, Free Men, Free Labor, Free Territory and Frémont." Despite its large reservoir of antislavery sentiment, the Republican party initially had a very limited conception of the citizenship rights of blacks. Even so, the Republicans were considerably more sympathetic to Afro-Americans than were the Democrats. Their differences appear in sharp relief in the words of two Illinois politicians, Democrat Stephen A. Douglas and Republican Abraham Lincoln.

Basing his assessment partially on the Declaration of Independence, Lincoln opposed the Dred Scott decision in 1857 and urged his fellow Republicans to preach "with whatever ability they can, that the negro is a man; that his bondage is cruelly wrong, and that the field of his oppression ought not to be enlarged." Unlike Lincoln, Stephen Douglas did not believe slavery was a moral issue. Supporting the Dred Scott decision and insisting repeatedly that the Negro was an "inferior being," Senator Douglas asserted in 1858 that

I believe that this government of ours was founded, and wisely founded, upon the

white basis. It was made by white men, for the benefit of white men and their posterity, to be executed and managed by white men. . . . I am utterly opposed to any amalgamation on this contingent. . . . The Negro is not a citizen, cannot be a citizen, and ought not be a citizen.

CIVIL WAR DEVELOPMENTS

On the eve of the Civil War, blacks confronted a Democratic party that denied rights of any kind to Negroes, slave or free, and a Republican party that denied them all political rights. Republican leaders asserted that free Negroes were human beings with civil rights to life, liberty, and property, but without the right to participate in politics. Women, children, unnaturalized foreigners, and Negroes had natural rights but not political rights. Even the Republican position was unacceptable to H. Ford Douglass, a runaway slave and an abolitionist orator, who told a Massachusetts audience in July, 1860, that no party deserved their votes "unless that party is willing to extend to the black man all the rights of a citizen." But other blacks, like Frederick Douglass and John Rock, supported the Republicans, and black conventions throughout the North endorsed Republican candidates. When choosing between the Republicans and Democrats, the Republicans were the only logical alternative.

When the Civil War started, free blacks believed that general abolition would be one step on the road to political and civil rights. They also knew that enlisting blacks into the military service was the fastest route to abolition. They encouraged the enlistment of blacks in the service and exerted every effort to convert what began as a war to save the Union into a war to free the slaves. They urged the War Department to accept black troops and organized volunteer black regiments in their own states. As the war continued and a great movement of slaves away from their masters ensued, they opposed any effort to solve the black problem short of abolition.

Free Negroes disagreed with most of Lincoln's early plans for the disposition of blacks, including his plan for compensated emancipation and colonization elsewhere. A joint resolution of April 10, 1862, provided that the United States would cooperate with any state adopting a plan of gradual emancipation together with satisfactory compensation for the owners. A law passed in April, 1862, provided for the emancipation of slaves in the District of Columbia, with compensation not in excess of $300 paid to the owner of each slave. The law provided $100,000 to support voluntary emigration of freedmen to Haiti and Liberia. Lincoln called a prominent group of free blacks to the White House in August, 1862, and urged them to support colonization, and he instructed the State Department to inquire if various South American and African governments would be willing to accept blacks. Two places were regarded favorably by Lincoln: Panama and the Isle à Vache in the Caribbean. But most blacks knew that the Civil War offered the best opportunity for gaining equality in America. They continued to oppose colonization and, in fact, denounced such suggestions as stridently as they had earlier proposals. As Isaiah Wears, a prominent black Philadelphian, asserted, "To be asked, after so many years of oppression and wrong have been inflicted in a land and by a people who have been so largely enriched by the black man's toil, to pull up stakes in a civilized and Christian nation, and to go to an uncivilized and barbarous nation, simply to gratify an unnatural wicked prejudice emanating from slavery, is unreasonable and anti-Christian in the extreme."

Free blacks encouraged and supported Lincoln, however, in the antislavery aspects of his policy. They were thrilled when on June 19, 1862, he signed a bill abolishing slavery in the territories and on July 17 signed the Confiscation Act, setting free all slaves of disloyal masters who were found or fled into Union-held territory. As he prepared an Emancipation Proclamation to free all slaves in states in rebellion on January 1, 1863, antislavery delegations including blacks encouraged him to issue it. When Lincoln issued the proclamation on September 22, 1862, with a reminder of the availability of compensated emancipation and of the benefits of voluntary colonization, there was jubilation. The document was not all it could be, but it was a stride toward freedom and was eagerly embraced by blacks. As the *Christian Recorder,* official organ of the AME Church, announced, "It will be said that the President only makes provision for the emancipation of a *part* of an injured race, and that the Border states and certain parts of the rebel states are exempted from the relief offered to others by this most important document. We believe those who are not immediately liberated will be ultimately benefitted by this act, and that Congress will do something for those poor souls who will still remain in degradation. But we thank God and President Lincoln for what has been done, and take courage." The proclamation provided that "all persons held as slaves within any state, or designated part of the state, the people whereof shall be in rebellion against the United States, shall be then, thenceforward, and forever free." On December 31, 1862, blacks held watch meetings to see in not only the New Year but also emancipation. Emancipation, as Lincoln said, was "a fit and necessary war measure"; it helped to save the Union but it also had political consequences.

Black politicians worked to shape the politics of black people in the new atmosphere of freedom. They focused on general abolition and the enactment of measures giving some recognition of black citizenship during the war as a precondition for black political participation. The State Department issued a passport to Henry Highland Garnet in August, 1861, which stated that he was a "citizen of the United States." In response to a request as to whether a black could legitimately command a ship flying an American flag, since only citizens were permitted such commands, Attorney General Edward Bates advised Secretary of the Treasury Salmon P. Chase in 1862 that every free person born in the United States was "at the moment of birth prima facie a citizen." A measure providing for the acceptance of the testimony of black witnesses in federal courts was passed in 1864, and in March, 1865, a bill permitting blacks to carry the mails became national law. Congress admitted blacks to its visitors' galleries during the Civil War, public lectures at the Smithsonian Institution were opened to blacks for the first time, blacks were invited to public receptions at the White House, and in February, 1865, John Rock was admitted to the bar of the U.S. Supreme Court. But as Frederick Douglass said in December, 1863, "Our work will not be done until the colored man is admitted as a full member in good and regular standing in the American body politic."

In Louisiana, where Union victories came early, the suffrage question did not wait until the end of the war. Free men of color in New Orleans insisted on obtaining the right to vote as a condition of the restoration of Louisiana to the Union. They submitted a petition to President Lincoln in March, 1864, reminding the nation of their service in the War of 1812 and the Civil War and asking that "the right of suffrage may be extended not only to natives of Louisiana of African descent, but also to all others, whether born slave or free, especially those who have vindicated their right to vote by bearing arms, subject only to such qualifications as shall equally affect the white and colored citizens." In response, Lincoln wrote to Louisiana Governor Michael Hahn, "I barely suggest for your private consideration whether some of the colored people may not be let in as, for instance the very intelligent, and especially those who have fought gallantly in our ranks."

Northern free Negroes also actively pushed the suffrage issue. In October, 1864, 144 blacks from eighteen states, meeting in Syracuse, New York, in a National Convention of Colored Citizens of the United States, issued an address to the people of the United States, written by Frederick Douglass, which asserted, "We want the elective franchise in all the states now in the union, and the same in all such states as may come into the union hereafter. . . . The position of that right is the keystone to the arch of human liberty; and without that the whole may at any moment fall to the ground; while, with it, that liberty may stand forever. . . ."

POLITICAL POWER DURING RECONSTRUCTION

The leadership for blacks in their struggle for political power would come, at first, largely from that articulate class of leaders before the war led by Frederick Douglass, the most prominent black political leader until his death in 1895. These leaders understood that the true meaning of freedom was not automatically encompassed by the Thirteenth Amendment's declaration that neither slavery nor involuntary servitude shall exist in the United States. Slavery could be defined narrowly, and merely lifting the shackles could be enough; slavery could be defined broadly, and political enfranchisement might be one result of the amendment. But as the Nashville *Colored Tennessean* asserted in August, 1865, blacks expected whites to

> Deal with us justly. Tell us not that we will not work, when it was our toil that enriched the South. Talk not to us of a war of races, for that is to say you intend commencing to butcher us, whenever you can do so with impunity. All we want is the rights of men. Give us that and we shall not molest you. We do not intend leaving this country. No land can be fairer in our eyes, than the sunny one beneath whose skies we have lived. We were born here. Most of us will die here. We are Americans and prouder of the fact than ever. Deal justly with us. That's all we want. That we mean to have, come what may!

Despite the views of blacks, abolition was narrowly defined by southern whites, who enacted legislation designed to insure the continued exploitation of blacks as a permanent underclass. No southern state provided for black suffrage or office holding, and many of the same whites who were bulwarks of the Confederacy were picked to lead this new Old South. The Lincoln and Johnson plans of Reconstruction did not require black suffrage. The only national concession to the needs of blacks seemed to be a relief agency, the Freedmen's Bureau.

Douglass and other black leaders objected strongly to what they regarded as the reestablishment of slavery. Practical Republicans became concerned that their party could never grow and hold power with an unreconstructed Democratic party in control in the South. Northern industrialists were eager to exploit the cheap labor and markets of the South—to modernize the southern economy—and were not interested in the mere reestablishment of the old plantation system. By the time Congress met in December, 1865, it was ready to create a Joint Committee on Reconstruction to inquire into the condition of the southern states and to make recommendations for a new policy.

Two major pieces of legislation, the Freedmen's Bureau Extension Bill and the Civil Rights Act of 1866, were vetoed by President Andrew Johnson, who also condemned a proposed Fourteenth Amendment which provided for civil equality. The resulting fight between Johnson and Congress, including the overriding of his vetoes and the enactment of the Fourteenth Amendment, paved the way for congressional control of Reconstruction. Congress passed its own Reconstruction Act in 1867, disfranchising participants in the rebellion and enfranchising blacks, with elections held under the supervision of the Union Army. The beginning of congressional Reconstruction presented the opportunity for blacks to become elected political officials.

Congressional Reconstruction established martial law in the South and provided that, on the basis of universal male suffrage, a convention in each state was to draw up a new constitution acceptable to Congress. No state would be readmitted to the Union until it ratified the Fourteenth Amendment. Former rebels who could not take the iron-clad oath of allegiance were disfranchised after Congress overrode Johnson's veto of the legislation.

Each of the constitutional conventions called in the southern states had black members, but blacks were in a majority only in South Carolina and Louisiana. In most states, blacks constituted a small minority. In six states, native whites were in the majority. Some black members were slaves and others free, some were emigrants from the North, and many were veterans of the Union Army. The blacks who spoke in the conventions took a moderate conciliatory position toward white Confederates, even supporting their enfranchisement.

In South Carolina's constitutional convention the subject of political rights of former Confederates stimulated heated debate. True to their affection for the principles of the Declaration of Independence, blacks refused to vote to disfranchise whites. Black delegate R. C. DeLarge offered a resolution to petition Congress to remove all political disabilities from citizens of the state. Francis Cardozo thought this was an opportunity for blacks to show that "although our people have been oppressed and have every inducement to seek revenge, although deprived of education and learning," they could rise above "all selfishness and exhibit a Christian universality of spirit." The Charleston *Advocate* explained in May, 1867, that "in the great work of reconstruction we should scorn the idea of the white or black man's party. . . . All should be admitted to equal rights and privileges in church and state whatever may be their race or color. . . . we should all live together in peace and harmony. . . ."

The state constitutions approved by the Reconstruction conventions were much more progressive than the constitutions of antebellum days. They abolished property qualifications for voting and holding office; some abolished imprisonment for debt. Slavery was abolished formally in all constitutions, and some eliminated race distinctions in real property law. In every constitution universal male suffrage was enacted, except for certain classes of former Confederates. Public school systems and modernized local government administrative machinery were also included. These constitutions were apparently so highly regarded that even when Reconstruction was overthrown by white supremacists, their basic provisions were maintained.

During congressional Reconstruction, blacks obtained the traditional fruits of political participation. They held public office and wielded some political power and influence in each state, although they were never in control in any, even where they constituted a majority of the population. In South Carolina whites always had a majority in the senate and there was always a white governor, but there were eighty-seven blacks and forty whites in the first legislature. There were two black lieutenant governors, Alonzo J. Ransier in 1870 and Richard Gleaves in 1872, and two black speakers of the house, Samuel J. Lee in 1872 and Robert B. Elliott in 1874. Francis L. Cardozo, who had been educated at the University of Glasgow, was secretary of state from 1868 to 1872 and treasurer from 1872 to 1876.

In Louisiana between 1868 and 1896, there were 133 black members of the legislature, 38 senators, and 95 representatives. Most who served between 1868 and 1877 were veterans of the Union Army and educated free men of color before the war. But some were former slaves. John W. Menard was elected to Congress but denied a seat. Oscar Dunn, P. B. S. Pinchback, and C. C. Antoine served as lieutenant governors. Pinchback

was acting governor for forty-three days in 1873 when Governor Henry C. Warmoth was impeached.

In national politics between 1869 and 1901, two blacks served in the U.S. Senate and twenty in the House of Representatives. The two senators were Hiram R. Revels and Blanche K. Bruce, both of whom represented Mississippi. Revels was born free in North Carolina in 1822. He migrated to Indiana, Ohio, and Illinois, receiving his education at a Quaker seminary in Indiana, a black seminary in Ohio, and Knox College in Illinois. While living in Illinois, he was ordained a minister in the AME Church at Baltimore in 1845. Revels was in Baltimore when the Civil War began and assisted in organizing the first two Maryland black regiments. In 1863 he moved to St. Louis, founded a school for freedmen, and helped recruit a black regiment there. He went to Vicksburg, Mississippi, in 1864 to work with the Freedmen's Bureau provost marshal in managing the affairs of freedmen. Revels also served as pastor of the Bethel AME Church in Vicksburg. He was elected as a compromise candidate to the state senate in 1869 and was elected by the state senate to fill the seat previously occupied by Jefferson Davis in the U.S. Senate. He served one year in the Senate in 1870, during which he supported the removal of all political disabilities from former Confederates, appointed a black to West Point, and obtained the admission of black mechanics to work in the U.S. Navy Yard. At the end of his term, Revels became president of Alcorn A & M University, established as a segregated institution of higher education for blacks.

Blanche K. Bruce, elected to the U.S. Senate in 1874, was the only black who served a full term in the Senate until the election of Edward Brooke from Massachusetts in 1966. Unlike Revels, Bruce was born a slave in Virginia. He escaped from his master in St. Louis when the Civil War came. He studied for several years and in 1869 went to Mississippi, where he entered politics. He served as tax collector, sheriff, and superintendent of schools. In the Senate he took an interest in both race-related matters and matters of general interest. He spoke in support of P. B. S. Pinchback when Pinchback was denied a seat in the Senate in a contest over irregularities in his election. He worked diligently with the Manufactures, Education, and Labor Committee and the Pensions Committee and chaired a committee that conducted a careful investigation into the causes for failure of the Freedmen's Bank.

The first of the twenty blacks to serve in the U.S. House of Representatives were seated in 1869. There were eight from South Carolina, four from North Carolina, three from Alabama, and one each from Georgia, Mississippi, Florida, Louisiana, and Virginia. James H. Rainey and Robert Smalls, both of South Carolina, each served five consecutive terms. John R. Lynch of Mississippi and J. T. Walls of Florida both served three terms. Their activities in Congress did not differ substantially from those of white congressmen. Most of them had served in some state political capacity before being elected to the House. They fought for such local issues as rivers and harbors legislation, as well as civil rights and education measures. Overall, ten of the blacks who served in Congress between 1869 and 1890 were drawn from the old free Negro caste. On the local level, 43 of the 102 who held office in Virginia between 1867 and 1890 had been free before the war. Of the 59 black delegates in the 1868 South Carolina constitutional convention, at least 18 were former free Negroes; another 14 had been born free in other parts of the nation. All but 20 of the 111 black delegates to the Louisiana Republican Convention in 1865 were free-born. But the most influential and successful black Reconstruction politician in South Carolina, Robert Smalls, was born and lived out his antebellum life as a slave, and Oscar Dunn, a former Louisiana slave, was as significant a figure in politics as P. B. S. Pinchback.

Most blacks who were influential during Reconstruction had been urban slaves, blacksmiths, carpenters, clerks, or waiters in hotels and boarding houses. A few of them had been favored body servants of influential whites. Some had been preachers, lawyers, or teachers in the free states or in Canada. Others were self-educated free men like Robert Carlos DeLarge, the tailor from Charleston who was the best parliamentarian in the South Carolina convention. P. B. S. Pinchback had only a common school education, and Oscar James Dunn was a plasterer.

Black politicians learned a very significant lesson during Reconstruction: the limits of coalition politics and the limits of the officeholders they elected. Northern politicians who enacted Reconstruction measures wanted black participation in the state governments but not black control. They wanted reform but not an economic revolution. They were not prepared to sanction the expropriation of white-owned property in order to give property to blacks. Northerners wanted middle-class, white-dominated governments operated on business principles, not an overthrow of capitalism and white control. Generally, black politicians were in accord with these views. Some, such as James T. Rapier of Alabama, were separated from the black masses by their own interests. Others, such as Francis Cardozo, who kept reminding his colleagues of the necessity of not "impairing the obligations of contracts," were prisoners of their own education. Men such as Beverly Nash of South Carolina spoke eloquently in the defense of voting and officeholding privileges for the very Confederates who were at that moment preparing for the destruction of blacks who dared participate in the political process.

There were dissenters from the black political strategy of coalition politics. The Pure Radicals in Louisiana urged blacks to take power into their own hands. But forty-six-year-old Oscar James Dunn, a former slave who managed to manipulate power for the

Pure Radicals for three years as lieutenant governor, died a month before a crucial effort to impeach the incumbent governor in November, 1871.

THE OVERTHROW OF RECONSTRUCTION

By the time Reconstruction was overthrown completely in 1877, blacks had voted, held office, and wielded some influence in the political system. In addition, the Fourteenth and Fifteenth Amendments gave permanent legal recognition to black citizenship and outlawed denial of the right to vote for racial reasons. But the continued enfranchisement of whites meant that if they could by force or fraud prevent blacks from voting in opposition to them, they would regain power. The Republican party discovered that it could maintain power in national affairs even while letting the Democrats regain power in the South. Through duplicity, bloodshed, riot, and murder, whites forced blacks out of the political arena while the national government acquiesced. Reconstruction unraveled even as it began; by 1877 it was at an end.

The three enforcement acts passed by Congress in 1870–71, under the authority of the Fifteenth Amendment, seemed to ensure protection for blacks in the enjoyment of their political rights. The laws provided for extensive enforcement machinery, including authority for the president to call out the Army and Navy and to suspend the writ of habeas corpus if necessary. The acts permitted states to restrict suffrage on any basis except race or color. But between 1870 and 1896, when the bulk of this legislation was repealed, 7,372 cases were tried and hundreds of offenders, who were never brought to trial, were arrested. Despite this pre-1896 activity, the disfranchisement of blacks proceeded successfully. After 1874, enforcement efforts gradually declined altogether. The white South remained opposed, the white North was not interested, and the Supreme Court soon decided that most of the federal efforts to punish individual violations of voting rights were unconstitutional. Local officials arrested and punished blacks, who complained to harassed federal officials. The few federal troops who were stationed in the South were not used to enforce the law. Additionally, Congress failed to provide adequate funds to finance the federal courts and officials refused to undertake serious enforcement. Many federal officials disagreed with the effort and were not willing to attempt enforcement. The protection of black voting rights in the South was not a national priority.

As the federal government continued to ignore white terrorism in the South, blacks spoke out against the perfidy of the Republican party. The *Colored Citizen* of Fort Scott, Kansas, in October, 1878, said, "The Democrats of the South are determined that the colored voters shall either be Democrats or not vote at all." T. Thomas Fortune in the New York *Globe* in October, 1883, expressed the view that "we have the ballot without any law to protect us in the enjoyment of it. . . . The Democratic Party is a fraud—a narrow-minded, corrupt, bloody fraud; the Republican Party has grown to be little better."

Political participation by blacks became increasingly fraught with dangerous consequences. A variety of so-called legal measures, including gerrymandering, poll tax requirements, and elaborate election procedures, applied in fact only to blacks, were instituted to keep most blacks permanently disfranchised. By 1889, blacks had been practically eliminated from Southern politics. Rather than a temporary setback, the overthrow of Reconstruction marked a long-term withdrawal from political power.

BLACK RECONSTRUCTION FAILS IN SOUTH CAROLINA

A closer look at the Reconstruction experiences of blacks and their political leadership in South Carolina provides an example of the successes and failures of political participation.

If black political participation during Reconstruction could succeed at all in improving social and economic conditions for blacks, it should have succeeded in South Carolina. Blacks were a distinct majority of the population and their political leadership was stronger in both numbers and influence than in any other state, but they were not able to maintain political power. As Thomas Holt explains in his *Black Over White, Negro Political Leadership in South Carolina During Reconstruction,* one reason for the failure lay in the origins of black leadership. Divisions between the free-born mulatto *petit bourgeoisie* and slave-born blacks and mulattoes emerged quickly in the leadership group. Out of a total of 255 Negroes elected to state and federal offices between 1868 and 1876, one in four had been free before the war and one of every three was a mulatto. Almost one in three owned some real estate, and 46 percent possessed some form of wealth, real or personal. One-fifth had combined property holdings in excess of $1,000; 11 percent had more than $1,000 in real property alone. Only 15 percent had no property at all. Sixty-five percent were literate, and 10 percent were professionally or college trained. Ministers and teachers predominated among the professionals, but ten of these lawmakers were or became lawyers during their terms of office. Those engaged in agriculture were the next largest group, and more of these appear to have been landowners than field hands.

Although it might appear that intraracial color prejudices between mulattoes and blacks were the basis for the divisions which inhibited political power, the divisions were in fact due to class differences. The free Negro class before the war, although hedged about with restrictions, was in a better economic position than was the slave class. Free Negroes were wealthier, better educated, and in many ways better prepared for political competition than were slaves. Slaves manumitted before the war were often provided with cattle, land, or other property, and many of them were the mulatto products of unions between white planters and slave women. Therefore, those with greater resources happened to be mulattoes, and some of the hostility between blacks and mulattoes resulted from their different class positions. Many of the black leaders freed during the war had served in the Army and had acquired enough financial resources to gain economic ground on the old free Negro class. In any event, all black legislators of whatever color had a constituency consisting largely of illiterate ex-slaves, upon whom they relied for continued power and who expected some improvement in their condition in return for bestowing that power.

Another significant factor which prevented the exercise of black power was the way in which blacks became politicians. The new politicians, black and white, were novices, but blacks had absolutely no experience in partisan politics. Most of the antebellum history of blacks had been spent trying to gain access to politics. The Freedmen's Bureau, the Army, and the missionary societies and churches provided whatever political experience they had gained in establishing a constituency. What these three institutions provided was a job, an opportunity for developing leadership qualities, and a pattern of public contacts, but these opportunities fell far short of the kind of local experience required for quick, effective action as a state or national political official.

These particular black officials were not able to convert a base of 60 percent of the population into political control in South Carolina. The population base was quickly converted into a majority in the legislature and control of the offices of secretary of state, lieutenant governor, adjutant general, secretary of the treasury, speaker of the house, and president pro tem of the state senate. But blacks never held the offices of governor, U.S. senator, comptroller general, attorney general, and superintendent of education, or more than one of the three positions on the state supreme court. In the legislature blacks were very successful in controlling some of the key committees in the general assembly until 1874. When it came to executive branch appointments, however, blacks early adopted the policy of supporting whites, because they had real or presumed contacts in the North and because of the urgings of their northern white supporters. This was one reason why black leaders never even considered pushing a black for governor, a position that required contacts with northern centers of power. "We don't want a colored Governor," Martin Delany insisted in the June 25, 1870, *Daily Republican.* "Our good sense tells us differently."

Not until the spring of 1870 did blacks in South Carolina fully realize that they had to have a larger portion of the appointed positions and of those elected by the legislature before they could develop a strong political organization. The *Daily Republican* reported on June 24, 1870, that Robert DeLarge had announced at a celebration in Charleston that blacks were thankful to the Republican party, but "some impudent scoundrels in the party now say, 'You want too much; you want everything.' We placed them in position, we elected them and by our votes we made them our masters. We now propose to change this thing a little, and let them vote for us." He was followed by Alonzo Ransier and Martin Delany, who expressed their support for this new approach. The result was an increase in political offices for blacks.

The failure to control the governorship was a significant problem for blacks. The governor appointed most local officeholders, including county treasurer, auditor, jury commissioner, and trial justices. The economic insecurity of many Republicans, which led even professional men to need part-time political appointments, increased the power of the governor. Even local newspapers, dependent on contracts to publish laws and governmental announcements, could be manipulated by the governor.

Although blacks normally dominated the apparatus for running the election campaigns, their control was tenuous. The largely black state central committee, the party convention, the county chairmen, and the union leagues organized the freedmen. The party central committee was responsible for raising and distributing campaign funds. But when black leaders ignored the policy of not electing blacks to conspicuously high offices and elected a black chairman to the state central committee, an agent of the Republican National Committee who was in South Carolina in 1868 simply advised the national party to bypass the central committee. The funds should instead be sent directly to the four congressional district campaign committees.

Federal patronage for local offices was controlled by the senior U.S. Senator and the local Congressman. The collector of the port of Charleston was the most important post, because the collector could hire a number of workers. Blacks were never able to gain control of the custom house patronage, because no black was ever elected Senator. Overall, blacks failed to control another avenue for developing a political machine and lost one of the most important traditional fruits of political participation.

On issues that could have crippled their white opponents, black members of the legislature showed a lack of resolve. They rejected confiscation of land and redistribution to the freedmen. They also withheld support from a measure that would have used tax collection as a measure for ending white control of land, even though Richard H. Cain explained that if the large landowners "are obliged to sell their lands the poor man will have a chance to buy."

The weaknesses of origins, interests, experience, and reliance on northern Republicans created conditions in which the Republicans and blacks lost power to the Democrats in South Carolina in 1876. President Rutherford B. Hayes' decision to withdraw federal troops in April, 1877, merely ratified a result that had already taken place. The Democrats had, through violence, intimidation, and the aid of certain Republicans including the governor, undermined the Reconstruction regime and taken control of the state. The Republicans' division over legislative policy and patronage was the very ingredient needed to consolidate political power. Daniel Chamberlain, elected Republican governor in 1874, consciously adopted a policy of destroying existing Republican alliances and forming a Democratic-Republican coalition which he could control. Chamberlain asserted that he was merely bent on decreasing corruption in government. Even so, the cuts in programs and budgets made by Chamberlain undermined Republican political support and his insistence on appointing Democrats to many local offices further destroyed the party. Chamberlain became the darling of the Democrats.

In July, 1876, the Hamburg massacre of a black militia company during an attack by whites on a barracks in which the militia was barricaded ushered in more violence and marked the end of Republican rule in South Carolina. Wade Hampton was the Democratic gubernatorial candidate and his militia, called the "Red Shirts," forced Republican officials to resign their offices and took over effective control of local government. In a similar situation in 1870, Governor Robert K. Scott had mobilized the black militia long enough to carry the election. But under Chamberlain's policies, the militia, a constant irritant to whites, had been unused and practically disarmed. Indeed, there is some evidence that the white clubs obtained guns from the state arsenal. By the time the disputed election was settled in favor of Hampton and federal troops were removed, the result was a foregone conclusion.

It can be argued that greater unity among the Republicans would have prevented the overthrow of Reconstruction. The preconditions for such unity at that time, however, are difficult to find. To expect more experienced black politicians is a self-evident contradiction, and to expect stronger northern white support of black control of politics is to expect more radical views than even the most radical Republicans then espoused. Not only did black politicians fail significantly to improve the conditions of their black constituency, they did not even receive all of the patronage and influence that are the usual concomitants of political power. However, given the general inexperience of black politicians, the perfidy of white Republicans like Chamberlain in the South, and the unwillingness of northern Republicans to support black control, it is phenomenal that blacks were as successful as they were.

POST-RECONSTRUCTION DECLINE IN POLITICAL PARTICIPATION

Once Reconstruction was over and black voters were largely driven from politics in the South, their absence exacerbated the problem of class divisions among white voters. In the 1880s depressed economic conditions for poor farmers led them to join radical agrarian organizations. The Southern Farmers' Alliance of whites was joined by a Colored Farmers' National Alliance and Cooperation Union in 1886. Radical leaders such as Tom Watson in Georgia began preaching solidarity for poor black and white farmers. The Populist party tried in 1892 to protect blacks in the exercise of the franchise, to insure equal application of voting procedures, and to gain the black vote. The Democrats retaliated first by trying and failing to make an alliance with the Populists and then by forcing blacks who worked for them to vote Democratic. The Democrats also resorted to riots and murder.

Facing such violence, Populists and Republicans gained control of the North Carolina legislature in 1894, and blacks were able to vote and hold office in the eastern black belt of the state. Blacks served as deputy sheriffs, policemen, and aldermen. This resurgence of black power was temporary. Democrats complained that even when they controlled black voters, this made for corruption in politics. The Populists feared that they would not always be able to control blacks if blacks were permitted to behave as allies, and they equally feared Democratic control of black voters and efforts to disfranchise poor whites. Even Tom Watson supported a constitutional amendment excluding blacks from the franchise. Poor whites, the planter class, and industrialists joined in forcing blacks out of the political arena in the 1890s. State after state formally disfranchised blacks by the discriminatory use of "reading and understanding clauses," by writing rigid educational and property tests into their constitutions, and by enacting "grandfather clauses" which enfranchised only those whose fathers and grandfathers were qualified to vote on January 1, 1867— that is, whites only. The disfranchisement of blacks was regarded by whites as necessary. White Democratic primaries and legalized racial segregation became the rule. The last black member of Congress in the nineteenth century, George H. White of North Carolina, was elected in 1896. Not until the 1960s would black political participation again become a significant factor in southern politics.

Despite the disfranchisement of blacks in the South, a few blacks were appointed to "Negro jobs" in the government in exchange for their support of the Republican party in national nominating conventions. Frederick Douglass, for example, was appointed marshal of the District of Columbia (1877), recorder of deeds (1881), and minister to Haiti (1889–91). Attempted black rebellion against the legal structure which resulted in political powerlessness and Jim Crow rule was quickly suppressed, with military force when necessary. Black organizations such as the Afro-American League and the Niagara Movement, which drew their membership from leading black newspapermen, ministers, educators, and former politicians, protested against this

continued oppression, but the white majority did not regard alleviating the plight of blacks as a high priority.

Most blacks who clung to the hope of political participation as a solution to racial discrimination and as a route to equal social and economic opportunity continued to support the party of Lincoln, the Republicans, between 1877 and the New Deal. As a group of Wisconsin blacks said in 1892, they knew the Republicans did not protect them but they were "yet unfailing in their devotion to this party and its principles." There was, essentially, no place else to go. Some Republicans continued to believe that the party had something to gain from the large black population that lived in the South until the turn of the century, but the party, in fact, did very little to enable blacks to vote. In every presidential election in the late nineteenth century, the GOP platform reiterated the wrongs of the defeated South and Republican support for ending the oppression of blacks. But these rhetorical flourishes, along with the "Negro jobs" in the government, were about all the Republicans were willing to do. In 1890 the House of Representatives passed its last serious effort to legislate protection of voting rights—the Lodge Federal Elections Bill. The measure was, however, abandoned in the Senate by the Republicans, who wished to gain Democratic support for high tariff and silver legislation. Southern black Republicans could exercise influence only in the national nominating conventions, when they were permitted to become delegates, which depended upon their support for the preferred candidate, usually the incumbent.

BOOKER T. WASHINGTON'S INFLUENCE
Blacks who had so eagerly rushed to vote in the elections during Reconstruction soon developed habits of nonparticipation in its aftermath. In states where blacks could vote and where they existed in sufficient numbers, black political participation achieved some limited results. In the northern states, after

the Supreme Court declared the Civil Rights Act of 1875 unconstitutional in 1883, blacks succeeded in obtaining the passage of state civil rights laws. But most blacks were in the South, and it was in the South that their efforts to vote were extinguished. The government in Washington, D.C., seemed very distant and no longer interested in their plight. There were few opportunities to develop a tradition of voting and amassing other political resources such as income, wealth, status, knowledge, and military prowess. Schools for black children in the South taught the basic symbols and rituals of the nation, including loyalty, but they were poor places to learn the role of political participant. This situation was one in which Booker T. Washington, who said he did not believe in political involvement, could practice his particular brand of politics. His politics included loyalty to the nation, a belief that blacks were passive figures who were inactive in political affairs and for whom such affairs had little importance.

Washington believed that political rights for blacks could be obtained only after wealth and hard work had gained the respect of whites and that political rights were not a precondition for economic advancement. Washington's reputation grew until he became the power broker between blacks and whites. His position with whites was threatened temporarily when they learned that he had accepted an invitation to have dinner at the White House with President Theodore Roosevelt. Washington was, however, ensconced solidly as the black patronage dispenser. Any black who wanted a federal appointment had to obtain his stamp of approval.

Washington's influence was obvious. President William McKinley spoke at Tuskegee Institute in 1898 during a visit scheduled for the purpose of addressing the Alabama legislature. President Theodore Roosevelt openly relied on Washington's advice in appointing both blacks and whites to southern posts. He wrote to a friend in 1903 that his black

appointees "were all recommended to me by Booker T. Washington." Washington's influence, however, seemed to result overall in only a small number of black appointees. Roosevelt appointed T. Thomas Fortune, editor of the New York *Age,* to a special commission to investigate conditions in U.S. insular possessions. He also selected William Henry Lewis, a graduate of the Harvard Law School, to be assistant U.S. attorney for Massachusetts. When Theodore Roosevelt, on one of his southern tours in the fall of 1905, spoke at Tuskegee, he echoed Booker T. Washington's philosophy of self-help and emphasized the duty of blacks to make war against all crime, especially that committed by other blacks.

Booker T. Washington enjoyed the same close relationship with Roosevelt's successor, President William Howard Taft. He helped Taft persuade Dr. William D. Crum, whose appointment as collector of customs at Charleston in 1903 had been opposed by whites and had never been permanently confirmed by the Senate, to resign in March, 1910. Upon Washington's advice, Taft appointed Whitefield McKinlay collector of customs for Georgetown, D.C., in 1909 and promoted William H. Lewis to be Assistant Attorney General in March, 1911, the highest post held by a black to that date.

Washington, a complex personality, covertly supported efforts to prevent disfranchisement while espousing his public philosophy of economics first, politics second. He provided financial support for court cases attacking disfranchisement provisions in Louisiana's constitution. He contributed money to the political cause in Alabama and Maryland. In 1903 and 1904 he "spent at least four thousand dollars in cash, out of my own pocket . . . in advancing the rights of the black man." He believed it was best to keep these activities secret in order to maintain the confidence of whites in his leadership role, but he made sure that his behind-the-scenes activities were known by black leaders. Washington wanted to keep the support of blacks while he maintained the confidence of whites, so that he could be unchallenged leader of the black community in all quarters. His behavior was consistent in that he wanted to mitigate legal discrimination if he could but did not believe it would end until economic self-sufficiency and black assimilation to white standards had been achieved.

Some black spokesmen and organizations, in the spirit of the antebellum convention movement, still pushed for the right to vote. They continued to believe that political power was necessary for economic and social advancement and for ending racial discrimination. It was not just that the black leaders had already achieved economic status and wanted political rights for themselves; they saw politics as a way for the masses of blacks to vote themselves into equality of economic opportunity. From opportunity would flow an improvement in status. They saw Washington as an "Uncle Tom" who sold their political rights in exchange for power for himself.

The convention movement soon became a vehicle for vocal opposition to Booker T. Washington. In 1890 three major conventions were held and in January, 1890, T. Thomas Fortune founded the Afro-American League in Chicago. Fortune, a native of Florida, came North to undertake a career as editor in 1880. He was the leading black journalist from the mid-1880s until he sold the New York *Age* to Fred R. Moore and Booker T. Washington in 1907.

In February, 1890, J. C. Price, the president of Livingstone College in Salisbury, North Carolina, who had just been elected vice president of the Afro-American League, chaired a convention in Washington, D.C., which organized a Citizens Equal Rights Association. Both groups were beset with internal rivalry and friction and became inactive. The Afro-American League, however, was resumed in 1898 as the Afro-American Council and met annually for ten years thereafter until its

membership dispersed into the Niagara Movement and the National Association for the Advancement of Colored People (NAACP). Through these various groups the convention movement was extended from its antebellum origins.

Booker T. Washington soon gained control of the Afro-American Council, which therefore became "conservative in all of its actions" insofar as political rights were concerned. Washington worked aggressively behind the scenes, using money and influence to gain control of the council so that, by the 1902 convention, Washington's secretary, Emmett J. Scott, could say in truth, "We control the council now." But their control was short-lived. William Monroe Trotter, editor of the *Boston Guardian,* provided effective newspaper criticism of Washington's leadership. Other influential critics of Washington, including W. E. B. Du Bois, soon emerged openly. In the spring of 1903 Du Bois' *The Souls of Black Folk* appeared, including the essay on "Mr. Booker T. Washington and Others," which provided a rallying point for the opposition.

Blacks in leadership roles in this period emphasized political rights as a means of achieving an end to Jim Crow and lynching. They paid little attention to the economic issues that the black masses faced. Perhaps Booker T. Washington's insistence that economic advancement could be made in the absence of political rights led the advocates of political rights to insist the reverse: that political rights were supreme and that economic equality would result when the political cause was won. T. Thomas Fortune reiterated his 1887 position on the Negro in politics in December, 1905, in the *Colored American Magazine*—that blacks should be independent voters. If northern blacks voted without adhering specifically to a particular party, "the vast body of disfranchising and separation laws which now cumber the statute books of the Southern states would never have been adopted." He thought, "In a democracy a citizen without a vote would have every other civil and political right denied him."

Despite Washington's "dirty tricks," including depriving critics of jobs, arranging to have some of them sued for libel, placing spies in their midst, and subsidizing the black press to prevent attacks on him, some of his critics formed the Niagara Movement in 1905. Their Declaration of Principles publicized the duty of blacks to engage in self-improvement efforts but indicated, "We believe in manhood suffrage and believe that no man is so good, intelligent or wealthy as to be entrusted wholly with the welfare of his neighbors." The movement, organized in response to a call issued by Du Bois to combat Washington's policy, successfully penetrated the Afro-American Council, which became by October, 1906, a protest voice against ballot restrictions, Jim Crow, and violence. Bishop Alexander Walters, who as president of the group in 1898 was preaching conciliation ("Let us improve our morals, educate ourselves, work, agitate and wait on the Lord") was asserting in 1906, "It is nonsense for us to say peace! peace! where there is no peace. . . . We use diplomatic language and all kinds of subterfuges; but the fact remains that the enemy is trying to keep us down and we are determined to rise or die in the attempt."

However, the victory of the Niagara Movement in taking over the Afro-American Council led to the decline of both. Washington effectively cut his opponents off from sources of support and publicity. But the black radicals took advantage of the support of a small group of prominent white progressives, who provided the backing for the founding of the NAACP in 1910. Oswald Garrison Villard, John Milholland, and other white progressives backed the organization of the NAACP, which had only one black offlcial at first, W. E. B. Du Bois, who edited *Crisis,* but the membership was chiefly composed of educated blacks. Villard had long been friendly with Washington and had raised $150,000 for the Tuskegee endowment, but he believed more aggressive efforts were needed to advance the cause of blacks. He invited Washington to the conference that led to the founding of the NAACP, but Washington declined. With the beginning of the NAACP the torch of the convention movement had been effectively passed to an organization determined to gain black civil and political rights in the courts and in Congress.

SUPPORTING THE DEMOCRATIC PARTY

Blacks had threatened time and time again to become independent voters, which would mean abandoning the Republican party, but no viable alternative appeared. Some southern conservative blacks supported the Democratic party, and northern blacks sometimes advocated cooperation with them. The Populist movement resulted in large numbers of blacks voting Democratic as whites applied economic pressure, fraud, and intimidation. Sometimes the support was willingly given. During the 1880s and 1890s in the black counties of Mississippi and South Carolina, fusion—dividing offices between black Republicans and white Democrats, giving blacks a few legislative seats and unimportant local posts—was widely practiced. In Georgia, AME Bishop Henry M. Turner sided with the Cleveland Democrats in 1889 and was rewarded when Hoke Smith, Secretary of the Interior, appointed three of Turner's close relatives to office.

Some northern blacks supported the Democrats. Peter H. Clark, a high school principal in Cincinnati, supported them because, as he said in 1885, he did not think blacks should have their vote "concentrated in one party." They must indicate a willingness to be flexible on political issues. George Downing, one of the best-known black workers in the struggle for citizenship rights of the period, broke with the Republicans in 1883 because he wanted "more than one party anxious, concerned, and cherishing the hope that at least part of that vote may be obtained."

In 1883 President Chester Alan Arthur's policy of siding with white independents and southern liberal white Republicans caused considerable black dissatisfaction with the Republican party and renewed interest in the Democrats. At the 1883 Negro convention in Louisville, so much concern was expressed that Frederick Douglass defended the party's position but called himself "an uneasy Republican," saying, "If the Republican Party cannot stand the demand for justice and fair play it ought to go down." In Massachusetts, James M. Trotter repudiated the party and resigned his political appointment as assistant superintendent of the registered letter department in the Boston post office. Later President Grover Cleveland appointed him recorder of deeds for the District of Columbia. Massachusetts Democratic Governor Benjamin F. Butler, in return for a substantial black vote, appointed Harvard Law School graduate and former member of the state legislature George L. Ruffin judge of the Charleston City Court, the first black judge in the North.

There were sizeable groups of black Democrats in New York, Cleveland, and other cities, all advising a split of the black vote or independence of black voters as the best political policy. But by the early 1890s most of those who had joined the Democrats had returned to the Republican fold. George Downing had become critical of the Democrats by 1891. T. McCants Stewart, a Charlestonian, graduate of the University of South Carolina and its law school during Reconstruction, and now a resident of New York, returned to the Republicans in 1895 after being frozen out of a job by objecting Democrats.

In the December, 1905, issue of the *Colored American Magazine,* T. Thomas Fortune argued that black voters were needed by the Republicans in the northern and western states, but since blacks always voted Republican they were taken for granted. Afro-American persistence got "nothing but crumbs from party success. A few offices of the lowest grade are here and there given to it, for the most part such offices as white partisans do not want. Afro-Americans have the strength of a giant and use it as a child."

J. Milton Waldron, Alexander Walters, and William Monroe Trotter supported the Democrats in 1908. In 1912 there was increasing discussion of the possibility of defection to the Progressive party or the Democrats. Woodrow Wilson met with Trotter and Waldron, and eventually a letter to Walters containing views conciliatory toward blacks but without specifics was circulated as Wilson's position on the race question.

W. E. B. Du Bois, then editor of *Crisis,* insisted in December, 1910, that blacks should vote, but independently: "No intelligent man should vote one way from habit." In August, 1912, he recommended Woodrow Wilson to the 500,000 blacks who could vote in the North. He asserted, "You could easily sell your votes for an Assistant Attorney General, a Register of the Treasury, a Recorder of Deeds, and a few other black wooden men whose duty it is to look pleasant, say nothing, and have no opinions that a white man is bound to respect. Do not do it." Blacks should ask for the abolition of interstate Jim Crow transportation, an end to peonage, the enforcement of the Fourteenth Amendment, "cutting down the representation in Congress of the rotten boroughs of the South," and national financial aid for all elementary public schools without regard to race. He knew Wilson was a southerner, but Taft was "utterly lacking in initiatives or ideals" and had done nothing on race issues. Wilson, "a cultured scholar," would do better "if he became President by grace of the black man's vote." The best choice was Eugene Debs, who "stands squarely on a platform of human rights regardless of race or class," but he could not be elected. Therefore, voting for Wilson was the best option. Many more blacks voted against the GOP, although there is controversy about the number of defectors.

As President, however, Wilson proved to be extremely hostile to black interests. He even expanded racial segregation among federal employees in several government departments, including the Bureau of Engraving and Printing, the Treasury Department, and the Post Office. Strong and prolonged protests ensued, but Wilson conferring with a delegation led by Trotter in November, 1914, defended segregation as in the best interest of both races and said it would continue. Wilson, in following the usual patronage policy, dismissed or accepted the resignations of black officeholders including William H. Lewis, but he only reluctantly appointed other blacks to office. He did reappoint Robert H. Terrell judge of the District of Columbia Municipal Court in February, 1914, and he appointed James J. Curtis as minister to Liberia in 1915. These were the only two black appointments made during his first term.

The experience with Wilson confirmed the unattractiveness of a Democratic alternative, but the election results in 1920 made the Republican option even worse. The Republicans picked up support in the border states, even carrying Tennessee. Party leaders, focusing on attracting southerners, made strong efforts to purge the party of the stigma of association with blacks. When Warren Harding was elected, James Weldon Johnson of the NAACP discussed the issues of disfranchisement, the Ku Klux Klan, lynching, and the necessity for black appointments with him, but it did not seem to have beneficial results. Harding, who was rumored to have black ancestry, knew little and cared less about the race question. For example, he had never heard of Tuskegee or Booker T. Washington. He finally did send a message to Congress asking them to outlaw lynching, but he never really pressed for the passage of such legislation,

which would have been doubtful even with his support.

EFFORTS TO GAIN VOTING RIGHTS IN THE SOUTH

Black voters in the South continued to fight to gain the right to vote. Succeeding in having grandfather clauses outlawed in 1915, the NAACP carried the legal burden. In 1925 blacks united in making a test of the southern white primary law, beginning with Texas. The Supreme Court unanimously declared the white primary laws unconstitutional in March, 1927. Texas and other states responded by enacting new evasive legislation which was eventually declared illegal. Meanwhile, the black citizen in the South faced, as James Weldon Johnson described it in 1929, "the grim determination of the Southern politicians never to allow him to take part in politics—his education, economic progress and moral fitness, notwithstanding—and the specter of force, violence and murder lurks not far behind." Not only plebeian demagogues like Senators J. Thomas Heflin of Alabama and Cole Blease of South Carolina but such aristocratic statesmen as Senator Carter Glass of Virginia expressed the southern determination to disfranchise blacks. Glass was quoted as saying, "The people of the original thirteen Southern states curse and spit upon the Fifteenth Amendment and have no intention of letting the Negro vote." Southerners obeyed the letter of the law, "but we frankly evade the spirit thereof—and propose to continue doing so. White supremacy is too precious a thing to surrender for the sake of a theoretical justice that would let a brutish African deem himself the equal of white men and women in Dixie."

ADJUSTMENTS AFTER THE NORTHERN MIGRATION

As black oppression and disfranchisement persisted in the South, large numbers of blacks migrated to the North after the turn of the century. Greater economic opportunity and the possibility of political participation seemed in the offing. But the opportunities to advance through politics were not as available as they seemed. When blacks migrated North they, like the earlier immigrants from Europe, were confronted with established political organizations. They had to compete for political power with other groups who still insisted on their share of the fruits. In return for votes, black newcomers, like groups before them, received political favors, material assistance, and low-paying jobs.

Blacks in the cities expressed strong interest in politics at the grass roots level. Very quickly a large number of associations and organizations, including the Urban League and the NAACP, evolved. But the issues the masses of blacks faced—discrimination in jobs, services, and housing, for example—did not dissipate even when blacks became an increasingly large portion of the electorate.

Blacks had to attempt to gain power in the cities within the context that already existed. If there was no white boss or white machine, there could be no black machine. In Chicago blacks gained the greatest immediate success because there was a machine. Blacks moved into a concentrated area of the city where, led by black political boss Edward Wright, they became a major cog in the Republican machine of Mayor Bill Thompson. In order to consolidate Republican power in the ward, the Republicans backed Oscar DePriest, who was elected in 1915 to the city council. Blacks were served by Thompson's machine. Jobs, intervention with the police, and payoffs on election day worked to consolidate machine support in the black wards. By 1928 DePriest had been elected to Congress. Black political power developed in Chicago because blacks were concentrated residentially in one or two wards, and because Mayor Thompson saw the importance of bringing blacks into politics, as another group in a city of ethnic groups, to support his machine.

During the ten years after Thompson's election, blacks gained increasing power in city politics. Black assistant corporation counsels, city prosecutors, and one assistant state's attorney were appointed. Aldermen and members of the state legislature, in addition to DePriest's elevation to Congress, were elected. Blacks took over the second and third ward machines. DePriest got involved in politics while he was earning a living by painting and decorating and a friend asked him to attend a political meeting one night. As the vote remained evenly divided for rival candidates, he approached one of the candidates and suggested that he would give him two additional votes if he supported DePriest for secretary. After the man refused, DePriest made the same offer to his rival, who accepted.

DePriest learned that the ward organization, with its committeeman at the top dispensing campaign funds and responsible to the county organization for delivering the vote and its precinct captains at the bottom, was the most important political organization in Chicago. The machine protected illegal businesses, arranged licenses and zoning exceptions for votes, and provided small services—Christmas baskets, picnics, parties, and jobs for the voters. DePriest organized a group of precinct captains for bargaining with Martin B. Madden, the white committeeman of the second ward. He began to make money from real estate and kept close ties with Madden. Three times when blacks ran for alderman, he supported Madden's white candidate for the same office. Then Madden supported him for his 1914 election as alderman. After DePriest won, he began organizing his own people's movement to sponsor him as an independent candidate. After his candidates lost in four tries at office, he supported Bill Thompson in the 1928 election. Thompson made him committeeman of the now black-dominated third ward. DePriest used his power to support his longtime crony Madden in his bid for reelection to Congress, even though a young black lawyer, college graduate and World War I veteran William L. Dawson, was running against him in the primary.

Dawson made the election, in part, an issue of race, pointing out that Madden did not even live in the district, and "he is a white man." Thompson was denounced when he went into the black community to support Madden. As he spoke, "the stomping became deafening." DePriest, pleading party regularity, continued to support Madden, who was successfully nominated. When Madden died between his nomination and the general election, DePriest ran for the seat himself. He won with the support of Mayor Thompson, who asserted:

> When he died there came some Judas from Washington and said to me, "We don't want a Negro Congressman. You're the man that can keep a Negro out of Congress." I said, "If I'm the one man who can keep a Negro out of Congress, then, by God, there'll be one there."

DePriest became the first black Congressman since George H. White of North Carolina left in 1901, and he remained in Congress for three terms.

When the Depression made it possible for the Democratic organization in Chicago to elect a mayor, blacks were already a significant factor in politics and the Democratic machine wanted their support. Edward Kelly, who was elected mayor by the city council upon the death of Anton Cermak, began to build a strong permanent Democratic organization. William L. Dawson, a black maverick Republican still active in the city council, wanted to advance politically; he switched to the Democratic party. Kelly gave him control of all patronage in the second ward and Dawson began to build a black machine, with himself as undisputed leader, to deal with the white citywide machine. Dawson, a shrewd politician, began with his second ward base and by 1949 was boss of the entire South Side. What Dawson did was to take over the black voters already organized by

Thompson, DePriest, and Madden and to turn them into a black Democratic machine. The machine elected Arthur Mitchell to Congress in 1934 and then Dawson himself in 1942.

Blacks found it more difficult to gain a share of political power in other cities. New York had even more blacks than Chicago and had a machine system, even though it was weaker than the one in Chicago. But there was no black district leader in Tammany Hall until 1935. In 1917 blacks had elected Edward A. Johnson to the state assembly, but a larger share of offices came slowly. New York districts were larger than Chicago wards, and there was less opportunity for a concentration of black voters. A district could have significant numbers of blacks, Italians, and Jews all competing for offices and power. The single vote possessed by the district in Tammany Hall would have to be split into three one-third votes. When blacks began to enter the Tammany organization at the district level in the 1930s, the city machine was under heavy attack. Mayor Fiorello LaGuardia, elected in 1933, led a successful movement that displaced the power in Tammany Hall with control by the mayor and the board of estimate. Blacks, then, entered Tammany Hall just when the posts there were decreasing in value. No strong black leader emerged; blacks were used by other factions one against the other. When a strong black leader, Adam Clayton Powell, Jr., ran for the twenty-second congressional district seat, created in 1944 specifically for a black, the Democratic district leader was so weak that he was overruled in the central party organization's decision to support Powell. But by the 1950s, Powell and his followers were even able to defeat regular organization candidates in the Democratic congressional primary and in three district leaders' contests.

INFLUENCE IN NATIONAL POLITICS IN THE 1920s

While blacks in New York and Chicago tried to gain a share of local power, at the national level blacks had little influence in the South or in the Republican party in the North. Blacks continued to recognize appointive office as a political resource, but they wanted more than "Negro jobs" in the government.

Some blacks continued to be critical of even the patronage rewards of party loyalty. Among the most consistent of the critics was the Socialist editor of the *Messenger,* A. Philip Randolph, who wrote repeatedly during the 1920s explaining the "causes for the political backwardness of the Negro." Reviewing these causes in November 1917, Randolph wrote words that he would reiterate in the 1920s:

> One of the most prominent of . . . [the causes] is his slavish and foolish worship of the Republican Party, which has pursued a policy of giving "big Negro leaders," the proverbial "job." . . . The Negro has not realized that, while a few leaders rode into jobs by pledging the support of the Negro voter to cunning, conniving, deceptive, and reactionary Republican politicians, the masses of colored voters and people were without civil protection and that they were growing lean and hungry, while the little Negro peanut politicians grew sleek and fat. . . . Fleas don't protect dogs, nor will big Negro leaders or white politicians protect the defenceless Negro.

W. E. B. Du Bois agreed with Randolph.

Du Bois despaired of any possible President making a difference and began admonishing blacks in 1920 to focus on local and congressional elections. In January, 1921, in *Crisis,* he advised of the necessity for disregarding the "chronic colored office seeker." He knew that after Harding's inauguration "he will be besieged by black men who want to be Recorder of Deeds, Register of the Treasury, Assistant Attorneys General and Fifteenth Auditor." These people would assert that "recognition of the Negro is the aim and object of the Negro vote." He wanted blacks to make it clear that voting was not for the purpose of providing "bread and butter for

a few unemployed politicians who have been vociferous during the campaign." Instead, blacks should tell Harding that they wanted an end to lynchings, disfranchisement in the South, and Jim Crow everywhere.

But the Bronx and Manhattan Non-Partisan League wanted to expand the traditional pattern. They asked President Harding in February, 1921, to appoint a black Attorney General. Even though some might think their request paradoxical, they believed that "today the 12,000,000 colored citizens of this country are represented in no position of honor or emolument in this Government." James C. Waters, Jr., of Hyattsville, Maryland, was even more explicit when on March 1, 1921, he wrote in a letter to the editor of the New York *Times* that blacks needed a different type of federal appointee. "All we have," he asserted, "is one appointee 5,000 miles away in a fever infested section of Africa, a Recorder of Deeds in the District of Columbia, a customs officer at New Orleans, and a Collector of Revenue at New York. . . ." He thought blacks should be appointed to powerful jobs like those on the Interstate Commerce Commission, the Federal Trade Commission, and the like. He asked, "Is the colored man to be used only when there's need for cannon fodder and his sister only when there's need for a scrubwoman?"

As the 1920s wore on, some blacks became increasingly critical of party loyalty. A group called the National Democratic Negro Conference Committee, represented by Oscar H. Waters, P. Hampton White, Harvey E. B. Davis, Bishop George A. McGuire, the Right Rev. E. B. Robinson, Alexander Manning, William Bailey, and Perry Brown, announced in Washington on January 17, 1924, that blacks should give "careful consideration" to their vote in the upcoming campaign. The Republican party "has used the Negro as the great football of our American politics." The party was "brazenly, openly, defiantly, trafficking in and traducing the Negro's civic and civil rights as one of the means of retaining control of the government." As the Republican party remained unresponsive to pleas for black patronage and support for civil rights, blacks continued to discuss the best approach to political participation and the role black voters should play in the conservative politics of the 1920s. *Opportunity,* the official publication of the Urban League, noted in February, 1924, that "the tendency appears to be to take more and more interest in local politics." Blacks could see "the civic advantages which come largely through politics such as better educational facilities, police protection, better sanitary conditions, etc." W. E. B. Du Bois in February, 1922, used the absence of schools, sidewalks, and public facilities in Mississippi communities as an example of the discrimination which proceeded from the absence of political power. He therefore lamented the fact that "some persons continue to admonish the Negro that political power is not omnipotent and that without it much may be done to uplift the people; while with it much may be left undone." In July, 1924, he advised blacks, "You don't really care a rap who is president. Republican presidents are just about as bad as Democratic and Democratic presidents are little better than nothing." But he told them that they should carefully select Congressmen and local officials without regard to party.

In January, 1926, S. L. Corrothers, pastor of Roosevelt Memorial Temple and president of the National Independent Voter Association of America, maintained that blacks had derived little benefit from their loyalty to Republicans over the years. A few "menial jobs" and a mention of civil rights were "given to the Negro to make him believe he was receiving some attention." He was convinced that there would be "a halt in this unqualified support of Republican policies." The shift Corrothers saw was only gradual.

As Republicans openly bid for white support in the South, they removed the little influence which prominent blacks had possessed in national nominating conventions by recognizing local white leaders in their stead. The Republican party in the South had been a federal officeholding oligarchy. The bosses carried handpicked delegations to Republican national conventions and used them as pawns in securing continued federal patronage in the South. The states were controlled by the Democrats and the federal offices by the Republican bosses. Now blacks were being excluded from even that minimal share of power. The stage was set for increasing defections from the GOP.

In 1928, Herbert Hoover carried Florida, Kentucky, North Carolina, Tennessee, Texas, Virginia, and West Virginia, capitalizing on southern antipathy toward Roman Catholic, "wet" or anti-prohibition Al Smith. Some black voters defected to Smith, but to no avail. After Hoover's victory, he began to discuss publicly the desire to build up the Republican party in the South, which meant catering to whites at the expense of black aspirations for equal treatment.

However, black voters in the North began to rely upon their strength to lobby for black causes. Their opposition, added to that of labor groups, tipped the vote against Circuit Court Judge John J. Parker, which resulted in the rejection of his nomination to the Supreme Court by the Senate in 1930. Blacks organized to help defeat those senators who had voted for Parker's confirmation, including Henry J. Allen of Kansas, Roscoe McCulloch of Ohio, and Samuel Shortridge of California, when they ran for reelection in 1932. In the defeat of Parker, the NAACP reported in April, 1931, "the bench was kept free of a man who had publicly flouted the wartime constitutional amendment . . . expressing opposition to the Negro's participation in politics." Beyond the constitutional issues, "a body blow was struck at the lily white policy, by which the Hoover administration proposed to conciliate southern white sentiment by sacrificing the Negro and his rights." Franklin D. Roosevelt's candidacy in the midst of the Depression offered an opportunity for many blacks to desert the Republican party, although many stayed with the party of Lincoln until the 1936 election.

During the 1920s and early 1930s the Communist party actively attempted to mobilize blacks. The party sent black visitors, such as Claude McKay, to Russia, where they were warmly welcomed. The Communists called for revolutionary action by black and white workers, applying their theory of nationalism for ethnic minorities in the Soviet Union to a proposal for "self-determination for the Black Belt." They also ran candidates for local and national offices, helped to organize boycotts of businesses which refused to hire blacks in Harlem, and took every opportunity to champion the cause of blacks. A black man, James W. Ford, was the vice presidential candidate on the Communist party ticket in 1932, 1936, and 1940, but not many blacks took the symbolic step of voting for him. The Communist party organizers worked assiduously to gain black adherents during the 1930s and some blacks, including Angelo Herndon, a young Birmingham, Alabama, coal miner, joined the cause. Herndon became a party organizer and was convicted and sentenced to eighteen to twenty years on a chain gang for allegedly inciting blacks in Georgia to insurrection in 1932. Until he was freed by the Supreme Court, the Communists made an international issue not only of his conviction but also of the convictions of nine young blacks for allegedly raping two white women on a freight train near Scottsboro, Alabama, in 1931. New trials were ordered for the Scottsboro boys, but they were convicted again and sentenced to up to ninety-nine years.

The Communists in the 1930s developed a tactic which they utilized persistently throughout the twentieth century—that of attempting to combine with black organizations in a united front against racism. After the National Negro Congress was organized in 1936, they worked to gain some control over its activities, and worked with the congress' president, A. Philip Randolph. Black opposition to the Communist party was based on pragmatism. As James Weldon Johnson said, "Placing our stake on the chance of solving our problem by gaining security through a communistic revolution is taking odds that are infinitely long." Marcus Garvey, holding similar views, wrote in the *Blackman* in 1933: "We would prefer the Communists carrying out their programme by themselves, and then in their success admit the Negro to the right of partaking in the benefits of the new system which they seek to establish, rather than placing the onus on the Negro at this early stage, making him a target of an organized political opposition. . . . The whole world is in arms against Communism. For the Negro, therefore, to lead in the crusade against the present order . . . [is] placing a terrible handicap on his head."

SHIFTING TO THE DEMOCRATIC PARTY IN THE 1930s AND 1940s

Herbert Hoover tried hard to inspire black voters to stick with his party in the 1932 presidential election by using traditional tactics. He sent a message to the May, 1932, NAACP convention lauding the continued progress of blacks since the Civil War. He met with 200 loyal black voters in Washington, who pledged their loyalty to him and he to the cause of civil rights. But after Senator Robert LaFollette, in a long speech at the convention, criticized Hoover for not doing enough to relieve unemployment, Walter White predicted that the black vote would be balanced in November. White insisted that "the old practice of handing out a few dollars to a group of discredited and powerless white and Negro politicians is futile." Unfortunately, "neither of the likely candidates of the major political parties stirred his blood."

The Republicans had to answer for Judge Parker and their silence on lynching and unemployment. Blacks would remember Roosevelt's "boast" that he wrote the constitution of Haiti when it was invaded by American marines, and they would be "suspicious to the extreme" of his support by the South. Increasingly, according to White, blacks understood "that the inequalities which made possible the concentration of enormous wealth in the hands of a few while the vast majority of the world are on the ragged edge of starvation has many of its roots in the exploitation of the brown and yellow people in Africa, India, the Far East, the United States." Black voters would be interested not only in the presidency but also in electing "an intelligent and liberal" Congress and state and local officials who would consider their welfare.

Blacks did not shift quickly to support Democrats, despite the Republican party's failure to protect their interests. Franklin D. Roosevelt was little known outside New York, and his service in the staunchly segregationist Wilson administration did not speak well for him. Also, having John Nance Garner of Texas as his running mate did not help in the black wards. In Chicago, only 23 percent of the black vote was for Democrats in the 1932 election. Blacks in the most depressed areas changed party allegiance the slowest. Personal loyalty to Republican precinct captains and officials whose machine had delivered in the past, and the influx of new migrants from the South who brought their long-held fondness for Republicans with them, seemed to influence the poorer black voters to remain Republican longer.

Throughout the 1930s more and more black leaders called for Afro-American voters to support the Democratic Party. Among them was Marcus Garvey, who declared in August 1936:

The Republicanism of America is too cunning, too crafty, to be of real beneficial

use to the Negro. It only uses the Negro for convenience. Its philosophy is poor, its humanity is poorer. In fact, it has nothing today to recommend it to a people who are seeking a way out from the oppression of those who are seated in power. . . . Sooner or later the American Negro will declare himself. In that event it will need a man with the philosophy and humanity of Roosevelt to bridge the great gulf between crackerdom and real democracy. American Negroes, therefore, should support solidly the democratic standard bearer and send him back to the White House with flying colors.

Black voters responded to the pleas of Garvey and other leaders as well as the "philosophy and humanity" of Roosevelt. By 1936 Roosevelt, in Chicago, for example, received 49 percent of the black vote and by 1940, 52 percent. Blacks were grateful for Roosevelt's programs to alleviate unemployment. Franklin and Eleanor Roosevelt, aware of the growing importance of the black vote, invited blacks to social events at the White House and let it be known that Robert L. Vann of the Pittsburgh *Courier* and other blacks were frequently sought after for advice. Mrs. Roosevelt, who was an intimate friend of Mary McLeod Bethune, was often photographed with her and other blacks.

The long-standing practice of having at least one black adviser and appointing blacks to patronage positions—the "Negro jobs"—in the government was expanded and modified. Roosevelt had an enlarged group of black advisers on racial matters in governmental departments, who constituted a black cabinet: Mary McLeod Bethune as director of the Negro Affairs Division of the National Youth Administration, Robert L. Vann as special assistant to the Attorney General, and Robert Weaver as adviser in the Department of the Interior. Weaver served in a variety of governmental posts and in 1966 he became the first black official cabinet member when the Housing and Home Finance Agency became the Department of Housing and Urban Development. In addition to the black advisers, the number of blacks in the Civil Service increased substantially, although even until the 1980s the majority of blacks were in the lowest skilled and unskilled brackets, with a few in the top grades of government service.

In the 1940s black legislators and local judges, both Democratic and Republican, became commonplace in northern communities where there were large numbers of blacks. However, a large percentage of black officeholders and voters were Democrats.

While the number of blacks holding office grew along with the increase in black voters, certain political changes in cities where there were large numbers of blacks dimmed their future political prospects. In Chicago, where the Dawson machine seemed safely empowered, the Democrats elected a reform mayor, Martin Kennelly, in 1947. Kennelly gave up control of the machine and began using the Civil Service Commission to make appointments. The machine deteriorated to the extent that by 1951 Democratic votes fell off sharply. By 1955, Dawson and the party leaders dumped Kennelly in favor of Richard J. Daley, a party man and a regular member of the inner circle of the county central committee. After Daley won, patronage positions increased somewhat, but Daley decided that he would develop a new political style. His machine would rule, but he would appoint "blue ribbon" newspaper-endorsed candidates for major offices. This meant a diminution of power for Dawson's machine, which was thoroughly disliked by the major papers. Also, Daley's new civic projects such as urban renewal and crime reduction through police harassment affected the black wards most harshly. Dawson found that the few blacks appointed to prestigious boards and commissions were not often his machine-backed candidates.

Blacks fared much worse politically in Detroit and Los Angeles than in Chicago. In both cities politics was nonpartisan. In Detroit, black voters were organized by the United Automobile Workers Union, to which most of the black workers belonged. Most workers learned to vote the union ticket and to vote across racial lines. In addition, city council members were elected at large, which meant that not until 1957 was a black candidate found who could get enough votes citywide to be elected. The possibility of a black mayor and council majority had to await the decline of white population and votes in the city.

Blacks persisted in their loyalty to the Democratic party, but the payoff in terms of appointments was disproportionately small. Blacks had helped the Democrats to destroy the Republican machines, but they did not react to these new events by changing their allegiance again to the Republicans.

Black support for Roosevelt did not prevent racial discrimination in the administration of relief programs, in employment opportunities in the defense industry, and segregation in the armed forces during Roosevelt's presidency. A. Philip Randolph, in calling for a march on Washington in 1941, began to emphasize the need for protest to complement political participation. He asserted, "In this period of power politics, nothing counts but pressure, more pressure, and still more pressure, through the tactic of broad, organized, aggressive mass action behind the vital and important issues of the Negro." If blacks would march, the President would be forced to respond politically. Roosevelt's response in issuing Executive Order 8802 in June, 1941, providing for equal employment in defense industries, proved the efficacy of Randolph's approach.

As the NAACP began to win a large number of cases involving unconstitutional discrimination in education, housing, and voting, the organization increasingly emphasized the importance of actually voting on Election Day to achieve civil rights objectives. In celebrating the drift of blacks from devotion to the Republican party into the Democratic camp, the NAACP in December, 1943, asserted, "The Negro knows that his voting strength in seventeen or more states with 281 or more votes in the electoral college gives him the potential balance of power in any reasonably close national election and in many state and local elections his vote no longer belongs to any one party." David Cartwright, in applauding the black shift to Roosevelt in 1936 as a sign of "greater political maturity," had warned in the pages of *Crisis* that blacks should not become tied to the Democratic party. Continued support of the Democrats would only result in "creation of another Negro political caste whose members will serve as perpetual decoys of the Negro masses." But his warning was ignored, and soon the black vote was as firmly tied to the Democratic party as it had been to the Republicans earlier.

President Harry S. Truman, continuing the trend developed by Roosevelt, seemed to respond to his black constituency. He appointed a committee in 1946 to inquire into the condition of civil rights and make recommendations. Their report, "To Secure These Rights," called for positive programs to provide for legal equality. Truman ordered the desegregation of the armed forces and issued an order in 1948 requiring fair employment in the federal service.

The events surrounding World War II had accelerated the trend toward black participation in political and governmental affairs. By 1948, more than 2,500,000 blacks in the North and West voted and more than 600,000 blacks were registered to vote in twelve southern states. In 1948 there were six black members of city councils in the nation and thirty-three members of state legislatures, including two senators. More than a dozen black judges and magistrates presided over courts, and there were two black Congressmen. As another recognition of his black constituency, Truman affirmed Roosevelt's appointment of Mary McCleod Bethune, Mordecai W. Johnson, president of Howard University, and W. E. B.

Du Bois and Walter White of the NAACP as delegates to the United Nations. Ralph Bunche went as a member of the official State Department staff. Bunche became director of the UN Trusteeship Council and won the Nobel Peace Prize in 1950 for his service as UN mediator in the Palestine dispute. He served as Deputy Secretary General of the UN until his death in 1971. Although it became evident very quickly that the UN would not intervene in U.S. race relations or even in cases of colonialist and neocolonialist oppression in Africa, blacks were usually a part of the American UN delegation.

The formation of the Dixiecrat party to oppose Truman in the 1948 election did not deter Truman from his civil rights policy, and he kept the Progressive party nominee, former Vice President Henry A. Wallace, from making inroads into the black vote. At the NAACP annual meeting in Kansas City in June, Loren Miller suggested that blacks were "pro-Truman" but they would be "pro-Wallace" if Wallace were a factor. At the same meeting, Henry Lee Moon, director of research for the NAACP, predicted an "influential" black vote in several southern states in the fall elections. James Herman of Atlanta pleaded passionately for the black vote to go to Wallace, but Dowdal H. Davis, editor of the *Kansas City Call*, insisted that blacks could not "solve their problems by looking to Russia," and Austin T. Walden, an Atlanta lawyer, stated that "the Negro belongs" in the Democratic party "for practical reasons." When the votes were counted, Wallace carried not one state and black voters were strongly in the Truman column. By the 1952 election, a majority of black voters voted for Adlai Stevenson even while Dwight D. Eisenhower was being elected President.

THE EFFECT OF THE 1950S AND 1960S CIVIL RIGHTS MOVEMENTS

In 1954, William L. Dawson was elected to Congress from Illinois for his seventh term, and Adam Clayton Powell, Jr., was serving his sixth term. That year Charles Diggs was elected from Detroit. By 1964, there were six blacks in the House of Representatives; by 1974 there were seventeen. Blacks were increasingly appointed to posts other than the "Negro jobs" in the government. In 1949 William H. Hastie was appointed to the U.S. Court of Appeals, Third Circuit. Thurgood Marshall was appointed to Circuit Court in 1961, resigned in 1965 to become Solicitor General, and was appointed to the Supreme Court in 1966. The environment in which these advances in political participation took place included Supreme Court decisions protecting voting rights and promoting school desegregation, the Montgomery bus boycott and the emergence of the Rev. Martin Luther King, Jr., the passage of the Civil Rights Act of 1957, the rise of nation-states in Africa, and the sit-ins and civil rights marches of the 1960s.

The boycott and arrests in Montgomery, Alabama, and resistance to the Supreme Court school desegregation decision in *Brown* v. *Board of Education* became issues in the 1956 presidential campaign. When Adlai Stevenson made what seemed to be a weak civil rights statement in February, Roy Wilkins of the NAACP criticized him for not insisting on immediate integration. Stevenson, in clarifying his statement, said he supported integration but "no child can be properly educated in a hostile environment." He thought too rapid government interference might "delay progress." He still received strong support from black voters while Eisenhower was being reelected. In 1957 President Eisenhower sent federal troops to Little Rock, Arkansas, to enforce a desegregation decision at Central High School and to keep order when faced with Governor Orville Faubus' opposition. The first civil rights bill to be enacted by Congress since 1875 was proposed by President Eisenhower in 1957. The act authorized the federal government to bring a civil suit in its own name to obtain injunctive relief when a person was denied or threatened in his right to vote and created

a civil rights division under an Assistant Attorney General in the Department of Justice. It also created the U.S. Commission on Civil Rights from its forerunner, President Truman's Committee on Civil Rights, authorized to investigate denials of the right to vote, to study and collect information concerning legal developments constituting a denial of equal protection of the laws, and to appraise the laws and policies of the federal government with respect to equal protection. The Civil Rights Commission held hearings on black voting in several cities, North and South, and found that blacks were being regularly denied the right to vote by certain white southern registrars. In 1960 another civil rights bill was passed to strengthen voting rights enforcement.

The 1960 presidential nominating conventions and election took place in the midst of the direct action ferment. Roy Wilkins warned both parties before their conventions that they should adopt a civil rights posture "without equivocation." For "equivocation will insure the equivocation of Negro voters in the choosing of party designees in the November election." During the Democratic Convention, the NAACP organized a civil rights rally in which about 6,000 blacks booed Lyndon B. Johnson when Oscar Chapman, who came to represent him, tried to speak, and then they barely let John F. Kennedy speak for himself.

When Chapman mentioned former President Harry S. Truman, who had said that the nonviolent sit-ins in the South were "Communist inspired," loud booing erupted again. But the booing was soon transformed into support. Mordecai Johnson was a voice crying in the wilderness when he told the National Colored Women's Club shortly before the election that "we still do not have a political party that we as a group can trust." Neither party had done anything, according to Johnson, to "give the American Negro an Equal Right to Work."

Three famous black leaders. From left to right, Adam Clayton Powell, Malcolm X, and Dick Gregory.

In the 1960 election, John F. Kennedy won the presidency with significant support from blacks. In the crucial states of Illinois and Michigan, black voters held the balance of power. Kennedy consolidated support in the campaign by interceding when Martin Luther King, Jr., was jailed after a sit-in in a restaurant in an Atlanta, Georgia, department store. He campaigned openly for black votes, criticizing his opponent for inaction. When the returns were in, black voters received some of the traditional rewards for their support. As President, Kennedy appeased Senators from the South by appointing a number of white racist federal judges, but he also appointed large numbers of blacks to federal jobs, including Thurgood Marshall to the Second Circuit and Wade McCree to the District Court for Eastern Michigan. He appointed Carl T. Rowan as Deputy Assistant Secretary of State and later Ambassador to Finland, and

Clifton R. Wharton as Ambassador to Norway and Mercer Cook as Ambassador to Niger. He appointed two black U.S. Attorneys and several blacks to presidential commissions. Overall, the percentage of blacks in federal employment increased, but some agencies still had no blacks at all, and the majority of blacks were still in the lowest ratings.

As the sit-ins, marches, demonstrations, and violent opposition to them continued in 1963, President Kennedy proposed a civil rights bill to Congress in March which became bogged down and seemed likely not to pass. A march for jobs and freedom on August 28, 1963, drew 200,000 people to Washington, but Congress did not move on the bill until after Kennedy's assassination on November 22, 1963, when Lyndon B. Johnson made it "must" legislation. The act, passed early in 1964, gave the Attorney General additional power to protect citizens against discrimination and segregation in voting, education, and the use of public facilities. It established an Equal Employment Opportunity Commission (EEOC) and extended the life of the Commission on Civil Rights. It forbade discrimination in federally assisted programs, with the termination of assistance for failure to comply. The lesson blacks learned reinforced A. Philip Randolph's view at the time of the proposed 1941 march on Washington: protest is an essential ingredient of political success.

President Kennedy and his brother, Attorney General Robert Kennedy, strongly favored a massive voter registration campaign, believing that until blacks became voters, southern Congressmen would not vote for significant civil rights legislation. They also wanted to dissuade blacks from protesting by focusing their attention more directly on political participation. Also, they knew the importance of black voters to Kennedy's election and wanted to create a massive increase of black Democratic voters before the 1964 election. With White House support, CORE, SNCC, SCLC, the NAACP, and the Urban League embarked on a Voter Education Project (VEP) in April, 1962. Designed to last two and one-half years, it cost $870,000, nearly all of which came from the Taconic and Field foundations and the Stern Family Fund. Wiley Branton, the attorney from Pine Bluff, Arkansas, who had been counsel in the Little Rock cases, was appointed to head the project. The VEP was hampered from the start by a Kennedy policy of urging voter registration but failing to protect civil rights activists and blacks attempting to register in order to appease southern whites.

In Mississippi the Council of Federated Organizations (CORE and the NAACP), led by Aaron Henry, Robert Moses, and David Dennis, worked to register blacks. They did so despite the withdrawal of VEP assistance in 1963, when it became evident that few blacks would be able to register. In 1964 the Mississippi effort focused on making a challenge to the regular Mississippi delegation at the 1964 Democratic Convention. The idea was to dramatize the illegal exclusion of blacks from politics by running black candidates for Congress in the Democratic primaries. Blacks tried to participate in precinct and county conventions and run independent candidates in the general election with the notion of unseating the all-white delegation at the National Convention. Late in April a statewide Mississippi Freedom Democratic party (MFDP) convention was held, and Aaron Henry was elected chairman. Four party candidates ran for Congress in the June primaries but were defeated, since few blacks could vote. Blacks who were registered were turned away when they tried to participate in precinct meetings. In August delegates were elected by the MFDP to the National Convention with Henry as chairman. At the convention, Lyndon B. Johnson and Hubert Humphrey arranged a compromise in which the credentials committee seated the regulars, and decided that the two MFDP delegates could be seated as delegates at large. Henry, moved by claims by King, Joseph Rauh, and Bayard Rustin that it was a symbolic victory, wanted to accept. But the entire delegation rejected the compromise and walked out. To them it was just one more failure of the national party to protect them in the South. Fannie Lou Hamer, a Mississippi sharecropper and one of the delegates of the MFDP to the National Convention who had earlier run as one of the four congressional candidates, believed that the experience would make blacks work harder in politics in Mississippi. The people would support the decision not to compromise "because we didn't have anything to compromise for. . . ." She was disconcerted by the lack of support of "other leaders of the Movement." She attended one meeting, where she said she "wouldn't dare think of" accepting a compromise. Thereafter she "wasn't allowed to attend the other meetings. It was *quite* an experience."

With nowhere else to go, those blacks who voted still voted for Lyndon Johnson in the 1964 election.

White hostility to civil rights enforcement did not end after Johnson's overwhelming victory over Barry Goldwater, and the marches and violence continued. The murder of black and white civil rights workers continued in some areas of the South. President Johnson federalized the Alabama National Guard to protect the demonstrators on a march from Selma to Montgomery to push for additional voting rights legislation. Local civil rights workers were faced with strong opposition, economic sanctions, and murder. After the march itself, a white woman from Detroit, Viola Liuzzo, was killed as she transported passengers from Montgomery back to Selma. Lyndon Johnson sent Congress a proposal for a voting rights act which Congress passed quickly in 1965. The act authorized the Attorney General to use federal examiners to register voters, and it suspended literacy tests and other devices in states and counties where less than 50 percent of the adults had voted in 1964. Alabama, Georgia, Louisiana, Mississippi, South Carolina, Virginia, parts of North Carolina, Alaska, and some counties in Arizona, Idaho, and Hawaii were covered by the act. By year's end, nearly 250,000 new black voters had registered, and blacks won seats in the Georgia legislature and in several southern city councils.

President Johnson expanded the policy of appointing blacks to federal posts as a reward for black political support. He appointed Mercer Cook to Senegal, Hugh Smythe to Syria, Franklin Williams to Ghana, Elliott Skinner to Upper Volta, and Patricia Harris to Luxembourg as ambassadors. He appointed Wade McCree to the Circuit Court and Thurgood Marshall to be Solicitor General and then Justice of the Supreme Court; Robert C. Weaver as Secretary of the new Housing and Urban Development Department; Hobart Taylor to the board of the Export-Import Bank; Andrew Brimmer to the Federal Reserve Board; and Walter Washington as Mayor of Washington, D.C.

SENSING THE LIMITS OF POLITICAL PARTICIPATION IN THE 1970S

Somewhere along the way, many blacks became bitter about the possibility of achieving equality even though there was more political participation than ever before. When did this pessimism become endemic? Perhaps the bitterness began when, a month after the march on Washington, four black children were killed in a church bombing in Birmingham. Or it could have been when the protest movement moved North and northern whites who had loved and supported blacks while they protested in the South began to draw careful distinctions between de facto segregation in the North, which was legal because unintended, and de jure segregation in the South, which was bad, to protect their own race and class interests. Or it could have been that blacks had heard too many whites warning them that to demand affirmative action for blacks would be to betray the American principles of democracy and to engage in reverse discrimination against whites. Perhaps it was the repeated warnings of Malcolm X that all of America was the South, or the assassination of the Kennedys and Martin Luther King, Jr., or seeing white people kill not only black rebels in the riots of the 1960s but also their own children in antiwar demonstrations. The net effect was to heighten the sense of the contradictions in American society; blacks sensed the limits of political participation.

By 1966, even as blacks in the South began to vote and participate in politics in large numbers, they began to recognize the limited rewards of suffrage. The problem of overcrowded housing in the cities in the North, a black unemployment rate twice as high as that of whites, and the segregation of black children in inferior schools seemed not to change much as a result of voting and office holding.

Some blacks reacted by turning against police and property in a veritable rash of riots in the 1960s, beginning with the violence in the Watts area of Los Angeles in August, 1965. The move of Martin Luther King, Jr., North in 1965 in order, as he put it, to halt "the increasing segregation in the North" met with hostility from whites and criticism from some blacks who did not believe the social and economic problems they faced would be solved by Christian charity and peaceful demonstration. The assassination of King on April 4, 1968, set off a series of riots and lootings in more than 100 cities by blacks who had seen King's efforts as at least promising some resolution to their plight.

Malcolm X, a year before his death in February, 1965, predicted that the events of the 1960s and the civil rights movement were making blacks "more politically mature." In echoing views expressed earlier by W. E. B. Du Bois, Walter White, and others, he said blacks saw that they could hold the balance of power in certain elections, as in the Kennedy-Nixon 1960 election, "yet when the Negro helps that person get in office the Negro gets nothing in return. All he gets is a few appointments. A few handpicked Uncle Tom handkerchief head Negroes are given big jobs in Washington, D.C., and then those Negroes come back and try and make us think that that administration is going to lead us to the promised land of integration. And the only ones whose problems have been solved have been those handpicked Negroes. A few big Negroes got jobs who didn't even need the jobs. They already were working. But the masses of black people are still unemployed."

Blacks in the civil rights movement who had been closely involved with registering voters had become more and more disillusioned after full equality seemed beyond their reach. They believed that public officials would not enforce laws even after they were passed. They began to believe that blacks must reject coalitions with whites and find some

other way to gain equality. Black leadership in black organizations became the watchword.

When Stokely Carmichael became Chairman of the Student Nonviolent Coordinating Committee (SNCC), he had an answer for the politically mature blacks Malcolm had described. Carmichael explained, "traditionally, for each new ethnic group, the route to social and political integration into America's pluralistic society, has been through the organization of their own institutions with which to represent their communal needs within the larger society." The oldest civil rights organizations both disavowed partisan political activity and relied on coalitions with liberal whites to make gains. Carmichael asserted that this approach would not work because "the political and social rights of Negroes have been and always will be negotiable and expendable the moment they conflict with the interests of our 'allies.'" The result of such coalition policies was that a few "qualified assimilated blacks could get good jobs." If blacks followed his advice and organized in their own communities to control them, their "chief antagonists" would be in the South the overtly racist Democratic party, and in the North the equally corrupt big city machines. He pointed out that when Kennedy and Johnson embarked upon registering black voters, what they really wanted to do was "to register Democrats." The black leaders enlisted in the cause were told to "go home and organize your people into the local Democratic party—*then* we'll see about poverty money and appointments." One result was that blacks were more closely tied to the Democratic party than ever for fear of losing poverty money, and black leaders knew they were "vote deliverers, more responsible to the white machine and the white power structure, than to the community they allegedly represent."

Some blacks continued to be "vote deliverers," while others cast deciding votes in local and national elections and the Democratic party responded to the black voting

Scene from the 1972 National Black Convention, with the Reverend Jesse Jackson and Mayor of Gary, Indiana, Richard Hatcher joining in the singing during opening ceremonies.

bloc by significantly increasing the number of black delegates to the 1972 Democratic National Convention. Some supported black Congresswoman Shirley Chisholm in her unsuccessful campaign for the Democratic presidential nomination in 1972. Others responded to the call for black political organization by participating in the National black Political Convention in Gary, Indiana, in March, 1972. Congressman Charles L. Diggs of Michigan, Mayor Richard Hatcher of Gary, and black poet LeRoi Jones (Imamu Amiri Baraka) issued the official call for the convention of more than 2,700 delegates and 4,000 alternates and observers. The black political agenda released by the leaders of the convention in May, 1972, contained a poor people's platform, model pledges for black and nonblack candidates who wanted black support, the outline of a voter registration bill, and a bill for community self-determination. Its provisions opposing school busing and

United States support of Israel were denounced by Hatcher and Diggs, who feared appearing to approve continued segregation and the loss of Jewish political support. Black politicians saw supporting an independent party as a means of gaining leverage within the Republican and Democratic parties and not as a real alternative. By the 1972 elections, most blacks who ran for office and voted were still in the Democratic column as Richard Nixon swamped George McGovern at the polls.

Despite the ascendancy of Richard Nixon and his active southern policy and disinterest in civil rights, black concentration in urban districts and continued black voting in the South led to some gains. The numbers of black elected officials increased year by year. By 1974 more than 200 blacks sat in 37 state legislatures and 17 in Congress—one Senator from Massachusetts, Edward Brooke (the only Republican), and four women, Shirley Chisholm of New York, Barbara Jordan of Texas, Yvonne

Braithwaite Burke of California, and Cardiss Collins of Illinois. In 1966 there was no black mayor of any major American city, but by 1974 blacks had served as mayors of a number of small southern towns as well as Cleveland, Los Angeles, Gary, Newark, and Washington, D.C. After Nixon was forced to resign for the crimes of Watergate, in January, 1975, Gerald Ford appointed William T. Coleman, Jr., a distinguished Philadelphia lawyer, as Secretary of Transportation, the second black cabinet Secretary in the nation's history.

In May, 1975, there were 3,503 blacks in elective offices, but there were more than 500,000 elected officials in the United States—287 elected officials for every 100,000 people—and the 3,503 black elected officials added up to only 16 for every 100,000 people. The South, which had 53 percent of the total black population, had 55 percent of the black elected officials. Blacks saw that litigation, political participation, and the protest movement had helped to remove legal racial discrimination, but they began to believe that 11 or 15 percent of the total population could not, even with a few white allies, vote the nation into a benevolent democracy. Even white liberals were opposed to the fundamental changes in the economic system required to improve the lot of the black masses. Blacks celebrated the number of black mayors until they noticed that the economic power of the cities was controlled by whites and that whites who could afford to moved to the suburbs and then began establishing metropolitan governments to prevent black political control of additional cities. But, of course, it took the experiences of the 1960s and 1970s to make black people realize the limits of political participation to change the predicament of the masses. Even the Congressional Black Caucus soon confessed the limits of its effectiveness. The theme of their fifth anniversary dinner in 1975 was "from changing institutions to using institutions." Time, the crush of routine congressional business, the need to

tend to problems in their own widely differing districts, and the task of trying to make gains for blacks in the face of a declining economy and what they saw as a hostile Ford administration and an indifferent Congress all contributed to making them "more realistic," the members said.

As the political campaign leading to the 1976 presidential election proceeded, some blacks were determined this time to make their political participation result in substantial benefits to the black community. The Democrats seemed sure to defeat the Republicans in the presidential election after Watergate. Andrew Young, Congressman from Georgia, bet early on Jimmy Carter, reconstructed Governor of Georgia, and provided crucial support for him in the Florida Democratic primary and thereafter. After Carter was nominated, blacks gave him critical votes accounting for his margin of victory over President Gerald Ford in the November election. Carter responded as no President had before in distributing the traditional rewards of political support to his black constituency. He named Andrew Young as Ambassador to the UN, Patricia Harris as HUD Secretary (and later Health and Human Services Secretary), Wade McCree as Solicitor General, Drew Days as Assistant Attorney General for Civil Rights, Eleanor Holmes Norton as Chair of the EEOC, at least one black to a subcabinet post in each of the cabinet departments, and a record number of black federal judges. Andrew Young quickly succeeded in refurbishing America's image in black Africa and extending Henry Kissinger's policy of appearing to support black opposition to the white Rhodesian government. Kissinger's policy and Congressional opposition to United States support of the new regime in Angola, even though it was pro-Communist, was designed to contain Communist influences among the guerillas fighting in Southern Africa.

Soon the blacks' enchantment with President Carter began to dissipate. They saw more clearly than ever before that the traditional rewards for political support did not solve their economic problems. Black unemployment remained twice as high as for whites, and unemployment among black youth was at an all-time high. In addition, President Carter's National Security Advisor, Zbigniew Brzezinski, attacked Andrew Young's support of guerrilla movements in southern Africa as being supportive of Russian expansion in the continent. Young was quickly reined in by Secretary of State Cyrus Vance and the President.

Hard times for blacks seemed marked by a plethora of reverse discrimination cases in which whites struck out against affirmative action programs that were only beginning to bear fruit. When the case of *Bakke* v. *University of California* brought the issue before the U.S. Supreme Court, blacks strenuously pushed the effort to have the Justice Department in the person of Wade McCree, the black Solicitor General, file an *amicus curiae* brief in support of affirmative action. After weeks of behind-the-scenes struggle, the administration took a pro-affirmative action position. As one White House staffer put it, "The President could not solve the economic problems of blacks cheaply, but the brief did not cost anything."

The first black Assistant Attorney General for Civil Rights, Drew S. Days, and the black chair of the EEOC, Eleanor Holmes Norton, asserted that they did not believe affirmative action programs would be deterred by the *Bakke* decision. Significantly, President Carter issued no statement on the subject at first. At an already scheduled meeting of black political appointees on the day of the decision, Andrew Young, as the most senior official present, was urged to ask the President to issue a strong statement of support for affirmative action efforts directed toward blacks. Young refused and advised that none of those present should urge such an action on the President since "it is not our role to tell the President what to do." Black White House staffers announced that their recommendations

that the President issue a statement were overruled by Stuart Eizenstat, the President's Assistant for Domestic Policy, and his deputy, Bert Carp. They reported that Carp explained to them that "white people have rights also" and that the President needed to worry about alienating Jews and other white voters who would be displeased by a presidential statement supporting strong affirmative action efforts for blacks.

A few days later Drew S. Days, in answer to a press question, did express concern about the absence of a statement from the President. Shortly thereafter the President responded to the demands of his black constituency. He issued a memorandum to heads of executive departments and agencies that "the recent decision by the Supreme Court in *Bakke* enables us to continue these efforts [affirmative action] without interruptions." He wanted "to make certain that, in the aftermath of *Bakke* you continue to develop, implement and enforce vigorously affirmative action programs." Ralph Perotta, executive director of the National Italian-American Foundation, saw in the *Bakke* decision that "affirmative action will be opened up to a lot of other groups that have not benefitted before." He planned to ask that the federal civil rights laws be refocused to conform to his view of the decision.

When the Supreme Court decided the *Weber* case in 1979, upholding the right of an employer to train blacks for higher positions to achieve affirmative action goals even if it meant bypassing a white with greater seniority, civil rights advocates were gleeful. They had feared the Court would impose limitations on employment efforts just as the *Bakke* case had limited affirmative action in higher education admissions policy. At least the court left the door open for novel solutions to the employment problems of blacks.

Toward the end of the 1970s, blacks were having great difficulty in reaping the benefits of political participation, in particular their crucial support of President Carter in the 1976 election. The President had trouble convincing Congress to accept his urban employment and social services programs designed to help blacks concentrated in the cities. Congress seemed more concerned with the complaints of their constituents about high taxes and waste in federal programs and by 1980 became obsessed with the need to balance the budget while increasing support for Defense Department programs.

Surely voting had some beneficial effects. In several southern states, enforcement of the Voting Rights Act of 1965 made blacks a significant factor in state and local politics. A fall 1978 Gallup poll reported that blacks had made considerable progress in American society in the fifteen years since the march on Washington. Prejudice toward a black presidential candidate had declined substantially. Seventy-seven percent of Americans, as opposed to 43 percent fifteen years before, were willing to vote for "a qualified black" for President.

The benefits of black political participation were still mixed. In 1976 about 57 percent of whites of voting age voted, but only 45 percent of blacks did so. Of the estimated 9,024,800 blacks registered to vote on November 7, 1976, about 64.1 percent voted. The 1976 results showed that in the presidential election, black voters were safely locked in the Democratic columns but not automatically so in congressional, state, and local races. Prognosticators who had labeled American voters, particularly black voters, apathetic before the election were surprised. There was a steady decline of black voter participation from 1968 through the presidential primaries in 1976, but several factors worked to change apathy to involvement again. Blacks who had become completely disenchanted about achieving social and economic gains through the political system came to believe during Richard Nixon's two terms that, in the absence of a revolution, some political influence was to be preferred

to none at all. In the aftermath of the 1960s rebellions and the suppression of black revolutionary movements by the federal government, a revolution seemed entirely beyond reach.

As early as May, 1976, a group of black leaders who represented major national, civic, religious, fraternal, labor, and civil rights organizations, convinced that the time was right to use voting for social and economic gains, met in Washington, D.C., to devise a strategy to combat voter apathy. They created the Nonpartisan National Coalition on Black Voter Participation. As the summer progressed, labor unions, civil rights groups, and the Atlanta-based VEP linked to mobilize the black vote. Registrations increased, and one result was that for Jimmy Carter, as the Joint Center for Political Studies reported, "the bottom line was black votes." The structure of the electoral college and the concentration of black voters in key states provided opportunities for blacks to exercise leverage in a presidential election.

While the long struggle to gain the right to vote resulted in the traditional benefits of political participation, blacks registered disappointment with their status, and their social and economic problems appeared intractable. Black members of Congress reported that constituents often did not feel that their representatives were solving housing and unemployment problems. Black mayors reported that not enough was being done to provide economic support in their cities. The continued complaints underscored the limits of political participation. Increased black participation in politics did result in more black officeholders, some increase in government contracts to blacks and black institutions, more public service job programs, and more obvious enforcement of civil rights. But no amount of participation seemed to precipitate a redistribution of national income or jobs or other changes that would solve the problems the masses of blacks face in their lives.

As the public increasingly focused on the politics of the 1980 presidential election, black prospects for reaping the benefits of political participation worsened. By September, 1979, Andrew Young was no longer with the Carter administration, although at the 1978 Black Caucus dinner the President had announced that Young would be in his administration as long as he wanted to stay. Young resigned after Israeli protests over his meeting with Palestine Liberation Organization (PLO) representatives to try to influence the course of a UN vote on the Middle East.

Young's violation of the government's prohibition against meetings with the PLO, maintained since the Nixon administration, led to his departure. Black reaction was fierce and fast. The Congressional Black Caucus, chaired by Cardiss Collins of Illinois, informed President Carter that he was not invited to speak at their annual dinner in September, 1979. The Rev. Joseph Lowery, president of the Southern Christian Leadership Conference (SCLC), Walter Fauntroy, Congressman from Washington, D.C., and other SCLC members accepted an invitation to visit Yasir Arafat and the PLO in Lebanon, as did the Rev. Jesse Jackson, national president of Operation People United to Save Humanity (PUSH), on a separate mission. In doing so, Lowery, Fauntroy, and Jackson incurred the wrath of American Jews, and Jackson, who had seemed to become President Carter's favorite black leader, suddenly found himself to be persona non grata at the White House. Benjamin Hooks and Vernon Jordan tested the waters and then withdrew into silence or lamentations regarding the excursions by their brothers into the Palestinian issue, which could be better left to the State Department. Although Lowery, Fauntroy, and Jackson asked to see Prime Minister Menachim Begin of Israel and Jackson stopped off in Israel for a visit before visiting the Palestinians, their requests were denied. Andrew Young and Jesse Jackson pointed out that if Begin could meet with Prime Minister John Vorster of South Africa, he could certainly find reasons to meet with them.

Suddenly on October 13, 1979, after Bayard Rustin wrote several pieces denouncing his brethren for visiting the Palestinian terrorists without mentioning that Begin himself was a terrorist, and after Hooks announced that blacks should not meddle in foreign policy, Begin decided to receive a group of black civil rights leaders, including Rustin and representatives of the National Urban League, the NAACP, and various labor unions. Rustin said, "We owe it to the people of Israel to show that there are a variety of views in the U.S. and that ours is the major one."

After Vernon Jordan added fuel to the fire by publicly criticizing the leaders who had visited the PLO, a hastily called meeting of the Black Leadership Forum on Wednesday night, October 24, criticized Jordan and Rustin for attacking other black leaders and issued a statement denouncing attacks by Jews and others on blacks who criticized the failure of Israel to make peace with the Palestinian Arabs. Throughout the controversy, President Carter stood on the sidelines and did not explain the "resignation" of Andrew Young.

The opening of Senator Edward Kennedy's official challenge to President Carter for the Democratic party nomination could have been the signal for blacks to join the Kennedy bandwagon. But the leadership in the Congressional Black Caucus and the civil rights groups was hesitant to take the risk of supporting a challenge to an incumbent President. Some supported President Carter, a few opted for Kennedy, and others organized a black political convention in Richmond, Virginia, in late February, 1980, to update an agenda reiterating the economic and social needs of the black community. In an increasingly conservative political climate, so disinterested were the presidential candidates in the influence of black leadership over the black vote that none of them appeared when invited to speak before the convention.

Despite their economic concerns, blacks supported Carter after his nomination because Republican nominee Ronald Reagan offered no economic program to meet the unemployment crisis directly and promised weaker civil rights enforcement. Ronald Reagan, dubbed a "racist" by Carter, won by a landslide, while about 85 percent of the black vote went to Carter. When Republicans won not only the presidency but control of the Senate, the Congress could not be expected, as in the Nixon era, to reject cuts in the budgets of social programs for which blacks were major beneficiaries. Also, long-time civil rights opponent Senator Strom Thurmond replaced Edward Kennedy as Chairman of the Senate Judiciary Committee, which controls the confirmation of federal judges. Senator Orrin Hatch of Utah replaced Harrison Williams as Chairman of the Subcommittee on Labor and Human Resources, which controls many social programs and the confirmation of the officials who manage them. Furthermore, Hatch, a strong opponent of civil rights, succeeded Birch Bayh as chairman of the Judiciary Subcommittee on the Constitution, which controls civil rights agencies and legislation.

As blacks reflected on the strategies they might use to address the political changes, they saw increasingly that direct action, protest, whether violent or nonviolent, was an essential ingredient of successful political action. But the political action did not improve the overall black condition. Even the new coalition-building politics had worked in the economic arena only to the extent that the goals did not require inordinate sacrifices on the part of any other members of the coalition. Unfortunately, the goals sought by the masses of blacks would require economic and status sacrifices on the part of whites.

Part IX *Key Terms and Essay/Discussion Questions*

KEY TERMS

Political culture

American democracy

Institutional racism

Three-fifths Compromise

Toussaint L'Ouverture

Missouri Compromise

Thirteenth Amendment

Fourteenth Amendment

Fifteenth Amendment

Crispus Attucks

Mary McCleod Bethune

NAACP

SNCC

Shirley Chisolm

Affirmative Action

Civil Rights Movement

Black Power Movement

Federalism

States' rights

Dred Scott case

Civil War

Reconstruction

Frederick Douglass

Hiram R. Revels

Blanche K. Bruce

Rutherford B. Hayes

Booker T. Washington

Oscar DePriest

Claude McKay

Martin Luther King, Jr.

Malcolm X

Jesse Jackson

Barbara Jordan

National Black Political Convention

Mississippi Freedom Democratic Party

Bakke *v.* University of California

ESSAY/DISCUSSION QUESTIONS

1. The contradiction between America's ideal of democracy and the practice of black oppression is fundamental to this nation's political culture and is a motivating force in the historic African American struggle for social change. Discuss.

2. How have southern whites historically benefitted from the federalist structure of the American political system?

3. What were the circumstances under which free African Americans both disagreed with and supported President Abraham Lincoln during the Civil War?

4. What is the significance of Reconstruction and its overthrow to African American political history? What political lessons can be drawn from these experiences?

5. How did Booker T. Washington respond to the political disenfranchisement of African Americans following Reconstruction?

6. When and why did African Americans become largely supportive of the Democratic Party?

7. It can be argued that the Black Power movement erupted as a result of frustrations with the Civil Rights movement. Compare and contrast the two movements by examining their leaders, ideologies, and organizations. What were the strengths and weaknesses of each movement?

Part IX *Supplementary Readings*

Allen, Robert L., *Reluctant Reformers: The Impact of Racism on American Social Reform Movements,* Washington, D. C.: Howard University Press, 1974.

_____, *Black Awakening in Capitalist America: An Analytic History,* Garden City: Doubleday and Company, Inc., 1969.

Anthony, Earl, *Picking Up the Gun: A Report on the Black Panthers,* New York: The Dial Press, 1970.

Assefa, Hizkias, and Paul Wahrhaftig, *The Move Crisis in Philadelphia: Extremist Groups and Conflict Resolution,* Pittsburgh: University of Pittsburgh Press, 1990.

Barker, Lucius J., and Ronald W. Walters, eds., *Jesse Jackson's 1984 Presidential Campaign: Challenge and Change in American Politics,* Urbana: University of Illinois Press, 1989.

Barker, Lucius J., and Jesse J. McCorry, Jr., *Black Americans and the Political System,* Cambridge: Winthrop Publishers, Inc., 1976.

Barnett, Marguerite R., and James A. Hefner, eds., *Public Policy for the Black Community,* New York: Alfred Publishing Company, 1976.

Boskin, Joseph, *Urban Racial Violence in the Twentieth Century,* Beverly Hills: Glencoe Press, 1969.

Boyte, Harry C., *Common Wealth: A Return to Citizen Politics,* New York: The Free Press, 1989.

_____, and Frank Riessman, eds., *The New Populism: The Politics of Empowerment,* Philadelphia: Temple University Press, 1986.

Branch, Taylor, *Parting the Waters: America in the King Years, 1954–63,* New York: Simon and Schuster, 1988.

Brisbane, Robert H., *The Black Vanguard: Origins of the Negro Social Revolution, 1900–1960,* Valley Forge: Judson Press, 1970.

Browning, Rufus P., Dale R. Marshall, and David H. Tabb, eds., *Racial Politics in American Cities,* New York: Longman, 1990.

_____, *Protest Is Not Enough: The Struggle of Blacks and Hispanics for Equality in Urban Politics,* Berkeley: University of California Press, 1984.

Bunche, Ralph J., *The Political Status of the Negro in the Age of FDR,* Chicago: The University of Chicago Press, 1973.

Bush, Rod, ed., *The New Black Vote: Politics and Power in Four American Cities,* San Francisco: Synthesis Publications, 1984.

Button, James W., *Blacks and Social Change: Impact of the Civil Rights Movement in Southern Communities,* Princeton: Princeton University Press, 1989.

Carmichael, Stokely, and Charles V. Hamilton, *Black Power: The Politics of Liberation in America,* New York: Random House, 1967.

Carson, Clayborne, *In Struggle: SNCC and the Black Awakening of the 1960s,* Cambridge: Harvard University Press, 1981.

Chisholm, Shirley, *Unbought and Unbossed,* Boston: Houghton Mifflin Company, 1970.

Clarke, John Henrik, ed., *Marcus Garvey and the Vision of Africa,* New York: Vintage Books, 1974.

———, ed., *Malcolm X: The Man and His Times,* New York: Collier Books, 1969.

Clavel, Pierre, and Win Wiewel, eds., *Harold Washington and the Neighborhoods: Progressive City Government in Chicago, 1983–1987,* New Brunswick: Rutgers University Press, 1991.

Conant, Ralph W., *The Prospects for Revolution: A Study of Riots, Civil Disobedience, and Insurrection in Contemporary America,* New York: Harper's Magazine Press, 1971.

Cone, James H., *Martin and Malcolm and America: A Dream or a Nightmare,* Maryknoll: Orbis Books, 1991.

Cronon, Edmund D., *Black Moses: The Story of Marcus Garvey and the Universal Negro Improvement Association,* Madison: The University of Wisconsin Press, 1966.

Cruse, Harold, *Plural But Equal: Blacks and Minorities in America's Plural Society,* New York: William Morrow and Company, 1987.

Dionee, E. J., Jr., *Why Americans Hate Politics,* New York: Simon and Schuster, 1991.

Duberman, Martin B., *Paul Robeson,* New York: Alfred A. Knopf, 1988.

Durden-Smith, Jo, *Who Killed George Jackson?* New York: Alfred A. Knopf, 1976.

Duster, Alfreda M., ed., *The Autobiography of Ida B. Wells,* Chicago: The University of Chicago Press, 1976.

Dymally, Mervyn M., ed., *The Black Politician: His Struggle for Power,* Belmont: Duxbury Press, 1971.

Edsall, Thomas B., and Mary D. Edsall, *Chain Reaction: The Impact of Race, Rights, and Taxes on American Politics,* New York: W. W. Norton and Company, 1991.

Farmer, James, *Lay Bare the Heart: An Autobiography of the Civil Rights Movement,* New York: Arbor House, 1985.

Forman, James, *The Making of Black Revolutionaries,* New York: The Macmillan Company, 1972.

Franklin, John H., and August Meier, eds., *Black Leaders of the Twentieth Century,* Urbana: University of Illinois Press, 1982.

Greider, William, *Who Will Tell the People: The Betrayal of American Democracy,* New York: Simon and Schuster, 1992.

Garrow, David J., *Bearing the Cross: Martin Luther King, Jr., and the Southern Christian Leadership Conference,* New York: William Morrow and Company, Inc., 1986.

————, *Protest at Selma: Martin Luther King, Jr., and the Voting Rights Act of 1965,* New Haven: Yale University Press, 1978.

Goldman, Peter, *The Death and Life of Malcolm X,* New York: Harper and Row, Publishers, 1973.

Hamilton, Charles V., *Adam Clayton Powell, Jr.: The Political Biography of an American Dilemma,* New York: Atheneum, 1991.

————, *The Black Experience in American Politics,* New York: G. P. Putnam's Sons, 1973.

Harland, Louis R., *Booker T. Washington: The Wizard of Tuskegee, 1901–1915,* New York: Oxford University Press, 1983.

Hayes, Floyd W. III, "Governmental Retreat and the Politics of African-American Self-Reliant Development: Public Discourse and Social Policy," *Journal of Black Studies,* Vol. 22, No. 3 (March 1992), pp. 331–348.

Haywood, Harry, *Black Bolshevik: Autobiography of an Afro-American Communist,* Chicago: Liberator Press, 1978.

Henderson, Lenneal J., Jr., *Black Political Life in the United States: A Fist as the Pendulum,* San Francisco: Chandler Publishing Company, 1972.

Henry, Charles P., *Culture and African American Politics,* Bloomington: Indiana University Press, 1990.

Holden, Matthew, Jr., *The Politics of the Black 'Nation,'* New York: Chandler Publishing Company, 1973.

Holt, Rackham, *Mary McLeod Bethune,* New York: Doubleday and Company, 1964.

Jackson, Byran O., and Michael B. Preston, eds., *Racial and Ethnic Politics in California,* Berkeley: Institute of Governmental Studies/University of California, 1991.

Jones, Charles E., "The Political Repression of the Black Panther Party: The Case of the Oakland Bay Area," *Journal of Black Studies,* Vol. 18, No. 4 (June 1988), pp. 415–434.

————, "United We Stand, Divided We Fall: An Analysis of the Congressional Black Caucus Voting Behavior, 1975–1980," *Phylon: The Review of Race and Culture,* Vol. 48, No. 1 (1987), pp. 26–37.

Karagueuzian, Dikran, *Blow It Up!: The Black Student Revolt at San Francisco State and the Emergence of Dr. Hayakawa,* Boston: Gambit, Inc., 1971.

Katznelson, Ira, *City Trenches: Urban Politics and the Patterning of Class in the United States,* New York: Pantheon Books, 1981.

King, Mel, *Chain of Change: Struggles for Black Community Development,* Boston: South End Press, 1981.

Kornweibel, Theodore, Jr., *No Crystal Stair: Black Life and the Messenger, 1917–1928,* Westport: Greenwood Press, 1975.

Litwack, Leon, and August Meier, eds., *Black Leaders of the Nineteenth Century,* Urbana: University of Illinois Press, 1988.

Logan, Rayford, *The Betrayal of the Negro: From Rutherford B. Hayes to Woodrow Wilson,* New York: Collier Books, 1965.

Lomax, Louis E., *The Negro Revolt,* New York: Signet Book, 1963.

McAdam, Doug, *Freedom Summer,* New York: Oxford University Press, 1988.

_____, *Political Process and the Development of Black Insurgency, 1930–1970,* Chicago: The University of Chicago Press, 1982.

McLellan, Vin, and Paul Avery, *The Voices of Guns,* New York: G. P. Putnam's Sons, 1977.

Malcolm X, *The Autobiography of Malcolm X,* New York: Grove Press, Inc., 1964.

Mann, Eric, *Comrade George: An Investigation into the Life, Political Thought, and Assassination of George Jackson,* New York: Perennial Library, 1974.

Marable, Manning, *Race, Reform, and Rebellion: The Second Reconstruction in Black America, 1945–1990,* 2d. Ed., Jackson: University Press of Mississippi, 1991.

_____, *W. E. B. Du Bois: Black Radical Democrat,* Boston: Twayne Publishers, 1986.

_____, *Black American Politics: From the Washington Marches to Jesse Jackson,* London: Verso, 1985.

Marine, Gene, *The Black Panthers,* New York: Signet Books, 1969.

Martin, Tony, *Race First: The Ideological and Organizational Struggles of Marcus Garvey and the Universal Negro Improvement Association,* Westport: Greenwood Press, 1976.

Martin, Waldo E., Jr., *The Mind of Frederick Douglass,* Chapel Hill: The University of North Carolina Press, 1984.

Morris, Aldon D., *The Origins of the Civil Rights Movement: Black Communities Organizing for Change,* New York: The Free Press, 1984.

Naison, Mark, *Communism in Harlem During the Depression,* Urbana: University of Illinois Press, 1983.

Omi, Michael, and Howard Winant, *Racial Formation in the United States: From the 1960s to the 1990s,* New York: Routledge and Kegan Paul, 1986.

O'Reilly, Kenneth, *"Racial Matters": The FBI's Secret File on Black America, 1960–1972,* New York: The Free Press, 1989.

Parker, Frank R., *Black Votes Count: Political Empowerment in Mississippi After 1965,* Chapel Hill: The University of North Carolina Press, 1990.

Patterson, William L., *The Man Who Cried Genocide: An Autobiography,* New York: International Publishers, 1971.

Pfeffer, Paula F., *A. Philip Randolph, Pioneer of the Civil Rights Movement,* Baton Rouge: Louisiana State University Press, 1990.

Pohlmann, Marcus D., *Black Politics in Conservative America,* New York: Longman, 1990.

Preston, Michael B., Lenneal J. Henderson, Jr., and Paul L. Puryear, eds., *The New Black Politics: The Search for Political Power,* New York: Longman Inc., 1987.

Reed, Adolph L., Jr., *The Jesse Jackson Phenomenon: The Crisis of Purpose in Afro-American Politics*, New Haven: Yale University Press, 1986.

Rivlin, Benjamin, ed., *Ralph Bunche: The Man and His Times*, New York: Holmes and Meier, 1990.

Savitch, H. V., and John C. Thomas, eds., *Big City Politics in Transition*, Newbury Park: Sage Publications, Inc., 1991.

Shapiro, Herbert, *White Violence and Black Response: From Reconstruction to Montgomery*, Amherst: University of Massachusetts Press, 1988.

Shepperd, Gladys B., *Mary Church Terrell, Respectable Person*, Baltimore: Human Relations Press, 1959.

Sitkoff, Harard, *A New Deal for Blacks: The Emergence of Civil Rights as a National Issue*, New York: Oxford University Press, 1978.

Smith, J. Owens, *The Politics of Racial Inequality: A Systematic Comparative Macro-Analysis from the Colonial Period to 1970*, Westport: Greenwood Press, 1987.

Stone, Chuck, *Black Political Power in America*, Chicago: The Bobbs-Merrill Company, 1968.

Walters, Ronald W., *Black Presidential Politics in America: A Strategic Approach*, Albany: State University of New York Press, 1988.

Stone, Clarence N., *Regime Politics: Governing Atlanta, 1946–1988*, Lawrence: University Press of Kansas, 1989.

Vincent, Theodore G., *Black Power and the Garvey Movement*, Berkeley: Rampart Press, nd.

Walton, Hanes, Jr., *Invisible Politics: Black Political Behavior*, Albany: State University of New York Press, 1985.

_____, *Black Political Parties*, New York: The Free Press, 1972.

_____, *Black Politics: A Theoretical and Structural Analysis*, Philadelphia: J. B. Lippincott Company, 1972.

Weisbord, Robert G., *Genocide?: Birth Control and the Black American*, Westport: Greenwood Press, 1975.

Weiss, Nancy J., *Whitney M. Young, Jr., and the Struggle for Civil Rights*, Princeton: Princeton University Press, 1989.

Wells-Barnett, Ida, *On Lynchings*, New York: Arno Press, 1960.

Wilson, William J., *Power, Racism, and Privilege: Race Relations in Theoretical and Sociohistorical Perspectives*, New York: The Macmillan Company, 1973.

Zinn, Howard, *SNCC: The New Abolitionists*, Boston: Beacon Press, 1965.

Ideology and the Culture of Ambiguity

America's "sacred texts"—which include at least the Declaration of Independence, the Federalist Papers, the U. S. Constitution, and Abraham Lincoln's Gettysburg Address—set forth such enlightened principles as freedom, equality, justice, morality, community, and democratic government. Yet, the trans-Atlantic slave trade, and the resultant large population of African and African-descended slaves in America, contradicted those lofty principles. The post-emancipation period of segregation and racism further exposed the inconsistency between democratic theory and practice. In this society, where the negative characterization and exclusion of African American women and men has been so institutionalized—while the institutions are apparently so admirable—African Americans have been the victims of such paradox. They have had simultaneously to engage in an external struggle with their white oppressors and in an internal battle with themselves. This is the coercive and seductive power of cultural hegemony!

The articles in this section focus on some of the historic and contemporary dilemmas and ideological struggles confronting African American men and women—in particular, those problems posed by Euro-American cultural hegemony. Therefore, attention has been directed to internal contradictions.

W. E. B. Du Bois' essay, "Of Our Spiritual Strivings," is a classic statement of the existential condition of the African American, or what it means to be an African-descended American. Written on the eve of the twentieth century, it is a deeply moving essay in which Du Bois seeks to reveal, as much as his rationalist orientation will allow, the innermost soul of African Americans. He uses the veil as his essential metaphor and theme, symbolizing white American imposition of physical separation (segregation) and psychological-attitudinal separation (racism). For Du Bois, white power excludes and dehumanizes African Americans and turns them into a "problem." And since whites do not recognize African Americans' essential humanity, they speak to and act unintelligently toward them; this reinforces how thoroughly all African Americans are excluded from the American social order.

Yet, a veil is a single entity possessing two sides. In the moment that it separates them, it also links them. Hence, African Americans also are intricately woven into America's social fabric. The African American is both excluded from and included in the American social dynamic, and this is the source of the African American predicament. For Du Bois, this results in a bifurcated sensibility, or divided self. African Americans experience double consciousness, an identity crisis, in which they are burdened with the clash between their African cultural heritage and social outlook and the values promulgated by white American cultural domination. For African Americans, the struggle for self-consciousness is interrupted and shaped by their oppressors' consciousness, so even when African Americans look at themselves or each other, they do so, according to Du Bois, from the negative standpoint or world view of white American cultural hegemony.

Since it is this clash of African and American cultures that constitutes African Americans' internal dilemma, the resultant "spiritual striving" is the struggle to blend the two dimensions of the divided self. Du Bois seems to be suggesting that African Americans' search for self-consciousness is a search for wholeness, and it also is a historic struggle for African American humanity within the larger American social dynamic.

In the essay "Assessing Black Neoconservatism," Cornel West probes the meaning of the recent rise to prominence of African American neoconservatives during the age of Reaganism. Although African American conservatism is not a new phenomenon—its genealogy can be traced back at least to the nineteenth century—West suggests that the emergence of the new African American conservatives in the current period has resulted from (1) the decline of United States global economic and military dominance, (2) the fundamental change in the American economy, and (3) the collapse of the moral infrastructure of America's urban working-class and impoverished communities.

After World War II there was an expanding African American middle class and a concomitant rise of professionals and elected officials, buttressed largely by affirmative action policies. West points out that although African American neoconservatives are themselves beneficiaries of affirmative action policies, they now have come to assault these programs in lock-step with their fellow white conservative ideologues. Attacking affirmative action policies and programs as racially biased, conservatives advocate hiring solely on the basis of merit. Yet, West argues, African American neoconservatives' advocacy of race-free employment hiring policies actually rationalizes continued employment discrimination against African Americans.

West argues that the decline of the manufacturing-based economy of the first half of this century and the rise of the services-based economy of the last half have severely affected the employment status of African Americans. Because most are skilled and unskilled industrial workers, African Americans have experienced tremendous job losses as a result of America's economic transformation. African American neoconservatives attack the argument of traditional African American liberal leaders that racism is the sole cause of the dramatic increase of poverty and attendant social problems in urban communities. Traditional African American liberal leaders continue to call on government for solutions to these difficulties. Neoconservatives argue that racial discrimination alone cannot explain these growing social difficulties, contending that government may well be their cause. According to West, African American neoconservatives thus have unmasked the crisis of traditional African American leadership. However, West states that the African American masses have not endorsed or legitimized the neoconservatives' support for the Reaganite economic policies and programs. When neoconservatives blame African American individuals and communities themselves for the occurrence of social and moral dislocations, they ignore the reality that a credible jobs program can help fight urban poverty. West points out however, that the welfare state cannot solve the economic, social, and cultural disarray in urban impoverished communities. In fact, he argues that neither African American liberal nor neoconservative elites speak to the needs and aspirations of the African American masses.

Patricia Hill Collins' article, "The Social Construction of Black Feminist Thought," sets forth an African American women's standpoint about the meaning of oppression and what women can and should do to resist it. Along the way, she articulates the political and epistemological issues that shape the social construction of African American feminist thought. In discussing the African American women's perspective, Collins argues that their everyday acts of resistance to oppression negate the assumption that the oppressed identify with their oppressors. She proposes that African American women's concrete political and economic situation has resulted in their unique life experiences, which have inspired a distinctive African American feminist consciousness. Since that consciousness comes out of concrete experiences, an oppressed group thinks about and operates in the world differently from an oppressor group.

Collins notes that African American feminist thought is the intellectual's specialized knowledge that articulates the existing, taken-for-granted knowledge of African American women. It is not some new set of ideas or perspectives but is a rearticulation of already present African American women's consciousness. In order to grasp and then express this particular standpoint, Collins contends that the traditional Eurocentric masculinist approach to validating or disproving knowledge claims must be set aside. As an example, Collins refers to the positivist approach to knowledge validation, which she finds inadequate because it is objectivist, unemotional, and adversarial.

As an alternative, Collins put forward an Afrocentric feminist epistemology—a theory of knowledge based fundamentally on the shared life experiences of people of African descent. Additionally, since African American women also share a gender experience, Collins also incorporates a feminist perspective into her proposal for an Afrocentric feminist theory of knowledge. She suggests that an Afrocentric feminist epistemology includes the following elements: (1) concrete experience or wisdom within an African American institutional or organizational context as a criterion for meaning; (2) dialogue, more particularly call and response discourse, employed to assess knowledge claims; (3) the ethic of caring—the value of personal expressiveness, the appropriateness of emotion, and the capacity for empathy; and (4) the ethic of accountability.

O water, voice of my heart, crying in the sand,
   All night long crying with a mournful cry,
As I lie and listen, and cannot understand
     The voice of my heart in my side or the voice of the sea,
  O water, crying for rest, is it I, is it I?
    All night long the water is crying to me.

Unresting water, there shall never be rest
   Till the last moon droop and the last tide fail,
And the fire of the end begin to burn in the west;
     And the heart shall be weary and wonder and cry like the sea,
  All life long crying without avail,
    As the water all night long is crying to me.
         ARTHUR SYMONS

Of Our Spiritual Strivings

W. E. B. DU BOIS

BETWEEN ME AND THE OTHER world there is ever an unasked question: unasked by some through feelings of delicacy; by others through the difficulty of rightly framing it. All, nevertheless, flutter round it. They approach me in a half-hesitant sort of way, eye me curiously or compassionately, and then, instead of saying directly, How does it feel to be a problem? they say, I know an excellent colored man in my town; or, I fought at Mechanicsville; or, Do not these Southern outrages make your blood boil? At these I smile, or am interested, or reduce the boiling to a simmer, as the occasion may require. To the real question, How does it feel to be a problem? I answer seldom a word.

And yet, being a problem is a strange experience,—peculiar even for one who has never been anything else, save perhaps in babyhood and in Europe. It is in the early days of rollicking boyhood that the revelation first bursts upon one, all in a day, as it were. I remember well when the shadow swept across me. I was a little thing, away up in the hills of New England, where the dark Housatonic winds between Hoosac and Taghkanic to the sea. In a wee wooden schoolhouse, something put it into the boys' and girls' heads to buy gorgeous visiting-cards—ten cents a package—and exchange. The exchange was merry, till one girl, a tall newcomer, refused my card,—refused it peremptorily, with a glance. Then it dawned upon me with a certain suddenness that I was different from the others; or like, mayhap, in heart and life and longing, but shut out from their world by a vast veil. I had thereafter no desire to tear down that veil, to creep through; I held all beyond it in common contempt, and lived above it in a region of blue sky and great wandering shadows. That sky was bluest when I could beat my mates at examination-time, or beat them at a foot-race, or even beat their stringy heads. Alas, with the years all this fine contempt began to fade; for the worlds I longed for, and all their dazzling opportunities, were theirs, not mine. But they should not keep these prizes, I said; some, all, I would wrest from them. Just how I would

From *Souls of Black Folk* by W. E. B. Du Bois, Penguin Books, 1989. (First published by A. C. McClurg & Co., 1903.)

do it I could never decide: by reading law, by healing the sick, by telling the wonderful tales that swam in my head,—some way. With other black boys the strife was not so fiercely sunny: their youth shrunk into tasteless sycophancy, or into silent hatred of the pale world about them and mocking distrust of everything white; or wasted itself in a bitter cry, Why did God make me an outcast and a stranger in mine own house? The shades of the prison-house closed round about us all: walls strait and stubborn to the whitest, but relentlessly narrow, tall, and unscalable to sons of night who must plod darkly on in resignation, or beat unavailing palms against the stone, or steadily, half hopelessly, watch the streak of blue above.

After the Egyptian and Indian, the Greek and Roman, the Teuton and Mongolian, the Negro is a sort of seventh son, born with a veil, and gifted with second-sight in this American world,—a world which yields him no true self-consciousness, but only lets him see himself through the revelation of the other world. It is a peculiar sensation, this double-consciousness, this sense of always looking at one's self through the eyes of others, of measuring one's soul by the tape of a world that looks on in amused contempt and pity. One ever feels his twoness,—an American, a Negro; two souls, two thoughts, two unreconciled strivings; two warring ideals in one dark body, whose dogged strength alone keeps it from being torn asunder.

The history of the American Negro is the history of this strife—this longing to attain self-conscious manhood, to merge his double self into a better and truer self. In this merging he wishes neither of the older selves to be lost. He would not Africanize America, for America has too much to teach the world and Africa. He would not bleach his Negro soul in a flood of white Americanism, for he knows that Negro blood has a message for the world. He simply wishes to make it possible for a man to be both a Negro and an American,

without being cursed and spit upon by his fellows, without having the doors of Opportunity closed roughly in his face.

This, then, is the end of his striving: to be a co-worker in the kingdom of culture, to escape both death and isolation, to husband and use his best powers and his latent genius. These powers of body and mind have in the past been strangely wasted, dispersed, or forgotten. The shadow of a mighty Negro past flits through the tale of Ethiopia the Shadowy and of Egypt the Sphinx. Throughout history, the powers of single black men flash here and there like falling stars, and die sometimes before the world has rightly gauged their brightness. Here in America, in the few days since Emancipation, the black man's turning hither and thither in hesitant and doubtful striving has often made his very strength to lose effectiveness, to seem like absence of power, like weakness. And yet it is not weakness,—it is the contradiction of double aims. The double-aimed struggle of the black artisan—on the one hand to escape white contempt for a nation of mere hewers of wood and drawers of water, and on the other hand to plough and nail and dig for a poverty-stricken horde—could only result in making him a poor craftsman, for he had but half a heart in either cause. By the poverty and ignorance of his people, the Negro minister or doctor was tempted toward quackery and demagogy; and by the criticism of the other world, toward ideals that made him ashamed of his lowly tasks. The would-be black *savant* was confronted by the paradox that the knowledge his people needed was a twice-told tale to his white neighbors, while the knowledge which would teach the white world was Greek to his own flesh and blood. The innate love of harmony and beauty that set the ruder souls of his people a-dancing and a-singing raised but confusion and doubt in the soul of the black artist; for the beauty revealed to him was the soul-beauty of a race which his larger audience despised, and he could not articulate the message of another people. This waste of double aims, this seeking to satisfy two unreconciled ideals, has wrought sad havoc with the courage and faith and deeds of ten thousand thousand people,—has sent them often wooing false gods and invoking false means of salvation, and at times has even seemed about to make them ashamed of themselves.

Away back in the days of bondage they thought to see in one divine event the end of all doubt and disappointment; few men ever worshipped Freedom with half such unquestioning faith as did the American Negro for two centuries. To him, so far as he thought and dreamed, slavery was indeed the sum of all villainies, the cause of all sorrow, the root of all prejudice; Emancipation was the key to a promised land of sweeter beauty than ever stretched before the eyes of wearied Israelites. In song and exhortation swelled one refrain—Liberty; in his tears and curses the God he implored had Freedom in his right hand. At last it came, suddenly, fearfully, like a dream. With one wild carnival of blood and passion came the message in his own plaintive cadences:—

> *"Shout, O children!*
> *Shout, you're free!*
> *For God has bought your liberty!"*

Years have passed away since then,—ten, twenty, forty; forty years of national life, forty years of renewal and development, and yet the swarthy spectre sits in its accustomed seat at the Nation's feast. In vain do we cry to this our vastest social problem:—

> *"Take any shape but that, and my*
> *firm nerves*
> *Shall never tremble!"*

The Nation has not yet found peace from its sins; the freedman has not yet found in freedom his promised land. Whatever of good may have come in these years of change, the shadow of a deep disappointment rests upon the Negro people,—a disappointment all the more bitter because the unattained ideal was unbounded save by the simple ignorance of a lowly people.

The first decade was merely a prolongation of the vain search for freedom, the boon that seemed ever barely to elude their grasp,—like a tantalizing will-o'-the-wisp, maddening and misleading the headless host. The holocaust of war, the terrors of the Ku-Klux Klan, the lies of carpet-baggers, the disorganization of industry, and the contradictory advice of friends and foes, left the bewildered serf with no new watch-word beyond the old cry for freedom. As the time flew, however, he began to grasp a new idea. The ideal of liberty demanded for its attainment powerful means, and these the Fifteenth Amendment gave him. The ballot, which before he had looked upon as a visible sign of freedom, he now regarded as the chief means of gaining and perfecting the liberty with which war had partially endowed him. And why not? Had not votes made war and emancipated millions? Had not votes enfranchised the freedmen? Was anything impossible to a power that had done all this? A million black men started with renewed zeal to vote themselves into the kingdom. So the decade flew away, the revolution of 1876 came, and left the half-free serf weary, wondering, but still inspired. Slowly but steadily, in the following years, a new vision began gradually to replace the dream of political power,—a powerful movement, the rise of another ideal to guide the unguided, another pillar of fire by night after a clouded day. It was the ideal of "book-learning"; the curiosity, born of compulsory ignorance, to know and test the power of the cabalistic letters of the white man, the longing to know. Here at last seemed to have been discovered the mountain path to Canaan; longer than the highway of Emancipation and law, steep and rugged, but straight, leading to heights high enough to overlook life.

Up the new path the advance guard toiled, slowly, heavily, doggedly; only those who have watched and guided the faltering feet, the misty minds, the dull understandings, of the dark pupils of these schools know how faithfully, how piteously, this people strove to learn. It was weary work. The cold statistician wrote down the inches of progress here and there, noted also where here and there a foot had slipped or some one had fallen. To the tired climbers, the horizon was ever dark, the mists were often cold, the Canaan was always dim and far away. If, however, the vistas disclosed as yet no goal, no resting-place, little but flattery and criticism, the journey at least gave leisure for reflection and self-examination; it changed the child of Emancipation to the youth with dawning self-consciousness, self-realization, self-respect. In those sombre forests of his striving his own soul rose before him, and he saw himself,—darkly as through a veil; and yet he saw in himself some faint revelation of his power, of his mission. He began to have a dim feeling that, to attain his place in the world, he must be himself, and not another. For the first time he sought to analyze the burden he bore upon his back, that dead-weight of social degradation partially masked behind a half-named Negro problem. He felt his poverty; without a cent, without a home, without land, tools, or savings, he had entered into competition with rich, landed, skilled neighbors. To be a poor man is hard, but to be a poor race in a land of dollars is the very bottom of hardships. He felt the weight of his ignorance,—not simply of letters, but of life, of business, of the humanities; the accumulated sloth and shirking and awkwardness of decades and centuries shackled his hands and feet. Nor was his burden all poverty and ignorance. The red stain of bastardy, which two centuries of systematic legal defilement of Negro women had stamped upon his race, meant not only the loss of ancient African chastity, but also the hereditary weight of a mass of corruption from white adulterers, threatening almost the obliteration of the Negro home.

A people thus handicapped ought not to be asked to race with the world, but rather allowed to give all its time and thought to its own social problems. But alas! while sociologists gleefully count his bastards and his prostitutes, the very soul of the toiling, sweating black man is darkened by the shadow of a vast despair. Men call the shadow prejudice, and learnedly explain it as the natural defence of culture against barbarism, learning against ignorance, purity against crime, the "higher" against the "lower" races. To which the Negro cries Amen! and swears that to so much of this strange prejudice as is founded on just homage to civilization, culture, righteousness, and progress, he humbly bows and meekly does obeisance. But before that nameless prejudice that leaps beyond all this he stands helpless, dismayed, and well-nigh speechless; before that personal disrespect and mockery, the ridicule and systematic humiliation, the distortion of fact and wanton license of fancy, the cynical ignoring of the better and the boisterous welcoming of the worse, the all-pervading desire to inculcate disdain for everything black, from Toussaint to the devil,—before this there rises a sickening despair that would disarm and discourage any nation save that black host to whom "discouragement" is an unwritten word.

But the facing of so vast a prejudice could not but bring the inevitable self-questioning, self-disparagement, and lowering of ideals which ever accompany repression and breed in an atmosphere of contempt and hate. Whisperings and portents came borne upon the four winds: Lo! we are diseased and dying, cried the dark hosts; we cannot write, our voting is vain; what need of education, since we must always cook and serve? And the Nation echoed and enforced this self-criticism, saying: Be content to be servants, and nothing more; what need of higher culture for half-men? Away with the black man's ballot, by force or fraud,—and behold the suicide of a race! Nevertheless, out of the evil came something of good,—the more careful adjustment of education to real life, the clearer perception of the Negroes' social responsibilities, and the sobering realization of the meaning of progress.

So dawned the time of *Sturm und Drang:* storm and stress today rocks our little boat on the mad waters of the world-sea; there is within and without the sound of conflict, the burning of body and rending of soul; inspiration strives with doubt, and faith with vain questionings. The bright ideals of the past,—physical freedom, political power, the training of brains and the training of hands,—all these in turn have waxed and waned, until even the last grows dim and overcast. Are they all wrong,—all false? No, not that, but each alone was over-simple and incomplete,—the dreams of a credulous race-childhood, or the fond imaginings of the other world which does not know and does not want to know our power. To be really true, all these ideals must be melted and welded into one. The training of the schools we need to-day more than ever,—the training of deft hands, quick eyes and ears, and above all the broader, deeper, higher culture of gifted minds and pure hearts. The power of the ballot we need in sheer self-defence, else what shall save us from a second slavery? Freedom, too, the long-sought, we still seek,—the freedom of life and limb, the freedom to work and think, the freedom to love and aspire. Work, culture, liberty,—all these we need, not singly but together, not successively but together, each growing and aiding each, and all striving toward that vaster ideal that swims before the Negro people, the ideal of human brotherhood, gained through the unifying ideal of Race; the ideal of fostering and developing the traits and talents of the Negro, not in opposition to or contempt for other races, but rather in large conformity to the greater ideals of the American Republic, in order that some day on American soil two world-races may give each to each those characteristics both so sadly lack. We the darker ones come even now not altogether empty-handed: there are to-day no truer exponents of the pure human spirit of the Declaration of Independence than the American Negroes; there is no true American music but the wild sweet melodies of the Negro slave; the American fairy tales and folklore are Indian and African; and, all in all, we black men seem the sole oasis of simple faith and reverence in a dusty desert of dollars and smartness. Will America be poorer if she replace her brutal dyspeptic blundering with light-hearted but determined Negro humility? or her coarse and cruel wit with loving jovial good-humor? or her vulgar music with the soul of the Sorrow Songs?

Merely a concrete test of the underlying principles of the great republic is the Negro Problem, and the spiritual striving of the freedmen's sons is the travail of souls whose burden is almost beyond the measure of their strength, but who bear it in the name of an historic race, in the name of this the land of their fathers' fathers, and in the name of human opportunity.

And now what I have briefly sketched in large outline let me on coming pages tell again in many ways, with loving emphasis and deeper detail, that men may listen to the striving in the souls of black folk.

Assessing Black Neoconservatism

CORNEL WEST

HE PUBLICATION OF THOMAS SOWELL'S *Race and Economics* in 1975 marked the rise of a novel phenomenon in the United States: a visible and aggressive black conservative assault on traditional black liberal leadership. The promotion of conservative ideas is not new in Afro-American history. The preeminent black conservative of this century—George S. Schuyler—published a witty and acerbic column in the influential black newspaper, *The Pittsburgh Courier,* for decades and his book *Black and Conservative* is a minor classic in Afro-American letters. Similarly, the reactionary essays (some of which appeared in *Readers' Digest*) and Republican party allegiance of the most renowned Afro-American woman of letters, Zora Neale Hurston, are often overlooked by her contemporary feminist followers. Yet Sowell's book still initiated something new—a bid for conservative hegemony in black political and intellectual leadership in the post–civil rights era.

This bid is as yet highly unsuccessful though it has generated much attention from the American media. The most salient figures are Thomas Sowell, a senior fellow at the Hoover Institution on War, Revolution, and Peace at Stanford University; Glenn C. Loury, a professor at Harvard's Kennedy School of Government; Walter E. Williams, a professor of economics at George Mason University; J. A. Parker, president of the Lincoln Institute for Research and Education Inc.; Robert Woodson, president of the National Association of Neighborhood Enterprises; and Joseph Perkins, editorial writer for *The Wall Street Journal.* Despite minor differences between them, these major figures of the new black conservatism are all supportive of the basic policies of the Reagan administration, such as its major foreign policies, opposition to affirmative action, abolition or lowering of adult minimum wage, the establishment of enterprise zones in inner cities, and the vast cutbacks in social programs for the poor.

These black publicists are aware of the irony of their positions; that is, their own upward social mobility was, in large part,

From *Prophetic Fragments* by Cornel West. Used by permission of the Wm. B. Eerdmans Publishing Company, Grand Rapids, Michigan.

made possible by the struggles of the liberal civil rights movement and more radical black activists they now scorn. They also realize that black liberalism is in deep crisis. This crisis, exemplified by the rise of Reaganism and the decline of progressive politics, has created the new intellectual space that their black conservative voices (along with nonblack ones) now occupy.

The emergence of the new black conservatives is best understood in light of three fundamental processes in American society and culture since 1973: the eclipse of uncontested postwar U.S. predominance in world markets and military power, the structural transformation of the American economy, and the breakdown of the moral fabric in communities throughout the country, especially in black working poor and underclass neighborhoods.

The end of the unprecedented postwar economic boom in 1973 resulted in the decline of American hegemony around the world on the economic and military fronts. The symbolic events here were the oil crisis, principally owing to the solidarity of OPEC nations, and the loss of the Vietnam War. In addition, increasing economic competition from Japan, West Germany, and other nations brought an end to unquestioned U.S. economic power. The resultant slump in the American economy undermined the Keynesian foundation of postwar American liberalism: economic growth along with state regulation and intervention on behalf of disadvantaged citizens.

The principal argument of American conservatives, both black and white, holds that state regulation and intervention on behalf of disadvantaged citizens (as opposed to military buildup or corporate contracts in agricultural production) stifles economic growth. As the economic slump deepened and liberal solutions failed, conservative views seemed to be the only alternatives. Needless to say, more radical democratic socialist perspectives are too marginal in American political culture to be even seriously entertained by politicians.

With the loss of the Vietnam War, self-doubts about U.S. military might provoked conservative rhetoric about the need for a renewed military buildup and reevaluation of foreign aid to U.S. allies. This rhetoric surfaced during the Carter administration with regressive tax policies supporting escalating military budgets. The major beneficiaries were domestic weapons-producing corporations and countries such as Chile, Honduras, Afghanistan, and, above all, Israel (after the fall of the Shah in Iran).

The impact of the end of the postwar economic boom on Afro-Americans was immense. To no surprise, it more deeply affected the growing black working poor and underclass than the expanding black middle class. Issues of sheer survival loomed large for the former; while the latter continued to seize opportunities in education, business, and politics. Most middle class blacks consistently supported the emergent black political class—elected black officials on the national, state, and local levels—primarily to insure black upward social mobility. But a few began to feel uncomfortable about how their white middle class peers viewed them—mobility by means of affirmative action breeds tenuous self-respect and questionable peer acceptance for many middle class blacks. The new black conservatives voiced these feelings in the form of attacks on affirmative action programs (after they had achieved their positions by means of such programs), thereby joining a louder chorus of nonblack neoconservatives.

This quest for full-fledged middle class respectability on meritorious rather than political grounds cannot be overestimated in the new black conservatism. Their failure or success to gain respect in the eyes of their white peers deeply shapes certain elements of their conservatism. In this regard, they simply want what most Americans want—to be judged by the quality of their skills not the color of their skin. Surprisingly, they overlook the fact that affirmative action policies were political responses to the pervasive refusal of most white Americans to judge black Americans by the quality of their skills rather than the color of their skin.

Furthermore, the new black conservatives assume that without affirmative action programs white Americans will make meritorious choices rather than race-biased ones. Yet they have adduced absolutely no evidence for this. Hence they are either politically naive or simply unconcerned with black mobility. Most Americans realize that job-hiring choices are both meritorious *and* personal choices. And this personal dimension often is influenced by racist perceptions. Therefore the pertinent question is never "merit vs. race" regarding black employment but rather merit and race-bias against blacks *or* merit and race-bias with consideration for blacks. Within the practical world of U.S. employment practices, the new black conservative rhetoric about race-free meritorious criteria (usually coupled with a dismantling of enforcement mechanisms) does no more than justify actual practices of racial discrimination against blacks. And their claims about self-respect should not obscure this fact. Nor should such claims be separated from the normal self-doubts, insecurities, and anxieties of new arrivals in the American middle class. It is worth noting that most of the new black conservatives are first generation middle class persons—offering themselves as examples for how well the system works for those willing to sacrifice and work hard. Yet, in familiar American fashion, genuine white peer acceptance still seems to escape them. And their conservatism still fails to provide this human acceptance. In this way, white racism still operates against them.

Another crucial area related to the eclipse of postwar U.S. hegemony in the world is that of foreign policy. The new black conservatives rightly call attention to the butchery

of bureaucratic elites in Africa who rule in the name of a variety of ideologies. Yet they reserve most of their energies to support U.S. intervention in Central America and prevailing U.S. policies toward Israel. Their relative silence regarding the "constructive engagement" U.S. policy with South Africa is revealing. Although most of the press attention they receive has to do with their provocative views on domestic issues, I suggest that their widespread support by Reaganite conservatives and Jewish neoconservatives has to do with their views on U.S. foreign policies.

This is so because an ideological glacier shift is occurring in black America regarding the role of America in the world. An undeniable consequence of the civil rights movement and Black Power ideology in the sixties has been a growing identification of black Americans with other oppressed peoples around the world. This has less to do with skin color and more to do with similar social location, political position, and experiences of oppression by European peoples. Just as many blacks sympathize with Polish workers and Northern Irish Catholics (despite problematic Polish-black and Irish-black relations in Chicago and Boston respectively), so more and more blacks are cognizant of South African oppression of its native peoples, Chilean and South Korean repression of their citizens, and Israeli oppression of Palestinians. This latter identification deeply upsets and worries conservatives in America. In fact, the oppositional potential and radical consequences for domestic issues of this growing black radical international consciousness— usually dubbed anti-Americanism by the vulgar right—frightens the new black conservatives. For they find themselves viewed in many black communities as mere apologists for pernicious U.S. foreign policies.

The second fundamental process in American society that helps us better to understand the new black conservatives is the structural transformation of the U.S. economy.

A contracting manufacturing sector and expanding service sector of the labor market yield limited opportunities for semiskilled and unskilled workers. Coupled with this decline of a major source of black employment (i.e., industrial jobs) is the most crucial transformation in the U.S. economy affecting black Americans in the past three decades: the mechanization of southern agriculture. For example, thirty-five years ago 50 percent of all black teenagers worked as agricultural workers, with more than 90 percent of them in the South. As these jobs disappeared, the black unemployment problem in urban centers surfaced. The recent deindustrialization of northeastern and midwestern cities has exacerbated this problem. And with the stiff competition for jobs given the entrance of new immigrants and white women into the labor market, semiskilled and unskilled black workers find it difficult, if not impossible, to find employment. So by 1980, 15 percent of all black men between twenty-five and sixty-four years of age reported to the Census Bureau that they had earned nothing whatsoever the previous year. The only option is often military enlistment (the U.S. Army is almost one-third black).

The new black conservatives rightly perceive that the dominant perspectives of traditional black liberal leadership cannot address these basic structural changes in the American economy. The notion that racial discrimination is the sole cause of the prevailing predicament of the black working poor and underclass is specious. Furthermore, the idea that the courts and government can significantly enhance their plight by enforcing laws already on the books is even more spurious. White racism indeed is pernicious and potent—yet it cannot fully explain the socioeconomic position of the majority of black Americans.

The crisis of black liberalism—liberalism supported by most black elected officials—is the inability to put forward visions, analyses, and programs that can ameliorate the plight of the black working poor and underclass. The new black conservatives highlight this crisis by trying to delegitimate and discredit traditional black liberal leadership. They claim the NAACP, National Urban League, Black Congressional Caucus, and most black mayors are guided by old-fashioned, anachronistic, outdated and ineffective viewpoints. The overriding aim of the new black conservatives is to undermine this leadership and replace it with black republicans like themselves who downplay governmental regulation and intervention and instead stress market mechanisms and success-oriented values in black communities.

Yet the new black conservatives have been unable to convince black Americans that conservative ideology and Reaganite policies are morally acceptable and politically advantageous. The vast depoliticization and electoral disengagement of blacks already suggest a disenchantment with black liberal leadership and a general distrust of American political processes. And for a downtrodden and degraded people with limited options, any alternative seems to be worth a try. Nonetheless, black Americans systematically reject the arguments of the new black conservatives. This is so neither because blacks are duped by liberal black politicians nor because blacks worship the Democratic party. Rather it is because most blacks conclude that while racial discrimination is not the sole cause of their plight, it certainly is one among various causes of their social location. Most black Americans view the new black conservative assault on traditional black liberal leadership as a step backward rather than forward. Black liberalism indeed is inadequate, but black conservatism is unacceptable This negative perception partly explains the reluctance of the new black conservatives to engage in rational debates on public forums with black liberals and leftists in the black community and their eagerness to do so in the mass media. A few even go as far as to portray themselves as courageous embattled critics of a black liberal "establishment"—while their salaries, honorariums, and travel expenses are paid by the most well-endowed and conservative foundations and corporations in the country.

The most salutary effect of the new black conservatives on public discourse is to highlight the breakdown of the moral fabric in the country and especially in black working poor and underclass communities. Jesse Jackson's PUSH and other black organizations have focused on the issue in the past. The new black conservatives have made it their obsession and thereby given it national attention. Unfortunately, they view this urgent set of problems in strictly individualistic terms— ignoring the historical background and structural context of the present situation. They claim that the decline of such values as patience, hard work, deferred gratification, and self-reliance have resulted in high rates of crime, increasing early unwed pregnancies and relatively uncompetitive academic performances of black youth. And certainly these sad realities must be candidly confronted.

Nowhere in their writings do the new black conservatives examine the pervasive sexualization and militarization of images promoted in the mass media and deployed by the advertising industry in order to entice and titillate consumers. Since the end of the postwar economic boom, new strategies have been used to stimulate consumption—especially strategies that project sexual activity as instant fulfillment and violence as machismo identity aimed at American youth. This market activity has contributed greatly to the disorientation and confusion of American youth—and those with less education and opportunities bear the brunt of this cultural chaos. Ought we to be surprised that those black youth outside the labor market, devalued by white ideals of beauty of Madison Avenue, marginalized by decrepit urban schools, and targeted by an unprecedented drug invasion (begun during the politically engaging sixties) have high crime and unwed pregnancy rates? My aim here is neither to provide excuses for black behavior nor absolve blacks of personal responsibility. But when the new black conservatives accent black behavior and responsibility in such a way that present-day structural and cultural realities of black people are ignored, they are playing a deceptive and dangerous intellectual game with the lives and fortunes of disadvantaged people.

To hold individual black persons responsible for their actions is imperative; to ignore what these individuals are up against—such as sexualization and militarization of images in the mass media over which they have no control—is invidious. We indeed must criticize and condemn immoral acts of black people but we must do so cognizant of those option-limiting structural features of circumstances in which people are born and under which they live. By overlooking this, the new black conservatives fall into the trap of blaming the bulk of black poor people for their predicament. To make this grand analytical mistake for the polemical purpose of attacking traditional black liberal leadership is to debase intellectual discourse about the disadvantaged in America. Needless to say, the lives of the disadvantaged depend more on the quality of this discourse than on those of us who partake in this discourse.

This polemical purpose guided by ideological blinders is exemplified in the new black conservative attempt to link the moral breakdown of poor black communities to the expansion of the welfare state. For them, the only structural features of the black poor situation are the negative role of the state and the positive role of the market. An appropriate question to these descendants of slaves sold at the auction block is: Can the market do any wrong?

They claim that transfer payments to the black needy engenders a mentality of dependence which undercuts values of self-reliance and that the required living arrangements for these payments undermines the black poor family. They hold that only an unregulated market can support values of independence and a strong family. The new black conservatives fail to see that the welfare state was the historic compromise between progressive forces for broad subsistence rights and conservative forces for unregulated markets. Therefore it should come as no surprise that the welfare state possesses many flaws, shortcomings, and imperfections. I do believe that the reinforcing of "dependent mentalities" and harm done to poor families are two of them. But simply to point out these rather obvious shortcomings does not justify cutbacks in the welfare state. This is so because in the face of high black unemployment, these cutbacks will not promote self-reliance or strong black families but rather produce even more black cultural disorientation and more devastated black households.

The only feasible alternative to the welfare state is more jobs for poor people—and the private sector is simply uninterested and unwilling to provide these jobs. It is simply not in their economic interests to do so, even if they can pay "third world"—i.e., subminimum—wages. Again the political naiveté or unconcern with black enhancement is manifest in the claims of the new black conservatives. Within the practical world of American politics, to attack the welfare state without linking this attack to a credible jobs program (more than likely supported by the public sphere) is to delimit the already limited options black poor people have to survive and live. To go as far as some new black conservatives have done and support the elimination of nearly every federal benefit program for the nonelderly poor (as put forward in Charles Murray's *Losing Ground*) is to serve as ideological accomplices to social policies that have genocidal effects on the black poor. The welfare state has not and cannot win a war on poverty, yet it has and

does sustain some boats that would sink given the turbulent condition of unemployment. To cut the lifelines of the latter in order to make an ideological point against black liberal elites is to follow a heartless political perspective that exacerbates an already deplorable situation.

Yet even effective job programs do not fully address the cultural decay and moral disintegration of poor black communities. Like America itself, these communities are in need of cultural revitalization and moral regeneration. There is widespread agreement on this need by all sectors of black leadership. But neither black liberalism nor the new black conservatism adequately speaks to this need. Black liberals and conservatives simply fail to come to terms with the existential meaninglessness and personal despair throughout Afro-America.

Presently, the major institutional bulwarks against such meaninglessness and despair are Christian churches and Moslem mosques. These churches and mosques indeed are fighting an uphill battle and serve as the few spaces of refuge against the terrors of urban ghetto life. Yet even they cannot counter the pervasive influence of sexual and violent images of mass media upon black people, especially black youth. I am convinced that those few prophetic black churches—with rich cultural and moral resources and a progressive political perspective—possess the kind of model it takes to meet the present crisis. That is, they affirm the humanity of black poor people, accent the capacities of black poor people, and keep alive a sense of resistance to the status quo. Unfortunately, there are not enough of these institutions to overcome the crisis.

What then are we to make of the new black conservatives? First, the narrowness of their viewpoints reflects the narrowness of the liberal perspectives with which they are critically obsessed. In other words, their major object of criticism, black liberals, circumscribes their critique. In fact, the relative lack of vision, analyses, and programs—especially the ignor-ing of crucial structural features of the black poor situation—of both black liberals and conservatives make them mirror-images of each other. The basic narrowness of both groups reveals an internal fight within the black middle-class elite as well as the parochial character of the fight itself—a parochialism inseparable from the highly limited alternatives available in contemporary American politics. Second, the new black conservatives signify a healthy development to the degree to which they call attention to the crisis of black liberal-ism, thereby encouraging black politicians and activists to entertain more progressive solutions to structural problems of social injustice in American society. Third, the next crucial terrain for black conservative attacks on tradi-tional black liberal leadership will be that of U.S. foreign policy. The visible role of the NAACP and black elected officials in the anti-apartheid movement cannot but come under more ideological assault by the new black conservatives. This assault can only intensify as black liberal leaders find it more and more difficult to pass the conservative litmus tests for pro-Americanism in foreign affairs: uncritical support for U.S. policy toward Israel and U.S. intervention in Central America.

The widening of this split between hege-monic black liberal leaders and black conser-vative critics may facilitate more principled and passionate political discourse in and about black America. I am confident that if more rational debates are held, with conservative, liberal and left voices heard, the truth about the predicament of the black poor can be more easily ascertained—with a few valuable insights of the new black conservatives incorporated into a larger progressive perspective which utterly rejects their unwarranted conclusions and repugnant policies. I suspect such a rational dialogue would unmask the new black conservatives to be what they really are: rene-gades from and critics of black liberalism owing to the limits of this liberalism, yet also highly rewarded and status-hungry ideologues unwill-ing to interrogate the narrow limits of their own new illiberalism. This parasitic relation with their black liberal foes and patronage relation with their white illiberal friends would be a farce if enacted on stage—but given the actual roles they play in present-day America, there is too much at stake to be simply amused.

The Social Construction of Black Feminist Thought

PATRICIA HILL COLLINS

SOJOURNER TRUTH, ANNA JULIA Cooper, Ida Wells Barnett, and Fannie Lou Hamer are but a few names from a growing list of distinguished African-American women activists. Although their sustained resistance to Black women's victimization within interlocking systems of race, gender, and class oppression is well known, these women did not act alone.[1] Their actions were nurtured by the support of countless ordinary African-American women who, through strategies of everyday resistance, created a powerful foundation for this more visible Black feminist activist tradition.[2] Such support has been essential to the shape and goals of Black feminist thought.

The long-term and widely shared resistance among African-American women can only have been sustained by an enduring and shared standpoint among Black women about the meaning of oppression and the actions that Black women can and should take to resist it. Efforts to identify the central concepts of this Black women's standpoint figure prominently in the works of contemporary Black feminist intellectuals.[3] Moreover, political

and epistemological issues influence the social construction of Black feminist thought. Like other subordinate groups, African-American women not only have developed distinctive interpretations of Black women's oppression but have done so by using alternative ways of producing and validating knowledge itself.

A BLACK WOMEN'S STANDPOINT

The Foundation of Black Feminist Thought

Black women's everyday acts of resistance challenge two prevailing approaches to studying the consciousness of oppressed groups.[4] One approach claims that subordinate groups identify with the powerful and have no valid independent interpretation of their own oppression.[5] The second approach assumes

This essay originally appeared in *Signs: Journal of Women in Culture and Society,* Vol. 14, No. 4, Summer 1989, a publication of the University of Chicago Press.

that the oppressed are less human than their rulers and, therefore, are less capable of articulating their own standpoint.[6] Both approaches see any independent consciousness expressed by an oppressed group as being not of the group's own making and/or inferior to the perspective of the dominant group.[7] More important, both interpretations suggest that oppressed groups lack the motivation for political activism because of their flawed consciousnecs of their own subordination.

Yet African-American women have been neither passive victims of nor willing accomplices to their own domination. As a result, emerging work in Black women's studies contends that Black women have a self-defined standpoint on their own oppression.[8] Two interlocking components characterize this standpoint. First, Black women's political and economic status provides them with a distinctive set of experiences that offers a different view of material reality than that available to other groups. The unpaid and paid work that Black women perform, the types of communities in which they live, and the kinds of relationships they have with others suggest that African-American women, as a group, experience a different world than those who are not Black and female.[9] Second, these experiences stimulate a distinctive Black feminist consciousness concerning that material reality.[10] In brief, a subordinate group not only experiences a different reality than a group that rules, but a subordinate group may interpret that reality differently than a dominant group.

Many ordinary African-American women have grasped this connection between what one does and how one thinks. Hannah Nelson, an elderly Black domestic worker, discusses how work shapes the standpoints of African-American and white women: "Since I have to work, I don't really have to worry about most of the things that most of the white women I have worked for are worrying about. And if these women did their own work, they would think just like I do—about this, anyway,"[11] Ruth Shays, a Black inner city resident, points out how variations in men's and women's experiences lead to differences in perspective: "The mind of the man and the mind of the woman is the same. But this business of living makes women use their minds in ways that men don't even have to think about."[12] Finally, elderly domestic worker Rosa Wakefield assesses how the standpoints of the powerful and those who serve them diverge: "If you eats these dinners and don't cook 'em, if you wears these clothes and don't buy or iron them, then you might start thinking that the good fairy or some spirit did all that. . . . Black folks don't have no time to be thinking that. . . . But when you don't have anything else to do, you can think like that. It's bad for your mind, though."[13]

While African-American women may occupy material positions that stimulate a unique standpoint, expressing an independent Black feminist consciousness is problematic precisely because more powerful groups have a vested interest in suppressing such thought. As Hannah Nelson notes, "I have grown to womanhood in a world where the saner you are, the madder you are made to appear."[14] Nelson realizes that those who control the schools, the media, and other cultural institutions are generally skilled in establishing their view of reality as superior to alternative interpretations. While an oppressed group's experiences may put them in a position to see things differently, their lack of control over the apparatuses of society that sustain ideological hegemony makes the articulation of their self-defined standpoint difficult. Groups unequal in power are correspondingly unequal in their access to the resources necessary to implement their perspectives outside their particular group.

One key reason that standpoints of oppressed groups are discredited and suppressed by the more powerful is that self-defined standpoints can stimulate oppressed groups to resist their domination. For instance, Annie Adams, a southern Black woman, describes how she became involved in civil rights activities.

> When I first went into the mill we had segregated water fountains. . . . Same thing about the toilets. I had to clean the toilets for the inspection room and then, when I got ready to go to the bathroom, I had to go all the way to the bottom of the stairs to the cellar. So I asked my boss man, "What's the difference? If I can go in there and clean them toilets, why can't I use them?" Finally, I started to use that toilet. I decided I wasn't going to walk a mile to go to the bathroom.[15]

In this case, Adams found the standpoint of the "boss man" inadequate, developed one of her own, and acted upon it. In doing so, her actions exemplify the connections between experiencing oppression, developing a self-defined standpoint on that experience, and resistance.

The Significance of Black Feminist Thought

The existence of a distinctive Black women's standpoint does not mean that it has been adequately articulated in Black feminist thought. Peter Berger and Thomas Luckmann provide a useful approach to clarifying the relationship between a Black women's standpoint and Black feminist thought with the contention that knowledge exists on two levels.[16] The first level includes the everyday, taken-for-granted knowledge shared by members of a given group, such as the ideas expressed by Ruth Shays and Annie Adams. Black feminist thought, by extension, represents a second level of knowledge, the more specialized knowledge furnished by experts who are part of a group and who express the group's standpoint. The two levels of knowledge are interdependent; while Black feminist thought articulates the taken-for-granted knowledge of African-American women, it also encourages all Black women to create new self-definitions that validate a Black women's standpoint.

Black feminist thought's potential significance goes far beyond demonstrating that Black women can produce independent, specialized knowledge. Such thought can encourage collective identity by offering Black women a different view of themselves and their world than that offered by the established social order. This different view encourages African-American women to value their own subjective knowledge base.[17] By taking elements and themes of Black Women's culture and traditions and infusing them with new meaning, Black feminist thought rearticulates a consciousness that already exists.[18] More important, this rearticulated consciousness gives African-American women another tool of resistance to all forms of their subordination.[19]

Black feminist thought, then, specializes in formulating and rearticulating the distinctive, self-defined standpoint of African-American women. One approach to learning more about a Black women's standpoint is to consult standard scholarly sources for the ideas of specialists on Black women's experiences.[20] But investigating a Black women's standpoint and Black feminist thought requires more ingenuity than that required in examining the standpoints and thought of white males. Rearticulating the standpoint of African-American women through Black feminist thought is much more difficult since one cannot use the same techniques to study the knowledge of the dominated as one uses to study the knowledge of the powerful. This is precisely because subordinate groups have long had to use alternative ways to create an independent consciousness and to rearticulate it through specialists validated by the oppressed themselves.

THE EUROCENTRIC MASCULINIST KNOWLEDGE-VALIDATION PROCESS[21]

All social thought, including white masculinist and Black feminist, reflects the interests and standpoint of its creators. As Karl Mannheim notes, "If one were to trace in detail . . . the origin and . . . diffusion of a certain thought-model, one would discover the . . . affinity it has to the social position of given groups and their manner of interpreting the world."[22] Scholars, publishers, and other experts represent specific interests and credentialing processes, and their knowledge claims must satisfy the epistemological and political criteria of the contexts in which they reside.[23]

Two political criteria influence the knowledge-validation process. First, knowledge claims must be evaluated by a community of experts whose members represent the standpoints of the groups from which they originate. Second, each community of experts must maintain its credibility as defined by the larger group in which it is situated and from which it draws its basic taken-for-granted knowledge.

When white males control the knowledge-validation process, both political criteria can work to suppress Black feminist thought. Since the general culture shaping the taken-for-granted knowledge of the community of experts is one permeated by widespread notions of Black and female inferiority,[24] new knowledge claims that seem to violate these fundamental assumptions are likely to be viewed as anomalies.[25] Moreover, specialized thought challenging notions of Black and female inferiority is unlikely to be generated from within a white-male-controlled academic community because both the kinds of questions that could be asked and the explanations that would be found satisfying would necessarily reflect a basic lack of familiarity with Black women's reality.[26]

The experiences of African-American women scholars illustrate how individuals who wish to rearticulate a Black women's standpoint through Black feminist thought can be suppressed by a white-male-controlled knowledge-validation process. Exclusion from basic literacy, quality educational experiences, and faculty and administrative positions has limited Black women's access to influential academic positions.[27] Thus, while Black women can produce knowledge claims that contest those advanced by the white male community, this community does not grant that Black women scholars have competing knowledge claims based in another knowledge-validation process. As a consequence, any credentials controlled by white male academicians can be denied to Black women producing Black feminist thought on the grounds that it is not credible research.

Those Black women with academic credentials who seek to exert the authority that their status grants them to propose new knowledge claims about African-American women face pressures to use their authority to help legitimate a system that devalues and excludes the majority of Black women.[28] One way of excluding the majority of Black women from the knowledge-validation process is to permit a few Black women to acquire positions of authority in institutions that legitimate knowledge and to encourage them to work within the taken-for-granted assumptions of Black female inferiority shared by the scholarly community and the culture at large. Those Black women who accept these assumptions are likely to be rewarded by their institutions, often at significant personal cost. Those challenging the assumptions run the risk of being ostracized.

African-American women academicians who persist in trying to rearticulate a Black women's standpoint also face potential rejection of their knowledge claims on epistemological grounds. Just as the material realities of the powerful and the dominated produce separate standpoints, each group may also have distinctive epistemologies or theories of knowledge. It is my contention that Black female scholars may know that something is true but be unwilling or unable to legitimate their claims using Eurocentric masculinist criteria for consistency with substantiated knowledge and Eurocentric masculinist criteria for methodological adequacy.

For any particular interpretive context, new knowledge claims must be consistent with an existing body of knowledge that the group controlling the interpretive context accepts as true. The methods used to validate knowledge claims must also be acceptable to the group controlling the knowledge-validation process.

The criteria for the methodological adequacy of positivism illustrate the epistemological standards that Black women scholars would have to satisfy in legitimating alternative knowledge claims.[29] Positivist approaches aim to create scientific descriptions of reality by producing objective generalizations. Since researchers have widely differing values, experiences, and emotions, genuine science is thought to be unattainable unless all human characteristics except rationality are eliminated from the research process. By following strict methodological rules, scientists aim to distance themselves from the values, vested interests, and emotions generated by their class, race, sex, or unique situation and in so doing become detached observers and manipulators of nature.[30]

Several requirements typify positivist methodological approaches. First, research methods generally require a distancing of the researcher from her/his "object" of study by defining the researcher as a "subject" with full human subjectivity and objectifying the "object" of study.[31] A second requirement is the absence of emotions from the research process.[32] Third, ethics and values are deemed inappropriate in the research process, either as the reason for scientific inquiry or as part of the research process itself.[33] Finally, adversarial debates, whether written or oral, become the preferred method of ascertaining truth—the arguments that can withstand the greatest assault and survive intact become the strongest truths.[34]

Such criteria ask African-American women to objectify themselves, devalue their emotional life, displace their motivations for furthering knowledge about Black women, and confront, in an adversarial relationship, those who have more social, economic, and professional power than they. It seems unlikely, therefore, that Black women would use a positivist epistemological stance in rearticulating a Black women's standpoint. Black women are more likely to choose an alternative epistemology for assessing knowledge claims, one using standards that are consistent with Black women's criteria for substantiated knowledge and with Black women's criteria for methodological adequacy. If such an epistemology exists, what are its contours? Moreover, what is its role in the production of Black feminist thought?

THE CONTOURS OF AN AFROCENTRIC FEMINIST EPISTEMOLOGY

Africanist analyses of the Black experience generally agree on the fundamental elements of an Afrocentric standpoint. In spite of varying histories, Black societies reflect elements of a core African value system that existed prior to and independently of racial oppression.[35] Moreover, as a result of colonialism, imperialism, slavery, apartheid, and other systems of racial domination, Blacks share a common experience of oppression. These similarities in material conditions have fostered shared Afrocentric values that permeate the family structure, religious institutions, culture, and community life of Blacks in varying parts of Africa, the Caribbean, South America, and North America.[36] This Afrocentric consciousness permeates the shared history of people of African descent through the framework of a distinctive Afrocentric epistemology.[37]

Feminist scholars advance a similar argument. They assert that women share a history of patriarchal oppression through the political economy of the material conditions of sexuality and reproduction.[38] These shared material conditions are thought to transcend divisions among women created by race, social class, religion, sexual orientation, and ethnicity and to form the basis of a women's standpoint with its corresponding feminist consciousness and epistemology.[39]

Since Black women have access to both the Afrocentric and the feminist standpoints, an alternative epistemology used to rearticulate a Black women's standpoint reflects elements of both traditions.[40] The search for the distinguishing features of an alternative epistemology used by African-American women reveals that values and ideas that Africanist scholars identify as being characteristically "Black" often bear remarkable resemblance to similar ideas claimed by feminist scholars as being characteristically "female."[41] This similarity suggests that the material conditions of oppression can vary dramatically and yet generate some uniformity in the epistemologies of subordinate groups. Thus, the significance of an Afrocentric feminist epistemology may lie in its enrichment of our understanding of how subordinate groups create knowledge that enables them to resist oppression.

The parallels between the two conceptual schemes raise a question: Is the worldview of women of African descent more intensely infused with the overlapping feminine/Afrocentric standpoints than is the case for either African-American men or white women?[42] While an Afrocentric feminist epistemology reflects elements of epistemologies used by Blacks as a group and women as a group, it also paradoxically demonstrates features that may be unique to Black women. On certain dimensions, Black women may more closely resemble Black men, on others, white women, and on still others, Black women may stand apart from both groups. Black feminist sociologist Deborah K. King describes this phenomenon as a "both/or" orientation, the act of being simultaneously a member of a group and yet standing apart from it. She suggests that multiple realities among Black women yield a "multiple consciousness in Black women's politics" and that this state of belonging yet not belonging forms an integral part

of Black women's oppositional consciousness.[43] Bonnie Thornton Dill's analysis of how Black women live with contradictions, a situation she labels the "dialectics of Black womanhood," parallels King's assertions that this "both/or" orientation is central to an Afrocentric feminist consciousness.[44] Rather than emphasizing how a Black women's standpoint and its accompanying epistemology are different than those in Afrocentric and feminist analyses, I use Black women's experiences as a point of contact between the two.

Viewing an Afrocentric feminist epistemology in this way challenges analyses claiming that Black women have a more accurate view of oppression than do other groups. Such approaches suggest that oppression can be quantified and compared and that adding layers of oppression produces a potentially clearer standpoint. While it is tempting to claim that Black women are more oppressed than everyone else and therefore have the best standpoint from which to understand the mechanisms, processes, and effects of oppression, this simply may not be the case.[45]

African-American women do not uniformly share an Afrocentric feminist epistemology since social class introduces variations among Black women in seeing, valuing, and using Afrocentric feminist perspectives. While a Black women's standpoint and its accompanying epistemology stem from Black women's consciousness of race and gender oppression, they are not simply the result of combining Afrocentric and female values—standpoints are rooted in real material conditions structured by social class.[46]

Concrete Experience as a Criterion of Meaning

Carolyn Chase, a thirty-one-year-old inner city Black woman, notes, "My aunt used to say, 'A heap see, but a few know.'"[47] This saying depicts two types of knowing, knowledge and wisdom, and taps the first dimension of an

Afrocentric feminist epistemology. Living life as Black women requires wisdom since knowledge about the dynamics of race, gender, and class subordination has been essential to Black women's survival. African-American women give such wisdom high credence in assessing knowledge.

Allusions to these two types of knowing pervade the words of a range of African-American women. In explaining the tenacity of racism, Zilpha Elaw, a preacher of the mid-1800s, noted: "The pride of a white skin is a bauble of great value with many in some parts of the United States, who readily sacrifice their intelligence to their prejudices, and possess more knowledge than wisdom."[48] In describing differences separating African-American and white women, Nancy White invokes a similar rule: "When you come right down to it, white women just *think* they are free. Black women *know* they ain't free."[49] Geneva Smitherman, a college professor specializing in African-American linguistics, suggests that "from a black perspective, written documents are limited in what they can teach about life and survival in the world. Blacks are quick to ridicule 'educated fools,' . . . they have 'book learning' but no 'mother wit,' knowledge, but not wisdom."[50] Mabel Lincoln eloquently summarizes the distinction between knowledge and wisdom: "To black people like me, a fool is funny—you know, people who love to break bad, people you can't tell anything to, folks that would take a shotgun to a roach."[51]

Black women need wisdom to know how to deal with the "educated fools" who would "take a shotgun to a roach." As members of a subordinate group, Black women cannot afford to be fools of any type, for their devalued status denies them the protections that white skin, maleness, and wealth confer. This distinction between knowledge and wisdom, and the use of experience as the cutting edge dividing them, has been key to Black women's survival. In the context of race, gender, and class oppression, the distinction is essential since knowledge without wisdom is adequate for the powerful, but wisdom is essential to the survival of the subordinate.

For ordinary African-American women, those individuals who have lived through the experiences about which they claim to be experts are more believable and credible than those who have merely read or thought about such experiences. Thus, concrete experience as a criterion for credibility frequently is invoked by Black women when making knowledge claims. For instance, Hannah Nelson describes the importance that personal experience has for her: "Our speech is most directly personal, and every black person assumes that every other black person has a right to a personal opinion. In speaking of grave matters, your personal experience is considered very good evidence. With us, distant statistics are certainly not as important as the actual experience of a sober person."[52] Similarly, Ruth Shays uses her concrete experiences to challenge the idea that formal education is the only route to knowledge: "I am the kind of person who doesn't have a lot of education, but both my mother and my father had good common sense. Now, I think that's all you need. I might not know how to use thirty-four words where three would do, but that does not mean that I don't know what I'm talking about . . . I know what I'm talking about because I'm talking about myself. I'm talking about what I have lived."[53] Implicit in Shays's self-assessment is a critique of the type of knowledge that obscures the truth, the "thirty-four words" that cover up a truth that can be expressed in three.

Even after substantial mastery of white masculinist epistemologies, many Black women scholars invoke their own concrete experiences and those of other Black women in selecting topics for investigation and methodologies used. For example, Elsa Barkley Brown subtitles her essay on Black women's history, "how my mother taught me to be an historian in spite of my academic training."[54] Similarly, Joyce Ladner maintains that growing up as a Black woman in the South gave her special insights in conducting her study of Black adolescent women.[55]

Henry Mitchell and Nicholas Lewter claim that experience as a criterion of meaning with practical images as its symbolic vehicles is a fundamental epistemological tenet in African-American thought-systems.[56] Stories, narratives, and Bible principles are selected for their applicability to the lived experiences of African-Americans and become symbolic representations of a whole wealth of experience. For example, Bible tales are told for their value to common life, so their interpretation involves no need for scientific historical verification. The narrative method requires that the story be "told, not torn apart in analysis, and trusted as core belief, not admired as science."[57] Any biblical story contains more than characters and a plot—it presents key ethical issues salient in African-American life.

June Jordan's essay about her mother's suicide exemplifies the multiple levels of meaning that can occur when concrete experiences are used as a criterion of meaning. Jordan describes her mother, a woman who literally died trying to stand up, and the effect that her mother's death had on her own work:

> I think all of this is really about women and work. Certainly this is all about me as a woman and my life work. I mean I am not sure my mother's suicide was something extraordinary. Perhaps most women must deal with a similar inheritance, the legacy of a woman whose death you cannot possibly pinpoint because she died so many, many times and because, even before she became your mother, the life of that woman was taken. . . . I came too late to help my mother to her feet. By the way of everlasting thanks to all of the women who have helped me to stay alive I am working never to be late again.[58]

While Jordon has knowledge about the concrete act of her mother's death, she also strives for wisdom concerning the meaning of that death.

Some feminist scholars offer a similar claim that women, as a group, are more likely than men to use concrete knowledge in assessing knowledge claims. For example, a substantial number of the 135 women in a study of women's cognitive development were "connected knowers" and were drawn to the sort of knowledge that emerges from first-hand observation. Such women felt that since knowledge comes from experience, the best way of understanding another person's ideas was to try to share the experiences that led the person to form those ideas. At the heart of the procedures used by connected knowers is the capacity for empathy.[59]

In valuing the concrete, African-American women may be invoking not only an Afrocentric tradition, but a women's tradition as well. Some feminist theorists suggest that women are socialized in complex relational nexuses where contextual rules take priority over abstract principles in governing behavior. This socialization process is thought to stimulate characteristic ways of knowing.[60] For example, Canadian sociologist Dorothy Smith maintains that two modes of knowing exist, one located in the body and the space it occupies and the other passing beyond it. She asserts that women, through their child-rearing and nurturing activities, mediate these two modes and use the concrete experiences of their daily lives to assess more abstract knowledge claims.[61]

Amanda King, a young Black mother, describes how she used the concrete to assess the abstract and points out how difficult mediating these two modes of knowing can be:

> The leaders of the ROC [a labor union] lost their jobs too, but it just seemed like they were used to losing their jobs. . . . This was like a lifelong thing for them, to get out there and protest. They were like, what do you call them—intellectuals. . . . You got

the ones that go to the university that are supposed to make all the speeches, they're the ones that are supposed to lead, you know, put this little revolution together, and then you got the little ones . . . that go to the factory everyday, they be the ones that have to fight. I had a child and I thought I don't have the time to be running around with these people. . . . I mean I understand some of that stuff they were talking about, like the bourgeoisie, the rich and the poor and all that, but I had surviving on my mind for me and my kid.[62]

For King, abstract ideals of class solidarity were mediated by the concrete experience of motherhood and the connectedness it involved.

In traditional African-American communities, Black women find considerable institutional support for valuing concrete experience. Black extended families and Black churches are two key institutions where Black women experts with concrete knowledge of what it takes to be self-defined Black women share their knowledge with their younger, less experienced sisters. This relationship of sisterhood among Black women can be seen as a model for a whole series of relationships that African-American women have with each other, whether it is networks among women in extended families, among women in the Black church, or among women in the African-American community at large.[63]

Since the Black church and the Black family are both woman-centered and Afrocentric institutions, African-American women traditionally have found considerable institutional support for this dimension of an Afrocentric feminist epistemology in ways that are unique to them. While white women may value the concrete, it is questionable whether white families, particularly middle-class nuclear ones, and white community institutions provide comparable types of support. Similarly, while Black men are supported by Afrocentric institutions, they cannot participate in Black women's sisterhood. In terms of Black

women's relationships with one another then, African-American women may indeed find it easier than others to recognize connectedness as a primary way of knowing, simply because they are encouraged to do so by Black women's tradition of sisterhood.

The Use of Dialogue in Assessing Knowledge Claims

For Black women, new knowledge claims are rarely worked out in isolation from other individuals and are usually developed through dialogues with other members of a community. A primary epistemological assumption underlying the use of dialogue in assessing knowledge claims is that connectedness rather than separation is an essential component of the knowledge-validation process.[64]

The use of dialogue has deep roots in an African-based oral tradition and in African-American culture.[65] Ruth Shays describes the importance of dialogue in the knowledge-validation process of enslaved African-Americans: "They would find a lie if it took them a year . . . the foreparents found the truth because they listened and they made people tell their part many times. Most often you can hear a lie. . . . Those old people was everywhere and knew the truth of many disputes. They believed that a liar should suffer the pain of his lies, and they had all kinds of ways of bringing liars to judgement."[66]

The widespread use of the call and response discourse mode among African-Americans exemplifies the importance placed on dialogue. Composed of spontaneous verbal and nonverbal interaction between speaker and listener in which all of the speaker's statements or "calls" are punctuated by expressions or "responses" from the listener, this Black discourse mode pervades African-American culture. The fundamental requirement of this interactive network is active participation of all individuals.[67] For ideas to be tested and validated, everyone in the group must participate. To refuse to join in, especially if one really disagrees with what has been said is seen as "cheating."[68]

June Jordan's analysis of Black English points to the significance of this dimension of an alternative epistemology.

> Our language is a system constructed by people constantly needing to insist that we exist. . . . Our language devolves from a culture that abhors all abstraction, or anything tending to obscure or delete the fact of the human being who is here and now/ the truth of the person who is speaking or listening. Consequently, *there is no passive voice construction possible in Black English.* For example, you cannot say, "Black English is being eliminated." You must say, instead, "White people eliminating Black English." The assumption of the presence of life governs all of Black English . . . every sentence assumes the living and active participation of at least two human beings, the speaker and the listener.[69]

Many Black women intellectuals invoke the relationships and connectedness provided by use of dialogue. When asked why she chose the themes she did, novelist Gayle Jones replied: "I was . . . interested . . . in oral traditions of storytelling—Afro-American and others, in which there is always the consciousness and importance of the hearer."[70] In describing the difference in the way male and female writers select significant events and relationships, Jones points out that "with many women writers, relationships within family, community, between men and women, and among women—from slave narratives by black women writers on—are treated as complex and significant relationships, whereas with many men the significant relationships are those that involve confrontations—relationships outside the family and community."[71] Alice Walker's reaction to Zora Neale Hurston's book *Mules and Men* is another example of the use of dialogue in assessing knowledge claims. In *Mules and Men*, Hurston chose not to become a detached observer of the stories and folktales

she collected but instead, through extensive dialogues with the people in the communities she studied, placed herself at the center of her analysis. Using a similar process, Walker tests the truth of Hurston's knowledge claims: "When I read *Mules and Men* I was delighted. Here was this perfect book! The 'perfection' of which I immediately tested on my relatives, who are such typical Black Americans they are useful for every sort of political, cultural, or economic survey. Very regular people from the South, rapidly forgetting their Southern cultural inheritance in the suburbs and ghettos of Boston and New York, they sat around reading the book themselves, listening to me read the book, listening to each other read the book, and a kind of paradise was regained."[72]

Their centrality in Black churches and Black extended families provides Black women with a high degree of support from Black institutions for invoking dialogue as a dimension of an Afrocentric feminist epistemology. However, when African-American women use dialogues in assessing knowledge claims, they might be invoking a particularly female way of knowing as well. Feminist scholars contend that males and females are socialized within their families to seek different types of automony, the former based on separation, the latter seeking connectedness, and that this variation in types of autonomy parallels the characteristic differences between male and female ways of knowing.[73] For instance, in contrast to the visual metaphors (such as equating knowledge with illumination, knowing with seeing, and truth with light) that scientists and philosophers typically use, women tend to ground their epistemological premises in metaphors suggesting speaking and listening.[74]

While there are significant differences between the roles Black women play in their families and those played by middle-class white women, Black women clearly are affected by general cultural norms prescribing certain familial roles for women. Thus, in terms of the role of dialogue in an Afrocentric feminist epistemology, Black women may again experience a convergence of the values of the African-American community and woman-centered values.

The Ethic of Caring

"Ole white preachers used to talk wid dey tongues widdout sayin' nothin', but Jesus told us slaves to talk wid our hearts."[75] These words of an ex-slave suggest that ideas cannot be divorced from the individuals who create and share them. This theme of "talking with the heart" taps another dimension of an alternative epistemology used by African-American women, the ethic of caring. Just as the ex-slave used the wisdom in his heart to reject the ideas of the preachers who talked "wid dey tongues widdout sayin' nothin'," the ethic of caring suggests that personal expressiveness, emotions, and empathy are central to the knowledge-validation process.

One of three interrelated components making up the ethic of caring is the emphasis placed on individual uniqueness. Rooted in a tradition of African humanism, each individual is thought to be a unique expression of a common spirit, power, or energy expressed by all life.[76] This belief in individual uniqueness is illustrated by the value placed on personal expressiveness in African-American communities.[77] Johnetta Ray, an inner city resident, describes this Afrocentric emphasis on individual uniqueness: "No matter how hard we try, I don't think black people will ever develop much of a herd instinct. We are profound individualists with a passion for self-expression."[78]

A second component of the ethic of caring concerns the appropriateness of emotions in dialogues. Emotion indicates that a speaker believes in the validity of an argument.[79] Consider Ntozake Shange's description of one of the goals of her work: "Our [Western] society allows people to be absolutely neurotic and totally out of touch with their feelings and everyone else's feelings, and yet be very

respectable. This, to me, is a travesty. . . . I'm trying to change the idea of seeing emotions and intellect as distinct faculties."[80] Shange's words echo those of the ex-slave. Both see the denigration of emotion as problematic, and both suggest that expressiveness should be reclaimed and valued.

A third component of the ethic of caring involves developing the capacity for empathy. Harriet Jones, a sixteen-year-old Black woman, explains why she chose to open up to her interviewer: "Some things in my life are so hard for me to bear, and it makes me feel better to know that you feel sorry about those things and would change them if you could."[81]

These three components of the ethic of caring—the value placed on individual expressiveness, the appropriateness of emotions, and the capacity for empathy—pervade African-American culture. One of the best examples of the interactive nature of the importance of dialogue and the ethic of caring in assessing knowledge claims occurs in the use of the call and response discourse mode in traditional Black church services. In such services, both the minister and the congregation routinely use voice rhythm and vocal inflection to convey meaning. The sound of what is being said is just as important as the words themselves in what is, in a sense, a dialogue between reason and emotions. As a result, it is nearly impossible to filter out the strictly linguistic-cognitive abstract meaning from the sociocultural psycho-emotive meaning.[82] While the ideas presented by a speaker must have validity, that is, agree with the general body of knowledge shared by the Black congregation, the group also appraises the way knowledge claims are presented.

There is growing evidence that the ethic of caring may be part of women's experience as well. Certain dimensions of women's ways of knowing bear striking resemblance to Afrocentric expressions of the ethic of caring. Belenky, Clinchy, Goldberger, and Tarule point out that two contrasting epistemological orientations characterize knowing—one, an epistemology of separation based on impersonal procedures for establishing truth, and the other, an epistemology of connection in which truth emerges through care. While these ways of knowing are not gender specific, disproportionate numbers of women rely on connected knowing.[83]

The parallels between Afrocentric expressions of the ethic of caring and those advanced by feminist scholars are noteworthy. The emphasis placed on expressiveness and emotion in African-American communities bears marked resemblance to feminist perspectives on the importance of personality in connected knowing. Separate knowers try to subtract the personality of an individual from his or her ideas because they see personality as biasing those ideas. In contrast, connected knowers see personality as adding to an individual's ideas, and they feel that the personality of each group member enriches a group's understanding.[84] Similarly, the significance of individual uniqueness, personal expressiveness, and empathy in African-American communities resembles the importance that some feminist analyses place on women's "inner voice."[85]

The convergence of Afrocentric and feminist values in the ethic-of-care dimension of an alternative epistemology seems particularly acute. While white women may have access to a women's tradition valuing emotion and expressiveness, few white social institutions except the family validate this way of knowing. In contrast, Black women have long had the support of the Black church, an institution with roots in African past and a philosophy that accepts and encourages expressiveness and an ethic of caring. While Black men share in this Afrocentric tradition, they must resolve the contradictions that distinguish abstract, unemotional Western masculinity from an Afrocentric ethic of caring. The differences among race/gender groups thus hinge on differences in their access to institutional supports valuing

one type of knowing over another. Although Black women may be denigrated within white-male-controlled academic institutions, other institutions, such as Black families and churches, which encourage the expression of Black female power, seem to do so by way of their support for an Afrocentric feminist epistemology.

The Ethic of Personal Accountability

An ethic of personal accountability is the final dimension of an alternative epistemology. Not only must individuals develop their knowledge claims through dialogue and present those knowledge claims in a style proving their concern for their ideas, people are expected to be accountable for their knowledge claims. Zilpha Elaw's description of slavery reflects this notion that every idea has an owner and that the owner's identity matters: "Oh, the abominations of slavery! . . . every case of slavery, however lenient its inflictions and mitigated its atrocities, indicates an oppressor, the oppressed, and oppression."[86] For Elaw, abstract definitions of slavery mesh with the concrete identities of its perpetrators and its victims. Blacks "consider it essential for individuals to have personal positions on issues and assume full responsibility for arguing their validity."[87]

Assessments of an individual's knowledge claims simultaneously evaluate an individual's character, values, and ethics. African-Americans reject Eurocentric masculinist beliefs that probing into an individual's personal viewpoint is outside the boundaries of discussion. Rather, all views expressed and actions taken are thought to derive from a central set of core beliefs that cannot be other than personal.[88] From this perspective, knowledge claims made by individuals respected for their moral and ethical values will carry more weight than those offered by less respected figures.[89]

An example drawn from an undergraduate course composed entirely of Black women, which I taught, might help clarify the uniqueness of this portion of the knowledge-validation process. During one class discussion, I assigned the students the task of critiquing an analysis of Black feminism advanced by a prominent Black male scholar. Instead of dissecting the rationality of the author's thesis, my students demanded facts about the author's personal biography. They were especially interested in concrete details of his life such as his relationships with Black women, his marital status, and his social class background. By requesting data on dimensions of his personal life routinely excluded in positivist approaches to knowledge validation, they were invoking concrete experience as a criterion of meaning. They used this information to assess whether he really cared about his topic and invoked this ethic of caring in advancing their knowledge claims about his work. Furthermore, they refused to evaluate the rationality of his written ideas without some indication of his personal credibility as an ethical human being. The entire exchange could only have occurred as a dialogue among members of a class that had established a solid enough community to invoke an alternative epistemology in assessing knowledge claims.[90]

The ethic of personal accountability is clearly an Afrocentric value, but is it feminist as well? While limited by its attention to middle-class, white women, Carol Gilligan's work suggests that there is a female model for moral development where women are more inclined to link morality to responsibility, relationships, and the ability to maintain social ties.[91] If this is the case, then African-American women again experience a convergence of values from Afrocentric and female institutions.

The use of an Afrocentric feminist epistemology in traditional Black church services illustrates the interactive nature of all four dimensions and also serves as a metaphor for the distinguishing features of an Afrocentric feminist way of knowing. The services

represent more than dialogues between the rationality used in examining biblical texts/stories and the emotion inherent in the use of reason for this purpose. The rationale for such dialogues addresses the task of examining concrete experiences for the presence of an ethic of caring. Neither emotion nor ethics is subordinated to reason. Instead, emotion, ethics, and reason are used as interconnected, essential components in assessing knowledge claims. In an Afrocentric feminist epistemology, values lie at the heart of the knowledge-validation process such that inquiry always has an ethical aim.

EPISTEMOLOGY AND BLACK FEMINIST THOUGHT

Living life as an African-American woman is a necessary prerequisite for producing Black feminist thought because within Black women's communities thought is validated and produced with reference to a particular set of historical, material, and epistemological conditions.[92] African-American women who adhere to the idea that claims about Black women must be substantiated by Black women's sense of their own experiences and who anchor their knowledge claims in an Afrocentric feminist epistemology have produced a rich tradition of Black feminist thought.

Traditionally, such women were blues singers, poets, autobiographers, storytellers, and orators validated by the larger community of Black women as experts on a Black women's standpoint. Only a few unusual African-American feminist scholars have been able to defy Eurocentric masculinist epistemologies and explicitly embrace an Afrocentric feminist epistemology. Consider Alice Walker's description of Zora Neale Hurston: "In my mind, Zora Neale Hurston, Billie Holiday, and Bessie Smith form a sort of unholy trinity. Zora *belongs* in the tradition of Black women singers, rather than among 'the literati.' . . . Like Billie and Bessie she followed her own road, believed in her own gods, pursued her own dreams, and refused to separate herself from 'common' people."[93]

Zora Neale Hurston is an exception for, prior to 1950, few Black women earned advanced degrees, and most of those who did complied with Eurocentric masculinist epistemologies. While these women worked on behalf of Black women, they did so within the confines of pervasive race and gender oppression. Black women scholars were in a position to see the exclusion of Black women from scholarly discourse, and the thematic content of their work often reflected their interest in examining a Black woman's standpoint. However, their tenuous status in academic institutions led them to adhere to Eurocentric masculinist epistemologies so that their work would be accepted as scholarly. As a result, while they produced Black feminist thought, those Black women most likely to gain academic credentials were often least likely to produce Black feminist thought that used an Afrocentric feminist epistemology.

As more Black women earn advanced degrees, the range of Black feminist scholarship is expanding. Increasing numbers of African-American women scholars are explicitly choosing to ground their work in Black women's experiences, and, by doing so, many implicitly adhere to an Afrocentric feminist epistemology. Rather than being restrained by their "both/and" status of marginality, these women make creative use of their outsider-within status and produce innovative Black feminist thought. The difficulties these women face lie less in demonstrating the technical components of white male epistemologies than in resisting the hegemonic nature of these patterns of thought in order to see, value, and use existing alternative Afrocentric feminist ways of knowing.

In establishing the legitimacy of their knowledge claims, Black women scholars who want to develop Black feminist thought may encounter the often conflicting standards of three key groups. First, Black feminist thought must be validated by ordinary African-American women who grow to womanhood "in a world where the saner you are, the madder you are made to appear."[94] To be credible in the eyes of this group, scholars must be personal advocates for their material, be accountable for the consequences of their work, have lived or experienced their material in some fashion, and be willing to engage in dialogues about their findings with ordinary, everyday people. Second, if it is to establish its legitimacy, Black feminist thought also must be accepted by the community of Black women scholars. These scholars place varying amounts of importance on rearticulating a Black women's standpoint using an Afrocentric feminist epistemology. Third, Black feminist thought within academia must be prepared to confront Eurocentric masculinist political and epistemological requirements.

The dilemma facing Black women scholars engaged in creating Black feminist thought is that a knowledge claim that meets the criteria of adequacy for one group and thus is judged to be an acceptable knowledge claim may not be translatable into the terms of a different group. Using the example of Black English, June Jordan illustrates the difficulty of moving among epistemologies: "You cannot 'translate' instances of Standard English preoccupied with abstraction or with nothing/nobody evidently alive into Black English. That would warp the language into uses antithetical to the guiding perspective of its community of users. Rather you must first change those Standard English sentences, themselves, into ideas consistent with the person-centered assumptions of Black English."[95] While both worldviews share a common vocabulary, the ideas themselves defy direct translation.

Once Black feminist scholars face the notion that, on certain dimensions of a Black women's standpoint, it may be fruitless to try to translate ideas from an Afrocentric feminist epistemology into a Eurocentric masculinist epistemology, then the choices become clearer. Rather than trying to uncover universal knowledge claims that can withstand the translation from one epistemology to another, time might be better spent rearticulating a Black women's standpoint in order to give African-American women the tools to resist their own subordination. The goal here is not one of integrating Black female "folk culture" into the substantiated body of academic knowledge, for that substantiated knowledge is, in many ways, antithetical to the best interests of Black women. Rather, the process is one of rearticulating a preexisting Black women's standpoint and recentering the language of existing academic discourse to accommodate these knowledge claims. For those Black women scholars engaged in this rearticulation process, the social construction of Black feminist thought requires the skill and sophistication to decide which knowledge claims can be validated using the epistemological assumptions of one but not both frameworks, which claims can be generated in one framework and only partially accommodated by the other, and which claims can be made in both frameworks without violating the basic political and epistemological assumptions of either.

Black feminist scholars offering knowledge claims that cannot be accommodated by both frameworks face the choice between accepting the taken-for-granted assumptions that permeate white-male-controlled academic institutions or leaving academia. Those Black women who choose to remain in academia must accept the possibility that their knowledge claims will be limited to those claims about Black women that are consistent with a white male worldview. And yet those African-American women who leave academia may find their work is inaccessible to scholarly communities.

Black feminist scholars offering knowledge claims that can be partially accommodated by

both epistemologies can create a body of thought that stands outside of either. Rather than trying to synthesize competing worldviews that, at this point in time, may defy reconciliation, their task is to point out common themes and concerns. By making creative use of their status as mediators, their thought becomes an entity unto itself that is rooted in two distinct political and epistemological contexts.[96]

Those Black feminists who develop knowledge claims that both epistemologies can accommodate may have found a route to the elusive goal of generating so-called objective generalizations that can stand as universal truths. Those ideas that are validated as true by African-American women, African-American men, white men, white women, and other groups with distinctive standpoints, with each group using the epistemological approaches growing from its unique standpoint, thus become the most objective truths.[97]

Alternative knowledge claims, in and of themselves, are rarely threatening to conventional knowledge. Such claims are routinely ignored, discredited, or simply absorbed and marginalized in existing paradigms. Much more threatening is the challenge that alternative epistemologies offer to the basic process used by the powerful to legitimate their knowledge claims. If the epistemology used to validate knowledge comes into question, then all prior knowledge claims validated under the dominant model become suspect. An alternative epistemology challenges all certified knowledge and opens up the question of whether what has been taken to be true can stand the test of alternative ways of validating truth. The existence of an independent Black women's standpoint using an Afrocentric feminist epistemology calls into question the content of what currently passes as truth and simultaneously challenges the process of arriving at the truth.

Notes

1. For analyses of how interlocking systems of oppression affect Black women, see Frances Beale, "Double Jeopardy: To Be Black and Female," in *The Black Women*, ed. Toni Cade (New York: Signet, 1970); Angela Y. Davis, *Women, Race and Class* (New York: Random House, 1981); Bonnie Thorton Dill, "Race, Class, and Gender: Prospects for an All-Inclusive Sisterhood," *Feminist Studies* 9, no. 1 (1983): 131–50; Bell Hooks, *Ain't I a Woman? Black Women and Feminism* (Boston: South End Press, 1981); Diane Lewis, "A Response to Inequality: Black Women, Racism, and Sexism," *Signs: Journal of Women in Culture and Society* 3, no. 2 (Winter 1977): 339–61; Pauli Murray, "The Liberation of Black Women," in *Voices of the New Feminism*, ed. Mary Lou Thompson (Boston: Beacon, 1970), 87–102; and the introduction in Filomina Chioma Steady, *The Black Woman Cross-Culturally* (Cambridge, Mass.: Schenkman, 1981), 7–41.

2. See the introduction in Steady for an overview of Black women's strengths. This strength-resiliency perspective has greatly influenced empirical work on African-American women. See, e.g., Joyce Ladner's study of low-income Black adolescent girls, *Tomorrow's Tomorrow* (New York: Doubleday, 1971); and Lena Wright Myer's work on Black women's self-concept, *Black Women: Do They Cope Better?* (Englewood Cliffs, N.J.: Prentice-Hall, 1980). For discussions of Black women's resistance, see Elizabeth Fox-Genovese, "Strategies and Forms of Resistance: Focus on Slave Women in the United States," in *In Resistance: Studies in African, Caribbean and Afro-American History*, ed. Gary Y. Okihiro (Amherst, Mass.: University of Massachusetts Press, 1986), 143–65; and Rosalyn Terborg-Penn, "Black Women in Resistance: A Cross-Cultural Perspective," in Okihiro, ed., 188–209. For a comprehensive discussion of everyday resistance, see James C. Scott, *Weapons of the Weak: Everyday Forms of Peasant Resistance* (New Haven, Conn.: Yale University Press, 1985).

3. See Patricia Hill Collins's analysis of the substantive content of Black feminist thought in "Learning from the Outsider Within: The Sociological Significance of Black Feminist Thought," *Social Problems* 33, no. 6 (1986): 14–32.

4. Scott describes consciousness as the meaning that people give to their acts through the symbols, norms, and ideological forms they create.

5. This thesis is found in scholarship of varying theoretical perspectives. For example, Marxist analyses of working-class consciousness claim that "false consciousness" makes the working class unable to penetrate the hegemony of ruling-class ideologies. See Scott's critique of this literature.

6. For example, in Western societies, African-Americans have been judged as being less capable of intellectual excellence, more suited to manual labor, and therefore as less human than whites. Similarly, white women have been assigned roles as emotional, irrational creatures ruled by passions and biological urges. They too have been stigmatized as being less than fully human, as being objects. For a discussion of the importance that objectification and dehumanization play in maintaining systems of domination, see Arthur Brittan and Mary Maynard, *Sexism, Racism and Oppression* (New York: Basil Blackwell, 1984).

7. The tendency for Western scholarship to assess Black culture as pathological and deviant illustrates this process. See Rhett S. Jones, "Proving Blacks Inferior: The Sociology of Knowledge," in *The Death of White Sociology*, ed. Joyce Ladner (New York: Vintage, 1973), 114–35.

8. The presence of an independent standpoint does not mean that it is uniformly shared by all Black women or even that Black women fully recognize its contours. By using the concept of standpoint, I do not mean to minimize the rich diversity existing among African-American women. I use the phrase "Black women's standpoint" to emphasize the plurality of experiences within the overarching term "standpoint." For discussions of the concept of standpoint, see Nancy M. Hartsock, "The Feminist Standpoint: Developing the

Ground for a Specfically Feminist Historical Materialism," in *Discovering Reality,* ed. Sandra Harding and Merrill Hintikka (Boston: D. Reidel, 1983); 283–310, and *Money, Sex, and Power* (Boston: Northwestern University Press, 1983); and Alison M. Jaggar, *Feminist Politics and Human Nature* (Totowa, N.J.: Rowman & Allanheld, 1983), 377–89. My use of the standpoint epistemologies as an organizing concept in this essay does not mean that the concept is problem-free. For a helpful critique of standpoint epistemologies, see Sandra Harding, *The Science Question in Feminism* (Ithaca, N.Y.: Cornell University Press, 1986).

9. One contribution of contemporary Black women's studies is its documentation of how race, class, and gender have structured these differences. For representative works surveying African-American women's experiences, see Paula Giddings, *When and Where I Enter: The Impact of Black Women on Race and Sex in America* (New York: William Morrow, 1984); and Jacqueline Jones, *Labor of Love, Labor of Sorrow: Black Women, Work, and the Family from Slavery to the Present* (New York: Basic, 1985).

10. For example, Judith Rollins, *Between Women: Domestics and Their Employers* (Philadelphia: Temple University Press, 1985); and Bonnie Thornton Dill, "'The Means to Put My Children Through': Child-Rearing Goals and Strategies among Black Female Domestic Servants," in *The Black Woman,* ed. LaFrances Rodgers-Rose (Beverly Hills, Calif.: Sage Publications, 1980), 107–23, report that Black domestic workers do not see themselves as being the devalued workers that their employers perceive and construct their own interpretations of the meaning of their work. For additional discussions of how Black women's consciousess is shaped by the material conditions they encounter, see Ladner (n. 2 above); Myers (n. 2 above); and Cheryl Townsend Gilkes, "'Together and in Harness': Women's Traditions in the Sanctified Church," *Signs* 10, no. 4 (Summer 1985): 678–99. See also Marcia Westkott's discussion of consciousness as a sphere of freedom for women in "Feminist Criticism of the Social Sciences," *Harvard Educational Review* 49, no. 4 (1979): 422–30.

11. John Langston Gwaltney, *Drylongso: A Self-Portrait of Black America* (New York: Vintage, 1980), 4.

12. Ibid., 33.

13. Ibid., 88

14. Ibid., 7.

15. Victoria Byerly, *Hard Times Cotton Mill Girls: Personal Histories of Womanhood and Poverty in the South* (New York: ILR Press, 1986), 134.

16. See Peter L. Berger and Thomas Luckmann, *The Social Construction of Reality* (New York: Doubleday, 1966), for a discussion of everyday thought and the role of experts in articulating specialized thought.

17. See Michael Omi and Howard Winant, *Racial Formation in the United States* (New York: Routledge & Kegan Paul, 1986), esp. 93.

18. In discussing standpoint epistemologies, Hartsock, in *Money, Sex, and Power,* notes that a standpoint is "achieved rather than obvious, a mediated rather than immediate understanding" (132).

19. See Scott (n. 2 above); and Hartsock, *Money, Sex, and Power* (n. 8 above).

20. Some readers may question how one determines whether the ideas of any given African-American woman are "feminist" and "Afrocentric." I offer the following working definitions. I agree with the general definition of feminist consciousness provided by Black feminist sociologist Deborah K. King: "Any purposes, goals, and activities which seek to enhance the potential of women, to ensure their liberty, afford them equal opportunity, and to permit and encourage their self-determination represent a feminist consciousness, even if they occur within a racial community" (in "Race, Class and Gender Salience in Black Women's Womanist Consciousness" [Dartmouth College, Department of Sociology, Hanover, N.H., 1987, typescript], 22). To be Black or Afrocentric, such thought must not only reflect a similar concern for the self-determination of African-American people, but must in some way draw upon key elements of an Afrocentric tradition as well.

21. The Eurocentric masculinist process is defined here as the institutions, paradigms, and any elements of the knowledge-validation procedure controlled by white males and whose purpose is to represent a white male standpoint. While this process represents the interests of powerful white males, various dimensions of the process are not necessarily managed by white males themselves.

22. Karl Mannheim, *Ideology and Utopia: An Introduction to the Sociology of Knowledge* (New York: Harcourt, Brace, 1936, 1954), 276.

23. The knowledge-validation model used in this essay is taken from Michael Mulkay, *Science and the Sociology of Knowledge* (Boston: Allen & Unwin, 1979). For a general discussion of the structure of knowledge, see Thomas Kuhn, *The Structure of Scientific Revolutions* (Chicago: University of Chicago Press, 1962).

24. For analyses of the content and functions of images of Black female inferiority, see Mae King, "The Politics of Sexual Sterotypes," *Black Scholar* 4, nos. 6–7 (1973): 12–23; Cheryl Townsend Gilkes, "From Slavery to Social Welfare: Racism and the Control of Black Women," in *Class, Race, and Sex: The Dynamics of Control,* ed. Amy Smerdlow and Helen Lessinger (Boston: G. K. Hall, 1981), 288–300; and Elizabeth Higginbotham, "Two Representative Issues in Contemporary Sociological Work on Black Women," in *But Some of Us Are Brave,* ed. Gloria T. Hull, Patricia Bell Scott, and Barbara Smith (Old Westbury, N.Y.: Feminist Press, 1982).

25. Kuhn.

26. Evelyn Fox Keller, *Reflections on Gender and Science* (New Haven, Conn.: Yale University Press, 1985), 167.

27. Maxine Baca Zinn, Lynn Weber Cannon, Elizabeth Higginbotham, and Bonnie Thornton Dill, "The Cost of Exclusionary Practices in Women's Studies," *Signs* 11, no. 2 (Winter 1986): 290–303.

28. Berger and Luckmann (n. 16 above) note that if an outsider group, in this case African-American women, recognizes that the insider group, namely, white men, requires special privileges from the larger society, a special problem arises of keeping the outsiders out and at the same time having them acknowledge the legitimacy of this procedure. Accepting a few "safe" outsiders is one way of addressing this legitimation problem. Collins's discussion (n. 3 above) of Black women as "outsiders within" addresses this issue. Other relevant works include Franz Fanon's analysis of the role of the national middle class in maintaining colonial systems. *The Wretched of the Earth* (New York: Grove, 1963); and William Tabb's discussion of the use of "bright natives" in controlling African-American communities, *The Political Economy of the Black Ghetto* (New York: Norton, 1970).

29. While I have been describing Eurocentric masculinist approaches as a single process, there are many schools of thought or paradigms subsumed under this one process. Positivism represents one such paradigm. See Harding (n. 8 above) for an overview and critique of this literature. The following discussion depends heavily on Jaggar (n. 8 above), 355–58.

30. Jaggar, 356.

31. See Keller, especially her analysis of static autonomy and its relation to objectivity (67–126).

32. Ironically, researchers must "objectify" themselves to achieve this lack of bias. See Arlie Russell Hockschild, "The Sociology of Feeling and Emotion: Selected Possibilities," in *Another Voice: Feminist Perspectives on Social Life and Social Science,* ed. Marcia Millman and Rosabeth Kanter (Garden City, N.Y.: Anchor, 1975), 280–307. Also, see Jaggar.

33. See Norma Haan, Robert Bellah, Paul Rabinow, and William Sullivan, eds., *Social Science as Moral Inquiry* (New York: Columbia University Press, 1983), esp. Michelle Z. Rosaldo's "Moral/Analytic Dilemmas Posed by the Intersection of Feminism and Social Science," 76–96; and Robert Bellah's "The Ethical Aims of Social Inquiry," 360–81.

34. Janice Moulton, "A Paradigm of Philosophy: The Adversary Method," in Harding and Hintikka, eds. (n. 8 above), 149–64.

35. For detailed discussions of the Afrocentric worldview, see John S. Mbiti, *African Religions*

and Philosophy (London: Heinemann, 1969); Dominique Zahan, *The Religion, Spirtuality, and Thought of Traditional Africa* (Chicago: University of Chicago Press, 1979); and Mechal Sobel, *Trabelin' On: The Slave Journey to an Afro-Baptist Faith* (Westport, Conn.: Greenwood Press, 1979), 1–76.

36. For representative works applying these concepts to African-American culture, see Niara Sudarkasa, "Interpreting the African Heritage in Afro-American Family Organization," in *Black Families,* ed. Harriette Pipes McAdoo (Beverly Hills, Calif.: Sage, 1981); Henry H. Mitchell and Nicholas Cooper Lewter, *Soul Theology: The Heart of American Black Culture* (San Francisco: Harper & Row, 1986); Robert Farris Thompson, *Flash of the Spirit: African and Afro-American Art and Philosophy* (New York: Vintage, 1983); and Ortiz. M. Walton, "Comparative Analysis of the African and the Western Aesthetics," in *The Black Aesthetic,* ed. Addison Gayle (Garden City, N.Y.: Doubleday, 1971), 154–64.

37. One of the best discussions of an Afrocentric epistemology is offered by James E. Turner, "Foreword: Africana Studies and Epistemology; a Discourse in the Sociology of Knowledge," in *The Next Decade: Theoretical and Research Issues in Africana Studies,* ed. James E. Turner (Ithaca, N.Y.: Cornell University Africana Studies and Research Center, 1984), v–xxv. See also Vernon Dixon, "World Views and Research Methodology," summarized in Harding (n. 8 above), 170.

38. See Hester Eisenstein, *Contemporary Feminist Thought* (Boston: G. K. Hall, 1983). Nancy Hartsock's *Money, Sex, and Power* (n. 8 above), 145–209, offers a particularly insightful analysis of women's oppression.

39. For discussions of feminist consciousness, see Dorothy Smith, "A Sociology for Women," in *The Prism of Sex: Essays in the Sociology of Knowledge,* ed. Julia A. Sherman and Evelyn T. Beck (Madison: University of Wisconsin Press, 1979); and Michelle Z. Rosaldo, "Women, Culture, and Society: A Theoretical Overview," in *Woman, Culture, and Society,* ed. Michelle Z. Rosaldo and Louise Lamphere (Stanford, Calif.: Stanford University Press,

1974), 17–42. Feminist epistemologies are surveyed by Jaggar (n. 8 above).

40. One significant difference between Afrocentric and feminist standpoints is that much of what is termed women's culture is, unlike African-American culture, created in the context of and produced by oppression. Those who argue for a women's culture are electing to value, rather than denigrate, those traits associated with females in white patriarchal societies. While this choice is important, it is not the same as identifying an independent, historic culture associated with a society. I am indebted to Deborah K. King for this point.

41. Critiques of the Eurocentric masculinist knowledge-validation process by both Africanist and feminist scholars illustrate this point. What one group labels "white" and "Eurocentric," the other describes as "male-dominated" and "masculinist." Although he does not emphasize its patriarchal and racist features, Morris Berman's *The Reenchantment of the World* (New York: Bantam, 1981) provides a historical discussion of Western thought. Afrocentric analyses of this same process can be found in Molefi Kete Asante, "International/Intercultural Relations," in *Contemporary Black Thought,* ed. Molefi Kete Asante and Abdulai S. Vandi (Beverly Hills, Calif.: Sage, 1980), 43–58; and Dona Richards, "European Mythology: The Ideology of 'Progress,'" in Asante and Vandi, eds., 59–79. For feminist analyses, see Hartsock, *Money, Sex, and Power.* Harding also discusses this similarity (see chap. 7, "Other 'Others' and Fractured Identities: Issues for Epistemologists," 163–96).

42. Harding, 166.

43. D. King (n. 20 above).

44. Bonnie Thornton Dill, "The Dialectics of Black Womanhood," *Signs* 4, no. 3 (Spring 1979): 543–55.

45. One implication of standpoint approaches is that the more subordinate the group, the purer the vision of the oppressed group. This is an outcome of the origins of standpoint approaches in Marxist social theory, itself a dualistic analysis of social structure. Because

such approaches rely on quantifying and ranking human oppressions—familiar tenets of positivist approaches—they are rejected by Blacks and feminists alike. See Harding (n. 8 above) for a discussion of this point. See also Elizabeth V. Spelman's discussion of the fallacy of additive oppression in "Theories of Race and Gender: The Erasure of Black Women," *Quest* 5, no. 4 (1982): 36–62.

46. Class differences among Black women may be marked. For example, see Paula Giddings's analysis (n. 9 above) of the role of social class in shaping Black women's political activism; or Elizabeth Higginbotham's study of the effects of social class in Black women's college attendance in "Race and Class Barriers to Black Women's College Attendance," *Journal of Ethnic Studies* 13, no. 1 (1985): 89–107. Those African-American women who have experienced the greatest degree of convergence of race, class, and gender oppression may be in a better position to recognize and use an alternative epistemology.

47. Gwaltney (n. 11 above), 83.

48. William L. Andrews, *Sisters of the Spirit: Three Black Women's Autobiographies of the Nineteenth Century* (Bloomington: Indiana University Press, 1986), 85.

49. Gwaltney, 147.

50. Geneva Smitherman, *Talkin and Testifyin: The Language of Black America* (Detroit: Wayne State University Press, 1986), 76.

51. Gwaltney, 68.

52. Ibid., 7.

53. Ibid., 27, 33.

54. Elsa Barkley Brown, "Hearing Our Mothers' Lives" (paper presented at the Fifteenth Anniversary Faculty Lecture Series, African-American and African Studies, Emory University, Atlanta, 1986).

55. Ladner (n. 2 above).

56. Mitchell and Lewter (n. 36 above). The use of the narrative approach in African-American theology exemplifies an inductive system of logic alternately called "folk wisdom" or a survival-based, need-oriented method of assessing knowledge claims.

57. Ibid., 8.

58. June Jordan, *On Call: Political Essays* (Boston: South End Press, 1985), 26.

59. Mary Belenky, Blythe Clinchy, Nancy Goldberger, and Jill Tarule, *Women's Ways of Knowing* (New York: Basic, 1986), 113.

60. Hartsock, *Money, Sex and Power* (n. 8 above), 237; and Nancy Chodorow, *The Reproduction of Mothering* (Berkeley and Los Angeles: University of California Press, 1978).

61. Dorothy Smith, *The Everyday World as Problematic* (Boston: Northeastern University Press, 1987).

62. Byerly (n. 15 above), 198.

63. For Black women's centrality in the family, see Steady (n. 1 above); Ladner (n. 2 above); Brown (n. 54 above); and McAdoo, ed. (n. 36 above). see Gilkes, "'Together and in Harness'" (n. 10 above), for Black women in the church; and chap. 4 of Deborah Gray White, *Ar'n't I a Woman? Female Slaves in the Plantation South* (New York: Norton, 1985). See also Gloria Joseph, "Black Mothers and Daughters: Their Roles and Functions in American Society," in *Common Differences: Conflicts in Black and White Feminist Perspectives,* ed. Gloria Joseph and Jill Lewis (Garden City, N.Y.: Anchor, 1981), 75–126. Even though Black women play essential roles in Black families and Black churches, these institutions are not free from sexism.

64. As Belenky et al. note, "Unlike the eye, the ear requires closeness between subject and object. Unlike seeing, speaking and listening suggest dialogue and interaction" (18).

65. Thomas Kochman, *Black and White: Styles in Conflict* (Chicago: University of Chicago Press, 1981); and Smitherman (n. 50 above).

66. Gwaltney (n. 11 above), 32.

67. Smitherman, 108.

68. Kochman, 28

69. Jordan (n. 58 above), 129

70. Claudia Tate, *Black Women Writers at Work* (New York: Continuum, 1983), 91.

71. Ibid., 92.

72. Alice Walker, *In Search of Our Mothers' Gardens* (New York: Harcourt Brace Jovanovich, 1974), 84.

73. Keller (n. 26 above); Chodorow (n. 60 above).

74. Belenky et al. (n. 59 above), 16.

75. Thomas Webber, *Deep Like the Rivers* (New York: Norton, 1978), 127.

76. In her discussion of the West African Sacred Cosmos, Mechal Sobel (n. 35 above) notes that Nyam, a root word in many West African languages, connotes an enduring spirit, power, or energy possessed by all life. In spite of the pervasiveness of this key concept in African humanism, its definition remains elusive. She points out, "Every individual analyzing the various Sacred Cosmos of West Africa has recognized the reality of this force, but no one has yet adequately translated this concept into Western terms" (13).

77. For discussions of personal expressiveness in African-American culture, see Smitherman (n. 50 above); Kochman (n. 65 above), esp. chap. 9; and Mitchell and Lewter (n. 36 above).

78. Gwaltney (n. 11 above), 228.

79. For feminist analyses of the subordination of emotion in Western culture, see Hochschild (n. 32 above); and Chodorow.

80. Tate (n. 70 above), 156.

81. Gwaltney, 11.

82. Smitherman, 135 and 137.

83. Belenky et al. (n. 59 above), 100–130.

84. Ibid., 119.

85. See ibid., 52–75, for a discussion of inner voice and its role in women's cognitive styles. Regarding empathy, Belenky et al. note: "Connected knowers begin with an interest in the facts of other people's lives, but they gradually shift the focus to other people's ways of thinking. . . . It is the form rather than the content of knowing that is central. . . . Connected learners learn through empathy" (115).

86. Andrews (n. 48 above), 98.

87. Kochman (n. 65 above), 20 and 25.

88. Ibid, 23.

89. The sizable proportion of ministers among Black political leaders illustrates the importance of ethics in African-American communities.

90. Belenky et al. discuss a similar situation. They note, "People could critique each other's work in this class and accept each other's criticisms because members of the group shared a similar experience. . . . Authority in connected knowing rests not on power or status or certification but on commonality of experience" (118).

91. Carol Gilligan, *In a Different Voice* (Cambridge, Mass.: Harvard University Press, 1982). Carol Stack critiques Gilligan's model by arguing that African-Americans invoke a similar model of moral development to that used by women (see "The Culture of Gender: Women and Men of Color," *Signs* 11, no. 2 [Winter 1986]: 321–24). Another difficulty with Gilligan's work concerns the homogeneity of the subjects whom she studied.

92. Black men, white women, and members of other race, class, and gender groups should be encouraged to interpret, teach, and critique the Black feminist thought produced by African-American women.

93. Walker (n. 72 above), 91.

94. Gwaltney (n. 11 above), 7.

95. Jordon (n. 58 above), 130.

96. Collins (n. 3 above).

97. This point addresses the question of relativity in the sociology of knowledge and offers a way of regulating competing knowledge claims.

Part X *Key Terms and Essay/Discussion Questions*

KEY TERMS

Double consciousness	*Epistemology*
New black conservatives	*Eurocentric masculinist epistemology*
Black liberalism	*Positivist methodology*
Black feminist thought	*Afrocentric epistemology*
Black women's standpoint	*Afrocentric feminist epistemology*
Knowledge validation process	

ESSAY/DISCUSSION QUESTIONS

1. According to W. E. B. Du Bois, African Americans are burdened with an agonizing duality that affects their self-image and their historic struggle for freedom. What is the nature of this duality? Why does oppression give rise to some form of duality? How can this contradiction be resolved?

2. In several places in his essay, Du Bois uses the metaphor of the "veil." What meaning do you think he gives to this term?

3. How is Du Bois' essay an indictment of white America's cultural domination of African Americans?

4. According to Cornel West, what conditions contributed to rise of black neoconservatism in the 1980s? What are the strengths and weaknesses of the ideas put forward by the new black conservatives?

5. Patricia Hill Collins argues that all social thought reflects the interests and standpoint of its creators; therefore, the justification of knowledge claims is not a natural or objective process. Rather, it is highly political and involves intellectual and social conflict and struggle. What is her criticism of white male epistemological dominance and how can black feminist thought challenge that dominance?

6. Why is an Afrocentric feminist epistemology important, in Collins' view, and what are the elements of her theory of knowledge?

7. It is commonly thought in America that freedom and justice are individually based ideals. However, upon closer examination, it is evident that in this nation political rights, obligations, and privileges are group based for they historically have been connected to race, sex, and class. Do you agree or disagree with this proposition? Develop an argument in support of or in opposition to this statement.

Part X *Supplementary Readings*

Andersen, Margaret L., and Patricia Hill Collins, eds., *Race, Class, and Gender: An Anthology*, Belmont: Wadsworth Publishing Company, 1992.

Asante, Molefi K., and Abdulai S. Vandi, eds., *Contemporary Black Thought: Alternative Analysis in Social and Behavioral Science*, Beverly Hills: Sage Publications, 1980.

Bennett, Lerone, Jr., *The Challenge of Blackness*, Chicago: Johnson Publishing Company, Inc., 1972.

Betts, Raymond F., *The Ideology of Blackness*, Lexington: D. C. Heath and Company, 1971.

Boggs, James, *Racism and the Class Struggle*, New York: Monthly Review Press, 1970.

Boggs, James, and Grace L. Boggs, *Revolution and Evolution in the Twentieth Century*, New York: Monthly Review Press, 1974.

Boulward, Marcus H., *The Oratory of Negro Leaders: 1900–1968*, Westport: Negro Universities Press, 1969.

Breitman, George, ed., *By Any Means Necessary: Speeches, Interviews and a Letter by Malcolm X*, New York: Pathfinder Press, Inc., 1970.

_____, ed., *Malcolm X Speaks: Selected Speeches and Statements*, New York: Grove Press, Inc., 1965.

Carmichael, Stokely, and Charles V. Hamilton, *Black Power: The Politics of Liberation in America*, New York: Random House, 1967.

Carter, Stephen L., *Reflections of an Affirmative Action Baby*, New York: Basic Books, 1991.

Chrisman, Robert, and Nathan Hare, eds., *Pan-Africanism*, Indianapolis: The Bobbs-Merrill Company, Inc., 1974.

Cleage, Albert B., Jr., *Black Christian Nationalism: New Directions for the Black Church*, New York: William Morrow and Company, Inc., 1972.

_____, *The Black Messiah*, New York: Sheed and Ward, 1968.

Cleaver, Eldrige, *Soul on Ice*, New York: McGraw-Hill Book Company, 1968.

Collins, Patricia Hill, *Black Feminist Thought: Knowledge, Consciousness, and the Politics of Empowerment*, Boston: Unwin Hyman, 1990.

Cone, James H., *For My People: Black Theology and the Black Church*, Maryknoll: Orbis Books, 1988.

_____, *The God of the Oppressed*, New York: Harper San Francisco, 1975.

_____, *A Black Theology of Liberation*, Philadelphia: J. B. Lippincott Company, 1970.

_____, *Black Theology and Black Power*, New York: The Seabury Press, 1969.

Cross, William E., Jr., *Shades of Black: Diversity in African-American Identity*, Philadelphia: Temple University Press, 1991.

Crouch, Stanley, *Notes of a Hanging Judge: Essays and Reviews, 1979–1989*, New York: Oxford University Press, 1990.

Cruse, Harold, *Plural But Equal: Blacks and Minorities in America's Plural Society*, New York: William Morrow and Company, Inc., 1987.

_____, *Rebellion or Revolution?* New York: William Morrow and Company, 1968.

_____, *The Crisis of the Negro Intellectual*, New York: William Morrow and Company, 1967.

Davis, Angela, *Women, Culture, and Politics*, New York: Random House, 1989.

_____, *Women, Race, and Class*, New York: Random House, 1981.

Delany, Martin R., *The Condition, Elevation, Emigration and Destiny of the Colored People of the United States*, New York: Arno Press, 1969.

Du Bois, W. E. B., *The Gift of Black Folk*, New York: Washington Square Press, 1970.

_____, *The Souls of Black Folk*, Grennwich: Fawcett Publications, 1953.

Epps, Archie, ed., *The Speeches of Malcolm X at Harvard*, New York: William Morrow and Company, Inc., 1968.

Essien-Udom, E. U., *Black Nationalism: A Search for Identity in America*, Chicago: The University of Chicago Press, 1962.

Fanon, Frantz, *Black Skin, White Masks*, New York: Grove Press, Inc., 1967.

_____, *The Wretched of the Earth*, New York: Grove Press, Inc., 1965.

Foner, Philip S., ed., *The Voice of Black America*, 2 Vols., New York: Capricorn Books, 1975.

Forman, James, *Self-Determination and the African American People*, Seattle: Open Hand Publishing, 1981.

_____, *The Making of Black Revolutionaries*, New York: The Macmillan Company, 1972.

Frazier, E. Franklin, "The Failure of the Negro Intellectual," in Joyce A. Ladner, ed., *The Death of White Sociology*, New York: Vintage Books, 1973, pp. 52–66.

_____, *Black Bourgeoisie: The Rise of a New Middle Class in the United States*, New York: Collier Books, 1962.

Giddens, Paula, *When and Where I Enter: The Impact of Black Women on Race and Sex in America*, New York: Bantam Books, 1984.

Giroux, Henry A., "Postmodernism as Border Pedagogy: Redefining the Boundaries of Race and Ethnicity," in Giroux, eds., *Postmodernism, Feminism, and Cultural Politics: Redrawing Educational Boundaries*, Albany: State University of New York Press, 1991, pp. 217–256.

Goldberg, David T., ed., *Anatomy of Racism*, Minneapolis: University of Minnesota Press, 1990.

Goodman, Benjamin, ed., *The End of White World Supremacy: Four Speeches by Malcolm X*, New York: Merlin House, Inc., 1971.

Harding, Vincent, *Hope and History: Why We Must Share the Story of the Movement*, Maryknoll: Orbis Books, 1990.

Hare, Nathan, "The Challenge of a Black Scholar," in Joyce A. Ladner, ed., *The Death of White Sociology*, New York: Vintage Books, 1973, pp. 67–78.

_____, *The Black Anglo-Saxons,* New York: Marzani and Munsell, Publishers Inc., 1965.

Hooks, Bell, *Yearning: Race, Gender, and Cultural Politics,* Boston: South End Press, 1990.

_____, *Talking Back: Thinking Feminist, Thinking Black,* Boston: South End Press, 1989.

_____, *Feminist Theory: From Margin to Center,* Boston: South End Press, 1984.

_____, *Ain't I a Woman: Black Women and Feminism,* Boston: South End Press, 1981.

Hooks, Bell, and Cornel West, *Breaking Bread: Insurgent Black Intellectual Life,* Boston: South End Press, 1991.

Hull, Gloria T., Patricia B. Scott, and Barbara Smith, eds., *All the Women Are White, All the Blacks Are Men, But Some of Us Are Brave: Black Women's Studies,* Old Westbury: The Feminist Press, 1982.

Itabari, Njeri, *Every Good-Bye Ain't Gone: Family Portraits and Personal Escapades,* New York: Times Books, 1990.

Jackson, George L., *Blood in My Eye,* New York: Random House, 1972.

_____, *Soledad Brother,* New York: Coward-McCann, Inc., 1970.

Jacques-Garvey, Amy, ed., *Philosophy and Opinions of Marcus Garvey,* New York: Atheneum, 1969.

James, C. L. R., *Spheres of Existence: Selected Writings,* London: Allison and Busby Limited, 1980.

_____, *The Future in the Present: Selected Writings,* Westport: Lawrence Hill and Company, 1977.

Johnson, James W., *Negro Americans, What Next?* New York: The Viking Press, 1935.

Jordan, Jennifer, "Cultural Nationalism in the 1960s: Politics and Poetry," in Adolph Reed, Jr., ed., *Race, Politics, and Culture: Critical Essays on the Radicalism of the 1960s,* Westport: Greenwood Press, 1986, pp. 29–60.

Karenga, M. Ron, *Essays on Struggle: Positions and Analysis,* San Diego: Kawaida Publications, 1978.

McDowell, Deborah E., "New Directions for Black Feminist Criticism," in Elaine Showalter, ed., *The New Feminist Criticism: Essays on Women, Literature, and Theory,* New York: Pantheon Books, 1985, pp. 168–185.

McLaughlin, Andree N., "Black Women, Identity, and the Quest for Humanhood and Wholeness: Wild Women in the Whirlwind," in Joanne M. Braxton and Andree N. McLaughlin, eds., *Wild Women in the Whirlwind: Afra-American Culture and the Contemporary Literary Renaissance,* New Brunswick: Rutgers University Press, 1990, pp. 147–180.

Marable, Manning, *Blackwater: Historical Studies in Race, Class Consciousness and Revolution,* Dayton: Black Praxis Press, 1981.

_____, *From the Grassroots: Social and Political Essays Towards Afro-American Liberation,* Boston: South End Press, 1980.

Meier, August, *Negro Thought in America, 1889–1915: Racial Ideologies in the Age of Booker T. Washington,* Ann Arbor: The University of Michigan Press, 1963.

Merod, Jim, *The Political Responsibility of the Critic,* Ithaca: Cornell University Press, 1987.

Moraga, Cherrie, and Gloria Anzaldua, eds., *This Bridge Called My Back: Writings by Radical Women of Color,* New York: Kitchen Table/Women of Color Press, 1983.

Nkrumah, Kwame, *Africa Must Unite,* New York: Frederick A. Praeger, Publisher, 1963.

Noble, Jeanne, *Beautiful, Also, Are the Souls of My Black Sisters: A History of the Black Woman in America,* Englewood Cliffs: Prentice-Hall, Inc., 1978.

Ofari, Earl, *"Let Your Motto Be Resistance": The Life and Thought of Henry Highland Garnet,* Boston: Beacon Press, 1972.

Padmore, George, *Pan-Africanism or Communism: The Coming Struggle for Africa,* London: Dennis Dobson, 1956.

Robinson, Cedric J., *Black Marxism: The Making of the Black Radical Tradition,* London: Zed Press, 1983.

Said, Edward W., "Orientalism Reconsidered," in Francis Barker, Peter Hulme, Margaret Iversen, and Diana Loxley, eds., *Literature, Politics, and Theory,* New York: Methuen, 1986, pp. 210–229.

Scheer, Robert, ed., *Eldridge Cleaver: Post-Prison Writings and Speeches,* New York: Random House, 1969.

————, *The World, the Text, and the Critic,* Cambridge: Harvard University Press, 1983.

Smith, Barbara, "Toward a Black Feminist Criticism," in Elaine Showalter, ed., *The New Feminist Criticism: Essays on Women, Literature, and Theory,* New York: Pantheon Books, 1985, 186–199.

————, ed., *Home Girls: A Black Feminist Anthology,* New York: Kitchen Table/Women of Color Press, 1983.

Steele, Shelby, *The Content of Our Character,* New York: St. Martin's Press, 1990.

Stuckey, Sterling, *Slave Culture: Nationalist Theory and the Foundations of Black America,* New York: Oxford University Press, 1987.

————, ed., *The Ideological Origins of Black Nationalism,* Boston: Beacon Press, 1971.

Thomas, Tony, *Black Liberation and Socialism,* New York: Pathfinder Press, 1974.

Turner, James E., "Foreword: Africana Studies and Epistemology; a Discourse in the Sociology of Knowledge," in James E. Turner, ed., *The Next Decade: Theoretical and Research Issues in Africana Studies,* Ithaca: Cornell University Africana Studies and Research Center, 1984, pp. v–xxv.

Wallace, Michele, *Invisibility Blues: From Pop to Theory,* New York: Verso, 1990.

————, "Modernism, Postmodernism and the Problem of the Visual in Afro-American Culture," in Russell Ferguson, Martha Gever, Trinh T. Minhha, and Cornel West, eds., *Out There: Marginalization and Contemporary Cultures*, Cambridge: The MIT Press, 1990, pp. 39–50.

_____, *Black Macho and the Myth of the Superwoman*, New York: The Dial Press, 1979.

Washington, James M., ed., *A Testament of Hope: The Essential Writings of Martin Luther King, Jr.*, San Francisco: Harper and Row, Publishers, 1986.

West, Cornel, "The Postmodern Crisis of the Black Intellectuals," in Lawrence Grossberg, Cary Nelson, and Paula Teichler, eds., *Cultural Studies*, New York: Routledge, 1992, 696–705.

_____, *The American Evasion of Philosophy: A Genealogy of Pragmatism*, Madison: The University of Wisconsin Press, 1989.

_____, "Marxist Theory and the Specificity of Afro-American Oppression," in Cary Nelson and Lawrence Grossberg, eds., *Marxism and the Interpretation of Culture*, Urbana: University of Illinois Press, 1988, pp. 17–33.

_____, *Prophetic Fragments*, Trenton: Africa World Press, 1988.

_____, "The Dilemma of the Black Intellectual," *Critical Quarterly*, Vol. 29, No. 4 (Winter 1987), pp. 40–52.

_____, *Prophesy Deliverance: An Afro-American Revolutionary Christianity*, Philadelphia: The Westminster Press, 1982.

Williams, Patricia J., *The Alchemy of Race and Rights*, Cambridge: Harvard University Press, 1991.

Willingham, Alex, "Ideology and Politics: Their Status in Afro-American Social Theory," in Adolph Reed, Jr., ed., *Race, Politics, and Culture: Critical Essays on the Radicalism of the 1960s*, Westport: Greenwood Press, 1986, pp. 13–27.

Winston, Henry, *Class, Race and Black Liberation*, New York: International Publishers, 1977.

_____, *Strategy for a Black Agenda: A Critique of New Theories of Liberation in the United States and Africa*, New York: International Publishers, 1973.

Woodson, Carter G., ed., *Negro Orators and Their Orations*, New York: Russell and Russell, 1969.

Name Index